The
Black Abolitionist
Papers

Board of Editorial Advisors

The
Black Abolitionist
Papers

VOLUME IV
The United States, 1847–1858

C. Peter Ripley, *Editor*
Roy E. Finkenbine, *Associate Editor*
Michael F. Hembree, *Assistant Editor*
Donald Yacovone, *Assistant Editor*

The University of North Carolina Press
Chapel Hill and London

© 1991 The University of North Carolina Press

The paper used in this book meets the guidelines for
permanence and durability of the Committee on Production
Guidelines for Book Longevity of the Council on Library
Resources.

Printed in the United States of America

95   94   93   92   91   5   4   3   2   1

Library of Congress Cataloging-in-Publication Data
(Revised for vol. 4)

The Black Abolitionist papers.

Includes bibliographical references and indexes.
Contents: v. 1. The British Isles, 1830–1865—
v. 2. Canada, 1830–1865—v. 4. The United States,
1847–1858.
1. Slavery—United States—Anti-slavery movements—
Sources.   2. Abolitionists—United States—History—19th
century—Sources.   3. Abolitionists—History—19th
century—Sources.   4. Afro-Americans—History—
to 1863—Sources.   I. Ripley, C. Peter, 1941–   .
E449.B624   1985   973′.0496   84-13131
ISBN 0-8078-1625-6 (v. 1)
ISBN 0-8078-1698-1 (v. 2)
ISBN 0-8078-1926-3 (v. 3)
ISBN 0-8078-1974-3 (v. 4)

The preparation and publication of this volume were made possible in part by grants from the Program for Editions and the Division of Research Programs of the National Endowment for the Humanities, an independent federal agency, and by grants from the National Historical Publications and Records Commission, The Florida State University, the Ford Foundation, and the Rockefeller Foundation.

Contents

Illustrations xiii

Acknowledgments xv

Abbreviations xvii

Editorial Statement xxi

Documents

Illustrations

Acknowledgments

The Black Abolitionist Papers Project is made possible through the substantial contributions of the project staff, university administrators, librarians and curators of research facilities, professional colleagues, and supporters at funding agencies and foundations.

The project editors—Roy E. Finkenbine, Michael F. Hembree, and Donald Yacovone—prepared this volume. They evaluated hundreds of documents; wrote, revised, and rewrote notes and headnotes; and brought a rare blend of intellectual curiosity, scholarly dedication, and enormous hard work to the considerable task at hand. With good humor and a shared sense of mission they made the process rich and rewarding.

Support from The Florida State University, the National Endowment for the Humanities, the National Historical Publications and Records Commission, the Ford Foundation, and the Rockefeller Foundation made possible the preparation of this volume. Vice-President Augustus Turnbull and William R. Jones at Florida State; Kathy Fuller and David Nichols at NEH; Roger Bruns, Mary Giunta, Sarah Jackson, and Richard Sheldon at NHPRC; Sheila Biddle at the Ford Foundation; and Alberta Arthurs, James O. Gibson, and Lynn Szwaja at the Rockefeller Foundation always made me feel welcome.

We wish to acknowledge the scholars, manuscript curators, repository directors, and librarians who responded to our inquiries for elusive information and allowed us to publish documents from their collections: Clifton Johnson of the Amistad Research Center; Karl Kabelac of the Department of Rare Books and Special Collections at the University of Rochester; Theresa Vann of New York City; the Special Collections staff at the George Arents Research Library of Syracuse University; James R. Lynch of the American Baptist Historical Library; Ron Wyly of the Memorial Library at the State University of New York–Cortland; Pat Michaelis of the Kansas State Historical Society; Alma J. Smith of the Rhode Island Black Heritage Society; the staff of the National Library of Jamaica; and Michael Meier, Michael Knapp, Charlotte Palmer Seely, and Marjorie Ciarlante of the National Archives staff. The interlibrary loan staff of The Florida State University Library was enormously helpful.

At Florida State, Associate Vice-President Thomas S. McCaleb, Director of the Black Studies Program William R. Jones, and Dean Charles F. Cnudde of the College of Social Sciences were always there with the right answers for the difficult situations. Sherry Phillips and Kay Sauers of the dean's office and Shamuna Malik of the Black Studies Program supervised our budgets and administrative paperwork with a helpful and cooperative spirit, for which I am very grateful.

Daniel Disch indexed research materials and performed a variety of project tasks. John L. Parker, Jr., kept us current in the world of word processing technology. Christopher Meyer prepared the manuscript for electronic publication with a sophisticated hand, a faultless eye for detail, and a devotion to precision that made us all look good.

The Editorial Board continues to provide sound advice and scholarly insight. Jerome Stern critiqued the headnotes and refereed our editorial decisions, providing the assistance we have come to rely on so heavily after four volumes.

Martha, John P., Mary Ann, Jerry, Joe, Phil, Dan, Jim, and Hal helped make it happen.

Tallahassee, Florida   C. P. R.
June, 1990

Abbreviations

Newspapers, Journals, Directories, and Reference Works

AA	*Aliened American* (Cleveland, Ohio).
AAM	*Anglo-African Magazine* (New York, New York).
AANYLH	*Afro-Americans in New York Life and History.*
ACAB	James Grant Wilson and John Fiske, eds., *Appletons' Cyclopaedia of American Biography*, 6 vols. (New York, New York, 1888–89).
AM	*American Missionary* (New York, New York).
AP	*Albany Patriot* (Albany, New York).
ASB	*Anti-Slavery Bugle* (Salem, Ohio; New Lisbon, Ohio).
ASRL	*Anti-Slavery Reporter* (London, England).
BB	*British Banner* (London, England).
BDAC	*Biographical Directory of the American Congress, 1774–1971* (Washington, D.C., 1971).
BH	*Boston Herald* (Boston, Massachusetts).
BP	*Boston Post* (Boston, Massachusetts).
CA	*Colored American* (New York, New York).
CBD	J. O. Thorne and T. C. Collocott, eds., *Chambers Biographical Dictionary*, rev. ed. (Edinburgh, Scotland, 1984).
CD	*Cortland Democrat* (Cortland, New York).
CF	*Christian Freeman* (New York, New York).
CJH	*Canadian Journal of History.*
CP	*Chatham Planet* (Chatham, Ontario, Canada).
CR	*Christian Recorder* (Philadelphia, Pennsylvania).
CWH	*Civil War History.*
DAAS	Randall M. Miller and John David Smith, eds., *Dictionary of Afro-American Slavery* (Westport, Connecticut, 1988).
DAB	Allen Johnson and Dumas Malone, eds., *Dictionary of American Biography*, 20 vols. (New York, New York, 1928–36).
DAH	*Dictionary of American History*, rev. ed., 8 vols. (New York, New York, 1976–78).
DAHB	Mark R. Lipschutz and R. Kent Rasmussen, eds., *Dictionary of African Historical Biography*, 2d ed. (Berkeley, California, 1986).
DANB	Rayford W. Logan and Michael R. Winston, eds., *Dictionary of American Negro Biography* (New York, New York, 1982).

DH	*Delaware History.*
DM	*Douglass' Monthly* (Rochester, New York).
DNB	Sir Leslie Stephen and Sir Sidney Lee, eds., *Dictionary of National Biography*, 22 vols. (London, England, 1885–1901; reprint, 1921–22).
E	*Emancipator* (Boston, Massachusetts; New York, New York).
EIHC	*Essex Institute Historical Collections.*
ESF	*Elevator* (San Francisco, California).
FDP	*Frederick Douglass' Paper* (Rochester, New York).
FI	*Friends' Intelligencer* (Philadelphia, Pennsylvania).
FJ	*Freedom's Journal* (New York, New York).
FJB	*Freedman's Journal* (Boston, Massachusetts).
G	*Gazette* (Cleveland, Ohio).
GSB	*Gerrit Smith Banner* (New York, New York).
GUE	*Genius of Universal Emancipation* (Mt. Pleasant, Ohio; Greeneville, Tennessee; Baltimore, Maryland; Washington, D.C.; Hennepin, Illinois).
HTECW	Patricia L. Faust, ed., *Historical Times Illustrated Encyclopedia of the Civil War* (New York, New York, 1986).
IC	*Impartial Citizen* (Syracuse, New York; Boston, Massachusetts).
ISHSJ	*Illinois State Historical Society Journal.*
JAC	*Journal of American Culture.*
JAS	*Journal of American Studies.*
JER	*Journal of the Early Republic.*
JNH	*Journal of Negro History.*
JQ	*Journalism Quarterly.*
JSH	*Journal of Southern History.*
JW	*Journal of the West.*
Lib	*Liberator* (Boston, Massachusetts).
LS	*Liberty Standard* (Hallowell, Maine).
MH	*Michigan History.*
MIAS	*Monthly Illustrations of American Slavery* (Newcastle-upon-Tyne, England).
MissH	*Missionary Herald* (Boston, Massachusetts).
ML	*Mirror of Liberty* (New York, New York).
MSt	*Morning Star* (Dover, New Hampshire).
MT	*Mirror of the Times* (San Francisco, California).
MVHR	*Mississippi Valley Historical Review.*
NASS	*National Anti-Slavery Standard* (New York, New York).
NAW	Edward T. James, ed., *Notable American Women, 1607–1950: A Biographical Dictionary*, 3 vols. (Cambridge, Massachusetts, 1971).

NBDES   *Daily Evening Standard* (New Bedford, Massachusetts).
NCAB   *National Cyclopaedia of American Biography*, 61 vols. to
            date (New York, New York, 1898–).
NECAUL   *National Enquirer and Constitutional Advocate of
            Universal Liberty* (Philadelphia, Pennsylvania).
NEQ   *New England Quarterly.*
NEW   *National Era* (Washington, D.C.).
NHB   *Negro History Bulletin.*
NI   *Northern Independent* (Auburn, New York).
NP   *National Principia* (New York, New York).
NSt   *North Star* (Rochester, New York).
NYCJ   *New York Colonization Journal* (New York, New York).
NYT   *New York Tribune* (New York, New York).
NYTi   *New York Times* (New York, New York).
OHSPR   *Ontario Historical Society Papers and Records.*
P   *Philanthropist* (Mt. Pleasant, Ohio; New Richmond,
            Ohio; Cincinnati, Ohio).
PA   *Pacific Appeal* (San Francisco, California).
PF   *Pennsylvania Freeman* (Philadelphia, Pennsylvania).
PFW   *Provincial Freeman* (Windsor, Ontario, Canada; Toronto,
            Ontario, Canada; Chatham, Ontario, Canada).
PH   *Pennsylvania History.*
PL   *Palladium of Liberty* (Columbus, Ohio).
PMHB   *Pennsylvania Magazine of History and Biography.*
PMHS   *Proceedings of the Massachusetts Historical Society.*
PP   *Pine and Palm* (Boston, Massachusetts; New York, New
            York).
PtL   *Patriot* (London, England).
RA   *Rights of All* (New York, New York).
RDA   *Rochester Daily Advertiser* (Rochester, New York).
RDD   *Rochester Daily Democrat* (Rochester, New York).
RE   *Richmond Enquirer* (Richmond, Virginia).
RIF   *Rhode Island Freeman* (Providence, Rhode Island).
RIH   *Rhode Island History.*
RR   *Rochester Republican* (Rochester, New York).
SDS   *Syracuse Daily Standard* (Syracuse, New York).
SDSt   *Daily Star* (Syracuse, New York).
SFMC   *Morning Call* (San Francisco, California).
SJ   *Syracuse Daily Journal* (Syracuse, New York).
SL   *Signal of Liberty* (Ann Arbor, Michigan).
SV   *Saturday Visiter* (Pittsburgh, Pennsylvania).
TG   *Globe* (Toronto, Ontario, Canada).
VF   *Voice of the Fugitive* (Sandwich, Ontario, Canada;
            Windsor, Ontario, Canada).
WAA   *Weekly Anglo-African* (New York, New York).

WC	*Western Citizen* (Chicago, Illinois).
WPHM	*Western Pennsylvania Historical Magazine.*

Manuscript Repositories

AHMS-ARC	American Home Missionary Society Papers, Amistad Research Center, Tulane University, New Orleans, Louisiana.
AMA-ARC	American Missionary Association Archives, Amistad Research Center, Tulane University, New Orleans, Louisiana.
CaOLU	University of Western Ontario, London, Ontario, Canada.
CaOTAr	Ontario Provincial Archives, Toronto, Ontario, Canada.
CaOTP	Metropolitan Toronto Central Library, Toronto, Ontario, Canada.
DHU	Moorland-Spingarn Research Center, Howard University, Washington, D.C.
DLC	Library of Congress, Washington, D.C.
DNA	National Archives, Washington, D.C.
MB	Boston Public Library and Eastern Massachusetts Regional Public Library System, Boston, Massachusetts.
MiU	William L. Clements Library, University of Michigan, Ann Arbor, Michigan.
NjR	Archibald Stevens Alexander Library, Rutgers University, New Brunswick, New Jersey.
NN-Sc	Schomburg Center for Research in Black Culture, New York Public Library, New York, New York.
NRU	Rush-Rhees Library, University of Rochester, Rochester, New York.
NSyOn	Local History and Genealogy Department, Onondaga County Public Library, Syracuse, New York.
NSyU	George Arents Research Library, Syracuse University, Syracuse, New York.
PHi	Historical Society of Pennsylvania, Philadelphia, Pennsylvania.
PU	Van Pelt Library, University of Pennsylvania, Philadelphia, Pennsylvania.
RHi	Rhode Island Historical Society, Providence, Rhode Island.

Editorial Statement

The Black Abolitionist Papers Project began in 1976 with the mission to collect and publish the documentary record of black Americans involved in the movement to end slavery in the United States from 1830 to 1865. The project was conceived from an understanding that broad spans of Afro-American history have eluded scholarly attention because the necessary research materials are not readily available. Many personal papers, business records, newspapers, and other documentary sources simply have not survived. Materials that have endured are often inaccessible because they have not been systematically identified and collected. Except for several small manuscript collections of better-known black figures (usually those that continued to be public figures after emancipation),[1] the letters, speeches, essays, writings, and personal papers of black abolitionists have escaped professional attention. The same is true of antebellum black newspapers.

But the publications of individual historians demonstrated that black abolitionist documents could be unearthed.[2] The black documents that

1. See Mary Ann Shadd Cary Papers, Public Archives of Canada (Ottawa, Ontario), DHU, and CaOTAr; Shadd Family Papers, CaOLU; Rapier Family Papers, DHU; Daniel A. Payne Papers, Wilberforce University (Wilberforce, Ohio); Anderson R. Abbott Papers, CaOTP; John M. Langston Papers, Fisk University (Nashville, Tennessee); Ruffin Family Papers, DHU; Amos G. Beman Papers, Yale University (New Haven, Connecticut); Charles Lenox Remond Papers, Essex Institute (Salem, Massachusetts) and MB; William Still Papers, Rutgers University (New Brunswick, New Jersey); Jacob C. White, Jr., Papers, PHi; Frederick Douglass Papers, DLC, NN-Sc, and DHU; Alexander Crummell Papers, NN-Sc; James T. Holly Papers, General Theological Seminary (New York, New York); J. W. Loguen File, NSyU; Paul Cuffe Papers, New Bedford Free Public Library (New Bedford, Massachusetts). Of these, only the Cary, Cuffe, Remond, Douglass, and Beman collections have significant antebellum documents.

2. A number of black abolitionist documents were reprinted before this project began its work in 1976: Carter G. Woodson, ed., *Negro Orators and Their Orations* (Washington, D.C., 1925), and *The Mind of the Negro as Reflected in Letters Written during the Crisis, 1800–1860* (Washington, D.C., 1926); Dorothy B. Porter, ed., "Early Manuscript Letters Written by Negroes," *JNH* 24:199–210 (April 1939); Benjamin Quarles, ed., "Letters from Negro Leaders to Gerrit Smith," *JNH* 27:432–53 (October 1942); Philip S. Foner, ed., *The Life and Writings of Frederick Douglass*, 5 vols. (New York, N.Y., 1950–75); Howard H. Bell, ed., *Minutes of the Proceedings of the National Negro Conventions, 1830–1864* (New York, N.Y., 1969); Dorothy Sterling, ed., *Speak Out in Thunder Tones: Letters and Other Writings by Black Northerners, 1787–1865* (New York, N.Y., 1973). Pioneer scholarship on the subject that further suggested the availability of documents includes a number of articles on antebellum black Canadian fugitive communities by Fred Landon that appeared in the *Journal of Negro History* and *Ontario History* during the 1920s and 1930s; Dorothy B. Porter, "Sarah Parker Remond, Abolitionist and Physician," *JNH* 20:287–93 (July 1935), and "David M. Ruggles, an Apostle of Human Rights," *JNH* 28:23–50 (January 1943); Herbert Aptheker, *The Negro in the Abolitionist Movement* (New York, N.Y.,

enriched those books and articles were not located in a single collection, repository, or newspaper in any quantity. They were found scattered in the manuscript collections of others (usually whites involved in nine-teenth-century reform movements) and in newspapers of the day (usually reform papers but also in the traditional press). Clearly, a significant body of black abolitionist documents survived, but it seemed equally certain that locating the documents would require a thorough search of large numbers of newspapers and a systematic review of a wide range of historical materials, particularly the papers of white individuals and in-stitutions involved in the antislavery movement.

An international search for documents was the first phase of the Black Abolitionist Papers Project. A four-year collection process took the proj-ect to thousands of manuscript collections and countless newspapers in England, Scotland, Ireland, and Canada as well as in the United States. This work netted nearly 14,000 letters, speeches, essays, pamphlets, and newspaper editorials from over 200 libraries and 110 newspapers. What resulted is the documentary record of some 300 black men and women and their efforts to end American slavery.[3]

The Black Abolitionist Papers were microfilmed during the second phase of the project. The microfilmed edition contains all the primary documents gathered during the collection phase. The seventeen reels of film are a pristine presentation of the black abolitionist record.[4] The microfilmed edition offers materials that previously were uncollected, unidentified, and frequently unavailable to scholars.

1941); Benjamin Quarles, *Frederick Douglass* (Washington, D.C., 1948); Philip S. Foner, *Frederick Douglass* (New York, N.Y., 1950); Benjamin Quarles, "Ministers without Portfo-lio," *JNH* 39:27–43 (January 1954); Leon F. Litwack, *North of Slavery: The Negro in the Free States, 1790–1860* (Chicago, Ill., 1961); William H. Pease and Jane H. Pease, *Black Utopia: Negro Communal Experiments in America* (Madison, Wis., 1963); Benjamin Quarles, *Black Abolitionists* (London, 1969); William Edward Farrison, *William Wells Brown: Author and Reformer* (Chicago, Ill., 1969); Robin W. Winks, *The Blacks in Canada: A History* (New Haven, Conn., 1971); Jane H. Pease and William H. Pease, *They Who Would Be Free: Blacks' Search for Freedom, 1830–1861* (New York, N.Y., 1974); Floyd J. Miller, *The Search for a Black Nationality: Black Emigration and Colonization, 1787–1863* (Urbana, Ill., 1975); Richard Blackett, "In Search of International Support for African Colonization: Martin R. Delany's Visit to England, 1860," *CJH* 10:307–24 (De-cember 1975). Several examples of early research on black abolitionists were reprinted in John H. Bracey, Jr., August Meier, and Elliott Rudwick, eds., *Blacks in the Abolitionist Movement* (Belmont, Calif., 1971).

3. This project has not collected or published documents by Frederick Douglass. Douglass's papers are being edited and published by John W. Blassingame and the staff of the Freder-ick Douglass Papers Project at Yale University.

4. The Black Abolitionist Papers are on seventeen reels of film with a published guide and index (New York, N.Y.: Microfilming Corporation of America, 1981–83; Ann Arbor, Mich.: University Microfilms International, 1984–). The guide contains a description of the collection procedures.

Now in its third phase, the project is publishing a five-volume series of edited and annotated representative documents. Black abolitionist activities in the British Isles and in Canada are treated in separate volumes; three volumes will be devoted to black abolitionists in the United States. The volume organization was suggested by a systematic review of the documents. The documents made clear that black abolitionists had a set of broadly defined goals and objectives wherever they were. But the documents also demonstrated that black abolitionists had a set of specific goals and actions in England, another set in Canada, and a third in the United States.

The U.S. volumes are treated as a series. A single introduction, which appears in volume III, introduces the series. Notes to the documents are not repeated within the U.S. volumes.

The microfilmed and published editions are two discrete historical instruments. The 14,000 microfilmed documents are a rich Afro-American expression of black life in the nineteenth century. Those black voices stand free of intrusion by either editor or historian. The microfilmed edition presents the collected documents. The published volumes are documentary history. Substantial differences separate the two.

The five volumes will accommodate less than 10 percent of the total collection, yet the volumes must tell the ambitious history of a generation of black Americans and their involvement in an international reform movement that spanned thirty-five years in the United States, the British Isles, and Canada. We reconstructed that story by combining documents with written history. A thorough reading of the documents led us to the major themes and elements of black abolitionist activity—the events, ideas, individuals, concepts, and organizations that made up the movement. Then we sought documents that best represented those elements. But given their limited number, the documents alone could only hint at the full dimensions of this complex story. The written history—the volume introduction, the headnotes that precede each document, and the document notes—helps provide a more complete rendition by highlighting the documents' key elements and themes.

The documents led us to yet another principle that governs the volumes. Antislavery was a critical and persistent aspect of antebellum black life, but it cannot correctly be separated from the remainder of black life and culture. Antislavery was part of a broad matrix of black concerns that at times seemed indistinguishable from race relations in the free states, black churches and schools in northern cities, black family life, West Indian immigration, African missionary work, fugitive slave settlements in Canada, and a host of other personal, public, and national matters. Ending slavery was but the most urgent item on the crowded agenda of the black Americans represented in these volumes.

A number of considerations influenced the selection of specific documents published in the volumes. The most important was the responsibility to publish documents that fairly represent the antislavery goals, attitudes, and actions of black abolitionists and, to a lesser extent, that reveal their more personal concerns. There were other considerations as well. We wanted to present documents by as many black abolitionists as possible. We avoided the temptation to rely on the eloquent statements of just a few polished professionals. We sought to document immediate antislavery objectives (often dictated by local needs and issues) as well as broad goals. A mix of document types—letters (both public and private), essays, scientific pieces, short autobiographical narratives, impromptu remarks, formal speeches, circulars, resolutions, and debates—was selected for publication.

We resisted selecting documents that had been reprinted before our work began. But occasionally when a previously published document surfaced as a resonant black expression on an issue, topic, or incident, it was selected for publication. And, with the release of the Black Abolitionist Papers on microfilm, all the documents are more available than in the past. We often found different versions of the same document (usually a speech that appeared in several newspapers). When that happened, we selected the earliest published version of the most complete text. The cluster of documents around particular time periods and topics mirrors black abolitionist activities and concerns. The documents are arranged chronologically within each volume. A headnote introduces each document. The headnote provides a historical context for the document and offers information designed to enhance the reader's understanding of the document and black abolitionist activities.

Notes identify a variety of items that appear within the documents, such as people, places, events, organizations, institutions, laws, and legal decisions. The notes enrich and clarify the documents. People and events that are covered in standard biographical directories, reference books, or textbooks are treated in brief notes. We have given more space to subjects on which there is little or no readily available information, particularly black individuals and significant events and institutions in the black community. A full note on each item is presented at the first appropriate point in the volume. Notes are not repeated within the volume. Information that appears in a headnote is not repeated in an endnote. The index includes references to all notes.

We have listed sources at the end of notes and headnotes. When appropriate, source citations contain references to materials in the microfilmed edition; they appear in brackets as reel and frame numbers (3:0070 reads reel 3, frame 70). The titles of some sources are abbreviated (particularly newspapers, journals, and manuscript repositories); a list of abbreviations appears at the front of the volume.

The axiom that "less is better" governed the project's transcription of documents. Our goal was to publish the documents in a form as close to the original as possible while presenting them in a fashion that enabled the reader to use them easily.

In the letters, the following items are uniformly and silently located regardless of where they appear in the original: place and date, recipient's name and address, salutation, closing, signature, marginal notes, and postscripts. In manuscript documents, idiosyncratic spelling, underlining, and quotation marks are retained. Words that were crossed through in the original are also retained.

The project adopted the following principles for documents found in published sources (newspapers, pamphlets, annual reports, and other nineteenth-century printed material): redundant punctuation is eliminated; quotation marks are converted to modern usage; obvious misspellings and printer's errors are corrected; printer's brackets are converted to parentheses; audience reaction within a speech is treated as a separate sentence with parentheses, for example, (Hear, hear.). We have let stand certain nineteenth-century printing conventions such as setting names or addresses in capital or italic letters in order to maintain the visual character of the document. A line of asterisks signals that material is deleted from a printed document. In no instance is black abolitionist material edited or deleted; but if, for example, a speech was interrupted with material extraneous to the document, the irrelevant material is not published.

The intrusive *sic* is rarely used. Brackets are used in their traditional fashion: to enclose information that we added and to indicate our inability to transcribe words or phrases with certainty. Some examples: we bracketed information added to the salutation and return address of letters; we bracketed material that we believe will aid the reader to comprehend the document, such as [illegible], [rest of page missing]; and we bracketed words and phrases that we believe appeared in the original but are uncertain about because of the quality of the surviving text. We have used brackets in the body of documents sparingly and only when necessary to avoid confusing the reader. We have not completed words, added words, corrected spelling, or otherwise provided material in the text of manuscript documents except as noted above.

Our transcription guidelines for manuscript documents differ slightly from those we used for printed sources. We took greater editorial liberties with documents from printed sources because they seldom came to us directly from a black abolitionist's hand. Speeches in particular often had a long editorial trail. Usually reporters wrote them down as they listened from the audience; in some cases this appeared to be done with precision. For example, William Farmer, a British abolitionist and newspaper reporter, was an accomplished stenographer who traveled with William Wells Brown and took down his speeches verbatim, then made them available to the local press. More often, a local reporter recorded speeches in a less thorough fashion. Speeches and letters that black abolitionists sent to newspapers were apt to pass through the hands of an editor, a publisher, and a typesetter, all of whom might make errors in transcription. Because documents that were reprinted in newspapers often had sections changed or deleted, we have attempted to find the original publication of printed documents.

Our transcription guidelines were influenced by the availability of all the documents in the microfilmed edition. Microfilmed copies of the original documents give the reader ready access to unedited versions of the documents that appear in the published volumes.

The
Black Abolitionist
Papers

1.
William Wells Brown to Samuel May, Jr.
9 August 1847

The effectiveness of the antislavery movement depended upon sustained labor at the local level, where funds were raised to print newspapers and pamphlets, arrangements were made for visiting lecturers, and new antislavery societies were organized. Black and white antislavery women assumed responsibility for much of that gritty, hard work. William Wells Brown, one of the movement's most articulate spokesmen, described and praised the efforts of antislavery women in a 9 August 1847 letter to Samuel May, Jr., the general agent of the Massachusetts Anti-Slavery Society. Brown had been lecturing for several months throughout Massachusetts and western New York, supported in part by proceeds raised at women's antislavery fairs. Brown's judgment about the importance of women in the antislavery movement was shared by other black abolitionists such as Robert Purvis, William C. Nell, Frederick Douglass, and Charles L. Remond, who also worked closely with antislavery women, encouraged their efforts, and valued their contributions to the cause. William Edward Farrison, *William Wells Brown: Author and Reformer* (Chicago, Ill., 1969), 103, 109–15; Benjamin Quarles, *Black Abolitionists* (London, England, 1969), 177–80.

FITCHBURG, [Massachusetts]
Aug[ust] 9, 1847

MY DEAR FRIEND MAY:[1]

You have, I doubt not, heard of our meeting at New Bedford;[2] it was well attended, and I think did some good for the cause. The colored people of New Bedford are in advance of the colored people of any other place that I have visited in the State. I came from there directly to Leominster,[3] and in the evening a large audience assembled at the Unitarian church, and a more attentive one I have never spoken to.

On the following Thursday, the females formed an anti-slavery sewing circle[4] for the purpose of aiding the next Boston *Fair;*[5] and I doubt not but their labor will be appreciated by the friends of the cause in and about Boston, and am more and more convinced of the propriety of invoking the aid of females to the slave's cause. Their sewing circles will have a salutary effect upon all who attend them. Nothing looks more cheering to me than to see a circle of women working with their own hands for the redemption of their enslaved countrymen. And why should they not labor for the downfall of slavery? Are not more than a million of females driven daily to the sugar, the cotton, the rice and tobacco plantations of the South? Are they not denied the marriage rite? Is not

Jesus crucified every day on the plains of the South, in the person of the unprotected slave? I never fail to urge upon the women the discharge of their duty to the slave. Some ask, "What can we do?"—"There is a majority against having anything done in our town," &c. But they should understand that the success of our cause does not depend upon the majorities; and if it did, the fact that a majority are against us, does not make them right or us wrong. They should recollect that it was a majority which passed the Stamp Act, and the Tea Tax, which smiled upon the persecutions of Galileo, which stood about the stake of Servetus, which administered the hemlock to Socrates, which called for the crucifixion of Jesus.[6] But that did not make those acts right.

And then they should take a view of the past, and see what has been accomplished by the aid of women. They should recollect that it was a woman that put in motion the machinery by which 800,000 of our brethren obtained their freedom in the West Indies; by a woman Rome obtained her liberty; by a woman the plebeians acquired the Consulate; by a woman, when the city was trembling with the vindictive exile at its gates, it was saved from that destruction which no other influence could avert.[7] Such evidences as these should strengthen their hands, and cause them to labor with redoubled energy, until the last chain shall fall from the limb of the last slave, not only in America, but in the world. Yours for the oppressed,

WM. W. BROWN[8]

Liberator (Boston, Mass.), 3 September 1847.

1. Samuel May, Jr. (1810–1899), a Unitarian clergyman from Leicester, Massachusetts, became a key member of William Lloyd Garrison's Boston antislavery circle in the early 1840s. He served as the general agent of the Massachusetts Anti-Slavery Society from 1847 to 1865, arranging conventions, procuring speakers, making travel arrangements, and frequently lecturing before antislavery audiences. In 1875 he was elected to the Massachusetts legislature. *NCAB*, 29:244; Lawrence J. Friedman, *Gregarious Saints: Self and Community in American Abolitionism, 1830–1870* (Cambridge, England, 1982), 45.

2. New Bedford blacks met at City Hall on 1 August 1847 to celebrate West Indian emancipation. Two meetings were held. Brown probably refers to the evening meeting, reputed to be the largest antislavery gathering in the city's history, at which he, James N. Buffum, and black abolitionist Jeremiah B. Sanderson spoke. *Lib*, 16 July, 20 August 1847.

3. Brown spoke at Leominster, Massachusetts, on 2 August 1847, while on a lecture tour for the Massachusetts Anti-Slavery Society. *Lib*, 30 July, 6 August 1847.

4. The Leominster Anti-Slavery Sewing Circle was formed in August 1847. At first Frances H. Drake, the city's most active female abolitionist, encountered serious opposition to her efforts to enlist local women in the antislavery cause. But the society eventually prospered. During the 1850s, it held antislavery fairs

to aid the Massachusetts Anti-Slavery Society and sponsored speakers such as Lucy Stone, Wendell Phillips, and Thomas W. Higginson. *Lib*, 16 July 1847, 28 February 1851, 10 December 1852, 3 March 1854, 27 November 1857.

5. Members of the interracial Boston Female Anti-Slavery Society began organizing antislavery fairs, or bazaars, in 1834. The event, which was held just before Christmas, quickly became a standard fund-raising method for antislavery societies across the North and in Britain. By the mid-1840s, the fair (then known as the Boston Anti-Slavery Bazaar) was usually held in a large meeting place such as Boston's Faneuil Hall. Entertainment and refreshments were provided, and abolitionists came to regard the bazaar as a significant social event—a time to renew friendships, win converts to the cause, and hold preliminary strategy sessions before the annual January meeting of the Massachusetts Anti-Slavery Society. The $65,000 collected from 1834 to 1857 served as a source of power and influence for Boston's abolitionist women and assisted local black institutions, funded lecture tours and legal actions, and supported antislavery publications such as the *Liberator* and *National Anti-Slavery Standard*. Although the Boston bazaar ceased after 1857, antislavery fairs remained popular into the 1860s. *Lib*, 3 May 1839; Walter M. Merrill and Louis Ruchames, eds., *The Letters of William Lloyd Garrison*, 6 vols. (Cambridge, Mass., 1971–82), 2:4, 10, 195, 408, 420, 699, 716–17, 3:135–36, 228, 239, 242, 397, 400, 452, 469, 517, 539; Benjamin Quarles, "Sources of Abolitionist Income," *MVHR* 32:63–76 (June 1945).

6. The author cites several instances of injustice or oppression that underscore the "tyranny of the majority." Britain's Parliament enacted new tax laws—the Stamp Act (1765) and the Tea Act (1773)—that angered American colonists and helped cause the American Revolution. The Catholic Inquisition forced Galileo Galilei (1564–1642), an Italian scientist, to recant his theories of astronomy and tried and executed Michael Servetus (1511–1553), a Spanish theologian, for religious heresy. Socrates (ca. 470–399 B.C.), a Greek philosopher, was convicted of treason by an Athenian jury but chose to take poison rather than face the sentence of permanent exile. According to the biblical account, Jesus faced charges of treason and was crucified by popular acclaim (ca. 30 A.D.).

7. Brown refers to events from contemporary history and ancient Roman legend in which women played a central role. The first eloquent plea for immediate emancipation was made in *Immediate, Not Gradual Emancipation* (1824) by Englishwoman Elizabeth Heyrick. Her uncompromising pamphlet mobilized public antislavery sentiment in Britain, leading to passage of the Emancipation Act of 1833 that ended slavery in the British West Indies. Hersilia, the wife of Romulus, Rome's legendary founder, intervened to end the war with the Sabines. An account in book 1 of Livy's *History of Rome* tells of the suicide of Verginia, whose death prompted riots by the common citizens of Rome. When the army sided with the rioters, the aristocratic elite were forced to admit plebeians to the ruling Consulate. Later, when Coriolanus threatened to destroy Rome, his mother and his wife dissuaded him. For their efforts, the Roman Senate erected a "temple to the Fortunes of Women" in their honor. Brown probably gleaned much of this information from the two-volume *History of the Condition of Women, in Various Ages and Nations* (1835) by abolitionist Lydia Maria Child.

8. William Wells Brown (ca. 1814–1884) was born in Lexington, Kentucky,

the son of Elizabeth, a slave woman, and a white relative of her owner. After twenty years in slavery, Brown escaped to freedom in January 1834. He spent the next two years working on a Lake Erie steamboat and running fugitive slaves into Canada. In the summer of 1834, he met and married Elizabeth Spooner, a free black woman; they had three daughters, one of whom died shortly after birth. Two years after his marriage, Brown moved to Buffalo, where he began his career in the abolitionist movement by attending meetings of the Western New York Anti-Slavery Society, boarding antislavery lecturers at his home, speaking at local abolitionist gatherings, and traveling to Cuba and Haiti to investigate emigration possibilities.

Brown's abolitionist career reached a turning point in the summer of 1843, when Buffalo hosted a national antislavery convention and the National Convention of Colored Citizens. Brown attended both meetings, sat on several committees, and became friends with a number of black abolitionists, including Frederick Douglass and Charles Lenox Remond. Brown joined these two in their appeal to the power of moral suasion, their rejection of black antislavery violence (particularly the course espoused by Henry Highland Garnet in his "Address to the Slaves"), and their boycott of political abolitionism. Brown's expanded service to the antislavery movement, his increasing sophistication as a speaker, and his growing reputation in the antislavery community brought an invitation to lecture before the American Anti-Slavery Society at its 1844 annual meeting in New York City; in May 1847, he was hired by the Massachusetts Anti-Slavery Society as a lecturing agent. He moved to Boston and by the end of the year had published the successful *Narrative* of his life.

In October 1849, Brown began a lecture tour of Britain. A mix of personal and political motives kept him abroad until 1854. He was exhilarated by the tour, found time to write, and enjoyed the benefits of reform society. Brown was also trying to recover from the dissolution of his marriage. Quite as important, passage of the Fugitive Slave Law of 1850 made it dangerous for the escaped slave to return to the United States. Concern for his safety prompted British abolitionists to purchase his freedom in 1854.

When Brown did return, he had written *Clotel*, the first novel published by an Afro-American, and was finishing *St. Domingo*, a volume that suggests his growing antislavery militancy. The publication of those works, as well as a travelogue, a play, and a compilation of antislavery songs, established his reputation as the most prolific black literary figure of the mid-nineteenth century. During 1861–62 he was a lecturing agent in Canada West and the Northeast for James Redpath's Haytian Emigration Bureau. For the remainder of his life, Brown lived in the Boston area, producing three major volumes of black history and continuing to travel, lecture, and write. He completed his last book, *My Southern Home: Or, the South and Its People*, in 1880. Farrison, *William Wells Brown*.

2.

Report by the Committee on a National Press of the National Convention of Colored People and Their Friends

Presented at the Liberty Street Presbyterian Church
Troy, New York
6 October 1847

Black abolitionists regarded a national black press as an essential instrument in shaping Afro-American life and culture. But in the mid-1840s, blacks published only a few poorly financed newspapers. During the 1847 black national convention at Troy, New York, James McCune Smith, George B. Wilson, and William H. Topp addressed this problem. Their report, which was largely Smith's work, summarized the vital functions a national press could serve—as a symbol of racial unity, as a communications link between black communities, as a public voice to counter racist diatribes and proslavery myths, and as a necessary component in forging an independent role in the antislavery movement. The delegates approved the report, although a few raised practical considerations, questioning whether scarce resources were better directed toward existing local black newspapers. Establishing a national black press remained an elusive goal, but two months after the Troy convention, black abolitionists found the assertive, independent voice they sought when Frederick Douglass published the first issue of his *North Star. Proceedings of the National Convention of Colored People, and Their Friends, Held in Troy, N.Y., on the 6th, 7th, 8th and 9th October, 1847* (Troy, N.Y., 1847), 5–8; Jane H. Pease and William H. Pease, *They Who Would Be Free: Blacks' Search for Freedom, 1830–1861* (New York, N.Y., 1974), 115–19.

REPORT OF THE COMMITTEE ON A NATIONAL PRESS.

It being admitted that the colored people of the United States are pledged, before the world and in the face of Heaven, to struggle manfully for advancement in civil and social life, it is clear that our own efforts must mainly, if not entirely, produce such advancement. And if we are to advance by our own efforts (under the Divine blessing), we must use the means which will direct such efforts to a successful issue.

Of the means for advancement of a people placed as we are, none are more available than a Press. We struggle against opinions. Our warfare lies in the field of thought. Glorious struggle! God-like warfare! In training our soldiers for the field, in marshaling our hosts for the fight, in leading the onset, and through the conflict, we need a Printing Press, because a printing press is the vehicle of thought—is a ruler of opinions.

Among ourselves we need a Press that shall keep us steadily alive to our responsibilities, which shall constantly point out the principles which should guide our conduct and our labors, which shall cheer us from one end of the land to the other, by recording our acts, our sufferings, our temporary defeats and our steadily approaching triumph —or rather the triumph of the glorious truth "Human Equality," whose servants and soldiers we are.

If a Press be not the most powerful means for our elevation, it is the most immediately necessary. Education of the intellect, of the will, and of character, is doubtless a powerful, perhaps the most powerful, means for our advancement; yet a Press is needed to keep this very fact before the whole people, in order that all may constantly and unitedly labor in this, the right direction. It may be that some other means might seem even more effectual than education; even then a Press will be the more necessary, inasmuch as it will afford a field in which the relative importance of the various means may be discussed and settled in the hearing of the whole people, and to the profit of all.

The first step which will mark our certain advancement as a people, will be our Declaration of Independence from all aid except from God and our own souls. This step can only be taken when the minds of our people are thoroughly convinced of its necessity and importance. And such conviction can only be produced through a Press, which shall show that although we have labored long and earnestly, we have labored in too many directions and with too little concert of action; and that we must, as one man, bend our united efforts in the one right direction in order to advance.

We need a Press also as our Banner on the outer wall, that all who pass by may read why we struggle, how we struggle, and what we struggle for. If we convince the world that we are earnestly and resolutely striving for our own advancement, one half the battle will already be won, because well and rightly begun. Our friends will the more willingly help us; our foes will quail, because they will have lost their best allies—our own inertness, carelessness, strifes and dependence upon others. And there is no way except through a Press—a National Press—that we can tell the world of our position in the path of Human Progress.

Let there be, then, in these United States, a Printing Press, a copious supply of type, a full and complete establishment, wholly controlled by colored men; let the thinking writing-man, the compositors, pressman, printers' help, all, all be men of color; then let there come from said establishment a weekly periodical and a quarterly periodical, edited as well as printed by colored men; let this establishment be so well endowed as to be beyond the chances of temporary patronage; and then there will be a fixed fact, a rallying point, towards which the strong and the weak amongst us would look with confidence and hope; from which would flow a steady stream of comfort and exhortation to the weary strugglers, and of burning rebuke and overwhelming argument upon those who dare impede our way.

The time was when a great statesman exclaimed, "Give me the song-making of a people and I will rule that people." That time has passed away from our land, wherein the reason of the people must be assaulted and overcome; this can only be done through the Press. We have felt, and bitterly, the weight of odium and malignity wrought upon us by one or two prominent presses in this land; we have felt also the favorable feeling wrought in our behalf by the Anti-Slavery Press. But the amount of the hatred against us has been conventional antipathy; and of the favorable feeling has been human sympathy. Our friends sorrow with us, because they say we are unfortunate! We must batter down those antipathies, we must command something manlier than sympathies. We must command the respect and admiration due men, who, against fearful odds, are struggling steadfastly for their rights. This can only be done through a Press of our own. It is needless to support these views with a glance at what the Press has done for the downtrodden among men; let us rather look forward with the determination of accomplishing, through this engine, an achievement more glorious than any yet accomplished. We lead the forlorn hope of Human Equality; let us tell of its onslaught on the battlements of hate and caste; let us record its triumph in a Press of our own.

In making these remarks, your Committee do not forget or underrate the good service done by the newspapers which have been, or are now, edited and published by our colored brethren.[1] We are deeply alive to the talent, the energy and perseverance, which these papers manifest on the part of their self-sacrificing conductors. But these papers have been, and are, a matter of serious pecuniary loss to their proprietors; and as the proprietors are always poor men, their papers have been jeopardized or stopped for the want of capital. The history of our newspapers is the strongest argument in favor of the establishment of a Press. These papers abundantly prove that we have all the talent and industry requisite to conduct a paper such as we need; and they prove also, that among 500,000 free people of color, no one man is yet set apart with a competence for the purpose of advocating with the pen our cause and the cause of our brethren in chains. It is an imposition upon the noble-minded colored editors; it is a libel upon us as a free and thinking people, that we have hitherto made no effort to establish a Press on a foundation so broad and national that it may support one literary man of color and an office of colored compositors.

The importance and necessity of a National Press, your Committee trust, are abundantly manifest.

The following plan, adopted by the Committee of seven,[2] appointed by the Convention with full power, is in the place of the Propositions proposed by the Committee of three:

1st. There shall be an Executive of eleven persons, to be denominated the Executive Committee on the National Press for the Free Colored People of the United States, viz:

2nd. *Massachusetts*—Leonard Collins, James Mars;[3] *Connecticut*— Amos G. Beman,[4] James W. C. Pennington; *Kentucky*—Andrew Jackson;[5] *New York*—J. McCune Smith, Chas. B. Ray, Alex. Crummell; *New Jersey*—E. P. Rogers;[6] *Pennsylvania*—Andrew Purnell,[7] George B. Vashon; of which Committee James McCune Smith of New York shall be Chairman, and Amos G. Beman of Connecticut, Secretary.

3rd. The members of this Committee residing in the city of New York shall be a Financial Committee, who shall deposit, in trust for the Executive Committee, in the "New York Seamen's Bank for Savings"[8] all the funds received by them from the Agents.

4th. No disposition shall be made of the funds by any less than a two-thirds majority of the whole Committee.

5th. The Committee shall hold stated meetings once in six months, and shall then publish an account of their proceedings, the receipts, and from whom all sums are sent to them by the Agents.

6th. The Rev. J. W. C. Pennington of Connecticut shall be the Foreign Agent of the National Press, and the Agents shall always be ex-officio members of the Committee.

7th. The remuneration of Home Agent shall be 20 per cent; of the Foreign Agent 30 per cent on collections made.

8th. The meetings of the Committee shall take place in the city of New York.

9th. The Agents shall report and remit to the Committee, at least once a month for the Home, and once in two months for the Foreign Agent.

10th. Members of the Committee from any two States may call an extra meeting thereof by giving the Chairman and Secretary thirty days notice.

Respectfully submitted,

J. McCUNE SMITH
G. B. WILSON[9]
WM. H. TOPP[10]

Proceedings of the National Convention of Colored People, and Their Friends, Held in Troy, N.Y., on the 6th, 7th, 8th and 9th October, 1847 (Troy, N.Y., 1847), 18–21.

1. More than a dozen black newspapers were founded during the two decades preceding the Troy convention. They all struggled under adverse financial conditions, and some ceased publication after only a few issues. The New York City-based *Freedom's Journal* (1827–29) and the *Colored American* (1837–41) were

the most successful and influential of these papers. Several short-lived black journals appeared in the early 1840s; the most notable were Martin R. Delany's *Mystery* (Pittsburgh) and David Jenkins's *Palladium of Liberty* (Columbus). Black newspapers still publishing at the time of the 1847 convention included Willis Hodges's *Ram's Horn* (New York City), Henry Highland Garnet's *National Watchman* (Troy), and Stephen Myers's *Northern Star and Freeman's Advocate* (Albany). Pease and Pease, *They Who Would Be Free*, 113–16; *Convention of Colored People . . . in Troy* (1847), 9.

2. A seven-man committee was appointed to "carry out the intention of the Convention in adopting said [press] report." The members were James McCune Smith, Zedekiah J. Purnell, James Mars, J. W. C. Pennington, Andrew Jackson, Leonard Collins, and Amos G. Beman. *Convention of Colored People . . . in Troy* (1847), 9.

3. James Mars (1790–ca. 1870) was born in North Canaan, Connecticut, to slave parents; his father, Jupiter Mars, was a Revolutionary War veteran. Mars's parents and sister were emancipated by their owner in 1798, but as part of the arrangement, Mars and his brother were indentured until age twenty-five. Mars served a Norfolk, Connecticut, farmer until 1815 and continued to do farm labor before moving to Hartford in the early 1830s with his wife and two children. Despite his slave background and a "broken and unsteady" education, Mars rose to a position of leadership in the Hartford black community. He was a founder and deacon of the Talcott Street Congregational Church, was active in the Connecticut State Temperance Society of Colored People, and participated in local efforts to support the black press and the Union Missionary Society. Mars won an important antislavery victory when he initiated a successful suit in the Connecticut courts to prevent a slave from being forced to accompany her master when he decided to return to Virginia. Frustrated by the legal inequality that blacks faced in Connecticut, Mars moved his family to Pittsfield, Massachusetts, in the late 1840s. Within four years, his wife and sixteen-year-old son had died of illness. Three of his sons became mariners, and one served in the Union navy during the Civil War. Mars published his narrative, *Life of James Mars, A Slave*, in 1864. James Mars, *Life of James Mars, A Slave* (Hartford, Conn., 1864), 1–38; David O. White, *Connecticut's Black Soldiers, 1775–1783* (Chester, Conn., 1973), 50–51; CA, 9 November 1839, 25 July, 19 September 1840, 15 May 1841 [3:0261, 0534, 0623, 4:0011].

4. Amos Gerry Beman (1812–1874) was the son of Jehiel C. Beman, a black abolitionist clergyman in Middletown, Connecticut. The younger Beman was privately tutored before attending several schools, including Oneida Institute (1835–36). He taught in Hartford while a candidate for the ministry, then moved to New Haven in June 1838 to serve the Temple Street Colored Congregational Church. Beman became an avid advocate of temperance and moral improvement and sponsored local educational lectures, library clubs, protective associations, and "elevation meetings"; in 1841 he organized the New Haven Literary and Debating Society. He also helped found the Connecticut State Temperance Society of Colored People and wrote a series of newspaper articles on the subject for the *Colored American*.

A vigorous abolitionist, Beman became one of the most important spokesmen for Connecticut's black community during the 1840s and 1850s. When the

American Anti-Slavery Society divided in 1840, he helped found the American and Foreign Anti-Slavery Society and served on its executive committee. He understood the importance of a dynamic black press and edited the short-lived *Zion's Wesleyan* in 1842. Elected president of the 1843 black national convention in Buffalo, he used his position and his oratory to help defeat a resolution by Henry Highland Garnet that sanctioned slave violence. As the 1840s wore on, Beman devoted increasing amounts of time to the struggle against slavery and for black civil rights. He led the black suffrage movement in Connecticut, made his church a station on the underground railroad, and counseled disobedience to the Fugitive Slave Law of 1850. Delegates to the 1853 black national convention in Rochester elected him to the National Council of the Colored People—an executive committee meant to serve as the convention's administrative arm—and the Manual Labor School Committee.

Beman faced personal tragedy in 1856–57 when his wife and two of his four children died of typhoid fever. He remarried in 1858. That same year, he was appointed pastor of the Fourth Colored Congregational Church of Portland, Maine. Beginning in July 1859, he served for a year as an agent of the American Missionary Association; he traveled throughout the Northeast, lecturing, raising funds, and assessing the state of the black church. After 1860 Beman supported himself and his family by filling a series of short-term ministerial appointments, by working for the freedmen in Tennessee, and by advising the African Civilization Society's freedmen's school project in Washington, D.C. His contributions to black civil rights were honored in 1872 when he was appointed chaplain to the Connecticut legislature. Robert A. Warner, "Amos Gerry Beman, 1812–1874: A Memoir on a Forgotten Leader," *JNH* 22:200–221 (April 1937); *Lib*, 7 January, 7 July, 11, 25 August 1832, 11 May, 11 August, 7 September, 2 November 1833, 2 March, 3 December 1836, 8 September 1843, 26 September 1856, 9 September 1864 [1:0092, 0218, 0283, 0341, 0651, 0751, 4:0660, 15:0517]; *FDP*, 22 July 1853, 8, 29 September, 13, 27 October 1854, 12 January, 4 May, 14 September 1855 [8:0373, 9:0072, 0133, 0168, 0374, 0578, 0832]; Amos G. Beman to Lewis Tappan, 11 October 1841, 27 September 1843, AMA-ARC [4:0251, 0673].

5. Andrew Jackson (1814–1848), a Methodist clergyman and antislavery lecturer, was born to an emancipated slave near Bowling Green, Kentucky, but was enslaved when his mother's freedom was contested and annulled by the local courts. After serving George Wall, a Methodist preacher, for twenty years, he was hired out to a series of masters, who worked him on turnpike construction projects. Jackson was eventually sold to Perry Claypoole, a tobacco farmer. In August 1842, when his master ordered him to marry a slave woman or be sold, he decided to escape. During his flight through Illinois, he was jailed as a fugitive but fled again. Within several months, he joined his brother in Wisconsin and, at the urging of family and friends, began lecturing for the antislavery cause. After attending the 1843 black national convention in Buffalo, Jackson decided to settle in Syracuse. Although completely illiterate upon his arrival in New York, he obtained a rudimentary education and developed his writing skills. In 1847 he published his *Narrative and Writings*, which consisted of a brief account of his slave experiences, anecdotes, sermons, poems, letters to a former master, and runaway notices from southern newspapers. It yielded "a handsome profit."

Jackson spent 1846–47 giving antislavery and temperance lectures, singing antislavery songs, and selling reform literature in churches and schoolhouses throughout western New York, Pennsylvania, and New England. While on a lecture tour in July 1848, he drowned in the Connecticut River near Putney, Vermont. *SJ*, 27 July 1848; *Narrative and Writings of Andrew Jackson, of Kentucky* (Syracuse, N.Y., 1847).

6. Elymus Payson Rogers (1815–1861), a Presbyterian clergyman, educator, and poet, was born near Madison, Connecticut. Tracing his roots to an African great-grandmother, whose slave ship was wrecked off the Connecticut coast in the early eighteenth century, he grew up with a strong sense of African identity. His parents were pious Christians who urged him to return and preach the gospel in their ancestral home. From 1835 to 1841, Rogers studied for the ministry at two abolitionist schools in upstate New York—Gerrit Smith's Peterboro Manual Labor School and Beriah Green's Oneida Institute. Hired at Smith's recommendation to teach in a black public school in Rochester, he alternated for five years between that job and his studies at Oneida. While in Rochester, Rogers became involved in antislavery activities, served as a subscription agent for the *Colored American*, and attended the 1840 black state convention. During this time, he met and married Harriet E. Sherman, a local woman.

After graduating from Oneida in 1841, Rogers became principal of a black school in Trenton, New Jersey. He taught and studied theology there until 1844, when he was licensed to preach. Rogers served Witherspoon Street Presbyterian Church in Princeton for two years, then accepted a call to the Plane Street Presbyterian Church in Newark, where he remained until 1860. The congregation grew rapidly under his zealous and industrious care and soon became one of the leading parishes in the presbytery. Rogers used his church work to pursue antislavery goals. He was an active member of the Evangelical Association of the Colored Ministers of Congregational and Presbyterian Churches, an abolitionist organization, and in 1857 persuaded his presbytery to denounce the Dred Scott decision. Rogers also wrote two volumes of antislavery verse, *A Poem on the Fugitive Slave Law* (1855) and *The Repeal of the Missouri Compromise Considered* (1856), and regularly published poems about slavery in the black press.

Rogers never abandoned his family goal of doing African missionary work. In 1859 he joined the African Civilization Society, attracted by the organization's emphasis on converting the continent to Christianity. One year later, he decided to visit West Africa at his own expense to establish an AfCS settlement and to investigate opportunities for an American Missionary Association station in Abeokuta. He sailed from New York City with two assistants in early November and arrived in Sierra Leone in about a month. After visiting the coastal villages of Liberia for five weeks, he died in Liberia before reaching Abeokuta, still believing that "there is a bright future for poor Africa." Joan R. Sherman, *Invisible Poets: Afro-Americans of the Nineteenth Century*, 2d ed. (Urbana, Ill., 1989), 21–26; Floyd J. Miller, *The Search for a Black Nationality: Black Emigration and Colonization, 1787–1863* (Urbana, Ill., 1975), 229–31; *CA*, 21 November 1840, 6 March 1841 [3:0712, 0925]; Philip S. Foner and George E. Walker, eds., *Proceedings of the Black State Conventions, 1840–1865*, 2 vols. (Philadelphia, Pa., 1979–80), 1:5; *WAA*, 7 October, 12, 26 November 1859, 11 May 1861.

7. The committee probably refers to Zedekiah J. Purnell, a Philadelphia dele-

gate involved in the convention's deliberations on the black press. A freeborn hairdresser, he belonged to St. Thomas's African Episcopal Church and was a member of one of the black community's most prominent families. Purnell's interest in the black press dated from the late 1830s, when he encouraged local support for the *Colored American* and served as a manager of the Demosthenian Institute, a black literary society that published its own journal. In the 1840s, he became involved in the protest against black disfranchisement, attended the 1841 black state convention, and joined in the call to revive the black national convention movement. *CA*, 13 October 1838, 5 December 1840, 8 May 1841 [2:0616, 3:0730, 1024]; *E*, 4 August 1842 [4:0457]; Foner and Walker, *Proceedings of the Black State Conventions*, 1:116; "Black Organizational Members, Sorted by Name," Philadelphia Social History Project, PU; Census Facts collected by Benjamin C. Bacon and Charles Gardner, 1838, Education and Employment Statistics of the Colored People of Philadelphia, 1856, Pennsylvania Abolition Society Papers, PHi.

8. The Seamen's Bank for Savings was located in New York City's Wall Street financial district. Chartered in 1829 to encourage savings among workers in the maritime trades, it operated under the supervision of the American Seamen's Friend Society. The *Colored American* urged black seamen to patronize the bank because of its nondiscriminatory policies. Clarence G. Michalis, *"Seamen's Bank": 125 Years in Step with New York* (New York, N.Y., 1954), 9–12; *Lib*, 20 July 1833; *CA*, 16 May 1840.

9. George B. Wilson, a black sailor, lived in New York City in the 1830s and 1840s. He worked to bring the exploitation and threats of enslavement faced by black seamen to public attention. Drawn into the broader movement for black civil rights after 1840, he attended local suffrage meetings and county and state conventions. Wilson also supported the attempt to revive the black national convention movement in 1840 and later served as a delegate to the 1847 black national convention at Troy, New York. After the Troy convention, he abandoned the sea and purchased one hundred acres of land from Gerrit Smith in upstate New York; he established a farm there in 1850. Willard B. Gatewood, Jr., ed., *Free Man of Color: The Autobiography of Willis Augustus Hodges* (Knoxville, Tenn., 1982), 80; *New York City Directory*, 1844; *Convention of Colored People . . . in Troy* (1847), 3, 6.

10. William H. Topp (1812–1857) of Albany, New York, was a successful, self-educated free black tailor of mixed African, Indian, and German ancestry. A respected community leader with a lifelong commitment to united black action and to reform, he participated in several local, state, and national black conventions, often as an officer or committee member. He served as president of the New York State Council of the Colored People (1854) and was a member of the National Council of the Colored People (1855)—short-lived coordinating bodies established to advance the status of blacks. Topp's name frequently appeared on remonstrances emanating from the Albany black community, where he assisted Stephen Myers in local underground railroad operations. Although an active member of the American Anti-Slavery Society and a friend and admirer of William Lloyd Garrison, Topp was a pragmatist in his approach to abolitionism and energetically pursued black political rights and activities. In 1852 he supported Free Soil presidential candidate John P. Hale and attempted to rally the Liberty

party behind him. Topp's reform interests included women's rights and integrated education; his support for the latter led him to oppose Frederick Douglass's 1853 proposal to establish a black industrial college, a position that injured the friendship between the two reformers. Topp urged free blacks to remain in the United States, as he considered colonization and emigration schemes to be tantamount to abandoning the slave. His health failed in 1857, and he died of consumption on 11 December. *E*, 10 December 1840 [3:0740]; *ASRL*, 30 June 1841 [4:0085]; *NSt*, 3 December 1847, 14, 21 January, 11, 18 February 1848, 19 January, 7 September 1849 [5:0054, 0957, 6:0135]; *FDP*, 15 January, 12 February, 10 September, 15 October 1852, 25 November 1853, 3 February, 25 August 1854, 25 May 1855 [7:0356, 0419, 0780, 8:0501, 0640]; *ASB*, 13 November 1852, 25 February 1854, 19, 26 May 1855 [9:0664]; *Lib*, 19 March 1852, 8 January 1858; *NASS*, 29 January 1846, 28 February, 19 December 1857 [5:0152]; Martin R. Delany, *The Condition, Elevation, Emigration and Destiny of the Colored People of the United States* (Philadelphia, Pa., 1852; reprint, New York, N.Y., 1969), 102; Merrill and Ruchames, *Letters of William Lloyd Garrison*, 4:379, 380–81; Foner and Walker, *Proceedings of the Black State Conventions*, 1:5–25, 54–75, 79–84 [7:0018]; Quarles, *Black Abolitionists*, 219.

3.
Thomas Van Rensellaer to Editor,
Monthly Illustrations of American Slavery
28 November 1847

The Mexican War heightened black abolitionist awareness of the federal government's role in expanding slave territory and protecting the institution. Thomas Van Rensellaer offered his observations on the war in a 28 November 1847 letter to *Monthly Illustrations of American Slavery*, a journal published by Quaker abolitionists Henry and Anna Atkins Richardson in Newcastle-upon-Tyne, England. From 1847 to 1850, this modest enterprise reprinted letters and accounts of slavery from American abolitionists in an attempt to mobilize British public opinion. Van Rensellaer's letter described the disastrous economic and human consequences of the war for both Mexico and the United States. By the end of the decade, black abolitionists, including Van Rensellaer, Frederick Douglass, and Henry Highland Garnet, explicitly linked the war to the extension of slavery; they all agreed that the "slave power"—those interests committed to protecting and expanding slavery—thoroughly dominated the federal government. *MIAS*, 1 January 1848, 1 May 1850 [5:0549]; Clare Taylor, ed., *British and American Abolitionists: An Episode in Transatlantic Understanding* (Edinburgh, Scotland, 1974), 301; John W. Blassingame, *The Frederick Douglass Papers*, ser. 1, 3 vols. to date (New Haven, Conn., 1979–), 1:308, 419; Joel Schor, *Henry Highland Garnet: A Voice of Black Radicalism in the Nineteenth Century* (Westport, Conn., 1977), 77, 88, 90–91.

New York, [New York]
Nov[ember] 28th, 1847

THE war that has been made on poor, helpless Mexico by this country is productive of evil, and nothing but evil. Our wicked government took such an extravagant position on the Oregon question with England, that they wrought the people up to *war heat*, and finding that England was not to be trifled with, they changed their destination from Oregon to Mexico; supposing that Mexico would be easy game, they eagerly sallied upon that unhappy republic, knowing nothing of the geography of the country or the capacity of their prey to defend itself.[1]

This war has already cost us nearly 100,000,000 of dollars, and the lives of about 50,000 Americans by sword and pestilence, and no nearer gaining a peace than at the beginning.[2]

This war has had the effect of raising the price of articles consumed by the poor; and not only so, but it is filling the land with widows and orphans; it is opening a floodgate through which to introduce a thousand paupers that will have to be supported by oppressing the poor to raise revenue to pay for pensions. Its effects on Mexico are still worse, because she is poor and ignorant, and compared with us, weak. Her peaceful villages and walled cities are battered down by our heavy artillery, and their helpless women and children slaughtered by hundreds, and left to seek shelter among the wild beasts of the forest. "Shall not I be avenged on such a nation as this?"[3] saith God.

Thos. Van Rensellaer

Monthly Illustrations of American Slavery (Newcastle-upon-Tyne, England), 1 January 1848.

1. Both the United States and Britain had claimed the Oregon country, a vast unsettled region extending from California to Alaska, since 1818. President James K. Polk aroused expansionist sentiment by demanding the Oregon country in his March 1845 inaugural address. In the year that followed, the United States and Britain came closer to armed conflict than at any time since the War of 1812. But in June 1846, after the beginning of the Mexican War, the two nations agreed to a treaty setting the boundary between the United States and the British North American Provinces at the forty-ninth parallel.

2. Van Rensellaer correctly estimates the financial cost of the Mexican War but greatly inflates the toll in human lives. Military expenditures exceeded $97,000,000, and about thirteen thousand American soldiers died during the war. Although Van Rensellaer wrote this letter two months after the conclusion of the fighting, the war did not officially end until the U.S. Senate ratified the Treaty of Guadalupe Hidalgo in March 1848. As part of the agreement, the United States paid another $18,000,000 to the Mexican government.

3. Van Rensellaer paraphrases Jeremiah 5:9, which was a divine warning to the Israelites for their immorality and corruption: "Shall I not punish them for these things? says the Lord; and shall I not avenge myself on such a nation."

4.
Essay by Joseph C. Holly
17 April 1848

By the late 1840s, black abolitionists had accepted the idea that slave-holding interests—the "slave power"—corrupted the South, animated racial prejudice in the North, and threatened American democracy; slavery had, in the words of one black leader, "pervaded every crevice and cranny of society." Joseph C. Holly, brother of emigration advocate James T. Holly, provided one of the more perceptive analyses of the slave power theory. His 17 April 1848 essay in the *North Star* described "the unhallowed connection and criminality of the North in relation to slavery." Holly argued that, from the nation's beginning, the North had conceded governmental authority to the South and assumed the financial burdens associated with slavery. In making these substantial political and economic concessions, the North had lost much of its sovereignty and forsaken its first principles of freedom and justice. The threat of the "slave power," as portrayed by Holly and other abolitionists, became a central theme in American politics during the 1850s. *NASS*, 19 May 1855 [9:0658]; David Brion Davis, *The Slave Power Conspiracy and the Paranoid Style* (Baton Rouge, La., 1969), 62–86.

April 17th, 1848
BROOKLYN, [New York]
American Slavery—its Effects upon the
Rights and Interests of the North
"If a people assist in fastening one end of a chain around the limbs of another, inevitable fate will sooner or later fasten the other end around their own necks."

We rejoice that it is an immutable law of Providence, in the regulation of human affairs, to order that individuals or communities cannot disregard and trample upon the rights of others without affecting their own rights and interests; that he has established the indivisibility of the human race an identity of their interest. We need no more infallible illustration of the workings of this Providential law than is presented in reviewing the unhallowed connection and criminality of the North in relation to slavery, and the effects of that institution on the rights and interests of the North.

In the formation of a constitution for the government of the confederacy, the North did not only mortgage every particle of its soil as a hunting ground for the bloodhounds of slavery, biped and quadruped, to dog the track of, and worry the panting fugitive from the worse than deathlike vale of Southern oppression; they did not only pledge every strong arm at the North to go to the South in case the slaves, goaded by oppression, should imitate the "virtues of their forefathers," and vindicate their rights by subscribing to the doctrine of Algernon Sydney—that "resistance to tyrants is obedience to God"[1]—and crush them in subjection to their galling yoke; but in the spirit of compromise and barter, stipulated that the slaveholder should have additional power in proportion as he became the great plunderer of human rights, the more insolent to the great declaration of fundamental principle, the substratum of all democratic institutions.

They agreed, in Art. 1st, Section 2d, of the Constitution, that representatives, and direct taxes, shall be apportioned among the several States which may be included within this Union, according to their respective numbers, which shall be determined by adding to the whole number of free persons, including those bound to service for a term of years, and excluding Indians not taxed, three-fifths of all other persons.

This provision allows slaveholders to count every five of their victims as three freemen in the apportionment of representatives to the popular branch of Congress—a representation which the lamented late John Q. Adams declared was an outward show, a representation of persons held in bondage;[2] in fact, a representation of the masters—the oppressor representing the oppressed—an exemplification of the art of committing the lamb to the tender custody of the wolf. By this arrangement, a slaveholder claiming two hundred of his fellow beings as property, "in a government professedly free," has the same weight in the national council as one hundred and twenty of his Northern brethren.

The advantage that the North supposed they would derive as a consideration for this bargain, was that the South should contribute in like proportion to the support of the government; "but here they got their foot in it," for armed with this overwhelming and consolidating political power, the South soon departed from this system, and *decreed* the indirect tax system, by which they threw the burden of supporting government almost entirely upon the shoulders of the North. The adoption of the impost system almost relieved the South from a partition in the support of government, as the principal ports of importation, as well as the principal consumption of imported goods are at the North. It is pretty well known that the laboring class at the South do not luxuriate in cloths and silks, wines and teas from abroad; and with these facts before him, one may venture to guess, though no Yankee, who contributes most to the support of government; so our Yankee pedlar sold his budget of political power for naught.

Having shorn Sampson of his locks, Delilah set about to get the green wisps wherewith to bind him;[3] the first that presented itself to her comprehensive vision was Louisiana. It was in vain that Jefferson, "who was not overscrupulous," declared that the Constitution was framed for the

government of territory defined to be United States territory by the treaty
of 1783; that the framers of that instrument never contemplated in its
provisions the admission of England, Holland, or any foreign State into
the Union. For a time our Sampson struggled. The North stood up boldly
for the Constitution;[4] but the coy maiden insisted on having this jewel to
decorate her casket,[5] and what could he do—poor impotent soul—but
yield; and thus was the constitutional barrier broken down, and the
South strengthened and secured for a time in her political ascendancy.
But owing to the influence of slavery upon the industrial classes, the tide
of emigration rolled North-westward, where it would not come in competition with that institution. Territorial governments were springing up
as if by magic of a wand, and knocking for admission into the confederacy of States;[6] the Northern Sampson's locks were growing out, and
Delilah was fearful of losing her power over him. The Constitution having been broken down, it was an easy matter to march through the
breach. Florida and Texas were other wisps to bind the North with—
were other jewels to decorate the political casket of the South. Against
each of these the North made a *faint* resistance; passed any number of
"rhetorical" resolves, well guarded with compromising "buts and ifs,"
and might have exclaimed, "Thy genius has triumphed, oh Delilah!"
And Sampson bows him to the dust; for these resolves were as impotent
as the famous "white man's resolution" in relation to President Polk's
indemnity will prove to be.[7]

But in the national Constitution are incorporated some guarantees for
freedom—the right of speech, the freedom of the press, the right of a
citizen of one State to the privileges and immunities of citizenship in
another State; these have been carried out extensively at the North; for
although the hand of violence has been raised against those that should
dare be so bold as to contend for a practical application of the principles
of "76," the sons of the South may stand over the very graves of those
who struggled and fell in defence of these principles, on the very spot
enriched by their patriot blood, and insult their hallowed memory by
declaring that "slavery is the cornerstone of democracy," that "all communities must settle down into classes of employers and laborers, and
that the former will sooner or later own the latter,"[8] and no hand of
violence will be raised against them. This is right. We want no weapons
but those of truth and right to combat these deluded sophistries, even
when backed by the learning, talents and sagacity of the Calhouns,
McDuffies and Rhetts,[9] or any other of the "model" republicans of
the Palmetto State. Cannons, brickbats, clubs and proscription, are the
weapons of tyranny and wrong.

But should any descendant of those who fought for liberty when it
meant something else than a "rhetorical flourish," who felt as the French
Republicans of '48 (honor to them!) felt, that liberty is the boon of

heaven, the birthright of man.[10] Go to South Carolina or most any of the slaveholding States, and advocate a practical application of these principles to the toiling masses; we are informed by modern democrats that "they will be seized upon, tried and hung, in spite of the interference of all governments, not excepting the general government of the United States."[11]

In 1812, this government contended with the most powerful maritime nation on the globe for "free trade and sailor's rights," the immunity of national flags, and yet in several of the Southern States, in violation of the Constitution, citizens, seamen from the North, are imprisoned, and if their captains, after being unjustly deprived of their services, will not pay the ransom of slavery, they are sold as chattels. The fact that they stand upon an American vessel, with an American commander, with the world-renowned stripes and stars floating above their heads, is no indemnity against such outrage.

Old Massachusetts, among whose granite hills are lurking whatever principle of freedom that remains to the degenerate sons of the pilgrim fathers, felt aggrieved at this treatment. With a Faneuil Hall and a Boston harbor in her, how could she fail to see that the right to imprison one of her citizens involved the right to imprison another, and with these old-fashioned, obsolete views, she sent commissioners to South Carolina and Louisiana to take cognizance of such cases, with a view of bringing them before the supreme tribunal for adjudication. But these ambassadors, on this peaceful and lawful mission, were driven from the soil of a sister State (!) by threats of violence, and one who felt his puritanic blood, and was not easily affrighted, was promised a coat of tar and feathers to assist him in making his flight, by a committee of Southern gentlemen! And thus was the sovereignty of a State insulted, in the person of her representative, and her constitutional rights trampled under foot.[12] Had some barbarous state in the Indian Archipelago, or in the Gulf of Mexico, refused to acknowledge the aristocratic titles of some American agent, the thunders of the Northern would cooperate with the Southern line in pronouncing vengeance upon the barbarians, and the cry of indemnity for the past and security for the future would resound through the executive and legislative halls, and be re-echoed in every grog-shop throughout the land. The Constitution is everything in its compromises in favor of the peculiar institution, but nothing in its guarantees for freedom.

When a Northern member, on the presentation of the Constitution of the State of Florida for the ratification of Congress, very politely suggested that one of its provisions conflicted with the national Constitution, a Southern representative rose with that air of command and arrogance peculiar to Southerners, and said: "We of the South sometimes find it necessary to enact laws for our personal safety, and when we find it so necessary, we care not how many clauses there are in *your constitu-tion* allowing or disallowing it, we will enact them." The Constitution is but another proof of the futility of any attempt at compromise between liberty and slavery, right and wrong; they are incompatible, incongruous, and wrong must ever strengthen at the expense of right.[13]

Having shown some of the effects of slavery upon the rights and lib-erty of the North, we will now present some few statistics of pecuniary consideration for prudent, calculating Yankees. It has been estimated, by those well calculated to know the relative proportion that the contribu-tion of the North to the national treasury by the impost system,[14] is that of three to one; and it must be recollected that all territories that have been purchased, and all wars in support of them, have been paid for out of the nation's "purse"; and it must be further recollected, that all such territory has been exclusively for one section; that slavery, that labor-degrading institution, has been established in them, and the self-respect-ing, working freemen of the North have been effectively excluded from any benefit of occupation, whil'st it was purchased out of the product of their industry. And now let us make a few calculations of the cost of these territories to the North:

Louisiana purchase	$ 15,000,000
Florida purchase	5,000,000
Texas' public debts	15,000,000
Mexican purchase and responsibility	18,000,000
Black Hawk war	9,000,000
Seminole war	20,000,000
Florida war	15,000,000
Mexican war, about	100,000,000
Total amount	$227,250,000[15]

Of this enormous sum, the North contributes one hundred and sev-enty million, two hundred and fifty thousand dollars, or three-fourths of the whole. This is indeed paying pretty dearly for the privilege of uphold-ing slavery, catching fugitives, and being tarred and feathered, to say nothing of the extra bills in the way of disabled soldiers, and widows of soldiers, made pensioners by these wars; but Jonathan[16] is a good-natured soul, and is content to call this national "glory." There can be no diversion of the national treasure for the improvement of rivers and harbors by which the hardy, industrious free-laborers of the North-west may be enabled to bring their products to a market on the seaboard, without jeopardizing life and property. Oh no! the Executive, the em-bodiment of slavery, wants it to sustain the national honor, and fight for a piece of Mexico. I am forcibly impressed with the truthfulness of the declaration of the Hon. J. R. Giddings,[17] that if the North cease to give pecuniary support to slavery, it would die of starvation in a single twelve months.

J. C. H.[18]

North Star (Rochester, N.Y.), 12 May 1848.

1. Holly incorrectly attributes this phrase to Sydney. It first appeared in the 14 December 1775 issue of the *Pennsylvania Evening Post* as the concluding line of an epitaph written for John Bradshaw, who presided over the commission that sentenced Charles I of England to death in 1649. Thomas Jefferson later used the motto on his personal seal.

2. In 1843 John Quincy Adams introduced a congressional measure to abolish the three-fifths clause of the U.S. Constitution. The bill stirred acrimonious debate but quickly died in committee. Adams called the clause a "fatal drop of Prussic acid in the Constitution." Samuel Flagg Bemis, *John Quincy Adams and the Union* (New York, N.Y., 1956), 446–47.

3. Holly refers to the biblical tale of the Israelite hero, Samson, from Judges 13–16. Samson, whose long hair was the source of incredible strength, frequently routed the Philistines in battle. In order to defeat him, the Philistines sent Delilah, an attractive woman, to seduce him. She cut his hair while he slept, bound him, and delivered him to his enemies.

4. The growth of American territory during the antebellum years raised constitutional questions. In 1803 the United States purchased the Louisiana Territory—an area of some 828,000 square miles—from France for $15,000,000. At first President Thomas Jefferson worried that the Constitution did not specifically authorize the acquisition of vast new lands and the incorporation of foreign citizens. But in time, even though Federalist leaders in New England charged that the Louisiana Purchase was a blatant attempt to expand the power of the Jeffersonians, slavery, and the South, Jefferson adopted a more pragmatic course. Louisiana was admitted as a slave state in 1812. In 1820 the petition for Missouri statehood raised the question of whether slavery would be allowed or prohibited in states carved from the rest of the Louisiana Purchase. As a compromise, Missouri was admitted as a slave state, and slavery was permitted in the Arkansas Territory but prohibited in the remaining territory north of latitude 36°30'. This so-called Missouri Compromise settled the question of slavery's extension until the Mexican War.

5. Holly refers to a small ornamental box, usually used to hold jewels or other valuables. Holly's "coy maiden" is the slave South, and the "jewels" are new slaveholding territories.

6. As American settlers moved westward in the 1830s and 1840s, population growth in the Northwest Territory and the northern part of the Louisiana Purchase prompted the admission of Michigan (1837), Iowa (1846), and Wisconsin (1848) as free states. In 1841 wagon trains began carrying American settlers into Oregon country, which was organized as the Oregon Territory in 1848.

7. Both Florida and Texas were admitted as slave states in 1845. The question of Florida statehood stirred only minor opposition, but Whig leaders strongly resisted Texas annexation, and abolitionists repeatedly denounced it as part of a

southern effort to expand slavery. Holly's mention of a "white man's resolution" refers to the Wilmot Proviso, a rider attached to the 1846 appropriations bill that funded the Mexican War. The measure, which was introduced by David Wilmot, a Democratic congressman from Pennsylvania, would have banned slavery from any territory acquired from Mexico as a result of the conflict. Many northern congressmen supported Wilmot's amendment as means of keeping both blacks and slavery out of western lands. Although the proviso was defeated, it fueled an impassioned national debate over slavery.

8. Holly paraphrases two statements by proslavery apologists that supported the theory that slavery was a positive good. The first came from an 1835 speech by George McDuffie to the South Carolina legislature. McDuffie argued that slavery was the foundation of a republican social order because it eliminated the tendency toward centralized governments, despotism, aristocracy, and other factors inimical to liberty. The second appeared in numerous speeches by John C. Calhoun between 1837 and 1850. Calhoun argued that society naturally divided into classes, an idea that found fullest expression in his posthumously published *Disquisition on Government* (1851). William S. Jenkins, *Pro-Slavery Thought in the Old South* (Chapel Hill, N.C., 1935), 78, 285–87.

9. South Carolinians John C. Calhoun, George McDuffie, and Robert Barnwell Rhett were among the South's most ardent and articulate defenders of slavery. Calhoun (1782–1850) was secretary of war during the War of 1812, vice-president in the administrations of John Quincy Adams and Andrew Jackson, U.S. senator (1832–43, 1845–50), and secretary of state. His political philosophy became the foundation for the South's theory of states' rights. McDuffie (1790–1851), another vigorous advocate of nullification, served his state in the House of Representatives and as governor, before sitting in the Senate (1842–46). Rhett (1800–1876), a close ally of Calhoun, represented southern interests in Congress from 1837 to 1860 and eventually helped lead the secession movement. *DAB*, 3:410–19, 12:34–36, 15:526–28.

10. The French Revolution of February 1848 ended monarchical rule and established a republican government based on universal manhood suffrage.

11. After 1830 southern whites were increasingly intolerant of antislavery activities. Disregarding constitutional guarantees of freedom of speech, many southern communities formed vigilance committees that suppressed open discussion of slavery by pressuring local postmasters to seize and burn antislavery publications, by intimidating editors and public speakers, and by harassing individuals believed to be sympathetic to the antislavery cause. Abolitionists in the South were often jailed, whipped, tarred and feathered, or banished for their "incendiary" actions. Russell B. Nye, *Fettered Freedom: Civil Liberties and the Slavery Controversy, 1830–1860* (East Lansing, Mich., 1949), 139–55.

12. Holly refers to a series of events relating to seamen's rights. Britain refused to recognize American neutrality during the Napoleonic Wars with France. Beginning in 1805, British naval vessels harassed U.S. shipping and threatened American sailors with impressment—being removed from merchant ships and forced to labor in the British navy. These violations of maritime rights helped cause the War of 1812. With a touch of irony, Holly compares British actions to the black seamen's acts, southern state laws requiring that free black sailors be imprisoned while their vessels remained in port and making their employers

liable for all costs of detention. Enforcement of these acts outraged antislavery leaders and led to diplomatic clashes with Britain, which employed many black sailors in its merchant fleet. Massachusetts officials requested federal intervention and, when Congress failed to respond, sent Samuel Hoar to South Carolina (1844) and Henry Hubbard to Louisiana (1845) to protest the odious practice and to challenge the laws in the courts. Mobs in Charleston and New Orleans forced both agents to return home before they could complete their tasks. Philip M. Hamer, "Great Britain, the United States, and the Negro Seamen's Acts, 1822–1848," *JSH* 1:19–28 (February 1935).

13. Holly paraphrases remarks made in 1845 by Senator William S. Archer of Virginia in a congressional debate over a bill to grant statehood to Florida and Iowa. Archer was responding to Rufus Choate of Massachusetts and George Evans of Maine, who objected to the proposed Florida constitution because it contained provisions that discriminated against free blacks. *Congressional Globe*, 1 March 1845, 379–80.

14. During the nineteenth century, tariffs (or the impost system) were a major source of federal revenue. Because of the North's commercial dominance, it paid a disproportionate percentage of these revenues.

15. Holly lists American territorial acquisitions during the antebellum period. These included the Louisiana Purchase (1803), the Florida Cession (1819), and the annexation of Texas (1845), in which the United States assumed the public debts of the former republic. By the Treaty of Guadalupe Hidalgo (1848), which ended the Mexican War, the United States agreed to pay Mexico $15,000,000 for the cession of 500,000 square miles of land and assumed $3,250,000 in claims by American citizens against Mexico. Several of these acquisitions led to warfare with Indian tribes in those regions, including the Black Hawk War (1832) in the upper Mississippi valley, the Seminole War (1817–18), and the Florida or Second Seminole War (1835–42).

16. "Brother Jonathan" was a popular nineteenth-century term for the United States. It is used here in reference to the North.

17. Joshua Reed Giddings (1795–1864) represented Ohio in the U.S. Congress from 1838 to 1858, first as a Whig, then as a Free Soiler and Republican. One of the first abolitionists elected to Congress, he assisted John Quincy Adams during the gag law controversy, opposed Texas annexation, repudiated the Mexican War, and regularly denounced proslavery legislation. James Brewer Stewart, *Joshua R. Giddings and the Tactics of Radical Politics* (Cleveland, Ohio, 1970).

18. Joseph Cephas Holly (1825–1855), the elder brother of black emigrationist James T. Holly, was born to free black parents in Washington, D.C. In 1844 the Holly family moved to Brooklyn. Joseph found work there as a shoemaker, gradually became involved in the antislavery movement, and in 1848 began to write articles on slavery for Frederick Douglass's *North Star*. The Holly brothers moved to Burlington, Vermont, in 1850 and established a bootmaking business with financial assistance from Lewis Tappan. Although they held diametrically opposed views on the emigration issue, they began to lecture together. Joseph attacked the colonization movement and his brother's emigration beliefs; he declared that by adopting either course, blacks would abandon the slave, sustain American racism, and signify a lack of faith that justice could be achieved in the United States. He led local protests against the American Colonization Society

and repeatedly affirmed his claim to American citizenship. Holly assured black audiences: "We can't be coaxed, cheated, hissed, or kicked out of our country."

Holly embodied the broad scope and varied nature of black abolitionism. He lectured both independently and for the American Anti-Slavery Society, attacked racism as strongly as he condemned slavery, promoted the black press, assisted fugitive slaves, and helped raise money to purchase slave families. Although he declared that "our improvement mainly depends upon our own efforts," he urged white abolitionists to help blacks become independent farmers, factory workers, and professionals. Like other black leaders of the period, he avoided ideological rigidity. Holly supported political abolitionists, while personally identifying with many Garrisonian principles. He backed the Garrisonian interpretation of the U.S. Constitution as a proslavery document but upheld Douglass's right to an opposing viewpoint. And even though he embraced moral suasion, he revered Toussaint L'Ouverture and Nat Turner and defended slave violence.

Holly continued to work with Douglass and canvassed Vermont as an agent for *Frederick Douglass' Paper*. In early 1852, he moved to Rochester, New York. As a leader of the local black community, he directed efforts to coerce city officials to hire black teachers, organized black voters, and was elected to the New York State Council of the Colored People. Holly also became a prolific antislavery poet. His verse appeared in *Frederick Douglass' Paper*, in the *Voice of the Fugitive*, and in a volume entitled *Freedom's Offering* (1853). When Holly died in January 1855 after a prolonged bout with tuberculosis, Douglass mourned his passing as a great loss to the antislavery cause. Blassingame, *Frederick Douglass Papers*, 2:514n; David M. Dean, *Defender of the Race: James Theodore Holly, Black Nationalist Bishop* (Boston, Mass., 1979), 3–7, 15, 20; *NSt*, 18 May 1849, 1 February 1850 [5:1092]; *FDP*, 9 October 1851, 22 January, 12 February, 11 March, 15 April 1852, 28 October 1853, 1 September, 15 December 1854, 12 January 1855 [7:0138, 0367, 0451, 0512, 8:0464, 9:0055]; Joseph C. Holly to William H. Seward, 26 October 1853, Seward Papers, NRU [8:0461]; Joseph C. Holly to William Lloyd Garrison, 31 December 1851, Anti-Slavery Collection, MB [7:0243]; *VF*, 9 September, 18 November 1852 [7:0829].

5.
Samuel Ringgold Ward to John H. Thomas, Ebenezer F. Simons, and Hiram Gillet
16 September 1848

Antislavery political parties offered blacks leadership opportunities denied to them in the major parties and in national antislavery organizations. Blacks enjoyed an unprecedented level of involvement in the Liberty party after its creation in 1840. As early as 1841, black leaders Theodore S. Wright, Charles B. Ray, and John J. Zuille served on the party's central nominating committee. Henry Highland Garnet and Samuel Ringgold Ward were leading stump speakers in party campaigns between 1840 and 1844. Ward later edited the *Impartial Citizen*, a party newspaper. Not all black leaders supported antislavery third parties, but all understood the symbolic value of black men seeking political office in the United States. On 14 September 1848, Ward was nominated for a seat in the New York legislature by a Liberty party convention at Cortland, New York, a gathering that he chaired. His letter of acceptance, written two days later to party officials, reflected the party's central concern with slavery and its broadening interest in black suffrage, temperance, land reform, and debtors' rights. David E. Swift, *Black Prophets of Justice: Activist Clergy before the Civil War* (Baton Rouge, La., 1989), 134; *LS*, 14 September 1843 [4:0669]; *CD*, 23 April, 9 September 1848.

Cortlandville, [New York]
Sept[ember] 16, 1848

GENTLEMEN:[1]

That partiality of your recent convention, which did me the honor, to place my name before the electors of this county for a seat in the Assembly, receives as it deserves my warmest thanks. You are aware, however, that could my own voice have prevailed in that convention, a different result would have been arrived at. But submitting to the will of those with whom it has always been my pleasure to act politically, I deem it due to the party with whom you and the convention represent, that you should have a full and explicit statement of the political views and principles of your candidate. As some two weeks will elapse before I shall have opportunity to address my fellow-citizens in the several towns in this county, this duty seems to be the more imperative.

I agree with any and all of my fellow-citizens who deprecate the existence of human slavery, over territory now free. We as a nation could never look the civilized world in the face, if, after having by Congress and Treaty, acquired an immense territory of country, now free—free by the Imperial Decree of a semi-barbarous people through their Government—we should establish in that territory a system of oppression and slavery, "the vilest that ever saw the sun." I am decidedly in favor of our State Legislature's maintaining its solemn and repeated expressions of emphatic dissent to the establishing of slavery in our newly acquired territory either by "extension" or "diffusion." But while I am so fully of the belief that slavery ought not to be established in New Mexico and California, I am equally clear in the opinion that that clause of the "Wilmot Proviso," so called, which provides for the recovery of fugitive slaves,[2] is irreconcilable alike with the dictates of our holy religion, and the most precious provisions of the Federal constitution, and to the sentiments of our common humanity as frequently exhibited in the enlightened, patriotic, and progressive state of public opinion on this subject. If therefore, I were a member of our State Legislature, while I should use my utmost influence for the passage of resolutions instructing our senators and representatives in Congress to wield the power intrusted to them, so as if possible to prevent the extension or diffusion of slavery, I should at the same time, protest most heartily against any bill, or any clause of a bill, which should contain the odious, anti-republican and anti-christian provision referred to.

I am in favor of the immediate abolition of slavery in the District of Columbia; and I believe the great state of New York, through her Legislature, ought as speedily as possible to place her influence in an unequivocal position on this important subject. So I think New York ought at once to express the most solemn protest against the inter-state traffic in slaves, who, though they be slaves, are American-born citizens and subjects of the same great plan of redemption upon which the hopes of us all are based.

It is important, too, in my opinion, that our relations with the republic of Hayti should be placed upon such a basis as would relieve our commerce with that Republic from the inconveniences to which it is now subject, in consequence of the unjust treatment of our Government towards Hayti. We acknowledged the independence of Texas within a few weeks of the battle of San Jacinto,[3] though Texas proved herself, in less than eight years, incapable of maintaining that Independence—and indeed, incapable of maintaining continued existence as an independent Republic. Why should Hayti, who has maintained her independence half a century—two-thirds of the time that we have maintained our own—be treated in a manner so markedly different? New York, whose commerce with Hayti is greater than that of any other State in the Union, should be foremost in the efforts necessary to induce our Government to treat our sister republic, Hayti, according to the claims of justice and propriety.[4]

Among the local subjects demanding speedy action in a reformatory direction, at the hands of our State Legislature, is

1. The passage of a law prohibiting the sale of intoxicating drinks, as a beverage, in any quantities whatever, and the visiting upon the dealer the expenses accruing to the county and state from his traffic. I mean the expenses of the maintenance of Paupers, and the prosecutions of criminals, where such expenses arise out of intemperance. If elected, I should, at the earliest practicable moment, bring this matter before the Legislature, and endeavor to secure in its behalf the aid of the strong, the good, and the true.

2. I am not clear as to whether the present constitution provides for the alleviation of the clause, in that document, which limits the Right of Suffrage in the case of colored citizens. If such provision is made, I am in favor of its immediate use; if not, I pledge myself to use all of my moral and political power, whether in or out of office, for the restoration of that right to the 40,000 citizens now unjustly deprived of it, at the earliest practical period.[5]

3. The passage of a law placing the homestead of a debtor beyond the reach and control of a creditor. As many reasons, in my opinion, exist for the passage of such a law as for the abolition of imprisonment for debt, or for the exemption of certain property, by the laws now in being. Nor could I, as a citizen, or legislator, give my influence in behalf of the continued existence of that law which places a poor man on the limits, in default of paying court costs and lawyers' fees. Our courts and lawyers ought to have the same power over debtors as have other creditors, and no more.[6]

Finally, I have the honor to rank myself among those who are laboring to bring about that reform in legislation which shall forever prohibit speculations in the public lands. The sooner our State and National governments assume and maintain their God-given relations to the poor and the landless, and decree to them homes, and refuse one great domain, and prohibit the onwership of more than from one to two hundred acres thereof by any one individual, the better.

With this frank expression of my political sentiments, gentlemen, you are at liberty to do as you shall see proper, and if it shall occur to you desirable, for any reasons whatever, to throw them in a public manner before the electors of the county, you have my consent to your doing so. Your obedient servant,

S. R. WARD

Cortland Democrat (N.Y.), 16 September 1848.

1. John H. Thomas (1818–?), an attorney, Ebenezer F. Simons (1794–?), a tanner, and Hiram Gillet (1804–?), a farmer, served together on the Cortland County central committee of the Liberty party in 1848. All three were of New England background. Thomas, who was also active in statewide party affairs, edited the *Liberty Party Paper* and served on the party's state and national central

committees. He supported the temperance movement, helped establish the Syracuse Vigilance Committee, and aided in the well-known October 1851 rescue of fugitive slave William "Jerry" McHenry. U.S. Census, 1850; *IC*, 4 July 1849, 6, 13 February, 12 June, 26 October 1850 [6:0397, 0521, 0651]; *SDS*, 7 October 1850 [6:0603]; *FDP*, 26 June 1851 [6:0979]; Samuel Ringgold Ward, *Autobiography of a Fugitive Negro* (London, 1855; reprint, New York, N.Y., 1968), 398–417.

2. In the spring of 1848, while Congress debated the Wilmot Proviso, Senator Andrew Pickens Butler of South Carolina introduced a separate bill to strengthen the Fugitive Slave Law of 1793. Although the bill received little attention at the time, it was reintroduced by Senator James Mason of Virginia two years later and became the Fugitive Slave Law of 1850. Thomas D. Morris, *Free Men All: The Personal Liberty Laws of the North, 1780–1861* (Baltimore, Md., 1974), 131–32.

3. Ward is mistaken. American recognition of Texas did not follow "within a few weeks" of the defeat of Mexican forces by the Texas militia at San Jacinto on 21 April 1836. Although the American public extended sympathy and support, formal recognition of the Lone Star Republic was delayed by President Andrew Jackson until after the 1836 presidential election. The United States formally recognized Texas independence on 3 March 1837, Jackson's last day in office.

4. Although Haiti declared its independence in 1804, the U.S. Congress repeatedly refused to extend diplomatic recognition, even after many European nations had done so. This created obstacles for commerce, but despite impediments, Haiti and the United States developed extensive trade relations during the antebellum period. Southern states, fearing the seditious influence of Caribbean free blacks in their ports, tended to discourage direct commerce with Haiti. As a consequence, most of the trade went through northern ports, most notably New York City. The exigencies of the Civil War finally compelled Congress to grant formal recognition to Haiti in 1862. Rayford Logan, *The Diplomatic Relations of the United States and Haiti, 1776–1891* (Chapel Hill, N.C., 1941), 112, 191–207, 277, 298, 302–7.

5. After considerable debate, the 1846 New York state constitutional convention voted to retain the property restrictions on black suffrage that had been mandated in the 1821 state constitution. This required blacks to own at least $250 in real property to be eligible to vote. In deference to the advocates of expanded suffrage, the convention submitted the new constitution and the issue of unrestricted black franchise to a statewide referendum. But New York voters rejected equal suffrage by more than a two to one majority. Phyllis F. Field, *The Politics of Race: The Struggle for Black Suffrage in the Civil War Era* (Ithaca, N.Y., 1982), 41–61.

6. The Stillwell Act of 1831 abolished imprisonment for debt in New York state, except in cases where the creditor alleged fraud. Because of this clause, some debtors continued to be imprisoned through the 1880s. Ward's remark concerning debtors being placed "on the limits" refers to the common practice of requiring convicted debtors to reside within "prison bounds," a restricted area outside the prison. Peter J. Coleman, *Debtors and Creditors in America* (Madison, Wis., 1974), 118–19.

6.
Mary Ann Shadd Cary to Frederick Douglass
25 January 1849

Traditional avenues to leadership positions—politics, business, and the professions—were usually circumscribed or closed to blacks. Black leaders often established their credentials through community activities and organizations, especially the church. As a result, the black clergy wielded enormous influence. Yet many ministers lacked formal education and training in theology, relying instead on conversion experiences to validate their call to the pulpit. These less sophisticated clergymen tended to emphasize spiritual matters, while ignoring the social and political problems of the black community. This troubled some members of the educated black elite. Mary Ann Shadd Cary, a young black teacher, discussed contemporary black leadership in a 25 January 1849 letter to the *North Star*. She expressed concern that the black convention movement, which was guided by some of the most capable black leaders of the day, had such limited influence. But her harshest criticism fell on the black clergy. Cary rebuked uneducated ministers for "their gross ignorance and insolent bearing" and for neglecting pressing temporal issues, particularly civil rights. Frederick Douglass and other black abolitionists shared Cary's viewpoint; they criticized the clergy for their accommodating tone and submissive behavior toward injustice and oppression. These charges sometimes stemmed from anticlerical sentiment or opposition to separate churches, but the most persistent criticism came from educated, abolitionist clergymen such as Daniel Payne, William Watkins, Charles B. Ray, and Samuel R. Ward, who competed with the uneducated clergy for influence in the black community. *CA*, 17, 24 June, 1 July 1837, 27 January 1838 [2:0077, 0088, 0095, 0367]; *VF*, 17 December 1851, 4 November 1852 [7:0225, 0815]; *NSt*, 25 February 1848.

WILMINGTON, [Delaware]
Jan[uary] 25, 1849

FREDERICK DOUGLASS:

Though native of a different State, still in anything relating to our people, I am insensible of boundaries. The statement of Rev. H. H. Garnet which appeared in the *North Star* of the 19th inst., relative to the very wretched condition of thirty thousand of our people in your State,[1] and your willingness to listen to suggestions from anyone interested, has induced me to send you these lines, which I beg you to insert if you think worthy.

The picture he drew, sir, of thirty thousand, is a fair representation of many more thousands in this country. The moral and intellectual debasement portrayed, is true to the life. How, in view of everything, can it be otherwise? We bring a heavy charge against the church and people of this country, which they themselves can hardly deny; but have we not been, and are we not still, "adding fuel to the flame"; or do our efforts, to the contrary, succeed as we have reason to expect? We are not satisfied with the result in every way—maybe we have reason for not being. With others, I have for some time doubted the efficiency of the means for the end. Do you not think, sir, that we should direct our attention more to the farming interest than hitherto? I suggest this, as concerning the entire people. The estimation in which we would be held by those in power, would be quite different, were we producers, and not merely, as now, consumers. He, sir, proposed a Convention without distinction of caste —a proposition which no doubt will be acceptable, because by exchanging views with those who have every advantage, we are materially benefitted. Persons likely to associate with our people in such manner, are generally educated people, and possessed of depth of sentiment. Their influence on us should not be lightly considered. We have been holding conventions for years[2]—have been assembling together and whining over our difficulties and afflictions, passing resolutions on resolutions to any extent; but it does really seem that we have made but little progress, considering our resolves. We have put forth few practical efforts to an end. I, as one of the people, see no need for our distinctive meetings, if we do not do something. We should do more, and talk less. What intellectually we most need, and the absence of which we most feel, is the knowledge of the white man, a great amount of which, by intercourse in public meetings, &c., we could glean, and no possible opportunity to seize upon which should be allowed to escape. Should not the importance of his literature upon us, and everything tending to add to his influence, be forcibly impressed, and we be directed to that course? The great fault of our people, is in imitating his follies; individual enterprise and self-reliance are not sufficiently insisted upon. The influence of a corrupt clergy among us, sapping our every means, and, as a compensation, inculcating ignorance as a duty, superstition as true religion—in short, hanging like millstones about our necks, should be faithfully proclaimed. I am willing to be convinced to the contrary, if possible; but it does really seem to me that our distinctive churches and the frightfully wretched instruction of our ministers—their gross ignorance and insolent bearing, together with the sanctimonious garb, and by virtue of their calling, a character for mystery they assume, is attributable more of the downright degradation of the free colored people of the North, than from the effect of corrupt public opinion; for, sir, notwithstanding the cry of prejudice against color, some think it will vanish by a change of condition, and that we can, despite this prejudice, change that condition.

The ministers assume to be instructors in every matter, a thing we would not object to, provided they taught, even in accordance with the age; but in our literature, they hang tenaciously to exploded customs (as if we were not creatures of progress as well as others), as they do in everything else. The course of some of our high priests, makes your humble servant, and many others, think money, and not the good of the people, is at the bottom. The great aim of these gentlemen now, is secrecy in all affairs where our spiritual welfare is being considered. Our conferences, they say, are too public. The open-stated people and laymen learn, as they should not, the transactions in conference and sessions, of these men of God. Depend upon it, sir, "men love darkness rather than light, because their deeds are evil."[3] One thing is clear; this hiding the light under a bushel, is not, to those who dare think, very satisfactory; their teaching tends to inculcate submission to them in all things. "Pay no attention to your perishing bodies, children, but get your souls converted; prepare for heaven. The elective franchise would not profit you; a desire for such things indicates worldly-mindedness." Thus any effort to a change of condition by our people is replied to, and a shrinking, priest-rid people, are prevented from seeing clearly. The possibility of final success, when using proper means, the means to be used, the possibility of bringing about the desired end ourselves, and not waiting for the whites of the country to do so, should be impressed on the people by those teachers, as they assume to be the only true ones; or at least there should be no hindrance to their seeing for themselves. Yours for a better condition,

M. A. SHADD[4]

North Star (Rochester, N.Y.), 23 March 1849.

1. Henry Highland Garnet's 12 January 1849 letter to the *North Star* argued that black self-improvement depended upon religious institutions. He claimed that the thirty thousand New York blacks living west of Albany were too widely dispersed, because of the effects of racism, to adequately support churches. He called for an interracial convention to promote religious activity among western New York blacks and the establishment of a state society to sponsor agents and missionaries to the western counties. The convention was never held. *NSt*, 19 January 1849.

2. Black national conventions were held annually between 1830 and 1835 in Philadelphia and New York. A rejuvenated national convention movement organized meetings at Buffalo (1843), Troy (1847), and Cleveland (1848). Several state conventions were also held during those years.

3. Cary quotes from John 3:19.

4. Mary Ann Shadd Cary (1823–1893) was the oldest of thirteen children born to free blacks Abraham and Harriet Shadd of Wilmington, Delaware. Abraham Shadd, a prosperous shoemaker and respected political activist, was a leader of the black convention movement, an anticolonizationist, and an early member of the American Anti-Slavery Society. The Shadds were devoted to education,

and Mary Ann began her studies by attending a school for free blacks sponsored by the African School Society of Wilmington. After moving to West Chester, Pennsylvania, in the mid-1830s, the Shadds enrolled Mary Ann in a Quaker-owned private school for free blacks, where she was tutored by Quaker antislavery activist Phoebe Darlington. For the next twelve years, Mary Ann Shadd Cary taught at black schools in the mid-Atlantic region and in New York City. Her experiences led her to publish *Hints for the Colored People of the North* (1849), an analysis of the manner by which the northern political economy repressed blacks. The pamphlet began Cary's lifelong examination of the interrelationship between economics and racism.

In 1851 Cary immigrated to Canada West with her brother Isaac and her father, hoping to assist blacks fleeing there after passage of the Fugitive Slave Law of 1850. Settling in Windsor, she opened a school for blacks and wrote *Notes on Canada West* (1852), an immigration guide for fugitives. In March 1853, she joined with Samuel Ringgold Ward to publish the first edition of the *Provincial Freeman*, a newspaper addressed to Canadian blacks. A year later, she helped transform the paper into a regularly published, Toronto-based weekly. Between 1854 and 1857, Cary, the first black woman newspaper editor in North America, dominated the journal despite staff and location changes. She used the paper to express her commitment to integration, her criticism of self-segregated black Canadian communities, and her vision of Canada as a permanent place of settlement. She also attacked corruption and mismanagement among the black and white leaders of the Canadian fugitive slave community.

In January 1856, Mary Ann married Thomas J. Cary, a Toronto businessman and antislavery activist who died in 1860. The Carys had two children. From 1860 to 1863, Mary Ann Shadd Cary operated a black school at Chatham. She also penned numerous letters to the *Weekly Anglo-African* and *Liberator* and edited Osborne P. Anderson's memoir, *A Voice from Harpers Ferry* (1861). During the last years of the Civil War, she recruited black soldiers for the Union army. Cary moved to Detroit in 1864 and continued to teach. After settling in Washington, D.C., in 1869, she served as principal of a black grammar school (1872–84) and continued her reform activities as a suffragist and as an advocate of black economic self-sufficiency. In 1883 Cary received a law degree from Howard University. *NAW*, 1:300–301; *DANB*, 552–53; Harold Hancock, "Mary Ann Shadd Cary: Negro Editor, Educator, and Lawyer," *DH* 15:187–94 (April 1973); Jim Bearden and Linda Jean Butler, *Shadd: The Life and Times of Mary Shadd Cary* (Toronto, Ontario, 1977).

7.
William Wells Brown to Francis W. Bird
19 April 1849

Black abolitionist lecturers usually reached their largest audiences when they operated under the auspices of an established white antislavery society that had the resources necessary to finance, organize, and promote a tour. But experienced black abolitionists often assumed managerial responsibilities for newcomers to the antislavery lecture circuit, particularly fugitive slaves. Benjamin F. Roberts coordinated Henry "Box" Brown's New England tour in 1850, and William Wells Brown introduced William and Ellen Craft to antislavery audiences. The Crafts were celebrities in antislavery circles for their daring escape from Georgia slavery during the Christmas holidays of 1848. For the first five months of 1849, Brown arranged their tour and accompanied them throughout eastern Massachusetts. His 19 April 1849 letter to Francis W. Bird, an East Walpole antislavery politician, demonstrates how their lectures were announced and promoted. The Crafts gave a series of five speeches, which Brown scheduled in Norfolk County, south of Boston, during late April. After being threatened by slave catchers in 1850, the Crafts fled to England, where Brown rejoined them to orchestrate a British tour. *Lib*, 20 April 1849; Farrison, *William Wells Brown*, 136; R. J. M. Blackett, *Beating against the Barriers: Biographical Essays in Nineteenth-Century Afro-American History* (Baton Rouge, La., 1986), 96–98.

> 21 Cornhill
> [Boston, Massachusetts]
> April 19th, [18]49

My Dear friend:[1]

I have appointed a meeting for your place, to be held on Sunday evening April 29th. The "Georgia Fugitives"[2] will be with me. I will leave the getting up of the meeting with you. If I can find an Express, I will send you a few hand bills.

[If] you think fit, you can have a meeting during the day. We shall be at Walpole, on Saturday evening, and should like to have a meeting there and go to your place[,] E. Walpole, on Sunday morning. I will send bills enough for both places. Will you please see to it. Faithfully your friend

> Wm. W. Brown

P.S. The Liberator is just from press and I find a mistake made as regards my being at your place. It says East Walpole Saturday 28th, that is wrong. I am to be at Walpole on Saturday, and at E. Walpole on Sunday. Yours in haste,

> W. W. B.

Miscellaneous Manuscripts, Houghton Library, Harvard University, Cambridge, Massachusetts. Published by permission.

1. Francis W. Bird (1809–1894), a successful paper manufacturer and anti-slavery politician from East Walpole, Massachusetts, served several terms in the state legislature and helped form the Massachusetts Republican party. His "Bird Club," a regular gathering of local political abolitionists, dominated statewide Republican politics throughout the 1860s. Bird promoted black rights, worked closely with the state's black abolitionist leaders, and aided the Boston Vigilance Committee. Merrill and Ruchames, *Letters of William Lloyd Garrison*, 4:458; Eric Foner, *Reconstruction: America's Unfinished Revolution, 1863–1877* (New York, N.Y., 1988), 469, 482; Friedman, *Gregarious Saints*, 229, 244–47; *NASS*, 4 March 1865 [15:0771].

2. Brown refers to fugitive slaves Ellen and William Craft. Ellen Craft (1826–1890) was born in Clinton, Georgia, the daughter of her master and his slave Maria. At age eleven, she was given to her mistress's daughter as a wedding present and sent to Macon, Georgia, to live. There she met William Craft (1824–1900). William's family had been sold to pay their master's debts, and William had been mortgaged to a local banker, then apprenticed to a cabinetmaker. William and Ellen devised an ingenious plan to escape slavery, and on the day after Christmas 1848, they executed it. Ellen, whose complexion was nearly white, disguised herself in the clothes of a young southern gentleman. She wore tinted glasses, put a poultice on her face, and wrapped her arm up in a sling to prevent being asked for a signature. Then, under the pretext of seeking special medical treatment in Philadelphia, Ellen and William, who acted as her servant, began a thousand-mile journey to freedom. They took a train to Savannah and then alternated between trains and ships, narrowly avoiding detection on several occasions during their four-day journey.

In late January 1849, the Crafts moved to Boston, where William found work as a carpenter and Ellen as a seamstress. They soon joined William Wells Brown on the antislavery lecture circuit and became two of the most celebrated fugitive slaves in American reform circles. In mid-October 1850, when two slave catchers appeared in Boston to take them back to slavery, the Crafts were hidden by black abolitionist Lewis Hayden. After being "officially" married by Theodore Parker, they fled Boston on 7 November in the company of Samuel May, Jr. They traveled to Portland, Maine, then on to Nova Scotia, and finally sailed to safety in England.

The Crafts spent the next nineteen years as English residents. Early in 1851, they again joined William Wells Brown for a series of lectures to British antislavery audiences, counterpointing Brown's analysis of slavery with the narrative of their daring escape. Between 1851 and 1854, they lived at Ockham School in Surrey, a vocational training institute, where they learned to read and write in return for vocational teaching services. The first of their five children was born at Ockham. In 1854 William returned to the lecture circuit to champion the free produce movement. During the mid-1850s, William and Ellen settled in West London where they entertained many black abolitionists who were touring England. In 1859 they helped form the Garrison-influenced London Emancipation

Society. One year later, they published their narrative, *Running a Thousand Miles for Freedom*.

Throughout the 1860s, Ellen worked for freedmen's aid societies and women's rights associations in England. William spent a number of years in Whydah, Dahomey, as an agent for the African Aid Society, a group concerned with promoting education, trade, and free labor cotton production. He founded a successful vocational school in 1865 and directed it until 1867. In 1869 the Crafts returned to the United States and settled in Cambridge, Massachusetts. By 1875 they had established a cooperative agricultural community and school on eighteen hundred acres of land in Byron County, Georgia—the homeland from which they had escaped twenty-seven years earlier. William Craft and Ellen Craft, *Running a Thousand Miles for Freedom* (London, 1860); *NAW*, 1:396–98; Blackett, *Beating against the Barriers*, 87–137.

8.
Circular by the Provisional Committee
of the *Impartial Citizen*
August 1849

Throughout the antebellum era, black newspapers struggled to survive.
Limited subscription lists and scant advertising revenues kept them de-
pendent upon the generosity and goodwill of the reform community.
Black women's groups were important sources of support. The Women's
Association of Philadelphia and the North Star Association of Rochester
aided Frederick Douglass's *North Star*. In July 1849, black women from
New York state formed the Provisional Committee to raise money for
Samuel Ringgold Ward's *Impartial Citizen*. One month later, they published a circular announcing plans to hold a fair. The advertisement
strengthened a call for funds by highlighting the importance of the black
press. The committee netted $34 for the *Impartial Citizen* at its mid-
September event. Through a variety of activities—fairs, sewing circles,
and church societies—black women advanced the antislavery cause, and
supporting the black press was one of their most significant contributions. *NSt*, 7 September 1849, 5 September 1850, 23 January 1851
[6:0137, 0570]; *IC*, 25 July, 19 September 1849, 26 October 1850
[6:650–51].

Aug[ust] 1849
FAIR IN AID OF THE *IMPARTIAL CITIZEN*
That the press should be sustained when it boldly and fearlessly advocates our rights, and when it really and truly represents us, is evident to
all. That a Reform Paper like the *Impartial Citizen*[1] cannot sustain itself
without the aid of its friends, has been demonstrated too often and too
clearly to admit of a shadow of a doubt. And that it is the duty of
Reformers to contribute of their means, time and talents for the sustenance of such a Press is equally unquestionable.

Feeling in some measure the force of these truths, the undersigned
have determined, with the Divine assistance, to hold a FAIR to aid the
self-sacrificing Editor and Publisher of the *Impartial Citizen*, in the City
of Syracuse, on the 11th, 12th, and 13th days of September next (during
the time of the State Agricultural Fair),[2] in the Lecture Room of the
Congregational Church.

The friends not only of SAMUEL R. WARD, but of the three millions
of slaves, and the six hundred thousand nominally free colored citizens,
with whom he is identified, and in whose behalf he has for years toiled,
the friends of Liberty, and Human Progress, the friends of Christ and His

crushed and insulted and outraged Poor, are earnestly entreated to give us their countenance and encouragement on the occasion.

During the evenings there will be speaking and singing of a superior order.

"Come over and help us."

MARY A. JEFFREY } Geneva
JULIA W. CONDOL }

Mrs. J. W. QUINCEY, Auburn

Mrs. J. C. FOSTER } Syracuse
Mrs. J. W. LOGUEN }

MALVINA R. SEARS, Newark, N.J.

Mrs. C. HIGHGATE, Albany

MARTHA M. WRIGHT, Geneva

JULIA W. GARNET, Peterboro

CHARLOTTE DUFFIN, Geneva

Mrs. JOHN PETERSON, N. York[3]

Articles intended for the Fair may be sent to any of the above named ladies, or to Seymour King, Esq., Syracuse.[4]

JULIA W. GARNET, Directress
MARY A. JEFFREY, Treasurer
MARTHA M. WRIGHT,
Corresponding Sec'y

Impartial Citizen (Syracuse, N.Y.), 5 September 1849.

1. The *Impartial Citizen*, which began publication in Syracuse on 14 February 1849, was the product of a merger between Samuel Ringgold Ward's Cortland (N.Y.) *True American* and Stephen Myers's Albany *Northern Star and Freeman's Advocate*. The semimonthly sheet carried news of antislavery, temperance, and other reform movements in western New York. Ward reported on his lecture tours and presented his personal views on political, social, and religious issues. Myers ended his affiliation with the *Citizen* in June 1849, and at that time, Ward converted the paper into a weekly Liberty party organ. By the end of its first year, the *Citizen* had seventeen hundred subscribers (out of the two thousand Ward thought necessary to insure its success). Delinquent subscribers created financial difficulties, which were only partially alleviated by donations from abolitionist Gerrit Smith and women's antislavery fairs. Despite financial problems, Ward and his assistant Seymour King published the paper in Syracuse through 19 June 1850, suspended publication briefly, and resumed on 10 July 1850 in Boston. Ward considered merging the *Citizen* with *Frederick Douglass' Paper*. Instead he discontinued publication in 1851, declared bankruptcy, and moved to Canada. Although Jermain W. Loguen, a former subscription agent for the *Citizen*, accused Ward of defrauding subscribers, Ward asserted that the paper failed because less than one-tenth of the subscribers had paid, and many stopped subscriptions "without paying up arrearages." *IC*, 28 February, 14 March, 17 June,

25 July, 5 December 1849, 13 February, 19 June, 14 September, 7 December 1850; Ronald K. Burke, "The *Impartial Citizen* of Samuel Ringgold Ward," *JQ* 49:759–60 (Winter 1972); *NSt*, 5 June, 30 October 1851; *PF*, 19 June 1851; *FDP*, 26 June, 30 October 1851; *VF*, 29 July 1852 [7:0677]; Quarles, *Black Abolitionists*, 88.

2. In 1841 the New York State Agricultural Society began sponsoring annual agricultural fairs to promote agriculture and animal husbandry and to educate farmers about new tools and techniques. The 1849 fair, which was held in Syracuse in early September, attracted a large number of black visitors from throughout western New York. Wayne C. Neely, *The Agricultural Fair* (New York, N.Y., 1935), 78, 95; *IC*, 5, 26 September 1849.

3. The women of the committee—most of them wives of black ministers, teachers, barbers, and laborers—shared antislavery work with their husbands. The majority were young, were freeborn in the North, and had recently become active in the abolitionist movement. Those few with greater experience in the movement, and whose husbands were prominent activists, took the lead.

Julia Ward Williams Garnet (1811–1870), the committee's director, was born in Charleston, South Carolina, but moved to Boston at an early age. After studying briefly at Prudence Crandall's school in Canterbury, Connecticut, and the Noyes Academy in Canaan, New Hampshire, she taught for several years in Boston. She married Henry Highland Garnet in 1841; only a daughter, Mary, survived childhood. In addition to organizing fund-raising bazaars for the *Impartial Citizen*, Julia Garnet presided over the Free Labor Bazaar, which accompanied the 1851 World Peace Congress in London, England. When the Garnets moved to Stirling, Jamaica, in 1852, she directed the Female Industrial School there. After their return to New York City in the mid-1850s, she operated a store at 174 West Thirtieth Street. Following emancipation, she did relief work among the freedmen in Washington, D.C.

Several other women had substantial local or regional antislavery experience. Caroline Storum Loguen (1817–1867), who married Jermain Wesley Loguen in 1840, helped her husband aid and protect fugitive slaves and spoke at First of August celebrations in Syracuse. Julia Condol (1825–?), the only unmarried woman on the committee, was originally from New England; her family had been prominent there in black temperance and moral reform efforts during the 1830s. She served as president of the Ladies' Sewing Society of Geneva, which organized fairs to benefit Henry Highland Garnet's antislavery endeavors. Mary A. Jeffrey (1810–?), the committee's treasurer, was a native of New Jersey. She was president of the Geneva Ladies' Anti-Slavery Society, which helped sponsor black lecturers like Frederick Douglass. Jeffrey represented Ontario County, New York, at the 1853 black national convention at Rochester and later served as treasurer of the county auxiliary of the National Council of the Colored People. Martha Wright, Jeffrey, Eliza G. Peterson (1815–1874), and Charlotte Duffin (1831–?) were the wives of abolitionists active at the state level. Richard Wright, Jason Jeffrey, John Peterson, and James W. Duffin took part in black state and national conventions and in the campaign to expand black suffrage in New York. The work of Hannah Highgate (1820–?), Catherine Quincey (1821–?), Malvina Sears (1820–?), Harriet Foster (1827–?), and their husbands—Charles Highgate, Joseph Quincey, William Sears, and John C. Foster—was more localized. *CR*, 22

January 1870; *CA*, 14 November 1840, 22 May, 21 August 1841; *IC*, 25 July 1846, 3 October 1849; *FDP*, 24 June, 16 December 1853; Martin Burt Pasternak, "Rise Now and Fly to Arms: The Life of Henry Highland Garnet" (Ph.D. diss., University of Massachusetts, 1981), 54–56, 60, 112–13, 120–21, 244; Schor, *Henry Highland Garnet*, 124–26; Foner and Walker, *Proceedings of the Black State Conventions*, 2:4–13, 37–41, 54–75, 99–101; *Minutes of the National Convention of Colored Citizens: Held at Buffalo, on the 15th, 16th, 17th, 18th and 19th of August 1843* (New York, N.Y., 1843), 10; *Proceedings of the Colored National Convention, Held in Philadelphia, October 16th, 17th and 18th, 1855* (Salem, N.J., 1856), 6–7; U.S. Census, 1850; *NSt*, 22 September 1848.

4. Seymour King operated an employment agency in Syracuse and was the authorized agent for several reform journals and causes, including Samuel R. Ward's *Impartial Citizen*, Jane G. Swisshelm's Pittsburgh *Saturday Visiter*, and the Ladies' Literary and Progressive Improvement Society of Buffalo. He also attended black conventions and occasionally accompanied Ward on lecture tours of western New York state. *IC*, 10, 17 October 1849, 6 February 1850; *NSt*, 22 February 1850 [6:0408]; *SDS*, 24 September 1850 [6:0568].

9.
James McCune Smith to Gerrit Smith
6 February 1850

The interracial bond between philanthropist Gerrit Smith and black abolitionists was closer and more enduring than any other in the antislavery movement. Henry Highland Garnet called him "the unflinching friend of my people," and no white reformer did more to justify such praise. His friendships with black leaders were founded upon personal respect, a spirit of equality, and shared concerns. Smith liberally financed black organizations and the black press, operated a manual labor school for blacks, loaned money and opened his home to black acquaintances, and spoke out on civil rights questions. He particularly admired black physician James McCune Smith of New York City. When Gerrit Smith announced in 1846 that he would donate 120,000 acres of his own land near North Elba, New York, to black settlers, he turned to his black colleague for assistance and advice. He hoped to encourage the elevation of free blacks by making them independent, landowning farmers. James McCune Smith promoted the scheme and helped select settlers. His 6 February 1850 letter to Gerrit Smith conveys the warmth of their relationship and their hopes for the North Elba settlement. Despite their efforts, poor soil, a harsh climate, and the inexperience of many black settlers kept most grantees from taking possession of the land. Ralph V. Harlow, *Gerrit Smith, Philanthropist and Reformer* (New York, N.Y., 1939), 61–62, 232, 241–58; Benjamin Quarles, ed., "Letters from Negro Leaders to Gerrit Smith," *JNH* 27:432–53 (October 1942); Swift, *Black Prophets of Justice*, 39–40, 73–74, 140, 155, 163–64, 168–69, 255, 260, 275, 334, 336.

New York, [New York]
Feb[ruary] 6, 1850

Dear friend:

Your letter last month found me stricken with grief for the loss of my first born, my dear little Amy. After a year of ailment, at times painful and distressing, always [obscure,] and which she bore with child-like patience, it pleased God to take her home to the company of Cherubs who continually do Praise Him. You have been afflicted in like manner and know the bitterness of it;[1] for one thing I feel deeply grateful; her mind was serene to the last, and intelligently hopeful of a Blessed Immortality. She died on Christmas eve and lacked 5 days of six years of age. My dear wife was sorely afflicted, and until within a few days I have dreaded a permanent dependency; she is growing more cheerful however,[2] and we both live, in the hope of meeting our dear little one where there will be no more sickness, nor pain[,] nor parting forevermore.

1. James McCune Smith

Courtesy of Schomburg Center for Research in Black Culture, The New York Public
Library, Astor, Lenox and Tilden Foundations

In September last, in company with Mr. Wm. P. Powel I visited Essex & Franklin Counties, and would have written you long ago about our very pleasant excursion had my heart not been heavy with Amy's approaching death.

We found in North Elba, about sixty colored persons in all, of all ages and sex. As a general thing the parties had not enough money at the outset, and had failed in making up the deficiency partly from the backwardness of the season and partly from having waited too long for Mr. John Browns team. They were however cheerful, many of them hardy and industrious; a fine talk they made too, about their feeling of independence, when I fear they were a little too dependent upon Mr. Brown's meal bin.[3] They had put up several good log houses, and I suppose by this time have made a pretty fair [fallow]. What struck me most was the evident impulse the old settlers had received; I think more clearing had been done within a year in ~~To[wnship]~~ 12, than in any three years together of late. We held an Anti-slavery church meeting and day meeting at good old Deacon Osgood's (where we tarried) and they talked of erecting a church on the Peterboro platform.[4]

I felt myself a "lord indeed" beneath the lofty spruce and maple and birch, and by the [tr]awling brook, which your Deed made mine, and would gladly exchange this bustling anxious life for the repose of that majestic country, could I see the way clear for a livelihood for myself & family. I am not afraid of physical labor; but do not think it would be prudent to risk sustenance in my personal labor in the farming line; and this country is yet too sparse to give support to a physician. Unless therefore, and until, I can make enough to secure an income of $400 per annum, I must defer settling in Essex County.

As we went north thro' township 11 and 10, we found (along a superbly rough stump and corduroy road) here and there colored settlers making the woods ring with the music of their axe strokes; of course we broke down, got lost in the woods, and became deeply indebted to Mr.—
—— of lot 204, To[.] 10 for assistance and direction, he is a Vermonter who purchased this lot from you and is doing very well.

We found the travel from Merrils to Port Kent very good; out of 36 miles, some 17 are good plank roads.[5]

To return to Township 12. Mr Henderson,[6] a shoe-maker from Troy had his sign hanging out (the first and only in the township) and appeared to drive a good business. Mr. Landrine[7] has cleared about two acres, and was vainly st[r]iving to reach water, by well digging. He has since given up in despair, and is now in this city wishing to sell his lot (which he bought from you) at $4 per acre. Mr. Drummond[8] also whose wife & children are in ~~To~~ 11 on a clearing of 4 or 5 acres, is miserably idling his time here, if not criminally. Could we get about 200 settlers in North Elba, and then cut off all communication with the city (burn the galleys) things could be made to prosper.

Brother Ray[9] and myself are anxiously and earnestly endeavouring to complete our list; and will in a short time forward you nearly all the names, except for Suffolk County, in which we find it hard to [select].

Mr. Levere[10] of this city visited Hamilton County in October and brought some exciting news of mineral wealth; what he thought silver, turned out to be pretty good Plumbago[11] of nearly the same value as silver; the mineral is in township 3; and you will greatly oblige me by stating whether the state has any reserved right to minerals found on said lands.

Please give our best regards to your family[12] & believe me sincerely & gratefully yours

J. McCune Smith

P.S. has your [local] ailment received any benifit from Homeiopathy?[13]

Gerrit Smith Papers, George Arents Research Library, Syracuse University, Syracuse, New York. Published by permission.

1. Two of Gerrit Smith's children died at an early age—a daughter, Ann (1830–1835), and a son, Fitzhugh (1824–1836). Harlow, *Gerrit Smith*, 16–17, 41.

2. Malvina Barnet Smith, the wife of James McCune Smith, continued to be active in the affairs of New York City's black community. She served on a subscription committee for the *North Star* and promoted adult education for local women. *NSt*, 4 May 1849 [5:1085]; *WAA*, 24 November 1860 [13:0005].

3. John Brown (1800–1859), a failed businessman and antislavery zealot, believed in racial equality, helped blacks resist the Fugitive Slave Law, and worked closely with black abolitionists. During 1849–51 he and his family lived at North Elba, New York, on 244 acres of land obtained from Gerrit Smith. Brown helped his destitute black neighbors clear their lands and determine their boundary lines, taught them how to farm, and brought in supplies to sustain them through lean times. He hoped to make North Elba into a model black community. Brown, who considered himself God's providential instrument to end slavery, earned a reputation for violence in the bloody guerrilla war that raged between free-state and slave-state factions in Kansas in 1856. In October 1859, after months of planning, he led a twenty-one-man assault against the federal arsenal at Harpers Ferry, Virginia, in the hope of sparking widespread slave insurrection. The effort failed and Brown was captured, tried, and executed in December. But his actions incited passions across the nation and helped propel the North and South toward civil war. Stephen B. Oates, *To Purge This Land with Blood: A Biography of John Brown* (New York, N.Y., 1970); Benjamin Quarles, *Allies for Freedom: Blacks and John Brown* (New York, N.Y., 1974).

4. Smith and Powell met with local abolitionists at the home of Iddo Osgood (1780–?), a white farmer, to discuss the formation of a Union church in North Elba. The Union church movement, an antislavery comeouter sect, was an effort to allow abolitionists to reconcile their religious and political lives. Forty Union churches with about one thousand members were eventually organized in upstate New York and western New England during the 1830s and 1840s. Under the leadership of Gerrit Smith, William Goodell, Beriah Green, and Smith's circle of

antislavery friends in Peterboro, New York, many Union churches were virtual auxiliaries of the Liberty party and made antislavery voting a membership requirement. U.S. Census, 1850; John R. McKivigan, *The War against Proslavery Religion: Abolitionism and the Northern Churches* (Ithaca, N.Y., 1984), 95–96, 129, 147–48.

5. Upon leaving Franklin County, Smith and Powell traveled through the village of Merrill, on the northeastern portion of Upper Chateaugay Lake in Clinton County, New York, about twelve miles from the Canadian border. They proceeded thirty-six miles southeast to Port Kent, on the western shore of Lake Champlain in the northeastern corner of Essex County.

6. James H. Henderson (1816–?), a native of Virginia, settled in New York City in the 1830s. He operated a "Boot and Shoe Manufactory" and in 1840 founded an evening school for adults and children at the Second Colored Presbyterian Church. In the early 1840s, Henderson moved to Troy, New York, where he represented local blacks at the 1847 black national convention held there and joined the statewide campaign to expand black suffrage. Henderson's interest in farming was sparked by Gerrit Smith's offer to set aside large tracts of land in upstate New York for a black settlement. In 1849 he moved with his wife and five children to the Smith lands near North Elba. U.S. Census, 1850; *CA*, 11 May, 14 September 1839, 7 November 1840; *NASS*, 29 January 1846 [5:0152]; *AP*, 13 March, 17 November 1846 [5:0184, 0288]; *CF*, 5 May 1843 [4:0566]; *NSt*, 5 February 1849 [5:0976].

7. Benjamin Landrine, a New York City black, had worked with the New York Committee of Vigilance and had been involved in efforts to sustain the *Colored American* in the late 1830s and early 1840s. *E*, 1 March 1838 [2:0392]; *ML*, July 1838 [2:0510–11]; *CA*, 2, 16 October 1841 [4:0232, 0266].

8. Samuel A. Drummond worked as a laborer in New York City before moving to the North Elba settlement. After an unsuccessful attempt at farming, he returned to New York City in 1850. His home was attacked during the July 1863 draft riots. *New York City Directory*, 1842, 1844; Gatewood, *Free Man of Color*, 80; *PA*, 9 September 1863.

9. Charles B. Ray.

10. George W. Levere (1820–1886) pastored St. Paul's Congregational Church in Brooklyn during the 1850s and early 1860s. He demonstrated a lifelong commitment to black voting rights by opening his church to black suffrage meetings, supporting the suffrage plan of the 1855 black state convention in New York, and serving as an officer of the New York State Suffrage Association and other suffrage organizations. Levere urged blacks to vote for John C. Frémont, the Republican presidential candidate, in the 1856 election. Like many black ministers, he nurtured an abiding interest in African missions. He was an early supporter of the African Civilization Society, and later as its president, he helped reorganize the society and redirect its program to the educational needs of the freedmen. Following the Emancipation Proclamation, Levere urged blacks to enlist in the Union army in order "to stand up against the outrages heaped upon them by the brutal portion of society." In 1864 he was named chaplain of the Twentieth U.S. Colored Infantry, which was stationed in Louisiana and Texas. In addition to his duties as regimental chaplain, he became a regular correspondent to the *Weekly Anglo-African* and an outspoken advocate for black soldiers and

freedmen. After the war, Levere served a black congregation in Knoxville, Tennessee, before ending his ministry at the Zion Presbyterian Church in Charleston, South Carolina. Miller, *Search for a Black Nationality*, 263; *FDP*, 14 September 1855 [9:0832]; *Lib*, 1 October 1858 [11:0379]; *WAA*, 24 September 1859, 24, 31 March, 19 April, 23, 30 June 1860, 22 March 1862, 30 May 1863, 12 March, 4 June 1864, 19, 26 August 1865 [12:0593, 0600, 0602, 0710, 16:0121]; Benjamin Quarles, *The Negro in the Civil War* (Boston, Mass., 1953), 164; *CR*, 18 June 1864, 21 October 1886 [15:0405].

11. Plumbago is another name for graphite.

12. In 1850 Gerrit Smith's family included his wife, Ann Carol Fitzhugh of Rochester, New York, whom he married in 1822, and two children—Elizabeth (b. 1822) and Green (b. 1842). Harlow, *Gerrit Smith*, 16, 42.

13. Homeopathic medicine, which originated in Germany about 1800, treated disease by artificially inducing symptoms of a weaker ailment. It flourished in the United States after 1830 but declined by the 1890s. Harvey Green, *Fit for America: Health, Fitness, Sport, and American Society* (New York, N.Y., 1986), 7–8.

10.
Speech by Samuel Ringgold Ward
Delivered at Faneuil Hall
Boston, Massachusetts
25 March 1850

Congressional debate over the adoption of the Fugitive Slave Law moved black abolitionists toward a consensus on political matters during the spring of 1850. The threat posed by the pending legislation minimized all other political issues. Now the key question was where a politician stood on the controversial bill. Blacks had once regarded Daniel Webster as a "great and eloquent" statesman, but over the years they had seen the "cords of party" restrain him on the issue of slavery. His infamous "Seventh of March Speech," which endorsed the fugitive slave bill on the floor of the U.S. Senate, confirmed for them his "recreancy to Freedom." In the weeks following the address, abolitionists condemned Webster in print and censured him at mass meetings. Samuel Ringgold Ward spoke before an anti-Webster rally at Boston's Faneuil Hall on the evening of 25 March 1850. He vilified Webster and other northern politicians who supported the bill. At the same time, he praised Senator William H. Seward who opposed Webster's call for compromise. Ward concluded that if the notorious bill became law, blacks should claim the "right of Revolution." *Lib*, 12 February 1831, 29 March, 5 April 1850 [1:0029]; *CA*, 16 February 1839, 29 August 1840 [3:0008, 0596]; *NSt* 24 March 1848 [5:0601].

I am here tonight simply as a guest. You have met here to speak of the sentiments of a Senator of your State whose remarks you have the honor to repudiate. In the course of the remarks of the gentleman who preceded me, he has done us the favor to make honorable mention of a Senator of my own State—Wm. H. Seward.[1] (Three hearty cheers were given for Senator Seward.)

I thank you for this manifestation of approbation of a man who has always stood head and shoulders above his party, and who has never receded from his position on the question of slavery. It was my happiness to receive a letter from him a few days since, in which he said he never would swerve from his position as the friend of freedom. (Applause.) To be sure, I agree not with Senator Seward in politics, but when an individual stands up for the rights of men against the slaveholders, I care not for party distinctions. He is my brother. (Loud cheers.)

We have here much of common cause and interest in this matter. That infamous bill of Mr. Mason,[2] of Virginia, proves itself to be like all other propositions presented by Southern men. It finds just enough of North-

ern dough-faces[3] who are willing to pledge themselves, if you will pardon the uncouth language of a backwoodsman, to lick up the spittle of
the slavocrats, and swear it is delicious. (Applause.)

You of the old Bay State—a State to which many of us are accustomed
to look as to our father land, just as we all look back to England as
our mother country—you have a Daniel who has deserted the cause of
freedom. We, too, in New York, have a "Daniel who has come to judgement," only he doesn't come quite fast enough to the right kind of judgement. (Tremendous enthusiasm.) Daniel S. Dickinson[4] represents someone, I suppose, in the State of New York; God knows, he doesn't
represent me. I can pledge you, that our Daniel will stand cheek by jowl
with your Daniel. (Cheers.) He was never known to surrender slavery,
but always to surrender liberty.

The bill of which you most justly complain, concerning the surrender
of fugitive slaves, is to apply alike to your State and to our State, if it
shall ever apply at all. But we have come here to make a common oath
upon a common altar, that that bill shall never take effect. (Applause.)
Honorable Senators may record their names in its behalf, and it may
have the sanction of the House of Representatives; but we the people,
who are superior to both Houses and the Executive too (hear, hear), we
the people will never be human bipeds, to howl upon the track of the
fugitive slave, even though led by the corrupt Daniel of your State, or the
degraded one of ours. (Cheers.)

Though there are many attempts to get up compromises[5]—and there is
no term which I detest more than this, it is always the term which makes
right yield to wrong; it has always been accursed since Eve made the first
compromise with the devil.[6] (Repeated rounds of applause.) I was saying, sir, that it is somewhat singular, and yet historically true, that when-
soever these compromises are proposed, there are men of the North who
seem to foresee that Northern men, who think their constituency will not
look into these matters, will seek to do more than the South demands.
They seek to prove to Northern men that all is right and all is fair; and
this is the game Webster is attempting to play.

"O," says Webster, "the will of God has fixed that matter; we will not
re-enact the will of God."[7] Sir, you remember the time in 1841, '42, '43
and '44, when it was said that Texas could never be annexed. The design
of such dealing was that you should believe it, and then, when you
thought yourselves secure, they would spring the trap upon you. And
now it is their wish to seduce you into the belief that slavery never will go
there, and then the slaveholders will drive slavery there as fast as possible. I think that this is the most contemptible proposition of the whole,
except the support of that bill which would attempt to make the whole
North the slavecatchers of the South.

You will remember that the bill of Mr. Mason says nothing about color. Mr. Phillips, a man whom I always loved (applause), a man who taught me my hornbook on this subject of slavery,[8] when I was a poor boy, has referred to Marshfield. There is a man who sometimes lives in Marshfield,[9] and who has the reputation of having an honorable dark skin.[10] Who knows but that some postmaster may have to sit upon the very gentleman whose character you have been discussing tonight? (Hear, hear.) "What is sauce for the goose, is sauce for the gander." (Laughter.) If this bill is to relieve grievances, why not make an application to the immortal Daniel of Marshfield? (Applause.) There is no such thing as complexion mentioned. It is not only true that the colored men of Massachusetts—it is not only true that the fifty thousand colored men of New York may be taken—though I pledge you there is one, whose name is Sam Ward, who will never be taken alive (tremendous applause)—not only is it true that the fifty thousand black men in New York may be taken, but anyone else also can be captured. My friend Theodore Parker[11] alluded to Ellen Craft. I had the pleasure of taking tea with her, and accompanied her here tonight. She is far whiter than many who come here slave-catching. This line of distinction is so nice that you cannot tell who is white or black. As Alexander Pope used to say, "White and black soften and blend in so many thousand ways, that it is neither white nor black."[12] (Loud plaudits.)

This is the question, Whether a man has a right to himself and his children, his hopes and his happiness, for this world and the world to come. That is a question which, according to this bill, may be decided by any backwoods postmaster in this State or any other. O, this is a monstrous proposition; and I do thank God, that if the Slave Power have such demands to make on us, that the proposition has come now—now, that the people know what is being done—now that the public mind is turned toward this subject—now that they are trying to find what is the truth on this subject.

Sir, what must be the moral influence of this speech of Mr. Webster on the minds of young men, lawyers and others, here in the North? They turn their eyes towards Daniel Webster as towards a superior mind, and a legal and constitutional oracle. If they shall catch the spirit of this speech, its influence upon them and upon following generations will be so deeply corrupting, that it never can be wiped out or purged.

I am thankful that this, my first entrance into Boston, and my first introduction to Faneuil Hall,[13] gives me the pleasure and privilege of uniting with you, in uttering my humble voice against the two Daniels, and of declaring, in behalf of our people, that if the fugitive slave is traced to our part of New York State, he shall have the law of Almighty God to protect him, the law which says, "Thou shalt not return to the master the servant that is escaped unto thee, but he shall dwell with thee in thy gates, where it liketh him best."[14] And if our postmasters cannot maintain their constitutional oaths, and cannot *live* without playing the pander to the slave-hunter, they need not *live at all*. Such crises as these leave us to the right of Revolution, and if need be, that right we will, at whatever cost, most sacredly maintain. (Mr. Ward sat down amidst rapturous applause.)

Liberator (Boston, Mass.), 5 April 1850.

1. William Henry Seward (1801–1872), the leader of the Whig party in New York state, was elected governor in 1838 and went to the U.S. Senate in 1848. An outspoken critic of slavery, he supported black rights and privately assisted opponents of the Fugitive Slave Law. After unsuccessfully seeking the Republican presidential nomination in 1856 and 1860, he served as secretary of state in the administrations of Abraham Lincoln and Andrew Johnson (1861–69), coordinating the delicate Civil War diplomacy with European nations and negotiating the 1867 purchase of Alaska from Russia. *DAB*, 16:615–21.

2. Ward refers to a bill introduced in the U.S. Senate by James Murray Mason (1798–1871), a slaveholding legislator and diplomat from one of Virginia's leading families. The bill, which became known as the Fugitive Slave Law of 1850, was meant to address slaveowner dissatisfaction with federal procedures for the return of fugitive slaves. One of five enactments passed in September of that year and collectively termed the Compromise of 1850, the new law created the position of U.S. commissioner (a federal hearing officer with final authority over extradition proceedings in northern state courts), ordered state and federal authorities to cooperate in capturing fugitives, and imposed a $1,000 fine or six-month prison sentence on anyone who aided a runaway. It made the slave certification hearing an administrative, rather than a judicial, procedure; as a result, blacks were unable to testify on their own behalf and had no right to counsel or a habeas corpus hearing. Northern free blacks regarded the law as a severe threat to their freedom, and abolitionists used the law to rouse northern antislavery sentiment and to reinvigorate local vigilance committees. The Fugitive Slave Law and the controversy it provoked moved the North and South closer to war. *DAB*, 12:364–65; Stanley W. Campbell, *The Slave Catchers: Enforcement of the Fugitive Slave Law, 1850–1860* (Chapel Hill, N.C., 1968), 15–25.

3. "Doughface" was a term used by abolitionists to describe northern politicians, particularly Democrats, who sympathized with slavery and the political defenders of the institution.

4. Daniel Stevens Dickinson (1800–1866), a New York City lawyer and legislator, actively opposed antislavery measures and supported the Compromise of 1850 as a member of the U.S. Senate (1844–51). Although a conservative Democrat for most of his career, Dickinson became a Republican and a vigorous supporter of the Lincoln administration and its policies during the Civil War. *DAB*, 5:294–95.

5. In January 1850, with the slavery crisis threatening to dissolve the Union, Senator Henry Clay of Kentucky presented a series of compromises to Congress that offered concessions to both the North and the South. Senator Stephen A. Douglas of Illinois shepherded an omnibus bill incorporating the various concessions through the legislative process. In September, after months of impassioned debate, Congress approved the bill, which is usually known as the Compromise of 1850. The measure admitted California as a free state, enacted a stricter

fugitive slave law (the Fugitive Slave Law of 1850), permitted territorial governments to be organized in the remainder of the Mexican cession without restrictions on slavery, assumed the war debts of Texas in exchange for the state relinquishing its claim to lands in the New Mexico Territory, and abolished the slave trade in the District of Columbia. Holman Hamilton, *Prologue to Conflict: The Crisis and Compromise of 1850* (Lexington, Ky., 1964).

6. Ward refers to the biblical tale of the fall of man in Genesis 3:1–14, in which Eve and Adam "compromise with the devil" by defying a divine commandment to refrain from eating the fruit of the tree of knowledge.

7. Ward paraphases a remark from Daniel Webster's famous 7 March 1850 speech in the U.S. Senate in defense of the Compromise of 1850. Webster argued that it was unnecessary to restrict the expansion of slavery into the American Southwest because climatic conditions would prevent the institution from thriving there. He concluded that he "would not take pains uselessly to reaffirm an ordinance of nature, nor to reenact the will of God." Maurice G. Baxter, *One and Inseparable: Daniel Webster and the Union* (Cambridge, Mass., 1984), 415.

8. Ward acknowledges his intellectual debt to the speeches and writings of Wendell Phillips.

9. Earlier in the meeting, Wendell Phillips made a speech contrasting Daniel Webster's support of the Compromise of 1850 with his earlier opposition to the expansion of slavery. He pointed to an 1848 address that Webster made in Marshfield, Massachusetts, condemning the annexation of Texas as a major factor in the institution's growth. Webster owned a home, 1,200-acre estate, and law office in Marshfield, a village near the Atlantic coast, about twenty-five miles south of Boston. *Lib*, 29 March 1850; Baxter, *One and Inseparable*, 282–84, 459.

10. Ward alludes to Daniel Webster's swarthy complexion, a source of frequent comment by abolitionists.

11. Theodore Parker (1810–1860) was a celebrated Massachusetts Unitarian clergyman, a brilliant theologian, and an ardent abolitionist. He led formal opposition to the Fugitive Slave Law in Boston, sheltered local fugitive slaves such as William and Ellen Craft, and backed John Brown's attempt to incite a slave insurrection at Harpers Ferry. To restore his failing health and to avoid prosecution for his role in Brown's raid, Parker moved in 1859 to Florence, Italy, where he died of tuberculosis. Henry Steele Commager, *Theodore Parker: Yankee Crusader* (Boston, Mass., 1947).

12. Ward paraphrases lines from *An Essay on Man* (1734) by English poet and essayist Alexander Pope. Epistle 2, lines 205–6, read:

> If white and black, blend, soften, and unite
> A thousand ways, is there no black or white?

13. Faneuil Hall, a public market and meeting hall in Boston, was erected in 1742 as a gift to the town by Peter Faneuil, a wealthy merchant. It earned the sobriquet "Cradle of Liberty" as the site of public protests against Britain in the decade before the American Revolution. Reform meetings were often convened there during the nineteenth century. *DAH*, 2:487.

14. Ward loosely quotes a decree by Moses in Deuteronomy 23:15–16 on sanctuary for fugitive slaves.

11.
William Still to James Miller McKim
8 August 1850

Blacks dominated underground railroad and vigilance committee work. A courageous few regularly smuggled slaves out of the upper South. Many more assisted fugitives once they arrived in the North. Underground railroad workers protected thousands of runaways; provided them with food, clothing, shelter, money, transportation, and legal assistance; and helped them reach safe haven. A network linked black communities across the North, but it was strongest along the Atlantic seaboard. William Still, a fugitive slave and a key figure in the eastern region, bore primary responsibility for aiding fugitive slaves coming through Philadelphia. Working out of the office of the Pennsylvania Anti-Slavery Society, he routinely interviewed escaped slaves in order to sift out impostors and to assess the needs of the worthy. On 2 August 1850, while querying a former slave, he was astonished to find his brother Peter staring him "too full in the face to . . . dispute the evidence for one moment." Peter Still had spent forty-eight years in bondage in Kentucky and Alabama, until he purchased his freedom from his master. William Still related a poignant account of this reunion in an 8 August letter to James Miller McKim, the editor of the *Pennsylvania Freeman*. Robert Brent Toplin, "Peter Still versus the Peculiar Institution," *CWH* 4:340–49 (December 1967); William Still to [?], 7 August 1850, Still Papers, NjR [6:0553].

> *Anti-Slavery Office*
> *Phila*[delphia], [Pennsylvania]
> *Aug*[ust] 8th, 1850

Dear Sir:[1]

As you desired that I should make a statement of some of the most prominent facts in relation to the late wonderful discovery of my lost brothers, I submit the following brief account.

On the 2d inst., two men came into this office, one of whom I recognized, the other was an entire stranger. My acquaintance introduced the stranger to me by the name of Peter Freedman,[2] of Alabama. The object of Peter's visit was merely referred to by my acquaintance, when Peter commenced his own story in an earnest and simple manner. Peter said that he was from Alabama. His visit here was for the purpose of seeing if he could gain some information or instruction how he might find out his people. He stated that he and an older brother had been stolen away from somewhere in this direction, about 41 or 42 years ago, when he was a boy only about six years old. Since that time he had been utterly

2. Peter Still
From William Still, *Underground Railroad* (Philadelphia, 1872)

excluded from all knowledge of his parents, having never even so much as heard a word from them or any of his relatives. I enquired of Peter what course he expected to pursue in order to gain the information he wished? He replied that it was his intention to have notices written and read throughout the colored churches of this city. I then inquired of him if he knew the names of his parents? To which he replied that his father's name was Levin and his mother's Sidney; he did not know their last names. By this time I was much surprised and interested at the remarks made by the stranger, and I continued to put such questions to him as I thought would, most likely, throw light upon the subject. I again desired him to repeat over the names of his parents and older brother, and he at once complied with my request. By this time I perceived that a most wonderful story was about to be disclosed; however I continued to ask questions respecting his being carried away, &c. I was then anxious to have my impressions verified by facts that could not be contested or disproved. I enquired of him if he knew the name of no other person, except those already mentioned? He answered that he knew a white man by the name of S. G.,[3] who lived near his parents—recollected of playing with this white man's children, &c. When the name of the white man was announced my doubts all fled, and the fact was confirmed to my satisfaction, that an own dear brother whom I had never before seen was before me. There was no evading the evidence; all the names rehearsed, and the circumstances connected therewith, were familiar to me, having heard my parents speak of them very frequently. Besides I could see in the face of my newfound brother the likeness of my mother. My feelings were unutterable, and I was obliged to exert all my mental powers in order to conceal them. Thought after thought crowded my mind in relation to the past history of my parents, especially in connection with the interest felt for the two lost boys. After I had been convinced of the startling fact that Peter was my own brother, so sudden was the occurrence that I at once concluded to keep the whole matter to myself, until after I could get the chance of consulting with my sister, which I intended to do that evening. But after a moment's reflection my mind changed, as I could see no good reason for withholding the secret from him any longer. I was then anxious for the friend who came with Peter to leave, as I preferred to be alone when I divulged the secret of my discovery to him. I told my acquaintance that he need not wait any longer, that I would take charge of Peter &c. At least one hour had elapsed before I revealed to my brother one word of what I had discovered. After my acquaintance left the office I took Peter and seated myself by his side, and commenced to make a brief explanation of what had been to us both a few moments before a profound mystery. I told him that I could tell him all about his kinsfolks. At this expression he seemed surprised, but not at all excited; I continued by telling him that he was an own brother of mine, and gave

him the names of my parents &c. To relate the particulars of our interview is quite unnecessary.

That you may better understand the story, I must go back and tell you
what I never mentioned to you before, that my parents were once slaves.
They lived in the State of Maryland, but feeling a strong desire for liberty
they were not slack in taking measures to procure it. My father deliberately (as I have often heard him say), resolved that he would rather die
than live a slave. By demonstrating his disposition to his owner upon the
subject, he was allowed the privilege of purchasing himself rather low,
which he accepted, and by the earnings of his own hands he soon paid
the sum demanded, and of course obtained his "free papers." At this
time my father was only about twenty-one years of age. In the meanwhile
he was married to my mother, who was a slave. My parents had four
children, and the desire of freedom rested so heavily upon the mind of
my mother, that she in concert with my father concluded that their only
hope of enjoying each other's society, depended altogether upon mother's
making her escape. Their plans all being laid they soon found themselves
in the State of New Jersey. But before mother had long enjoyed what she
had so eagerly sought after, and what she prized so highly (liberty), she
and all four of her children were pursued, captured, and carried back to
Maryland, from whence they had fled. For a while after my mother was
taken back, she was kept confined of nights in a garret, to prevent her
from making a second effort for freedom; but it was all to no purpose.
Before she had been back three months she made a second flight, taking
her two youngest, which were girls, and leaving her two oldest boys,
Levin and Peter. I shall never forget hearing my mother speak of the
memorable night when she last fled. She went to the bed where her two
boys, Levin and Peter, were sleeping—kissed them—consigned them into
the hands of God and took her departure again for a land of liberty. My
mother's efforts proved successful, though at the heartrending consideration of leaving two of her boys to the disposal of slaveholders. Those
unfortunate boys were sold soon after my mother's escape. All that she
ever heard of them afterwards was, that they had been sold far south.
But I shall not have time nor space now to dwell a great while longer
upon particulars. I doubt not but what you will be interested to know
something of the early career of Levin and Peter.

Peter related to me the following circumstances in regard to himself.
He recollected to have missed his mother, and wanted to go to her. They
said he should go to her—that they were going to take him and his
brother to her. This deception was used in order to quiet them of course.
But instead of being placed in the hands of their mother, when at their
journey's end, they were placed in the hands of a slaveholder in Kentucky. Thirteen of their youthful years were passed away in Kentucky, in

a manner that I have no need of describing. They were then sold into the State of Alabama, where they were subjected to the painful necessity of passing through the hands of several owners. Levin died about nineteen years ago, and was buried by his surviving brother Peter. Within the last two years Peter, through much entreaty, prevailed upon a gentleman to purchase him, with a view to let him work out his freedom. The price for Peter was $500. Through his industry and economy, by working of nights and using all possible activity, in doing extra jobs by day, he managed to accumulate the whole amount required for himself. As soon as he had accomplished the anxious task of paying the last dollar for himself, the lifelong wish of his heart prompted him to make enough money to defray his expenses of a tour in search of his people, for whom he felt the warmest affection; although he was so young at the time when separated from his parents as not to know even their last names. He had also endured the burthens of slavery with all its ills for forty-three long years, yet he had not yielded his hopes of seeing the land from whence he had been sold, nor of again greeting that mother who gave him birth. The distance he travelled was about 1500 miles. He arrived in this city on the first of this month, on the 2d he found his brother in the place and manner above mentioned; on the 3d he was conveyed to my mother's in New Jersey, by two of my sisters who reside here. He found his mother, five brothers and three sisters.[4]

I shall not attempt to describe the feelings of my mother and the family on learning the fact that Peter was one of us; I will leave that for you to imagine. You are probably aware that my father has been dead for seven years. Unfortunately brother Peter has a wife and three children in slavery. He has gone back to Alabama with the earnest hope of being able to liberate his wife and children, by purchasing them, that being his only chance. His attachments to his family are so strong, that when I intimated to him—if he could not get them, I supposed he would leave them and come North—he instantly replied that he "would as soon go out of the world as not to go back and do all he could for them."

There are two very remarkable incidents connected with this development, which I must state to you before I close my letter, viz. The name of the white man referred to, and remembered so correctly by my brother Peter, was that of his original owner, though the boys were too young to know that fact. The name of my mother had always, after her escape from slavery, been kept concealed, and she was known only by a different one, for reasons which will readily occur to you. When I glance over those wonderful circumstances connected with the history of these unfortunate brothers, I am utterly astonished. But I cannot stop now to tell you the feelings of my heart in reference to those enslaved brothers and the enslaved generally. I have already said more than I had intended; still my account seems but brief. But you are too well acquainted with slavery and its woes not to be able to judge in reference to what I have been obliged to omit. Your obedient servant,

WM. STILL[5]

Pennsylvania Freeman (Philadelphia, Pa.), 22 August 1850.

1. James Miller McKim (1810–1874) worked with William Still and the General Vigilance Committee of Philadelphia to protect and aid fugitive slaves during the 1850s. A founding member of the American Anti-Slavery Society, he left the Presbyterian ministry in 1836 to devote himself entirely to abolitionism and served as the corresponding secretary of the Pennsylvania Anti-Slavery Society for twenty-five years. McKim helped recruit black soldiers during the Civil War and assisted in relief and educational efforts for the freedmen. Merrill and Ruchames, *Letters of William Lloyd Garrison*, 4:92.

2. Peter Still (1801–1868) was born to slave parents on Maryland's eastern shore. His father, Levin Steel, soon purchased his freedom. When his mother, Sidney (later called Charity Still), escaped to New Jersey in 1807, she was forced to leave her two sons—Peter and Levin—in bondage. Their original owner, Saunders Griffin, promptly sold them into slavery in Lexington, Kentucky. Because of their youth, the two boys were unaware of their last name and believed that they had been kidnapped. Their new owners were John Fisher and Nat Grist, who operated brickyards in Lexington. About 1820 they were taken to Alabama where Levin died in 1831. Peter served several masters near Florence and Tuscumbia in the northwestern part of the state, although he was often hired out for various tasks. At age twenty-five, he married Levina, a slave from a neighboring plantation. They had three children—Peter, Jr., Levin, and Catherine. Hired out to a local bookseller in 1846, Peter began saving his earnings to emancipate himself. In 1849 after becoming the slave and close friend of Joseph Friedman, a local Jewish merchant, he was permitted to buy his freedom. Still adopted the name Peter Freedman, bade farewell to his family, and set out to find his parents. In 1850, after a chance meeting with his brother, black abolitionist William Still, at the Philadelphia Anti-Slavery Office, he was reunited with his mother and surviving brothers and sisters.

Once free, Still began a five-year struggle to bring his wife and children out of slavery. Seth Concklin, an enigmatic underground railroad activist, helped them escape to Vincennes, Indiana, but they were recaptured and returned. Still then attempted to purchase them, but B. McKiernan, their owner, demanded $5,000 in payment. Armed with letters of certification from J. Miller McKim, Harriet Beecher Stowe, and other prominent abolitionists, Still lectured and collected funds throughout New York and New England for the next two years. After reaching his goal in October 1854, he worked through Florence businessman John Simpson to complete his family's purchase and have them brought north. About that time, Kate E. R. Pickard, a white teacher who had befriended Still while an Alabama slave, began writing a book about his experiences. Fearing for the liberty and safety of his mother, brothers, and sisters, who were legally considered fugitive slaves, Still was uncertain about the project. He repeatedly denied Pickard's requests for family information—facts that would have facilitated completion of the volume. Pickard finally published Still's tale in *The Kidnapped and the Ransomed* (1856) but was obliged to omit many facts, distort others, and ultimately confine herself to his "personal recollections," including his story about being kidnapped into slavery. Still spent the remainder of his life in relative obscurity on a ten-acre truck farm near Burlington, New Jersey. He was a leading member of the local black Baptist church. Still died of pneumonia in January 1868. *NASS*, 1 February 1868; Toplin, "Peter Still versus the Peculiar Institution," 340–49; Kate E. R. Pickard, *The Kidnapped and the Ransomed* (Syracuse, N.Y., 1856; reprint, New York, N.Y., 1941), 19–20, 28–32; William Still, *The Underground Railroad* (Philadelphia, Pa., 1872; reprint, Chicago, Ill., 1970), 18–19.

3. Still refers to Saunders Griffin, Peter Still's first owner.

4. At the time of Peter Still's escape, his mother Charity lived in Burlington, New Jersey. Three sisters—Mahalah Thompson, Kitturah Willmore, and Mary Still—were residents of Philadelphia. His brothers included William and Charles W. Still of Philadelphia, John N. Still of Brooklyn, and James Still of Medford, New Jersey. A fifth brother, Samuel Still (1807–1875), farmed near Burlington. In addition to William and John, both prominent figures in the antislavery movement, two other siblings became well known. Mary Still (1808–1889) operated a private school for black children in Philadelphia from the late 1840s through the Civil War. After the war, she raised funds to aid the freedmen and taught at American Missionary Association schools in Beaufort, South Carolina (1865–68), and Jacksonville, Florida (1869–72). She was active in the women's activities of the African Methodist Episcopal church. James Still (1812–1882) practiced medicine in Medford, New Jersey, for more than thirty years. A popular, self-taught physician, he manufactured and marketed his own remedies and was famous for his cancer treatments. He recounted his own history in the *Early Recollections and Life of Dr. James Still* (1877). Toplin, "Peter Still versus the Peculiar Institution," 343; U.S. Census, 1850; *A Statistical Inquiry into the Condition of the People of Colour, of the City and Districts of Philadelphia* (Philadelphia, Pa., 1849), 21 [5:0913]; *CR*, 16 March 1882, 31 January 1889; *WAA*, 26 August 1865; Clara Merritt De Boer, "The Role of Afro-Americans in the Origin and Work of the American Missionary Association, 1839–1877" (Ph.D. diss., Rutgers University, 1973), 297, 495, 509; Mary Still to the Board of the American Missionary Association, 27 November 1868, AMA-ARC; Herbert M. Morais, *The History of the Afro-American in Medicine* (Cornwells Heights, Pa., 1978), 21–23; James Still, *Early Recollections and Life of Dr. James Still* (Philadelphia, Pa., 1877), 15, 29–30, 41–43, 47, 68–69, 161, 248–49.

5. William Still (1821–1901), a Philadelphia businessman, writer, and civic leader, directed one of the most vital links in the underground railroad. He was born in New Jersey, the youngest of eighteen children of a former slave, Levin Steel, who changed his name to Still to protect his wife, a fugitive slave. The younger Still moved to Philadelphia in 1844 and found employment as a mail clerk and janitor for the Pennsylvania Anti-Slavery Society. His continued efforts for self-education, his commitment to antislavery, and his concern for fugitive slaves led to increasing responsibilities in the society. In 1852 he was appointed chairman of the General Vigilance Committee of Philadelphia. Still reorganized and reinvigorated the committee by building a network of safe hiding places for

fugitives in the city's black community, by raising funds for fugitives, and by carefully monitoring the activity of slave catchers in Pennsylvania. Under his direction, the committee aided almost eight hundred fugitive slaves before the Civil War. Still's attention to detail and his careful record keeping contributed to his organizational and managerial achievements. As chairman of the vigilance committee, he recorded the personal history of each fugitive slave assisted by the committee. He later used this information to write *The Underground Railroad* (1872), an account that described the courage of fugitives and the extensive free black participation in the slave rescue efforts.

Still maintained close contacts with former slaves who had settled in Canada. In the 1850s, he acted as an agent for the black Canadian newspapers—Henry Bibb's *Voice of the Fugitive* and Mary Ann Shadd Cary's *Provincial Freeman*. He toured Canada West in 1855 to examine the condition of black communities and gather information to refute charges that fugitive slaves were unable to cope with freedom. Still also operated a boardinghouse in Philadelphia, and after the Civil War, he became a successful coal merchant. He dedicated much of his later life to improving the welfare of Philadelphia blacks. In 1859 he initiated a successful eight-year struggle to end discrimination on city streetcars. Two years later, he helped found and finance the Pennsylvania Social, Civil, and Statistical Association—an organization that sponsored cultural events and collected information and statistics on the city's black community. Still's civic leadership was evident in his work on behalf of several religious, social, and charitable organizations. He was a member of the Freedmen's Aid Commission, helped establish the Mission Sabbath School and a black Young Men's Christian Association, served on the Philadelphia Board of Trade, and was a director of black institutions for the aged and orphaned. Still's writings—his vigilance committee journal, pamphlets, and personal correspondence—remain a valuable source of nineteenth-century Afro-American history. *DANB*, 573–74; Larry Gara, "William Still and the Underground Railroad," *PH* 28:33–43 (January 1961); *VF*, 16 December 1852; *PFW*, 15 April 1854.

12.
William P. Newman to Frederick Douglass
1 October 1850

Passage of the Fugitive Slave Law of 1850 marked a dramatic and difficult moment for black abolitionists. The law's threat of arbitrary arrest and enslavement caused them to rethink abolitionist ideology, tactics, and goals; the federal government's growing complicity in sustaining slavery compelled them to question fundamental assumptions about the nation's institutions and political principles. Their analyses and recommendations helped set the tone for the black community's response. In a 1 October 1850 letter to Frederick Douglass's *North Star*, William P. Newman expressed a profound loss of faith in the federal government. He found the government's conduct so corrupt that he questioned whether "the Devil [would not] do well to *rent out hell* and move to the United States?" Newman, a Baptist clergyman and former student at Oberlin College, set aside his Christian pacifism and declared it his "fixed and changeless purpose to kill any so-called man who attempts to enslave me or mine." He urged blacks to pursue a course of militant resistance, implored fellow Christians to come to the aid of anyone threatened by the slave catchers, and encouraged both groups to agitate for the repeal of the legislation. Newman's call for resistance, rescue, and repeal was echoed by black abolitionists in churches, meeting halls, and antislavery journals throughout the North. Pease and Pease, *They Who Would Be Free*, 206–50; Quarles, *Black Abolitionists*, 197–215.

CLEVELAND, O[hio]

Oct[ober] 1, 1850

FREDERICK DOUGLASS:

On arriving here, I find no little excitement about the "Fugitive Slave Bill." Since President Fillmore "has unchained the tiger," by the use of his pen, on the 18th of Sept.,[1] exerting his power for the *glory* of God and the *liberty* of man, I have felt an ardent desire to have some religious-political watchman "tell us what the signs of promise are," for the world is expressing its opinion freely respecting that enlightened and Christian enactment called the "Fugitive Slave Bill," the sentiment of which is doubtless the result of the inspiring influence of his Satanic Majesty, the climax of his infernal wickedness.

It seems to me that the world has misunderstood, till the sitting of the last United States Congress, what the real and true mission of that government is. Is it not a mission of bonds and death? Our race has been taught to think that it was to be the example of all coming human governments, it being itself the model of heaven, as soon as it should ACT

3. Armed resistance to the Fugitive Slave Law of 1850 at Christiana, Pennsylvania, September 1851

From William Still, *Underground Railroad* (Philadelphia, 1872)

upon the principle that "there is a higher power than the Constitution." But all must confess, that were all legislative governments to follow the example it has set of late, that earth would be anything else than human.

It may properly be asked, would not the Devil do well to *rent out hell* and move to the United States, and rival, if possible, President Fillmore and his political followers? *If* he can beat them at the game of sin, the change will be well. Would not fallen angels make wise and humane Senators, compared with Cass, Clay and Webster?[2] The fugitive slave might have rejoiced had these men have had the experience of a lost being, or Fillmore the soul of Satan. The world must be convinced that damned spirits would do better and honor more the representative hall, than such men as Bissell, Brown, Buel, Eliot, Fuller, Gilbert, Hibbard, Mann, Miller and Walden.[3] God grant that

> Their names may rot
> On the scroll of time.

We are proud to say that even fugitive slaves pity the nation that makes colored men slaves and white men kidnappers. But I pity the MAN who willingly becomes such a slave and beast of burden, for

> God has a bolt unhurled
> For such in store.

I have often been struck with the great contrast between King James of England and President Fillmore of America.[4] One withstood the corrupting influences of irreligion—resisting demagogues, priests and the pope—writing for God and in behalf of man—giving the Bible to the poor, and sustaining its humane and God-established institutions. The other floats on the popular current of infidelity and oppression—opposing the truth, unless humanity be a lie, and seeking to sunder every cord that rivets creature to creature, and the finite to the Infinite. Also the different influence of these two men upon their fellow-creatures. James's right position, decision of character, and virtuous actions, bound the good will of his subjects to him with ligaments of eternal love—fixing the foundation of his throne not in the pleasure of any despot, but in the confidence and affection of his loyal people. But Fillmore's heartless position, indecision of character, and the want of a virtuous soul, have rendered him despicable in the eyes of the good, and contemptible in the just opinion of the bad. In seeking to please tyrants, he has lost the favor of all. And alas, the true church of Christ can no longer pray for the success of his truckling administration. It has given their souls to the oppressor, and their bodies to the prison, if they dare do their duty in obedience to Christ. In view of such facts, it is my candid conviction that the record of the infernal regions can exhibit no blacker deeds than the American archives, and the accursed Fugitive Slave Bill. Upright humanity cannot uphold the hand that signed that bill of abominations, unless it first does violence to its own nature. God is against the man who owns the hand. He is weighed in the balance, and found wanting. Such men as do him honor,

> The Devil fears,
> And slaves hate.

This truth will be exemplified, I believe, in certain parts of the country, in the attempts to take back to slavery and to death—yes, in the American hell itself—the dejected, poor, and panting fugitives. In honor of humanity, I am proud to say that Patrick Henry's motto is mine—"Give me Liberty or give me Death." I am frank to declare that it is my fixed and changeless purpose to kill any so-called man who attempts to enslave me or mine, if possible, though it be Millard Fillmore himself. To do this, in defence of personal liberty, to my mind, would be an act of the highest virtue, and white Americans must be real hypocrites if they say not to it—amen!

Do they not *saint* the spirits of '76 for their noble defence of their inalienable rights? Why then damn me for doing the same? 'Tis the 4th of July. Hark! What means that cannon's roar? 'Tis the joyful voice of a free people, eulogizing the man who exterminated tyrants, and gave to the American colonies freedom. Why, on a public day, those oratoric sounds, falling from human oracles—those words that burn—words mingled with eloquence divine—words that raise the dead? They are because of deeds done by our country's fathers, when they were oppressed and wronged. Such words tell how they obtained their earthly heritage, and independence for ourselves, pleasure for our families, and liberty forever for our hopeful posterity. Who that is oppressed himself, is not ready to do the like deeds for his race to come? Life is naught to lose. I am ready, willing, and should rejoice to die; and I glory in the fact that so many of my brethren in tribulation are of the same mind, and feel determined to be sacrificed rather than be enslaved. God grant that their number may be increased a thousand fold. Then shall tyrants know,

> Thrice armed is he
> Who hath his quarrel just.[5]

And now, friends of the beloved Jesus, can you and will you stand quietly and see your Savior kidnapped in the person of his poor? Remember, if you suffer it to be done unto one of the least of his brethren, you suffer it to be done unto him.

Professors of religion, can you and will you permit, silently, the American Congress to pass a bill bidding all its citizens to aid in the enslaving of the Son of God? It is your duty to let the word "repeal! *repeal!!*

REPEAL!!!" go forth, backed up by the Christian's motto, "resistance to tyrants is obedience to God."

And you, my brethren, the objects of hate and the victims of oppression, can you and will you allow yourselves to be made the dupes of despots and the slaves of tyrants, without resisting even to death? I hope not. Disgrace not your nature. Be not recreant to your God. Allow not posterity to curse thy memory and disown thy name for a base submission to avaricious knaves.

That you may "show yourself a MAN," is the constant and ardent prayer of Your brother in bonds,

W. P. NEWMAN[6]

North Star (Rochester, N.Y.), 24 October 1850.

1. Millard Fillmore (1800–1874), who was president of the United States from 1850 to 1853, signed the Fugitive Slave Law on 18 September 1850. A professional politician, he had served in the New York state legislature and in the U.S. Congress before being elected vice-president on the Whig ticket in 1848. He became president upon the death of Zachary Taylor on 9 July 1850. Fillmore's support and enforcement of the Fugitive Slave Law damaged his political career. *DAB*, 6:380–82.

2. Lewis Cass of Michigan, Henry Clay of Kentucky, and Daniel Webster of Massachusetts were major supporters of the Compromise of 1850 (including the Fugitive Slave Law) on the floor of the U.S. Senate. Cass (1782–1866), a conservative Democrat, had been the party's presidential candidate in 1848. After serving in the Senate (1845–48, 1849–57), he became secretary of state in the administration of James Buchanan. Clay (1777–1852), a slaveholding Whig, had been in the forefront of American politics for over thirty years. In 1820 and again in 1850, he negotiated Union-preserving compromises between proslavery politicians and their adversaries. Clay was an unsuccessful candidate for the presidency in 1824, 1832, and 1844. *DAB*, 3:562–64, 4:173–79.

3. Newman refers to ten northern members of the U.S. House of Representatives who voted for the Fugitive Slave Law of 1850. William Harrison Bissell of Illinois, William J. Brown of Indiana, Alexander W. Buel of Michigan, Thomas J. D. Fuller of Maine, Edward Gilbert of California, Harry Hibbard of Vermont, Job Mann of Pennsylvania, John Krepps Miller of Ohio, and Hiram Walden of New York were Democrats. The only Whig mentioned was Samuel Atkins Eliot of Massachusetts. These congressmen were regularly rebuked in antislavery broadsides during the early 1850s. *BDAC*, 595–96, 652, 663, 905, 976, 1000, 1113, 1334, 1411, 1867; Hamilton, *Prologue to Conflict*, 195–200; Langston Hughes, Milton Meltzer, and C. Eric Lincoln, eds., *A Pictorial History of Blackamericans* (New York, N.Y., 1983), 44.

4. Newman contrasts the religious activities of James I of England to Fillmore's endorsement of the Fugitive Slave Law. James I (1566–1625) ascended to the English throne in 1603. He repressed both Puritans and Catholics and vigorously defended the Church of England, which provoked widespread discontent.

He also penned several volumes on theological themes and is best remembered for authorizing the King James translation of the Bible.

5. Newman quotes from act 1, scene 3, of William Shakespeare's *Henry VI, part 2*:

> What stronger breastplate than a heart untainted!
> Thrice is he armed that hath his quarrel just,
> And he but naked, though locked up in steel,
> Whose conscience with injustice is corrupted.

6. William P. Newman (1815–1866) was born a slave in Richmond, Virginia, but escaped from bondage in the 1830s. He eventually settled in Ohio and, after a year of study at Oberlin College (1842–43), was ordained a Baptist clergyman. During the next two years, he pastored the Union Baptist Church in Cincinnati and did itinerant preaching in Zanesville and Chillicothe. About this same time, he became involved in Ohio antislavery activities, attended two black state conventions, and served as a subscription agent for David Jenkins's *Palladium of Liberty*.

In 1845 Newman accepted an appointment in Canada West from the American Baptist Free Mission Society. Arriving at the Dawn settlement in June, he took charge of the British-American Institute and assumed secretarial duties on the Dawn executive committee. His insistence on financial accountability led to confrontations with Dawn agents Hiram Wilson and Josiah Henson. Frustrated by affairs at Dawn, Newman resigned in September 1846 and returned to Cincinnati, where he again served his old congregation and briefly acted as an agent for the Colored Orphan Asylum. But he continued to criticize the conduct of Wilson and Henson and brought Dawn's condition to public attention. When responsibility for Dawn fell to the ABFMS in 1850, Newman returned to Canada West and assisted Rev. Samuel H. Davis in managing the British-American Institute. His work at Dawn ended when British abolitionist John Scoble assumed control of the institute in 1852. Newman then settled in Toronto where he pastored Baptist congregations for the next seven years and engaged in antislavery and civil rights work. He served as secretary of the Canadian Anti-Slavery Baptist Association and the Provincial Union Association and helped lead the black struggle for equal access to the province's public schools. In 1855 Newman accepted the editorship of the *Provincial Freeman*, a position that gave him a forum to express his political conservatism, his opposition to begging practices, and his militant abolitionism. He remained at that post for one year.

Newman became pessimistic about black prospects in Canada West during the late 1850s. Black minority status, the persistence of racial prejudice, and the Canadian climate convinced him that the Afro-American destiny lay beyond the North American continent. Unimpressed by Martin R. Delany's Niger valley venture, he looked to the Caribbean and traveled to Haiti as an ABFMS missionary in 1859 to investigate the feasibility of black immigration there. His initial reports were positive, but by the summer of 1860, he offered a more skeptical assessment, criticizing Haiti's military government, Catholic faith, and liberal social customs. By the time Newman returned to Canada West in late 1861, he was a staunch opponent of Haitian settlement. Believing that blacks had no stake in the outcome of the Civil War, he promoted Jamaican immigration during the early war years. But by 1864 he had returned to his former position at the Union Baptist Church in Cincinnati, enthused by the new opportunities that Reconstruction offered. He attended the National Convention of Colored Men (1864) and served as an officer of the National Equal Rights League. Newman led an attempt to merge black and white Baptists into an interracial, egalitarian denomination, but this ambitious work had only begun when he died of cholera in 1866. James Melvin Washington, "The Origins and Emergence of Black Baptist Separatism, 1863–1897" (Ph.D. diss., Yale University, 1979), 33, 43, 53, 62, 70, 72–74, 79–83; *E*, 1 September 1842; *P*, 18 October 1843 [4:0685]; *PL*, 27 December 1843, 1 May, 16 October 1844 [4:0712]; *CF*, 27 November 1845 [5:0114]; Robin W. Winks, *The Blacks in Canada: A History* (New Haven, Conn., 1971), 164–65, 196–203; William H. Pease and Jane H. Pease, *Black Utopia: Negro Communal Experiments in America* (Madison, Wis. 1963), 71–77; *ASB*, 21 January 1848 [5:0559]; *NSt*, 22 December 1848, 9 March 1849, 21 October 1852 [5:0862]; *WC*, 29 October 1850 [6:0654]; *VF*, 15 January, 9 April 1851, 23 September, 21 October 1852 [6:0878]; *Lib*, 4 March 1853 [8:0154]; Donald George Simpson, "Negroes in Ontario from Early Times to 1870" (Ph.D. diss., University of Western Ontario, 1971), 868–69; *PFW*, 24 March 1853, 15, 29 April, 24 June, 1 July, 9 August, 2, 23 September, 14 October 1854, 13, 20 January, 30 June, 22, 29 August, 15, 22 September, 22 December 1855, 19 April 1856 [8:0175, 9:0018, 0110, 0139, 0787, 0807, 0833]; William P. Newman to Egerton Ryerson, 7 March 1852, 13 January 1856, Ryerson Papers, CaOTAr; *WAA*, 23 July 1859, 23 June 1860, 31 August, 30 November 1861, 4 January, 29 March 1862 [11:0865, 12:0807, 13:0718, 0942, 14:0058, 0203]; *PP*, 31 August, 14 September 1861 [13:0715, 0753]; *CP*, 19 July, 20 December 1859, 22 March, 21 June 1860 [11:0862, 12:0304, 0583, 0804]; *Proceedings of the National Convention of Colored Men, Held in Syracuse, N.Y., October 4, 5, 6, and 7, 1864* (Boston, Mass., 1864), 6.

13.
Resolutions by a Committee of Philadelphia Blacks
Presented at the Brick Wesley
African Methodist Episcopal Church
Philadelphia, Pennsylvania
14 October 1850

The Fugitive Slave Law provoked an outpouring of protest in the black community. Throughout the fall of 1850, northern blacks in unprecedented numbers attended hundreds of gatherings in dozens of cities to express their outrage and their determination to resist the law. Joshua B. Smith, a black caterer, demonstrated the prevailing mood when he brandished weapons at the podium of a Boston assembly. On 14 October, hundreds of Philadelphia blacks met in mass protest at the Brick Wesley African Methodist Episcopal Church. A committee of thirteen men, who ranged from members of the working class to members of the elite, drafted ten resolutions describing the seriousness of the threat and conveying the militancy of the black response. They challenged the legality and morality of the law and vowed to "resist to the death" any attempts at enforcement. After a brief debate, the resolutions were unanimously adopted. In rejecting the law and affirming the right of self-defense, Philadelphia blacks typified the way in which the Fugitive Slave Law mobilized entire black communities. *NASS*, 10, 31 October 1850 [6:0606–11]; *IC*, 28 September, 26 October 1850 [6:0589, 0652]; *SJ*, 19 October 1850 [6:0620]; *PF*, 31 October 1850 [6:0657]; *SDS*, 27 September 1850 [6:0588].

Whereas, the Declaration of American Independence declares it to be a self-evident truth, "that all men are created equal, and are endowed by their Creator with certain inalienable rights, among which are life, liberty, and the pursuit of happiness"; and whereas, the Constitution of the United States, Art. 1, sect. 9, declares that "the privilege of the writ of habeas corpus shall not be suspended"; and in Art. 5 of the Amendments, that "no person shall be deprived of life, liberty, or property, without due process of law"; and whereas, the late Fugitive Slave Bill, recently enacted by the Congress of the United States, is in clear, palpable violation of these several provisions; therefore,

1. Resolved, That while we have heretofore yielded obedience to the laws of our country, however hard some of them have borne upon us, we deem this law so wicked, so atrocious, so utterly at variance with the principles of the Constitution; so subversive of the objects of all law, the protection of the lives, liberty, and property of the governed; so repugnant to the highest attributes of God, justice and mercy; and so horribly

cruel in its clearly expressed mode of operation, that we deem it our sacred duty, a duty that we owe to ourselves, our wives, our children, and to our common nature, as well as to the panting fugitive from oppression, to resist this law at any cost and at all hazards; and we hereby pledge our lives, our fortunes, and our sacred honor so to do.

2. Resolved, That we deem the laws of God at all times paramount to any human laws; and that, in obedience to the command, to "hide the outcast, and betray not him that wandereth,"[1] we shall never refuse aid and shelter and succor to any brother or sister who has escaped from the prison-house of Southern bondage, but shall do all we can to prevent their being dragged back to a slavery inconceivably worse than death.

3. Resolved, That whenever a Government "frameth mischief by law," or "decrees unrighteous decrees,"[2] or concentrates all its power to strengthen the arm of the oppressor to crush the weak, that Government puts itself in an attitude hostile to every principle of justice—hostile to the liberal spirit of the law, hostile to that God who "executeth righteousness and judgment for all that are oppressed."[3]

4. Resolved, That in our resistance to this most cruel law, we appeal to our own boasted Declaration of Independence, to the inherent righteousness of our cause, to the moral sense of enlightened nations all over the world, and to the character of that God, who by a series of the most astounding miracles on record, declared his sympathy for the oppressed and his hatred of the oppressor.

5. Resolved, That feeling the need in this trying hour of the Wisdom that erreth not, and the arm that is invincible to defend and guide us, we therefore call upon all the colored pastors of our churches in the Free States (so called) to set apart the first Monday night in each month for public prayer and supplication, that the hearts of this people may be so turned to the weak and the oppressed, that the operation of this cruel law may be powerless, and that the time may soon come when "liberty shall be proclaimed throughout ALL the land unto ALL the inhabitants thereof."[4]

6. Resolved, That we will hold up to the scorn of the civilized world that hypocrisy which welcomes to our shores the refugees from Austrian tyranny, and at the same time would send the refugees from American Slavery back to a doom, compared with which, Austrian tyranny is mercy.[5]

7. Resolved, That we endorse, to the full, the sentiment of the Revolutionary patriot of Virginia, and should the awful alternative be presented to us, will act fully up to it—"Give me Liberty or give me Death."[6]

8. Resolved, That a Committee be appointed to draft an appeal to the citizens of the Commonwealth of Pennsylvania, setting forth the Anti-Republican, Anti-Christian, Anti-human nature of the Fugitive Slave Bill, and asking of them their sympathy and succor.

9. Resolved, That having already witnessed to some extent the cruel operations of this law; having felt such anguish as no language can describe in seeing the wife flying from her home and the embraces of her husband, and the husband compelled to fly from his wife and helpless children, to gain that security in the land of a Monarchy which they could not enjoy in this Republic;[7] we ask, calmly and solemnly ask, the American people, "What have we done to suffer such treatment at your hands?" And may we not, in the sight of that God with whom there is no respect of persons, appeal to your sense of justice and mercy to have this most cruel law repealed as soon as Congress shall reassemble, and in the meantime may we not ask you to create, by all lawful means, such a public sentiment as shall render its operation upon us powerless?

10. Resolved, That, not in the spirit of bravado, neither of affected unconsciousness to the cruelties of public sentiment and law, in regard to our unfortunate and abused race, but seeing clearly, and knowing fully, the unjust prejudice existing against us, and using only those moral means of truth, sufficient as we deem them by a certain process, to the "pulling down the stronghold" of the injustice and wrong that now afflict us; yet in view of the unheard of atrociousness of the provisions of this infernal FUGITIVE SLAVE BILL, we solemnly declare before the Most High God, and the world, to resist to the death any attempt to enforce it upon our persons, adopting fully the noble sentiment of the Irish Patriot—

Whether on the scaffold high,
Or on the battle's van,
The fittest place where man can die,
Is where he dies for man.[8]

COMMITTEE[9]
Dr. J. J. G. Bias
Robert Purvis
J. C. Bowers
A. Whipper
Isaiah Wears
J. W. Stokes
Mr. Shelly
John P. Burr
Thomas Kinnard
James Henderson
P. Tillman
H. Hazell
Wm. Nickless

Pennsylvania Freeman (Philadelphia, Pa.), 31 October 1850.

1. The committee paraphrases Isaiah 16:3, which advises sanctuary for Moabite refugees: "Give counsel, grant justice; make your shade like the night at the height of noon; hide the outcasts, betray not the fugitive."

2. The committee quotes from Psalms 94:20 and Isaiah 10:1. The passage from Psalms is a prayer for deliverance from political oppression: "Can wicked rulers be allied with thee, who frame mischief by statute." The prophet Isaiah also condemns abuse of political power: "Woe to those who decree iniquitous decrees, and the writers who keep writing oppression."

3. The committee quotes from Psalms 103:6.

4. The committee quotes from Leviticus 25:10, in which Moses is divinely instructed about the establishment of a "year of jubilee."

5. The committee contrasts federal enforcement of the Fugitive Slave Law of 1850 with the enthusiastic reception accorded Louis Kossuth, the leader of the Hungarian independence movement, in the United States. Forced into permanent exile after the collapse of the Revolution of 1848, Kossuth toured the United States in 1849 and 1851, drawing widespread acclaim. But abolitionists condemned him after failing to enlist his aid in the antislavery struggle. Donald S. Spencer, *Louis Kossuth and Young America: A Study of Sectionalism and Foreign Policy, 1848–1852* (Columbia, Mo., 1977).

6. The committee refers to Patrick Henry.

7. The committee refers to the thousands of fugitive slaves who fled to the British North American Provinces, particularly Canada West, in reaction to the Fugitive Slave Law.

8. The committee quotes from "The Place to Die" by Michael J. Barry (1817–1889), an Irish poet and magistrate. The poem was originally published in the 28 September 1844 issue of the Dublin *Nation*.

9. The committee of thirteen charged with drafting these resolutions reflected the broadly based opposition of Philadelphia blacks to the Fugitive Slave Law. The more prominent members—Robert Purvis (1810–1898), John C. Bowers, John P. Burr (b. 1792), and James J. G. Bias (d. 1860)—had been established leaders of the local black community since the early 1830s. They were also well known beyond Philadelphia because of their participation in state and national conventions, moral reform organizations, and the antislavery movement. They undoubtedly guided the committee's deliberations and were largely responsible for the tone and content of the resolutions. Several younger members—Isaiah C. Wears, the son of Josiah C. Wears; Alfred P. Whipper (b. 1830), the younger brother of William Whipper; and William Nickless (b. 1829), the son of Samuel Nickless—represented the rising generation among Philadelphia's black elite. In contrast, baker James Henderson (1814–1863) and laborers Henry Shelly (b. 1811), Peter Tillman (b. 1815), and Henry Hazell had no previous record of antislavery activism or community leadership. Thomas Kinnard, a former slave, and John W. Stokes (1816–1862), a cake vendor, had come to the city from Maryland. Both had some prior involvement in the antislavery movement. Although most of the members of the committee remained in Philadelphia after 1850, doing what they could to blunt the effects of the Fugitive Slave Law, Whipper, Kinnard, and Stokes eventually left for the black settlements in Canada West. In December 1852, Purvis, Burr, and Wears helped organize Philadelphia's General Vigilance Committee. U.S. Census, 1850; *NECAUL*, 7 September

1837; *PP*, 13 July 1861, 13 February 1862; *WAA*, 12 November 1859, 10 January 1863; *Lib*, 29 November 1861, 3 January 1862; Harry C. Silcox, "The Black 'Better Class' Dilemma: Philadelphia Prototype Isaiah C. Wears," *PMHB* 113:47, 64 (January 1989); C. Peter Ripley et al., eds., *The Black Abolitionist Papers*, 3 vols. to date (Chapel Hill, N.C., 1985–), 2:332–33n, 459n; Still, *Underground Railroad*, 636.

14.
Exchange between H. Ford Douglas
and William Howard Day
at the Second Baptist Church
Columbus, Ohio
16 January 1851

The Fugitive Slave Law forced blacks to rethink a wide range of issues, including race, citizenship, and their future in the United States. One of the more divisive questions was the influence of slavery on the U.S. Constitution—the very foundation of American government. The Fugitive Slave Law seemed to confirm the Garrisonian view that the Constitution was a proslavery pact—"a covenant with death and an agreement with hell." In mid-January 1851, Ohio blacks debated the nature of the document at their state convention in Columbus. Chaired by David Jenkins, a local black leader, this was the first state black gathering since the passage of the Fugitive Slave Law. The delegates approved three strongly worded resolutions condemning what one black abolitionist called this "abomination of all abominations." In the course of debate, an exchange ensued between two young Cleveland blacks, H. Ford Douglas and William Howard Day, when the former introduced a resolution stating that "no colored man can consistently vote under the United States Constitution." Douglas argued that the proslavery character of the document made participation in the American political process a violation of antislavery principles. He pointed to the Fugitive Slave Law to justify his position. Day challenged Douglas's contention by making a distinction between the democratic principles embodied in the Constitution and the way it was construed by proslavery politicians. After lengthy discussion, the delegates rejected Douglas's resolution by a twenty-eight to two vote. *Minutes of the State Convention of the Colored Citizens of Ohio, Convened at Columbus, Jan. 15th, 16th, 17th, and 18th, 1851* (Columbus, Ohio, [1851]), 7–12 [6:0741–44]; Blackett, *Beating against the Barriers*, 298.

Mr. Chairman:

I am in favor of the adoption of the resolution. I hold, sir, that the Constitution of the United States is pro-slavery, considered so by those who framed it, and construed to that end ever since its adoption. It is well known that in 1787, in the Convention that framed the Constitution, there was considerable discussion on the subject of slavery. South Carolina and Georgia refused to come into the Union, without the Convention would allow the continuation of the Slave Trade for twenty years. According to the demands of these two States, the Convention submitted to that guilty contract, and declared that the Slave Trade should not be prohibited prior to 1808.[1] Here we see them engrafting into the Constitution a clause legalizing and protecting one of the vilest systems of wrong ever invented by the cupidity and avarice of man. And by virtue of that agreement, our citizens went to the shores of Africa, and there seized upon the rude barbarian, as he strolled unconscious of impending danger, amid his native forests, as free as the winds that beat on his native shores. Here we see them dragging these bleeding victims to the slave ship by virtue of that instrument, compelling them to endure all the horrors of the "middle passage,"[2] until they arrived at this asylum of western Liberty, where they were doomed to perpetual chains. Now, I hold, in view of this fact, no colored man can consistently vote under the United States Constitution. That instrument also provides for the return of fugitive slaves. And, sir, one of the greatest lights now adorning the galaxy of American Literature declares that the "Fugitive Law" is in accordance with that stipulation—a law unequalled in the worst days of Roman despotism, and unparalleled in the annals of heathen jurisprudence. You might search the pages of history in vain to find a more striking exemplification of the compound of all villainies! It shrouds our country in blackness; every green spot in nature is blighted and blasted by that withering Upas. Every monument of national greatness, erected to commemorate the virtuous and the good, whether its foundation rests upon the hallowed repositories that contain the ashes of the first martyrs in the cause of American Liberty, or lifts itself in solemn and majestic grandeur, from that sacred spot where the first great battle of the Revolution was fought, no matter how sacred the soil, whether fertilized by the blood of a Warren,[3] or signalized by the brilliant and daring feats of Marion![4] We are all, according to Congressional enactments, involved in the horrible system of human bondage; compelled, sir, by virtue of that instrument, to assist in the black and disgraceful avocation of recapturing the American Hungarian[5] in his hurried flight from that worse than Russian or Austrian despotism, however much he may be inspired with that love of liberty which burns eternal in every human heart. Sir, every man is inspired with a love of liberty—a deep and abiding love of liberty. I care not where he may dwell—whether amid the snows of the polar regions, or weltering beneath an African sun, or clanking his iron fetters in this free Republic—I care not how degraded the man—that Promethean spark[6] still lives, and burns, in secret and brilliant grandeur, upon his inmost soul, and the iron rust of slavery and uninterrupted despotism, can never extinguish it. Did not the American Congress, professing to be a constitutional body, after nine months' arduous and patriotic legislation, as Webster would have it, strike down in our persons the writ of *Habeas Corpus* and *Trial by Jury*[7]—those great bulwarks of human freedom, baptized by the blood, and sustained by the patriotic exertions of our English ancestors.

The gentleman from Franklin (Mr. Jenkins), alluded to the Free Soil candidate for Governor.[8] I will here state that I had the pleasure, during the Gubernatorial campaign, to hear Mr. Smith make a speech in opposition to the "Fugitive Law," in which he remarked that it was humiliating to him to acknowledge that our forefathers did make a guilty compromise with Slavery in order to form this Union; and so far as the validity of that agreement was concerned, he felt that it was not binding upon him as a man, and that he never would obey any law which conflicts with that higher law,[9] that has its seat in the bosom of God, and utters its voice in the harmony of the world.

Mr. Douglas[10] having taken his seat, Mr. Day[11] of Lorain obtained the floor, and addressing the President, in substance said:

I cannot sit still, while this resolution is pending, and by my silence acquiesce in it. For all who have known me for years past, know that to the principle of the resolution I am, on principle opposed. The remarks of the gentleman from Cuyahoga (Mr. Douglas), it seems to me, partake of the error of many others who discuss this question, namely, of making the *construction* of the Constitution of the United States the same as the Constitution itself. There is no dispute between us in regard to the proslavery action of this government, nor any doubt in our minds in regard to the aid which the Supreme Court of the United States has given to Slavery, and by their unjust and, according to their own rules, illegal decisions; but *that* is not the Constitution—they are not that under which I vote. We, most of us, profess to believe the Bible; but men have, from the Bible, attempted to justify the worst of iniquities. Do we, in such a case, discard the Bible, believing as we do that iniquities find no shield there?—or do we not rather discard the false opinions of mistaken men in regard to it? As someone else says, if a judge makes a wrong decision in an important case, shall we abolish the Court? Shall we not rather remove the *judge*, and put in his place one who will judge righteously? We all so decide. So in regard to the Constitution. In voting, with judges' decisions we have nothing to do. Our business is with the Constitution. If it says it was framed to "establish justice," it, of course, is opposed to injustice; if it says plainly "no person shall be deprived of life, *liberty*, or property, without due process of law," I suppose it means it, and I shall avail myself of the benefit of it. Sir, coming up as I do, in the midst of three millions of men in chains, and five hundred thousand only half free, I consider every instrument precious which guarantees to me liberty. I consider the Constitution the foundation of American liberties, and wrapping myself in the flag of the nation, I would plant myself upon that Constitution, and using the weapons they have given me, I would appeal to the American people for the rights thus guaranteed.

Mr. Douglas replied by saying:

The gentleman may wrap the stars and stripes of his country around him forty times, if possible, and with the Declaration of Independence in one hand, and the Constitution of our common country in the other, may seat himself under the shadow of the frowning monument of Bunker Hill, and if the slaveholder, under the Constitution, and with the "Fugitive Bill," doesn't find you, then there doesn't exist a Constitution.

Yes, resumed Mr. Day, and with the Constitution I will *find* the "Fugitive Bill." You will mark this, the gentleman has assumed the same error as before, and has not attempted to reply to my argument. This is all I need now say.

Mr. President:

I do not intend to make a speech, but merely to define my position on this subject, as I consider it one of no ordinary importance.

I perfectly agree with the gentleman from Cuyahoga (Mr. Douglas), who presented this resolution, that the United States Constitution is pro-slavery. It was made to foster and uphold that abominable, vampirish and bloody system of American slavery. The highest judicial tribunals of the country have so decided. Members, while in the Convention and on returning to their constituents, declared that Slavery was one of the interests sought to be protected by the Constitution. It was so understood and so administered all over the country. But whether the Constitution is pro-slavery, and whether colored men "can consistently vote under that Constitution," are two very distinct questions; and while I would answer the former in the affirmative, I would not, like the gentleman from Cuyahoga, answer the latter in the negative. I would vote under the United States Constitution on the same principle (circumstances being favorable), that I would call on every slave, from Maryland to Texas, to arise and assert their *liberties*, and cut their masters' throats if they attempt again to reduce them to slavery. Whether or not this principle is correct, an impartial posterity and the Judge of the Universe shall decide.

Sir, I have long since adopted as my God, the freedom of the colored people of the United States, and my religion, to do anything that will effect that object, however much it may differ from the precepts taught in the Bible, such as "Whosoever shall smite thee on thy right cheek, turn to him the other also"; or "Love your enemies; bless them that curse you, and pray for them that despitefully use you and persecute you." Those are the lessons taught us by the religion of our white brethren, when they are free and we are slaves; but when their enslavement is attempted, then, "Resistance to Tyranny is obedience to God." This doctrine is equally true in regard to colored men as white men. I hope, therefore, Mr. President, that the resolution will not be adopted, but that colored men will vote, or do anything else under the Constitution that will aid in effecting our liberties, and in securing our political, religious and intellectual elevation.

Minutes of the State Convention of the Colored Citizens of Ohio, Convened at Columbus, Jan. 15th, 16th, 17th, and 18th, 1851 (Columbus, Ohio, [1851]), 8–11.

1. The problem of slavery framed much of the debate at the Constitutional Convention in 1787. James Madison jotted in his private notes that "the institution of slavery and its consequences formed a line of discrimination" between northern and southern delegates. One slaveholding delegate remarked that southern states wanted guarantees that "their Negroes may not be taken from them." Led by delegates from Georgia and South Carolina, the proslavery group won important concessions on taxation, representation, fugitive slaves, and the slave trade. According to article 1, section 1, of the Constitution, the importation of slaves could not be abolished for twenty years. The U.S. Congress ended the slave trade in 1808. Paul Finkelman, *An Imperfect Union: Slavery, Federalism, and Comity* (Chapel Hill, N.C., 1981), 23–24.

2. The term "middle passage" referred to the forced transatlantic voyage of slaves from West Africa to the New World. The forty- to sixty-day sea passage, the first stage of slavery, was usually characterized by barbaric treatment, malnutrition, disease, and death. Some ten to twelve million slaves were brought to the New World between 1451 and 1870.

3. Joseph Warren (1741–1775), a Boston physician, abandoned a successful practice to further the rebel cause in the American Revolution. In May 1775, he was elected president pro tempore of the Second Continental Congress. Following his death one month later at the Battle of Bunker Hill, he became a martyr and a symbol of the Revolutionary cause. *DAB*, 19:482–83.

4. Francis Marion (1732–1795) of South Carolina, a lieutenant colonel in the Continental Army during the American Revolution, earned the nickname "the Swamp Fox" for his resourceful guerrilla tactics. *DAB*, 12:283–84.

5. Douglas compares the situation of fugitive slaves to that of Louis Kossuth and other Hungarian nationalists who fled to the United States after the combined armies of Austria and Russia crushed the Revolution of 1848.

6. Douglas refers to Prometheus, a figure in Greek mythology who brought the gift of fire to mankind. He has become synonymous with resistance to tyranny and injustice.

7. Douglas refers to Daniel Webster and the debate in the U.S. Congress over the Fugitive Slave Law of 1850.

8. Edward Smith was the Free Soil candidate for governor of Ohio in 1850. He was overwhelmingly defeated. Originally a Methodist clergyman, Smith served as an itinerant preacher in the denomination's Baltimore Conference. But in 1841, shortly after being selected presiding elder for the Pittsburgh Conference, he broke with the Methodists over the slavery issue. He then joined the Wesleyan Methodist church, a comeouter sect. Smith gravitated to the Liberty party in the early 1840s and edited the Pittsburgh *Spirit of Liberty* (1841–43), a party organ. He also wrote several abolitionist tracts and compiled *Uncle Tom's Kindred* (1853), a ten-volume collection of antislavery literature. Lucius C. Matlack, *The History of American Slavery and Methodism from 1780 to 1849 and History of the Wesleyan Methodist Connection in America* (1849; reprint, New York, N.Y.,

1971), 226, 272–81; Theodore C. Smith, *The Liberty and Free Soil Parties in the Northwest* (New York, N.Y., 1897), 183–85; William B. Gravely, "Research Log for Institutional History of Northern Black Churches, 1787–1860," 1981–82, unpublished ms. in the editors' possession.

9. Abolitionists seized upon the doctrine of higher law as their most effective argument against the institution of slavery and the legal apparatus that supported it, including the U.S. Constitution. According to antislavery theorists, natural law endowed men with certain inalienable rights, which human laws could not rescind. Slavery, they argued, contradicted those rights and should be resisted. The doctrine was frequently applied to the Fugitive Slave Law of 1850. David Brion Davis, *The Problem of Slavery in the Age of Revolution, 1770–1823* (Ithaca, N.Y., 1975), 268–96, 317–34, 401–3, 504–21; Dwight L. Dumond, *Antislavery: The Crusade for Freedom in America* (New York, N.Y., 1966), 81–82, 231–33.

10. Hezekiah Ford Douglas (1831–1865) was born a slave in Virginia. He escaped from bondage in 1846, settled in Cleveland, and obtained employment as a barber. Although self-educated, his later speeches indicate that he acquired a remarkable mastery of the Bible, classical literature, history, drama, and poetry. Despite his youth, Douglas established himself in the Ohio black community. His handsome appearance and exceptional oratorical talents, which he displayed at black state conventions during the early 1850s, also attracted attention among white abolitionists. Douglas's hatred of American slavery and racial prejudice and his perception that the Constitution was a proslavery document convinced him that blacks owed no allegiance to the United States. By 1852 he was a confirmed emigrationist. He played an influential role at the 1854 and 1856 meetings of the National Emigration Convention in Cleveland. At the latter gathering, he was appointed to the movement's General Board of Commissioners. Between the two sessions, Douglas moved to Chicago, where he helped revitalize Illinois's black state convention movement and led protests against the state's black laws.

In early 1856, Douglas became coproprietor of the *Provincial Freeman*. His earlier work as a Cleveland subscription agent for Henry Bibb's *Voice of the Fugitive* had convinced him that black success in Canada West would help uproot the institution of slavery. Douglas viewed this as a chance to contribute to that success. He assumed little editorial responsibility but contributed articles and toured Canada West and the northern United States to enlist subscribers. He viewed the separate black institutions he found in Canada West as unnecessary and urged black Canadians to become full and loyal British citizens, a position that made him unpopular among some black Canadians. A disillusioned Douglas returned to Chicago in late 1858 and, within a few months, became an agent of Congressman Francis P. Blair's Central American Land Company, which promoted black settlement on the isthmus. After Blair's scheme failed, Douglas returned to antislavery lecturing. At the invitation of abolitionist Parker Pillsbury, he made an extensive antislavery lecture tour of New England in 1860, much of it as a lecturing agent of the Massachusetts Anti-Slavery Society. His speeches during this tour demonstrated a more militant tone and advocated violent overthrow of slavery. In January 1861, Douglas returned to Chicago as the midwestern agent for James Redpath's Haytian Emigration Bureau. The Civil

War interrupted his Haitian efforts, and enthused by this prospect for a violent end to slavery, he enlisted in the Ninety-fifth Regiment of Illinois Infantry Volunteers in July 1862. The light-skinned Douglas was one of only a few blacks to serve in a white regiment during the war. In 1863 he was authorized to raise an independent black company. It was mustered in during early 1865, saw only limited fighting, and was mustered out within a few months. Douglas is believed to have been the only black officer to lead troops into combat during the war. After the war, Douglas attempted to establish a restaurant in Atchison, Kansas, but weakened by malaria, he died in November 1865. Robert L. Harris, Jr., "H. Ford Douglas: Afro-American Antislavery Emigrationist," *JNH* 62:217–34 (July 1977).

11. William Howard Day (1825–1900), one of Ohio's foremost black abolitionists, was born in New York City. His father died in 1829, leaving the family in difficult circumstances; his mother eventually consented to his adoption by J. P. Williston, an ink manufacturer and reformer from Northampton, Massachusetts. Williston raised Day in a strict but benevolent manner, provided for his education, and apprenticed him in the print shop of the *Hampshire Herald*, a local newspaper. Day's own experiences in an interracial household convinced him that racial integration was possible in American society. He entered Oberlin College in 1843, the only black in a class of fifty students. When he graduated four years later, he had already earned a reputation as a spokesman for Ohio blacks. A committed political abolitionist, he endorsed the Liberty and Free Soil parties, led the struggle to overturn Ohio's black laws, and lobbied for black suffrage before the state legislature and the 1850–51 state constitutional convention. Day was a prominent figure at several black state and national conventions, and in 1853 he represented Ohio blacks on the National Council of the Colored People.

Day began a career in journalism in 1850 as a reporter and editor for the Cleveland *True Democrat*. In April 1853, he founded his own newspaper, the *Aliened American*, which spoke for western blacks chafing under direction of eastern black leaders. Day broke with the eastern leadership and joined Martin R. Delany's western faction at the 1854 and 1856 national emigration conventions in Cleveland. Although he had previously opposed emigration, he announced that he "would not discourage individuals who are disposed to emigrate to Africa or the West Indies." The demise of the *Aliened American*, the persistence of northern racial prejudice, and poor health soon prompted him to move to Canada West, where he farmed and wrote occasional pieces for the *Provincial Freeman*. Later as president of the General Board of Commissioners for the National Emigration Convention in Chatham (1858), his ambivalence led the commissioners to offer only a tepid endorsement of Delany's Niger Valley Exploring Party.

In the summer of 1859, Day accompanied William King, the founder of the successful Elgin community, on a fund-raising tour of Britain. When he returned to the United States in 1863, he settled in New York City and edited the *Zion Standard*, the organ of the African Methodist Episcopal Zion church. After the Civil War, he served as general secretary of the Freedmen's American and British Commission (1866) and as superintendent of schools for the Freedmen's Bureau in Maryland and Delaware (1867–68). Day moved to Harrisburg in the 1870s and published *Our National Progress*, a widely circulated weekly devoted to black issues and Republican politics. His involvement in local Republican politics waned in the 1880s, but he continued his religious and educational activities, serving as general secretary of the AMEZ General Conference (1876–96) and as a member of the board of education for the Harrisburg public schools. In recognition of his community service and standing, Day received an honorary doctor of divinity degree in 1887 from Livingstone College. *AA*, 9 April 1853 [8:0208]; Miller, *Search for a Black Nationality*, 180–225; Blackett, *Beating against the Barriers*, 287–386.

15.
Speech by Sojourner Truth
Delivered at the Universalist Church
Akron, Ohio
29 May 1851

Antebellum black women suffered the double restraints of racism and sexism. During the 1830s, Maria W. Stewart stretched the limits of traditional gender roles by delivering public lectures. But few black women directly challenged the social restrictions of womanhood until the 1850s when Mary Ann Shadd Cary, Frances Ellen Watkins Harper, Sarah P. Remond, Margaretta Forten, Harriet Purvis, and dozens of others joined the nascent women's rights movement. Few black women combined abolitionism and feminism as effectively as Sojourner Truth, a former slave from New York's Hudson River valley. Like many other women abolitionists, she came to feminism by way of the antislavery lecture platform. Truth's rejection of domesticity frequently sparked popular outrage, but her Dutch accent, powerful voice, infectious humor, and "whole-souled, earnest gestures" captivated audiences. This was the case on 29 May 1851, when she spoke before a women's rights convention at the Universalist Church in Akron, Ohio. In this, the earliest known version of her most famous address, Truth proved to the scores of men and women in the audience that she was "a match for most men." *NASS*, 15 May 1844; *ASB*, 7, 14, 21 June 1851; *Lib*, 13 June 1851; Dorothy Sterling, ed., *We Are Your Sisters: Black Women in the Nineteenth Century* (New York, N.Y., 1984), 120–21, 176–78.

May I[1] say a few words? Receiving an affirmative answer, she proceeded; I want to say a few words about this matter. I am a woman's rights. I have as much muscle as any man, and can do as much work as any man. I have plowed and reaped and husked and chopped and mowed, and can any man do more than that? I have heard much about the sexes being equal; I can carry as much as any man, and can eat as much too, if I can get it. I am as strong as any man that is now. As for intellect, all I can say is, if woman have a pint and man a quart—why can't she have her little pint full? You need not be afraid to give us our rights for fear we will take too much, for we can't take more than our pint'll hold. The poor men seem to be all in confusion, and don't know what to do. Why children, if you have woman's rights give it to her and you will feel better. You will have your own rights, and they won't be so much trouble. I can't read, but I can hear. I have heard the bible and have learned that Eve caused man to sin. Well if woman upset the world, do give her a chance to set it right side up again. The Lady has spoken about Jesus, how he never spurned woman from him, and she was right. When Lazarus died, Mary and Martha[2] came to him with faith and love and besought him to raise their brother. And Jesus wept—and Lazarus came forth. And how came Jesus into the world? Through God who created him and woman who bore him. Man, where is your part? But the women are coming up, blessed be God, and a few of the men are coming up with them. But man is in a tight place, the poor slave is on him, woman is coming on him, and he is surely between a hawk and a buzzard.

Anti-Slavery Bugle (Salem, Ohio), 21 June 1851.

1. Sojourner Truth (ca. 1797–1883), or Isabella Van Wagener as she was known during the early part of her public career, was born a slave in Hurley, Ulster County, New York. She married another slave named Thomas and bore five children. Truth passed through several owners and suffered repeated beatings before running away in 1827, the year preceding the emancipation of New York's slaves. About 1829, after the death of her husband, she arrived in New York City, found work as a domestic servant, and began having mystical experiences. She assisted an unorthodox preacher named Elijah Pierson in his ministry to the city's prostitutes. In May 1832, she met another eccentric street preacher named Robert Matthew. One year later, Truth moved with Pierson and Matthew to a utopian settlement called Zion Hill in Sing Sing, New York. But Pierson's murder soon disrupted the commune. Having lost all her personal belongings in the Zion Hill fiasco, Truth returned to domestic work in New York City for eight or nine years, until mystical experiences again drew her into preaching. When an 1843 revelation instructed her to "go east" and preach, she adopted the name Sojourner Truth and ventured by foot through Long Island and Connecticut, speaking to whatever crowds she could attract. She attended several Millerite meetings and adopted their apocalyptic beliefs.

In her travels through southern New England, Truth met abolitionist George Benson, who introduced her to William Lloyd Garrison and the antislavery movement. In 1850 she moved to Salem, Ohio, made the office of the *Anti-Slavery Bugle* her headquarters, published her narrative, and began to deliver antislavery lectures. She soon became extremely popular with northern audiences. Truth was introduced to the women's rights movement, a cause she continued to champion after the Civil War. She settled in Battle Creek, Michigan, in the mid-1850s. Truth solicited supplies for black troops during the Civil War and, in December 1864, became a counselor for the National Freedmen's Relief Association at a refugee settlement in Arlington Heights, Virginia. Her experiences there prompted her to pursue the establishment of an all-black state, and in 1870 she petitioned President Ulysses S. Grant for government assistance to settle blacks on western public lands. The president did not accommodate her request, but her actions helped to stimulate the exodus of blacks to Kansas and Missouri during the late 1870s. Truth continued to preach religion, black rights, women's suffrage, and temperance to white audiences until 1875, then returned to Battle Creek, where she remained until her death. *NAW*, 3:479–81; *Narrative of So-*

journer Truth, A Northern Slave, Emancipated from Bodily Servitude by the
State of New York, in 1828 (Boston, Mass., 1850).

2. Truth refers to an account in Luke 16:19–36 in which Jesus interceded on behalf of his friends Mary and Martha and raised their brother, Lazarus, from the dead.

16.
Jermain Wesley Loguen to Frederick Douglass
11 August 1851

The Fugitive Slave Law and the widespread public protest it provoked helped revitalize the antislavery movement. The law brought the issue of slavery and the slave power directly before the northern public, arousing a sentiment that astonished leaders on both sides of the issue. Although initially disheartened by passage of the "bloodhound bill," black abolitionists grew optimistic when northern public opinion turned against the law and the antislavery movement gained an unprecedented measure of approval. The reform press scarcely found space to print the flood of articles and letters responding to the act. Black antislavery speakers found larger, more enthusiastic audiences awaiting them on the lecture circuit. Jermain Wesley Loguen reported on the success of his own recently completed tour in an 11 August 1851 letter to *Frederick Douglass' Paper*. He expressed surprise that the "public ear was so ready and willing to hear on American Slavery." Loguen recognized that northern resentment of the Fugitive Slave Law offered an opportunity to reshape public opinion on the slavery question and only lamented that the demand for lecturers greatly exceeded the number in the field. *Lib*, 18 October, 1 November 1850; James Brewer Stewart, *Holy Warriors: The Abolitionists and American Slavery* (New York, N.Y., 1976), 153–54.

SYRACUSE, [New York]
Aug[ust] 11th, 1851

MY DEAR FRIEND DOUGLASS:

I have no congratulations to offer to you on account of your new position in the anti-slavery field at the present time.[1] I think that I am one of those that have admired your course from my first acquaintance with you some eight or nine years since. I always regarded you as candid and honest in your course, let others say what they may. I, today, regard you the same Frederick Douglass that I did in former years, candid and honest in your purpose, and true to the poor slave in all his wrongs and degradation. I have feelings of gratitude always to God for raising up such men, and especially at such a time as the present where it calls men everywhere to be true to God and his poor, as it does at this time of great distress in this country. Dear friend, I should like to give you some account of my travels for the last two months, and the meetings that we have attended in the time, but I will not intrude on your readers at this time with such a detail of facts. I left Syracuse the first of June, and travelled south-west to Pa. Passing through some nine counties of this

4. Jermain Wesley Loguen

From Jermain Wesley Loguen, *The Rev. J. W. Loguen, As a Slave and As a Freedman*
(Syracuse, 1859)

State, holding meetings more or less in them all. In Chautauqua I spent some two weeks passing into Pa. some part of the time (where we had some grand meetings). We had glorious meetings through all the counties in which I stopped for that purpose. We found many and true friends on the way, that have been made so by the wicked Fugitive Slave Law. I never saw the time during the last ten years that I have been in the anti-slavery field, when the public ear was so ready and willing to hear on American Slavery. The Fugitive Slave Bill had a good effect in making the people willing to hear on the subject, and I hope it will drive them to action, as action is what we need at present. I never had a better hearing.

O that we had twenty-five living, traveling lecturers in the field at this time! They might do a world of good for the long neglected slave. But we have but few, as you know, in the field at present. Many of our strong and true men are out of the country at this the time of great distress and need of their labors.[2] Would to the Lord that they were all on the ground with their sword and battle axes in hand, to do battle against the foul monster of hell! They might do much for their country. As weak a brother as I am in the cause, I have calls enough for five men at this time if I could fill them all, but I am but one man and poor at that, but will do what I may for the good cause in my way. I would that we could have force sufficient to commence a war upon this State, by the way of hold-ing conventions in every county in this State, this fall. We might, by so doing, make a great change in favor of equal rights. Will you let us hear from your strong pen on the subject, if you think proper? All I think we need now, to do a great work in this country for the slave, are true friends and concert of action. If this we can have, then we may defy the infernal Fugitive Slave Bill, and through God, make it a dead letter. And if a few of us are carried back, then I believe we will make it hot for them even in the prison house of woe, as I hope our brother Henry Long is doing at this time.[3] I, under God, am determined to stand my ground and fight until the war shall end. I take your paper, and read it with much delight every week. The name is a mere matter of taste; the princi-ple is the thing. I am, truly yours,

J. W. LOGUEN[4]

Frederick Douglass' Paper (Rochester, N.Y.), 21 August 1851.

1. Loguen refers to Frederick Douglass's recent conversion to political aboli-tionism and his adoption of an antislavery interpretation of the U.S. Constitu-tion, both of which caused conflict with Garrisonians.

2. Several noted black abolitionists left the United States in the early 1850s, some to escape enforcement of the Fugitive Slave Law, others to further the antislavery cause in Britain or Canada West. At the time of Loguen's letter, Henry "Box" Brown, William Wells Brown, William and Ellen Craft, Alexander Crum-

mell, Henry Highland Garnet, Josiah Henson, and William P. Powell were residing in England; Henry Bibb and Samuel R. Ward had settled in Canada West.
Ripley et al., *Black Abolitionist Papers*, 1:571–73, 2:108–12, 177–80.

3. Henry Long, a fugitive slave from Alexandria, Virginia, was arrested in
New York City in early January 1851. Local abolitionists tried to free him
through the courts. The Union Safety Committee, a group of New York City
merchants, feared that the South would interpret such a ruling as an act of bad
faith and funded the claimant's case. On 8 January, a federal commissioner
ordered that Long be returned to Virginia. He was led through the streets on his
way back to slavery by an escort of two hundred policemen. Despite threats by
black and white abolitionists to resist the Fugitive Slave Law, no attempt was
made to free Long, and he was returned to slavery at government expense. Once
in Virginia, he was resold and taken to Georgia. Campbell, *Slave Catchers*, 116–
17, 199; *NSt*, 16 January 1851.

4. Jermain Wesley Loguen (1813–1872), a noted black abolitionist, underground railroad agent, and African Methodist Episcopal Zion clergyman, was
born in Davidson County, Tennessee. His slave name was Jarm Logue. He was
the son of a slave mother and a white slaveholder, David Logue. When Logue
sold mother and son to a brutal master, the slave determined to obtain his
freedom. About 1835 Quakers in Kentucky and southern Indiana helped him
escape to Hamilton, Upper Canada. There he learned to read and worked for a
time as a lumberjack, hotel porter, and farmer before settling in western New
York state. After studying at the Oneida Institute for three years, he opened
schools for black children in Utica and Syracuse. Loguen was ordained into the
AMEZ clergy in 1842. About that time, he changed his name, adopting Wesley
in honor of the famous Methodist leader. During the following decade, he became a leading AMEZ preacher and founded six churches in western New York.
In the 1850s, he also did itinerant preaching throughout the region with American Missionary Association support.

During the early 1840s, Loguen began to work closely with Frederick Douglass to aid and protect fugitive slaves escaping through the area. He managed
underground railroad activities in Syracuse in the latter part of the decade and
stepped up this work after passage of the Fugitive Slave Law of 1850. Indicted
for his participation in the October 1851 fugitive slave rescue of William "Jerry"
McHenry at Syracuse, Loguen fled to St. Catharines, Canada West. He did missionary work and temperance lecturing among the fugitive slaves there under the
direction of Hiram Wilson. The Anti-Slavery Society of Canada also engaged him
to give several antislavery speeches in Toronto. Loguen returned to Syracuse in
late 1852 and resumed his underground railroad activities. He managed the
Fugitive Aid Society, a local vigilance committee, throughout the 1850s and
devoted all his time to this work after 1857. His pleas for international assistance
generated nearly $400 a year for the society from British antislavery women. He
claimed to have assisted nearly fifteen hundred fugitive slaves in the decade
before the Civil War.

Loguen was an outstanding antislavery orator and a leading black activist.
Originally a Garrisonian moral suasionist, he moved toward support of political
antislavery by the late 1840s. He joined the Liberty party remnant about 1850,

helped direct its work through 1854, and two years later abandoned it for the Radical Abolition party. After passage of the Fugitive Slave Law, he became more militant, urging local abolitionists to resist that law at any cost and to make Syracuse an "open city" for fugitive slaves. By 1854 he openly supported use of violent means to end slavery, and he eventually recruited men for John Brown's Harpers Ferry raid, although no evidence exists to indicate that he was involved in the planning of the raid. Loguen was a reformer of broad vision, as evidenced by his concern for temperance and women's rights and his work among the poor and prisoners in Syracuse. He summarized his antebellum activities in *The Rev. J. W. Loguen, As a Slave and As a Freeman* (1859), which was well received by the abolitionist community. After the Civil War, he concentrated his efforts on doing missionary work and establishing AMEZ churches among southern freedmen. Elected to an AMEZ bishopric in 1868, he directed denominational efforts in the upper South and border states during the middle years of Reconstruction. In 1872 Loguen was named to take charge of AMEZ missionary efforts on the Pacific coast, but he died in Saratoga Springs, New York, before leaving for the new position. *DANB*, 404–5; *NYT*, 1 October 1872; William J. Walls, *The African Methodist Episcopal Zion Church: Reality of the Black Church* (Charlotte, N.C., 1974), 573–74; Pease and Pease, *They Who Would Be Free*, 235, 293n; Hiram Wilson to George Whipple, 24 November 1851, AMA-ARC; Ian C. Pemberton, "The Anti-Slavery Society of Canada" (M.A. thesis, University of Toronto, 1967), 39; Quarles, *Black Abolitionists*, 80, 93, 154, 157–59, 178, 188, 210–11, 238.

17.
Essay by William P. Powell
[August 1851]

Although black abolitionists were far more willing than their white colleagues to cooperate with abolitionists of a different ideological stripe, they sometimes disagreed over antislavery ideology, tactics, and goals. In May 1851, Frederick Douglass's long-simmering feud with the Garrisonians intensified when he openly rejected two of the Garrisonians' firmly held tenets—that abolitionists should not participate in the political process and that the U.S. Constitution sanctioned slavery. Douglass's public conversion to political antislavery and a belief that the Constitution was not a proslavery document precipitated a quarrel that resounded through the black community for nearly a decade. It shocked black Garrisonians such as Robert Purvis and William C. Nell, coming as it did on the heels of the Fugitive Slave Law, which seemed to confirm the immorality of the nation's political system. Douglass rebuked his black critics as "contemptible tools" of William Lloyd Garrison. William P. Powell, a zealous New York Garrisonian, used the merger of Douglass's *North Star* with the *Liberty Party Paper* as the occasion for a satirical essay condemning Douglass's newfound antislavery faith. Employing an astronomical metaphor, he concluded that the antislavery brilliance of the *North Star* had been "*Eclipse*[d]." John S. Rock to Gerrit Smith, 8 March 1859, Gerrit Smith Papers, NSyU [11:0637–38]; *NASS*, 14 August 1851 [7:0059]; Robert Purvis to William Lloyd Garrison, 12 September 1853, Anti-Slavery Collection, MB [8:0437]; William C. Nell to Amy Post, 12 August, 20 December 1853, 20 January 1854, Post Papers, NRU [8:0397–98, 0518–22, 0603–5].

THE NORTH STAR

In my last notice of the unfortunate catastrophe which happened to this worthy planet, I said that the "result of the collision is, that it (the *North Star*) had lost its *attraction*, and is now in the hands of the Tinker,"[1] and that its future usefulness depends materially upon his skill in star-mending. All things considered, he has, no doubt, done as well as he could to repair the damage; still he *fails* to make the *substitute* give a sure and certain guide to that class who were wont to gaze upon its sublime brightness. The lame attempt of the *North Star* in its vaulting ambition, to borrow light from the twins, *Conscience* and the *Constitution*, without consulting the Prophets, *Moses* of Andover, and *Daniel* of Marshfield, who discovered the twins in the year of Grace 1850,[2] is sufficient evidence of its ill success. There is, however, some consolation left for those who are waiting the termination of the *Eclipse*. By the latest news received, August 7th, two celebrated Political *savans*, Smith and Spooner, have invented three smoked optical instruments[3] and sent 500 to the Rochester emporium, for the benefit of those who have weak eyes, through which they might see the *change*, and believe. These new modern invented telescopes are capital things as long as they last. It will require the aid of *Boreas*[4] to puff them in the market, and then they won't *sell*.

What can be done to please this refractory luminary? If the moral world (for whose benefit the *North Star* was ostensibly created) should differ in opinion as to which of the two planets they would *prefer* to shine, and object to be the transferred subjects of the newfangled substitute, without a name to *live* by, or even one to *die* for, why, forsooth, the *tinker* threatens all such with excommunication, without benefit of clergy. Charging us with "sinister efforts" to secure "the patronising smiles of"—who? Why, the very class he is now making his chief study to please. They that live in glass houses should be careful how they throw stones. And then, too, we are charged with "ingratitude"—to whom?[5] Why, to the *North Star*, which has left its *orb*, to give place to a substitute of doubtful magnitude. Ingratitude! indeed!! What does this pugnacious substitute mean? Does it mean that it is the only planet in the moral universe in existence for *our* special good, and that *we* ought to fall down and worship this new bantling, baptizing it in the name of Smith, of Spooner, and of Webster, the *unholy trinity* of Conscience and the Constitution? If this is the kind of light we are to have from the Vatican at Rochester, the sooner the Pope leaves the chair of Saint Editor, the better; for neither Free Soil bayonets nor Liberty Party cohorts (now reduced to a corporal's guard)[6] will enable His Holiness to hold his seat against the will of his once faithful, but now deserted, vassals.

WILLIAM P. POWELL

National Anti-Slavery Standard (New York, N.Y.), 14 August 1851.

1. Powell refers to the June 1851 merger of the *North Star* and John Thomas's *Liberty Party Paper* to form *Frederick Douglass' Paper*, an antislavery weekly edited and published by Frederick Douglass in Rochester, New York. Like his *North Star*, which began publication in December 1847, the new journal printed political and antislavery news, correspondence from readers, and probing editorials by Douglass. It also offered black abolitionists an important forum for debate and treated black issues and activities ignored by the white antislavery press. Douglass's journal gave blacks an independent and influential voice in shaping the antislavery movement in the decade before the Civil War.

Subsidies from white philanthropists, especially Gerrit Smith, allowed *Frederick Douglass' Paper* to meet expenses during its first two years, but after 1853 it suffered continual financial problems. Despite a circulation of more than four thousand, delinquent subscribers made Douglass dependent upon external sources. British abolitionist Julia Griffiths, the paper's business manager, regularized its finances, sponsored fairs, mailed personal appeals, tapped the Rochester Ladies Anti-Slavery Society, and produced *Autographs for Freedom*, an antislavery giftbook, to raise funds. She returned to Britain in 1857 to generate additional donations. Douglass also drew upon a variety of black sources, including women's groups, public meetings, and several talented but unpaid local correspondents. And he spent over $12,000 of his own money to keep the paper alive. To counter mounting debts, he began publishing *Douglass' Monthly* for British subscribers in June 1858 and reduced the size of *Frederick Douglass' Paper* one year later. Douglass stopped publication of the *Paper* in July 1860, but he continued to produce the *Monthly* through August 1863. Benjamin Quarles, *Frederick Douglass* (Washington, D.C., 1948), 84–98; *NSt*, 2 February 1849 [5:0963–64]; *FDP*, 26 June, 4 December 1851, 10 June 1852, 12 August, 30 December 1853, 13 January 1854 [7:0214, 0622, 8:0532, 0826–27].

2. Powell underscores his damning criticism of Frederick Douglass by linking him with Moses Stuart and Daniel Webster, men who had earned the contempt of abolitionists by their support of the Compromise of 1850. Stuart (1780–1852), a renowned biblical professor at Andover Theological Seminary in Massachusetts, wrote *Conscience and the Constitution, with Remarks on the Speech of Webster on Slavery* (1850), which defended Webster's 7 March 1850 speech in support of the Union and the Compromise of 1850 (including the Fugitive Slave Law). Webster, in turn, praised Stuart's pamphlet in subsequent addresses. *DAB*, 18:174–75; Wendell Phillips Garrison and Francis Jackson Garrison, *William Lloyd Garrison, 1805–1879: The Story of His Life*, 4 vols. (New York, N.Y., 1885–89), 3:278; Blassingame, *Frederick Douglass Papers*, 1:114–15.

3. Powell probably refers to three of the many tracts and pamphlets by Gerrit Smith and Lysander Spooner on the antislavery nature of the U.S. Constitution. Among Smith's works were his *Letter of Gerrit Smith to Henry Clay* (1839) and *Letter of Gerrit Smith to S. P. Chase on the Unconstitutionality of Every Part of American Slavery* (1847). Spooner (1808–1887), an eccentric Boston lawyer, created a stir with *The Unconstitutionality of Slavery* (1845). It was widely reprinted and became an important piece of Liberty party campaign literature and the focus of bitter debate among abolitionists. *DAB*, 17:466–67.

4. "Boreas" is a Latin term for the north wind.

5. Powell refers to the newspaper war waged between the Garrisonians and Frederick Douglass after his May 1851 announcement that he had adopted an antislavery interpretation of the U.S. Constitution. Relations between Douglass and his antislavery colleagues had become strained in 1847 when he moved to Rochester, New York, and began publishing the *North Star*. In mid-1851 his increasingly independent course, the merger of his journal with the *Liberty Party Paper*, and his defense of political abolitionism brought accusations of apostasy in the Garrisonian press, especially from the *Pennsylvania Freeman*. Douglass justified his actions, announcing that only "mean-spirited and despotic persons" would deny him the right to change his views and to publish his own paper. He became convinced that blacks would receive favorable treatment from Garrisonians only when they acted submissively. "If [a black man] dares to show manliness enough to think for himself, as to his field and mode of labor," he declared, "he must be denounced." Garrison denied the charges, claiming that he contin-

ued to admire Douglass's talents, and wished his paper success, but relations between the two men rapidly degenerated into a permanent breach. *FDP*, 24 July 1851; *PF*, 5, 25 June 1851; *Lib*, 4 July 1851; Quarles, *Frederick Douglass*, 70–79.

6. Most Liberty party adherents joined the Free Soilers during the 1848 campaign, but a vocal minority rejected the limited abolitionism of the Free Soil platform. Under the leadership of Gerrit Smith, this remnant convened in 1848 and 1852 and nominated a slate of Liberty party candidates for national office. Richard H. Sewell, *Ballots for Freedom: Antislavery Politics in the United States, 1837–1860* (New York, N.Y., 1976), 163–64, 246n.

18.
Samuel Ringgold Ward to Joseph C. Hathaway
15 September 1851

Most black abolitionists recognized the importance of political action, but they disagreed over which party—Whig, Liberty, or Free Soil—could best fight slavery and advance civil rights. Political purists, such as Henry Highland Garnet, James McCune Smith, J. W. C. Pennington, and Samuel Ringgold Ward, argued that all blacks were morally obliged to support the Liberty party because it alone endorsed emancipation and black rights. Ward contended that a vote for any other party was a vote for slavery and racism. His 15 September 1851 letter to Joseph C. Hathaway, the secretary of an upcoming Liberty party convention at Buffalo, New York, explained his conviction that the party should remain resolute on the slavery issue and not erode its moral foundation with political compromises. *CA*, 17 November 1838 [2:0654]; *NASS*, 27 March 1851 [6:0864]; James Oliver Horton and Lois E. Horton, *Black Bostonians: Family Life and Community Struggle in the Antebellum North* (New York, N.Y., 1979), 87; *NSt*, 1 September 1848; *FDP*, 26 August 1853 [8:0419–20]; James McCune Smith to Gerrit Smith, 12 May 1848, J. W. C. Pennington to Gerrit Smith, 6–7 November 1852, Gerrit Smith Papers, NSyU [5:0633–34, 7:0821].

RAVENNA, Ohio
Sept[ember] 15, 1851

MY DEAR SIR:[1]
I find that I am obliged to deny myself the pleasure of attending your Convention.[2] On my own account, I have abundant reason to regret this. In the Convention, however, no such poor and obscure man as myself can be missed.

I take the liberty of addressing this line to suggest a word, on two or three points of some practical importance.

1. *In regard to our platform of principles.* My hope is that it shall be both radical and catholic. Insisting upon the inalienable rights of all men, and the equality of the whole brotherhood of the human race, denying the validity and the legality of any and all constitutions, enactments, compromises, compacts, and decisions which conflict with the doctrine of the inalienable rights of all men, it is to be hoped that we shall meanwhile insist upon nothing as a test of party fellowship, which does not necessarily conflict with this doctrine, and that we shall be ready and willing to cooperate with all who honestly embrace it, and who are willing to study its relations, and apply it to the entire range of civil duties.

But to yield up, compromise, or hold in abeyance, any of our great vital principles, for the sake of making it easy for others to unite with us, would be not only wounding to the hearts of those most devoted to our cause, but detrimental, also, to the very success which we should seek by such means. We learned a valuable lesson in 1848.[3] Too many of our old coadjutors hastened to nominate and to vote for a Presidential candidate, who, within less than fourteen months of his nomination, and in less than ten months of his being voted for, was a member of one of the most corrupt pro-slavery parties that ever consented to, and aided in, the crushing and enslavement of man. That deed of folly, though done with the best of intentions, on the part of our brethren, ought to be a perpetual admonition to us, that we depend much less upon numbers than upon the integrity and steadfastness with which we shall maintain our principles. If we have a hearty and cordial belief in the principles which underlie our Heaven-originated cause, let us not be in haste to gather numbers, at the expense of the truth. The divine word assures us that "he that believeth shall not make haste," and also that "he that believeth shall not be made ashamed."[4] Let us neither be ashamed of the paucity of our numbers, nor be in haste to increase them.

2. *As to Candidates.* The eyes of many, in my opinion, a great majority of the true and faithful, are turned towards our beloved Gerrit Smith as the standard-bearer of our ranks in the coming campaign. None can better represent our principles, in civil or social matters, than he. But for his unconquerable repugnance to being a candidate, it would seem unwise to convene and adjourn, without the placing of his great name before the people, as the representative and embodiment of our principles, and a rebuke to the character of opposing candidates, and a protest against the truckling spirit of compromise which is working the ruin of our country.

It is a source of great joy, however, that we are not destitute of great names, bourne by good men. No party in the country, of whatever pretensions, will seek the elevation of better men than William Goodell, James H. Collins, George W. Johnson, Lindley M. Moore, or Samuel Aaron.[5] Either of these gentlemen, as a nominee for Vice President, or, in case of Mr. Smith's irrevocable declinature for President, would form a ticket of which we might well be proud. What is most important, in my judgement, is the naming of men who are true-bred, unwavering, intelligent in the history and relations of the cause of freedom, and self-sacrificing in their devotion to the cause. What we should chiefly seek to avoid is the nominating of some halfway compromise candidate, to accommodate whom, we must lower our standard after the manner of October, 1847.[6] May the God whom we serve save us from all such folly!

3. Allow me to say a word concerning *the aspects of our cause in*

several of the States. In Maine, the Free Soil Party[7] is but the old Liberty Party, with a very small addition from the two pro-slavery parties. It were not difficult, if tried, to cooperate and harmonize with our friends in Maine. In New Hampshire there is a growing anti-slavery sentiment among the Free Soilers, but the leaders of the party never were abolitionists. There is, consequently, more of the spirit of compromise, and less of radical tendency, in that State. The Free Soilers of Connecticut have so low a standard of action that but little may be hoped of them. Free Soil in that State, is but little else than modified, but not converted, spurious democracy. In Vermont and Massachusetts, the Free Soilers are not yet tired of uniting with Democrats for the sake of sharing in the results of victories which neither could achieve without the aid of the other. Rhode Island abolitionism always had the misfortune to be, as is abolitionism elsewhere in New England, too much attached to the tariff to be at liberty to embrace radical ideas of reform.[8]

In the West, there are brighter signs of hope. Illinois is with us. Wisconsin is fighting for the same principles as ourselves. The mass of the Free Soilers of Ohio spurn the tendencies toward the Democratic party exhibited in the Southern, and the Whig-wise tendencies of some leading minds in the Northern part of that State.[9] A paralytic stupor sits upon the bosoms of Michigan, Indiana, Iowa, New Jersey, and Pennsylvania.

4. *Laborers are needed.* They are needed in the last named States. In many portions of the free States, the need of men to talk about our principles to the honest, laboring masses is but too apparent—too evident. Many of our best lecturers are abroad. Others will leave soon. The temptation to leave the country is greater, from the fact that compensation is so poor at home. Would that some more liberal plan could be adopted by the Convention, and recommended to the national committee, securing the employment of able young men (it were better that they be unmarried), to carry our principles to the people in all the free States.

Suffering from the disappointment of not being able to be with you, and praying for the Divine blessing on your deliberations, I am, dear sir, Your obedient servant,

SAMUEL R. WARD

Frederick Douglass' Paper (Rochester, N.Y.), 25 September 1851.

1. Joseph C. Hathaway (1810–?), a prosperous Farmington, New York, farmer, was secretary of the 1851 Liberty party convention. Active in antislavery and temperance activities, he helped found the New York State Anti-Slavery Society, served as president of the Western New York Anti-Slavery Society, joined black abolitionists William Wells Brown and Charles L. Remond on lecture tours of western New York, and acted as general agent for the American Anti-Slavery Society. Although a Garrisonian, Hathaway cooperated with political abolitionists in the Whig and Liberty parties and worked with Frederick Douglass and

Gerrit Smith to oppose the Fugitive Slave Law. U.S. Census, 1850; *FDP*, 25 September, 9 October 1851; Joseph C. Holly to William Lloyd Garrison, 31 December 1851, Anti-Slavery Collection, MB [7:0243]; *RDD*, 2 October 1835 [1:0632]; *NASS*, 23 May 1844, 12 December 1846, 14 January, 11 February 1847 [4:0810, 5:0284, 0359, 0369]; *PF*, 29 August 1850 [6:0559]; Alice H. Henderson, "The History of the New York Anti-Slavery Society" (Ph.D. diss., University of Michigan, 1963), 333–34.

2. The 1851 Liberty party convention, which met on 17–18 September at Buffalo, adopted the "radical and catholic" platform that Ward desired. During the early 1850s, the Liberty party remnant attempted to increase its public appeal by expanding its platform beyond abolitionism. It courted black voters and encouraged the participation of women; the 1851 convention admitted nearly twenty women as delegates. Its platform condemned colonization and clerical moderation on the slavery issue and supported civil rights for blacks and women, temperance, peace, land reform, and free trade. *FDP*, 26 June, 31 July, 25 September 1851.

3. Most Liberty party members supported Martin Van Buren, the presidential candidate of the Free Soil party, in 1848. Van Buren, a former president and Democratic party leader, was accepted by Liberty men with apprehension. His later return to the Democratic fold confirmed charges by abolitionists such as Gerrit Smith and William Lloyd Garrison that he could not be trusted. John Niven, *Martin Van Buren: The Romantic Age of American Politics* (New York, N.Y., 1983), 566–600.

4. Ward quotes from Isaiah 28:16 and Romans 10:11.

5. Ward praises five key figures in the Liberty party. William Goodell had established a reputation as an editor of antislavery journals and the author of several works arguing the unconstitutionality of slavery. James H. Collins (?–1854) moved in 1833 from Oneida County, New York, to Chicago, where he became one of the city's most successful lawyers and foremost abolitionists. He served as president of the Illinois State Anti-Slavery Society, assisted the underground railroad, and defended Owen Lovejoy for his participation in a fugitive slave case. Active in both the Liberty and Free Soil parties, Collins represented Chicago at Illinois's first Liberty party convention and served on the party's national committee. In 1848 he represented Cook County at the founding meeting of the Free Soil party in Buffalo; two years later, he ran unsuccessfully as a Free Soil candidate for Congress. George W. Johnson (1810–?), a Buffalo attorney, temperance advocate, and abolitionist, was also a member of the Liberty party's national committee. In 1851 he ran for attorney general of New York on the Liberty party ticket. Lindley Murray Moore, a Quaker abolitionist from Rochester, New York, was a leading member of the Western New York Anti-Slavery Society and an agent for the underground railroad. In 1851 he ran as the Liberty party candidate for New York state comptroller. Samuel Aaron (1800–1865) was a Baptist clergyman, educator, temperance advocate, and abolitionist from Sugar Grove, Pennsylvania. Although a Garrisonian and a member of the board of managers of the American Anti-Slavery Society, he cooperated closely with the Liberty party. U.S. Census, 1850; Edward Magdol, *Owen Lovejoy: Abolitionist in Congress* (New Brunswick, N.J., 1967), 41–46, 88, 95, 118; John M. Palmer, ed., *The Bench and Bar of Illinois*, 2 vols. (Chicago, Ill., 1899), 2:603, 608–10; N. Dwight Harris, *The History of Negro Servitude in Illinois*

and the *Slavery Agitation in That State, 1719–1864* (1904; reprint, New York, N.Y., 1969), 148, 165, 180; Smith, *Liberty and Free Soil Parties*, 230; Nancy A. Hewitt, *Women's Activism and Social Change: Rochester, New York, 1822–1872* (Ithaca, N.Y., 1984), 92; *NEW*, 20 May 1847 [5:0422]; *FDP*, 26 June, 25 September, 9 October 1851, 26 August 1853 [6:0979]; *NSt*, 5 September 1850 [6:0570]; *NASS*, 22 January 1846 [5:0151]; Wilbur H. Siebert, *The Underground Railroad from Slavery to Freedom* (New York, N.Y., 1898), 414; McKivigan, *War against Proslavery Religion*, 203; *ACAB*, 1:1.

6. Ward refers to the 1847 Liberty party convention, which met on 20–21 October in Buffalo. Delegates debated the party's platform and its selection of a presidential candidate for 1848. Finally, they chose maverick Senator John P. Hale of New Hampshire, a tardy convert to their cause. Although most Liberty party members endorsed the selection, some grumbled that the candidate came from a "class of slippery politicians." Hale eventually withdrew his candidacy and supported the newly formed Free Soil party in the 1848 campaign. Sewell, *Ballots for Freedom*, 132–38, 154–56.

7. As Ward indicates, the background and antislavery commitment of the membership of the Free Soil party varied from state to state. The Free Soil party, which was founded in August 1848, brought together disgruntled Whigs and Democrats, Liberty party men, and a scattering of unaffiliated abolitionists, all united in their opposition to the extension of slavery into new western territories. The anti-extension stance of the Free Soilers signaled an important shift in American politics. But many abolitionists repudiated the party because of its failure to endorse emancipation or to condemn the Fugitive Slave Law. Black abolitionists criticized its unwillingness to promote civil rights. The party named former president Martin Van Buren as its presidential candidate in 1848; although he polled only 10 percent of the popular vote, eleven Free Soil candidates were elected to Congress. The party dwindled after the 1848 election, and most Free Soilers became Republicans by the mid-1850s. Sewell, *Ballots for Freedom*, 152–98, 202–30, 239–45.

8. Many political abolitionists, including Free Soilers and Liberty party members, endorsed free trade by the late 1840s. But in New England, efforts to reduce tariffs distressed many opponents of slavery. This was particularly true in Rhode Island, where the economy had become increasingly dependent upon textile and metal manufacturing after 1830. Most abolitionists in the state, including leaders of the largely Garrisonian Rhode Island Anti-Slavery Society, supported protective tariffs. Sewell, *Ballots for Freedom*, 112–19, 143, 160–61, 245, 292; John S. Gilkeson, *Middle-Class Providence, 1820–1940* (Princeton, N.J., 1986), 44.

9. The controversy over the Fugitive Slave Law of 1850 temporarily revived the Free Soil party in the West. Illinois Free Democrats (as party members were increasingly called) worked with former Liberty party men and other abolitionists to fight enforcement of the law. Free Soilers in Wisconsin held a mass convention in 1851 to oppose the measure and cooperated with Whigs to elect an antislavery governor. In Ohio party members organized mass rallies throughout the state and worked with antislavery Whigs to elect Benjamin F. Wade, an outspoken critic of slavery, to the U.S. Senate. But they failed to increase the party's vote totals in other state elections. Smith, *Liberty and Free Soil Parties*, 226–41, 265.

19.
Proceedings of a Meeting of Rochester Blacks
Convened at the Memorial African Methodist
Episcopal Zion Church
Rochester, New York
13 October 1851

Northern black communities responded forcefully and quickly to the
threat posed to their liberty and safety by the Fugitive Slave Law. Local
blacks, many with no previous antislavery experience, held rallies, organized vigilance committees and private militias, raised funds for the
legal defense of alleged fugitives, and vowed to resist slave catchers
and federal efforts to enforce the law. On 13 October 1851, Rochester
blacks gathered at the Memorial African Methodist Episcopal Zion
Church to establish a vigilance committee. Just twelve days earlier, federal marshals had seized suspected fugitives in neighboring cities. In
sounding the "tocsin of alarm" and organizing to protect themselves,
Rochester blacks followed the example of Syracuse abolitionists, whose
aggressive vigilance organization had recently rescued the fugitive William "Jerry" McHenry from federal authorities. Quarles, *Black Abolitionists*, 197–222, 229; *SDS*, 24, 27 September 1850; *SDSt*, 3 October
1851.

Pursuant to call a large meeting was held at the Zion church[1] on Monday evening October 13th, 1851:
   J. P. Morris[2] was called to the chair and Wm C. Nell appointed secretary.
   The Chairman in stating objects of the meeting detailed a history of
the recent causes of excitement consequent upon enforcement of the
Fugitive Slave Law[3] and urged its consideration upon the friends assembled that a union of effort might be created for the aid and defence of
those liable to be thus victimized.
   Wm C. Nell submitted the following preamble and resolutions:

   Whereas, The tocsin of alarm now being sounded in the City of
   Rochester presaging the "Hunting of Men" in the valley of the
   Genesee—the consternation already visible by the seperation of
   Husbands and Fathers from thier wives and little ones—and all
   interesting Home associations together with the Knowledge that on
   the side of our oppressors there is power, <u>might</u> with <u>them</u> making
   <u>right</u>, and hense a liability of Kidnapping and arresting the nominally free equally with those who guided by the North Star have
   declared thier independence of slavery, we feel impelled in this the

hour of peril to convene together for devising ways and means to preserve our lives and liberties, and of presenting that declaration of purpose to the hearts and consciences of all who love liberty for Man the wide world over, therefore

Resolved, That we constitute ourselves a vigilance committee to give immediate notice to the citizens of an arrest and to the extent of our abilities aid those claimed as Fugitive Slaves.

Resolved, That the system of American Slavery—the vilest that ever saw the sun—is a violation of every sentiment of christianety, and the antipodes of every dictate of humanity. The Slaveholders pretentions to property in Man are of no more weight than those of the midnight assassin or pirate on the high seas. "God made all men free—free as the birds that cleave the air or sing on the branches—free as the sunshine that gladdens the earth—free as the winds that sweep over sea and land—free at his birth—free during his whole life—free to day—this hour—this moment"

> God having willed us free
> Though Man wills us slaves
> We will as God wills
> Gods will be done.

Resolved, That in view of the imminent danger present and looked for we caution every colored Man, woman and child to be careful in thier walks through the highways and byways of the City by day and doubly so if out at night—as to where they go[,] How they go, and who they go with to be guarded on side, off side, and all sides—as watchful as Argus with his hundred eyes, and as executive as was Briareus with as many hands,[4] if siezed by any one, to make the air resound with the signal word that all within hearing may know and witness the deed[,] the deed over which angels weep and Demons exult for Joy.

Resolved, That any commissioner who would deliver up a victim to his claimant under the Heaven defying Fugitive Slave Law would have delivered up Jesus Christ to his persecutors for one third of the price that Judas Iscariot did.

Resolved, That in the event of any Commissioner of Rochester being applied to for remanding a Fugitive we trust he will emulate the example of Judge Harrington of Vermont and be satisfied with nothing short of a bill of sale from the Almighty.[5]

The above were advocated by the mover—Isaac Gibbs[6]—Lloyd Scott,[7] and Several others, when on motion the entire were adopted and thier publication in the Rochester city papers requested.[8]

After the appointment of Finance and Relief Committees the meeting adjourned[,] pledged one and all to remember that eternal vigilance is the price of liberty!

J. P. Morris   Chairman

Wm. C. Nell   Secretary

Post Papers, Rush-Rhees Library, University of Rochester, Rochester, New York. Published by permission.

1. Memorial African Methodist Episcopal Zion Church was organized in the early 1830s by Rev. Thomas James. His antislavery activism, and that of members Frederick Douglass, Harriet Tubman, and Jacob P. Morris, soon made it a common meeting place for Rochester's black leaders. Douglass briefly published the *North Star* in the church's basement. Tubman often hid fugitive slaves in the church, and many attended services there. But from 1849 to 1856, the congregation was the center of controversy because it allowed a segregated public school to use the basement for classes. Douglass organized a successful boycott of the school and often criticized church leaders in his journal. Memorial AMEZ Church continued to serve the local black community into the twentieth century. Howard W. Coles, *The Cradle of Freedom: A History of the Negro in Rochester, Western New York and Canada* (Rochester, N.Y., 1942), 96, 109, 128–29; Musette S. Castle, "A Survey of the History of African Americans in Rochester, 1800–1860," *AANYLH* 13:14–23 (July 1989).

2. Jacob P. Morris (1820–?), a Rochester barber, helped direct local efforts to assist fugitive slaves during the 1850s. Although his attempt to organize a formal vigilance committee ultimately failed, he cooperated with Frederick Douglass and other local black and white abolitionists to provide for the care and transportation of refugees arriving in the city. As a result of this work, and Rochester's proximity to Canada West, the city became a key point on the underground railroad. Morris also served on the executive committee of the Western New York Anti-Slavery Society. He participated in several black state and national conventions, demonstrating his commitment to black voting rights and elevation. At the 1843 black national convention in Buffalo, Morris voted against Henry Highland Garnet's "Appeal to the Slaves" and its endorsement of slave violence. He joined other local black leaders in making preparations for the 1853 black national convention, which was held in Rochester. Morris left Rochester for California in early 1854. U.S. Census, 1850; *Lib*, 5 March 1852; Siebert, *Underground Railroad*, 414; *CA*, 1 August 1840 [3:0545]; *NASS*, 29 January 1846, 27 January 1848 [5:0152–53, 0562]; *RR*, 9 November 1848 [5:0822]; *FDP*, 10, 17 June 1853, 24 March 1854 [8:0293, 0311]; *Convention of Colored Citizens . . . at Buffalo* (1843), 10, 19 [4:0636, 0641]; Frederick Douglass, *Life and Times of Frederick Douglass*, rev. ed. (Boston, Mass., 1892; reprint, New York, N.Y., 1962), 266–67.

3. The "recent causes of excitement" to which Morris refers were undoubtedly the events surrounding the rescue of a fugitive slave, William "Jerry" McHenry (?–1853), in Syracuse twelve days earlier. McHenry had escaped from his owner, John McReynolds of Madison County, Missouri, and was working as a cooper in Syracuse when he was arrested on 1 October 1851 under the terms of the Fugitive Slave Law of 1850. Local abolitionists—including Gerrit Smith, Samuel J.

May, and Jermain W. Loguen of the local vigilance committee—hastily planned his rescue. That afternoon an interracial mob broke into the local jail, freed McHenry, and spirited him away to Kingston, Canada West, where he remained until his death.

Federal authorities hoped to make an example of the rescuers. An 18 February 1851 proclamation by President Millard Fillmore had stated that those who aided such rescues would be prosecuted for obstructing the Fugitive Slave Law. The U.S. attorney for New York, James R. Lawrence, attempted to bring treason charges against the rescuers but failed to accumulate the necessary evidence. A grand jury indicted twenty-six men, including twelve blacks, for rioting. Samuel R. Ward was implicated because he had visited McHenry on the day of his arrest and had delivered a speech to the waiting crowd. Nine of the accused blacks, including Ward and Loguen, escaped to Canada West. Three whites were brought to trial but none were convicted. The only black to stand trial, Enoch Reed, was convicted under the Fugitive Slave Law of 1793, thus thwarting the federal effort to make an example of the rescuers through enforcement of the 1850 law. The Jerry rescue became one of the most celebrated fugitive slave incidents of the 1850s. Campbell, *Slave Catchers*, 154–57; Ward, *Autobiography of a Fugitive Negro*, 117–18.

4. Argus, a hundred-eyed beast that guarded the goddess Hera, and Briareus, one of three beasts with a hundred hands, were figures in Greek mythology.

5. The resolution refers to Theophilus Herrington (?–1813), a justice of the state supreme court in Vermont from 1803 until his death. He was remembered by abolitionists for his refusal in an 1807 case to order the return of a fugitive slave unless the claimant could "show a grant from God Almighty." *NASS*, 18 March 1847 [5:0394]; Merrill and Ruchames, *Letters of William Lloyd Garrison*, 2:41; William C. Nell, *The Colored Patriots of the American Revolution* (Boston, Mass., 1855; reprint, Salem, N.H., 1986), 124–25.

6. Isaac C. Gibbs (1804–?), a black Rochester cartman, was a native of New Jersey. He was involved in local temperance activities during the 1830s and later served as a delegate to the 1843 black state convention. U.S. Census, 1850; *RDA*, 21 January 1831 [1:0031]; *AP*, 3 October 1843 [4:0676].

7. Lloyd Scott (1813–?), a black clothing merchant in Rochester, came to the city from Maryland. He was active in the affairs of the local black community, including education. Scott joined other local blacks in making preparations for the 1853 black national convention held in Rochester and, after the gathering, helped organize the National Council of the Colored People. He became interested in Haitian immigration during the late 1850s and, in October 1861, settled in Haiti with his wife and six children. U.S. Census, 1850; *NSt*, 25 August 1848; *FDP*, 17 June 1853, 1 September 1854 [8:0311]; *PP*, 14 December 1861.

8. The resolutions were published in the 23 October 1851 issue of *Frederick Douglass' Paper*.

20.
Black Laws in the West

Abner H. Francis to Frederick Douglass
[October 1851]

Petition of California Blacks to the
California State Legislature
20 February 1862

The American frontier beckoned to settlers with the promise of social equality and economic opportunity. Yet blacks migrating westward found no escape from the political and legal discrimination that plagued them in the East. During the early 1850s, several western states—Indiana, Illinois, Iowa, and California—passed laws to discourage or prohibit blacks from settling within their borders. In October 1851, black abolitionist Abner H. Francis reported to *Frederick Douglass' Paper* on the Oregon Territory's settlement law. He described how his brother, O. B. Francis, a black merchant in Portland, was threatened with expulsion from the territory after a rival white businessman filed a complaint. Blacks in California faced similar obstacles. State statutes denied blacks the vote, forbade interracial marriages, prohibited black participation in the state militia, and restricted black testimony in the courts. The testimony laws were particularly galling because they made blacks vulnerable to unscrupulous white businessmen. In 1852 California blacks began a decade-long struggle to repeal the testimony laws. They held protest meetings, gathered in state conventions, and flooded the state legislature with petitions. The following petition, submitted in February 1862, accompanied two bills calling for repeal of the laws. Both bills passed the state assembly but failed in the senate. The testimony laws were not repealed until March 1863. Elizabeth McLagan, *A Peculiar Paradise: A History of Blacks in Oregon, 1788–1940* (Portland, Oreg., 1980), 23–29; Philip M. Montesano, "Some Aspects of the Free Negro Question in San Francisco, 1849–1870" (M.A. thesis, University of San Francisco, 1967), 34–45; Rudolph M. Lapp, *Blacks in Gold Rush California* (New Haven, Conn., 1977), 186–238.

My Dear Friend:

Since my last letter to you,[1] mailed at San Francisco, I had in part written out two communications intended for publication. Before their completion, I was brought to the knowledge of the fact, and experienced the result of an existing law in this "free territory" of Oregon,[2] so unjust and devilish in all its features, that I waive other matter that you may immediately give publicity to the facts relating to it. After a two months' tour from Buffalo via New York, to Chagres, through New Granada, Mexico, California and Oregon, I concluded, in connection with my brother, to locate for a time in Oregon. In accordance therewith, we rented a store and commenced business at a very heavy expense. After the expiration of ten days, I was called away for three weeks. Shortly after my departure, my brother was arrested through the complaint of an Englishman (said, by some, not to be naturalized), on charge of violating one of the laws of the territory. And what do you suppose was the crime? That he was a negro, and that one of the laws of the "free" territory forbid any colored person who had a preponderance of African blood from settling in the territory. He was tried before a Justice of the Peace, and, I must say, very generously given six months to leave the territory. The law says thirty days. The second day after my return, Sept. 15th, the complainant, not being satisfied with the past decision, carried the case up to the Supreme Court, Judge Pratt presiding. Before his Judgeship we were summoned. After a formal hearing, establishing the fact of negro identity, the court adjourned, to meet the next morning at 9 o'clock. At the hour appointed, the room was crowded, showing much feeling of indignation and wrath against the complainant. Judge Tilford, late of San Francisco (a Kentuckian), appeared as counsel for the defense. To be brief, he conducted the case with the ability and skill rarely seen by the legal profession, showing, by the constitution of the United States, the right of citizens of one state to enjoy the right of citizens in another. To be understood upon this point, his argument rested that citizens of one state had a right to enjoy the same privileges that the same class of citizens enjoy in the state which they visit. This he contended was the understanding or meaning of that article in the constitution. He demanded for us, under this clause, all the rights which colored people enjoyed in the territory prior to the passage of this law. (Those in the territory at the time of the passage of this law are not affected by it.) He then took the position, and clearly proved it, that the law was unconstitutional, on the ground that the law made no provision for jury trial in these arrests, showing that any person, no matter how debased, had the power to enter complaint against any colored persons and have them brought before any petty Justice of the Peace and commanded to leave the territory. Did space permit, I should gladly follow the Judge further in this branch of his interesting argument. At the close of it, the whole house appeared to feel that the triumph was complete on the part of the defendants, that unconstitutionality of the law must be conceded by Judge Pratt. But alas! self-interest or selfishness led him to *attempt* to override the whole argument, and prove the constitutionality of the law; and it is none the less true that we now stand condemned under his decision, which is to close up business and leave the territory within four months. This decision produced considerable excitement. Some said the scoundrel (the complainant) ought to have a coat of tar, while the mass have agreed to withhold their patronage from him, as desire of gain had led him to proceed against us. The people declare we shall not leave at the expiration of the time, whether the Legislature repeal the law or not. Petitions are now being circulated for its repeal.[3] The member from this district, Col. King,[4] one of the most influential men in the house, declares, as far as his influence can go, it *shall* be repealed at the commencement of the session, which takes place on the first of December next. Thus you see, my dear sir, that even in the so-called *free* territory of Oregon, the colored American citizen, though he may possess all the qualities and qualifications which make a man a good citizen, is driven out like a beast in the forest, made to sacrifice every interest dear to him, and forbidden the privilege to take the portion of the soil which the government says every citizen shall enjoy. Ah! when I see and experience such treatment, the words of that departed patriot come before me, *"I tremble for my country when I remember that God is just, and that his justice will not always sleep."*[5] I find, upon examination, that more than half of the citizens of Portland were ignorant of any such law. The universal sentiment is *that it shall be repealed.* God grant that this may be the case. If I have been one who, though suffering severely, has had the least agency in bringing about this repeal, I shall freely surrender, and be well pleased with the result. Yours for equal rights, equal laws and equal justice to all men,

A. H. FRANCIS[6]

Frederick Douglass' Paper (Rochester, N.Y.), 13 November 1851.

To The Honorable, The Senate and Assembly of the State of California:

The undersigned, natives of the United States, and residents of the State of California, respectfully represent unto your Honorable bodies, that the Statutes of the State of California, prohibiting persons of one-half or more of negro blood from being witnesses in an Action or Proceeding to which a white person is a party, and prohibiting persons who have one-eighth part or more of negro blood from giving evidence in favor of, or against, any white person, in a criminal Action, ought, in the opinion of your Petitioners, to be repealed.

That said Statutes are unjust and oppressive both to the white and the black. That crime often goes unpunished for the reason that the only witnesses to its commission are persons disabled by these statutes from testifying.

That the honest white man is also estopped from the use of the existing evidence of persons of color to legitimate transactions.

That pretended and fraudulent claims and evidences of indebtedness are often placed in the hands of white men, purporting upon their face to have arisen in due course of business, against colored persons, for the purpose of excluding colored evidence of payment or satisfaction; and these claims are often sued upon and the amounts recovered.

Your Petitioners are of opinion that Judges and Jurors ought to be allowed to judge of the weight which should be given to the evidence of colored persons, and that they <u>should</u> be as capable of determining whether a <u>black</u> man is speaking the truth, as a <u>white</u> man.

We believe that the exclusion of the testimony of a race of men, is never necessary, unless of a race held as slaves, or of one having an Idolatrous Religion. That the exclusion of the testimony of the descendants of Africans, in the United States, commenced as in incident to slavery, and should be discontinued with it.

In presenting this Petition, we respectfully suggest, that justice and an impartial administration of the laws, both in civil and criminal cases, demands that the 3d clause of Section 394 of the Civil Practice Act, and the 14th Section of An Act Entitled An Act concerning Crimes and Punishments, Should be Repealed.[7]

And your Petitioners will ever pray.

Petitions to the State Assembly, 1862, California State Archives, Sacramento, California. Published by permission.

1. Francis probably refers to one of three July 1851 letters that he wrote to Frederick Douglass from San Francisco. They were later published in *Frederick Douglass' Paper* under the title "Sketches from California." *FDP*, 16, 23, 30 October 1851.

2. Oregon's territorial legislature passed a black exclusion law in 1844. Intended to assuage white fears that black settlers might have a seditious influence on the Native American population, it was repealed before taking effect. In September 1849, the legislature approved a second exclusion law, which closed Oregon's borders to black settlers but allowed blacks already living in the territory to remain. Oregon blacks petitioned the legislature for exemption and repeal of the law, and only one black was banished from the territory under its provisions. Revisions of the legal code voided the law in 1854, but it became part of the state constitution by popular vote in 1857. Although later nullified by the Fourteenth Amendment, the exclusionary clause remained in the Oregon constitution until 1926. McLagan, *Peculiar Paradise*, 23–31.

3. In August 1851, O. B. Francis was arrested under Oregon's black exclusion law on a complaint filed by several white residents of Portland. On 11 September, the case was heard by Orville C. Platt, Sr. (1819–1891), controversial associate justice of the Oregon Supreme Court from 1849 to 1852. Francis was defended by Franklin Tilford, a prominent San Francisco attorney and politician during the 1850s. Despite Tilford's argument that Oregon's exclusion law was unconstitutional, Platt ordered Francis to leave the territory within four months. When the territorial legislature convened in December, a petition was presented asking that

both Francis brothers be exempted from the exclusion law. It was signed by 211 leading residents of Oregon, including two territorial officials and Thomas J. Dryer, the editor of the *Portland Oregonian*. Although several legislators tried to amend the law to allow blacks to remain in the territory by posting good behavior bonds, it remained intact. But the law went largely unenforced, and the Francis brothers stayed in Portland until the end of the decade. Quintard Taylor, Jr., "A History of Blacks in the Pacific Northwest, 1788–1970" (Ph.D. diss., University of Minnesota, 1977), 66; *NCAB*, 38:101; Malcolm Clark, *Eden Seekers: The Settlement of Oregon, 1818–1862* (Boston, Mass., 1981), 228–35, 245, 251–54, 270–75; John M. Myers, *San Francisco's Reign of Terror* (Garden City, N.Y., 1966), 69–70.

4. "Colonel" William M. King (1800–1869), a Portland merchant and civic leader, was the Democratic speaker of the Oregon territorial legislature in the early 1850s. Clark, *Eden Seekers*, 245.

5. Francis quotes from query 18 of Thomas Jefferson's *Notes on the State of Virginia* (1785).

6. Abner Hunt Francis (1812–1872) was born and reared on a farm near Flemington, New Jersey. After obtaining a rudimentary education at the local common school, he moved to Poughkeepsie, New York, and acquired a knowledge of bookkeeping and the tailoring trade. Although barely an adult, Francis had established a clothing business in Trenton, New Jersey, by 1830. He led local blacks in protests against the American Colonization Society, served as a subscription agent for the *Liberator*, and raised money for a proposed black manual labor college. Trenton blacks acknowledged Francis's leadership skills by naming him a delegate to the 1833 and 1834 black national conventions.

Excited by economic opportunities in western New York, Francis moved to Buffalo in 1836. He reestablished his clothing business and, together with partners James Garrett and Robert Banks, became one of the city's leading black businessmen. Francis took part in the activities of the local black community, chairing meetings, speaking at First of August celebrations, and joining the Buffalo Library Association, a black literary society. He also gained a reputation as a black abolitionist and frequently served on the business committee of the Western New York Anti-Slavery Society. A leading figure in the statewide campaign to expand black suffrage, Francis helped organize the first black state convention for that purpose, attended the 1840 and 1841 conventions, coordinated the suffrage campaign that emerged from them, and corresponded with Governor William H. Seward on the subject. Francis represented Buffalo interests at the 1843 and 1848 black national conventions and coauthored the address that emerged from the 1848 gathering. A vocal advocate of the black press, he contributed considerable financial support to the *Colored American* and served as local agent for that paper, the *Palladium of Liberty*, and the *North Star*. In 1850 Francis urged Buffalo blacks to resist the Fugitive Slave Law.

Francis and his wife Lynda left for the Oregon Territory in mid-1851, and, despite the territory's black exclusion laws, they operated a boardinghouse in Portland. Within a few years, he opened a successful mercantile business with his old partner, James Garrett; by 1860 he had accumulated holdings valued at $36,000. Francis established a close relationship with black merchants in San

Francisco and even participated in the civil rights campaigns in California. Because of growing intolerance for Oregon's black laws, Francis moved to Victoria, Vancouver Island, in late 1860. The sale of his Portland business resulted in a loss that forced him to declare bankruptcy. But he established a thriving grocery and provisions business in Victoria, gained a reputation for integrity and ability, and in 1865 became the first black elected to the city council. Francis remained in Victoria until his death. U.S. Census, 1850; *PA*, 12 April 1862, 4 July 1863 [14:0243, 0943]; *Lib*, 17 December 1831, 5 January, 9 March 1833, 4 January 1834, 27 October 1848 [1:0138]; *Minutes and Proceedings of the Third Annual Convention for the Improvement of the Free People of Colour* (New York, N.Y., 1833), 3 [1:0294]; *Minutes of the Fourth Annual Convention for the Improvement of the Free People of Colour* (New York, N.Y., 1834), 8 [1:0466]; *Buffalo City Directory*, 1836–39; *NSt*, 29 December 1848, 10, 24 August 1849, 24 October 1850 [5:0872, 6:0073, 0095, 0646]; *CA*, 27 July 1839, 28 March, 25 April, 13 June, 4 July 1840, 9 January, 13 March, 4, 11, 18 September 1841 [3:0154, 0356, 0400, 0456, 0508, 0824, 0949, 4:0185, 0211]; *NASS*, 29 January 1846, 8 October 1847 [5:0503]; Foner and Walker, *Proceedings of the Black State Conventions*, 1:5, 8–10, 13; *IC*, 28 November 1849 [6:0226]; *Convention of Colored Citizens . . . at Buffalo* (1843), 10 [4:0636]; *Report of the Proceedings of the Colored National Convention, Held at Cleveland, Ohio, On Wednesday, September 6, 1848* (Rochester, N.Y., 1848), 4 [5:0770]; *SL*, 16 January 1843 [4:0525]; *VF*, 18 June 1851 [6:0976]; McLagan, *Peculiar Paradise*, 88–89; *ESF*, 1 December 1865; James W. Pilton, "Negro Settlement in British Columbia, 1858–1871" (M.A. thesis, University of British Columbia, 1951), 208.

7. In 1850 the California legislature passed an act preventing blacks, mulattoes, Native Americans, and Chinese from testifying in criminal cases involving whites. One year later, a second law extended the proscription to include civil proceedings. These testimony laws became the focus of a civil rights struggle by California blacks. In 1852 San Francisco blacks petitioned the legislature for repeal; dozens of petitions soon followed from other black communities around the state. From 1855 to 1857, California blacks convened annual state conventions to offer a unified voice and to coordinate statewide petition campaigns. The legislature amended the law regarding criminal cases in 1855 to allow blacks to act as witnesses in certain instances; but five years later, the California Supreme Court again disallowed black testimony against white litigants. California blacks renewed their efforts against the testimony laws in 1862. Early the following year, the legislature removed restrictions against black testimony but kept them in effect against Native Americans and Chinese. Lapp, *Blacks in Gold Rush California*, 192–209; Montesano, "Free Negro Question in San Francisco," 34–44.

21.
John N. Still to Henry Bibb
3 February 1852

Condemned as intellectually inferior by whites and relegated to the economic margins, blacks found their opportunities and aspirations severely limited. Most working blacks served as bootblacks, sailors, stevedores, waiters, domestic servants, or in similar occupations. During the 1850s, a new generation of black leaders counseled more ambitious and self-reliant attitudes in the economic world. Men such as Martin R. Delany and John N. Still, a Brooklyn clothing merchant and political activist, wanted blacks to work free of white restraints. "White men are producers—we are consumers," observed Delany when he urged blacks to pursue racial elevation by increasing black economic might. Still voiced a similar argument in a 3 February 1852 letter to Henry Bibb. Social advancement would be impossible, he argued, without changing economic goals. He chided blacks for using their limited resources to support churches and benevolent associations while ignoring business ventures. Seeking autonomous economic action and a more practical orientation, Still called for the black community to produce "more financiers and not so many ministers." Pease and Pease, *They Who Would Be Free*, 128–31; *PF*, 20 May 1854 [8:0832]; *FDP*, 9 June 1854 [8:0864].

> Brooklyn, [New York]
> Feb[ruary] 3, 1852

Dear BIBB:

I occasionally get to see your little sheet,[1] and I am much pleased with it. I think it aims more directly at what we need than any paper we have had yet, I mean the investigation and introduction of practical money-making operations. We want more financiers and not so many ministers, at least not "of the same sort." Heretofore we have been principally engaged in building churches and making ministers; we have but few producers, but few manufacturers, and, I may say, no financiers. The various institutions among us are nonproductive in their tendency and operations. We have yet to learn to talk, think and act with some specific object in view—to aim at the accomplishment of some definite thing. Our sons and daughters should be taught to commence the career of life with that settled and fixed determination, and the result would be the same as with English, Irish, Dutch, or any others; but those who have no definite aim cannot expect to do the world nor themselves any good. Communities and nations work out their redemption and elevation just in proportion to the development of undivided energy, determination or patriotism among them. Where these traits are not found in individuals, they cannot be found in the community in which they live—and where they cannot be found in the community, it is in vain they will be sought in the nation. True, we, the colored people, have objects of desire, but we have no settled policy, no determination to do any one thing—no organized efforts, or companies or agencies executing the will, and using the capital of corporate bodies, or individuals, in which might be profitably invested the hard earned monies of our cooks, stewards, whalemen and others, whose lives and avocations will not allow them to learn the nature of trade and how to protect their interest from the long practised and unscrupulous speculator. It is often said that we have not the money to do business, but I think it is not so much the want of money, as the knowledge of using it advantageously. We have 500 per cent more money than we know how to render productive. In all the principle cities of the north, we have deposited in the hands of the whites thousands and tens of thousands of dollars. This truth reflects discredit on us—we must learn to use our own monies.

If some of those gentlemen who have roamed the country arguing theoretical questions, in the pay of our friends, the abolitionists, had been half the time investigating practical moneymaking questions, we think they would have made more money for themselves, more for our people, and, in the main, done more good.

It is strange, but true, that all the institutions we have formed and made so much ado about, consume a great deal, but produce nothing. We have universally established Odd Fellowship, Masonry, Good Samaritans, Rechabites, Sons of Temperance, &c.;[2] their principles are all good, the same to be found in any church; but they occupy a great deal of time and consume a great deal of means, and leave us but little wiser, or but little better off. But why shall we not have "Building and accumulating fund associations"? "Protective union associations," "Borrowing and loaning associations." The time and means spent with the latter would, in a few years, prove a blessing, while those of the former, many of them, are kept up but two or three years, and then abandoned. I am convinced that our reading, writing, thinking, talking and lecturing, and conventions, must be directed more to practical operations.

What is doing in a public way in this direction, you may learn better from the papers than from me. I shall embrace an occasional opportunity to write you, and in future will say more about New York, as I suppose many of your readers are from here and would like to hear the news.

J. N. S.[3]

Voice of the Fugitive (Sandwich, Canada West), 26 February 1852.

1. Still refers to the *Voice of the Fugitive*, a biweekly antislavery journal published by Henry Bibb, a fugitive slave. The contrast between Bibb's personal correspondence and the newspaper's polished prose suggests that Mary E. Bibb, his well-educated wife, played a major editorial role. Bibb published the first issue on 1 January 1851 in Sandwich, Canada West. The paper soon obtained a wide readership by creating a network of subscription agents in Canada West, Ohio, Michigan, Pennsylvania, New York, and New England. Within a year, it boasted one thousand subscribers and was widely quoted in abolitionist journals. As the title implies, the *Voice* spoke for fugitive slaves in both Canada West and the northern United States. It reported extensively on the condition of Canadian fugitives and promoted the immediate abolition of slavery, temperance, black education, black agriculture, Canadian immigration, and moral reform in numerous editorials by Bibb. The paper functioned as the official organ of the Refugee Home Society and informed readers of the progress of the society's organized black settlements; but it also became embroiled in the controversies that arose from the society's fund-raising and relief activities. The *Voice* underwent several changes in 1852. In April Bibb moved his offices to Windsor, Canada West. Two months later, James Theodore Holly became coeditor and coproprietor. In December Bibb announced that the paper would be renamed the *Voice of the Fugitive and Canadian Independent*. But in October 1853, the office of the *Voice* burned to the ground. Although Bibb informed readers that the paper "is not dead," publication was suspended. Bibb's death the following year prevented it from being revived. *VF*, 1 January 1851, 22 April, 17 June, 16 December 1852; Winks, *Blacks in Canada*, 395–97; Simpson, "Negroes in Ontario," 168, 171–74; *Lib*, 28 October 1853 [8:0461].

2. Fraternal societies were among the earliest organizations formed by free blacks in the decades following the American Revolution. Prince Hall and fourteen other Boston blacks founded the first black Masonic lodge—African Lodge No. 1—in 1776. Because white lodges in the United States denied admission to blacks and refused to recognize black lodges, the African Lodge received its formal charter from the Grand Lodge of England in 1787. Encouraged by this example, blacks in other eastern cities, including Philadelphia and New York City, soon formed Masonic lodges. Through the efforts of Richard H. Gleaves of Philadelphia, dozens of black Masonic lodges were also organized in the West after 1846. Blacks participated in similar fashion in the Independent Order of Odd Fellows, organizing separate branches in the 1840s, then obtaining recognition from the Grand United Order of Odd Fellows of England. By the early 1850s, there were about thirty black Masonic lodges and ten Odd Fellows lodges in the United States. Other fraternal societies organized by antebellum blacks also functioned as moral reform or mutual aid associations. Although blacks were usually excluded from the Sons of Temperance and the Independent Order of Rechabites (named for a biblical nomadic sect that abstained from wine), a few independent black branches were formed. Groups like the Order of Good Samaritans and Daughters of Samaria, the Daughters of Africa, and the Heroines of Jericho offered black women the opportunity to participate in auxiliary sororal organizations. Blacks who participated in fraternal societies developed leadership skills and affirmed their social standing in the black community.

Many leading black abolitionists joined these organizations. Mary Ann Clawson, *Constructing Brotherhood: Class, Gender, and Fraternalism* (Princeton, N.J., 1989), 129–35; Leonard P. Curry, *The Free Black in Urban America, 1800–1850: The Shadow of the Dream* (Chicago, Ill., 1981), 208–12; Ian R. Tyrrell, *Sobering Up: From Temperance to Prohibition in Antebellum America, 1800–1860* (Westport, Conn., 1979), 209–10; Quarles, *Black Abolitionists*, 97–99.

3. John Nelson Still (1815–?), the brother of black abolitionist William Still, settled in Brooklyn by 1840 and became one of the city's leading black businessmen. With his partner, John P. Anthony, he operated a tailoring shop, a secondhand clothing store, and a barber supply business that served black barbers throughout New York state. Still was a founding member and lay leader of Siloam Presbyterian Church. He joined David Ruggles in calling for the National Reform Convention of Colored Citizens at Hartford in 1840. Criticized by leading blacks who opposed moral reform, he avoided an active role in protest activities for nearly a decade. But passage of the Fugitive Slave Law of 1850 prompted Still's return to public life. He became a key figure in the local underground railroad and publicly urged blacks throughout the state to resist the law by whatever means necessary.

During the early 1850s, Still advocated a program of racial unity and economic nationalism as the keys to black advancement. He urged blacks to form their own businesses, financial institutions, press, and artisans unions as a means of improving the situation of the race. He promoted these ideas through black newspapers, at black state and national conventions, and as a member of the New York State Council of the Colored People. Still—a correspondent, financial backer, and agent for five black newspapers—thought the press would be the most effective tool in rallying blacks behind his program. But worsening race relations and the ineffectiveness of integrationist leaders moved him toward the emigrationist camp. Attracted to Martin R. Delany's ideas, he signed the call for the first National Emigration Convention (1854), which brought criticism from local black leaders. He later attended the 1856 National Emigration Convention in Cleveland but soon abandoned his advocacy of the movement.

In 1855 Still traveled with a "Diorama of Uncle Tom's Cabin," which illustrated scenes from the novel and from Afro-American history—including black military service in the American Revolution and the War of 1812, the Haitian Revolution, and contemporary black leaders. He sold his various enterprises in 1857 and began a teaching career. After working in black public schools at Brooklyn and Macedonia, New York, he moved to Shrewsbury, New Jersey, in 1861. A decade earlier, Still had expressed support for blacks settling on the Gerrit Smith lands in upstate New York; now he urged blacks to locate in rural New Jersey and to adopt an agrarian life-style. He had retired from public life by the beginning of the Civil War. Still, *Life of Dr. James Still*, 15; *Brooklyn City Directory*, 1850–57; *FDP*, 24 July 1851, 27 January, 3 February, 17 March, 7 April 1854, 4 May 1855 [8:0624, 0640, 0684, 0723]; Harold X. Connolly, *A Ghetto Grows in Brooklyn* (New York, N.Y., 1977), 10, 14; *NASS*, 9 July 1840; *CA*, 25 July 1840 [3:0534]; Foner and Walker, *Proceedings of the Black State Conventions*, 1:55–63, 73, 78, 83, 88; *IC*, 5 October 1850; *Lib*, 4 April 1851 [6:0875]; *Proceedings of the Colored National Convention, Held in Rochester,*

July 6th, 7th and 8th, 1853 (Rochester, N.Y., 1853), 25 [8:0338]; Martin R. Delany, *Official Report of the Niger Valley Exploring Party* (Leeds, England, 1861), 6 [13:0309]; Miller, *Search for a Black Nationality*, 166; *PFW*, 25 November 1856 [10:0386]; *WAA*, 14 July, 29 December 1860, 27 April 1861 [12:0878, 13:0078, 0481].

22.
Resolutions by a Meeting of New Bedford Blacks
Convened at the Third Christian Church
New Bedford, Massachusetts
16 February 1852

The Fugitive Slave Law revived the flagging colonization movement. The American Colonization Society refilled its treasury, recruited new members, restored wayward auxiliaries to the fold, and persuaded a few white abolitionists to reconsider their opposition to colonization. Several state legislatures endorsed Liberian settlement, and a few appropriated funds. But in community after community, as blacks met to protest the Fugitive Slave Law, they restated their opposition to African colonization. They insisted that the combination of oppressive legislation and the promise of relief implicit in colonization coerced free blacks to abandon their American homeland. On 16 February 1852, New Bedford blacks packed the Third Christian Church to reiterate their "solemn protest" against the ACS. Resolutions drafted by a committee of local blacks censured the colonization movement and blamed its resurgence on the Fugitive Slave Law. After obtaining the unanimous approval of those assembled, the officers of the meeting—Ezra R. Johnson, William Jackson, John Bush, and Daniel B. Davis—signed the resolutions and prepared them for publication. P. J. Staudenraus, *The African Colonization Movement, 1816–1865* (New York, N.Y., 1961), 242–45; Leon F. Litwack, *North of Slavery: The Negro in the Free States, 1790–1860* (Chicago, Ill., 1961), 252–58; *FDP*, 10 June 1852 [7:0623]; *SJ*, 21 March 1853 [8:0172].

Whereas, the American Colonization Society has been for the past twenty years in a rapid state of decline, and considered by its friends beyond the reach of restitution, but through the influence of that infamous enactment, the Fugitive Slave Bill, has encouraged its supporters to hope that one more struggle can be made before the monster gives up the ghost, we, the thirteen hundred colored citizens of New Bedford, do reiterate our solemn protest, which was uttered more than twenty years ago, in this time-honored building, against the wicked devices of that iniquitous system;[1] and we now declare to the world our unalterable determination to abide by the policy of nonintervention with all that relates to the American Colonization Society, now and forever. Therefore,

Resolved, That in whatever light we view the Colonization Society, we discover nothing in it but terror, prejudice and oppression; that the warm and beneficent hand of philanthropy is not apparent in the system, but the influence of the Society on public opinion is more prejudicial to the interest and welfare of the people of color in the United States, than slavery itself.

Resolved, That the Society, to effect its purpose, the removal of the free people of color (not the slaves) through its agents, teaches the public to believe that it is patriotic and benevolent to withhold from us knowledge and the means of acquiring subsistence, and to look upon us as unnatural and illegal residents in this country; and thus, by force of prejudice, if not by law, endeavor to compel us to embark for Africa and that, too, apparently, by our own free will and consent.

Resolved, That as great a nuisance as we may be in the estimation of that Society, we yet have a hope in Him who has seen fit to continue our existence through days worse than—which we do not fear—which emboldens us, as peaceable citizens, to resolve to abide the issue of coming days in our native land, in which we ask no more than the age in which we live demands, and which this nation, as republicans and Christians should not refuse to grant.

Resolved, That we urge our brethren throughout the Free States to express in public their oft-repeated declaration, not to countenance, under any circumstances, the claims of this Society, let the advice come from what source it may; for it is fraught with evil inconceivable, and we do not consider any man a friend to our race who would recommend it.

Resolved, That as citizens of the Bay State, for the support of these resolutions, with a firm reliance on the protection of Divine Providence, we do mutually pledge to each other our lives, our fortunes, and our sacred honor, not to support the American Colonization Society. Here are our earliest and most pleasant associations, here is all that binds man to earth and makes life valuable. If Colonizationists desire to better their condition by emigrating to Africa, the field is open to them; we do not intend to fight their battles in Bassa Cove or Fish Town;[2] our duty as colored Hungarians[3] is plain before us; here we were born, here we will live, by the help of the Almighty, and here we will die, and let our bones lie by our fathers.

Voted, that the proceedings of this meeting be signed by the officers, and be published in the papers of this city, the *Liberator* and *Commonwealth* of Boston.[4]

Liberator (Boston, Mass.), 27 February 1852.

1. On 23 January 1832, New Bedford blacks held a mass meeting at the Third Christian Church to protest the actions and objectives of the American Colonization Society. They claimed to see "nothing but terror, prejudice and oppression" in its schemes. The gathering was chaired by Richard C. Johnson, a local merchant, Garrisonian abolitionist, and the patriarch of a family of black antislavery activists. His son, Ezra R. Johnson, presided over the 16 February 1852 meeting.

William Lloyd Garrison, *Thoughts on African Colonization* (Boston, Mass., 1832; reprint, New York, N.Y., 1969), part 2, 50–51; *NBDES*, 5 November 1850; *PA*, 18 July 1863; Nell, *Colored Patriots*, 90–91.

2. Bassa Cove and Fishtown were small colonial settlements, about thirty miles apart, located southeast of Monrovia on the Liberian coast.

3. The authors compare the efforts of black abolitionists to the independence struggle of Louis Kossuth and other Hungarian nationalists in 1848.

4. The Boston *Commonwealth*, the official organ of the Massachusetts Free Soil party, first appeared in 1851 when local political abolitionists purchased Elizur Wright's *Chronotype* and merged it with two other Boston antislavery journals. John Gorham Palfrey and Francis Bird edited the paper, initially with Wright's managerial and editorial assistance. The *Commonwealth* continued publication until 1854. Lawrence B. Goodheart, "Elizur Wright, Jr., and the Abolitionist Movement, 1820–1865" (Ph.D. diss., University of Connecticut, 1978), 174; Friedman, *Gregarious Saints*, 247–50.

23.
J. W. C. Pennington and the Colonization of Africa

J. W. C. Pennington to Editors, New York Independent
23 March 1852

J. W. C. Pennington to George Whipple
August 1853

The resurgence of the colonization movement focused attention on Africa in the early 1850s. Amid renewed calls for black settlement in Africa, J. W. C. Pennington offered fresh, insightful observations about the future of the continent. His 23 March 1852 letter to the New York *Independent* examined the significance of European imperialism for the colonization debate. Pennington pointed out that British settlement in South Africa undermined colonizationist claims that the races must live apart, in separate lands. He further noted that British imperialism had brought British troops into Africa and concluded that black Americans should not leave their homes only to be "impaled on British bayonets" in a "Saxonized" Africa. In an August 1853 letter to the editor of the *American Missionary*, Pennington discussed the relationship between European imperialism and Christian missions in Africa. Pennington, a founder and president of the Union Missionary Society with a long-standing interest in African missions, believed that Christian missions could safeguard African peoples from European exploitation; but he worried that these same missions might be used as a wedge to open the African interior to further colonial expansion. His analysis anticipated the course of European imperialism in Africa during the late nineteenth century. Blackett, *Beating against the Barriers*, 22–26, 33; *AM*, September 1853.

NEW YORK, [New York]
March 23, 1852

MESSRS. EDITORS:[1]

Some time since a Congregational brother, an excellent friend of mine, asked me if my views had been modified in regard to the African Colonization scheme. I said they had not. He remarked that he thought the late recognition of the Liberian government by several European powers[2] entitled the subject to a reconsideration from me. It so happened that I had commenced, previously to that, a course of reading and research upon the whole African question, the result of which is likely to be very different from what my friend may have expected.

1. In regard to the actions of European governments toward the Li-

berian government, they are good as far as they go; still one cannot help lacking confidence in their good intentions. Who can trust in Louis Napoleon's good intentions, when he has his heel on the necks of 30,000,000 Frenchmen? Who will give him the hand of fellowship? And as for the King of Prussia, let him repent of the unmanly act by which he robbed 50,000,000 Germans of their liberal Constitution and continues to divide their necks with his despotic neighbors of Russia and Austria.[3]

2. But again, look at the present doings of Great Britain in Africa! Take the account your correspondent gives under date of October 3d, 1851, from Port Natal. He says, "the tide of emigration is towards the interior."[4] What emigration? White emigration from Great Britain. Well, but I thought there were no white men in Africa! So it has been represented. Well, how is it? I thought white men could not live in Africa. That has also been represented. But it now comes out that thousands of white men are not only living there, but the number is on the increase, and they are pushing for the interior! They are Saxonizing Africa! But what is still more to be reflected upon is that the Saxon has taken up an anti-African position even in that land where they have been admitted by the sufferance of the natives.

Your correspondent says of the natives, "The fact that they are split up into petty tribes, nearly all of which are at variance with each other, is apparently the safeguard of the Colony. The least resistance to government manifested by one tribe, is quickly made known by their prejudiced and revengeful neighbors, and government employs those natives as tools for punishing the rebels." In a letter to Joseph Sturge, recently published in the *British Banner*, Mr. Cobden says there is no evidence that the British government or people have paid one farthing for the lands for which they are now fighting the Kaffirs of South Africa.[5] Yet these men are treated as rebels, though upon their own sacred soil. Major General Somerset has been sent out with fresh troops panting with high notions of national glory and ambition for Saxon progress in the land of Ham![6] At the last accounts, up to the 25th of January last, the British bayonets were carrying everything before them. "About 30,000 head of cattle had been taken from the Kaffirs, and they had been driven into an uninhabited tract of land in the Bushman country of some 4,000 square miles."[7]

This is British recognition in Africa! "Consistency, thou art a jewel!" How then can we trust the motives of the British government? Not only does it thus treat every African tribe as rebels who will not bow and own Victoria[8] as their superior, but it will send no governor or agent anymore who has any humane or anti-slavery leaning. None but men who will represent John Bull,[9] with sword and red coat, and who will chase the natives, "cry havoc and let slip the dogs of war."[10] Hence it is now found that the Briton going to Africa loses all his kindly and generous feelings for the Negro, and becomes a government ghost to haunt every tribe that has a goodly tract of land; and to treat as rebels everyone among them who offers the slightest resistance. The Kaffirs have flogged the British four times during the last eighteen months. For this the poor fellows may expect to pay severely enough, as John Bull has rallied strength and inspired himself with wrath. And besides, let it be borne in mind he is fighting for *beef* as well as land.

Now, you push us in this country, and we must get out of your way. We must go to Africa. Well, when we look to Africa, there we see the Saxon doing his old work, firing dwellings, stealing land, shooting men and women, and seizing cattle by the thousand. John Bull and Jonathan[11] between them seem determined to place us in the position of the extravagant Scotchman who had his candle lighted at both ends. And I submit whether this is not asking too much of good nature that we should furnish candle for you to burn at both ends? And then another serious reflection is that the whites are disseminating that most terrible vice, drunkenness. Your correspondent says of the English emigrants: "To drown their grief and disappointment many take to the fatal cup; and I was lately informed by a clergyman of this place, that he had attended within a few months, fifty funerals, a majority of which were those of inebriates." How appalling! I need not comment. One woe (the Slave Trade) has passed over my fatherland; but another and a still more terrible is at hand at this rate!

But if the doctrine of Colonization is to be insisted upon according to the plan of a correspondent of the *New York Tribune* writing from Lindenwood, Missouri, Sept. 20, 1851, and published in that paper, March 19, 1852![12] what will be the result? You say we must separate from the Saxon by going to Africa. But the Saxon is there! The real, land-stealing, unscrupulous, overreaching Saxon is even in Africa, and is pushing his way into the interior!

Do you say that on our going to Africa he will be recalled? What security do you give us of that? Is the doctrine of intervention to be extended to Africa? John Bull is there knee-deep in his war-boats, with cocked hat, red coat, sword, &c. &c., for the campaign. Or do you say the Continent of Africa is large, and that we must share it with the whites who are there? Then you give up the doctrine of a separation of the races—the fundamental maxim of Colonization. These difficulties are presenting themselves to the minds of intelligent colored men; and I confess I should like to see how candid Colonizationists will undertake to remove them.

J. W. C. Pennington

Independent (New York, N.Y.), 8 April 1852.

Sir:[13]

I have been greatly interested in the project spoken of in your last for a new Mission in Egypt.[14]

About the time, or soon after the formation of the U.M.S.[15] I recollect to have had a conversation with that excellent ex-Missionary, Rev. Josiah Brewer, now Principal of the Middletown, Ct. Female Seminary[16] in which he broached the whole subject of missions to that region of the world, giving his views of the kind of agencies required. My reading and observations have of late years, been directed to that field—to the whole interior of Africa; and I am satisfied that Colonies on the Coasts, and the interferences of foreign governments, present the most deadly obstacles to the progress of the Gospel in Africa.

On the West you have the Americans and the British—the latter has now already the possession of the mouth of every navigable river on the Western Coast; Notwithstanding the boasted Independent Republic of Liberia is on that western Coast. You have the British also on the North Coast. South East you have the French; South you have the British again.

Colonists invariably fall out with the natives, and home governments side with the Colonists against the natives. This has ever been the great misfortune of Africa, and is at this present moment.

Take South Africa, the last point mentioned. Some months ago I had my attention drawn to the heading of the news in several of the Daily papers—"Very interesting from the Cape of Good Hope." On dropping my eyes down the Columns in search of the "interesting," I saw these items: "A sharp and sangunary Conflict occured between the 6th regiment, and a large body of Kaffirs."[17]

> It is stated to be the intention of the governor to erect forts near the mountain passes of the Kaffirs, and thus Compell them to abandon them.
>
> Sandilhi, the chief of the Kaffirs had again sued for peace, but the governor replied that he would not treat with him while there was a single Kaffir upon the South side of the River Kei. The Cape papers greatly rejoice at this descision, believing that their old adversary will be driven into Central Africa, and the Kaffir lands be annexed to the Colony.[18]

It will be seen from this what is in reserve for Central Africa. The bayonet is to peirce even to her bowels!

Governments are all of a peice. I always But we [should] make a distinction between governments and people. I know it is a maxim, that people are to be judged of by their laws, legislators and rulers. But this is not always true right. The British Christian people are ashamed and sick of the cruel Conduct of their government. They have remonstrated in every way, and on every fitting occassion; and yet still the oppressions and abuses of government continue.

There is reason to believe that there will be war between the blacks and the whites in Africa for a hundred years to come.

So little sense of justice has been shown those who have represented Christian governments in Africa, that the confidence of the native Tribes has been greatly shaken, even in well intended efforts for their good. But, there is an evil of still greater magnitude. On the one hand, the natives are dispossessed of many important points along their Coast. They have [lost] several of their important commercial streams, such as the Niger, The Callibery, The Bonny, and The Camiroan. These waters all leading ~~deep~~ far into the interior, and destined to be of great commercial value are already, as far as explored, in the hands of the British government, which has trading stations—another name for forts—about their mouths.[19]

This governmental operation will go on. As fast as desirable points are discovered along the banks, possessions will be gained. So that ages hence the natives will find themselves a[r]med off in every direction by foreign forces. The effect of this is easily foreseen. There will be Conflicts for water rights. Nor will the evil stop here. It will soon be found, that many parts of the interior are more healthy than the seaboard, on these unscrupulous parties, will attempt to seize. Already the saxon Colonists are penetrating from the South.

Looking at our subject from these points of view there is ~~something~~ much that is gloomy in the prospect. Any missionary scheme to interior Africa should certainly have but one grand aim—namely the <u>evangelization</u> of the people and their existing governments. Let the native Kings and their subjects be taught to know, that "there is another King, one Jesus," and let them continue to hold and exercise their authority subject to His authority, or in other words let them become Christian Theocracies.

The plan, now so highly lauded in this country, of Republicanising Africa will prove mischievious, anti missionary, and revolutionary. Besides countries, or nations ~~or~~ and governments are naturally jealous of each other's movements. What one government or party may do another will claim the right to do. If a handful of colonists may go from one Country, and seize lands, lay hands upon the persons of the existing Kings, suspend their governments, and annex their territory and populations, another, and another will do the same. And thus under the garb of Civilization the whole Country, and people become common plunder.

Our missions to the interior of Africa then, must not only continue strictly anti Slavery, and anti war, but they must take decided stand ~~against~~ in favor of the natives against the foreign plunderer[s] and revolutionaries beginning to enter the country in such numbers from all sides.

The idea that missions can only be sustained in connexion with some colony or by the potent name of some foreign Ruler, is mischievious in practice, and false in theory. Let our missionaries respect the governments in Africa which honorably protect them and recognise and respect their missions; and let them not remain neutral when these governments and their people are politically and unjustly ~~insulted~~ treated; and the interior of the Country can be taken for Christ, with far less expense of time[,] means, loss of life, and with less jealousy than would be occasioned by any of the present methods of operation.

J. W. C. Pennington

American Missionary Association Archives, Amistad Research Center, Tulane University, New Orleans, Louisiana. Published by permission.

1. The New York *Independent*, a Congregationalist weekly founded in 1848, was managed during its first decade by an editorial board consisting of three prominent clergymen—Joseph P. Thompson and Richard S. Storrs of New York City and Leonard Bacon of New Haven. The actual editorial work was performed by Thompson and assistant editor Joshua Leavitt. When Henry Ward Beecher and Theodore Tilton assumed control in the late 1850s, the paper was a sectarian sheet with a circulation of seventeen thousand. They broadened its scope, strengthened its abolitionist outlook, and made it the leading religious newspaper in the nation. By 1870 the *Independent* had seventy-five thousand subscribers. Louis Filler, "Liberalism, Anti-Slavery, and the Founders of the Independent," *NEQ* 27:293–306 (September 1954); James M. McPherson, *The Abolitionist Legacy: From Reconstruction to the NAACP* (Princeton, N.J., 1975), 25.

2. Soon after Liberia became an independent republic in 1847, President Joseph J. Roberts embarked on a European tour and received assurances of diplomatic recognition from several countries. By 1852 Britain, France, and Prussia had concluded treaties of amity and commerce with the new nation. C. Abayomi Cassell, *Liberia: History of the First African Republic* (New York, N.Y., 1970), 156–59, 175, 178, 215, 229, 231.

3. Pennington refers to the authoritarian actions of two European heads of state. Louis Napoleon, the president of the French Republic, initiated a successful coup d'état in 1851 and soon declared himself Emperor Napoleon III. In 1849 Frederick William IV, the king of Prussia, rejected a proposal that would have unified many of the German states under a constitutional monarchy. Pennington laments that the German people remained divided under the domination of Prussia, Russia, Austria, and several German states.

4. Pennington refers to "From Our Correspondent in South Africa," which appeared in the 18 March 1852 issue of the *Independent*. This 3 October 1851 letter by "J. T.," a regular correspondent of the paper in Port Natal (now Durban), noted increasing agricultural settlement, as well as commercial and missionary interest, in the South African interior. Because of this, he expressed uncertainty that peaceful relations would continue with the indigenous Zulu tribesmen in the region.

5. An 8 January 1852 letter by Richard Cobden, a member of the British Parliament, to Birmingham abolitionist Joseph Sturge appeared thirteen days later in the *British Banner*. "The real question," Cobden asked Sturge, "is what title have Englishmen to the possessions of the land of the Caffres?" *BB*, 21 January 1852.

6. Western Christianity had long assumed that blacks were descended from Ham, Noah's third son in the biblical account in Genesis 9–10. Pennington uses the common nineteenth-century identification of Africa as the "land of Ham." Winthrop D. Jordan, *White over Black: American Attitudes toward the Negro, 1550–1812* (Chapel Hill, N.C., 1968), 17–20.

7. The nineteenth-century expansion of British colonial settlement in South Africa brought white settlers into frequent conflict with the Xhosa and other indigenous Bantu tribes, commonly called "Kaffirs" (a derisive term meaning "infidel") by the British. Both sides engaged in raids and counter-raids over cattle, their most prized commodity. Occasionally this conflict escalated into open warfare between British troops and Bantu warriors, which became known collectively as the Kaffir Wars. In 1847 Sir Henry "Harry" Smith, the new governor of the Cape Colony, initiated an aggressive annexation policy and attempted to extend British authority over the Xhosa. Sandile (1820–1878), a Xhosa chieftain who had led an unsuccessful campaign against the British in 1846, responded by renewing the warfare in 1850. Sir George Cathcart, who replaced Smith as governor in January 1852, vigorously pursued the war to a close. By the end of the year, British forces under Major General Henry Somerset (?–1853) had driven Sandile and his followers out of British-held territory and into an area previously inhabited only by primitive hunter-gatherers known as Bushmen. *DAHB*, 204, 218–19; Robert Godlonton and Edward Irving, *Narrative of the Kaffir War, 1850–1851–1852* (London, 1851; reprint, Cape Town, South Africa, 1962).

8. Pennington refers to Queen Victoria (1819–1901), the constitutional monarch of Britain and the British Empire from 1837 until her death.

9. "John Bull" was a standard nineteenth-century term or symbol for Britain.

10. Pennington quotes from act 2, scene 1, of William Shakespeare's play *Julius Caesar*, in which Brutus decides to battle against Marc Antony: "Cry 'Havoc!' and let slip the dogs of war."

11. Pennington refers to "Brother Jonathan," a symbol for the United States.

12. A 20 September 1851 letter from Lindenwood, Missouri, appeared in the 19 March 1852 issue of the *New York Tribune*. Written by "GCS," it advocated colonization and reprinted sections of Thomas Jefferson's *Notes on the State of Virginia* (1785) that reflected the Founding Father's views on slavery and race. "GCS" believed that Jefferson's observations supported the judgment that blacks posed a danger to the future of the United States and had to be colonized.

13. George Whipple (1805–1876), one of the Lane rebels, studied at Oberlin College and was appointed professor of mathematics there in 1838. He helped found the Western Evangelical Missionary Society and in 1846 became corresponding secretary of the newly organized American Missionary Association, a position he held for thirty years. Whipple was responsible for editing and publishing the AMA's monthly paper, the *American Missionary*, which contained reports of the organization's activities, missionary correspondence, and news of the antislavery movement. *AM*, November 1876; Clifton H. Johnson, "The

American Missionary Association, 1846–1861: A Study in Christian Abolitionism" (Ph.D. diss., University of North Carolina, 1959), 253–72.

14. Encouraged by travel reports about Egyptian Christians, the American Missionary Association sent Charles F. Martin to Egypt in the fall of 1854. He was commissioned to establish a permanent mission and to study the language and religion of the Copts, a variety of Christianity found in Egypt and Ethiopia. Poor health forced him to return home after three years. Because the AMA focused its attention on home missions during and after the Civil War, an Egyptian mission was never reestablished. Johnson, "American Missionary Association," 398–401.

15. Pennington refers to the founding of the Union Missionary Society in August 1841.

16. Josiah Brewer (1796–1872), a Congregational clergyman, was an advocate of abolitionism, pacifism, and international mission work. From 1830 to 1838, he labored in Asia Minor for the American Board of Commissioners for Foreign Missions, introducing educational reforms and establishing the region's first newspaper. After returning to the United States, he edited the *Union Missionary Herald* (1842), helped found the Union Missionary Society and the American Missionary Association, and served on the AMA's executive committee (1846–63). Brewer and his wife, Emilia, opened the Middletown Female Seminary in 1850. About one hundred women attended the school, which continued under the Brewers' control until 1856 and was disbanded in 1868. *ACAB*, 1:370; De Boer, "Afro-Americans in American Missionary Association," 26, 37–38, 580; *AM*, January 1873; *History of Middlesex County, Connecticut, with Biographical Sketches of its Prominent Men* (New York, N.Y., 1884), 132; *Catalogue of the Middletown Female Seminary* (Middletown, Conn., 1851); Arnold M. Paul, "David J. Brewer," in *The Justices of the United States Supreme Court, 1789–1969: Their Lives and Major Opinions*, ed. Leon Friedman and Fred L. Israel, 5 vols. (New York, N.Y., 1969), 2:1515–16.

17. The Sixth (Royal First Warwickshire) Regiment of Foot, a British infantry unit, was headquartered at Fort Peddie, on Cape Colony's eastern frontier. The regiment saw action in several engagements with Xhosa warriors during the Kaffir Wars.

18. When the last of the Kaffir Wars ended in 1853, the Xhosa had been pushed north of the Great Kei River, slightly beyond Cape Colony's eastern frontier. Pennington suggests that the British press in South Africa favored this outcome.

19. Pennington refers to the Niger River and the Cross River, the only two navigable river systems flowing into the Gulf of Guinea on the West African coast. Because of their commercial importance, Britain attempted to gain control over them during the 1850s. The Niger is a major river system extending over twenty-five hundred miles through West Africa. Two outlets of the Niger delta, the Kalibari and the Bonny, were usually identified as separate rivers on nineteenth-century maps. The Cross and several other streams that drain the Cameroon highlands flow into a large estuary 150 miles east of the Niger delta. The major trading centers of Brass, Kalibari, Bonny, and Old Calabar were located on these rivers. David Northrup, *Trade without Rulers: Pre-Colonial Economic Development in South-Eastern Nigeria* (Oxford, England, 1978), 11, 177–223.

24.
Robert Purvis to Oliver Johnson
24 April 1852

The publication of *Uncle Tom's Cabin* (1852), an antislavery novel by
Harriet Beecher Stowe, was a major event in antebellum American culture. More than a million copies were sold in the United States during
its first seven years in print. Black leaders recognized the book's enormous antislavery value and believed that it would reach a far broader
audience than any previous abolitionist tract or slave narrative. But
many blacks reeled at the novel's endorsement of colonization. Robert
Purvis, a prominent black Garrisonian, believed that his white allies
failed to appreciate the seriousness of Stowe's mistake; the *Pennsylvania
Freeman* concluded that the book's antislavery influence would outweigh any damage that the "unfortunate chapter" on colonization
might do. Purvis's 24 April 1852 letter to the *Freeman*, written less than
a month after the publication of *Uncle Tom's Cabin*, offered a black
abolitionist view of the book and reminded white reformers of their
duty to repudiate colonization in all its forms. Harriet Beecher Stowe,
Uncle Tom's Cabin; or, Life Among the Lowly, ed. Ann Douglas (New
York, N.Y., 1981), 9; Philip S. Foner, *History of Black Americans*, 3
vols. to date (Westport, Conn., 1975–), 3:114–15; *FDP*, 6 May 1853
[8:0239]; *PFW*, 22 July 1854.

> *Byberry,* [Pennsylvania]
> *April* 24th, 1852

Friend Johnson:[1]
I have just finished reading Uncle Tom.[2] What a portraiture of the
infernal system! I felt as my excited feelings carried me with accelerated
pulse through the thrilling incidents of the narrative, that by its reading
slavery would be cursed of all men, and that a speedy and mighty change
in the nation's sentiment toward the cause of freedom and the rights of
man would be effected. The review of *The Liberator* in the matter of
Colonization, led me to apprehend some disappointment.[3] But the tame-
ness of Mr. Garrison's remarks left me unprepared for the terrible blow
which the closing chapter of this otherwise great book inflicted. "Alas!" I
exclaimed, "save us from our friends." The imposture in the chapter
referred to should cause its condemnation as pernicious to the well-being
of the colored people in this country. It is *African Colonization un-
masked*, while the unbecoming thing at Hayti, and her noble self-eman-
cipated inhabitants, as well as the gratuitous "concluding remarks," as to
fitness for Liberia, gave evidence of a heart which needs to be cleansed
and purified from that "prejudice and scorn" which are somewhat

shared by the author in common with "Miss Feely"[4] and the American people.

ROBERT PURVIS

Pennsylvania Freeman (Philadelphia, Pa.), 29 April 1852.

1. Oliver Johnson (1809–1889), an accomplished antislavery journalist and a trusted associate of William Lloyd Garrison, helped found the New England Anti-Slavery Society and often edited the *Liberator* in Garrison's absence. After assisting Horace Greeley on the *New York Tribune* (1844–48), he edited three Garrisonian journals—the *Anti-Slavery Bugle, Pennsylvania Freeman,* and *National Anti-Slavery Standard.* Johnson worked for several New York City newspapers after the Civil War. Merrill and Ruchames, *Letters of William Lloyd Garrison,* 2:xxv–xxvi.

2. *Uncle Tom's Cabin; or, Life Among the Lowly* (1852) was the first novel by nineteenth-century American author Harriet Beecher Stowe. Initially printed in forty serial installments in the *National Era,* it was soon republished as a book, sold more than three hundred thousand copies the first year, and was made into a popular stage drama in Britain and the United States. A fictionalized indictment of slavery, the book helped crystallize northern sentiment against the institution. Southern reviewers vilified Stowe and challenged the accuracy of the book's depiction; some thirty anti-Tom novels appeared in the South. Stowe wrote *The Key to Uncle Tom's Cabin* (1853) to provide documentary evidence to refute her detractors. *DAAS,* 709; William R. Taylor, *Cavalier and Yankee: The Old South and American National Character* (New York, N.Y., 1961), 307.

3. William Lloyd Garrison sympathetically reviewed *Uncle Tom's Cabin* in the 26 March 1852 issue of the *Liberator.* He predicted that the book would have great influence but regretted its support for colonization and questioned its inference that there was "one law of submission and non-resistance for the black man, and another law of rebellion and conflict for the white man."

4. Purvis refers to Miss Ophelia St. Clare, a fictional character in *Uncle Tom's Cabin.* She is the New England cousin of a southern slaveholding family. Although slavery offends her sense of domestic propriety, she harbors racial prejudice and lacks real concern for the slaves.

25.
Martin R. Delany to Frederick Douglass
10 July 1852

The Fugitive Slave Law and other discriminatory enactments rekindled black interest in emigration during the 1850s. Martin R. Delany established himself as emigration's leading spokesman with the publication of *The Condition, Elevation, Emigration and Destiny of the Colored People of the United States* (1852). The volume offered an alternative to the integrationist position espoused by Frederick Douglass and most other black abolitionists. Delany revived the idea of black nationality, arguing that racial progress was inexorably tied to the existence of a strong black nation beyond the United States. He looked to Central and South America as possible emigration sites and even considered Africa, although he vigorously rejected the American Colonization Society's Liberian settlement scheme. *Condition* was criticized by the white antislavery press and received equivocal treatment at the hands of black editors. The *Aliened American* generally praised the work but objected to its pessimistic tone and emigrationist message. The *Voice of the Fugitive* welcomed its observations on Canada yet largely ignored the remainder of the book. *Frederick Douglass' Paper* passed over the book in silence. In a 10 July 1852 letter, Delany hinted that Douglass's antiemigrationist stance might have been the reason for the oversight. Despite this equivocation, Delany's volume was widely recognized as a primer for the black emigration movement by the end of the decade. It remains a valuable and original contribution to black literature and social thought. Miller, *Search for a Black Nationality*, 125–33; Victor Ullman, *Martin R. Delany: The Beginnings of Black Nationalism* (Boston, Mass., 1971), 140–51; Delany, *Condition of the Colored People*, 4–5; AA, 9 April 1853 [8:0219–20]; VF, 3 June 1852.

NEW YORK CITY, [New York]
July 10, 1852

SIR:

I send you for publication, an interesting paper, written evidently by a competent person, one very intelligent upon the subject, as a contribution to the *National Intelligencer* (of Washington City, D.C.), giving a statistic summary of the five States of CENTRAL AMERICA.[1] Of course, anything said in commendation of this paper, every due allowance is made for the peculiar *Anglo-Saxon prejudices* of the writer, in his allusion to the "superiority" of the white race, a fact well worthy of remark, that wherever found, this same *Anglo-Saxon* race, is the most inveterate enemy of the *colored races*, of whatever origin—whether African, Mongolian, Malayan, or Indian. This is substantially true (to which there are always individual exceptions) but is not really the case with any *other* race of the Caucasian type. You will find by this writer's own acknowledgement, that the greater part of the inhabitants of the country are colored people, there being more *whites* in proportion in the little State of Costa Rica, than in any other of the States, and these fall far in the minority.

I am deeply interested in this subject—and you will not charge me with the "egotism," with which a distinguished statesman was charged during the Mexican War with the United States, who said, that he had "studied Humboldt[2] forty years ago"—when I say, that I am equally, if not more familiar with the subject of these countries, than the most of colored men, having made them a matter of thought, for more than seventeen years, at which time (being very young) I introduced the subject before the young people,[3] and have never since abandoned it. But for my views upon this subject, I refer you and the reader to a work, recently published by myself, on the *Condition, Elevation, Emigration, and Destiny of the Colored People of the United States.* This work, a copy of which I sent you in May, on its issue, has never been noticed in the columns of your paper. *This* silence and neglect on your part was unjustifiable, because in noticing it, it was not necessary that you should implicate yourself either with the *errors* or *sentiments* therein contained. You could have given it a circulating notice, by saying such a book had been written by me (saying anything else about or against it you pleased), and let those who read it pass their own opinions also. But you heaped upon it a cold and deathly silence. This is not the course you pursue towards any issue, good or bad, sent you by white persons; you have always given them some notice. I desire not here to make an undue allusion, but simply to be treated as justly as you treat them. I care but little, what white men think of what I say, write, or do; my sole desire is, to benefit the colored people; this being done, I am satisfied—the opinion of every white person in the country or the world, to the contrary notwithstanding. This, I believe, so far, my book has accomplished—at least, the *colored people* generally are pleased with it, and that is all I desire in this case. It is true, there are some white men and women whose good opinions I desire and esteem; but these are few—good and tried friends. The remarks I make concerning your neglect, will also apply to Mr. Henry Bibb.[4] I may add, that when it was my province to conduct a *Journal,*[5] I always took pleasure in noticing anything to enhance either of your interests. But no matter.

I desire that our people have light and information upon the available means of bettering their condition; this they must and shall have. We never have, as heretofore, had any settled and established policy of our own—we have always adopted the policies that white men established for themselves without considering their applicability or adaptedness to us. No people can rise in this way. We must have a position, independently of anything pertaining to white men as nations. I weary of our miserable condition, and [am] heartily sick of whimpering, whining and snivelling at the feet of white men, begging for their refuse and offals existing by mere sufferance. You will please give this an insertion, in any part of the paper, so that the letter and article appear in the same number. Yours for God and Humanity,

M. R. DELANY[6]

Frederick Douglass' Paper (Rochester, N.Y.), 23 July 1852.

1. Delany refers to an article that appeared without attribution in the 5 July 1852 issue of the Washington *National Intelligencer*. A survey of economic, social, and political conditions in Guatemala, Salvador, Honduras, Nicaragua, and Costa Rica, it stressed promising developments, while noting problems arising from the heritage of colonialism and the lack of democratic traditions. The essay was reprinted along with Delany's letter in the 23 July issue of *Frederick Douglass' Paper*.

2. Alexander von Humboldt (1769–1859), a German naturalist, was considered a foremost authority on the politics and geography of Latin America. He explored the region between 1799 and 1804 and published his observations in the *Personal Narrative of Travels to the Equinoctial Regions of the New Continent* (1814–29). *CBD*, 700–701.

3. In 1836 Delany penned "A Project for an Expedition of Adventure, to the Eastern Coast of Africa," which he later published as an appendix to *The Condition, Elevation, Emigration and Destiny of the Colored People of the United States* (1852). The essay, an early expression of his ideas on black nationality, argued that black Americans could not advance under white oppression. It urged black leaders to explore possibilities for settlement in East Africa but also suggested that they look to "all such places as might meet the approbation of the people," including South America, Mexico, and the West Indies. Delany probably first delivered these remarks before a meeting of the Theban Literary Society, an organization of young Pittsburgh blacks devoted to intellectual improvement. Delany, *Condition of the Colored People*, 9–10; Ullman, *Martin R. Delany*, 21–27.

4. Delany was mistaken in his assertion that Henry Bibb's *Voice of the Fugitive* had also ignored his book. The 3 June 1852 issue of the *Voice* gave Delany's *Condition* a limited but generally favorable review.

5. Martin Robinson Delany published the *Mystery* in Pittsburgh from September 1843 to January 1848. Several local black leaders—including John B. Vashon, Henry Collins, and Lewis Woodson—contributed assistance and financial support. Early issues of the antislavery journal emphasized the local concerns of Pittsburgh blacks, but Delany later expanded its size and scope to appeal to a wider audience. He also created a network of subscription agents in more than sixty cities throughout the North. Despite competition from two Ohio black newspapers—the *Disfranchised American* in Cincinnati and the *Palladium of*

Liberty in Columbus—the *Mystery* apparently drew a large readership in Ohio and western Pennsylvania. Persistent financial problems, caused in part by a libel suit, eventually forced Delany to relinquish ownership of the paper to a publishing committee of local blacks. He left the *Mystery* in early 1848 to work with Frederick Douglass's *North Star*. The publishing committee continued to produce the journal, but without Delany's editorial direction, it could not be sustained. It ceased publication by the end of the year. Ullman, *Martin R. Delany*, 44–88; *NSt*, 21, 28 January, 11 August 1848 [5:0560, 0568, 0748]; *Mystery*, 16 April 1845, 16 December 1846; *PL*, 1 May 1844 [4:0797]; *ESF*, 19 April 1873.

6. Martin Robinson Delany (1812–1885), the leading advocate of black nationalism and emigration during the antebellum period, was born in Charlestown, Virginia, to a free black woman and her slave husband. As a child, he heard his grandmother tell tales of her African homeland. When his mother was caught educating her five children, she was forced to resettle the family in Chambersburg, Pennsylvania. Delany moved to Pittsburgh at age nineteen, enrolled in Lewis Woodson's African Educational Society School, and soon began a three-year apprenticeship with a local doctor. He directed several black self-help organizations, aided fugitive slaves, led local attempts to recover the franchise for Pennsylvania blacks, and worked for the Liberty party. Delany edited his own antislavery weekly called the *Mystery* from 1843 to 1848, then joined Frederick Douglass as coeditor of the *North Star*. Two years later, he resigned and returned to his Pittsburgh medical practice. Although rejected by a number of medical schools, Delany was accepted at Harvard College in 1850, but student protests forced his dismissal from the program after a single term. Such evidences of American racism made him increasingly radical. He became attracted by the prospects for slave violence, the theme of *Blake; or The Huts of America*, a novel that he wrote and serialized in the black press between 1859 and 1862.

In 1852 Delany published *The Condition, Elevation, Emigration and Destiny of the Colored People of the United States*—a brief for emigration and black nationalism. Although attacked by the white antislavery press and black integrationists such as Frederick Douglass, the volume struck a responsive chord among many blacks and helped provoke a growing emigration sentiment. In August 1854, Delany brought together 106 black leaders at the first National Emigration Convention in Cleveland to consider immigration to Central America, South America, or the West Indies. He moved to Canada West in early 1856 and planned a second convention, which met in Cleveland that August and marked a new direction in emigration thought. Delany now focused on Africa. From 1856 to 1858, he made plans to launch the Niger Valley Exploring Party, an agency for establishing a free labor settlement in West Africa. Delany and Philadelphia teacher Robert Campbell visited the Niger valley region in 1859 and concluded a treaty for land with the *alake* (king) of Abeokuta. Delany spent the next three years telling audiences in Britain, Canada, and the United States of his African plans and experiences.

When emancipation became federal policy in 1863, Delany turned his attention to the Union war effort. He recruited soldiers for black regiments and promoted a plan to arm slaves behind Union lines. In 1865 he obtained a commission as a major in the U.S. Army, becoming the first black field officer to serve in the war. Sent to Charleston, he raised two regiments of former slaves before the war ended. Delany remained in South Carolina after the war as an agent for the Freedmen's Bureau. From 1870 to 1875, he was active in Republican party politics in the state, serving part of that time as a trial judge in the Charleston courts. When Reconstruction failed, Delany promoted a short-lived emigration project called the Liberian Exodus Joint Stock Steamship Company. He also wrote *Principia of Ethnology* (1879), an examination of the African role in world civilization. Delany retired to Wilberforce, Ohio, in the early 1880s. *DANB*, 169–72; Ullman, *Martin R. Delany*; Miller, *Search for a Black Nationality*, 116–225, 265–67; Dorothy Sterling, *The Making of an Afro-American: Martin Robinson Delany, 1812–1885* (Garden City, N.Y., 1971), 48–55.

26.
Granville B. Blanks to Editor, *Syracuse Daily Journal*
12 August 1852

Emigration attracted free blacks of every station in the decade before
the Civil War. Their willingness to leave the United States revealed a
profound loss of hope for racial progress. Granville B. Blanks, a Michigan free black, offered his own bleak assessment of American race relations in a 12 August 1852 letter to the *Syracuse Daily Journal*. Drawing
on experience gained from his travels in the northern and border states,
Blanks determined that it was "impracticable, not to say impossible, for
whites and blacks to live together, and upon terms of social and civil
equality." He concluded that black emigration offered the only solution
to the racial impasse. Although Blanks approved of emigration sites in
Central America and the Caribbean, he focused on West Africa, particularly the recently founded Republic of Liberia. Blanks emphasized that
his preference for Liberia was based solely on personal judgment, not
on a connection with the American Colonization Society. His call for
emigration was a practical presentation that reflected the sentiment of
thousands of blacks who left for Africa, Haiti, or Canada West during
the 1850s and early 1860s. Miller, *Search for a Black Nationality*, 93–
169.

SYRACUSE, [New York]
Aug[ust] 12, 1852

SIR:[1]

I desire through your columns to make a few statements to the citizens
of Syracuse, and to the public in general. I am a colored man, now forty
years of age. I was born in Virginia, a free man, my father having purchased his freedom and that of my mother before my birth. About sixteen years ago I removed to Michigan, in which state I have since resided, with the exception of an absence for the most part of the last two
years.

The question of the condition and prospects of the colored race is one
which has long been agitating the public mind. The position of this
government in relation to this portion of its population has afforded a
theme for discussion the most intense and exciting both in this and other
lands. The passage of the Fugitive Slave Law in 1850 aroused my mind
and excited in me a purpose to examine for myself what would be the
probable future history of my people. This examination has led me to
certain conclusions which by your permission I desire here to express.

In the first place it is my deliberate conviction that, with our present
Constitution and prejudices, it is impracticable, not to say impossible,

for the whites and blacks to live together, and upon terms of social and civil equality, under the same government. In a mixed community, the white man has a superiority, and the black man is forced into a subordinate condition. Disabilities thus lie upon him which, with very rare exceptions, have crushed down the whole colored population of this country. Many of these disabilities are of such a nature, that no change of legal enactments, no force of education, no favor of public sentiment seems adequate to remove them, for they originate in the actual distinctions of the two races, which have been constituted by another than human power. Under this view of the subject I see no possible alternative for the mass of the colored population now, but a state of continual degradation or a removal to some land where they may hope to attain a condition of permanent freedom and of progressing civilization. Yet the negro is a *man*, although downtrodden. He must have, like the white man, a country he can call his own, where he may enjoy the opportunity of developing all his faculties under those just and equal laws which God has given to all mankind. And in passing, allow me to state that after long consideration I have adopted the opinion that the western coast of Africa, and especially the Republic of Liberia, offers the most controlling inducements to our emigration. Other regions, I know, have been mentioned, as Canada, the West India Islands and Central America, but a glance at the present condition of Africa and the prospect of her future civilization and christianization, together with the instrumentalities to be employed in an enterprise so noble and Godlike, will serve to show the paramount motives to our people which lie in that direction. I am not, however, pleading for the American Colonization Society, or for any other organization, as I am connected with none of any description. I hope all these associations will do good, and promote the paramount welfare of humanity. Nor have I been bought up by any individual or set of individuals to put forth these sentiments. Not all the money in the country could purchase these convictions, deliberately formed in my own mind, and not only from my own sad personal experience, but also from a close and attentive observation of the condition of my colored brethren in this nation. From that spirit of cupidity and that mercenary influence which is so prevalent and polluting, and which, while it corrupts the laws and customs of the American people, at the same time casts its dark suspicions on the purest motives and the most disinterested actions, I desire to be delivered. If any judge that the black man cannot think and feel for himself without the bribe of the designing, and without being bought, as his labor, and even his body and his soul are bought for the comparatively paltry considerations of filthy lucre, I hope the time will come when we shall demonstrate the libel of such an opinion.

It is true, I differ widely from many of my oppressed people who are longing for deliverance, but my judgement is formed in candor, and not,

I hope in the bitterness of prejudice. It is painful for me to hold sentiments which others and especially those of my own race may feel bound to oppose—but if I stand alone, I cannot do otherwise than proclaim my honest convictions. Every day's experience has confirmed me in those convictions. I have been traveling now for a period of 18 months in various portions of the country, and the facts I have gathered up and not any delusive imagination are the basis on which I establish my opinions. In the State of Kentucky last summer I saw free colored men competent to do business and anxious to obtain a livelihood, but laboring under those distressing inequalities which must inevitably attend them among the white people. I found them, in many respects, surpassed by another class of colored men who were naturally no more adequate or enterprising, but who being slaves derived even from their masters a protection to labor, which is denied to the free people of color in that State. This advantage I do not ascribe to the system of slavery as such, but to the more humane disposition of certain masters in spite of the system itself. These are reasons which lead me to believe that the two races cannot, even if both were free, continue together in a condition of social and civil equality. To illustrate this more in detail, I will give, out of an abundance of similar proofs, one or two instances.

While in Louisville, Kentucky, I became acquainted with a colored man, an industrious and excellent mechanic. In conversation with him, I learned that he had once been worth a considerable property, but the tide of public prejudice was such as to render it impossible for him to compete with those of the same class of white laborers, or to secure the same degree of confidence or the same amount of patronage. The result was, he had become reduced in purse and dejected in spirit, and would gladly have left the place for some asylum where labor and economy shall be as sacred in the person of the black man as in that of the white man. I will specify a single other instance. A man in Louisville had bought himself from his master, a hardware merchant in that city, and was desirous to do business for himself. But such was the known prevalent disposition of the white men to tyrannize over the black, he stipulated with his master to extend to him that protection in his everyday business, now that he was free, which he would have enjoyed in the service of his master had he remained a slave. He provided himself with a horse and cart and became a drayman. Soon after, having been employed to cart goods to a certain place by another white man, his employer under the impression that he was a free negro doing business for himself, insisted that he should take such an amount of loading each time as it was plainly beyond the strength of his horse to draw. Upon this requisition the drayman remonstrated, at which his employer commenced the most outrageous abuse of him, threatening personal violence. The drayman soon left the cart standing there with the unreasonable load and called his old master to his aid. And when it appeared by a legal stipulation the drayman had still the protection of his master, then and then only were things set to rights and the poor drayman suffered to take such loads as it was possible for his horse to draw. This may be regarded of no account, but it is to my mind a circumstance similar to numberless others which prove beyond a question the existence of those difficulties which stand ever in the way of the black man in this country.

After leaving Kentucky, I resolved to visit those parts of the country where the sentiments of the white people were said to be more favorable to the interests of the colored people. I went into the Western States for the purpose of observing their condition in that section and noting the degree of progress to which they had attained. I invariably found them laboring under the same burdens. I then returned through the Eastern and older States where Slavery as a legal system had been longest abolished[2] and where I was entitled to expect a more improved condition and a greater equality of privilege among the colored people, but in this I have been mainly disappointed. I have found but one or two colored men, and those in the city of New York, who have even the appearance of that prosperity and position which belong to the white citizen. I find then the colored population of this country, as a whole, in a most abject and degraded condition. They are mostly in ignorance and corrupted by many vices. Even the most enterprising and active of them, hold subordinate and menial positions. Some few there are like FREDERICK DOUGLASS, or PROFESSOR ALLEN,[3] or DR. PENNINGTON,[4] who may have partially risen above the obstacles which beset us, but even these men are compelled to mortifications which the white man knows nothing of, while the great mass of our people are totally shut out from the immunities and regards of the highest circles of society.

In view of this, to what conclusions could I, or any rational person, or any lover of his race, come upon this subject other than those I have already formed! I feel a deep interest in the future welfare of my colored brethren. I wish to see them in a condition where they can emulate any other portion of humanity in all the great interests of human life. I am persuaded they cannot do so, as long as they remain among the whites. It is my solemn judgment that they must have a country and laws and privileges of their own, in order to take that rank among the people of the earth to which they are entitled to aspire. Holding these sentiments, can I stand by in silence with folded arms, and look upon the certain degradation and ruin of the colored people, without an effort to relieve them. Too keenly do I feel in myself and too clearly do I see in my brethren the evils of our condition, and as long as strength endures I cannot rest, [b]ut must with my whole heart labor for the redemption of the colored race, feeling sacredl[y] bound to proclaim these opinions everywhere by my obligations to myself, my people and my God. Truly, your obedient servant,

G. B. BLANKS[5]

Syracuse Daily Journal (N.Y.), 14 August 1852.

1. Vivus W. Smith (1804–1881), a local politician and civic leader, edited the *Syracuse Daily Journal* during this period. He and his brother, Silas F. Smith, had established the paper in 1844 and forged it into Syracuse's first successful daily. It reflected his Whig (later Republican) views and antislavery leanings. Smith and his three brothers dominated journalism in central New York, and the family continued to control the *Daily Journal* until its 1899 demise. *SJ*, 7 February 1871, 12 April 1893; Card File, NSyOn.

2. Blanks refers to those seven among the original thirteen states—New Hampshire, Massachusetts, Connecticut, Rhode Island, New York, New Jersey, and Pennsylvania—that abolished slavery during or shortly after the American Revolution. Two other states in the Northeast, Vermont (1791) and Maine (1820), had been admitted as free states.

3. William G. Allen (1820–?) was born in Virginia to a free mulatto mother and a Welsh immigrant father. He spent most of his youth in Norfolk; when both parents died, he was adopted by a prosperous free black family at Fortress Monroe. Allen attended a black elementary school in Norfolk, until it was closed in the wake of Nat Turner's insurrection (1831). About 1840 he enrolled in Oneida Institute in Whitesboro, New York. Attendance at the college, a center of abolitionist activity, drew Allen into the antislavery movement. Upon graduation in 1843, he moved to Troy, New York, where he taught school, helped Henry Highland Garnet edit the short-lived *National Watchman*, joined the Liberty party, and attended the 1847 black national convention.

Allen moved to Boston in 1847 where he clerked and read law in the office of Ellis Gray Loring. He joined with local black leaders to protect fugitive slaves, served as secretary of the Boston Colored Citizens Association, and supported black efforts in Canada West. Gaining a reputation as an expert on black history and literature and the destiny of the African race, Allen lectured on these subjects and compiled a pamphlet entitled *Wheatley, Banneker, and Horton* to aid his audiences. In December 1850, he joined the faculty of New York Central College in McGrawville, an interracial and coeducational school based on abolitionist and manual labor principles. He became friends with a white student named Mary King, and in late 1852, the two decided to marry. When mob violence threatened to prevent this interracial union, the couple married in New York City and sailed for Britain in April 1853.

The Allens spent their first seven years of exile living in London (1853–56) and Dublin (1856–60) and raising the first three of their seven children. During this time, Allen earned a modest income as a tutor and as a lecturer on Africa, American slavery, and educational reform. He also published two narratives of his life, which focused on northern white reaction to his interracial marriage. In 1860 the Allens returned to London, where William participated in local abolitionist activities, including the work of the London Emancipation Committee and the John Anderson Committee. He also continued his interest in educational reform, particularly the rehabilitation and retraining of juvenile delinquents.

In the summer of 1863, with the help of British abolitionist Harper Twelve-trees, he opened the Caledonian Training School in Islington, England. Even after the Civil War, the bitterness that the Allens felt toward American racial prejudice kept them from returning home. Allen's school closed about 1868, but his wife organized a small training facility for girls in Islington. This school also closed after a few years, and by 1878 the Allens had returned to London. Throughout their years in Britain, they remained in a precarious financial situation, dependent upon the regular assistance of antislavery friends. R. J. M. Blackett, "William G. Allen: The Forgotten Professor," *CWH* 26:39–52 (March 1980); William G. Allen, *A Short Personal Narrative* (Dublin, 1860), 5–34; William G. Allen, *American Prejudice Against Color: An Authentic Narrative, Showing How Easily the Nation Got into an Uproar* (London, 1853), 1–107; William G. Allen to Gerrit Smith, 24 January 1854, Gerrit Smith Papers, NSyU [8:0001, 0608, 12:0383]; *Lib*, 2 February 1848, 10 November, 20 December 1850; *NSt*, 6 July 1846; *PtL*, 8 August 1853; *ASRL*, 2 November 1863.

4. J. W. C. Pennington.

5. Granville B. Blanks (1812–?) was born in Virginia, the son of former slaves who had purchased their freedom. He settled in southern Michigan about 1836, living initially in Monroe and Jackson. Blanks was a resident of nearby Marshall during the 1840s and represented local blacks at the 1843 black state convention. Aroused by passage of the Fugitive Slave Law, he visited black communities throughout the border states and the North during the early 1850s. Because of the prejudice and poverty he encountered during these travels, he urged blacks to immigrate to West Africa. Blanks later returned to Michigan and settled in Battle Creek. In 1861 he embraced Haitian emigration and announced that he would tour black communities to promote the scheme. Although he anticipated going to Haiti, he was living in Ann Arbor, Michigan, during the Civil War. *CA*, 12 June, 4 December 1841 [4:0057, 0319]; Foner and Walker, *Proceedings of the Black State Conventions*, 1:183–88; *WAA*, 4 May 1861, 3 December 1864 [13:0506].

27.
Essay by Jacob C. White, Jr.
29 December 1852

Anglo-American abolitionists theorized that an organized boycott of slave-produced goods would reduce the profitability of slavery and help destroy the institution. Although the free produce movement proved ineffective as an antislavery tactic, it allowed abolitionists to avoid the taint of complicity with slavery. Many black abolitionists embraced free produce. Henry Highland Garnet and Frances Ellen Watkins Harper lectured for the cause during the 1850s. In Philadelphia, where Quaker concern for free produce extended back into the eighteenth century, blacks offered enthusiastic support. They established a free produce society in 1831, and black leaders William Whipper and Jacob C. White, Sr., later operated free produce stores. This interest sometimes crossed several generations. Fifteen-year-old Jacob C. White, Jr., a student at the Lombard Street School in 1852, continued his father's advocacy of free produce. His 29 December essay reminded local blacks that boycotting cotton, sugar, rice, tobacco, and other slave-grown goods was part of their obligation to the "down-trodden and oppressed slave." Ripley et al., *Black Abolitionist Papers*, 1:149–51; Sterling, *We Are Your Sisters*, 160; *GUE*, January, February, May 1831; *Lib*, 28 May 1831; Foner, *History of Black Americans*, 2:249; Harry C. Silcox, "Philadelphia Negro Educator: Jacob C. White, Jr., 1837–1902," *PMHB* 97:78–79 (January 1973).

[December] 29, [18]52
The Inconsistency of Colored People using Slave Produce
By Jacob C. White Jr.[1]
It is a fact that is (or should be) well known, by every Colored American that there are now upwards of three millions of slaves in the "United States of America." It is a fact that should also be known, that they can only remain slaves, so long as the slave trade is encouraged; or in other words, so long as their masters have sale for the Cotton, the Sugar, the rice, the Tobacco, or whatever it may be that the slaves are forced to cultivate for sale. What would be the object in the masters having slaves to work from day to day, if he could not dispose of the products of their labor? It could not possibly be an advantage to him to have them toiling to accumulate something that he could not sell, and that he would consequently have no use for; and when he found that such was really the case and that it was useless for him to [ha]ve slaves, their emancipation, and the compensation ~~of~~ to them or some other persons for their labor, would probably be the result. I do not mean to intimate however that if

the colored people were all to abstain from the use of slave products, that the abolition of Slavery would be the result. But I do say that they would be [abiding] with consistency if [they] were to make it a rule not to use any products but those of compensated labor; for as a general thing, [they] are in favor of the abolition of Slavery and maintain that they are friends to the down-trodden and oppressed slave, while at the same time they are using means to keep the ~~slave~~ him in slavery. If there were but two Stores in this city and one sold Free produce and the other slave produce, I doubt that there could be found one colored person in fifty that would put themselves to the least trouble in order to patronize the store that sold the Free produce. And while they utter maledictions against the slaveholders, and cry against the system of slavery as an infernal system, they at the same time encourage the slave holder to continue his business.

Leon Gardiner Collection, Historical Society of Pennsylvania, Philadelphia, Pennsylvania. Published by permission.

1. Jacob C. White, Jr. (1837–1902), the son of a wealthy black businessman and abolitionist, grew up among Philadelphia's black elite. He learned to read and write at the Lombard Street School, a black public institution. But much of his education came within the White household—local black leaders like Robert Purvis and William Whipper were frequent guests, current intellectual and moral issues were regularly discussed, and religious and antislavery journals abounded. From 1853 to 1857, White attended the Institute for Colored Youth, a local training school for black teachers, where he studied under the tutelage of Charles L. Reason and Ebenezer Bassett. His fellow students recognized him as a skilled essayist and speaker. He continued these interests as a founder and leading member of the Banneker Institute, a society of young Philadelphia blacks devoted to intellectual improvement. White served as its secretary (1854–59), organized its meetings, gave occasional lectures, and helped forge it into an important black forum.

After reaching adulthood, White became a leader of the Philadelphia black community. His most notable contributions came in the field of education. After graduating from the Institute for Colored Youth, he taught mathematics there for seven years. From 1864 to 1896, he served as principal of the Roberts Vaux Primary School, a position that made him the foremost black educator in the city. White also maintained ties with his alma mater and helped many of its black graduates find teaching positions. He worked tirelessly to ease racial strains when Pennsylvania schools were integrated in the 1880s.

Like his father, White figured prominently in the economic and social life of black Philadelphia. He acquired a substantial income from several business ventures, managed his father's cemetery business, and established a joint stock company to promote investments in the local black community. And he adopted his father's commitment to abolitionism, temperance, and moral reform. He served as the local subscription agent for the *Weekly Anglo-African*, and his weekly order of five hundred copies proved a major source of financial support for the black antislavery journal. Although never strongly committed to black emigration, he served as Philadelphia agent for the *Pine and Palm* and local bureau chief for the Haytian Emigration Bureau. During the Civil War, White encouraged blacks to enlist in the Union army. After the war, he worked for black voting rights as secretary of the Pennsylvania Equal Rights League and joined the struggle against racial discrimination as a member of the Pennsylvania Social, Civil, and Statistical Association. After 1872 White's interest in civil rights organizations waned. But he remained important in local black educational and cultural activities. During the 1890s, he led efforts to establish the Douglass Hospital, a medical and nurse's training facility for the city's black community. Silcox, "Philadelphia Negro Educator," 75–98; Jacob C. White, Jr., to Thomas Hamilton, 7 February 1860, Leon Gardiner Collection, PHi [12:0478].

28.
William J. Wilson to Frederick Douglass
5 March 1853

As black leaders struggled to forge an independent place in the antislavery movement, many recognized the value of nurturing a separate black identity and culture. The *Hyperion*, a short-lived paper edited by Jonas H. Townsend, argued that black cultural nationhood was a necessary prerequisite to political and social equality. Even Frederick Douglass, James McCune Smith, and other integrationists conceded the essential role of "complexionally distinct institutions." The writings of Brooklyn educator William J. Wilson provide thoughtful commentary on this question. Wilson regularly corresponded with *Frederick Douglass' Paper* under the pseudonym "Ethiop" during the 1850s. His 5 March 1853 letter recounted a recent visit to New York City. Wilson observed in the daily routine of urban life the subtle ways in which white cultural hegemony destroyed black self-esteem, confidence, and resolve. He called for greater black initiative in literature and the arts: "We must begin to tell our own story, write our own lecture, paint our own picture, chisel our own bust." Only then, he argued, could blacks develop the clear, confident sense of personal and collective identity necessary for racial progress. Pease and Pease, *They Who Would Be Free*, 251–52; *Colored National Convention . . . at Cleveland* (1848), 17–19 [5:0777–78]; *FDP*, 5 February 1852 [7:0402].

BROOKLYN HEIGHTS, [New York]
March 5th, 1853
DEAR DOUGLASS:
    You know my fondness for rambling. The country affords pleasure; the city, if nothing else abundant, information. If the country gives vigor to the spirits, the city induces many profitable reflections. Hence, if I go to the country often, I perambulate the city oftener, and even venture, occasionally, into Gotham.[1] Well, I went over to that mysterious city the other day, and the first salutation from a wag was, "there goes Ethiop." Set that down to your account, my dear sir.
    I was in Gotham, and saw much, but shall speak of little that I saw. Among other things, I was strongly attracted by some fine specimens of daguerreotypes in oil, hanging in a Broadway stair passage; and in my minute examination of them without heeding, found I had wound my way up the ample and tastefully hung stairs, where I was confronted by a very polite gentleman, inviting me within a splendid chamber, artistically hung with the finest specimens of daguerrean likenesses in oil, and other-

wise perhaps in the country. Likenesses thus taken in oil are so accurate, so lifelike, that they seem to be life itself. The individual is before you. There is no mistaking it. The Gallery, let me say, was no other than the distinguished PLUMBE'S,[2] and Ethiop was strongly solicited by that gentlemanly proprietor to sit for a miniature. The next time he goes to Gotham, he thinks he will submit. A little incident occurred while in this establishment worth mentioning. Two well dressed colored *lads*, about fifteen years of age, came swaggering in, and, though with a strong flavor of black Broadway (*alias* Church Street) about them—sporting large box coats, tight pants and patent boots, and a Havana[3] each, coupled with their swaggering air—yet I soon detected that one was employed in the establishment. What struck me most, was the careless indifference, and insolence of manner with which he received some special directions of the proprietor, and I could but conclude that it was one of the reasons why, with our young men, it was situation today, and evacuation tomorrow.

I again found myself in Broadway. Incidents in this great thoroughfare are numerous enough—sights so plentiful that they completely bewilder the common countryman; and shall I confess it, they so bewildered me, fresh as I was from the *Heights*, that I have but a confused idea of what I did see. I remember to have found myself peering within a cellar, at the door of which, among some fine specimens of statuary, stood in solemn majesty *"the Father of our country,"* pallid, pensive, beckoning me in. I entered, and became so deeply absorbed in the wonders around me, that it was some moments before I became aware of the presence of an extraordinary image, bolt upright before me—one of the old masters, truly, said I, as I looked up. It was the proprietor, an Italian, whose head would have given the painter or sculptor more delight than any one of the fine models of his own *studio*.

But to return; there stood Franklin and Adams, Lafayette and Jefferson, and Clay and Webster; the gods and goddesses were there, and the Queen of England was there, and so was the Emperor of France; but I found not the Emperor of Hayti, nor of Dahomey, nor the President of Liberia, nor any other distinguished *black*.[4] I enquired for one or two—Toussaint L'Ouverture,[5] Boyer[6] and Faustin I.[7] The reply of the old Italian, after a shrug of his shoulders, was "they no sell in this country." I asked for some who had distinguished themselves in the country. "They no sell," was the same reply. "Washington he sell, Franklin he sell, and," pointing to some others, "they sell," said he. "I have there," said he, pointing to a box, "busts of great colored men of West Indies, for go there; sell well there; no sell here." No demand has been made, thought I, as I rushed out of his place into the street.

The result of all this, upon my mind, may be summed up in a few words. A radical change in the process of our development is here demanded. At present, what we find around us, either in art or literature, is made so to press upon us, that we depreciate, we despise, we almost hate ourselves, and all that favors us. Well may we scoff at black skins and woolly heads, since every model set before us for admiration has pallid face and flaxen head, or emanations thereof. I speak plainly. It is useless to mince this matter. Every one of your readers knows that a black girl would as soon fondle an imp as a black doll—such is the force of this species of education upon her. I remember once to have suddenly introduced one among a company of twenty colored girls, and if it had been a spirit the effect could not have been more wonderful. Such scampering and screaming can better be imagined than told. As simple as these slight incidents may seem at first sight, they lie at the bottom of half our difficulties. No, no; we must begin to tell our own story, write our own lecture, paint our own picture, chisel our own bust (I demand not caricatures but correct emanations), acknowledge and love our own peculiarities if we have any. Ever so little done in these directions is worth more than all we have ever done, assimilative of the whites since creation, or can do till the end of time. The encouragement and self-reliance it will inspire will do more to push us forward than all the speculations about our "manifest destiny," &c., that has emanated from the brains of all the fools, white or black, in Christendom.[8] Now is the time to begin to cultivate among us both a taste for the arts and sciences themselves, before we become more deeply immersed in the rougher affairs of life. Our present peculiar situation well calculates us for their highest perfection. But I must break off here to resume the subject.

Some rich and spicy events have occurred in Gotham since my last. I shall speak of them hereafter. Enough for the present to say, that the moral *teachings* of Church St. and St. Philip's Row, and the rival claims of the leaders of the black *ton*,[9] to become the *instructors*, formed the staple of the budget.

I learn from a reliable source here, that it is in contemplation to send *Sam Ward* to England—that means is to be provided for his support while there. The object of this is, that his strong arm may hoe the good seed sown there by *Uncle Tom*, and otherwise culture the stock and the blade till the full ear comes. Who better than this man, provided he keeps proper command over his inner-self, is calculated for the task?[10] Yours truly,

ETHIOP[11]

Frederick Douglass' Paper (Rochester, N.Y.), 11 March 1853.

1. Gotham is a popular nickname for New York City.
2. John Plumbe (1809–1857), a Welsh-born railroad entrepreneur, began a second career as a daguerreotypist in 1840. Within five years, he owned a large studio and gallery in New York City with branches in thirteen cities. In 1846 he

began to market a series of portraits called "Plumbeotypes," which were painted engravings based on his daguerreotypes of prominent Americans. Many of these were reprinted in popular magazines. *DAB*, 15:11–12; Harold Francis Pfister, *Facing the Light: Historic American Portrait Daguerreotypes* (Washington, D.C., 1978), 20–21, 38.

3. Wilson refers to Havana cigars, those made partly or entirely from Cuban-grown tobacco.

4. While in the studio, Wilson observed busts of George Washington, Benjamin Franklin, John Adams, the Marquis de Lafayette, Thomas Jefferson, Henry Clay, Daniel Webster, the gods and goddesses of ancient Greece and Rome, Queen Victoria of Britain, and Napoleon III of France. He notes with regret that he saw no busts of black leaders, such as Joseph J. Roberts of Liberia, King Gezo of Dahomey, and Faustin I of Haiti.

5. Toussaint L'Ouverture (ca. 1746–1803) led a bloody slave uprising in 1791 in the French colony of St. Domingue (now Haiti). After becoming an ally of France, he was named lieutenant governor and eventually assumed dictatorial control over the island. French forces invaded St. Domingue, captured L'Ouverture in 1802, and imprisoned him in France. C. L. R. James, *The Black Jacobins: Toussaint L'Ouverture and the San Domingo Revolution*, 2d ed. (New York, N.Y., 1963), 90–365.

6. Jean-Pierre Boyer (1778–1850), a French-educated mulatto, became president of Haiti in 1818. He reunited the country, which had been politically divided for several years, extended government control over the entire island of Hispaniola, and won diplomatic recognition from France. In 1824 Boyer invited black Americans to settle in Haiti and offered transportation and land grants to those who came. An 1843 coup forced him into exile. Roland I. Perusse, *Historical Dictionary of Haiti* (Metuchen, N.J., 1977), 10, 17–19, 27–28.

7. Faustin Soulouque (1785–1867), a slave who rose to the rank of general in the Haitian army, became president of Haiti in 1847. Two years later, he proclaimed himself Emperor Faustin I, but he was overthrown in 1859 and forced to flee to France. Perusse, *Historical Dictionary of Haiti*, 97.

8. The popular term "manifest destiny" was coined in 1845 by John L. O'Sullivan, the editor of the influential *United States Magazine and Democratic Review*, to describe a belief in the inevitability of American expansion across the entire continent. By the spring of 1853, some black leaders had begun to talk in similar terms about the future of their race. Martin R. Delany discussed his thoughts on the "destiny of the colored race" in *The Condition, Elevation, Emigration and Destiny of the Colored People* (1852). Wilson suggests that blacks should not depend on a belief in their "manifest destiny"—that progress in race relations was inevitable—but should be self-reliant and work hard to develop their own culture.

9. Wilson contrasts two groups within New York City's black elite that competed for cultural leadership of the black community. He uses Church Street, a major thoroughfare through the city's black neighborhoods in the 1850s, to represent those concerned with fashion and style. In a letter in the 14 April 1854 issue of *Frederick Douglass' Paper*, he described their "flashy" dress and frequent social gatherings, which were characterized by music, dancing, gaiety, and the drinking of alcoholic beverages. Wilson employs St. Philip's Episcopal

Church, a congregation located on nearby Centre Street from 1819 to 1856, to symbolize the sobriety, thrift, and attention to moral and intellectual improvement promoted by many older black leaders. Rhoda G. Freeman, "The Free Negro in New York City before the Civil War" (Ph.D. diss., Columbia University, 1966), 218–19, 393.

   10. In April 1853, the Anti-Slavery Society of Canada sent Samuel R. Ward to Britain to lecture and raise funds to aid the fugitive slaves in Canada West. The society hoped that his tour would take advantage of the antislavery sentiment stirred in Britain by the appearance of *Uncle Tom's Cabin* the previous year. "Tom-mania" swept through Britain, and the novel sold a million copies there within eight months. The antiabolitionist London *Times* admitted that a copy could be seen in the hands of every third traveler in English railway stations. Even Lord Palmerston, who claimed not to have read a novel in thirty years, read the book three times. Ripley et al., *Black Abolitionist Papers*, 2:20; Betty Fladeland, *Men and Brothers: Anglo-American Antislavery Cooperation* (Urbana, Ill., 1972), 350–52, 370.

   11. William Joseph Wilson (1818–?) regularly corresponded with *Frederick Douglass' Paper* under the pseudonym "Ethiop" during the 1850s. His letters and articles discussed a variety of topics in black life and culture, ranging from serious analyses of the need for a distinct racial identity to humorous glimpses of the black convention movement. Wilson was born and reared near Shrewsbury, New Jersey, where his family operated an oyster boat. He opened a bootmaking shop in New York City during the late 1830s. In 1837 he married Mary Ann Garret Marshall, a local black. Later that year, he became involved in the campaign to expand black suffrage in New York state; he continued to play an active role in that struggle over the following two decades, addressing mass meetings, organizing local suffrage conventions, coordinating petition drives, and leading local suffrage rights organizations. Wilson further influenced the franchise movement as a delegate to the 1854 and 1855 black state conventions and a member of the board of managers of the New York State Suffrage Association. He participated in a number of New York City–based organizations during the 1850s, including the American League of Colored Laborers and the Committee of Thirteen, which was organized by local black leaders to curtail enforcement of the Fugitive Slave Law and hinder the reviving colonization movement. Wilson represented local interests at the 1853 and 1855 black national conventions.

   Wilson's primary contributions were in the area of black education. He became a teacher in Brooklyn's black schools about 1842 and was named principal of Colored Public School No. 1 later in the decade. As a leading figure in the Society for the Promotion of Education among Colored Children, he worked to increase black access to local schools, to encourage black school attendance, and to operate black charity schools. He also opened a library and reading room in the city to provide opportunities for learning to black adults. In 1863 Wilson resigned his principalship and moved to Washington, D.C. From 1863 to 1866, he taught at various freedmen's schools, including an American Missionary Association institution. He also lectured and served as a trustee and executive committee member at Howard University in the early 1870s.

   Wilson remained a national figure during Reconstruction, dominating the 1869 black national convention and helping to found the Colored National

Labor Union. Commissioned as cashier of the local branch of the Freedman's Savings Bank, he threw his energy into the venture, publicizing the branch in the local black community and in Richmond. But his faulty accounting procedures led to a $40,000 deficit, and he left the bank under suspicion in 1874, shortly before it failed. Out of work, Wilson unsuccessfully appealed for another AMA post and lived the remainder of his life in poverty and relative obscurity. U.S. Census, 1850; *FDP*, 17 June 1852, 15 December 1854 [7:0635]; *CA*, 14 January, 19 August, 2 September, 18 November, 30 December 1837, 19, 26 December 1840, 2, 16 January, 20 November 1841 [2:0152, 0167, 3:0753, 0761, 0809, 0836, 4:0308]; *NASS*, 29 January 1846 [5:0152]; Foner and Walker, *Proceedings of the Black State Conventions*, 1:79–88, 96; Freeman, "Free Negro in New York City," 46, 353; George Walker, "The Afro-American in New York City, 1827–1860" (Ph.D. diss., Columbia University, 1975), 168, 221; *NSt*, 13 June 1850; Carleton Mabee, *Black Education in New York State: From Colonial to Modern Times* (Syracuse, N.Y., 1979), 54, 63–67, 123, 129, 155, 188; De Boer, "Afro-Americans in American Missionary Association," 304–8, 538–44, 665n, 761n; Carl T. Osthaus, *Freedmen, Philanthropy, and Fraud: A History of the Freedman's Savings Bank* (Urbana, Ill., 1976), 17, 25, 45, 105, 168, 181, 229, 233; Rayford W. Logan, *Howard University: The First One Hundred Years, 1867–1967* (New York, N.Y., 1969), 53, 64, 66, 75; Philip S. Foner and Ronald W. Lewis, *The Black Worker: A Documentary History from Colonial Times to the Present*, 8 vols. (Philadelphia, Pa., 1978–84), 47, 131–32; Philip S. Foner and George E. Walker, eds., *Proceedings of the Black National and State Conventions, 1865–1900*, 1 vol. to date (Philadelphia, Pa., 1986–), 27, 344–81; William J. Wilson to George Whipple, 27 November 1874, AMA-ARC.

29.
Editorial by William Howard Day
9 April 1853

American territory grew dramatically during the 1840s as a result of diplomacy and conquest. Most white Americans justified expansion under the empire-building slogan of "manifest destiny," a belief in the inevitable and divinely ordained spread of the United States across the entire continent. President Franklin Pierce invoked the concept of "manifest destiny" in his 4 March 1853 inaugural address. He quieted long-standing fears over the Republic's unrestrained growth by reassuring Americans that the nation's geographic expansion had not compromised its democratic principles. William Howard Day, the editor of the *Aliened American*, rejected Pierce's confident assessment. In an editorial written one month after the inauguration, Day offered a moral critique of American expansionism. He contrasted Pierce's rhetoric about American freedom and justice with the reality of American slavery and discrimination, arguing that it was inappropriate to talk about "devotion to freedom" when the nation's slave population continued to increase. Day reminded his readers that a nation's progress should not be measured by territorial expansion but by its "advances in education, in general intelligence, and in a strict sense of justice." James D. Richardson, ed., *A Compilation of the Messages and Papers of the Presidents, 1789–1897*, 10 vols. (Washington, D.C., 1897), 5:197–203.

President Pierce's Inaugural

The Inaugural Message of President Pierce, although in some of its rhetoric obnoxious to criticism, generally reads well. The manner, too, of the *delivery* of the Inaugural is said by those who heard it to have been capital.

The President's allusion to the severe affliction which had befallen his family is touching. He however dispels the idea of the necessity of any special leniency to his new position, for he enters upon it, he says, "with nothing like shrinking apprehensions."

He calls our attention to the increased duties of an administration of today, on account of the "changes which have occurred . . . in territory, in population, and in wealth," and here adverts to a question perhaps in its bearing more important than any other to a nation, and which he says, "has been the subject of earnest thought and discussion on both sides of the ocean." That question is—"Whether the elements of inherent force in the Republic have kept pace with its unparalleled progression?"

What *are* the elements of inherent force in the Republic? As we glean them from the Message, they are: 1st. A consciousness of strength even

5. William Howard Day
From B. F. Wheeler, *Cullings from Zion's Poets* (Mobile, 1907)

in weakness; 2nd. A desire to reduce theory to practice; 3rd. An energy; and 4th. A devotion to freedom. And the President seems to suppose the question so discussed "on both sides of the ocean," to be entitled to an affirmative answer. We beg leave to say we do not so see it. We admit that there was a consciousness of strength in the Revolution. We admit that the founders of the Republic believed sufficiently in self-government, to adopt the republican principle; and that they felt that the country was safe in pursuing a certain policy. Still, if we rightly recall the memories of those days, this "expansion" of territory was one of the very evils feared by them. It was upon this ground, we take it, that "less than sixty-three years ago, the Father of this Country made the recent accession of the important State of North Carolina to the Confederation of the United States, one of the subjects of his special consideration."[1] That this was true to a marked extent, President PIERCE afterwards virtually admits by saying—"the actual working of our system has dispelled a degree of solicitude *which at the outset disturbed bold hearts and far-reaching intellects.*" He then says—"The apprehension of dangers from extended territory, multiplied States, accumulated wealth and augmented population, has proved to be unfounded"; and therefore concludes that this one "element of inherent force"—a consciousness of strength—remains still, and that, so far, these elements "have kept pace with our unparalleled progression" in territory. It seems to us, this conclusion is a begging of the question. In the minds of not a few of the people of the Republic there is "apprehension of dangers" still, from the extension already secured, and from the extension towards our *"manifest destiny"*—namely, the securing of all this continent. Extension or expansion is not a sign of strength. It *may be* the sure mark of weakness. England, the moment this country was severed from it, was stronger than before. A country or a government is strong not as it progresses in territory, but as that country develops its own resources, as it advances in education, in general intelligence, and in a strict sense of justice. Let these be absent, as to an alarming extent they are absent here, and expansion is but an evil. Says the Inaugural, "Although comparatively weak, the new-born nation was intrinsically strong. Inconsiderable in population and apparent resources, it was upheld" (not by expansion of territory, but) "by a broad and intelligent comprehension of rights, and an all-pervading purpose to maintain them, stronger than armaments." *There*, as we have said, was its power, and in proportion as that "comprehension of rights" *is* "broad and intelligent," will our present government and country be powerful, and "a consciousness of strength" be induced, even in weakness.

2. We do not see that as a nation we have reduced our theories to practice in proportion as we have extended our territory.

3. We are glad to admit that there is some ground for President PIERCE'S idea that *energy*—one of the "elements of inherent force in the Republic"—has kept pace with our progression. And well has he expressed it: "The stars upon your banner have become nearly three fold their original number; your densely populated possessions skirt the shores of two great oceans." Yet what kind of an energy has it been? There *is* an energy silent as the grave, and yet powerful enough to bring life from dull clods—*innate* energy; in a national sense, energy or force of character. There *is* an energy like that of flame, sparkling, crackling, dazzling, dying. We have had an energy without; but have not had its counterpart within. Increment without has not been based upon a fixed, pure principle within. Things understood, agreed upon by the Fathers of the Government have been boldly disregarded, and a one-sided, selfish policy made the basis of nearly all our increase since. While this *directive* energy is wanting, we feel that the President overlooks a vital point, when he says—"the policy of my administration will not be controlled by any timid forebodings of evil from expansion."

4. Nor do we believe that our Government has shown devotion to freedom. Mere devotion to preservation of the Republic may not be devotion to freedom, however much nations of the old world may be cheered by the Republican principle. Our devotion to freedom is not evinced in this way. The law of *self-preservation* may continue the Republic, and yet that Republic deliberately tramples upon man's most sacred rights. We believe the Founders of the Government intended devotion to Freedom. Said FRANKLIN, "That mankind are all formed by the same Almighty Being, alike objects of His care, and equally designed for the enjoyment of happiness, the Christian religion teaches us to believe, and the political creed of the Americans fully coincides with the positions."[2] Yet that political creed has been violated, continually. While at the commencement of the Government, the rights of five-hundred thousand human beings were wrested; according to the last census, the number is represented to be thirty-one-hundred thousand, showing an increase, since 1776, of twenty-six-hundred thousand—an increase, during seventy-six years, at the rate of thirty-five thousand, two hundred and twenty-nine, annually. This increase of slaves—not freemen—in this professedly free Government, especially when, at that early day, it was believed slavery would die out, is startling, and speaks of anything else than a "devotion to Freedom." Now, instead of barely existing in thirteen States, Slavery grows rampant in sixteen, to say nothing [two words illegible] over our territories. Another remarkable fact, from which we may prove our "devotion to Freedom," is that of the States in which Slavery exists, nine are new ones.[3] Our Government has not then spoken, as President Pierce intimates it has, for "the largest rational liberty."

We think, therefore, that the President has occupied a wrong standpoint in making up a conclusion that "the elements of inherent force in the Republic have kept pace with our unparalleled progression."

With the following extract we are especially pleased; whether the President means all his words convey, remains to be seen:

> The great objects of our pursuit as a people are best to be attained by peace, and are entirely consistent with the tranquillity and interest of the rest of mankind. With the neighboring nations upon our continent we should cultivate kindly and fraternal relations. We can desire nothing in regard to them so much as to see them consolidate their strength and pursue the paths of prosperity and happiness. If, in the course of their growth, we should open new channels of trade and create additional facilities for friendly intercourse, the benefits realized will be equal and mutual.

Upon the subject of the protection of American citizens, the Message is explicit and frank. "The rights which belong to us as a nation, are not alone to be regarded, but those which pertain to every citizen in his individual capacity at home and abroad, must be sacredly maintained." We trust this is not mere verbiage. And to show its sincerity, we hope this Administration will apply the principle in the State Department, so that passports will not be denied to American citizens going abroad.[4] We believe, with the President, that "good citizens may well claim the protection of good laws, and the benign influence of good government."

In reference to our "involuntary servitude," or American Slavery, and its support, the Message does not disappoint us. Mr. PIERCE'S course in Congress, his course in New Hampshire politics, his course as to the National Slavocratic platform, all led us to suppose him prepared to maintain the constitutionality of Slavery, and of the enactments to defend it. We are, therefore, not surprised to hear the President say—"I hold that the laws of 1850, commonly called the Compromise Measures, are strictly constitutional and should be carried into effect." Still, we protest against his apparent anxiety to soothe the wounds of the South, and to pass over so lightly, the action of the South in favor of Disunion—a blow at the whole country—and that, too, when he feels that "with the Union his best and dearest earthly hopes are endeared." The President forgot, or if he did not forget, cared not to remember, that the South, for whom he was pleading, tramples every day upon the Constitutional rights of free citizens. Let certain citizen-sailors of Massachusetts, or Ohio, go to the port of Charleston or New Orleans, and the common Constitution, spreading its aegis from the St. Johns to the Pacific, and guaranteeing that "citizens of each State, shall be entitled to all the rights and immunities of citizens of the several States," is overridden by a State enactment, or a borough ordinance.[5] Why did not President PIERCE, as

the President of the *Whole*, remember *these* things? Even DANIEL WEB-
STER, on the notable 7th of March, said that these offenses of the South
were "impracticable and oppressive."[6] President PIERCE's desire for justice should expend itself where justice and the Constitution are violated.
The Compromise Measures were themselves infringements upon our
common rights, for Mr. CLAY himself admitted before the Kentucky
Legislature, that in them the South had been the gainer.[7] There is a
North, and that North has rights as sacred as those of the other portion of the Union; and while we are willing to give to that other portion
all belonging to it, we are unwilling, where the States are equal, and
the North, by its own action, in the minority, that the South should be
held up as the great National Martyr, and the North as the National
Aggressor.

There is a Constitution—let it be strictly construed. There is a majesty
of Law—let it be the law of the Constitution. There is a Popular Voice—
it should speak for the Constitution. *That*, whether it "strengthen the
fraternal feeling of all the members of our Union" or not, should be
applied to our General and State Governments. Then will the desire of
our Fathers be attained, namely: "to establish justice, to provide for the
common defense, and to secure the blessing of Liberty to us and our
posterity."

We here close our article already longer than we intended, but as curt
as the circumstances seemed to justify. Many points we have purposely
omitted. We have devoted the space we have to spare, to the bearing of
the Message upon vital points, and especially to its bearing upon Human
Freedom. We close with the emphatic language of the President: "Preeminently the power of our advocacy reposes in our example; but no
example, be it remembered, can be powerful for lasting good, whatever
apparent advantage may be gained, which is not based on eternal principles of right and justice."

Aliened American (Cleveland, Ohio), 9 April 1853.

1. In 1789 North Carolina ceded its trans-Appalachian lands (now Tennessee)
to the federal government. Fearing that disgruntled frontiersmen would ally with
Spanish colonial officials in the West, President George Washington moved to
solidify control over the region. He persuaded Congress to create the new Southwest Territory in 1790 and worked to remove the causes of western discontent by
pursuing free navigation of the Mississippi River and peace with southeastern
Native American tribes. Ray Allen Billington, *Westward Expansion: A History of
the American Frontier*, 3d ed. (New York, N.Y., 1967), 206, 233–35.

2. Day quotes from an antislavery memorial presented to the U.S. House of
Representatives by the Pennsylvania Abolition Society on 12 February 1790. The
society's president, Benjamin Franklin, authored and signed the document. Mat-

thew T. Mellon, ed., *Early American Views on Negro Slavery* (Boston, Mass., 1934; reprint, New York, N.Y., 1969), 20–24.

3. Of the original thirteen states, six—Delaware, Maryland, Virginia, North Carolina, South Carolina, and Georgia—failed to abolish slavery during the post-Revolutionary decades. Congress admitted nine new slave states before the Civil War. These included Kentucky (1792), Tennessee (1796), Louisiana (1812), Mississippi (1817), Alabama (1819), Missouri (1821), Arkansas (1836), Florida (1845), and Texas (1845). Slavery was also permitted in the District of Columbia and several western territories.

4. Prior to 1857, when the Dred Scott decision denied black claims to American citizenship, the State Department had no official policy on passports for blacks traveling abroad. This led to erratic and inconclusive practices. Secretary James Buchanan skirted the problem in 1847 by issuing special certificates to blacks on a case-by-case basis. Two years later, Secretary John M. Clayton ruled that neither these certificates nor federal protection would be granted to blacks unless they were the servants of American diplomats. As the number of black abolitionists traveling abroad increased during the 1850s, the State Department faced a corresponding rise in black requests for passports. Many blacks obtained official authorization, either in the form of passports or special certificates, but their ability to do so often depended upon the rights granted by an applicant's home state or the assistance of influential whites. Between 1857 and 1861, black applications for passports were consistently rejected. This policy caused states like Massachusetts to issue their own passports to "denationalized" black citizens. Litwack, *North of Slavery*, 49–57.

5. Day refers to enforcement of the black seamen's acts.

6. In his famous 7 March 1850 speech before the U.S. Senate, Daniel Webster criticized the South for several offenses that aggravated sectional tensions. These included insisting upon the expansion of slavery, resorting to "fire-eating" rhetoric, making insulting comparisons between slavery and northern factory labor, and imprisoning black seamen. Baxter, *One and Inseparable*, 415.

7. Henry Clay addressed a special joint session of the Kentucky legislature at Frankfort in November 1850. He defended the Compromise of 1850 as a necessary measure to protect slavery and prevent the dissolution of the Union. Glyndon G. Van Deusen, *The Life of Henry Clay* (Boston, Mass., 1937), 414.

30.
William J. Watkins to Editor, *Boston Herald*
22 April 1853

Blacks argued that their service in America's wars affirmed their right to full citizenship. They pointed to a proud military record—fighting with Andrew Jackson to defend New Orleans during the War of 1812 and assuming "their full proportion of the sacrifices and trials of the Revolutionary War"—to support their claim. But federal policy prohibited blacks from joining state militias and effectively barred them from regular enlistment in the U.S. Army, Navy, and Marines. Black leaders challenged these restrictions. In 1852 sixty-six Boston blacks petitioned the Massachusetts legislature for authorization to organize their own militia company. Their request was denied. When they reintroduced the petition in early 1853, Robert Morris and William J. Watkins testified before the Committee on the Militia on the role played by blacks in the Revolution and War of 1812. They assured legislators that favorable action on the petition would "elicit our undying, indissoluble" allegiance. But in mid-April, the committee withdrew the petition from consideration. A few days later, in a letter to the *Boston Herald*, Watkins expressed his disappointment and disgust at the committee's action. One year later, Boston blacks formed their own militia unit, the Massasoit Guards, without legislative approval. *NASS*, 30 October 1845 [5:0086–87]; Nell, *Colored Patriots*, 7–10, 101–11; Litwack, *North of Slavery*, 31–33; Quarles, *Black Abolitionists*, 230; *BH*, 18 April 1853.

April 22, 1853

MR. EDITOR:[1]

The Committee on the Militia have at length "asked leave to withdraw," and the colored citizens of Massachusetts are still arrayed among the lunatics, paupers, and common drunkards of this time-honored Commonwealth. Now, is this just, fair, and honorable? What right have the Committee to "ask leave" of the Legislature to disregard a petition, upon the merits of which we have an *inalienable* right to demand a full, fair, and impartial hearing? We call upon this Committee, as our servants, as servants of the people, to inform us why they have insulted us, for so we regard the treatment our petition has elicited. Now this Committee have, in our opinion, acted just as they *intended* to act before they heard the arguments of the gentlemen who advocated the claims of the petitioners. They could, we believe, have brought in their report as well before the hearing as afterward. The so-called hearing was, to all intents and purposes, a humbug—a legislative farce. During the play, the faces of the Committee were ever and anon elongated to an almost indefinite tension, and we really thought they had forgotten our complexion, and were inwardly digesting the merits of the petition. They seemed to be very nice young men indeed, particularly the Chairman, who, before we commenced our remarks, very politely desired us to "hurry up the cakes," as he had other business to attend to; and during the hearing, one of the Committee, at least, took leave "to withdraw."

Now I, as an individual, believe that no one has a right, morally speaking, to shoot his brother through the heart or blow out his brains; but if the Committee have the right, then "Jonas W. Clark and sixty-five others" have the right also. And if companies composed of foreigners can obtain charters, why, most assuredly, native-born American citizens ought to be able to obtain the same without any difficulty.

We are, Mr. Editor, treated as men when we commit any crime against the "majesty" of the law; we are admitted to the jails and prisons of the Commonwealth, but when we petition for protection in the exercise of any legal right, and ask to be placed in a position in which we shall be able to show ourselves as men, and honorable men, and thereby give the lie to the *American* doctrine of our innate inferiority; when we wish to demonstrate our capacity to cope successfully with anybody else in the "wide, wide world," then our Committee on the Militia beg leave to "withdraw" from the field. O *tempora! O mores!*[2]

Well, *they* may take leave to withdraw, but *we* never. We recommend to their especial and pious consideration the parable of the unjust judge which they will find recorded in the 18th chapter of Luke.[3] We intend, God willing, by our "continual" praying, to weary the "unjust judge," and possibly, he will "avenge" him of his "adversary." We have colored lawyers, physicians, and teachers; why not colored soldiers?

But we understand there was one Free Soiler on that Committee. Where is *his* report? Echo answers WHERE? Does he, too, beg leave to withdraw? Where are his anti-slavery predilections, his notions of "equal rights," his hatred of tyranny, irrespective of the source whence it emanates, and regardless of the complexion of its victims? All gone by the Board. We *did* hope that *he* would show forth his love by his works. We care nothing about that sympathy which shows itself in profuse lacteal demonstrations, and then stabs us to the vitals; which, while it salutes us by the endearing cognomen of "brethren," in action virtually repudiates the affinity existing between us as the children of one common father.

Verily, verily, I say unto you, *such* Free Soilism is infinitely worse than rampant pro-slaveryism. The latter elicits our intensified hate—the former, our superlative contempt, and from its tender mercies we invoke the good Lord to deliver us.

Just now, the old adage, "All is not gold that glitters,"[4] recurs to my mind most forcibly. In conclusion, we would inform the Committee that we are by no means disheartened. They shall hear from us again, and we trust they will yet manfully "stand by the fire," and not beg leave to "retreat."

W. J. WATKINS[5]

Boston Herald (Mass.), 23 April 1853.

1. The *Boston Herald*, a penny paper with Whig leanings, was owned and edited by John M. Barnard during the 1850s. Established by abolitionist William J. Snelling in 1846, the paper grew to a circulation of fifty-four thousand by 1860. Frank Luther Mott, *American Journalism: A History, 1690–1900* (New York, N.Y., 1962), 239, 480.

2. Watkins quotes a Latin phrase that means, "O the times! O the manners!"

3. Watkins alludes to a biblical allegory in Luke 18:1–8, in which Jesus uses a parable about an "unjust judge" who eventually gives in to the incessant pleadings of a widow to reassure the disciples of the power of prayer.

4. Watkins paraphases a common proverb of Greek origin.

5. William J. Watkins (ca. 1826–?) was born to free black parents William and Henrietta Watkins in Baltimore. Although a machinist by trade, he occasionally taught at the Watkins Academy, his father's school, during his early years. Watkins moved to Boston by 1849 and became involved in local underground railroad and civil rights efforts. He petitioned for the formation of black militia companies, pushed for the integration of the city's public schools, and advocated immediate abolitionism. Watkins broke with the Garrisonians during the early 1850s over the issue of political antislavery; he was active in Free Soil and Republican party politics throughout the remainder of the decade and labored diligently for the extension of black suffrage in New York state. After his break with the Garrisonians, he aligned himself with Frederick Douglass, moved to Rochester in 1853, and served as associate editor of *Frederick Douglass' Paper* for several years. About the same time, he began to actively participate in the women's rights and black convention movements.

Watkins's extended tour of New York and Pennsylvania in the spring of 1854 earned him a reputation as a tireless, articulate, and persuasive antislavery speaker. His antislavery critique was directed primarily at the free black community, which he admonished for its petty factionalism bred by separate institutions. Watkins lamented the apathy among northern blacks and urged them to be more militant in defense of their civil rights. He advocated slave violence in certain circumstances. Toward the end of the decade, Watkins abandoned his earlier antiemigrationism and joined the Haitian immigration movement. During 1861 he toured Canada West and Michigan as an agent for James Redpath's Haytian Emigration Bureau, recruiting prospective settlers. Watkins, who had earlier antagonized black Canadians with his persistent opposition to Canadian immigration, now attracted even sharper criticism. After the demise of the HEB in late 1862, he returned to Boston, studied law, and became one of the first blacks admitted to the legal profession in the United States. He died in the early 1870s. *FDP*, 24 March, 9, 16 December 1853, 24 March, 14, 28 April, 30 June, 14 July, 18, 25 August, 8 September 1854, 12 January, 2, 16, 23 February, 2 March, 4, 25 May, 24 August 1855 [9:0011]; Blassingame, *Frederick Douglass Papers*, 2:442n; Leroy Graham, *Baltimore: The Nineteenth-Century Capital* (Lanham,

Md., 1982), 126–30; Bettye J. Gardner, "William Watkins: Antebellum Black Teacher and Anti-Slavery Writer," *NHB* 39:623–25 (September–October 1976), 623; *Colored National Convention* . . . *in Philadelphia* (1855), 6, 10; *Lib*, 7 September 1849, 20, 27 December 1850, 28 November, 5 December 1851, 9 January 1852, 13 May 1853, 23 August 1861 [13:0706]; *PP*, 13 July, 7, 21 September 1861, 4 September 1862 [13:0742, 0766]; *WAA*, 9, 30 November, 14 December 1861 [13:0844, 0886, 0943]; *TG*, 27 June 1861 [13:0603].

31.
Martin R. Delany, John C. Peck, William Webb, and Thomas Burrows to Editor, Kingston *Morning Journal* 31 May 1853

Black communities across the North cooperated to prevent kidnappings of both fugitive slaves and free blacks. In 1853 a Tennessean named Thomas J. Adams convinced Alexander Hendrickure, a mulatto youth from Jamaica, to accompany him to the United States. Adams enticed Hendrickure with new clothing and tales of California gold, even though Hendrickure had been similarly tempted by another American kidnapper more than a year before and was returned home by British officials in New York. The two men landed in Philadelphia and on the evening of 27 May boarded a westbound train. Local abolitionists telegraphed ahead to Pittsburgh where an impromptu vigilance committee met Adams and Hendrickure at the train station the following day. With the help of local authorities, they forced Adams to abandon his claim to Hendrickure and flee the city. Unaware of Adams's plans to sell him into slavery, Hendrickure protested when the two were separated. But when advised of Adams's real motives, Hendrickure "was profuse in expressions of joy and gratitude at his escape." On 31 May, Martin R. Delany, John C. Peck, William Webb, and Thomas Burrows wrote black leaders in Jamaica, warning them of a "regular system of *decoying, kidnapping and selling into hopeless bondage, in the United States, the free subjects of Great Britain.*" *SV*, 4 June 1853.

PITTSBURGH, [Pennsylvania]
May 31st, 1853

Sir:[1]

On Saturday afternoon of May 28th, a telegraphic dispatch was received from Philadelphia, in this city, to the effect that one *Thomas J. Adams,*[2] of Nashville, Tennessee—a slaveholding State—had brought from Kingston, Jamaica, W. I., with him, a colored youth, then en route for the South, by the name of Alexander Hendrickure—*Hendrickson* was the name given in the dispatch.

On the receipt of which intelligence, the undersigned, with three other friends, repaired immediately to the depot located on Eighth and Liberty streets, just as the train of cars from the East reached its terminus. From the hindmost car, among the last of the passengers who got out, was a handsome, well-dressed mulatto youth, called in Jamaica a *brown* in complexion.

On approaching him and demanding his name, a finely dressed white man came forward, ordering the youth away, answering in a manner peculiar to the upstart American *slave trader: "That boy belongs to me!"* His assumption was at once denied, and the youth taken hold of by one of us, and placed in charge of a faithful officer, Mr. John Fox, the police-man of the depot, who took him, in company with the kidnapper, to the St. Clair hotel, corner of St. Clair and Penn streets,[3] to await the proceed-ings of a legal issue.

An application was immediately made to the Hon. Judge Williams,[4] one of the Justices of the Bench of the District Court for the Western District of Pennsylvania; but owing to the lateness of the hour at which the intelligence was received, and the day being Saturday, business was closed in the public offices, and the officers generally scattered about and difficult to find. The Judge also resided some way out of the city, and it was therefore full half-past ten o'clock in the evening before a writ of *habeas corpus* was sued out.

Officer Fox having the youth in custody at the hotel, the writ was placed in the hands of Robert Hague,[5] Esq., High Constable of Pitts-burgh, an excellent and efficient officer, who delivered Alexander into the hands of his friends who awaited the issue at the hotel door. The purport of the writ was to bring the kidnapper, Thomas J. Adams, before the Hon. Judge Williams at ten of the clock on Monday morning the 30th. The youth being delivered up, Adams consequently fled the same evening, and has not since been seen nor heard from. We have placed Alexander, the youth, in the family of one of the undersigned, Mr. John Peck,[6] where he will be provided for and comfortably faring as a member of the family, and shall remain, awaiting the requisition of the British Consul at Philadelphia or his friends in Jamaica. Alexander is decidedly a youth of great promise.

We have closely and carefully conversed with and examined Alexander Hendrickure, and making all due allowance for his age—which is four-teen years—qualifications, opportunities, inaccuracies, and discrepan-cies; yet the facts which he has imparted to us, told in his simple, boyish, and peculiarly native manner, developed to us the key to important and startling truths, as connected with the American steamers touching Ja-maica, and probably other British West India Islands.

In the winter of 1851–2, this same youth was decoyed by an American, and induced to leave Jamaica for the United States, the vessel in this instance touching at Norfolk, Virginia, where the man with whom he embarked from Jamaica went ashore on business (it may have been to make arrangements to sell him) and overstaying his time, was left, Alex-ander being taken to New York on board of the steamer, where, on application, he was provided for by the British Consul for the port of New York, and sent back to Jamaica. The *truth* of this last statement may easily be ascertained.

The inducements, he says, which led him from home each time, was a desire to make money, which are generally held out by the Americans on board of the steamers, in such a manner as to prove entirely successful. He was promised by the kidnapper, Thomas J. Adams, to be taken to Tennessee, where he had large quantities of cattle, to go from thence by the overland route to California, where he should become wealthy by his industry. He seemed not to have been aware, until now, of the existence of Slavery and the inequality between the white and colored people of the United States. There were three other youths besides himself, called Brown, John, and the other not recollected, all of whom were induced by Americans to leave Jamaica for this country, who came on the American Steamer *Uncle Sam*, on her last homeward trip from California. And these youths are now in different parts of the United States, having separated at New York, Alexander being destined for Tennessee.

He informs us that this is no uncommon occurrence; almost every American steamer which touches the island bring[s] away some colored youths to the United States, always predicated upon great promises of doing great things for them. In proof of this, the kidnapper Adams replied to us, when finding there was no alternative, that he had found the boy in Kingston, *half-naked* and *half-starved*, and brought him away to *provide* for him, and give him a *good home* in Cincinnati, Ohio. This was a sheer fabrication.

In addition to, and corroborative of these facts, Mr. S. L. C.,[7] a returned Californian, and respectable citizen of Pittsburgh, asserts that in his late passage from Jamaica, in the last trip of the *Illinois*, there were to his knowledge some two or three colored girls—two he is certain of—brought by American ladies, who purported that, after sojourning in the United States, they were to be taken to California. These Jamaica girls landed at New York in this month, and no doubt are still in the United States, and probably in slavery.

These facts appear, to us, to present startling disclosures, sufficient to induce the most thorough investigation; and to our minds there is no doubt but there is now being carried on by unprincipled Americans, citizens of the United States—Southerners it may be—a regular system of *decoying, kidnapping and selling into hopeless bondage, in the United States, the free subjects of Great Britian.* This is a new and alarming species of the slave trade, without precedent in the annals of history. A new feature in the foreign trade, carried on in the face of law and religion, without risk, danger or capital, where the victims are obtained for the mere expense of their passage. Nothing seems clearer to our minds than these facts.

Were these white children, the case would be different; but we can place no confidence in the pretensions of these Americans while they are studiously devising every mode of oppressing and getting rid of the native free colored people of their own country. And we now most earnestly call upon the colored people of the West Indies, and all others out of the United States, to be cautious, and never under any pretext whatever permit their children nor themselves to leave their native places to reside in the United States; as it is better to live on one banana or yam, and a cup of water a day, and be free, than be a slave anywhere, especially in this country, which is the worst and meanest upon which Heaven's sun ever shone. No colored person in the United States is really free; all are virtually and legally, if not abjectly, slaves. Bury your bones in the sunny clime of your own beautiful isles, rather than come to this *slaveholding, oppressing* country.

All of which we respectfully submit for your consideration. Subjoined are the notices of the leading daily journals,[8] many of which contain sentiments which we cannot endorse; yet all give some of the main facts, and show the spirit of the Pittsburgh press concerning such high-handed acts of infamy.

We cannot too highly commend the course of the counsel in the case, Messrs. J. M. Kirkpatrick and D. Reed,[9] for their untiring and faithful zeal in the case.

M. R. DELANY
JOHN PECK
WILLIAM WEBB[10]
THOMAS BURROWS
Committee

Saturday Visiter (Pittsburgh, Pa.), 4 June 1853.

1. The authors write to black legislators Edward Jordon and Robert Osborn, editors of the Kingston *Morning Journal*. After founding the journal in 1838, they edited it until 1863, making it into a political voice for Jamaica's sizable mulatto population. By the 1850s, it served as an organ of the City party, which also represented the island's reform-minded public officials and merchants. The *Morning Journal* ceased publication in 1875. Frank Cundall, ed., *Bibliographia Jamaicensis* (Kingston, Jamaica, 1902; reprint, New York, N.Y., 1971), 62; Philip D. Curtin, *Two Jamaicas: The Role of Ideas in a Tropical Colony, 1830–1865* (New York, N.Y., 1970), 58, 89, 182, 264n; John Bigelow, *Jamaica in 1850* (New York, N.Y., 1851), 24.

2. Thomas J. Adams (1808–?), a farmer, had lived in Montgomery County, Tennessee, north of Nashville, since 1840. U.S. Census, 1850.

3. John Fox was a member of the Pittsburgh police. He took Hendrickure into custody at the Pennsylvania Railroad depot on Water Street and transported him about ten city blocks to the St. Clair Hotel, a local landmark. *Pittsburgh City Directory*, 1850–54.

4. Thomas Williams (1806–1872), a prominent Pittsburgh attorney, was judge of the district court of Allegheny County during the 1850s. Active in local Whig and Republican party politics, he served several terms in the state legislature and

in the U.S. Congress (1863–69), where he managed the impeachment proceedings against President Andrew Johnson. *NCAB*, 8:469, 15:329.

5. Robert W. Hague was a member of the Pittsburgh police. The mayor appointed him high constable in 1852. *Pittsburgh City Directory*, 1850–52.

6. John C. Peck (1802–1875) ranks among western Pennsylvania's foremost antebellum black leaders. Born in Hagerstown, Maryland, he grew up in northern Virginia, where he obtained a rudimentary education from a Presbyterian clergyman. He settled in Carlisle, Pennsylvania, in 1821 and moved west to Pittsburgh sixteen years later. A successful entrepreneur—a barber, wigmaker, and perfumer and the owner of several businesses, including a clothing store and an oyster house—Peck acquired a comfortable home and the means to educate his children. Although raised in a black Catholic family, he converted to Methodism when eleven years old, began preaching in 1834 in the African Methodist Episcopal denomination, and eventually established Pittsburgh's Wylie Street AME Church. Peck's preaching, which was described as "not brilliantly eloquent" but practical and earnest, frequently carried an antislavery message. He criticized American churches for their lack of commitment to emancipation. In addition to his careers as a businessman and a clergyman, Peck participated in community organizations devoted to black education and moral reform. He served as a trustee of Avery College, a local black institution, from the 1850s until his death.

Peck was a black abolitionist and civil rights advocate of local, state, and national scope. During the early 1840s, he served on the executive committee of the Western Pennyslvania Anti-Slavery Society, often hosting meetings of the society in his home. He belonged to the publishing committee for Martin R. Delany's *Mystery*, a black antislavery journal. As president of the Philanthropic Society (a Pittsburgh vigilance committee), he played a major role in the local underground railroad, occasionally acting as an intermediary between fugitive slaves and their former owners. Peck also pursued racial equality as a leading figure in the black convention movement. After representing Carlisle blacks at the national gatherings of the 1830s, he joined the struggle for black voting rights in Pennsylvania in the latter part of the decade. Continuing his efforts for black suffrage over three decades, he worked through state and national conventions and the National Equal Rights League. Peck presided at the opening session of the 1853 black national convention at Rochester and promoted the conclave's goals as a cofounder and officer of the National Council of the Colored People. But slavery's growing influence over the federal government, the National Council's 1855 demise, and disunity among northern blacks left him discouraged. He concluded in the wake of the Dred Scott decision that blacks could only escape racial oppression by leaving the United States. Although he advocated black emigration and announced his intention of settling in Canada West, he remained in Pittsburgh until his death. *CA*, 12 April, 1 December 1838 [2:0456, 0662]; Ullman, *Martin R. Delany*, 18, 31, 45–47, 70; *NSt*, 21 December 1849 [6:0246]; *FDP*, 8 September 1854 [9:0073–74]; *PFW*, 25 April 1857 [10:0665]; *PP*, 21 December 1861 [13:0679]; *WAA*, 16 September 1865 [16:0215]; *CR*, 4 February 1865, 9 September, 4 November 1875 [15:0703]; Foner and Walker, *Proceedings of the Black State Conventions*, 1:106, 139

[4:0174, 15:0708]; *Minutes and Proceedings of the First Annual Convention of the People of Colour* (Philadelphia, Pa., 1831), 8, 15 [1:0080, 0083]; *Minutes and Proceedings of the Second Annual Convention for the Improvement of the Free People of Color* (Philadelphia, Pa., 1832), 3–28 [1:0171–84]; *Minutes of the Third Annual Convention* (1833), 3–26 [1:0294–306]; *Minutes of the Fourth Annual Convention* (1834), 9–16 [1:0467–70]; *Minutes of the Fifth Annual Convention for the Improvement of the Free People of Colour* (Philadelphia, Pa., 1835), 14–21 [1:0592–96]; *Colored National Convention . . . in Rochester* (1853), 6, 46 [8:0329, 0349]; *Convention of Colored Men . . . in Syracuse* (1864), 5, 29 [15:0539, 0551].

7. The committee probably refers to Samuel L. Cuthbert, a prominent merchant and real estate agent in Pittsburgh during the late 1840s and 1850s. *Pittsburgh City Directory*, 1841–54.

8. Delany enclosed accounts of the incident from five Pittsburgh newspapers: the *Daily Gazette, Evening Chronicle, Daily Commercial Journal, Daily Union*, and *Morning Post. SV*, 4 June 1853.

9. John M. Kirkpatrick and David Reed, prominent Pittsburgh attorneys, represented local blacks in several fugitive slave cases during the early 1850s. Kirkpatrick (1825–1898) later became district attorney of Allegheny County (1855–58), sat in the Pennsylvania legislature, and served as a county judge. He was a central figure in local Republican party politics during the late 1850s. R. J. M. Blackett, "Freedom, or the Martyr's Grave: Black Pittsburgh's Aid to the Fugitive Slave," *WPHM* 61:132 (April 1978); *NCAB*, 8:469; Michael F. Holt, *Forging a Majority: The Formation of the Republican Party in Pittsburgh, 1848–1860* (New Haven, Conn., 1969), 156–58, 180, 287.

10. William Webb (1812–1868) was born in Fredericksburg, Virginia, but spent his youth and early adulthood in Carlisle, Pennsylvania. An ordained African Methodist Episcopal clergyman, he twice represented congregations in the region at the denomination's General Conference. His involvement in local civic affairs included promoting temperance, presiding over the Young Men's Debating Society, organizing a black savings company, and acting as a subscription agent for the *Colored American*. Webb represented Carlisle at black state conventions in 1841 and 1848. In the early 1850s, he moved to Pittsburgh, opened a grocery store, and worked as a subscription agent for the *Provincial Freeman*. Frustrated by racism, he became a leading advocate of black emigration and joined with Martin R. Delany to organize the first National Emigration Convention, which met in 1854 at Cleveland.

Webb moved to Detroit about 1858, reestablished himself in the grocery business, and assumed a leadership position in the city's black community. He was active in local efforts to assist and protect fugitive slaves and participated in Refugee Home Society affairs. In 1859, in an effort to generate interest in John Brown's proposed insurrection, he hosted a meeting between Brown and local black leaders at his home. He later helped found Detroit's John Brown League. Webb cofounded the Michigan Freedmen's Aid Society after the Civil War. His autobiography was posthumously published as *The History of William Webb, Composed by Himself* (1873). U.S. Census, 1850; *CR*, 7 November 1868; Daniel A. Payne, *History of the African Methodist Episcopal Church* (Nashville, Tenn., 1891; reprint, New York, N.Y., 1968), 211, 249–50; Alexander W.

Wayman, *Cyclopaedia of African Methodism* (Baltimore, Md., 1882), 177; *CA*, 20 October 1838, 30 January 1841, 10 October 1842 [2:0622, 3:0865]; *NSt*, 1 December 1848 [5:0841]; Foner and Walker, *Proceedings of the Black State Conventions*, 1:110, 120; *FDP*, 25 November, 23, 30 December 1853 [8:0499, 0525, 0531]; *PFW*, 6 May 1854; *WAA*, 17 December 1859 [12:0299]; John C. Dancy, *Sand against the Wind* (Detroit, Mich., 1966), 44–45.

32.
Harriet A. Jacobs to Horace Greeley
19 June 1853

Slave women lived, as Henry Highland Garnet explained, "unprotected from the lust of tyrants." Although few black men spoke or wrote openly on the subject, black women indicted the institution of slavery with shocking tales of sexual exploitation. Sarah P. Remond informed audiences that the 800,000 mulattoes in the South were "the fruits of licentiousness" on the part of white masters. Harriet A. Jacobs, Louisa Picquet, and other slave autobiographers stunned readers with dramatic firsthand accounts of seduction, concubinage, and rape. But slave women were constantly aware of the need to balance credibility with discretion. Graphic accounts or personal details might offend middle-class sensibilities and humiliate the narrator. Jacobs, who had been forced into a sexual relationship with her former owner, felt compelled to refute a published piece by former first lady of the United States Julia Tyler on the positive effects of slavery on the black family. Her 19 June 1853 letter to the *New York Tribune*, written under the pseudonym "A Fugitive Slave," described the seduction of a fourteen-year-old slave girl by her master. Jacobs referred to the girl as her sister, but in reality the victim was a close friend. Jacobs might have told her own story; but as she later explained to Rochester abolitionist Amy Post, it was much easier for a woman to "whisper" of sexual abuses to a friend than to "record them for the world to read." Jacobs eventually revealed her own sexual mistreatment in slavery in *Incidents in the Life of a Slave Girl* (1861), which she published under the pseudonym "Linda Brent." Pease and Pease, *They Who Would Be Free*, 38–39, 41; Ripley et al., *Black Abolitionist Papers*, 1:23; Sterling, *We Are Your Sisters*, 18–31; Harriet A. Jacobs, *Incidents in the Life of a Slave Girl, Written by Herself*, ed. Jean Fagan Yellin (Cambridge, Mass., 1987), xix–xxi, 235–37.

SIR:

Having carefully read your paper for some months, I became very much interested in some of the articles and comments written on Mrs. Tyler's Reply to the Ladies of England.[1] Being a slave myself, I could not have felt otherwise. Would that I could write an article worthy of notice in your columns. As I never enjoyed the advantages of an education, therefore I could not study the arts of reading and writing, yet poor as it may be, I had rather give it from my own hand, than have it said that I employed others to do it for me. The truth can never be told so well through the second and third person as from yourself. But I am straying from the question. In that Reply to the Ladies of England, Mrs. Tyler said that slaves were never sold only under very peculiar circumstances. As Mrs. Tyler and her friend Bhains were so far used up, that he could not explain what those peculiar circumstances were, let one whose peculiar suffering justifies her in explaining it for Mrs. Tyler.

I was born a slave, reared in the Southern hot-bed until I was the mother of two children, sold at the early age of two and four years old. I have been hunted through all of the Northern States, but no, I will not tell you of my own suffering—no, it would harrow up my soul, and defeat the object that I wish to pursue. Enough—the dregs of that bitter cup have been my bounty for many years.

And as this is the first time that I ever took my pen in hand to make such an attempt, you will not say that it is fiction, for had I the inclination, I have neither the brain or talent to write it. But to this very peculiar circumstance under which slaves are sold.

My mother was held as property by a maiden lady; when she married, my younger sister was in her fourteenth year, whom they took into the family. She was as gentle as she was beautiful. Innocent and guileless child, the light of our desolate hearth! But oh, my great heart bleeds to tell you of the misery and degradation she was forced to suffer in slavery. The monster who owned her had no humanity in his soul. The most sincere affection that his heart was capable of could not make him faithful to his beautiful and wealthy bride the short time of three months, but every stratagem was used to seduce my sister. Mortified and tormented beyond endurance, this child came and threw herself on her mother's bosom, the only place where she could seek refuge from her persecutor; and yet she could not protect her child that she had borne into the world. On that bosom with *bitter tears* she told her troubles, and entreated her mother to save her. And oh, Christian mothers! you that have daughters of your own, can you think of your sable sisters without offering a prayer to that God who created all in their behalf? My poor mother, naturally high-spirited, smarting under what she considered as the wrongs and outrages which her child had to bear, sought her master, entreating him to spare her child. Nothing could exceed his rage at this, what he called impertinence. My mother was dragged to jail, there remained twenty-five days, with negro traders to come in as they liked to examine her, as she was offered for sale. My sister was told that she must yield, or never expect to see her mother again. There were three younger children; on no other condition could she be restored to them without the sacrifice of one. That child gave herself up to her master's bidding, to save one that was dearer to her than life itself. And can you, Christian, find it in your heart to despise her? Ah, no! not even Mrs. Tyler; for though we believe that the vanity of a name would lead her to bestow her hand where her heart could never go with it, yet, with all her faults and follies, she is nothing more than a *woman*. For if her domestic hearth is surrounded with slaves, ere long before this she has opened her eyes to the evils of slavery, and that the mistress as well as the slave must submit to the indignities and vices imposed on them by their lords of body and soul. But to one of those peculiar circumstances.

At fifteen, my sister held to her bosom an innocent offspring of her guilt and misery. In this way she dragged a miserable existence of two years, between the fires of her mistress's jealousy and her master's brutal passion. At seventeen, she gave birth to another helpless infant, heir to all the evils of slavery. Thus life and its sufferings were meted out to her until her twenty-first year. Sorrow and suffering had made its ravages upon her—she was less the object to be desired by the fiend who had crushed her to the earth; and as her children grew, they bore too strong a resemblance to him who desired to give them no other inheritance save Chains and Handcuffs, and in the dead hour of the night, when this young, deserted mother lay with her little ones clinging around her, little dreaming of the dark and inhuman plot that would be carried into execution before another dawn, and when the sun rose on God's beautiful earth, that broken-hearted mother was far on her way to the capitol of Virginia. That day should have refused her light to so disgraceful and inhuman an act in your boasted country of Liberty. Yet, reader, it is true, those two helpless children were the *sons* of one of your sainted Members in Congress;[2] that agonized mother, his victim and slave. And where she now is God only knows, who has kept a record on high of all that she has suffered on earth.

And, you would exclaim, Could not the master have been more merciful to his children? God is merciful to all of his children, but it is seldom that a slaveholder has any mercy for his slave child. And you will believe it when I tell you, that mother and her children were sold to make room for another sister, who was now the age of that mother when she entered the family. And this selling appeased the mistress's wrath, and satisfied her desire for *revenge*, and made the path more smooth for her young rival at first. For there is a strong rivalry between a handsome mulatto girl and a jealous and *faded* mistress, and her liege lord sadly neglects those little attentions for a while that once made her happy. For the master will either neglect his wife or double his attentions, to save him from being suspected by his wife. Would you not think that Southern women had cause to despise that Slavery which forces them to bear so much deception practiced by their *husbands*? Yet all this is true, for a slaveholder seldom takes a white mistress, for she is an expensive commodity, not submissive as he would like to have her, but more apt to be tyrannical; and when his passion seeks another object, he must leave her in quiet possession of all the gewgaws that she has sold herself for. But not so with his poor *slave victim*, that he has robbed of everything that could make life desirable; she must be torn from the little that is left to bind her to life, and sold by her *seducer* and *master*, caring not where, so that it puts him in possession of enough to purchase another victim. And such are the peculiar circumstances of American Slavery—of all the evils in God's sight the most to be abhorred.

Perhaps while I am writing this, you too, dear Emily, may be on your way to the Mississippi River, for those peculiar circumstances occur every day in the midst of my poor oppressed fellow-creatures in bondage. And oh ye Christians, while your arms are extended to receive the oppressed of all nations, while you exert every power of your soul to assist them to raise funds, put weapons in their hands, tell them to return to their own country to slay every foe until they break the accursed yoke from off their necks, not buying and selling; this they never do under any circumstances. But while Americans do all this, they forget the millions of slaves they have at home, bought and sold under very peculiar circumstances.

And because one friend of the slave has dared to tell of their wrongs you would annihilate her. But in *Uncle Tom's Cabin* she has not told the half.[3] Would that I had one spark from her storehouse of genius and talent, I would tell you of my own sufferings—I would tell you of wrongs that Hungary has never inflicted,[4] nor England ever dreamed of in this free country where all nations fly for liberty, equal rights and protection under your stripes and stars. It should be stripes and scars, for they go along with Mrs. Tyler's peculiar circumstances, of which I have told you only one.

A FUGITIVE SLAVE[5]

New York Tribune (N.Y.), 21 June 1853.

1. In December 1852, the New York press published an appeal by prominent Englishwomen that called upon the white women of the South to help abolish slavery. On 24 January 1853, former first lady Julia G. Tyler penned a lengthy rejoinder—"To the Duchess of Sutherland and the Ladies of England"—for the *Richmond Enquirer*. Ridiculing the appeal for its presumption and arrogance, she reminded its authors that proper women confined themselves to domestic concerns and did not engage in political debate. She also contrasted the condition of slaves with that of English factory workers, asserting that "the Negro of the South lives sumptuously in comparison with the 100,000 of the white population in London." Tyler's widely reprinted response elicited praise from southern newspapers and some northern journals like the *New York Times* and *New York Herald*. But it outraged abolitionists—the *Liberator* called it "trashy" and "decidedly vulgar." Horace Greeley denounced it in a lengthy editorial in the *New York Tribune*, and he questioned her authorship of the piece, suggesting that it might have been written by her husband, former president John Tyler. Robert Seager, *And Tyler Too: A Biography of John and Julia Gardiner Tyler* (New York, N.Y., 1963), 402–6, 622n; *RE*, 28 January 1853; *Lib*, 18 February 1853; *NYT*, 1 February 1853.

2. Jacobs probably refers to Samuel Tredwell Sawyer (1800–1865), with whom she had shared a similar relationship. Sawyer, an Edenton, North Carolina, lawyer, was elected to the U.S. Congress as a Democrat in 1837 and served a single term. In 1829 Jacobs attempted to resist the unwanted sexual advances of her master, Dr. James Norcom, by becoming Sawyer's mistress. She hoped he would purchase her and grant her freedom. The liaison produced two children, Joseph (b. 1829) and Louisa Matilda (b. 1833). Sawyer is represented as Mr. Sands in Jacobs's autobiography, *Incidents in the Life of a Slave Girl* (1861). *BDAC*, 1659; Jacobs, *Life of a Slave Girl*, xv, xxx–xxxi, 54–55, 125, 224, 268, 279.

3. Jacobs refers to Harriet Beecher Stowe and her authorship of *Uncle Tom's Cabin*.

4. Jacobs refers to the brutal suppression of the Hungarian independence movement by the armies of Russia and Austria in 1848.

5. Harriet Ann Jacobs (1813–1897) wrote three letters to the *New York Tribune* during the summer of 1853 under the pseudonym "A Fugitive Slave." Jacobs was born to slave parents in Edenton, North Carolina, but was orphaned as a young child. Her first mistress taught her to read. At age eleven, Jacobs became the slave of James Norcom, a local physician. As she matured, he subjected her to unrelenting sexual harassment. To escape his advances, she became sexually involved with a young white lawyer named Samuel Tredwell Sawyer. This relationship produced two children, Joseph and Louisa Matilda. In 1835 upon hearing that Norcom planned to put her two children to work at his plantation, she went into hiding. Although Sawyer bought the two children, Jacobs remained hidden for nearly seven years in a tiny crawl space above a storeroom in the home of her free black grandmother. During this time, she practiced writing and read extensively in the Bible.

In 1842 Jacobs escaped to the North and was reunited with her children. She found work in Brooklyn as a nursemaid in the family of literary editor Nathaniel Parker Willis. Norcom repeatedly visited the city in an attempt to locate Jacobs, forcing her to flee to Boston in 1844. During 1845–46, she accompanied the Willis family on a trip to Britain. Upon her return to the United States, Jacobs moved to Rochester to live with her brother John S. Jacobs, who was then lecturing for the antislavery movement. She joined a circle of antislavery activists and began working in the antislavery reading room that they had opened above the offices of Frederick Douglass's *North Star*. Jacobs voraciously read abolitionist literature. She lived for nine months in the home of Isaac and Amy Post; the latter became her confidante and urged her to make her story public. Jacobs returned to the Willis household in 1850. When the Norcom family continued to look for her, she persuaded Mrs. Willis to arrange her purchase.

Jacobs was eager "to be useful in some way" to the antislavery cause. She reconsidered Amy Post's suggestion that she tell her story and began to write her narrative, with the editorial assistance of her daughter Louisa and Lydia Maria Child. It was published in 1861 as *Incidents in the Life of a Slave Girl*. A British version, *The Deeper Wrong*, appeared the following year. These volumes made her a minor celebrity, and she used her influence to further relief efforts for the former slaves of the South. Jacobs and her daughter worked among the freedmen in northern Virginia and Washington, D.C. (1863–66), and Savannah, Georgia (1866–68), distributing clothing and supplies and organizing schools, nursing homes, and orphanages. She used the public press to report back to reformers on conditions in the South. In 1868 she returned to Britain to raise funds for a Savannah orphanage and home for the aged. Jacobs ran a boardinghouse in Cambridge, Massachusetts, in the 1870s and 1880s. During her final years, she went back to Washington, where she participated in the organizing meetings of the National Association of Colored Women. Jacobs, *Life of a Slave Girl.*

33.
Constitution of the National Council
of the Colored People
8 July 1853

Since the 1830s, black leaders had considered the idea of establishing a
permanent national association to link northern black communities and
coordinate their many reform efforts. In 1849 Frederick Douglass proposed a National League of Colored People "to grapple with the various
systems of injustice" which blacks faced. Two years later, the North
American Convention urged the formation of a "league of the colored
people of the North and South American continents, and of the West
Indies." Similar plans attracted widespread support during the early
1850s. In July 1853, black leaders met in Rochester, New York, to
adopt a constitution for a National Council of the Colored People.
Seeking to fulfill long-standing desires for a permanent national organization, they vowed that the council would undertake educational programs, sponsor economic cooperatives, establish a press, and enlarge
employment opportunities for blacks. They carefully balanced the racial
separatism implicit in the council's exclusively black composition with
its goal of racial integration. The National Council was the first serious
attempt to unify diverse black endeavors; although short-lived, it anticipated the goals and structure of many black national organizations established in the twentieth century. *RIF*, 19 May 1854 [8:0822]; *FDP*,
17 June, 15 July 1853; Pease and Pease, *They Who Would Be Free*,
251–54.

For the purpose of improving the character, developing the intelligence, maintaining the rights, and organizing a Union of the Colored
People of the Free States, the National Convention does hereby ordain
and institute the

NATIONAL COUNCIL OF THE COLORED PEOPLE[1]

ART. 1. This Council shall consist of two members from each State,
represented in this Convention, to be elected by this Convention, and
two other members from each State to be elected as follows: On the 15th
day of November next, and biennially thereafter, there shall be held in
each State, a Poll, at which each colored inhabitant may vote who pays
ten cents as a poll tax; and each State shall elect, at such election, delegates to State Councils, twenty in number from each State, at large. The
election to be held in such places and under such conditions as the public
meetings in such localities may determine. The members of the National
Council in each State shall receive, canvass and declare the result of such
vote. The State Council thus elected shall meet on the first Monday in

January, 1854, and elect additional members to the National Council, in proportion of one to five thousand of colored population of such State; and the members of Council, thus elected, to take office on the 6th day of July next, and all to hold office during two years from that date; at the end of which time another general election by State Council shall take place of members to constitute their successors in office, in the same numbers as above. The State Council of each State shall have full power over the internal concern of said State.

ART. 2. The members of the first Council shall be elected by this Convention, which shall designate out of the number, a President, Vice-President, Secretary, Treasurer, Corresponding Secretary, and Committee of five on Manual Labor School—a Committee of five on Protective Unions—of five on Business Relations—of five on Publications.

ART. 3. The Committee on Manual Labor School shall procure funds and organize said School in accordance with the plans adopted by this National Convention,[2] with such modifications as experience or necessity may dictate to them. The Committee shall immediately incorporate itself as an Academy under the general Committee of the State of ———, and shall constitute the Board of Trustees of the Manual Labor School, with full power to select a location in the State designated by the National Council, to erect buildings, appoint or dismiss instructors in the literary or mechanical branches. There shall be a farm attached to the School.

ART. 4. The Committee on Protective Unions shall institute a Protective Union for the purchase and sale of articles of domestic consumption, and shall unite and aid in the formation of branches auxiliary to their own.

ART. 5. The Committee on Business Relations shall establish an office, in which they shall keep a registry of colored mechanics, artisans and business men throughout the Union. They shall keep a registry of all persons willing to employ colored men in business, to teach colored boys mechanical trades, liberal and scientific professions, and farming; and, also, a registry of colored men and youth seeking employment or instruction. They shall also report upon any avenues of business or trade which they deem inviting to colored capital, skill, or labor. Their reports and advertisements to be in papers of the widest circulation. They shall receive for sale or exhibition, products of the skill and labor of colored people.

ART. 6. The Committee on Publications shall collect all facts, statistics and statements, all laws and historical records and biographies of the Colored People, and all books by colored authors. They shall have for the safekeeping of these documents, a Library, with a Reading Room and Museum. The Committee shall also publish replies to any assaults, worthy of note, made upon the character or condition of the Colored People.

ART. 7. Each Committee shall have absolute control over its special department; shall make its own bylaws, and in case of any vacancy occurring, shall fill up the same forthwith, subject to the confirmation of the Council. Each Committee shall meet at least once a month or as often as possible; shall keep a minute of all its proceedings, executive and financial, and shall submit a full statement of the same, with the accounts audited, at every regular meeting of the National Council.

ART. 8. The National Council shall meet at least once in six months, to receive the reports of the Committees, and to consider any new plan for the general good, for which it shall have power, at its option, to appoint a new Committee, and shall be empowered to receive and appropriate donations for the carrying out of the objects of the same. At all such meetings, eleven members shall constitute a quorum. In case any Committee neglect or refuse to send in its report, according to article 8th, then the Council shall have power to enter the bureau, examine the books and papers of such Committee, and in case the Committee shall persist in its refusal or neglect, then the Council shall declare their offices vacant, and appoint others in their stead.

ART. 9. In all cases of the meetings of the National Council, or the Committees, the travelling expenses (if any) of the members shall be paid out of their respective funds.

ART. 10. The Council shall immediately establish a bureau in the place of its meeting; and the same rooms shall, as far as possible, be used by the several Committees for their various purposes. The Council shall have a clerk, at a moderate salary, who shall keep a record of their transactions, and prepare a condensed report of the Committee for publication, and also a registry of the friends of the cause.

ART. 11. The expenses of the Council shall be defrayed by the fees of membership of sub-societies or Councils, to be organized throughout the States. The membership fee shall be one cent per week.

ART. 12. A member of the Council shall be a member of only one of the Committees thereof.

ART. 13. All officers holding funds shall give security in double the amount likely to be in their hands. This security to be given to the three first officers of the Council.

ART. 14. The Council shall have power to make such bylaws as are necessary for their proper government.

Proceedings of the Colored National Convention, Held in Rochester, July 6th, 7th and 8th, 1853 (Rochester, N.Y., 1853), 18–19.

1. The National Council of the Colored People, which was organized at the 1853 black national convention, reflected the long-standing desire of black leaders to establish a permanent national body to promote the interests of their race.

The convention charged the council with the task of "improving the character, maintaining the rights, and organizing a Union of the Colored People of the Free States." To accomplish this, two delegates from each state represented were to meet every six months to transact business. Ongoing council work was divided among committees responsible for a manual labor school, publications, business and employment, and other concerns. The National Council gained immediate and widespread support among blacks, who organized state councils and local auxiliaries across the North. Yet geographic and personal rivalries, disputes over the role of women in the organization, and ideological conflict between separatists and integrationists left both the state councils and the national leadership divided. The National Council met three times before its 1855 demise but never overcame a split between supporters of Frederick Douglass, who advocated a powerful black organization, and delegates from Boston and Philadelphia, who resented his leadership and rejected the council's racial exclusiveness. As its final act, the National Council called the 1855 black national convention in Philadelphia. Pease and Pease, *They Who Would Be Free*, 13, 140–42, 253–55; *FDP*, 18 March, 1 April, 6, 20 May, 24 June, 17 July, 26 August, 2 December 1853, 27 January, 3 February, 24, 31 March, 7, 21 April, 19 May, 28 July, 25 August 1854, 30 March, 18 May, 26 October 1855 [8:0626, 0640, 0708, 0723–24, 0749, 9:0041]; Ripley et al., *Black Abolitionist Papers*, 2:175–76; *Colored National Convention . . . in Philadelphia* (1855), 14–19, 33–34 [9:0885–87, 0894–95].

2. The proposal by the National Council of the Colored People to establish a manual labor school was one of many such plans that black leaders had endorsed since the early 1830s. Leading advocates of this effort included Frederick Douglass, James McCune Smith, John Peck, John Jones, Amos G. Beman, and James D. Bonner. They contended that because white artisans refused to accept black apprentices, a school of this type would offer blacks their only opportunity to learn the skilled trades necessary for social and economic independence. A committee appointed by the council drew up a plan to establish a manual labor school, to be called the American Industrial School, in western Pennsylvania. Students would be admitted without regard "to sex or complexion," and the curriculum would be equally divided between academics and trades.

The committee believed the school would become self-supporting but pledged to raise an initial endowment of $50,000—later reduced to $30,000. Hopes were buoyed by Harriet Beecher Stowe's promise to collect funds for this purpose in Britain. The plan initially generated considerable black enthusiasm, but divisions quickly surfaced. Black Garrisonians charged that the school would promote racial exclusiveness; Martin R. Delany denounced Stowe's affiliation with the scheme; others argued that the school was too expensive, impractical, or unnecessary. White philanthropists refused to contribute funds, and Stowe withdrew her offer of assistance by January 1854. The council attempted to rally black churches behind the school, but a lack of funds and continuing disunity among council members prompted the 1855 black national convention to abandon the plan. Pease and Pease, *They Who Would Be Free*, 136–43; *FDP*, 11, 18 March, 15 April, 6 May, 2 December 1853, 20 January, 24 March 1854, 18, 25 May 1855.

34.
The Douglass-Garrison Controversy
and the Black Community

William C. Nell to Frederick Douglass
13 August 1853

William C. Nell to Amy Post
20 December 1853

Resolutions by a Meeting of Chicago Blacks
26 December 1853

The independent course taken by black abolitionists caused racial and ideological strife and strained personal relations in the antislavery movement. Frederick Douglass's break with William Lloyd Garrison demonstrated the gravity of the conflict that resulted when blacks rejected white control and influence. Throughout the 1840s, white abolitionists prized Douglass for his slave background and charismatic appeal on the lecture circuit. But he soon outgrew the limited role they assigned to him, and as he matured as an author, editor, and antislavery theorist, he drifted away from Garrisonian principles. In 1851, when Douglass announced his adoption of political abolitionism and an antislavery interpretation of the U.S. Constitution, he touched off a decade-long battle with the Garrisonians. The controversy forced black abolitionists to choose sides. Black loyalty to Garrison was strongest in Boston and Philadelphia, yet even staunch Garrisonians such as William C. Nell, who condemned Douglass as an apostate, regretted the divisions and admired the black leader's immense talent. Nell's 13 August and 20 December 1853 letters describe the impact of the Douglass-Garrison feud on Boston blacks. Outside the eastern antislavery establishment, blacks defended Douglass, describing him as "our acknowledged leader and exponent." On 26 December 1853, Chicago blacks staged a mass meeting to respond to the growing conflict. Led by John Jones, William Smith, James D. Bonner, Byrd Parker, and Henry O. Wagoner, they adopted a series of resolutions denouncing the arrogance of white abolitionists and praising Douglass as the "able champion and defender of the rights of colored people." William C. Nell to Amy Post, 22 December 1853, 20 January 1854, Post Papers, NRU [8:0523–24, 0603–5]; *FDP*, 4 December 1851, 10 June 1852, 20 December 1853, 13 January 1854 [7:0214, 0622, 8:0532, 0826–27]; Blassingame, *Frederick Douglass Papers*, 2:349–50.

6. William C. Nell
Courtesy of the Massachusetts Historical Society

BOSTON, [Massachusetts]
August 13, 1853

MR. DOUGLASS:

In your paper of Aug. 12th, you have grossly misrepresented my sayings and doings at the meeting recently held in Boston. I, therefore, ask you to publish the following communication.

In the first place, I must express to you the surprise manifested here in view of the language of your editorial; for, at the meeting, you acquitted me of any dishonorable or personal motive in the presentation I felt called upon to make relative to your course, and, moreover, promised you would do all in your power to promote harmony and allay controversy; but the first development to your readers is applying to me the epithet, "contemptible tool."

You put words into my mouth which I never used. I did not say, "I am the injured party here; I am on trial." What I did say was, "I am the persecuted party"—persecuted, I meant, by yourself and Mr. Morris. I made no allusion to being "on trial," there being no occasion for it. I have no fears of any trial before a Boston audience.

As to your holding me up as a practical enemy of the colored people, my pen smiles at the idea. When are you going to commence the task of proving your assertion?[1]

I heed not your innuendoes nor your comments; I can wait the decision of an impartial community. But your readers should know what I said and did on that occasion, hence I submit my remarks, as offered.

REMARKS ON THE FIRST EVENING

MR. CHAIRMAN:[2]

Concurring, as I am happy to do, in the general train of remark which we have just heard from Mr. Douglass, I the more deeply regret his omission of another topic, which others beside myself anticipated his making some allusion to. But as neither himself nor any other person has done so, the duty seems to devolve upon me.

It is, of course, known to most of those present, that the time has been when Mr. Douglass sustained very friendly relations toward Mr. Garrison and the pioneer Society.[3] It is also well known that now that relation is changed, and within a few months past, his spirit seems more than ever alienated, and in his paper he has made use of language which to many, and certainly to me—when considering his former identity of interests with them—seems unkind, ungenerous and ungrateful. I say this more in sorrow than in anger; but as I have long and intimately known Mr. Douglass—been associated with him in the publication of his paper—familiar with him and the old Society in their day of harmony and cooperation—and, moreover, as I have, to persons present and elsewhere, in speaking of his paper, cheerfully commended, though not afraid to blame—it occurs to me that I am no less his friend than before, because I ask him to explain his new position. There are those here who desire it, and the words that he may offer may correct us if in error, and render his paper the more acceptable.

I have not risen to defend Mr. Garrison and his coadjutors; for, thank God! from me, and in this place, they need no defence. I have not risen to offend Mr. Douglass and his friends; to anything of that kind, I am opposed by my whole moral, mental and physical constitution. But here, in the city where Mr. Garrison and the pioneer Society are known and loved, it is fitting that an opportunity should be tendered for explanation.

SECOND EVENING

MR. CHAIRMAN:

I disclaim any wish or desire to curtail the list of subscribers for Mr. Douglass's paper. I would not blot from the moral firmament one anti-slavery star. The colored people of Boston, like those of other places, are very delinquent in supporting anti-slavery papers, for even the pioneer sheet, THE LIBERATOR, has not from them a tithe of the patronage to which it is preeminently entitled.[4] Let them all remain, to shed light on the slave's path to freedom. It is only because I would have *Frederick Douglass' Paper* emit a more friendly light, that I stand before you this evening.

Among the articles in Mr. Douglass's paper which I submit in justification of my statement, is that published by him May 27th, headed "Infidelity," followed with some of Mr. Garrison's comments in THE LIBERATOR of June 10th.[5]

This censure of the old Society, in consequence of the oft-exploded charges of infidelity against some of its agents, brings to my mind that most eloquent passage in the anti-slavery lectures of Mr. Douglass, a few years since: "Commend me to that infidelity which takes off chains, rather than to the Christianity which puts them on."

Mr. Douglass, on one occasion, dealt very unhandsomely with George Thompson; but as I have reason to believe he regretted the course he took and the language he used on that occasion, I will waive the reading of his remarks, and the comments of Mr. Thompson's friends in England.[6] But it seems appropriate that I should present, in this connection, what I then expressed in letters to my friends, and what I always feel when he utters an unkind word toward any of his old friends:

> My abiding feeling is one of sincere regret that George Thompson should have been attacked by a colored man, at least such an one historically as Frederick Douglass. He should have pondered *long* and *well*, before allowing his pen to indite or tongue to utter anything disparagingly of George Thompson.
>
> If there had been a crime committed, and a necessity for its exposure, the matter would present a wholly different aspect; as it

is, I think an indecent haste was exhibited in the performance of a very ungrateful act.

In Mr. D's paper of July 22, he calls upon Geo. W. Putnam of Lynn, who has recently become disaffected towards the Mass. Anti-Slavery Society, in a manner invoking a renewal of his warfare against them.[7]

But I care not to enlarge, or go into details. My object is not controversy, but simply a presentation of facts, for all parties interested.

Mr. Douglass remarked, that two or three more such speeches as were delivered here by Mr. Foss would heal the wound (which, after all, was not a very deep one), between him and his old friends.[8] Happy indeed would I be, Mr. Chairman, if my words on this occasion would be accepted in that light. Let us compare notes by the wayside—let Mr. D. cease his direct and indirect hostility toward his old friends, speak well of or laud to the skies any individuals or parties he may feel disposed to, discuss and argue with them, show his to be a more excellent way than theirs—all this is well and proper; but in doing this, let him not detract from and drag others down; for he and they, though honestly differing as to ways and means, can both work in a general way for the downfall of our common enemy, slavery.

WILLIAM C. NELL

Liberator (Boston, Mass.), 2 September 1853.

Boston, [Massachusetts]
Dec[ember] 20, 1853

Esteemed Friend Amy:

This is the anniversary of <u>yours</u> and my Birthday. How fitting that I should commen[ce] a letter to you on this day. I cannot write in full to you but will pen in some items preliminary to more beyond.

Ten O clock. Wednesday Eve 21st. Here I am all alone at the anti slavery office[9] having Just parted with Charles Lenox Remond and wife[10] at the [door]. They are en route home from the Fair.[11] They unite in sending love to you. Miss Wood[12] and others took a carriage. The Fair opened this morning, the [weather] truly auspicious, tonight a slight sprinkle of snow but now it is starlight. The reciepts of the Fair on this its first day has been $1134. I was delighted to meet Mrs. Coleman.[13] She also called here today and had a talk with Mr. Garrison and subscribed for the Liberator. She has gone out of town tonight but arrangements are made for her stopping in the City should she [like] to do so. Mrs. Stowe writes to Mr. Garrison as though F. D. belongs to the weaker party and must be forborne with. She has been rather favorably impressed by him and though admitting in some former correspondence his failings, she will of course aid him somewhat. She did say that F. D. must cease his warfare against the anti slavery friends, but whether this was a condition on which favors were to be conferred, I have no reliable information as she had as above intimated to Mr. Garrison. She sent a note stating her interview with Douglass.[14] Mr. Garrison and Mr. Phillips[15] will not take any special pains to correct matters, but let the developements all appear in thier due time. The presents of Mrs. Stowe are quite an attractive feature in the Bazaar. Wish you had visited Boston Just at this time. I have communicated some facts from your letter to Mr. Garrison, May, Wallcut, Jackson [&] Samuel J. May[16] also who find them and others of much use by way of answering questions often put to him.

Douglass held a meeting in Boston last Friday night but the presence of Chas. Lenox Remond changed the programme some and F. D. did not happen to acquire any new laurels. D's speech was mainly (with some incidental flings) on the elevation of Colored People and his impressions of the West[,] remarks in which any body would concur.[17] Remond entered the meeting before I did and was cheered by the audience and when Douglass sat down he was loudly called for. He replied briefly concurring with D. in the general remarks but [noting] that He was but a spectator [& thought] if he should speak at any length, it might mar the harmony [&] Douglass siezed on these words and evidently tried to make Remond appear as the aggressor but like an old soldier familiar with the tricks of the enemy, Charles maintained an advantageous, Manly and Dignified position all the way through. D. intimated with his smooth and characteristic style that if he could be convinced of having done wrong to Mr. R. or any one else in the meeting, He would meet them halfway. R. answered that if the glove was thrown down to him He accepted it cheerfully. D. disclaimed the Glove but rather termed it an Olive Branch. R. rejoined that D. was his enemy ~~but~~ and had defamed his character and added that if he was going into the Controversy, He should fight behind no Cowards Castle or Haystack. D. applied the term to his paper &c. A large majority were eager for the two to get fairly under way, but the lateness of the hour and other reasons prevented. D. said He must be in Rochester Monday night. Remond was ready to meet him any time and did come to Boston next day to ascertain whether He had remained over but Douglass was on his way homeward.

Douglass called upon the Brothers and Sisters to pray for Him, and finally closed with singing. Lewis Hayden declared himself Neutral. Some think him otherwise. Mr. Grimes[18] also, but they are the Men who are with him mostly when here. There are many here very anxious even now for a discussion between C. L. R. & F. D. The latter mentioned his paper the other eveng but had no time to do any thing about it. He, of course will get some subscribers but no matter What may be the result elsewhere[,] He cannot get the Colored People of New England to approve his conduct and especially Boston as you would have believed if present at our Garrison [Association] last Monday Eve.[19] Hayden,

Grimes, Remond present. Mr. Grimes told Mr. Garrison that Douglass felt sorry & wept because of the troubles. They also say that He promises to bury the Hatchet now. If he does it will only be because he thinks no more harm can be done with it. I doubted it, Judging from the past and so I told Mr. Grimes. He was surprised at my skepticism and spoke of repentance. I replied, Douglass may repent, but otherwise I have no confidence in him. I have known him longer than most of them. He can exhibit a sunny side, but I can not easily forget the shady side of his character.

[Wm. C. Nell]

Post Papers, Rush-Rhees Library, University of Rochester, Rochester, New York. Published by permission.

Whereas, at the anniversary meeting of the A. A. S. Society, held at Syracuse, N.Y., 1851, at which meeting our esteemed friend and brother, Frederick Douglass, whom we are free to acknowledge as a bold, faithful, and manly advocate of most, if not all, of the reformatory movements of the times; and, whereas, we especially regard him as the prominent leader, advocate, and exponent of the wrongs and demands of the colored people of the U.S. And whereas, at said meeting referred to, Frederick Douglass boldly and frankly announced his change of views and opinions, harmonizing with those of Lysander Spooner, Gerrit Smith, Rev. S. R. Ward, and William Goodell, in regarding the Constitution of the U.S. as an anti-slavery document.[20] And whereas, we conceive it to be, not only the right, but also the duty which every man owes to the cause of truth, justice and humanity, to change his views and opinions whenever he arrives at a deliberate and well settled conviction of his errors, that he should at once abandon the wrong and adopt the right.

And whereas, we have noticed with feelings of deep regret and mortification, for some months past, a number of articles, at different times, in the columns of the *Liberator, N. A. Slavery Standard, Penn. Freeman* and *Anti-Slavery Bugle*,[21] which are, in the opinion of this meeting, most cruel and unjustifiable attempts on the part of the conductors of those journals to destroy the influence and usefulness of Frederick Douglass as an anti-slavery reformer. And whereas, the able and dignified defence of Mr. Douglass against all those illiberal and personal attacks is, in the opinion of this meeting, a triumphant and complete vindication of his character as a true reformer and honorable man, therefore:

Resolved, That the unchristian and unfeeling articles in the journals referred to—the base and unscrupulous charges and insinuations so often made, intended to destroy, not only his influence as an Editor and a Lecturer, but also as a man and a Christian—merits and should receive the lasting and withering rebuke of all true friends of the rights of our oppressed people.

Resolved, That we regard Frederick Douglass as an able champion and defender of the rights of the colored people of the United States, and that they, the colored people, will promote their true interest by giving to his efforts as an editor and a lecturer their active sympathy and approval, and to his paper their generous support.

Resolved, That it is with surprise and regret that we find colored men of acknowledged intelligence and moral worth actually engaged in this vile crusade against one who has proved himself an ornament to, and a benefactor of, his race.

Resolved, That the sentiment put forth by Mr. Garrison, that the Anti-Slavery cause, both religiously and politically, has transcended the ability of the sufferers of American slavery and prejudice, as a class, to keep pace with it, or to perceive what are its demands, or to understand the philosophy of its operations, is insulting to the intelligence of colored men, and we are thus forced to stamp it with a unanimous disapproval.

Resolved, That we earnestly and respectfully invite the attention of the State Councils,[22] and of the colored people throughout the Free States, to examine, discuss, and make themselves familiar with the grand questions involved in this difficulty. 1st. The pro-slavery and anti-slavery character of the Constitution of the United States. 2dly. The circumstances connected with and immediately concerning Frederick Douglass' change of views and opinions on this subject. 3dly. The present difficulty growing out of the whole matter, and, lastly, that after examining thoroughly the whole affair, so as to be enabled to arrive at correct conclusions, we may then give an intelligent judgement, and assume a decisive position.

Resolved, That the invasion by the *Liberator* of the sacred privacy of the domestic relations of Mr. Douglass' family[23] should meet the frowns and execration of all honorable men; and that the resorting to such an undignified and unmanly course seems to evince the utter weakness of his tirade against Mr. Douglass.

Whereas, since it is pretty generally conceded that *"we mean to remain here"*—at least, the *"great body of our people"*—and work our destiny in this country, therefore,

Resolved, That in contending for our civil and political rights, we plant ourselves firmly upon the principles of the *Declaration of Independence* and the Preamble and the Constitution of the United States.

Chicago Daily Tribune (Ill.), 28 December 1853.

1. In a 6 August 1853 letter, which appeared six days later in *Frederick Douglass' Paper,* Douglass condemned Nell, Robert Purvis, and Charles L. Remond "as my bitterest enemies, and the *practical* enemies of the colored people." He charged that Nell had urged Boston blacks not to subscribe to his paper because he displayed "ingratitude and unkindness" toward William Lloyd Garrison. Nell

expressed surprise, contrasting the tone of Douglass's letter with his alleged behavior at meetings held earlier in the week. Boston blacks had assembled to hear Douglass on 2 August at the Twelfth Baptist Church and on 3–4 August at the First Independent Baptist Church. According to William J. Watkins, Robert Morris made an unprovoked and "most ungenerous and ungentlemanly attack" upon Nell at the final session. *FDP*, 12 August 1853; *Lib*, 12, 19, 26 August 1853; Blassingame, *Frederick Douglass Papers*, 2:440–50.

2. Robert Morris chaired the meeting at which Nell's remarks were made. It was held on 2 August 1853 at Boston's Twelfth Baptist Church. Blassingame, *Frederick Douglass Papers*, 2:441.

3. Nell refers to the American Anti-Slavery Society.

4. Nearly 150 black Bostonians, about 10 percent of the city's black population, subscribed to the *Liberator* during the 1830s. But this support declined dramatically by the late 1840s due to competition from other papers, the growing conflict between Frederick Douglass and William Lloyd Garrison, and the *Liberator*'s diminished reportage of local black news. Donald M. Jacobs, "William Lloyd Garrison's *Liberator* and Boston Blacks, 1830–1865," *NEQ* 44:261 (June 1971); Pease and Pease, *They Who Would Be Free*, 117.

5. Nell refers to an editorial in the 27 May 1853 issue of *Frederick Douglass' Paper* in which Douglass speculated that white Garrisonians Stephen S. Foster, Parker Pillsbury, and Henry C. Wright had avoided a recent meeting of the American Anti-Slavery Society in order to defuse charges that the society was a source of religious heresy. Douglass argued that the three should have ignored the allegations and attended the convention. William Lloyd Garrison reprinted the editorial with additional comments in the 10 June issue of the *Liberator*. He condemned Douglass's remarks as "supremely ridiculous" and equated them to the writing of the proslavery press. The three men, he declared, were absent for other reasons; Foster was housebound with illness, Pillsbury had boils, and Wright was struggling to meet publication deadlines.

6. Nell refers to one of many charges that Garrisonians leveled at Douglass at the height of their conflict. In 1852 they accused Douglass of calling English abolitionist George Thompson a drunkard. In response, Garrison wrote to Douglass's British friends and urged them to withdraw their support for his paper. Quarles, *Frederick Douglass*, 75–76.

7. The 22 July 1853 issue of *Frederick Douglass' Paper* reprinted a story from the Worcester *Massachusetts Spy* that charged that the Massachusetts Anti-Slavery Society had barred Rev. Daniel Foster, a MASS lecturer, from distributing copies of William Goodell's *Slavery and Anti-Slavery*, a tract for political abolitionism. Douglass believed the incident reflected Garrisonian intolerance. He erroneously linked the incident to a minor dispute between Samuel May, Jr., MASS general agent, and George W. Putnam, one of the society's traveling lecturers. Putnam expressed disappointment with May's conduct as coordinator of the lectures. In May 1853, the New England Anti-Slavery Convention discussed Putnam's complaints but expressed support for May and the society's agency committee. Putnam denied any dissatisfaction with the MASS; his dispute, he argued, was with its general agent. Although the convention failed to act on his complaints, Putnam claimed by September that he and the society had worked out a mutually satisfying arrangement. *Lib*, 3 June, 29 July, 16 September 1853.

8. Andrew Twombly Foss (1803–1875), a Baptist clergyman and abolitionist, was a lecturing agent for the Anti-Slavery Society of the Baptist Church (North), as well the American Anti-Slavery Society and its Massachusetts auxiliary. During August and September 1853, he spoke throughout eastern and central Massachusetts, taking care to avoid the battle between Douglass and the Garrisonians. Douglass probably referred to his speech at a 2 August meeting at Boston's Twelfth Baptist Church. Merrill and Ruchames, *Letters of William Lloyd Garrison*, 4:317; *Lib*, 29 July, 30 September 1853; *FDP*, 12 August 1853 [8:0399].

9. The Massachusetts Anti-Slavery Society and the *Liberator* shared an office at 21 Cornhill in Boston from 1846 to 1860. *Lib*, 13 November 1846, 11 May 1860.

10. Amy Matilda Remond (1809–1856) was the daughter of black abolitionist Peter Williams, Jr., of New York City. As a young woman, she married Joseph Cassey, a member of Philadelphia's black elite. She became prominent among antislavery women as a founding member of the Gilbert Lyceum, an officer of the Philadelphia Female Anti-Slavery Society and Philadelphia Women's Association, and a participant in the city's annual antislavery fairs. Following Cassey's death in 1848, she married Charles L. Remond and continued her antislavery work in Salem, Massachusetts. In 1853, after being ejected from a Boston theater, she challenged the theater's racial discrimination in court and won a favorable decision. The *Liberator* eulogized her in 1856, noting that "at the earliest period of the anti-slavery movement, she espoused it with zeal and devotion." *NSt*, 9 March 1849 [5:0997]; *NASS*, 20 December 1849 [6:0245]; *SJ*, 17 June 1853; *Lib*, 30 August 1856.

11. Nell refers to the twentieth annual Boston Anti-Slavery Bazaar, which was held during 21–31 December at Horticulture Hall on School Street. Although hampered by bad weather, the bazaar managed to raise $4,256. *Lib*, 16, 23, 30 December 1853, 20 January 1854.

12. Annie C. Woods (1831–?), a native of North Carolina, moved with her family to Philadelphia as a young child. She was sent to Salem, Massachusetts, to pursue an education in the city's racially integrated public schools. Woods was the sister-in-law of black abolitionist Robert Forten and a lifelong correspondent and confidante of Charlotte Forten, her niece. In 1854 she married John Webb of Philadelphia, the brother of black novelist Frank J. Webb. They settled near Trenton, New Jersey, and raised five children. After her husband's death in 1860, Woods returned to Philadelphia and served as assistant principal at the "Ragged School"—a vocational school for indigent and impoverished black children. Although she eventually remarried, she continued to teach in Philadelphia until the early 1880s. U.S. Census, 1860, 1870; Brenda Stevenson, ed., *The Journals of Charlotte Forten Grimké* (New York, N.Y., 1988), 69, 188, 210, 214, 234, 237–38, 296–97, 302, 317, 345, 359–60, 364, 381, 400, 443, 458, 503, 535, 556–57n; Gloria C. Oden, "The Journal of Charlotte Forten: The Salem–Philadelphia Years (1854–1862) Reexamined," *EIHC* 119:134–35 (April 1983); *PP*, 23 November 1861; *Philadelphia City Directory*, 1861, 1870–82.

13. Lucy N. Coleman (1817–1906), a Boston native, taught at a black school in Rochester during the early 1850s. After the 1852 death of her second husband, she embraced abolitionism, spiritualism, and women's rights and emerged as a prominent figure in local reform circles. Coleman toured the North as a

lecturing agent for the American Anti-Slavery Society. During the Civil War, she worked as a matron in the National Colored Orphan Asylum in Washington, D.C., and as superintendent of the city's black schools. *NCAB*, 4:229–30; Merrill and Ruchames, *Letters of William Lloyd Garrison*, 4:532; Hewitt, *Women's Activism and Social Change*, 184–86.

14. Harriet Beecher Stowe (1811–1896), a leading American novelist, profoundly influenced public debate about slavery with *Uncle Tom's Cabin* (1852). In 1853 she decided to use part of the proceeds from the sale of the book to establish a black school. Stowe initially intended to assist the American Industrial School, a black manual labor college promoted by Douglass. The black leader expected that she would donate $1,500 to the project from an Uncle Tom Fund collected in Britain. About this time, Stowe attempted to mediate the growing breach between Douglass and William Lloyd Garrison. Both men met separately with Stowe at her Andover, Massachusetts, home. Although her efforts improved their strained relationship, Stowe withdrew her support for Douglass's project in 1854, probably due to continuing Garrisonian opposition. *NAW*, 3:393–402; Quarles, *Frederick Douglass*, 130–31; Merrill and Ruchames, *Letters of William Lloyd Garrison*, 4:287.

15. Wendell Phillips.

16. Nell refers to William Lloyd Garrison, Samuel May, Jr., Robert F. Wallcut, Francis Jackson, and Samuel J. May—all prominent Garrisonian abolitionists. Wallcut (1797–1884), a Unitarian clergyman, served from 1846 to 1865 as the general agent and bookkeeper for the *Liberator*. He worked for the Freedmen's Aid Commission after the Civil War and in 1876 became a clerk in the Boston Customs House. Merrill and Ruchames, *Letters of William Lloyd Garrison*, 5:46.

17. Douglass spoke at a 16 December 1853 meeting at Boston's Twelfth Baptist Church. He addressed the situation of free blacks, urging united action and the formation of a "National Union" to advance black interests. Douglass warned that new waves of European immigrants were displacing blacks from their traditional occupations and advised them to learn new trades to gain "wealth, respectability, and independence." *FDP*, 30 December 1853.

18. Leonard A. Grimes (1815–1874) was one of the leading black clergy activists in antebellum Boston. Born to free parents in Leesburg, Virginia, he later moved to Washington, D.C., where he worked with the underground network to aid and protect escaping slaves. He was eventually arrested and sentenced to two years in a Richmond prison for helping a slave family to reach freedom. After completing his sentence, he returned to Washington, found work as a hackman, and joined the Baptist faith. In 1846 Grimes moved his family to New Bedford, Massachusetts, and entered the ministry.

Grimes served as pastor of Boston's Twelfth Baptist Church from 1848 until his death. Under his forceful leadership, the congregation, many of them fugitive slaves, grew in size and importance. But the Fugitive Slave Law of 1850 threatened the congregation when more than forty members were forced to flee to Canada. In response, Grimes made his church into a key station on the underground railroad. Members hid runaway slaves and raised funds to purchase blacks returned to slavery under the law. In several notable cases, including those of Shadrach, Thomas Sims, and Anthony Burns, Grimes participated in efforts to free members of his congregation being held as fugitives by federal authorities. Grimes gained a reputation as one of the most aggressive black abolitionists in the city. He avoided formal antislavery organizations, choosing instead to address local problems almost exclusively through his church. But his interests extended beyond Boston. Grimes was an outspoken opponent of southern slavery. He presided over meetings of the American Baptist Missionary Convention, represented Boston at the 1853 black national convention in Rochester, and criticized the African Civilization Society. With the outbreak of the Civil War, Grimes lobbied Governor John A. Andrew of Massachusetts to create a black Union regiment. When the Fifty-fourth Massachusetts Regiment was formed in 1863, Grimes recruited black troops throughout the state and held regular meetings to pray for those on the battlefield. He was offered the chaplaincy of the regiment but declined. After the war, Grimes worked with the Freedmen's Bureau to settle former slaves from Virginia in Boston. From 1866 to 1868, he met their boats, located temporary lodging, and found them employment. Grimes continued to promote relief work among the freedmen. At the same time, he conducted revivals that dramatically increased the size of his local congregation during the six years following the war. Horton and Horton, *Black Bostonians*, 41, 44, 47–49, 101, 107–12, 118, 121; William J. Simmons, *Men of Mark: Eminent, Progressive and Rising* (Cleveland, Ohio, 1887; reprint, New York, N.Y., 1968), 662–65; Robert C. Hayden, *Faith, Culture, and Leadership: A History of the Black Church in Boston* (Boston, Mass., 1983), 28–30; Elizabeth J. Pleck, *Black Migration and Poverty: Boston, 1865–1900* (New York, N.Y., 1979), 27–28.

19. The second annual meeting of the Garrison Association convened on 19 December 1853 at Boston's First Independent Baptist Church. The group was organized by black Bostonians in 1852 "for the special purpose of annually testifying the love and affection we cherish for the Pioneer, and unflinching advocate of Immediate Emancipation"—William Lloyd Garrison. Douglass argued that the association served no useful purpose. *Lib*, 6 January 1854; *FDP*, 23 December 1853.

20. The annual meeting of the American Anti-Slavery Society convened on 7 May 1851 in City Hall at Syracuse, New York. Many abolitionists hoped that the gathering would reunite the splintered antislavery movement to meet the threat posed by the Fugitive Slave Law. Attempts at harmony foundered when Edmund Quincy proposed that the society support only those papers that denounced the U.S. Constitution as a proslavery document. Frederick Douglass then gained the enmity of Garrisonians by announcing his conversion to political abolitionism and a belief in the antislavery nature of the Constitution. *Lib*, 23 May 1851.

21. The *Anti-Slavery Bugle*, the voice of Garrisonianism in the West, was the official organ of the Western Anti-Slavery Society. From 1845 until its 1861 demise, the journal carried news of the antislavery, temperance, peace, and anti–capital punishment causes to some fifteen hundred readers each week. The Salem, Ohio, paper was edited throughout most of its history by Benjamin S. Jones (1845–49, 1859–61) and Marius Robinson (1851–59). Joseph Anthony Del Porto, "A Study of American Anti-Slavery Journals" (Ph.D. diss., Michigan State College, 1953), 172–79, 290; *ASB*, 5 March 1859, 4 May 1861.

22. The authors of the resolutions refer to the State Councils of the Colored People.

23. Garrisonians blamed Julia Griffiths, Douglass's personal friend and editorial assistant, for causing the breech with their former friend. The *National Anti-Slavery Standard* denounced her as "a Jezebel whose capacity for making mischief between friends would be difficult to match." In its 18 November 1853 issue, the *Liberator* bluntly announced that Griffiths was the cause of marital discord in the Douglass household. Garrison later regretted his remarks on the subject, but he was likely correct, and Griffiths's exit from the Douglass home in late 1852 helped substantiate the charges. Quarles, *Frederick Douglass*, 105–7.

35.
Robert Purvis to Joseph J. Butcher
4 November 1853

Antislavery values guided the daily lives of black abolitionists. Robert Purvis, who owned two large farms in Byberry, Pennsylvania, near Philadelphia, mounted a personal campaign against segregated education when local officials bowed to white pressure and barred his children from the township's public schools. Already angered by a series of racial incidents during the fall of 1853, including his son's exclusion from Philadelphia's Franklin Institute, Purvis refused to pay the school assessment to tax collector Joseph J. Butcher. Purvis wrote abolitionist Charles C. Burleigh, confessing that "it seemed impossible to bear any longer this robbery of my rights and property, by those miserable serviles to the slave power." One day later, in a letter widely reprinted in the antislavery press, Purvis outlined for Butcher his reasons for refusing to pay the tax. At first Byberry officials exempted him from payment, but unwilling to keep one of the township's largest landowners off the tax rolls, they reversed their policy and integrated the schools. *PF*, 10 November 1853 [8:0472]; *Lib*, 21 September 1860; Janice Sumler Lewis, "The Fortens of Philadelphia: An Afro-American Family and Nineteenth-Century Reform" (Ph.D. diss., Georgetown University, 1978), 94–95.

> *Byberry*, [Pennsylvania]
> Nov[ember] 4th, 1853

Dear Sir:[1]

You called yesterday for the tax upon my property in this Township,[2] which I shall pay, excepting the "School Tax." I object to the payment of this tax, on the ground that my rights as a citizen and my feelings as a man and a parent have been grossly outraged in depriving me, in violation of law and justice, of the benefits of the school system, which this tax was designed to sustain. I am perfectly aware that all that makes up the character and worth of the citizens of this township, look upon the proscription and exclusion of my children from the Public School as illegal, and an unjustifiable usurpation of my right. I have borne this outrage ever since the innovation upon the usual practice of admitting *all* the children of the Township into the "Public Schools,"[3] and at considerable expense have been obliged to obtain the services of private teachers to instruct my children, while my school tax is greater, with a single exception, than that of any other citizen of the Township. It is true (and the outrage is made but the more glaringly and insulting), I was informed by a *pious Quaker* director, with a sanctifying grace, imparting doubtless an unctuous glow to his *saintly* prejudices, that a school in the village of Mechanicsville was appropriated for "*thine*." The miserable shanty, with all its appurtenances, on the very line of the township, to which this *benighted* follower of George Fox alluded,[4] is as you know the most flimsy and ridiculous sham which any tool of a skin-hating aristocracy could have resorted to, to cover or protect his servility. To submit by voluntary payment of the demand is too great an outrage upon nature, and with a spirit, thank God, unshackled by this, or any other wanton and cowardly act, I shall resist this tax, which before the unjust exclusion had always afforded me the highest gratification in paying. With no other than the best feeling towards yourself, I am forced to this unpleasant position, in vindication of my rights and personal dignity, against an encroachment upon them as contemptibly mean, as it is infamously despotic. Yours, very respectfully,

ROBERT PURVIS

Pennsylvania Freeman (Philadelphia, Pa.), 10 November 1853.

1. Joseph J. Butcher (1824–?), a New Jersey–born carpenter, also worked as the tax collector of Byberry, Pennsylvania. U.S. Census, 1850.
2. Following the Philadelphia race riot of August 1842, Robert Purvis moved his family to a large and elegant country estate in nearby Byberry. His extensive acreage made him one of the most highly taxed residents of the township. The Purvis family frequently hosted abolitionist friends and fugitive slaves in their Byberry home, gaining for it the name "Saints' Rest." *DANB*, 508–10; Joseph A. Boromé, "The Vigilant Committee of Philadelphia," *PMHB* 92:327 (July 1968).
3. In 1834 the Pennsylvania legislature established a general system of public education in the state. The law made no reference to race and technically allowed blacks to attend the school of their choice. But in practice, local school officials often refused to admit black children. An 1854 revision in the law required districts with twenty or more black students to maintain a separate black school. In the absence of a separate school, districts were required to admit blacks into white classrooms. Edward J. Price, "School Segregation in Nineteenth-Century Pennsylvania," *PH* 43:121–37 (April 1976).
4. George Fox (1624–1691), an English religious thinker, founded the Society of Friends, whose members were popularly known as Quakers.

36.
Charles L. Reason to Editor,
Philadelphia *Daily Register*
24 January 1854

Black abolitionists served as the racial conscience of the antislavery movement. They recognized that black and white abolitionists did not share the same sense of urgency on the issue of prejudice; black leaders found themselves regularly reminding white colleagues of their obligation to promote racial equality as well as end slavery. On the evening of 21 January 1854, Lucy Stone, a Massachusetts abolitionist and feminist, lectured on the subject of "Woman's Rights" to a large audience at Philadelphia's Musical Fund Hall even though the hall's managers refused to seat a group of blacks whom she had invited. At the close of her remarks, she condemned the managers. After the incident, Stone published a brief statement, explaining that news of the episode came to her too late to conveniently cancel the talk; she promised in the future to engage only those halls that admitted blacks. Black abolitionists found Stone's justification unsatisfactory. Frederick Douglass insisted: "We who have to endure the cuffs of proslavery can ill bear to be deserted by our friends." In the following letter, which originally appeared in the Philadelphia *Daily Register*, Charles L. Reason, who was among those expelled from the lecture, reproved Stone for failing to stand firm in defense of her friends and the principle of racial equality. *FDP*, 10, 17 February 1854 [8:0646]; *PF*, 19, 26 January 1854.

PHILADELPHIA, [Pennsylvania]
Jan[uary] 24th, 1854

To the Editor of the Daily Register:[1]
DEAR SIR:

There appeared in your paper of Monday, a card from Lucy Stone,[2] touching the exclusion of some of her friends from Musical Fund Hall,[3] on account of their color. She shields herself from blame for having lectured under the circumstances, on the ground that it was too late to alter the arrangements after the occurrence happened, and further, that at the end of her lecture, she entered her protest against the treatment they had received. Acknowledging our thanks for one of the complimentary tickets distributed by her own directions, we feel called upon at the same time to declare that we think she has failed to exonerate either herself, or the anti-slavery friends who secured the building for her, from a connexion with the proscription which denied us admission on Saturday evening. It is a notorious fact, made more so since the Hutchinson concerts, that colored persons are not permitted to enter Musical Fund

7. Charles L. Reason

Hall, under any circumstances.[4] The lessees are always required to abide by this condition. Indeed it is openly avowed that there are *two* fixed rules in the letting of that building: 1st, That no anti-slavery lecture shall be delivered; and 2dly, That no colored person may form a portion of any audience. The friends who hired the hall for Miss Stone, being long residents of Philadelphia, we think, ought to have known its history so well as not to have contracted for it without assuring themselves as to the position they and she would occupy. That this was in part known, is admitted in the card, where the Curator is represented as having said that he would "close the Hall rather than allow colored people to come in." When it is known that this threat was made to Lucy Stone and James Mott on the afternoon of Saturday, and that early in the morning of that day a forewarning was given them that the invited friends would be denied, the question is submitted, whether as an ultra-abolitionist, Lucy Stone could consistently lecture in that Hall, and *especially* whether, with the known regulations that govern it, her friends had a right to compromise their principles and hers by hiring it!

We do not make a complaint because of our personal ejection, nor that of our friends, for the proscription was intended to be general, and would have been meted out to all others of our class who might have presented themselves. But it does seem reasonable to us that abolitionists should be expected not to pay voluntarily for halls where the stipulations exact from them silence on the question of human freedom, and where, themselves being lecturers, the obligation is imposed upon them to side with our proscribers. Had these tickets not come from the hand of Lucy Stone herself, we should not have ventured the experiment of being admitted, for we knew too well the sternness of the tyranny that stood ready to exercise us; but, under the circumstances, we had a right to believe that we were under the protection of our friends. In this, as it turned out, we were deceived, and the mortification was ours, to see members of the anti-slavery Society[5] pass us at the door, to lose themselves in the throng of our embittered haters, who went rejoicingly to occupy the comfortable seats where they were sure they would in no wise "be elbowed by negroes."

Charles Sumner and Ralph Waldo Emerson refused, in 1845, to lecture before an institution that proscribed persons on account of complexion.[6] Is Lucy Stone or any Garrison Abolitionist of Philadelphia less true to us than these? We hope there will be a show of hands on this question, that we may know whether there is a common cause between us and the Abolitionists, or whether, as circumstances demand, they believe it their right to forsake us for the benefit of other reforms. Very respectfully,

CHAS. L. REASON[7]

Frederick Douglass' Paper (Rochester, N.Y.), 10 February 1854.

1. The Philadelphia *Daily Register* was published from 1847 through 1854. William Birney (1819–1907), the son of noted political abolitionist James G. Birney, edited the paper during its final two years. The younger Birney participated in the French Revolution of 1848, then served as a foreign correspondent for two New York City newspapers before coming to Philadelphia to edit the *Daily Register*. He shared his father's antislavery convictions. A brigadier general in the Union army during the Civil War, Birney recruited black troops in Maryland and the District of Columbia and eventually led them into battle. *A Checklist of Pennsylvania Newspapers: Philadelphia County* (Harrisburg, Pa., 1944), 197; *HTECW*, 61; Ira Berlin et al., eds., *Freedom: A Documentary History of Emancipation, 1861–1867*, 2 ser. to date (Cambridge, England, 1982), 2:184–86.

2. Lucy Stone (1818–1893), a popular antislavery lecturer and feminist, was a lifelong advocate of women's suffrage and marriage reform. She led the call for the first national women's rights convention in 1850. After the Civil War, she helped organize and direct the American Equal Rights Association and the American Woman Suffrage Association. During the 1870s and 1880s, Stone financed and edited the *Woman's Journal*. *NAW*, 3:387–90.

3. The Musical Fund Hall at the corner of Locust Street and Eighth Avenue was one of the foremost meeting places in antebellum Philadelphia. Built by the Musical Fund Society, it regularly hosted dances, orchestral concerts, operas, lectures, and other public gatherings from 1824 to 1857. Popular artists such as Jenny Lind, Ole Bull, Adelina Patti, and Madame Sontag often performed in the hall. Nathaniel Burt, *The Perennial Philadelphians: The Anatomy of an American Aristocracy* (Boston, Mass., 1963), 283, 460–63.

4. In 1849 Philadelphia authorities informed New Hampshire's "Singing Hutchinsons," an enormously popular family of antislavery vocalists, that it would not be possible to protect them from violence if blacks were allowed to attend their local concerts. When Robert Purvis attempted to hear them at the Musical Fund Hall, the manager threatened to cancel their performances unless policemen were posted at the doors to exclude blacks. The Hutchinsons rejected this policy, canceled their tour, and forfeited nearly $1,600. The Hutchinson family continued to be a fixture at antislavery gatherings, as they had since the mid-1840s; they often toured with black abolitionists Frederick Douglass and Robert Purvis. Two Hutchinson "tribes" toured during the late 1850s, but the family's popularity declined shortly after the Civil War. Carol Ryrie Brink, *Harps in the Wind: The Story of the Singing Hutchinsons* (New York, N.Y., 1947); *NSt*, 19 October 1849.

5. Reason refers to white members of the American Anti-Slavery Society and its auxiliary, the Pennsylvania Anti-Slavery Society.

6. In November 1845, Charles Sumner and Ralph Waldo Emerson rejected requests to lecture before the New Bedford Lyceum. Sumner (1811–1874), a prominent Massachusetts abolitionist, later led the Radical Republicans in the U.S. Senate. Emerson (1803–1882), a popular essayist, was the central figure in the Transcendentalist movement. Both were scheduled to speak, but upon learning that the lyceum refused membership to blacks and limited them to the gallery at its public lectures, they canceled their speeches and published letters condemning the offensive racial practices. New Bedford blacks responded by organizing

an interracial lyceum. *DAB*, 6:132–41, 18:208–14; *Lib*, 16 January 1846; Nell, *Colored Patriots*, 114.

7. Charles Lewis Reason (1818–1893) was born in New York City, the son of Haitian immigrants to the United States. Like his brothers, Patrick and Elmer, he was educated at the New York Manumission Society's African Free School. In 1832, when the society decided to employ an all-black staff at the school, Reason's academic accomplishments and special aptitude for mathematics led to his appointment as an instructor. He prepared for the Episcopal clergy but was denied admission to seminary because of his race. Instead he pursued a teaching career. In September 1849, Reason was appointed professor of literature and languages at New York Central College, an interracial institution in McGrawville. Three years later, believing that abolitionists had failed to keep "avenues of industrial labor" open to free blacks, denying them the opportunity to become "self-providing artisans," he left the college to direct Philadelphia's Institute for Colored Youth, a Quaker-sponsored coeducational school that taught vocational and academic subjects. He increased enrollment from 6 to 118 students, built a good library, and developed a popular lecture series. In 1855 he returned to New York City, where for the next thirty-five years he served as a teacher and principal in the black public schools.

Reason's lifelong advocacy of black self-help through education took many forms. He cofounded the Society for the Promotion of Education among Colored Children (1847), served on the education committee at the 1848 black national convention, and was appointed by the 1853 convention to a committee that investigated the feasibility of establishing a black manual labor college. Reason encouraged black adult education, was a leading figure in New York City's Phoenix Society, and urged blacks to support their own national press. A skilled writer, he contributed verse to the *Colored American* and later penned a forty-eight-stanza poem entitled "Freedom" for a published eulogy of Thomas Clarkson. Two of Reason's essays, "Caste Schools" (1850) and "The Colored People's 'Industrial College'" (1854), appealed for equal educational opportunities for his race.

A dedicated abolitionist and advocate of black rights, Reason opposed African colonization and joined numerous organizations devoted to ending slavery, gaining civil rights, and obtaining equal suffrage for blacks. As a founder and leader of the New York Association for the Political Elevation and Improvement of the People of Color, he helped obtain the right of jury trial in 1840 for blacks accused of being fugitive slaves. He later successfully lobbied the New York legislature to revoke the sojourner law, which guaranteed the right of unimpeded movement to slaveholders traveling through the state with their slaves. While in Philadelphia, he aided fugitives as a member of the General Vigilance Committee. Reason also helped organize several black national and state conventions and served as secretary of many of these gatherings. In 1848 he attended the Free Soil party's founding convention in Buffalo. Reason was a member of the local Citizens' Civil Rights Committee during the Civil War and continued his struggle against racial prejudice throughout the postwar decades as an active member of several black educational and protective organizations. *DANB*, 516–17; Anthony R. Mayo, "Charles Lewis Reason," *NHB* 5:212–15 (June 1942); Mabee, *Black Education in New York State*, 60–66, 83, 89–90, 105–8, 112, 121–28,

150, 153, 167–69, 201, 215, 218–20; *CA*, 19 August, 2, 23 September 1837, 15 March, 16 June, 1, 8 September, 6, 22 October, 16 December 1838, 14 September, 28 November 1840, 16, 30 January, 5, 19 June, 3, 10 July 1841 [2:0152, 0167, 0196, 0198, 0436, 0494, 0572, 0580, 0608, 0622, 0680, 3:0615, 0722, 0834, 0857, 4:0047, 0068, 0091, 0099]; *NSt*, 21 January 1848, 11 May 1849, 13 June, 24 October 1850; *PF*, 2 October, 9 December 1852, 7 April, 28 July 1853, 30 April 1854 [8:0199, 0706]; *IC*, 14 February 1849; *WAA*, 21 April, 26 May 1860, 2 November 1861 [12:0646, 0650, 0685, 0728]; *NASS*, 28 May 1864 [15:0362].

37.
Report by the Committee on Slavery
of the New England Conference
of the African Methodist Episcopal Church

Presented at the Bethel African Methodist Episcopal Church
Providence, Rhode Island
26 January 1854

Black churches were at the center of the antislavery movement. Ministers offered leadership, congregations provided essential support, and
church buildings served as abolitionist meetinghouses and stations on
the underground railroad. But prior to 1850, black denominations were
often more circumspect than their individual congregations, limiting
themselves to spiritual matters, or in the case of the African Methodist
Episcopal church, equivocating on the issue out of concern for their
congregations in the slave states. Events of the 1850s changed the relationship between black religious organizations and the antislavery
movement. In the wake of the Fugitive Slave Law and the Kansas-Nebraska Act, black denominations became militant opponents of slavery.
The African Methodist Episcopal Zion church denounced the institution at its 1852 annual conference; the American Baptist Missionary
Convention, which represented twenty-six northern black congregations, followed suit the next year; and the Evangelical Association of the
Colored Ministers of Congregational and Presbyterian Churches issued
antislavery protests later in the decade. Typifying this new forthright-
ness, the AME's New England Conference approved antislavery resolutions at its January 1854 assembly. Meeting in Providence, Rhode Island, these black clergymen drafted an unequivocal denunciation of
slaveholding, characterizing the practice as "the sum of all villainies."
Payne, *African Methodist Episcopal Church*, 334–45; Quarles, *Black
Abolitionists*, 81–84; James Melvin Washington, *Frustrated Fellowship:
The Black Baptist Quest for Social Power* (Macon, Ga., 1986), 34–40.

> *Providence*, [Rhode Island]
> *January 26th*, 1854
> To the Bishops and Annual Conference of the A. M. E. Church now in
> session in the City of Providence, R.I.:[1]

We, your committee to whom was referred the subject of slavery, beg
leave most respectfully to submit the following report as the result of our
deliberation:

WHEREAS, The slave power is bent on its course of systematic oppression and injustice towards our race, robbing us of our liberty, breaking

in upon the peace of our homes, carrying many of our dear friends from a land of liberty to that of cruel and merciless bondage, without due process of law, regardless of all the groans and tears of a Christian community;

AND WHEREAS, New slave territories have been added to it, wresting a large section of country from the domain of freedom, a section whose freedom from slavery rested upon a historic fact in the Annals of American Legislation,[2] but which has been denied by the slavery propaganda; therefore,

Resolved, That we, as a body, do, in the name of Almighty God, utter a solemn protest against slavery in all conditions, believing it to be the sum of all villainies—that is, take wrong, violence and injustice; take cruelty, hard-heartedness and contempt for the rights and interests of humanity; take fornication, adultery, concubinage of the different races of the human family, in all their acts—among all, there is none more cruel, more wicked, more unrighteous, than the cruel system of slavery. In its system are theft, robbery and murder. Add them all together, and the sum total will be slavery.

Resolved, That in the enactment and passage of the Fugitive Slave Law, and the more recent act, namely, the repealing of the Compromise of 1820, in the passage of the Nebraska Bill[3]—in these wicked and cruel acts are burning coals of fire, which will burn to the lowest hell. Over them all hovers the dark angel of night, covering them with the dark mantle of wickedness.

Resolved, That we have entire confidence in the promises of God to deliver the oppressed nations of earth from the thraldom of sin and slavery, and to establish righteousness and truth, life and liberty, to all the human race.

Resolved, That until our voices are heard no more we will wage a lifelong and sleepless warfare with the principles of slavery in all its varied forms.

Resolved, That we appoint a committee at this Conference, now in session, to wait on the Hon. William W. Hoppin, now Governor of this state,[4] and present to him a copy of our resolutions on the slavery question, and ask his influence in behalf of the colored citizens of this state, many of whom are members of our churches.

Voted that the committee consist of the Bishops of this Conference— Rt. Rev. Daniel A. Payne[5] and Rt. Rev. Willis Nazrey.[6]

REV. W. H. JONES, *Chairman*

W. M. WATSON   *Committee*

REV. G. A. STANFORD   *on*

C. H. PEARCE   *Slavery*[7]

REV. JAMES HYATT

Daniel A. Payne, *History of the African Methodist Episcopal Church* (Nashville, Tenn., 1891; reprint, New York, N.Y., 1968), 307–8.

1. Bishops Daniel A. Payne and Willis Nazrey presided over the 1854 annual gathering of the New England Conference, the youngest and smallest administrative conference in the African Methodist Episcopal denomination at that time. Organized in 1852, the conference represented 608 members in eight congregations from Connecticut to Maine. The AME (often called Bethel Methodist) church was a leading black denomination during the antebellum period. It came to life when discriminatory seating practices prompted black parishioners to withdraw from individual Methodist congregations in Baltimore (1787) and Philadelphia (1792) in favor of establishing their own semi-independent black Methodist churches. In 1816, seeking greater black control over congregational affairs, these congregations joined three other black churches in the mid-Atlantic states to found the AME church. The denomination grew rapidly, soon establishing foreign missions and a thriving publishing program for its religious materials. After emancipation, the AME actively competed for converts among black Methodists in the South and dramatically increased its numbers and influence. The denomination currently claims more than two million members. Payne, *African Methodist Episcopal Church*, 284–87, 294–95, 306–8; Carol George, *Segregated Sabbaths: Richard Allen and the Rise of Independent Black Churches, 1760–1840* (New York, N.Y., 1973), 51–119; Clarence E. Walker, *A Rock in a Weary Land: The African Methodist Episcopal Church during the Civil War and Reconstruction* (Baton Rouge, La., 1982), 4–5, 8–15, 19, 46–81, 99–103.

2. The committee refers to the 1820 Missouri Compromise line of 36°30′—the traditional demarcation between free and slave territory.

3. The committee refers to a bill introduced into the U.S. Congress in 1853 to organize two territories—Kansas and Nebraska—from the vast northern lands between Iowa and the Rocky Mountains. Southern senators protested because slavery would be prohibited in these new territories by the provisions of the Missouri Compromise (1820). The compromise, which granted statehood to Missouri and Maine in order to maintain the numerical balance between free and slave states, banned slavery in the remaining portions of the Louisiana Purchase north of 36°30′. In January 1854, Senator Stephen A. Douglas of Illinois overcame southern opposition to the bill by calling for the repeal of the Missouri Compromise. He proposed instead that "all questions pertaining to slavery in the Territories . . . be left to the people residing therein," a concept called "popular sovereignty." In May, after five months of bitter debate, Congress approved the Kansas-Nebraska Act. The new law angered many in the North, prompting the formation of the Republican party and pushing the nation even closer to civil war.

4. William W. Hoppin (1807–1890), a member of the Know Nothing party, served as governor of Rhode Island from 1854 to 1856. He opposed the Kansas-Nebraska Act and in 1856 urged the state legislature to call for the admission of Kansas as a free state. *DAB*, 5:227–28; Arline Ruth Kiven, *Then Why the Negroes: The Nature and Course of the Anti-Slavery Movement in Rhode Island, 1637–1861* (n.p., 1973), 72–73.

5. Daniel A. Payne (1811–1893) was the dominant figure in the African Methodist Episcopal denomination during the second half of the nineteenth century. He was born in Charleston, South Carolina, to free black parents, who provided for his early education. Payne established his own school in 1828 but was forced to close it when the South Carolina legislature prohibited the teaching of blacks. He left Charleston in 1835. After studying for two years at the Evangelical Lutheran Seminary in Gettysburg, Pennsylvania, he quit because of failing eyesight, obtained a license to preach, and in 1839 became the first black clergyman ordained by the Franckean Evangelical Lutheran Synod. Payne briefly served a white Presbyterian congregation in Troy, New York, then in 1840 he opened a coeducational school in Philadelphia. During this time, he became involved in the antislavery movement. He addressed the annual meeting of the American Anti-Slavery Society in 1837, helped the Vigilant Committee of Philadelphia protect fugitive slaves, spoke at First of August celebrations, and solicited financial support for the *Colored American*.

His hopes of serving a Lutheran parish never materialized, and in 1841 he joined the AME church. At first he hesitated to enter the black denomination because of the animosity of many members to an educated clergy. Payne's preference for formal, liturgical worship and well-trained ministers contrasted with the emotional, spontaneous style of many AME pastors and congregations. He worked to standardize AME worship, improve church education, and preserve a record of the denomination's history. This earned the respect of church leaders, and in 1852 he was named a bishop. Payne, more than any other individual, shaped the character and policies of the denomination. Under his leadership, the AME expanded its home and foreign missions, reorganized its publication department, and revived its periodical under a new name—the *Christian Recorder*. After the Civil War, he organized the AME's South Carolina Conference, which became the base for the denomination's rapid growth among the freedmen.

Payne also gained renown as an educator and author. During the late 1830s, he founded the Mental and Moral Improvement Society of Troy and participated in the American Moral Reform Society. Many of his poems, essays, speeches, and sermons were published in the black press. His autobiographical *Recollections of Seventy Years* (1888) and *History of the African Methodist Episcopal Church* (1891) are important contributions to black literature and valuable sources for nineteenth-century black history. In 1863 Payne was named president of Wilberforce University, the first black-controlled college in the United States. He made the institution solvent, attracted capable students and educators, and enhanced its reputation. Although he resigned the presidency of Wilberforce in 1876, he remained active in its administration until his death. An internationally recognized Methodist leader during his later years, Payne was a conspicuous figure in the World Parliament of Religions at the World's Columbian Exposition in Chicago (1893). *DANB*, 484–85; Milton C. Sernett, *Black Religion and American Evangelicalism: White Protestants, Plantation Missions, and the Flowering of Negro Christianity, 1787–1865* (Metuchen, N.J., 1975), 131–35; Minute Book of the Vigilant Committee of Philadelphia, 1839–44, Leon Gardiner Collection, PHi [3:0102]; *Lib*, 30 August 1839 [3:0186]; *CA*, 7, 14 October 1837, 28 September 1839, 7, 14 November, 12 December 1840, 3 April 1841 [2:0212, 0223, 3:0212, 0696, 0703, 0745, 0971]; *NECAUL*, 14, 21 September 1837 [2:0184, 0192–93].

6. Willis T. Nazrey (1808–1875), an African Methodist Episcopal bishop, was born to free black parents in Isle of Wight, Virginia. He worked as a mariner for several years before settling in New York City. After becoming an itinerant AME minister in 1840, he served congregations in the New York, Baltimore, and Philadelphia conferences. Nazrey's tireless and devoted labors culminated in 1852 in his election to an AME bishopric, which he used to introduce administrative reforms and to encourage denominational involvement in Canadian, Caribbean, and African mission work. He moved to Chatham, Canada West, to better supervise AME expansion in the Canadas, and in 1856 he was elected bishop of a newly organized denomination—the British Methodist Episcopal church. Nazrey devoted most of his time to administrative tasks—organizing and visiting congregations throughout Canada West and attending annual church conferences in the United States. He recruited subscribers for the *Provincial Freeman* during these travels. Nazrey endorsed Haitian emigration in the early 1860s and later served as an officer of the African Civilization Society. His position as a bishop of two denominations created a lingering controversy that was finally resolved with his resignation from the AME church in 1864. But Nazrey remained interested in American affairs and served as a director of the Lincoln Monument Association. Throughout his career, he was noted more for his businesslike manner and his "promptness and force of character" than his oratory or intellect. Wayman, *Cyclopaedia of African Methodism*, 4; Payne, *African Methodist Episcopal Church*, 127, 134, 138, 287–88, 292–93, 306–8, 382–83; Daniel A. Payne, *Recollections of Seventy Years* (Nashville, Tenn., 1888; reprint, New York, N.Y., 1969), 141, 144–45, 158; *CR*, 18 June 1864, 2 September 1875, 14 February 1901; *PFW*, 10 June 1854; *PP*, 6 July 1861; *ESF*, 28 July 1865 [15:1082].

7. All five members of the Committee on Slavery were recent additions to the African Methodist Episcopal clergy ranks, having been ordained between 1845 and 1852. William H. Jones (?–1915) was traveling book agent for the denomination's press. George A. Stanford was serving a congregation in Bridgeport, Connecticut. William M. Watson (1822–1888), Charles H. Pearce (1817–1887), and James Hyatt were itinerant ministers assigned to the New England Conference. At least three of these men had seen slavery firsthand—Pearce was born a slave in Queen Anne County, Virginia; Watson was born and reared in Sussex County, Delaware; Jones grew up in the free black community of Baltimore. These five went on to have varied careers. Hyatt and Stanford soon left the AME ministry, the latter because of allegations of spouse abuse. Watson served AME parishes in New Jersey until about 1880. Jones and Pearce accepted calls to churches in Chatham, Canada West, where they became instrumental in forming the British Methodist Episcopal denomination, which seceded from the AME in 1856. The two men became bitter rivals in the early 1860s. In 1865 Pearce moved to Florida, where he supervised AME missionary work among the freedmen, served in the state senate, and became a powerful figure in the Republican party. Jones toured Britain from 1865 through 1868, raising funds to aid the freedmen. He later did missionary work in Tennessee. Ripley et al., *Black Abolitionist Papers*, 2:487–89n; Payne, *African Methodist Episcopal Church*, 184, 199–200, 215, 255, 286, 306, 321; *CR*, 20 October, 17 November 1855, 13 September 1888.

38.
Editorial by William J. Watkins
10 February 1854

Blacks were bitterly disappointed by the hypocrisy they encountered within the antislavery movement. Many white abolitionists championed the idea of racial equality, but only a few accepted blacks as equal partners in the cause. White reformers generally hired blacks for menial tasks, if at all, and such an obvious contradiction between abolitionist theory and practice disturbed black leaders. William J. Wilson observed whites who espoused sympathy for blacks but spent "not one dollar to make a practical example of the capacity of a single colored man." William J. Watkins, a talented journalist with *Frederick Douglass' Paper*, found such duplicity intolerable. In a 10 February 1854 editorial, he argued that racism would not be eliminated as long as blacks were "mere hewers of wood and drawers of water." White businessmen who claimed reform principles had an obligation to employ blacks in meaningful positions, he maintained, yet they lacked the "moral courage" to exercise their beliefs, fearing it would hurt their businesses. Arguing that their failure to employ blacks perpetuated racial prejudice, Watkins challenged white abolitionists to "live out practically the doctrines they so faithfully promulgate." Pease and Pease, *They Who Would Be Free*, 85–86.

One Thing Thou Lackest

Nearly a quarter of a century has elapsed since the inception of the immediate emancipation movement in this country. A vast amount of money has been expended by the Abolitionists in developing the atrocious iniquity, the insatiable cupidity, the Anti-Republicanism of the Slave Power. Books, and tracts, and newspapers have been sent forth on their errand of light and love, but the slave still mingles his groans with the soul-harrowing screams of the American Eagle. Conventions have assembled and reassembled; they have resolved that the last fetter should be broken, and the slave should be a man; but "horses, slaves, and other *cattle*" are still sold, in the noonday, at public vendue; yes, they have, in their resolutions, placed us who are nominally free, upon the broad platform of Equality, and yet, we are still the victims of the relentless ferocity of pro-slavery hate.

Now, we have a word to say to the Abolitionists, who have pled our cause so eloquently; those who, for our sake, have become "of no reputation," and stood up manfully, despite the pitiless pelting of the raging storm. We gratefully appreciate their labors of love; they have done well and nobly. We have, as a people, been advised to repudiate our affinity with the Abolitionists of the country. But we know who are our friends, and who, our enemies; and we have drawn a broad line of distinction between them. What we have to say is addressed to no particular school of the Abolitionists, but to Medians and Parthians, and also to the dwellers in Mesopotamia; in a word, to all whose sympathies and affinities are on the side of universal liberty.[1] We despise the honied words of flattery. When the magnanimous Cromwell was about to sit for his picture, he was informed that an omission of the scars would enhance the comeliness of his features. "*Paint me as I am*," he indignantly replied, and the artist did so.[2]

We are men, conscious of the dignity of manhood, and as MEN, do we speak to the noble advocates of Freedom. Have we, then, in view of their efforts to ameliorate our condition, anything more to ask at their hands? Have we any accusation to bring against them? Any voice of complaint to utter?

To these plain interrogatories, we plainly answer YES. Come, brethren, let us reason together. But, in the first place, we would enquire, what have the Abolitionists not done, that they could do? What is the "*one thing*" which they still lack? We reply: *they lack a practical exemplification of the doctrines they inculcate.*

On the one hand, Colonizationists affirm that, in the inflexible economy of the Divine arrangement, it is ordained that the white and the black races cannot live together in this country, on terms of equality; that the "*black man must eventually go to the wall.*" They tell us that God has drawn a line of demarcation between them. They assume the position of our innate mental and moral inferiority. Prejudice against the black man, they affirm to be perfectly natural and, consequently, invincible. And their action is in perfect accordance with their expressed opinions. They appear to hate us with a perfect hatred. That they really believe what they affirm, we deny *in toto*; but it is a fact that the unmitigated severity of their treatment toward us, made manifest in their barbarous legislation, the object of which is to drive us from the country, is in exact conformity with the theory they promulgate.

Now, what is the doctrine of the Abolitionists? The equality of the races is the foundation stone of their theory. They affirm that "God hath made of one blood all nations, to dwell on all the face of the earth."[3] They thunder their terrible anathemas against those who deny the fact of our natural equality. They speak forth in terms of bitter reproach, and well merited denunciation, against the institution of those unnatural distinctions, founded upon the contingency of birth, fortune, education, or complexion. They not only deny the allegations of pro-slavery hate, concerning us, but affirm, as the result of their deliberate convictions, that we shall yet stand forth, in *this, the land of our birth*, a redeemed people. And we very naturally sympathize with them in the utterance of these sentiments, and have irrevocably determined to REMAIN HERE, and help them work out our salvation.

That there shall be no strife between us, we must perfectly understand each other. We, then, believe that this complexional distinction will never be annihilated, while we, *as a class*, occupy secondary positions in society. Our aspirations must be of an elevated character. It is folly in the extreme to talk about *living down* American prejudice, so long as we are regarded as mere hewers of wood and drawers of water. We must be something more than clay in the hands of the potter, to be moulded and fashioned according to his good will and pleasure. We must fill the same positions that white men occupy. We would have no one suppose that we are suppliants for favor; what we DEMAND is our unrestricted rights as freemen. Upon our merits, are we prepared to stand, or fall. If we are qualified to act as clerks in countinghouses, the doors should be thrown open. If we desire to teach our children trades, their complexion should be no barrier. Our lawyers, and physicians, and mechanics must be encouraged. Now, we do not expect our revilers, our virulent enemies, to take us into their countinghouses, their workshops, or have us write a recipe for *their* headache, or extract a tooth for them, or be their mouthpiece to the gentlemen of the Jury.

Upon whom, then, would we naturally suppose the responsibility rests? Why, upon the Abolitionists, those who sympathize with us in our affliction, and declare American Prejudice to be a heinous crime against God and man. Now, what are the facts in the case? Do the Abolitionists themselves act towards us as though they were devoid of prejudice against color, or condition? They do not. When the writer of this came to Boston, a few years ago, he found this prejudice at the North much more virulent than at the South. He read the following advertisement in the papers, and applied for the situation: "WANTED—A clerk who will be satisfied the first year, with a moderate salary. None but a first rate penman need apply," &c., &c. I was recommended to the advertiser by several well known gentlemen in Boston, and was told he was a good Abolitionist. I went into his countinghouse boldly, as a *man* would go. I made known my business. He looked at me and laughed, and virtually informed me I had mistaken my vocation. I told him I approached him as a friend, and that I took him to be an Abolitionist. "Who sent you here," he enquired. I handed him my "recommendations," which he read with much attention. Laughter was portrayed in every lineament of his countenance, when I informed him the object of my visit, but now his visage assumed a more somber aspect. His face reddened, *and so did mine*; his with shame, mine with indignation. He was the victim of an exigency he did not anticipate. He tested my ability, and upon my inquiring whether or not I complied with the requisition of the advertisement, he frankly replied, your COLOR IS THE ONLY OBJECTION. He told me the *time had not come yet* for colored men to apply for such situations; the prejudice against them precluded the possibility of success. But, said I, do you not cater to this wicked prejudice, when you "thrust me out on account of my complexion?" He sympathized with me, and was willing to do anything else for me in his power. I left him, having formed a rather unfavorable opinion of *his* Abolitionism.

Now, this is not an isolated instance. Such instances might be multiplied almost *ad infinitum.*

Now, the accusation we make, in candor and sincerity, against the Abolitionists, as a class, is that they lack the moral courage to *actualize* their ideas. They will not take us into their countinghouses, or workshops, for fear of "impairing their business." In a word, we are *colored* men in their estimation, and so are we in the estimation of "*crushers*" of Abolitionism.

Now if the Abolitionists wish to see this prejudice vanish like frostwork before the rising sun, they must begin the great work by "conquering *their* prejudices"; and live out practically the doctrines they so faithfully promulgate. But we must, for the present, close this article, asking for it a candid perusal.

W.

Frederick Douglass' Paper (Rochester, N.Y.), 10 February 1854.

1. Watkins equates the diversity within the antislavery movement to the international assembly in Jerusalem during the day of Pentecost described in Acts 2. The biblical account describes this assembly as consisting of "Parthians, and Medes, and Elamites, and the dwellers in Mesopotamia," and residents of other regions in the ancient world.

2. Oliver Cromwell (1599–1658) led the Puritan forces during the English Civil War, overthrew King Charles I, and ruled England with a dictatorial hand from 1651 until his death. Watkins paraphrases remarks by Cromwell that were recorded in Horace Walpole's massive *Anecdotes of Painting in England* (1762).

3. Watkins quotes from Acts 17:26.

39.
Charles L. Reason to "Fugitive Slaves and Their Friends"
1 March 1854

The ordeal of fugitive slaves did not end with their safe arrival in the free states. The continued threat of slave catchers called for caution, discretion, and even deception. To protect themselves and their families, fugitives assumed new identities, altered details in their personal histories, and hid their slave past even from their children in some cases. They exercised particular care in their correspondence with family and friends still in the South. Their caution was well placed. Southerners monitored mail from the North, censoring "incendiary" abolitionist literature and examining letters to free blacks for information about escaped slaves. Harriet A. Jacobs, a fugitive, inserted misleading information in her correspondence to protect herself and those who helped her escape. Charles L. Reason, a leading member of the General Vigilance Committee of Philadelphia, published the following notice in the 1 March 1854 issue of the *Pennsylvania Freeman* to warn "fugitives and their friends" about the risks of writing to free blacks in the South. He emphasized the danger to the recipient, who could be arrested and imprisoned on the *"mere suspicion"* of involvement in slave escapes. *DANB*, 631; Jacobs, *Life of a Slave Girl*, 128–32, 165–66, 190–201; Clement Eaton, *The Freedom of Thought Struggle in the Old South* (New York, N.Y., 1964), 89–117.

Phil[adelphia], [Pennsylvania]
March 1, 1854
TO FUGITIVE SLAVES AND THEIR FRIENDS
We desire to remonstrate, in the kindest spirit, against the custom which is becoming very common, of writing letters from Canada, and from places in the Northern and Eastern States, to free colored persons residing South, on matters touching fugitives who have made good their escape. Letters are frequently sent from fugitives themselves, who have left perhaps wives or children behind, begging that means may be adopted to favor *their* escape also. When it is remembered that the custom is very general at the South, and in some places uniform, *to open all letters addressed to colored persons*; and when, as it frequently happens, persons are called upon to finish a work which they had no hand in beginning; it will be seen how easily a father or husband may be snatched up by the law, and, on *mere suspicion*, made to drag out a tedious and miserable imprisonment. *Fugitive friends have no letters written South.* Your thoughtless act may break up forever the happiness of many a

8. Mob ransacking the Charleston, South Carolina, post office for antislavery literature

Courtesy of the American Antiquarian Society

family, besides preventing others, yet slaves, from effecting their escape. We hope that our advice will be made known to all interested, especially to those who are unable to read this caution; and that papers friendly to the oppressed will give this warning general circulation.

C. L. R.

Pennsylvania Freeman (Philadelphia, Pa.), 10 March 1854.

40.
Editorial by William J. Watkins
3 March 1854

Black abolitionists wavered between hope and despair during the 1850s. The Fugitive Slave Law, the Kansas-Nebraska Act, and other federal legislation were distressing setbacks to the antislavery cause. But as northern popular opinion turned against these statutes, a new enthusiasm and hopefulness infused the movement, and antislavery leaders eagerly awaited a swelling of the ranks. William J. Watkins shared this optimism. Returning from a lecture tour with "Anti-Nebraska written on [his] brow," he found public sentiment "wrought up to the highest pitch of enthusiasm" against the Kansas-Nebraska bill. In an editorial written for the 3 March 1854 issue of *Frederick Douglass' Paper*, Watkins predicted that the bill would have "a most salutary influence in working out the salvation of the American Slave." *FDP*, 10, 17, 24, 31 March, 14 April 1854 [8:0678, 0685–86, 0694, 0709–10, 0734].

Effect of the Nebraska Bill

Whether or not the infamous Nebraska Bill of Senator Douglas[1] will receive sufficient support from the craven hearted North, its introduction in Congress, at this eventful crisis, will have a most salutary influence in working out the salvation of the American Slave. Slaveholders and their apologists are unconsciously erecting a gallows upon which to hang themselves. They are doing much toward the overthrow of the foul system of slavery. They are, morning, noon, and night, developing its crushing cruelty, its savage iniquity. Their actions speak more loudly than words. They talk to the North of the danger accruing from the agitation of the question, and then when all the world is gazing at them, burn up human beings, and give their flesh to dogs! They speak through the press, and from the pulpit, of the humane and christianizing influence of the peculiar institution, and then do some dark and damning deed which gives the lie to their meaningless asseverations.

The friends of the Slave might travel thro' every State and County, and City and Town, and hamlet, north of Mason's and Dixon's line,[2] and endeavor by the "foolishness of preaching" to awake the slumbering North to a consciousness of the fearful aggression, the ever grasping cupidity of the Slave power; but both priest and Politician will write fanaticism on our brow, and bid us sound no note of warning, but sing and dance, and dream, for nought they see but what is bright and beautiful.

But when Senator Douglas, the Illinois Senator, and Mississippi slaveholder,[3] speaks, and evinces a determination to act out his speeches—when the proposition is seriously made to them to yield all the unorganized territory of the union to the ravages of the Slave power—when they behold the foul footprint of the rapacious monster upon their own hearthstones, and the solemn compact of their fathers about to be thrown to the winds, then it is that slavery becomes to them a terrible, tangible, inflexible reality. Hence, we behold the North at length awakened to a sense of danger. Senator Douglas hath touched her eyes, and they are opened. She now knows that the South cares for the North only on condition that she behaves herself, or in other words, consents to have the manhood "crushed" out of her.

This Nebraska swindle has set the mind of the North at work, and judging from the accounts of meetings held throughout the free States, denouncing the Bill and its advocates—Whig and Democratic meetings, attended and addressed by men whose lips were hermetically sealed in 1850, by the Baltimore Inquisition[4]—we rather think, that, upon the whole, God is making the wrath of man to praise him, in a way and manner of which we had not dreamed in our philosophy. The Bill, then, works like a charm. Let us all continue to hope. We have much to animate and encourage us. Agitation lives and breathes in an element of immortality. Its fires burn more fiercely now than ever. Our enemies are as restless as the troubled sea. They know retribution is on the wing. The clanking of the chain is heard. The slave will yet be free. His morn will yet appear, for the light hath, at last, shined into his dark habitation, and revealed a picture of cruelty and iniquity, the sight of which shall call forth the indignation of every lover of liberty throughout the world; and this indignation shall "clothe itself as with a garment,"[5] and sweep the monster of slavery into the dark abyss of ruin, as though a whirlwind had breathed upon it.

W.

Frederick Douglass' Paper (Rochester, N.Y.), 3 March 1854.

1. Stephen A. Douglas (1813–1861) represented Illinois in the U.S. Senate from 1847 to 1861. The diminutive Democrat played a central and controversial role in congressional debates over the Compromise of 1850, the Kansas-Nebraska Act, and other issues related to slavery. His name became closely identified with the concept of popular sovereignty, the belief that the people of a territory should decide if slavery would exist there. The famous Lincoln-Douglas debates (1858) assured his reelection to the Senate but doomed his bid for the presidency in 1860. *DAB*, 5:397–403.

2. The Mason-Dixon line symbolized the dividing line between the slave and free states. The name came from a survey completed in 1763 and 1767 by Charles Mason and Jeremiah Dixon, which settled boundary differences between Pennsylvania and Maryland.

3. In 1847 Stephen A. Douglas married Martha Martin, the daughter of a Lawrence County, Mississippi, slaveholder. One year later, she inherited her fa-

ther's sizable plantation and 142 slaves. Douglas managed the estate until 1857, in exchange for 20 percent of its annual income. Robert W. Johannsen, "Stephen A. Douglas and the South," *JSH* 33:29–30 (February 1967).

4. In June 1852, both the Democrats and the Whigs adopted platforms endorsing the Compromise of 1850 at their presidential nominating conventions in Baltimore. Watkins suggests that many northern politicians, who once thought the slavery question to have been settled by the compromise, were now speaking out against the Kansas-Nebraska Act (1854). David M. Potter, *The Impending Crisis, 1848–1861* (New York, N.Y., 1976), 141–42, 232–33.

5. Watkins paraphrases Psalms 104:6.

41.
Essay by Jacob C. White, Jr.
24 March 1854

The transformation of the black temperance movement reflected broader changes in black abolitionist thought. During the 1830s, black leaders viewed temperance in the context of moral reform, arguing that by abstaining from alcoholic beverages blacks would gain the respect of whites and thereby diminish prejudice. By the 1850s, black temperance advocates changed their appeal. Abandoning moral reform rhetoric, with its emphasis on white expectations, they placed the alcohol question in an explicit antislavery framework—by rejecting alcohol, blacks would demonstrate their commitment to the slave and the survival of the northern black community. In a 24 March 1854 essay, Jacob C. White, Jr., a rising member of Philadelphia's black elite, embodied the earnest views of this new generation of black leaders. Conscious of his responsibility to the black community, he urged blacks to live sober, virtuous lives, so that "they should have men to fight their battles, and contend with our enemies for our rights." Donald Yacovone, "The Transformation of the Black Temperance Movement, 1827–1854," *JER* 8:281–97 (Fall 1988).

Phil[adelphia], [Pennsylvania]
Mar[ch] 24th, 1854
What Rum is doing for the Colored People
We are all familiar with the effects produced by intoxicating liquors. We hear temperance lectures plainly setting forth the evils of intemperance and admonishing the youth to beware lest they should fall into the net which surrounds them on all sides, and become less than worthless to Society. Notwithstanding the admonitions which are daily given to our young men, we find them frequenting these earthly hells, not only throwing away the time which might be improved with great advantage both to themselves and to the people at large, but also throwing away their money for that which brings unto them nothing but want, misery, death, and eternal torment. A vast amount of good might be accomplished if the money spent by our young men, for liquors[,] was employed for the purpose of elevating our people and promoting the cause of education among them. Aside from this, the Respectable Groggeries are ruining the very class of our people to whom we are to look as warriors who are to fight for us for our liberty, and our rights, when the heads of our Fathers Shall be laid low in the silent tomb, and wrapped in the cold embrace of death (shall be those who are now so earnestly pleading for suffering humanity, and their immortal souls have taken their flight to receive the

recompense for the deeds done in the service of their people). If there is any people who have a good reason for advocating the passage of the "Maine Liquor Law," or some other kind of prohibitory liquor law,[1] it is the Colored people of this country: if for nothing but a matter of policy. So that they should have men to fight their battles, and contend with our enemies for our rights, which state of things cannot possibly exist if the grog shops are not Suppressed or some measures taken to reclaim our young men who have been so unfortunate as to become addicted to the habit of drinking rum. Let us then do all that we can to eradicate this evil, and put forth all our energies for the purpose of having the youth trained in such a manner that they will be fitted for usefulness when they grow up to be men & women. When this is accomplished we will see a marked difference in the Colored People of this country, in a political and social point of view.

Jacob C. White

Leon Gardiner Collection, Historical Society of Pennsylvania, Philadelphia, Pennsylvania. Published by permission.

1. The Maine Liquor Law (1851) prohibited the sale and manufacture of alcoholic beverages except by licensed agents for medical or industrial use. As the first state prohibition act, it provided a model for temperance advocates throughout the nation. By 1855 twelve northern and western states had enacted similar legislation. Tyrrell, *Sobering Up*, 252–89.

42.
Editorial by William J. Watkins
7 April 1854

Black and white abolitionists shared an uneasy awareness of their role as leaders of a reform movement. Most Americans viewed social reformers with ambivalence, suspicion, or even hatred. Ralph Waldo Emerson admired their quest for a better world but criticized their idealism, charging that it inevitably led to extremism, contentiousness, and narrowness of vision. William J. Watkins took a more laudatory view in his 7 April 1854 editorial in *Frederick Douglass' Paper*. During his recent antislavery lecture tour, which took him throughout western New York, he gained new insights about the qualities required of an effective reformer. Watkins accentuated the reformer's need for moral courage and perseverance in the face of apathy, adversity, and public hostility. David Brion Davis, ed., *Ante-Bellum Reform* (New York, N.Y., 1967), 11–18; *FDP*, 17 March, 21, 28 April, 12 May, 2, 9, 30 June, 28 July 1854.

The Reformer

Agitation has always been the life blood of all reformatory movements. These movements, in their inception and onward, have ever encountered the most virulent opposition. Man is so constituted that he adheres, with inflexible tenacity, to preconceived opinions. These cannot be attacked with impunity. The bold and dashing Reformer, who walks to and fro, with the besom of destruction in his right hand—whose business seems to be to scatter, tear, and slay, meets with opposition from almost every quarter. He lives in the tempest. He does not feed upon the oil and wine of popular sympathy, but upon the vinegar and gall of the people's hate. He beholds arrayed against him their seemingly invincible prejudices. He comes with his flaming sword, and must penetrate, if he would be successful in the end, the incrustations of ignorance, in which he finds imbedded, man's mental and moral organism. It requires a strong nerve, and potent arm, determined will, moral courage, strong powers of analysis, depth and breadth of comprehension, indomitable perseverance, correct judgement, and a worldwide heart, full of hope and love, to make an effectual Reformer, one whose tongue should sting like a thousand scorpions, and whose pen should manufacture words of fire, clothed with superhuman energy, and almost unearthly power.

A timid man can no more make a Reformer, than can an ass become a lion. A fearful man flees from his own shadow. The Reformer has to deal not with mere shadows, but with substances—substances, too, which assume a terrible aspect. Some men claim to be Reformers, who are

wholly destitute of that moral courage, which enables a man to speak
out the honest convictions of his soul. One may possess, to almost any
extent, *physical* courage, and know nothing experimentally of *moral*
courage. He may stand before the cannon's mouth, and laugh amid its
mighty thunderings; but at the same time, he may be afraid of the burning words of truth which would proceed from *his own mouth*, if suffered
to do so. Such a man is afraid of himself, and will never make a true
Reformer. This class of men are always found crying out lustily against
all true Reforms, and true Reformers. They fear the masses. They are
ever characterized by that spaniel-like obsequiousness, and lick-the-dust
servility, which are essential ingredients in that *un*manly compound, everywhere known by the name of coward. These poor souls must consent
to get out of the way at this crisis. It is suicidal for them to stand in the
way of the true Reformer, who, in his onward course, will most assuredly
crush them. O that their eyes were opened, that they might "see themselves as others see them!"[1]

We want more living men; of dead men, we have enough already. That
the number of the former may be abundantly multiplied is a "consummation devoutly to be wished"[2] by everyone who is in sympathy with the
true Reformer of the age.

W.

Frederick Douglass' Paper (Rochester, N.Y.), 7 April 1854.

1. Watkins borrows verses from "To a Louse" (1786) by Scottish poet Robert
Burns:

> O wad some power the giftie gie us
> To see oursels as others see us!

2. Watkins quotes from act 3, scene 1, of the play *Hamlet* by William Shakespeare.

43.
John N. Still to Frederick Douglass
18 April 1854

From 1853 through 1855, the National Council of the Colored People struggled to become a forceful representative body. Council leaders recognized the need for effective communication among local, state, and national black leaders and groups. John N. Still, who served on both the National Council and the New York State Council of the Colored People, explained this need in an 18 April 1854 letter to *Frederick Douglass' Paper*. He encouraged black communities to establish "committees of correspondence" and to support black newspapers. Such a network would disseminate vital information, forge unity, promote an exchange of views, place programs before the broader black community, generate support for common goals, and equip ordinary blacks with the "language and argument to meet [their] enemies." Still, a subscription agent and correspondent for several black newspapers, believed that this was the surest way for black leaders to "reach and benefit [their] constituents, and render them contributors to the cause." He offered brief descriptions of four black journals in the United States and Canada West and urged his readers to subscribe, reminding them that the black press needed their support. *FDP*, 15 July 1853, 20 January 1854 [8:0359–60, 0607, 0624].

> BROOKLYN, L[ong] I[sland], [New York]
> April 18, 1854

MR. EDITOR:

I wish, Sir, through the medium of your valuable journal, to address a few words, partly by way of suggestions, to my constituents. This, however, is not the plan of operations I had laid down; but necessity compels me to adopt it, which, upon the whole, may turn out to be the best one. As the propositions I may submit, or the suggestions, will afford an opportunity for private and more mature deliberation than if submitted in remarks at a meeting. I prefer this method of communication. Considering the time required to attend meetings, prepare matter, and meet every frivolous objection from those least inclined to act efficiently when the time for action comes, it is more than should be expected or asked by any constituency.

In view of these circumstances, I would suggest to my fellow citizens throughout the island to organize associations, or committees of correspondence, for the purpose of placing yourselves in a responsible relation to the National and State Council,[1] or their officers. This will entitle you, on your solicitation, to receive whatever desirable information you may wish from them. Some such arrangement is necessary; and if not made, there are thousands who will know no more about our movements five years hence, than they did five years ago. The State, I think, should have appointed an agent; in fact, but little can be effected without one. The idea that he would have to be paid, is, with some, an objection. A man that is not worthy of pay we don't want. You will please allow me further to suggest, that in the absence of an agent, we must endeavor to make the papers published by our worthy coadjutors supply their place. It is to *their* support, for your own benefit, that I wish most particularly to call your attention. The officers appointed to both the National and State Councils, are, many of them, at least, poor men, and compelled to pursue their daily avocations uninterruptedly. I repeat, therefore, it should not be expected of them to attend the Council sessions, and to travel about to lecture, and organize associations unpaid. Remember that you also have duties as well as they—duties which they *cannot* discharge. The business of the legislator is to plan, and the people to approve or disapprove, and execute.

The papers to which I alluded are four, which I do most impartially commend to your candid and unceasing patronage, as the easiest and best means of informing and aiding yourselves, and aiding the cause. My friends, you *must* become better informed on the subject of slavery, and our general condition in the North and South, and thro'out this continent. There is much to be obtained that would bring you up and encourage you to more energetic action. Besides, it would give you language and argument to meet your enemies. The very presence and exhibition of these papers, of which I have spoken, would often supply the place of argument and suppress the contemptuous indignity often hurled by cowards at the weak and defenceless. My friends you *must take the papers.* Those published by our own people are,

First—*Frederick Douglass' Paper*, by F. Douglass of Rochester, N. Y., which is now, I think, in its seventh volume, during which time, it has not, to my knowledge, missed a single week (being published weekly). It certainly is equal in variety, ability, and literary merit, with very few exceptions, to any of those published by the whites. It is devoted, specifically, to the anti-slavery cause. Among its correspondents, as I may say also of the others, are some of the best informed among our citizens, whose labors you cannot appreciate without reading their writings.

Second—*The Aliened American*,[2] by Wm. H. Day, of Cleveland, O.— quite a young man of marked ability and extensive literary acquirements. This paper is not yet a year old; but from its general management, its intelligent corps of male and female correspondents, has already found a place in the affections of the people, which can never be "alienated." It, too, is a weekly paper, and has been as punctual in its visits as the rising and setting sun.

Third—I must now refer you to Canada, "the land of the free and home of the fugitive." They have among them two papers, the same number that we have in the States. You, certainly, cannot be indifferent to *their* success. The former of these papers is edited by Henry Bibb,[3] a fugitive, and an unceasing advocate of our rights. I may say of the merit of this paper what I have said of the others. And in addition, I may say, also, that in it may be always found much important information in relation to our fugitive brethren—their general state and condition. It, also, commends itself to your support.

Fourth and lastly—*The Provincial Freeman*,[4] by the patriotic and inde-fatigable Samuel Ringgold Ward, also a "fugitive." This paper is aiming at the practical activities of labor. The ability that surrounds it is not surpassed by any of the above-mentioned. Though it has but recently commenced its career, it already exhibits, in its business arrangements, the character and the appearance of an old established journal. Those wishing to become informed in regard to Canada, its laws, government, and the general resources of the country, as well as the chances for enterprize, we can warrant will find such, prepared with care and atten-tion for the especial use of those wishing such information.

What I have said in regard to these papers has been entirely voluntary. But I had come to the conclusion, after mature deliberation, that it is the easiest way that I could reach and benefit my constituents, and render them contributors to the cause. Let us support the men now in the field advocating our cause and defending our rights; they are entitled to our support; and what is more, we need their counsel and instruction. We need their papers as the medium of exchanging our own views and plac-ing our plans before the people. My friends, consider this matter, and attend to it. I shall communicate such other matter from time to time as the case may require. I shall hope, in future, to be joined by my col-leagues, J. C. Morel[5] and Wm. J. Wilson, both of whom, however, I have some time since addressed on this subject, without any responses due from one gentleman to another.

If the Editors of *The Aliened American*, the *Voice of the Fugitive*, and *The Provincial Freeman* think this or any part of it of sufficient interest to the people to find a place in their columns, they will oblige me by its publication, and sending me a few extra copies. Your obedient servant,

JOHN N. STILL.

P.S. Persons wishing either of the above papers can procure sample copies of me, or any other information which will enable them to com-municate direct with their Editors for subscription. I hope as many as can will become subscribers to the papers of their choice.

J. N. S.

Frederick Douglass' Paper (Rochester, N.Y.), 28 April 1854.

1. Still refers to the National Council of the Colored People and its several state auxiliaries.

2. The *Aliened American*, a black-supported weekly edited and published by William Howard Day in Cleveland, emerged from the persistent efforts by Ohio blacks to establish a journal to speak for their interests. The initial issue appeared on 9 April 1853; regular publication began in August. Bearing the masthead, "Educate your children—and Hope for Justice," the *Aliened American* claimed to represent western blacks, independent of all political parties and factions. It not only sparked interest among Ohio blacks but was endorsed by the 1853 Illinois black state convention and drew praise from black communities throughout the North. Day, then only twenty-three years old, won recognition as a skilled editor and a promising black leader. He assembled an impressive list of contributors. His wife, Lucy Stanton Day, helped him publish the paper; Samuel R. Ward and J. W. C. Pennington served as corresponding editors; and Amos G. Beman and Martin R. Delany were regular correspondents. The paper attracted an unusual number of female correspondents, including Mary F. Vashon Colder, who wrote under the pseudonym "Fanny Homewood." Health problems forced Day's resignation in May 1854. The Ohio State Council of the Colored People purchased his interest in the paper and hoped to continue publication, but no additional issues appeared. Competition from other Ohio reform papers—especially the Cleveland *True Democrat*—and a lack of advertising revenue hastened its demise. The failure of the *Aliened American* left western blacks without a journal of their own for more than a decade. William Cheek and Aimee Lee Cheek, *John Mercer Langston and the Fight for Black Freedom, 1829–1865* (Urbana, Ill., 1989), 148, 215, 249; Blackett, *Beating against the Barriers*, 299–302; *AA*, 9 April 1853 [8:0213–14]; Foner and Walker, *Proceedings of the Black State Conventions*, 2:62; *NASS*, 31 March 1855 [9:0510]; *FDP*, 6 May 1853, 6 October 1854 [9:0132].

3. Still refers to the *Voice of the Fugitive*.

4. The *Provincial Freeman* began regular weekly publication during March 1854 in Toronto, Canada West. Samuel Ringgold Ward was nominal editor the first year, but Mary Ann Shadd Cary performed most editorial labors, and readers soon addressed their letters to the editor, "Dear Madam." In March 1855, the paper became the *Provincial Freeman and Weekly Advertiser*. Three months later when Cary began a lecture tour to raise subscriptions, she relinquished the editorship to William P. Newman. The following month, the *Freeman* permanently moved to Chatham. Newman left the paper in January 1856, and by May editorial responsibilities were divided between Cary, her brother Isaac Shadd, and H. Ford Douglas. This circle determined editorial policy for the next two years.

Although devoted to "Anti-Slavery, Temperance, and General Literature," the *Freeman* opened its columns to a wide range of interests and issues. It encouraged blacks to settle in Canada West, urged them to assume the rights and responsibilities of British citizenship, regularly criticized fund-raising efforts for the relief of Canadian fugitives (which it labeled "begging"), and chastised the Anti-Slavery Society of Canada for its inactivity. The editors initially opposed African and Caribbean immigration, but in the mid-1850s, they endorsed the black emigration movement and made the paper the official organ of the 1856 National Emigration Convention at Cleveland. The *Freeman* evidently suspended publication in late 1857, but Isaac Shadd revived it the following year. When Shadd was arrested in late 1858 for his part in a fugitive slave rescue, publication of the paper was again halted. By July 1859, Shadd was publishing the *Provincial Freeman and Semi-Monthly Advertiser* in Chatham. The paper's date of demise is uncertain, but it advertised in the *Weekly Anglo-African* through July 1860. By September 1861, the paper was defunct. Alexander L. Murray, "The *Provincial Freeman*: A New Source for the History of the Negro in Canada and the United States," *JNH* 44:123–35 (April 1959); *PFW*, 24 March 1853, 25 March, 9 September 1854, 10 March, 23, 30 June, 22 September 1855, 2, 23 February, 29 March, 10 May, 14 June 1856; Miller, *Search for a Black Nationality*, 157–60, 166; William Howard Day to Gerrit Smith, 21 June 1858, Gerrit Smith Papers, NSyU [11:0253–54]; *GSB*, 28 October 1858 [11:0393]; *WAA*, 30 July 1859, 14 July 1860; *PP*, 28 September 1861 [13:0774].

5. Junius C. Morel (?–1874) was born in North Carolina, the son of a planter and his female slave. He was educated in Philadelphia and, after traveling widely in America and abroad, settled in the city and married into the local black elite. In 1829 Morel began a long and distinguished reform career by becoming a local subscription agent for the *Rights of All*. Two years later, he formed a partnership with John P. Thompson to publish a black paper called *The American* in Philadelphia. Although this endeavor failed, Morel continued to support and correspond with black and antislavery papers. He opposed African colonization but endorsed black immigration to Canada as early as 1830. This led him to help organize the first black national convention later that year. He called the 1831 gathering to consider the same subject and authored a minority report favoring Canadian immigration. Morel played a prominent role in five of the first six black national conventions and called for the revival of the convention movement in 1840. He was also a leading member of the Philadelphia Young Men's Anti-Slavery Society.

As an outsider and a militant, Morel bristled under the dominance of Philadelphia's black elite. He condemned their "criminal apathy and idiot coldness." To circumvent elite control, he called for local delegates to national conventions to be elected by all blacks in the city. Although he accepted their moral reform principles, he criticized the leaders of the American Moral Reform Society for the "visionary" nature of their program, their ineffectiveness, and their refusal to address practical black issues in an aggressive fashion. Morel formed a "Political Association" to mobilize local blacks against disfranchisement efforts during the mid-1830s. But he found that "a vain temerity on the part of some, and a suicidal apathy on the part of others" doomed the effort. Frustrated by the conservatism and timidity of the elite, he abandoned the city for Harrisburg in 1837. Then after residing briefly in Newark, New Jersey, during the 1840s, he resettled in Brooklyn.

Morel became a noted black educator in Brooklyn. As principal of a black public school, he persuaded local school officials to allow whites to attend classes there from the early 1850s through the late 1860s. The success of this experiment in race-mixing vindicated black efforts to fully integrate the Brooklyn school system. After the Civil War, Morel helped edit a monthly student reader published by the African Civilization Society. Passage of the Fugitive Slave Law of 1850 reinvigorated Morel's activism. He joined the public outcry against the law, worked to protect local blacks threatened by its enforcement, and advocated black violence in defense of their rights. Morel again tried to revive the convention movement, joined efforts to establish the National Council of the Colored People, and represented Brooklyn blacks at the 1855 national convention. Although he flirted with emigration organizations, he defended black claims to American citizenship in the wake of the Dred Scott decision. He openly criticized President Abraham Lincoln's plans to resettle blacks in Central America and the Caribbean during the Civil War. Julie Winch, *Philadelphia's Black Elite: Activism, Accommodation, and the Struggle for Autonomy, 1787–1848* (Philadelphia, Pa., 1988), 66–67, 81, 85, 90–107, 110, 115, 123, 125–26n; *RA*, 16 October 1829; *Lib*, 12 March, 16 July 1831, 21 May 1832, 8 February 1834, 24 May 1844 [1:0067, 0091, 0158, 0394, 4:0812]; *NECAUL*, 17, 24 August 1836, 11 March, 2 November 1837 [1:0691, 0694–95, 0998, 2:0252]; *CA*, 3 May, 13 October 1838 [2:0464, 0616]; *FDP*, 26 February 1852, 10 June 1853, 20 January, 9 May 1854, 7 December 1855 [7:0439–40, 8:0606–7, 9:0974]; *NASS*, 10 October 1850, 3 April 1851 [6:0606–9]; *WAA*, 23 July, 15 October, 24 December 1859, 16 June 1860 [11:0869, 12:0801]; *ESF*, 9 June 1865, 7 March 1874 [15:0941]; Garrison, *Thoughts on African Colonization*, part 2, 36 [1:0088]; *Colored National Convention . . . in Philadelphia* (1855), 6 [9:0881]; "Black Organizational Members, Sorted by Name" Philadelphia Social History Project, PU; Junius C. Morel et al. to Abraham Lincoln, 25 November 1863, RG48.16, Records of the Secretary of the Interior Relating to the Suppression of the African Slave Trade and Negro Colonization, DNA [15:0062–75]; Mabee, *Black Education in New York State*, 86, 123, 126–27, 151–52.

44.
James McCune Smith to Frederick Douglass
4 May 1854

Black leaders struggled to speak with a common voice and to act with a shared sense of purpose. But conflicting interests and quarrels over strategy and tactics often hampered efforts at building a consensus. Clashes between integrationists and separatists, divisions based on skin color, bitter personal disputes, and the indifference of many in the black community worried black leaders. During the excitement accompanying the Kansas-Nebraska crisis, William J. Watkins found some black groups strangely "cold and dead"; the San Francisco *Mirror of the Times* criticized blacks who opposed community reform in favor of personal financial rewards. James McCune Smith, New York City's foremost black intellectual, regretted these differences and despaired that he led "an invisible people." In this 4 May 1854 letter to Frederick Douglass, Smith examined the divisions among blacks and concluded that they were caused by the differing circumstances of their oppression. *FDP*, 24 March, 17 November 1854 [8:0694, 9:0235–37]; *CA*, 17 June 1837 [2:0078]; *NSt*, 7 April 1848 [5:0613]; *MT*, 12 December 1857 [10:0968–69]; David W. Blight, "In Search of Learning, Liberty, and Self-Definition: James McCune Smith and the Ordeal of the Antebellum Black Intellectual," *AANYLH* 9:10–11, 18–19 (July 1985).

NEW YORK, [New York]
May 4th, 1854

Mr. Editor:

The great hindrance to the advancement of the free colored people is the want of unity in action. If we were to unite in the pursuit of any one object, I can imagine no possibility beyond our power to compass.

But we are not united as a people; and the main reason why we are not united is that we are not equally oppressed. This is the grand secret of our lack of union. You cannot pick out five hundred free colored men in the free States who equally labor under the same species of oppression. In each one of the free States, and often in different parts of the same State, the laws, or public opinion, mete out to the colored man a different measure of oppression; in Maine and Massachusetts, no political rights are denied him; the polls in election time, the churches and school houses (except in Boston, which hardly belongs to Massachusetts) are open to him and his; hence, by a natural course of events, Massachusetts abolished the old law which interdicted marriages between whites and blacks.[1] In Pennsylvania, on the contrary, the colored man has everything to contend for, in matters political, religious and social.[2] A colored gentleman of Boston, who was in Philadelphia last week, procured a ticket for Jullien's concert; he was refused admission at the door, and, on rating the doorkeeper in good set terms for the refusal, he was deprecatingly told "that the colored people of Philadelphia never thought of seeking admission to such entertainments!"[3] Midway between these extremes, we have New York, Ohio, Michigan and the northern part of Illinois, in which either statute law, or public opinion, accords some rights to, and withholds other rights from, the man of color.[4]

And in addition to these local oppressions, the free colored man, in the free States has other grades or gradations of oppression laid upon him. He is oppressed in the ratio of his complexion. The weight is laid heaviest on the purely black man, and is lightened as he approaches the caste of the purely white man. A thousand instances may be adduced to support this statement; it is a rule which has found its way into a decision of the Supreme Court of Ohio, and into the statute laws of Illinois and Virginia.[5] In our own ranks, the same rule has found expression in the contrariety of motive which sends Delany and Whitfield to seek to found a State in which, as the latter says, there shall be no distasteful amalgamation, but "black be the ruling element," while, on the other hand, Langston and Day claim their rights inside the Senate House in Ohio.[6]

Here, then, we have before us, the fact that there are various grades of oppression inflicted on our people; reduced to numerical exactness, I may safely assert that there may be counted two thousand distinct forms of oppression scattered among the hundred and seventy-six thousand free colored people in the free States.

The result is, that each man feels his peculiar wrong, but no hundred men together feel precisely the same oppression; and, while each would do fair work to remove his own, he feels differently in regard to his neighbor's oppression. For example, our yellow friends, Day and Langston, may vote at the next, as I believe they did vote at the last, general election in Ohio, under the quadroon decision of the Supreme Court of that State,[7] while our black friend Delany curses that decision as "infamous," and berates his yellow brothers aforesaid as "willing contributors to their own degradation," in voting under it. Day and Langston vote because they believe it their duty as *men* to avail themselves of all privileges within their reach; Delany denounces their act, because he is excluded by the very decision which grants them the privilege. Now, put the main question, can these three colored men in good and hearty faith earnestly unite in a common resistance to their diverse oppressions? Does not that Ohio decision pluck them asunder in the very springs and secret sources of action? And is it not the depth and bitterness of our oppression, when earnest men are thus rent apart by impulses they cannot control? And are we not forced to probe this difficulty to the very bottom and find the remedy, before we can be in position "*to do something* for the common elevation?"

Similarly cruel differences in oppression, in every variety of shade, ramify through the entire free colored population, and with similar results. Hence that want of unity in thought, action and resistance, which has distinguished us; for there must be common oppression to produce common resistance.

Hence, also, we have too long blamed ourselves with the want of union without sufficiently enquiring into the cause thereof. We have attributed to innate fault of character what really belongs to the circumstances which surround us—And now that we have traced our want of Union to this its real course—I mean unequal oppression—how shall we discover the remedy for our disunion? In reply to this question, it is idle to speculate about *ought to*; we must go down to the practical level of *can*; how *can* we become united? The underlying question, whether we ought to unite, as colored people, I will discuss hereafter; at present I assume that we ought so to combine.

If it be true that the main reason of our disunion lies in the fact that we are not equally oppressed, then we must seek to create within ourselves such a hearty hatred of all oppression that any wrong to one shall be a wrong to all; or, we must seek to find without ourselves some general form of oppression continuous in character, against which we may all, as one man, combine and continuously struggle until we are free and equal.

The first alternative is manifestly impossible at present, although it is the most desirable, and will be the necessary result of a combination found under the second alternative. And, in view of the second alternative, PUBLIC OPINION is the general form of oppression, continuous in character, against which we may rally and form persistent union. But we must be content to attack public opinion in detail; and each specific victory will strengthen our hands and perfect our organization for the next.

Public opinion is the King of today; and rules our land; yet we can conquer public opinion, because we have conquered it. Public opinion said we must go to Liberia; yet here we are, and it is granted by public opinion that here we will stay; so omnipotent is our combined *will* against the public *wish*. And yet, our opposition to the colonization scheme was rather instinctive (I use the word for want of a better) impulse, than aforethought combination: it was part of that innate love of soil which our *forbears* brought from Africa, and which renders indigenous negro-land the most impenetratable in God's earth. The Scotch thistle, celebrated in a *Latin* motto, was trodden down by Romans, and cut away from its native heath to make room for Roman bridges yet extant; but no hostile foot has maintained its foothold upon, no hostile *cohorts* have cut military roads through, negro-land! Yet the British maintain Empire in the (to European Constitution) equally pestilential India.[8]

Colonization, an oppression bearing equally upon us all; was resisted by us all: it compelled our union and thereby ensured its own defeat. Having, in this common resistance, learned the secret of our power, it is our duty to use it for our elevation and affranchisement.

If we look around us, we will find public opinion our oppressor in a thousand other matters; it broods over us from free Maine to slave Texas, nay—and let this be hindered well by our emigration brethren—it goes in advance of us to the uttermost parts of the earth and defends its tyranny over us on the grounds of our imbecility; it says we are "kicked" by it because "we've got no friends, *and ain't able to help ourselves.*" That is, we lack executive power.

We have borne enough, and well enough, already; it is time that we should "up boys and at them";[9] that is *do something*. We must do something to take away this reproach of imbecility; it does not matter so much what we do, whether we overrun Sonora, or create an Industrial School.[10] But, as brother Day says, this talk must be (CONTINUED IN OUR NEXT).[11]

Brother Day calls on me, by my own and two other names,[12] to "do battle" with him, touching the Industrial School. Now, Mr. Editor, if I knew a nice little brook with five smooth stones, and could get Philo to make me a sling, I would mix in with the he-biddy of *Dear Aliened*,[13] if there be such a one; but it should be an express'd condition that *hens* and shawls should be kept from the battleground. It is a pretty rural sight and sound to witness Brother Day gallanting Maria*, and Becky†, and Nancy‡, and Fanny§, over his barnyard,[14] astonishing them with his bantam strut and squeaky crowing, while he boastfully cries "*hens* you *are hens* and I know it"—now, Mr. Editor, could I have the heart to disturb that harmony? If tearful Fanny Homewood sat and listened to wailing Lucy Stone until she thought her to be brother Day, who could be so hardhearted as to ruffle a feather of brother Day's wings? It might be the death of her (Fanny, to wit):

Our excellent pastor of St. Philip's actually preaches against the Ne-braska Bill; and it is said that a distinguished vestryman is "down on him" ever since that sermon.[15] I have seen a letter from Providence, which states that Philo actually *fainted* on reading Charlotte K———'s last letter in your paper; as Philo is about to give the world renewed proofs of his sterling manhood,[16] I hope Charlotte will write no more at him; he can't be spared. Yours affectionately,

COMMUNIPAW.

---

*A Shanghai (with spurs?) hen.
†A speckled hen.
‡A Brahmpootra hen.
§A Guinea hen, crows also in the Spring, and wears *gaffs*.

Frederick Douglass' Paper (Rochester, N.Y.), 12 May 1854.

1. In 1786 the Massachusetts legislature passed a marriage law prohibiting blacks and Native Americans from intermarrying with whites. In 1831 William Lloyd Garrison began a campaign against the law, and antislavery societies throughout Massachusetts petitioned the legislature to end the marriage restriction. Aware of public sensitivity to the issue of racial intermarriage, Massachusetts blacks quietly supported the repeal efforts. The law was finally repealed in March 1843. Louis Ruchames, "Race, Marriage, and Abolition in Massachusetts," *JNH* 11:250–73 (July 1955).

2. Far-reaching legal and extralegal discrimination restricted black civil rights in antebellum Pennsylvania. A new state constitution in 1838 denied blacks the franchise. Blacks were usually excluded from schools, churches, and other public and private institutions, segregated on public conveyances, passed over for public employment, and victimized by periodic race riots. Most legal discrimination persisted in Pennsylvania until after the Civil War. Litwack, *North of Slavery*, 17, 84–87, 113, 162, 206–7.

3. Smith refers to an April 1854 concert in Philadelphia by Louis Antoine Jullien (1812–1860). The popular French conductor and composer toured the eastern United States during 1853–54 at the invitation of P. T. Barnum. He gave more than two hundred orchestral concerts, and, on several occasions, blacks were denied admission to his performances. Stanley Sadie, ed., *The New Grove Dictionary of Music and Musicians*, 20 vols. (London, 1980), 9:798–99; *Lib*, 16 December 1853.

4. A variety of legal restrictions circumscribed black civil rights in antebellum Ohio, Illinois, Michigan, and New York. State black laws required blacks to register and post surety bonds, impeded black settlement, prohibited black testimony in court, and limited or outlawed black suffrage. As Smith suggests, enforcement of these laws varied. In Detroit and Chicago, public opinion permitted free blacks to ignore many of these restrictions, while racial proscriptions were more strictly enforced in southern Illinois, where *de facto* slavery persisted well into the 1840s. Frank Quillin, *The Color Line in Ohio* (Ann Arbor, Mich., 1913), 36–37; Ronald P. Formisano, "The Edge of Caste: Colored Suffrage in Michigan, 1827–1861," *MH* 56:19–41 (Spring 1972); Elmer Gertz, "The Black Laws of Illinois," *ISHSJ* 56:454–73 (Autumn 1963); *FDP*, 18 March 1853.

5. States that enacted black laws had to determine the legal definition of race. That definition, which was based on color gradation, varied from state to state. The Ohio Supreme Court ruled in the case of *Polly Grey v. Ohio* (1831) that individuals of more than one-half white ancestry were legally white. Subsequent rulings in 1834 and 1842 reaffirmed this decision. In 1849 the Virginia legislature defined as black anyone with "one-quarter part or more negro blood." The Illinois General Assembly also employed the "one-quarter part" designation in an 1853 law restricting free black immigration into the state. Quillin, *Color Line in Ohio*, 24–25, 58–59; Kenneth M. Stampp, *The Peculiar Institution: Slavery in the Ante-Bellum South* (New York, N.Y., 1956), 195; Gertz, "Black Laws of Illinois," 454–73.

6. Smith contrasts two responses by black leaders to racial oppression during

the 1850s. Martin R. Delany and James M. Whitfield were leading advocates of black emigration and the creation of a separate black nation in Africa, Latin America, or the Caribbean. John Mercer Langston and William Howard Day urged blacks to remain in the United States and fight for their rights as citizens. Both failed to gain access to the Ohio state senate. In January 1854, Day was expelled from the press gallery; two months later, Langston was rebuffed when he attempted to present a memorial to the legislators. The incidents stirred protests by Ohio blacks. Miller, *Search for a Black Nationality*, 135–69; Blackett, *Beating against the Barriers*, 309; Cheek and Cheek, *John Mercer Langston*, 228–29.

7. Light-skinned Ohio blacks such as William Howard Day and John Mercer Langston were entitled to vote by the decision in *Edwill Thacker v. John Hawk and Others* (1842). When a Gallia County court refused to count Edwill Thacker's ballot in a local election, arguing that men of black ancestry could not be legal voters, Thacker, a mulatto, appealed to the Ohio Supreme Court. The higher court reversed the Gallia decision, citing earlier cases to demonstrate that individuals of more than one-half white ancestry were entitled to full citizenship rights in Ohio. Even so, many mulattoes continued to avoid the polls, fearing humiliation at the hands of election judges, who decided whether they were light-skinned enough to vote. Edwin M. Stanton, ed., *Reports of Cases Argued and Determined in the Supreme Court of the State of Ohio, in Bank* (Columbus, Ohio, 1855), 11:376–85; Cheek and Cheek, *John Mercer Langston*, 269–70.

8. Smith suggests that African peoples have an "innate love of soil," which prevented Africa from being effectively colonized. He compares African colonization to the Romans' failed attempt to expand into ancient Scotland during the first century A.D. Scottish defiance is celebrated in the Stuart family's coat of arms, which bears the Scotch thistle—Scotland's national emblem—and the Latin motto of the Scottish kings: "Nemo me impune lacessit" ("No one provokes me with impunity"). Smith also notes the rapid extension of British colonial power in India during the 1840s and 1850s, even though its climate approximated that of Africa.

9. Smith paraphrases a quote attributed to the Duke of Wellington at the battle of Waterloo (1815): "Up Guards and at them again!"

10. Smith urges blacks to take action—emigrate, establish the proposed American Industrial School, or act in an even more assertive fashion. He alludes to recent actions by American filibusterer William Walker who invaded Mexico's Baja California province and announced on 18 January 1854 that he was annexing Sonora province and establishing the Republic of Sonora, with himself as president. The Mexican army soon forced Walker to retreat to San Diego, where he surrendered to American authorities. Potter, *Impending Crisis*, 177–78, 193.

11. Smith does not appear to have written a second letter to *Frederick Douglass' Paper* on this subject.

12. During the 1850s, Smith regularly corresponded with *Frederick Douglass' Paper* and the *National Anti-Slavery Standard* under the pseudonym "Communipaw" (after Communipaw Flats, an area of New York City). He occasionally used the pseudonym "Wapinummoc"—"Communipaw" spelled backwards.

13. Smith alludes to a story from 1 Samuel 17:31–54, in which a young Israelite shepherd named David, armed with only a sling and five smooth stones from a nearby brook, killed the Philistine giant Goliath. He suggests that if he is to engage William Howard Day of the *Aliened American* in a war of words, he wants the pen of "Philo" on his side. "Philo" was the pseudonym of George T. Downing, the respected Providence, Rhode Island, correspondent for *Frederick Douglass' Paper*.

14. Smith sarcastically refers to editor William Howard Day and the many women who contributed to the publication of his Cleveland-based *Aliened American*. Lucy Stanton Day, his wife, and other Ohio black women assisted him in the journal office. Several women regularly corresponded with the paper under the pseudonyms "Maria," "Becky," "Nancy," and "Fanny Homewood." "Maria" was a New York City correspondent. "Fanny Homewood" was the pseudonym of Mary Frances Vashon Colder (1817–1854) of Pittsburgh, the daughter of black abolitionist John B. Vashon. Cheek and Cheek, *John Mercer Langston*, 249; *FDP*, 24 March, 6 October 1854 [8:0692–93, 9:0132].

15. Dr. William Morris, a white Episcopal clergyman, ministered to St. Philip's Episcopal Church in New York City from 1850 to 1860. The large black parish, which was founded in 1819, had been served during its first two decades by Rev. Peter Williams, Jr., a prominent black abolitionist. Led by white priests after 1840, the congregation lost much of its earlier antislavery fervor. Morris initially urged his black parishioners to obey the Fugitive Slave Law but later criticized federal policy on slavery and preached against the Kansas-Nebraska Act (1854). The "distinguished vestryman" who objected to Morris's new stance was probably either Philip A. White, George Lawrence, or Henry Scott; all three black leaders were conservative members of St. Philip's vestry board during the early 1850s. *WAA*, 4 February 1860; Benjamin F. De Costa, *Three Score and Ten: The Story of St. Philip's Church* (New York, N.Y., 1889), 12; Kenneth Cameron, ed., *American Episcopal Clergy* (Hartford, Conn., 1970), 10; *FDP*, 29 April 1852.

16. In the 3 March 1854 issue of *Frederick Douglass' Paper*, a letter by Pittsburgh correspondent "Charlotte K———" mentioned "Philo" and criticized black Odd Fellows lodges for their "hypocrisy and humbug." "Philo" (George T. Downing) responded three weeks later with a defense of the Odd Fellows. *FDP*, 2 December 1853, 3, 24 March 1854 [8:0505, 0674–75, 0692–93].

45.
Editorial by William J. Watkins
2 June 1854

The Fugitive Slave Law dissolved lingering black doubts about the efficacy and morality of violence. Because the law threatened the liberty
and safety of both fugitives and northern free blacks, black abolitionists
advocated forceful resistance, comparing their call to arms to the actions of the Founding Fathers during the American Revolution. Jermain
W. Loguen urged blacks to "smite down Marshals and Commissioners"
who attempted to enforce the act; Frederick Douglass declared that
"making two or three dead slave holders" was the best way to render
the law ineffective. William J. Watkins discussed the use of violence
against slave catchers in a 2 June 1854 editorial in *Frederick Douglass'
Paper*. It was written one week after Boston abolitionists killed a deputy
marshal in a failed attempt to rescue Anthony Burns, a Virginia runaway. Watkins defended the bloodshed, claiming that blacks had the
right and obligation to "kill the man who would dare lay his hand on
us, or on our brother, or sister, to enslave us." The threat to black life
and liberty posed by the Fugitive Slave Law moved Watkins to ask,
"Who are the Murderers?" Jermain Wesley Loguen, *The Rev. J. W.
Loguen, As a Slave and As a Freeman: A Narrative of Real Life* (Syracuse, N.Y., 1859; reprint, New York, N.Y., 1968), 402; *SDS*, 24, 27
September 1850; George Thompson to Ann Warren Weston, 7 March
1851, Anti-Slavery Collection, MB; Campbell, *Slave Catchers*, 125–27.

Who are the Murderers?

RIOTS AT BOSTON—The opponents of the Fugitive Slave Law,
murdered a Deputy U.S. Marshal, on Friday night, in order to
prevent the delivery of a slave to his master. See telegraph head.
Rochester American[1]

Slavery is murder in the highest degree. Every slaveholder is a murderer, a wholesale murderer. Those who apologise for them are worse
than murderers. If one of these midnight and noonday assassins were to
rush into the house of a white man, and strive to bind him hand and
foot, and tear God's image from his brow, and be shot in the attempt, no
one would characterize the act as murder. Not at all. It would be considered an act of righteous retribution. The man who sent a bullet through
the tyrant's heart would be almost extravagantly lauded. This would be
done, we remark, if the man to be enslaved, or murdered, which is the
same thing, were a white man. Now take the following case. A colored
man is living quietly in Boston, one mile from Bunker Hill Monument.
He is a free man, for God created him. He stamped HIS image upon him.

KIDNAPPING
AGAIN!!

A MAN WAS STOLEN LAST NIGHT BY THE

Fugitive Slave Bill COMMISSIONER!

HE WILL HAVE HIS

MOCK TRIAL

ON SATURDAY, MAY 27, AT 9 O'CLOCK,

In the Kidnapper's 'Court,' before the Hon. Slave Bill Commissioner,

AT THE COURT HOUSE, IN COURT SQUARE.

SHALL BOSTON STEAL ANOTHER MAN?

Thursday, May 25, 1854.

9. Poster announcing the seizure of Anthony Burns

Slavery has well nigh murdered him. He has contrived to break loose from its iron grasp. He is pursued by his murderers. The hall of justice has become a den of thieves. A man leaves the honorable occupation of driving horses, and consents, for a "consideration," to be appointed Deputy Marshal, consents to be invested with power to rob him of his God-given rights. The miserable hireling is shot in the attempt. Is that man a murderer who sent the well-directed bullet through his stony heart? He would not be so considered if the parties were white. If he be a murderer, then was Gen. Washington; then were all who wielded swords and bayonets under him, in defence of liberty, the most cold-blooded murderers. We believe in peaceably rescuing fugitive slaves if it can be peaceably effected; but if it cannot, we believe in rescuing them forcibly. We should certainly kill the man who would dare lay his hand on us, or on our brother, or sister, to enslave us. We would feel no compunction of conscience for so doing. We cannot censure others for doing what we would be likely to do, under the same circumstances, ourselves.

W.

Frederick Douglass' Paper (Rochester, N.Y.), 2 June 1854.

1. This news story appeared in the 30 May 1854 issue of the *Daily American*, a newspaper published between 1844 and 1857 in Rochester, New York. It referred to a 26 May attempt to rescue Anthony Burns, a fugitive slave from Virginia, who had been arrested in Boston under the provisions of the Fugitive Slave Law. An interracial mob led by abolitionists Thomas W. Higginson, Martin Stowell, and Lewis Hayden stormed the Municipal Court House, where Burns was being held. During the unsuccessful attack, a deputy, James Batchelder, was fatally stabbed. Although nine of the rioters were arraigned for his murder, none were ever convicted. Winifred Gregory, *American Newspapers, 1821–1936* (New York, N.Y., 1937), 488; David R. Maginnes, "The Case of the Court House Rioters in the Rendition of the Fugitive Slave Anthony Burns, 1854," *JNH* 56:31–43 (January 1971).

46.
The Battle against Streetcar Segregation

Testimony of Elizabeth Jennings
Presented by Peter S. Ewell at the
First Colored Congregational Church
New York, New York
17 July 1854

Resolutions by James R. Starkey
Delivered at a Meeting of the Young Men's Association
San Francisco, California
14 August 1854

Northern blacks often risked personal safety to defy racist practices. The Third Avenue Railroad Company of New York City excluded blacks from its horse-drawn streetcars, the chief form of urban transportation in the 1850s. On 16 July 1854, Elizabeth Jennings, a black teacher, attempted to board one of the company's cars on her way to church services. When she refused the driver's order to leave the car, she was forcibly ejected. The next day, local blacks gathered at the First Colored Congregational Church to protest the incident. Peter S. Ewell, the meeting's secretary, read Jennings's personal account of the affair; she was unable to attend due to injuries suffered during the episode. The meeting appointed a committee to investigate the possibility of legal recourse. Jennings eventually sued the streetcar company for damages and was awarded $225 and the right to ride. The decision was widely hailed as a victory over Jim Crow transportation, and it prompted local black leaders to organize the Legal Rights Association to encourage and finance court challenges against those companies that continued to exclude blacks. A month after the incident, members of the black Young Men's Association of San Francisco met to express their sympathy and support for Jennings. James R. Starkey offered a resolution denouncing the actions of the Third Avenue Railroad Company. This protest by San Francisco blacks against an act of discrimination across the continent underscored the unity and common concerns among black communities in the free states. *NYT*, 19 July 1854; Blackett, *Beating against the Barriers*, 60–62; Lapp, *Blacks in Gold Rush California*, 188–90.

Sarah E. Adams and myself[1] walked down to the corner of Pearl and Chatham Sts.[2] to take the Third Ave. cars. I held up my hand to the driver and he stopped the cars, we got on the platform, when the conductor told us to wait for the next car; I told him I could not wait, as I was in a hurry to go to church (the other car was about a block off). He then told me that the other car had my people in it, that it was appropriated for that purpose. I then told him I had no people. It was no particular occasion; I wished to go to church, as I had been going for the last six months, and I did not wish to be detained. He insisted upon my getting off the car; I told him I would wait on the car until the other car came up; he again insisted on my waiting in the street, but I did not get off the car; by this time the other car came up, and I asked the driver if there was any room in his car. He told me very distinctly, "No, that there was more room in my car than there was in his." Yet this did not satisfy the conductor; he still kept driving me out or off of the car; said he had as much time as I had and could wait just as long. I replied, "Very well, we'll see." He waited some few minutes, when the drivers becoming impatient, he said to me, "Well, you may go in, but remember, if the passengers raise any objections you shall go out, whether or no, or I'll put you out." I answered again and told him I was a respectable person, born and raised in New York, did not know where he was born, that I had never been insulted before while going to church, and that he was a good for nothing impudent fellow for insulting decent persons while on their way to church. He then said I should come out and he would put me out. I told him not to lay his hands on me; he took hold of me and I took hold of the window sash and held on; he pulled me until he broke my grasp and I took hold of his coat and held on to that, he also broke my grasp from that (but previously he had dragged my companion out, she all the while screaming for him to let go). He then ordered the driver to fasten his horses, which he did, and come and help him put me out of the car; they then both seized hold of me by the arms and pulled and dragged me flat down on the bottom of the platform, so that my feet hung one way and my head the other, nearly on the ground. I screamed murder with all my voice, and my companion screamed out "you'll kill her; don't kill her." The driver then let go of me and went to his horses; I went again in the car, and the conductor said you shall sweat for this; then told the driver to drive as fast as he could and not to take another passenger in the car; to drive until he saw an officer or a Station House. They got an officer on the corner of Walker and Bowery,[3] whom the conductor told that his orders from the agent were to admit colored persons if the passengers did not object, but if they did, not to let them ride. When the officer took me there were some eight or ten persons in the car. Then the officer, without listening to anything I had to say, thrust me out, and then pushed me, and tauntingly told me to get redress if I could; this the conductor also told me, and gave me some name and number of his car; he wrote his name Moss[4] and the car No. 7, but I looked and saw No. 6 on the back of the car. After dragging me off the car he drove me away like a dog, saying not to be talking there and raising a mob or fight. I came home down Walker St., and a German gentleman followed, who told me he saw the whole transaction in the street as he was passing; his address is Latour, No. 148 Pearl St., bookseller. When I told the conductor I did not know where he was born, he answered, "I was born in Ireland." I made answer it made no difference where a man was born, that he was none the worse or better for that, provided he behaved himself and did not insult genteel persons.

I would have come up myself, but am quite sore and stiff from the treatment I received from those monsters in human form yesterday afternoon. This statement I believe to be correct, and it is respectfully submitted.

ELIZABETH JENNINGS

New York Tribune (N.Y.), 19 July 1854.

Whereas, We have learned by the New York *Tribune* of July 19th, that two colored ladies, ELIZABETH JENNINGS and SARAH E. ADAMS, were violently ejected from a *public* conveyance into the street by a ruffianly Irish driver in the city of New York, solely on account of their color, while on their way to *Church,* upon the Sabbath; and,

Whereas, We cannot believe that such outrages upon the rights and persons of intelligent and upright citizens will be sanctioned by the public, when they shall be made aware of their preparation, but that they will denounce and command that such outrages shall no longer be permitted; therefore,

Resolved, That we have read with deep interest the proceedings of the meeting of colored citizens of New York, in relation to the brutal treatment Misses JENNINGS and ADAMS were subjected to, and heartily approve the course pursued by our brethren at that meeting, and sympathize with the ladies, who were the subjects of the treatment complained of; and we say to our friends, even from the distant shores of the Pacific, that we, with them, do, and will ever protest against this, and like injustice on all proper occasions, and resist it by all proper means, by appealing to justice and importuning public sentiment until we secure our rights.

Frederick Douglass' Paper (Rochester, N.Y.), 22 September 1854.

1. Elizabeth Jennings (1830–?), the daughter of black abolitionist Thomas L. Jennings, taught in New York City's black public schools during the 1850s and 1860s. She also promoted adult education and served as organist for the First Colored Congregational Church. Jennings married Charles Graham in June 1860. U.S. Census, 1850; *PFW*, 10 March 1855 [9:0476]; *WAA*, 30 June, 24 November 1860 [13:0005]; *NP*, 13 August 1863 [14:1008].

2. Pearl and Chatham streets were located on the lower east side of Manhattan Island.

3. Jennings had traveled some six blocks north when she was forcibly ejected at the corner of Walker and Bowery streets.

4. Edward Moss was a carman for the Third Avenue Railroad Company of New York City. *New York City Directory*, 1848–51.

47.
William H. Newby to Frederick Douglass
10 August 1854

Black cultural life flourished in the 1850s. Communities outside the
South boasted of hundreds of churches, schools, lodges, literary societies, benevolent associations, and temperance organizations. Despite
systematic oppression, urban blacks achieved a sufficiently high level of
economic success to finance these institutions. San Francisco's black
community, the largest and most prosperous on the Pacific coast, typified the vibrancy of free black culture. Local black residents had
amassed nearly $5 million in property during the gold rush and used
their resources to support a wide variety of institutions and organizations. William H. Newby, who regularly corresponded with *Frederick
Douglass' Paper* under the pseudonym "Nubia," reported on these developments in a 10 August 1854 letter. He informed Douglass that he
could not fathom "the progress made by the colored people in this city
within the short space of two years." Written to impress blacks in the
East, Newby's report offered a revealing statement of free black achievements. Litwack, *North of Slavery*, 178–86; Foner, *History of Black
Americans*, 2:196, 223, 237–50, 265–67; Lapp, *Blacks in Gold Rush
California*, 223–25, 263.

SAN FRANCISCO, [California]
Aug[ust] 10th, 1854

MR. EDITOR:

Your not being in the receipt of any regular correspondence from
California, and knowing your great interest in all that concerns the welfare of "our people," has induced me to pen this epistle. You can form no
idea of the progress made by the colored people in this city within the
short space of two years. We have three churches—one Baptist and two
Methodist.[1] The two Methodist churches are filled regularly with large
and intelligent audiences. The St. Cyprian is on Jackson St.; it is the
largest of the three. Its interior is as handsome as any church in the city.
It is presided over by the Rev. Mr. Ward[2] (a nephew of Samuel R. Ward)
and the Rev. Darius Stokes.[3] Both of these gentlemen are eminently
qualified to fill the positions they occupy. Mr. Stokes is regarded here as
a very eloquent man; his memory is surprising, and his language chaste
and elegant. The Stockton St. Church (Methodist) is presided over by the
Rev. Mr. Moore.[4] He is, perhaps, the best scholar of color in the State.
His sermons are looked upon as learned effusions. He is a very instructive preacher, and is doing much good.

We have one Literary Association—the "San Francisco Athenaeum."

To this institution we are greatly indebted. It has given tone and character to Society. It requires its members to be moral and intelligent. The doings of the Society are published quarterly, and are characterized with great ability. Their library is small, but well selected, comprising about 800 volumes, besides periodicals, magazines, and papers from every part of the world. The Annual Report of the Institution showed an accession of 70 members, and the receipts of about $2000.[5] We have one public school of color; it numbers about fifty children. Mr. Moore is the teacher. All this, Mr. Editor, has been effected, and much more, by the much despised blacks. We suffer many deprivations, however. We have no oath against any white man or Chinaman. We are debarred from the polls. The Legislature refused to accept our petition for the right to testify in courts of justice against the whites;[6] but notwithstanding all these drawbacks, we are steadily progressing in all that pertains to our welfare. Your valuable (or rather invaluable) paper is much sought after. Many persons have sent on for it, but have never received it. This must be attributed to the Post Office here, as persons are in the habit of receiving the paper, who have never subscribed for it.

There was a demonstration made in behalf of the *North Star*, or *Douglass' Paper*, here recently, which resulted in some forty or fifty subscribers, and the selection of Mr. Collins of Pittsburgh as agent;[7] and we hope for the future to be edified by the columns of your paper, on the arrival of every mail.

The First of August was celebrated here very spiritedly by addresses from several gentlemen.[8] Mr. Ward made us believe that we were listening to his great namesake and relation, Samuel R. Ward. His remarks were characterized by great force of expression. He said, "we had met to dig the grave of Slavery." He urged resistance, mental and physical, to every encroachment of our rights and liberties. His remarks called forth much applause. Mr. Sanderson, recently from New Bedford (who, by the way, is a most eloquent speaker), gave us a history of the antislavery parties in England and America. Mr. Townsend[9] and Mr. Newby[10] also made addresses. The former gentleman is President of the Athenaeum, and is a regular graduate of one of the Eastern Colleges. We have a large number of respectable ladies here, and their influence is felt and acknowledged.

San Francisco presents many features that no city in the Union presents. Its population is composed of almost every nation under heaven. Here is to be seen at a single glance every nation in miniature. The Chinese form about one-eighth of the population. They exhibit a most grotesque appearance. Their "unmentionables" are either exceedingly roomy or very close fitting. The heads of the males are shaved, with the exception of the top, the hair from which is formed into a plaited tail, resembling "pigtail tobacco." Their habits are filthy, and their features totally devoid of expression. The whites are greatly alarmed at their rapid increase. They are very badly treated here. Every boy considers them lawful prey for his boyish pranks. They have no friends, unless it is the colored people, who treat everybody well, even their enemies.[11] But I must close this already too long letter. Yours, &c.,

NUBIA

Frederick Douglass' Paper (Rochester, N.Y.), 22 September 1854.

1. San Francisco blacks organized three churches during the early 1850s. In 1852 Rev. John J. Moore established the Stockton Street African Methodist Episcopal Zion Church, which grew rapidly under his leadership. Later that year, thirteen local blacks founded the Third Baptist Church. The congregation remained small until 1857, when it obtained a regular pastor; until that time, services were led by Joseph Davenport, a member and lay preacher from New Orleans, although local African Methodist Episcopal clergymen occasionally preached. In 1854 Rev. Barney Fletcher organized the St. Cyprian AME Church. Before the year was out, Rev. T. M. D. Ward came to serve as pastor, with Rev. Darius Stokes as his assistant. It soon became the largest black congregation in the city and opened a school in its basement. Fletcher returned in 1856, but many parishioners left during his tenure and St. Cyprian soon closed its doors. The Stockton Street and Third Baptist churches remained major forces in the political and cultural life of black San Francisco for decades. Lapp, *Blacks in Gold Rush California*, 159–62, 167.

2. Thomas Myers Decatur Ward (1823–1894) was a leading figure in the African Methodist Episcopal church during the nineteenth century. He was born in Hanover, Pennsylvania, and reared on a nearby farm by slave parents who had fled to freedom a few months before his birth. In 1843 he moved to Philadelphia, attended a Quaker night school, and joined the AME church. Four years later, he was ordained an AME clergyman. Ward served congregations in Connecticut, Binghamton (New York), and Boston and became the first secretary of the AME's New England Conference.

In early 1854, Ward left to do missionary work in California. After serving as pastor of the St. Cyprian and Little Pilgrim churches in San Francisco, he was named a traveling missionary elder for the state. In this role, he organized and reviewed the progress of dozens of new AME churches. At the same time, he acted as traveling agent for the *Pacific Appeal*, a San Francisco black journal, and wrote numerous articles on social and religious themes for the paper. Ward was increasingly recognized as a leader of the state's growing black community. He worked with other black leaders to fight California's testimony laws and to obtain the franchise, promoted temperance, and represented San Francisco at the 1855 black state convention. At the 1865 convention, Ward chaired the Committee on Industrial Pursuits and produced a report urging blacks to enter business, industry, and professional occupations in order to increase their economic clout.

Ward lobbied the AME to create a California Conference during the 1860s. He achieved this goal in 1868 and was elected the first bishop of the new conference. This involved the enormous task of superintending AME parishes in California, Oregon, and British Columbia. He traveled more than fourteen thousand miles during his first year in the post. In 1872 he was reassigned to a bishopric in the southeastern United States. While there, he established himself as "an orator of the first class" and often wrote for the *AME Church Review*. For the final ten years of his life, Ward was in charge of AME work in Arkansas, Louisiana, and Indian Territory. A strong supporter of higher education for blacks, he played a major role in establishing three denominational colleges during this time. Montesano, "Free Negro Question in San Francisco," 58–62; Wayman, *Cyclopaedia of African Methodism*, 8; ACAB, 6:355; Payne, *African Methodist Episcopal Church*, 285–86; CR, 14 June 1894; Foner and Walker, *Proceedings of the Black State Conventions*, 2:112–30, 168–98.

3. Darius P. Stokes (?–ca. 1864) was described by his contemporaries as an eloquent preacher and skilled debater. Born in Baltimore, he served African Methodist Episcopal congregations there from 1841 to 1849, for a time as Daniel Payne's assistant at the Bethel AME Church. While in the city, he gained a reputation as one of the "first officers" of a black underground railroad network that helped hundreds of slaves escape from the Chesapeake region. Stokes left for Sacramento, California, in 1849, but soon returned home after an unsuccessful attempt to found a congregation among blacks who had followed the gold rush. As Bethel's pastor, he reestablished himself as one of the city's foremost black leaders. He briefly flirted with the colonization movement, taking the lead in organizing Maryland's first black state convention (1852), which endorsed Liberian settlement. He was assaulted by a mob of Baltimore blacks, who stormed the gathering after hearing news of its sentiments.

Stokes returned to Sacramento in 1853. The following year, he became an assistant pastor at the St. Cyprian AME Church in San Francisco, where he helped support himself by working as a whitewasher and a scrap dealer. Stokes claimed to have established fourteen AME churches during his California years. He participated in the statewide struggle for equal rights as a delegate to the 1855 and 1856 black state conventions. He died in Virginia City, Nevada. Wayman, *Cyclopaedia of African Methodism*, 157; Payne, *African Methodist Episcopal Church*, 134, 155, 208–11; ESF, 22 September 1865 [15:0225]; *Lib*, 9 March 1849; Lapp, *Blacks in Gold Rush California*, 95, 108, 158, 245; Graham, *Baltimore*, 153–54; FDP, 6 August 1852, 22 September 1854; NYCJ, September 1852 [7:0718]; VF, 26 August 1852; Foner and Walker, *Proceedings of the Black State Conventions*, 2:112–24; PA, 30 May, 6 June 1863, 12 March 1864 [14:0878, 15:0278].

4. John Jamison Moore (1804–1893) was born to slave parents in Berkeley County, Virginia. Originally named Benjamin Clawson, he changed his name when he escaped to Pennsylvania with his parents during his youth. After embracing religion in 1833, Moore prepared for a preaching career by employing private tutors in Latin, Greek, Hebrew, and theology. In 1839 he began itinerant preaching in Pennsylvania, Maryland, and Ohio. A dynamic pulpit orator, he was considered an outstanding black preacher. Ordained into the African Methodist Episcopal Zion ministry in 1842, he spent the following decade serving AMEZ congregations in Philadelphia and Baltimore. Moore left Baltimore in 1852 for San Francisco, where he established the first AMEZ congregation west of the

Mississippi River. His activism helped energize the nascent California black community. Moore opened and directed the city's first black school, agitated for appropriation of public funds for black education, and opposed the state's black laws. He penned numerous newspaper articles on local black politics and edited and published the *Lunar Visitor*, a black monthly. A participant in the 1855, 1856, and 1865 California black state conventions, he served on various black state committees, and at the 1865 state convention, he urged California blacks to adopt a militant rhetoric in defense of their civil rights.

But Moore's concern extended beyond the local black community. He was a frequent antislavery speaker. He made several extended visits to investigate conditions in the black communities at Victoria, Vancouver Island (1859), and in the Cariboo mining region of British Columbia (1863–64). During the Civil War, he served as corresponding secretary of the California Contraband Relief Association and also did missionary work among Native Americans in California. A leading AMEZ cleric after the war, he was elected to the bishopric in 1868 and returned east to lead an effort to unite his denomination with the African Methodist Episcopal church. When that failed, he directed his energy to missionary work among the freedmen in the South, and during the latter years of Reconstruction, he organized numerous churches in North Carolina, Georgia, and the Bahama Islands. In 1877 Moore was appointed to direct the AMEZ's publishing efforts; two years later, he traveled to England and successfully solicited funds for that purpose. He personally authored a number of AMEZ publications, including a catechism and a denominational history, and edited *The A.M.E. Zion Sunday School Banner* during the 1880s. Moore spent his last years in Salisbury, North Carolina. Walls, *African Methodist Episcopal Zion Church*, 129, 141, 149, 164–66, 199–200, 204, 212, 249, 268, 302, 337–38, 353, 360, 402, 437, 463, 478, 576–77, 632; Douglas H. Daniels, *Pioneer Urbanites: A Social and Cultural History of Black San Francisco* (Philadelphia, Pa., 1980), 64, 113; *G*, 12 December 1885; Foner and Walker, *Proceedings of the Black State Conventions*, 2:112–14, 126, 130, 133–35, 152, 169–71, 178, 192, 196, 201; *PA*, 16 August 1862, 17 January, 11 July, 25 September 1863, 20 February 1864 [14:0446, 0699, 0950, 1067, 15:0251]; *San Francisco City Directory*, 1863.

5. The San Francisco Athenaeum was organized in July 1853 by Jacob Francis, William H. Newby, Jonas H. Townsend, and other prominent local blacks. The society's meeting place became the cultural and intellectual center for the local black community. Members debated major racial and political issues, including "the merits of the controversy between the old antislavery party and the Liberty Party." Within a year, the Athenaeum had attracted eighty-five members, established a library and reading room, and raised $2,000 among local white businessmen. It later publicized local black accomplishments, initiated California's black state conventions, and started the *Mirror of the Times*, the city's first black newspaper. Membership and activity began to decline in late 1857, and despite Newby's attempts to rejuvenate the society, it perished the following year. Lapp, *Blacks in Gold Rush California*, 99–102, 211, 262; *PA*, 20 June 1863 [14:0926–27].

6. California blacks struggled against a wide range of legal and extralegal proscriptions. State law restricted black testimony in the courts, denied blacks

the vote, forbade interracial marriages, and prohibited black participation in the state militia. Three times during the 1850s, the California legislature nearly passed bills prohibiting black immigration into the state. These bills would have required blacks already in the state to register and to carry free papers at all times. In many areas, blacks faced segregation by custom or local ordinance in schools, churches, theaters, hotels, restaurants, and public conveyances. Lapp, *Blacks in Gold Rush California*, 126–38, 148–54, 236–40, 268–69; Daniels, *Pioneer Urbanites*, 107; Eugene H. Berwanger, "The 'Black Laws' Question in Ante-Bellum California," *JW* 6:205–20 (April 1967).

7. Henry M. Collins (1819–1874) was born in Pittsburgh, the son of African Methodist Episcopal clergyman Samuel Collins. After working for several years as a steamboat steward on the Ohio River, he began to invest in various building and real estate ventures and became one of the foremost developers in Pittsburgh. In the early 1840s, he established himself as a leader of the local black community. He worked for black suffrage at the 1841 black state convention, served on the publishing committee of Martin R. Delany's *Mystery*, and aided fugitive slaves passing through the city.

Collins moved to San Francisco in 1852 and assumed a prominent position among the city's burgeoning black population. Although employed as a steward by the California Steam Navigation Company, and later as a janitor in the Merchant's Exchange, he became one of California's wealthiest black businessmen. Using the investment knowledge he had gained in Pittsburgh, Collins acquired extensive property holdings in San Francisco; he later founded and directed the black Savings and Land Association, which accumulated capital for land speculation throughout the state. He also organized several profitable trading expeditions to the gold-mining camps near Victoria, Vancouver Island.

Although "not gifted as a public speaker," Collins gained respect for his leadership skills, forthright manner, and business expertise. He helped finance and manage the construction of three black churches in San Francisco, served as a trustee of the St. Cyprian AME Church, and took the lead in organizing the Livingstone Institute—a society that fostered black education. He continued to promote the black press, serving as local subscription agent for *Frederick Douglass' Paper* and on the publishing committee of the *Mirror of the Times*, a San Francisco paper. Collins provided vital leadership for the civil rights struggle in California. He served as treasurer of a statewide black executive committee and participated in the 1855, 1856, and 1857 black state conventions. A contemporary called him one of the "prime movers" behind these gatherings. Collins suffered great tragedy in his personal life. Nine of his ten children died at an early age. His wife, Elizabeth, moved to Ohio in 1865, while he remained in California until his death. *PA*, 25 September 1863, 12 March 1864, 27 June, 18, 25 July 1874 [14:1067, 15:0276]; Lapp, *Blacks in Gold Rush California*, 99, 188, 219, 265; *ESF*, 30 June, 1 December 1865 [15:0983, 16:0491]; Delany, *Condition of the Colored People*, 104–5; Foner and Walker, *Proceedings of the Black State Conventions*, 1:116, 2:112–203.

8. On the evening of 1 August 1854, San Francisco blacks gathered at the Stockton Street African Methodist Episcopal Zion Church to commemorate West Indian emancipation. The program began with recitations by several stu-

dents, followed by a brief but rousing speech by Rev. T. M. D. Ward. Jonas H. Townsend, William H. Newby, Jeremiah B. Sanderson, and John C. Jenkins offered brief remarks. *FDP*, 20 October 1854.

9. Jonas Holland Townsend (?–1872) graduated from Waterville (now Colby) College in Maine. By the early 1840s, he was a leading figure in the black community of Albany, New York. Townsend represented local blacks at the 1843 black national convention in Buffalo, where he endorsed Henry Highland Garnet's militant "Address to the Slaves"; later that year, he attended the black state convention in Rochester. Although he urged blacks to work for change through the political process, his disavowal of minor antislavery parties prompted critics to label him "a colored Whig." In 1849 he began a career in journalism when he started the *Hyperion* in New York City. One contemporary described it as a "gratifying exception to the mass of papers started in this country by persons of color, both as regards its size, and the ability with which it is conducted." But the publication soon ceased when Townsend joined an all-black mining association headed for the California gold fields.

After arriving in San Francisco, Townsend established himself as a spokesman for the city's black community. With Mifflin W. Gibbs, he initiated a prolonged, statewide campaign to overturn restrictions on black testimony in the courts. He helped found the San Francisco Athenaeum, a local black cultural and intellectual society. And he proved to be a key figure at the 1855, 1856, and 1857 black state conventions. As chairman of a statewide black executive committee, he provided vital leadership for the civil rights struggle of California blacks. In response to calls by the Athenaeum and the 1855 convention, he helped establish the *Mirror of the Times*, the first black newspaper in the state. He edited the journal from 1856 to 1858, forging it into a mouthpiece for the equal rights campaign.

Townsend returned to New York City near the end of the decade. He continued his journalistic endeavors, writing for the *Anglo-African Magazine* and editing *Frederick Douglass' Paper* during Douglass's 1859 tour of Europe. He also continued to fight for black voting rights as a member of the New York State Suffrage Association and secretary of the 1858 black suffrage convention. Townsend worked in the New York Customs House after the Civil War. In the early 1870s, he moved to Brazoria, Texas, and became involved in local Republican party politics. He was selected as a Republican presidential elector in 1872. Montesano, "Free Negro Question in San Francisco," 22–25; *AP*, 26 January, 3 October 1843 [4:0529, 0676]; *NSt*, 15 September 1848, 3, 10 August 1849; *Lib*, 30 March 1849; *IC*, 5 December 1849; *FDP*, 23 November 1855; *AAM*, March 1859; *WAA*, 22 October 1859, 24 March 1860, 28 December 1861; *PA*, 2 June 1863; *ESF*, 28 May 1869, 25 August 1872; Lapp, *Blacks in Gold Rush California*, 13, 39, 194, 266; Foner and Walker, *Proceedings of the Black State Conventions*, 1:99, 2:112–27, 132–65.

10. William H. Newby (1828–1859) was born in Virginia to a slave father and free black mother. When Newby's father died during his childhood, his mother moved the family to Philadelphia. Young Newby studied in the city's segregated public schools, joined the Philadelphia Library Company of Colored Persons, and learned the hairdresser's trade. Increasingly dissatisfied with his occupation, he became a daguerreotypist in 1845 and pursued that career with some success

until moving to California in 1851. Newby dominated the emerging cultural life of the San Francisco black community in the 1850s. He was a skilled debater and an active Mason. In 1853 he joined with Jonas H. Townsend and other local black leaders to organize the San Francisco Athenaeum, the first black literary association in the state. It functioned as a forum for debating racial issues. In 1856 Newby and Townsend established the *Mirror of the Times,* a local black paper devoted to the discussion of national black concerns. Both men edited the paper; Newby acted as traveling agent. Writing under the pseudonym "Nubia," he regularly reported on the San Francisco black community in letters to *Frederick Douglass' Paper.*

Newby was a dominant figure in California's early black state conventions. He represented San Francisco blacks at the 1855 and 1856 gatherings, where he pressed for racial unity, urged action against the state's testimony laws, and recommended the development of a state black press. Newby helped coordinate the statewide petition campaigns for black rights that emerged from the conventions. He created a stir at the 1856 convention by questioning black allegiance to the United States. As the decade wore on, he became increasingly attracted to emigration and explored the idea in several letters to *Frederick Douglass' Paper.* In the fall of 1857, he accepted a position as private secretary to the French consul in Haiti. Newby had contracted tuberculosis and thought the Haitian climate might restore his health. But after arriving there in early 1858, he found that the consul had died and left him without employment. He returned home in a weakened condition and endeavored to resuscitate the Athenaeum, which had become moribund during his absence. Finding that task too great, he organized the Dillon Literary Association, believing that such a body was vital to the life of the local black community. That organization also failed, a victim of his growing sickness and eventual death. *PA,* 20 June 1863 [14:0926–27]; Lapp, *Blacks in Gold Rush California,* 100–101, 189–90, 211–12, 223–24, 263; Foner and Walker, *Proceedings of the Black State Conventions,* 2:110–66.

11. In 1849 Chinese immigrants began to arrive in San Francisco in large numbers. Chinatown, a distinct Chinese neighborhood, soon developed. The dramatic growth of the Chinese population, their distinctive culture, and the disease and crime that plagued their neighborhood alarmed and angered many local whites. They were frequently subjected to public insults and abuse. Because of a state law that prohibited their testimony in the courts, they were particularly vulnerable to acts of fraud, thievery, and violence. Most white workingmen viewed the Chinese as an economic threat. Responding to these fears, the California legislature often considered, but never passed, laws restricting Chinese immigration. San Francisco blacks rarely mistreated the Chinese, but their views were mixed. The local black press frequently criticized them, and in 1867 the *Elevator* called for a prohibition of further immigration from the Asian mainland. Gunther Barth, *Bitter Strength: A History of the Chinese in the United States, 1850–1870* (Cambridge, Mass., 1964), 57–156.

48.
William Whipper to Frederick Douglass
[October 1854]

The transformation of William Whipper's views on the origins and nature of American racism paralleled the course of black abolitionist
thought. During the 1830s, Whipper embodied the black community's
widespread devotion to moral reform. Prejudice against blacks, he explained in 1837, "*arises not from the color of their skin, but from their
condition.*" He advised blacks to conform to white expectations—to improve their mental, moral, and economic situation—as the surest means
to change white racial attitudes. But by the 1850s, most black leaders
had abandoned moral reform and rejected the "condition" argument as
"fit only to be used by our oppressors." Reflecting this change, Whipper
now blamed racism on white ignorance. He believed that blacks had little power to alter race relations—American racism was ingrained, instinctive, and likely to endure for generations. Not all blacks shared
Whipper's pessimism. A few persistent moral reformers continued to
promote the "condition" argument. The following October 1854 letter
from Whipper to Frederick Douglass was part of this ongoing debate
among black leaders. In it, Whipper defended his current view that
"complexion . . . and nothing else" caused racial prejudice. *CA*, 24 June
1837, 23 February 1839 [2:0091, 3:0012]; *FDP*, 19 January, 2 February, 13 April, 8 June 1855 [9:0393, 0420–21, 0535–36, 0687].

MR. EDITOR:

What is prejudice, its cause, and against what is it applied? Some say
against "*complexion,*" others "*condition.*" Is it either or any one of
them? The learned doctors disagree; and it is not likely that any of them
will be able to prescribe a cure, until they have found out the true nature
and cause of the disease.

I was amused on reading the running debate on this subject, as reported in the *Standard* of the 7th inst.[1]

W. W. Brown commences by stating that "prejudice" originated in the
slave States, because slavery exists there; that it applies to *condition*, not
color; that the latter is the mark that instances the condition. The condition of slaves is a general condition, they all being denied the right of self
control. But how will Mr. Brown's argument apply to the condition of
the colored people in the free States? Is not their condition as special and
variable as the whites, among whom they reside? He says that "he did
not feel it in England, but on landing at Philadelphia, was driven out of
an omnibus on account of it."

Now, if Mr. B. had landed in Boston instead of Philadelphia, and "entered an omnibus," he would, doubtless, have been without an illustration for his argument.[2] Boston and Philadelphia are both in "free States," and equally connected with the slave power by the Constitution and laws of the federal government. Now, if the *cause* of prejudice was against the condition of Mr. B., why did he not receive the same treatment in England and Boston, as in Philadelphia?

I regret that we have not a full report of the debate. The Rev. Beriah Green,[3] it is said, poured forth a stream of philosophy on the subject; and I readily grant, that if this "prejudice" was found in philosophy, he is the very man to explain its "cause and effect." But unfortunately for this distinguished speaker and profound thinker, it does not repose in the sacred sepulchre of philosophy. Its foundation is in man's selfish nature, pride and ambition, which rule and govern his worst passions. It grows spontaneous, inflates the instincts of the ignorant, and directs the minds of the learned. It has a home at the fireside and the altar. It follows men to the loftiest heights of ambition, and down to the deepest grave. It nerves the arm of the despot, and nestles in the affections of the patron saint. It is of antiquated birth, and witnessed the slaying of the Egyptian by Moses.[4] It is older than kings or constitutions. It is not physical in its nature, and can only become the patron of governments by adoption.

Mr. Green says, "this colorphobia is what in Europe is called caste, and in the Bible, respect of persons. The color is of no account. It is only the index of slavery, and despised for that cause." What! the color of no account, and yet the index of slavery. Why, the index of a book is of great importance to the reader, and so is the "color" to the slaveholder. If it was not for the "color," the fugitive slave law would be rendered nugatory. The color is despised, because it is the index of slavery, under a slaveholding government. This appears very extraordinary. It would be but fair to suppose that those who were favorable to the institution of slavery would *love* the complexion that designated the victims over whom they hold despotic control; and that those who hated slavery would hate the index that pointed to it. If this supposition be founded in truth, it furnishes a reason why "prejudice" is stronger against colored persons in the free, than in the slave States. But let us agree for the sake of argument that "color" is the index of slavery, and that "prejudice against color" (as we call it, says Frederick Douglass) is an emanation from it. Is it logical to believe that it can exist after the cause is renovated? Let us suppose that "chattel slavery" shall be abolished by natural and State legislation tomorrow, will any sane mind believe for a minute that this natural edict will obliterate this prejudice by the same "fell swoop"? Certainly not—Will not this "color be of some account as an index" to the State governments as it is now to the governments of the "free States," as a standard to disqualify the colored people from the rights and privileges of the elective franchise, to erect "negro pews" to debar them from equal privileges in colleges, schools, trades, the arts and sciences, the social circle, the halls of legislature, the jury box, the forum, public conveyances, &c.?

In my opinion, the power that this prejudice *now* exerts in the few States is not dependent on the foetid breath of slavery, but that the people of those Commonwealths are capable of perpetuating it after slavery is abolished. Therefore, I am unable to comprehend the doctrine that this prejudice has its origin in "chattel slavery," or that it will be obliterated by its abolition. I think the discovery will yet be made that this prejudice is of very ancient birth, that it has pursued different nationalities down the long catalogue of ages, that it is older than American slavery and that the latter derived its existence from an organic action of the former. I intended to notice the arguments of the other speakers, but my sheet is full.

W. W.

Frederick Douglass' Paper (Rochester, N.Y.), 3 November 1854.

1. Whipper refers to a debate during a 29 September 1854 special meeting of the American Anti-Slavery Society held at City Hall in Syracuse, New York. William Wells Brown posited that American racial prejudice originated in the slave states, because slavery existed there. Beriah Green later expanded on Brown's remarks. Arguing that "colour is of no account," he pointed to Brown's contention to bolster his claim that condition was the cause of prejudice. A lengthy dispute then ensued between Green and Charles L. Remond, who asserted that "this question of colour is the pivot on which the whole question turns." *NASS*, 7 October 1854.

2. By the mid-1850s, blacks and whites in Boston enjoyed "the privilege of being squeezed up" together in omnibuses and public stages. Although most common carriers had enforced Jim Crow restrictions during the previous decade, they had voluntarily ended the practice by this time. *Lib*, 16 March 1860; Horton and Horton, *Black Bostonians*, 68.

3. Beriah Green (1795–1874), an early immediatist, chaired the 1833 convention that organized the American Anti-Slavery Society. From 1833 to 1844, he was president of Oneida Institute, an interracial college in Whitesboro, New York. Green became a leading figure in the Liberty party and the Union church movement during the early 1840s. After leaving Oneida, he served a local Congregational church until 1867. *DAB*, 7:539–40; McKivigan, *War Against Proslavery Religion*, 147.

4. Whipper refers to a story from Exodus 2:11–15, in which Moses, a Jew, kills an Egyptian overseer for brutally beating a Jewish slave.

49.
Speech by William Wells Brown
Delivered at the Horticultural Hall
West Chester, Pennsylvania
23 October 1854

At the core of the black abolitionist message was a belief in the intimate bond between slavery and prejudice. Black leaders sometimes disagreed over the precise nature of that relationship, but all agreed that both were equally malevolent and must be opposed by the larger antislavery movement. William Wells Brown, a former slave who had encountered discrimination in the North, spoke on the subject with an authority that came from personal experience. He invoked black abolitionism's twin themes at the 23 October 1854 annual meeting of the Pennsylvania Anti-Slavery Society, which convened in the Horticultural Hall at West Chester, Pennsylvania. With the Quaker abolitionist James Mott in the chair, Brown took his place at the podium and excoriated the hypocrisy of American race relations. He reiterated a standard litany of black abolitionist charges—the evils of slavery and the slave trade, the complicity of American Christianity and republicanism in perpetuating slavery, and the unequal treatment of free blacks in the North. Although Brown saw evidence that northern public opinion was "beginning to be aroused" against slavery, he reminded whites in the audience of their obligation to fight prejudice. *NASS,* 4 November 1854.

Mr. Chairman and Ladies and Gentlemen:

The short time that I shall occupy your attention will be devoted more particularly to considering the condition and past treatment of the slaves and free people of colour in this country. With all the boasted philanthropy and Christianity of the people of this Republic, the coloured race has received at their hands treatment scarcely equalled by that of any people the world has ever known. Introduced into the colonies more than two centuries ago, bought and sold from generation to generation, they have indeed become the "hewers of wood and drawers of water."[1] You have all heard of the horrors of the African slave trade. I do not know that I had a just idea of its horrors until I heard them depicted in the House of Commons in England, and I am sure that no countryman of mine would have been willing to have been identified on that occasion as a dealer in human beings. A great mistake was made by the fathers of this country when they incorporated the slave trade in the Constitution of the country, allowed the slave representation in Congress, and gave to the slaveholder the right to hunt his victims in the free States.[2] It was believed that Christianity and Republicanism would wipe out the foul

Engraved by J.C. Buttre.

Wm. W. Brown.

10. William Wells Brown
Courtesy of the Historical Society of Pennsylvania

blot, but such has not been the result. On the contrary, the number of slaves has increased from a little more than half a million to three and a half millions. The African slave trade was abolished after a certain time, but a worse than the African slave trade continued to exist. The internal slave trade, it is true, has not the middle passage and the drowning of its victims; but the black race has, to some extent, become refined by intercourse and commingling of blood with the Anglo-Saxon, so that they feel more sensitively the separations of families, sundering of ties and other cruelties which are inseparable from the system. A hundred thousand slaves are taken from the slave-raising to the slave-consuming States every year.[3] What a tale to tell future generations about the people of this country! Professors of Christianity, members of the popular religious denominations, engaged in raising, selling, buying and whipping men and women on their plantations! Go into a southern market and see men and women sold in lots to suit purchasers, and then place yourselves in their condition, if you would feel for them as you ought. Place your wife, daughter or child in their position, to be struck off to the highest bidder, if you would realize their wrongs and sufferings. Indifference from our own friends and relations is sad; it is terrible indeed to the sensitive bosom. Then think of the slave mother who sees her child placed in the market and knows that that child is sold by its father. This is no fancy picture; we know that such scenes do take place every day. Why do I stand before you, Mr. Chairman, tonight, not an African nor an Anglo-Saxon, but of mixed blood? It is attributable to the infernal system of American slavery. My father is a slave-owner, and at his instance was I sold on a southern plantation.[4]

They tell us that the slave is contented and happy.[5] I heard a gentleman travelling between New York and Philadelphia remark about his old slaves being cared for and watched over. It reminded me of what I saw in the Isle of Wight[6]—a donkey enjoying a degree of liberty that no other animal was allowed to enjoy. For thirty years that donkey had drawn water from a very deep well and was now a pensioner. He was allowed his penny loaf of bread every day and full range of the premises, and he was strutting around like a duke; but, alas, his limbs were so stiff that he could scarcely move; his best days had been spent in a treadmill, drawing water, and he was hobbling about in his decrepitude. And so it is with the human donkeys in the South; if one poor slave lives to be so old and infirm that he is unfit to labour, he is pensioned off like this superannuated donkey.[7] Should that fact weigh a single moment upon the minds of intelligent persons in favour of enslaving a race because they happen to have skins not coloured like your own?

We cannot tell the evils that exist in the southern States. Like the painter who stands idle by the side of his picture, waiting for the crowd to go out before lifting the screen from the canvas, for fear of frightening his visitors with the unfinished work, so we must wait and let the future historian complete the picture. I know that, after having spent twenty years as a slave, one would suppose that I might relate the evils that I witnessed. And so I might. I might stand here for hours and tell you what I saw, and felt, and know, but now is not the time. The time has passed for devoting ourselves to such a purpose. We need not go out of the free States to see its cruelties. They are all about us. Look at the coloured people of the free States, thrown out of your schools, your churches and your social circles, deprived of their political rights and debarred from those avenues of employment that are necessary to a proper maintenance of themselves and families. We find the degrading influences of slavery all about us. Pennsylvania deprives the black man of the elective franchise, and so does New York, except with a property qualification. In most of the northern States, he is looked upon as something to be knocked and kicked about as they see fit. There were two passengers on board the *Atlantic* when I returned from Europe, who had ridden with me on the same car from London to Liverpool, and we enjoyed the same privileges on board the steamer. They were foreigners and I an American; and when they landed in this country, they were boasting that they had arrived at a land of liberty where they could enjoy religious and political freedom. I, too, might have rejoiced, had I not been a coloured man, at my return to my native land; but I knew what treatment to expect from my countrymen—that it would not be even such as was meted out to those foreigners, and I rejoiced only to meet my anti-slavery friends. We all started to walk up the streets of Philadelphia together; we hailed an omnibus; the two foreigners got in; I was told that "niggers" were not allowed to ride.[8] Foreigners, mere adventurers, perhaps, in this country, are treated as equals, while I, an American born, whose grandfather fought in the revolution,[9] am not permitted to ride in one of your fourth-rate omnibuses. The foreigner has a right, after five years' residence, to say who shall be President, as far as his vote goes, even though he cannot read your Constitution or write his name, while 600,000 free coloured people are disfranchised. And then you talk about equality and liberty, the land of the free and the home of the brave, the asylum of the oppressed, the cradle of liberty! You have the cradle, but you have rocked the child to death.

I think I have a right to speak of the shortcomings of the people of this country. I stand here as the representative of the slave to speak for those who cannot speak for themselves, and I stand here as the representative of the free coloured man who cannot come up to this convention. I saw not long since in one of your papers a statement that a coloured American had applied to an American Consul in a foreign land for a passport and it was denied him; the Consul would not admit that he was a citizen of the United States, and he was obliged to go without a passport. When

I wished to leave this country, through the aid of my eloquent friend, Wendell Phillips, I secured a paper from the State of Massachusetts showing that I was a citizen of this country. I went to Mr. Davis, the Secretary of Abbott Lawrence, and asked for my passport. I was told that I was not an American citizen. I produced my paper and said that if he refused me a passport I would get one from the English government and would sail under foreign colours. I knew I could get one from the English government, because I had been offered it. The Secretary was ashamed and turned round and made out my passport.[10] He was afraid I would go before the English public, where the anti-slavery feeling was so strong, and make the fact known that the American Minister in England refused to recognize my citizenship.

There is no parallel in history to the treatment of the coloured people in this country; certainly none in the present. Tell me of any nation treating any portion of their subjects as we are treated. We are told by the colonizationists that we must be sent out of the country—that we are not citizens of it. If I am not a citizen of the United States, pray, are you? Did your father not come from another country? We were brought here by force, it is true (I speak not now as an Anglo-Saxon, as I have a right to speak, but as an African), but that fact does not alter our birthright. And you are willing to acknowledge the citizenship of the foreigner no matter how ignorant or degraded; but because I am a shade darker than you, you disfranchise me. I am ashamed when I hear men talking about the national honour of this country being insulted by the Spaniards, or Cubans, just as if we had any national honour to be insulted![11] A nation that enslaves and scourges one-sixth part of its people talking about national honour! Go to the South and see Methodist carting Methodist to the market and selling him, Baptist whipping Baptist, and Presbyterian purchasing Presbyterian, and Episcopalian tying chains upon the limbs of Episcopalian, and then talk about national character and honour! I know these are hard sayings, but they are true and must be told, and they are the best friends of their country who sound the alarm. You need not be startled at our motto, "No Union with Slaveholders"; this nation has within it the elements of disunion.[12] And are you not, after all, as much in favour of disunion as I am? Where are your rights, guaranteed by the Constitution to every citizen? Where is the right of free locomotion in the slave States? Go into the southern States an avowed enemy of slaveholding, and are you free? I point you to the murdered Lovejoy; to Burr, Work and Thompson spending four or five years in a Missouri prison; to Torrey pining away in a southern prison; to Fairbanks now in a Kentucky penitentiary; to Delia Webster persecuted and imprisoned in the same State; to Mrs. Douglass shut up in a Virginia jail, and all because they did not think as slaveholders think.[13] Can you be as free in South Carolina as the South Carolinian can be in

Pennsylvania? He can walk the streets of Philadelphia or New York and say what he pleases, and he is protected, while a southern Senator threatens a northern man with hanging upon the tallest tree if he shows himself in Mississippi, simply because he speaks his thoughts on the subject of freedom. And when you send a man to the South to test by law this very right of the citizens of any State to all the immunities of the citizens of the several States under the Constitution, to bring it before one of the Courts of the United States in the South to be adjudicated, he is expelled from the State by mob violence.[14]

I thank God, Mr. Chairman, that this question of American slavery is no longer a question between the black man and the slave-owner, but a question between the people of the North and South. You have allowed them to enslave the black man, to extend the institution and to make the whole North a hunting ground for their slaves, until the people of the free States can endure it no longer, and the North is now fairly pitted against the South. Look at your political parties torn asunder by the slavery issue[15]—and I am glad of it. Look at your religious denominations divided on the same question[16]—and I am glad of it. The great issue is beginning to be between the North and South. The people of the South have always looked upon the people of the North as their pliant tools, and I am glad to see the North becoming aware of it. You welcome the fugitive from European oppression, and, after shaking hands with him and congratulating him for his escape, you turn to catch the fugitive from American oppression and return him to his chains.[17] And when you could find no better man to welcome, you welcomed John Mitchel, who is ready to join in the chase with you.[18] Four hundred thousand foreigners come here every year, and you welcome them, while you drive the coloured American from your very doors.

But the people of the North are beginning to be aroused, and the cry of "disunion," which they have heretofore hated so much to hear, is practically becoming their watchword. The North is arrayed against the South, and you know it, and you are become practically co-workers with us. If you do not go as far as we do, you follow in the wake, and are coming up. Men that were Democrats and Whigs ten years ago are disunionists today, and Democrats and Whigs of today will be disunionists before the next ten years roll round. You have fostered slavery until you find yourselves enslaved. It was the sentiment of a distinguished writer that no man could put a chain upon the limbs of another without fastening a chain upon his own. You have helped the slaveholder put chains upon his slave until he has fettered his own limbs, and you are now beginning to see it.

I stand here tonight a freeman only by the act of British philanthropists. I left this country a slave; I returned a freeman.[19] I am not indebted to my birth, or to your Constitution, or to your Christianity, or to your philanthropy for it. Am I then indeed an American citizen, or am I a foreigner? Call me what you please, I am nevertheless a freeman; and yet I feel scarcely more free than I did twenty years ago when I was working on Price's plantation. I felt then that I had as good a right to my freedom as the man who claimed me as his property, and, acting under that conviction, I started for the North. I could not help thinking, while abroad, of the treatment I had received in this country at the hands of the American people, and I asked myself, why is it that I can put up at one of the best hotels in Liverpool, or London, or Paris, or Rotterdam, and not in Philadelphia? Why is it that I can ride in the coach, or omnibus, or railcar, or steamboat, in Great Britain or on the continent, and enjoy the same privileges that any man enjoys, while I cannot do it here? It is not because of the colour of my skin, but because of the influence of slavery. My daughters were kept out of school in the State of New York, and would have been brought up in ignorance in this country, and so I resolved to take them away from this liberty-loving country and educate them under a monarchical government and institutions. They go abroad and they are received and treated according to their merits and not according to their colour, and today one of them, the daughter of an American slave, teaches a school of Anglo-Saxons, and the other is preparing herself, under another monarchical government, France, to follow the same employment.[20] You talk about the despotism of Napoleon III,[21] and yet your own countrymen escaping from American despotism can find protection under his throne. I could walk free and protected in any part of the Kingdom of Great Britain, but I dared not set foot on American soil until some southern scoundrel first received $300 for me. You have not a single foot of soil in all this republic on which I could have stood a year ago and said I was a freeman, though born and brought up here, and descended from ancestors who fought in the American revolution for American liberty. I know there is oppression abroad; I am not blind to the fact that in all the governments of Europe there is more or less oppression, but before we talk of the oppression of other countries, let us look at our own; before you put out your hands to welcome the victims of foreign oppression, wash them clean so that the blood of the slave may not contaminate the hand of the foreigner. Before you boast of your freedom and Christianity, do your duty to your fellowman.

National Anti-Slavery Standard (New York, N.Y.), 4 November 1854.

1. "Hewers of wood and drawers of water" is used in the Old Testament to refer to servants or slaves. Josh. 9:21–23.

2. Delegates to the 1787 Constitutional Convention approved three provisions dealing with slavery. Article 1, section 2, of the U.S. Constitution, better known as the three-fifths clause, provided that three-fifths of the slave population

should be counted in apportioning taxes and representation in the U.S. House of Representatives. Article 1, section 9, prohibited Congress from interfering with the importation of slaves until 1808. Article 4, section 2, provided for the return of fugitive slaves. This clause appeared to leave enforcement to the states but was refined when Congress enacted the Fugitive Slave Law of 1793, providing a legal mechanism for the return of escaped slaves. Alfred H. Kelly and Winifred A. Harbison, *The American Constitution: Its Origins and Development*, 3d ed. (New York, N.Y., 1963), 262–63.

3. The U.S. Congress banned the importation of slaves in 1808, but a surplus of slaves in the upper South and a growing demand for slaves in the developing cottonlands of the lower South caused a dramatic expansion of the domestic slave trade during the early nineteenth century. A network of professional slave traders and large slave-trading depots emerged in key cities of the upper South. Some 600,000 slaves were removed from the older slave states to the newer slave states of the deep South and Texas in the three decades before the Civil War; slave traders were responsible for 20 to 25 percent of this movement. *DAAS*, 684–89.

4. Brown's father was probably George W. Higgins of Fayette County, Kentucky. Higgins was a cousin of Brown's master, Dr. John Young, and was "connected with some of the first families in Kentucky." Farrison, *William Wells Brown*, 5–6.

5. To counter antislavery propaganda and calm southern fears of slave insurrection, proslavery apologists promulgated the image of the docile and contented bondsman. They charged that nature made blacks unfit for freedom and claimed that slaves found happiness and fulfillment only in slavery. The contented slave thesis complemented southern views of slavery as a "positive good" and formed a central element of proslavery thought. George M. Fredrickson, *The Black Image in the White Mind: The Debate on Afro-American Character and Destiny, 1817–1914* (New York, N.Y., 1971), 52.

6. Brown probably visited the Isle of Wight, about three miles off the coast of southeastern England, while lecturing in the port city of Southampton during 8–9 July 1850. *Lib*, 9 August 1850.

7. The treatment of aged slaves varied from paternalistic concern to appalling abuse and neglect. Many were "retired" and provided a small allowance or permitted to remain on the plantation, where they acquired positions of respect in the slave community. Local whites, not wanting aged slaves to become a public charge, also reminded masters of their responsibilities. Despite custom and public opinion, many owners merely manumitted their elderly slaves and left them to survive on their own under the harshest of circumstances. Eugene D. Genovese, *Roll, Jordan, Roll: The World the Slaves Made* (New York, N.Y., 1972), 519–23.

8. This incident took place in Philadelphia on the afternoon of 26 September 1854, immediately after Brown's arrival from Britain aboard the *City of Manchester*. William Wells Brown, *Sketches of Places and People Abroad* (Boston, Mass., 1855), 311–14.

9. Brown's maternal grandfather, a slave named Simon Lee, fought with a Virginia regiment during the American Revolution. He expected to gain his freedom in exchange for military service, but after the war, he was honorably discharged and returned to his master. Nell, *Colored Patriots*, 223.

10. In mid-1849, Wendell Phillips helped Brown obtain a certificate from

William B. Calhoun, the Massachusetts secretary of state, that permitted Brown to travel abroad. On 31 October, he visited the American legation in London to obtain a passport before proceeding on to France. John C. B. Davis (1822–1907), the secretary of the legation from 1849 to 1852, granted his request. Davis served under Boston merchant Abbott Lawrence (1792–1855), who was then the American ambassador to Britain. Nell, *Colored Patriots*, 323–26; *DAB*, 5:134–36, 11:44–46.

11. Brown refers to contemporary diplomatic tensions between Spain and the United States. On 28 February 1854, Spanish authorities in Cuba seized an American merchant ship, the *Black Warrior*, for technical violations of port regulations. The incident sparked widespread indignation in the United States; President Franklin Pierce asked Congress for authority "to vindicate the honor of our flag." Although an ultimatum was issued demanding an apology and payment of a sizable indemnity, Pierce eventually allowed Spanish authorities to settle the affair directly with the ship's owners.

12. Brown quotes the disunionist motto of the American Anti-Slavery Society, which first appeared in the 17 March 1843 issue of the *Liberator* and was adopted by the society at its 1844 annual meeting. Garrisonians dissociated themselves from any relationship with slavery and the institutions that directly or indirectly gave it support, including the federal government. Aileen S. Kraditor, *Means and Ends in American Abolitionism: Garrison and His Critics on Strategy and Tactics* (New York, N.Y., 1969), 199–200.

13. Brown refers to eight individuals considered martyrs for the antislavery cause. Elijah P. Lovejoy (1802–1837), the antislavery editor of the Alton (Ill.) *Observer*, was killed in 1837 by a mob intent on smashing his press. James Burr, Alanson Work, and George Thompson of Quincy, Illinois, were arrested in Missouri in 1841 for helping slaves escape to Illinois. Although sentenced to twelve years in the state penitentiary, they were released by 1846. Political abolitionist Charles T. Torrey (1813–1846) of Massachusetts was arrested in Baltimore in 1844 for his extensive underground railroad work. He died in a Maryland prison while serving a six-year sentence. In 1846 Methodist clergyman Calvin Fairbanks (1816–1898) and schoolteacher Delia Ann Webster (1818–1904) were imprisoned for helping black abolitionist Lewis Hayden escape from slavery in Kentucky. Although Webster was quickly freed, Fairbanks served four years before being pardoned. Both returned to their underground work. Fairbanks was imprisoned a second time and not released until 1864. Norfolk authorities arrested seamstress Margaret Douglass in 1853 for operating a school for free blacks in violation of state law. She served one month in the city jail. Merrill and Ruchames, *Letters of William Lloyd Garrison*, 2:328–29, 332, 410; Clyde S. Kilby, "Three Antislavery Prisoners," *ISHSJ* 52:419–30 (Autumn 1959); *DAB*, 6:247, 11:434–35, 18:495–96; Marion Tinling, ed., *Women Remembered: A Guide to Landmarks of Women's History in the United States* (Westport, Conn., 1986), 159; Philip S. Foner and Josephine F. Pacheco, *Three Who Dared: Prudence Crandall, Margaret Douglass, Myrtilla Miner—Champions of Antebellum Black Education* (Westport, Conn., 1984), 57–95.

14. Brown refers to the treatment of Massachusetts officials Samuel Hoar and Henry Hubbard when they attempted to challenge the constitutionality of the black seamen's acts in the courts of South Carolina and Louisiana.

15. Events of the early 1850s sparked a realignment of America's party system.

Battles over the Compromise of 1850 fractured Whig unity in 1852. The Kansas-Nebraska Act, which came before the Senate in January 1854, prompted the rise of a new political organization. Angered by Democratic support for the expansion of slavery in the West, anti-Nebraska Democrats, Conscience Whigs, Free Soilers, and old Liberty party men came together later that year to form the Republican party. The new party's commitment to the principle of nonextension attracted many abolitionists. William E. Gienapp, *The Origins of the Republican Party, 1852–1856* (New York, N.Y., 1987), 13–271.

16. By 1845 America's three major evangelical Protestant denominations had broken apart over the issue of slavery. The Presbyterian church separated into New School and Old School factions in 1837, ostensibly over matters of doctrine. But sharp divisions over slavery figured significantly in the schism. Methodists formally divided over slavery in 1844, although a sizable antislavery group had seceded one year earlier to establish the Wesleyan Methodist church. In 1845 Baptists south of the Mason-Dixon line repudiated the moderate antislavery views of their northern brethren and formed the Southern Baptist Convention. Although Episcopalians, Catholics, Lutherans, Disciples of Christ, and other major denominations had articulate activists on both sides of the slavery debate, most managed to avoid disruption until the Civil War. C. C. Goen, *Broken Churches, Broken Nation: Denominational Schisms and the Coming of the Civil War* (Macon, Ga., 1985), 66–107, 134.

17. Brown refers to enforcement of the Fugitive Slave Law of 1850.

18. John Mitchel (1815–1875), an Irish journalist and nationalist, was deported to a Tasmanian penal colony because of his radical politics in 1850. He escaped and surfaced in New York City in 1854 as the publisher of the *Citizen*. An unabashed advocate of slavery, he soon gained national notoriety and lectured throughout the South. Mitchel edited newspapers in Knoxville and Richmond during the Civil War era. He returned to Ireland in 1874. Blassingame, *Frederick Douglass Papers*, 1:139–40n; *Lib*, 27 January, 3 February, 17 March 1854.

19. Brown went to Britain in 1849 as a fugitive slave. After the enactment of the Fugitive Slave Law of 1850, he faced the very real possibility of arrest and reenslavement if he returned to the United States. To eliminate this threat, British abolitionists raised $300 to buy his freedom from his former master, St. Louis merchant and steamboat owner Enoch Price. Working through a Boston agent, Ellen Richardson of Newcastle, England, completed the purchase in April 1854. Farrison, *William Wells Brown*, 238–42.

20. Brown refused to allow his two daughters, Clarissa (b. 1836) and Josephine (b. 1839), to enroll in Buffalo's segregated public school system. To do so, he insisted, "would have been to some extent giving sanction to the proscriptive prejudice." In 1845 he moved to Farmington, a center of antislavery activities in western New York, so that his daughters could learn in an integrated environment. In July 1851, Brown sent Clarissa and Josephine abroad. They studied for a year at a seminary in Calais, France, then enrolled at the Home and Colonial School in London. After eighteen months of study, they received teaching certificates. In early 1854, both obtained positions as schoolmistresses in England—Clarissa at Berden, near London; Josephine at Plumstead in Woolwich. Later

that year, Josephine went back to France to continue her education. She returned to the United States in 1855 and accompanied her father on antislavery lecture tours of New England. After writing *Biography of an American Bondsman, by His Daughter* (1856), an account of her father's life, she rejoined her sister in England. Farrison, *William Wells Brown*, 66–67, 93–94, 192–97, 245, 270–75; Mabee, *Black Education in New York State*, 183–84.

21. Charles Louis Napoleon Bonaparte (1808–1873) was elected president of France in 1848. Four years later, he proclaimed himself Emperor Napoleon III and assumed dictatorial powers. His reign, which was marked by mass imprisonments, suppression of the press, and bloody repression of popular resistance, ended with Prussia's conquest of France in 1870.

50.
Editorial by William J. Watkins
22 December 1854

Americans of the mid-nineteenth century celebrated the growth of their democratic institutions and heralded their mission to serve as a model republic for the rest of the world to emulate. George Bancroft, the foremost American historian of the period, captured the popular spirit with his declaration that the United States was "bound to allure the world to Liberty by the beauty of its example." Black abolitionists found little justification for such nationalist sentiment. They chafed at the arrogance and hypocrisy of a nation that proclaimed democratic principles while sanctioning racial oppression and perpetuating slavery. Black leaders worked to expose the myth of American freedom. "Our Influence Abroad," an editorial by William J. Watkins in the 22 December 1854 issue of *Frederick Douglass' Paper*, challenged Bancroft's idyllic vision of American destiny. Watkins explained to his readers that America's patriotic rhetoric was rendered meaningless by the reality of 3,500,000 blacks living in permanent bondage. Frederick Merk, *Manifest Destiny and Mission in American History* (New York, N.Y., 1963), 261–66; Blassingame, *Frederick Douglass Papers*, 2:359–88.

Our Influence Abroad

"Our country is bound to allure the world to Liberty by the beauty of its example."—*George Bancroft.*

The utterance of such a sentiment, at this cold season of the year, is rather ill-timed, and altogether inappropriate. It must have died on the ears of Mr. Bancroft's audience, the moment it was uttered. The people naturally expect, in the course of human events, to be compelled to listen to such rhetorical flourishes on the Fourth of July, when everybody knows that Truth has taken leave of absence, not being willing to have a part or lot in the claptrap oratory of that festive day.

If the Lecturer was speaking ironically, why, then, it was well enough; but if he presumed upon the gullibility of his hearers, and palmed this nonsense upon them as Truth, his conduct is very reprehensible.

"*Our country is bound to allure the world to Liberty by the beauty of its example!*" So said George Bancroft, Esq., in his Historical Oration recently delivered in the city of New York.[1]

We would suggest a slight alteration in the phraseology of this sentence. In order that it may speak the truth, it should read, "Our country is bound to allure the world to *Slavery!*"

Is not this a slaveholding nation? One unacquainted with the facts of the case would judge from this choice sentence we have quoted that this is a land of Freedom, unpolluted by the foul footprints of the Tyrants who arrogate to themselves the power to "crush out" the humanity of millions, and reduce them to a level with the brute. "Allure the world to *Liberty*," indeed! What is the example of the United States? Where is its beauty? Is there anything very beautiful in whipping women, burning them with red hot irons, setting bloodhounds upon their track, tearing their infant children from them, and selling them with horses and other cattle? Is there anything very beautiful in *this* example? This is a government which makes it a crime, punishable with fine and imprisonment, for a man or woman to feed the hungry, and clothe the naked. No man can be a Christian and obey its demoniacal enactments. Would Mr. Bancroft have the world imitate the example of the United States, when she snatched a minister of the cross from his Heaven-appointed labors, and by the help of rum, and bayonets, and cannons, and men lost to all sense of shame, or honor, thrust him into the hell of Slavery?[2] The *beauty* of its example! Is there anything beautiful in theft, and murder, and prostitution, and all the black catalogue of American Slavery? Anything specially beautiful in our chains, and thumbscrews, and bloodhounds, and branding irons? Anything very delectable in the contemplation of the slave code? O what a beautiful example does America set before the world! But Mr. Bancroft says we are alluring the world to Liberty. How? By legislating in favor of Slavery? By pulling down the old barns of Slavery, and building greater? Where has Mr. Bancroft been living that with all his wisdom and erudition he has not found out that the great object of this Government, *as developed in its policy*, is the extension, the consolidation, and the perpetuity of a system of robbery, and plunder, and oppression, aptly characterized the vilest that ever saw the sun.

The nation is ruled by a horde of despots, who would, if possible, hurl the Eternal from his throne, in order to get at the heart's blood of the negro. The influence of the American Government abroad is only an influence for evil. Our theory is well enough; but our practice is as far removed from it as the east is from the west. While making loud professions in behalf of Liberty, no nation under Heaven is so powerful an ally of Despotism. We are a hissing and a byword among all civilized nations. Even the heathen blushes at our inconsistencies. We may preach about Freedom forever; but until the three and a half millions of men, women and children, now writhing in the dust, are emancipated from their thraldom, all our nonsensical rhodomontade about free thought, and free discussion, and free institutions—all the unmeaning twaddle of Fourth of July orators concerning the "beauty of our example"[3]—will be regarded by the "world," to which Mr. Bancroft alludes, as a sounding brass, and a tinkling cymbal.[4]

W.

Frederick Douglass' Paper (Rochester, N.Y.), 22 December 1854.

1. George Bancroft (1800–1891), an influential American historian, made these remarks as part of an address entitled "The Necessity, the Reality, and the Promise of the Progress of the Human Race," which he delivered at the 20 November 1854 semicentennial celebration of the New-York Historical Society in New York City. Like most of his historical works, this speech expressed his faith in the divine mission of the American people and the providential nature of their government. George Bancroft, *Literary and Historical Miscellanies* (New York, N.Y., 1855), 516; *DAB*, 1:564–70.

2. Watkins refers to the arrest, trial, and reenslavement of Anthony Burns under the provisions of the Fugitive Slave Law of 1850.

3. Patriotic orations were the central event in antebellum Fourth of July celebrations. Marked by a distinctive rhetoric, these speeches became known for their bravado, boosterism, and justification of national purpose. The *North American Review* observed in 1857 that "our usual synome for bombast and mere rhetorical flourish is 'a Fourth of July oration.' " Daniel J. Boorstin, *The Americans: The National Experience* (New York, N.Y., 1965), 387–90.

4. Watkins draws from 1 Corinthians 13:1, "Though I speak with the tongues of men and of angels, and have not charity, I am become as sounding brass or a tinkling cymbal."

51.
Editorial by James McCune Smith
20 January 1855

The bonds between the American Anti-Slavery Society and black leaders, dramatically weakened over two decades, nearly broke apart in the 1850s. Black abolitionists insisted that the AASS had deserted its first principles. The society's founding documents expressed a commitment to equal justice and opportunity, but blacks had learned over the years that AASS members were more willing to espouse these ideas than to act upon them. In December 1854, this growing strain provoked a series of charges and countercharges between James McCune Smith and the editors of the *National Anti-Slavery Standard*, the AASS's official newspaper. Smith contended that few blacks remained in the "old organization" due to the racism of its white members, and he pointed to systematic job discrimination to make his case. The *Standard* rejected Smith's allegations, declaring that blacks who avoided the AASS were "either pro-slavery in feeling, or indifferent to the wrongs of the slave," and insisting that the AASS would not "make places for Dr. Pennington, a *minister of a slaveholding Church* and such mali[gn]ers as Dr. Smith and Frederick Douglass" if it meant unemployment for white friends. In a 20 January 1855 editorial in *Frederick Douglass' Paper*, Smith lamented the discord between black and white abolitionists, noting that "the twain ought to be, but are not, one flesh." Smith reminded Garrisonians that blacks had been abolitionists before the AASS existed, had helped to sustain the society through its early years, and would continue to participate in the antislavery movement. *NASS*, 13 January 1855.

NEW YORK, [New York]
Jan[uary] 20th, 1855
The reciprocal relations of the Free Colored People and the American Anti-Slavery Society form a subject of intense interest at this moment; it is admitted that these two classes of persons stand aloof from each other; they ought to be allied and bound together by hooks of steel—for the one class is Anti-Slavery by the seal of God upon their brows, the other class is Anti-Slavery by that "new birth" wherewith noble and energetic natures have been awakened to a sense of the sin and shame wherewith Slavery curses the land—the twain ought to be, but are not, one flesh.

The why and the wherefore of this disseverance is a serious question, it is not answered by the statement that the Colored People are governed by Pro-Slavery influences. In the light which Anti-Slavery has shed upon them, if they remain Pro-Slavery, then is one Anti-Slavery argument silenced—to wit, that this portion of God's creatures are fit for Freedom, even in part.

The statement of the organ of the American Anti-Slavery Society "that the colored people have ever kept aloof from the Anti-Slavery movement," would help solve the question, if it were a true statement; but it is not. For there was a time when the colored people were identified with that movement—nay, they almost began the present movement; they certainly antedated many of its principles. In 1810, while New York was yet a slave State, a long array of colored men marched through this city, in open day, bearing a banner inscribed with the portrait of a colored man, and the words

Am I not a Man and a Brother?[1]

And they did this in spite of the earnest remonstrances of the abolitionists of that day. In 1813, when Pennsylvania was about to enact a law requiring every colored person to be registered, the law was opposed in a series of brilliant letters written by "a man of color," letters containing sentiments promulgated twenty years afterwards as new Anti-Slavery truth. They may be found reprinted in the *Freedom's Journal* for March 1828, a paper edited by Rev. S. E. Cornish and J. B. Russwurm, colored men.[2] The statement of the "Organ" is not true, moreover, because the very sun in the Anti-Slavery firmament which that "Organ" adores, was nurtured into warmth, clothed with lustre and shot up into midair by the hot sympathies of colored men's bosoms. William Lloyd Garrison and the *Liberator* owe their evangel to the free colored people; he thought material and material aid, in the early darkest days of both, came largely from the colored people. Garrison's *Thoughts on Colonization* are but splendid comments on principles announced many years before, and lived up to till the present moment by the colored people. Mr. Garrison came on one platform, and remains on it, in this matter, in which the eloquence of words belongs to him, of action to us; our action antedating his words, and giving force to them; our action embracing a new principle, grander than that announced by the *Mayflower*'s people when they landed on Plymouth Rock. It is the principle of resisting oppression on the spot, against all odds, in contradistinction to the principle of flying from oppression.

In beginning his warfare against slavery, in the first number of the *Liberator*, like Jackson on the eve of battle before New Orleans, Mr. Garrison made his last appeal to

OUR FREE COLORED BRETHREN

Your moral and intellectual elevation, the advancement of your rights, and the defence of your character will be a leading object of our paper. We know that you are now struggling against wind and tide, and that "adversity has marked you for its own," yet among three hundred thousand of your number some patronage may be given. We ask and expect but little; that little may save the life of the *Liberator*.[3]

How this "appeal" was met may be inferred from the fact that during the first four years of its existence five-sixths of the most active agents for the *Liberator* (the names are contained in its columns) were colored men. The Bells (Fylbel), Hogarths, Stewart in New York; the Bemans in Connecticut; the Pompeys and Johnsons (not Oliver) in Massachusetts; the Casseys, Vashons, Whippers and Pecks in Pennsylvania; and Watkins in Baltimore,[4] were the colored men who planted the *Standard* and unfurled the *Oriflamme*[5] of the incipient gathering "host" in the period of its young helplessness. It is quite refreshing to look over the *Liberator* of those days, and read how prettily Mr. Garrison writes of Mr. Purvis[6] as "a young colored gentleman" (twenty odd years after a "colored man") and of meetings of "gentlemen of color" at Rochester, New York, Philadelphia, &c., &c., to support and circulate the *Liberator*. "All went merrily as a marriage bell"[7] in this honeymoon of the Anti-Slavery movement, the smiles, caresses, blandishments, and terms of fondness were tossed backwards and forwards—reciprocally—so assiduously that although Mr. Garrison sometimes "blushed" at an unusually warm hug, it was hard to tell which loved the other most, Mr. Garrison the Colored People, or the Colored People Mr. Garrison. Mr. Garrison advised colored conventions, national and annual, for the elevation of the Colored People; they were held; he attended them; gave some good advice and received some.[8]

But all at once "a change came o'er, &c., &c." On this good, warm soil the *Liberator* had grown beyond the measure of colordom; these agents' names were erased from its columns. And on Jan. 3d, 1835, came

A NOTICE TO SUBSCRIBERS

Mr. Benjamin Bacon (white man) is appointed General Agent to the *Liberator*[9]—All monies due for past subscriptions to our paper must be paid to us. All due from the commencement of the present volume must be paid to him, &c.

GARRISON & KNAPP

Also,

PHILADELPHIANS—TAKE NOTICE!

The New England Anti-Slavery Society[10] having constituted the subscriber sole agent of the *Liberator* for this city, &c., &c.

Signed, ARNOLD BUFFUM (White man.)[11]

Where are the colored gentlemen agents now? Out of the forty who had stood by the *Liberator* and upheld it in the day of its struggling adversity, was there no one fit for the office of agent when that office *paid*? There were dozens, but they were passed over whenever money began to flow in, and white men placed in their stead; and this course of conduct, call it Garrisonism, or what you will, has ever marked the subsequent history of the "host." Talk of colored men's ingratitude to Mr. Garrison, why the sheerest mite of gratitude, not to say the manly feeling on his part, would have led him to select a colored man for his agent when it did pay, in return for what they had done when it did not pay to be agent.

Who pushed colored men off that platform?

This historical view of the reciprocal relations, &c., &c., is a subject so rich and interesting that I will continue it. Enough has been said to show that the colored people have *not* always held aloof from the Anti-Slavery movement.

Wendell Phillips' lecture at the Tabernacle was attended by about thirteen hundred people,[12] Henry Ward Beecher's by a thousand more. Neither speaker seemed at ease. I think both, in view of Messrs. Storrs' and Bellows' efforts, aimed too high.[13] There was a constraint about Mr. Phillips, which took away that smooth fine polish with which his spoken words are wont to cut the air. Mr. Beecher read his lecture, which he should never do; blunt outness must ever be his forte. On the same night when Mr. Beecher lectured, there was gathered in Shiloh Church some seven hundred of "our people" listening to a complimentary concert to Professor Jackson, on Paganini; he *can* play on the violin.[14] The *elite* of New York and Philadelphia gave brilliancy to the vocal and instrumental music. It passed off splendidly, except that Fylbel, like Olly at the Tabernacle,[15] would get on the platform and throw sheep's eyes at the pretty girls. Yours,

COMMUNIPAW

Frederick Douglass' Paper (Rochester, N.Y.), 26 January 1855.

1. Smith probably fuses several events in his memory. New York City's African Society for Mutual Relief, which was organized in 1808, held annual parades from 1810 until about 1830 to commemorate its incorporation by the state. On 5 July 1827, black benevolent societies staged a mass parade through the streets of New York City to celebrate the end of slavery in New York state. Wearing a cocked hat, brandishing a sword, and riding on horseback, black abolitionist Samuel Hardenburgh led the procession, followed by a banner bearing the phrase, "Am I not a man and a brother?" This phrase was borrowed from a popular cameo by eighteenth-century English abolitionist Josiah Wedgewood, which also depicted a kneeling slave with chained hands. *FDP*, 16 February 1855 [9:0441]; Henry Highland Garnet, *A Memorial Discourse* (Philadelphia, Pa., 1865), 24–25 [15:0728]; Curry, *Free Black in Urban America*, 198–200; Fladeland, *Men and Brothers*, 49.

2. Smith refers to *Letters from a Man of Colour* (1813), a pamphlet written by James Forten of Philadelphia in response to a bill before the Pennsylvania legisla-

ture to ban black immigration into the state. The measure would have required blacks to register and carry certificates; those found without them would be defined as indigent and sold into slavery. Forten argued that the bill would not only restrict black freedom but limit the liberty of all Americans. *Freedom's Journal*, the first black newspaper in the United States, later reprinted the pamphlet in its February and March 1828 issues. The New York City–based weekly appeared from March 1827 to March 1829 under the editorship of Samuel E. Cornish and John B. Russwurm. James Forten, *Letters from a Man of Colour on a Late Bill Before the Senate of Pennsylvania* (Philadelphia, Pa., 1813), 1–11 [16:1095–1100]; *FJ*, 22, 29 February, 7, 14, 21 March 1828; Bella Gross, "*Freedom's Journal* and the *Rights of All*," *JNH* 17:241–88 (July 1932).

3. Smith compares William Lloyd Garrison's appeal in the 1 January 1831 issue of the *Liberator* to the one issued by General Andrew Jackson on 3 December 1814, a month before the Battle of New Orleans. Jackson called on Louisiana free blacks to enlist in his forces in exchange for the same pay and bounty that white soldiers received.

4. Some twenty to thirty blacks served as subscription agents for the *Liberator* during its first four years. These included Philip A. Bell of New York City, George Hogarth of Brooklyn, John G. Stewart of Albany, Jehiel C. Beman of Middletown (Conn.), Edward J. Pompey of Nantucket (Mass.), Richard C. Johnson of New Bedford, Joseph Cassey of Philadelphia, John B. Vashon of Pittsburgh, James P. Whipper of Pottsville (Pa.), John Peck of Carlisle (Pa.), and William Watkins of Baltimore. Some proved vital to the paper's success. Speaking of Cassey, Garrison later conceded that "if not for his zeal, fidelity, and promptness with which he executed his trust, the *Liberator* would not have completed its first [year]." *Lib*, 31 August 1831, 10 March, 25 August 1832, 28 January 1848.

5. An oriflamme, meaning golden flame in French, is a banner or symbol that inspires courage or devotion.

6. Robert Purvis.

7. Smith quotes from canto 3, stanza 21, of Lord Byron's *Childe Harolde's Pilgrimage*.

8. William Lloyd Garrison attended and addressed the 1831 and 1832 black national conventions. In 1831 he spoke on education and, together with white abolitionists Simeon S. Jocelyn and Arthur Tappan, submitted a plan for a black manual labor college. The following year, he debated R. R. Gurley of the American Colonization Society, urging delegates to reject the colonization movement. *Minutes of the First Annual Convention* (1831), 5–6 [1:0078–79]; *Minutes of the Second Annual Convention* (1832), 9 [1:0174].

9. Benjamin C. Bacon (1803–1874), a Boston abolitionist, helped found the New England Anti-Slavery Society. During the mid-1830s, he served as office agent for the *Liberator* and secretary of the Anti-Slavery Depository, where he managed the sale of antislavery books. Bacon later moved to Philadelphia, joined the Pennsylvania Anti-Slavery Society, and helped black abolitionist Charles W. Gardner compile an 1838 census of the city's black community. Merrill and Ruchames, *Letters of William Lloyd Garrison*, 1:387; *The Present State and Condition of the Free People of Color of the City of Philadelphia* (Philadelphia, Pa., 1838), 40 [2:0334].

10. The New England Anti-Slavery Society was founded in January 1832 by William Lloyd Garrison, Oliver Johnson, Arnold Buffum, and seven other New England abolitionists. During the next three years, the society battled colonizationists, distributed antislavery tracts, sent lecturing agents throughout New England, organized local auxiliaries, and sponsored Garrison's 1833 trip to England. The NEASS soon grew into a strong and vigorous regional organization and attracted support from several black societies, including the Massachusetts General Colored Association, and from Susan Paul, John Remond, and other prominent black leaders. The *Liberator* served as the society's official organ. By 1835 the rise of the American Anti-Slavery Society and the organization of state societies in Maine, New Hampshire, and Vermont forced the NEASS to confine its operations to Massachusetts. Changing its name to the Massachusetts Anti-Slavery Society to reflect this new reality, it continued to exert considerable influence throughout New England, acting as a bellwether of Garrisonianism until after the Civil War. Roman J. Zorn, "The New England Anti-Slavery Society: Pioneer Abolition Organization," *JNH* 43:157–76 (July 1957); *First Annual Report of the New England Anti-Slavery Society* (Boston, Mass., 1833), 7.

11. Arnold Buffum (1782–1859), a Providence, Rhode Island, hatter, was the first president of the New England Anti-Slavery Society. He moved to Philadelphia in 1834 and served as a subscription agent for the *Liberator*. During the early 1840s, Buffum lectured to antislavery audiences throughout Ohio and Indiana, published the New Garden (Ind.) *Protectionist*, and rejected his earlier Garrisonianism for political abolitionism. Merrill and Ruchames, *Letters of William Lloyd Garrison*, 1:147, 2:123; *DAB*, 3:241–42.

12. Wendell Phillips lectured during the evening of 9 January 1855 at Broadway Tabernacle in New York City. He observed that twenty-five years of antislavery agitation had failed to confine slavery and urged abolitionists to adopt more aggressive measures. Phillips praised participants in the Christiana slave riot (1851), in which a slaveholder was killed. *NASS*, 20 January 1855.

13. Popular local clergymen Henry Ward Beecher, Richard S. Storrs, and Henry W. Bellows had recently spoken at the Broadway Tabernacle as part of a lecture series sponsored by the New York Anti-Slavery Society. Beecher (1813–1887) was the pastor of Plymouth Congregational Church in New York City; Storrs (1787–1873), also a Congregationalist, served Brooklyn's Church of the Pilgrims; Bellows (1814–1882) ministered to the First Unitarian Church in New York City and later founded the United States Sanitary Commission during the Civil War. Storrs lectured on 29 November 1854 on the conflict between slavery and republicanism. Bellows spoke on 2 January 1855, blaming northern public opinion for slavery's continued existence. Beecher's address on 16 January warned against the growing influence of the slave power. Before long, he averred, the North "will be but a fringe to a nation whose heart will beat in the South." *DAB*, 2:129–35, 169, 18:100–101; *NASS*, October 1854–January 1855.

14. On 16 January 1855, black violinist William Jackson performed selections by Italian virtuoso Niccolò Paganini at a concert in the First Colored Presbyterian Church (also known as Shiloh Church) in New York City. Members of the New York City and Philadelphia black elite were in the audience. Jackson, who performed with black dance bands locally and in Boston from the 1830s to the

1860s, was ranked by Martin R. Delany "among the leading musicians of New York City and . . . the most skillful violinists of America." Eileen Southern, ed., *Biographical Dictionary of Afro-American and African Musicians* (Westport, Conn., 1982), 198, 309; Delany, *Condition of the Colored People*, 124.

15. Smith compares Philip A. Bell to Oliver Johnson, the editor of the *National Anti-Slavery Standard*, who frequently chaired antislavery meetings at Broadway Tabernacle.

52.
Testimony by Lewis Hayden
Delivered at the Massachusetts State House
Boston, Massachusetts
13 February 1855

In seeking an effective strategy to curtail enforcement of the Fugitive Slave Law, black abolitionists fought for the enactment of personal liberty laws—state statutes that guaranteed due process for all citizens, including runaway slaves. On 13 February 1855, the Joint Special Committee on Federal Relations of the Massachusetts legislature heard testimony from interested parties on a pending personal liberty bill. The hearings took an unusual turn when John W. Githell, an Alabama slaveholder, rose to speak in defense of slavery. He repeated the standard proslavery arguments—slaves were well treated and contented; only the worst slaves ran away from their masters. Githell conceded that slavery would eventually be abolished but argued in favor of compensated emancipation. When he finished, Lewis Hayden, a local black leader and former Kentucky slave, refuted Githell's remarks point by point. Several newspapers carried accounts of this rare public debate between a slaveholder and a fugitive slave. A correspondent for the *New York Evening Post* witnessed the proceedings and contrasted Githell's illiteracy and ineptitude with Hayden's eloquence and quiet dignity: "To look and listen to the product of slavery on a white freeman and of freedom on a colored slave . . . was such a sermon as [no minister] could have preached." The Massachusetts legislature enacted a state personal liberty law in June. *Lib*, 23 February, 2 March 1855; *FDP*, 2 March 1855 [9:0466]; Morris, *Free Men All*, 160–73.

Mr. Chairman and Gentlemen of the Committee:[1]
    I am happy to have an opportunity to say a few words at this time, though unexpectedly called upon. The Gentleman who last spoke,[2] and myself,[3] are both from the South. The principal difference between us is that Mr. Githell was born in a free State surrounded by the sweet influences of free schools, free churches, and a free Bible; whereas I was born a slave upon a plantation, brought up under the humiliating influences of the slave driver's lash. It is true, sir, I sometimes of my own free will, and sometimes by compulsion, attended what my brother calls "a church" and heard the "Missionary" to whom he has alluded preach that Gospel which is so peculiar to the South—"*Servant obey thy master!*" This is the sum total of the "Gospel" which slaves have preached unto them.[4]
    I have always said, Mr. Chairman, that you get here the poorest speci-

11. Lewis Hayden

mens of slaves. My brother Githell asserts it as a fact and thereby he and myself are agreed. Now, sir, you have all seen Frederick Douglass, Mr. Brown,[5] and other fugitive slaves, and if they are among the worst specimens then you need have no fear of letting loose those now in bondage! (Sensation and applause.) I should like to ask that gentleman, who has been allowed to walk our streets in peace, to enter our halls of justice, and to appear before a Legislative Committee to enter his protest against the enactment of a law to protect fugitive slaves, if Wm. Lloyd Garrison would be allowed to go down to Alabama and go before a similar Committee to that which I am now addressing, and enter his protest against the imprisonment of free colored seamen?[6] (Applause, but no reply from the slaveholder.)

Mr. Githell has told you, gentlemen, that God in his own good time will abolish slavery. This is true, and he will most probably do this through the free agency of his children who have been blessed with a free Gospel. The gentleman from Alabama does not seem to have confidence in the announcement made in the U.S. Senate, by Mr. Clay,[7] some years since, that "By the bleaching process slavery was to die out."

Mr. Hayden concluded his eloquent remarks by a direct appeal to Mr. Githell, to know how he could stand up in an enlightened community, and before God, and claim fifty human beings as his slaves, each of whom is as much entitled to his freedom as Mr. G.

Massachusetts Spy (Worcester, Mass.), 21 February 1855.

1. O. W. Albee of Marlboro chaired the seven-member Joint Special Committee on Federal Relations of the Massachusetts legislature. A man of mild antislavery leanings, he represented Middlesex County in the state senate. *FDP*, 18 May 1855 [9:0056]; *Lib*, 23 February 1855, 30 January 1857, 18 December 1863.

2. Hayden followed John W. Githell, who lived near Jacksonville in northeastern Alabama. He claimed to own fifty slaves. *FDP*, 9 March 1855.

3. Lewis Hayden (1811–1889) was born a slave in Lexington, Kentucky, and his sufferings under the peculiar institution became the foundation for a distinguished antislavery career. His mother was beaten into insanity for refusing the sexual advances of her owner, his family was sold on the auction block, and Hayden was swapped for a pair of carriage horses. Determined and resourceful, he taught himself to read from discarded newspapers and a Bible. In 1844 Hayden, his wife Harriet, and their son escaped to Canada West. But early the next year, they resettled in Detroit in order to become more involved in the antislavery movement. Hayden opened a school there for black children, raised funds to build a black Methodist church, and began antislavery lecturing. Dissatisfied with his place at the movement's periphery, he moved to Boston in 1846.

By virtue of his uncompromising nature and immense energy, Hayden quickly became a leader of Boston's black community. He worked comfortably with individuals of all stations and served as a liaison between working-class blacks and white abolitionists. A member of the Boston Vigilance Committee, he played a key role in the day-to-day work of aiding and protecting escaped slaves in the city and made his Beacon Hill home into a center of local underground activities. Hayden personally sheltered and fed hundreds of fugitives. His actions in the case of the celebrated fugitives William and Ellen Craft revealed his willingness to use any means to thwart enforcement of the Fugitive Slave Law. "Armed to the teeth," Hayden and several other blacks fortified themselves inside his home. When slave catchers arrived to seize the Crafts, they found Hayden waiting at his front door with two kegs of gunpowder and a torch. He led the successful rescue of Shadrach (1851) and the failed attempt to free Anthony Burns (1854). Ably defended by abolitionist lawyers, Hayden escaped conviction for his role in the Shadrach rescue and avoided prosecution in the Burns case. He later became an ally of John Brown and helped him raise money and recruits for his ill-fated Harpers Ferry raid.

When Hayden's clothing store failed in 1858, the new Republican administration appointed him as a messenger in the office of the Massachusetts secretary of state. He held this post for the remainder of his life, and it allowed him to make many political acquaintances. He soon became a close friend of John A. Andrew, the governor of Massachusetts during the Civil War. Hayden pressed for black enlistment in the conflict and claimed credit for persuading Andrew to organize the Fifty-fourth and Fifty-fifth Massachusetts regiments. Hayden was an important figure in black freemasonry, which absorbed much of his time after the war. He was grand master of the local Prince Hall Lodge, fought to integrate the National Grand Lodge of Masons, and traveled to Virginia and South Carolina to promote freemasonry and establish lodges among the freedmen. In 1873 Hayden was elected to the Massachusetts state senate. During his later years, he played a role in founding the Boston Museum of Fine Arts and actively supported the temperance and women's rights movements. *DANB*, 295–97; Stanley J. Robboy and Anita W. Robboy, "Lewis Hayden: From Fugitive Slave to Statesman," *NEQ* 46:591–613 (December 1973); Horton and Horton, *Black Bostonians*, 55, 80, 100, 124; Blackett, *Beating against the Barriers*, 91–95.

4. Obedience to masters was a major theme in the sermons and writings of antebellum southern clergymen. Southern theologians drew heavily from the letters of St. Paul—particularly Ephesians 6:5–8, Colossians 3:22, and Philemon—to provide a biblical justification for slave obedience. Methodist, Baptist, and Presbyterian missionaries carried this message to the plantation, simultaneously soothing the concerns of slaveholders and promoting docility, honesty, and loyalty among slaves. Sernett, *Black Religion and American Evangelicalism*, 73–78.

5. William Wells Brown.

6. Hayden refers to enforcement of the black seamen's acts.

7. Henry Clay.

53.
Jermain Wesley Loguen to Frederick Douglass
[March 1855]

Black abolitionists carried the antislavery message throughout the North. Even well-established leaders such as Frederick Douglass, William Wells Brown, and Jermain Wesley Loguen spoke in isolated villages as part of their professional responsibilities. Loguen, a clergyman who managed the aggressive Fugitive Aid League of Syracuse, included lecture tours of upstate New York among his many tasks. Although public indifference and the ordeals of travel in the backcountry often tested Loguen's antislavery resolve, he was unmatched at moving lethargic or even hostile audiences. "Slavery never looked more foul, cold blooded and fiendish," remarked Frederick Douglass, than when Loguen "portrayed the sale and carrying away of his sister's children." Loguen's March 1855 letter to Douglass described his tour through rural Delaware and Otsego counties, near the Catskills. He was astonished to discover how little the antislavery movement had touched most people in this region. After speaking at a white Methodist church, one woman thanked Loguen for ending the "nearly quarter of a century" that her minister "had kept her so long in the dark." *FDP*, 17 February, 23 June, 25 August 1854, 4 January, 11 May 1855 [8:0895, 9:0632–33]; *NASS*, 11 March 1855; *SJ*, 24 November 1860; *NI*, 8 October 1857.

Dear Sir:

I am at present laboring in our common cause among the rough hills of Delaware. I find many warm hearts that respond to the truth, and [are] touched with the story of the slave's wrongs. The portion of the county in which I have been laboring is noted for its prompt attendance at these meetings. Men and women often travel miles to listen to a lecture on slavery. A strong desire is felt by many to see and hear a fugitive slave, and thus my meetings are largely attended.

I have held two meetings in the village of Franklin—the locality of the Delaware Institute. The last was the largest I have attended for a long time; and I felt encouraged in my mark. We have many true friends in Franklin. There is a "Ladies' Anti-Slavery Society" here, which is in a flourishing condition, and accomplishing much good. Would to God that woman's voice might everywhere be raised against the damning wrongs which crush our race. How eloquent might it be in hastening the hour of our deliverance. Mrs. Stilson, President of the above Society, and her husband, are truehearted friends of our cause.[1] I saw on their table one striking proof of their devotion to the slave, viz: *Frederick Douglass' Paper*. Wherever this paper is read, I find men and women whose hearts are true to the slave—who labor for the colored man's good as well as the white man's. In this they differ widely from many I have found of late, who are very willing to work in the name of the slave, if *the thing pays*, and the pay goes directly to *their pockets*. The colored man is "all right"; he is a "good *nigger*" so long as he will worship at their shrine, and pour money into their coffers; but let him only presume to think and act for himself, like an independent and accountable being, and above all to put his own penny into his own pocket, and he is no longer a "good *nigger*"! Away with such arrant hypocrisy, that would save a man from the clutches of the slavedriver only to fasten upon him the shackles of another despotism! I am sick of all *such* friends of the slave. The less we have of them the better. From such we may well pray to be delivered. Years ago, while a toiling slave in Tennessee, I resolved, that with the help of God, and the energies he had given me, I would cast off the chain and be a slave no longer. "Liberty or Death!" never came from a more earnest breast than when I uttered it there before my God! My residence in the North has not diminished, but has rather strengthened the firm resolve I then took. I will be no man's slave, be he called friend or foe— be he in a church or out. God helping me, I will be a MAN—I will wear no chain!

I have also passed through a portion of Otsego Co. since I left home, and had some fine meetings and, what is better, found a few sterling friends. Alas! I found many, too, who are temporizing—"policy men"— men only about half "dyed in the wool." While thinking this over, the words of that great, and noble, and pure man, GERRIT SMITH (how many hearts beat joyfully at the mention of that name), came to my mind. He says in his letter to Wendell Phillips: "I admit that it requires only a small number of right-minded persons to sustain the American anti-slavery cause, and carry it forward to victory, and that even this small number cannot be supplied."[2] Alas! that in so holy a cause these words should be true. O consistency! thou art a jewel; would that thy lights were not so rare.

But, notwithstanding these discouragements, our hearts are often made glad by finding honest persons, who are laboring for universal freedom. In these two counties, I find what is rare, devoted ministers to the Gospel who preach against manstealing as well as against sheep stealing, and against the atrocious cruelties of woman-whipping and cradle robbing in America, as well as in any other part of the world. Among these noble ministers, I found Elder J. N. Adams and Elder George Post, both Baptists,[3] with many of other churches. Would to God that *all* the ministers were as true as these. Slavery would soon be numbered among the things that were and are not. They are *do* ministers as well as *say* ministers; and our Savior says, "Inasmuch as ye have *done* it"[4]—not inasmuch as ye have *said* it.

I have spoken two or three times every Sunday, and with a few exceptions, every evening through the week, for the last three weeks; and I feel to go on in God's great name, doing battle for our bruised and downtrodden brethren. As I have before said to you, dear friend, I say again—we want more true soldiers in the field, who are not afraid to die, if need be, in our great cause—men and women, too, who feel the cause at heart sufficiently to stand alone, with God's help, and fight on and ever, and not quit the field nor be frightened by persecutions, prejudice, disagreement with so called friends, Fugitive Slave Bills, slave hounds, kidnappers, or any other instruments of the devil; but who will stand with sword in hand, contending for God and liberty! Let them not wait for some church or society to send them forth and push them onwards. Let the love of justice and truth, the cries of bleeding humanity persuade them forth, and God will sustain them. Every man and woman must be within himself an embodiment of all a church or society can be for good. For myself, I am willing to cooperate with others, so long as I can do so and maintain my manhood. Beyond that I will not go.

I am now getting up Fugitive Slave Societies wherever I may, to stand by every fugitive who will take a stand in the free States and maintain it at all hazards. *The time has come for us to stop running!* Such as can not nerve themselves up to this, and feel like going to another land, we must help; but we want everyone to feel that it is his duty to stand; and we want those who come in with us to feel like standing by them. We have some true hearts enlisted already, and we hope to have many more. Let such remember that God will bless the right and the true.

I would like to say to the slaveholders and all others, just here, that the Underground Railroad was never doing a better business than at present. We have had as many as sixteen passengers in one week in this city—I speak officially, as the agent and keeper of an Underground Railroad Depot. Let them come; we have some true hearts ready to receive them, and God will raise up more.

I send you a copy of our Constitution and Bylaws. Please give them an insertion in your good paper.[5] "Speak the Truth—God defend the Right."[6] Truly yours,

J. W. LOGUEN

Frederick Douglass' Paper (Rochester, N.Y.), 6 April 1855.

1. The Ladies Anti-Slavery Society of Franklin, New York, had some forty members, who regularly assisted the work of black abolitionist Frederick Douglass and contributed clothing to the Fugitive Aid League of Syracuse. Lucia Stilson (1812–?) was the society's president. She and her husband, Ansel F. Stilson (1814–1857), a merchant and Liberty party backer, were key figures in local antislavery and underground railroad efforts. *FDP*, 18 May 1855 [9:0651];

SDS, 19 December 1856 [10:0434]; *CD*, 9 September 1848; *NASS*, 28 February 1857.

2. Loguen quotes from Gerrit Smith's 20 February 1855 letter to Wendell Phillips. Smith lamented the failures of the antislavery movement, attacked intolerance among reformers, and defended his political abolitionism and brief career in the U.S. Congress. *Lib*, 16 March 1855.

3. Joseph N. Adams (ca. 1818–1886) and George F. Post, both ordained Baptist clergymen, ministered to small congregations in Otsego and Delaware counties from the 1840s through the 1880s. At the time of Loguen's visit, Adams was serving the Croton Baptist Church near Franklin and Post was at nearby East Meredith. James R. Lynch of the American Baptist Historical Society, letter to editors, 10 April 1990.

4. Loguen quotes from Matthew 25:40, in which Jesus identifies with and urges concern for the poor and oppressed: "Inasmuch as ye have done it unto one of these my brethren, ye have done it unto me."

5. Loguen refers to the constitution of the Fugitive Aid League of Syracuse, which was reprinted with his letter in the 6 April 1855 issue of *Frederick Douglass' Paper*. The document established a structure for the organization, outlined its purpose, and stated its commitment to aid and protect fugitive slaves "by every means that may be necessary." As the agent of the league, Loguen provided food, clothing, shelter, and other assistance to hundreds of fugitives fleeing through the city. He successfully solicited donations of money and supplies from dozens of churches and women's antislavery societies in Britain and New York state. Later known as the Fugitive Aid Society, the league continued to operate into the early years of the Civil War. *NI*, 8 October 1857 [10:0860]; *FDP*, 12 March 1858; *SJ*, 13 September 1858 [11:0367]; *SDS*, 28 January 1860 [12:0459].

6. Loguen quotes from part 2, act 2, scene 3, of the play *Henry VI* by William Shakespeare.

54.
James McCune Smith to Gerrit Smith
31 March 1855

Evidence to a commitment to racial equality was the litmus test for black abolitionists. They carefully monitored the words and actions of white reformers, politicians, and other public figures, praising those who advocated equal rights and censuring those who fell short of that mark. Black leaders believed that the battle to destroy American prejudice required vigilance, which occasionally compelled them to reprimand their friends. Even though the relationship between several black leaders and Gerrit Smith was as personally close as any in the antislavery movement and blacks benefited from Smith's benevolence, they corrected the Peterboro, New York, philanthropist whenever he strayed from the principle of equality. James McCune Smith's March 1855 letter criticized racist statements by William H. Seward, a moderate opponent of slavery, and chided Gerrit Smith for his failure to do the same. Two years later, when Gerrit Smith wrote in the *New York Tribune* that the "mass of the blacks are ignorant and thriftless," James McCune Smith repudiated the charge and reminded his good friend of the damage his careless remarks did to all blacks. "You surely owed it to your own fame, to say nothing of us," he wrote in a personal note, "to have ascertained, by the direct examination of facts that your statement was true, before you ventured to make it." John S. Rock to Gerrit Smith, 28 December 1857, James McCune Smith to Gerrit Smith, 9 April 1858, Gerrit Smith Papers, NSyU [10:0982–84, 11:0200–201]; *NYT*, 12 August 1857.

New York, [New York]
March 1, 1855

Dear Friend:

My wife and I often talk of our visit to Peterboro as a pleasure in store for us, and which I hope we may enjoy before winter is past. My heart yearned to you in the midst of our deep affliction; and now, when the first sharp bitterness is past, there is no one I would rather commune with among men, than you. I seem suddenly to have leaped over along period of life: [anon]. Oh it is sad to have no children playing round the hearthstone.[1] I try, and may God give me the grace to succeed, to look into other little glad eyes and listen to other little glad voices; and I try to reason myself out of the selfishness that they are not mine. Oh that meeting hereafter!

I thank you for your letter to Wendell Phillips;[2] it is is clear, pointed and timely, to those who understand; but the hebetude of party is so universal an ailment, that few are able, to understand you, even if they would. You can well afford to be misunderstood by this generation; the next, or whichever next shall find man swelling beyond the institutions of to day will abundantly appreciate and bless you.

March 31. Still more do I thank you for your letter to Senator Seward. It must be the Old Puritan blood in me that leaps up at fair and faithful blows laid on regardless of any thing but the bare truth. My spiritual quarrel with Seward began in the very act for which you commend him. In defending Freeman, he used an expression about "inferiority of race" which I can forgive in no man; and I gave up all hope of him when I read that sentence,[3] because no man can fight the true Anti-Slavery fight who does not believe that all men are equal socii.[4] Hence I have waged war against the Garrisonians, and will, until they admit this doctrine. It is a strange omission in the Constitution of the American Anti-Slavery Society that no mention is made of Social Equality either of slaves or Free Blacks, as the aim of that Society.[5]

We are not entirely idle down this way. A new "Abolition Society" is just forming to Abolish Slavery by means of the Constitution;[6] or otherwise. The last two words I squeezed into the preliminary Resolution; and should there be any quarrel in the future as to the meaning of them, I mean fight. So you will please preserve this note as a sort of Madison Paper.[7]

William Goodell, Wm. E. Whiting,[8] Elder Ray[9] and others are framers of this new Society.

We colored men are organizing a society to raise a fund to test our legal rights in traveling &c. &c. in the Courts of Law.[10] Oh that I could infuse an "Esprit du Corps" in my black brethrens!

But I must close this letter, lest I let it lay by another month. I often puzzle my brains to fathom the cause of Horace Greeley's especial malignity against you & cannot.[11] Is it that his own soul is in torment to see a man living up to his convictions?

Have you seen any thing half so eloquent, lately, as our friend Miss Griffiths rejoinder to the Anti-Slavery Advocate?[12]

I have an opinion that one half the opposition to Women's Rights arises from a half defined dread of women's keen eloquence; I would stand up, in fair fight with any living man, but I have a wholesome dread of Abby Kelly's tongue[13] or any like it.

My wife is quite under the weather; if she is well enough, I will try and reach Peterboro this month.

Please give our best regards to your lady & family. Sincerely and gratefully yours

James McCune Smith

Gerrit Smith Papers, George Arents Research Library, Syracuse University, Syracuse, New York. Published by permission.

1. The three remaining children of James McCune and Malvina Barnet Smith —Frederick Douglass (b. 1850), Peter Williams (b. 1852), and Anna Gertrude (b. 1850)—died between 13 August and 19 September 1854. *FDP*, 6 October 1854.

2. Smith refers to Gerrit Smith's 20 February 1855 letter to Wendell Phillips, which is mentioned in the preceding document.

3. On 13 March 1855, Gerrit Smith wrote a letter to William H. Seward criticizing the latter's 23 February speech on the Fugitive Slave Law before the U.S. Senate. Although the New York philanthropist praised Seward's earlier efforts on behalf of blacks, he repudiated his racial views and denounced his moderate antislavery stance. Only the color of the victims, Smith declared, permitted Seward to tolerate such an unjust law and to encourage gradual emancipation.

Seward advocated civil and political equality for blacks, while rejecting the idea of racial equality. He expressed these views during the murder trial of William Freeman (1824–1847), an Auburn, New York, native of mixed black, Indian, and French lineage. After being wrongfully convicted of stealing a horse, Freeman was beaten mercilessly by prison guards until he went insane. Upon his release, he killed a family that he believed to be responsible for his imprisonment. Seward defended Freeman and argued that he should never have been tried because of his mental state. Seward's eloquent reasoning was widely circulated as *Argument in Defense of William Freeman* (1847). *FDP*, 10, 23 March 1855; Glyndon G. Van Deusen, *William Henry Seward* (New York, N.Y., 1967), 93–97.

4. "Socii" is an archaic term meaning colleagues or associates.

5. The American Anti-Slavery Society's 1833 constitution did not pledge signatories to social equality among the races but did commit the organization to work for black elevation and the elimination of racial prejudice, so that blacks might, "according to their intellectual and moral worth, share an equality with the whites, of civil and religious privileges." "Constitution of the American Anti-Slavery Society," 4 December 1833, American Anti-Slavery Society Papers, DLC [1:0353].

6. The New York City Abolition Society was founded on 15 March 1855 by William Goodell, Arthur and Lewis Tappan, William E. Whiting, James McCune Smith, and other local members of the moribund American and Foreign Anti-Slavery Society. The organization was devoted to ending slavery through the political process and to obtaining civil and economic equality for blacks. Most members, including Smith and Goodell, viewed the U.S. Constitution as an antislavery document. When the American Abolition Society was created six months later, it adopted verbatim the constitution of the New York organization. M. Leon Perkal, "American Abolition Society: A Viable Alternative to the Republican Party?" *JNH* 65:58–59 (Winter 1980).

7. Smith refers to "Notes of Debates in the Federal Convention of 1787 Reported by James Madison," which was posthumously published in H. D. Gilpin's edition of *The Papers of James Madison* (1840). Since that time, these so-called "Madison Papers" have been used to determine the original intent of the framers of the U.S. Constitution on various issues, including slavery. William M. Wiecek, *The Sources of Antislavery Constitutionalism in America, 1760–1848* (Ithaca, N.Y., 1977), 239.

8. William E. Whiting (?–1882), a committed political abolitionist, was a key figure in the American and Foreign Anti-Slavery Society. In 1855 he joined the newly organized American Abolition Society and served as treasurer of its auxiliary, the New York City Abolition Society. Whiting helped direct the American Missionary Association from 1846 until his death. *AM*, July 1882; *FDP*, 27 April 1855; McKivigan, *War against Proslavery Religion*, 220; Perkal, "American Abolition Society," 59.

9. Charles B. Ray.

10. Smith refers to the Legal Rights Association, which was founded in the early months of 1855 by J. W. C. Pennington, Amos N. Freeman, and other New York City blacks. Encouraged by Elizabeth Jennings's successful discrimination suit against the Third Avenue Railroad Company, they created the organization to sponsor legal action against other segregated carriers. It continued to finance such cases, with limited success, through the remainder of the decade. Blackett, *Beating against the Barriers*, 60–62.

11. Smith alludes to the controversy between Horace Greeley's *New York Tribune* and Gerrit Smith over the Kansas-Nebraska Act. In July 1854, the paper erroneously charged that Smith, while serving in Congress, had missed a crucial vote on the measure because it occurred after his 9:00 P.M. bedtime. Gerrit Smith demanded a retraction, which Greeley grudgingly printed in the *Tribune*. Harlow, *Gerrit Smith*, 333–34.

12. Smith refers to a 28 March 1855 letter by Julia Griffiths in response to an editorial in the *Anti-Slavery Advocate*, a Garrisonian monthly published in Dublin, Ireland. The exchange was part of the continuing conflict between Garrisonians and the supporters of Frederick Douglass. The *Advocate* had criticized Griffiths's Rochester Ladies Anti-Slavery Society for supporting *Frederick Douglass' Paper*, condemned Douglass for "depreciating" the American Anti-Slavery Society, and disparaged the letters of "Communipaw" as "disgraceful to the writer, and no credit to the paper or its editor." Griffiths defended Douglass as the best spokesman of the oppressed and maintained that "Communipaw's" correspondence needed no defense. She reminded the *Advocate* editors that the RLASS's financial support for Douglass's paper was necessitated by the Garrisonians' withdrawal of support from Douglass. *FDP*, 30 March 1855; Howard Temperley, *British Antislavery, 1833–1870* (London, 1972), 239.

13. Abby Kelley Foster, a skilled antislavery lecturer, was renowned for her forceful rhetoric and powerful voice. *NAW*, 1:648.

55.
Uriah Boston to Frederick Douglass
April 1855

Although most black abolitionists were committed to racial integration, they disagreed on how to best achieve that goal. Frederick Douglass, William J. Wilson, James McCune Smith, and like-minded leaders believed that true integration required a black "declaration of independence." In order to live with whites on equal terms, they argued, blacks must first develop self-reliance and a strong sense of racial pride. Other blacks had a difficult time reconciling integration with the idea of racial distinction. They were made uneasy by calls for a distinct black identity and argued that accentuating racial differences set black and white Americans apart, giving credence to colonizationist claims that blacks would be better off in Africa. Uriah Boston entered this debate by responding to the writings of "Ethiop" (Wilson) and "Communipaw" (Smith). In an April 1855 letter to *Frederick Douglass' Paper*, he insisted that to claim American citizenship, blacks must abandon racial distinctions. Boston's comments revisited the intractable dilemma of Afro-American duality—the apparent contradiction between integration into American society and the need to affirm a separate black consciousness. *FDP*, 5 March 1853, 9 March 1855 [8:0163, 9:0472–73]; *Convention of Colored People . . . in Troy* (1847), 19; *Colored National Convention . . . at Cleveland* (1848), 19–20.

POUGHKEEPSIE, [New York]
April 1855

DEAR SIR:

Allow me to present a few thoughts with regard to the position always held, as far as I know, by Ethiop, and recently taken, as I think, by Communipaw. I allude to their position of preserving and maintaining the African identity of the colored people of the United States. Did I not know personally "Ethiop" and "Communipaw," I should suspect that they were colonizationists in disguise, urging the colored people to preserve their identity with the African race, that thereby the propriety and necessity of African colonization might be made to appear most plain to all men, without dispute and without contradiction. This would so appear, 1st: because if the colored people are in fact Africans, what business, it may be asked, have these three millions of inferior degraded Africans here in the United States trying to mix themselves up with 24 or 30 millions of whites? You cannot mix nationalities, nor can you mix black and white; and if you could mix black and white, what benefit could possibly result to either party, while each would preserve its identity. But "Ethiop" and "Communipaw" would not have the colored people imitate nor mix with the whites. They would have them contend with each other. Just think of it! Three millions of Africans contending with 24 millions of Americans—for what? Why, for the rights of American citizens, politically, socially and religiously. What an idea that is. I desire to have no part in such a contest. I hope no one desires it. It would be more fatal to the colored race than the brave and daring charge of the British Light Brigade at Balaklava. Nay, more, the foolish daring of the British Light Brigade[1] would be justly considered an act of wisdom compared with the conduct of 3 millions Africans charging 24 millions Americans on the ground selected by the Americans themselves. One such charge would result in the annihilation of the African Brigade, with no prospect of recruits.

The true policy, in my opinion, for the colored people to pursue is, lessen the distinction between whites and colored citizens of the United States. We are American citizens by birth, by habit, by habitation, and by language. Why, then, wish to be considered Africans. "African churches" —African schools will do, while nothing better is to be had. These will do very well in Africa, but not in the U.S. The presumption with most people is that no man is a proper citizen of one certain country while he claims at the same time to be a citizen of any other country. It therefore seems out of place and [un]reasonable to claim to be Americans, and at the same time claim to be Africans. Common sense would seem to dictate that if we are American citizens, then we are in our own country of right; but, on the other hand, if we be Africans, then surely our country is Africa. For my part, I claim to be an American citizen, and also claim to be a man. When I claim to be anything else, I trust I shall evince my bravery and wisdom by taking my proper place, whether it be in Africa or elsewhere. "Colored Americans" will do in the United States, but "Africans" never. I shall be greatly mistaken if the free colored people of this country shall consent to be packed and labelled for the African market by "*Ethiop*" and "*Communipaw*."

URIAH BOSTON[2]

Frederick Douglass' Paper (Rochester, N.Y.), 20 April 1855.

1. The Battle of Balaklava, fought on 25 October 1854, was one of the major clashes of the Crimean War. Although the combined Anglo-French forces won the battle, Balaklava became known for an ill-fated British cavalry assault against Russian artillery emplacements—a disaster immortalized in Alfred Tennyson's poem, "The Charge of the Light Brigade."

2. Uriah Boston (1815–?) was born in Pennsylvania. By the late 1830s, he operated a barber shop in Poughkeepsie, New York, where he was the dominant figure in the black community over the next two decades. Boston and his wife Violet were devoted advocates of a strong black press. They collected donations,

recruited new subscribers, and served as agents for the *Colored American* in the early 1840s; later, Boston regularly corresponded with *Frederick Douglass' Paper*. He believed that the black press was a major factor in stimulating black activism. And he challenged editors such as Horace Greeley of the *New York Tribune* who questioned black ability in the white press. Boston was best known for his role in the campaign to expand black suffrage in New York state. From 1840 to 1846, he led the Dutchess County Suffrage Committee, which coordinated petition drives and worked with black leaders throughout the state. In 1855 he formed and directed Poughkeepsie's Political Suffrage Association, a New York State Suffrage Association auxiliary, which led the local fight for an equal franchise. Boston was a regular fixture at black state conventions, participated in the 1853 black national convention, and served on the New York State Council of the Colored People. When he failed to attend the 1855 black state convention, Philip A. Bell commented that "there is a vacancy in our conventions, when Uriah Boston is not present." His activism declined after the mid-1850s, but New York blacks acknowledged his contributions by naming him a vice-president of the NYSSA at the end of the decade.

Boston's reform philosophy and program were complex and often contradictory. He worked closely with Frederick Douglass but frequently criticized the Rochester editor's statements and actions. Although he supported Douglass's endorsement of political abolitionism and the antislavery nature of the U.S. Constitution, he was an avowed disunionist. Boston generally worked through separate organizations, but he often condemned distinct black institutions and identity. A lifelong advocate of moral reform, who believed that prejudice was caused by condition, he was also one of the leading political activists in New York state. As early as 1840, he urged blacks: "Let our motto be ACTION, ACTION, *energetic, untiring and continued action.*" U.S. Census, 1850; Simmons, *Men of Mark*, 1114; *CA*, 6 June, 4 July, 12 September, 21, 28 November 1840, 2, 9, 16 January, 21 August, 11 September, 2 October 1841 [3:0450, 0512, 0615, 0716, 0722, 0808, 0823, 0839, 4:0163, 0192, 0231]; *AP*, 3 October 1843 [4:0679]; *NASS*, 29 January 1846 [5:0152]; *FDP*, 1, 15, 22 April, 24 June, 22 August, 9 September, 9 December 1853, 19 January, 20 April, 20 July, 31 August, 14, 28 September, 5 October 1855 [8:0227 0277, 0314, 0393, 0435, 9:0546, 0748, 0817, 0832, 0849, 0859]; Foner and Walker, *Proceedings of the Black State Conventions*, 1:81, 89; *Colored National Convention . . . in Rochester* (1853), 25 [8:0338]; *WAA*, 31 March 1860 [12:0600].

56.
John Mercer Langston to Frederick Douglass
April 1855

Individual black achievements carried immense symbolic value. The singing voice of Elizabeth T. Greenfield ("The Black Swan"), the intellect of James McCune Smith, the eloquence of Frederick Douglass, and the skillful renderings of the black past by William C. Nell swelled racial pride and challenged white beliefs about black inferiority. The election of black men to political office marked another breach in the wall of American racism. In March 1855, black lawyer John Mercer Langston was nominated by the Independent Democrats to be clerk of Brownhelm Township, near Oberlin, Ohio. Local voters, agitated by proslavery violence in the Kansas Territory, rallied behind Langston's candidacy. On 2 April, he became the first black elected to political office in the United States. Black abolitionists derived great promise from this small victory. Ironically, the light-skinned Langston was able to run for office because Ohio statute defined him as white. But he boldly described himself as black, and in the following letter to *Frederick Douglass' Paper*, he proudly announced his victory as evidence of the "steady march of the Anti-Slavery sentiment." Cheek and Cheek, *John Mercer Langston*, 259–62.

I have a news item for you. On the 2nd of this month, we held our elections. In our township, we had three distinct parties, and as many independent tickets. The Independent Democrats were wise for once, at least, in making and sticking to their own nominations. But more than this, and a thing which also exhibits their wisdom and virtue, they put upon their ticket the name of a colored man, who was elected clerk of Brownhelm Township by a very handsome majority indeed. Since I am the only colored man who lives in this township, you can easily guess the name of the man who was so fortunate as to secure this election. To my knowledge, the like has not been known in Ohio before. It argues the steady march of the Anti-Slavery sentiment, and augurs the inevitable destruction and annihilation of American prejudice against colored men. What we so much need just at this junction, and all along the future, is political influence; the bridle by which we can check and guide to our advantage the selfishness of American demagogues. How important, then, it is that we labor night and day to enfranchise ourselves. We are doing too little in this direction. And I make this charge against white Anti-Slavery persons, as well as colored ones. I hope that before a great while, we will all amend our ways in this particular.

JOHN MERCER LANGSTON[1]

Frederick Douglass' Paper (Rochester, N.Y.), 20 April 1855.

1. John Mercer Langston (1829–1897), an attorney, abolitionist, and postwar politician, was born in Louisa County, Virginia, to Ralph Quarles, a planter, and Quarles's manumitted slave, Lucy Langston. Quarles provided for the Langston children in his will, and, after the death of their parents in 1834, they moved to Ohio. John was raised and educated by white foster parents in Chillicothe. In 1844 he entered Oberlin College, where he earned bachelor's and master's degrees. Langston pursued theological studies, which he abandoned for legal training, and after reading law under Philemon Bliss, an Elyria judge, he passed the Ohio bar examination in 1854.

Langston established a prosperous law practice in nearby Brownhelm. Discouraged by American race relations, he embraced emigrationist ideas by the early 1850s. But he astonished delegates at the 1854 National Emigration Convention in Cleveland by advocating integration and offering an optimistic assessment of the possibilities for racial equality in the United States. Langston fought for black progress by participating in a wide range of antislavery activities. He presided at local and state black conventions, organized reform societies, protected fugitive slaves along Ohio's underground railroad, challenged the state's black laws, worked to improve black education in Ohio, encouraged the growth of black businesses, and advocated a strong black press. Langston, active in local politics, ran successfully for township clerk in 1855. His victory made him the first black American elected to public office by popular vote. Three years later, he organized the Ohio State Anti-Slavery Society, an independent statewide black association that fought slavery and barriers to racial progress. By the end of the decade, Langston and his brothers—Gideon and Charles—were major figures in Ohio abolitionism. Increasingly militant, he anticipated a violent national conflict over the issue of slavery and aided John Brown's plans to foment slave insurrection but decided against participating directly in the Harpers Ferry raid.

During the Civil War, Langston established his reputation as a national black leader. He recruited troops for the Union army's black regiments and encouraged the work of soldiers' aid societies. The 1864 black national convention acknowledged his growing stature by naming him president of the newly founded National Equal Rights League. Langston embarked on a distinguished career in education and politics after the war. He toured the South as inspector-general of the Freedmen's Bureau, advocating political equality and economic opportunity for the freedmen. Langston founded and became the first dean of the law department at Howard University in 1868; he later served as the university's acting president. Following two years as president of Virginia Normal and Collegiate Institute, he accepted an appointment as consul general to Haiti in 1887. Upon his return to Virginia, he won a contested election for a seat in the U.S. House of Representatives. Langston was admired for his intellect and persuasive oratory and was characterized as having an "aristocratic style and a democratic temperament." Late in life, he recounted his lengthy public career in an autobiography, *From the Virginia Plantation to the Nation's Capitol* (1894). *DANB*, 382–84; Cheek and Cheek, *John Mercer Langston*.

57.
John W. Lewis to Frederick Douglass
16 April 1855

The growing importance of antislavery politics during the mid-1850s encouraged many black abolitionists. Amid despair over federal slavery policy, they found reason for optimism in the electoral successes of the Republican party, with its promise to halt the spread of slavery. For John W. Lewis, a Baptist clergyman and antislavery lecturer, the reaction of the southern press to Republican victories in the 1855 elections underscored antislavery progress. His 16 April 1855 letter to *Frederick Douglass' Paper* disputed the charge that abolitionists had hindered slave emancipation by alienating northern moderates and making slaveholders even more intransigent. He cited a *Mobile Evening News* (Ala.) editorial as evidence that abolitionism was a powerful moral and political force that southerners feared. The editorial credited the success of Republican senatorial candidates to the growing influence of the antislavery movement and advised that the South should be prepared for its eventual separation from the Union. Heartened by this admission from the proslavery press, Lewis vowed to "gird the anti-slavery armor closer, and face the storm." Pease and Pease, *They Who Would Be Free*, 203.

ST. ALBANS, V[ermon]t
April 16, 1855

MY DEAR DOUGLASS:

The question has often been asked by the pro-slavery press and pulpit—What have the abolitionists of the North done to benefit the poor bondman of the South, or to aid in the downfall of American slavery? And the charge has often been made that their course has been so fanatical as to exasperate the slaveholder and rivet the fetters tighter on the galled limbs of the slave. By their argument, many kindhearted men and women at the North have been kept back from doing what their consciences dictated to them as duty to their suffering fellowmen. But, thank God! the time has fully come when light cannot be kept back from the people. They now see great importance attached to the anti-slavery enterprise. That cause is no longer in embryo; it is no longer weak and unprotected before the merciless rage of an infuriated mob; it no longer has to sit in silence to meet the scoff and menace of base political demagogues in the halls of national or state legislation. Its strength in manliness, in moral power, dare face the mightiest champion of the slave power, and speak for right in defence of impartial freedom, in a voice that cannot be misunderstood, and that makes many a Southern dough-face quail. State after State, in the annual elections, are now bending before the mighty power of abolitionism. The South sees it and fears it; for, as the mighty host moves on, bearing the banner of freedom, justice is their guide and equal rights is their rallying cry. No wonder that there is fear in the Southern camp. The following extracts I copy from an article which lately appeared in the Mobile *News*,[1] one of the ablest and far-seeing of the Southern opponents of the Northern spirit of abolitionism. It is surely significant. The editor says:

> The success of abolitionists in the recent election of United States Senators from the North and north-west is ominous.[2] The party which, twenty years ago was ridiculed in the North for its insignificance in numbers and its fanaticism, and treated with contempt in the South, now controls the political destiny of States like New York. In the East, West and North, the reverberation of their cannon echo from hill and valley. The fiendish joy of their host, their bonfires and rockets luridly glare upon their cold sky and snow-clad earth, in commemoration of victory. Along road, river and lake, upon the sea shore and mountain, from old Massachusetts to Wisconsin, shout answers from their jubilant followers.

This is language that cannot be misunderstood. It shows that there is potency in the anti-slavery of the North, to call forth such a growl from this Southern watchdog of slavery. But he says further:

> The election of several abolition Senators is not the triumph of men. Mr. Seward's and Mr. Wilson's election[3] is no exponent of individual success; it is the exponent of a great moral power; it is the pulsation of the heart of a great revolution which has been gathering slowly, but with accelerated progress. If, then, the election of abolition Senators is an index of a revolution in the North, and not of individual success—and if it be true that revolutions never go backwards—what is the South to do? She must look to no party of men north of Mason & Dixon's line for safety. She must not expect it in the Constitution. The South must prepare to rely upon herself, for abolitionism will, at no distant day, put her out of the pale of the Union.

No one can read such talk as the above, from a Southern press, without feeling assured that there is trouble in the camp somewhere. But hear him further:

> Seward and Wilson are but flies on the massive wheel of the car of juggernaut, which will soon crush all, North and South, that comes in its resistless way. It is not Seward and Wilson that is to be feared; it is ideas that live, that revolutionize, not men. Let not the South be limited in her view, and lose sight of a great revolution in watching the success of men.

Now, sir, I never felt more encouraged to gird the anti-slavery armor closer, and face the storm, than when I read the above article coming from a Southern press. Thank God the friends of freedom have "not labored in vain!" The anti-slavery enterprise will not fail to accomplish its great mission; it is an important mission. The destiny and happiness of millions depend upon its success. Our confidence is too strong in the Infinite God to doubt for a moment. The agonizing wails of the millions of poor bondmen will not be unheeded by Him. The anti-slavery enterprise has His approbative seal, accompanied by the faithful prayers of thousands. It has poured a flood of light into the South already; and, wielding its power over the ballot box, it shakes the citadel of despotism in this nation. When Southern editors begin to cry out like the above, and stand aghast with fear, then let Northern political demagogues and doughfaces beware, for justice and truth are on their track and will soon overtake them; and woe betide the men that fall before the car of impartial freedom. Well may the South say, it is not Seward or Wilson that is to be feared, but those living ideas, those noble principles that lie at the foundation of the great revolution. Even my friend Frederick Douglass is but human. Simply as a man, he is not to be feared. But on freedom's platform, in *the name of God* and humanity, ideas go out from him that accelerate the progress of reform. It is so with every reformer. If so, then no one is excusable in any circumstance from doing something in this great work. The editor of the Mobile *News* says, *"Revolutions never go backward."* It is so, and here is our encouragement.

One word, sir, about our season here. We are now having beautiful weather overhead, but the mark of old winter is all around us. Our mountain roads are, in some places, filled up three feet deep in snowdrifts, and in other places, a foot deep in mud; and woe betide the poor pedestrian who attempts to travel Vermont when winter is breaking up his position, as a powerful spring sun compels him to evacuate his quarters among us. Well, as in freedom, so in the weather, we look for better days to come. Yours as ever,

JOHN W. LEWIS

Frederick Douglass' Paper (Rochester, N.Y.), 4 May 1855.

1. The *Mobile Evening News*, an independent daily founded in 1851, was edited by local politician Charles C. Langdon. The paper was a leading defender of southern interests. Harriet E. Amos, *Cotton City: Urban Development in Antebellum Mobile* (University, Ala., 1985), 229; Rhoda C. Ellison, *History and Bibliography of Alabama Newspapers in the Nineteenth Century* (University, Ala., 1954), 118–19.

2. Both abolitionists and Republican organizers were encouraged by the 1855 senatorial elections. Several politicians with antislavery leanings were called to the U.S. Senate. Iowa and Wisconsin each elected anti-Nebraska men. The New Hampshire legislature chose antislavery Whig James Bell and longtime Free

Soiler John P. Hale. Maine selected William P. Fessenden, an antislavery Whig, and Hannibal Hamlin, an anti-Nebraska Democrat. Massachusetts named Henry Wilson, a Know Nothing politician with antislavery principles. William H. Seward was reelected as a Republican in New York. And anti-Nebraska Democrat Lyman Trumbull won a Senate seat from Illinois. Sewell, *Ballots for Freedom*, 259–60, 266, 271–74; Gienapp, *Origins of the Republican Party*, 172–79.

3. The *Mobile Evening News* refers to the 1855 election of William H. Seward and Henry Wilson to the U.S. Senate. Wilson (1812–1875), a prominent Massachusetts lawyer, editor, and politician, served in the Senate from 1855 to 1873, first as an antislavery advocate before the Civil War, then as a Radical Republican during Reconstruction. He was President Ulysses S. Grant's running mate in the successful 1872 campaign. *DAB*, 20:322–24.

58.
Speech by William Wells Brown
Delivered at the Cincinnati Anti-Slavery Convention
Cincinnati, Ohio
25 April 1855

Black antislavery lecturers elicited a wide variety of public responses, ranging from apathy, suspicion, and open hostility to congeniality and enthusiasm. They were greeted as foreign dignitaries in the British Isles, where they dined with royalty, mingled with the aristocracy, and addressed distinguished assemblies. As black speakers toured through the northern states, they were sometimes feted by local white reformers and extended a degree of hospitality to which they were unaccustomed. Along with these warm receptions came subtle pressures to restrain their militancy and soften their antislavery rhetoric—to ingratiate rather than agitate. William Wells Brown raised the subject of abolitionist "etiquette" in a 25 April 1855 speech before the Cincinnati Anti-Slavery Convention, an annual Garrisonian gathering sponsored by local antislavery women. Brown related to the interracial audience an amusing incident that had occurred during his early years on the antislavery lecture circuit. His host and hostess, a conservative Methodist minister and his wife, surprised Brown with their courtesy and amiability. He was temporarily distracted by these unexpected social pleasantries, until a chance recollection about his life as a slave refocused his attention on the serious business of abolitionism. Ripley et al., *Black Abolitionist Papers*, 1:14–17, 33–35; *NASS*, 26 September 1844 [4:0924]; Farrison, *William Wells Brown*, 265–67.

Wm. Wells Brown was then introduced to the audience. He commenced by saying that we were here to comment on the doings of our fathers. If his audience thought he referred to black fathers they were mistaken—neither did he refer to white fathers. We were a mixed people (Mr. Brown is a light Mulatto, with a broad nose, but except this and the kink in his hair, not of decidedly African features). Slavery had no legal existence till the convention of 1787 gave it legal existence, protection.[1] Here our fathers had failed to carry out the principles of the great Declaration. His white fathers had deprived him of the privilege of appealing to the black race for his ancestry, but he was a type representing both races, and would for the moment throw aside his African ancestry, and appeal to his Anglo-Saxon.

The prophet Jeremiah had asked, can the Ethiopian change his skin?[2] as though it were an impossible thing; but the slaveholders of this day had found a way of changing the Ethiopian's complexion, and they were doing it mighty fast too.

He had often heard his old master[3] say he wanted to get rid of slavery, but never heard him say that he wanted to get rid of him, and when he ran away he gave him the best evidence that he did not.

He then alluded to the recent instances of a conviction in New York for engaging in the slave trade.[4] This trade was still carried on between the slave-consuming and slave-raising States, and the only mistake in this case was that the man went to the coast of Africa instead of Virginia for his slaves. Had he done the latter, he might have pursued his business religiously, and been a respectable member of a Southern church.

He then alluded to the recent work of Dr. Adams, of Boston, on Slavery. The Doctor had visited the South, and been affected by its great hospitality. Dr. Fuller, of South Carolina, had received him with so much kindness that the very next morning after his arrival, in writing home, he says: "A slight frost has nipped my Anti-Slavery."[5] The effect of this hospitality he illustrated by an anecdote. Shortly after his escape from Slavery, he went to lecture in a certain town in Massachusetts. The clergyman of the place, who was very conservative, at first refused the use of his vestry room, or even to announce the lecture from the pulpit; but afterwards, as a matter of policy, proffered both the church and the hospitality of his house to the lecturer. The speaker did not like to accept the latter, because the clergyman belonged to the same church with his 'ole massa, and he had a good many hard things to say in his lecture about him and the church, but he buttoned up his coat, and resolved to go and do his duty. This was just after he had left slavery, and he had not gotten rid of his awe of the white man, or learned to look him in the face.

When he entered, the lady of the house met him kindly, and set out the rocking chair for him. Such a rocking chair he had never seen before. It had a kind of spring wire, gutta-percha, India rubber bottom, and when he got into it he began to tremble and shake all over, and his head swam so that he had to hold on to the framework to keep from falling out. The lady remarked, "It's a pleasant day, Mr. Brown." His confusion by all this kindness was so great he could only say, "Thanky, maam." "Hope we'll have a pleasant evening." "Thanky, maam." "We need a stirring up here." "Thanky, maam." The lecturer thought—what a good woman! I'll cut out some of the hard things I was going to say about her church. Mr. Marshall then came down, "Brother Brown, how do you do? I'm very glad to see you, be seated Brother Brown." He hadn't been used to being called Brother Brown by the white men, and thought, "What a good man, I'll scratch a little more off."

At tea, he was seated by the lady's right hand, and had an extra lump of sugar in his tea; and that made him scratch a little more off. After tea, the lady called—"Harriet, my dear, can't you play for Mr. Brown?"

There he sat rocking in his chair—his head swimming—the piano going; had resolved to scratch it all off, and had entirely forgotten his duty. But he had a bond of sympathy with the slave that Dr. Adams had not. The little girl Harriet reminded him that he once had a sister; that she was torn from him and sent South; that he had not dared remonstrate, or even call her sister.[6] The kindness of the lady whose hospitality he was enjoying brought to mind his mother, from whose caresses he had been torn, and she sent he knew not whither, never to see her boy's face again. He resolved to do, and did his duty.

Anti-Slavery Bugle (Salem, Ohio), 5 May 1855.

1. Delegates to the 1787 Constitutional Convention in Philadelphia agreed to count slaves as three-fifths of a person in apportioning taxes and representation in the U.S. House of Representatives, to enable owners of slaves to recover them from other states, and to prohibit Congress from abolishing the African slave trade before 1807.

2. Jeremiah 13:23.

3. Brown apparently refers to his original owner, Dr. John Young of Lexington, Kentucky. Young moved to the Missouri Territory in 1816 and eventually served in the state's first legislature. In 1827 he purchased a three-thousand-acre farm near St. Louis, where Brown worked briefly as a house servant. Young regularly hired Brown out, then sold him in 1833 to Samuel Willi, a St. Louis tailor, who resold him later that year to Enoch Price, a local commission merchant and steamboat owner. Farrison, *William Wells Brown*, 8–42.

4. Brown probably refers to the February 1855 conviction of a Captain Smidth in the U.S. Circuit Court at New York City. Smidth, the captain and owner of the brig *Julia Moultan*, had sailed from the port of New York to the West African coast and purchased five hundred slaves. He then traveled to Cuba, sold his cargo, and burned the vessel. Smidth was initially tried in November 1854 but claimed exemption from American law as a citizen of Hanover, Germany. *NYTi*, 10 November 1854; *NASS*, 3 March 1855; Helen T. Catterall, ed., *Judicial Cases Concerning American Slavery and the Negro*, 5 vols. (Washington, D.C., 1936), 4:403.

5. Nehemiah Adams (1806–1878), a Boston Congregationalist clergyman, toured the South in early 1854. After returning home, he published *A South-Side View of Slavery* (1854), which presented slavery in a positive light. Adams condemned abolitionists, asserting that the South would eventually end slavery through peaceful means. While in Beaufort, South Carolina, he visited Richard Fuller (1804–1876), a slaveholding Baptist minister and leading proslavery apologist. *DAB*, 1:93–94, 7:62–63; Anne C. Loveland, *Southern Evangelicals and the Social Order, 1800–1860* (Baton Rouge, La., 1980), 66, 198–99, 214–17.

6. Brown's sister, Elizabeth, was a house servant on the farm of Dr. John Young near St. Louis. She was sold to Isaac Mansfield, a local tinner, in the late 1820s, then resold in 1833 to a Mississippi planter. Brown last saw his sister in a St. Louis jail, while she was awaiting transfer to Natchez. Farrison, *William Wells Brown*, 9, 20, 35.

59.
Speech by James McCune Smith
Delivered at the First Colored Presbyterian Church
New York, New York
8 May 1855

Antebellum black leaders endorsed a broad reform agenda that included
emancipation, racial equality, universal manhood suffrage, temperance,
and opposition to Jim Crow laws and practices. While they sometimes
quarreled over strategy and tactics, no one disputed the evils of slavery
and racism, and few questioned the need for independent black action.
Their concerns, declared James McCune Smith, extended "from the
mere act of riding in public conveyances, up to the liberation of every
slave in the land . . . embracing a full and equal participation, politically
and socially, in all the rights and immunities of American citizens."
Smith spoke these words at an 8 May 1855 meeting of the National
Council of the Colored People, which convened at the First Colored
Presbyterian Church in New York City. He presided over the gathering
and opened its first session with the following address. His audience included Frederick Douglass, Philip A. Bell, and Stephen Myers from New
York state and a handful of other black leaders from Pennsylvania, New
England, and Illinois. Smith reminded them of their responsibility to
"*do their own thinking,*" to lead their race in the struggle for freedom,
and not to rely on their white colleagues. "It is emphatically our battle,"
he told members of the council, "no one else can fight it for us." Smith's
sentiments reflected the thrust of the black abolitionist movement in the
1850s. *NYT,* 9, 10, 11 May 1855; *ASB,* 19 May 1855 [9:0663–64].

GENTLEMEN:
    You are assembled to fulfill the duties imposed on you by a Conven-
tion of the colored people, assembled at Rochester in July 1853, by
which Convention you were duly appointed "for the purpose of improving the character, developing the intelligence, maintaining the rights, and
organizing a Union of the colored people of the free States."[1] The hundred and seventy thousand souls who compose the free colored people of
the free States occupy a position in regard to human progress of greater
importance and responsibility than any like number of individuals on the
face of the globe. The great question of human brotherhood is brought
to a direct test in our persons and position; the practicability of democratic institutions, their ability to overcome the last vestige of tyranny in
the human heart, the vincibility of caste by Christianity, the power of the
gospel, the disenthrallment of three millions of bleeding and crushed
slaves; all these issues lend their weight and rest their decision very

greatly, if not entirely, on the free colored people of the free States. This weight of responsibility is enough to make men shrink therefrom; but we cannot avoid it if we would. The influence of our land and its institutions reaches to the uttermost parts of the earth; and go where we may, we will find American prejudice, or at least the odor of it, to contend against. It is easiest, as well as manliest, to meet and contend with it here at the fountainhead; nor can we cease affecting these great issues by inactivity; the case is going on, whether we labor or not; and our inactivity will only help deciding it against us and these, and true principles, which it would seem the Providence of God that we are set apart to uphold. Although we may not readily see it, our position is not a hopeless one; it is full of promise. It sometimes happens in great moral, as in great physical battles, that certain divisions of men, by simply maintaining a fixed position, even without striking an active blow, will conduce to the victory; in like manner, by simply maintaining our numbers, and our senses, and our Christianity under the waves of oppression and practical infidelity that have vainly beaten against us, we have done our appointed service in the land where we dwell. But the hour has come for us to take a direct and forward movement. We feel and know it. Just as in 1817 there was a spontaneous movement among our brethren of that generation, with one voice to oppose the Colonization movement,[2] so in this year 1855, throughout the length of the land, do we feel roused to take an active and energetic part in the great question of Liberty or Slavery. We are awakened, as never before, to the fact that if slavery and caste are to be removed from the land, we must remove them, and move them ourselves; others may aid and assist if they will, but the moving power rests with us. Gentlemen, the direction of this newly-awakened power rests greatly with you. Untrammeled by any of the influences that curb or straiten other benevolent or deliberative organizations, you may bring forward, discuss and adopt such plans of movement as may seem best. One or two primary considerations are all I will venture. First, it is important that you thoroughly organize all the colored people; we cannot spare the aid of a single man, or woman, or minor capable of thinking. Then you should adopt means to lay your plans of organization or cooperation before every individual among our people. This can be done by the agency of lectures and of the Press. We must distinctly keep before the people the fact that our labors consist in something beside the declaration of sentiments. We must act up to what we declare. And so closely does oppression encompass us that we can act constantly in behalf of our cause by simply maintaining for ourselves the rights which the laws of the land guarantee to us in common with all citizens. From the mere act of riding in public conveyances, up to the immediate and entire abolition of Slavery in the slave States, the laws of the land and the Constitution of the country are clearly on our side. And that man is a traitor to Liberty and a foe to our Humanity who maintains or even admits that we or any other human beings may be held in slavery on account of the color of skin, or for any reason short of the committing of crime. And from the mere act of riding in public conveyances, up to the liberation of every slave in the land, do our duties extend—embracing a full and equal participation, politically and socially, in all the rights and immunities of American citizens. If these our duties are weighty, we have the means to perform them. Our cause is inseparably wrapped up with every genial reform moving over the land.

> Freedom, hand in hand with labor,
> Walketh strong and brave;
> On the forehead of his neighbor
> No man writeth slave!

The States which have legislated in behalf of the Temperance reform have also made movements toward recognizing our rights as citizens thereof. But efforts on our own part have helped toward this good result; in Massachusetts, mainly by efforts of some colored citizens, one a member of this Council, the last vestige of caste in Public Schools has been abolished. In Connecticut, on the petition of her colored citizens, led by a member of this Council, both Houses of the Legislature have done their share toward granting us equal suffrage, and the Governor has recently strongly recommended the same. In New York, through the efforts of a member of this Council and the President of our State Council, aided by the moving eloquence of another member of our Council, the Legislature passed a vote of equal suffrage—a vote for which during the past twenty years we have petitioned and struggled in vain. In Pennsylvania, a strong and able effort has been made to obtain the franchise by our colored brethren, and not without some signs of success. Even in Illinois, hitherto covered with deeper infamy in caste than any other State, there are signs that the labors of her intelligent and energetic colored citizens have not been in vain.[3] Gentlemen, these cheering and grand results have followed the almost isolated labors of less than a hundred colored men; I had almost said of five. What may we not do if we secure the hearty, earnest and steady cooperation of ten thousand such men! If a hundred colored men have struck these blows under which Slaveocracy reels and staggers, how easily will ten thousand overthrow that atrocious system. We have the men and the spirit, and a favorable public sentiment; let us address ourselves to the work of organization. The time is come when our people must assume the rank of a first-rate power in the battle against caste and Slavery; it is emphatically our battle; no one else can fight it for us, and with God's help we must fight it ourselves. Our relations to the Anti-Slavery movement must be and are changed. Instead of depending upon it, we must lead it. We must maintain our citizenship and manhood in every relation—civil, religious and social—throughout the land. The recognition of our manhood throughout this land *is* the Abolition of Slavery throughout the land. One of the means of elevation left in your care by the Rochester Convention is an Industrial School;[4] and a plan by which our rising youths may forsake menial employments for mechanical and mercantile occupations. The accomplishment of both these objects is within our ability. Among the wants which we labor under as a class, there is not the want of money. We do not even in half our proportionate numbers occupy the Almshouses in the free States.[5] During the profound distress which existed during the past winter, we were not in any degree the distressed or starving class. And statistics will be presented to this Council, showing that as a mass, in the free States, we occupy a middle position between the rich and the poor. Not only could the hundred thousand free colored people of Pennsylvania and New York easily establish and richly endow an Industrial School; but I could name ten men among us who could do it without sensible loss to their abundance of means. This Industrial School should, like the rest of what we do, be our own movement, done by our own means. We will make both character and reputation in establishing it. We have, there-fore, gentlemen, a cause, and the men and the means to carry it on; may you be endowed with true wisdom for the accomplishment of the great purpose for which you are now met together.

New York Tribune (N.Y.), 9 May 1855.

1. The Colored National Convention of 6–8 July 1853 met at Corinthian Hall in Rochester, New York. Nearly 170 delegates from ten northern states attended the proceedings to examine, discuss, and approve numerous resolutions concern-ing the condition of free black life in the United States. Four goals dominated. The delegates, particularly Frederick Douglass, who drafted the meeting's decla-ration of sentiments, rejected the resurgent efforts of the American Colonization Society and, by implication, recent calls for black emigration. Delegates stressed the need for northern blacks to better understand their own political economy and to erect institutions addressing their economic and educational needs. They supported the creation of a manual labor college to train black students in the liberal and mechanical arts. And convinced that efforts to develop black-directed institutions must begin with the formation of a separate national organization, delegates established the National Council of the Colored People, drafted its constitution, and elected its executive committee. Pease and Pease, *They Who Would Be Free*, 123, 139–40, 150, 253–55; *Colored National Convention . . . in Rochester* (1853), 3–57 [8:0327–54]; *FDP*, 15 July 1853.

2. Free blacks had not been of "one voice" on the colonization question in 1817, as Smith suggests. After initially expressing some interest in colonization during that first year, free blacks in Philadelphia, the District of Columbia, and Richmond led the general opposition to the American Colonization Society. By the late 1820s, Philadelphia blacks had invented a "spirit of 1817" myth—the

popular notion that free black rejection of colonization had been both immediate and complete. Marie Tyler McGraw, "Richmond Free Blacks and African Colonization, 1816–1832," *JAS* 21:209 (August 1987); Winch, *Philadelphia's Black Elite,* 38–39.

3. Between 1851 and 1855, the legislatures of Maine, Massachusetts, Rhode Island, Vermont, Michigan, Connecticut, New York, Indiana, Delaware, and Iowa prohibited the sale of alcoholic beverages. Smith saw encouraging signs that blacks in these and other states were gaining their civil and political rights. His expectations were heightened by several black initiatives then in progress. In April 1855, after a lengthy lobbying effort by Boston blacks under the leadership of William C. Nell, a member of the National Council of the Colored People, the Massachusetts legislature abolished segregated schools throughout the state. Amos G. Beman, another member of the National Council, directed an 1854–55 petition drive for suffrage by Connecticut blacks, which the legislature rejected despite Governor William T. Minor's recommendation that blacks be enfranchised. Stephen Myers, a member of the National Council, and William H. Topp, the president of the state council, led a similar movement in New York state, which was part of a campaign that began in 1837. In February 1855, Frederick Douglass spoke eloquently before the New York state legislature on the subject. The lower house endorsed elimination of the state's property qualification for black voters, but the state senate tabled the bill in April. A pamphlet by a committee of "Colored Citizens of Philadelphia," calling for the restoration of black voting rights in Pennsylvania, renewed hopes in that state. About the same time, Chicago blacks John Jones, James D. Bonner, and Henry O. Wagoner led a campaign for equal suffrage in Illinois, a state notorious for restricting black rights. Despite these efforts, laws restricting black suffrage remained in effect in Connecticut, New York, Pennsylvania, and Illinois until the ratification of the Fifteenth Amendment (1869). Tyrrell, *Sobering Up,* 260; Horton and Horton, *Black Bostonians,* 75; *FDP,* 23 February, 13, 20 April, 8 June 1855; Litwack, *North of Slavery,* 70–93; Field, *Politics of Race,* 91–93.

4. Smith refers to the proposed American Industrial School.

5. Smith worked hard to refute charges by proslavery apologists that free blacks were disproportionately dependent on public welfare. In 1844 he had reported to the *New York Tribune* that Philadelphia blacks contributed far more to public welfare than they received and that a smaller percentage of New York City blacks were in public almshouses than whites. Available records suggest a more complex picture. The proportion of blacks dependent on charity varied from city to city, fluctuating with changes in both the economy and local relief policies. Blacks comprised nearly 18 percent of New York City's institutionalized poor in 1849—six times greater than their proportion of the city's residents. In the early 1850s, the number of blacks in Philadelphia and Albany almshouses was only slightly larger than their percentage of the local population. In Boston the rate was actually much smaller. *NASS,* 8 February, 18 April 1844; Curry, *Free Black in Urban America,* 120–35.

60.
Barbara Ann Steward to Frederick Douglass
29 May 1855

Sharing the traditional American faith in education as a vehicle for social and economic advancement, black leaders promoted a variety of
training programs, particularly the manual labor schools that emerged
as a component of the moral reform movement during the 1830s. But
education took on new meaning for the black community in the 1850s,
becoming a symbol of the movement toward autonomy and self-eleva-
tion. A committee appointed by the National Council of the Colored
People drew up a plan for an institution to be called the American Industrial School. Frederick Douglass, James McCune Smith, John Peck,
and other champions of the school argued that it would offer blacks
their only opportunity to learn the skilled trades needed for independence and progress. In May 1855, after intense debate over the wisdom
of establishing a racially exclusive school, members of the National
Council approved the plan by a seven to five vote. Barbara Ann Steward, a black teacher and antislavery lecturer, was disappointed by the
council's weak endorsement. A delegate to the 1853 black national convention that organized the council, she believed that the school could
provide the skills necessary to lift blacks out of poverty and produce the
next generation of black leaders. Steward's enthusiasm resulted largely
from her own vision of the narrowing opportunities for blacks in the
United States. Talented and well-educated, she was disheartened by the
unwillingness of whites to employ blacks, regardless of ability, in anything but menial labor. She saw evidence of this in her own experience.
"I have spent all my life in educating my head," she explained in a 29
May 1855 letter to Frederick Douglass, "and the brightest prospect I
have today for the future . . . is to sail for Monrovia on the coast of Africa." *NYT,* 8, 9, 10 May 1855; *FDP,* 24 March 1854 [8:0691].

CANANDAIGUA, [New York]
May 29th, 1855

MR. DOUGLASS:

I was both surprised and pained to learn, on taking up your paper, that
the INDUSTRIAL COLLEGE had a majority of but two, and I was mortified to find that men who were familiar with all the outlines of the
proposed plan should oppose it. It seems incredible that they should so
far forget the position we occupy as to do such a thing. We are an
unsettled, unstable people, destitute, in a great measure, of homes that
we can call our own; looked down upon, by our more favored fellowmen, as ignorant and degraded. Unacquainted with the mechanical arts,

in all the agricultural fairs, while others are hurrying to the place of exhibition with skilful and ingenious articles to exhibit, we are unrepresented. Thousands and thousands of intelligent fathers and mothers, whose children are as dear to them as those of their more white neighbors, lay down upon their pillow at night with their minds burdened with care. What shall I do with my children? is the uppermost thought. If a porter shop is to be the highest station in life to which my son can aspire; the gentleman's kitchen the only place my daughter can find employment, then what is the use of educating them? The more ignorant they are, the better they will be suited with their condition. And is it not too true? We see fine intelligent youths of both sexes idling around in the Spring, waiting for the boats to run, or the Springhouses to open. Hundreds of young men, with educations that might admit them into any office as clerks, at good salaries, if they were not so unfortunate (in the eyes of the world) as to be black, are found engaged in the most menial employments as mere drudges. Their labors are such they must be kept steadily to work, and when six o'clock comes they cannot leave off, like other young men engaged in mechanical employment, and have time at their disposal. They must keep steady at work till late at night; then they hurry to the enticing saloon and theatre, and spend their time in indulging in intoxicating drinks. And on the Sabbath, it is the same routine of labor; and when that is done, worn out and tired, they feel little like entering churches, and encountering the gaze of persons who wonder at their impudence in coming; but will rather ensconce themselves in some snug corner among their comrades, where the exhilarating glass is passed around, and cards close the scene, and the fourth commandment is broken. Oh! can it be that there are men so traitorous to the best interests of their people as to say we do not want to live differently from that? *"There are places enough now open where colored youths can learn trades,"* some say. But I should like to have these places specified more definitely; and if there are workshops enough open on terms of perfect equality, where all the workmen will instruct a colored boy, irrespective of color, why then I shall take my stand on the opposing ground too. And *if* there are *now* workshops enough in this country, where every colored youth can get a trade, then I am ashamed of my people.

I am daily meeting with those who are entirely ignorant of the plan of the Industrial College. They think it is merely an institution where the attention is paid to educating the head. And almost in anger they will toss their head and say, "Yes, a fine business to think of my son or daughter going to college, and I in the washtub." Or, "Yes, my boy, I guess, has education enough to black boots and shoes." And when I explain to them (as I always try to do), I have seen their eyes sparkle with joy, they cannot believe it to be true. And yet men will say that they are opposed to it, when they have sent forth no lecturers on the subject.

Think you that slavery would be the all-engrossing subject, as it is, if there had been no Douglasses, Wards,[1] Garnets,[2] bearing on their own persons the severity of the lash of slavery, and feeling perhaps too sensitively its degradation? In any other way of escape than trades, I have no faith. As to a mere knowledge of books, I have no faith in it. I do not say that I undervalue education, for I think every child should be kept in school till twelve or fourteen years old at least. But a mere knowledge of books, without a trade of some kind, is useless, as the colored people are situated now. I have spent all my life in educating my head, and the brightest prospect I have today for the future, and the most advantageous offer I have ever had, is to sail for Monrovia on the coast of Africa in October next. But I must stop, *not* for want of words, but because I would not trespass on your time. Yours in the great cause of our elevation,

BARBARA ANN STEWARD[3]

Frederick Douglass' Paper (Rochester, N.Y.), 1 June 1855.

1. Samuel Ringgold Ward.
2. Henry Highland Garnet.
3. Barbara Ann Steward (1836–1861), a teacher and antislavery lecturer of some repute, was the daughter of black abolitionist Austin Steward. Although born in Canada West, she lived most of her life near Rochester, New York. During the mid-1850s, she toured western New York and New England, impressing audiences with her eloquent and persuasive speeches. Blacks in Ontario County, New York, selected Steward as one of their nine delegates to the 1853 black national convention in Rochester. Later that year, she helped organize a western New York auxiliary of the National Council of the Colored People. She also attended the 1855 black state convention in Troy, but when delegates objected to the presence of a woman delegate, her name was stricken from the rolls. Steward was also frustrated by the limited number of employment opportunities open to educated black women. She was convinced by her own experience that vocational training at a manual labor college would best serve black needs. Turning down an offer to teach in Liberia, she accepted a position at a black public school in Wilkes-Barre, Pennsylvania. Steward developed an interest in the Haitian emigration movement, and in the spring of 1861, she announced her intention of visiting Haiti to assess the prospects for permanent settlement. Illness prevented her from making the trip, and she died later that year. U.S. Census, 1850; Ripley et al., *Black Abolitionist Papers*, 2:64n; *FDP*, 24 June, 16 December 1853, 1 June, 14 September, 19 October, 9 November 1855 [9:0679, 0826]; *WAA*, 21 April 1860, 18 May, 14 December 1861; *PP*, 9 November 1861 [13:0881].

61.
William C. Nell to Wendell Phillips
8 July 1855

Black intellectuals believed that black history and memory fostered Afro-American identity and advanced the struggle against slavery and racial prejudice. They invoked the black past to support their call for freedom, equality, and citizenship. No one did this more convincingly than William C. Nell. During the 1850s, Nell organized annual Crispus Attucks celebrations to commemorate black contributions to American independence and composed several historical works, including *Colored Patriots of the American Revolution* (1855). That volume, the result of careful scholarship and the innovative use of oral sources, is generally considered the first serious attempt to write Afro-American history. It recorded black military service in the American Revolution and War of 1812, which had been "quietly elbowed aside," and gave historical justification of black claims to American citizenship. Nell's work made a powerful abolitionist statement to both white and black audiences at a time when the federal government was denying the birthright of black Americans. His 8 July 1855 letter to Wendell Phillips discussed his struggle to publish the volume and conveyed his certainty that it would present "*colored* antislavery." *Colored Patriots* exemplified the spirit of black abolitionism in the 1850s—a militant call for greater independence and an emphasis on racial pride. *DANB*, 472–73; Earl E. Thorpe, *Black Historians: A Critique* (New York, N.Y., 1971), 33–35; *FDP*, 23 February 1855; William C. Nell, *Property Qualification or No Property Qualification: A Few Facts* (New York, N.Y., 1860), 3–24 [12:0341–52]; Nell, *Colored Patriots*.

Boston, [Massachusetts]
July 8, 1855

Respected Friend:

At Framingham on the 4th inst. while I was meditating about my book, your kind enquiries and suggestions were quite apropos. As answer to the same, I have noted down the following as definite knowledge of my hopes and plan for thier realization.

I foresaw that I should need some pecuniary aid in publishing the edition augmented and improved so far beyond its two predecessors.

My experience in this attempt has been a long, complicated, and wearisome one—the successes of which have been indeed few and far between.

C. F. Hovey[1] declined without as I thought suppose giving the subject much thought.

COLORED PATRIOTS

OF THE

AMERICAN REVOLUTION,

WITH SKETCHES OF SEVERAL

DISTINGUISHED COLORED PERSONS:

TO WHICH IS ADDED A BRIEF SURVEY OF THE

Condition and Prospects of Colored Americans.

By WM. C. NELL.

———

WITH AN INTRODUCTION BY

HARRIET BEECHER STOWE.

———

BOSTON:

PUBLISHED BY ROBERT F. WALLCUT.

1855.

12. Frontispiece to William C. Nell,
Colored Patriots of the American Revolution
(Boston, 1855)

Geo. R. Russell[2] I recieved no answer from and several others whom for various considerations I anticipated favor turned the cold shoulder upon me.

I procured copies of the facsimilie and the illustrations and my Circulars[3] in part, for this purpose. I ventured to hope that Mrs. Stowe might consider it within the embrace of certain Foriegn donations. She in a polite note expressed otherwise, though Dr. Rogers[4] told me she presented him 150 dollars for his Book. His being thus aided and mine being rejected is a problem not easily solved. She has promised me the introduction which I presume I may obtain.[5]

J. P. Jewett[6] recommended me to the artist who has already recieved from me nearly his 35 dolls. for wood cuts. Chandler[7] I yet owe 25 dolls. for the Facsimilies. I have made quite an outlay in correspondence[,] Journeyings, Documents and other facilities. And as my business yet renders but scanty Cash supplies my path is far from being a smooth one. I have recieved aid as follows:[8]

$		Pledges	
T. T. Bouve	10—	Francis Jackson	10
F. A. Sumner	5—	S. G. Howe	2
B. C. Clark	5—	Samuel May Jr.	
Richd. Clapp	5	has volunteered a	
	25 (all appreciated)	donation of——	

Several have subscribed thier dollar and many promise—also, agencies have been solicited.

Ball's Panorama—Services as Ticket, Newspaper and Door agency occupied much time and to the present has made no Cash equivalent.[9]

Antioch College Scholarship[10] [word illegible] which I confidently expected 20—failed me. And the Equal School Rights movement has taked my time and money too, and even now I am on a mission to the Parents to facilitate the Superintendents transferring the Scholars.[11]

Had it not been for these drawbacks of time and money, my own Special interests would have been further advanced. These are the facts no matter how various or caustic should be the Commentary.

I never felt more moved to accomplish any object than now to publish my Book and I have abundant reasons for knowing that it is needed and that it will pay for itself amply. Aside from the military facts, the other departments dovetailed in [are] what will be attractive and instructive to Colored people, and anti-slavery friends. To ~~those~~ new converts they will be serviceable in the political campaign now sounding its Battle cry over the country.

The Boston Bee and Post have lately been discussing Irish valor and antecedents.[12] This compilation will show the world Colored American Valor and antecedents.

The question of <u>Colored</u> antislavery is fully set forth and used up by examples and precepts, many of them from the armory of the champions now arrayed on the opposite side though not in a manner calculated to brooke a controversy. Individuals and facts associated with the early Colonial history of Colored Massachusetts Citizens and prominent servants of other States, each of which is a nucleus for many cherished memories, will all help its circulation. Langston, Day and others in Ohio[13] and good names in New York, Pennsylvania and Connecticutt are pledged to assist its sale. Each name and every past has its use. The various parties among Colored people will here discover something of local attractiveness contributing towards general elevation.

To abandon this publication now, after my flourish of trumpets[,] is a greater stroke of disappointment and mortification than my philosophy can endure, more than it shall be subjected to unless Destiny removes me speedily from active life. I will go to New York State and sell my Gerrit Smith lands[14] to speculators and make all other possible sacrifices first. But I am persuaded this need not be, for a hundred or more dollars for a basis can be soon raised by a few friends if you will render me your influence in the following plan.

Address my Circulars or substance condensed with an addenda of your own as Treasurer soliciting sums as loans or donations. The work can be put to press and by instalments the obligation shall be promptly redeemed.

I am desirous for you and Mr. Garrison[15] to review the Manuscript feeling assured that the Book as a whole will meet your concurrant approbation. If I did not feel sure that with the solicited aid the plan would succeed I should not urge it upon your attention. As ever, I remain Gratefully Yours,

William C. Nell

Crawford Blagden Collection of the Papers of Wendell Phillips, Houghton Library, Harvard University, Cambridge, Massachusetts. Published by permission.

1. Charles Fox Hovey (1807–1859), a Boston merchant, embraced Garrisonian abolitionism in 1845 and served on the executive committees of the American Anti-Slavery Society and its Massachusetts auxiliary during the following decade. He used his considerable wealth to promote a wide range of reforms. Merrill and Ruchames, *Letters of William Lloyd Garrison*, 4:8–9.

2. George Robert Russell (1800–1866), the son of the American diplomat Jonathan Russell, was the mayor of West Roxbury, Massachusetts, during the 1850s. After amassing considerable wealth in the China trade, he retired in 1835 and devoted his time to literary study and Whig, Free Soil, and Republican politics. Russell was a major contributor to the Boston Vigilance Committee. U.S. Census, 1850; Theodore Lyman, "Memoir of George Robert Russell," *PMHS* 18:280–81 (December 1880); Merrill and Ruchames, *Letters of William Lloyd Garrison*, 4:334–35.

3. Nell probably refers to a circular reprinted in the 25 May 1855 issue of the *Liberator*, which solicited advance orders for his forthcoming book, *Colored Patriots of the American Revolution* (1855).

4. Edward Coit Rogers (1835–1856), a Massachusetts abolitionist and spiritualist, had recently published *Letters on Slavery, Addressed to the Pro-Slaverymen of America* (1855) in Boston. It appeared under the pseudonym O. S. Freeman. W. Stewart Wallace, *A Dictionary of North American Authors* (Toronto, Ontario, 1951), 388.

5. As promised, Harriet Beecher Stowe penned a brief introduction to the 1855 edition of Nell's *Colored Patriots of the American Revolution*.

6. John Punchard Jewett (1814–1884), a Boston publisher and bookseller, issued the first book-length edition of Harriet Beecher Stowe's *Uncle Tom's Cabin* (1852). He published many other works on theological, historical, and reform themes. Jewett's numerous contacts with reformers and individuals in the publishing world prompted Nell and other authors to seek his advice. His business collapsed during the Panic of 1857, and in 1866, after several more failed ventures, he opened a bookstore in New York City. *DAB*, 10:69.

7. Nell probably refers to John G. Chandler, an engraver and lithographer in Boston during the 1850s. *Boston City Directory*, 1850–57.

8. Nell received financial support from several respected Massachusetts businessmen, reformers, and philanthropists. Thomas T. Bouvé (1815–1896), a wealthy Boston iron merchant and amateur naturalist, regularly contributed to the Boston Vigilance Committee. Francis A. Sumner (1802–?) operated an academy for boys in Stoughton. Benjamin Cutler Clark, a Boston shipping magnate, was an early supporter of Haitian emigration whose *Plea for Haiti* (1853) was widely reprinted. During the Civil War, Clark supported the Massachusetts Colonization Society's plan to voluntarily resettle blacks in the West Indies. Richard Clapp (1780–1861), a Dorchester tanner, held several local political offices and served as president of his city's antislavery society. Francis Jackson and Samuel May, Jr., were leading figures in both the American Anti-Slavery Society and its Massachusetts auxiliary. Samuel Gridley Howe (1801–1876), a Boston political abolitionist who directed the Perkins Institution for the Blind from 1832 until his death, raised funds for John Brown's Harpers Ferry raid and promoted the United States Sanitary Commission during the Civil War. *ACAB*, 1:332; *NCAB*, 7:506–7; U.S. Census, 1850; Treasurer's Account Book of the Boston Vigilance Committee, Siebert Collection, MB [6:0620, 0629, 0634, 0639, 0640]; *Lib*, 22 October 1847; Joseph E. Garland, *Boston's North Shore: Being an Account of Life Among the Noteworthy, Fashionable, Wealthy, Eccentric and Ordinary, 1823–1890* (Boston, Mass., 1978), 44, 122–26; *PP*, 6 February 1862; Merrill and Ruchames, *Letters of William Lloyd Garrison*, 2:713; *DAB*, 5:296–97.

9. Nell served as a local agent for a panorama created by black daguerreotypist James Presley Ball of Cincinnati, Ohio. Exhibited during the spring and summer of 1855 at Amory Hall in Boston, it included scenes of American cities, cotton plantations, the slave trade, and natural wonders such as the Mississippi River and Niagara Falls. An illustrated volume, *Ball's Splendid Mammoth Pictorial Tour of the United States* (1855), was published to promote the exhibition. One year later, Ball successfully toured with his panorama in Europe. *Lib*, 11

May 1855; *FDP*, 13 April 1855; James deT. Abajian, *Blacks in Selected Newspapers, Censuses and Other Sources: An Index to Names and Subjects*, 5 vols. (Boston, Mass., 1976), 1:96–97.

10. Working out of the *Liberator* office, apparently without compensation, Nell solicited applications from qualified black students for an academic scholarship to attend Antioch College, a coeducational, abolitionist school in Yellow Springs, Ohio. *Lib*, 11 May 1855.

11. Nell played a prominent role in the struggle to integrate Boston's public school system during the 1840s and early 1850s. In April 1855, the Massachusetts legislature abolished racially separate schools throughout the state. During the months that followed, Nell worked with local school administrators to ease and expedite the relocation of students from the all-black Smith School into newly integrated classrooms. Horton and Horton, *Black Bostonians*, 70–75.

12. The 6 June 1855 issue of the *Boston Bee* printed a nativist attack on Irish character, which claimed the Irish lacked bravery in battle and had assisted the British forces during the American Revolution. "Argus," an anonymous correspondent, responded to the piece in "Irish Antecedents," a series of seven articles that appeared in the *Boston Post* over the following month. "Argus" defended Irish military heroism, denied that they had fought against the American rebels, chronicled Irish contributions to American society and culture, and repudiated the notion that only those peoples that "have a natural capacity for servility remain enslaved." *BP*, 20, 27, 28, 29 June, 11, 12, 13 July 1855.

13. Nell anticipated assistance from John Mercer Langston, William Howard Day, and other black abolitionists in Ohio.

14. In 1846 Gerrit Smith decided to grant tracts of land of forty to sixty acres each to three thousand blacks living in New York state. Nell was deeded a tract in December 1847, while assisting Frederick Douglass with the *North Star* in Rochester. William C. Nell to Gerrit Smith, 28 December 1847, Gerrit Smith Papers, NSyU [5:0543].

15. William Lloyd Garrison.

62.
Uriah Boston to Frederick Douglass
[August–September 1855]

Disunionist sentiment grew among black abolitionists during the 1850s. Events of the decade—the Fugitive Slave Law, the Kansas-Nebraska Act, attempts to annex Cuba as a slave territory, the campaign to reopen the African slave trade, and the Dred Scott decision—convinced many black leaders that slaveholding interests had an intractable hold on the federal government. Dissolution of the Union, once unthinkable to all but a few, now emerged as a worthy antislavery goal. Most blacks who favored disunionism did so out of despair that the nation's attitudes toward slavery and racism could ever be reformed, not to demonstrate personal purity or ideological commitment, as was common among white Garrisonians. Robert Purvis embraced disunionist sentiment because he believed that under the U.S. Constitution "the colored people are nothing, and can be nothing but an alien, disfranchised and degraded class." Uriah Boston, a Poughkeepsie, New York, barber and political activist, promoted disunionism as an essential antislavery tactic. In two letters, written to *Frederick Douglass' Paper* during August and September 1855, he expressed his views on the "dissolution of the Union" and the demise of slavery. *Lib*, 10 January 1851, 22 May 1857 [6:0726, 10:0688]; *ASB*, 11 April 1857 [10:0644]; *FDP*, 22 April 1853, 19 January, 20 April 1855 [8:0227, 9:0393, 0546]; *CA*, 6 June 1840, 16 January 1841 [3:0450, 0839]; *NASS*, 29 January 1846 [5:0152]; *WAA*, 31 March 1860 [12:0600].

MR. EDITOR:

As I have seen nothing original in your paper on the much and long-talked of dissolution of the Union, and having some thoughts that may be of interest to your readers, I deem the present a fit time to express them. Our friends, Hon. Daniel Webster and Henry Clay, used all possible means to save the Union, up to their last moment; the first by his magic influence in speech and act, the latter by tears, speeches and compromises. But though these two of the great, if not the greatest, American statesmen used their combined influence and efforts to save this Union, yet, present appearances do indicate, that the Union is not yet out of danger. Indeed things look as though they were just coming to a crisis. This crisis will come, if the South mean what they have declared, and the North are true to their interests. This crisis will be brought about in the application of Kansas to be admitted to the Union as a Slave State.[1]

Now, let us see what would be the results of the dissolution of the Union. Your readers will judge of the correctness and probabilities of the statements here made. Here they are:

1. The first result of a dissolution would be the weakening of the Slave Power, by the withdrawal of the sixteen Northern free States,[2] containing a population of 18 or 20 millions, and leaving 15 Slave States with a population of four or five millions to sustain Slavery. In other words, now, 25 millions of people sustain, and suffer the disgrace for sustaining, the worst system of slavery ever known, certainly the worst of the 19th century; then this disgrace would fall upon the guilty parties only, namely the slaveholding States. This would be a great change for the better, inasmuch as we are professedly (as free States would then really be), the freest nation on earth.

We then would be the great example of all nations aspiring to become free.

2. The second result would be a final release of the Northern States from the enormous expenses incurred by the general or federal government in promoting slave interests. These expenses are enormous considering the free population of the Slave States.[3]

3. The third beneficial result to the free States would be that they would be freed from the unpleasant and disagreeable agitation of the slavery question, and its developments, such as ministers of Christ advocating the constitutionality of the fugitive slave Law,[4] and the duty of citizens to catch, and send back to bondage, the panting fugitive. Many disgusting things of this sort would end with the dissolution of the Union. The whole question would be taken out of Church and State, and we would be relieved from the heart-sickening, demoralizing sight of otherwise seemingly good men proving themselves knaves in order to prove themselves constitutionally good citizens. The above results would accrue to the North from dissolution of the Union, and all very desirable, because really beneficial—durably so.

But there are others of not so pleasant a character, which would be felt directly by the South.

1. The slaves would flee without let or hinderance in every direction. Thousands of people who now refuse to assist fugitives to escape would then openly and freely assist them. The fugitives would find open and avowed friends in all quarters, and any and all of the free States would be as safe as Queen Victoria's dominions.[5] (The colored population of the free States would increase in ten years 50 per cent, if not 100 per cent. It would put the colored churches in a flourishing condition.)

2. A second result to the South would be slave insurrections. These disturbances would be excited and encouraged by Indians, Mexicans and Yankees. By Indians, and Mexicans, to retaliate for the injuries done them; and by the Yankees, as a matter of policy, to get slavery off the continent, and to encourage free labor and to make it honorable and praiseworthy.[6]

The final and grand result would be that slavery would be abolished—

it would end sooner by the dissolution of the Union than it will if the Union continues, and all the States where Slavery now exists would come into the Union again, thus constituting one great and free Republic. There can be but little doubt of this, where we reflect that now Slavery is protected by the whole power of the federal government, and it would only be sustained then by the power of the Slave States, a power too weak to suppress the discordant elements of its own existence.

In view of the facts here stated, and others that might be stated, I would ask why should citizens of the free States shudder at the oft-repeated threat of dissolutions?

U. B.

Frederick Douglass' Paper (Rochester, N.Y.), 31 August 1855.

MR. EDITOR:

Your kind notice of my first communication on this subject, the objections made by you to the position taken, or which is the same thing, to the results cast up by me, and a desire I cherish to benefit what I can my fellow beings, prompts me to reply to your objections;[7] let me make myself understood, as that is important. To this end, I remark, 1st. While the South have not ceased to threaten the North with the cry of dissolution, Northern Representatives in Congress, and Northern political leaders, have not failed when called to an account for their treachery to freedom, to make it the scapegoat for all their political sins. Here lies the secret of our failures on the Slavery question; and we suffer ourselves to be humbugged and fooled by this Southern scarecrow. The South should be made to understand that the Union is of more value to them, than it is to the North. My opinion is that if the South really believed and felt conscious that the Northern people desired to have the Union dissolved, we would hear no more about dissolution from that quarter. It was this opinion that prompted my former communication. And now, I will briefly notice your objections. 1st. There is but a very small portion of the 5 millions Southerners who can use "bayonets," and a smaller portion still, who would use them against the slaves. It is estimated that there are 250,000 slaveholders in the South. This is the highest estimate I have seen. But admit this to be a true estimate, we may safely conclude that many of these are unfit to take part in any effort to put down slave insurrections. Others would flee, the instant danger was apprehended; others again are timid and tender. On the other hand, the slaves are hardy, being used to rough usage, and though ignorant, they are brave, and would, if properly led and controlled by some daring leader, be too formidable a force for any army of high-lived slaveholders, that [c]ould be brought against them. In addition to this, there are many of the whites there, who would take sides with the slaves. There are others from the

North that would be glad of an opportunity to aid the slaves for freedom's sake; others, for plunder, and others again out of ill will toward the stiff aristocracy of the South. Combine all these and they would never fail to break every yoke. Secondly, with regard to the welfare of the slaves, they would be placed in a position to be benefited. Some would be benefited, others would not. On the whole, I believe even the slaves would be benefited by an insurrection, whether it would succeed or fail. I do not say that I desire this, but I do believe that we would witness an insurrection within ten years after the dissolution of the Union that would shake the very foundation of the slave system. I repeat, I do not desire such an event, but as the South make such a hobby of dissolution, and as this would follow as one of the results of dissolution, I should not regret it, but should feel to rejoice over it upon the principle of divine authority, as it is written: "woe unto the wicked, for the reward of his hands shall be given him, and he shall eat the fruit of his doings."[8] I believe in divine justice as well as in divine benevolence, and one of the strongest convictions of my Christian faith is, that I shall be able cheerfully to say Amen, to God's punishment of the incorrigibly wicked. "Then the wicked shall cease from troubling, and the weary shall be at rest, and the servant shall be released from his master."[9]

The last and only objection remaining to be noticed is the one relative to "accessions to colored churches," with regard to which, permit me to say, that, though I should rather see no distinctive organizations of "colored people," yet, as they are already existing, and that according to the will of the greater portion of the people, as the best that can be had at the present, I can see no reason why they should not be improved, both in numbers and respectability. The only result that I at present cheerfully acquiesce in, and heartily desire, is the grand final result—the destruction of slavery. The others are the means to an end. I cannot see how anyone can doubt that the speedy downfall of slavery would follow the dissolution of the Union. Slavery is a system of weakness and, if left to maintain itself, must die. This is especially true of American slavery, at this age. Why ask for proof to a self-evident fact. A man fatally diseased at the vitals is diseased in every limb; so is a system, and slavery being a system thus diseased, must die. If you say it is a healthy, sound system, then I shall be willing to dissect it, and prove its unsoundness. This I think you will not say, and therefore I drop the matter for the present.

As I said before, I believe slavery is a weak system, and it has, within itself, the elements of death. It is a sick thing, kept alive by its connection with the North. Now, if this sick thing would behave itself, I would bear with it, but seeing it will give us no peace, but is all the while rumpusing, and boasting of its deeds of daring, and its strength, I say cut it loose and let us see what will come of it. Slavery reminds me of an aged piece of poetry, which personifies a certain personage who did live, but did live hard. It runs thus:

> Hunty-bunty on the wall,
> Hunty-bunty got a fall,
> All the doctors in the land,
> Couldn't make Hunty-bunty stand.[10]

Let me add in conclusion, that I hope "all the doctors in the land" will let "Hunty-bunty" alone, and use their skill to better purpose. At all events I hope the better portion of the family will consent to let "Hunty-bunty" have his own way, let him go out and try his weakness. Respectfully,

U. B.

Frederick Douglass' Paper (Rochester, N.Y.), 28 September 1855.

1. Throughout early 1855, antislavery and proslavery settlers streamed into Kansas in anticipation of the 30 March territorial elections. Through fraudulent practices, supporters of slavery won the election and convened their own legislature, which adopted a repressive set of statutes for the protection of slavery. In December free-state men held their own election and set up a rival government. Both factions planned to apply for statehood. Boston believed that the conflict over Kansas statehood, including efforts by Congress to determine the legitimate territorial government, would precipitate a crisis threatening the Union. Potter, *Impending Crisis*, 200–208.

2. Those states that outlawed slavery before the Civil War were referred to as free states. In 1855 they included Maine, New Hampshire, Vermont, Massachusetts, Rhode Island, Connecticut, New York, New Jersey, Pennsylvania, Ohio, Indiana, Illinois, Michigan, Wisconsin, Iowa, and California.

3. Boston repeated a charge made by abolitionists since the 1830s. They maintained that slavery would die without northern support. The expense of maintaining armed forces and the direct and indirect costs of guaranteeing the South's domestic tranquillity were, abolitionists charged, disproportionately borne by the North, which had the largest share of the nation's population. Dissolution of the Union would throw that burden back on the South and help end slavery.

4. Although several famous American clergymen protested against the Fugitive Slave Law, the vast majority in nearly every major denomination defended the legislation and urged obedience. Most maintained that disobedience to one law endangered all laws and that the preservation of the Union depended upon northern compliance with the controversial act. McKivigan, *War against Proslavery Religion*, 153–54.

5. Boston refers to the protection from slave catchers that Britain granted to fugitive slaves fleeing to the British North American Provinces, particularly Canada West.

6. Boston suggests that Native Americans, Mexicans, and northerners had all been victimized by southern expansionism and would encourage and assist slave revolt.

7. Douglass published his objections in the 31 August 1855 issue of *Frederick Douglass' Paper*, the same issue in which Boston's first letter on disunionism appeared. He rejected Boston's position as "unsafe, unsound, and unwarrantable." Disunionism, he argued, would neither weaken the South nor absolve the North of its complicity in the perpetuation of slavery. Douglass believed that breaking apart the Union would not make slave escapes easier or encourage slave insurrections. He invited Boston to respond. *FDP*, 31 August 1855.

8. Boston paraphrases Isaiah 3:10–11.

9. Boston quotes from Job 3:17 and 19.

10. Boston recites a variation of "Humpty-Dumpty," a popular nursery rhyme.

63.
William J. Wilson to "My Dear Cousin M——"
[October 1855]

Black state and national conventions were benchmarks in the struggle
for racial equality and justice. These gatherings offered black leaders
an opportunity to exchange ideas, devise strategies, formulate goals,
foster new programs, and seek common ground. Reports of the convention proceedings were published as pamphlets or serialized in reform
newspapers and usually consisted of delegate rosters, resolutions, vote
counts, committee reports, and perhaps one or two notable speeches.
Although these official summaries are valuable historical records of
black abolitionism, they seldom impart the spirit of the conventions—
the rancor and tensions, the humor and congeniality, or the passion and
resolve. Writing under the pseudonym "Ethiop," William J. Wilson reported on the 1853 and 1855 black national conventions for *Frederick
Douglass' Paper*. His correspondence captured the unique personalities,
the animated debates, and some surprising events. The following letter
from Wilson to his "Dear Cousin M——," an anonymous relative,
was the second in a five-part series on the 1855 Philadelphia convention. Wilson described the "magic" of Robert Purvis's voice and the polished debating skills of a young Isaiah C. Wears. He marveled at the
ability of Mary Ann Shadd Cary, the only female delegate, to captivate
the entire assembly with the force of her appeal for black settlement in
Canada West. And he depicted Frederick Douglass's imposing presence
at the podium, noting that even an unexpected visitor—Robert Tyler,
the son of former president John Tyler—left the session deeply moved
by Douglass's remarks. Wilson's correspondence offers a rare, personal
glimpse of the conduct of antebellum black conventions. *FDP*, 22 July,
5, 19, 26 August 1853, 26 October, 9, 23 November, 7 December 1855
[8:0371–72, 0391, 0418, 0423, 9:0908, 0922–23, 0954–55, 0974–75].

MY DEAR COUSIN M——:
    In my last I said that Quietude is one feature of Philadelphia. Cleanli-
ness is another. You might take your morning meal upon any stoop
almost in the town, without the slightest degree of qualmishness. But
what was a greater marvel to me, and would, I know, much amuse you,
were these same little, low, white, unrailed stoops, placed two and two
together, square after square, as far as the eye could reach; and when the
stoops recede from view, rows of plain, white window-shutters, and
semi-circular topped doors obtrude themselves upon the eye as it glances
upwards to the eaves. The red fronts, too, made of genuine Philadelphia
brick, present plainness itself; for, let me tell you, Philadelphia brick in

Philadelphia is not Philadelphia brick in New York, or the trowel and the mason's hand do not make such artistic use of them. Here and there you may find an innovation, in the shape of an Upper-Tendom[1] New York house, forming a small gorgeous picture, set in plain frame, composed of Philadelphia houses. Occasionally, a square, nearly, of these innovations, *larger pictures* present themselves to the eye; and, though refreshing to the stranger, they seem as it were to receive the rebukes and frowns of their plainer, white-stooped, white-windowed neighbors.

Then, again, there is such an evenness of sidewalk. I searched an hour, one morning, in vain for a hillock or valley, to give relief to the weariness of the eye. A level brick floor, at every stride, was my only compensation. Philadelphia, upon the whole, presents to the eye of the stranger a kind of holidayish or Sunday appearance. Or, better, it resembles a clean, neat, white-cravated, straight-coated, broad-brimmed, double-chinned, portly, sturdy old *Quaker*, attired in his Sunday best and meeting-going. There is no bustle, no confusion, no clatter, no jostling down to *Change*, no rolling aristocratically up from thence with folded arms and princely air, in splendid *turnouts* after three o'clock. All is, comparatively, as quiet as the bosom of Nature. Notwithstanding, Philadelphia has features of admiration. One morning, long before Veritas and a Rev. friend[2] (who lodged in the same chambers with me) had made their *toilet*, I strolled into one of these parks. Nothing could be more delightful to my feelings than to see the little squirrels, black, white and gray, skipping from branch to branch, and playfully bounding amid the green and golden leaves of the majestic trees, and chattering to each other, and coming down to the greener turf, and paying their respects to the little children, and kind dames, and venerable sires, and receiving their morning repasts from their hands. But, my dear M———, I am wandering from my way.

"We are ready," said Veritas, as he buttoned up closely his coat, pulled on his gloves, and at the same time pulled our Rev. friend by the buttonhole. So, taking the hint, I straightened up my own shirt collar, drew on my gloves—yes, my dear M———, drew on my gloves, and with them repaired to Franklin Hall.[3] We entered; but the promptness of the Rochester assembly[4] was not apparent here. So far from hastily grouping in, and to business, as did the memorable gathering of '53, the members came straggling in, one by one, and listlessly took their seats. For the purpose of whiling away the morning hour, rather than anything else, permission was granted to an old gentleman from Norristown, Pa., whom I soon learned was the Rev. Mr. Hunt, to make a speech.[5] Whatever the few members who heard it, thought of it, one thing is certain—it deserved better of the Convention than the early morning delivery it received. He called on the Convention to recommend practical measures—to recommend to the people to obtain lands, and engage, as do white men, in Agriculture, and be no longer consumers, merely, but producers as well. There was, he said, sufficient material among the people to do anything for their highest good, if properly directed. Thus, for more than a half an hour, did a speech, replete with sound, practical advice, fall like dead weight from the lips of the venerable speaker, while here and there a pert dandy might be seen fidgeting in his seat like a puny worm.

Anon, the delegates were assembled, and quiet was restored. The men of mark, though seemingly eyeing each other like so many chess players, indulged each in his favorite amusement. E. V. Clark, who had considerably wrecked his brain in the production of a voluminous, but capital, Report,[6] looked charmingly grave. Remond[7] chatted gallantly with the *ladies*; Purvis[8] talked polishedly. Douglass[9] discoursed earnestly and seriously amid a circle of a few friends in one corner of the Hall. Nell[10] looked quietly on, while the tall and angular form of Dr. Rock,[11] like the Irishman's flea, was seen in different parts of the Hall, almost at the same time—putting your finger on him there, and he was not there. Bell[12] looked pensive—while Stephen Smith[13] looked earnest. Whipper[14] moved about thoughtfully and quietly. Topp[15] wore rather an air of dissatisfaction—while young Downing[16] looked for once pale and disconsolate. Wears[17] fidgeted nervously—while the Rev. Messrs. Grimes and Beman,[18] the elder, smiled benignly upon all around. It was a space of beautiful, and I may say profitable suspense; and it may be that the President, Rev. A. G. Beman, of Conn., than whom a more urbane and dignified gentleman could not have been selected—I say, it may be that he arranged this suspension the better to sharpen the delegates for what was in store for them—for, after rubbing his hands, and, as I thought, with some zest, he called the Convention to order. Some unimportant business was disposed of—after which, Prof. Reason,[19] Chairman of the Business Committee, rose and announced that he had several important documents to present, one of which he read. Here a dozen young members sprang to their feet at once, though they scarcely knew what for. The truth was, I suspect, they had prepared, before leaving home, elaborate speeches, but had hitherto been so obscured by the greater lights, that they had not, as yet, shone out. Rap! rap! went the President's gavel. Mr. President! Mr. President! was the loud acclaim. Rap! rap! goes the hammer again. Order is at length restored. "I move that the document be adopted," says one. "Second the motion," says another. Here at least twenty jumped up, each shouting Mr. President! Mr. President! while the old and tried members gave each other looks, mingled with vexation, sorrow and laughter. One white man came to me, and angered me somewhat by saying, and ashamed I am to repeat it, "Why don't your folks learn to behave themselves, as other people, and before you meet in Convention, learn how to do business?" The President assigned, this time, the floor to Captain J. J. Simons,[20] remarking, at the same time, that he had been two days in earnest endeavor to obtain it. No one seemed more disappointed than the Captain; for, after he obtained the floor, it seemed to me, he knew neither what to do with it or say on it; and after a few flourishing remarks, and a few flourishes with a huge roll of paper which he held in his hand, he quietly sank down in his seat. I suspect the Captain was taken unawares.

Prof. Reason now presented another billet. It was quickly disposed of, and yet another and another. At last he rather quietly announced that he had a communication from a Mr. Handy, of Baltimore, on the subject of African Colonization.[21] My dear cousin M———, you are, I know, accustomed to the torrent, the tornado, and the storm, as they sweep through your native forests; but the storm raised by this announcement, and the presence of this document in the house, you can form no conception of. The members took fire in every direction, and the whole house was in a blaze. No bombshell, thrown at the seige of Sebastopol,[22] ever created a greater sensation. The Rev. Mr. Adams,[23] of Philadelphia, fairly flashed lightning from out his cloud of eloquent warmth—while Dr. Gray,[24] of New Haven, thundered and lightninged both. His was a noble burst. Could you have heard it! Dr. Gray had no sooner ceased, than nearly one-half of the Convention sprang to their feet at once. Here was a scene that Hogarth[25] might have envied, but never could have painted. All the detestation of the system of African Colonization—all the contempt for its aid[er]s and abettors—all the horror—all the holy hatred for anything that ever looked like the damnable system—and all the conception of fixed determination to plant our own trees on American soil, and repose beneath the shade thereof, were visible in every face. There were those, however, who were for treating the document with, at least, some respect—some by reading it—and others by returning it to the *author* with a flea in his ear. The President gave the floor to P. A. Bell, of New York, who seems to have been among the latter number. Someone moved that the document be kicked under the table. Bell, with great vehemence, and in Shakespearian style exclaimed, "Oh consistency thou art a jewel"; and then drew from his breeches' pocket a little pamphlet some twenty odd years old, and read therefrom a speech of his own making in the same TOWN in opposition to Colonization;[26] notwithstanding, he was for respectful treatment of the document. This roused to the utmost tension Remond. Fiercer than any lion from his den, and greedy for his prey, he came forth. Small in stature and almost feminine in organization, it was scarcely possible to believe that the thoughts, the voice, and the utterer, held communion together. Downing now got the floor, and moved that the document be not returned to the correspondent, as no delegate, he hoped, would pay the three cents postage, but that it be *burned*. This was potent; and for a moment feeling and excitement reigned supreme. Rev. J. M. Williams,[27] of Brooklyn, called for the matches; someone else—"Veritas," I think—ran after tinder. The point was pressed; the deed accomplished! Dr. Smith,[28] out of respect, attempted to stay it; Purvis stirred the flame, and Douglass looked grave. Bell tried to snatch the burning fragments from the pile in vain, while Downing, Watkins,[29] and others, rubbed their hands joyfully over the black and smouldering embers. Poor Mr. Coates,[30] a white man—a merchant, a man of wealth, and a Colonizationist looked like a dying man, the very object of pity and misdirection. Could the ceiling have opened, as did the earth, to swallow Dathan of the *Israelitish* camp,[31] he (Coates) would gladly have skulked therein to return no more. Thus fared African Colonization in the Philadelphia Convention in 1855.

> Ye little thought, ye firey folks,
> The cheil was 'mong you taken notes.

More anon. Yours truly,

ETHIOP

Frederick Douglass' Paper (Rochester, N.Y.), 9 November 1855.

1. "Upper tendom" refers to the world of the upper ten thousand—the highest social class. The term had recently been popularized in *New York: Its Upper Ten and Lower Million* (1854) by celebrated American novelist George Lippard. Mitford M. Mathews, *Dictionary of Americanisms on Historical Principles* (Chicago, Ill., 1951), 1802–3.

2. The identity of "Veritas"—a black Brooklyn resident and popular correspondent of *Frederick Douglass' Paper* and the *Aliened American*—cannot be determined. Wilson's "Rev. friend" was probably Brooklyn clergyman George W. Levere. *FDP*, 5 May, 6, 28 July, 22 September 1854 [8:0773, 0909, 0943, 9:0100].

3. The 1855 black national convention assembled in Franklin Hall, a large meetinghouse near the intersection of Sixth and Arch streets in Philadelphia. *Colored National Convention . . . in Philadelphia* (1855), 3.

4. Wilson refers to the 1853 black national convention, which met in Rochester, New York.

5. Thomas P. Hunt (1795–?), a black Presbyterian clergyman, addressed the 1855 black national convention on "the advantages of Agricultural pursuits." A Virginia native, he pastored the African Presbyterian Church in Newark, New Jersey, during the late 1830s but left this position in 1840 to do missionary work among recent black American settlers in Trinidad. The widespread poverty and disease he encountered on the island convinced him that emigration was a failure. After the death of his wife, he returned to the United States along with thirty-eight other discouraged and destitute black emigrants. Hunt worked as a subscription agent for the *Mirror of Liberty*, then served Presbyterian congregations in Reading and Norristown, Pennsylvania, during the 1850s. Despite his misfortunes in the Caribbean, he retained an interest in black agrarianism. Hunt

operated his own farm and backed a proposal for an organized black settlement in upstate New York known as the Florence Farming and Lumber Association. Writing to the *Impartial Citizen*, he urged blacks to seek their future on farms in the American West. U.S. Census, 1850; *Colored National Convention . . . in Philadelphia* (1855), 7, 27 [9:0881, 0891]; *Newark City Directory*, 1835–39; *CA*, 30 September 1837, 18 April, 19 September 1840, 2 January, 20 May 1841 [2:0207, 3:0389, 0620, 0810, 0868]; *IC*, 28 March 1849, 20 February 1850 [5:1013, 6:0404]; *NASS*, 6 February 1841 [4:0022].

6. Edward V. Clark (1813–?), a prominent black businessman in antebellum New York City, presented the delegates with a detailed statistical report on black involvement in the trades and professions. Clark, a jeweler and watchmaker, had provided civic leadership to the New York black community for over two decades. An officer of the Philomathean Society and the African Society for Mutual Relief, he served on the publication committee of the *Colored American* and supported other black newspapers with his business advertisements. A devoted advocate of black voting rights, he campaigned for suffrage expansion through the New York Political Association in the 1830s and continued the struggle as a member of the New York City and State League Association in the 1850s. Clark tempered his politics with a businessman's pragmatism. He counseled discretion and restraint during the intense protests against the Fugitive Slave Law of 1850. A delegate to the 1853 black national convention, he later joined Frederick Douglass, James McCune Smith, and others in organizing the National Council of the Colored People. Clark developed a particular interest in black economic issues, which he pursued as a member of the executive committee of the American League of Colored Laborers and a participant in the convention movement. U.S. Census, 1850; Delany, *Condition of the Colored People*, 106–7; *Colored National Convention . . . in Philadelphia* (1855), 6, 14–24; *CA*, 22 February, 29 April, 19 August 1837, 13 January, 15 December 1838 [1:0952, 2:0038, 0354, 0679]; *FDP*, 16 December 1853, 20 January, 3 February 1854 [8:0607, 0641]; *PFW*, 26 May 1855 [9:0673]; *ASB*, 27 July 1856 [10:0258]; *WAA*, 17 March 1860, 16 March 1861; *NASS*, 10 October 1850 [6:0609]; *Colored National Convention . . . in Rochester* (1853), 5 [8:0328].

7. Charles L. Remond.

8. Robert Purvis.

9. Frederick Douglass.

10. William C. Nell.

11. John S. Rock was a black lawyer, physician, and abolitionist from Boston.

12. Philip A. Bell (1808–1889), one of the foremost black journalists of the nineteenth century, was born in New York City and educated at the African Free School. Bell's public career as an abolitionist and a community leader began in the early 1830s. Over the next two decades, his activities touched virtually every facet of black life in New York City. He was an early member of the American Anti-Slavery Society, served as the city's first *Liberator* agent, and promoted moral reform as chairman of the Philomathean Society and a director of the Phoenix Society. Bell attended three black national conventions during the 1830s. He later represented New York City blacks on the National Council of the Colored People. From his early opposition to colonization to his criticism of

black emigration proposals shortly before the Civil War, Bell urged black Americans to remain in the United States and demand their full rights as American citizens. His efforts to assist and protect fugitive slaves early in his career anticipated the work of the New York Committee of Vigilance. In the 1850s, as a member of the Committee of Thirteen, he and other prominent local blacks coordinated protests against the Fugitive Slave Law, colonization, and racial discrimination. Bell furthered the voting rights movement as a leader of the New York Political Association during the 1830s. He toured the state, urging blacks to organize petition and lobbying campaigns to expand black suffrage. Two decades later, he fought for the equal franchise through black state conventions and the New York State Suffrage Association.

Bell began his career in journalism in January 1837 as proprietor of the *Weekly Advocate*, which soon became the *Colored American*, one of the most important black newspapers of the antebellum period. He remained integrally involved with both the business and editorial aspects of the publication until 1840. Together with Samuel E. Cornish, he shaped the *Colored American*'s aggressive advocacy of black initiative and political action. After the paper's demise, Bell operated an "intelligence office"—a private employment service for black workers. He corresponded regularly with the *Liberator*, *Frederick Douglass' Paper*, and other antislavery journals, often using the pseudonym "Cosmopolite." After moving to San Francisco, California, in 1857, he resumed his work as a journalist, editing the *Pacific Appeal* with Peter Anderson in 1862, then founding his own newspaper, the *Elevator*, three years later. Bell's papers functioned as a voice for blacks in the West, but they also offered a valuable source of black history because of the editor's frequent recollections of the antislavery struggle. Bell participated in Republican party politics during Reconstruction, working to keep "the colored voters in unbroken harmony in state, municipal, and national elections." The Republican party rewarded his efforts in 1880 by appointing him assistant sergeant-at-arms of the California senate. Throughout a distinguished journalistic career that spanned five decades, financial security eluded Bell; he lived his last years completely destitute. *DANB*, 38–39; *SFMC*, 27 April 1889; *Lib*, 4 March 1831, 16 February 1853 [1:0243]; *CA*, 19 August, 4 November 1837, 2 June 1838, 5 October 1839 [2:0258, 3:0217]; *FDP*, 7 April 1854 [8:0723]; *PA*, 21 June 1862; Daniels, *Pioneer Urbanites*, 114–15.

13. Stephen Smith (ca. 1797–1873), a Philadelphia businessman, philanthropist, and clergyman, was born in Dauphin County, Pennsylvania, the son of a slave woman. At the age of five, he became the indentured servant of Thomas Boude and eventually managed Boude's business concerns in Columbia, Pennsylvania. Smith purchased his freedom in 1816 and established a lumber business in Columbia. In the 1830s, he formed a partnership with William Whipper and expanded his business. By the late 1840s, Smith had amassed a fortune of several hundred thousand dollars in coal and lumber reserves, Philadelphia real estate, railroad cars, and stock investments.

Smith's leadership of Columbia's black community was based on his abolitionism as well as his wealth. He acted as a subscription agent for *Freedom's Journal* and the *Rights of All* and organized local protests against colonization. Together with Whipper, he operated the local station of the underground railroad—an important link in the escape route for slaves coming from Maryland. His lumberyard provided a haven and temporary employment for fugitives on their way north. Smith's antislavery activities and economic standing in Columbia made his business the target of antiblack violence during the 1830s. His multifaceted career also included work as a pastor in the African Methodist Episcopal church. Ordained in 1831, he preached at several black churches in Columbia and Philadelphia. Like Whipper, he demonstrated a strong commitment to temperance and moral reform.

Smith's activism reached beyond the local community. He represented Columbia at the 1834 and 1835 black national conventions, helped his business partner organize the American Moral Reform Society, joined the nascent Pennsylvania Anti-Slavery Society in 1837, promoted black voting rights as a delegate to the 1841 and 1848 black state conventions, and served on the National Council of the Colored People. In 1843 he moved to Philadelphia and purchased Robert Purvis's house, which functioned as a gathering place for black and white reformers, including the historic 15 March 1858 meeting at which John Brown informed four key black abolitionists of his plan to instigate a slave insurrection in the South.

During the Civil War, Smith encouraged black enlistment in the Union army and raised funds to aid the freedmen at Port Royal, South Carolina. He continued to work for black voting rights after the war as president of the Pennsylvania Equal Rights Association. Throughout his life, Smith used his substantial wealth to support AME congregations and other local black institutions, including the Institute for Colored Youth, Olive Cemetery, and the Home for Aged and Infirm Colored Persons. Martin R. Delany described Smith as "decidedly the most wealthy colored man in the United States," and Smith's name was frequently invoked by abolitionists to highlight free black achievements. *DANB*, 566; Delany, *Condition of the Colored People*, 95–96; Garrison, *Thoughts on African Colonization*, part 2, 31–33; Payne, *African Methodist Episcopal Church*, 103–4; *FDP*, 22 July 1853 [8:0373]; *PF*, 8 December 1853 [8:0509]; *Colored National Convention . . . in Rochester* (1853), 6–7 [8:0329]; *Colored National Convention . . . in Philadelphia* (1855), 3–8 [9:0877–79]; *CR*, 5 April 1862, 20 April 1865 [14:0212, 15:0901]; *PA*, 16 May 1863 [14:0863].

14. William Whipper.

15. William H. Topp.

16. George Thomas Downing (1819–1903)—one of the wealthiest black businessmen and most persistent defenders of black rights during the Civil War era—was born in New York City and attended Hamilton College in upstate New York. In 1841 his marriage to Serena De Grasse united two of the city's leading black families. With his father, abolitionist Thomas Downing, he operated an oyster house and catering service that became a city landmark. By 1854 he had additional businesses in Providence and Newport, Rhode Island, including a hotel valued at $40,000. From the late 1830s, father and son worked together in black antislavery, educational, and political organizations in New York City.

The younger Downing waged a prolonged war against the American Colonization Society and black emigrationist schemes. In 1852 Downing and a delegation of black leaders met with Governor Washington Hunt and convinced him to abandon plans to appropriate state funds for the colonization movement. Downing denounced colonization as a threat to black liberty and safety, charging that it was designed "to oppress, to harass, and to dampen the aspirations of free coloured men." He discredited any black organization that cooperated with the ACS but reserved his greatest animosity for Henry Highland Garnet and the African Civilization Society. To Downing, Garnet's emigration movement was "kin to the old colonization scheme," a charge he repeated to white antislavery leaders such as Gerrit Smith and William Lloyd Garrison. Downing also organized New York City blacks against the AfCS, arguing that it was indistinguishable from the old ACS. The conflict between Downing and Garnet grew so intense that even after Garnet redirected his energies into freedmen's education during the 1860s, Downing remained distrustful.

From 1857 to 1866, Downing led a campaign against segregated schools in Rhode Island. Maintaining that racism sustained both slavery and racially separate education, he financed the movement, organized meetings, published pamphlets, and petitioned the state legislature to outlaw the practice. Downing moved to Boston in 1860 but continued his efforts in Rhode Island, finally achieving victory over segregationists after the Civil War. Later in Washington, D.C., he and Frederick Douglass led a delegation of black spokesmen who personally urged President Andrew Johnson to adopt a more vigorous Reconstruction policy. Downing advised prominent Republican politicians, including his friend Charles Sumner, and used his position as restaurateur for the House of Representatives to lobby for civil rights, abolition of Jim Crow railroad cars, opening the Senate gallery to blacks, and adoption of the District of Columbia's 1873 public accommodations law. He broke with the Republicans in 1883 to support the northern wing of the Democratic party. *DANB*, 187–88; *NASS*, 22 January 1852 [7:0363–64]; *WAA*, 24 September 1859 [12:0062]; George T. Downing to William H. Seward, 9 February 1857, Seward Papers, NRU [10:0539]; Freeman, "Free Negro in New York City," 49n, 54–56, 131–32, 176, 236–37, 325–28n, 352–53, 369, 430–32; Walker, "Afro-American in New York City," 26, 37–38, 50, 53, 166–67, 178, 221–25, 234; Irving Bartlett, *From Slave to Citizen: The Story of the Negro in Rhode Island* (Providence, R.I., 1954), 53, 55; Lawrence Grossman, "George T. Downing and Desegregation of Rhode Island Public Schools, 1855–1866," *RIH* 26:98–105 (November 1977); Cheek and Cheek, *John Mercer Langston*, 427–34; Schor, *Henry Highland Garnet*, 157–58, 167, 186, 202–4; James H. Whyte, *The Uncivil War: Washington during the Reconstruction, 1865–1879* (New York, N.Y., 1958), 251–52, 257–58; Douglass, *Life and Times*, 382, 387.

17. Isaiah C. Wears (1822–1900), a Philadelphia barber and Republican politician, was born to free black parents in Baltimore. A few years later, the family moved to Philadelphia. Wears continued the abolitionist work of his father, Josiah C. Wears, who had provided leadership for the city's first vigilance committee during the 1830s. The younger Wears opposed black disfranchisement and colonization in the mid-1840s, helped organize the General Vigilance Committee, and participated in several black state and national conventions, where he gained recognition as a skilled speaker and debater. He criticized black emigration proposals, including those of the African Civilization Society. Initially hesitant to endorse black participation in the Civil War—he referred to the conflict as "the great slaughter house of government"—by the fall of 1862, Wears was

encouraging Pennsylvania blacks to go to Rhode Island or Kansas, states that accepted black enlistment.

Wears's stature in the Philadelphia black community increased during the Reconstruction years. He served as president of the Pennsylvania Social, Civil, and Statistical Association; worked through the Pennsylvania Equal Rights League to challenge racial discrimination on city streetcars; and in 1869 addressed the Judiciary Committee of the U.S. Senate on the black enfranchisement issue. Wears had openly endorsed the Republican party by 1859; after the war, his reputation as a party stalwart and his ability to mobilize black voters for the party made him an important political figure. His "tonsorial saloon" at the corner of Randolph and Poplar streets provided a political forum for Philadelphia blacks. Following the assassination of Octavius V. Catto in 1871, Wears became the city's leading black Republican politician. Yet for all his achievements, he never received a nomination from his party for political office. Late in the century, Wears served with distinction on several influential civic committees. Silcox, "Black 'Better Class' Dilemma," 45–66; *NSt*, 15, 22 June 1849 [6:0014, 0017]; *PF*, 9 December 1852 [7:0851]; *PFW*, 28 March 1857 [10:0596]; *WAA*, 7 October, 5, 26 November, 24 December 1859, 2 November 1861 [12:0015, 0197, 0240, 0319, 13:0867]; *PA*, 27 September 1862 [14:0516]; Roger Lane, *Roots of Violence in Black Philadelphia, 1860–1900* (Cambridge, Mass., 1986), 55, 58, 61, 68, 148–49.

18. Wilson refers to Leonard A. Grimes and Jehiel C. Beman.

19. Charles L. Reason.

20. J. J. Simons, who resided in New York City in the 1850s, was often called "Captain" because of his involvement in local black militia units. Active in the movement to expand black voting rights, he attended state suffrage conventions at Troy in 1855 and 1858 and sat on the executive committee of the New York State Suffrage Association. Simons vigorously opposed colonization and emigration. At one state convention, he proposed outfitting two ships to bring back black settlers dissatisfied with life in Liberia. He later joined other New York City blacks in condemning the African Civilization Society. Simons, who was known as one of "John Brown's lieutenants," apparently jeopardized the secrecy of the planned Harpers Ferry raid in 1859 with indiscreet public statements about a project to invade the South and free the slaves; while addressing a newly organized black militia in Philadelphia, Simons said northern blacks would march through the region with "a bible in one hand and a gun in the other." *FDP*, 14 September 1855 [9:0826]; Foner and Walker, *Proceedings of the Black State Conventions*, 1:88, 90, 99; *WAA*, 27 August 1859, 31 March, 21 April, 19 May 1860 [11:0975, 12:0600, 0646, 0710]; *Autobiography of Dr. William Henry Johnson* (1900; reprint New York, N.Y., 1970), 194–96.

21. James Anderson Handy (1826–1911), a colonization advocate, was a leader of the Baltimore black community during the nineteenth century. The son of working-class free blacks Ishmael and Nancy Handy, he obtained a limited education, then spent three decades working in the Baltimore shipyards. An eloquent orator and a tireless organizer, he became a spokesman for local free blacks. He founded several beneficial societies, including the Good Samaritans and the Nazarites, which rapidly expanded throughout the Chesapeake region. A

leading black voice of the colonization movement, he chaired the 1852 Maryland black state convention, which endorsed Liberian settlement. Seven years later, Handy formed the Emigrant Association to help blacks flee worsening race relations in the city for Africa, the Caribbean, Canada, or the North. After the Civil War, he urged local blacks to settle in the West and endorsed the 1879 Exoduster movement to Kansas. Handy enthusiastically joined the Republicans during Reconstruction, and in 1871 he campaigned as the party's candidate for the state legislature.

Handy played a leading role in the African Methodist Episcopal denomination during and after the war. He joined Bethel AME Church in Baltimore in 1853 and was soon recognized as one of the congregation's "most talented sons." Licensed to preach in 1860, he served congregations in Washington, D.C., and Portsmouth, Virginia, then supervised AME mission work in the Carolinas during the early years of Reconstruction. He returned to Baltimore in 1871 but continued to be active in denominational affairs as an officer of the Missionary Society and a member of the commission that reunited the AME and British Methodist Episcopal churches (1880). He was rewarded for this work in 1892 by being named bishop of an AME district consisting of Maryland, the District of Columbia, Virginia, North Carolina, Haiti, and San Domingo. Handy authored a popular volume entitled *Scraps of African Methodist Episcopal History* (1902). He retired from the ministry in 1908 in "enfeebled condition." *Crisis*, November 1911; Graham, *Baltimore*, 156, 200, 229, 235, 238, 278–79, 289; *NYCJ*, September 1852 [7:0718–19]; *CR*, 18 October 1854, 22 April 1871 [9:0153]; Charles S. Smith, *A History of the African Methodist Episcopal Church* (Philadelphia, Pa., 1922; reprint, New York, N.Y., 1968), 3, 49, 55, 60, 79, 81, 88, 93, 133, 202, 259, 286.

22. The Anglo-French siege of Sebastopol (currently Sevastopol), a heavily fortified Russian port on the Black Sea, was one of the major military maneuvers of the Crimean War. Despite extensive artillery bombardment, Russian forces resisted the siege from October 1854 to September 1855 before they withdrew.

23. Ennals J. Adams, a Presbyterian clergyman, began his ministerial career in the African Methodist Episcopal church but left the denomination in 1853 to serve the Central Presbyterian Church in Philadelphia. He participated in a wide variety of community activities, from lecturing before the Banneker Institute to attending the 1855 black national convention in Philadelphia. Adams ministered to congregations in Hartford, Connecticut, and Buffalo, New York, before succeeding Elymus P. Rogers at the Plane Street Presbyterian Church in Newark, New Jersey, in September 1861. Turning his attention to African missions in the late 1850s, he lectured on Africa and African culture in New York City and served as an agent for the African Civilization Society. In 1862 he became involved with the American Missionary Association's Mendi Mission in West Africa. Adams worked for two years as a pastor and teacher at Good Hope Station on Sherbro Island, Sierra Leone.

In 1865 missionary work among the freedmen drew Adams back to the United States. He labored briefly for the AMA in Beaufort, South Carolina, then attempted to reestablish a black Congregational church in Charleston. Despite hostility between Adams and the local freedmen, he became a strident voice for black rights as an editor of the weekly *Charleston Journal* (1866) and a local

Republican leader. From 1875 to 1880 he supervised the Avery Institute, a black school. Adams later returned to Philadelphia and retired from the ministry. Payne, *African Methodist Episcopal Church*, 294; Richard P. McCormick, "William Whipper: Moral Reformer," *PH* 43:44–45n (January 1976); *Colored National Convention . . . in Philadelphia* (1855), 7, 13 [9:0881, 0884]; Miller, *Search for a Black Nationality*, 263; *CR*, 7 December 1861 [13:0956]; *WAA*, 14 September, 2 October 1861 [13:0795]; *AM*, July, November 1864, January, August 1865; *FJB*, December 1866; Thomas Holt, *Black over White: Negro Political Leadership in South Carolina during Reconstruction* (Urbana, Ill., 1977), 89.

24. Samuel T. Gray (?–1864), an African Methodist Episcopal Zion clergyman and physician, began his ministry in the Pittsburgh area and then served an AMEZ congregation in New Haven, Connecticut, in the 1840s and early 1850s. In 1847 Gray purchased 150 acres of land from Gerrit Smith in upstate New York, but he apparently never settled there. Two years later, he attended the Connecticut black state convention and coauthored its appeal for black voting rights. Gray also represented New Haven at the 1853 and 1855 black national conventions. He achieved notoriety among black clerics for his unsuccessful attempt to reunify the African Methodist Episcopal and AMEZ denominations in 1856. Later in the decade, he took charge of the Zion African Methodist Church in New York City, where he continued his work for black suffrage. Gray completed his ministry at the Wesley Zion Church in Washington, D.C. Although he apparently lacked a medical degree, he was highly regarded for his therapeutic practices and knowledge of herbal medicine. *CA*, 29 June 1839 [3:0129]; *WAA*, 5 May 1860, 2 July 1864; David H. Bradley, *A History of the AMEZ Church*, 2 vols. (Nashville, Tenn., 1970), 1:11–12, 150; Foner and Walker, *Proceedings of the Black State Conventions*, 2:20–33; *New Haven City Directory*, 1853.

25. William Hogarth (1697–1764), an English painter and engraver, was famous for his graphic and often amusing depictions of British society. *DNB*, 9:977–91.

26. Bell probably read from *An Address to the Citizens of New-York* (1831), which he had coauthored. The anticolonization pamphlet had emerged from a 25 January 1831 meeting held by New York City blacks to register their protest against the activities of the New York State Colonization Society. Garrison, *Thoughts on African Colonization*, part 2, 13–17.

27. James Morris Williams (1823–1880), an African Methodist Episcopal clergyman, was born in Westchester, New York. Ordained an elder by the AME's New York Conference in 1851, he served congregations in New Brunswick, (N.J.), Albany, Philadelphia, Brooklyn, and Newark (N.J.) during his ministerial career. Because of his extensive organizational and administrative work, he was regarded within the denomination as the "father of the New Jersey Conference." Williams participated in the movement to expand black voting rights in New York state. He represented Albany blacks at the 1851 black state convention and later attended the 1855 black national convention at Philadelphia. *CR*, 15 July 1880; Wayman, *Cyclopaedia of African Methodism*, 183; Payne, *African Methodist Episcopal Church*, 255; *Brooklyn City Directory*, 1855–56; *Colored National Convention . . . in Philadelphia* (1855), 6 [9:0881].

28. James McCune Smith.

29. William J. Watkins.

30. Benjamin Coates (1806–1887), a Philadelphia wool merchant, was a prominent member of the American Colonization Society. He wrote *Cotton Cultivation in Africa* (1858) to generate interest in black agricultural settlement in West Africa and endorsed both Martin R. Delany's Niger Valley Exploring Party and Henry Highland Garnet's African Civilization Society. Despite his colonizationist views, Coates attempted to remain active in the antislavery movement. Merrill and Ruchames, *Letters of William Lloyd Garrison*, 4:598n; *FDP*, 17 September 1858; *FI*, 7 May 1887.

31. Wilson refers to the biblical account in Numbers 26:9–11 of Dathan, a dissident who challenged Moses and Aaron for leadership of the Israelites. As divine punishment, he and his followers were destroyed in an earthquake.

64.
Uriah Boston to Frederick Douglass
[December 1855]

Antislavery advocates competed with proslavery theorists to shape northern public opinion. Defenders of slavery constructed an elaborate mythology to make their case—slaves were racially inferior, lived comfortably under benevolent white ownership, and preferred bondage to freedom. Boston clergyman Nehemiah Adams, in *A South-Side View of Slavery* (1854), sought to contest abolitionist arguments and soften slavery's image by asserting that southern legal codes did not accurately reflect slave life; among several examples, Adams noted that even though slaves could not legally own property, some did. Black abolitionists, many of them former slaves, personally refuted such fables. In a December 1855 letter to Frederick Douglass, Uriah Boston contested the proslavery claim that slaves lived better than free blacks. He outlined six advantages held by northern free blacks: they could own property, acquire an education, legally marry, work for themselves, testify in court, and travel freely. Boston repudiated the anecdotal style of proslavery thinkers such as Adams by informing his readers that the South not only denied slaves the right to own property but made them property. Nehemiah Adams, *South-Side View of Slavery; or, Three Months at the South, in 1854* (Boston, Mass., 1854), 20–40, 50–52.

DEAR SIR:

We often hear it said that the slaves are better off than the free colored people in the free States. No one who is acquainted with the facts in the case can believe this. It can do no harm to lay a few of these facts before the people, which I now propose to do, and which I will do with your permission, believing that no one who reads these facts will retain any such belief a moment thereafter. Here are the facts:

1. The laws of the slave States do not only deny the right of the slaves to hold property, but make them property; while the free colored people are free to acquire property of every sort, and to any extent with all others.[1]

2. The slaves are prohibited by law to educate themselves; while the free colored people in the free States are not only allowed education, but encouraged to embrace the opportunity of getting a good education free of charge.

3. The slaves have no legal right to wife or children; while the free colored people have not only the legal right to both these, but are protected in all the rights pertaining thereto.[2]

4. The slaves labor for others life long; the free colored people in the

free States labor for themselves, with the legal right to collect the just reward of their labor.

5. In the free States, the colored man's oath is good legal testimony in all cases whatever against or in favor of anybody, rich and poor;[3] while in the slave States, the meanest and most worthless white man can kick, abuse, and even kill any colored man or woman, and nothing can be done about it, unless some white person will swear to the fact. I have seen things of this sort with my own eyes.

6. In the free States, colored people may travel where and how they please, without molestation; while in the South, even in Maryland and the District of Columbia, they cannot travel a mile anywhere without "a pass" or in the care of some white man.[4] I had a friend of the first character and standing visit me not long since, and my heart sank within me when this friend told me, with apparent composure, that he was "passed" from office to office, and from man to man, until finally he was handed over and into the hands of an old Irishman, who, instead of signing his name to the "pass," had to make his —| |—, and who took charge of him to see that he went out of the city and State in the "Jim Crow" car. And yet the Southerners ask the Northerners why they don't treat the free colored people better? But I ask again, which of the two classes are the best off, the colored people in the free States, or the colored people in the slave States? Who will dare say the latter? Much more I want to say on this subject, and may say hereafter; but for the present I must close, with the hearty belief that the above facts encourage us to labor on in our progress with hearty good cheer.

U. B.

Frederick Douglass' Paper (Rochester, N.Y.), 14 December 1855.

1. Slaves had no legal right to own property, but local custom and compliant masters often permitted them to keep private gardens or domesticated animals to supplement their diets and to make and sell handcrafted items. Despite various exclusionary statutes, free blacks were allowed to hold property virtually everywhere except the Oregon Territory, which forbade them to own real estate. Genovese, *Roll, Jordan, Roll*, 30–31; Litwack, *North of Slavery*, 93.

2. Southern state laws defined slaves as the property of their masters and permitted slaveowners a virtually unrestricted right to dispose of their chattels as they wished. Because slave marriages were not recognized by law, slave families were frequently separated by sale, forced migrations, estate settlements, and the giving of gifts. In some areas of the South, one in every six or seven slave marriages ended on the auction block. Herbert G. Gutman, *The Black Family in Slavery and Freedom, 1750–1925* (New York, N.Y., 1976), 128–33, 145–55, 285–90, 317–19, 354–59.

3. Boston was mistaken in his assertion that northern blacks could give legal testimony "in all cases." Several free states—Illinois, Indiana, Iowa, and Califor-

nia—prohibited free blacks from testifying in cases involving whites. The Ohio legislature had rescinded its ban on black testimony in 1849. Litwack, *North of Slavery*, 93–94.

4. Although free black travel was unregulated in the North, southern states restricted the movement of both slaves and free blacks within their borders. Slave travel was carefully monitored through a written pass system, in which masters usually indicated the slaves' destination, time of return, and permission to travel without supervision. Slaves were required to present their passes to any white person on demand. Free blacks were compelled to carry papers verifying their status or risk arrest and enslavement. Slave passes and free papers were frequently forged, despite statutes outlawing the practice. Stampp, *Peculiar Institution*, 149, 208; Ira Berlin, *Slaves without Masters: The Free Negro in the Antebellum South* (New York, N.Y., 1974), 93–94.

65.
Stephen A. Myers to Gerrit Smith
22 March 1856

For black abolitionists, independence meant new strategies, new tactics, and new initiatives. Some struggled to expand black rights by taking their case directly before state legislatures; they circulated petitions, corresponded with sympathetic politicians, and, when permitted, testified before various legislative bodies. John Mercer Langston and William Howard Day brought the demands of Ohio blacks to the attention of their legislators. Charles L. Remond, William J. Watkins, and Robert Morris testified against Jim Crow laws before committees of the Massachusetts legislature. Stephen A. Myers of Albany, New York, one of the most effective abolitionist lobbyists, became acquainted with prominent politicians through his work as a journalist, temperance advocate, and manager of local underground railroad activities. These personal contacts allowed him to influence the New York legislature on black concerns. In a 22 March 1856 letter to Gerrit Smith, Myers described his lobbying efforts on behalf of the New York State Suffrage Association to eliminate the $250 property qualification for black suffrage and his attempts to defeat a bill to appropriate state funds for the New York State Colonization Society. Cheek and Cheek, *John Mercer Langston,* 228–29; Quarles, *Black Abolitionists,* 175–76, 181, 230; *WAA,* 13 August 1859 [11:0928]; Field, *Politics of Race,* 94–100.

> AntiSlavery office
> 168 third street
> Albany, [New York]
> March 22, 1856

Sir:
    I have been striving hard this winter with the members of the Senate assembly and Legislator to recommend an amendment to the Constitution of this state so as to strik off the property qualifycation, and let us vote on the same footing of the white mail citizens. So as to hav it one more handed down to the people I hav got Senetor Cuyler some weeks a go to get up a resolution in the senat[1] wich is now under discusin and will com up again on monday or tuesday. I shall hav one up in the assembly in a few days. I hav recieved partitions from Colerd men from differant sections of the state wich I hav presented to Senate and assembly. I hav devided the partitions in the two houses. The partitions hav about 1600 names all together.[2] I hav also devoted my time to defeat the Collenization bill to appropriate five thousand dollars to the colenization Society.[3] I hav gotten about sixty members pledged to go against it

13. Stephen A. Myers
From I. Garland Penn, *The Afro-American Press and Its Editors*
(Springfield, Mass., 1891)
Reproduced with the cooperation of The Florida State University Libraries

on a final vote. It now under discussion. When it comes up again thy will iether vote it down or strike out the inacting clause wich will eventually kill the bill. Their is one thing that I am sorry to say: two thirds of my people want energy and more perseveranc. At the state convention of Colerd Citizens at troy[4] it fell to me to be as one of the agents of the Suffrage association[5] to attend the Capitol during the seting of the legislator. Thy were to furnish funds from the differant portions of the State to pay expenes during the winter. Thy hav not yet forwarded the first Cen Cent for that purpos. The only aid I hav received has been from Fredrick Douglas. My people want a great deal done but thy are not willing to make any sacrifices. Yor speech at the Capitol on the Canses Kanses question last thursday night a week has left a lasting impresion on the people. It has been all the talk sinc you Sir made that famous speech. Their has been over fifty members of the Senate and assembly spoken to of your speech and dozens of our citizens hav talked to me of your speech and say that it was one of the greaest speeches made by any in the Capitol. The people say that you compleetily anhialated Judge Northrap.[6] The Judge has spoken to me two or three time on that subject. The Judge says that he did not wish to speak but he was forced out unprepared. He said he thought that you was rather hard on him and is willing to admit that you are a sound and strong argurer. He said Mr Smith wanted to giv him a hard rap because he was a going to support Mr Filmore.[7] He said Mr Smith took that oppertunity to do it before a large audianc. He says never the less he likes Mr Smith. He says that you do not talk anything only what you practic and says that your check for three thousand dollars[8] is the impuls of your noble Heart. And he says that your life is crowned with hundreds of Charitable acts. The members of assembly plague the Judge because he could not answer you. I forwared you Sir one of the curculars that the Collenization agent is a curculating in the Senate and assembly. I hav had sinc Mr Smith was in our city [six] fugitives from Maryryland. They were more destitute of [c]lothing than any that hav reached here for many winters. The letter sir that you wrote to Topp and me[,] I hav never seen it. Topp and me differ a litle on the Garrison question. I am rather more favorable to Mr Douglass veiues and not to Mr Garrisons. Theirefore we differ.[9] I remain your Humble Servat,

Stephen Myers

Gerrit Smith Papers, George Arents Research Library, Syracuse University, Syracuse, New York. Published by permission.

1. Myers refers to Samuel Cuyler (1808–?), a Wayne County farmer and Republican who served in the New York state senate during the 1850s. Active in western New York antislavery circles as early as the 1840s, he advocated equal rights and black suffrage. At Myers's request, Cuyler introduced a measure in the

legislature to amend the state constitution by removing the property requirements that restricted black suffrage. The bill died, gaining only three other Republican votes. Cuyler reintroduced the measure one year later; although approved by the senate, it was defeated in the state assembly. U.S. Census, 1850;
PF, 9 January 1840; Field, *Politics of Race,* 94–95, 98–99, 103.

2. Acting as the agent of the New York State Suffrage Association, Myers
presented at least nineteen petitions bearing sixteen hundred names to the state
legislature in 1856. Field, *Politics of Race,* 94.

3. Myers refers to the New York State Colonization Society, an American
Colonization Society auxiliary founded in 1817. The society declined during the
early 1820s but revived in 1829 with the assistance of Gerrit Smith. Smith's
repudiation of colonization and the rise of immediate abolitionism during the
1830s disrupted the society. The NYSCS prospered once again under the direction of John B. Pinney, a Presbyterian clergyman, during the late 1840s, when it
published the *New York Colonization Journal* and purchased the families of
many freed slaves, provided they remove to Liberia.

Beginning in 1851, the NYSCS made several attempts to secure state funding
for African colonization. A coalition of New York City blacks and prominent
white abolitionists defeated the first attempts. The society renewed its efforts in
early 1856, petitioning the state legislature for $10,000. The measure passed the
assembly but died in the senate. A revised bill was quickly resubmitted with an
amendment calling for the incarceration of all blacks who refused to leave the
state within twelve months. The legislation met vigorous opposition in the assembly, where it was denounced as a proslavery measure. Later in the decade, the
NYSCS worked with the African Civilization Society and black emigrationists
such as Martin R. Delany. After the Civil War, it supported black college students
and promoted Liberian education, operating as a trust until 1964 when it turned
over its remaining resources to the Phelps-Stokes Fund. Eli Seifman, "A History
of the New York State Colonization Society" (Ph.D. diss., New York University,
1965); *NYCJ,* March–April 1856; Miller, *Search for a Black Nationality,* 184–
85, 197–99.

4. Myers refers to the 4 September 1855 black state convention at Troy, New
York. Black leaders called the meeting to launch a campaign against the state's
property requirements for black suffrage. The convention adopted resolutions
condemning the restrictions, founded the New York State Suffrage Association
to coordinate the campaign, appointed five agents to deliver suffrage lectures
throughout the state, and named two others to lobby the state legislature. Foner
and Walker, *Proceedings of the Black State Conventions,* 1:88–98.

5. The New York State Suffrage Association directed the statewide campaign
to expand black voting rights in the late 1850s. It sought to eliminate the property qualifications for black voters established by the 1821 state constitution.
New York's black leaders organized the NYSSA at the 1855 state convention at
Troy. Although the NYSSA held yearly meetings and established dozens of auxiliaries, interest in the organization waned by the end of the decade, only to be
reinvigorated by the 1859–60 campaign to secure a statewide referendum on the
question of equal suffrage. Through the lobbying efforts of Stephen A. Myers,
William J. Watkins, and James McCune Smith, the legislature put the question
before the voters in November 1860. Dozens of new suffrage clubs and NYSSA

auxiliaries were formed during the campaign—forty-eight in New York City and eighteen in Brooklyn alone. Watkins, Myers, Smith, Frederick Douglass, James N. Gloucester, and others conducted lecture tours, disseminated thousands of pamphlets, obtained funding from white philanthropists, and secured the cooperation of New England's black leaders in a vigorous campaign to sway the state's white electorate. The NYSSA staked its appeal upon the black role in securing national independence, free black social progress and educational efforts, and natural rights arguments. Defeated at the polls, the NYSSA abandoned its activities. Foner and Walker, *Proceedings of the Black State Conventions,* 1:88–98; Freeman, "Free Negro in New York City," 144–53; Walker, "Afro-American in New York City," 183–86; *DM*, October, November, December 1860 [12:1023]; *WAA*, 15 September 1859, 31 March, 28 April, 5, 19 May, 30 June 1860 [12:0600, 0604]; Nell, *Property Qualification or No Property Qualification* [12:0341–52]; James McCune Smith, "An Address of the New York City Suffrage Committee," 24 August 1860, Gerrit Smith Papers, NSyU [12:0967–70].

6. Gerrit Smith spoke to supporters of the Free Kansas movement on 13 March 1856 in the state assembly chamber at Albany, New York. He argued that the Kansas crisis offered an unprecedented opportunity to attack slavery. Richard H. Northrop, a local attorney, responded to Smith's speech. Although he claimed to oppose slavery and denounced the Fugitive Slave Law as "odious," he rejected Smith's call for the immediate end of slavery and advocated an apprenticeship program to prepare blacks for freedom. Smith defended immediatism as the only practical antislavery posture, maintaining that anything less than complete emancipation meant perpetual slavery. *Lib*, 28 March 1856; *Albany City Directory*, 1845–52.

7. In 1856 Millard Fillmore was the presidential candidate of the American party, more commonly known as the Know-Nothings.

8. Earlier in the month, Smith had donated $3,000 to the New York State Kansas Committee, one of many such bodies organized throughout the North to support antislavery forces in the Kansas Territory. Harlow, *Gerrit Smith*, 348, 350–62, 391.

9. Although both Myers and William H. Topp of Albany supported political abolitionism and cooperated in the campaign to expand the franchise in New York, they differed in their attitude toward William Lloyd Garrison and his views. Topp supported Garrison and the American Anti-Slavery Society. Myers rejected Garrisonianism, worked closely with opponents of Garrison such as Gerrit Smith and Frederick Douglass, and campaigned for Whig and Republican candidates. Ripley et al., *Black Abolitionist Papers*, 2:162–63n; *FDP*, 7 March 1856.

66.
William Still and the Underground Railroad

Joseph C. Bustill to William Still
24 March 1856

William Still to Elijah F. Pennypacker
2 November 1857

Black workers on the underground railroad faced dangerous and difficult circumstances. They struggled to balance the need for secrecy with demands for efficient operation. The Fugitive Slave Law enlarged the burden by greatly expanding the number of runaways seeking freedom and increasing the threat posed by slave catchers and federal authorities. Yet black activists managed to protect most fugitive slaves who came under their care. In southeastern Pennsylvania, blacks and white Quakers maintained one of the best-organized sections of the railroad. The following letters by Joseph C. Bustill and William Still shed light on typical operations during 1856–57. Bustill helped establish the Fugitive Aid Society (later renamed the Harrisburg Vigilance Committee) shortly after moving from Philadelphia to Harrisburg in 1856. He forwarded runaways along the Reading Railroad, which passed near the Phoenixville home of Quaker abolitionist Elijah F. Pennypacker, some twenty miles from Philadelphia. After sheltering the escaped slaves in his house, Pennypacker usually sent them on to Still, the agent of the General Vigilance Committee of Philadelphia. Five days after Still's 2 November 1857 letter, his Quaker friend advised him that forty-three fugitives had "passed through our hands" in the past two months. R. C. Smedley, *History of the Underground Railroad in Chester and the Neighboring Counties of Pennsylvania* (Lancaster, Pa., 1883), 206–15; Siebert, *Underground Railroad*, 79; Charles L. Blockson, ed., *The Underground Railroad* (New York, N.Y., 1987), 236–37; Still, *Underground Railroad*, 24–25, 220–22, 332–34.

HARRISBURG, [Pennsylvania]
March 24, [18]56

FRIEND STILL:

I suppose ere this you have seen those five large and three small packages I sent by way of Reading, consisting of three men and women and children. They arrived here this morning at 8½ o'clock and left twenty minutes past three. You will please send me any information likely to prove interesting in relation to them.

Lately we have formed a Society here, called the Fugitive Aid Society. This is our first case, and I hope it will prove entirely successful.

14. William Still
From William Still, *Underground Railroad* (Philadelphia, 1872)

When you write, please inform me what signs or symbols you make use of in your dispatches, and any other information in relation to operations of the Underground Rail Road.

Our reason for sending by the Reading Road, was to gain time; it is expected the owners will be in town this afternoon, and by this Road we gained five hours' time, which is a matter of much importance, and we may have occasion to use it sometimes in the future. In great haste, Yours with great respect,

Jos. C. Bustill[1]

William Still, *The Underground Railroad* (Philadelphia, Pa., 1872), 24–25.

Phila[delphia], [Pennsylvania]
Nov[ember] 2nd, [1857]

[Dr Sir:][2]

With regard to those unprovided for, I think it will be safe to send them on any time toward the latter part of this week. Far better it will be for them in Canada, this winter, where they can procure plenty of work, than it would be in Pa., where labor s will be scarce and hands plenty, with the usual amount of dread & danger hanging over the head s of the Fugitive. From the place where the ten you referred to came, fourty four ~~have~~ have left within the last two weeks—16 of whom we have passed on, I trust safely.

After the middle of this week, I think you might venture to send them to us in "Small parcels"—that is, not over four or 5 in a company.

If convenient, you will confer a favor by droping us a few lines informing us by what hour & train the arrivals will come. Yours truly,

Wm Still

Elijah F. Pennypacker Papers, Friends Historical Library, Swarthmore College, Swarthmore, Pennsylvania. Published by permission.

1. Joseph C. Bustill (1822–1895), a teacher and underground railroad agent, was the youngest son of black abolitionist David Bustill of Philadelphia. Educated in local private schools, he was respected as a "polished writer and convincing speaker" and a committed antislavery activist. Bustill became involved in vigilance committee work at age seventeen and reportedly assisted more than one thousand fugitive slaves during the 1840s and 1850s. After an unsuccessful attempt to open a clerical office in Philadelphia, he moved in 1856 to Harrisburg, where he taught in the public schools, collected subscriptions for the *Weekly Anglo-African*, and continued to aid fugitive slaves. Leading the Harrisburg Vigilance Committee during the late 1850s, Bustill personally forwarded hundreds of fugitives to Reading, Philadelphia, and Auburn, New York.

Bustill became attracted to the Haitian emigration movement in the early 1860s. He recruited prospective emigrants and organized a settlement company known as the "Geffrard Industrial Regiment." But gloomy reports by blacks returning from Haiti prompted many in Bustill's band to balk on the eve of departure in April 1862, causing Bustill to abandon his settlement plans. In 1864 he returned to Philadelphia, where he served as a trustee of the African Civilization Society and joined in efforts to create a new black organization—the National Equal Rights League. Bustill attended the 1864 black national convention at Syracuse, New York; at Pennsylvania's black state convention the following year, he was appointed secretary of the state auxiliary of the National Equal Rights League. Following the Civil War, Bustill remained active in several local community organizations, including the Banneker Institute, the Masons, and the First African Presbyterian Church. Anna Bustill Smith, "The Bustill Family," *JNH* 10:641–43 (October 1925); *NSt*, 8 February 1850; Still, *Underground Railroad*, 24–25, 220–22, 332–34; *WAA*, 3 September 1859, 26 April 1862 [14:0276]; *PP*, 28 December 1861, 2, 23 January 1862; *CR*, 18 June 1864 [15:0405]; *Convention of Colored Men . . . in Syracuse* (1864), 5 [15:0539]; Foner and Walker, *Proceedings of the Black State Conventions*, 1:139–60.

2. Elijah F. Pennypacker (1804–1888), a Quaker abolitionist, feminist, and temperance advocate, was president of the Pennsylvania Anti-Slavery Society. He served in the Pennsylvania legislature from 1831 to 1836 before abandoning politics because of his nonresistance principles. Pennypacker's Phoenixville home was a regular stop on the underground railroad. *DAB*, 14:446.

67.
William Whipper to Gerrit Smith
22 April 1856

After four decades of struggling against the colonization movement, black abolitionists viewed with suspicion any effort at resettlement beyond the United States. Emigration was equated with abandoning the slave and renouncing black claims to American citizenship. But events of the 1850s caused many blacks to rethink the issue. Beginning with Martin R. Delany's *Condition, Elevation, Emigration and Destiny of the Colored People of the United States* (1852), blacks demonstrated greater tolerance for emigration programs. William Whipper, for years a faithful integrationist and anticolonizationist, reflected the changing mood. In a 22 April 1856 letter to Gerrit Smith, he announced his current outlook on the emigration question by arguing that emigration was a reasonable response by a persecuted and dispossessed people. To refute Smith's claim that those who "quit America" were forsaking the slave, he pointed to the "practical antislavery work" being carried on by blacks in Canada West. Whipper, Delany, and other emigrationists believed that black success outside the United States would have a powerful "reflex influence" on American race relations—it would demonstrate black abilities and the inherent injustice of American racial policies. By the end of the decade, black leaders had organized three national emigration conventions that promoted black settlement in Canada, Africa, Central and South America, and the Caribbean. Delany, *Condition of the Colored People*, 159–208; Ripley et al., *Black Abolitionist Papers*, 2:228–331; Miller, *Search for a Black Nationality*, 134–69; *PFW*, 24 March 1853 [8:0172].

Columbia, [Pennsylvania]
April 22, 1856

Dear Sir:

Frederick Douglass' paper of the 11th inst contains your speech on the "Right of Suffrage" deliver'd at Albany Feby 28th 1856,[1] and in it I find the following remarkable passage viz "Those blackmen disgrace themselves and their race, and disgrace human nature, who quit America, in order to better their fortunes elsewhere, and who desert their own bruised and bleeding people to identify themselves with another people." I would be much pleased if that you would give the public, and especially "black men" a more full explanation of your views on that subject.

If the position you assume be correct, then every "blackman" who leaves America for the purpose of "benefiting his condition" should be branded like Cain,[2] and labelled a "Vagabond" unfit for the society of

Christians & be placed beyond the pale of humanity because he has committed the impardonable sin of "degrading human nature." I can conceive the force of your assertion as an argument against African Colonization, but I cannot comprehend how your pure, liberal and philanthropic mind, can justify the utterance of such anathema's against a "blackman" leaving a Country whose crushing influence, moral, civil and religious[,] aims at the extinction of his manhood.

The spirit of free emigration has in all ages, promote[d] the progress and development of the oppressed, and must this agent of ~~civilat~~ civilization be denied to the "blackman" when by the simple act of crossing our Western Lakes,[3] he can obtain and enjoy an equality of rights and priviliges under a government whose principles, policy, and practical Justice is more pure than our own.

Nor will I consent to stop here. I am prepared to assert and prove that there are many "black men" who have removed to the Canada's, are doing a more practical antislavery work than they were capable of performing in the States. These men so far from being refugee's from duty, or crime are aiding the progress of Civilization in their new home, and demonstrating the Capacity of the "blackman" to enter into and pursue the arts of Civilized life (when removed from the precincts of republican despotism) which creates a nations resources, augments her power and embellishes her name and character.

But I will not enter into a discussion of the subject at present as I am yet unwilling to believe that the sentiments I have quoted will receive the ~~mature~~ sanction of your Judgement. I remain yours for liberty, Justice & Equality,

Wm Whipper

Gerrit Smith Papers, George Arents Research Library, Syracuse University, Syracuse, New York. Published by permission.

1. Gerrit Smith addressed the New York state legislature on 28 February 1856. He urged the body to remove the suffrage restrictions on blacks in order to combat racial prejudice and prove to the South that blacks could live successfully in freedom. The speech was later published as *Gerrit Smith on Suffrage. His Speech in the Capitol, Albany, February 28th 1856* ([1856]). Field, *Politics of Race*, 96.

2. According to the biblical account in Genesis 4:1–15, Cain murdered his brother Abel out of jealousy and was marked by God as punishment.

3. Whipper refers to the thousands of fugitive slaves who were crossing over or around the Great Lakes into Canada West.

68.
Charles B. Ray to Gerrit Smith
29 April 1856

The practice of buying slaves to secure their freedom evoked controversy in antislavery circles. Many white abolitionists worried that traf-
ficking in slaves legitimized the institution and argued that the practice
should not be encouraged, regardless of its worthy intent. But black
leaders were less troubled by the moral ambiguity of the act and accepted its practical necessity. They frequently marshaled the limited resources of the black community for this purpose. In 1855 Rev. Leonard
A. Grimes and the members of his Twelfth Baptist Church in Boston
collected funds and arranged the purchase of well-known fugitive Anthony Burns, who had been returned to slavery the year before. Other
black leaders, such as Charles B. Ray, the corresponding secretary of the
New York State Vigilance Committee, enlisted the generosity and goodwill of white reformers to aid scores of fugitives and their families. This
29 April 1856 letter from Ray to Gerrit Smith, concerning the protracted case of Eliza Hamilton and her family, demonstrates how black
leaders orchestrated these purchases. Horton and Horton, *Black Bostonians*, 110–11; Freeman, "Free Negro in New York City," 90–91; Ripley et al., *Black Abolitionist Papers*, 1:327–29.

> New York, [New York]
> April 29, 1856

My dear Friend:
  You will remember that, in the month of July, when you were at Washington in Congress,[1] that a Mr Larkin[2] called on you, with a Certificate
of Deposit for $800—procured by me, payable to your order, with which
to purchase a Sister of Mr Larkin, then a slave in Virginia, and that you
purchased, or secured her Emancipation. She came here with Mr Larkin
and has resided in Brooklyn & Saratoga since then. Her name is Eliza
Hamilton. She left three children in Slavery, one of them a girl now 21
years of age. Since then, the Master has deceased, and the widow, to save
the girl from falling into other hands, retained her, and gave a mortgage
of her, the boys were sold. The widow has written to the Mother, that
she will be unable to meet this mortgage, and wishes that she would
endeavour to raise the money, and thus secure the freedom of the girl.
She is evidently anxious the girl should be free, anxious that the Mother
should have her with her. The price is $800. Mrs Hamilton called on me
to day, with her papers &c. I have had so many of these cases but
recently, (this is only the 2d to day) that I not only have used myself up,
but my friends, and I must have some respite, more on their account than

Document 68

on mine, for I cannot keep calling all the time. Anxious however to do something for her, I thought and promised her, I would write to you about her case. She has only about one Hundred dollars. Whether it will be in your power to do any thing for her in the way of money or not, you can help her, by stating the fact that you purchased her over your signature, for a book, in which I am going to copy her papers, to be entered there. It would doubtless be of great service to her. You will let me hear from you at your earliest convenience. I hope you are all well. Best regards of myself & wife to your family. Truly Yours,

Charles B. Ray

Gerrit Smith Papers, George Arents Research Library, Syracuse University, Syracuse, New York. Published by permission.

1. Gerrit Smith served in Congress from March 1853 until August 1854, when he resigned due to the pressure of his "far too extensive private business" and his disgust with congressional politics. Harlow, *Gerrit Smith*, 312–35.

2. Ray probably refers to Abraham W. Larkin, a Brooklyn black who later served as secretary of the Young Men's Literary Association and on the board of directors of the African Civilization Society. *WAA*, 2 June 1860, 5, 19 April 1862; Henry Highland Garnet et al. to Gerrit Smith, 16 February 1859, Gerrit Smith Papers, NSyU [11:0587].

69.
Speech by William Wells Brown
Delivered at the City Assembly Rooms
New York, New York
8 May 1856

The personal experience of black abolitionists allowed them to understand the subtle and pervasive impact of slavery upon life in the North.
William Wells Brown touched on this theme in an address before the annual meeting of the New York Anti-Slavery Society on 8 May 1856.
Sydney H. Gay chaired the gathering, which convened at the City Assembly Rooms in New York City. After discussing the effects of slavery
on southern white culture, Brown turned to the "workings of slavery
. . . throughout the North." He noted how southern politicians intimi-
dated their northern colleagues in Congress and how the children of
southern planters brought the "rough edges" of slavery to northern
schools and colleges. Brown recounted several encounters with racial
discrimination in the North, contrasting that treatment with the acceptance he had experienced in Europe. Most members of Brown's audience of Garrisonians had heard before how slavery degraded both servant and master in the South; but many of them were struck by Brown's
charge that they too were influenced by slavery. Farrison, *William Wells
Brown*, 145–76.

Mr. Chairman, Ladies and Gentlemen:
    Those of you who have been here during yesterday and today will bear
witness that the several speakers have hesitated not to declare the truth
as it regards the iniquity of slavery. It can scarcely be expected, however,
that those of us who understand the workings of slavery in the Southern
States will bring before you the wrongs of the slave as we could wish.
Language will not allow us; and if we had the language, the fastidious-
ness of the people would not permit our portraying them. Slavery has
justly been termed the crime of crimes. Man cannot inflict upon his
fellowman a greater crime than to enslave him, for by so doing he not
only injures his fellowman, but himself. It is not possible for one part of
mankind to enslave another portion without injuring themselves. That
may be seen in the workings of slavery in this country.
    Everyone who speaks of the condition of the slave will tell you of his
ignorance and degradation. This ignorance and debasement necessarily
affects the master. The master may get education and refinement, but his
relation to the slave is such that he is contaminated. Those of us who
have lived in slavery could tell you privately what we cannot tell you
publicly of the degradation in the domestic circle of the master. I could

tell you of the ignorance of the white people as well as the black. The white children are brought up with the black children; it is not possible to separate them; hence the ignorance and degradation that is found among the slave population communicates itself to them. The child grows up to the age of ten or twelve years; then the master discovers that that son or daughter must be removed to a part of the country where the rough edges that intercourse with the slave children has imparted may be rubbed off. The young man is sent off to the North to get an education;[1] and in coming to your Northern seminaries of learning, among your own sons, he must neccessarily rub off those rough edges upon them. And the same is true with regard to the slaveowner's daughter. Thus your children partake of this degradation, vice and ignorance. This is one of the results of your toleration of such a system. A distinguished writer has justly said that no one can fasten a chain upon the limbs of his neighbor without afterwards inevitably fastening the other end upon his own neck. This is exemplified not only in the slaveholder at the South, but in the people of the North, who have folded their arms and permitted this iniquity to live.

You have, no doubt, all of you, read of the riot that occurred, some three months since, among the students of Columbia College, South Carolina, in which the students drove the police back to their stations, and at length demanded the chief of the police, that they might sacrifice him to their ferocity; and when the mayor had called out the militia, they could do nothing, and the chief of the police was murdered, with two other policemen.[2] That was a legitimate fruit of slavery. The young white boy is brought up with these ferocious passions. He has been accustomed to kick and drive the black slave about; and when he meets with white persons, he considers them his inferiors, and his passions break forth on the slightest provocation. Northern men complain that they send men to Congress and they exhibit no backbone—that they don't face the music in the halls of Congress. To send your Northern men to Congress, there to meet the bully, the duelist, the woman-scourger, the gambler, the murderer, is like taking your little son from the country and sending him to the city, where he finds a thousand rude boys who insult and abuse him. Men in the South who are accustomed to flog old men and young women, and to sell children from the mother's breast, are more than a match for your Northern man when it comes to bullying and threats. To talk about a good slaveholder is a contradiction. A good slaveholder is a bad man, a Christian slaveholder an infidel, a just slaveholder a thief, for to rob a man of himself is the greatest theft that a human being can commit. The South is the great Sodom of this country. I hold in my hand an advertisement taken from the New Orleans *Picayune*,[3] by which you may see the evidence of what I assert, coming from the slaveholder himself.

$20 REWARD.—Ran away from the plantation of the under-signed the negro man SHADRACK, a preacher, five feet nine inches high, about forty years old, and stamped N. E. upon the breast and having both small toes cut off. He has a very dark complexion, with eyes small but bright, and a look quite insolent.

The slaveowner has the audacity to say that his slave has a look quite insolent. I rather think if the Rev. Dr. Nehemiah Adams, who has just been reelected as a member of the Board of Directors of the Tract Society,[4] and who thinks the slaves are so happy, contented and always look so smiling, should happen to be sold down South, be stamped with the letters "N. E.," and have his toes cut off—I rather think he would look quite as insolent as that "very dark-complexioned" man mentioned in this advertisement. (Laughter and applause.)

I saw in a newspaper published in my town, St. Louis—for I happen to have come from among the "border ruffians" (laughter)—an editorial announcement that a man who owned a slave there, a short time since, had caused that slave to be branded upon the right cheek with the words "slave for life,"[5] and the editor spends a great deal of invective and indignation upon this owner of the slave, saying that the slave was a good servant and had committed no offence to merit such treatment. The crime of this victim was being born with a white skin, for the editor tells us that he had straight hair and would pass for a white man. Being white, it was easy for him to escape, and hence the necessity of branding these words on his cheek, so as to prevent his running away. Perhaps, too, he had too much Anglo-Saxon blood in him to be a submissive slave, as Theodore Parker would say.

Such are the workings of slavery. A slave must always be made to know his place; if it were not so, he could not be kept in his chains. We see the effects of slavery everywhere throughout the North. I saw an illustration of it today in your own city. A very nice-looking coloured lady, a stranger in this city, no doubt, who was not aware that on Sixth Avenue they have cars expressly for coloured people,[6] entered a car that stopped to take in some other ladies. She was rudely thrust from the platform by the conductor and told that it was not the car for her to ride in. She was considerably lighter in complexion than myself, and perhaps as white as some that were seated in the car.

Some year and a half ago, I landed in this city from a British steamer, having just left England,[7] after having been abroad in different countries in Europe for a number of years, where I was once never reminded that I was a coloured person, so that I had quite forgotten the distinction of caste that existed in democratic America. I walked into an eating-house. I had scarcely got my hat off when the proprietor told me I could not eat there. Said I, "I have got a good appetite, and if you will give me a trial, I rather think I will convince that I can." "But," said he, "it is not allowable." I did not know what to make of it; I had been away five years, and had forgotten the great power of slavery over the North. I felt insulted. I walked into another eating-house. The proprietor asked me what I wanted. I said I wanted my dinner. "You can't get it here; we don't accommodate niggers." That was twice I was insulted. I went into a third, with a like result. I then went and stood by a lamppost for some five minutes. I thought of the nineteen years I had worked as a slave; I thought of the glorious Declaration of Independence; I looked around me and saw no less than seven steeples of churches; and I resolved I would have my dinner in the city of New York. (Applause.) I went to another restaurant. I made up my mind what I would do. I saw a vacant plate at a table; I took aim at it. I pulled back the chair, and sat down, turned over the plate, and stuck my knife in something. I was agitated, and did not know what it was, until I got it on my plate, when I found it was a big pickle. (Laughter.) At any rate I went to work at it. The waiter stared at me. Said I, "Boy, get me something to eat." He stared again, walked to the proprietor, and said something to him, came back and helped me. When I got through my dinner, I went up to the bar, and handed the proprietor a dollar. He took it, and then said, "You have got the greatest impudence of any nigger I have seen for a great while (laughter); and if it hadn't been that I didn't want to disturb my people sitting at the table, I would have taken you up from that table a little the quickest." "Well, sir," said I, "if you had, you would have taken the tablecloth, dishes and all with me. Now, sir, look at me; whenever I come into your dining saloon, the best thing you can do is to let me have what I want to eat quietly. You keep house for the accommodations of the public; I claim to be one of that public."

Some twenty days after that, I was about to start for Boston; I hadn't time to go to that saloon, so I went to a confectionery establishment, and thought I would do with a little pastry. I walked in; a young woman, who attended, came up and said she, "Can't accommodate you, sir." I paid no attention to her, but picked up a knife, and pitched into a piece of pie. Said she, "We can't accommodate you, sir." Said I, "This is very good pastry." (Laughter.) Then said she, "We don't accommodate niggers." Said I, "Did you make this?" (Laughter.) I finished my piece of pie, and then a second piece. By and by another lady came to me, and said, "Sir, we don't accommodate niggers." Said I, "You give very good accommodations; I shall always patronize you." I finished my third piece of pie, and asked for a glass of soda water. Says she, "Just leave my place, and I will charge you nothing." Said I, "Madam, I expect to pay wherever I get accommodation, but I can't pay for this until you give me a glass of soda water." So I took a chair and sat down, saying I was in no hurry; for I concluded to wait and go on the next train. As soon as she saw I was determined to stay, she said, "You may have your soda water." I drank it and walked out. Now that grated very hard on my feelings, after being away so long, and forgetting almost everything about the way coloured people were treated in this country.

Such are the workings of slavery, and yet, with all your boasted benevolence and religion, there is scarce a pulpit in New York that has a word to say against these wrongs. (Applause.) Still, such is the compromising character of the American people, that the time will probably come when colourphobia will become the subject of compromise, even with this religious sentiment. Not long since, a coloured man of great wealth came to visit a merchant in one of our Eastern cities, who, by a business connection with this coloured man, had acquired a considerable fortune. The merchant knew he must treat him kindly, and so he invited him to his house, and on Sunday he asked him to go to his church. It was one of the fine churches where a coloured face is never seen inside, except, perhaps, to do some menial work. The pew was near the pulpit. When the merchant, with his black friend, entered the pew, the congregation stared. There was no mistake about its being a black man. The minister entered his pulpit and commenced the services. He didn't discover the black man until he got into the midst of his sermon. It disconcerted him, and he could not go on. He lost his place in his sermon, hesitated, and at length had to slip secondly, and go to thirdly. He made a botch of it and concluded. As soon as service was over, a neighbour of the merchant came to him, and asked him what he meant by bringing a nigger into the church. "Why, it is my pew," said the merchant. "Is that any reason why you must insult the whole congregation?" said the man. "Yes, but he is an educated man," the merchant replied. "What of that?" said the man, "he is black." "But, sir, he is a correspondent of mine, and is worth a million of dollars." "Worth what!" "A million of dollars." "I beg pardon, introduce me to him." (Laughter and applause.)

Ladies and gentlemen, you may think lightly of these insults and annoyances which the coloured people have to endure, but they are felt keenly by us. And if there were nothing else for the people of the North to do, they have got enough to revolutionize the public sentiment in this respect. You see nothing of this hatred abroad. A black man is treated in Europe according as he behaves, and not according to his colour. This feeling is one of the great hindrances to the abolition movement. The Colonization Society[8] fosters this hatred and makes itself one of the great props of slavery. There are churches that refuse to open their doors for a meeting in behalf of the slave, but throw them wide open to the Colonization Society, and yet pretend that they are opposed to slavery and in favour of elevating the black man.

The American Anti-Slavery Society is the only one, of all the various societies, of whatsoever name, that meet this week in this city, that goes for the abolition of slavery.[9] Our work is to look after humanity and try to lift it up in the person of the downtrodden slave. I feel that if those in the Southern States with whom I am identified by complexion could only know of the sentiment and feeling which animates those who take part in this great cause, they would put up their prayer to God for our success. (Applause.)

I speak not for the purpose of making any display of eloquence or rhetoric. Whenever I come before a cultivated audience like this, I remember that I was nineteen years a slave, and never had a day's schooling in my life, and yet that it is a duty I owe to my enslaved countrymen, to those who are bound to me by tenderest ties, to my God and to my country, to labour in the cause of humanity and remember those in bonds as bound with them. And if I can be the means of helping to remove a single obstacle out of the way of the anti-slavery cause, I shall feel well paid. (Applause.)

National Anti-Slavery Standard (New York, N.Y.), 16 May 1856.

1. Despite sectional tensions, many children of the planter class attended northern academies, colleges, and military schools during the antebellum period. Particularly popular were Princeton, Harvard, Yale, and the U.S. Military Academy at West Point. By the 1850s, southerners constituted nearly one-half of the graduates of West Point and one-third of those at Princeton. John Hope Franklin, *A Southern Odyssey: Travelers in the Antebellum North* (Baton Rouge, La., 1976), 56–72.

2. Brown evidently had read exaggerated reports of the "guard house riot" that occurred on 17–18 February 1856 in Columbia, South Carolina. An altercation between the town marshal and a few students from South Carolina College escalated into a tense confrontation between five militia companies and a hundred armed students. The crisis ended when a popular faculty member intervened and persuaded the students to return to the college. Daniel Walker Hollis, *University of South Carolina*, 2 vols. (Columbia, S.C., 1951), 1:194–99.

3. The New Orleans *Picayune*, which was founded in 1837, regularly published notices of runaway slaves and slaves for sale. The *Picayune* merged with the *Times-Democrat* in 1914. Mott, *American Journalism*, 249–50, 636.

4. The American Tract Society, an influential evangelical organization founded in 1825, printed and distributed millions of religious pamphlets and books throughout the nation. Control of the society lay with a publishing committee of clergymen, each holding a veto over the printing of any work. Throughout the 1850s, Rev. Nehemiah Adams of Boston, an apologist for slavery, served on the committee, which refused to publish antislavery tracts. The large Boston auxiliary broke away in 1858 and produced its own antislavery pamphlets, but the American Tract Society remained silent on the slavery question until the Civil War. McKivigan, *War against Proslavery Religion*, 77–78, 120–24, 188.

5. Brown refers to an undated piece from the *St. Louis Gazette*, which he recorded in his *Narrative*: "A wealthy man here had a boy named Reuben, almost white, whom he caused to be branded in the face with the words 'A slave for

life.'" *Narrative of William W. Brown, A Fugitive Slave* (Boston, Mass., 1848), 59.

6. The Sixth Avenue Railroad Company of New York City restricted black passengers to separate Jim Crow streetcars. After the formation of the Legal Rights Association in 1855, local blacks frequently attempted to sit in cars reserved for whites and were ejected. Despite these actions and numerous challenges in the courts, the company refused to abandon its policy until after the Civil War. Freeman, "Free Negro in New York City," 108–12.

7. Brown is mistaken. After returning from Britain on the *City of Manchester*, he disembarked at Philadelphia, not New York City, on 26 September 1854. Brown, *Sketches of Places and People Abroad*, 311–14.

8. Brown refers to the American Colonization Society.

9. During the "anniversary week" of 4–10 May 1856, dozens of American benevolent and reform societies convened their annual meetings in New York City. These included Bible and tract societies, the American Colonization Society, peace groups, education and prison reformers, the Young Men's Christian Association, Sunday school unions, and national health reform conventions. The American Anti-Slavery Society and its auxiliary, the New York Anti-Slavery Society, were the only two abolitionist organizations that met during this week. Ripley et al., *Black Abolitionist Papers*, 1:96; *Lib*, 2, 16 May 1856.

70.
Jermain Wesley Loguen to Hiram Mattison
13 August 1856

Black abolitionists engaged in a protracted struggle with American churches over the slavery question. No major denomination denounced the institution before the Civil War, and many of them condemned abolitionism, to the distress of black leaders. Even though Methodists split along sectional lines in 1844, in no small measure because of slavery, antiabolitionist sentiment continued to dominate that church's northern wing. Methodist policy-making bodies censured members who gave antislavery speeches, refused to ordain ministerial candidates with antislavery leanings, suspended outspoken abolitionist clergymen, and squelched debate over slavery in the denominational press. Although Methodist leader Rev. Hiram Mattison helped move the denomination in an antislavery direction, his clash with Jermain Wesley Loguen in the summer and fall of 1856 demonstrated that even prominent clerical abolitionists were not exempt from slavery's influence. Loguen's 13 August 1856 letter was part of a lengthy and bitter public exchange between the two men, sparked by Mattison's refusal to allow Loguen to collect funds for the underground railroad from his Adams, New York, congregation. Mattison enumerated several reasons for denying Loguen's request—he claimed not to know Loguen, did not want his quarterly conference disrupted, and opposed "collecting funds for any such objects." Loguen rejected the explanation as a contemptuous falsehood and condemned Mattison's statement that the Fugitive Slave Law was "the law of the land, as much so as the postal and revenue laws." Mattison subsequently denounced Loguen as "an itinerant beggar" who pocketed the money he collected and lied about his slave past. Ironically, the 18 December 1856 issue of the *Northern Independent*, Mattison's own journal, described Loguen as an "active and efficient agent of the underground railroad . . . himself a fugitive, and intimately acquainted with all the horrors of . . . slavery." McKivigan, *War against Proslavery Religion*, 46–47, 52–53, 84–87, 170–72; *Correspondence between Rev. H. Mattison and Rev. J. W. Loguen, on the Duty of Ministers to Allow Contributions in the Churches in Aid of Fugitive Slaves* (Syracuse, N.Y., 1857).

Syracuse, [New York]
Aug[ust] 13, 1856

REV. H. MATTISON:[1]

I have read in the Jefferson County *News*, your letter regarding me and my mission,[2] and those like me who escape from slavery, and assist others to escape. I read it with sadness, but not disappointment, because the knowledge I acquired of your character during my brief visit to you Sabbath before last, prepared me to expect such an article, if you were so imprudent as to put your justification on paper.

Now, mark me, it is not because money can not be had for an anti-slavery Gospel and the fleeing slave without your aid, that I apply to you, but because of the *inconsistency of your position and principles.*

On the Saturday before this Sunday, you say, your "Quarterly Conference"[3] discussed the subject of collections "*for foreign objects*," and determined that none should be taken in your church—at least until your "*church debt was provided for.*" I necessarily infer you came to this result in anticipation of my arrival, announced in the letter you received from Rev. Mr. Hunt,[4] of Pulaski. Sir, it is in vain for ministers and conferences, at this day, to attempt to shut up the hearts of God's people against feeding the hungry, and clothing the naked who are pressing in great numbers through Syracuse, and stretching out their hands for charity in their flight from bondage.

But could you bring your people to submit to restraints upon their compassionate sympathies, and to succumb to the rule that "no Methodist may take collections in the churches, other than the annual collections without the *order of the conference* and the *consent of the trustees*" in respect to some wretched "usage" which classes mercy to the slave with "*foreign objects*"—could you persuade your church and the church of the country that aid to the slave and hostility to slavery are *foreign* to the aims of the Methodist church, your success would only prove that you and your church were the enemies of humanity, and accursed of Heaven. Your people, the Methodists of the North, will submit to no such usage or sentiment.[5] In *their* name I protest against your heartless policy, and your more heartless and absurd theology, which I propose to consider. There is no class of people more free than Methodists to open their doors to me, and to contribute to my aims. It is news to the ministers and churches of Western New York that contributions to this most pressing charity are *foreign* to the Methodist Church, and that they may without discrediting religion and honor, interpose their "*present church debt*" and "*corporate liabilities*" against the claims of humanity.

You conclude your cold-blooded argument on this point, if argument it is, thus—"I was willing all should contribute, individually, as I suggested, and as many did." Yes, they did, but it was without encouragement from you. You stood in the way of their sympathies. Your whole treatment of me corresponds with your confession.

"I (Mattison) did not desire him (Loguen) to visit my church on that day, if at any time."

Why did you not write me at Syracuse and say so, as you were requested by Mr. Hunt? Why hold a conference on Saturday to ignore me, without acquainting me with your wishes? To tell your church members they may help the suffering slave "individually," but not as Christian Methodists under your charge, is a grant which takes more than it gives. It assumes that as Methodists they are your subjects, and that as individuals your license is a necessary or proper condition precedent to their action. It implies a sovereignty of the will, founded on a distinction between a Methodist and a man. It assumes that it is wrong to do as a Methodist what it may be dutiful to do as a man. It separates Christianity from the man, and of course annihilates it. It merges the man in the Methodist, and annihilates him also.

Sir, I am a Methodist—an humble preacher of the most abject class, and in the name of that class cowardly ignored, in the name of Methodism dishonored, and religion perverted, I protest against your position and conclusions. Take from your church individual men and women, with their gifts, and what remains of it and its charities? Why, Sir, do you suppose your church is a mere *external* thing—an outside bauble for you to handle and the world to look at, separated from the kernel and soul within? For shame! Cease such unmanly quibbles—they are unworthy of you.

But you are *"not in favor of traveling agents to collect funds for such objects"*—No object is worthy of support, you say, that is not endorsed by *"the Conferences and Presbyteries."* Pray, Sir, did you ever ask the Conference to make up a purse or move the churches to provide bread, lodging and clothing for my suffering countrymen? Did you ever hear of such a thing being suggested to a Presbytery? If the people of Syracuse did not employ me or somebody else to do it—if they depended on the Conferences and Presbyteries—if they waited for *you* to do it, would not my fugitive brothers have perished by hunger and cold by thousands? Sir, your whole article, if it means anything at all, means that you would desert my poor brethren and leave them to perish.

And now, Sir, I come to your last and most important position, which to my mind shows your first reasons to be mere evasions. You think your duty as a citizen and a Christian forbids you *"to assist slaves to run away."* Would you think so if yourself, or your wife, or mother, or child were a slave? Does *your* religion forbid you to do unto others as you would have them do unto you? You say "you had never heard of Mr. Loguen before." And had you not thrown yourself across the track of public feeling in behalf of my outraged mother, brothers and people, you might have never heard of him again. I could have suffered the past to relapse into forgetfulness.

But you say, "The fugitive slave law is the law of the land, as much so as the postal and revenue laws."

"It is made a crime to assist a slave to flee from bondage."

"Is it wise for me, as a minister, publicly to set the laws of my country at defiance, and expose myself to their penalties, by taking a collection in my church to assist slaves to run away?"

Were these the words of a Northern doughfaced politician, or a slave-holding congressman, they would not surprise me—but they are your words—the words of a Northern Methodist preacher, and therefore they surprise me. Dare you say that slave laws do not conflict with the laws of God? If they do conflict with the laws of God, you, a clergyman, should be the last person to say they are valid as "the postal and revenue laws" are. If you say they obligate you and me, then you say God approves them—then you say that "Law," which is ordained of heaven to protect rights, may destroy rights—that Legislation can change the truth into a lie and break up the foundation upon which all law reposes.

But it is your concluding argument which most astonishes me. I insert it in your own words:

> But suppose a minister were to preach in the morning from I Peter, ii. 13–15—"Submit yourself to every ordinance of man for the Lord's sake; whether it be to the king, as supreme; or unto Governors, as unto them that are sent by him for the punishment of evil doers, and for the praise of them that do well. For so is the will of God," &c.; how would it look for him to take up a public collection in the afternoon to maintain a systematic organization, whose avowed object is to violate and resist the law of the land? Or suppose he read in one of his public scripture lessons, the passage, Titus iii. 1, "Put them in mind to be subject to principalities and powers (civil authorities), to obey magistrates," &c., and then proceed to advise a collection to resist "principalities" and disobey "magistrates"? Or suppose further he had read for the instruction and guidance of his flock, the council of Paul to the Church of Rome: Rom. xiii. 1—"Let every soul be subject unto the higher powers (civil authorities). For there is no power but of God. Whosoever therefore resisteth the power, resisteth the ordinance of God; and they that resist shall receive to themselves damnation!" Would it become him as a minister to take up a collection in his church for the avowed purpose of "resisting the power"?

What if the apostles—what if Moses and Aaron, and Daniel and Elijah had adopted this wretched doctrine, and obeyed rulers, who, in a scriptural sense, are not men or magistrates, but "principalities and powers" of Hell, instead of obeying God! Why, your argument strikes at all righteousness, and blots out the only feature of the Bible which makes it merciful, sublime, and Godlike. When commanded to teach no more in Christ's name, the apostle said, "we ought to obey God rather than men," and a worldly wise one rose and said, "refrain from these men— lest happily ye be found fighting against God."[6] It was through disobedience to the Kings of Egypt and Babylon, and other false rulers, that the government of Jehovah was preserved in the Jewish dispensation. It is owing to such disobedience in the Christian dispensation that it has been preserved ever since, and that light and knowledge, liberty and religion, progress and civilization exist on the earth. These are the "Principalities and Powers"—"the Rulers of the darkness of this world"—"the spiritual wickedness in high places," against which the apostles "wrestled."[7] And now am I to be told in the latter part of the nineteenth century, when all Christendom is in arms against those infernal Principalities and Powers, that I must welcome them "for the Lord's sake"? Will you make me believe that the villain who raised his gory lash from my bleeding body, and who now holds it over the backs of my poor mother, brothers and sisters—that the scoundrels who made and execute the fugitive slave law, who chase my famishing countrymen through the States, are the ministers of the most High God, and that we ought to submit quietly to be tortured, and robbed, and murdered, "for the Lord's sake," and if we resist them we must be damned? Does my Lord and Saviour subject me to such powers? Sir, you don't understand the Scriptures. The very fact that there are "higher powers ordained of God,"[8] implies that there are lower powers ordained of Hell—that the former only are to be recognized as "the Powers that be," and the latter to be recognized as no Powers at all; "after the doings of the latter ye shall not do—neither shall ye walk in their ordinances."[9] Are you a teacher in Israel and not understand these things?

But I have done. I may not trespass further on these columns. If you think I have spoken too plainly, and even severely, remember I am a slave, and hold my freedom only by setting the laws and ordinances which you respect in open defiance. Yours, &c.,

J. W. LOGUEN

Correspondence between Rev. H. Mattison and Rev. J. W. Loguen, on the Duty of Ministers to Allow Contributions in the Churches in Aid of Fugitive Slaves (Syracuse, N.Y., 1857), 9–13.

1. Hiram Mattison (1811–1868) served Methodist pulpits in upstate New York and later in New York City, where he established the comeouter St. John's Independent Methodist Church. Although he opposed Loguen's efforts to collect funds for fugitive slaves, he frequently spoke against slavery, advocated the exclusion of slaveholders from church membership, worked to sever ties between slavery and Methodism, and published antislavery tracts, most notably *The Impending Crisis of 1860* (1858). He also edited a Methodist antislavery organ called the *Northern Independent.* Mattison was a key figure in the Church Anti-Slavery Society during the Civil War. *DAB*, 12:423; McKivigan, *War against Proslavery Religion*, 142, 171, 191–92, 213; *Correspondence between Rev. H. Mattison and Rev. J. W. Loguen*, v, 42.

2. Loguen refers to a 29 July 1856 letter by Hiram Mattison to the editor of the *Jefferson County News*, a paper published in Adams, New York. *Correspondence between Rev. H. Mattison and Rev. J. W. Loguen*, 5–8.

3. Loguen refers to the quarterly meeting of the Methodist Black River Conference, which convened on 26 July 1856 at Syracuse, New York. *Correspondence between Rev. H. Mattison and Rev. J. W. Loguen*, 17–19 [10:0283–84].

4. Loguen mistakenly refers to a Rev. Hunt. In 1856 Rev. William Jones was serving the Methodist congregation at Pulaski, New York. On 21 July, he wrote a letter to Hiram Mattison, noting Loguen's willingness to speak in the Methodist church at Adams. Jones urged Mattison to write to Loguen at Syracuse if he desired his services. *Correspondence between Rev. H. Mattison and Rev. J. W. Loguen*, 17–18 [10:0283–84].

5. Many northern Methodists were active abolitionists. Gilbert Haven, Hiram Mattison, and other clergymen revived denominational debate over slavery by the 1850s. During the decade, the antislavery movement attracted thousands of new adherents among Methodists, particularly in New England, western New York, and the upper Midwest. Dissatisfied with the progress of the cause in the church, some members broke away and joined the Wesleyan Methodist church or the Free Methodist church, both comeouter sects. Although abolitionists continually prodded the denomination to expel slaveholders, the Methodist General Conference refused to view slaveholding "as grounds for expulsion from membership" until 1860. McKivigan, *War against Proslavery Religion*, 170–72.

6. Loguen alludes to a story in Acts 5:29–40. Warned against public preaching, Peter and other early Christians responded that they "ought to obey God rather than men." After hearing their answer, a prominent rabbi named Gamaliel counseled Jews in Jerusalem to refrain from harming them, lest they "be found even to fight against God."

7. Loguen borrows from Ephesians 6:12; "For we wrestle not against flesh and blood, but against principalities, against powers, against the rulers of the darkness in this world, against spiritual wickedness in high places."

8. Loguen paraphrases Romans 13:1–2.

9. Loguen paraphrases Leviticus 18:3.

71.
Robert Campbell and Philadelphia Racism

Robert Campbell to the Board of
Managers of the Franklin Institute
12 November 1856

Robert Campbell to Alfred Cope
17 November 1856

Blacks made antislavery statements by refusing to compromise with racist practices. They personally challenged acts of discrimination, testifying to their courage, conviction, and commitment to equality. Sarah M.
Douglass withdrew from a Quaker congregation rather than suffer the
indignity of the "negro pew." Robert Purvis refused to pay his property
tax when his children were barred from attending the public schools. A
third Philadelphian, Robert Campbell, demonstrated his abolitionist resolve in an 1856 incident involving one of the city's foremost cultural
institutions. Campbell, an instructor at the Institute for Colored Youth,
sought to improve his scientific knowledge by enrolling in a lecture series at the Franklin Institute. At first, the managers of the institute ignored his request. Campbell challenged their actions in a 12 November
note. To avoid setting the precedent of permitting black enrollment,
they offered Campbell a complimentary ticket for the series. In a 17
November letter to Philadelphia philanthropist Alfred Cope, a trustee
of the Institute for Colored Youth, Campbell indicated that he would
refuse the offer because it did not address the Franklin Institute's policy
of racial exclusion. *DANB*, 186–87, 508–10; Blackett, *Beating against
the Barriers*, 144–49.

Institute for Cold Youth[1]
Lombard St.
11 mo. 12d., 1856
Gentlemen:[2]
　　Complying with the terms of your advertisement, I during the preceding fortnight made application to the actuary of your institution to purchase a season ticket. On three or four occasions I was told that the
tickets were not ready, but that there was no necessity for one until after
the introductory week. I consequently attended those lectures unmo-
lested. On last Monday evening I again applied, when after some attempt
to evade a direct refusal I was told that no ticket could be sold to me. I
inquired what the objections were, and received the very emphatic reply
of "color."

My object, gentlemen, in this note is simply to ascertain whether you endorse the action of your agent in his refusal. I may here assert, by the way, that I was induced to seek access to your lectures by no other than a desire to be profited by them. Yours &c.,

Robt. Campbell[3]

Richard Humphreys Foundation, Friends Historical Library, Swarthmore College, Swarthmore, Pennsylvania. Published by permission.

Institute [for Colored Youth]
[Philadelphia], [Pennsylvania]
11 mo. 17d., [18]56

Respected Friend:[4]

I sought to purchase a ticket of admission to the Lectures of the Franklin Institute, but was refused by the actuary of that institution on account of "color." I subsequently wrote to the Board of Managers, inquiring whether they endorsed the conduct of their agent. Without replying directly to my note, they, it seems, agreed that "under the circumstances" of my being a teacher in an incorporated institution &c. they would present me with a ticket.

I have seriously considered whether, "under the circumstances" I could accept it, and have concluded that I could not without making a sacrifice of principle. Simply as a respectable individual they are unwilling to grant what I seek; but as they would admit gratis, "Mr. Jones'" servant, under the circumstance of his being Mr. Jones' servant so would they admit me.

Yet sir, were they in the habit of presenting complimentary tickets to teachers, I would accept it. They are not; and I shall be no exception.

The loss I will experience in these lectures is considerable, but the path of duty to my persecuted and proscribed brethren is evident, when I weight that loss against the compromise. If the Managers of that institution deem it wrong for respectable men of different complexions to partake of knowledge in common, then let them as scientific men, let them as the assured instructors of the people, fearlessly proclaim it. I could then pity the distortion of their judgment, but would respect their honesty. On the other hand, if they do not, why cater to the weakness and prejudice of the vulgar—why on any pretense evade a direct issue in this matter? Most respectfully yours,

Robt. Campbell

Richard Humphreys Foundation, Friends Historical Library, Swarthmore College, Swarthmore, Pennsylvania. Published by permission.

1. The Institute for Colored Youth, one the most important black schools in nineteenth-century Philadelphia, was constructed in 1852 in the heart of the

city's black community. It was the most successful of several black academies built from the 1832 bequest of Richard Humphreys, a Quaker philanthropist and businessman. Charles L. Reason served as principal until late 1855. He instituted a rigorous classical curriculum, established a library and lecture series open to local blacks, and attracted a respected black faculty. Grace A. Mapps headed the school's female department, and her cousin, Sarah Mapps Douglass, directed its elementary classes. The ICY quickly earned a statewide reputation for academic excellence. Under the leadership of Ebenezer Bassett, who followed Reason as principal, the institute became a center for civic and reform activity among black Philadelphians. He replaced many of the scientific lectures with those of a more political nature, inviting Frederick Douglass, Alexander Crummell, Henry Highland Garnet, and other black abolitionists to speak. In 1863 ICY became a local headquarters for recruiting black soldiers. It also produced dozens of black teachers for the city's segregated public schools and for freedmen's schools in the South. In 1869 Fanny Jackson, a black teacher from Oberlin College, succeeded Bassett. She made teacher training the school's primary mission and replaced its traditional curriculum with manual labor education based on Booker T. Washington's Tuskegee model. In 1903 the institute moved to nearby Cheyney, Pennsylvania, and later became Cheyney State University— part of Pennsylvania's public system of teachers' colleges. Linda Marie Perkins, "Quaker Beneficence and Black Control: The Institute for Colored Youth, 1852– 1903," in *New Perspectives on Black Educational History*, ed. Vincent P. Franklin and James D. Anderson (Boston, Mass., 1978), 19–43.

2. A twenty-four-member board of managers directed the affairs of the Franklin Institute for the Promotion of the Mechanic Arts, the foremost champion of technological development in the antebellum United States. The Philadelphia-based institute was founded in 1824 to benefit poor and disadvantaged artisans, but its managers, who came from the city's economic elite, allied the organization with manufacturing interests. They sponsored an ambitious program of public lectures, education, research, publications, library and museum facilities, and popular industrial fairs. Bruce Sinclair, *Philadelphia's Philosopher Mechanics: A History of the Franklin Institute, 1824–1865* (Baltimore, Md., 1974).

3. Robert Campbell (1829–1884) was born in Kingston, Jamaica, the son of a mulatto mother and a Scotsman. As a young man, he worked as a printer's apprentice and attended a teacher-training college before becoming a parish schoolmaster in Kingston. Campbell resettled his family in Central America in 1852, but a year later he took a job at a small printing shop in Brooklyn. In 1855 he accepted an appointment as instructor of natural sciences, geography, algebra, and Latin at the Institute for Colored Youth in Philadelphia. Campbell also promoted adult education at the Banneker Institute and offered evening science lectures for the broader black community. Several encounters with racial prejudice and friendships with local black abolitionists moved him toward antislavery activism. In 1857 he participated in a fugitive slave rescue.

Troubled by American racial mores, Campbell became increasingly receptive to proposals for African and Caribbean immigration. In 1858 he joined Martin R. Delany's Niger Valley Exploring Party and went to New York City to solicit funds for the project. Writing in March 1859 in the *Anglo-African Magazine*, he suggested that black political equality and personal distinction could only be achieved in a black republic. Unable to secure financing in the United States, Campbell journeyed to Britain. There he received government and private support, particularly from the Manchester Cotton Supply Association, a group interested in fostering the development of alternative, free labor cotton sources. Campbell sailed for West Africa in late June. Six months later, after exploring inland, he and Delany negotiated a land treaty with Egba chieftains. Both men traveled to Britain in May 1860, hoping to secure funds and recruits for their proposed African settlement; Campbell later continued this effort in the United States. He published two works about his African journey: *A Few Facts Relating to Lagos, Abbeokuta and Other Sections of Central Africa* (1860) and *A Pilgrimage to My Motherland and an Account of a Journey among the Egbos and Yorubas of Central Africa* (1860).

In February 1862, Campbell settled with his family in Lagos, West Africa. He remained there, becoming the only major African immigration advocate of the 1850s to remain on the continent. From June 1863 to December 1865, he published an independent weekly called the *Anglo-African*. Throughout his remaining years, Campbell worked to improve the cultural and economic life of Lagos. He organized and promoted several local scientific and literary societies, undertook a series of commercial ventures, and served in a number of minor political posts. From 1858 until his death, he displayed an unflagging commitment to the advancement of Africa. Blackett, *Beating against the Barriers*, 139–82.

4. Alfred Cope (1806–1875), a Philadelphia Quaker merchant, served on the board of managers of the Institute for Colored Youth from 1842 until his death. A favorite of ICY's black faculty, he personally recruited black instructors, financed cash prizes for outstanding graduates, donated $10,000 to the school's building fund, and provided leadership indispensable to its operations. Cope supported other black causes, including the African Civilization Society, and funded the graduate education of physicist Edward Bouchet, the first black American to earn a Ph.D. U.S. Census, 1850; Perkins, "Quaker Beneficence and Black Control," 25; Blackett, *Beating against the Barriers*, 155.

72.
Remarks by William H. Newby
Delivered at St. Andrew's
African Methodist Episcopal Church
Sacramento, California
10 December 1856

Blacks demonstrated their patriotism during the Republic's early years—they shouldered arms in America's wars and boasted of the country's democratic principles. But in the 1840s, after decades of slavery and prejudice, some black leaders began to question their duty to the nation. Commenting on an Anglo-American diplomatic crisis in 1842, the *People's Press* called on blacks to remain neutral in the event of war; the editors pointed to the sacrifices blacks had made in the American Revolution and the War of 1812 and asked: "Shall we a third time kiss the foot that crushes us?" The government's proslavery course during the 1850s sharpened the debate. California blacks confronted the issue of loyalty and citizenship at their 1856 state convention, which met during 9–13 December at St. Andrew's African Methodist Episcopal Church in Sacramento. On the second day, the business committee submitted a series of resolutions, including one that offered a seemingly innocuous national tribute: "We hail with delight its onward progress; sympathize with it in its adversity; and would freely cast our lot in the fortunes of battle, to protect her against foreign invasion." A debate followed. William H. Newby, a prominent San Francisco black, spoke against its adoption, then several delegates followed with supporting and opposing arguments. The convention ultimately rejected an amended form of the resolution by a twenty-nine to twenty-seven vote. *E*, 31 March 1842; *NASS*, 11 September 1845 [5:0074]; *Proceedings of the Second Annual Convention of the Colored Citizens of the State of California* (San Francisco, Calif., 1856), 41–47 [10:0402–6].

I am opposed to the language of this resolution, "that we hail with delight its onward progress." No man can expect me to do this. A country, whose prosperity and wealth has been built upon our sweat and blood, to say we hail its progress with delight, is to make ourselves ridiculous; to tell this to America—to the world—is to volunteer the acknowledgement of a degree of servility, that would make us undeserving of the sympathy and respect of just men.

"We freely cast in our lots in the fortunes of battle, to protect against foreign invasion." This may be patriotism—but patriotism may be a vice; in a white man—a freeman, it may be worthily indulged; as an American, the events of his country's history, and the circumstances of her present condition, may indeed stir within him sentiments of pride and love of country; but to the colored people, what is the history of the past, in America, but the history of wrongs and cruelties such as no other people upon the face of the earth have been forced to endure? The same institutions that bless the white man, are made to curse the colored man.

Shall we say "we will protect against foreign invasion?" God knows I speak advisedly—I would hail the advent of a foreign army upon our shores, if that army provided liberty to me and my people in bondage. This may be thought ultra, but in saying it I am influenced by the same motives and spirit which influenced Henry,[1] when he said to the burgesses of Virginia, "give me liberty, or give me death!"—words that made men's blood move fast within them, and caused them instinctively to clutch the handles of their swords.

Henry was thought at first to be bold and ultra; but history regards him as a brave and noble man. We are wronged; let us declare it openly to the world. England has done her duty towards us; she has abolished slavery in her colonies, and is doing what she can to destroy the system from the earth.[2] In the great conflict of opinion that is stirring the nations, her example, her influence is on the side of freedom.

Would we, could we do battle against England? There is in men an innate sense of justice—we feel it; let us not stultify ourselves. I trust the resolution will not be adopted.

Proceedings of the Second Annual Convention of the Colored Citizens of the State of California (San Francisco, California, 1856), 42.

1. Patrick Henry.
2. Newby refers to the Emancipation Act of 1833 (which ended slavery in the British Empire), the international influence of British abolitionists, and the vigorous efforts of the British navy to enforce diplomatic agreements outlawing the African slave trade.

73.
Essay by William Still
17 January 1857

The Fugitive Slave Law made America's judicial system a sympathetic ally of the slaveholders. It denied blacks basic legal rights, such as a jury trial and the right to be represented by an attorney, and established a process for the smooth and speedy return to slavery of accused fugitives. Even experienced abolitionist lawyers were often powerless to impede the combined will of slaveowners and the courts. In this 17 January 1857 account, which was probably written for publication in the *Provincial Freeman*, William Still narrates the case of Henry Tiffney, a young black Philadelphian arrested for theft—a common ploy of slave catchers—in the heart of the city's black community. Tiffney was brought before federal fugitive slave commissioner David Paul Brown, Jr., and alleged to be Michael Brown, the escaped servant of William H. Gatchell, Sr., of Baltimore. During the two-day hearing, Gatchell's son and slave catcher John Graham appeared as claimants, and several local blacks, including abolitionist J. J. G. Bias, testified that Tiffney was free and had lived in the city for at least six years. Ignoring the black testimony, the commissioner ordered Tiffney "returned" to the Gatchell household. Philadelphia blacks were outraged by the commissioner's handling of the case. Unprotected by the law and rebuffed by the courts, many black abolitionists challenged the Fugitive Slave Law through extralegal means, including violence. *NASS*, 24 January, 14 February 1857 [10:0542].

Slave Case!
Since penning the above, the Slave Hunters have been in our mids[t], and a promising looking young man of 25 years of age has been thrust back to bondage!

On the 15th inst., while walking along one of our streets, obviously unconscious of Kidnappers of or Slave Catchers, Henry Tiffney who had been known here for the Several years, was arrested as he states, on the charge of stealing, and was hurried before a United States Commissioner, where a different offence was alledged. John Graham, of Baltimore, Agent for the Claiment, James Crossen, John Jenkins and a man by the name of Stewart, Deputy United States Marshalls,[1] are intitled to the "bad pre-eminence" of doing the business of blood hounds, in this Case.

The scheme of the Slave Catchers, now being fully reveald and the ill fated victim wholly in the power of the Commissioner & the atrocious Claiment, no time was to be lost in proving Henry Tiffney to be the property of Wm. H. Gatchell, Sr., of Baltimore, Md., which was done with marked alacrity by Wm. H. Gatchell, Jr.,[2] and the Said John Graham.

Anxious to witness the Commissioners mode of operation, and to show my sympathy for the unfortunate man, I resolved to be an eye witness throughout the entire hearing. Before the hearing Commenced however, by the request of Wm. S. Peirce, Esq.[3] ~~his~~ counsel for the prisoner, I availed myself of the priviledge of a brief interview with him. But being surrounded by his captors of course, I could glean but little— indeed he was positively forbidden by one of the Deputy Marshalls to have ~~no~~ interview with any person whatever, except his counsel. Horror stricken as he was however he told me distinctly that he "had rather die than go back!"

The hearing lasted for two whole days, closing this evening at 8 oclock.

It is needless to say that the Hunters, and their counsel, Daniel Dougherty, Esq.[4] & Mr. Commissioner Brown[5] were a whit behind the notorious Edward D. Engraham, Judge Kane, & Geo. F. Alberti, & Co., in carrying out the Fugitive Slave Law to the "fullest extent!"[6]

The 2nd day, Colored people were generally excluded from the Court Room. Mr. Peirce very ably denounced this proceedure, and argued that the doors should be thrown open to all, and that no "Star ~~Chambers~~ proceedings" should be tolerated, &c.[7] Whereupon the Marshall arose & stated that he had ordered the doors closed, because ~~he~~ threats of a ~~Rescuse~~ had been made the day before, which he had heard himself. The Commissioner asked him if he would "make an affidavit of that fact"— "No!" he replied indignantly.

To avoid delay probably, at this instant, the head Slave Catcher, Graham, volunteered to make the called for oath, which of course was readily admitted and the doors kept closed as before.

Thus the reader may easily judge how utterly unfairly the hearing was conducted; what a slim chance there really must have been for the prisoner; and indeed how perfectly easy ~~it~~ the most inhuman monsters can be accommodated, even in Philadelphia.

Some half Dozen Colored witnesses testified positively that they had known him well for years, for at least one year before it was alledged that he escaped, but it all availed nothing.

The Commissioner "owed a solem duty to the Constitution & the Union!" hence made out the "warrent" and delive~~d~~red him into the hands of his tormentors, to be carried back to hopeless bondage.

The alledged Fugitive, was very faithfully and ably defended by ~~Wm~~ Mr. Pierce, who to his honor be it said never fails to be found on the side of the weak & oppressed—whoever may oppose.

Now, in ~~the~~ Conclusion shall it be told that this Commissioner is the son of David Paul Brown, who has been the eloquent & able champion ~~of~~ and advocate for the oppressed for so many many years;[8] whose scathing denounciations of Slave holders, menstealers, Slave Catchers and their infamous tools on the Bench or at the Bar, have caused them so frequently to tremble and turn pale with shame! Yes with deep regret and feelings of mortification & Shame it must be acknowledged that this same Commissioner who issued the warrant for the arrest of Henry Tiffney, and also signed the same which doomed him for ever to bondage, is ~~one~~ his son. Hence forth therefore this atrocious act ~~with~~ will be an ~~everthe~~ everlasting disgrace in the estimation of all good people to both the son & sire.

W. S.

Philadelphia, [Pennsylvania]
January 17, 1857

Mary Ann Shadd Cary Papers, Ontario Provincial Archives, Toronto, Ontario, Canada. Published by permission.

1. Still lists the four slave catchers involved in Henry Tiffney's arrest. John Graham was employed by the private detective agency of Potee and McKinley in Baltimore. James Crossin and John Jenkins were deputy U.S. marshals in Philadelphia during the 1850s. On three occasions in 1853–54, local abolitionists charged Crossin and Jenkins with assault and battery with deadly intent when they attempted to arrest fugitive slaves. Each time they were acquitted. Crossin later worked at the U.S. Mint. The "Stewart" to whom Still refers was probably Joseph Stewert of the Philadelphia police. *Baltimore City Directory*, 1856–60; *Philadelphia City Directory*, 1854–60; Campbell, *Slave Catchers*, 139–41.

2. William H. Gatchell, Sr., an attorney, and his son, William H. Gatchell, Jr., lived in the same Baltimore household. The younger Gatchell represented his father's interests as claimant and chief witness in the Tiffney case. *Baltimore City Directory*, 1856–60.

3. William S. Pierce (1825–?) was a wealthy Philadelphia attorney and an active member of the Pennsylvania Anti-Slavery Society. He regularly defended blacks threatened with enslavement under the Fugitive Slave Law of 1850 and helped represent those arrested in the Christiana affair. U.S. Census, 1850; *PF*, 27 January 1853; *WAA*, 1 October 1859, 19 May 1860 [12:0097, 0718]; Still, *Underground Railroad*, 381, 593.

4. Daniel Dougherty, an Irish immigrant, worked as an attorney in Philadelphia throughout the 1850s. He was active in the local Democratic party. *Philadelphia City Directory*, 1850–60; *NASS*, 31 January 1857.

5. David Paul Brown, Jr. (1829–1869), a Philadelphia attorney, became federal fugitive slave commissioner for Philadelphia in 1854 upon the death of Edward D. Ingraham. He earned the animosity of the local black community for his enforcement of the Fugitive Slave Law. John Hill Martin, *Martin's Bench and Bar of Philadelphia* (Philadelphia, Pa., 1883), 252; *NASS*, 14 February 1857 [10:0542]; *WAA*, 19 May 1860 [12:0718].

6. Still compares the actions of Daniel Dougherty and David Paul Brown, Jr., to those of Edward D. Ingraham, John K. Kane, and George F. Alberti—three

other Philadelphians renowned for their enforcement of the Fugitive Slave Law. Ingraham (1793–1854), an attorney and legal scholar, was among the first Pennsylvanians named as a federal fugitive slave commissioner. He remained in that position until his death, earning the enmity of local blacks, particularly for his role in deputizing slave catchers and issuing treason charges in the wake of the Christiana affair. Kane (1795–1858), a prominent jurist and Democratic party figure, served briefly as attorney general of Pennsylvania before his 1846 appointment to the U.S. District Court in Philadelphia. He heard several fugitive cases, including the trial of the Christiana rioters, and urged the use of federal troops to prevent fugitive slave rescues. Alberti (1801–?), a dentist, was frequently hired by southern claimants to hunt for fugitive slaves. The local black community labeled him a "notorious kidnapper." *ACAB*, 3:350–51; Jonathan Katz, *Resistance at Christiana: The Fugitive Slave Rebellion, Christiana, Pennsylvania, September 11, 1851, A Documentary Account* (New York, N.Y., 1974), 74–75, 128, 333n; Still, *Underground Railroad*, 362, 366, 377; *NCAB*, 11:190; Campbell, *Slave Catchers*, 97, 133, 140–43, 153; U.S. Census, 1850; *PFW*, 22 December 1855 [9:0986].

7. On 17 January 1857, G. M. Wynkoop, a U.S. deputy marshal, prevented black observers from entering the courtroom where Henry Tiffney's case was being heard. Defense attorney William S. Pierce compared Wynkoop's behavior to that of the Star Chamber, a royal prerogative court in Tudor-Stuart England that denied defendants basic rights of English common law. *NASS*, 31 January 1857; M. M. Knappen, *Constitutional and Legal History of England* (Hamden, Conn., 1964), 317–19, 425.

8. David Paul Brown, Sr. (1795–1872), of Philadelphia, a respected trial lawyer and prolific playwright, became an active abolitionist in the 1830s. Local blacks praised him for defending the Christiana rioters and representing numerous individuals arrested as fugitive slaves. But in the late 1850s, they were outraged when Brown excused the actions of his son, David Paul Brown, Jr., then employed as a federal fugitive slave commissioner, and represented Ellen B. Wells of St. Louis in her libel suit against black abolitionist William Still. *DAB*, 3:111–12; *Lib*, 30 July 1836 [1:0677]; *CA*, 20 February 1841 [3:0904]; *PF*, 27 January 1853; *NASS*, 14 February 1857 [10:0542]; *WAA*, 2, 30 June 1860 [12:0775, 0843, 0844]; Still, *Underground Railroad*, 381, 593.

74.
Speech by Robert Purvis
Delivered at the City Assembly Rooms
New York, New York
12 May 1857

The U.S. Supreme Court's decision in the case of *Dred Scott* v. *Sanford* dealt a devastating blow to hopes for racial progress. Chief Justice Roger B. Taney's written opinion that Afro-Americans "had no rights which a white man was bound to respect" left blacks stunned and disheartened. William Still reported that some Philadelphia blacks felt "hopelessly doomed," while others saw only a "faint prospect" for improvement. Another black abolitionist characterized the ruling as one in which "slavery is made 'the supreme law of the land' and all descendants of the African race denationalized." Speaking before the annual meeting of the American Anti-Slavery Society on 12 May 1857, two months after the decision was issued, Robert Purvis conveyed the prevailing mood of resentment, anger, and despair. William Lloyd Garrison chaired the session, which attracted some two thousand abolitionists to the City Assembly Rooms in New York City. A furious Purvis informed his audience that he was now convinced that the U.S. Constitution was a proslavery document to which blacks owed no allegiance. Other black leaders shared Purvis's pessimism and outrage, when, in the wake of the Dred Scott decision, black abolitionism reached its most discouraging moment. Pease and Pease, *They Who Would Be Free*, 240–44; Quarles, *Black Abolitionists*, 230–35; *PFW*, 28 March, 25 April 1857 [10:0596, 0663]; *NASS*, 18 April, 16, 23 May 1857.

Mr. Chairman:

In allowing my name to be published as one of the speakers for this morning, which I have consented to do, at the earnest request of the Committee,[1] it is due to myself to say that I have acted with great reluctance. Not that I am not deeply interested in this cause, nor that I have not clear convictions and strong feelings on the subject. On the contrary, my interest is too intense for expression, and my convictions and feelings are so vivid and overpowering that I cannot trust myself in attempting to give them utterance. Sir, I envy those who, with cooler blood or more mental self-command, can rise before an audience like this, and deliberately choose their words and speak their thoughts in calm, measured phrase. This is a task, sir, to which I am not adequate. I must either say too much or too little. If I let my heart play freely and speak out what I think and feel, I am extravagant, as people call it. If I put a curb on my feelings and try to imitate the cool and unimpassioned manner of others,

I cannot speak at all. Sir, how can any man with blood in his veins, and a heart pulsating in his bosom, and especially how can any coloured man, think of the oppression of this country and of the wrongs of his race, and then express himself with calmness and without passion. (Applause.)

Mr. Chairman, look at the facts—here, in a country with a sublimity of impudence that knows no parallel, setting itself up before the world as a *free country*, a *land of liberty!*, "the *land of the free*, and the *home of the brave*," the "*freest country in all the world!*" Gracious God! and yet here are millions of men and women groaning under a bondage the like of which the world has never seen—bought and sold, whipped, manacled, killed all the day long. Yet this is a *free country!* The people have the assurance to talk of their *free institutions*. How can I speak of such a country and use language of moderation? How can I, who, every day, feel the grinding hoof of this despotism, and who am myself identified with its victims? Sir, let others, who can, speak coolly on this subject; I cannot, and I will not. (Applause.)

Mr. Chairman, that I may make sure of expressing the precise sentiment which I wish to present to this meeting, I will offer a resolution. It is one which I had the honour of presenting to a meeting lately held in the City of Philadelphia, but to which I did not speak as I could have desired,[2] for the reasons which I have already stated. The resolution is as follows:

> Resolved, That to attempt, as some do, to prove that there is no support given to slavery in the Constitution and essential structure of the American Government is to argue against reason and common sense, to ignore history and shut our eyes against palpable facts; and that while it may suit white men, who do not feel the iron heel, to please themselves with such theories, it ill becomes the man of colour, whose daily experience refutes the absurdity, to indulge in any such idle phantasies.

Mr. Chairman, this resolution expresses just what I think and feel about this newfangled doctrine of the anti-slavery character of the American Constitution. Sir, with all due respect to the Hon. Gerrit Smith, who is a noble and a good man, and one whom, from my soul, I honour with all due respect—I say to the nobleminded, largehearted Gerrit Smith, I must say, that the doctrine of the anti-slavery character of the American Constitution seems to me one of the most absurd and preposterous that ever was broached. It is so contrary to history and common sense, so opposite to what we and every man, and especially every coloured man, feel and know to be the fact, that I have not patience to argue about it. I know it is said that the word "slave" or "slavery" is not to be found in the document. Neither are these words to be found in the Fugitive Slave law. But will any man pretend, on this account, that that infamous statute is an anti-slavery statute, or that it is not one of the most atrocious and damnable laws that ever disgraced the annals of despotism. (Applause.) I know, sir, that there are some fine phrases in the Preamble about "establishing justice" and "securing to ourselves and our posterity the blessings of liberty." But what does that prove? Does it prove that the Constitution of the United States is an anti-slavery document? Then Mr. Buchanan's late Message was an anti-slavery document, and Mr. Buchanan himself a great Abolitionist.[3] Then were all the Messages of your contemptible President Pierce[4] anti-slavery documents, and your contemptible President Pierce was not contemptible, but a much misunderstood and misrepresented Abolitionist. If these fine phrases make the Constitution anti-slavery, then all the Fourth of July orations delivered by pro-slavery doughfaces at the North, and Democratic slave-breeders at the South, all these are anti-slavery documents. Sir, this talk about the Constitution being anti-slavery seems to me so utterly at variance with common sense and what we know to be facts that, as I have already intimated, I have no patience with it. I have no particular objection, Mr. Chairman, to white men, who have little to feel on this subject, to amuse themselves with such theories; but I must say that when I see them imitated by coloured men, I am disgusted! Sir, have we no self respect? Are we to clank the chains that have been made for us, and praise the men who did the deed? Are we to be kicked and scouted, trampled upon and judicially declared to *"have no rights which white men are bound to respect,"* and then turn round and glorify and magnify the laws under which all this is done? Are we such base, soulless, spiritless sycophants as all this? Sir, let others do as they may, I never will stultify or disgrace myself by eulogizing a government that tramples me and all that are dear to me in the dust. (Applause.)

Sir, I treat as an absurdity, an idle phantasy, the idea of the Constitution of this American Union being anti-slavery; on the contrary, I assert that the Constitution is fitting and befitting those who made it—slaveholders and their abettors—and I am free to declare, without any fears of successful contradiction, that the Government of the United States, in its formation and essential structure as well as in its practice, is one of the basest, meanest, most atrocious despotisms that ever saw the face of the sun. (Applause.) And I rejoice, sir, that there is a prospect of this atrocious government being overthrown, and a better one built up in its place. I rejoice in the revolution which is now going on. I honour, from the bottom of my soul, I honour this glorious Society for the part, the leading part, it has taken in this noble work. My heart overflows with gratitude to the self-sacrificing men and women of this Society who have been pioneers in this cause—men and women who, from the beginning till this time, in storm and whatever of sunshine they have had, through evil report and good report, have stood by the side of the slave and unfalteringly maintained the rights of free men of colour. Sir, I cannot sufficiently express, the English language has not words strong enough to express, my admiration of the Abolitionists of this country, and my gratitude to them for what they have done for the confessedly oppressed coloured people in it. And in saying this, I believe I utter the sentiments of all the true coloured men in the country. I know, sir, there are coloured men, some of them occupying prominent places before the public, who lose no opportunity of traducing and misrepresenting the character and course of the Garrisonian Abolitionists; but, sir, these are men without principle, men who are actuated by the basest selfishness, and in whose hearts there is not a spark of genuine love for the cause of freedom. They value anti-slavery not for what it is in itself, or for what it is doing for the slave, but for what it does or fails to do for themselves personally. Sir, I should be ashamed and mortified to believe that these men represented truly the views and feelings of the people of colour in this country. They do not.

But, Mr. Chairman, I am getting away from the subject of the resolution; and, as I have occupied more time than I intended, I will bring my remarks to a close at once, making way for one who, though following after, is greatly preferred before us—one upon whom no higher praise can be pronounced than the simple enunciation of his name—Wendell Phillips. (Applause.)

National Anti-Slavery Standard (New York, N.Y.), 23 May 1857.

1. Purvis spoke at the request of the executive committee of the American Anti-Slavery Society.

2. This is one of four resolutions on the proslavery nature of the U.S. Constitution that Purvis presented at a 2 April 1857 meeting in Philadelphia. The gathering at Israel Congregational Methodist Church had been called by local blacks to respond to the U.S. Supreme Court's decision in *Dred Scott* v. *Sanford*. After Purvis, Charles L. Remond, and others spoke to support the resolutions, they were quickly adopted. *ASB*, 11 April 1857 [10:0644].

3. Purvis refers to the 4 March 1857 inaugural address of President James Buchanan, in which Buchanan discussed the pending decision of the U.S. Supreme Court in *Dred Scott* v. *Sanford* and concluded that it would solve the crisis over the extension of slavery into the territories. Buchanan (1791–1868), a Pennsylvania Democrat, had a lengthy career in national politics as a member of Congress, secretary of state during the Mexican War, and minister to Russia and Britain. Elected to the presidency in 1856 with the overwhelming support of the South, he strictly enforced federal laws on slavery. During his last months in office, Buchanan witnessed the beginnings of Southern secession. *DAB*, 3:207–14.

4. Franklin Pierce.

75.
Speech by Edward Scott
Delivered at the Roger Williams Freewill Baptist Church
Providence, Rhode Island
6 October 1857

Slavery and racism shaped a distinct black theological perspective. By the 1850s, many black clergymen viewed abolitionism as part of their gospel mandate—their sermons carried antislavery messages, and their churches were centers of abolitionist activity. Rev. Edward Scott, a black pastor in Providence, Rhode Island, discussed the differences between black and white clergy during a session of the Freewill Baptist Anti-Slavery Society on 6 October 1857. Rev. C. O. Libby from Parsonsfield, Maine, presided over the meeting, which convened in a local white church. After two white ministers endorsed moral suasion in their comments, Scott was asked to respond. Scott, a fugitive slave, employed personal examples to denounce the hypocrisy of slaveholding Christians, the inadequacy of clerical pacifism, and the silence of northern missionary societies. Although Scott praised fellow Freewill Baptists for their stance on antislavery and black rights, he reminded them that should they deviate from those principles, they would hear from "poor Edward." Monroe Fordham, *Major Themes in Northern Black Religious Thought, 1800–1860* (Hicksville, N.Y., 1975), 11–51; *MSt*, 14, 21 October 1857.

Mr. President:

It has been said by some of our learned men that the slaves, if emancipated, would not be able to take care of themselves. Now, do I not look as though I took care of myself, Mr. President? Look at me well, and see if I don't look as though I took pretty good care of myself. So much for that argument. I've stove it all in pieces. (*A Voice.* Was Bro. Scott[1] ever emancipated?) No, I ran away, taking leg bail. I was thinking, while Bro. Dunn was speaking,[2] of Christianity among slaveholders. Now, I am a kind of President of the Underground Railroad, and once helped to get one of Henry Clay's slaves away. He used to drive old Henry round. A few years before he ran away, he said his master thought he experienced religion. But all he could say was, "whereas I was once blind, now I see. And yet," said the runaway, "he sold my son." Good Christian still. I tell *you*, Mr. President, I believe but little in the religion of the South. My old mistress was one of the greatest Christians you ever saw. Why, she was brimful of religion. I want to tell you just how she used to serve me. She used to tie me to the bedpost and whip me. I remember one time, just as she was doing it, the minister came in. And O you ought to have seen the long face she put on as she said, "they are so bad, I am obliged to correct them." And so the minister prayed. And heaven knows, I was all the time praying that the devil would take both woman and minister. I have known much of religion in the South. In many places, where the blacks are to be preached to, the smallest boy can tell what the text is to be. They have got it by heart—"*Servants be obedient to your masters.*" So time serving are Southern ministers. And many at the North are not two cents better. Mr. President, you all know that I am a fugitive. And knowing what I know of slavery, and feeling what I have felt of it, if called upon to go back to it, I would say, "give me liberty or give me death." This is the doctrine preached down there in *Pond Street.*³ Ministers preach against fighting. That is very well. But in the name of God, how can fugitives join the Peace Society, with Judge Taney at their back?⁴ White folks' religion won't do for black folks anyhow. The devil is at our heels every day in the shape of slaveholders.

Mr. President, a few weeks ago I sat in that great gathering in this city of all the great ministers in the country. I watched their prayers, and heard not one of them pray for the sin of our nation. I looked at them, and was so wicked—I confess it to you, but I would not to one of those creatures—that I said in my heart, O you palefaced hypocrites! They had agreed to keep still, and did.⁵ Send missionaries to the heathen, and shed great crocodile tears as big as your fist! In the name of God, how is it that God calls so many to preach to the heathen, and none to the South? This is a puzzler to me. I should think somebody would be called to take their lives in their hands and preach to the heathen of the South.

Today while standing here as a representative of three millions of my brethren, I feel grateful as a man and as a Christian that my lot was ever cast among Freewill Baptists.⁶ And now all I want is that you should take this subject right home to yourselves. Go with me for a moment into the South. You are sitting with your family around your fireside. A being walks in, in the shape of a man, and begins to feel of the hands and head of your boy and girl, and says to your boy, "I have bought you, you must go with me." How would you feel, mothers and fathers? Now take this matter right home to yourselves.

I have often told some of you how I was taken and carried on board the slave ship. When I was thirteen years old, a man put handcuffs on me, and carried me on board the *Sea King* (?) on Norfolk river. O, I thought if I could only see mother once more, I should be willing to go. But, alas! of this I was deprived; but in an unexpected moment, a young man came to the hold of the vessel and said, "Edward, your father is alongside." And there was my old greyheaded father in a canoe. Said he, "Edward, is that you?" "It is," I answered, and I dropped my head over the bulwark and mingled my tears with his in the river. And I remember what he said to me. "My child, I can do nothing for you. Get religion.

Get the religion of Jesus Christ, and then if we meet no more here, we will meet where there is no slavery." *No slavery!* And sometimes when I think of it, knowing that the old man, and mother too, died in the triumphs of faith, and see the sin of this nation, I am almost ready to say,

> Fly swiftly round ye wheels of time,
> And bring the joyful day.

Brethren, I feel safe among you. No other denomination in the United States, I think, takes so decided anti-slavery ground as you. We shall all have equal rights in heaven. You have a fine church here without a Jim Crow pew. You always give me a seat, but should you ever turn a cold shoulder to poor Edward, he will tell you of it.

Morning Star (Dover, N.H.), 21 October 1857.

1. Edward Scott (ca. 1812–1864), a black Freewill Baptist clergyman, was one of the leading antislavery activists in antebellum Providence, Rhode Island. He was born to slave parents at Norfolk, Virginia. At about age thirteen, he was separated from his family and sent to the slave market at New Orleans, but he soon stowed away on a vessel bound for New York City. After living for a time in York, Maine, he joined the Freewill Baptist denomination and began preaching throughout New England. He was ordained in 1845 and served the Second Freewill Baptist Church in Providence from that time until 1864. Scott also worked as a clock repairer as his parishioners were too poor to support him. The black working-class congregation grew quickly under his leadership and became a center for local antislavery activities. Although he joined other local black clergymen in defending separate churches, he strongly supported George T. Downing's efforts to integrate the public schools of Rhode Island.

Working outside of traditional antislavery organizations, Scott acquired a reputation as one of the city's leading abolitionists. He organized local First of August celebrations and directed efforts to aid and protect fugitive slaves in the city. In 1848 he helped organize the Rhode Island Committee of Vigilance, which used his church as a base of operations. When the Fugitive Slave Law was passed in 1850, Scott rallied local blacks and persuaded them to "use every means" to protect those threatened by the enactment. He was popularly regarded as a "kind of President of the Underground Railroad." Scott influenced the antislavery sentiments of his denomination through his participation in the Freewill Baptist Anti-Slavery Society. At the organization's 1850 meeting, he publicly revealed his fugitive slave status for the first time and persuaded the society to advocate militant resistance to the Fugitive Slave Law. With the coming of emancipation, Scott felt "specially called" to do mission work among the former slaves in the South. In April 1864, he resigned his charge and accepted an American Missionary Association assignment in South Carolina. After laboring briefly in Beaufort, he and his wife Mary operated a mission school and farm for the freedmen at nearby Parris Island. Scott was surprised by the destitute condition of the blacks there and troubled by the cultural differences he encountered, but he hoped to positively influence the "rising generation." He died less than six months after leaving Providence. U.S. Census, 1850; Gideon A. Burgess and J. T. Ward, *Free Baptist Cyclopaedia* (Chicago, Ill., 1889), 589; *MSt*, 21 October 1857; Robert G. Sherer, Jr., "Negro Churches in Rhode Island before 1860," *RIH* 25:21–22 (January 1966); *Providence City Directory*, 1847–56; Edward Scott Manuscripts, Newspaper Clipping File, RHi [5:0780, 1053, 7:0107, 10:0754, 11:0303, 0604]; *WAA*, 10 August 1861; Norman A. Baxter, *History of the Freewill Baptists: A Study in New England Separatism* (Rochester, N.Y., 1957), 97–98; Edward Scott to American Missionary Association, 28 February 1864, George T. Day to George Whipple, 29 February 1864, Edward Scott to William E. Whiting, 10 June 1864, Edward Scott to George Whipple, 12 May, 22 July 1864, AMA-ARC [15:0262–63, 0348, 0397, 0461–63].

2. Ransom Dunn (1818–1900), a Boston clergyman and key figure in the Freewill Baptist Anti-Slavery Society, urged the audience to employ moral suasion, arguing that "our anti-slavery work yet has chiefly to do with conscience." Before coming to Boston, Dunn had served Freewill Baptist churches in northern New England and done extensive missionary work in the Midwest. He later became president of Hillsdale College in Michigan. *MSt*, 14 October 1857; Ransom Dunn Papers, Michigan Historical Collections, Bentley Historical Library, MiU; *Lib*, 17 November 1843; Baxter, *History of Freewill Baptists*, 80, 90.

3. The Second Freewill Baptist Church at the corner of Pond and Angle streets was among the most militant black institutions in antebellum Providence. The working-class congregation had the distinction of being the only black Freewill Baptist church in New England before 1880. It was organized in 1835 by Rev. John W. Lewis and ten local blacks as the Abyssinian Freewill Baptist Church. After worshiping in other churches and rented halls for six years, they built a small meetinghouse and adopted a new name. Edward Scott served as pastor between 1845 and 1864; under his leadership, the congregation grew to eighty members and became a key point on the underground railroad. The Second Freewill Baptist Church battled declining membership and persistent financial problems after the Civil War but continued to serve the local black community for several decades. Sherer, "Negro Churches in Rhode Island," 20–22; "African Church in Providence, R.I.," 9 April 1849, Newspaper Clipping File, RHi [5:1053]; *WAA*, 3 September 1865; Baxter, *History of Freewill Baptists*, 159n.

4. Several Providence clergymen belonged to the Rhode Island Peace Society, a small but active organization founded in 1818 by local Quakers that advocated pacifist principles and the efficacy of nonresistance as a defensive technique. Scott contended that pacifism would be ludicrous for blacks when they were denied due process by the Fugitive Slave Law of 1850, which was consistently upheld by Chief Justice Roger B. Taney and the U.S. Supreme Court. Like other local black leaders, he counseled violent resistance to slave catchers. Peter Brock, *Radical Pacifists in Antebellum America* (Princeton, N.J., 1968), 185–87, 270; Robert J. Cottrol, *The Afro-Yankees: Providence's Black Community in the Antebellum Era* (Westport, Conn., 1982), 92; "Meeting of Colored Citizens," 23 September [1851], Newspaper Clipping File, RHi [7:0107].

5. Scott refers to the annual meeting of the American Board of Commissioners for Foreign Missions, which convened during 8–11 September 1857 at the Beneficent Congregational Church in Providence. Over four hundred clergymen, mostly Congregationalists, attended, including prominent American divines such

as Richard S. Storrs, Leonard Bacon, and the notorious Nehemiah Adams. As at other ABCFM gatherings, delegates consistently avoided discussion of the slavery question. *MissH*, October 1857; McKivigan, *War against Proslavery Religion*, 112–18.

6. The Freewill Baptist denomination was founded in 1780 by Benjamin Randall, a New Hampshire tailor influenced by the preaching of George Whitefield and a belief in the freedom of the will and the possibility of universal atonement. The new denomination grew by 1830 to more than twenty-one thousand members throughout the North. Largely a revivalistic lay movement, it appealed primarily to farmers, artisans, and the urban working class. Freewill Baptists actively opposed slavery and intemperance and did extensive missionary and educational work among southern freedmen after the Civil War. In 1911 the denomination merged with the American Baptist Convention, the major body of northern Baptists. Baxter, *History of Freewill Baptists*.

76.
George E. Stephens to Jacob C. White, Jr.
8 January 1858

A majority of active black abolitionists were freeborn in the North, lacked a personal knowledge of slavery, and acquired information about the institution by reading antislavery literature or hearing the testimony of former slaves. Those few who ventured South were unprepared for the realities of life there. When George E. Stephens, a Philadelphia cabinetmaker traveling on board a U.S. Coast Survey vessel, visited Charleston, South Carolina, in December 1857, he was seized by local authorities under provisions of the state's Negro Seamen's Act, which required that all free black sailors be incarcerated for the duration of their stay in port. Later released through the intervention of the ship's captain, he spoke with slaves and observed slavery and the domestic slave trade firsthand. Stephens described these experiences in an 8 January 1858 letter to Jacob C. White, Jr., a close friend and fellow Philadelphian. He advised White that, regardless of what he had learned about slavery, "you must become a witness yourself." Stephens later returned to South Carolina with invading Union forces during the Civil War. Remembering his earlier visit to Charleston, he hoped to burn the city with "Greek fire" and dig rebel graves "beneath its smoldering ruins." Pease and Pease, *They Who Would Be Free*, 288–89; *WAA*, 10 October 1863.

> U.S. Steamer Walker[1]
> Pensacola, Fl[orida]
> January 8th, 1858

Dr Sir:

Two months have elapsed since I bade adieu to my friends in Philadelphia. I have since my departure visited the ports of Charleston, S.C., Key West[,] Cedar Keys and this place. I have doubled Cape Hatteras, passed in sight of Cape Moro light,[2] and am safe and sound upon the Northern shore of [the] Gulf of Mexico. Two months is an age to be without "news from home." I have not received a single line from any one in Phil. since our good ship weighed anchor at Phil. I have written [several] to my Friends. But they have all forgotten me. I have received 3 letters from my wife (she is in York). She informs me informs me of her own and the Boys good health.

I must first tell you of my adventures in Charleston. On the 25th of Nov. the Walker dropped down the Delaware, to the Breakwater on the 27th put to sea, bound for Charleston, at which place we arrived on the second of december. My duty on board this ship required that I should go on shore. The laws of South Carrolina forbade my doing so. The day after I arrived I was ordered ashore, and obeyed. No one observed me, particularly. I of course continued to go on shore until the 15th when as I was walking up King street I was seized by the minions of the accursed slave power, and arraigned before the mayor of the city, for merely treading upon the soil that Slavery blights. Fortunately for me, a young gentleman, an acquaintance of Captain Hueger (the Cap't of the Walker), saw the arrest and informed him immediately of the condition of affairs. The Captain rendered securities and I was released.[3] This is one item. You sir have not perhaps been south of Masons and Dixson line, and Judge slavery therefore by the testimony you receive. You must witness it in all its loathsomeness. You must become a witness yourself. On the 5th of Dec. I was seated in the stearn sheets of one of our boats going on shore. As I neared the wharf I saw a crowd of half clad, filthy looking men[,] women and children to go on bord the Savanna steamer. Poor wreches. 3 or 4 overseers[4] stood around. I took my stand[,] noticed every feature that I could get suffeceantly near for the purpose. In all that vast number, 2 or 300, I did not notice one smile. All were moody[,] silent[,] sorrowful. I see in this gang both sexes and all ages from the sucking Babe to the decrepid old, all bartered and sold to the rice swamp.[5] I walked up the street, passed the post office[,] turned up a large throughafare, the name of which I know not. The first thing that attracted my especial was a large sighn <u>Negroes and</u> lands for sale, with all kinds of farming impliments. I passed on a little farther and I see a large open room[,] over the door Broker's office. But you must understand that this means, A Negro Seller.[6] Two or 3 half-starved looking wreches were seated around. The very Earth seemd to tremble for the guilt of the oppressor. I walked on and came to a large cemetery. This told me that death lays his icy hands on many a guilty head, and is the avenger of many a vile wrong—the finger of God is laid upon Charleston. Every stone[,] every Avenue, bears upon it the mark of decay—lean squalid wobegone slaves dressed in lindsey-wolsey.[7] Broken carts, with Emaciated steads (mules), present the most ridiculous appearance. I did not see a stout fat looking Colored man during [word crossed out] my stay in the above place.

A few days after my perambulation about the streets of Charleston, I met a young man by the name of McKinley—with whom I have become acquainted in Phil.[8] I wished him to take a cigar with me, he told me he would accept it but that he dare not smoke in the sto[re]. He informed me that it was against the law, for a Colored man to smoke a cigar or walk with a cane in the streets of Charleston. And if the streets (sidewalk) are crowded the negro must take the ~~near~~ middle of the street. I met several white men, they did not pretend to move an inch—so I had always to give way to them. I have been informed since that if I had run against one of them, they would have had me flogged.[9] Poor wreches.

Little do they accomplish by such trivial proscriptions, such miserable oppressions serves not one single degree to curb the spirit of even a crushed and injured African.

One can witness here what education can effect. The Blacks here invariably believe that white men are superior not meerly mentally, but physically. I had occassion to have some clothes washed and called on an old woman for that purpose. I found that this woman was a slave. Several little white children were running about the house, and whenever she called them she always prefixed master or mistress. I could not stand this and reprimanded her. She was perfectly astonished, commenced and argument with me to prove that these children were entitled to this distinction. By way of a caution she told me I must not talk this way— some of the people might overhear me and tell master. My space is almost consumed. I must conclude with the conclusion that Charleston is a vast conglomeration of Negroes, rice and filth. In a word the half-way house on the pathway of wrong to the region of the dammed.

Trusting that you are well, and that I may hear from you soon. I remain very truly yours,

G. E. Stephens[10]

P.S. Direct your letters to me on board the Walker, Brashere City, St. Marys Parish, La.[11]

Jacob C. White, Jr., Papers, Moorland-Spingarn Research Center, Howard University, Washington, D.C. Published by permission.

1. The *U.S.S. Walker*, an iron-hulled steamer, was constructed in 1845 for the Revenue Cutter Service. Transferred to the U.S. Coast Survey in 1852, it regularly recorded wind speed, water and air temperatures, water depth, current speed and direction, and other data along the Atlantic and Gulf coasts of the United States. It sank off the New Jersey shore in 1860. Paul H. Silverstone, *Warships of the Civil War Navies* (Annapolis, Md., 1989), 145; Log Book, U.S. Coast Survey Steamer *Walker*, 1854–55, RG 23, Records of the Coast and Geodetic Survey, DNA.

2. On its voyage from Philadelphia to Pensacola, the *U.S.S. Walker* passed Cape Hatteras, the site of a major lighthouse on the North Carolina coast. Along the way, it visited the port of Charleston and refueling stations at Key West and Cedar Key, Florida. While rounding the southern tip of Florida, the *Walker* passed within view of Morro lighthouse at the entrance to the harbor at Havana, Cuba.

3. As Stephens walked up King Street, the major north-south thoroughfare in antebellum Charleston, he was arrested under provisions of the state's Negro Seamen's Act (1822). He was taken before the mayor's court, which was presided over by Charles Macbeth, a prosperous attorney and Charleston's mayor from 1857 through the end of the Civil War. Macbeth rigorously enforced state and local black laws and led a movement to expel or reenslave the city's free blacks. Stephens was released after Lieutenant Thomas B. Huger, captain of the *Walker*,

posted the bond required by the Negro Seamen's Act. Huger (1820–1862), a member of one of Charleston's leading families, served in the U.S. Navy from 1835 until the Civil War; he was killed in 1862 while serving with the Confederate navy in the lower Mississippi valley. Michael P. Johnson and James L. Roark, eds., *No Chariot Let Down: Charleston's Free People of Color on the Eve of the Civil War* (Chapel Hill, N.C., 1984), 93–96, 103–6, 127; *NCAB*, 5:13; Isaac Toucey to Thomas B. Huger, 29 September 1859, Correspondence of Alexander Dallas Bache, Superintendent of the Coast and Geodetic Survey, 1843–65, DNA.

4. Overseers supervised field labor and administered slave discipline on antebellum southern plantations.

5. Ninety-six percent of the rice produced in the United States during the 1850s was grown in a narrow band of tidal swamplands along coastal North Carolina, South Carolina, and Georgia. Because of the backbreaking labor involved and the various diseases native to the region, most of it was planted, cultivated, and harvested by slaves. *DAAS*, 644–47.

6. Stephens walked up East Bay Street, a major thoroughfare that paralleled the wharves along the Cooper River. After passing the Old Post Office and Exchange, he probably headed west on Broad Street where he would have passed the offices of at least ten brokers who bought and sold slaves. These included the Shingler Brothers at 7 Broad Street and Louis D. DeSaussure at 23 Broad Street, probably the two brokers to whom Stephens refers. Frederic Bancroft, *Slave Trading in the Old South* (New York, N.Y., 1959), 165–96.

7. Linsey-woolsey is a coarse sturdy fabric woven from wool and linen.

8. Stephens refers to William J. McKinlay (1835–?), a wealthy member of Charleston's mulatto elite who was probably educated in Philadelphia during the late 1840s. McKinlay taught at a Freedmen's Bureau school in Orangeburg, South Carolina, after the Civil War. He joined the Republican party and was elected as a delegate to the state constitutional convention of 1868. From 1868 to 1870, he represented Charleston in the state legislature, voting with white conservatives on economic issues and with the Radical Republicans on civil rights questions. In 1874 he joined other black businessmen to build the Charleston and Sullivan's Island Railroad, which connected the city with several of the Sea Islands. McKinlay continued to influence local Republican party politics once Reconstruction ended. Holt, *Black over White*, 37n–38, 71, 149–50, 165, 236; Alrutheus A. Taylor, *The Negro in South Carolina during Reconstruction* (New York, N.Y., 1924), 291.

9. In their daily lives, Charleston's free blacks guarded against breaches of racial etiquette that might be considered acts of insolence, such as failing to remove a hat or neglecting to yield the sidewalk to a passing white. Local ordinances forbade free blacks to smoke a cigar or pipe or to carry a cane in public. Offenders received twenty lashes and forfeited the cigar, pipe, or cane to any white who seized it from them. Michael P. Johnson and James L. Roark, *Black Masters: A Free Family of Color in the Old South* (New York, N.Y., 1984), 48–49; Marina Wikramanayake, *A World in Shadow: The Free Black in Antebellum South Carolina* (Columbia, S.C., 1973), 69.

10. George E. Stephens (1832–1888), a Philadelphia cabinetmaker, was the son of free blacks from Virginia. In 1854 he helped found the Banneker Institute, a black literary and debating society that served as a training ground for the new

generation of local black leaders that emerged during the decade. From 1857 to 1859, Stephens worked for the U.S. Coast Survey as a carpenter and laborer aboard the *U.S.S. Walker*. An articulate and aggressive spokesman for black rights, Stephens helped shape the black response to the major events of the Civil War era. In early 1861, he urged northern blacks to join slaves in a violent insurrection. When war broke out, Stephens counseled blacks to withhold their support for the Union cause until they were accepted into the military on an equal basis with whites. During 1861–62, he traveled with the Army of the Potomac as a reporter for the *Weekly Anglo-African*. As he chronicled the conflict between Union and Confederate forces and the freedmen, Stephens determined that blacks would exercise a decisive influence upon the course of the war, eventually compelling the Lincoln administration to fight slavery. "The eternal logic of facts," he declared, "tells me that the negro henceforth and forever, holds the balance of power in this country."

In March 1863, after recruiting black troops for two months, Stephens enlisted in the Fifty-fourth Massachusetts Regiment; he was soon promoted to sergeant. Although wounded during the assault on Battery Wagner, he later took part in battles at Olustee, Florida, and Boykin's Mills, South Carolina. His many wartime letters to the *Anglo-African* reflected the mood of the black troops, particularly their resentment over the government's failure to grant them equal pay and the relentless prejudice of white soldiers. Stephens's criticisms probably prompted Brigadier General Quincy A. Gilmore's warning against comments on military matters in the press by black troops. Although Governor John A. Andrew of Massachusetts approved Stephens's promotion to first lieutenant in July 1865, the War Department rejected it because of his race.

Stephens was mustered out of service in August 1865 and returned to Philadelphia. In 1867 he established a freedmen's school near Port Royal, Virginia, supported by Philadelphia's Union League. Later that year, Stephens and his wife Susan organized the Tilghman School at Tappahannock, Virginia, with the assistance of several freedmen's aid associations. His involvement in local politics, clashes with the Freedmen's Bureau, and competition for financial support caused conflict between Stephens and other teachers at the school. After defaulting on accumulated debts, he left Virginia in January 1870. Three years later, he moved to Brooklyn and opened an upholstery shop. Wounds received at Fort Wagner plagued Stephens during his last years, and he died of hepatitis in April 1888. *WAA*, 26 November 1859, 17 February, 22 December 1860, 26 January 1861, 18 January, 1 February, 5, 26 April 1862; Compiled Military Service Records, Quincy A. Gilmore Circular Letter, 7 August 1863, Company Letterbooks, Fifty-fourth Massachusetts Regiment, File 392-Box 306, RG 94, Adjutant General's Office, U.S. Colored Troops, DNA; Pension File #517251, Certificate 382825, RG 15, DNA; George E. Stephens to Orlando Brown, 24 October 1867, George E. Stephens to Rev. R. M. Manly, 5 February 1869, Unregistered Letters, E-3826, Records of the Superintendent of Education for Virginia, James Johnson to Orlando Brown, 31 December 1867, Letters Received, Records of the Assistant Commissioner of Education for Virginia, E-3798, Teachers' Monthly School Reports, October 1868, April 1869, E-3831, List of Teachers in the Field, January 1869, Letters Received, Records of the Superintendent of Education, E-154, RG 105, Bureau of Refugees, Freedmen and Abandoned Lands, DNA; Betty

Mansfield, "The Fateful Class: Black Teachers of Virginia's Freedmen, 1861–1882" (Ph.D. diss., The Catholic University of America, 1980), 170–71, 220, 365–66.

11. Brashear City, Louisiana, was located at a widening of the Atchafalaya River on the Gulf of Mexico. Established in 1850, it became the western terminus of a railroad link to New Orleans and a key port for merchant steamers bound for Galveston and other Texas harbors. It was renamed Morgan City in 1876. Harry Hanson, ed., *Louisiana: A Guide to the State*, rev. ed. (New York, N.Y., 1971), 387–88.

77.
The Gloucester Family and John Brown

James N. Gloucester to John Brown
19 February 1858
9 March 1858

Elizabeth A. Gloucester to John Brown
18 August 1859

John Brown's October 1859 raid on the federal arsenal at Harpers Ferry, Virginia, was the antislavery crusade's most dramatic and violent moment. The raid had special meaning for black abolitionists. Brown had maintained close ties with leading blacks since the 1840s. More than thirty blacks attended the May 1858 convention at Chatham, Canada West, which planned the government to be put in place after Brown's insurrection. Five blacks fought at Harpers Ferry. Countless others offered moral and financial support. James N. Gloucester, a Brooklyn clergyman, and his wife Elizabeth were steadfast Brown supporters in the years before the raid. In a 19 February 1858 letter, Rev. Gloucester gave Brown his "heartiest consent and cooperation," while counseling him on the difficulties of mobilizing the free black population to support such a perilous and uncertain undertaking. On 9 March, he expressed his willingness to see violence employed on behalf of the slaves. Elizabeth Gloucester also encouraged Brown and sent him $25 in an 18 August 1859 letter. Benjamin Quarles, *Allies for Freedom: Blacks and John Brown* (New York, N.Y., 1974), 15–81.

Philadelphia, [Pennsylvania]
Feb[ruary] 19, 1858

Most Esteemed Friend:

Being called away from home by death—to Philadelphia—I have not as yet sent any answer to your first communication. I do so now. I was pleased to hear from you at last after so long silence. I thought perhaps you might have passed to your more immediate field of Premeditated Labour—having not seen or heard anything from you, for so long a time—but I rejoice that you are still, in life and health—with the same vigorous hopes as formerly. Your very commendable ~~Letter~~ measure to deliver the slave, has yet my heartiest consent and cooperation. I have never as yet faltered, in my previous asserted interest to you in the matter. All I need is the clear, inteligent watch-word of that Gallant Hero— distinguished in former triumphs—and then in David Crocket style.[1] I can go ahead, but you speak in your Letter of the people. I fear there is little to be done in the masses. The masses suffer for the want of inteligence—and it is difficult to reach them in a matter like you propose. So far as is necessary to secure their cooperation, the Colored People are impulsive—but they need Sagacity—Sagacity to distinguish their proper course.

They are like a Bark at sea without a commander or rudder ready to catch port—or no port just as it may be—and it is so difficult to strike a line to meet them. No one knows better than Mr. Douglass the truth of this. But however, I do not despair, I only note it—as it may form a part of the history of your undertakings—and that it may not otherwise dampe ardor.

I wish you sir Gods speed in your Glorious work—may nothing arise to prevent accomplishing. Your intended visit to this city will be cheering. Please to make my house your home. I am not at home now but will be in a few days. Your sincere Friend,

James N. Gloucester[2]

John Brown Collection, Manuscripts Department, Kansas State Historical Society, Topeka, Kansas. Published by permission.

Brooklyn, [New York]
March 9, 1858

Captain Brown:

Esteemed Sir, I regret that I cannot at this time be with you and friends convened in Philadelphia[3] but you have my heartiest wish, with all the true friends here, for your success.

I hope sir, you will find in that city, a large response—both in money and men—Pepared at your command to do battle to that ugly foe.

I am more and more convinced that now the day and now the hour, and that the proper mode is at last suggested, practically.

Long enough have we had this great evil in our land discussed in all its possible aspects. Long have we applied to it, as we have thought[,] all those the moral means that enlightened men are capable. But yet this evil, as a system[,] remains the same. They have not phased it, as yet, in one material point.

What then shall we do, is the only sensible question—to every true lover of God and man. Shall we go on—and still prosecute under these means—and thus as we have done for years signally fail, or shall we in the Language of that noble Patriot of his country (Patrick Henry), now use those means that God and nature has placed within our power. I hope Sir to this sentiment sir in Philadelphia there is but one response—for in that city reside some noble men and women whose hearts are always warmed and cheered at every rising hope for the slave. But Sir your measure anticipates not only for the abject slave, but to those colored men, north and south, who are but virtually <u>slaves</u>. There is in ~~no~~ truth no <u>black man</u>, north, or south of <u>mason</u> and <u>Dixion</u> Line—a <u>free-man</u> whatever be his wealth, position, or worth to the <u>world</u>. This is but the result of that <u>hellish system</u>, against which every honest man and <u>woman</u> in the Land should be combined. I hope Sir you will be able, assisted by those Eminent Gentlemen who accompany you—to make these things plain—and take their hold upon the Philadelphia mind, and join with you, in holy Energy and Combat against <u>the all damnable foe</u>. Let them see the Little Book[4] you presented to me, and so disipate their doubts and fears.

Please to put me down for (25) more to begin with. Yours for strug-gling universal rights,

J. N. Gloucester

P.S. Please to read to the friends assembled if thought best.

John Brown Collection, Manuscripts Department, Kansas State Historical So-ciety, Topeka, Kansas. Published by permission.

BROOKLYN, [New York]
Aug[ust] 18, 1859

Esteemed Friend:

I gladly avail myself of the opportunity afforded by our friend, Mr. F. Douglass, who has just called upon us previous to his visit to you,[5] to inclose to you for the cause in which you are such a zealous laborer a small amount, which please accept with my most ardent wishes for its and your benefit.

The visit of our mutual friend Douglass has somewhat revived my rather drooping spirits in the cause; but seeing such ambition and enter-prise in him, I am again encouraged. With best wishes for your welfare and prosperity, and the good of your cause, I subscribe myself, Your sincere friend,

MRS. E. A. GLOUCESTER[6]

P.S. Please write to me. With best respects to your son.[7]

Anglo-African Magazine (New York, N.Y.), December 1859.

1. David Crockett (1786–1836) was a popular hero of the American frontier who died defending the Alamo in February 1836. *DAB*, 4:555–56.

2. James Newton Gloucester was the son of John Gloucester, a prominent black Presbyterian clergyman in Philadelphia. The younger Gloucester was born in the city and worked as a clothes dealer there in the late 1830s. Like his father and brothers, Jeremiah and Stephen, he later entered the ministry; throughout his career, he filled Presbyterian pulpits in New York state, most of the time with the support of the American Home Missionary Society. After serving Buffalo and Brooklyn congregations during the early 1840s, Gloucester did mission work among the blacks of Brooklyn. His efforts resulted in the establishment of

Siloam Presbyterian Church, one of the leading black congregations in the city. Gloucester and his wife Elizabeth also accumulated considerable rental property and other real estate in Brooklyn. In late 1859, Gloucester left the city to serve the Liberty Street Presbyterian Church in Troy, but he returned after four years. He was a key figure in the Evangelical Association of the Colored Ministers of Congregational and Presbyterian Churches during this time.

Gloucester supported the abolitionist and temperance movements, opened his churches to reform lecturers, and attracted strident parishioners such as William J. Wilson and John N. Still. He had joined the antislavery cause during his Philadelphia years. In the early 1840s, he urged racial unity as a natural prerequisite to black advancement, published his ideas in a pamphlet called *Union* (1843), and used it to promote the revival of the black national convention movement. At the 1843 black national convention at Buffalo, Gloucester chaired the Committee on the Condition of the Colored People, which accumulated data on the size, wealth, employment, and cultural organizations of black communities throughout the North. He was a strong advocate of the black press, and in 1849 he briefly edited his own temperance paper called the *Delevan Union*.

The coming of the Civil War raised Gloucester's hopes for racial advancement. One of a handful of black abolitionists who worked closely with John Brown in the months preceding the Harpers Ferry raid, he openly endorsed John Brown's course once it failed. He believed that a sectional conflict would greatly advance civil rights and urged blacks to "hold on with a vigorous, preserving, unyielding grasp [to] your destinies." He criticized the advocates of emigration, particularly Henry Highland Garnet and the African Civilization Society, for giving up hope. As president of the American Freedmen's Friend Society in Brooklyn he supervised one of the most active relief organizations during the Civil War. Gloucester continued to live in Brooklyn through the 1880s. Connolly, *A Ghetto Grows in Brooklyn*, 10; *Philadelphia City Directory*, 1837; Curry, *Free Black in Urban America*, 187; *New York City Directory*, 1842–44; Samuel H. Cox to Milton Badger, 6 June 1845, James N. Gloucester to the American Home Missionary Society, 1 November 1848, N. S. S. Beman to Milton Badger, 17 February 1860, AHMS-ARC [5:0816]; Pease and Pease, *They Who Would Be Free*, 118, 293; *NP*, 24 September 1863 [14:1065–66]; *WAA*, 3, 24 September, 5 November 1859, 31 March, 14, 28 April 1860, 12 January 1861, 20 February 1864 [12:0010, 0069, 0195, 0597, 0631, 0657, 13:0190]; Winch, *Philadelphia's Black Elite*, 191n, 213n; James N. Gloucester, *Union: An Address on its Importance and Benefits to the People of Color* (New York, N.Y., 1843); *Convention of Colored Citizens . . . at Buffalo* (1843), 23, 36–39 [4:0643, 0649–51]; *VF*, 1 January 1851; *NSt*, 4 May, 29 June 1849 [5:1085]; Quarles, *Allies for Freedom*, 39–40; Quarles, *Black Abolitionists*, 242; James N. Gloucester to Frederick Douglass, 27 August 1888, Frederick Douglass Papers, DLC.

3. Gloucester refers to a 16 March 1858 meeting between John Brown and leading black abolitionists at the Philadelphia home of Stephen Smith, a wealthy black businessman and antislavery activist. Although Brown had invited many black leaders, only Smith, Frederick Douglass, Henry Highland Garnet, and William Still attended the session, where they probably heard an appeal for men and money to assist the planned Harpers Ferry raid. Quarles, *Allies for Freedom*, 39–41.

4. Gloucester may refer to a draft copy of John Brown's "Provisional Constitution and Ordinances for the People of the United States," which was intended to provide the structure for a temporary government following the Harpers Ferry raid. Brown wrote the document at Frederick Douglass's home in January 1858, then obtained the approval of his supporters at their May gathering in Chatham, Canada West. William Howard Day later published the work in booklet form. Quarles, *Allies for Freedom*, 39, 47–51.

5. Frederick Douglass visited the Gloucester home in Brooklyn en route to a meeting with John Brown at Chambersburg, Pennsylvania. Escorted by Shields Green, he delivered Elizabeth Gloucester's letter and $25 donation to Brown on 19 August 1858. Quarles, *Frederick Douglass*, 177.

6. Elizabeth A. Gloucester (1820–1883), a Richmond, Virginia, native, was the wife of Rev. James N. Gloucester of Brooklyn. An accomplished businesswoman, she operated her own furniture store and made a comfortable income by buying and selling real estate. She also served as the director of the Colored Orphan Asylum, promoted adult education for local blacks, and assisted her husband in various church functions. U.S. Census, 1850; Quarles, *Allies for Freedom*, 39–40; *WAA*, 24 March, 24 November 1860, 30 November 1861, 26 April 1862 [13:0005].

7. Gloucester probably refers to John Brown, Jr. (1821–1895), the eldest son of abolitionist martyr John Brown. Although active in the Kansas free-state movement, he did not participate in the Harpers Ferry raid but did tour the Northeast and Canada West, soliciting funds, weapons, and recruits for the cause. Brown commanded a company in the Union army during the Civil War. Oates, *Purge This Land with Blood*, 16, 84–87, 117, 120–32, 282–83, 316.

78.
Speech by Charles L. Remond
Delivered at Mozart Hall
New York, New York
13 May 1858

Black abolitionists lost faith in the American government during the years leading up to the Civil War. The downward course of federal policy in the 1850s, culminating in the Dred Scott decision, shattered black hopes that the government might become an instrument for abolishing slavery. Charles L. Remond, speaking before the annual meeting of the American Anti-Slavery Society on 13 May 1858, voiced the profound discouragement and political alienation that many blacks experienced. Surveying fifty years of antislavery activity, Remond spoke about failure, not progress. Pointing to the dramatic increase in the number of slave states and the pervasive influence of the slave power, he described white Americans as "destitute of feeling, and destitute of principle" on the slavery question. Remond's pessimistic assessment forced him to conclude that the dissolution of the Union was both necessary and inevitable. *Lib*, 12 March, 21 May 1858 [11:0176].

MR. CHAIRMAN, LADIES AND GENTLEMEN:

I have listened to a series of resolutions[1] every way important in their character, and involving many questions and considerations upon this great subject which must more or less interest all who are present; and congratulating, Mr. Chairman, as I do, yourself, and the members of this Society, and the friends of this cause, upon the numbers and character of this audience, I do not propose, at this time, and under the circumstances by which we are surrounded, to occupy but a very few moments of the time, in the hope that others that I see, both upon my right hand and upon my left, will take some part in the deliberations of this meeting.

Not long since, I happened to attend a public demonstration in Massachusetts, where I believe I chanced to be the only person of color present. I did not expect, by any means, to be called upon to say a word, for the gathering was somewhat out of my line; and I cannot well understand why I was called upon to speak, unless it was to give *color* to the occasion. (Laughter and applause.) I am here this morning, Mr. Chairman, not only to give color to this occasion—and a pretty deep one at that— but to give my most hearty approval of the resolutions to which we have listened. (Applause.)

I have heard, sir, something of the present religious awakening, or "revival,"[2] in the resolutions, and something in the sentiment around us; but I have discovered also the revival of a custom which I had hoped had

15. Disunion pledge form

From Langston Hughes, Milton Meltzer, and C. Eric Lincoln, eds., *A Pictorial History of Blackamericans*, 5th rev. ed. (New York, 1973) become obsolete in our country—that no matter what was said, or where said, we could scarcely expect to call forth a hiss. Hence, sir, in witnessing the "revival" of this particular American custom at this time, I am led to suppose that the work we have yet to do is greater than we had contemplated. But I propose to ask the attention of the audience for a few moments to that resolution of the series which looks to the overthrow of the American Government and of the American Union, in their present form, and character, and spirit.

I care but little, sir, about any other view of this subject at the present time, because, at the end of a quarter of a century,[3] I discover that all efforts, of whatever kind, or in whatever spirit manifested, have proved complete failures, so far as the progress of the cause of universal liberty is concerned in our country, and the practical demonstration of genuine republicanism, to say nothing about the character of the religion of our country. Feeling, then, the pressure of this failure—that all attempts, from the old gradual Abolition Society, of which Benjamin Franklin was a member and an officer,[4] down to the last phase of anti-slavery, have proved vain, and that in, or through, or over them all, American slavery has grown, and the number of its victims increased from one million to nearly four—of course, I have nothing to hope for in those directions; and having nothing to hope for in those directions, it seems to me that the only course left us to pursue is the one proposed by the Society with which I am happy to be identified. And so far from having my judgment swerved an iota, so far from having a single feeling or impulse changed by anything which has been said by professed or non-professed Abolitionists, in opposition to the proposition for a dissolution of the Union, I am, as I before remarked, more deeply strengthened and confirmed in the feasibility of the plan as it has been suggested.

I give as my reasons some facts which cannot have failed to come under the observation of all who are present, together with some historical facts which, perhaps, have not been so strikingly noticed as they deserve to be by every well-wisher of his country and the cause of universal freedom.

If, Mr. Chairman, I shall go back but fifty years, I shall mark—as every other man has done—where American slavery stood at that time, what part the leading men in our country were taking in it, where the press stood, where the pulpit stood, and where the public sentiment was to be found upon the subject. If I shall go back even no further than the time I have mentioned, I need not remain ignorant in regard to the sentiment which was then extant in the nation respecting this subject; and whether I take my stand upon the history of that day or at the present moment in the City of Washington, I am forced into a belief in the same truth, to wit, that the American people are destitute of feeling, and destitute of principle, in regard to this question. The scenes which have transpired on the soil of Kansas, as well as those which have transpired in the American Congress,[5] go to prove this, if the doctrines held by many Doctors of Divinity do not prove it.

Where, sir, are the colored people of the United States?—and I refer to them only as an illustration. Where do they stand? Why, sir, so far as the masses of the American people are concerned, they have no place in their regard, they have no place in their esteem. And when I make this remark, I want to say that it applies strictly to every other man and every other woman in our country, be their complexions what they may, if they have a regard for the principles which underlie our glorious movement. Then, I repeat, that the friends of universal freedom in this country have no hope for the emancipation of the slave, or for the rescue of the cause of liberty, but by the adoption of this plan, and that at the speediest moment.

In the District of Columbia, we know there exist a large number of laws, all for the purpose of recognizing slavery. If they were confined to Washington, I should not have a word to say on this occasion; if they were confined to the State of Virginia, I might not; but when I am made to feel that the same class of laws does really exist, in spirit, in every State of this Union, I do insist, now as before, that our question or cause comes before and into the hands of every man within the limits of this and of every other State in the country, and as direct as it comes before and into the hands of every colored man.

This, Mr. Chairman, leads me to remark that the question of anti-slavery and pro-slavery in the United States is not the black man's question; that the question of slavery and anti-slavery is practically an American question—all the way American, from beginning to end—and especially with every *decent* American. It strikes me that if justice was done in this country upon this subject, we should have a class of criminals arraigned before the gaze of the world such as few of us have presumed to anticipate; and I long for the time when men shall be driven from their present hiding places, in the excuses, in the concessions, in the compromises which they make, in the reasons which they are giving, from time to time, upon this subject. Dr. Cheever has very recently, in his allusion to scenes in Kansas, and to the conduct of American Congressmen, made the remark that this Kansas controversy has been carried on, from beginning to end, in reference to the white men in that Territory (as the resolution implies), and that the sin of American slavery has not been touched.[6]

Sir, I am glad that Dr. Cheever has so expressed himself—for many will believe the remark coming from that source who, it seems to me, have not cared to notice the same truth when uttered from this platform.

All that I can make out of the last effort of Dr. Cheever is, that he adopts the platform of the American Anti-Slavery Society, without identifying himself personally with our movement.

Now, what I want to call attention to is this: that men who have gone the entire round of social reforms, who have been conversant with everything written, published or spoken on this subject, have not felt themselves called upon until so recently to utter these truths which have been uttered by other voices so long, but have ignored them, so far as their presence at our meetings, their influence and their testimony are concerned.

One other remark in this connection. There are those who believe that that man is a good anti-slavery man who goes for freedom in Kansas, but does not recognize the existence of slavery in any of the slave States. I wish to take this opportunity to say that I ignore as heartily the sentiment or the feeling of any and of all men who, looking at this subject from such a standpoint, profess the slightest interest in the colored men of this country. Our friend Mr. Garrison, in the resolutions he has read, has told us that, step by step, in everything that should entitle a man to his freedom, to citizenship, to the popular respect of a nation, in everything that should call forth the regard of a great and growing people, the colored people have demonstrated their capabilities; and yet there are reformers in this nation, who go for the non-extension of slavery into Kansas, who look with allowance upon the existence of slavery in the nation. Sir, this is temporizing—this is fragmentary—this is selfish; it is local, and I abhor it. It is in close affinity with the spirit of the American party,[7] which I equally abhor; and I earnestly hope that, if, during the series of meetings on which we have just entered, no other impression shall be made upon those who are present, they shall at least be forced to the conviction that the friends of this Society are in earnest, solemn earnest, in their purpose to dissolve the American Union and break into a thousand pieces the American Government, for the emancipation of the black men of this country, as the greatest and best means for the emancipation of the cowardly whites in the same nation. (Applause and hisses.) I no longer limit my remarks to the black men when I speak of slaves in this nation; for if I should go south of Mason and Dixon's line tomorrow, I might, in my humble judgment, ransack society, day and night, and not be able to find a more veritable slave in the blackest bondman on the darkest Southern plantation, than I hold the Hon. Edward Everett to be in every particular which constitutes true manhood. (Loud applause, mingled with hisses.) Mr. Chairman, those who hiss in this audience pay me the highest possible compliment. (Laughter and applause.) I remarked, when I rose, that whether we search into the records of the past or look into the present, no man can fail to see that, as our country has grown in years, American slavery has grown in num-

bers, in cruelty, in everything calculated to degrade its victims, and outrage humanity at large; and when I bear in mind that into the American
Union, since its formation, there have been some seven slave States admitted, and that in the Constitution of the State of Arkansas may be
found a clause which declares that slavery shall never be abolished
within its borders,[8] I inquire whether the Union into which these States
have been admitted, whether the Constitution that has recognized them,
whether the Government that has endorsed them, are not, each and all of
them, complete failures upon the great question of Republicanism, Democracy, and Liberty? I hold that they are; and that we want no stronger
proof that our Union, and Government, and Constitution are failures
than that one fact alone. But when I bear in mind that this Union, as now
constituted, of and by some thirty-one or thirty-two States, is a slaveholding Union, that the District of Columbia, which should constitute
the heart of the nation, is a slaveholding district, and that no man before
me, whether black or white, as a man, can exercise any other rights there
than the blackest slave may exercise, I say I have here another proof of
the total failure of this Republic, under its present institutions. And when
I bear in mind that black men may be burnt in one State, and white men
may be shot down in another, for their love of freedom, I assert this
Union to be a failure. And when I remember that, standing in Philadelphia a few days ago, I saw a noble woman who obtained her freedom by
allowing herself to be placed in a box scarcely larger than a coffin, and,
secreted in that way, was brought from one of our Southern States into
the State of Pennsylvania, the only breathing air she obtained coming
through a small hole bored by a pair of scissors in her own hands,[9] then I
again declare, before God, that the American Union is a failure. (Applause.) And when I pass from the city of Philadelphia, the residence of a
Rush and a Franklin,[10] and go to the Queen City of the West,[11] and am
there told by the counsel of another woman that a more heroic effort for
freedom was never made by mortal man than that of Robert Garner and
his wife to secure their liberty, and remember that they were dragged out
of that city at noonday and hurried back to bondage,[12] I again make the
declaration that the American Union is a failure. And then, when I go to
Boston, in my own State of Massachusetts, and find such men as Edward
Everett, Rufus Choate and Robert C. Winthrop as silent as a gravestone
in regard to this question of slavery,[13] I assert that to be even a stronger
proof of the failure of this Union.

Sir, I might stand here and pile fact upon fact of the same character,
until they should be higher than the hall, but I will not detain the audience longer than simply to refer to one other fact (as I will call it) which
has come under the notice of many very recently. It is this: I do not know
that I need to ask this audience whether they consider me a man or not. I
do not care what people consider me. I think the American people are

coming to one conclusion, and that is, that whether they call the black people men or not, they are fast proving it in this nation; and the last and the best proof of it is—and this is the fact to which I am now about to call attention—that when the decision of Judge Taney was made,[14] silence, generally speaking, characterized the nation. The blow, of course, was one struck at everything near and dear to us as a people, and the impression generally prevailed that the colored people would hold meetings, from one end of the country to the other, to protest against that decision, thus signifying an anxiety on their part to know whether the doctrine there laid down was to be allowed or not. The significant fact to which I would call attention is, that no portion of the American people have evinced greater carelessness with regard to that decision than the colored people themselves. I look upon this as a good sign, if we may at all go by contraries in this country; and if they would be as careless about many other decisions to which I might refer, I believe the day of their redemption would come to them sooner than it otherwise will. Now, I do not wish to be misunderstood in this particular, and perhaps I shall make my meaning clearer if I say, there are certain decisions which have been given by judges in this country, there are certain acts which have been passed by certain Legislatures in this country, there have been some positions taken by the American Congress in regard to the colored people, which I am glad to know that colored persons are careless of; and I long for the time to come when the American slave shall be so careless of his master south of Mason and Dixon's line that he will wake up some morning and resolve to go about his business, as if there were not an oppressor in the wide world; and, if he shall be resisted in the step he shall then take, that he shall be ready to say to those who would enslave him, "I am a man! If you doubt it, we will measure arms. God and Freedom shall be my watchword!" When that hour shall have come, the American people will be ready, if they are not now, to subscribe to the doctrine, at once and forever, "NO UNION WITH SLAVEHOLDERS!" (Applause.)

Liberator (Boston, Mass.), 21 May 1858.

1. William Lloyd Garrison had proposed eighteen resolutions for the consideration of the delegates. They denounced slavery, rebuked American churches for their moderation on the issue, repudiated the Dred Scott decision, condemned the Chinese coolie business as a slave trade, supported free-state settlers in the Kansas Territory, and censured federal efforts to impose slavery there. *Lib*, 14 May 1858.

2. Sparked by the Panic of 1857, religious revivals swept across the North in early 1858. William G. McLoughlin, *Modern Revivalism: Charles Grandison Finney to Billy Graham* (New York, N.Y., 1959), 163–64.

3. The American Anti-Slavery Society, which was founded in 1833, had just completed twenty-five years of antislavery work.

4. Remond refers to the Pennsylvania Abolition Society, a Quaker-dominated organization founded in 1775 and revived in 1784. Benjamin Franklin was an early president of the society, which advocated the gradual abolition of slavery, promoted black education, sponsored relief efforts for free blacks, offered legal counsel to kidnapping victims and fugitive slaves, and petitioned Congress to end the slave trade. Arthur Zilversmit, *The First Emancipation: The Abolition of Slavery in the North* (Chicago, Ill., 1967), 159, 162–64, 206–8.

5. Passage of the Kansas-Nebraska Act (1854) initiated the rapid development of the Kansas Territory by proslavery and free-state settlers. Each group sought to dominate the political process leading to statehood and thereby determine whether Kansas would be admitted as a slave or free state. By 1855 the struggle had erupted into civil war, making the territory a symbol of sectional controversy and earning it the sobriquet "Bleeding Kansas." The Kansas question prompted heated debate on the floor of the U.S. Congress. Remond may refer to the brutal caning of Senator Charles Sumner by South Carolina congressman Preston Brooks on the floor of the Senate during May 1856 in response to Sumner's earlier antislavery speech, "The Crime against Kansas."

6. George Barrell Cheever (1807–1890), a Congregational clergyman and abolitionist, was a prominent opponent of the Fugitive Slave Law and the Kansas-Nebraska Act. Cheever helped found the Church Anti-Slavery Society in 1859 but was best known for his *Guilt of Slavery and the Crime of Slaveholding* (1860), a scholarly rebuttal of the idea that the Bible sanctioned slavery. Remond refers to a recent speech by Cheever on the Kansas question, which was reprinted in the 7 May 1858 issue of the *Liberator*. Cheever charged that the House of Representatives had opposed the Lecompton Constitution for the proposed state of Kansas, not out of concern over the "injustice and wickedness of enslaving *the blacks*," but because it refused to force the document on the territory "*without the consent of white people.*" *DAB*, 4:48–49; McKivigan, *War against Proslavery Religion*, 137.

7. The American party was founded in 1849 and by 1854 had become a major political force. Most members were disaffected Whigs, former Democrats, and native-born workers fearful of competition from poorly paid immigrants. Dubbed Know-Nothings because of their secretiveness, members generally endorsed immigration restriction, anti-Catholicism, and temperance. Many Know-Nothings held moderate antislavery views. The party split into northern and southern wings in 1856 over the question of slavery in the territories and soon declined.

8. Arkansas was admitted as a slave state in 1836. Article 9, section 1, of the original state constitution prohibited the legislature from emancipating slaves without their owners' consent and from preventing immigrants from bringing their slaves with them. During congressional debate over the admission of Arkansas, Congressman Benjamin Swift of Vermont claimed that the document "made the institution of slavery perpetual." Abolitionists often repeated this charge. Lonnie J. White, *Politics on the Southwestern Frontier: Arkansas Territory, 1819–1836* (Memphis, Tenn., 1964), 1, 191–95.

9. The young woman, a domestic servant for a wealthy Baltimore family, was placed in a box by a local free black and shipped to abolitionists in Philadelphia during the winter of 1857–58. After living in the William Still household for several weeks, she was forwarded on to Canada West. Still, *Underground Railroad*, 632–35.

10. Remond refers to early Philadelphia abolitionists Benjamin Rush and Benjamin Franklin.

11. Cincinnati, Ohio, was often referred to as "the Queen City of the West" during the antebellum period.

12. Remond refers to a fugitive slave case involving Simon Garner, Jr., his wife Margaret, and their four children, who escaped from Boone County, Kentucky, in January 1856 but were soon captured in Cincinnati's free black community. Their owners requested that they be returned under the provisions of the Fugitive Slave Law of 1850. Local antislavery attorney John Joliffe acted as chief counsel for the Garner family during hearings before a federal fugitive slave commissioner. The case created a public sensation because of an unusual instance of slave violence. At the moment of capture, Margaret Garner killed one of her children and attempted to slay the other three rather than see them reenslaved. The commissioner eventually ruled in favor of the slaveowners, and the Garner family was sent back to Kentucky. Margaret Garner was sold further South, effectively thwarting the attempts of Ohio officials to extradite her on a murder charge. Julius Yanuck, "The Garner Fugitive Slave Case," *MVHR* 40:47–66 (June 1953).

13. Edward Everett, Rufus Choate, and Robert C. Winthrop were conservative Massachusetts politicians who attempted to maintain good relations with the South by avoiding discussion of the slavery question. Everett (1794–1865) was a Unitarian clergyman, a diplomat, and a renowned orator. He served several terms in the U.S. Congress and became the vice-presidential candidate of the Constitutional Union party in 1860. Choate (1799–1859), a distinguished jurist, served in the state legislature and the U.S. Congress during the 1830s and 1840s. He was a staunch supporter of the Fugitive Slave Law. Winthrop (1809–1894) was also a lawyer. After serving in Congress from 1840 to 1851, including a term as Speaker of the House, he was defeated for reelection to the Senate by Charles Sumner in 1851, largely due to his mild opposition to the Fugitive Slave Law. Winthrop served as chairman of the Peabody Educational Fund after the Civil War. Potter, *Impending Crisis*, 237; *DAB*, 4:86–90, 6:223–26, 20:416–17.

14. Remond refers to Chief Justice Roger B. Taney and the decision of the U.S. Supreme Court in the case of *Dred Scott* v. *Sanford* (1857).

79.
Resolutions by Lloyd H. Brooks
Delivered at the Third Christian Church
New Bedford, Massachusetts
16 June 1858

Discouraged and frustrated, blacks searched for an effective response to the Dred Scott decision. The U.S. Supreme Court had produced a legal opinion, not a statute that could be challenged in practice, lobbied against in state legislatures, or overturned in the courts. The ruling's indeterminate nature left blacks with few options. Charles Langston advised fellow blacks: "Ours is the poor privilege to protest, to remonstrate, to beg, to weep; here ends our power." Powerlessness and indignation were the watchwords at protest meetings across the North. New York blacks, paraphrasing Chief Justice Roger B. Taney's language, censured the ruling as "a foul and infamous lie which neither black men nor white men are bound to respect." Boston blacks inaugurated the first annual Crispus Attucks Day celebration, where they commemorated black heroes of the American Revolution to give historical justification to their citizenship claims. The character of these responses reflected black vulnerability in the face of federal tyranny, but it also revealed seething militancy and growing unity. New Bedford blacks registered their protest against the decision at a 16 June 1858 meeting at the Third Christian Church. The assembly unanimously adopted the following resolutions, which were submitted by local black leader Lloyd H. Brooks. *Lib*, 26 February, 12 March 1858 [11:0173–76]; Quarles, *Black Abolitionists*, 230–35; Pease and Pease, *They Who Would Be Free*, 240–44; Foner and Walker, *Proceedings of the Black State Conventions*, 1:99–101, 2:96–104.

Whereas, For many years all of the Southern, and a majority of the Northern States, have by their legislation increased in acts of hostility and malignity towards the colored people of this country, as evinced by the repeated and continued passage of oppressive, disfranchising and expatriating laws. And
Whereas, The general government of these United States, the object of whose existence is declared to be to protect the weak, and to secure the blessings of liberty to the whole people, have not only from time to time sanctioned these flagitious outrages, but has itself become the patron of all these, and the perpetrators of the most highhanded injustice ever inflicted upon an unoffending and unprotected people. And
Whereas, We believe the designs of this Government upon the free colored people to be threefold, *i.e.*—1st, their enslavement; 2d, their

forcible expatriation; 3d, their final extirpation; all with the sole view of rendering our enslaved brethren more secure in their chains. And

Whereas, The colored people of this country have ever proved themselves worthy of the confidence and respect of their countrymen, by their daring bravery in behalf of the country at the times of her greatest peril, "that tried men's souls,"[1] and their loyalty to its interests and general welfare in the time of peace as well as war, in all the aspects of life. Therefore,

Resolved, That the infamous "Dred Scott" decision[2] is a palpably vain, arrogant assumption, unsustained by history, justice, reason or common sense, and merits the execration of the world as a consummate villainy.

Resolved, That the indifference manifested by a majority of the professed Christian ministers and churches, relative to our condition in this country, is clearly demonstrative of their true character and policy on the great question of human rights.

Resolved, That the attempt of the United States Supreme Court to stigmatize us is the legitimate result of the efforts of leading divines and statesmen to dispute our claim to the Fatherhood of God, and to the equal blessings growing out of that relationship.

Resolved, That we believe the design, now more than ever before, is to make our grievances permanent, by greatly multiplying the disabilities under which we labor; nevertheless, we are determined to remain in this country, our title and right being as clear and indisputable as that of any class of people.

Resolved, That we feel, as we express, the deepest gratitude to all of our friends individually and collectively for all they have done or said in behalf of our oppressed race, either from the pulpit or the church, through the press or political action, or anti-slavery and abolition societies, and pledge them all our consistent, hearty cooperation in the future.

Resolved, That we neither recognize nor respect any laws for slavery, whether from Moses, Paul, or Taney. We spurn and trample them all under our feet as in violation of the laws of God and the rights of men.

Resolved, That slavery does not exist as a right, and has no guarantee but in usurpation, might and brute force, the many and strong oppressing the few and weak; and were we equal in numbers, no attempt would be made to enslave us, nor to deny us the respect due to our manhood.

Resolved, That there ought to be a general mutual understanding between the colored people of this continent, and that immediate measures ought to be taken to bring about this desirable object.

Resolved, That it is the imperative duty of every colored preacher, minister, or pastor, to call the attention of those under his influence to their true condition, and urge them to unite in all practicable means and measures for the obtainment of our rights.

Resolved, That we request our brethren in every city, town, and village, to hold similar meetings, and that petitions and memorials be gotten up by our people in every church or society, and circulated for signatures; and that we begin and continue to petition and memorialize Congress until our grievances are heard and redressed.

Resolved, That we will endeavor to use all honorable means to induce that interchange of harmonious action which is so indispensable to the promotion and establishment of our national rights as natives of the United States of America.

Resolved, That as no attempt for human freedom was ever successful unless perfect union existed in the ranks of the oppressed, we consider it a paramount duty for all *lovers of liberty* to join in waging a war of annihilation against every vestige of oppression under which we are now suffering.

And further *Resolved*, That the object for which this meeting was called may be more fully carried into effect, this meeting issues a call for a Mass. State Convention to be held in this city, Aug. 2d, 1858.[3]

Liberator (Boston, Mass.), 9 July 1858.

1. Brooks quotes from number 1 of Thomas Paine's *The American Crisis* (1776–83), a series of political pamphlets written in defense of the American struggle for independence.

2. Brooks refers to the decision of the U.S. Supreme Court in the case of *Dred Scott v. Sanford* (1857). Dred Scott, a Missouri slave, had sued his owner, John F. A. Sanford, contending that he should be free because a previous master had allowed him to reside in Illinois and the Minnesota Territory from 1834 to 1838. The Court not only denied Scott's claim but rejected Congress's authority to legislate on the issue of slavery in the territories. Chief Justice Roger B. Taney declared that slave property was protected by the due process clause of the Fifth Amendment to the Constitution. This overturned both the underlying premise of the Missouri Compromise (1820) and the concept of "popular sovereignty" contained in the Kansas-Nebraska Act (1854). Writing for a majority of the justices, Taney also held that blacks could not be American citizens and argued that the U.S. Constitution presumed them to be "so inferior that they had no rights which a white man was bound to respect." Abolitionists and free blacks reacted vigorously to the Dred Scott decision because it limited the authority of a free state to exclude slavery within its borders, denied black claims to American citizenship, and allowed the spread of slavery into the territories—thus upsetting the fragile balance between slave and free states. Don Fehrenbacher, *The Dred Scott Case: Its Significance in Law and Politics* (New York, N.Y., 1978).

3. A state convention of Massachusetts blacks met at City Hall in New Bedford during 2–3 August 1858. Delegates rejected the Dred Scott decision as a

"palpable violation" of the U.S. Constitution, reiterated their claims to American citizenship, and appointed a committee to petition the state legislature and U.S. Congress on the subject. John Freedom, Solomon Peneton, William Berry, and Lloyd H. Brooks—the leading figures at the 16 June meeting that approved the above resolutions—represented New Bedford blacks at the convention. Foner and Walker, *Proceedings of the Black State Conventions,* 2:96–107.

80.
Anthony Burns to William Lloyd Garrison
[July 1858]

The myth that blacks were unfit for freedom informed most proslavery propaganda. Apologists for slavery argued that if slaves were freed they would become a social burden, destined for the almshouse, the asylum, the prison, or the continued care of paternalistic whites. The proslavery press regularly invoked this image, sometimes by making erroneous charges about the condition of well-known former slaves. Black abolitionists were quick to challenge these stories. Ellen Craft wrote from England to quell a rumor that, weary of freedom, she desired to return to her master. "I had much rather starve in England, a free woman," she informed the proslavery press, "than be a slave for the best man that ever breathed upon the American continent." Other fugitives published open letters to their former owners to disabuse the public of the notion that they were dissatisfied with freedom. Anthony Burns wrote William Lloyd Garrison during the summer of 1858 to refute published reports that he had been convicted of robbery and was incarcerated in a Massachusetts penitentiary. To the contrary, Burns proudly described his progress in freedom—his studies at Oberlin College and Fairmount Theological Seminary and his plans to tour the North with an antislavery panorama. Garrison reprinted Burns's letter in the 13 August issue of the *Liberator*. Ripley et al., *Black Abolitionist Papers*, 1:330–31, 2:65–67, 217–21.

Dear Sir:
    Having seen a piece from Richmond (Va.) paper stating that I ~~was~~ am in the Massachusetts Penitentuary,[1] I avail myself of the opportunity to say that the accusation is lie without a father. I am not, nor niether have I been, nor do I expect to be, unless some one should attempt to deprive me of my liberty as before. Then I would enforce the Motto of Patrick Henry, liberty or death. Again if such had been the case, I should only fall back to the midest of such a class of Individuals as I was among before my escap from the South.
    That of liars, Cradlerobers, Thieves, Murderers, Idolators and Whoremongers, such as ought to be in a Penitentuary, for the murdered fathers, mothers, Sisters & Brothers, of the South. ———I now call for the attention of the public to the place where I have been residing since my return from the South. I have for two years, been prossecuting my studies in Ohio at Oberlin Institute ~~the light of the World,~~ and since that time at Fairmount Theo. Seminary, Cincinnati Ohio. [I'm] striving hard with the aid of my friends to store my mind with that knowledge which I have

been deprived of by Slavery. &c. I have no doubt but what that I shall find friends enough with aboundent means, who will aid me in my noble Object.

And as I am making a preporation to Travel with a Pan-orama, Titled the Grand Moving Marror—scenes of real life[,] Startling and Thrilling Incidents, degradation & Horrors of American Slavery, for the purpose of selling my Book, a Narritive, giving full account of my life in Slavery, from ChildHood with many other facts connected with the System of Slavery.[2] The proceeds of which to enable me to complet my Studies. At which time friends will have the opportunity of seeing, hearing, Reading, and knowing for themselves.

The propriators of the Pan-orama, Mrss. A. Herriman, Longley &c. Garscland, ———— of Lewiston Maine.[3] I have no doubt but there are some, who would beglad If the above report was true. The Gentleman who thus informed the pl public that I am in Mass. Penitentuary wished to be kicked into notice, Who like Balaam's Ass, which would not have spoken If his master had not give him such an awful Lashing.[4] Who ever they may be, I can assure them that they shall not be kicked into notice me by me.

Anthony Burns of Boston Mass.[5]

P.S. Please publish this & accomadate yours truly friend.

Anthony Burns

1. This rumor was circulated by several Virginia newspapers. The Fredericksburg *Virginia Herald* reported that a "reliable gentleman who has recently been north" had informed the editors that Burns was incarcerated in a Massachusetts penitentiary "for the crime of robbery." *NASS*, 26 June 1858.

2. Burns toured New England with a panorama called the "Grand Moving Mirror of Slavery" during the fall of 1858. The "narrative" to which he refers is probably *Anthony Burns, A History* (1856), a biography written by Charles Emery Stevens. Burns had sold more than three hundred copies of that volume while studying at Oberlin College. *Lib*, 17 September 1858.

3. Burns's panorama was owned by A. Herriman, Josiah P. Longley, and Alonzo Garcelon of Lewiston, Maine. Little is known of Herriman, but Longley and Garcelon were community leaders. Longley (1829–?) operated a sizable harness manufacturing business in the town from 1847 through the 1880s. Garcelon (1813–1906), a physician, founded and edited the *Lewiston Falls Journal* and played a major role in the establishment of Bates College. He served in the state legislature as a Free Soiler and a Republican during the 1850s. In 1879 Garcelon was elected governor of Maine. *Leading Business Men of Lewiston, Augusta and Vicinity* (Boston, Mass., 1889), 49; U.S. Census, 1860; *DAB*, 7:131–32; Baxter, *History of Freewill Baptists*, 141–42.

4. Burns alludes to the biblical account of Balaam, a Mesopotamian diviner, in

Numbers 22:7–34. Balaam beat his mule with a staff when he refused to move, prompting the mule to speak. Burns implies that the proslavery informant, like Balaam's ass, responded to provocation. In this case, the Virginia press published the erroneous notice of Burns's imprisonment due to the growing influence of the antislavery message.

5. Anthony Burns (1834–1862) was born to slave parents in Stafford County, Virginia. At age six, he became the property of Colonel Charles F. Suttle, a local shopkeeper and deputy sheriff. Suttle hired out the young slave as a domestic servant and laborer. During this time, Burns joined the Baptist faith and secretly learned to read. In February 1854, he stowed away on a ship bound for Boston. Upon reaching the city, he obtained employment as a cook, then worked in a clothing store owned by Coffin Pitts, a local black abolitionist. Suttle traced Burns to Boston, obtained a federal warrant for his arrest, and seized him on 24 March under provisions of the Fugitive Slave Law. Abolitionist lawyers, supported by the Boston Vigilance Committee, exhausted legal means to free Burns. When a federal commissioner ruled that the fugitive must be returned to slavery, an interracial mob led by white abolitionist Thomas Wentworth Higginson and Lewis Hayden stormed the courthouse where he was held and attempted to free him. The effort failed, and Burns was returned to Norfolk, Virginia, where he spent four months in the slave pen before being purchased by a North Carolina speculator. In February 1855, members of the Twelfth Baptist Church, of which Burns had been a member, purchased his freedom. A Boston woman sponsored his study at Oberlin College, where he remained through 1857, before taking further instruction at Fairmount Theological Seminary near Cincinnati, Ohio. He then briefly pastored a black congregation in Indianapolis but left because of local prejudice against free blacks. Burns settled in St. Catharines, Canada West, in 1860 and served the Zion Baptist Church there until his death. Charles Emery Stevens, *Anthony Burns, A History* (Boston, Mass., 1856); Campbell, *Slave Catchers*, 124–32; Samuel Shapiro, "The Rendition of Anthony Burns," *JNH* 44:34–51 (January 1959); *Lib*, 30 October 1857; Fred Landon, "Anthony Burns in Canada," *OHSPR* 22:162–66 (1925).

81.
Black Abolitionists and the Republican Party

Henry Highland Garnet and James W. Duffin
to Gerrit Smith
16 September 1858

William J. Watkins to Gerrit Smith
27 September 1858

Blacks welcomed the rise of the Republican party as an important sign of changing American opinion on the slavery question. The new party's rapid growth and its opposition to the extension of slavery convinced a majority of black leaders that it represented their best hope of retarding the advance of the slave power through practical politics. Pragmatic black leaders such as William J. Watkins campaigned widely for Republican candidates. Yet others, including Henry Highland Garnet, balked at embracing any party that fell short of abolitionism's central principles. They urged blacks to support antislavery third parties, despite their limited chances for success. The following letters from Garnet and Watkins to Gerrit Smith, a third-party candidate for governor of New York in 1858, reflect the divisions that arose among black leaders as they struggled to chart the best course to advance their rights in the late 1850s. *Lib*, 5 September 1856, 13 July 1860 [10:0286]; *FDP*, 26 August 1853, 9 November 1855 [8:0419–20, 9:0925]; *WAA*, 27 August 1859 [11:0976]; J. W. C. Pennington to Gerrit Smith, 6–7 November 1852, Gerrit Smith Papers, NSyU [7:0821]; Quarles, *Black Abolitionists*, 188–90.

> 52 Laurens St.
> New York, [New York]
> Sep[tembe]r 16, 1858

My Dear Bro.

I am deeply grieved. I have just returned with my friend J. W. Duffin[1] from the Colored Men's State Suffrage Convention held at Troy where they went for the Republican Party,[2] and condemned the Radical Abolitionists, and disapproved of your nomination.[3] There were some forty delegates, and only four or five of us stand by the truth, and fought for just, and righteous principles. There we stood, and there we intend to stand to the last. I could not have thought that [colored men] would [be] so blind to their best interests, and so [recreant] to the cause of Liberty. The convention was packed by Republican influences and only about four counties along the Hudson river were meagrely represented. There [were others] from New York—two voted right, and battled a day and a half in concert with Duffin from Ontaria, and Rev. Mr. Williams from Troy.[4] Yet this will go out as the opinion of the Colored people of the State. Therefore this is our proposition. To call a State Convention of Colored people at Rochester at an early date,[5] rallying the West, and your Friends in New York, and get your attendance to address us—and thus save the honour of our people, and show to the country that we will fight forever under the banner bearing the illustrious name of "Gerrit Smith." In this our friend J. W. Duffin fully, and heartily concurs. For the sake of truth, Law, and justice we must redeem the honour of our people from the base, and wicked committal of this miserable Convention. In order to do this we must have some means at hand—as the Republicans showered their money upon the Troy meeting. Many of your friends here are too poor to travel to Rochester. We want much to pay the fares of some ten or twelve friends from New York, a few from Albany[,] Troy, Schenectedy, Utica, Syracuse[,] Buffalo &c. I should like to start ten days before the meeting and muster the forces. Some of the best men of the state will cooperate. We will write to Douglass[6] today, who did not attend the Convention. Watkins, poor Watkins, went over to the enemy, and is employed as their agent to stump the State for the Republicans.

Write me your opion immediately and let me know your decision. My kind regards to Mrs. Smith.[7] Yours in the good cause, Signed,

Henry Highland Garnet

J. W. Duffin

P.S. Mrs. S. R. Ward, and son are with us on their way to Jamaica.[8]

H. H. G.

Gerrit Smith Papers, George Arents Research Library, Syracuse University, Syracuse, New York. Published by permission.

Rochester, [New York]

Sept[ember] 27, [1858]

Dear Friend:

I hope you have seen my letter, in the Tribune, The Hour and the Man,[9] has dealt unfairly, ungentlemanly, meanly with me.

Mr. Douglass has just handed me your letter, saying he wished he had seen me before sending it. You remark that I have sadly changed since my visit to Peterboro. Not at all, sir. I have no more changed my Rad. Abolition Principles than did the majority of Rad. Abolitionists who voted for Fremont,[10] and who will vote for the Republican nominee, in 1860. It is with me a question of Policy, as well as of Principle; and I maintain that we may when a great end is sought to be attained, consult the genius of Expediency, without sacrificing one iota of moral Principle. But I will not argue this question here. You know what can be said in favor, what can be said against this view. My object in writing to you was, simply, to inform you that I have not been "sold" to the "Prince of the State Regency,"[11] nor even hired by him or any one else to follow you around the Country. My meeting at the Falls (Glen's) was arranged by others, without any knowledge on my part of your proceeding me. I attend meetings got up for me, without any reference to who is to procede me. Thus I may follow you again. And I challenge any one who has heard any one of the twenty speeches I have already made during the present Campaign,[12] to quote a single sentence in which I have opposed you, or the views you entertain.

I wish you had been nominated by the Republican Party. As it is, I think my duty lies in the direction I have taken. My conscience approves me. I may be in the fog, but I think I bask amid the sunlight.

My respects to your good family. Yours, truly,

W. J. Watkins

Gerrit Smith Papers, George Arents Research Library, Syracuse University, Syracuse, New York. Published by permission.

1. James W. Duffin (1814–1874) was one of the leading black abolitionists in western New York. Born and reared in Le Roy, he married Charlotte Smith in 1834, and they settled in nearby Geneva later in the decade. Duffin organized First of August celebrations, served as secretary of the Geneva Colored Anti-Slavery Society, and urged members of the community to abstain from using the "products of slave labor." An advocate of moral reform, he guided the work of the Geneva Moral and Mental Improvement Society and promoted temperance among local blacks during the late 1830s. In 1843 he was elected vice president of the Delevan Union Temperance Society, a statewide black organization. Duffin also supported the black press and worked as a local agent for the *Colored American* and the *Palladium of Liberty* in the early 1840s. He represented Geneva blacks at the 1843 black national convention in Buffalo and served as the meeting's secretary. New York blacks later recognized his leadership by naming him to the New York State Council of the Colored People.

An early convert to political abolitionism, Duffin became a prominent figure in the struggle to expand black suffrage in the state. He joined the campaign by 1839 and, the following year, signed the call for a black state convention to discuss the suffrage issue. Over the next two decades, he helped coordinate the statewide fight for an equal franchise, recruited local suffrage activists, directed petition drives, and promoted suffrage work at black state conventions. He also led the Ontario County Suffrage Committee, which advanced the campaign at the local level. Duffin was an organizer of the New York State Suffrage Association in 1855 and served on its board of managers for the remainder of the decade. Critical of the Republican party, he endorsed antislavery third parties at the 1858 black state suffrage convention.

Disgusted by the continuing failure of New York blacks to gain equal suffrage, Duffin joined the Haitian immigration movement. In 1861 he recruited potential settlers in Geneva for a Haitian colony. Duffin, his wife, and their four youngest children left for Haiti in October; they settled in St. Marc and were initially excited about the place and business prospects there. Duffin worked hard to sustain the St. Marc colony and criticized those immigrants who returned. As of July 1862, he was determined "not [to] return to their former condition, upon any consideration." But family illness, business failure, and the inactivity of the Haitian government soon forced him to reconsider. After returning to New York late in the year, he became a critic of the Haitian experiment. Duffin lived his final decade in New York City. *ESF*, 18 April 1874; *CA*, 11 March 1837, 2 February, 18 May, 27 July, 2 November 1839, 6 June 1840 [2:0994, 3:0063, 0154, 0449]; *CF*, 29 June 1843; *PL*, 27 December 1843; *Convention of Colored Citizens . . . at Buffalo* (1843), 8 [4:0635]; *AP*, 3 October 1843 [4:0678]; Foner and Walker, *Proceedings of the Black State Conventions*, 1:5, 8–13, 37, 79–84, 92, 96, 99; *FDP*, 1 February 1856; *PP*, 13 July, 28 December 1861, 16 January, 27 February, 1, 22 May, 3, 17 July, 4 September 1862; *WAA*, 30 June, 23 July 1859, 13 April 1861, 22 February 1862, 10 January 1863; James W. Duffin to Gerrit Smith, 15 November 1861, Gerrit Smith Papers, NSyU [13:0897–98]; *Lib*, 12 June 1863.

2. The Suffrage Convention of the Colored Citizens of New York met at the Concert Hall in Troy on 14 September 1858. Thirty-seven delegates—and many female spectators—heard William J. Watkins present eight resolutions condemning the Dred Scott decision, defending black rights, asserting black claims to the franchise, and endorsing the Republican party as the most effective means to promote black interests. Although debate centered on the resolution endorsing the Republicans, a majority of the delegates supported the measure. Foner and Walker, *Proceedings of the Black State Conventions*, 1:99–101.

3. The Radical Abolition party was organized in 1855 by Lewis Tappan, Gerrit Smith, William Goodell, and other former members of the defunct American and Foreign Anti-Slavery Society, who envisioned it as a vehicle for political abolitionism. The party established a new antislavery newspaper called the *Radical Abolitionist*, held national conventions in Boston and Syracuse, and obtained encouraging endorsements from black leaders Frederick Douglass and James McCune Smith, but it failed to attract widespread abolitionist support. Although the New York–based party nominated Gerrit Smith for president and Samuel McFarland of Virginia for vice-president in 1856, it polled only 165 votes in the entire state. By 1858 it was moribund. But on 4 August of that year, a remnant met in Syracuse and nominated Gerrit Smith for governor of New York on the "People's State Ticket." Smith polled about five thousand votes in the fall election. Perkal, "American Abolition Society," 57–69; Bertram Wyatt-Brown, *Lewis Tappan and Evangelical War against Slavery* (Cleveland, Ohio, 1969), 332–34; Harlow, *Gerrit Smith*, 378–81.

4. Garnet refers to Rev. John A. Williams, who was then serving an African Methodist Episcopal Zion congregation in Troy, New York. At the 1858 convention, he spoke against resolutions expressing support for the Republican party. *Troy City Directory*, 1857–60; Foner and Walker, *Proceedings of the Black State Conventions*, 1:99–101.

5. A proposed Rochester convention to arouse black support for Gerrit Smith's

candidacy also received the endorsement of the 1858 black state convention in Troy. But it was apparently never held. *Lib*, 1 October 1858.

6. Frederick Douglass.

7. Ann Carol Fitzhugh Smith.

8. In late 1855, after completing an antislavery lecture tour in Britain, Samuel Ringgold Ward traveled to Jamaica, where he had been deeded fifty acres of land by an English philanthropist. His wife Emily and son Samuel, Jr., left Canada West and joined him in Kingston, Jamaica, three years later. Ronald Kevin Burke, "Samuel Ringgold Ward, Christian Abolitionist" (Ph.D. diss., Syracuse University, 1975), 82–86.

9. *The Hour and the Man* was one of two campaign periodicals that Gerrit Smith financed to publicize his 1858 campaign for governor of New York. It was edited and published in Cortland by local abolitionist John Thomas at a cost of $1,450. Harlow, *Gerrit Smith*, 380.

10. Most political abolitionists, including a large number of Radical Abolition party adherents, supported John C. Frémont, the Republican presidential candidate, in the 1856 election. Despite his limited antislavery commitment, abolitionists viewed Frémont as their best candidate. Frémont (1813–1890), a popular western explorer and military leader in the Mexican War, had served briefly in the U.S. Senate. He lost the 1856 election by a slim margin, winning all but five of the free states. During the Civil War, Frémont was removed from command of the Department of the West for emancipating captured slaves. He unsuccessfully challenged Lincoln for the Republican presidential nomination in 1864. Sewell, *Ballots for Freedom*, 284–90; *DAB*, 7:19–23.

11. Watkins adopts a term applied to Martin Van Buren and the Democratic political machine in New York state during the 1820s and 1830s. He probably refers to Thurlow Weed who, together with Senator William H. Seward, controlled the Republican party in the state in the late 1850s. He was often referred to as "Lord Thurlow." Glyndon G. Van Deusen, *Thurlow Weed: Wizard of the Lobby* (Boston, Mass., 1947), 234–36.

12. Watkins's speech at Glens Falls, New York, was one of many he made throughout the state for the Republican party in the fall of 1858. Watkins had been hired by the Republicans and authorized by that year's black state convention at Troy to solicit black support for Edwin D. Morgan, the Republican gubernatorial candidate. His speeches and Stephen Myers's Albany *Voice of the People* were part of a statewide effort by black Republicans. Although Morgan defeated Gerrit Smith and his Democratic opponent, he offered only tepid support for expanded black suffrage once in office. *GSB*, 19 October 1858; Henry Highland Garnet to Gerrit Smith, 10 September 1858, Gerrit Smith Papers, NSyU [11:0346–47]; *NASS*, 9 October 1858 [11:0385]; Walker, "Afro-American in New York City," 207–9.

82.
"Bury Me in a Free Land"
by Frances Ellen Watkins Harper

The 1850s witnessed a flowering of Afro-American literature. Blacks began to use fiction, poetry, and other forms of creative expression as instruments of antislavery protest. "The Heroic Slave" (1853), Frederick Douglass's short story about an insurrection aboard a slave ship, was one of the earliest works of black fiction. The black novel originated with William Wells Brown's *Clotel* (1853), Frank J. Webb's *The Garies and Their Friends* (1857), and Martin R. Delany's *Blake* (1859–62)—books with obvious abolitionist themes. The antislavery poetry of Joseph C. Holly, James Madison Bell, James M. Whitfield, Frances Ellen Watkins Harper, and other blacks filled the columns of reform newspapers and provided inspirational interludes at antislavery gatherings. Harper, a renowned speaker for the antislavery and women's rights movements, frequently incorporated poetry readings into her lectures, and she soon earned recognition as one of the foremost black poets of her time. Her verse was representative of antebellum reform poetry— occasionally poignant, often sentimental, always didactic. The following piece, "Bury Me in a Free Land," typified Harper's efforts to convey an antislavery message through verse. James Fulcher, "Black Abolitionist Fiction: The Formulaic Art of Douglass, Brown, Delany and Webb," *JAC* 2:583–97 (Winter 1980); Sherman, *Invisible Poets*, xv–xxxii, 62–74; Margaret Hope Bacon, " 'One Great Bundle of Humanity': Frances Ellen Watkins Harper (1825–1911)," *PMHB* 113:21–43 (January 1989); *PFW*, 7 March 1857 [10:0571].

BURY ME IN A FREE LAND
BY FRANCES ELLEN WATKINS[1]

You may make my grave wherever you will,
In a lowly vale or a lofty hill;
You may make it among earth's humblest graves,
But not in a land where men are slaves.

I could not sleep if around my grave
I heard the steps of a trembling slave;
His shadow above my silent tomb
Would make it a place of fearful gloom.

I could not rest if I heard the tread
Of a coffle-gang to the shambles led,
And the mother's shriek of wild despair
Rise like a curse on the trembling air.

16. Frances Ellen Watkins Harper
Courtesy of the Library of Congress

I could not rest if I heard the lash
Drinking her blood at each fearful gash,
And I saw her babes torn from her breast
Like trembling doves from their parent nest.

I'd shudder and start, if I heard the bay
Of the bloodhounds seizing their human prey;
If I heard the captive plead in vain
As they tightened afresh his galling chain.

If I saw young girls, from their mothers' arms
Bartered and sold for their youthful charms
My eye would flash with a mornful flame,
My death-paled cheek grow red with shame.

I would sleep, dear friends, where bloated might
Can rob no man of his dearest right;
My rest shall be calm in any grave,
Where none calls his brother a slave.

I ask no monument proud and high
To arrest the gaze of passers by;
All that my spirit yearning craves,
Is—bury me not in the land of slaves.

Anti-Slavery Bugle (Salem, Ohio), 20 November 1858.

1. Frances Ellen Watkins Harper (1825–1911), an antislavery speaker and women's rights advocate, became one of the foremost black literary figures of the nineteenth century. Born in Baltimore, the only child of free black parents, she was orphaned at an early age. She was reared by her uncle, William Watkins, who educated her at his school and infused her with abolitionist sentiment. Harper left Baltimore in 1850 to teach at Union Seminary, an African Methodist Episcopal school near Columbus, Ohio. Two years later, she secured a teaching position at Little York, Pennsylvania. Contact with William Still and other Philadelphia abolitionists intensified her antislavery feelings. Friends persuaded her to take up lecturing, and in 1854 she accepted a position with the Maine Anti-Slavery Society. She spoke throughout the North and Canada during the remainder of the decade, impressing audiences with her earnestness, eloquence, and extemporaneous abilities. Many thought her the "best female speaker on the subject of slavery." Harper also labored for the free produce movement and contributed a significant portion of her earnings to assist William Still in his efforts to aid and protect fugitive slaves. She openly sympathized with John Brown's actions and consoled Mary Brown, his wife, during the trial and execution of the abolitionist martyr.

In 1860 she married Fenton Harper of Cincinnati, Ohio, and invested her small savings in a farm near Columbus. When he died four years later, the estate settlement left her penniless and forced her to resume lecturing. Harper traveled across the South during Reconstruction, selling her poetry and speaking to groups of freedmen. She championed the cause of black suffrage and emphasized temperance, education, and economic self-reliance as the keys to racial progress. She recorded her observations on black life during these tours as *Sketches of Southern Life* (1872). Harper played an important role in several white-dominated women's organizations, including the Women's Christian Temperance Union and American Woman Suffrage Association. Although interested in a wide range of women's issues, she usually focused on the double burden of discrimination endured by black women. In 1896 she helped found the National Association of Colored Women.

Harper is best remembered for her contributions to Afro-American literature. She nurtured an early interest in the subject while working for the family of a Baltimore bookseller during the 1840s, then published several volumes of poetry, beginning with *Forest Leaves* (1845). Her *Poems on Miscellaneous Subjects* (1854) sold twelve thousand copies in the first four years. Although she wrote in the sentimental style typical of Victorian literature, Harper used her poetry to praise abolitionists, to expose the evils of slavery, and to highlight the ordeal and heroism of slave women. Titles such as "Slave Auction," "Eva's Farewell," and "Double Standard" reflect the antislavery and feminist content of her verse. She also wrote numerous articles for the antislavery press. "The Two Offers," a feminist piece in the *Anglo-African Magazine* (1859), was among the earliest short stories by a black author. *Iola LeRoy* (1892), her tale of a quadroon sold into slavery, was probably the second novel published by a black woman in the United States. *NAW*, 2:137–39; *DANB*, 288–90; Bacon, " 'One Great Bundle of Humanity,' " 21–45; Sterling, *We Are Your Sisters*, 159–64, 403–7; Still, *Underground Railroad*, 755–80.

83.
Stephen A. Myers to John Jay
17 December 1858

The effectiveness of underground railroad stations depended upon the courage, initiative, and managerial skill of individual black leaders. Working in the shadows of legitimacy, they maintained links with dozens of other activists across the North and courted the support of prominent white businessmen and political figures, even some who publicly repudiated abolitionism and supported the colonization movement. Stephen A. Myers directed underground efforts in Albany, New York, for more than twelve years, furnishing food, shelter, and safe passage to hundreds of fugitive slaves; between November 1857 and May 1858, at least 188 runaways reached Canada West as a result of his labors. His 17 December 1858 letter to reformer John Jay of New York City offers an unusually detailed account of his station. Finding eloquence in the simple statement of fact, Myers describes the routine of underground work, the routes of travel, and abolitionist contacts in surrounding cities and states. More important, he reveals the ongoing financial commitments he obtained from prominent Republican politicians and merchants in Albany and New York City. The skillful efforts of Myers and other black leaders secured freedom for thousands of fugitives in the years prior to the Civil War. *PA*, 11 January 1873; Stephen Myers to Francis Jackson, 22 May 1858, Anti-Slavery Collection, MB [11:0232]; *FDP*, 12 February 1858.

Antislavery offic[e]
No. 10 Lark St.
Albany, [New York]
Decem[ber] 17, 1858

Mr. John Jay:[1]
Sir your kinde letter came to hand on the 11th wich was written on the 9th[,] forwarded sir by you for the aid and comfort of fugitives. I thank you and it shall be faithfully appropriated for that object wich you specify. On the 6th Marcelus Custolow Colchester MD[,] on the 7th Wm Locks Oldchester MD[,] on the 10th evening 3 fugitives came in a vesel to New London and they were forwarded to me by T. Holly of Springfeild. Their names and places are Colchester Marryland[,] John Mical[,] James Sims[,] Peter Common & this being sir a central point they are sent to me by Francis Jackson of Boston when any arrive in Boston. Their is many that strays up here that does not come to through Philadelphia or New York.[2] Those I hav named above I hav sent on. Each passage to Syracuse is tow Dollars and fifty cents as the passage has risen. While

17. Fugitive slaves escaping from the eastern shore of Maryland
From William Still, *Underground Railroad* (Philadelphia, 1872)

they remain here I pay one shilling per night for Lodging[,] 18 cents each meal. I hav made it a ruel when I can to send them in the country amoung farmers. I will inform Mr. Jay what my arrangements are for my services. I receive ten per cent on each dollar I receive as I devote my wole time to this Business. The Committee of gentlemen who inspect my Books once a month agreed if I could not collect mony enough to make my services pay four Hunddred and fifty a year that they would assist me in getting that amount after my paying all Board and passages and forwarding them on. I give Mr. Jay a correct statement of the way that I manage my Business. I hav to colect evry Dollar myself and hav for the last nine years. In Philadelphia and in New [York] they hav a Different way to manage their Business. They rais their mony through antislavery societies and fairs. Unfortunately we hav no such society here[,] but the members of the republican party hav allways been very good to assist me. But I hav to colect from this one set of men all the time[,] come very hard on them some times. Mr. Weed gives me for that purpos about one hunddred Dollars per year. Govnor King has given about twenty five dollars a year[,] Mr. Wm. Nuton Deacon of the Baptist Church about thirty Dollars a year. Govnor Seward sends about fifteen Dollars a year[,] Mr. James Wadsworth about 20 Dollars a year[,] Simeon Draper about ten dollars a year[,] Mr. M. Grennell 20 Dollars a year[,] Mr. R. Minturn ten dollars a year[,] Mr. H. Greely eight a year[,] E. D. Morgan fifteen a year[,] Mr. Jams W. Beekman five dollars[,] Mr. J. P. Cummings of New York tewnty a year.[3] Mr. John Jay since 1851 if my memory serves me ~~hav~~ has give me your check on the Bank on the corner of Wall & William St.[4] for 20 dollars[,] and in 1852 you give me ten dollars at your offic[;][5] in 54 I was in New York[,] you gave your check on the same Bank for fifteen Dollars[;] in fifty six you gave at your offic ten dollars[,] and last winter in 1857 at the Capitol here Mr. Jay gave me ten dollars. When I called last sumer in New York to pay Mr. Jay a visit out of respect[,] without asking you presented me with a check on the same Bank for ten dollars[,] all for wich I thank Mr. Jay kindly for. If Mr. Jay should visit Albany this winter during the Legislato[r] I should like Mr. Jay to see our books[,] how much received and how much expended.

I will just give a statement of the number of fugitives that your father has sent here within the last eight years before his death:[6] 3 from Norfolk Va.[,] 2 from Alexandria[,] 2 from New Orleanes. Last tow he sent me were from North Carolia. The sevral checks your father sent me from time to time amounted to fifty Dollars on the Albany State Bank.[7] In his death all lost a true freind to humanity. And yet he rememered the poor fugitive in defianc of the Law. Yours very Respectfully,

Stephen Myers

supt of the underground RR

P.S. Durring the last 18 months we hav had more fugitives than we hav had in former times in tow years.

Jay Family Papers, Rare Book and Manuscript Library, Columbia University, New York, New York. Published by permission.

1. John Jay (1817–1894), the grandson of Chief Justice John Jay, was a prominent lawyer and reformer in New York City. He regularly represented blacks accused of being fugitive slaves, donated funds to the city's Colored Orphan Asylum, and helped organize the local Republican party. During the Civil War, he advocated emancipation, black enlistment, and creation of the Freedmen's Bureau. *DAB*, 10:10–11; Walker, "Afro-American in New York City," 94–95.

2. Fugitive slaves were often landed at New London, Connecticut, a whaling port with an active abolitionist presence, then routed up the Connecticut River valley to Springfield, Massachusetts. There they were aided by a militant, black-dominated vigilance committee led by Timothy H. Harley (1821–?) and fugitive Thomas Thomas. Harley, a barber, had moved to Springfield in 1853 from Kingston, New York, where he had been active in the black state conventions of the 1840s. In 1854 he was elected to the Massachusetts State Council of the Colored People. Harley forwarded hundreds of runaway slaves on to Stephen Myers at Albany. Francis Jackson and the Boston Vigilance Committee also sent fugitives to Albany through Springfield. Under the direction of Myers, the agent and superintendent, the interracial Albany Vigilance Committee fed, housed, protected, and transported hundreds of escaped slaves. Myers also maintained contact with underground railroad workers from Wilmington, Delaware, to Canada West. From Albany, most fugitives were sent west to Jermain W. Loguen and his collaborators at Syracuse. Horatio T. Strother, *The Underground Railroad in Connecticut* (Middletown, Conn., 1962), 131, 138, 172; Siebert, *Underground Railroad*, 125–26, 129, 132; Joseph Carvalho III, *Black Families in Hampden County, Massachusetts, 1650–1855* (Westfield, Mass., 1984), 17–18, 67; *CA*, 6 June 1840, 11 September 1841 [3:0450, 4:0195]; *AP*, 3 October 1843 [4:0679]; *Lib*, 28 July 1854; *Springfield City Directory*, 1862; *FDP*, 12 February 1858; Stephen Myers to Francis Jackson, 22 May 1858, Anti-Slavery Collection, MB [11:0232].

3. Myers and the Albany Vigilance Committee received financial support from leading Republicans throughout New York state. Many of these men had intimate ties with Thurlow Weed and William H. Seward, the leading figures in the statewide Republican organization. Weed (1797–1882), like his counterpart, Horace Greeley of the *New York Tribune*, was a prominent journalist. He published the Albany *Evening Journal* and used the paper to urge New Yorkers to aid fugitive slaves. Most of Myers's contributors were close friends of Weed in the New York City business community. Moses H. Grinnell (1803–1877) and Robert B. Minturn (1805–1866) were major shipping merchants. Merchants Simeon Draper (1804–1866) and Edwin D. Morgan (1811–1883) were leading party figures and close friends of Seward and Weed. Morgan, who served as state commissioner of immigration from 1855 to 1858, had been elected governor of New York the previous month. He replaced the outgoing governor, John Alsop King (1788–1867), a local banker and staunch opponent of the Fugitive Slave

Law. James W. Beekman (1815–1877) was a celebrated lawyer and philanthropist. John P. Cummings owned a lime mill and worked as a building contractor. From the 1830s on, Grinnell, Minturn, Draper, and Morgan had provided Weed with a steady source of funds for political campaigns. He repaid the favor by looking out for their interests in the legislature at Albany. Weed probably directed Myers to these prominent New York City businessmen. When Weed sought the restriction of the Fugitive Slave Law and the strengthening of personal liberty laws in 1860, he obtained their overwhelming support. Myers's other contributors included William Newton (1787–?), an Albany stoneware manufacturer and Baptist lay leader, and James S. Wadsworth (1807–1864), a large landowner in Livingston County. Van Deusen, *Thurlow Weed*, 77, 101, 107, 224, 266–67, 336; *DAB*, 8:5–6, 10:394–95, 13:32–33, 168–69, 19:308–9; U.S. Census, 1850; Amasa J. Parker, ed., *Landmarks of Albany County, New York* (Syracuse, N.Y., 1897), part 3, 349; *ACAB*, 2:229; *New York City Directory*, 1848–59; Hendrik Booraem V, *The Formation of the Republican Party in New York: Politics and Conscience in the Antebellum North* (New York, N.Y., 1983), 91, 118–19, 157, 202–3, 209–11, 244.

4. Myers probably refers to the Bank of America, which was located at 46 Wall Street. *New York City Directory*, 1851–58.

5. John Jay's law office was located at 20 Nassau Street in New York City. *New York City Directory*, 1848–60.

6. John Jay's father, William Jay, died in October 1858. *NYT*, 16 October 1858.

7. Myers refers to the New York State Bank at Albany, which was founded in 1803 and became one of the city's foremost financial institutions. Parker, *Landmarks of Albany County*, part 1, 364.

Index

Page numbers in boldface indicate the main discussion of the subject. Boldface numbers broken by a colon indicate notes in a previous volume in the series.

D1255983

BUSINESS ECONOMICS
Principles and Cases

Business Economics
Principles and Cases

MARSHALL R. COLBERG

Professor of Economics
Department of Economics
The Florida State University

DASCOMB R. FORBUSH

Professor of Economics
School of Management
Clarkson College of Technology

GILBERT R. WHITAKER, JR.

Associate Dean and
Professor of Business Economics
Graduate School of Business Administration
Washington University

 Fifth Edition   1975

RICHARD D. IRWIN, INC.   Homewood, Illinois   60430
Irwin-Dorsey International   London, England   WC2H 9NJ
Irwin-Dorsey Limited   Georgetown, Ontario   L7G 4B3

Fifth Edition

First Printing, May 1975

ISBN 0-256-01547-3
Library of Congress Catalog Card No. 74-27544
Printed in the United States of America

Preface

THIS BOOK combines text and case materials for use in courses in which economic analysis is applied to the solution of business problems. These courses, which may have such titles as Business Economics, Managerial Economics, or Economics of the Firm, are offered both by schools of business administration and by departments of economics. Such courses may serve either as alternatives for, or as complements to, traditional intermediate courses in microeconomics. The cases serve to get the student fully involved in the application of such basic economic concepts as opportunity cost, marginality, and profit or utility maximization as well as providing additional factual information about many types of business activity.

The authors have attempted to write the book for undergraduates who have had a course in principles of economics. With appropriate supplementation it is suitable for first year graduate students in business administration. Some prior training in accounting, finance, and statistics is desirable but not essential to an understanding of this volume. Mathematical formulations, apart from geometrical figures, are not emphasized except where necessary for precision, as in the case of capitalization formulas.

This is a very substantial revision of the fourth edition published in 1970. Among the changes are a new introductory chapter which can easily be read by students who may have missed the first class meeting. At the request of many instructors simple expositions of the theory of consumer choice and of linear programming have been added as appendixes for those who wish to assign (or skip) these materials. Some elements of human capital theory as it applies to the firm have been added. Concern for environmental protection, which can affect both the voluntary and involuntary actions of business enterprises, is reflected in new text material and cases dealing with social costs and consumerist

v

pressures. Nixon era price controls are included. The growth of international investment has led the authors to include multinational as well as domestic plant location determinants. Much updating of statistical and legal material has occurred in chapters dealing with such subjects as forecasting and antitrust actions.

Many new cases have been added, and some which were previously used have been updated. To some extent it has been possible to use the revealed preferences of professors who used earlier editions as a guide to retention or deletion of cases. A move in the direction of shorter cases has occurred because of this guidance.

It is believed that the present edition contains enough material for a full academic year of work in business economics. The book more usually has been adapted to courses lasting a single semester, trimester, or quarter by eliminating many cases and by skipping appendixes or chapters thought to be of less importance to course objectives.

An undertaking of this sort owes much to the work of others, and each of the authors has separate as well as joint obligations. Especially important among the latter are permissions to use case materials on the part of firms and to extract cases from published articles. Specific acknowledgements are made in the cases.

At The Florida State University, thanks are due to James P. King, Assistant Professor of Finance and former manager of the Elberta Crate and Box Company; to Leland Gustafson and Eugene Holshouser for permission to use their statistical demand studies; to Marjan Senjur for library research, and to several secretaries, notably Carol Bullock and Mrs. G. W. Jordan for indispensable work.

From Clarkson College, we thank John R. Tedford for helpful comments from his course experience and Virginia Smith for her competent secretarial work. We acknowledge gratefully the supplying of case material by John A. Larson of Brookings Institute and by Daniel H. Forbush.

At Washington University, thanks are due to Jess B. Yawitz, Assistant Professor of Business Economics and Finance, for material for a case and for several useful suggestions; to Lyn Pankoff for a critical review of the linear programming appendix; and to Gloria Becker, and Ruth Scheetz for typing assistance.

April 1975   MARSHALL R. COLBERG
                                                DASCOMB R. FORBUSH
                                                GILBERT R. WHITAKER, JR.

Contents

4. Demand Analysis for the Industry   96

Quantity and Price. Slope and Price Elasticity. Elasticity and Revenue. Computation of Price Elasticity. Quantity and Income. Quantity and Population. Quantity and Prices of Substitutes. Quantity and Advertising. Quantity and Stock. Empirical Demand Functions. Shifts in Demand and Supply.

APPENDIX TO CHAPTER 4: The Theory of Consumer Choice and the Demand for Products, 112

5. Demand Analysis for the Firm   137

Demand Facing a Monopolist. Some Qualifications. Demand Facing Pure Competitor. Pure Competition Is Uncommon. Demand under Oligopoly. Market Share. Demand Analysis and Forecasting Sales of a Firm.

6. Short-Run Private Costs of Production   163

Opportunity Cost. Production Possibilities for a Single Good. Fixed and Variable Costs. Relationship of Costs to Production Function. Hypothetical Cost Data. Average and Marginal Cost Curves. Output under Competitive Conditions. All or Nothing Decision. Adaptability and Divisibility of Plant. Statistical Cost Analysis.

APPENDIX A TO CHAPTER 6: Optimal Inventory Policy, 177
APPENDIX B TO CHAPTER 6: Linear Programming Methods and Cost Minimization, 179

7. Investment Decisions and Long-Run Cost   203

Flexibility of Plant. Size of Firm and Cost. Limited Production Run. Value of Equipment. Value of a Machine. Decision to Purchase a

Machine. Should a New Model Be Purchased? Alternative Formulation of Replacement Criterion. Revenue Considerations.

APPENDIX TO CHAPTER 7: The Abandonment Decision, 217

8. Capital Budgeting and Financing Capital Expenditures   226

Ranking Projects by Rate of Return. Supply of Capital Funds. Sources of Funds. Cost of Capital from Specific Sources. Cost of Debt. Cost of Preferred Stock. Cost of Common Stock. Cost of Internally Generated Funds. Overall Cost of Capital. Capital Structure. Supply Schedule for Capital Funds.

9. Production and Social Costs   250

Private Bargaining. Pollution and Common Property. Solution by Merger. Prohibition of Pollution. Regulation by Authorities. Taxes on Pollutants. Summary of Some Important Principles.

10. Employment of Human Resources   262

Marginal Productivity of Labor. Fixed Proportions. Monopolist's Demand for Labor. Monopsony. Bilateral Monopoly. Bilateral Monopoly in Labor Markets. Minimum Wage Laws. Training of Workers. Worker Alienation. Executive Incentives.

11. The Determination of Prices—Competition and Monopoly   286

COMPETITION: Very Short-Run Supply. Short Run and Long Run. MONOPOLY: Other Sources of Monopoly Power. Monopoly Demand. Marginal Revenue. Monopoly Price for Existing Supply. Short-Run Output and Prices. Long-Run Adjustments. Cartels. Taxation of Monopoly Profits.

APPENDIX TO CHAPTER 11: Pricing under Regulation, 300

12. Price Discrimination and Price Differentials   337

Definition of Price Differentials and Price Discrimination. Elements of Monopoly and Market Imperfection as Requisites for Discrimination. Separation of Markets as a Requisite for Price Discrimination when Price Differentials Are Involved. Perfect Price Discrimination. Discrimination by Customer Classification. Discrimination and Differentials when Products Are Differentiated. Geographic Price Discrimination. Basing-Point Pricing in Steel. Market Penetration. Price Differentials and Discrimination when Marginal Costs Differ. The Legality of Price Discrimination. The Social Acceptability of Price Discrimination.

13. Price Strategies When Sellers Are Few   375

Reactions to Price Changes under Oligopoly. Concentration of American Industry and Oligopoly. Pure and Differentiated Oligopoly. The Variety of Oligopolistic Situations as an Influence on Business Decisions. Cartelization or Formal Agreements. Price Leadership and Other Conventions. Emphasis on Policies That Are Difficult to Retaliate Against. Independent Action with Little Concern for Reactions.

14. Nonprice Aspects of Competition   426

Competition in Services and Other Terms of Trade. Types of Product Competition. Varieties of Sales Promotion. The Magnitude of Product and Selling Competition. An Economic Model of Product Differentiation. Sales Promotion and Economic Growth: An Illustrative Model. A Marginal Approach. Consumerism, Product, and Promotion Policies. The Game Theory Approach.

APPENDIX TO CHAPTER 14: Game Theory and Business Decisions, 439

1

The Challenge of Business Economics

ECONOMICS is the study of the optimal use of scarce resources to satisfy human wants. It consequently deals with both the extent to which labor and capital are employed and the way in which these factors are allocated among alternative goods and services. Economics is primarily a social science rather than one which has as its purpose the analysis of efficient behavior on the part of the individual business firm. Nevertheless, social economy requires that business enterprises be well located, be alert to the demands of consumers, be of efficient size, be operated efficiently, and be compelled by competition to pass on to buyers the advantages of their efficiency. A good deal of economic analysis is concerned, consequently, with principles of efficient action applicable to the firm. This book will discuss some of these principles and will present business cases the solution of which should be facilitated by the application of the associated analysis. A good businessman need not be an economist, but a knowledge of economics is likely to sharpen his thinking about his own firm's problems and sometimes will aid him in making wise decisions which would not otherwise be obvious. Certain types of business decisions are sufficiently difficult and important to justify use not only of all relevant theoretical analysis but also of expensive empirical investigation.

The Perspective and Decisions of Business Economics

Business economics is primarily concerned with the applicability of economic concepts and analysis to five types of decisions made by businesses: the selection of the product (or service), the choice of production methods, the determination of prices and quantities, the promotional

1

strategy, and the place (or location) decision. In brief, how can businessmen mind their p's and q's.

The perspective of business or managerial economics is quite different from that of conventional microeconomics in studying these decisions. The major interest of the latter is to predict equilibrium prices and quantities in demonstrating how resources are allocated to the production of goods and services throughout the economy. The firm is recognized as a leading actor on the economic stage but is typically a rather bloodless abstraction. It is usually convenient to assume that the firm seeks to maximize profit. Somewhat sophisticated revenue and cost functions lead to price and quantity predictions using this criterion. Whether a particular firm is successful or not is not usually a central issue in the analysis which is primarily concerned with industry or market performance.

The emphasis of business economics is on managerial decisions rather than on predicting the equilibrium position of an industry. Forecasting the probable outcomes of alternative actions is seen as part of this decision-making process. It is not necessary to assume the goal of profit maximization; part of the decision-making process is to determine the firm's objectives (and profit is likely to be important among them). The success of the particular firm is of considerable consequence to its managers and owners, though it may be of minor importance to the economy.

While the viewpoint of the participating manager is far different from that of the observing economist, the participant can make use of much of what the economist has noted: concepts such as marginal revenue and opportunity cost which have been developed by economists making deductions as to rational behavior; forecasting techniques such as leading indicators and regression analysis; analytical frameworks such as the classification of market structures; and institutional observations on the impact of antitrust policy or a minimum wage law.

Each of the types of decisions of primary concern to business economics has many manifestations:

1. The product decision may range from the launching of a major innovation following a long period of research, such as Du Pont's introduction of nylon, to a minor alteration in quality, like producing saltines as single crackers instead of blocks of four. It may be a routine annual decision such as whether to plant the "back forty" in soybeans or corn, or it may be almost never made, such as changing the formula of an established soft drink. It may be made by a new firm or an established firm, through a merger or by building a new plant.

2. *The Choice of Production Methods.* When highly generalized, this choice is the selection of the cost-minimizing combination of labor and capital necessary to produce a particular output and is dependent on the state of technology and the relative prices of the factors. In specific business cases it may involve changes as small as a switch to longer runs

and larger inventory holdings of replacement parts for equipment. On the other hand, it could involve a multibillion dollar switch to a newer technology such as the substitution of oxygen converters for open-hearth furnaces in the steel industry, which was substantially accomplished in the 1960s. Instead of the two (or three if land is included) factors of production in generalized economic analysis, the detailed decisions of firms will involve choices among the numerous types of labor, capital, land, raw materials, and intermediate goods. Nevertheless, the principles guiding factor substitution that will minimize cost are the same for two or one hundred factors.

3. *The Determination of Prices and Quantities.* Price and quantity can be viewed as two aspects of the same decision. For the pricetaker in a competitive market (for example, a cattle rancher), the decisions are entirely quantity decisions: the size of herd and the number of young steers sold to feeding lots at a particular time. Current and anticipated prices are information to guide the quantity decisions. For firms with sufficient market power to have some discretion over price, the quantity that can be sold will be determined by the price charged. When firms do formulate price policies, a close relationship is likely to exist with product and promotional decisions. A list price of $6,500 for a Cadillac Eldorado is determined after a sequence of decisions regarding particular product specifications and the image of the car that has been projected partly as a result of promotional strategy. The WEO (Where Economy Originates) program of A & P stores which involved an aggressive pricing policy in 1972–73 also reflected the promotional possibilities inherent in such a program when the public was highly concerned about inflation in food prices and a product policy which emphasized A & P's own brands.

4. *Promotional Strategy.* As long as the assumption of given, or at least exogenously determined, tastes and preferences of consumers is made, economic analysis has no place for a consideration of promotional expenditures. With the relaxation of this assumption, promotion, defined as expenditures made by the firms to shift demand curves, becomes important. Advertising expenditures involving such media as television, radio, magazines, newspapers, direct mail, and outdoor signs have run in the range of 3 percent to 4 percent of total consumption expenditures. Sales promotion also includes personal selling efforts such as the Avon lady, the Fuller Brush man, the drug company representative visiting doctors, and at least part of the time of system analysis experts representing computer companies.

5. *The Place (or Location) Decision.* Much of traditional economic analysis makes the simplifying assumption that the production and distribution of goods occurs at one point in space and thus does not bear on locational decisions. For most businesses, major locational decisions are relatively infrequent. New distribution outlets may be set up or a

warehouse system reorganized, but shifts in the location of major plants with long depreciation periods and established labor forces are infrequent. The importance of the decisions and the applicability of economic analysis with the spatial dimension added, as it has been in location, transportation, and regional economics, justify treating the place decision as the fifth of the types of decisions with which business economics is primarily concerned.

It has already been suggested that price, product, and promotional decisions may be closely interrelated. Other types of decisions are also interrelated; for example, a decision to substitute plastic for wood as a raw material for clothespins involves both product and production methods. The introduction of large-scale, high-density broiler production concentrated the location of broiler production geographically, notably in Georgia and the Delmara area.

The Importance of Business Decision Making in a Changing Society

It is important to the welfare of society that the decisions allocating resources to and using resources for production of goods and services be accomplished efficiently. Comparative studies of the underdeveloped and developed countries have indicated that a significant variable influencing the performance of an economy is the relative abundance of competent managers and business entrepreneurs. How well the "invisible hand" works in a market-governed economy will depend on the quality of individual decisions by producers and consumers. Low-cost, efficient production will not be assured by the competition among the firms in an industry unless at least a significant fraction of the individual firms are able to use technological and economic information to develop low-cost methods of producing wanted products. Competition among the inept does not produce the competent. The resources lost by an ill-conceived venture are not restored to society.

In a democratic society the perception the public has of how business enterprise is performing is important, although the public is not necessarily completely informed. Its perception also may be subjected to great swings in sentiment resulting from forces beyond businesses' control as indicated in Figure 1–1 which summarizes the results of Harris polls taken in 1966 and in December, 1972. The question asked of about 1,500 households in each year was, "I would like you to keep in mind the companies and management that make up American business. For each area I ask you about, I wish you would tell me your impression of the job that American business is doing in that area—excellent, pretty good, only fair, or poor." "Excellent" and "pretty good" were considered positive responses and "only fair" or "poor" negative responses in the tabulation given in Figure 1–1.

FIGURE 1–1

Trend in Positive Attitude toward Business

		Positive Rating		
		1972	*1966*	*Change*
1.	Developing new products through research...............69		92	−23
2.	Putting in latest improvements in machinery..............59		89	−30
3.	Building new plants to make economy grow..............55		78	−23
4.	Providing enough steady jobs for people.................48		76	−28
5.	Providing job openings for minorities...................49		57	− 8
6.	Paying good wages and salaries........................48		72	−24
7.	Paying out adequate dividends to stockholders............42		56	−14
8.	Providing stockholders with sound investment op-portunities..42		56	−14
9.	Bringing better quality products to American people........42		75	−33
10.	Offering young people chance to get ahead...............41		73	−32
11.	Dealing fairly with labor unions.......................41		56	−15
12.	Allowing people to use their full creative abilities..........34		62	−28
13.	Really caring about the individual......................22		39	−17
14.	Helping care for workers displaced by automation.........19		40	−21
15.	Keeping profits at reasonable levels.....................19		46	−27
16.	Keeping down cost of living...........................10		21	−11

Source: *Chicago Tribune*, syndication (1973).

Seventy-seven percent of the public felt that the policies of Nixon's second term ought to be tougher toward business, and only 1 percent thought the policies should be easier than those of the first term. Nixon's landslide victory a month before, however, suggested that the public had not provided a mandate for a change in policies toward business. Much of the dissatisfaction in the earlier 1970s with the performance of American business reflected the rather unpalatable combination of inflation of well over 3 percent per year[1] and unemployment of over 5 percent, phenomena largely outside of the control of individual businessmen. Nonetheless important challenges both for public policy and business decision making have arisen, and it is worth considering several of these.

The Challenge of Consumerism

New vitality has been added to a movement that has affected government regulation particularly in the period just before World War I and again in the 1930s—Ralph Nader and Nader's Raiders, young lawyers and others working with him on a series of exposés on business actions and government regulation. The major business decisions under attack

---

[1] The survey was taken before the 1973–74 surge in prices that raised the intermediate annual budget for an urban family of four 10.3 percent in a year (Bureau of Labor Statistics).

are those concerned with product and promotion. The major questions raised about products have been concerned with safety, particularly concerning automobiles and drugs. Nader first came to prominence in the early sixties with his book, *Unsafe at Any Speed*,[2] which focused particularly on the dangers of the Corvair, a General Motors compact car that was shortly discontinued. The resulting Motor Vehicle Safety Act has led to increasing controls such as seat-belt regulations, which may be leading to the compulsory buckling. Policy questions raised for business firms include not only the political problem of resistance to or support of safety legislation but this economic issue: how far should firms push the safety or other qualities of products, given the added costs involved in the face of social and market pressures, rather than mandatory laws?

Both product and promotional issues have been raised in the drug industry but have wider ramifications for other businesses. New drug legislation requiring stricter testing procedures followed the incident in which thousands of deformed babies were born in Europe (notably in Germany and Great Britain) as the result of the use of thalidomide, a new analgesic. The United States was spared not so much because of strong laws but because of the administrative firmness of one medical official. The effect of requiring fuller testing of drugs before public sale has been to materially reduce the rate of introduction of new drugs.

What is being asked of the drug industry and of American business in general is "fuller disclosure" of the relevant facts about products. For drugs, food additives, some cosmetic preparations, and so forth, full disclosure requires more knowledge about long-range side effects of materials ingested into the complex human body. For American industry as a whole, greater candor has been called for under such legislation as Truth in Lending and the Fair Packaging Act, under administration decrees such as the warning requirement on cigarette packages and advertising, under the threat of private damage suits using the common-law concept of warranty, and under voluntary programs such as unit pricing and listing nutritional content of foods. The increasing complexity of products and the variety of product choices suggests further moves away from "caveat emptor" or "let the buyer beware" doctrines, moves which on the whole should prove a welcome although sometimes inconvenient challenge for business. A fuller discussion of the economic aspects of and implications for product and promotional strategies of fuller disclosure developments is contained in Chapter 14.

The Challenge of the Environmental Movement

A broad range of business decisions are being conditioned by the several aspects of environmentalism. Decisions on production methods

---

[2] Ralph Nader, *Unsafe at Any Speed* (New York: Grossman, 1965).

must meet the clean air and pure water standards of state and federal acts. The economic case for charges per unit of pollutant which would confront the firm with increased costs in proportion to the effluent discharged has been largely rejected in favor of maximum discharge limits. The degree to which these maxima can be reduced over time will largely be a function of the success some business firms have in developing technology that will reduce pollution at costs that the public is willing to bear. It is easy to put the finger on corporations as polluters, but the ulimate cost of abatement must largely be carried by the consumers whose demands are being presently met by lower cost production methods that involve effluent discharges.

That product decisions of firms are and will be affected is most conspicuously illustrated in the challenge to auto manufacturers to meet the engine emission standards set by the Environmental Protection Agency under the Clean Air Act of 1970. Some observers were highly critical of the technological solution proposed by the auto companies of the catalytic converters, as being expensive to the consumer ($300 to $400 a car were estimates), unreliable, and costly in terms of fuel. Unfavorable comparisons were made with the progress made by the Japanese particularly in the Honda's stratified charge technology. Other types of product decision involve packaging. The growing dominance of the nonreturnable container for beer and soft drink was being questioned to the point of stringent legal restrictions, as in Oregon· and Vermont. The environmental issues raised by the nonreturnables include the contribution of such containers to the solid waste disposal problem, the visual desecration of roadways and parks by discarded containers, and the extra energy requirements of producing containers that were simply thrown away.

Serious questions continue to be raised about the increase in the demand for electricity, amounting to 7 percent a year in the United States for the decades since World War II. The rate of use of natural resources and the various forms of pollution accompanying such increases in resource consumption are aspects of the concern. Price-quantity decisions of electric utilities are being challenged, particularly on the grounds that step-rate structures that give lower rates to larger users tend to stimulate growth in power consumption.

The electric utilities are prime examples of new constraints on place decisions, though the structures extend to heavy industry in general and in some locations such as Greenwich, Connecticut, to light, smokeless industrial or commercial establishments whose presence would tend to increase population or automotive densities. The growth in zoning and land use restrictions, requirements for environmental impact studies, and in legal and political activities by environmentally concerned citizens add new complexities to location decisions.

The Provision of Equal and Challenging Employment Opportunities

There are two distinct strands to this important challenge to management decision making. The first is that of fairness in hiring and promotion so that equal opportunities are provided in all categories of employment to men and women regardless of race and ethnic background. The second is that of reducing what some observers have noted as increasing job alienation.

Both strands could be classified as influences on decisions involving production methods. Efforts to make jobs more meaningful could involve restructuring manufacturing processes to reduce the input of labor in purely repetitive, quasi-mechanical tasks epitomized by assembly-lines operation. Some means toward this end could be the substitution of automatic equipment, increasing job content to cover a broader range of operations, encouraging greater worker participation in restructuring operating procedures. To some observers the labor unrest at the Lordstown, Ohio, plant of General Motors has been symbolic of job alienation and management's efforts to cope with it. As a new plant in the early 1970s in a traditionally assembly-line industry with an unusually youthful work force, its difficulties were taken as representative of new conflicts.

It could be argued that pressures for equal opportunities in employment do not result in changes in production methods, since the same labor skills in a black or female form are being substituted for those of white males. In fact, however, the occupations in which female and black participation rates are the lowest are business-related professions such as accounting and engineering and in managerial occupations. Readjustments are likely to be called for by white males toward taking the technical advice of women or black professionals and orders from women or black managers. That the ability, training, and experience of those from economically underprivileged groups will be precisely the same is also in doubt. The long history of occupational exclusion from these occupations is likely to mean continued shortages of those educated for and experienced in these fields.

The place or location decisions of firms must also be influenced if equality of opportunity in a wide range of occupations is to be increased for black minorities (and to a lesser extent, for Spanish-speaking minorities). Most new manufacturing and retailing locations are being selected at the periphery of metropolitan areas. At the same time, black population growth is almost entirely occurring in the central cities (from 9.7 million in 1960 to 13.6 million in 1970). It is doubtful whether free market decisions of firms will be effective in equalizing employment opportunities to inner city ghetto residents without various subsidies that would influence locational decisions.

The Organization of Business Economics

Basic economic decisions that firms make have been outlined, and several challenges to how such decisions are made have been considered. It is now appropriate to look at the structure of an economic approach to the problems involved.

The success of a business enterprise depends on its ability to at least cover the costs of its operations with revenues. The concept of economic profits expresses the difference between relevant revenues and costs, and represents the logical starting point for Chapter 2. Business decisions look forward into an uncertain future, and so when profits are discussed the relationship with uncertainty must be recognized, and thus Chapter 2 is entitled "Uncertainty, Profits and Business Decisions." The future orientation of decision making makes it important that techniques for forecasting be given the early consideration of Chapter 3, "Forecasting Methods."

Economic analysis is firmly based in the concepts of demand and supply. Either could be taken up first; our choice has been for demand because economic forecasting has given particular attention to the forecasting of demand functions in which the quantity demanded of a product is determined by the key decision variables of price and promotion as well as such externally determined variables as income and population. The sequence chosen of first looking at the demand for industries (Chapter 4) and then the demand for firms (Chapter 5) reflects a frequent forecasting practice of businesses in which a forecast for the economy as a whole precedes the forecast for the industry, which in turn serves as a framework for forecasting the firm's share of the market.

Chapters 6–10 are concerned with the costs that determine the ability of a firm to be an effective supplier for various quantities of production. The student should recall the economist's technique of keeping some variables constant while the behavior of others is being examined, and should recognize that the short-run costs referred to in Chapter 6 are those incurred when plant and technology are taken as fixed. A broader choice of production methods becomes available when capital inputs are allowed to vary, as in Chapter 7. Meeting recent environmental concerns about the total social costs are part of the agenda of Chapter 9. For this purpose firms may be required to develop new technologies as well as to alter output level or plant size.

Chapter 8, "Capital Budgeting and Financing Capital Expenditures," stresses the key time dimension of business decision making in which capital resources are invested in time periods prior to the realization of the benefits in the form of revenues or cost savings. Together with Chapter 7, it presents key concepts included in such courses as engineering economics and managerial finance. Chapter 10, "Employment of Human

Resources," is a logical successor, since production essentially requires the combination of capital and human resources.

The economist uses hypotheses or laws about supply and demand to predict the prices and quantities of outputs. Chapters 11–15 bring together demand and supply concepts as a framework which firms may use in determining their price-quantity, promotional, and product decisions. Chapter 11 considers the basic economic models of competition and monopoly for the determination of prices and quantities. The following chapters deal with decisions for which these models must be elaborated or otherwise modified. The pricing problem faced by firms includes not only that of price level but also of price structure, so Chapter 12 deals with price differentials and price discrimination. Neither the competitive nor monopoly model is entirely satisfactory for the determination of price strategy when sellers number more than one and less than many, and thus Chapter 13 is concerned with price strategies when sellers are few. The possibilities of altering demand through product policies and promotional decisions are considered in Chapter 14. A strong trend toward increasing the scope of a business firm's activities, particularly through conglomerate mergers, reached a peak in the late 1960s. Chapter 15, "Product Line Policy and the Conglomerate Firm," examines economic considerations behind this development.

The place or location decision which was only incidentally touched upon in previous chapters is the subject of explicit consideration in Chapter 16. Not only is this a key decision for business but it is one that has become of increasing interest to public policy with the greater interest in urban and regional planning and with the postwar magnitude of direct investment abroad.

Throughout the text, government regulation has been recognized as an important constraint on business decision making. The final chapter on governmental parameters to business decisions both acts as a reference for considering such constraints during previous parts of the course and as a concluding note on public policies designed to influence present and future business decision making.

Uncertainty, Profits, and Business Decisions

THE SUBJECT MATTER of this chapter is interrelationships between uncertainty, profits, and business decisions in standard economic analysis and in business decision theory. An introductory section on uncertainty precedes a discussion of the distinction between accounting and economic profits with the key concept of opportunity costs. A review of general economic theories of profits which have implications for business strategy follows. All stress departures from the static model of pure competition and see economic profits as resulting from dynamic forces in the economy and, under some definitions, from monopolistic elements.

An illustrative example contrasting a graphic supply and demand approach to an output decision and a payoff matrix is used first to show an approach to business decision making under the three assumptions of certainty, uncertainty, and risk. This example is further developed to show how a utility measure that is more inclusive than monetary profits could be used as the criterion for business decision making.

Finally, the chapter ends with a discussion of a variety of ways in which business firms transform or reduce uncertainties and risks resulting from possible price fluctuations, with hedging in commodities markets as an example.

Only Uncertainty Is Certain

It is often said that nothing is certain except death and taxes. In an important sense, not even these qualifications need be made. The entire institution of life insurance is based on the uncertainty of the date of death of the individual in comparison with the calculability of mortality rates for large numbers of persons within various age groups. Also, the amount and nature of the taxes, which will be assessed by governmental bodies, are often important uncertainties of life.

If the future could be known with certainty, correct economic decisions could be made by everyone. The worker could know precisely where and how to earn the largest income, the business executive would know in advance the outcome of alternative ventures which he might undertake, and the investor would be fully cognizant of the relative desirability of the various investment opportunities open to him. Decision making would not be difficult, and professional decision makers (business executives) would not be highly paid. Investment in a newly formed uranium mining company would be as safe as investment in a well-established utility company.

In the actual world the existence of uncertainty causes future incomes to be imperfectly predictable. Often it is possible for the individual to choose between receiving income which is definite in amount according to terms either of a contract or of an unwritten agreement, or receiving income which depends, instead, on the outcome of the economic activity in which he participates. In the first case the individual can be fairly sure as to what his income will be in the near future, while in the second case the degree of predictability is lower. A fisherman, for example, may work for a regular daily wage or, alternatively, may share in the proceeds of the sale of the catch. The latter arrangement is very common because of the unusually high degree of uncertainty regarding the production function (relation of output to input) in the fishing industry. Similarly, a manager may be employed at a specific salary rate by a chain grocery store or, alternatively, may operate his own store where the return for his labor and capital investment depends on the success of the operation. Similarly, a person wanting to invest funds in a particular corporation may become a bondholder, a preferred stockholder, or a common stockholder. In the first case, he would be a creditor of the firm, receiving interest in a fixed annual amount. His income would not depend on the success of the firm except that a sufficiently unprofitable situation might endanger both his receipt of interest and the safety of his principal. As a preferred stockholder the degree of uncertainty of his return would be somewhat lower, while as a common stockholder the investor faces the greatest degree of uncertainty, both as to return and as to safety of principal.[1]

---

[1] Over a long period of time, however, common stock may offer the investor more nearly a guarantee of stability or gain in *real* income and real value of principal. This is traceable primarily to the propensity of governments to follow inflationary monetary and fiscal policies.

Hired and Self-Employed Resources

Labor contracted at a specific wage or salary rate, a rented building or machine, and funds borrowed from bondholders or banks may conveniently be considered to be examples of "hired" resources from the point of view of the firm. Labor secured on an income-sharing basis, including that contributed by owners of the enterprise, and capital contributed by stockholders, partners, or individual proprietors may be termed "unhired" or "self-employed" resources or factors of production. Persons who dislike uncertainty are likely to take steps to receive their income primarily as a contractual return, while those with less aversion to uncertainty are more willing to receive a larger proportion of their income on a noncontractual basis.

In a profit-oriented economic system the payments to hired factors of production are based on the estimated marginal revenue productivity of these resources—that is, on the additional revenue which firms expect to secure from the sale of the additional output attributable to a unit of a resource, other productive inputs remaining unchanged in amount. Since contractual payments must be arranged in advance, and since firms compete with one another in hiring factors of production, the payments to hired resources reflect businessmen's anticipations as to the worth of these resources. In business, as elsewhere in life, expected and realized situations frequently differ. If a favorable turn of events—a sudden increase in people's willingness to spend their money for goods and services, for example—causes firms' incomes to exceed expectations, increased residuals are left over after all costs have been deducted from gross income. An unfavorable turn of events, or overoptimism on the part of businessmen in bidding up the prices of factors of production, will reduce the size of the residuals which remain to firms after paying for all hired inputs. The "self-employed" or "unhired" resources receive their incomes out of these amounts which remain after hired resources are paid off at contractual rates.

Accounting and Economic Profit

The accountant designates as "profit" or "net income" (before taxes) the amount which is left over out of gross income after all payments to hired factors. The economist points out that further deductions must be made from this amount in order to get a somewhat less arbitrary picture of the success of the firm's operations in any period. The accountant's measurement, while suited to the purpose for which it is made, is greatly affected by the extent to which resources are remunerated on a contractual basis. Other things being equal, the greater the extent to which the needed resources are hired rather than self-employed, the lower will be the net income shown in the accounting records. In order to avoid this arbitrary element, the cost of self-employed resources, evaluated by determining what they could earn if employed on a contractual basis instead, must also be deducted. The alternative earnings of unhired factors are often called "implicit costs." Hence, deduction of implicit as well as explicit costs from gross income gives "economic profit." Deduction of explicit costs alone gives accounting profit.

The above distinction is of great practical importance because of the existence of a heavy federal tax on corporation "profits." Often, it is possible for a firm to raise additional capital funds by selling either bonds or common stock. If it sells bonds, the funds are "hired," and the interest paid is an explicit cost of doing business. If, instead, stocks are sold, the funds are owned, and there is no explicit interest cost which can be deducted in arriving at accounting profit. There is an implicit cost involved in that the funds raised by selling stock could instead have earned some contractual rate in an alternative employment. By selling stock instead of bonds, the corporation subjects itself to a larger corporate income tax. In recent years, many firms have raised additional capital funds by means of bonds rather than stock, in order to secure this tax advantage. In other cases, firms have converted preferred stock into bonds for the same reason.[2]

Economic profits are of primary significance when calculated for the future. It is the prospect (not the achievement) of such profits that is seen by the economist as directing businessmen to employ resources in their "best," that is, most profitable, use. Profits are estimated for the relevant future alternatives in determining this use. Thus in Case 2–1, Cows or Condominiums, the Vermont dairyman should consider the potential return from selling his land as a cost in computing the profitability of continuing the dairy business.

In contrast, accounting profits are figured for the course of action actually taken. They, therefore, measure past or historical costs for the one alternative actually followed rather than estimating possible future gains for many alternatives.

The distinction between economic and accounting profit is also of importance in either evaluating the worth of an enterprise which is for sale or deciding whether an enterprise should be continued. Typically, the individual enterpriser contributes his own labor and some capital to

---

[2] In order not to affect the relative desirability of different types of securities from the corporation's point of view, a corporate income tax could theoretically be levied on economic profit rather than accounting profit. In practice, however, a knotty problem of calculating appropriate alternative contractual rates of return on securities would exist. A simpler alternative would be elimination of interest as a cost in computing net profit for income tax purposes.

the operation of his firm. This involves an implicit cost, since his labor and capital could, alternatively, earn income elsewhere on a contractual basis. Since no explicit cost is involved, the enterpriser is unlikely to show any cost on his books for the use of his own resources. If the firm is offered for sale, it becomes important for a potential buyer to keep in mind the exclusion of these costs. Since the alternative earning power of the buyer's labor may differ from that of the labor of the previous owner, the best appraisal of the desirability of making the purchase may involve the use of the buyer's alternative income-earning possibilities rather than those of the previous operator. Like all decisions of this sort, the decision regarding purchase of a business involves *anticipated* rather than past incomes, and these anticipations are fraught with uncertainty. In the absence of better information, however, anticipations may have to be based on past performance.

In order to decide whether a somewhat marginal enterprise is worth continuing, the businessman may do well to think in terms of an "economist's balance sheet." Such a balance sheet would value individual assets according to their income-earning potential in other uses, that is, according to their present market prices. Historical costs, which provide the basis for the accountant's balance sheet, would not enter into consideration. If the total market value of such individually evaluated assets exceeded their value as a whole to the enterprise, as calculated from future earnings prospects, the indicated decision is to liquidate the business by selling assets separately. The process of discounting anticipated future earnings of the business as a whole in order to find the present value of its net assets (assets minus liabilities) will be discussed in some detail in a later chapter.

Even if the decision is to remain in business, this way of thinking about the "opportunity cost" of retaining assets may lead to useful decisions. For example, the present market value of an asset may be so high that the firm in question should sell the asset and replace it with a cheaper one. This is especially likely to happen with land that is vacant or that supports a well-depreciated building. A periodic check of its value to other possible users might lead a firm to a more rational decision on whether this particular parcel of land should remain in the business.

One of the pressures that has resulted in the movement of firms to the rural fringes of metropolitan areas is that rising land values in more central locations make the land asset too valuable for continuation of its present use. Higher property taxes that usually accompany such increases in land value add to the pressure to act. One recreational industry that has been particularly affected is that of the private golf course. In the face of a rapid growth in the number of golfers, the number of golf courses has remained relatively constant, essentially because well-located suburban courses are sold off for residential and commercial development as the land becomes literally too valuable for the land-extensive game of the Scots. The result: escalating greens fees and increased congestion with lineups at 5:00 A.M. on weekends for an early tee off at public urban courses.

The implicit opportunity costs of alternative uses of a scarce resource may prove to be a financial solace to firms faced with unfavorable shifts in demand. For example, the scarce waterfront property that was an indispensable part of a northern New England boys' or girls' camp may now be valued at $150 a foot for second-home use. For a camp owner struggling against competition from European tours and specialized sports camps for a youth market impatient with reveilles and woodcraft, $150,000 for lake frontage could be substantial inducement for early exit.

Uncertainty Theory of Profit

If the future were always perfectly predictable, the income received by a factor of production would be the same whether it were remunerated on a contractual or on a residual basis. Persons paid on the former basis would not be willing to accept less than they could get as residual claimants; and similarly, those receiving residual incomes would not accept less than they could earn at contractual rates. In the actual, uncertain world, there is usually a difference between the income which resources earn on a contractual and self-employed basis—that is, economic profits (positive or negative) usually exist. In a year of especially good business, for example, economic profits generally are likely to be positive. Most stockholders will receive better rates of return than bondholders, while persons in business for themselves may do better, on the average, than if they had worked for someone else. In a year of depressed business activity the situation is likely to be just the opposite—that is, economic profits will frequently be negative.

Since there would be no economic profits in a perfectly predictable and competitive economy, uncertainty is the basic reason for the existence of profits. It is necessary, however, to distinguish between true uncertainties and those more manageable uncertainties which can be insured against. Examples of the latter are uncertainty as to the duration of life, uncertainty as to whether a particular house will burn, and uncertainty as to whether a car or truck will be involved in an accident. If statistical probabilities have been worked out with sufficient accuracy to make it possible for a company to sell insurance against occurrences of a particular contingency, a definite contractual payment by the firm to the insurance company will guard against financial loss on this account. The late Professor Frank Knight termed such insurable uncertainties "risks," in order to distinguish them from the uninsurable uncertainties which must be faced by those who receive their incomes on a noncontractual basis. The two types of uncertainties can also be usefully distinguished as "transformable" and "nontransformable," the former being those which can be avoided at a definite cost by means of insurance or other types of hedging (to be described later in this chapter), and the latter being those which cannot be sidestepped by the businessman by means of transformation into a definite cost.[3] Shifts in tastes, inventions, discoveries of new natural resources, and interruptions in the state of peace or war are changes which can neither be anticipated nor be insured against. They are examples of the true uncertainties which cause economic profits —positive and negative—to exist.

Profits, Liquidity, and Uncertainty

Professor Boulding frames the uncertainty theory of profit in liquidity terms.[4] He emphasizes that the ownership of goods of any sort—factories, inventories of finished products, goods in process—involves the sacrifice of liquidity. That is, an alternative on the part of the owner would be the holding of cash instead of goods. Boulding points out that even holding cash involves risk of loss because the general price level may go up, thereby reducing the real value (purchasing power) of a stock of cash. He believes, however, that greater risk is involved in holding any particular good because the good may not only decline in value because of a fall in the general level of prices but it may also decline because of supply-demand conditions peculiar to that commodity.[5] Also, the holding of liquid purchasing power permits the snapping-up of bargains which may become available and quick entry into fields where innovations offer a favorable opportunity. Because of these advantages of liquidity, Professor Boulding has stated that profits can be considered to be the necessary reward to induce firms to hold goods, and he points out that this ownership of goods is indispensable to the existence of enterprise. It should be noted that this theory hinges on uncertainty regarding future prices; consequently, it is logically a part of the broader uncertainty theory of profit.

Innovation Profits

The innovation theory of profits is concerned with the impact of changes which occur with the passage of time. Perhaps the most widely

---

[3] J. F. Weston, "A Generalized Uncertainty Theory of Profit," *American Economic Review*, March 1950, p. 44, suggests this terminology.

[4] K. E. Boulding, *Economic Analysis* (New York: Harper & Bros., 1948), pp. 429–31.

[5] It should be noted, however, that the modern tendency of government to follow inflationary monetary and fiscal policies reduces the riskiness of holding goods and increases the chance of loss by holding cash.

known statement of the theory is that of the late Professor Schumpeter, who attributed economic profits to innovations made by businessmen.[6]

The innovation theory can be described as follows: A firm introduces a new product or a new idea which provides an existing product at a lower cost; or differentiates its product which results in a wider acceptance by consumers; or promotes various combinations of these ideas which gives the firm an advantage over its competitors. As a result, the firm enjoys an economic surplus from this advantage. Eventually, either new firms are attracted to the field by the profits of the successful firm, or competitors produce close substitutes and thus reduce the sales of the innovator. Or competitors may adopt the cost-reducing methods of the innovating firm, causing the latter to lose its temporary advantage. All this requires the passage of time; but when the adjustment has worked itself out, the advantageous position of the innovating firm has been lost, and its economic surplus has disappeared. As the number of firms adopting the innovation or producing a sufficiently close substitute increases, the profits of all firms tend to decline.

Such a theory implies the freedom of new firms to enter the field without restriction other than that imposed by time—a lag during which the profits of innovation can be received. So long as such a condition exists and all potential competitors possess complete knowledge of past events in the business world, no firm can enjoy innovation profits indefinitely.

The innovation theory is logically part of the broader uncertainty theory of profit. Innovations in methods and products are one of the great unpredictables which cause positive and negative economic profits to exist. If innovations could be fully foreseen, they would not have this effect. All firms would be ready to introduce a new production method, for example, as soon as it was available, and no special advantages would accrue from the method. Since such prediction is not possible, and since adjustments take time, innovations would occasion profits even if our economic system were highly competitive in all respects.

Monopoly Profits

While "negative profits" or "losses," in the sense of less than normal returns, are about as common as positive profits in fully competitive situations, monopoly is often a source of more persistent profits. Cartel agreements, whereby firms in a particular field set prices above the competitive level, are an important source of profit. Exclusive franchises are common in the utility and transportation fields; and these, of course,

---

[6] Joseph S. Schumpeter, *The Theory of Economic Development* (Cambridge, Mass.: Harvard University Press, 1934), chap. 5.

confer monopoly power on their owners. While public regulation of privately owned transportation and utility systems may prevent franchise holders from securing very large profits, such public regulation often is not sufficiently effective to prevent above-normal returns. Also, monopoly profits are frequently made by governments which sell such commodities as electric power and water in noncompetitive situations, such profits frequently being used as a partial substitute for taxes.

The limitations that government antitrust policy places on private attempts to gain monopoly profits are discussed in Chapter 17. The government, however, sanctions grants of monopoly power for limited periods in the case of patents on inventions and for copyrights for books, musical compositions, and plays.

Product differentiation by such means as trade names, distinctive packaging, and highly publicized differences (real or fictitious) from rival commodities give some degree of monopoly power to a great many firms. This source of monopoly profits is often less dependable than that of a franchise or patent, and heavy advertising may be necessary to maintain the advantage over time. However, the importance of a well-known slogan, picture, or package should not be underestimated.

A particularly advantageous location can also bring monopoly profits to a firm. This is especially likely to be true if the site is owned by the enterprise itself, since otherwise the rental charged by the owner is apt to be so large as to make the location no more favorable than some poorer site which could be rented more cheaply. However, if the enterpriser in question—say, a clothing retailer—owns the store and the land, he could, alternatively, lease this property to another firm and secure a favorable rental income. Monopoly profits due to locational advantages are, consequently, difficult to distinguish from rental income.

Innovation and monopoly theories of profits are somewhat related. Temporary monopoly power often results from an innovation in product, production technique, marketing, location, or advertising. This sort of monopoly power tends to diminish unless further innovations by the firm outpace the efforts of competitors to take advantage of the same profitable new avenues.

Business Decisions, Economic Analysis, and Uncertainty

The process of decision making is one of making a choice among alternatives. Were there no uncertainty or risk in predicting the outcome of a decision, no ambiguity in measuring the desirability of the results, and no difficulty in listing all the possible courses of action, it would be a very simple process. A payoff table of the following sort could be constructed. The alternative actions could be listed vertically, and the results of each action could be listed next to the alternative:

Choice	Payoff
1	a
2	b
3	c

If b were larger than a or c, choice 2 would be made.

Classical economic analysis of the static equilibrium type takes this relatively simple form. The firm is assumed to maximize measurable profits. Many alternative courses of action in the form of different price and output combinations are shown quite succinctly with demand and cost curves from which profit consequences are easily derived. No specific provision, however, is made for uncertainty. The economist recognizes, of course, that the firm's forecasts of demand and cost functions may be faulty, especially under changing circumstances. The economic theories of profit (except for monopoly profit) discussed earlier in this chapter rest heavily on the entrepreneurial role in operating under uncertainty. The standard equilibrium analysis, however, is designed to show the eventual price-output adjustment to given demand and supply conditions. It assumes that knowledge of these given conditions would, over time, perhaps with some trial and error, be sufficient to establish specific demand and cost functions.

For business managers in a dynamic economy, demand and cost functions will never be known with certainty. The very conditions underlying a particular equilibrium are continually being transformed. A range of outcomes to a particular business decision is a possibility. Estimates of the demand for his product are at best central points of a comparatively narrow range of possibilities.

Assume a very simple case of a firm that is considering three strategies: to expand, maintain, or reduce output. It conceives of three discrete states of nature which would affect the outcome of its decision, an upturn in business conditions, stability, or a downturn. It calculates the profit possibilities of each strategy under each state of nature as shown in Figure 2–1.

FIGURE 2–1

	State of Nature		
Strategy	Upturn	Stability	Downturn
1. Expand output......................	$20,000	$5,000	$ − 10,000
2. Maintain output...................	12,000	6,000	-0-
3. Contract output..................	4,000	3,000	2,000

Decision Making under Certainty

Suppose it is assumed that stability conditions are certain and that the profit consequences of the strategies are correctly specified. The indicated decision would be to maintain output and obtain a profit of $6,000. Two reservations must be made. One, the question of whether expected profits would necessarily be the measure in which the payoff matrix was expressed, will be discussed later. The second is that of whether unlisted strategies are available which would be more profitable than those specified. The cost and revenue curves used by the economist cover a multitude of possible variations in product specifications, promotion and production methods. A real problem for management is the range and number of alternatives it can afford to evaluate.

Decision Making under Risk and the Concept of Expected Profits

If the outcome is unknown and the firm does not choose to act as though it were certain, two different cases can be assumed: decision making under risk and decision making under uncertainty. The distinction is this. Risk is used to designate a situation where the particular outcome is unknown but there is a substantial basis for estimating the probabilities (p) for a number of possible outcomes. Uncertainty is used to designate a situation where there is no basis for expecting one rather than another of the universe of possible outcomes.

Under conditions of risk, it is possible to compute the expected profits from a particular strategy by the following formula:

$$E = p_i G_i + p_2 G_2 + \ldots + p_n G_n$$

where E is expected profit, and G_1, G_2, $\ldots$, G_n represent the payoffs (gains) resulting from the various possible outcomes (or "states of nature"). The series $p_1 + p_2 \ldots + p_n$ equals 1, since it is assumed that one of the possible outcomes will occur though which one will occur is uncertain.

If the probabilities of various states of nature were estimated at 0.6 for an upturn, 0.3 for stability, and only 0.1 for a downturn, the expected profits could be evaluated as follows:

$$E(1) = 0.6(20,000) + 0.3(5,000) + 0.1(-10,000) = \$12,500$$
$$E(2) = 0.6(12,000) + 0.3(6,000) + 0.1(0) \qquad = \$\ 9,000$$
$$E(3) = 0.6(4,000) \ \ ^` + 0.3(3,000) + 0.1(2,000) \qquad = \$\ 3,500$$

The strategy that maximizes expected profits is that of expanding output.

Decision Making under Uncertainty

Suppose now that the decision maker is completely uncertain about the state of nature, that is which outcome is the most likely. What criteria might he use? A number of decision criteria that might be chosen have been suggested, but we will deal with just two.[7]

One approach is to make the assumption associated with LaPlace and Bayes that in the absence of other information, all of the possible states of nature are equally likely. Under this assumption, expected profits can be computed as suggested above. They are at a maximum of $6,000 for maintaining output. Two difficulties should be noted in the application of this approach to business decisions.

First, the listing of the possible states of nature may be incomplete. In this illustrative example, there is an element of arbitrariness in selecting only three business conditions. Depending upon what additional possibilities were included, the expected profits would be estimated differently. In typical examples from another book,[8] "war," "peace," and "depression" or "perfect weather," "variable weather," and "bad weather" have been included as the three possible states of nature, and yet the gradations in each of these sets are many. For example, depression could include the almost imperceptible break in growth in early 1967 (called a mini-recession) and the Great Depression of the 1930s with many other possibilities such as the recession of 1970 accompanied by continued inflation.

Second, even if all possibilities were listed, information is likely to be available that would suggest greater probabilities for one outcome than another. This point is important to keep in mind in reading this chapter, which makes the distinction between uncertainty, in which no knowledge is available as to the probabilities of possible outcomes, and risk, in which although the outcomes are unknown, their probabilities of occurrence can be calculated. Many, if not most, business problems fall between the two. Probabilities are not known, but the outcome is not completely uncertain either. Much business information gathering and forecasting is designed to reduce the uncertainty and make the decision more nearly one that deals with manageable risks.

The Use of Criteria Other than Maximization of Profits

One of the criteria most frequently suggested for decision making under uncertainty is the miximin, that is, the maximization of the

---

[7] The student who is interested in a further discussion of decision theory will find both a summary discussion and further references in chaps. 4 and 5 of D. W. Miller, S. Martin, K. Starr, *Executive Decisions and Operations Research* (Englewood Cliffs, N.J.: Prentice-Hall, Inc., 1960); and in chap. 24 of W. Baumot, *Economic Analysis and Operations Research*, 2d ed. (Englewood Cliffs, N.J.: Prentice-Hall, Inc., 1965).

[8] Miller, et al., *Executive Decisions*, chap. 5.

minimum level of profits, or more generally of utility expected. If this were applied to the payoff matrix of Figure 2–1, it would be noted that the poorest result from each strategy would result from a downturn. The best payoff for this would be $2,000 for the strategy of contraction; and if it used the maximin criterion, the firm would elect this course. Every other strategy could, under some outcome, result in greater losses. This could be termed the criterion of pessimism. Its counterpart, the criterion of optimism, would be the maximax, that is, to maximize the maximum profits. Expansion would be the maximax decision.

An absolute measure of profits does not necessarily measure the total of utility that is involved to the decision maker. The application of the maximin criterion above to a payoff matrix implies that the certainty of some minimum level of profits could take precedence over the assumption of the maximization of profits. Another more relevant payoff matrix could be expressed in terms of utility which could embrace more than the magnitude of profits.

Assume that the owner of this hypothetical firm had the following concept of measuring his preferences:

1. A dollar of profits in the range of $0–$10,000 represented one unit of utility.
2. Profits above $10,000 added 0.5 units of utility per dollar of profits; each dollar of loss was equivalent to −1.5 units of utility.
3. The act of expansion itself was worth 1,000 units of utility; a decision to contract represented a negative 2,000 units of utility; maintaining output represents 500 units of utility.

The payoff matrix in utility units would now look as shown in Figure 2–2.

FIGURE 2–2

| | State of Nature or Outcome | | |
Strategy	Upturn	Stability	Downturn
1. Expand output	16,000	6,000	−14,000
2. Maintain output	11,500	6,500	500
3. Contract output	2,000	1,000	-0-

The student should confirm these choices: under equally likely probabilities, or under maximin criterion, that "maintain output" would be chosen; with very small probabilities of a downturn and significant possibilities of an upturn that expansion would be chosen; and that contracting output would never be chosen.

A Recapitulation

1. Economic analysis has traditionally used models that assumed maximization of profits by firms and has been successful in many of its predictions from such analysis.

2. In business economics, where much of our concern is with the decisions of particular managements and we have further information as to what constitutes utility to the firm, it is not necessary to assume such maximization as the only criterion. We would, however, expect the profit consequences of decisions to be an important part of decision-making analysis, and the economist would predict in market structures approaching perfect competition that the failure to maximize profits would threaten the continued existence of the firm.

3. In the condition of complete uncertainty about what will be the outcome of a business strategy, maximizing profit expectations would be impossible because the weighting of the predicted results of possible outcomes depends upon probability estimates. A rational, but pessimistic, decision criterion in this case could be the maximin.

4. Business managers are likely to seek information which will reduce, though probably not eliminate, the uncertainty and make possible probabilistic estimates as to the likelihood of various results. Such estimates would permit at least rough evaluations of the expected profits or utilities resulting from following various strategies to be made from payoff tables, and decisions may be said to be made under conditions of risk.

5. When adopting the apparatus of equilibrium economic analysis to the managerial decision-making process, it will frequently be useful to recognize the demand, supply, and cost curves as functions that fall within a range of possibilities. Although possible positions may be continuous through the range, a payoff table that reduces many possibilities to a few as in our illustrative case can be a useful simplification.

The Transforming of Uncertainties

As was pointed out earlier, it is useful to distinguish between "transformable" and "nontransformable" uncertainties. The latter provide the basic explanation for the existence of profits in an economy of private, competitive industry. Nevertheless, a good deal of knowledge and judgment are required by businessmen in order to successfully and economically transform the types of uncertainties which are avoidable at a certain cost. The time and effort which must be spent in this type of activity vary a great deal from business to business. One process of transforming uncertainties into definite costs can be called "hedging."

Hedging, in essence, involves the purposive holding of two opposite positions at the same time. Roughly, it can be described as betting in two opposite ways at the same time. The purchase of insurance is of this nature and can be thought of as hedging. When a businessman buys fire insurance, he is, essentially, betting that a fire will occur on his premises; the insurance company is betting that this will not happen. Even if the fire does occur, the directors of the insurance company are unlikely to be dismayed because the company will undoubtedly win its bets with numerous other persons who bought fire insurance, and the successful wagers would at least offset the unsuccessful ones. As the owner of a building and its contents, the businessman is, of course, hoping that no fire will occur, since this would bring financial loss. In order to protect himself in this position, he must take an opposite stand—that is, he must bet that a fire will occur. Whatever the actual outcome, he should not fare too badly, since he will have converted an important uncertainty into a definite cost—the cost of the insurance premiums.[9]

Long and Short Positions

Hedging in the business world primarily consists of taking offsetting "long" and "short" positions. This strategy is appropriate when the firm is forced into one position as an incident to doing business. If the position is a dangerously speculative one, it is conservative to hedge against it, thereby incurring a small, certain cost rather than risking a large loss that could result from price changes.

An individual is in a "long" position whenever he owns any commodity, security, or other valuable asset. His hope is then that the asset will increase in money value as a result of the operation of supply-demand forces.[10] His fear is that market forces will reduce the value of his asset. On the other hand, a person in a "short" position hopes that the market price will decline rather than rise, since he has made a contract to deliver a commodity, security, or other asset at a future date for a specific price. The more cheaply he can purchase the asset when the delivery date rolls around, or the more cheaply he can produce it in time to meet the delivery requirement, the larger his gain will be. A contractor, for

---

[9] Even apart from the consequences of the disruption of business, the insured person is apt not to recover his entire loss, since insurance companies normally do not sell policies to cover the whole value of inflammable property. To do so might place too much temptation in the way of some policyholders to win their bets with the company. Even beneficiaries of life insurance policies have been known to take steps to secure the proceeds prematurely.

[10] It is also possible to be long on money itself. This occurs whenever a cash balance is held. The hope of the individual is then that the purchasing power of the cash will increase—that is, that prices will fall. Conversely, one is "short" on money when in debt, since it is necessary to make future delivery of principal and interest to a creditor.

example, who has agreed to construct a building, road, or other project for a specified sum may be considered to be in a "short" position with respect to that asset. One of his problems, once that contract has been signed, is that the cost of materials, labor, and other inputs may increase during the construction period, so as to make the job an unprofitable one. In order to hedge against this contingency, he must take a long position with respect to the needed inputs.

He may, for example, sign a lease to rent the needed equipment at a specified price for the period of construction; or alternatively, he may buy the equipment. He may attempt to secure a contract with the labor unions involved, which will make his labor costs more predictable. With respect to materials, he has two alternatives: (1) he may buy all of the necessary materials ahead of time, storing them until needed; or (2) he may contract to have them delivered to him at specified prices at specified future dates. Either way, he would have a hedge against an increase in their price. Once the contractor has assumed correct "long" positions on most of the inputs required for construction of the project, he would be fairly well hedged against unfavorable price changes. He would have transformed some uncertain costs into predictable ones.

Futures Markets

Hedging operations on the part of businessmen in many lines of activity are made possible by the existence of organized markets in which commodities are traded both at "spot" or "cash" prices for immediate delivery and at "futures" prices for deferred delivery. Futures contracts are regularly made for some dozens of relatively homogeneous and storable commodities such as wheat, corn, oats, lard, cottonseed oil, cotton, cocoa, coffee, refrigerated eggs, Maine potatoes, lead, zinc, and copper. In the month of April, for example, Mr. A may contract to buy, and Mr. B to sell, a specified quantity of wheat during the month of December at a specified price. The seller has the option of making delivery on any day within the month of December, delivery actually taking the form of delivery of warehouse receipts for the commodity. Mr. B also has the option of delivering any of several grades of wheat rather than just a specified grade; and a discount or premium from the agreed price then is effective, since the agreed price relates to a standard grade.

The financial pages of certain newspapers regularly carry quotations of both spot and futures prices. In April, for example, prices of spot, May, July, September, and December wheat are quoted. Since quoted futures prices are based on anticipated demand-supply conditions in those future months, they may be thought of as traders' present expectations as to what spot prices will be for the same grade when those months roll around. In an uncertain world, these expectations are seldom entirely correct. The constant changes in futures prices reflect the buying and selling actions which are constantly taking place, the price movements generally being in the direction of more correctly reflecting the cash prices which will actually prevail in the future months, since later quotations are based on later information. Quoted futures prices are, therefore, likely to be a good forecast of price movements. If, for example, May coffee is selling at 55 cents, July coffee at 51 cents, September coffee at 47 cents, and December coffee at 45 cents a pound, a housewife can look forward with some confidence to a reduction in the cost of coffee in her budget.

Spot and Futures Prices

The "spot" or "cash" market for a commodity differs in important ways from the futures market. Whereas a futures contract can usually be satisfied by delivery of several grades of the commodity, a spot transaction pertains to the transfer of a specific lot of a specific grade to one of many possible locations. When a spot transaction is made, the buyer actually wants to receive delivery of the commodity, and delivery will be made unless the contract is canceled by subsequent agreement between the two parties. On the other hand, most of the buyers of futures do not actually want to take delivery on these contracts, nor do sellers usually want to make actual delivery. Instead, the buyer of a futures contract usually "offsets" this contract by a similar futures sale prior to delivery time; if the price has gone up, he makes a gain equal to the difference in price (less commissions and taxes). Similarly, the seller of a futures contract usually offsets the contract with a purchase of futures prior to delivery time; he gains if the purchase can be made at a lower price than he has sold for, and he loses in the opposite case. A commodities exchange such as the Chicago Board of Trade acts as a clearing house paying the gainers and collecting from the losers.

Speculation and Arbitrage

The futures market is a great convenience to both speculators and hedgers, since the actual commodity need not be handled, and since buyers and sellers normally do not have to be concerned about selection of the specific grade, place of delivery, and other details. A speculator who believes that a presently quoted futures price is too low—that is, that demand will be stronger in relation to supply than present quotations indicate—is likely to *buy* a futures contract. If his expectation is correct, he can later offset this purchase with a similar sale at a higher price. On the other hand, a speculator who believes that a presently quoted futures price is too high can *sell* futures, profiting by a later offsetting purchase if his "bearish" expectation turns out to be correct.

Instead of attempting to take advantage of a change in a single price over time, a speculator may, instead, attempt to turn to his advantage a difference between two prices when that difference appears to be out of line. Suppose that a study of market conditions suggests strongly that July oats futures are underpriced relative to September oats. This would suggest an arbitrage transaction in which July oats would be bought and September oats would be simultaneously sold. It would then not matter whether the more normal differential were established by a rise in the price of July oats, by a fall in September oats, or any other combination of change, so long as a smaller difference in price came to be established. The arbitrager would gain on either the long or the short transaction and lose or break even on the other one, but his gain would exceed his loss. Similarly, an improper differential between two markets—say, between the New York and New Orleans cotton markets—could be turned into an arbitrage profit by a simultaneous purchase in the relatively low market and a sale in the relatively high market.

The arbitrager can be considered to be "betting two ways at once." His action differs, however, from that of the hedger in that the latter is forced to assume one of his positions (make one of his bets) as an incident to carrying on his regular line of business activity. The arbitrager takes both of his positions as a speculative matter. In practice, it is often impossible to characterize an individual as purely a hedger or purely an arbitrager on a particular transaction, since a hedger is not averse, of course, to making an arbitrage profit, whenever possible, in the process of protecting himself against an adverse price change.

Hedging by Selling Futures

A wheat farmer, contemplating his growing crop in July, realizes that he is an involuntary speculator in wheat on the "long" side. He may decide to hedge by selling September wheat, perhaps in about the quantity he expects to harvest in that month. By taking this action, he has, roughly speaking, already sold his growing crop at a specific price for delivery at harvest time, and he is in no danger of suffering a speculative loss between July and September. Actually, he is unlikely to deliver his own wheat on the futures contract; he will probably offset his short position in late August or September by buying September futures in the same amount he had previously sold. Then he will sell his own wheat in the cash market.

If we assume that the quantity of wheat involved was 10,000 bushels and make certain price assumptions, the transactions can be summarized as shown in Figure 2–3.

In the situation pictured, the farmer would be glad that he hedged, since he has a net gain of $29,750, whereas his crop would have brought him $25,000 if he had not hedged. The cash price of wheat declined 50

FIGURE 2–3

Date	Events	Receipts and Payments
July 20	Farmer has growing wheat with estimated yield of 10,000 bushels in September. Wishing to assure himself the September futures price of $3 (spot price is also $3), he sells futures contract for 10,000 bushels. He puts up margin of $3,000 and pays commission of $200.	September futures receipts................. $30,000 Commission payment....... 200
Sept 20	Spot and futures prices have declined to $2.50. Farmer sells wheat in spot market (10,000 bushels). He buys September futures for $2.50. He pays off margin loan with 10 percent annual interest.	Cash receipts............. 25,000 September futures payments................. 25,000 Interest payment.......... 50
	Result: Farmer nets $25,000 for wheat plus $4,750 on futures contract.	Net..................... 29,750
	Note: Had cash and futures prices increased to $3.25 he still would have netted $29,750 rather than the $32,500 with no hedge.	

cents a bushel between July 20 and September 20, but this was offset by the 50-cent decline in September futures over the same period. The protection received from this sort of hedging is based on the fact that cash and futures prices generally move in the same direction. These two prices may, however, not move by the same amount; consequently, the hedger is apt to either make a speculative gain or suffer a loss of moderate proportions.[11] If the price of cash wheat had increased from, say, $3 per bushel on July 20 to $3.25, the farmer would have had a larger net income by not hedging. The existence of government price supports at some designated percentage of "parity" may make hedging by farmers less necessary. (However, both spot and futures prices can fall below support levels.) The price-support program thus places part of the speculative risk of a price decline on the shoulders of the taxpayers.

Hedging is practiced extensively by certain types of processors. For example, the practice has expanded in recent years in the case of southern textile mills. These mills buy spot cotton early in the season and sell cotton futures as a hedge. Offsetting futures purchases are made as orders are received for textiles. This gives them substantial protection against losses on their long position in cotton. If cotton has declined in

[11] Actually, the farmer did not engage in a pure hedging transaction, since he was short on mature wheat but long on immature wheat prior to harvest time. If he had held wheat in storage and had sold wheat futures in the same amount, the long and short positions would have been more definitely offsetting. With a growing crop, an unfortunate hailstorm could have left him short.

price between the time it is purchased and a textile order is received, the mill may have to quote a price on textiles which reflects the lower price of cotton. In this case, however, a profit will be made on the futures transactions, and this may equal or even exceed the reduction in revenue occasioned by the need to cut the price of textiles.

Miscellaneous Hedges and Other Strategies to Reduce Uncertainties

Such businessmen as bakers, bottlers of soft drinks, coffee and cocoa importers, flour millers, cold-storers of eggs, cottonseed and soybean crushers, copper smelters, and many others make extensive use of hedging. Often, the choice of whether to hedge at all, and if so, what sort of hedge to use hinges on the relation between spot and futures prices. If futures prices appear to be abnormally low relative to spot prices, it may not be wise to hedge by selling futures; the chance of their declining further may be too poor. In this situation, it may be best to attempt to arrange short and long positions which call instead for purchasing the underpriced futures.

In a more general sense, a great many types of protective actions by individuals and business organizations seek to reduce uncertainty. Diversification of an investment portfolio among the stocks of various corporations, between stocks and bonds, between long-term and short-term bonds, and between securities and cash holdings is one such strategy. The use of general-purpose machine tools rather than highly specialized tools or of convertible rather than nonconvertible equipment is a hedge against the uncertainties of demand. Similarly, the production of many commodities rather than of just one may be a useful hedge. The hiring of executives with several capabilities instead of highly specialized men is similar to the use of convertible rather than specialized equipment.

The use of options to buy or sell can reduce a firm's commitment and thus the potential risk. For example, a real estate developer may purchase an option to buy for a particular price over a specified time period. For a small sum it can eliminate the uncertainty as to future price changes or the risk of tying up large amounts of capital in an unsuccessful attempt to complete a parcel of land for future development. Case 2–2 deals with such a land option.

The use of put (sell) and call (buy) options on stock have increased substantially since an organized market was initiated by the Chicago Board of Trade in 1972. Such options have both hedging and speculative uses as presented in Case 2–6.[12]

---

[12] See C. B. Franklin and M. R. Colberg, "Puts and Calls: A Factual Survey," *Journal of Finance,* March, 1958, for additional information, including option arbitrage and functions of the conversion house.

CASE 2–1. Cow Pastures or Condominiums *

Until 1960 there were more cows than people in Vermont. As a matter of fact after 1830 Vermont's population had never changed by as much as 5 percent in a decade—the major demographic development was the heading south or west of most of the natural increase in population. Between 1960 and 1970 a population explosion by Vermont's very modest standards occurred. The number of Vermonters increased by 14+ percent, slightly more than the national average, and accompanying this population surge was a great increase in land valuations.

As for the cow pastures of northern Vermont it was the increase in land values that counted. It was not necessary for people to commit themselves to vigorous winters and limited full-time employment opportunities of the Green Mountain state for its land to become more valuable. The potential of nearby ski slopes in the winter, air-conditionless summers, woodland trails, and mountain vistas when contrasted with the congestion and pollution of Megalopolis increased the demand for second homes and land on which something eventually might be built. Many are capable of being moved by a view of Mt. Mansfield to the southwest and Jay Peak to the north such as found around Morrisville, Vermont. The inflation of the late sixties and early 1970s enhanced the values of tangibles such as land; and the four-lane ribbons of concrete and asphalt named Interstate 89 and Interstate 91 promised seven-hour access from New York and five hours from Boston.

The production function of a northern Vermont farm can be largely described in terms of this same land. Given one acre of land for hay and another acre of land for grazing plus 3,000 pounds of purchased grain, a Holstein can give close to 15,000 pounds of milk a year. After allowing for all out of pocket expenses plus depreciation, the yearly monetary yield per acre averaged $100 at prices prevailing in the late 1960s and early 1970s.

To be more specific take the Vermont farm of Mr. Aiken, which encompasses 225 acres of Lamoille County in northern Vermont. Aiken maintained 75 dairy cows on the 150 acres suitable for hay and pasture.

Since Vermont is the least horizontal of the 50 states, 75 acres of Aiken's hilly land yielded only $5 an acre for maple sugar and pulpwood. In order to maintain a herd of 75 cows with family labor, Mr. Aiken had to invest considerable capital in hay loaders, milking machines, sterilizers, and so forth, buildings and fences as well, amounting to $75,000 in de-

---

* This case is designed to be representative of frequent choices made in northern New England. The characters are fictional, and the facts rest on some familiarity with the region. Part of the idea for the case came from "Cows and Cambodia" published in Edward Hoagland's *Walking the Dead Diamond River* (New York: Random House, Inc., 1973).

preciated value. The market value of the portable, salable equipment was only $40,000 should the land be taken out of dairy farming. Aiken's labor skills were specialized toward dairying; and with the limited industrial labor market in Vermont (what he considers the fleshpots and beehives a few hundred miles to the south and east have no attraction for him), the market value of his alternative employment was only $5,000 annually. Aiken recognized that his dairy business was a bit risky. The per capita consumption of milk had not been moving favorably; despite reasonable contributions to the campaigns of Nixon and his opponents, the milk price support program had not always compensated for unfavorable changes in the milk-grain price ratio; hay crops varied with precipitation; and mastitis and Bang's disease remained around as possible cattle afflictions. No less than 10 percent would seem to be the risk-equivalent return to be used in looking at alternative investments.

In 1971 Ecological Condominiums & Open Spaces, Inc., made an offer for the Aiken farm of $90,000 exclusive of salable equipment. The $400 an acre was in line with the bids it was making elsewhere in the area. E.C. & O.S. was a relatively ethical and responsible operator in a field not noted for burning-bush honesty and extraordinary environmental concern. Standards were called for since Vermont, concerned with the land speculation and population increases, had strict land use controls by comparison with the nation's standards. The developers' general plan was to buy 4,000 reasonably contiguous areas at $400 an acre and establish a recreational-retirement community with an eventual 1,600 residential units, about half of them in clustered condominiums. This arrangement made the provision of central facilities such as sewage disposal economical and was to be balanced by leaving a quarter of the area completely undeveloped except for riding and walking trails. If all went reasonably well the corporation could expect to net about $1,250 an acre on the sales of the land, the yield running anywhere from a significant minus amount for such necessary amenities as a golf course, $500 an acre for a steep 20-acre plot (which might be just enough to find a level area for house and septic system), to $15,000 an acre for prime locations in a shopping center. The $5,000,000 prospective net for land costing $1,600,000 would seem to be a handsome return, but the corporation recognized it would have another million and a half in capital tied up before the dollar inflow from land and condominium sales could be expected to offset the continuing development expenses needed. Thus it would be unreasonable to expect to complete the sale of the land in less than ten years.

When Mr. Aiken was approached the corporation had already secured the key parcels it needed to start and it was operating openly, since preliminary plans had already been submitted to town and state governments. The plans were flexible enough so that no particular farm was necessary (some operating farms in the area would be an advantage to the corporation providing local color and added green space). Thus Aiken had no particular bargaining power on price. He knew there were opportunities for selling a few of his most desirable acres for more than $400, but his acreage that was redundant to farming was far from the road. He saw no desecration to the land in development per se and was confident that the ecological people were probably better than most. He did think it would be a bit strange to operate a farm in an area with a peak population of 5,000 rather than 300.

In brief Aiken felt he could approach the decision on the basis of economic profitability without emotional involvement. He started out by including tax consequences, but after getting into a muddle on capital gains, which would depend on the cost of a new house and income averaging, and so forth, he decided to look at the problem before taxes. This made some economic sense because the income tax advantages of keeping the farm were approximately offset by the fact that there was an excellent chance that the new assessor would increase his land taxes and that substantial barn and fence repair would reduce his future operating net below the present. As he was completing his calculations, Mrs. Aiken called down to remind him that a roof over their heads should be considered part of the farm income. Mr. Aiken put down $1,500 (heating and maintenance costs were very high for the old house) and concluded that while this made the calculation close, economic profitability favored selling.

The next morning his neighbor stated he wasn't selling. His calculations were pretty much the same, except that he left out the opportunity cost for receipts received from the land sale on the grounds that in view of inflation and the pressure from city folk for country homes, prices for land would rise 10 percent a year in the future. Mr. Aiken was only partly convinced—he knew of cases where the appreciation had been even greater, but most of these had been for scarce property: lakefront, hilltop with spectacular mountain view and proven water, or a quiet street in a desirable community near Burlington and Essex Junction where IBM had located. When the ecological man called later in the day he indicated his indecision and was told that while the base price would not be increased, the corporation would be glad to buy an option to purchase the farm in five years for the $90,000. Five thousand dollars would be paid now and for each of the next four years, and then the corporation would pay the full $90,000 or drop the commitment leaving Mr. Aiken the land to use or sell as he saw fit. The $5,000 a year and the right to farm would be guaranteed for five years.

Questions

1. Show why it was economically unprofitable to continue to farm the land under the initial assumptions.

2. Was the neighbor's decision correct on the basis of his assumption of a 10 percent annual rise in land valuation?
3. Was the option deal probably a better one for both Aiken and the company than the original offer?

CASE 2–2. Haloid to Xerox

In 1972 Xerox, Inc., had sales of $2,419,103,000 and its net income of close to a quarter of a billion dollars amounted to $3.16 and permitted a dividend payment of $0.84 for each of 78,500,000 shares of stock. During the first half of 1973 the price per share of Xerox stock sold in a range of $140 to $170 as sales rose 22 percent and profits 21 percent over the year before.

In 1935 the Haloid Company had sales of $1,232,596 and its net income of $145,530 amounted to $4.85 a share. This permitted a dividend payment of $2 for each of 30,000 shares of stock. Each of these shares, if held from 1935 to 1973, would have become 540 shares of Xerox stock. In 1936, after a three-to-one stock split, a public offering of 55,000 new shares brought $20 a share which helped to finance the purchase of the Rectigraph Company, the producer of a photocopy machine, to add to Haloid's capacity to produce 10 miles of 41-inch photographic paper a day.

Chester F. Carlson, a physicist and patent attorney, produced his first xerographic image in 1938 and received a patent on his process in 1940. He was unable to interest any business firm (IBM was one he visited) in his electrostatic, dry writing process (in Greek, zeros means "dry" and graph is the Greek stem of "write"). In 1944 Battelle Memorial Institute in Columbus did undertake the expensive job of perfecting the process in return for 60 percent of any proceeds that developed.

A Haloid vice president read about xerography in a technical magazine; and in 1947 the company president, John C. Wilson, arranged a patent license with Battelle and shortly afterward negotiated exclusive commercial rights to xerography in return for financing research at Battelle.

The first Xerox copy machine, designed to make masters for offset printing, was introduced in 1949. All but a handful of Americans turned down the chance to become millionaires (not until 1954 were there more than 1,500 Haloid stockholders). Haloid's stock sold in a range of $14–$22 despite the increase of its sales to $7,723,651 and modest national coverage (for example, in *Time* of November 1, 1948) of its rights in xerography. Haloid badly needed funds to finance research and market development and was successful in selling 47,183 shares of common stock (at $28.50 to its shareholders and $29.50 to outsiders), and over two million dollars' worth of convertible preferred stock in 1950 (almost all of this preferred issue was converted to 68,000-odd common shares in 1954).

Nineteen fifty-four was also the year in which Haloid arranged to buy outright all of some 100 Battelle patents on xerography for what amounted by 1965 to 5,400,000 shares (1973 basis) of Xerox. Mr. Carlson, who received 40 percent of the proceeds, was finally able to resign from his position in a patent law office. In 1956 Rank-Xerox was formed with a 50 percent Haloid interest to handle the world market. In 1957 the 914 copier, which could copy individual documents of up to 9 × 14 inches (hence the name), was developed. This was the machine Haloid had been seeking for decisive penetration into the photocopy market. The marketing job seemed too formidable for a small company so Haloid sought IBM as a distributor. But IBM rejected this second chance after receiving a research report that "prospects for such a big expensive unit were dim."[13]

Haloid split its stock four for one, changed its name first to Haloid-Xerox in 1957 and then to Xerox Corporation in 1961, and prepared a merchandising plan for the 914. It decided to lease the copier for $95 a month plus 3½ cents for each copy above 2,000 a month. To meet capital requirements it borrowed heavily, including debentures convertible to stock. It marketed its last issue of common stock by granting rights to its current stockholders to buy additional shares of the split stock at $24.

By 1961 it was clear that the 914 was a mint. The average user made 10,000 copies a month and paid annual rentals of $4,000 on a machine costing $2,500 to manufacture with a conservative depreciation period of five years. Plans were made to launch a smaller copier, the 813, and a copy duplicator, the Xerox 2400, numbered after its hourly production rate. The ability to reproduce nonchemically and on ordinary paper vastly expanded the market for copying, an expansion underestimated by the company president when he looked forward to only a 15 percent to 20 percent annual increase in xerography products after 1962 and an eventual goal of $1,000,000,000 sales in a broader communications market. To reach that goal the company acquired companies with publishing and reproduction interests. Xerox moved into the computer field with the acquisition of Scientific Data Systems in 1969, a product addition that had not yet led to profits in 1973. (IBM almost concurrently inaugurated the production of copiers.) The original Carlson patents had run out by 1962, but by then Xerox had built a structure of 250 improvement patents to protect its position.

---

[13] William Hammer, "There Isn't Any Profit Squeeze at Xerox," *Fortune*, July, 1962, pp. 151 ff.

In January, 1973, the FTC filed a complaint against Xerox alleging the monopolization of the copier market. The complaint sought unrestricted licensing of all Xerox patents and know-how, divesture of the Rank-Xerox in which Xerox now held 51 percent control, and permission for other companies to maintain and service copiers leased to Xerox customers. In its 1973 report the company stated, "We consider the Commission's case without merit," in explaining its refusal to negotiate a consent settlement. "What is really at issue here is the right of any organization to earn success through the creativity, imagination, and dedication of its people. . . . It is in effect an attack on the very foundation of the patent system. . . . Moreover, given the fact that there are already 50 competitors in the U.S. market alone . . . the Commission's charges are in our view without foundation."

The 1973 report also stressed the following recent or new products: the Xerox 7000 reduction duplicator, the color copier, Cyclex 400 (a copier-duplicator paper from 100 percent recycled materials), the Xerox 400 telecopier-transceiver for facsimiles, Xeroradiography (a dry process for X-ray pictures), and the Xerox 530 (a general-purpose computer).

Very large rewards have been paid to Xerox stockholders—to some extent in dividends and to a greater extent in capital appreciation. Exhibit 2–2A is designed to show the origins of the roughly 78.5 million shares of Xerox stock outstanding in 1972. The first category, 1935 initial holders, owned shares that have since been split into 540 shares: 1936, three for one; 1955, three for one; 1959, four for one; 1963, five for one; 1969, three for one. The $20 a share average price in 1935 can be

EXHIBIT 2–2A

	No. of 1972 Shares	Multiplier (1972 shares ÷ initial issue)	Price per 1972 Share
Initial holders (1935 or before)	16.2	540	0.09[†]
Purchases or conversions to stock:	(38.8)	. . .	. . .
1936 stock sale @ $20	9.3	180	0.11
1950 stock sale @ $29.50	8.5	180	0.15
1954 conv. 1950 pref. @ $35.80	12.3	180	0.20
1960 stock sale @ $24	5.0	15	1.60
1963 conv. 1960 deb. @ 100	2.2	15	6.66
1966–67 conv. 1964 deb. @ 92	1.5	3	30.67
Stock for patent rights to Battelle and Anderson (1955–65)	5.4	3–60	*
Stock options to executives 1960 to date	3.3	15[‡]	0.85[‡]
Stock for acquisitions:	(14.8)	. . .	. . .
Scientific data systems, 1969	10.0	1	100.00[†]
All others, 1962–72	4.8	1–15	*

* Various.
† Based on average market value for year.
‡ Various. The figures given represent an option to purchase a share in 1960 for $12.75.

divided by 540 to get approximately $0.09 as the price of a 1973 share in 1935. To put it the opposite way, the holder of one share in 1935 could have sold 540 shares in 1973 for $81,000. In addition, such a holder of one share in 1935 would have received $123 in dividends from 1936 to 1962 and $2,370 from 1963 to 1972 (after the 914 copier had become an established success).

The second category represents the sale of additional shares of stock either directly or indirectly through the issuance of convertible preferred stock and debentures. This financing was used for expansion into the photocopy machine business (1936), the xerox duplicating business and xerography research (1950), and xerox copiers and continuing research (1960–64). All such purchases were rewarding to the investors with prices for a 1973 share ranging from 0.11 in 1936, 0.20 in 1954, and $30.67 in 1966–67.

The other categories are the shares exchanged in compensation for the patent rights of Battelle and inventor Anderson (5,400,000 shares); the stock options used to reward executives (3,300,000 shares); and the 14,800,000 shares exchanged in the acquisition of companies, which includes the ten million shares for Scientific Data Systems, the yet-to-be-profitable foothold in the computer industry.

Many current stockholders acquired these shares by simple purchases of already issued stock. As late as 1953 this could be done for $0.19 a 1973 share or less; in the later 1950s the range was $0.36 to $2.50; from 1960 to 1967 the range was $1.50 to $33. Only in 1968 was the price over $50 ranging upward to the 1973 price of $150.

Exhibit 2–2B shows that the company's rapid growth continued from 1963 to 1972.

EXHIBIT 2–2B

Xerox: Ten Years in Review
(columns 1–4 in millions)

	(1) *Operating Revenues*	*(2)* *Net Income*	*(3)* *Equity*	*(4)* *R&D*	*(5)* *Income ÷ Average Equity*	*(6)* *Income per Share*	*(7)* *Dividends per Share*
1963........	$ 176	$ 23	$ 85	$ 15	34.4%	$0.39	$0.08
1964........	318	44	155	24	36.4	0.68	0.14
1965........	549	66	229	38	34.2	0.92	0.20
1966........	752	87	326	53	31.2	1.20	0.31
1967........	983	106	474	51	26.6	1.42	0.40
1968........	1,224	129	601	60	24.0	1.88	0.50
1969........	1,483	161	738	84	24.1	2.08	0.58
1970........	1,719	188	893	98	23.0	2.40	0.65
1971........	1,961	213	1,052	104	21.9	2.71	0.80
1972........	2,419	250	1,253	132	21.7	3.16	0.84

Questions

1. Suppose you had purchased 100 shares of Xerox stock in 1935 or in 1950, or in 1960 and held for sale in 1973, what would your rewards have been? Would you have performed any service to justify these returns? Why would the rewards be so much less if you bought in the 1970s?
2. Consider the services performed by other groups who received or bought Xerox stock: the 1935 holders of Haloid stock, the executives who received stock options, the stockholders of acquired firms, persons who bought Haloid or Xerox stock over the counter or on the N.Y. Stock Exchange (starting in 1961). For what, if anything, were they rewarded?
3. How would the various profit theories discussed in this chapter pertain to Xerox profits?
4. Did Xerox make economic or pure profits in the 1963–73 period (assume a rate of return on capital of 6 percent)? Is there any evidence these were diminishing?

CASE 2–3. Broadway (A)

In the postwar period, the theatrical production on Broadway was a risky and uncertain business. The profits on a few hits each year sometimes exceeded and sometimes fell below that of the losses of the many failures, depending upon whether the successful plays were so outstanding that the realization from such ancillary enterprises as national tours and recording, movie and television rights was great. Exhibit 2–3A

EXHIBIT 2–3A

	Number of Productions	Average Profit or Loss	Total Profit or Loss
Total losses	42	$ — 150,000	$ —6,300,000
Partial losses	6	— 50,000	— 300,000
Moderate hits	9	180,000	1,620,000
Smash hits	3	1,700,000	5,100,000

summarizes outcomes for a representative season. Simplifications such as having an average cost of $150,000, even though musicals would generally cost more and straight plays less, have been used. The outcomes for investors are approximations for a 60-production year.

Investor George Tompkins considered whether to invest $15,000 for a 10 percent share in a new production. Assume his alternative was to keep the $15,000 in short-term government bonds at 4 percent annual interest. Since it would take a prolonged run and subsequent sale of other rights to realize the profits on a smash hit, interest should be calculated for a three-year period.

Questions

1. Suppose the probabilities of the four summarized outcomes were computed on the basis of past experience. What decision would have maximized expected profits?
2. How might theatrical productions continue to command new capital even though economic losses exceeded economic profits?
3. The 1973–74 theatrical season was particularly bad. Out of 46 productions only 10 had prospects of financial success, and there were no smash hits. An alternative riskless investment in treasury notes yielded 8 percent. Assume the unsuccessful plays averaged a loss of $200,000 and that the successes eventually would average profits of $500,000. Was it surprising that producers found it increasingly difficult to raise money for new shows? Explain.

CASE 2–4. Broadway (B)

It is not surprising that in a business with the high uncertainty of success of the theater, interesting methods of sharing the risk and uncertainty develop. The producer, in effect the business manager, has traditionally not been paid a fixed salary but shares 50 percent of the profits after the investors have been repaid. The investors who supply the capital, faced by great uncertainties, relinquish this 50 percent share since confidence in the producer's ability to better the usual odds is important in inducing them to invest. Conditioning any payment to the producer on profits also reduces the cost of production and thus the amount of their capital at risk.

Other key factors to the success of the production, the stars, the authors, and the director, also may accept compensation partially or wholly based on the success and thus profitability of the show. This is illustrated in Exhibit 2–4A which gives the weekly operating budget for the famous musical "South Pacific" in its original Broadway run.

The actual terms agreed to may well reflect the degree to which different elements in the theatrical production are thought to increase the probability of success. Rodgers and Hammerstein had just had a tremendous success with "Oklahoma," whose producers, the Theatre Guild, had to give the investors 60 percent instead of the usual 50 percent of the profits because of the doubts with which its success was viewed.

The triumph of "Oklahoma" enabled Rodgers and Hammerstein to

EXHIBIT 2–4A

Weekly gross exclusive of federal taxes at capacity.............	$50,600
Theater rental—25% of first $40,000 and 25% of any gross over $50,000 (these are unusually favorable terms; the theater often receives as much as 35% with none of the gross exempted)......	10,150
Authors' 10% of gross (Rodgers, 4½%; Hammerstein, 4½%; Michener, 1%)..	5,060
Director (Logan), 2½%....................................	1,265
Stars' 14% of gross (7% to Ezio Pinza, 7% to Mary Martin, as against $2,000 weekly guarantee).........................	7,085
Operating expenses—rest of cast, publicity, share of stage crew, musicians, ice, and advertising (the theater is responsible for some of these costs)......................................	16,000
Net, of which 50% goes to the producers, 50% to the backers (investors)...	11,000
	(approximate)

claim 60 percent of the producer's share while another 27 percent of this share went to Joshua Logan, a director with a string of successes. The producer contracted for only 13 percent of this usual share and depended for his profits largely on his role as the backer who put up much of the $225,000 initial investment.

Questions

1. What weekly gross for "South Pacific" would allow the production to break even (draw a break-even chart with dollars of cost on the vertical axis and dollars of revenue on the horizontal axis)? How did the percentage arrangements reduce the risk of an early closing of the show?
2. Why is the distinction between profits and returns to other factors of production not very clear-cut in the theatre? What were the returns received by the various factors of production at the break-even point and at capacity?

CASE 2–5. James Barkley, Grain Merchant

In February, 1963, James Barkley, a member of the Chicago Board of Trade, headed his own firm and was one of a decreasing number of individual grain merchants in Chicago. While Chicago retained its leading position as a market for commodities futures, the volume of cash grain sent to Chicago for sale had greatly diminished in the postwar period.

Barkley specialized in oats. His customers used the grain for animal feeding, and he particularly concentrated on selling oats to feed dealers serving horse-racing stables. He depended upon his skill and knowledge of the grain to make favorable purchases. He then had the grain processed by a local elevator to upgrade it into types that would meet the preferences of his customers. A typical transaction would incur the following costs per bushel of oats:

1.50 cents—Elevation (paid for unloading car into elevator bin, weighing, subsequent reloading, etc.).

0.50 cents—Clipping (paid for shearing off oat beards from kernels; this process raises the weight per bushel several pounds).

0.75 cents—Cleaning.

0.25 cents—Inspection and weighing (paid to state and to the Board of Trade weighmaster).

1.00 cent —Shrinkage (actually, this could be as high as 3 percent or as low as zero, depending on process used).

Four cents of the usual 6-cent margin Barkley sought thus had to be paid out. He estimated that one of the 2 cents remaining would be net for him after the payment of office, telephone, printing, and other expenses. Not all lots would require exactly the same processing. Some might be given a recleaning, others would be bleached (while the horses might not distinguish dark oats, certain owners valued lightness). While frequently Barkley was able to sell his oat purchases immediately, he found it desirable to carry an inventory of from four to ten carloads to meet sudden demands of customers. Full carrying charges, including storage and financing, typically were 1¾ cents per bushel per month, but Barkley had obtained storage from his elevator in return for the oat clips.

It was a real challenge to keep the firm going at an acceptable net; and for the last few years, Barkley had fallen short of his annual target of 400 carloads (1,000,000 bushels of oats). Thus, he supplemented his main business by occasionally handling special lots of other feed grains, by occasionally speculating in other commodities, and by clearing futures transactions for other grain firms. He almost invariably hedged his own purchases of oats by selling an equivalent amount in the futures market. He did not, however, customarily hedge his basic inventory requirement of four carloads or 10,000 bushels.

On February 19, he purchased two carloads of oats (a total of 5,000 bushels) at "two over" which he hoped to sell in a few days at "eight over" after the oats had been clipped and cleaned. If not hedged, this would bring his long position to six carloads. Cash grain was quoted in terms of the nearest futures (see Exhibit 2–5A); thus, "two over" meant a price of 73½ cents, since the March futures were then quoted at 71½. He could finance the purchase partly through a bank loan and partly from his own limited capital (the banks were willing to finance the whole purchase only if the transactions were hedged).

EXHIBIT 2–5A

Closing Futures Prices for March Delivery of Oats:
February 19–March 5, 1953–63
(cents per bushel)

	February 19*	High within Period	Low within Period	March 5*
1953	73¼	75⅛	73⅛	73¾
1954	76⅛	77⅞	74	77¾
1955	75¾	75¾	71⅞	72⅛
1956	64	64	59⅝	60½
1957	75⅞	76	74⅜	75¼
1958	65⅜	66⅜	63⅛	66⅜
1959	64½	66	64½	64½
1960	73½	75¾	73	75¼
1961	63	63¾	62⅜	62⅜
1962	62	65⅛	61⅞	65⅛
1963	71½			

* Or nearest date on which market was open.
Sources: Board of Trade of the City of Chicago and *The Wall Street Journal.*

Barkley had been bullish about the commodity market in general. In his January 23 letter to his regular customers, he had stated that "there is not too much in the present picture to give much comfort to a bear." The short-run oats picture also was fairly tight, and cash grain deliveries in Chicago were slow. But March futures for oats had fallen from 73¾ on January 23 to the current 71½. The relative price of corn was still favorable, and it would be substituted for oats by some feeders. In terms of weight equivalent, corn at $1.25 would be about equal to oats at 71½, but the March futures for corn were actually selling at $1.17.[14]

Conflicting advice was being given by two leading market bulletins. One noted, as to oats: "A very slow local trade. A prominent local long was seen as a seller late in the week. Would stay on the sidelines." The other stated: "The oat market followed the lead of corn and allied feeds, showing a modest gain for the week. Oats appear to be a buy at current levels."

Barkley had no strong opinion about how the market for March futures would move, in view of the mixed evidence. Before following his usual practice of selling in the most current futures market, he did look over the chart of the range in which March futures had moved over the last five years on the relevant dates. These figures are shown in Exhibit 2–5A.

---

[14] Actually, a bushel of oats is a weight measure, 32 pounds to a bushel. The grades Barkley sold after clipping weighed 40 pounds or more to a bushel and thus would be measured as 1.25 or more bushels. The standard for corn is 56 pounds per bushel.

Questions

1. Do you think Barkley should hedge his two-carload purchase?

   It is suggested that you set up a payoff matrix with the two strategies, hedge or not hedge, and with five possible outcomes for future prices for changes of: over −3 cents; −3 cents to −1⅛ cents; −1 cent to 1 cent; +1⅛ cents to +3 cents; and over 3 cents. Use −5 cents, −2 cents, 0, +2 cents, +5 cents as representative figures for figuring the payoffs of the outcomes which can be expressed as dollar contributions to fixed costs and profits. Hedging costs can be taken as $5 (for a nonmember of the Board of Trade they would be several times this figure). Assume Barkley's price reflects the futures price.

   a. Consider the maximin criteria.
   b. Consider expected profits using equal probabilities for each outcome. Then use the experience of the last ten years to assign probabilities in figuring expected profits.
   c. Is Barkley's past policy of hedging necessarily inconsistent with profit maximization?

2. What is the probable reason for not hedging his basic inventory of four carloads?

3. What are the hedging transactions required at the time of purchase and at the time of sale of the oats? What relationship between futures and cash prices is necessary if all price risk is to be avoided?

CASE 2–6. Puts, Calls, and Straddles

Call options had become relatively familiar to American investors in the mid-1970s partly because of the newly established Chicago Board of Trade's Option Exchange which handled these options on over 30 leading stocks. Put options as well as call options are also offered by specialized brokers in New York who are members of the Put & Call Brokers and Dealers Association.

A "call" is an option to buy a security at a specified price, usually close to the current market price, for a designated period in the future. The usual unit is 100 shares. A common period for the option to buy is the six months necessary to establish capital gain income tax treatment. Shorter periods are frequent, and longer periods may also be used. The Chicago Board has standardized the termination of option contracts in January, April, July, and October with three contract periods outstanding at any one time. For example, a call which gave the option to buy 100 shares of Polaroid stock for a share price of $40 in January, 1975, sold for $962.50 on June 12, 1974. A similar call for October, 1974, at $737.50 was also available.

The "put" is the opposite of the "call." The option is one to sell stock at a designated price by a specified future date. On June 13, 1974, Thomas, Haab & Potts, a brokerage firm, advertised a six-month put entitling the holder to sell Polaroid stock at $41 a share for $687.50. The "straddle" combines a put option with a call. The buyer of a straddle made up of a call and a put at the prices mentioned would require either a fall in the price of Polaroid to below $25 or a rise to almost $57 to recover his combined option costs. The greatest use of this option is likely to be made by a stockholder who sells both a put and call as in the case of Mr. Callison below. A particular buyer is likely to want either the call or the put, but seldom both.

To show how puts may be used to reduce risk, let's look at the situation of Mr. Anderson. He is attracted by the prospects of a rise in the price of stock X and purchases 100 shares for $60 a share. He is quite uncertain that the rise will be immediate and without substantial downward fluctuations. He therefore buys the option to sell the 100 shares for $60 during the next six months. In the matrix of Exhibit 2–6A we have

EXHIBIT 2–6A

Mr. Anderson's Decision

	Profit Outcome if Price of Stock in Six Months Is:						
	$30	*$40*	*$50*	*$60*	*$70*	*$80*	*$90*
Buy X Stock............	−3,000	−2,000	−1,000	0	1,000	2,000	3,000
Buy X Stock and Put.....	− 525	− 525	− 525	−525	475	1,475	2,475

shown his prospective gain for prices from $30 to $90. The first line shows the results from buying the stock only, and the second line gives the results of following the stock purchase plus $525 paid for the put. Actually, there are many intermediate prices for which the stock might sell in six months; nevertheless, a very good approximation of his gains and losses is possible by lumping all of the intermediate possibilities into these seven outcomes. If his expected gains considering each of the seven outcomes are assumed as equally likely, the second course of action involving the put has the higher expected profits. If you give very large probability to the prices from $60 to $90, Mr. Anderson as a profit maximizer would not purchase the put, although if his goal was to maximize the minimum profit to be expected, he would still wish to use the option.

Mr. Bunderson considered different alternatives in making a similar decision (see Exhibit 2–6B. As an alternative to buying 100 shares of stock X for $6,000, he considered the possibility of purchasing an option to buy, that is a call, that would run for just over six months. Such an option would limit his losses to $600 and reduce prospective gains by the

EXHIBIT 2–6B

Mr. Bunderson's Decision

	Profit Outcome if Price of Stock in Six Months Is:						
	$30	$40	$50	$60	$70	$80	$90
Buy X Stock	−3,000	−2,000	−1,000	0	1,000	2,000	3,000
Buy a Call on X Stock	− 600	− 600	− 600	− 600	400	1,400	2,400
Buy Ten Calls on X Stock	−6,000	−6,000	−6,000	−6,000	4,000	14,000	24,000

same amount. It then occurred to him that by using the whole $6,000 for ten calls he could open up possibilities of very large gains if the stock rose to 80–90.

Clearly, options are being used speculatively with the potential long position being extended rather than offset with the call option if this third course is followed.

The selling of options represents a way of increasing returns on a stock portfolio with the acceptance of some risk from price fluctuations. The payoff matrix for Mr. Callison shown in Exhibit 2–6C illustrates the general prospects from options sold in a particular period but may give an exaggerated idea of the relative gains and losses since a recommendation of put and call brokers is that "No more than 20 percent of the dollar value of options sold should expire in any one month. This would prevent undue risks caused by short-term market fluctuations."[15] For simplicity in the decision matrix, no dividends have been put in and the assumption has been made that the investor in effect maintains his portfolio holdings in face of declines and rises in the stock prices. The possibilities of increased return in the stock can readily be seen. For example, if dividends were $240, a call option that was not exercised would add $600 and two such six-month options could be sold in a year bringing income to $1,440 a year.

EXHIBIT 2–6C

Mr. Callison as the Investor Who Sells Options

	Profit Outcome if Price of Stock in Six Months Is:						
	$30	$40	$50	$60	$70	$80	$90
(A) Hold Stock	0	0	0	0	0	0	0
(B) + Sell Call	600	600	600	600	−400	−1,400	−2,400
(C) + Sell Put	−2,475	−1,475	−475	525	525	525	525
(D) + Sell Straddle	−1,875	− 875	125	1,125	125	− 875	−1,875

[15] "The ABC's of Puts and Calls" (New York: Goodrich & Sons, Inc., 1969), p. 8.

Questions

1. Evaluate each of the decision matrices on the basis:
    a. Equal probabilities for each of the seven prices;
    b. Probabilities of 0.05, 0.10, 0.20, 0.30, 0.20, 0.10, and 0.05 for the outcomes from $30 to $90; (*c*) probabilities of 0.01, 0.04, 0.15, 0.25, 0.25, 0.20, 0.10 for the outcomes from $30 to $90 and for (*d*) 0.10, 0.20, 0.25, 0.15, 0.04, and 0.01 for the outcomes from $30 to $90.
2. Compare the profit-maximizing decision with the maximin decision for the three men under the probability assumptions of (*a*), (*b*), (*c*), and (*d*) above.
3. Which decisions would represent a shifting of uncertainty; which represent a speculative willingness to undertake greater uncertainties?

chapter **3**

Forecasting Methods

IN THE PREVIOUS chapter it was pointed out that many businessmen protect themselves from unfavorable price changes by hedging. If hedging is "pure"—that is, if it does not include an element of speculation—a forecast is not necessary, because the businessman is protected regardless of which way the relevant price moves. For most business decisions, however, no perfect hedge is available, and reasonably accurate forecasting is necessary for profitable operations. The typical businessman must often "stick his neck out," and careful forecasting can help him keep ahead.

Forecasting is not always carried out as an explicit function, but it is necessarily implicit in numerous decisions which must be made within the firm. If forecasting is not a centralized, explicit activity, there is danger that, in effect, important forecasts will be made by persons who are not in the best position to engage in this activity. For example, the sales forecast may be implicit in decisions made by an order clerk using rule-of-thumb methods, rather than taking advantage of all available information which could be brought to bear on the problem.[1]

While business economists and management consultants engage in many kinds of analysis, such as plant location, pricing, financing, and so forth, most of them are active to some degree in economic and business forecasting. Economic forecasting applies to *general* business activity such as movements of national income, aggregate industrial production or employment, total exports or imports, or fluctuations in security price indexes. Business forecasting pertains more directly to the activity of a particular industry or firm, consisting of short- and long-term forecasts of sales, price forecasts for important raw materials and equipment,

---

[1] This is suggested by Carl A. Dauten, *Business Fluctuations and Forecasting* (Cincinnati: South-Western Publishing Co., 1954), p. 6.

availability of resources at plant sites under investigation, and a host of other matters of specific interest. The separation between economic and business forecasting is not always sharp, however, and the two are frequently intertwined in the same forecasting process. For example, a forecast of industry sales is dependent on an economic forecast of general business conditions. In turn a firm's forecast of its sales uses the industry projection as well as such specific factors as it own promotional campaigns or new products. The firm's sales may be highly correlated with the sales of the industry of which it is a member, but this relation does not necessarily hold, especially over the longer run (during which new firms may enter or leave the field). In view of this difficulty of classification, no sharp division will be drawn in this chapter between economic and business forecasting. Instead, several popular methods of forecasting, which are applicable to both general and specific prediction, will be discussed separately. Chapter 4 will consider in greater detail the role of demand analysis in forecasting.

Uses of Forecasting

Economic forecasting is quite obviously of value to the federal government to the extent that prevailing policy is to use fiscal and monetary measures to prevent or moderate depressions and severe price inflation. Substantial changes in federal spending and taxing may take many months to put into effect, especially if Congress is not in session at the "right" time. This means that a serious downturn in business would have to be predicted far ahead of time if fiscal measures were to prevent its actual occurrence. Monetary policy can be changed more quickly, but may have lags in taking effect and is, therefore, also dependent on effective forecasting.

The deliberate use of monetary and fiscal policy to prevent undesirable fluctuations in overall economic activity and prices suggests an interesting problem in verification of the accuracy of forecasts. A correct forecast of a depression would appear to have been incorrect if prompt and adequate governmental efforts actually prevented its occurrence. Yet the forecast would in fact have been instrumental in preventing the depression. Therefore, assumptions regarding effects of policy maneuvers should be included in economic forecasts.

The same caution in evaluating the accuracy of a forecast must be exercised when an individual firm is large enough to affect by its own actions the event which is predicted. A forecast of an insufficient capacity to meet demand in five years might itself be sufficient to cause a firm to build enough new capacity to meet the demand. (This self-defeating effect of the forecast would be amplified if rival firms were induced by the firm's actions to expand their plant capacity also.) Usually, however, the individual firm is not sufficiently important to affect the outcome by its own reactions to a forecast. If forecasting should indicate a general rise in raw material prices, for example, the power of the individual firm to prevent such a price rise would be negligible.

Forecasting has many applications within the firm. As has already been suggested, plant expansion (or contraction) plans should be based on a long-term forecast of demand for output.[2] In order to be fully relevant for this purpose, a forecast should cover the period during which fixed capital equipment provides economic services. In making decisions about inventory holding, short-term price movements are of great importance. Normally, an expected increase in price makes it advantageous to build up stocks (provided carrying costs are not too great). In general, an expectation of inflation makes it desirable for a firm to place itself in more of a debtor position by actions such as borrowing and reducing its holding of cash and accounts receivable. A forecast of general deflation makes it desirable for the firm to attain more of a creditor position by building up cash, accounts and notes receivable, and other assets whose value is fixed in dollars, and to substitute common stock for bonds in its own capital structure.[3]

Forecasting the appropriate rate of production for a number of months into the future may be extremely important as an aid to procurement of materials and components which must be ordered far in advance of their use. The same is true of workers who require a period of training before they are useful to a company. On the other hand, ordinary supplies and unskilled labor may usually be purchased as the need arises, and forecasting is of less importance in relation to their acquisition.

Projection and Extrapolation Methods

Probably the most common way of forecasting the future is simply to construct a chart depicting the actual movement of a series and then to project (extrapolate) the apparent trend of the data as far into the future as is desired for the purpose at hand. The projection is usually a straight line, but it may be curvilinear. This is sometimes classified as a "naive" method of forecasting, since it is based on no particular theory as

---

[2] The term "output" should be considered to comprehend not only the product of a manufacturing firm but also the services furnished by a retailer or wholesaler, the transportation furnished by a truck or train, the housing services provided by apartment buildings, and so forth.

[3] An interesting empirical study of the effect of debtor and creditor positions on a firm is described by Reuben A. Kessel, "Inflation-Caused Wealth Redistribution: A Test of a Hypothesis," *American Economic Review*, March, 1956, p. 128. He found that the debtor-creditor hypothesis has predictive usefulness. Kessel's results are in keeping with the idea that there is more "leverage" behind a stock when the company also has bonds outstanding.

to what causes the variable to change, but merely assumes that forces which have contributed to change in the recent past will continue to have the same effect. Trend projectors are often able to show a high percentage of forecasts which are correct (in direction, at least), but the method has the serious defect of missing sudden downturns or upturns —just the changes which it is most important to predict correctly.[4]

On the other hand, trend projection may be the only available method when the variable under consideration is affected by a *large number of factors*, the separate influence of which cannot readily be measured because of lack of data, lack of time, or other reasons. For example, the analyst may have a feeling that a series is affected by the general growth of the economy as population increases, capital accumulates, and technology improves. If he has confidence in this general underlying growth, he may feel, quite rationally, that the observed upward trend in the series in which he is interested will continue. His simple extrapolation is then not entirely naive. However, provided the necessary data were available—on time—he might make a more reliable forecast by using more complicated methods.

In using any forecasting method it is important that the analyst be familiar with the field in which he is working. It would be ridiculous to predict January sales of retail toys by measuring the increase of sales in December over November and projecting the result.

Trend projections may be made graphically, using only a pencil and ruler, or mathematically, by methods of curve fitting. In Figure 3–1 a simple example of graphic "eyeball" trending is illustrated. Actual domestic factory shipments of wringer washers for the period 1950–66 are plotted. As can be seen, this product declined in sales over this period. Two alternative projections have been drawn with a ruler using a dotted line. It is clear that the farther into the future they are drawn the more the two projections will diverge. This growing divergence emphasizes the importance of choosing correctly from among the many alternative projections possible when using trends alone. For long-term predictions, therefore, analysis of underlying demand factors should be a more accurate method, trend projections being extremely useful for the very short run.

It should be noted that different analysts could draw quite different trend projections from the same body of data. Some comparability can be achieved through the use of mathematical methods of curve fitting. These methods involve fitting to the data equations which meet the criterion of minimizing the difference between actual data points and the trend equation. A simple illustration of this technique appears in

---

[4] This is pointed out by Charles F. Roos in a useful article, "Survey of Economic Forecasting Techniques," *Econometrica*, October, 1955, p. 366.

FIGURE 3–1

"Eye-Ball" Trend Projection

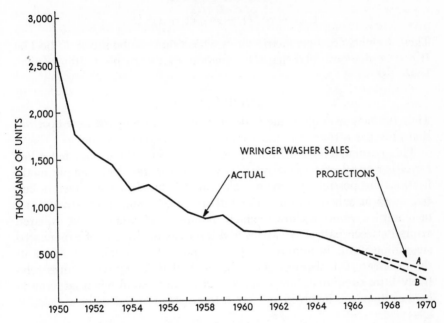

Chapter 4. More on the subject can be found in many basic statistics texts.[5] It must be noted that the particular mathematical function selected and the time span of past data will alter in significant ways the prediction obtained from trend projections.

Another extrapolation method used frequently is exponential smoothing.[6] This method uses the entire past data series available, but assigns weights to past observations, greatest weight being given to the most recent observation. This method is based upon the familiar notion of a geometric series. Thus, if we let S_t represent actual sales in period t and $\hat{S}_t$ represent the exponentially smoothed value of sales for period t, and α equal a smoothing weight, we can write the following expression:

$$\hat{S}_t = \frac{S_t + (1 - \alpha) S_{t-1} + (1 - \alpha)^2 S_{t-2} + \ldots}{1 + (1 - \alpha) + (1 - \alpha)^2 + \ldots}$$

---

[5] For example, see William A. Spurr and Charles P. Bonini, *Statistical Analysis for Business Decisions* (rev. ed.; Homewood, Ill.: Richard D. Irwin, Inc., 1973). See also Roger Chisholm and Gilbert R. Whitaker, Jr., *Forecasting Methods* (Homewood, Ill.: Richard D. Irwin, Inc., 1971).

[6] See R. G. Brown, *Statistical Forecasting for Inventory Control* (New York: McGraw-Hill, Inc., 1959).

This says that one can obtain an estimate of the average value of sales by weighting all past observations with the set of weights:

$$1, (1 - \alpha), (1 - \alpha)^2, (1 - \alpha)^3, \ldots$$

These weights are a geometric series whose sum can be shown to be $1/\alpha$. It can be demonstrated that the equation above can be written equivalently as:

$$\hat{S}_t = \alpha S_t + (1 - \alpha) S_{t-1}$$

Thus the new average value is determined by α times the new observation plus $1 - \alpha$ times the last estimate of the average value.

This particular formulation of exponential smoothing does not allow for either trend or seasonal variation. However, relatively ·simple modifications are possible which can take care of this deficiency. Determination of α is usually done on a trial and error basis using alternative values of α until a value is chosen which minimizes the sum of the squared errors between past observations and forecasts made. Use of exponential smoothing virtually requires that a computer be available to do all of the necessary calculations. Once the method is set up, it requires relatively little computer storage space and is very useful when large numbers of items are involved and rapid forecasts are needed.

Leading Indicators

As has been suggested, a shortcoming of linear projection methods as forecasting techniques is that they necessarily fail to foresee the vital turns, downward and upward, in the series under consideration. It is these turns which call for the most important changes in inventory policy, hiring policy, capital budgeting, debtor-creditor position adjustment, and other matters. A great deal of statistical research has been devoted to the problem of finding "leading indicators," that is, sensitive series which tend to turn up or down in advance of other series. The value of such indicators (if reliable) is obvious. If one could discover a series which would reliably lead stock or commodity price indexes, it would not be difficult to become rich (providing that this method of prediction did not come into general use; in that event, it would cease to lead these speculative prices). Actually, stock prices themselves have been found to be significant leading series for industrial production and for other important indicators of business health. For example, the stock market crash of 1929 preceded the calamitous depression of the 1930s. However, stock market price movements reflect the opinions and actions of speculators and investors; and the more basic question still remains as to what information affects, or should affect, the opinions of the most alert and best informed speculators.

In 1950 Dr. Geoffrey Moore of the National Bureau of Economic Research tested the cyclical behavior of over 800 statistical series. He selected 18 monthly and 3 quarterly series which appeared to be outstanding business indicators. These are not all leading indexes, however; some are coincident with business fluctuations, and others lag behind general business activity. In October, 1961, the Bureau of the Census began publication of *Business Cycle Development,* a monthly publication giving up-to-date information on the indicators which have been identified as leading, roughly coincident, and lagging.[7]

In Figure 3–2 the concept underlying the indicators is illustrated. The vertical lines represent the peak and trough of a general business cycle which has been identified. Line *A* represents an indicator which leads

FIGURE 3–2

Economic Indicators Illustrated

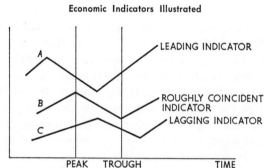

the general cycle by peaking in advance of the general peak and by also reaching its trough in advance of the general trough. Line *B* represents a roughly coincident indicator which peaks and troughs simultaneously with the general cycle. Line *C* represents a lagging indicator which peaks and troughs after the general cycle.

Data for representative leading indicators for the years 1961–72 are indicated in Case 3–4 (page 83). One difficulty is immediately apparent: The indicators often point in different directions at the same time, so that until their movements become substantial in magnitude and similar in direction, it is hard to know where they are leading. Nevertheless, a downturn of some of these indicators after a consistent rise might at least warn the businessman that a general turn is more likely than before. A downturn of a substantial number might well be a signal for action in

---

[7] A revised list of indicators was published in 1967 by the National Bureau of Economic Research. See Geoffrey H. Moore and Julius Shiskin, *Indicators of Business Expansions and Contractions,* Occasional Paper 103 (New York: National Bureau of Economic Research, 1967). The name of the publication of indicators has been changed to *Business Conditions Digest.*

anticipation of lower prices and reduced business activity. The indicators should not be utilized in a mechanical way but rather as one basis for judging coming business conditions. Their use requires alertness in watching for first publication of an index and for anticipating movements before they are published. For example, industrial stock averages are published daily as well as monthly.[8]

Econometric Methods

The most elegant (and sometimes the best) method of forecasting is by the use of econometrics. This term covers a variety of analytical techniques, most of them being a blending of economics, statistics, and mathematics. Econometric models of the entire economy are constantly being worked upon and improved. These models contain among their variables such factors as net investment, consumption, government expenditures, taxes, and net export or import balance, since these are key determinants of national income. To the extent that some of the determining variables can be predicted, an econometric model may be useful in forecasting such overall measures of economic activity as gross national product and national income. If, for example, it could be shown by statistical study of the past that investment in one year is largely determined by profits of the previous year and that consumption is heavily influenced by the amount of liquid savings accumulated before January 1 of the year in question, the econometrician could use these relationships in his forecasting model. If past relationships continued to hold true (which may be a big "if"), he could make a usefully accurate prediction.

In recent years great progress has been made in the development and predictive usefulness of econometric model building for the American economy. Models have been developed which capture more of the detail of the complex economy and which utilize quarterly data for more timely reporting of results.[9] Further, these new models are constructed so that various policy alternatives can be tried out in model environment to reveal possible results of such policies if they were actually employed. *Business Week* regularly publishes predictions which are made with a quarterly model of the economy developed by Lawrence Klein at the

---

[8] See Arthur M. Okun, "On the Appraisal of Cyclical Turning-Point Predictors," *Journal of Business*, April, 1960. For a corporation's use of indicators, see Robert L. McLaughlin, "Leading Indicators: A New Approach for Corporate Planning," *Business Economics*, May, 1971.

[9] See D. B. Suits, "Forecasting and Analysis with an Econometric Model," *American Economic Review*, March, 1962, pp. 104–32; J. S. Dusenberry, G. Fromm, L. R. Klein, and E. Kuh, eds., *The Brookings Quarterly Econometric Model of the United States* (Chicago: Rand McNally Co., 1965).

Wharton School. The Office of Business Economics of the Department of Commerce has also developed an econometric model.[10]

One recent econometric forecasting model that has proved useful is one developed at the Federal Reserve Bank of St. Louis. Its basic assumption is that change in the money supply is the most important determinant of future aggregative economic activity. The model consists of relatively few equations as these models go and has developed a creditable track record in prediction.[11] The student who is interested in this model should refer to the publications of the Federal Reserve Bank of St. Louis, which also publishes a large number of periodic reports on monetary variables that are of great value to business and economic forecasters.

Development of a relatively dependable econometric model for the U.S. economy is a difficult problem, and one which requires constant attention. In each period, as new observations are secured, the equations must be recomputed so that "structural change will manifest itself as it occurs."[12]

Much simpler statistical and econometric techniques are frequently valuable, especially for forecasting which is of narrower scope than an economywide model. Suppose one is interested in forecasting total expenditures on recreation. Demand analysis would suggest that of the variables which probably influence such expenditure, disposable personal income should be an outstanding candidate.[13] From publications of the U.S. Department of Commerce, one could secure the data shown in Figure 3–3. These could then usefully be plotted against one another, as in Figure 3–4.

It is apparent that there has been a close correlation between disposable personal income and consumer expenditures on recreation. This close correlation is apparent over a period, spanning over 40 years and is remarkable for its consistency. This sort of simple correlation analysis may help a businessman understand the forces which affect his sales and, perhaps, help him in his planning for the future. To the extent that forecasts of disposable personal income are available, these could readily be translated into forecasts of recreation expenditures on an overall basis.

---

[10] A Quarterly Econometric Model of the United States: A Progress Report," *Survey of Current Business,* May, 1966.

[11] Leonall C. Andersen and Jerry L. Jordan, "Monetary and Fiscal Actions: A Test of Their Relative Importance in Economic Stabilization," *Review,* Federal Reserve Bank of St. Louis, November, 1968. Also see Leonall C. Andersen and Keith M. Carlson, "A Monetarist Model for Economic Stabilization," *Review,* Federal Reserve Bank of St. Louis, April, 1970.

[12] Lawrence R. Klein, *Econometrics* (Evanston, Ill.: Row, Peterson & Co., 1953), p. 264.

[13] Chapter 4 will further develop this topic, but a brief introduction will be given here.

FIGURE 3–3

Recreation and Disposable Income
(in billions)

Year	DPI	Expenditures on Recreation
1929	83.3	4.3
1933	45.5	2.2
1940	75.7	3.8
1945	150.2	6.1
1950	206.9	11.1
1955	275.3	14.1
1956	293.2	15.0
1957	308.5	15.3
1958	318.8	15.8
1959	337.3	17.4
1960	350.0	18.3
1961	364.4	19.5
1962	385.3	20.5
1963	404.6	22.2
1964	438.1	24.6
1965	473.2	26.3
1966	511.9	28.9
1967	546.3	30.8
1968	591.0	33.6
1969	634.4	36.9
1970	691.7	40.7
1971	746.0	42.7
1972	797.0	47.8

Source: U.S. Office of Business Economics, *The National Income Accounts of the U.S.*, 1929–65, Supplement to the Survey of Current Business (Washington, D.C.: Government Printing Office, 1966). *Survey of Current Business*, July 1966 issues.

This would be done by locating the predicted disposable personal income on the horizontal scale and moving up to the straight line in Figure 3–4.

Other factors which might, in theory, affect expenditures on recreation should also be investigated. If, for example, the age distribution of the population and the average number of hours worked per week should also be found to be significant, the analyst might make a multiple regression study (using familiar statistical techniques) to discover their past effect on recreation expenditures. If these relationships were to remain reasonably constant in the near future, and if some forecast of the independent variables could be secured,[14] the regression equation so derived would make possible a forecast of recreation expenditures.[15]

[14] It would not be difficult, for example, to forecast the age distribution of the population in the near future, since these people would already be living, and since death rates are quite predictable.

[15] Discussion of the economic theory of demand which would help in the choice of variables is postponed to the next chapter.

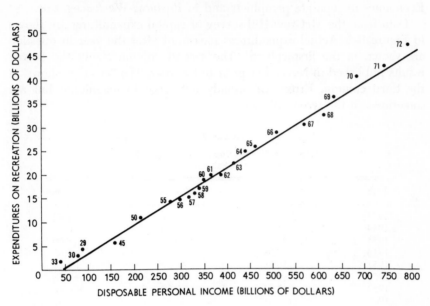

FIGURE 3–4

Expenditures on Recreation Follow Disposable Personal Income

Survey Methods

It has been pointed out that the forecaster who wishes to make optimum use of econometric methods must constantly recompute his equations as later data become available. Also, he should be willing to incorporate the work of others into his own system if he has reason to believe that their estimates are better than those which he could make or if this procedure is worthwhile as a timesaver. Similarly, he should be willing to substitute the results of intentions surveys on such matters as planned investment and consumption if he feels that such data are more accurate than those which he can compute from past relationships. On the other hand, the analyst is free to use computed relationships if he does not have sufficient faith in the predictive value of a survey.

Intentions surveys have increased in popularity in recent years as a basis for forecasting important economic variables. The Department of Commerce and the Securities and Exchange Commission conduct a joint quarterly survey in order to ascertain recent and anticipated expenditures for plant and equipment: The McGraw-Hill Department of Economics makes highly publicized surveys of planned investment of the larger companies in the larger industries. These companies not only account for a very substantial part of total investment but also are likely to have more carefully formulated plans than smaller firms, and greater ability actually to effectuate investment decisions. Data on actual and planned investment are published by the McGraw-Hill Department of Economics in separate pamphlets and in *Business Week* magazine.

Data from the McGraw-Hill survey of capital expenditures are shown in Figure 3–5. Actual expenditures measured after the year in question are shown in the first column. The second column shows the survey results published in November prior to the year. The "error" is shown in the third column. Errors are usually not large in magnitude but are sometimes in the wrong direction.

FIGURE 3–5

Actual and Planned Capital Spending, 1953–67
(in billions)

Year	Actual*	Planned†	Difference
1953	28.32	26.50	−1.82
1954	26.83	26.50	−0.33
1955	28.70	20.70	−8.00
1956	35.08	33.40	−1.68
1957	36.96	40.20	+3.24
1958	30.53	36.10	+5.57
1959	32.54	33.00	+0.46
1960	35.68	37.30	+1.62
1961	34.37	35.07	+0.70
1962	37.31	35.84	−1.47
1963	39.22	38.15	−1.07
1964	44.90	40.72	−4.18
1965	54.42	46.86	−7.56
1966	63.51	54.87	−8.64
1967	65.47	63.82	−1.65
1968	67.76	65.05	−2.71
1969	75.56	69.23	−6.33
1970	79.71	76.71	−3.00
1971	81.21	82.46	+1.25
1972	88.44	87.02	−1.42

* Expenditures for new plant and equipment (excluding agriculture). Source: *Economic Indicators*, July, 1973.
† From various November issues of *Business Week*. Data is listed in the preceding year.

Requirements Forecasting

An important and very common type of sales forecasting is quite obviously open to all firms selling materials or components to other firms which set up production schedules for end items. Firms which regularly supply General Motors with components can clearly gauge their future sales prospects by securing the General Motors output schedules —assuming, of course, that these schedules are sufficiently "firm," that General Motors will not decide to make its own components, and that the company in question will continue to get the General Motors business.

In recent years an allied form of forecasting has become possible to the extent that the federal government establishes production programs and schedules. During World War II, for example, President Roosevelt called for the production of 60,000 military airplanes in 1942 and 125,000 in 1943. These goals were followed by detailed production schedules which were supposed to add up to these totals. (Actually, they did not, especially for 1942.) From the detailed schedules of airplane production the federal statisticians were able to compute requirements for aluminum, engines, propellers, radio equipment, and thousands of other components. To the extent that end-product schedules were realistic for airplanes and other munitions, the detailed requirement schedules gave firms producing materials and components an excellent forecast of their own sales possibilities.

A similar situation existed just after the war, when the veterans' emergency housing program was put into effect by Congress. Unlike the wartime munitions programs, this program did not call for government purchase of the end product. Rather, it was an attempt to use priority ratings, allocation orders, limitation orders applied to less essential construction, subsidies on building materials, and other unusual measures to secure the rapid construction of homes for purchase by veterans. To the extent that realistic housing schedules were set up by the government (and here, too, schedules tended to be overoptimistic), it was possible for industries supplying such materials as brick, tile, nails, wallboard, and clay sewer pipe to compute their probable sales to the housing industry.

When the federal government formulated its huge interstate highway program, it became possible for the portland cement industry, asphalt industry, aggregates producers, pipe producers, steel industry, and others to make approximate calculations of their probable sales in support of this tremendous program. An advantage of this sort of program from the view of materials suppliers is its recessionproof nature. In fact, a business recession would probably increase their sales on this account, since the highway program would very likely be speeded up as an emergency public work.

A firm in one of these categories faces a number of problems in forecasting its sales as related to a government production program:

1. The end-item schedules usually reflect a combination of political, administrative, and economic considerations. They are likely to be placed deliberately too high in order to stimulate private firms to set their sights high. Often, the end-item schedules reflect more what government officials believe is required than what can actually be produced within the specified time period.

2. The firm may not get its share of the industry sales in support of a government program. (Or it may be able to get more than its share.)

3. There are usually some opportunities for substitution of one ma-

terial for another. Computation of requirements is complicated by this possibility, since there is usually no set "bill of materials" which can be depended upon. Portland cement and asphalt are important examples of substitute materials.

4. "Pipeline" requirements create difficulties. It is necessary for producers not only to turn out the materials and components needed for incorporation in end items, but also to build up inventories at various stages in the transportation-production process. In part, these inventories are needed to "fill the pipeline" so that a steady input into end items can be secured. These inventory needs are often especially difficult to predict.

In general, as government activities have come to loom larger in our economy, it has become more and more important for firms in many lines to gear their activities to government procurement programs or to government scheduling of some private activities. This requires a sort of forecasting and suggests the importance of following not only federal government activities but also those of state and local governments. States usually budget on a two-year basis; some of the larger states, however, budget annually. Also, over 115,000 local governments have budgets.[16] An examination of available pertinent budgets may give valuable hints to the businessman as to sales possibilities. Budget proposals are usually not supported fully by legislative bodies, of course, so actual appropriations details may give more accurate (but less early) information. Further, the businessman may do well to follow the progress of bond issues of state and local governments, since these are often made for specific capital purposes and therefore have some predictive significance.

Loaded-Dice Techniques

Numerous other ways of looking into the future—some of which are more ethical than others—are based on getting information which is not generally available or on securing information sooner than other people get it. Simply knowing the status of the present and of the immediate past can be of great help in planning operations instead of, as in many situations, having to depend on facts that are weeks or even months old. For example, one use of computers by automobile and appliance manufacturers is keeping continual track of dealers' inventories so that the current rate of retail sales is known. A naive short-run forecast that next week's sales are going to be the same as this week's when current sales are known is probably superior to the most elaborate method of projection that depends on data that are several weeks old. An interesting

---

[16] George W. Mitchell, "Forecasting State and Local Expenditures," *Journal of Business*, 1954, p. 18.

historical example of the latter occurred in 1815. By using their own news service, the Rothschilds received advance news of the outcome of the Battle of Waterloo, which gave them their chance to make a fortune on the London Stock Exchange.[17]

A similar situation in which advance news has value to speculators occurs when the U.S. Department of Agriculture compiles its crop estimates in Washington, D.C. If the estimates are larger than had been expected, future prices will fall, and the speculator with advance news can profit by selling grain futures before the new estimates are publicly released. The opposite is true if the estimates are lower than had been expected. This situation has led some persons to attempt to communicate with cohorts outside the building as soon as the estimates have been assembled. It is said that a man was once caught passing a signal from a washroom by means of adjusting the height of the window shade. Strict security measures are employed by the Department of Agriculture to prevent the premature export of crop estimates from the building.

"Forecasting the forecast" obviously presents another possibility along these lines. If, for example, an individual were able to come up with a close approximation of his own to the federal crop estimate and were able to make the estimate soon enough, he might be in a position to make speculative profits. (Actually, the cost of gathering and analyzing the necessary data would, in this particular case, probably bring a net loss rather than a profit.)

Methods of securing advance information vary from those which merely require alertness to those which are downright dishonest. Alertness was displayed by Andrew Carnegie, who secured advance information on industrial production by counting the number of smoking chimneys.[18] A less clearly ethical way of forecasting land values is used in the oil industry, where men are regularly employed to watch the drill rigs of other companies through field glasses and to rush to the nearest phone to take up all available options on adjacent land if they see oil struck.[19]

At the bottom of the list ethically are a variety of sharp and often illegal practices which may be ways either of ascertaining what exists or of forecasting what is coming. Engineering employees of rival firms are sometimes asked in job interviews to answer questions designed to disclose products and processes rather than to ascertain fitness for employment. Telephone wires may be tapped or a tiny portable transmitter planted under an executive's desk. Or industrial secrets may be stolen in outright cases of breaking into and entering premises. It is strongly

---

[17] Cecil Roth, *The Magnificent Rothschilds* (London: Robert Hale, Ltd., 1939), p. 23, says that contrary to popular legend, Nathan Mayer Rothschild's news service was not based on pigeon post.

[18] "Business Forecasting," *Business Week*, September 24, 1955, p. 6.

[19] Richard Austin Smith, "Business Espionage," *Fortune*, May, 1956, p. 119.

recommended, however, that only the legitimate means of forecasting be studied further by the student.

CASE 3–1. Avery Screen Wire Products Company

In 1949 Walter Avery obtained a sales job with a local firm which sold and installed aluminum storm sash and doors and metal weather-stripping. He was quite successful in this business and in 1953 established his own sales firm in the same business.

His market at first consisted primarily of older residences and a few commercial buildings; but subsequently, he began to obtain contracts to provide metal doors and sash on new homes where the undertaking was not large. For the new homes and buildings, Mr. Avery purchased the standard-size doors and windows from a manufacturer of such items. On older homes, however, the window and door openings were often of variable sizes and seldom standard by modern dimensions. To provide metal sash and doors for the latter, he contracted with various small shops to make the items to order. This was rather expensive and allowed him only a small margin on his sales.

Mr. Avery observed that commercial and apartment buildings were also using more metal sash and doors as well as trim. He often lost bids on these jobs because of price and quantity involved. In order to obtain any of this business on a substantial scale, Mr. Avery was convinced he could only do so profitably if he produced his own doors and windows. He therefore set up a small shop to assemble his products. He purchased aluminum and steel extrusions and wire screen direct from metal fabricators, and glass from suppliers. This arrangement permitted him to bid on both residential and commercial buildings, since he could now supply not only in quantity but also to specification. Financing this operation presented some problems; but by pledging his construction awards with his bank, he was able to obtain sufficient working capital to handle the increased volume of sales.

The business prospered, and by 1957 the firm employed 60 persons and occupied rented quarters of approximately 30,000 square feet. In this same year the name of the firm was changed from John H. Avery, Contractor, to Avery Screen Wire Products Company. Early in 1957 Mr. Avery obtained a contract with a large mail-order and retail firm to manufacture metal windows and doors for it under the private brand name of the mail-order firm. In order to meet the increased sales resulting from this contract, the Avery company constructed a building to its specifications and installed some new and laborsaving equipment to increase production. One half the cost of this expansion was financed by the mail-order firm.

EXHIBIT 3–1A

AVERY SCREEN WIRE PRODUCTS COMPANY
Monthly Sales, Sash and Doors—January, 1954–May, 1961

Month	1954	1955	1956	1957	1958	1959	1960	1961
January......	$ 9,132	$ 22,891	$ 44,033	$ 72,004	$ 90,633	$ 100,344	$ 99,181	$ 96,555
February......	7,911	25,614	41,929	69,199	87,521	96,597	97,664	91,492
March......	8,204	24,572	39,051	68,044	84,319	93,885	94,118	89,532
April......	10,512	27,447	42,540	71,552	88,525	90,357	92,337	88,117
May......	19,327	31,551	45,880	78,439	93,995	93,433	93,889	88,913
June......	27,114	37,119	51,364	89,507*	96,197	99,518	97,414	
July......	31,215	40,336	57,002	94,962	99,562	103,655	102,937	
August......	22,461	46,111	63,099	95,101	103,212	105,541	106,004	
September......	18,314	51,210	68,553	97,210	105,527	107,555	108,954	
October......	19,761	51,040	74,500	97,235	106,329	107,348	109,033	
November......	20,411	51,115	74,266	96,404	107,374	106,591	108,181	
December......	21,515	47,229	75,427	95,891	104,193	103,284	105,910	
	$215,877	$456,235	$677,644	$1,025,548	$1,167,387	$1,208,108	$1,215,622	$454,609

* Includes sales to mail-order house under private brand.

EXHIBIT 3–1B

AVERY SCREEN WIRE PRODUCTS COMPANY
Monthly Sales "Metalfab" Buildings—April, 1958–May, 1961

Month	1958	1959	1960	1961
January................		$ 78,545	$ 128,665	$134,144
February..............		82,147	130,499	134,109
March................		89,515	132,557	135,007
April.................	$ 39,200	92,338	135,851	135,617
May..................	43,731	101,288	137,772	136,411
June.................	46,884	111,315	139,550	
July.................	57,102	127,882	148,662	
August...............	59,137	131,471	146,889	
September............	68,443	131,486	145,314	
October..............	73,877	132,007	145,110	
November............	72,896	131,218	142,199	
December............	73,459	130,449	139,322	
	$534,729	$1,339,661	$1,672,390	$675,288

The new plant offered many economies of production. Metal was now purchased directly from mills and fabricated by extruding machines in the plant. Also installed were two wire-weaving machines to produce several grades of wire screen. New-type cutting and forming machines were also installed. Although sales in 1957 exceeded $1 million, the new plant upon completion presented a problem of excess capacity. In an attempt to make use of this excess capacity, the company undertook to produce and market sash, doors, and trim under its own brand name of "Avery." These were sold through manufacturers' representatives and by 1959 were on sale in 31 states. In addition to doors, sash, and trim, the company in 1958 introduced prefabricated metal buildings ranging in size from 4 by 6 feet to 20 by 30 feet. The smaller buildings were used frequently by homeowners and small firms for auxiliary storage, while the larger buildings were used by construction firms for storage and garage purposes. The largest size was often used by farms and industrial firms, since several units could be erected and fastened together to make a building 20 feet wide and any desired length in multiples of 30 feet. The largest unit had a ridge-type roof and could be had in heights ranging from 9 to 17 feet. As shown in Exhibit 3–1B, sales of these buildings, sold under the trade name "Metalfab," exceeded the volume of sash, door, and trim.

Exhibit 3–1A shows monthly sales of sash, doors, and trim from 1954 through May, 1961. Exhibit 3–1B shows sales of "Metalfab" buildings of all sizes from April, 1958, through May, 1961. Exhibit 3–1C shows residential and nonresidential building contracts by months for all states from 1957 through May, 1961.

EXHIBIT 3–1C

Value of Construction Contracts Awarded, Nonresidential and Residential, 1957–61

(in millions)

Month	1957 Nonresidential	1957 Residential	1958 Nonresidential	1958 Residential	1959 Nonresidential	1959 Residential	1960 Nonresidential	1960 Residential	1961 Nonresidential	1961 Residential
January.	$ 914	$ 817	$ 759	$ 777	$ 818	$1,022	$ 801	$ 927	$ 813	$ 974
February.	820	875	751	727	704	1,073	698	988	804	870
March.	1,092	1,107	967	1,071	913	1,541	1,067	1,294	1,027	1,371
April.	838	1,232	958	1,240	1,187	1,831	1,048	1,480	1,050	1,454
May.	1,120	1,297	1,124	1,346	1,072	1,677	1,110	1,453		
June.	1,186	1,135	976	1,364	1,055	1,762	1,110	1,483		
July.	961	1,287	1,076	1,557	1,191	1,690	1,152	1,329		
August.	1,008	1,284	1,079	1,451	961	1,551	1,177	1,433		
September.	866	1,151	892	1,460	1,006	1,466	1,124	1,277		
October.	910	1,165	955	1,595	1,003	1,515	1,165	1,390		
November.	878	930	775	1,206	801	1,092	916	1,253		
December.	699	759	748	981	790	993	994	878		

Source: U.S. Department of Commerce.

In June, 1960, Mr. Avery was preparing to place orders for steel and aluminum plate, aluminum wire, and miscellaneous nuts, bolts, and screws to meet his coming year's needs. By placing his order for an entire year with arrangement for advanced deliveries, the firm was able to obtain substantial price advantages. In studying his sales for several years, Mr. Avery noted with concern that sales for the first four months of 1960 were lagging slightly behind 1959, whereas in the past each year had shown successively increasing sales.

During a discussion of the problem with his sales manager, the question of prices for the following year was considered. The sales manager suggested that perhaps the company should reduce its prices in order to stimulate sales. Mr. Avery stated that he was doubtful if a price reduction would result in increased sales.

Questions

1. Would you say that the variations in sales are the result of an emerging seasonal variation? Why? If you think there is evidence of seasonal variation, why had it not appeared in earlier years?
2. Is there evidence of cyclical fluctuation? What?
3. Test the data for any lead-lag relationship between the "value of construction contracts awarded" series and Avery's sales that could be useful for forecasting.
4. What price policy would you recommend, in view of the leveling off in sales?
5. What is the nature of demand for sash, doors, and trim?

CASE 3–2. Continental Radio and Television Corporation

In 1924 the Landle Electric Company was manufacturing a line of electric motors, condensers, switches, and transformers which it sold to other manufacturers and industrial users. In November of that year the company began to manufacture radio receiving sets and speakers. At the time, radio sets were a relatively recent invention, and it was the company's first venture into the consumer market. Distribution of these sets was made through wholesalers and jobbers.

The first models produced by Landle Electric were priced at $555, exclusive of aerial. Radio sets were well received by the public so that by 1928 there were several hundred companies producing more than a thousand different brands. The Landle company manufactured all the components for its sets except tubes, cabinets, and speakers. These were purchased from other manufacturers. The earliest sets were practically handmade, but by 1929 the company was using assembly-line operations. Sales in 1928 were more than 9,000 sets.

In July, 1927, largely because of its success in the consumer market with radios, the company began the manufacture and sale of electric refrigerators, another consumer item which had been introduced to the public within the preceding few years. Using its present facilities and some newly constructed ones, the company manufactured its own compressors and motors, but purchased the boxes from another manufacturer. Sales of refrigerators also expanded until the depression which began in 1929.

The Landle company suffered sharp declines in sales and profits immediately following the economic collapse in 1929. In addition, prices of all the items it produced declined approximately 50 percent. Price declines in radios, however, had begun in 1925; but this was due in large measure to technological improvements in both design and methods of production. Early in 1930 the company found itself with a large inventory on its own account as well as in the hands of its dealers. About 20 percent of the radio inventory was eventually junked because of obsolescence.

In 1934 Landle Electric Company merged with the Nadine Corporation, a producer of commercial refrigerators and milk coolers. In 1935 another merger was completed with a producer of home laundry equipment. Thereafter the company was known as the Continental Radio Corporation.

During World War II the company devoted almost all of its facilities to the production of military goods, manufacturing various types of electronic equipment. A limited quantity of repair parts was produced for its consumer line. In 1946, after reconversion to its line of industrial and consumer goods, the company was among the first to place television sets on the market. The name of the company was then changed to Continental Radio and Television Corporation. In 1947 the company added electric dryers, electric ranges, and home freezers to its line.

The initial stages of television production presented several problems. Whereas the company had originally made almost all of the component parts of its radio sets, it now made relatively few of them. Other than condensers, transformers, and switches, it purchased its parts from other producers and assembled the sets. Television parts were deeply involved in patent rights so that it was decided to purchase as many components as possible and to assemble the sets. Furthermore, as in its early experience in the production of radios, the company had to undertake expensive research in electronics to develop and produce many parts in television sets. It was anticipated that like radios, television sets would undergo considerable improvement in design and performance which would result in changes in methods of production. The company's 1947

EXHIBIT 3–2A

Wholesale Price Index of Television Receivers
(1947–49 = 100)

Month	1947*	1948*	1949*	1950*	1951*	1952*	1953†	1954†	1955†	1956	1957	1958	1959	1960	1961
January.........	..	..	..	..	..	..	74.5	73.5	69.0	69.7	69.9	71.2	70.2	69.0	69.3
February........	..	..	..	..	..	..	75.6	73.8	68.8	69.9	69.9	70.7	70.2	69.1	68.7
March...........	..	..	..	..	..	..	74.9	73.8	68.8	69.9	69.5	70.7	69.6	69.1	..
April...........	96.3‡	100.1‡	103.6‡	96.8‡	92.8‡	92.9‡	74.9	73.8	69.0	69.5	69.5	70.7	69.6	69.0	..
May.............	..	..	..	..	..	..	74.9	73.8	69.0	69.3	69.5	70.7	69.6	69.0	..
June............	..	..	..	..	..	..	75.0	70.6	68.8	69.1	69.7	70.0	69.6	69.0	..
July............	..	..	..	..	..	..	74.3	70.3	68.9	69.3	70.8	71.1	70.9	69.0	..
August..........	..	..	..	..	..	..	74.0	68.5	68.9	69.6	71.4	71.2	70.1	68.9	..
September.......	..	..	..	..	..	..	74.2	68.7	69.3	70.1	71.4	71.2	70.1	68.9	..
October.........	..	..	..	..	..	..	74.2	68.7	69.5	69.9	71.4	71.2	69.5	68.9	..
November........	..	..	..	..	..	..	74.2	69.2	69.5	69.9	71.4	69.3	69.2	68.9	..
December........	..	..	..	..	..	..	74.0	69.2	69.7	69.7	71.6	69.3	69.2	69.3	..

* Not available on a monthly basis.
† Prices of television sets only.
‡ Yearly average of radio, phonograph, and television sets.

sets were priced from $395 to $795, depending upon screen size and cabinet style. In 1950 the company's prices ranged from $209.95 to $495 for sets with much larger viewing screens and more efficient performance. By 1960 there had been further slight price reductions, the company's prices ranging from $199.95 for portable sets to $439.95 for console types. Some models were offered for as high as $795, but this was due to more luxurious cabinets and extras such as remote-control devices. As shown in Exhibit 3–2A, prices had remained fairly stable since 1955, although quality of service and performance had improved considerably.

In March of 1961 the sales manager was requested to provide a forecast of the number of television sets to be produced for the 1962 model year, together with suggested prices. Because so many of the components of sets were purchased from other manufacturers, it was necessary to place orders for the year's requirements in April for July delivery. New-model sets were usually introduced in September of each year. About two months' production was necessary to provide dealers with sufficient inventory at the time the new line was announced.

Continental Radio and Television Corporation sold all of its products in the national market, except for approximately 4 percent, which was exported. In the television market the company had accounted for about 7 to 12 percent of the total market and in 1961 anticipated a 10 percent share. Exhibit 3–2B shows shipment of television sets by the firm from 1947 through 1960. As indicated in Exhibit 3–2C, production of television sets experienced a phenomenal growth from 1947 to 1950, and then grew more slowly until 1955. Since 1956 the industry has failed to produce seven million sets annually. The large reduction in output in 1951 reflects restriction upon materials due to the Korean War.

In preparing his forecast, the sales manager was aware of several developments in the market. The rapid growth from 1947 to 1950 was clearly the result of the introduction of a new medium of communica-

EXHIBIT 3–2B

Shipment of Television Receivers, 1947–60

1947	7,152
1948	43,902
1949	135,307
1950	447,840
1951	376,999
1952	426,748
1953	577,264
1954	551,002
1955	681,745
1956	673,936
1957	659,481
1958	499,314
1959	601,578
1960	626,117

EXHIBIT 3–2C

Monthly Production of Television Receivers, 1947–60

Month	1947*	1948*	1949*	1950*	1951	1952
January...............	..	..	..	..	650,700	404,900
February..............	..	..	..	..	679,300	409,300
March................	..	..	..	..	870,000	510,600
April.................	..	..	..	..	500,000	322,900
May..................	..	..	..	..	406,000	309,400
June.................	..	..	..	..	352,500	361,200
July..................	..	..	..	..	148,900	198,900
August...............	..	..	..	..	146,700	397,800
September............	..	..	..	..	337,300	755,700
October..............	..	..	..	..	411,900	724,100
November............	..	..	..	..	415,300	780,500
December............	..	..	..	..	467,100	921,100
Total............	178,800	975,600	3,000,000	7,464,000	5,385,700	6,096,400

* Not available on a monthly basis.
Note: In March, 1961, Continental had trade information indicating that January and February production had been 367,900 and 444,400 receivers, respectively. Indications were that March production would be slightly under 500,000 sets.

tion. The growth was not dampened by the Korean War alone, but was limited by the fact that relatively few new television broadcasting stations had been approved by the Federal Communications Commission since 1948. A large number of applications was still pending, but new stations were usually approved only in areas where there was no station. Many areas had only one station so that the choice of programs was limited. After 1948 the Federal Communications Commission had approved a number of applications for ultrahigh-frequency stations; but in the sales manager's opinion, these had not been successful. Many of the ultrahigh-frequency stations shortly went out of business. It had been necessary to build sets which would receive high-frequency signals as well as ultrahigh-frequency signals, and also to produce adapters for sets which were manufactured prior to the establishment of ultrahigh-frequency stations. Very few of the adapters were sold.

Another factor in the market was that much of the replacement of sets sold from 1947 to 1955 had been fairly well completed. The earlier sets had small screens, required installation charges and, frequently, expensive service. Sets produced after 1954–55 had larger screens comparable in size to current models, required only nominal or no installation charge, and required less frequent service. Since 1954 the company had offered portable sets in several models, and these had sold more than other models in the complete line. The relatively recent introduction of stereo reproduction of records and magnetic tape was considered a major

EXHIBIT 3–2C (Continued)

1953	1954	1955	1956	1957	1958	1959	1960
719,200	420,600	654,600	588,300	450,200	434,000	437,000	526,500
730,600	426,900	702,500	576,300	464,700	370,400	459,500	503,500
810,100	599,600	831,200	680,000	559,800	416,900	494,000	549,500
567,900	457,600	583,200	549,600	361,200	302,600	389,300	422,600
481,900	396,300	467,400	467,900	342,400	267,000	431,900	422,200
524,500	544,100	590,000	553,000	543,800	377,100	571,000	518,900
316,300	307,000	344,300	336,900	360,700	275,000	350,400	268,900
603,800	633,400	647,900	612,900	673,700	507,500	547,400	462,300
770,100	947,800	939,500	894,200	832,600	621,700	808,300	678,900
680,400	921,500	759,700	820,800	662,000	495,600	706,600	500,000
561,200	858,500	631,700	680,000	574,600	437,800	560,800	429,800
449,800	833,400	604,600	627,000	573,500	414,900	593,200	405,500
7,215,800	7,346,700	7,756,600	7,386,900	6,399,200	4,920,500	6,349,400	5,688,600

Source: U.S. Department of Commerce.

factor of competition with the higher priced console and combination television sets.

In the mid-1950s, price cutting had broken out at the dealer level; and to some extent, it had been pushed back to the manufacturer's level. As indicated in Exhibit 3–2C, sales had been lagging since 1955, which had stimulated price concessions by dealers. The growth of discount houses had, in effect, obliterated the significance of suggested retail price by the manufacturer. In spite of this situation, Continental Radio and Television Corporation continued to publish a suggested list price for each model. Evidence of continued deterioration in prices is shown in Exhibit 3–2A.

In December, 1960, the company had an inventory on hand of 453 of the 1960 models, with 3,271 in dealer hands. This was not considered an undesirable level. The company had 67,449 of the 1961 models on hand, and there were 198,552 in dealer hands. The 1960 models would probably be cleared by price reductions. The problem of color television was not considered as serious as a few years earlier but was still a factor. In 1960 the company had produced and sold 6,000 color sets and had no inventory on hand of that model year. Included in the 1961 inventory above are approximately 16,000 color sets. The number of color telecasts was increasing, and it was anticipated that all of the three major television networks would be telecasting some part of their programs in color by 1963. Prices on color television sets had remained fairly constant, but the quality of color reception had been sharply improved, and they required far less frequent service.

As far as price considerations were concerned, the company anticipated increased costs of production. Almost all of its factory employees

EXHIBIT 3–2D

Disposable Income, Consumer Expenditures, Consumer Saving,
Gross Private Investment Annually, 1946–60
(in billions)

Year	Disposable Income	Consumer Expenditures	Consumer Savings	Gross Private Investment
1946	$160.6	$147.1	$13.5	$28.1
1947	170.1	165.4	4.7	31.5
1948	189.3	178.3	11.0	43.1
1949	189.7	181.2	8.5	33.0
1950	207.7	195.0	12.6	50.0
1951	227.5	209.8	17.7	56.3
1952	238.7	219.8	18.9	49.9
1953	252.5	232.6	19.8	50.3
1954	256.9	238.0	18.9	48.9
1955	274.4	256.9	17.5	63.8
1956	292.9	269.9	23.0	67.4
1957	308.8	285.2	23.6	66.1
1958	317.9	293.2	24.7	56.6
1959	337.3	314.0	23.4	72.4
1960	351.8	328.9	22.9	72.4

Source: U.S. Department of Commerce.

were union members, many of whom would seek new contracts during the year as present contracts expired. It was a foregone conclusion that labor costs would rise whether it be in the form of higher wages, fringe benefits, or both. It was anticipated that some reduction in the unit cost of production could be made in 1961 because of improved methods of production. In view of the present economic situation, it was recommended that no price changes be made for the 1962 model year.

The general business outlook itself was somewhat mixed. The index of industrial production had been declining since February, 1960, and the decline had continued into 1961. On the other hand, consumer disposable income had shown no such tendency. The Consumer Price Index had, however, continued to rise slowly but steadily throughout this same period. In the same period, private housing starts had also declined, while interest rates on mortgages as well as commercial loans had risen. There were some feelings of optimism, however, in that many economists predicted that the decline would come to an end in the summer of 1961 and a definite upturn would appear in the fall.

Exhibit 3–2D provides data on income, consumer spending, and saving. Exhibit 3–2E shows the amount of consumer installment credit outstanding, as well as that pertaining to durables other than automobiles. Exhibit 3–2F shows the cost of production of the two basic models of sets manufactured by Continental, as well as suggested list prices for the respective models.

EXHIBIT 3–2E

Consumer Credit Outstanding, 1954–60
(in millions)

Year	Total	Consumer Durables Other than Automobiles and Modernization
1954	$32,464	$ 6,751
1955	38,882	7,634
1956	42,511	8,580
1957	45,286	8,782
1958	45,544	8,923
1959	52,119	10,476
1960:		
January	51,468	10,386
February	51,182	10,254
March	51,298	10,192
April	52,353	10,281
May	52,991	10,339
June	53,662	10,462
July	53,809	10,452
August	54,092	10,477
September	54,265	10,543
October	54,344	10,625
November	54,626	10,715
December	56,049	11,215
1961:		
January	54,726	11,365
February	53,843	11,136

Source: U.S. Department of Commerce.

EXHIBIT 3–2F

Actual Costs, Models 110 and 210, Television Receivers, 1960 and 1961

Item	1960		1961*	
	Model 110	Model 210	Model 110	Model 210
Materials	$ 40.25	$ 29.82	$ 40.19	$ 29.67
Direct labor	21.26	18.97	21.70	19.05
Depreciation	2.04	2.02	2.06	2.03
Indirect labor	7.51	5.21	7.61	5.39
Factory overhead	3.34	2.99	3.39	3.08
Administrative and selling expense	2.39	2.10	2.40	2.20
Total cost	$ 76.79	$ 61.11	$ 77.35	$ 61.42
Suggested retail price	$299.95	$199.95	$299.95	$199.95

* Estimated.

Questions

1. Appraise the difficulties faced by Continental in forecasting in comparison with those of other business firms—for example, a gasoline refiner and distributor, and a building materials producer. Outline possible approaches to short-run forecasting for Continental after analysis of the data given.
2. What implications does your answer to Question 1 have for questions of business policy, such as the advanced ordering of set components?

CASE 3–3. Procter & Gamble*

Procter & Gamble produces a wide line of quality shortenings, of which the best-known retail brands are Crisco and Fluffo. Shortenings made for restaurant, bakers, and industrial use include such brand names as Primex, Sweetex, Pertex, Selex, Flakewhite, and Frymax.

For many years, Procter & Gamble's shortenings were made entirely from vegetable oils, such as soybean oil and cottonseed oil. Early in the 1950s, however, the company began to merchandise three brands that utilized lard as an ingredient. In the manufacture of these products, lard and soybean oil can be interchanged without downgrading the product. Furthermore, the percentage of lard used in the manufacturing process can be varied over a fairly wide range. For example, let us assume that in early 1959 the company could use a maximum of 20 tank cars of lard per week (60,000 pounds per tank car) when the price was favorable. When the price of lard was unfavorable, the soybean oil usage could be increased and the usage of lard reduced to six or seven tank cars per week.

Purchases of lard are made from a large number of packing houses. Most of these suppliers merchandise some of their lard in their own products. These products include lard sold in retail packages and lard sold to bakers, hotels, and so forth. A few packers also make shortening from mixtures of lard and vegetable oil. The packers' surplus lard production is sold as "loose" lard in tank cars. Procter & Gamble purchases loose lard in tank-car quantities, with delivery made one to three weeks after purchase. Contact with the sellers is maintained by telephone, plus an occasional visit. Some of the telephone contact is direct with sellers, but in other cases a broker acts as an intermediary. All of the sellers and brokers, of course, are in contact with other buyers. The price for each transaction is really a separate negotiation, and actual trading prices can fluc-

---

* This is one of a series of marketing problems prepared by Procter & Gamble, and the authors express appreciation to the company for permission to use it. Brand names, raw material names, market prices, freight rates, and lard production figures are actual. However, figures regarding the company's usage are hypothetical.

tuate from day to day or even from transaction to transaction. The trading prices are determined by the supply and demand conditions effective in the market at a given time.

Because of the nature of trading, it is impossible to quote a precise "market" price at any time. However, the loose-lard quotation on the Chicago Board of Trade is widely used as a market indicator by both buyers and sellers. A brief summary of these quotations is known in Exhibit 3–3A. The term "delivered Chicago basis" means that the seller allows freight from the origin to Chicago and the buyer pays the balance of the freight (see Exhibit 3–3B for actual freight rates for typical points). For example, lard purchased from Davenport, Iowa, at 9 cents per pound, delivered Chicago basis, would actually be delivered to Cincinnati, Ohio, at 9.59 cents per pound. (It should be noted that loose lard is hardly ever sold for future delivery, and speculation in the raw material is more likely to be accomplished by outright purchase. Physical possession of lard results in a carrying charge of about 5 cents per hundredweight per month.)

Procter & Gamble uses lard in Cincinnati, Ohio, and Dallas, Texas. Approximately two thirds of the usage is at Cincinnati, which is supplied from two areas. The first area includes most of western Ohio, Indiana, southern Illinois, and Kentucky. Lard from this area can normally be purchased, "delivered Cincinnati," at the Chicago loose-lard price, plus ¼ cent per pound. This area will normally supply the company with six or eight cars of lard per week during the heavy slaughter season, but only two or three cars per week during the late spring, summer, and early fall. The second supply area for Cincinnati includes Iowa, Minnesota, Wisconsin, and Nebraska. Normally, good quantities of lard can be purchased from points in this territory on a Chicago basis. Lard for Dallas comes from the Iowa-Nebraska area, with a little coming from local producers. Purchases of lard for Dallas from Iowa-Nebraska are normally on a Chicago basis. There is little lard produced west of Omaha and Kansas City.

Competitive manufacturers of shortenings are also able to use lard as an alternative for soybean oil. Chicago is an important production point for shortenings of this type, and buyers at this location can usually purchase lard delivered to their plants at the Chicago loose-lard quotation. Other manufacturers of shortening throughout the country use some lard, and it is believed that the majority of their purchases are made on a Chicago basis.

In order to convert crude fats into shortening, a series of processing operations is required. From a cost standpoint, there is little difference between the cost to convert soybean oil to shortening compared with the cost of processing lard, except for the loss of weight during the refining operation. The weight loss for lard is slightly over 2 percent,

Date	High	Low	Average of Daily Closes
1951–52:			
October	b 17⅝	a 13¾	16.40
November	n 15	b 12⅞	13.95
December	n 14⅞	a 12⅝	13.73
January	n 13⅞	12½	13.00
February	n 12⅜	10	11.46
March	n 11⅜	10	10.58
April	10¼	9¼	9.62
May	11½	9⅛	10.32
June	10⅞	9⅝	10.19
July	11½	b 9	9.89
August	10¼	n 8⅝	9.38
September	b 10	8¼	9.14
1952–53:			
October	n 8⅞	n 8⅛	8.48
November	b 8¾	8⅛	8.37
December	n 8¼	7¼	7.68
January	7¾	6⅞	7.23
February	8½	n 7	7.90
March	9½	n 8¼	9.07
April	9¾	n 8¾	9.26
May	10½	9⅞	10.32
June	10¼	8	9.13
July	12⅞	n 10	11.62
August	17¼	12¼	14.88
September	n 20	13	17.11
1953–54:			
October	n 17¼	14	15.79
November	15	n 13½	14.11
December	b 17	b 15½	15.98
January	a 16¼	14½	15.22
February	b 16⅜	b 15½	16.04
March	18⅛	15¾	16.91
April	n 20½	a 17⅝	18.86
May	n 18	16¼	17.11
June	n 17¼	n 14⅛	15.40
July	a 17	n 15½	16.19
August	n 18⅞	a 16	17.10
September	16⅝	n 14⅜	15.52
1954–55:			
October	b 15½	n 13¾	14.24
November	b 15¼	n 12⅜	13.76
December	12⅞	a 11¾	12.16
January	11⅞	11¼	11.51
February	n 11⅜	10⅝	10.99
March	b 11⅝	a 10⅝	10.87
April	n 12¼	n 11⅜	11.88
May	11¾	b 10½	11.18
June	n 11¼	n 10½	10.82
July	n 11¼	n 9¾	10.52

Date	High	Low	Average of Daily Closes
August	b 10⅝	b 9¼	9.91
September	n 11¼	n 9⅞	10.29
1955–56:			
October	n 12¼	n 9⅝	10.71
November	10⅜	n 9	9.89
December	9¼	8½	8.90
January	b 9¾	n 8½	9.01
February	n 10	n 9⅜	9.70
March	n 10⅛	n 9⅜	9.71
April	n 12	n 10	10.93
May	n 12¼	10¾	11.29
June	10¾	9⅞	10.18
July	n 11⅞	9¾	10.41
August	12¼	n 10½	11.42
September	n 12⅜	n 11⅛	11.87
1956–57:			
October	n 13	n 11½	12.20
November	13⅞	a 11⅜	12.66
December	n 14	n 12¾	13.45
January	n 14¼	n 13¼	13.97
February	n 14¼	13⅛	13.55
March	a 13¼	a 12¾	13.02
April	n 13¼	12½	12.87
May	12½	n 10¾	11.44
June	n 13	n 11¼	12.26
July	b 13	n 12⅝	12.86
August	n 13	n 11½	12.34
September	n 13⅛	n 11¼	12.38
1957–58:			
October	n 12 5/16	n 11½	11.94
November	n 11¾	11	11.22
December	n 11⅛	n 10¾	10.91
January	10⅞	10⅜	10.62
February	12⅞	10½	11.54
March	12	11⅜	11.65
April	11¾	11⅛	11.55
May	12	11½	11.67
June	12	11	11.51
July	12¾	11⅜	12.03
August	13⅜	12¼	13.01
September	12	11	11.47
1958–59:			
October	12½	11	11.65
November	11	10	10.46
December	10	8⅝	9.28
January	8⅞	8½	8.62
February	8⅝	8¼	8.49
March	8⅝	8¼	8.39

Note: The letter a means asked; b, bid; and n, nominal.

Sources: Data for 1951–57 highs and lows from annual reports of Board of Trade of the City of Chicago; 1958 highs and lows from *Procter & Gamble Chart Book;* monthly averages from *Procter & Gamble Chart Book.*

EXHIBIT 3–3B

Crude Rendered Lard Freight Rates, Effective March 4, 1959
(in cents per hundredweight)

			Destinations		
Origins	*Chicago*	*Cincinnati*	*New York*	*Dallas*	*Long Beach*
Illinois:					
Chicago................		64	130	118½	272
Indiana:					
Indianapolis.............	30	34	121		
Muncie..................	60	34	118		
Iowa:					
Davenport..............	29	88	143	130	260
Dubuque...............	29	90	144	134	260
Fort Dodge.............	52	115	170	130	260
Mason City.............	47	110	162	133	260
Storm Lake.............	61	124	178	134	260
Waterloo	41	104	157	132	260
Minnesota:					
Austin..................	47	110	162	134	260
Missouri:					
St. Joseph..............	63	122	174		236
Nebraska:					
Fremont................	70	133	186	104½	244
Ohio:					
Columbus...............	76	46	106		
Troy...................	70	39	114		
Wisconsin:					
Madison................	29	88	136	139	267

while the effective loss of weight for soybean oil is 7 percent. About half of the value lost is recovered in by-product form.

Procter & Gamble cannot be considered a speculative buyer of material since the company normally does not take extreme positions, either long or short. Generally, the company is willing to buy material fairly steadily as required and make its profit through manufacturing and merchandising. At times, however, the company will think that a market trend is fairly evident and under these circumstances will make some change in its owning position. In past years, Procter & Gamble has been quite successful in accumulating large supplies of lard during periods of low price.

On April 1, 1959, the price for soybean oil was 9¼ cents f.o.b. Decatur, Illinois (see Exhibit 3–3C). This converted to delivered prices of approximately 9½ cents Chicago, 9¾ cents Cincinnati, and 10 cents Dallas. On the same day, Chicago lard was 8⅝ cents. Using Iowa freight

EXHIBIT 3–3C

Chicago Soybean Oil Futures, March, 1959

(cents per pound)

		Futures				
Date	*Cash Spot*	*May*	*July*	*September*	*October*	*December*
March 2............	9.375	9.27	9.17	8.92	8.82	8.82
3............	9.375	9.27	9.18	8.94	8.83	8.83
4............	9.50	9.40	9.34	9.08	8.96	8.95
5............	9.50	9.31	9.24	8.99	8.85	8.85
6............	9.375	9.29	9.24	9.00	8.87	8.85
9............	9.375	9.28	9.23	8.99	8.84	8.82
10............	9.375	9.30	9.27	9.00	8.84	8.81
11............	9.50	9.39	9.34	9.04	8.88	8.85
12............	9.50	9.37	9.34	9.04	8.89	8.85
13............	9.375	9.30	9.26	9.00	8.90	8.86
16............	9.375	9.29	9.26	9.03	8.97	8.92
17............	9.375	9.28	9.25	9.03	8.96	8.92
18............	9.375	9.31	9.27	9.03	8.93	8.91
19............	9.25	9.23	9.20	8.94	8.83	8.82
20............	9.25	9.26	9.21	8.98	8.91	8.87
23............	9.25	9.22	9.17	8.96	8.89	8.85
24............	9.25	9.20	9.15	8.92	8.87	8.84
25............	9.25	9.19	9.14	8.91	8.86	8.84
26............	9.375	9.27	9.21	8.99	8.94	8.92
30............	9.375	9.29	9.25	9.07	9.02	8.98
31............	9.25	9.24	9.21	9.01	8.95	8.92
April 1............	9.25	9.19	9.16	8.94	8.88	8.85

Note: Cash spot basis: prompt or ten-day shipment.

rates, this made delivered prices about 9¼ cents Cincinnati and 9½ cents Dallas, which was a relatively attractive pricing situation for lard.

Lard prices had moved quite widely since World War II, creating a number of speculative possibilities (see chart, Exhibit 3–3D). The April 1, 1959, price was near the low of a two-year decline from 14 cents. There were some indications that the market was "bottoming out," and buying was fairly aggressive in late March. On the other hand, the commodity research section of the buying department prepared a report (Exhibit 3–3E) showing that hog slaughter for the rest of 1959 would exceed that of the same months in 1958. Hog slaughter follows fairly regular cycles, with production upswings lasting from 14 to 30 months. The estimates of lard production, stocks, and domestic consumption for the period February–September, 1959 (in Exhibit 3–3F), were also prepared by the commodity research section. These were based on the slaughter figures and on past consumption data. The lard export estimates

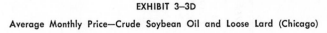

EXHIBIT 3–3D

Average Monthly Price—Crude Soybean Oil and Loose Lard (Chicago)

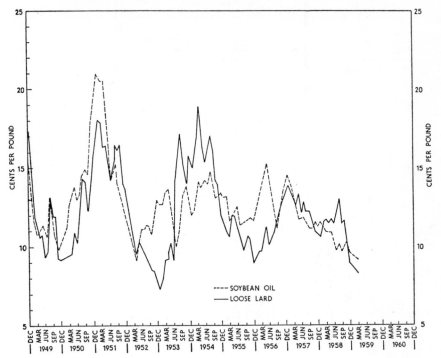

were based on a USDA survey of foreign demand and were believed to be accurate.

Soybean oil prices had also declined from the 14-cent level in early 1957 to the 9¼-cent level. This price had shown some signs of stability during March, and the company expected little price change until new crop prospects became known. The "intent to plant" report issued by the USDA on March 10 indicated a slightly higher acreage of soybeans more or less in line with a rising trend which began before the war. The summer growing weather would be the most important crop determinant. A poor yield would mean higher oil prices, while an excellent yield could reduce prices. The market effect of the weather would probably not be felt until August or September.

On April 1, 1959, the company owned about 10 weeks' supply of lard (200 carloads), all purchased after December, 1958. In order to insure uninterrupted factory schedules and be able to buy on an orderly basis, the company felt that a minimum of six weeks' ownership was necessary. The vice president for purchases and the manager of fats and oils purchasing met on April 1 to develop a position with respect to lard

EXHIBIT 3-3E
Commercial Hog Slaughter*
(thousands of head)

Month	1951–52	1952–53	1953–54	1954–55	1955–56	1956–57	1957–58	1958–59	1959–60
October	6,950	6,878	6,094	6,223	7,226	7,507	7,224	6,979	(7,700)†
November	7,856	7,099	6,649	6,969	8,100	7,705	6,536	6,227	(7,300)
December	8,285	8,777	6,452	7,409	8,672	6,790	6,603	6,955	(7,500)
January	8,415	7,764	5,874	6,810	8,038	6,880	6,714	7,030	
February	7,164	5,812	4,887	5,761	7,102	5,996	5,421	(6,728)	
March	7,140	6,232	5,648	6,714	7,514	6,381	5,793	(7,071)	
April	6,563	5,450	4,724	5,449	6,260	5,977	5,920	(6,700)	
May	5,622	4,548	4,205	5,098	5,865	5,866	5,301	(6,155)	
June	5,256	4,448	4,272	4,608	5,177	4,792	5,010	(5,550)	
July	4,657	4,106	4,123	4,197	5,064	5,032	5,162	(5,710)	
August	4,642	4,279	4,723	5,423	5,524	5,310	5,348	(5,780)	
September	5,479	5,078	5,769	6,158	5,967	5,997	6,165	(6,790)	
Total	78,029	70,471	63,420	70,819	80,509	74,233	71,197	(77,675)	(85,000)

* Commercial hog slaughter = all slaughter of hogs except slaughter on farms.
† Parentheses indicate estimate.

EXHIBIT 3–3F

Commercial Lard Situation in the United States
(in millions of pounds)

Date	Beginning Stocks	Production	Exports	Domestic Usage	Used in Shortening
1955–56:					
October...............	75	214	56	158	31
November.............	75	264	67	174	34
December.............	98	292	70	173	27
January...............	147	273	65	171	30
February.............	184	232	48	158	38
March................	210	254	62	169	36
April.................	233	207	59	155	39
May..................	226	199	69	145	43
June.................	211	180	45	143	29
July..................	203	170	42	153	25
August...............	178	172	41	168	40
September............	141	177	38	157	30
1956–57:					
October...............	123	228	47	198	46
November.............	106	247	47	203	56
December.............	103	226	48	169	44
January...............	112	226	38	199	47
February.............	101	198	36	151	37
March................	112	216	62	147	30
April.................	119	207	44	155	26
May..................	127	211	66	152	34
June.................	120	174	51	136	31
July..................	107	166	35	136	24
August...............	102	159	24	160	27
September............	77	173	31	150	22
1957–58:					
October...............	69	216	43	174	28
November.............	68	207	37	159	38
December.............	79	216	33	161	34
January...............	101	221	33	188	36
February.............	101	170	36	144	36
March................	91	177	36	147	32

purchases. One alternative considered was to extend the coverage of lard beyond the present position. The second alternative was to buy additional lard but to "hedge" this lard in the soybean oil futures market by selling futures contracts. Each purchase of lard would be offset by an equivalent "short" sale of July or September soybean oil futures on the Chicago Board of Trade. This would be profitable if soybean oil declined more rapidly than lard, since the profit on the short sale of soybean oil would be larger than the loss on lard. It would also be profitable if lard moved up more rapidly than soybean oil. A loss would occur, of course, if the spread between the two prices widened. The third and fourth

EXHIBIT 3–3F (Continued)

Date	Beginning Stocks	Production	Exports	Domestic Usage	Used in Shortening
April................. 85	188	22	164	30
May.................. 87	178	36	142	30
June................. 87	167	31	157	28
July................. 66	167	34	144	19
August.............. 55	158	27	136	17
September........... 50	182	25	161	17
1958–59:				
October............. 48	217	39	170	21
November........... 56	201	40	147	25
December........... 70	228	26	177	27
January............. 95	228	42	172	
February............109	211	38	159	
March..............123	231	40	175	
April...............139	224	45	170	
May................148	210	45	155	
June................158	196	40	160	
July................154	190	40	170	
August.............134	182	40	170	
September...........106	203	40	165	

Notes:

1. Commercial lard is all lard produced in the country except for lard from farm slaughter. The commercial lard production is reported by the USDA.

2. The figures on beginning stocks, exports, and used in shortening are collected by the Bureau of the Census from monthly questionnaires.

3. Beginning stocks include stocks of lard in all positions except lard in the hands of retailers and consumers.

4. The historical figures for domestic usage are determined by deduction, using the production, export, and stock figures.

5. The figures reported as used in shortening include only lard that is mixed with other fats to form a compound shortening and do not include lard that is used as lard. The quantity used in shortening is also included as a part of domestic usage.

6. All data are estimated for the period February–September, 1959.

possibilities would be to maintain the present lard position or to reduce it below the present level.

There was another alternative which was not seriously considered. This was the purchase of lard with hedge sales made on the Chicago Board of Trade drum-lard futures market. The manager of fats and oils purchasing did not like to be short on this market because of the difficult problem of making delivery if it became necessary. Deliveries are not usual on futures markets, but trading of drum lard is so limited that a "short" might find it preferable to deliver drummed lard instead of closing out his contract by a purchase. Delivery requires that drummed lard be put into cold storage at Chicago, and the company has no drumming or cold-storage facilities in Chicago and normally owns no lard in that city. Another reason was the lack of any normal or fixed relationship between loose-lard prices and drum-lard prices. For the purposes of this case, you may assume that the company was correct in not considering this alternative.

Questions

1. What decision should be made concerning lard ownership?
2. What forecast was required for your answer to Question 1? How did you make it? What alternative methods could be used with the data available? With other data that the company might have secured?

CASE 3–4. Leading Indicators and Cyclical Turning Points

Such has the interest been in the use of leading indicators to predict upturns and downturns in general business conditions that the U.S. Department of Commerce through its Bureau of the Census has published for several years *Business Conditions Digest,* a monthly available during the last week of the month following that of the data. Among other data it includes about 70 principal indicators—leading, coincident, and lagging—and draws heavily upon the pioneering work of the National Bureau of Economic Research in its selection of the indicators and in its presentation of analytical measures utilizing the indicators. Any business economist engaged in forecasting where general business conditions are important would find this publication a valuable source and would wish to be familiar with the National Bureau's work, summed up in the two volumes of *Business Cycle Indicators.*[20]

This case is designed to familiarize the student with both the possibilities and the pitfalls in using the leading indicators in forecasting. No one of the eight leading indicators for which data are presented in Exhibits 3–4A and 3–4B fully satisfies the following four criteria for the ideal indicator that forecasters would like to have: logical reasons for supposing the indicator will lead general business conditions, a long statistical record of leadership (both of these increase one's confidence that there should be a high probability of the lead relationship continuing), consistent periods of precedence by highs of the indicator before cyclical peaks and lows of the indicator before cyclical troughs, and substantial cyclical variation (as compared with irregular variation) in the leading series so that irregular movements will not be misinterpreted as harbingers of cyclical upturns and downturns.

This problem of substantial irregular movements plus the great variation in lead time for individual series from cycle to cycle has led forecasters to seek various ways of systematically combining consideration of several of the leading indicators. One simple method of combination

---

[20] Geoffrey H. Moore, ed. (Princeton: Princeton University Press, 1961). An updating and revision is contained in Geoffrey H. Moore and Julius Shiskin, *Indicators of Business Expansions and Contractions* (New York: Columbia University Press, 1967).

EXHIBIT 3-4A

Basic Data for Business Cycle Series, Eight Leading Indicators and Four Roughly Coincident Indicators January, 1961, through May, 1973

Date	(1) Average Work-week of Production Workers, Manufacturing (hours per employee)	(9) Construction Contracts Awarded for Commercial and Industrial Buildings (millions of square feet of floor space)	(13) Number of New Business Incorporations	(17) Ratio, Price to Unit Labor Cost Index, Manufacturing (1967 = 100)	(19) Index of Stock Prices 500 Common Stocks (1941–43 = 100)	(23) Index of Industrial Materials Prices (1967 = 100)	(24) Value of Manufacturers' New Orders, Machinery and Equipment Industries (billions of dollars)	(29) Index of New Private Housing Units Authorized by Local Building Permits (1967 = 100)	(43)* Unemployment Rate, Total (invert for cyclical indicator) (percent)	(47) Index of Industrial Production (1967 = 100)	(200) Gross National Product in Current Dollars, Quarterly Series (annual rate, billions of dollars)	(52) Personal Income (annual rate, billions of dollars)
1961:												
January	39.2	36.21	13,607	93.1	65	96.9	2.74	92.3	6.6	63.0	503.6	404.8
February	39.3	36.49	14,570	92.8	68	98.9	2.76	91.5	6.9	62.9		405.5
March	39.3	37.49	14,658	93.2	70	102.7	2.76	95.2	6.9	63.2		409.5
April	39.6	35.62	15,327	93.9	72	103.7	2.73	95.4	7.0	64.6	514.9	409.6
May	39.7	35.16	15,298	93.7	72	104.0	2.66	97.8	7.1	65.6		412.2
June	39.8	36.73	15,431	94.0	71	100.6	2.81	101.9	6.9	66.5		415.8
July	40.0	36.57	15,492	94.7	71	101.3	2.94	103.1	7.0	67.2	524.2	419.6
August	40.0	39.32	15,277	95.1	74	102.5	3.08	110.4	6.6	67.8		418.8
September	39.6	38.73	15,402	95.8	73	102.5	2.91	104.5	6.7	67.8		419.8
October	40.3	33.88	16,035	95.1	74	101.9	2.94	106.9	6.5	69.1	537.7	424.3
November	40.6	41.61	16,149	95.2	77	98.5	3.04	109.7	6.1	70.1		428.6
December	40.3	41.69	15,881	96.2	78	100.6	2.88	110.5	6.0	70.7		431.1
1962:												
January	40.0	38.70	15,599	95.3	75	102.5	3.06	106.8	5.8	70.2	547.8	430.7
February	40.3	42.75	15,758	95.6	76	100.2	3.27	113.7	5.5	71.3		433.7
March	40.5	45.90	15,670	95.4	76	100.0	2.92	108.0	5.6	71.7		437.2
April	40.7	42.72	15,372	94.5	74	97.9	3.20	117.6	5.6	71.8	557.2	439.8
May	40.5	44.64	15,245	94.3	69	97.4	3.02	108.7	5.5	71.8		440.8

June..............	40.4	41.16	14,947	93.9	61	95.0	2.97	109.9	5.5	71.6		441.8
July..............	40.5	40.56	15,171	94.6	62	93.8	3.00	113.2	5.4	72.3		443.4
August............	40.3	42.69	15,056	94.8	64	94.1	2.99	114.3	5.7	72.4	564.4	444.6
September.........	40.6	40.96	15,249	95.2	63	93.6	3.06	116.4	5.6	72.9		447.0
October...........	40.2	41.08	14,892	95.0	61	94.5	3.11	112.4	5.4	72.9		447.9
November..........	40.4	42.20	14,951	95.2	65	96.0	3.34	117.7	5.7	73.2	572.0	450.4
December..........	40.2	41.89	14,985	95.0	68	95.4	3.15	117.7	5.5	73.2		452.6
1963:												
January...........	40.4	44.61	14,924	95.1	71	95.1	3.21	114.7	5.7	73.6		457.6
February..........	40.3	45.11	15,390	95.6	72	94.7	3.29	111.4	5.9	74.3	577.4	455.7
March.............	40.4	39.42	15,563	95.6	71	94.0	3.34	115.6	5.7	74.9		457.6
April.............	40.2	40.23	15,305	96.7	75	94.1	3.35	118.4	5.7	75.5		458.4
May...............	40.5	47.00	15,682	96.8	76	94.8	3.49	124.1	5.9	76.4	584.2	461.2
June..............	40.5	51.39	15,536	96.9	76	93.5	3.33	123.6	5.6	76.8		464.2
July..............	40.5	45.78	15,431	96.1	75	93.8	3.36	121.4	5.6	76.4		465.6
August............	40.4	44.93	16,093	96.6	77	93.8	3.47	120.4	5.4	76.6	594.7	467.8
September.........	40.6	43.88	15,689	96.5	79	93.7	3.53	129.9	5.5	77.3		470.0
October...........	40.7	50.81	16,275	96.8	79	95.9	3.54	130.0	5.5	77.9		473.4
November..........	40.4	43.73	15,759	96.4	79	96.9	3.45	124.7	5.7	78.2	605.8	474.9
December..........	40.6	45.43	15,867	95.9	81	97.3	3.61	130.8	5.5	78.2		479.1
1964:												
January...........	40.0	50.88	15,993	97.7	83	98.1	3.94	119.1	5.6	78.8		482.4
February..........	40.6	49.10	16,326	96.9	84	98.1	3.52	132.6	5.4	79.3	617.7	484.6
March.............	40.6	48.65	15,917	96.5	86	98.5	3.77	120.7	5.4	79.5		486.8
April.............	40.8	49.12	16,132	97.2	87	102.0	3.72	116.2	5.3	80.6		490.1
May...............	40.7	46.86	16,473	97.1	88	100.5	4.12	119.4	5.1	81.2	628.0	493.0
June..............	40.8	49.99	16,282	97.0	87	101.0	4.23	117.7	5.2	81.5		495.0
July..............	40.7	53.40	16,550	97.4	91	102.1	3.90	119.9	4.9	81.9		498.4
August............	40.8	49.28	15,692	96.8	89	105.3	3.94	120.0	5.0	82.5	638.9	502.6
September.........	40.5	51.21	16,948	96.5	91	107.8	3.92	116.3	5.1	82.8		505.3
October...........	40.7	53.46	16,728	96.5	92	111.6	4.01	113.1	5.1	81.7		506.0
November..........	40.8	52.57	16,804	97.8	93	112.7	4.06	115.3	4.8	84.0	645.1	509.8
December..........	41.2	57.91	17,021	97.7	91	112.1	4.15	107.0	5.0	85.1		515.6
1965:												
January...........	41.1	53.00	16,784	98.8	94	110.2	4.13	116.2	4.9	85.7		518.8
February..........	41.3	55.12	16,854	98.5	94	110.3	4.06	108.9	5.1	86.1	662.8	519.4
March.............	41.4	54.77	17,131	99.0	94	112.7	4.40	111.3	4.7	87.1		522.9
April.............	41.0	57.74	16,664	99.4	96	116.2	4.34	106.8	4.8	87.3		525.9

EXHIBIT 3–4A (Continued)

Date	(1) Average Work-week of Production Workers, Manufacturing (hours per employee)	(9) Construction Contracts Awarded for Commercial and Industrial Buildings (millions of square feet of floor space)	(13) Number of New Business Incorporations	(17) Ratio, Price to Unit Labor Cost Index, Manufacturing (1967=100)	(19) Index of Stock Prices 500 Common Stocks (1941–43=100)	(23) Index of Industrial Materials Prices (1967=100)	(24) Value of Manufacturers' New Orders, Machinery and Equipment Industries (billions of dollars)	(29) Index of New Private Housing Units Authorized by Local Building Permits (1967=100)	(43)* Unemployment Rate, Total (invert for cyclical indicator) (percent)	(47) Index of Industrial Production (1967=100)	(200) Gross National Product in Current Dollars, Quarterly Series (annual rate, billions of dollars)	(52) Personal Income (annual rate, billions of dollars)
May	41.2	57.52	16,580	99.6	97	116.4	4.23	110.9	4.6	87.9	675.7	531.1
June	41.1	57.72	17,017	100.3	93	114.8	4.38	114.1	4.6	88.8		535.5
July	41.1	56.68	16,844	100.8	92	114.1	4.46	113.7	4.4	89.4		539.0
August	41.1	52.00	16,901	100.7	94	114.7	4.34	114.8	4.4	90.0	691.1	541.9
September	40.9	62.97	17,136	100.7	97	114.3	4.50	112.8	4.3	90.3		557.2
October	41.2	60.55	16,994	100.4	99	114.5	4.63	117.6	4.2	91.2		553.5
November	41.3	61.74	17,606	100.4	100	115.0	4.72	120.0	4.1	91.6	710.0	558.3
December	41.4	64.13	17,625	101.5	100	116.6	5.05	120.9	4.0	92.7		563.3
1966:												
January	41.4	62.29	18,087	102.0	102	120.0	4.79	121.8	4.0	93.8		565.3
February	41.7	70.42	17,451	101.5	101	122.4	5.25	106.5	3.8	94.7	729.5	570.8
March	41.5	67.99	17,266	102.2	97	123.0	5.17	113.4	3.8	96.0		574.9
April	41.5	68.28	17,057	101.5	100	121.0	5.33	105.2	3.8	96.4		577.8
May	41.5	64.00	16,644	102.3	94	117.8	5.37	99.1	3.9	97.4	743.3	579.6
June	41.4	65.85	16,577	102.0	94	117.9	5.31	87.9	3.8	97.9		584.7
July	41.3	63.54	16,074	102.7	93	118.3	5.57	85.7	3.8	98.6		588.4
August	41.4	63.52	16,343	101.9	88	111.3	5.20	80.6	3.8	98.7	755.9	593.1
September	41.3	64.40	15,764	102.5	85	108.5	5.46	71.1	3.7	99.5		597.0
October	41.2	54.76	16,233	102.0	84	105.9	5.36	67.9	3.7	99.6		601.6
November	41.2	64.42	16,206	100.7	88	105.5	5.15	67.7	3.6	99.6	770.7	605.6
December	40.9	60.21	16,583	101.0	88	105.4	5.19	68.3	3.8	99.7		607.8

1967:												
January	41.0	49.09	16,703	100.3	92	106.4	4.43	87.2	3.9	99.5		612.2
February	40.3	57.84	15,987	100.0	95	104.8	4.69	79.5	3.8	98.5	774.4	613.7
March	40.4	56.14	16,244	99.2	97	102.1	4.73	83.7	3.8	98.3		616.8
April	40.5	58.27	16,760	100.2	99	99.7	4.78	90.7	3.8	98.8		618.7
May	40.4	54.72	17,627	99.7	101	99.2	4.88	94.3	3.8	98.6	784.5	621.2
June	40.4	62.30	17,799	99.8	99	99.4	5.03	102.5	3.9	98.9		626.5
July	40.5	56.72	16,300	99.6	101	97.9	5.13	103.2	3.8	99.1		630.7
August	40.7	61.66	17,674	99.8	103	97.7	5.24	107.7	3.8	100.6	800.9	635.5
September	40.8	60.45	17,818	99.7	104	97.4	4.99	112.1	3.8	100.0		637.9
October	40.7	58.42	17,654	100.0	104	97.3	5.04	112.2	4.0	100.2		639.9
November	40.7	63.17	17,958	99.8	101	98.7	5.12	113.7	3.9	101.7	815.9	646.1
December	40.7	64.08	18,238	100.2	104	99.7	5.40	115.2	3.9	102.9		652.7
1968:												
January	40.2	64.51	18,061	100.0	103	99.4	5.06	103.3	3.7	102.8		656.1
February	40.9	61.39	18,041	100.0	99	99.1	6.42	117.6	3.8	103.8	834.0	663.8
March	40.7	66.61	18,538	99.5	97	99.7	7.14	120.1	3.7	103.9		672.1
April	40.1	47.09	18,663	100.1	104	97.9	6.88	112.7	3.5	104.0		675.0
May	40.9	66.96	18,723	99.4	106	95.7	6.83	113.7	3.5	105.5	857.4	681.3
June	40.9	66.35	18,839	99.6	109	95.2	6.34	113.9	3.7	106.0		687.4
July	40.9	71.65	19,407	99.6	109	94.0	6.77	117.8	3.7	105.9		692.9
August	40.7	66.15	19,947	99.1	107	94.5	7.23	118.9	3.5	106.2	875.2	697.5
September	41.0	61.59	20,582	98.2	110	95.7	6.53	128.3	3.4	106.5		703.1
October	41.0	79.63	21,093	98.0	113	97.1	7.84	124.5	3.4	106.5		708.0
November	40.8	69.70	20,890	98.3	115	99.9	7.15	125.9	3.4	107.7	890.2	712.7
December	40.7	71.47	20,619	97.4	116	100.3	7.36	121.7	3.4	107.5		717.2
1969:												
January	40.6	94.43	21,364	98.8	102	103.0	6.07	129.3	3.4	108.4		720.8
February	40.3	69.98	22,105	100.4	101	105.9	6.01	127.3	3.3	109.7	906.4	726.1
March	40.8	63.50	22,083	99.8	99	106.5	6.04	124.1	3.4	110.3		733.4
April	40.8	65.82	23,262	99.2	101	108.9	6.62	123.9	3.5	110.2		738.1
May	40.7	85.60	23,118	99.2	105	110.0	6.14	116.7	3.4	110.2	921.8	742.9
June	40.7	80.37	23,439	99.4	99	111.2	5.99	118.1	3.4	110.8		748.1
July	40.6	73.70	23,366	110.1	95	112.0	6.01	113.1	3.5	111.5		754.1
August	40.6	71.96	22,871	99.3	94	114.5	5.75	116.0	3.5	111.4	940.6	759.5
September	40.7	68.90	22,594	99.2	95	116.9	6.49	109.2	3.8	111.9		764.3
October	40.5	79.96	24,263	99.0	96	115.1	5.80	106.2	3.7	111.7		768.0
November	40.5	64.31	23,125	98.4	96	115.1	5.98	106.1	3.5	110.3	948.0	772.1
December	40.6	86.89	22,404	97.2	91	116.7	6.00	103.2	3.6	109.9		776.5

EXHIBIT 3–4A (Concluded)

Date	(1) Average Workweek of Production Workers, Manufacturing (hours per employee)	(9) Construction Contracts Awarded for Commercial and Industrial Buildings (millions of square feet of floor space)	(13) Number of New Business Incorporations	(17) Ratio, Price to Unit Labor Cost Index, Manufacturing (1967 = 100)	(19) Index of Stock Prices 500 Common Stocks (1941–43 = 100)	(23) Index of Industrial Materials Prices (1967 = 100)	(24) Value of Manufacturers' New Orders, Machinery and Equipment Industries (billions of dollars)	(29) Index of New Private Housing Units Authorized by Local Building Permits (1967 = 100)	(43)* Unemployment Rate, Total (invert for cyclical indicator) (percent)	(47) Index of Industrial Production (1967 = 100)	(200) Gross National Product in Current Dollars, Quarterly Series (annual rate, billions of dollars)	(52) Personal Income (annual rate, billions of dollars)
1970:												
January	40.3	88.86	22,196	96.7	90	118.9	6.76	93.1	3.9	107.8	958.0	781.2
February	40.1	80.95	22,968	97.3	87	119.5	7.13	98.0	4.2	108.2		784.7
March	40.1	67.11	21,181	97.2	89	118.7	6.52	99.2	4.4	108.1		791.2
April	40.0	64.00	21,745	96.7	86	118.2	6.68	107.3	4.7	107.7	971.7	810.0
May	39.8	58.19	22,046	97.0	76	117.5	7.09	116.4	4.8	107.7		804.4
June	39.9	54.47	21,984	97.3	76	114.8	6.66	115.9	4.8	107.9		804.0
July	40.1	70.45	21,896	96.6	76	112.4	6.95	116.0	5.0	107.6	986.3	808.0
August	39.8	61.04	21,841	97.1	78	111.2	6.67	122.2	5.1	107.5		812.9
September	39.4	60.16	22,194	96.0	83	110.5	6.66	125.0	5.4	106.3		819.2
October	39.5	51.71	21,604	96.3	84	109.5	6.64	137.1	5.5	103.7	989.7	816.7
November	39.6	54.00	22,381	96.1	84	108.8	6.48	131.6	5.8	102.8		818.3
December	39.6	54.69	22,071	96.7	90	106.4	7.43	154.9	6.1	104.9		824.4
1971:												
January	39.9	54.37	22,563	96.5	93	105.9	7.00	146.2	6.0	105.5	1,023.4	833.9
February	r 39.8	50.04	21,034	96.7	97	107.2	7.06	137.8	5.9	106.0		837.3
March	39.8	65.44	23,237	96.9	100	107.8	7.06	150.9	6.0	106.0		842.9
April	r 39.7	54.82	22,970	97.2	103	110.2	7.13	150.8	5.9	106.5	1,043.0	847.4
May	40.0	63.40	24,030	97.4	102	108.6	7.18	172.7	6.0	107.4		853.4
June	r 39.9	62.83	24,314	97.6	100	106.1	7.31	167.7	5.8	107.4		873.4
July	40.0	60.67	24,726	97.7	99	104.7	7.10	182.2	5.9	106.7		862.4

Month												
August	39.8	54.82	25,165	97.7	97	106.1	7.32	179.3	6.1	105.6	1,056.9	869.1
September	39.6	70.72	23,450	98.4	99	107.5	7.34	174.1	5.9	107.1		872.2
October	39.9	61.75	25,152	98.2	97	107.4	7.62	177.7	5.9	106.8		874.8
November	r 40.0	68.70	25,677	98.2	93	106.9	7.82	183.3	6.0	107.4	1,078.1	879.4
December	r 40.3	66.69	25,921	97.8	99	106.8	8.02	192.0	6.0	108.1		890.4
1972:												
January	40.1	59.65	24,871	97.9	103	110.7	7.90	193.2	5.9	108.7		898.9
February	r 40.5	66.72	25,055	97.6	105	113.0	8.15	180.2	5.8	110.0	1,109.1	908.5
March	40.4	66.68	26,862	98.1	108	117.2	8.30	175.9	5.9	111.2		913.6
April	r 40.7	65.53	26,681	98.3	109	119.5	8.70	174.5	5.8	112.8		919.4
May	40.5	81.95	26,243	98.5	108	124.3	8.93	171.3	5.8	113.2	1,139.4	924.0
June	r 40.6	70.51	26,303	98.3	108	123.8	8.98	185.9	5.5	113.4		922.9
July	40.6	67.74	26,815	98.8	107	123.7	8.95	184.8	5.6	113.9		932.9
August	40.6	75.65	26,420	99.2	111	124.6	8.90	196.1	5.6	115.1	1,164.0	940.0
September	40.8	74.69	26,798	99.4	109	124.8	9.73	198.5	5.5	116.1		946.8
October	40.7	74.61	27,417	99.3	110	128.1	9.62	194.2	5.5	117.5		964.8
November	r 40.8	82.67	26,387	99.6	115	131.6	9.70	187.5	5.2	118.5	1,194.9	976.2
December	40.7	78.82	27,614	100.7	118	134.8	9.99	H 208.3	5.1	119.2		982.9
1973:												
January	40.3	85.94	27,173	100.7	H 118	139.3	10.28	194.4	5.0	r 120.0		986.0
February	r 41.0	H 86.40	28,640	r 101.5	114	147.5	10.10	192.0	5.1	121.1	H 1,237.9	994.5
March	40.9	84.30	Hr 29,914	r 104.4	112	155.3	10.57	181.5	5.0	r 122.0		1,001.3
April	Hr 41.0	83.86	p 28,674	r 103.5	110	158.2	10.62	r 160.7	5.0	r 122.8		r 1,007.4
May	p 40.8	76.21	n.a.	Hp 105.3	107	H 162.9	Hp 10.67	p 163.6	H 5.0	Hp 123.4		Hp 1,012.2
June					105	169.8						

Notes: Numbers of columns denote the numbers given to the series in the source. Numbers 1–29 are NBER leading indicators, and numbers 43–52 and 200 are NBER roughly coincident series. All series are seasonally adjusted except 19, which displays no consistent seasonal variation.

* Beginning with 1972 data, 1970 Census is used as benchmark for the unemployment rate. Many such changes in calculation of statistical data are constantly made (such as change in base year) as more complete and current information becomes available. The forecaster must be alert to these changes and their effect on the data.

The letter r indicates revised; p, preliminary; n.a., not available; H, high to date.

Source: *Business Conditions Digest*, July, 1973, and historical tables in earlier issues.

EXHIBIT 3–4B

Dates of Peaks and Troughs of Business Cycles and Selected Leading and Coincident Indicators

		Peak	Trough	Peak
Dates of business cycles		Nov., 1948	Oct., 1949	Aug., 1954
		(37)*	(8)†	(13)
Corresponding dates for special business indicators:				
1.	Average workweek	n.s.c.	Apr., 1949	Apr., 1953
9.	Construction contracts	Mar., 1946	Aug., 1949	n.s.c.
13.	New business incorporations	July, 1946	Feb., 1949	n.s.c.
17.	Price per unit of labor	Jan., 1948	May, 1949	Feb., 1951
19.	Index of stock prices	June, 1948	June, 1949	Jan., 1953
24.	Value of manufacturers' new orders	Apr., 1948	Apr., 1949	Feb., 1951
29.	Index of new private housing	n.a.	n.a.	n.a.
43.	Unemployment rate (inverted)	Jan., 1948	Oct., 1949	June, 1953
47.	Index of industrial production	July, 1948	Oct., 1949	July, 1953
200.	Gross national product in current dollars	4th quarter, 1948	2d quarter, 1949	2d quarter, 1953
52.	Personal income	Oct., 1948	Oct., 1949	Oct., 1953

* Number in parentheses indicates months of expansion at peak.
† Number in parentheses indicates months of contraction at trough.
   Note: The letters *n.s.c.* indicate no specific cycle related to reference dates. The reference dates are those denoting the peaks and troughs of the general business cycle, and those selected by the National Bureau of Economic Research have come to have at least semiofficial standing. The letters *n.a.* indicate not available.
   Source: Appendixes A and B, *Business Cycle Developments*, May, 1963; *Business Conditions Digest*, June, 1973.

is a so-called "diffusion index"[21] in which 100 indicates that all of the series have risen, zero that all have fallen, and in general the index represents the percentage of the group of indicators that have risen during the period of consideration. Interpretation of such an index remains somewhat of an art. A low index number in an expansionary period that is sustained for a number of months should foreshadow a downward turning point, that is, a cyclical peak, while a high index number in a period of contraction should anticipate the upturn from a recession. How low or high, and how many months, remain matters of judgment. The forecaster is unlikely to rely solely on such an index which weigh all rises and falls equally regardless of the amplitude and duration of change or the significance he may attach to particular indicators. The data given in Exhibit 3–4B cover the May, 1960, downward

[21] The diffusion indexes presented in *Business Conditions Digest* are prepared from breakdowns of individual indicators into components rather than combinations of series. For example, stock prices are broken down into series for 82 industries, and the diffusion index shows what percentage of these have risen in a particular month. Therefore, we place quotation marks around "diffusion index" as used above.

EXHIBIT 3–4B (Continued)

Trough	Peak	Trough	Peak	Trough	Peak	Trough
Aug., 1954 (13)	July, 1957 (35)	Apr., 1958 (9)	May, 1960 (25)	Feb., 1961 (9)	Nov., 1969 (116)	Nov., 1970 (12)
Apr., 1954 n.s.c.	Nov., 1955 Mar., 1956	Apr., 1958 June, 1958	May, 1959 n.s.c.	Dec., 1960 n.s.c.	Oct., 1968 Nov., 1969	Sept., 1970 Nov., 1970
n.s.c.	Feb., 1956	Nov., 1957	Apr., 1959	Jan., 1961	Oct., 1969	Jan., 1971
Dec., 1953	Mar., 1957	Apr., 1958	May, 1959	Jan., 1961	Feb., 1969	Nov., 1970
Sept., 1953	July, 1956	Dec., 1957	July, 1959	Oct., 1960	Dec., 1968	June, 1970
Jan., 1954	Mar., 1957	Feb., 1958	May, 1959	Oct., 1960	Apr., 1969	Mar., 1970
n.a.	Feb., 1955	Feb., 1958	Nov., 1958	Dec., 1960	Feb., 1969	Jan., 1970
Sept., 1954	Mar., 1957	July, 1958	Feb., 1960	May, 1961	May, 1969	Aug., 1971
Apr., 1954	Feb., 1957	Apr., 1958	Jan., 1960	Jan., 1961	Sept., 1969	Nov., 1970
2d quarter, 1954	3d quarter, 1957	1st quarter, 1958	2d quarter, 1960	1st quarter, 1961	n.s.c.	n.s.c.
Mar., 1954	Aug., 1957	Feb., 1958	n.s.c.	n.s.c.	n.s.c.	n.s.c.

turning point and the February, 1961, upward turning point, as well as the difficult period for forecasts in the latter part of 1962; working with these data should permit the student to see some of the possibilities and difficulties in using a simple type of "diffusion index."

Questions

1. Consider each of the eight leading and four coincident indicators in Exhibits 3–4A and 3–4B as to whether there are logical economic reasons for expecting each to lead or coincide with the movements of general business.

2. Construct a "diffusion index" for the eight leading indicators from the data in Exhibit 3–4A for January, 1966, through May, 1973. Would such an index have helped you forecast the November, 1970, and the November, 1971, turning points? Do you find the index more reliable than the indicators individually? Note: In computing the percentage of the eight series which have risen, count unchanged series as half-rise and half-fall. The February, 1969, index will be 75, since six of the eight series rose.

3. As a business economist in the latter half of 1962, would you have found evidence for a cyclical downturn in these leading indicators?

4. At the time you are preparing this case, would you, on the basis of leading indicators, forecast a turning point? As a minimum, update the eight indi-

cators of the exhibits. You may wish to go beyond the preparation of a diffusion index of these and consider other techniques of smoothing and averaging and other series, particularly those presented in *Business Conditions Digest*.

CASE 3–5. Omega Corporation

The new business economist for the Omega Corporation had discovered a strong and significant relationship between quarterly changes in gross national product (seasonally adjusted, constant 1958 dollars) and the company's unit sales. Each 1 percent change in the GNP seemed to be associated with a roughly 3 percent change in unit sales when other factors were allowed for. Quarterly figures corresponded with the company's production planning period, and thus a quarter in advance represented the appropriate forecast period. In the spring of 1969 the economist was investigating the variations in real GNP preparatory to the recommendation of forecasting procedures. He decided first to work with various simple methods of forecasting (often termed "naive" or "agnostic") to see which could produce the greatest improvement over a random guess. He expected to use the best of the simple methods as a standard of comparison in order to evaluate whether the costs of a more elaborate approach (including the possible hiring of an outside economic consultant) would justify the expense. As a rough index to the cost of errors in forecasting GNP, he used the squares of the deviations of the quarterly percentage change "predicted" by each method from the actual percentage changes. The squares seemed more appropriate than the simple deviations because as a matter of business operations, Omega had the flexibility to adjust easily to small discrepancies in plans so that the cost of errors of increasing size would increase far more than proportionally. No distinction was made between plus or minus deviations (see Exhibit 3–5A, pages 94–95).

Questions

1. Approximate the "level of costs" of errors in forecasting by a random prediction. For this purpose a tolerable predicting process would be to number the universe of 82 quarterly predictions from 00 to 82 and use a table of two-digit random numbers to make a "prediction" for each quarter. Alternatively, slips with the changes could be made out, shuffled, and drawn, replacing the slip after each draw. Compute the squares of the deviations of the predicted percentage changes from the actual percentage changes.

2. Evaluate the following three "agnostic" methods of forecasting over the 22 quarters (first quarter of 1968 through second quarter of 1973) by cal-

culating the squares of the deviations of predicted from actual: (*a*) the assumption of no change (0 percent); (*b*) projection of a long-run trend (use a 0.9 percent quarterly change which is fractionally above the mean percent change and slightly less than the median change; (*c*) the assumption that the change from this quarter to the next quarter will be the same as the last quarter to quarter change which was observed. On the basis of this evaluation and any other pertinent considerations, which of these simple approaches would you recommend for future periods? Check your selection against data subsequent to that given in Exhibit 3–5A.

3. To get an idea of the possible savings of more sophisticated methods, the business economist assumed that the cyclical turning points could be predicted within the proper quarter. (These turning points are listed in Exhibit 3–4B, page 90). He used method (*c*) above, except that he substituted a forecast of 0 percent in the quarter of the turning point and forecast either a plus or a minus 2 percent change for the quarter following, depending upon the direction of the turn. Would a significant saving in "cost" result? (Again, use the criterion of the squares of the deviations of "predicted" from actual.)

EXHIBIT 3–5A

Quarterly Gross National Product, 1953–73
(seasonally adjusted—constant 1958 dollars)

Year	Gross National Product (billions)	Percent Change from Previous Quarter
1953:		
First quarter............................	412.1	
Second quarter...........................	416.4	1.0
Third quarter............................	413.7	−0.6
Fourth quarter...........................	408.8	−1.2
1954:		
First quarter............................	402.9	−1.4
Second quarter...........................	402.1	−0.2
Third quarter............................	407.2	1.2
Fourth quarter...........................	415.7	2.1
1955:		
First quarter............................	428.0	3.0
Second quarter...........................	435.4	1.7
Third quarter............................	442.1	1.5
Fourth quarter...........................	446.4	1.0
1956:		
First quarter............................	443.6	−0.6
Second quarter...........................	445.6	0.5
Third quarter............................	444.5	−0.2
Fourth quarter...........................	450.3	1.3
1957:		
First quarter............................	453.4	0.7
Second quarter...........................	453.2	0.0
Third quarter............................	455.2	0.4
Fourth quarter...........................	448.2	−1.6
1958:		
First quarter............................	437.5	−2.4
Second quarter...........................	439.5	0.5
Third quarter............................	450.7	2.5
Fourth quarter...........................	461.6	2.2
1959:		
First quarter............................	468.6	1.5
Second quarter...........................	479.9	2.4
Third quarter............................	475.0	−1.0
Fourth quarter...........................	480.4	1.1
1960:		
First quarter............................	490.2	2.0
Second quarter...........................	489.7	−0.2
Third quarter............................	487.3	−0.5
Fourth quarter...........................	483.7	−0.3
1961:		
First quarter............................	482.6	−0.2
Second quarter...........................	492.8	2.1
Third quarter............................	501.5	1.8
Fourth quarter...........................	511.7	2.0
1962:		
First quarter............................	519.5	1.5
Second quarter...........................	527.7	1.6
Third quarter............................	533.4	1.1
Fourth quarter...........................	538.3	0.9
1963:		
First quarter............................	541.2	0.5
Second quarter...........................	546.0	0.9

EXHIBIT 3–5A (Continued)

Year	Gross National Product (billions)	Percent Change from Previous Quarter
Third quarter	554.7	1.6
Fourth quarter	562.1	1.3
1964:		
First quarter	571.1	1.6
Second quarter	578.6	1.3
Third quarter	585.8	1.2
Fourth quarter	588.5	0.5
1965:		
First quarter	601.6	2.2
Second quarter	610.4	1.5
Third quarter	622.5	2.0
Fourth quarter	636.6	2.3
1966:		
First quarter	649.1	2.0
Second quarter	655.0	0.9
Third quarter	660.2	0.8
Fourth quarter	668.1	1.2
1967:		
First quarter	666.6	−0.2
Second quarter	671.6	0.8
Third quarter	678.9	1.1
Fourth quarter	683.6	0.7
1968:		
First quarter	692.6	1.3
Second quarter	705.3	1.8
Third quarter	712.3	1.0
Fourth quarter	716.5	0.6
1969:		
First quarter	721.4	0.7
Second quarter	724.2	0.4
Third quarter	729.2	0.7
Fourth quarter	725.1	−0.6
1970:		
First quarter	720.4	−0.6
Second quarter	723.2	0.4
Third quarter	726.8	0.5
Fourth quarter	718.0	−1.2
1971:		
First quarter	731.9	1.9
Second quarter	737.9	0.8
Third quarter	742.5	0.6
Fourth quarter	754.5	1.6
1972:		
First quarter	768.0	1.8
Second quarter	785.6	2.3
Third quarter	796.7	1.4
Fourth quarter	812.3	2.0
1973:		
First quarter	829.3	2.1
Second quarter	p 834.6	0.6

The letter p indicates preliminary.

chapter 4

Demand Analysis for
the Industry

ECONOMIC ANALYSIS can contribute substantially to understanding the factors which influence demand for the output of an industry. An industry may be thought of as a group of firms or plants which produce the same or similar products or services. This rather vague definition will suffice for most purposes and allow relatively unambiguous classification of firms into industries. It should be noted, however, that rigorous definition of an industry is quite difficult; the more substitutes a product has, the less clear-cut the industry description can be.

Demand analysis provides a basis for understanding the factors which influence consumer choice of particular products and services. Knowledge of these underlying factors allows a businessman either to react to expected changes in these factors or to change in an appropriate manner those factors which are under his control. Our prime concern is with the economic factors which influence demand; it should be noted that psychological and sociological factors are also of considerable importance.[1]

The quantity of a product which will be demanded by consumers can be viewed as related to (as a function of) its price, consumer income, population or other demographic factors, the prices of substitutes, and the existing stock of the good.[2] These major factors will be dealt with separately in this chapter, although in fact they are interrelated.

---

[1] For survey of a variety of research efforts, see Robert Ferber, "Research on Household Behavior," *American Economic Review*, March, 1962, pp. 19–63.

[2] Quantity $= F$ (price, income, population, prices of substitutes, stock). Expressed this way with the appropriate data, statistical estimates can be made of the demand function. The theoretical reasoning behind this assertion is explained in the appendix to this chapter.

Quantity and Price

For a great many analytical purposes, the price of a commodity may be considered the independent variable upon which the physical volume of sales depends. Other pertinent variables are then held constant for purposes of defining the demand function. (The student who has studied calculus may recognize that this is the process of finding the partial derivative of sales with respect to price of the same good, other variables being held constant.) The usual demand curve of economic analysis is a special case in which all variables except price of the commodity under consideration are placed in *ceteris paribus*—that is, in which other factors having an effect on sales are unchanged.

The inverse relationship between quantity demanded and the price of a commodity is, consequently, one that holds with great certainty *if* other major factors, such as those enumerated above, remain unchanged. A firm which raises the price of a good expects a decrease in volume of sales. If it actually sells more than in an equal time period before the increase, it is because some factor other than price caused an increase in demand. In this case an even greater gain in physical sales volume would have occurred if the price had not been raised.

A hypothetical demand schedule for wheat is shown in Figure 4-1. Since a great many farmers sell this commodity, the schedule pertains to the entire market rather than reflecting what any individual farmer could sell at the various alternative prices. In a highly competitive market the individual seller has no control over price. However, the state of market demand has a great influence upon the price which he will be able to command for his product. It should be noted that the demand schedule shown in Figure 4-1 is greatly simplified, showing price only at 50-cent intervals. Also, "wheat" is not a strictly homogeneous commodity (there being several grades), nor is it sold only in a single market. Further,

FIGURE 4-1

Market Demand Schedule

Row	Price of Wheat (per bushel)	Quantity Demanded (millions of bushels per month)	Value (millions of dollars)
A	$4.00	50	$200
B	3.50	60	210
C	3.00	70	210
D	2.50	80	200
E	2.00	90	180
F	1.50	100	150
G	1.00	110	110

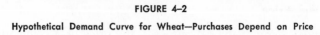

FIGURE 4–2

Hypothetical Demand Curve for Wheat—Purchases Depend on Price

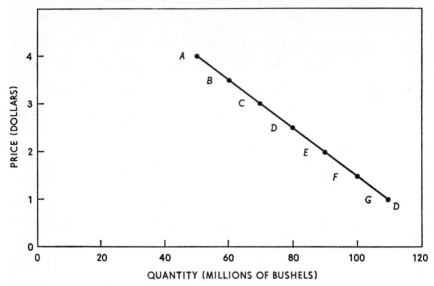

QUANTITY (MILLIONS OF BUSHELS)

"price" must relate to an average price per month; or alternatively the quantity demanded must be interpreted as the monthly rate of purchase which would take place at a particular price at a moment of time.

For analytical purposes, it is usually more convenient to convert the discrete demand schedule into a continuous demand curve. The market demand schedule of Figure 4–1 is plotted as a demand curve in Figure 4–2. Since the demand curve connects the various price-quantity combinations, it is drawn on the assumption that no irregularities occur between the plotted points. The hypothetical data used in this example provide a straight-line relationship between price and quantity purchased. An actual demand curve for wheat might exhibit some curvature; however, a straight-line relationship is more convenient to use, and most statistical demand studies for agricultural products have shown that a straight line fits the data about as well as more complex curves.

Slope and Price Elasticity

An examination of the demand schedule shows that a decrease in price of 50 cents per bushel is associated with an increase of 10 million bushels per month in quantity demanded. This relationship is unchanging throughout the demand schedule, giving the demand curve a slope of −5, that is, (−50 ÷ 10). This may be interpreted as meaning that a decrease of 5 cents a bushel will occasion an increase of one million bushels in the quantity purchased monthly.[3]

Although the physical volume of sales is related linearly to price, the same is not true of the value of sales. This is evident from an inspection of the Value column of Figure 4–1 (this column being the product of price and quantity). Except at the top of the table, smaller quantities are worth more to the sellers than larger quantities. This is because the *percentage* decrease from 100 million to 90 million bushels, for example, is smaller than the *percentage* increase in price from $1.50 to $2 per bushel; that is, a 10 percent decrease in quantity is associated with a 33⅓ percent increase in price, and this causes the smaller quantity to bring a higher monetary return to sellers.

The dependence of total value on the relative percentage change of quantity and price often makes the measure of "elasticity" of demand a more useful one than the measure of slope. Price elasticity of demand is defined as the ratio of the percentage change in quantity demanded to the corresponding percentage change in price. It is mathematically necessary, however, to take the ratios of very small (strictly, infinitesimally small) percentage changes in order to measure elasticity at a particular price.[4] Elasticity is therefore a relative measure of the responsiveness of quantity to changes in price. Along a downsloping straight-line demand curve, price elasticity of demand differs at every point and is negative in sign.

Elasticity and Revenue

Elasticity was defined in the last paragraph as the percentage change in quantity divided by the percentage change in price which resulted in that change in quantity. Reflection indicates that since the relationship between price and quantity with all other factors unchanged is an inverse one, that the measure of price elasticity computed will be negative. Thus, if price increases, quantity demanded would be expected to decrease.

It is customary to denote a computed measure of elasticity as relatively *elastic* when the percentage change in quantity is greater in ab-

---

[3] If this demand curve is considered to extend along the same straight line until it touches both axes, its equation becomes $P = 650 - 5Q$, where P (price) is measured in cents per bushel and Q (quantity) is in millions of bushels. The slope (-5) appears as the coefficient of Q.

[4] If $\dfrac{dq}{q}$ denotes a very small percentage change in quantity demanded and $\dfrac{dp}{p}$ denotes a very small percentage change in price, elasticity of demand $(E) = \dfrac{dq}{q} \div \dfrac{dp}{p}$. This is usually written $E = \dfrac{dq}{dp} \cdot \dfrac{p}{q}$.

solute terms than the percentage change in price, that is, when computed elasticity is greater than the absolute value of -1, for example, -2. A computed elasticity of -1 is denoted *unitary* elasticity. When the calculated value of elasticity is less than the absolute value of -1, for example, $-\frac{1}{2}$, demand is said to be relatively *inelastic*.

The relationship between total revenue and demand (average revenue) is shown in Figure 4–3 for a straight-line demand curve. In this case since total revenue is equal to price times quantity ($TR = pq$), then total revenue will be a parabola since $p = a - bq$ and $TR = pq = aq - bq^2$. As can be seen from the diagram, the parabola for total revenue starts at zero when quantity is zero and ends at zero when price is zero. In the diagram, the maximum value is reached where total revenue stops increasing as price decreases and begins to decrease for further reductions in price. Each of these regions of increasing, constant (maximum), and decreasing total revenue are related to the price elasticity of demand.

The ranges of elastic and inelastic demand and the point of unitary elastic demand are shown on Figure 4–3. Since where demand is elastic, a price decrease results in a more than proportionate increase in quantity, total revenue must be increasing. Also, where a decrease in price results in a less than proportionate increase in quantity, total revenue must be declining. Where there is a proportionate change in quantity as a result of a change in price, total revenue remains constant and the resulting elasticity measure is unitary.

FIGURE 4–3

Relationships among Total Revenue,
Average Revenue, and Elasticity

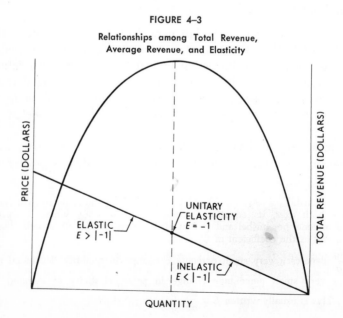

It is often the case in attempting to learn something about the elasticity of demand that the analyst does not have enough information to derive the whole demand curve and must rely on inferences about elasticity from observed changes in total revenues. The relationships discussed above provide the necessary clues to make such inferences.

Computation of Price Elasticity

Numerical computations of elasticity follow directly from the definition:

$$\text{Elasticity} = \frac{\text{Percentage change in quantity}}{\text{Percentage change in price}}$$

Strictly speaking, since elasticity is measured at a point, the changes should be very small to make the computation accurate. However, since the data are usually rough and prime interest is in knowing within limits how responsive quantity is to price changes, this approach provides a useful measure of elasticity. For example, suppose that as a result of a price decrease of 5 percent, quantity increases 10 percent, then

$$E = \frac{+10\%}{-5\%} = -2$$

The concept of arc elasticity allows one to compute an approximate measure of elasticity when only two observations on price and quantity are available. If p_1 and q_1 represent one observation and p_2 and q_2 the other, arc elasticity is calculated by

$$\text{Elasticity} = \frac{\dfrac{q_1 - q_2}{q_1 + q_2}}{\dfrac{p_1 - p_2}{p_1 + p_2}}$$

This computes the elasticity midway between the two points on a straight-line demand curve; thus the approximation is better the closer the two points are to each other.

Quantity and Income

When longer time periods are considered in discussing the demand for a product, price becomes only one of many factors which influence the quantities which consumers desire to purchase. Income is a factor of considerable importance in explaining the demand for many products over the longer run. It is conventional to treat income as a factor which shifts the demand curve. For most products, it is expected that increases in consumer income will result in a shift of the price-quantity relation-

FIGURE 4–4

Price, Income, Quantity Schedule

Year	Price (dollars)	Income (dollars per capita)	Quantity (thousands of units)
1...............	$1	$2,000	1,000
2...............	1	2,500	1,250
3...............	1	3,000	1,500
4...............	1	3,500	1,750
5...............	1	4,000	2,000

ship up and to the right. Figure 4–4 gives data on quantity, price, and income for a hypothetical product over five years.

In this exhibit price remains constant yet quantity continues to increase over time apparently due to the changes in per capita income. From these data, a chart which illustrates the relationship between quantity and income may be drawn. Figure 4–5 is such a chart.

If price and income both may vary then the chart shown in Figure 4–6 illustrates a price-quantity schedule which shifts as income changes. In order to *predict* the quantity for any point in time, it is necessary to know both the price and level of income. In this chart price and quantity are shown on the axes and each schedule represents a specified level of income.

In this discussion, the term income has been used rather vaguely. However, for particular products it may be quite important that great care be used in selecting the appropriate measure of income to relate to quantity. For example, if the concern is with the demand for tractors, then farm income may be the appropriate income measure while disposable consumer income may be the appropriate measure when studying automobile demand.

FIGURE 4–5

Relationship between Quantity and Income-Price Remaining Constant

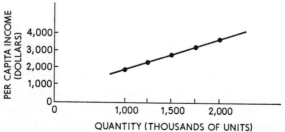

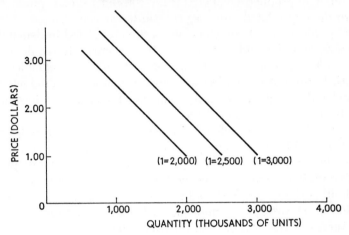

FIGURE 4–6

Increase in Income—Shifts Demand Upward

Quantity and Population

Another variable of considerable importance for demand studies when longer time periods are considered is population. Again, population may be considered as a variable which shifts the basic price-quantity relationships. In general, it is expected that the greater the population, the greater the demand for a product at a given price. That is, there is usually a positive relationship between population and quantity, all other variables holding constant.

There are many aspects of the population—that is, demographic characteristics—that may be of critical importance in long-run demand studies. The age distribution of the population is one such aspect. Thus, if half the population is under 25, a producer of geriatric supplies may want to plan diversification and a builder may want to give more attention to apartments than single-family homes. Actually, the analyst would want to look at more than just the median age in his analysis. Marriage rates, family formation, urban concentration, and many other demographic factors are relevant in long-run demand studies; and the economist who ignores these factors is courting disaster.[5] For medium range (five to ten years) demand forecasts, population is a very useful variable as all the potential heads of households are already born, making forecasts much easier.

---

[5] See Haskel Benishay and Gilbert R. Whitaker, Jr., "Demand and Supply in Freight Transportation," *Journal of Industrial Economics*, July, 1966, for a study using demographic variables.

Quantity and Prices of Substitutes

Although all products compete for the consumer dollar, products may be more directly related either as substitutes or complements. Complementary products are those which are positively related in demand, that is, an increase in demand for one leads to an increase in the demand for the other. For example, golf balls and golf clubs are complementary products. Fords and Chevrolets are substitute products. Products which are unrelated except in terms of competing for consumer income may generally be considered independent.

Except as an income effect, changes in the price of independent products should have little effect on the aggregate demand of a product. Changes in the prices of either substitute or complementary products may have profound effects. In general reduction in the price of a substitute, all other things equal, should reduce the demand for a product but reduction in the price of a complementary good should increase the demand. Increases should have the opposite effects.

Cross elasticity of demand is a measure which can be utilized to determine whether products are complements or substitutes. Price of the product itself and other independent variables are held constant. Cross elasticity is negative for products that are complements. For example, a decrease in the price of camera film will increase the demand for developing of film even when the price of this service is unchanged. On the other hand, cross elasticity is positive for close substitutes; for example, a decrease in the price of oleomargarine will tend to decrease the consumption of butter. In either case, cross elasticity can be measured (when proper data are available) by dividing the percentage change in the quantity sold of product X by the percentage change in the price of closely related product Y, *ceteris paribus*. A zero measure shows that the products are unrelated.

Quantity and Advertising

A firm or industry through its trade association may attempt to shift the demand curve through advertising expenditures. If successful, the result will be a change in the consumers' tastes and in their willingness to purchase additional units at the same prices. The shift obtained should give the same kind of pattern as that observed when income increases in Figure 4–6. Quality variation is also undertaken with the same purpose in mind.

Quantity and Stock

The effect of the existing stock of a good on current demand is most pronounced when the good being studied is a durable. However, some interesting studies have been done which use the notion of a stock as a proxy for tastes or habits.[6] For durable goods such as automobiles not only is the existing stock important, knowledge of the stock is helpful in predicting replacement demand and also in a real sense the existing stock is a substitute for new goods. Both of these aspects of stock should be taken into account in analyzing the demand for a durable.

Empirical Demand Functions

All of the variables discussed above and many more can affect the demand for a good or service. Recognition of the important factors can aid managers in making better informed judgment about the responsiveness of their products' demand to changes in these factors. Some of the factors such as price and promotion policy are to some extent controllable by a business. As to others they can only react or plan their reactions if they are forewarned about changes to come. More precise quantitative estimates of demand may be possible through empirical or statistical demand functions.

Shifts in Demand and Supply

The most common method of deriving statistical demand curves involves the use of time-series data on prices, sales, and other relevant variables.[7] The first step is usually to plot all of the price-sales data on a chart where price is measured vertically and quantity sold is measured horizontally. (This has become conventional, although theoretically it would be preferable to plot price, the independent variable, against the horizontal scale [X axis] and sales against the vertical scale [Y axis].) If the investigator is unusually fortunate, he can immediately draw the statistical demand curve merely by fitting a "regression" line to the price-sales data.[8] Even if the fit is very close and the regression line slopes nicely downward it may not be a demand curve, as will become apparent in the subsequent discussion.

In the case of a competitively produced commodity, each historically

---

[6] See H. S. Houthakker and Lester D. Taylor, *Consumer Demand in the United States, 1929–1970* (Cambridge, Mass.: Harvard University Press, 1966).

[7] Family budget data have been used by statisticians to derive demand curves for some consumer goods. This method will not be considered in the present chapter.

[8] Such a line of "best" fit may simply be drawn freehand in such a way as to minimize approximately the sum of the deviations of the plotted points from the regression line. Or mathematical methods such as the "least-squares" method may be employed. The least-squares method may minimize the sum of the squared vertical distances, squared horizontal distances, or squared perpendicular distances from the regression line.

FIGURE 4–7

Shifting Supply and Demand May Trace No Pattern

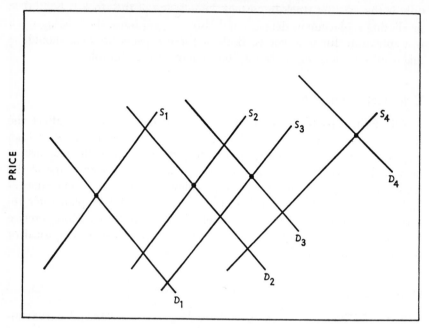

QUANTITY

recorded price-sales point can be considered to have been determined by the intersection of a supply and a demand curve. This is illustrated in Figure 4–7 for a hypothetical situation in which both the demand and the supply curves have shifted over a period of time. Each of the intersections (D_1 and S_1, D_2 and S_2, etc.) indicates a price which existed at one time during the period studied. It is clear that if the demand and supply curves have both shifted to the right, as suggested by Figure 4–7, the price-quantity data plotted by the statistician would not trace out a demand curve, a supply curve, or any of the other curves of economic theory.

On the other hand, if the situation has been that of Figure 4–8 in which the demand curve was stable over the period while the supply curve shifted to several different positions (due, for example, to different crop yields in successive years), the price-sales data would trace out the demand curve which the statistician is seeking.[9] If the demand curve shifted only slightly while the supply curve shifted substantially, the intersections would appear to follow a single demand curve but would

[9] The various possibilities are shown in a classic article by E. J. Working, "What Do Statistical Demand Curves Show?" *Quarterly Journal of Economics*, February, 1927, pp. 212–35.

FIGURE 4–8

Shifting Supply and Steady Demand—Intersections Trace a Demand Curve

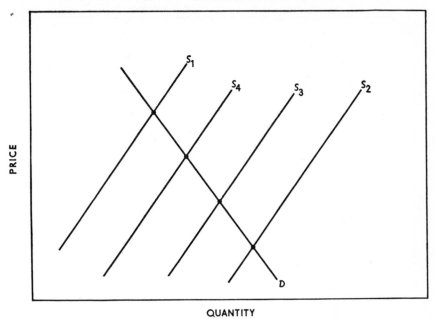

QUANTITY

not actually do so. If the supply curve were unchanged while the demand curve shifted, the price-sales data would trace out a supply curve.

In practice the demand curve usually shifts a good deal over the period for which the statistician has price-sales data. Numerous statistical devices are available for removing the shift and coming out with an approximation to the static demand curve of economic theory. A simple graphical method for accomplishing this end may be illustrated by its application to the hypothetical price-sales data of Figure 4–9. The "period" referred to is usually a year, but may be a shorter span of time. Price must refer to a weighted average for the period unless, of course, a single price persisted throughout the time interval.

As a first step in finding the influence of price on quantity sold, the analyst would probably plot these data as in Figure 4–10. At this point, he might be discouraged, because the plotted points do not even come close to falling along a negatively declining demand curve such as would be expected from a knowledge of the economist's "law of demand." Inspection of the original data reveals clearly, however, that there has been an upward trend in sales over the seven periods.[10] This is easily seen

---

[10] Trend is a "proxy" for all the factors other than price which may have caused the demand curve to shift over time. The assumed relationship is $q = f(p, t)$, where $q =$ quantity, $p =$ price, and t is the trend variable. This "shortcut" method is a two-step approach with trend removed in order to isolate the effect of price.

FIGURE 4–9

Hypothetical Price-Sales Data

Period	Quantity Sold	Price per Unit
1................	50	$ 9
2................	75	8
3................	65	15
4................	110	10
5................	150	7
6................	150	14
7................	200	9

FIGURE 4–10

Price-Sales Data—May Show No Pattern

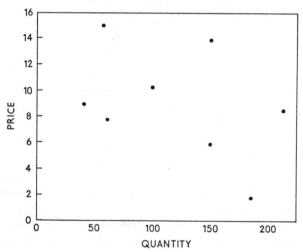

by reference to the fact that in period 1 a price of $9 was associated with sales of 50 units, while in period 7 the same price was coupled with sales of 200 units. One way of eliminating the trend in order to isolate the influence of price is to fit a trend line to the time series of sales. Such a line can be fitted freehand or, if more accuracy is desired, by the method of least squares.

If time is designated by X and quantity by Y, a straight-line fit which minimizes the sum of the squared vertical deviations can be obtained by solving the equations:

$$\Sigma y = na + b\Sigma x$$
$$\Sigma xy = a\Sigma x + b\Sigma x^2$$

Where n is the number of observations, a is the Y-axis intercept, and b is the slope of the regression line. The following table gives necessary data related to Figure 4–9:

X	Y	X^2	XY
1	50	1	50
2	75	4	150
3	65	9	195
4	110	16	440
5	150	25	750
6	150	36	900
7	200	49	1,400
28	800	140	3,885

Placing these values in the equations we have:

$$800 = 7a + 28b$$
$$3,885 = 28a + 140b$$

Multiplying each term in the first equation by 4 we get:

$$3,200 = 28a + 112b$$
$$3,885 = 28a + 140b$$

Subtracting the first equation from the second:

$$685 = 28b$$
$$b = 24.46$$

Substituting this value for b in either equation:

$$a = 16.45$$

Consequently the line of the best fit has the equation:

$$Y = 16.45 + 24.46X$$

This line can be readily plotted in Figure 4–11. It will hit the vertical axis at 16.45 (since $X = 0$). Suppose $X = 5$, then

$$Y = 138.75$$

Through these two points (or any other calculated two points) the regression line can be drawn.

The next step in a shortcut method of deriving a demand curve is to measure the vertical deviations of observations from the regression line. If the line in Figure 4–11 had been fitted by freehand means, the devia-

FIGURE 4–11

Sharp Upward Trend in Sales—Has Obscured Effect of Price

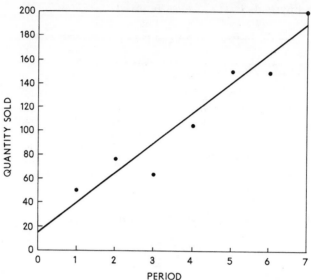

PERIOD

tions could be measured with a ruler. Since the line was fitted by least squares, the deviations can be found more accurately by comparing actual and calculated values of Y, as shown below:

X	Actual Y	Calculated Y	Deviation
1	50	40.91	+ 9.09
2	75	65.37	+ 9.63
3	65	89.83	−24.83
4	110	114.29	− 4.29
5	150	138.75	+11.25
6	150	163.21	−13.21
7	200	187.67	+12.33

The next step is to plot deviations against price. The underlying assumption is that the upward trend in quantity over time is due to such factors as growth of population and income. Consequently periods in which price was relatively high should exhibit sales below "normal," that is, below the fitted trend line, while low prices should have stimulated above-normal sales. (This relationship between price and deviations of sales works out nicely in Figure 4–12 because the data have been contrived to do so.) If a negative relationship does not appear at this point, the shortcut approach will not work for the commodity being investigated. It is possible that the difficulty is due to such factors as

FIGURE 4–12

Effect of Price Appears—Because Trend Has Been Removed

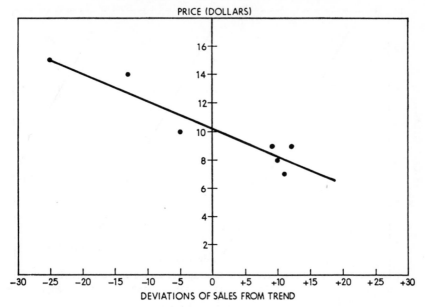

existence of a close substitute that has not been brought into the analysis. irregularity of factors such as disposable income or even poor data.

Although the line which has been fitted freehand in Figure 4–12 indicates the effect which price had on sales, it is not a demand curve because the full quantity demanded is not shown. It is necessary to add back the trend value of quantity for whatever time period a demand curve is to be estimated. The following calculation would be made to show demand curves for periods 1, 4, and 7. Any two price-deviation combinations on the regression line of Figure 4–12 will be satisfactory. Arbitrary prices 14 and 8 are used below:

	Trend Value	Deviation		Quantity	
		P = 14	*P = 8*	*P = 14*	*P = 8*
Period 1............	40.91	−20	+12	20.91	52.91
Period 4............	114.29	−20	+12	94.29	126.29
Period 7............	187.67	−20	+12	167.67	199.67

The end result is the shifting demand curve shown in Figure 4–13, plotted from the data in the right-hand columns. The upward shift of demand (which characterizes a great many actual commodities) should be taken into account in any attempt to judge current demand. A weak-

FIGURE 4–13

Upward Shifting Demand Curve—The Final Product of Analysis

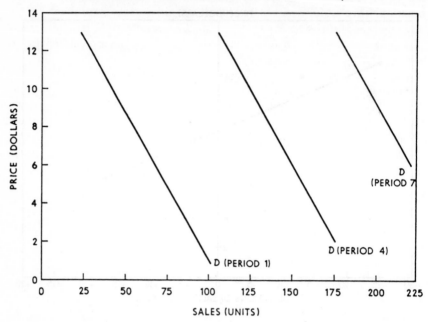

ness of the shortcut method employed is that all of the demand curves have the same slope. (The elasticity of demand at any given price diminishes, however, as the curve moves to the right). In spite of shortcomings, a shortcut method such as the one described above is recommended as providing a relatively quick check on whether more complicated methods will be likely to be worthwhile in any particular case.[11]

APPENDIX TO CHAPTER 4. The Theory of Consumer Choice and the Demand for Products

The economic theory of consumer behavior is developed from *three* basic assumptions. First, given various combinations of goods and services, a consumer (or household) is assumed to be able to rank these

[11] For additional information on the techniques of estimating and interpreting statistical demand equations, the reader is referred to William J. Baumol, *Economic Theory and Operations Analysis* (3d ed.; Englewood Cliffs, N.J.: Prentice-Hall, Inc., 1972), chap. 10; J. Johnston, *Econometric Methods*, (2d ed.; New York: McGraw-Hill Book Co., 1972); and Roger K. Chisholm and Gilbert R. Whitaker, Jr., *Forecasting Methods* (Homewood, Ill.: Richard D. Irwin, Inc., 1971), chaps. 7 and 8.

combinations in such a way that any one combination is either more satisfactory, less satisfactory, or equally satisfactory to any other combination. This ranking makes no statements concerning how much better one combination is over another, it only makes an ordering. Thus, given two different bundles of goods A and B, a consumer is assumed to be able to state:

> A is preferred to B, or
> B is preferred to A, or
> I am indifferent.

A second necessary assumption is that a consumer's preferences are consistent (transitive). Suppose there are three bundles of goods, A, B, and C, then the following statements must be true:

> A is preferred to B
> B is preferred to C,
> therefore,
> A is preferred to C.

The third necessary assumption is that the consumer's demand is not satiated. That is, he does not have so much of one or more products that he would not take any more regardless of the price.

From these basic premises the tastes of a particular consumer can be illustrated geometrically for two products or product combinations. To illustrate these preferences, a diagram which is called an indifference map is used. An example is shown in Figure 4–14.

This preference or indifference map represents the tastes or preferences of an individual consumer for goods X_1 and X_2. Consider first,

FIGURE 4–14

Indifference Map Illustrated

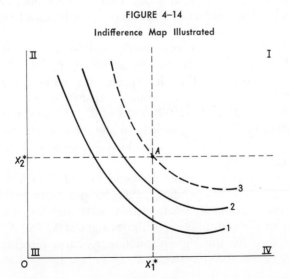

point A and the horizontal and vertical lines which arbitrarily divide the diagram or map into four quadrants. If point A represents the level of satisfaction a consumer can achieve by consuming X_1^* of X_1 and X_2^* of X_2, given the assumptions, some general statements about the diagram can be made. First, any point in quadrant I, including all points on the relevant sections of the dotted lines, represents a higher level of satisfaction to the consumer than that which he is enjoying at point A. This is true because any point in this area will represent more of one or both commodities than he is now receiving at point A. Any point in quadrant III represents a lower level of satisfaction than point A since less of one or both commodities is received by the consumer. Quadrants II and IV require closer examination since any point in these quadrants implies more of one commodity and less of the other commodity. It is possible to consider conceptionally picking points in these quadrants and asking the consumer whether the quantities represented by these points give him more, less, or the same satisfaction as point A. If all of those points which give equal satisfaction to that of point A are located, they may be connected with a line of equal satisfaction or an indifference curve. Every point on this curve therefore gives this consumer equal satisfaction.

This process may be repeated for any number of levels of satisfaction and plotted as indifference curves. Every point on the map lies on some indifference curve and, in general, the farther an indifference curve is away from the origin, the higher level of satisfaction it represents. In the diagram, we have drawn several such indifference curves. An important point to remember is that even though the curves bear higher numbers as we move away from the origin, they represent greater levels of satisfaction only in an ordinal sense. That is, curve number 2 represents a higher level of satisfaction than curve 1, but it cannot be said how much higher.

In order to determine the consumer's equilibrium position, his income, I, and the prices of the two commodities, P_1 and P_2, must be known. If it is assumed that he spends his entire income, then $I = P_1X_1 + P_2X_2$. This implies, for example, that if he spent his income only for X_2, he would purchase I/P_2 units of X_2. Or, he could purchase any combination of X_1 and X_2 as long as the total purchased does not exceed I. The area which indicates his possible purchases is the triangle $OX_2'X_1'$ in Figure 4–15.

Since the consumer is required to spend his entire income (we can consider saving a type of spending), then his purchases will be somewhere on the line segment $X_2'X_1'$. In order to maximize his satisfaction or total utility from the consumption of the two goods X_1 and X_2, the consumer desires to reach the highest indifference curve possible with his given income, I.

FIGURE 4–15

Budget Constraint

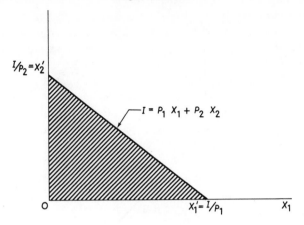

Here it is useful to spell out explicitly some additional properties of indifference curves. First, indifference curves cannot cross each other since to do so would result in a logical contradiction. This can be seen by assuming that two curves do cross as in Figure 4–16 and considering points A, B, and C. According to our basic postulates, B is preferred to A since it indicates that more of both X_1 and X_2 are consumed than at point A. But the consumer must be indifferent between A and C since they are on the same curve. He must also be indifferent between C and B since they are on the same curve. If this is true, then he must be in-

FIGURE 4–16

Indifference Curves Cannot Cross

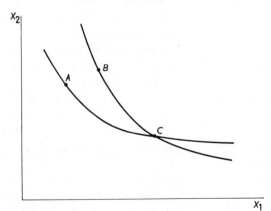

FIGURE 4–17

Consumer Maximizes Satisfaction

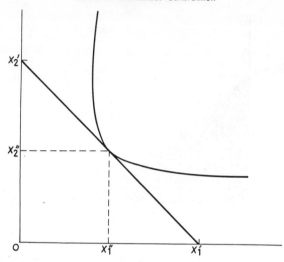

different between A and B and there is a contradiction. Hence, indifference curves may not cross.

A second property which is necessary if the two goods are not perfect substitutes, is that the marginal rate of substitution of X_2 for X_1 declines as the quantity of X_1 increases. That is, the consumer requires successively greater amounts of X_2 in exchange for an incremental decrease in the quantity of X_1. This property of diminishing marginal rate of substitution implies that indifference curves are convex to the origin of the indifference map.

Thus, if the indifference curves are convex to the origin and do not cross each other, our consumer can achieve his highest possible level of satisfaction where his budget restraint as expressed by $I = P_1X_1 + P_2X_2$ is just tangent to an indifference curve. This is illustrated in Figure 4–17. The consumer maximizes his satisfaction with his given income, and tastes as represented by the indifference map, with the given prices P_1 and P_2, by purchasing X_1'' units of X_1 and X_2'' units of X_2.

The slope of the budget restraint must equal the slope of the indifference curve at the point of tangency. This is the requirement for consumer equilibrium. The slope of the budget restraint is given by $X_2/X_1 = P_1/P_2$.[12] The slope of the indifference curve is given by the

---

[12] This can be shown by rewriting the equation of the budget restraint in the slope-intercept form:

$$X_2 = \frac{I}{p_2} - \frac{P_1}{p_2} X_1.$$

The minus signs have been omitted above since they appear on both sides of the equality.

FIGURE 4–18

Income and Substitution Effects

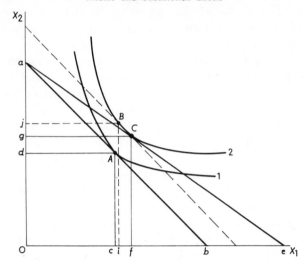

marginal rate of substitution of X_2 for X_1 which in turn is equal to the ratio of the marginal utility of X_1 to the marginal utility of X_2, the marginal utility being the utility gained from having an additional unit of a good.[13] Thus the equilibrium condition is given by:

The student should experiment with the effect of price changes on this equilibrium condition to see what purchase adjustments the consumer will make as prices change.

Next, consider the effects of a price change of X_1 on the consumer's purchase of X_1 as shown on the indifference map.

Figure 4–18 illustrates the results of a price reduction for good X_1. The consumer's income at the original prices of X_1 and X_2 is represented by line *ab*. At this income and these prices the consumer will purchase *c* units of X_1 and *d* units of X_2. A price reduction in X_1 allows the consumer to purchase a greater quantity of X_1 than previously, and his income is now represented by the line *ae*. At the new price for X_1, he will purchase *g* units of X_2 and *f* units of X_1. As a result of the price change, his consumption has moved from point *A* to point *C*, placing the con-

---

[13] This can be shown by considering two points on the same indifference curve which are very close to each other. The consumer achieves the same level of satisfaction at each point so the utility gained by the additional units of X_1, ΔX_1 must therefore be equal to the utility lost by giving up the units of X_2, ΔX_2. Therefore, $MU_{x_1} \Delta X_1 = MU_{x_2} \Delta X_2$. And,

$$\frac{\Delta X_2}{\Delta X_1} = \frac{MU_{X_1}}{MU_{X_2}}.$$

sumer on a higher indifference curve and enabling him to enjoy a higher level of satisfaction than before. This movement can be analyzed as the combination of two effects: one, an effect on the consumer's real income; and the second, a substitution effect toward the commodity which has become relatively cheaper.

The income effect can be·demonstrated by considering what income level would be required to move the consumer from indifference curve 1 to indifference curve 2 with no change in relative prices. This is illustrated in Figure 4–18 by the dashed income line parallel to income line *ab* and tangent to indifference curve 2 at point *B*. Thus a change in income which allowed a consumer to reach indifference curve 2 would result in the consumption of j units of X_2 and i units of X_1. But since the price of X_1 has been reduced, the consumer tends to substitute the product X_1 (which has become relatively less expensive) for the product X_2 (which has become relatively more expensive). This substitution effect results in the consumer's moving along the indifference curve from point *B* to point *C*, where he consumes g units of X_2 and i units of X_1. He substitutes $(f - i)$ units of X_1 for $(j - g)$ units of X_2. Thus the total change in the consumption $(f - c)$ of X_1 as a result of the reduction in price of X_1 may be considered to be the result of two effects: the income effect $(i - c)$ and the substitution effect $(f - i)$.

The next problem to consider is the derivation of an individual consumer's demand curve for a product from his indifference map. A demand curve or schedule is a relationship which shows the quantities of a product which a consumer is willing and able to purchase at various prices.

Figure 4–19 shows a consumer's indifference map for two products, X_1 and X_2. The objective is to derive the consumer's demand curve for product X_1. X_2 represents the rest of the consumer's purchases of goods, services, and savings, all of whose prices are assumed to remain the same. As before, the consumer spends his total income, I, for X_1 and X_2.

The upper diagram shows the consumer's indifference map for X_1 and X_2 along with the budget constraint for successively lower prices of X_1. Each of the tangencies of the indifference curves and the budget constraints are connected, and the resulting curve is called the price-consumption, or offer, curve. Each price of X_1 results in a different quantity of X_1 being purchased. These price-quantity combinations are transposed to the curve in the lower figure which is labeled "Demand for X_1." This demand curve indicates how many units of X_1 the consumer would purchase at various prices as long as all other prices remain the same and his income and tastes (indifference map) are unchanged.

Thus far the demand for X_1 for only one consumer has been considered. The total market demand for all consumers with given incomes and tastes can be obtained in theory by the summation of their individ-

FIGURE 4–19

Derivation of an Individual Consumer's Demand Curve for a Product

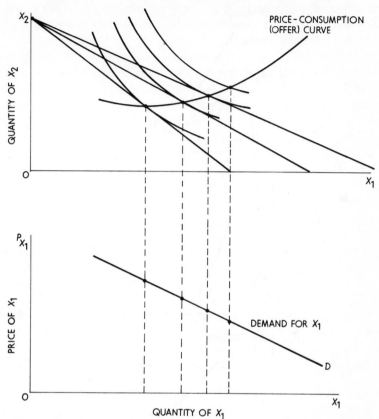

ual demands. This summation is illustrated for two consumers in Figure 4–20. The curves are summed horizontally, that is, for a given price the quantities demanded by each consumer are added to give total demand. This analysis suggests that price, income, population, and tastes are all relevant demand function variables.

Also, since all other prices were held constant, it is clear that changes in other prices, all other factors unchanged, would change the final demand curve. It is also apparent that different levels of consumer income would result in different final demand curves. The student should experiment with indifference curves and different incomes to see the final impact on market demand. The result of this analytical framework is that the market demand for a commodity X_1 is seen to be related not only to its own price but to other prices, income, population, and to tastes. This is the proposition which was asserted at the beginning of Chapter 4.

FIGURE 4–20

Market Demand for Two Consumers

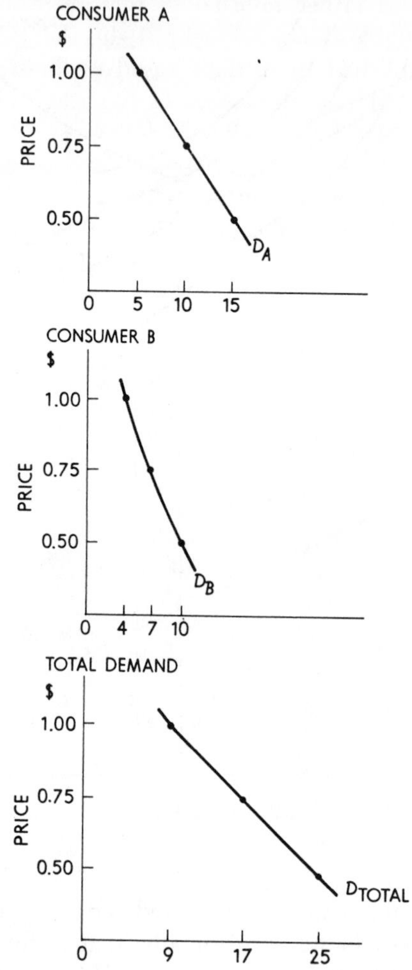

CONSUMER A

CONSUMER B

TOTAL DEMAND

CASE 4–1. Demand for Frozen Orange Concentrate[14]

The problem of deriving a statistical demand curve for an actual commodity, frozen orange concentrate, is illustrated in this case. A relatively new good, it was first produced and retailed during the 1945–46 orange crop season. Demand increased rapidly as consumers became

---

[14] This case is based largely on a study by Leland V. Gustafson in a Master's thesis at Florida State University, 1968. The writer has been assisted also by an earlier Master's thesis by Eugene C. Holshouser.

acquainted with the product and as retail stores installed the necessary refrigerated cabinets.

This commodity is rather unusual in that monthly retail sales and price data are available. Since October, 1949, the U.S. Department of Agriculture has published these data based on figures obtained under contract from the Market Research Corporation of America.[15] The monthly reports relate to four-week periods and are based on a sample of approximately 7,500 families. Quantity sold is then "blown up" in order to estimate sales for the entire country. It is likely that sales data are less accurate than price data. Ordinarily the use of monthly figures requires that adjustments be made for a regular seasonal fluctuation; however, no substantial seasonal pattern of sales exists for frozen orange concentrate. Monthly sales and price data are suitable in a statistical demand study and have the advantage of incorporating more up-to-date information than would a sufficient body of yearly data.

During most of the period since the end of World War II the demand for frozen orange concentrate has been increasing at a moderate rate due to population growth, favorable changes in consumer tastes and preferences, and the rise in disposable income. However, the freeze of 1962–63 in Florida caused a temporary downshift in demand for frozen orange concentrate by hurting its quality and by stimulating the development of substitutes such as Tang. (The high price of frozen orange concentrate due to the reduced orange crop would ordinarily have been a help in determining the demand curve; however, this is not the case when factors affecting supply also affect the demand schedule.) In an important sense the underlying factors determining sales of frozen orange concentrate changed because of the freeze. Consequently, the demand curve derivation shown in this case covers the period September, 1963, through March, 1966. Demand was again on the upswing during this 31-month period.

Some Problems in Statistical Measurement of Demand

Exhibit 4–1A shows the variables that were selected for close examination in the measurement of demand for frozen orange concentrate. It should be recognized that all of these data are subject to problems of measurement, that many other series have some relevance, and that problems of "multicollinearity" and "autocorrelation" exist.

Sales and price data are affected by the reliability of the small sample of families, by lack of complete homogeneity of orange concentrate both over a period of time and at any point in time, and by weighting

---

[15] *Consumer Purchases of Citrus, Fruit, Juice, Drinks and Other Products,* U.S. Department of Agriculture, Economic Research Service, in cooperation with Florida Citrus Commission (quarterly).

EXHIBIT 4–1A

Frozen Orange Concentrate and Related Data

Month	Consumer Purchases* (thousand gallons)	Retail Price* (cents per six-ounce can)	Disposable Personal Income† (annual rate, billion dollars)	Consumer Price Index‡ (1957–59 = 100)	U.S. Population § (millions)
1963:					
September............	3,222	28.0	408.3	107.1	189.8
October..............	3,238	27.7	411.6	107.2	190.0
November............	3,263	27.4	413.1	107.4	190.4
December............	3,240	27.8	417.3	107.6	190.6
1964:					
January..............	3,398	27.3	420.8	107.7	190.8
February.............	3,283	27.4	422.8	107.6	191.0
March...............	3,494	27.4	424.1	107.7	191.2
April................	3,649	27.0	430.8	107.8	191.4
May.................	3,527	25.7	434.3	107.8	191.6
June.................	3,551	25.7	435.9	108.0	191.9
July.................	3,349	25.6	437.3	108.3	192.1
August..............	3,290	25.6	440.7	108.2	192.3
September............	3,728	25.4	442.9	108.4	192.6
October..............	4,369	25.0	442.1	108.5	192.8
November............	4,090	25.2	445.9	108.7	193.1
December............	4,163	24.9	451.3	108.8	193.3
1965:					
January..............	5,076	22.8	450.6	108.9	193.5
February.............	5,046	21.3	450.4	108.9	193.7
March...............	4,931	21.1	453.0	109.0	193.8
April................	5,353	19.7	454.3	109.3	194.0
May.................	5,105	18.1	458.8	109.6	194.2
June.................	5,044	18.0	462.3	110.1	194.4
July.................	4,801	17.8	469.7	110.2	194.6
August..............	4,936	17.7	472.1	110.0	194.8
September............	5,596	17.4	476.1	110.2	195.0
October..............	5,675	17.3	480.5	110.4	195.2
November............	5,519	17.3	486.5	110.6	195.5
December............	5,507	17.5	491.5	110.0	195.6
1966:					
January..............	6,401	16.7	490.7	110.0	195.8
February.............	5,744	17.1	495.2	111.6	196.0
March...............	5,709	17.8	499.5	112.0	196.2

Sources:
* Market Research Corp. of America and U.S. Department of Agriculture.
† Calculated from data in *Survey of Current Business*, U.S. Department of Commerce.
‡ Bureau of Labor Statistics, as reported in *Survey of Current Business*.
§ Bureau of the Census, as reported in *Survey of Current Business*.

problems involved in getting an average retail price. Disposable personal income, like other aggregate measures of income, fails to pick up transactions which do not go through the market (e.g., housewives' services) and some that do go through the market (e.g., babysitting services). Personal taxes can be estimated only approximately on a monthly basis. The Consumer Price Index is especially vulnerable to quality changes in the commodities on which it is based, probably overstating the rise in the cost of living. Even population is measured only approximately, especially because census enumerators are unable to find many persons in the cities (particularly when welfare recipients fear that reporting their presence may be harmful to continued receipt of benefits). It is probable that the actual population of the United States is several million greater than official figures show. From the viewpoint of the present study there are problems also of relevance of total population to demand because age and geographical distribution also affect consumption. At the same time it should be realized that an excessively critical attitude toward available data will result in the loss of statistical studies which may be useful in prediction and interpretation of the real world.

The common statistical problem of multicollinearity refers to intercorrelation among independent variables. Such correlation makes it difficult to measure their separate influences on the dependent variables. Minimization of its influence requires careful selection of dependent variables. The problem of autocorrelation refers to the correlation of each item in a series with its succeeding item. Statistical methods used to reduce autocorrelation include the use of first differences (each item subtracted from the previous one) and removal of linear trends.

A useful way of reducing the number of independent variables in a demand study is sometimes found in the division of one series by another. For present purposes it was found desirable to divide both retail price and disposable personal income by the Consumer Price Index. (It was not found to be useful, however, to place sales on a per capita basis by dividing by population.) "Deflated" retail price data and "real" disposable personal income are shown in Exhibit 4–1B. These two series, along with consumer purchases, are the ones entering the regression equation as independent variables. (The equation has been fitted by means of least squares analysis, minimizing the sums of squared vertical deviations.)

$$Q = 2{,}779 - 172P + 12.6Y \tag{1}$$

where Q is consumer purchases in thousands of gallons per month, P is the deflated price in cents per 6-ounce can, and Y is real disposable personal income.[16]

Equation (1) shows that a 1-cent change in price brings about an opposite change in sales of 172.0 thousand gallons per month. A change of one billion in real disposable income brings about a change of 12.6 thousand gallons per month in the same direction.[17]

---

[16] The method of fitting such an equation is described in many good statistics books and in the references cited in footnote 11 on page 112.

[17] Both regression coefficients are significant at the 5 percent level. The coefficient of determination is 0.91, significant at the 5 percent level.

EXHIBIT 4–1B

Deflated Prices and Real Disposable Income

Month	Deflated Price*	Real Disposable Income†
1963:		
September	26.1	381.2
October	25.8	384.0
November	25.5	384.6
December	25.8	387.8
1964:		
January	25.3	390.7
February	25.5	392.9
March	25.4	393.8
April	25.0	399.6
May	23.8	402.9
June	23.8	403.6
July	23.6	403.8
August	23.7	407.3
September	23.4	408.6
October	23.0	407.5
November	23.2	410.2
December	22.9	414.8
1965:		
January	30.9	413.8
February	19.6	413.6
March	19.4	415.6
April	18.0	415.6
May	16.5	418.6
June	16.3	419.9
July	16.2	426.2
August	16.1	429.2
September	15.8	432.0
October	15.7	435.2
November	15.6	439.9
December	15.8	442.8
1966:		
January	15.0	442.1
February	15.3	443.7
March	15.9	446.0

* Retail price divided by Consumer Price Index.
† Disposable personal income divided by Consumer Price Index.

Since real disposable income shows mainly an upward trend during the period covered, the demand curve relating sales to price tends to move upward and to the right over time. If one wishes to measure elasticity of demand for frozen orange concentrate, it is necessary to specify which demand curve is to be used and also the price at which elasticity to to be calculated. If real income of 446.0 is substituted for Y in equation (1) we have:

$$Q = 8,399 - 172P \qquad (2)$$

Substituting 15.9 for *P* we have:

$$Q = 5,664 \tag{3}$$

(This estimated value of *Q* compares with and actual quantity of 5,709.)

To find elasticity of demand at a price of 15.9 the following formula can be employed:

$$E = \frac{dQ}{dP} \cdot \frac{P}{Q} \tag{4}$$

or

$$E = -172 \left(\frac{15.9}{5,664} \right) \tag{5}$$

solving

$$E = -0.45 \tag{6}$$

Since this computed price elasticity of demand is less than unity it is an example of "inelastic demand" at the prevailing price. From the point of view of the industry, a higher price would be more profitable. From the social point of view the situation appears to be favorable since quite a highly competitive situation appears to prevail.

Income elasticity of demand can also be computed from the formula

$$E = \frac{dQ}{dY} \cdot \frac{Y}{Q} \tag{7}$$

substituting,

$$E = 12.6 \left(\frac{446}{5,664} \right) = \frac{5,620}{5,664} = +0.99$$

The positive sign indicates that during the period covered, frozen orange concentrate was a "superior" good. A 1 percent increase in real income brought about approximately a 1 percent increase in sales of frozen orange concentrate.

Questions

1. The data listed in Exhibit 4–1C are for later years than the data used in developing the forecasting (demand) equation in the case. Use these data to forecast the demand for frozen orange concentrate for several additional months.
2. Using the additional data and any available computer program for regression analysis, recompute the demand equation for frozen orange concentrate. Are the coefficients stable? Why or why not?

EXHIBIT 4–1C

Frozen Orange Concentrate and Related Data

Month	Consumer Purchases* (thousand gallons)	Retail Price* (cents per six-ounce can)	Disposable Personal Income† (annual rate, billion dollars)	Consumer Price Index‡ (1957–59 = 100)	U.S. Population§ (millions)
1967:					
January	6,410	16.7	532.3	114.7	197.7
February	6,220	17.0	533.4	114.8	197.8
March	6,130	17.4	536.1	115.0	198.0
April	5,800	17.8	537.7	115.3	198.1
May	5,790	18.3	541.3	115.6	198.3
June	5,550	18.4	545.2	116.0	198.5
July	5,180	18.2	548.3	116.5	198.6
August	5,270	18.2	550.7	116.9	198.8
September	5,970	18.6	555.1	117.1	199.0
October	5,980	19.1	557.3	117.5	199.2
November	5,980	19.3	559.9	117.8	199.4
December	6,110	19.5	565.5	118.2	199.6
1968:					
January	6,380	19.7	568.3	118.6	199.7
February	5,840	20.6	574.9	119.0	199.8
March	5,190	21.4	581.8	119.5	200.0
April	5,070	21.7	584.1	119.9	200.1
May	5,310	21.2	588.4	120.3	200.3
June	5,390	20.3	592.7	120.9	200.4
July	5,200	20.0	593.3	121.5	200.6
August	5,230	20.0	595.6	121.9	200.8
September	5,990	19.9	600.4	122.2	201.0
October	6,080	19.7	604.5	122.9	201.2
November	6,210	18.9	606.0	123.4	201.4
December	6,460	19.8	609.6	123.7	201.5
1969:					
January	7,160	19.3	610.9	124.1	201.7
February	6,910	19.2	612.0	124.6	201.8
March	7,030	18.3	616.8	125.6	201.9
April	6,990	18.4	620.6	126.4	202.1
May	6,290	18.1	623.0	126.8	202.3
June	6,410	18.0	627.4	127.6	202.4

Sources:
* Market Research Corp. of America and U.S. Department of Agriculture.
† Calculated from data in *Survey of Current Business*, U.S. Department of Commerce.
‡ Bureau of Labor Statistics, as reported in *Survey of Current Business*.
§ Bureau of the Census, as reported in *Survey of Current Business*.

3. How would a decision maker who had to rely on forecasts of demand determine when he should recompute demand equations?

4. Are the elasticity estimates derived from your recomputed equations reasonably consistent with those reported in the case?

CASE 4–2. The Demand for Refrigerators[18]

Refrigerators are a long-lived consumer durable good. Existing homes are saturated with refrigerators, but failures can be expected to result in replacement purchases. New homes and apartments usually require additions to the total stock of refrigerators. Therefore, total demand can be considered to consist of two basic components—replacement demand and new owner demand. However, sales data do not indicate the reason why a particular customer is buying a refrigerator. Also, there are no registration data available such as there are for automobiles to provide a basis for estimating scrappage. An approximate method was required to separate sales data into these two components.

Annual shipments for replacement were estimated under the assumption that replacement demand (scrappage and replacement of existing refrigerators) was a probabilistic function of prior refrigerator purchases. In order to make estimates of replacements for recent periods, it was necessary to utilize annual refrigerator sales data from the year 1920. The assumption of probabilistic replacement implies that some small fraction of the refrigerators sold in 1920 will be scrapped in 1921, a somewhat larger percentage in 1922, and so forth. A probability distribution, the Wiebull distribution illustrated in Exhibit 4–2A, was assumed. By applying the theoretical replacement percentages to annual sales, the scrappage through time of a particular year's sales may be estimated. Repeating the process for each year's sales since 1920 and summing the annual scrappage figures obtained, an estimate was made of replacement demand for each year. This process was repeated with different probability distributions until results were obtained which provided a reasonable check with available census data. The distribution which worked best was one with an average life of 16 years as shown in Exhibit 4–2A. This 16-year average life also checked well against life estimates made by other researchers using other methods.[19]

Exhibit 4–2B (as shown on page 129) shows total refrigerator shipments for the period 1950–65, replacement demand estimated using the procedure outlined above and the resulting "apparent" new-owner demand which was obtained by subtracting replacement demand from total shipments.

Replacement demand was readily extended for forecasting purposes

---

[18] This case is based upon a study made in 1966 by the economic and market research department of the Whirlpool Corporation. It is used with their permission.

[19] Jean L. Pennock and Carol M. Jaeger, "Household Service Life of Durable Goods," *Journal of Home Economics,* January, 1964.

once the basic series had been developed in the manner described above. However, this left unresolved the problem of forecasting new-owner demand.

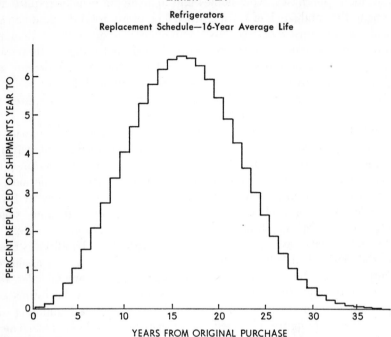

EXHIBIT 4–2A

Refrigerators
Replacement Schedule—16-Year Average Life

Forecasting new-owner demand was explained in the following manner:

The next step is the construction of an econometric model capable of explaining the observed variation in the new owner demand curve. At this point, the statistical technique of multiple regression analysis is employed.

A number of sets of independent variables were used to explain the fluctuations in new owner demand. The group finally selected consisted of (1) the total U.S. population age 20–34, (2) housing starts, (3) change in current dollar disposable personal income, and (4) the consumer price index for refrigerators.

The number of people between 20 and 34 represents the primary market of "first appliance" buyers since most people have established by age 34 an independent household which has already triggered the purchase of a *new* refrigerator somewhere in the economy. Since the new owner segment ex-

EXHIBIT 4–2B

Refrigerators
New-Owner Demand—Shipments—Replacement Demand

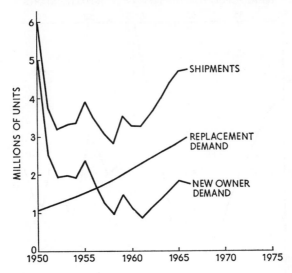

cludes replacement purchases by definition, this demographic variable is most important in explaining the historic new owner series. E&MR believes that the general weakness in appliance sales in the late fifties can be traced directly to the depression-caused falloff in young adults entering this critical consumer segment at that time. On the other hand, the continued expansion of this age group in the next decade creates a strong basis for "bullish" forecasts of new owner purchases for appliances, particularly refrigerators.

Change in disposable personal income was used to pick up the short-term swings in the economy that caused deviations around the underlying demographic trend in new owners. People's immediate economic expectations are an important determinant of whether they decide to purchase a durable good now or to wait. The change in disposable personal income is a gross measure of people's personal buoyancy in that their current expectations are based on their most recent experiences. The use of this economic variable helps to explain the 1959 resurgence of refrigerator shipments in the face of continued decline in the number of younger adults.

The correspondence between the "apparent" new owner series and a curve computed from the multiple regression analysis was improved through the addition of two supplementary variables. Housing starts insofar as they contain multifamily units with their near-saturation installation rates of 95 percent are directly related to new owner purchases. The refrigerator consumer price index, which exhibits the continued increase in refrigerator values for the consumer, although modest in its effect, applies the finishing touches to this explanation of the historic new owner's demand series.

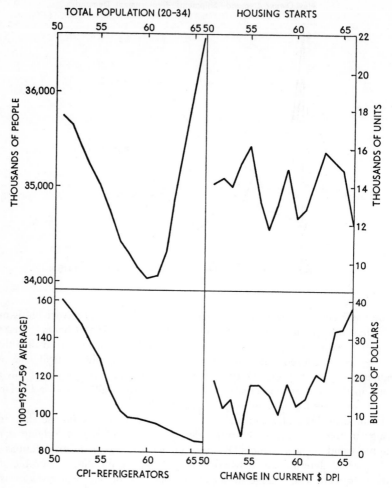

EXHIBIT 4–2C

Independent Variables for New-Owner Demand

The variation which was inherent in the independent variables is shown in Exhibit 4–2C.

Multiple regression analysis was performed using "apparent" new-owner demand as the dependent variable and the four independent variables discussed above. This resulted in the following multiple regression equation for predicted new-owner demand:

Apparent new owners (000 units) = 0.022 population
+ 0.7761 housing starts + 17.594 Consumer Price Index for
refrigerators + 33.286 disposable personal income − 2,812

EXHIBIT 4–2D

Refrigerators

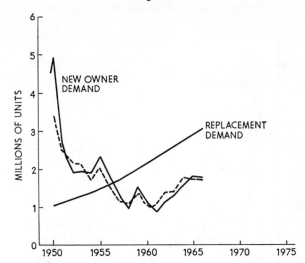

NEW OWNER DEMAND EXPLAINED AS A FUNCTION OF:
(1) POPULATION, AGE 20–34   (POP) (thousands)
(2) HOUSING STARTS   (HS) (thousands)
(3) REFRIG. CPI   (CPI) (percent)
(4) CHANGE IN OUR $ DPI   (DPI) (billions)
APP. NEW OWNERS = 0.0220 POP + 0.7761 HS + 17.594 CPI + 33.286 DPI − 2812

The numbers were the regression coefficients estimated for the independent variables and −2,812 was the regression constant. Thus, given predictions of the independent variables, predictions could be made for the dependent variable. Using the actual values of the independent variables and substituting them into the equation above gave the dashed line "fit" as shown in Exhibit 4–2D. This equation explained 92.5 percent of the variation in new-owner demand. The graph indicated a close fit of the "predicted" values to the actual values especially with respect to the major turning points in the series.

A ten-year forecast of refrigerator shipments was computed by recursively adding the annual projections of replacement and new-owner demand. Using refrigerator shipments from 1930 to 1967, replacement demand was projected for 1968. New-owner demand for 1968 was projected based upon substitution of forecasts of the independent variables in the estimating equation reported above. Refrigerator shipments for 1968 were projected as the sum of these two components. This 1968 shipment estimate became an input in estimating the 1969 replacement demand. Exhibit 4–2E shows these projected demands for the ten-year period through 1976.

EXHIBIT 4–2E

Refrigerators
Ten-Year Projection of Domestic Factory Shipments

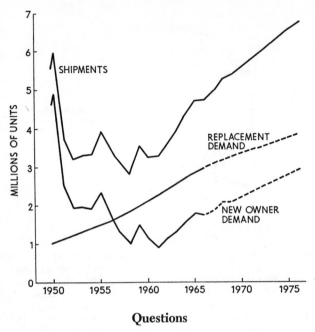

Questions

1. Exhibit 4–2F gives some additional values of the independent variables used in the new-owner demand equation. Substitute these into the equation and make forecasts of new-owner demand for these years.

EXHIBIT 4–2F

Independent Variable Data
1965–72

Year	Population Age 20–34 (thousands)	Total Private Housing Starts (thousands)	Annual Average Consumer Price Index Refrigerators (1957–59 = 100)	Disposable Personal Income (annual rate, billions)	Change in Disposable Personal Income
1965	34,750	1,472	80.4	473.2	
1966	34,900	1,165	80.0	511.9	38.7
1967	35,953	1,292	79.4	546.3	34.4
1968	37,612	1,508	80.1	591.0	44.7
1969	38,906	1,467	81.5	634.4	43.4
1970	41,278	1,434	83.1	691.7	57.3
1971	44,012	2,052	85.1	746.0	44.3
1972	45,572	2,357	85.1	797.0	51.0

2. Critically appraise the economic significance of the statistical results reported herein.
3. Exhibit 4–2G indicates a graphic extrapolation of the replacement demand

EXHIBIT 4–2G

Estimated Replacement Demand and Actual Sales
1965–71 (thousand units)

Year	Estimated Replacement Demand*	Refrigerator Sales
1965...............	2,879	4,678
1966...............	2,984	4,685
1967...............	3,097	4,576
1968...............	3,198	5,023
1969...............	3,287	5,246
1970...............	3,366	5,099
1971...............	3,438	5,551

* From extrapolation Weibull distribution.

and the actual data for refrigerator sales for the years indicated. Compare the forecasts you obtained in Question 1 with actual demand and appraise the results. How would you attempt to do better if the results are not "good"?

CASE 4–3. The Demand for Chickens and Broilers

The domestic sale of broilers has grown from 883,855,000 pounds in 1946 at an average price of 32.7 cents per pound to 10,823,889,000 pounds in 1971 at an average price of 13.7 cents per pound. On the other hand, the domestic sale of chickens has declined from 2,317,984,000 pounds in 1946 at an average price of 27.6 cents per pound to 1,168,197 pounds in 1971 at an average price of 7.7 cents per pound. Exhibit 4–3A presents price-quantity data for broilers and chickens from 1946 to 1966 inclusive.

Questions

1. Construct a statistical demand curve for chickens, for broilers.
2. Explain why the quantity of chickens consumed declined as the price fell.
3. What is your expectation about the cross elasticity of demand between broilers and chickens? Can it change over a period of time? Why?

EXHIBIT 4–3A

Domestic Sales of Broilers and Chickens, 1945–66

Year	Broilers* (1,000 pounds)	Price per Pound	Chickens (1,000 pounds)	Price per Pound
1946	883,855	32.7¢	2,317,984	27.6¢
1947	936,442	32.3	2,144,133	26.5
1948	1,126,643	36.0	1,803,759	30.1
1949	1,570,197	28.2	1,954,034	25.4
1950	1,944,524	27.4	1,858,998	22.2
1951	2,414,767	28.5	1,791,376	25.0
1952	2,623,934	28.8	1,637,026	22.1
1953	2,904,174	27.1	1,581,950	22.1
1954	3,236,248	23.1	1,508,118	16.8
1955	3,349,555	25.2	1,214,742	18.6
1956	4,269,502	19.6	1,156,673	16.0
1957	4,682,738	18.9	1,006,172	13.7
1958	5,430,674	18.5	1,037,339	14.0
1959	5,762,951	16.1	1,086,758	11.0
1960	6,020,417	16.9	866,173	12.2
1961	6,831,932	13.9	902,079	10.1
1962	6,907,076	15.2	920,132	10.2
1963	7,276,008	14.6	907,567	10.0
1964	7,521,269	14.2	936,634	9.2
1965	8,114,549	15.0	967,818	8.9
1966	8,992,614	15.3	1,034,053	9.7
1967	9,186,535	13.3	1,157,938	7.9
1968	9,331,987	14.2	1,097,426	8.2
1969	10,045,658	15.2	1,053,200	9.7
1970	† 10,820,908	13.6	† 1,128,453	9.1
1971	p 10,823,889	13.7	p 1,168,197	7.7

The letter p indicates preliminary.

* Commercial broilers are young chickens of heavy breeds to be marketed at 2 to 5 pounds live weight and from which no pullets are kept for egg production.

† Commercial broilers and chickens were changed to a December 1 through November 30 marketing year beginning with 1970 estimates.

Source: U.S. Department of Agriculture, *Agricultural Statistics, 1972* (Washington, D.C.: U.S. Government Printing Office), and earlier editions.

CASE 4–4. Problems in Demand Analysis for Industry

1. When the Hudson and Manhattan Railroad Company (which operates under the Hudson from New Jersey to Manhattan) raised its fare from 10 cents to 15 cents, passengers carried dropped off 15 percent in the first two days. The Lackawanna and Erie ferries, which offer free transportation to their commuting passengers (who constitute a large percentage of normal H-M traffic), had standing room only during rush hours.

a. Was the demand indicated to be elastic or inelastic?

b. Would you expect the elasticity to prove less or greater after a few days or weeks? After a year or two?

2. The average selling price of oxygen sold in containers decreased almost constantly between 1914 and 1954. In 1914 the price of oxygen

EXHIBIT 4–4A

Date	Total Sales (billions cubic feet)	Average Selling Price (cubic feet)	Wholesale Price Index (1947–49 = 100) Approximate
1914......................	0.83	$1.82	n.a.
1924......................	1.00	1.34	n.a.
1934......................	1.20	0.96	49.0
1942......................	7.50	0.51	64.0
1946......................	6.30	0.46	79.0
1947......................	8.60	0.43	100.0
1948......................	10.20	0.41	104.0
1949......................	9.20	0.42	97.0
1950......................	14.00	0.35	103.0
1953......................	15.50	0.34	110.0
1954......................	13.40	0.35	110.0

n.a.—not available.

per cubic foot was $1.82, and in 1954 it was 35 cents. Sales increased, so the question is whether the industry from the demand side at least was wise in reducing prices in view of the fact that during part of this period the price level was rising.

Study Exhibit 4–4A and determine what the situation is from the demand side.

3. An advertising program of $1,000,000 permitted the Generally American Company to increase volume, make larger profits, and charge a lower price to maximize profits on its major product. Diagram a situation which would make this possible.

4. As a result of an increase in the price of coffee from 80 cents to 95 cents per pound, the sales of tea increases from 500,000 pounds per week to 600,000 pounds. What is the cross elasticity of demand?

5. The Illinois Razor Strop Company was the leader of four producers in the industry and the only one whose sole product was strops. The president estimated that in 1948 two thirds of sales were to barbers and the rest to individuals.

Estimated sales of the industry and the number of producers active run as shown in Exhibit 4–4B.

EXHIBIT 4–4B

Year	Unit Sales	Number of Producers	Price*
1900..............	800,000	10	7.50
1915..............	1,750,000	11	11.00
1930..............	400,000	8	13.50
1945..............	100,000	5	15.00
1948..............	80,000	4	15.00

* Price to wholesalers per dozen of a typical medium-price strop.

What, if anything, should the president conclude about the price elasticity of demand? What is your position as to using a price-quantity graph here?

6. An increase in demand means a higher price. A higher price leads to decreased demand. An increased demand, therefore, is quivalent to a decreased demand. Comment.

chapter 5

Demand Analysis
for the Firm

In applying demand analysis to a firm, the analyst must take into account the markets in which the firm offers its product for sale. In the previous chapter *market* demand has been discussed. In this chapter primary attention will be focused on the price-quantity relationship for an individual firm. This analysis is concerned with the structure of the market in which the firm operates. Market structure means the competitive conditions in terms of the numbers of buyers and sellers which operate in the market for a good or service. The relevant market may be in a very narrow geographic region or may be international in scope. The analyst should take care to define as precisely as possible the nature of the market for which his analysis is concerned. An additional aspect of structure of importance in some industries is the degree of product differentiation which is present. Product differentiation often makes the definition of an industry quite difficult.

Demand Facing a Monopolist

Where the entire output of the commodity is accounted for by a single firm, it is clear that demand facing such a monopolistic seller is identical with the market demand. Monopoly demand curves consequently slope downward to the right.

It is useful, in analyzing the monopolist's economic behavior, to employ the concept of "marginal revenue" as well as that of the demand schedule. Marginal revenue is simply the *additional* revenue secured by a seller from the sale of an additional unit of product. (Strictly, the unit should again be infinitesimally small.)[1] If there were only one producer

---

[1] In terms of calculus, marginal revenue is the derivative of total revenue with respect to quantity, that is, the rate of change of total revenue.

of wheat—an unrealistic assumption but one which is no longer unimportant, since farmers attempt to act somewhat in concert through the federal farm program and by means of private marketing agreements— the market-demand schedule which we have been using would be the demand curve facing that firm. Marginal revenue from the sale of additional output would be found by taking the difference between successive total revenues and dividing these by the differences between successive quantities demanded. These calculations are shown in Figure 5–1.

In order to get the change in quantity and in total revenue for row A, it is necessary to assume that a quantity of 40 million bushels would have been demanded at a price of $4.50 per bushel. This would have yielded a total revenue of $180 million, and the difference between this amount and $200 million is $20 million. Division of $20 million by the quantity increase of 10 million bushels means that each additional bushel sold added an average of $2 to the sellers' aggregate revenue. In row D through row G, marginal revenue is negative, showing that additional units sold actually reduce the total income of sellers (make negative additions to income).

It is clear that a monopolist seeking to maximize his profits would not sell any units which, through their depressing influence on price, would reduce his total revenue. That is, the monopolist will not operate in the region of negative marginal revenue. His price will be set at $3.25 per bushel or higher, and his sales will be 65 million bushels per month or less. (The exact optimum cannot be defined until cost is brought into the picture. This will be done in a later chapter.) It is clear that he should operate in the region where demand is of unitary elasticity or higher, rather than where demand is inelastic. Although total revenue would be the same at quantities of 50 million and 80 million bushels, for example, the cost of producing the smaller amount would obviously be less.

FIGURE 5–1

Computation of Marginal Revenue

Row	(1) Price of Wheat (per bushel)	(2) Quantity Demanded (millions of bushels per month)	(3) Value (millions of dollars)	(4) Change in Quantity (millions of bushels)	(5) Change in Total Revenue (millions of dollars)	(Col. 5 ÷ Col. 4) Marginal Revenue per Bushel
A.........	$4.00	50	$200	10	$20	$2
B.........	3.50	60	210	10	10	1
C.........	3.00	70	210	10	0	0
D.........	2.50	80	200	10	− 10	− 1
E.........	2.00	90	180	10	− 20	− 2
F.........	1.50	100	150	10	− 30	− 3
G.........	1.00	110	110	10	− 40	− 4

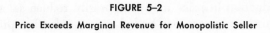

FIGURE 5–2

Price Exceeds Marginal Revenue for Monopolistic Seller

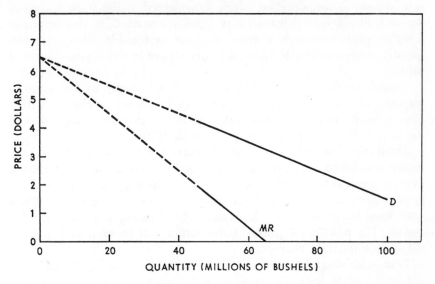

Demand and marginal revenue for the hypothetical wheat monopolist are shown in Figure 5–2. The dotted portions indicate the course of the curves at quantities below 50 million bushels, assuming that the same linear relationship holds true. It can be seen that marginal revenue is zero at a quantity of 65 million bushels. It was noted earlier that elasticity of demand is unitary at this quantity. Consequently, it is clear that unitary elasticity and a marginal revenue of zero exist at the same output. When demand is elastic, marginal revenue is greater than zero; while in the region of inelastic demand, marginal revenue is negative. The logic of this last relationship is not difficult to understand: When demand is inelastic, it is necessary to cut price sharply on all units in order to sell a little more; hence the additional sale will decrease the total value of sales—that is, bring in negative marginal revenue. These relationships between marginal revenue and elasticity should be compared and integrated with the discussion of the relationship between total revenue and elasticity considered in Chapter 4.

Some Qualifications

The demand curves which have been used so far show highly simplified "static" relationships which are especially useful in the economic theory of price determination. While they may also be useful to the businessman, it is likely to be important for him to keep in mind some complicating qualifications.

First, a reduction in price may temporarily reduce sales rather than increase them, since buyers may be led to expect further price cuts. This is a "dynamic" consideration which is neglected in the static theory of demand. Similarly, a price cut may "spoil the market" so that return to a higher price previously charged may not be feasible. Buyers are frequently more sensitive to changes in price than to the absolute level of price.

Second, even when some buyers immediately begin to buy more in response to a price cut, other buyers may be slower in changing their buying habits so that a considerable period of time may elapse before the full effect of the price change works itself out.

Third, the demand and marginal revenue curves which have been drawn assume that all buyers are charged the same price. Actually, it may be possible to sell additional units by reducing price only to a new group of buyers, or only on additional sales to existing customers. Block rates used by public utility firms are a good example of quantity discounts. The practice of price discrimination will be examined in some detail in a separate chapter.

Fourth, although it is theoretically irrational for a monopolist to sell in the region of inelastic demand—since he can gain revenue by raising price—he may still find it expedient to do so. By charging a less-than-optimum price, he may be able to discourage would-be competitors, build up consumer goodwill for the long run, and perhaps reduce the likelihood of prosecution under the federal antitrust laws. if he is selling in interstate commerce. (There are seldom laws against intrastate monopoly.)

Demand Facing Pure Competitor

Economists define "perfect" or "pure" competition as a situation in which there are so many sellers of a particular commodity that none can individually affect the price. In the absence of governmental interference, many agriculture commodities are produced under such conditions. Even today, truck-garden vegetables, poultry, eggs, and fish, for example, are often turned out by perfectly competitive firms.

Under pure competition the demand curve for the produce of the individual firm is simply a horizontal line drawn at the price determined in the market. That is to say, market price is determined by overall supply and demand and the individual firm can sell as much as it wishes at this price. It cannot charge more than the market price without losing all of its customers (who are assumed to be both rational and mobile) and need not, of course, accept less than the prevailing price.

The demand for the product of a purely competitive firm is represented in Figure 5–3. Such a horizontal curve is infinitely elastic along

FIGURE 5–3

Infinitely Elastic Demand Faces Perfectly Competitive Firm

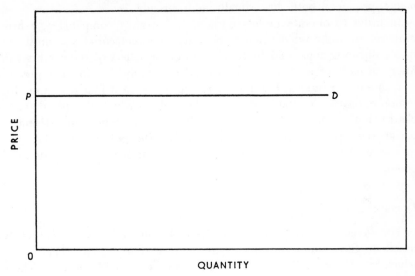

its entire range. The firm has no control over price and can be designated as a "price taker" rather than as a "price maker." (The latter term
is appropriate for a monopolistic firm.)

Pure Competition Is Uncommon

The case of pure competition is, in practice, much less common than
that of monopoly, when the latter term is used to cover all situations in
which the demand facing the individual firm is downsloping rather than
horizontal. Most firms have some power to fix prices, within limits, and
hence are not fully competitive with others. The amount of this price-
making power may be great—for example, in the case of a city-owned
electric utility system where the rates set by the munipical authorities
may be subject to no check by a regulatory commission. Or the amount
of price-making power may be severely limited by the existence of close
substitutes, as in the case of a seller of a particular breakfast cereal or
sardines.

Some writers use the term "monopolistic competition" to denote the
situation of a firm which has some monopoly power—due, perhaps, to
selling under a brand name which no one else can use—but which faces
the competition of more or less similar products. No clear line can be
drawn between monopoly and monopolistic competition, however, since
every monopolist faces some competition. The prewar Aluminum Com-

pany of America had great monopoly power in the production of this metal but nevertheless encountered a measure of competition from other metals produced both domestically and abroad.

In order to operate under conditions of perfect competition, a firm must sell an unbranded commodity (such as sweet corn) and must not be significantly separated spatially from other sellers of the same good. Many firms have a degree of locational monopoly due to their greater convenience to buyers. Vendors of refreshments at a football game, for example, have a separateness from other sellers which permits them to charge higher prices than those on the outside. Much advertising is designed simply to imprint brand names on the public mind, in order to lessen the severity of competition from similar or even identical goods.

Demand under Oligopoly

The demand curves which have been drawn so far were necessarily based on the assumption of *ceterus paribus*—that is, all other factors which would affect the quantity demanded were held constant. These include prices of competing products, incomes and their distribution, and consumers' tastes. Where there are only a few sellers of a particular commodity, however, this assumption is not useful. Instead, it must be recognized that each seller will carefully watch the action of his close competitors and frequently will react to any change which they make in price, quality, or selling effort. This is called an "oligopolistic" situation —the case of a few sellers. It is an extremely common real-world situation. Oligopolistic firms may turn out identical homogenous products (e.g., brass tubing, aluminum sheet, or copper wire); or they may sell closely related but somewhat dissimilar goods (e.g., trucks, airplanes, typewriters, or soap powder).

A single demand curve cannot depict the price-quantity relationship for a commodity sold oligopolistically. If price is changed, the response of sale depends heavily on the actions which close rivals are induced to take. If, for example, price is lowered by one firm but rivals choose to maintain their prices and quality unchanged, the amount which buyers will purchase from the price cutter is likely to expand quite sharply. If rivals match a price cut, sales of the first price cutter are likely to increase only moderately, since others will share in the larger total sales volume. If rivals more than meet a price cut, the physical volume sold by the first price cutter may even fall off.

A general picture of the demand situation under oligopoly can be shown graphically. Such a chart is suggestive only, since it cannot show the results of all of the possible combinations of action and reaction on the part of oligopolistic rivals. Figure 5–4 pertains to an individual firm which is assumed, first, to be charging price OP_1. If the firm then lowers

FIGURE 5–4

Oligopoly Demand Curves—Sales Depend on Rivals Reactions

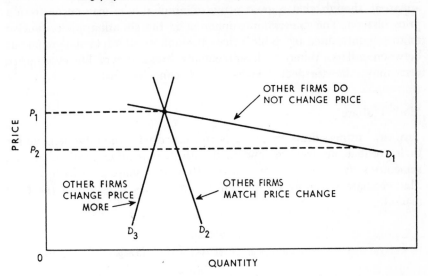

its price to OP_2 and its rivals do not change their prices, the physical sales of the price cutter may expand sharply, as indicated by curve D_1. (Since this curve is elastic between prices OP_1 and OP_2, total revenue received by the firm will rise.) If, instead, rival firms match the price cut, the volume of sales may expand only moderately, as indicated by D_2. (Since this curve, as drawn, is inelastic between prices OP_1 and OP_2, the dollar volume of sales would be down, despite the rise in physical volume.) It is even possible that the firm under consideration will encounter a positive sloping demand curve such as D_3. This is only likely if rivals more than match the first firm's price cut.

Above the original price OP the demand curves can be interpreted in a similar way. If our firm raises its price and its close rivals do not do so, sales may fall off quite sharply, as suggested by curve D_1. If the other sellers match the price increase, sales may fall off only moderately, as along D_2. If rivals should decide to raise their prices more than the first firm, that firm may enjoy higher physical and dollar sales, as indicated by D_3.

It is clear that there are so many possible combinations of oligopolistic price behavior (to say nothing of changes in such variables as quality, amount of advertising, premiums, credit terms, etc.) that demand curves for the individual firm are of limited usefulness. The same is not true of *market* demand curves for oligopolistic industries, however, and considerable effort has been expended in deriving statistical demand curves for such commodities as steel and cigarettes, where the number of producers is relatively small.

The consequences of the complex nature of demand under oligopoly will be examined in some detail in subsequent chapters. It is readily apparent, though, that a great many different results may ensue from a price change. The uncertainties inherent in the situation are conducive to the maintenance of stable prices through overt or tacit agreements between sellers. When such agreements break down, however, price wars may follow, especially when excess capacity exists.

Market Share

Many business firms are not only concerned with the total demand for their product but are also concerned with their relative position. In fact, some are said to be more concerned with market share than with profits.[2] Market share is simply the percentage one firm's sales are of the total market.

FIGURE 5–5

Price Differentials versus Market Share Changes

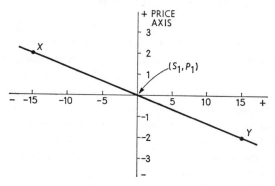

Market share elasticity may be defined as the responsiveness of the market share of a firm to changes in a competitor's price.

$$\text{Elasticity of market share} = \frac{\text{Percent change in market share of } A}{\text{Percent change in price of } B}$$

This concept is clearly related to the economists' measure of cross elasticity but conforms to the businessman's usual concern with market share.

A useful graphic device to illustrate market share response to price changes is given in Figure 5–5. In this diagram P_1 represents either a

---

[2] William J. Baumol, *Business Behavior, Value and Growth* (New York: Macmillan Co., 1948).

price differential of zero, or some customary differential such as the usual 2-cent differential between major and independent brands of gasoline which results in no change in market share. S_1 represents the firm's usual market share if the price and other factors remain the same. The vertical axis, therefore, shows deviations from zero or the customary differential while the horizontal axis shows the resulting changes in market share. Data for such curves may be available from historical records of a firm and if used with care may provide some very useful insights into pricing problems in a market with differential products.

Demand Analysis and Forecasting Sales of a Firm

The foregoing discussion has shown that only firms which are in imperfectly competitive markets can make really effective use of forecasting.[3] Competitive firms which can quickly adjust output should do so in response to changes in market price. The reasons for this will become more apparent after the role of costs is examined. Firms which have some ability to fix price and other promotional policies can make effective use of forecasting and the "if . . . then" reasoning which explicit consideration of the demand determining factors allows. However, it is clear that many firms must give explicit consideration to the potential actions and reactions of their competitors.

One example of how a firm may use an industry forecast is through market share analysis. If market share is usually 30 percent, then to the extent that all other firms' pricing and promotion policies are unchanged, next year's sales should be 30 percent of the industry forecast. Models which attempt to account for departures from no change policies can be developed and used.

CASE 5–1. Central Petroleum Products, Inc.

Central Petroleum Products, Inc., is a small integrated oil company operating in the states of Arkansas, Alabama, Louisiana, Mississippi, Tennessee, and Texas. The company purchases crude oil from independent producers but owns its own refineries, distribution system, storage facilities, and more than 65 percent of its retail outlets. Through these outlets the company offers for sale both regular and ethyl gasoline and a line of oils and lubricants under the brand name "Central." Included in

---

[3] A recent text which considers demographic, economic, sociological, and psychological models of demand and relates them to the firm is G. David Hughes, *Demand Analysis for Marketing Decisions* (Homewood, Ill.: Richard D. Irwin, Inc., 1973).

the line of oils are three grades of furnace and heating oils. These latter oils are sold by salesmen, and delivery is made through and directly from bulk storage plants.

The company has been in business since 1936 and since that time has built up a rather profitable business. In 1959 it owned and operated 211 stations and sold its products through 187 dealers throughout its territory. The volume of business produced by the independent dealers was relatively small. In 1957 they accounted for only 14 percent of the total gasoline and motor oil sales. While the company began its operations in El Dorado, Arkansas, where the home office is still located, its largest markets are Little Rock and Fort Smith, Arkansas; Memphis and Nashville, Tennessee; Birmingham, Alabama; Jackson, Mississippi; and Alexandria, Baton Rouge, and New Orleans, Louisiana. Approximately 60 percent of its retail sales is to customers in these cities. The balance of sales is in smaller cities and rural communities in the territory.

Since the company was primarily concerned with the marketing of gasoline, motor and fuel oils, and lubricants, the refining operations were somewhat, though not entirely, subordinated to the retail operations. In the refining process, several by-products were yielded as residuals which the company was not in a position to market. These by-products, such as asphalt, bunker oil, heavy lubricants, and similar products, were sold to other refiners or processors. The output of these products, therefore, depended primarily upon the company's need for gasoline and oil to meet customer demand. The company owned three refineries, all of which were modern and well maintained. From a barrel of crude oil, there was, within limits, a certain proportion which could be refined into gasoline, lubricating oils and greases, fuel oil of various grades, and other residual products. This meant that in the face of a strong demand for gasoline, there would be a certain output of the other products in the production of gasoline. The liquid by-products of the refining process, such as motor and fuel oils, required storage in tanks which had to meet certain safety requirements and be located in areas approved by public authorities. It was not possible, for example, to refine the correct proportions of gasoline and fuel oil in a continuous refining process. More gasoline was consumed in the spring, summer, and fall months than during the winter, while fuel oil of the lighter weights was consumed more heavily during the winter, with lighter demands during the summer season. This meant that the company had to provide storage facilities for gasoline during the winter and fuel oil storage during the summer. In almost all cases, separate facilities were necessary for the two products.

The market in which the company sold the by-products it did not use was one in which the company had no control over price. Prices of these products varied over a limited range, depending upon the demand and supply situation of the moment. The company sold these products immediately upon refining rather than face additional costs of storage. The revenues received for these by-products affected, to some extent, the revenues which were anticipated from gasoline and motor and fuel oils which the company hoped to receive in order to show a profit.

The retail market in which the company competed was dominated by the major oil companies, such as Shell, Standard Oil, Gulf, and others. Central sold about 8 percent of the gasoline and motor oil marketed in Memphis and New Orleans; about 6 percent in Jackson, Mississippi; 5 percent in Nashville, Tennessee; about 9 percent in Baton Rouge, Louisiana; and 14 percent in Little Rock, Arkansas. Central had always sold its gasoline at the prevailing market price, although there were several independent cut-rate gasoline outlets in almost all of the territory. The company had maintained the quality of its products on a level comparable to that of the major companies and had priced its products accordingly.

Whenever a price change was made in any of the urban areas, it was almost always initiated by one or more of the major oil companies. Central had always followed these price changes both upward and downward. Such changes usually involved a difference of only 1 or 2 cents per gallon. Occasionally, a new independent company would attempt to invade the cut-rate market and offer unbranded gasoline at 5 or 6 cents below the price of the major brands. Usually, the cut-rate prices were about 2 cents per gallon below the major brands. If the new company attempted to hold its price more than 2 cents below the major brands, there would usually be a price cut by the major companies to within at least 2 cents per gallon of the invading company. This situation would prevail until the invading company raised its prices to the prior level of cut-rate companies or until it left the market. Prices would then quite often return to the former prevailing level for major brands.

Occasionally, there would be a price cut by a major company; this usually did not precipitate a price war but often reflected the demand and supply situation in gasoline. Since the consumption of gasoline declined in the winter months but production continued during that season, gasoline stocks were usually pressing upon storage facilities in early spring unless it had been a mild winter, so that fuel oil production had been light, resulting in lower refinery runs. If gasoline supplies were pressing upon storage facilities, there might be a price reduction by a major company which was usually followed by all other companies, including Central. If storage facilities were adequate, there might be an upward adjustment of prices, since gasoline consumption would begin to rise in the spring and demand was met by current refining plus gasoline in storage. Central had never initiated a price change either upward or downward.

In February, 1958, Central found itself with a large carry-over of gasoline stocks in its Memphis and Little Rock markets. Not only were the storage tanks at the refineries practically filled, but the bulk stations were carrying more than normal supplies of gasoline. Asphalt, bunker oil, and a by-product used in the manufacture of synthetic rubber were in demand, and prices were slightly higher than usual. The company had an ample supply of crude oil but was unable to carry on refining operations on a large scale because of the storage problem.

The retail price of ethyl gasoline in Memphis at the time was 38.6 cents per gallon, and regular sold at 35.6 cents, including state and federal taxes. The same prices prevailed in Little Rock. In order to move the gasoline out of storage and into the market, the president of Central suggested to the sales manager that the company reduce the price of gasoline in Memphis and Little Rock by 5 cents per gallon. To this the sales manager objected, stating that a cut of this size would immediately bring about similar reductions by the major companies, with the result that little, if any, more gasoline would be sold, and the company would receive less for it. The president, on the other hand, believed that a reduction in the price would increase the sale of gasoline even if the major companies did meet the reduction. He argued that all the companies would sell more gasoline because of the lower price and that therefore Central would gain by a price reduction of the amount he suggested. The sales manager suggested that if there were to be a price reduction, it be no more than 1 cent per gallon, since he did not believe the major companies would follow such a small cut and the company

EXHIBIT 5–1A

CENTRAL PETROLEUM PRODUCTS, INC.
Sales of Gasoline—Memphis Market Area
Monthly, 1957

	Regular		Ethyl	
Month	*Gallons*	*Retail Price* per Gallon*	*Gallons*	*Retail Price* per Gallon*
January...................	687,000	33.6¢	297,000	36.6¢
February................	681,000	33.6	295,000	36.6
March...................	701,000	33.6	300,000	36.6
April....................	752,000	35.6	427,000	38.6
May.....................	955,000	35.6	469,000	38.6
June....................1,001,000		35.6	501,000	38.6
July....................1,021,000		35.6	500,000	38.6
August..................1,152,000		35.6	519,000	38.6
September...............1,099,000		30.6†	553,000	33.6†
October.................1,101,000		30.6†	574,000	33.6†
November................	921,000	35.6	497,000	38.6
December................	700,000	33.6	345,000	36.6

* Includes state and federal gasoline taxes.
† Price war lasting 57 days.

would then have a price advantage over the major companies. The president of Central was dubious about this policy, since he thought a reduction of only 1 cent would not stimulate the sale of gasoline sufficiently to help the company reduce its gasoline stock so that it could resume refining operations and again enter the market for the by-products.

Exhibit 5–1A shows the company sales in the Memphis market area by months for the year 1957, together with prevailing prices for both regular and ethyl grades. The same prices prevailed in Little Rock.

Questions

1. Would you recommend that Central initiate a price reduction at this time? If so, would you recommend the 5-cent or the 1-cent reduction?
2. Did the president think the demand for gasoline was elastic or inelastic? Why? The sales manager? Why? What is your opinion of the elasticity of the gasoline market?
3. Did the sales manager think the gasoline market for Central was elastic or inelastic? Why?
4. What is the nature of demand for gasoline? On the basis of your answer, would you say that the demand for gasoline is elastic or inelastic?
5. Would you say that the elasticity of demand for Central is greater or less than the elasticity of the total gasoline market? Why?

CASE 5–2. University of the Mid-West

University of the Mid-West was established in 1902 as a private non-profit educational institution to provide instruction in the arts and sciences. From an initial enrollment of 127 students, it has grown to its present enrollment of 5,400 students, of whom 611 are enrolled in the graduate school. The university is located near the center of a midwestern state in a small city of approximately 69,000 population.

The operations of the university include the provision and maintenance of living accommodations for 3,000 students in dormitories, 1,900 for men and 1,100 for women. Upperclass male students, married students, and graduate students are permitted to live in private homes in the city. Instruction is carried on in 11 buildings, which include classrooms, laboratories, and offices for faculty and administration. All of the buildings have been constructed from the proceeds of gifts and grants from individuals and foundations.

The university is governed by a self-perpetuating board of trustees consisting of 21 members. The administrative staff consists of the president, two vice presidents, and seven deans. The board is the policy-making body of the university, usually acting upon recommendations submitted to it by the faculty and administration through the president. All financial matters, including budget and fees, are subject to approval of the board.

The budget for the operation of the university is $12 million for the current academic year. Tuition is currently $900 per year, payable at the beginning of each semester. Less than 1 percent of the student body are part-time students; the remainder carry a full academic load. Tuition for graduate students is the same as for undergraduates. In the current year, student fees account for $4.86 million of income, dormitory receipts amount to $2 million, endowment income is anticipated to be $4 million, and gifts and miscellaneous receipts are expected to reach about $950,-000. Out of this income are expenditures for faculty salaries, which comprise almost one half of the total budget, dormitory and dining hall maintenance and expense, purchases of current supplies and equipment, scholarship funds, and general maintenance of buildings and grounds.

The size of the incoming freshman class each year depends upon available dormitory facilities, since the university does not permit freshmen and sophomores to live in other than university housing or in the few fraternity and sorority houses. These latter houses accommodate approximately 400 students. Thus the size of the freshman class varies from 1,200 to 1,400 students, depending upon space available. In addition to incoming freshmen, the university admits about 250 transfer students each year from other colleges and universities or junior colleges. The incoming freshman class is selected from among approximately 4,000 applicants. About 2,000 to 2,200 applicants are offered admission, which results in a net class of approximately 1,200 to 1,400. About 20 percent of the incoming freshman class are usually awarded scholarships to make it possible for them to meet the expenses of education. The university is fairly selective in its admissions policy, requiring better than average scholastic aptitude test scores as well as preference for high school seniors in the upper 25 percent of their class. This policy is generally known by high school counselors, and the admissions office advises in all of its publicity that students who do not meet these minimum requirements should not apply.

In spite of such admission requirements, about 10 percent of the freshman class do not return for their sophomore year, although this has not been due to academic reasons alone. Some have left for financial reasons, health, and other miscellaneous causes. Enrollment in the spring term has almost always been approximately 200 students less than in the fall term. Again, while academic reasons have been the chief cause, the other reasons cited above are also a factor.

The current tuition rate has been in effect since September, 1956. Within a radius of 175 miles, there are two large state universities.

Within a larger radius of 300 miles, there ar two other state universities. The highest tuition for state residents at any of these universities is $225 per year. The lowest rate is $150. The highest tuition for out-of-state students is $550 and the lowest $375 per year. Enrollment at University of the Mid-West in the 1956–57 academic year was 4,950 students, including graduate students. While enrollment has increased since that time to the present 5,400, an increase of slightly less than 10 percent, enrollment at the four state universities has risen by more than 30 percent. The last dormitory on the campus of University of the Mid-West was opened in September, 1956, at the beginning of that school year. This was a building providing housing for 425 students, and there were 81 vacancies in the building during the first year. The university could have accommodated more students until the academic year 1959–60, but it was unable to select additional students without seriously lowering its admission requirements. Since 1959–60, there have been no vacancies in the dormitories, and the available rooms and apartments in the city were practically fully occupied.

For the academic year beginning in September, 1962, the president, in the preparation of his budget, felt that a substantial increase in faculty salaries was long overdue. The salary scale was somewhat below that of other private schools of comparable size and, in some instances, substantially below that of the state universities. He estimated that a minimum increase of 10 percent was necessary to retain the present faculty as well as to attract new faculty members. In addition, there was need to provide additional fringe benefits in the way of additional retirement annuity, group life insurance, and improved health insurance. It was estimated that this would add $800,000 to the budget. There was also need to make upward adjustments in the compensation of the staff, which consisted of secretaries, clerks, and maintenance and service personnel. This would require an additional $150,000. In order to keep the library not only current in its book purchases but to expand its services, an additional $105,000 was required to finance additional book and periodical purchases, which had been somewhat restricted in the last two years. Increases in the costs of supplies and miscellaneous expenses were estimated at $95,000. There was also a need to increase the scholarship funds in order to attract better students who were unable to finance an education at Mid-West without assistance.

The long-term outlook for enrollment was optimistic. It was estimated that the number of students in college by 1970 would be approximately twice that of 1960. It was the immediate problem which was more serious. No substantial increase in enrollment at Mid-West was anticipated until the bulge of high school students to be enrolled in the colleges in 1964 to 1966. In order to permit an increase in enrollment, it would be necessary to construct additional dormitory space. It was

EXHIBIT 5–2A

Present and Proposed
Tuition Fees and Enrollments

Present and Proposed Rates	Current and Estimated Enrollment
$ 900	5,400
1,000*	5,300†
1,100*	5,150†
1,200*	5,050†

* Proposed.
† Estimated.

hoped that a donor could be found who would provide the funds for such a building; but at present, none was at hand. The president intended to propose to the board of trustees that if no donor could be found by the summer of 1963, the university make application to the College Housing Loan Fund, a government agency, for a loan to construct a dormitory which would house at least 450 students. It was estimated that the university could accommodate an additional 400 to 500 students without materially adding to its instructional and operating costs. In the meantime, it was necessary to obtain more funds to meet the need outlined above for the coming year.

Since the president foresaw no substantial additions to annual gifts from friends and alumni, he proposed an increase in tuition fees for the coming year. Together with his proposed budget, he submitted a pro-

EXHIBIT 5–2B

Tuition and Fees of Selected Private Colleges and
Universities in the United States

Institution	Tuition	Fees	Total
Beloit College	$1,275	....	$1,275
Brown University	1,600	....	1,600
Carleton College	1,150	$ 48	1,198
Cornell University	1,340	260	1,600
Dartmouth College	1,550	....	1,550
Denison University	1,100	150	1,250
Harvard University	1,446	74	1,520
Knox College	1,300	75	1,375
Lawrence College	1,275	20	1,295
Middlebury College	1,300	56	1,356
Mount Holyoke College	1,500	20	1,520
Pomona College	1,250	55	1,305
Princeton University	1,550	50	1,600
Stanford University	1,260	....	1,260
Swarthmore College	1,300	150	1,450
Syracuse University	1,370	100	1,470
Wellesley College	1,500	....	1,500
Yale University	1,550	....	1,550

posal to the board of trustees for a tuition increase based upon the estimates shown in Exhibit 5–2A.

Exhibit 5–2B shows tuition rates in effect at a selected number of private colleges and universities in the United States for the academic year 1961–62.

The president supported his proposal to the board with an observation that approximately 35 percent of the students at Mid-West came from the midwestern states, 25 percent came from the northeastern and middle states along the Atlantic seaboard, 20 percent from the far West and Northwest, and the remainder from the Southeast and Southwest, as well as 23 foreign countries. He recommended that a tuition increase of $300 per academic year be approved by the board.

Questions

1. Do you agree with the president's recommendations? Why?
2. Should short- or long-term considerations prevail in adjusting the tuition rates at this time? Explain.
3. Comment upon the elasticity of demand for enrollment at Mid-West.
4. Should the fact that Mid-West is a nonprofit educational institution have any effect upon the determination of tuition rates?
5. This case was written in the early sixties as student enrollment was increasing rapidly and as state institutions were expanding capacity to meet anticipated demand. If you were asked to prepare a tuition recommendation for the University of the Mid-West for 1975–76 and succeeding years, what data would you collect? How might your analysis differ from that you made for the period in the case?

CASE 5–3. Continental Airlines

In early November of 1961, Continental Airlines startled the air industry by proposing a cut-rate fare plan at a time when airline losses were shaping into a colossal $34.7 million. The plan called for a third, "no frills" jet class with fares 25 percent under conventional jet coach fares. The proposal came after four years of slow growth in airline traffic and at a time of jet overcapacity in the industry.

Airline traffic had grown at an average rate of 18 percent a year between 1950 and 1957, but slowed thereafter to 6 percent and had virtually stopped by 1961. The big question before the Civil Aeronautics Board, whose job it is to regulate the airlines in the public interest, was whether the lower fare would lure enough new passengers to increase air profits, or whether it would result in heavier losses for a number of air carriers. United Air Lines, the largest air carrier in the nation, led the fight against the proposed "economy class."

Continental's president, Robert Six, outlined the basic conflict as he saw it. "Underlying the multiple attacks on this plan to stimulate new air travel is the apparently common belief . . . that air transportation has lost its potential for further penetration of the competitive travel market." "However," said Six, "there is substantial evidence that growth has been retarded to a marked degree by the considerable increases in the level of fares that have occurred in the past several years. . . . Fare levels today are 16.4% higher in first-class and 34.8% higher in coach than they were in 1957, coincidently the last year in which the industry realized a substantial growth in traffic!"[4]

Continental rested its case upon the demonstration that its proposal would require only 2.4 percent of the intercity surface travel market (projected in passenger-miles) in its total market area to switch to air travel for the "economy plan" to break even.[5] Continental's position was stated to the Civil Aeronautics Board as follows:

At the present time, over 75% of our jet revenue passenger miles are in Club Coach service. We know that a portion of this traffic is business traffic that has been diverted from First Class. We do not believe very much of this business traffic will be diverted to the new "economy service," since it will be "Spartan" in nature. . . . In the Club Coach section of the aircraft, we will be providing 42 seats at a load factor of 50–55%, or approximately 40% of the traffic we are now carrying in this section with capacity reduced 50%. In the economy section, we anticipate a load factor of 60%, comprised of 25 to 30 passengers diverted from existing Club Coach service and 15 to 20 new passengers in the markets, attracted by new low fares. The new traffic will consist of the following:

1. Newly created traffic among the people now unwilling or unable to spend the time required to travel by surface means and unable to afford air travel at existing price levels.

2. More frequent travel among present air travelers due to reduced prices.

3. Travel diverted from surface transportation.

These load factors would result in a requirement for Continental Airlines to develop approximately 550,000 additional revenue passenger miles per day. Even assuming that no new travel is created, this represents a diversion from existing surface travel of only 2.4% of the [22.5 million daily estimated surface passenger miles in Continental's market area]. There is no question but that this modest diversion from surface transportation media will be realized with the planned reduction of fares.[6]

---

[4] *Forbes Magazine*, December 15, 1961, p. 16.

[5] Continental's area consisted of a rough triangle between Chicago, Los Angeles, and Houston, Texas, including (in addition to these cities) Kansas City, Denver, Dallas, Fort Worth, Oklahoma City, Albuquerque, Phoenix, and El Paso.

[6] *Brief of Continental Airlines* (CAB Docket Nos. 13163 et al.).

EXHIBIT 5–3A

Additional Traffic Necessary to Maintain Revenues under
Varying Assumptions if Entire Airline Industry
Established Economy Fares

	Assuming All Coach Traffic Diverted	*Retention of 40% of Coach Traffic*
Coach RPM's, 1961 (billions)	15.4	15.4
Yield (based on Los Angeles–Chicago)	0.05668	0.05668
Coach revenue (millions)	$872.9	$872.9
Percent coach revenue	0	40%
RPM's retained	0	6.2
Amount of coach revenue retained	0	$349.2
Amount of economy revenue needed	$872.9	$523.7
Economy yield (75% of coach)	0.04251	0.04251
Economy RPM's needed	20.5	12.3
Total RPM's	20.5	18.5
Additional RPM's needed (billions)	5.1	3.1

Source: *Brief of Continental Airlines* (CAB Docket Nos. 13163 et al.).

Exhibit 5–3A contains additional calculations by Continental as to needed traffic generation, assuming that the entire industry followed its lead.

A few days after Continental submitted its proposal, United and other companies issued formal protests before the CAB. United averred that demand for air travel now followed the general level of the economy and that the levels of consumers' incomes more nearly determined their willingness to travel. Continental replied: "Certainly the business recessions of 1958 and 1960 have played their part. How major a part they played is open to question as evidenced by the fact that air travel in 1954 and 1957 grew a healthy 13.6% and 13.2% respectively, in years also considered recession periods. . . . Why then are today's [November, 1961] levels of air travel not substantially greater since consumer income, after taxes, is at a record rate of $367.8 billions versus a level of $354.4 billions in 1960?"

EXHIBIT 5–3B

RPM'S in Billions

Length of Passenger Trip (miles)	*Percent Coach of Total Air Travel**
0–299	11.4
300–499	25.0
500–749	31.0
750–999	48.5
1,000–1,499	65.6
1,500–1,999	66.3
2,000–2,849	67.1

* CAB figures for 1960.

United also suggested that "for longer haul business travel, the distinguishing characteristics of air transportation such as speed and comfort provide a value so great, price is not, in United's opinion, a serious consideration." Continental replied: "The . . . table [shown in Exhibit 5–3B] . . . clearly illustrates that as the total dollar savings become larger, the more attraction it has for the traveling public."

In addition, Continental utilized *Fortune* magazine's 1959 airline study as a "demonstration that price consciousness when related to income plays heavily on demand for air travel, and that to induce these people to travel, a substantial reduction in existing levels of air fares must be made." The *Fortune* study indicated that air trips were taken by:

1. One out of every two adults with a family income of $15,000 and over.
2. One out of five adults with a family income of $10,000–$14,999.
3. One out of 10 adults with a family income of $7,500–$9,999.
4. One out of 14 adults with a family income of $6,000–$7,499.
5. One out of 20 adults with a family income of $5,000–$5,999.

However, United Vice President A. M. de Voursney, referring to Continental's position, later stated in a speech: "Proponents of the idea . . . that this huge automobile travel volume represents the future market for air travel . . . point out that . . . only 28% of the adult population have ever flown. But it is also true that . . . only 71% have ever taken a train trip, 48% have taken a bus trip, and only about 40% have ever stayed in a hotel room overnight."

DeVoursney continued: "If the airlines could capture a fraction of this market, it is reasoned, our traffic increase would be tremendous. Of course, you must realize that most of the market [intercity travel] is short haul; next, that it is highly seasonal; and that it is also a market in which the traveler takes along a lot of luggage. . . ."

Both sides claimed that they had evidence from past statistics to support their position concerning the importance of price in stimulating air travel. One of United's past arguments had been that when a 17 percent increase in fares was granted in February, 1958, the height of the recession, the increase had no appreciable effect on its passengers. Stated United:

As of February 5, there were 85,750 passengers holding advanced reservations . . . scheduled for departure after February 10, the effective date of the fare increases. . . . In an effort to advise each of these passengers, United . . . made 55,300 calls. In many instances it was possible to contact several passengers with one call and there were only a very limited number of passengers whom we were unable to reach. Only three passengers canceled reservations and only twelve . . . changed from first class to coach service. . . . It is unnecessary for me to discuss [CAB] Bureau Counsel's theories of what might happen in event of fare increase when we now have concrete evidence of what does happen. . . .[7]

United also introduced figures from which it concluded that "an analysis of traffic in the top 100 pairs of cities shows that in those markets in which coach service was introduced between March–September, 1953, and March–September, 1957, the growth in passenger traffic between these two periods was only 6.6% greater than in all other markets." Continental did not deny this, but replied that "by 1953 more than half of the top 100 passenger markets already had coach service." Continental therefore proceeded to analyze traffic in the leading markets prior to any introduction of coach service (see Exhibit 5–3C).

EXHIBIT 5–3C

Passengers

	Number of Markets	September, 1948	September, 1952	Percent Increase
Markets in which coach service was provided in 1952 but not 1948........	50	245,162	429,394	75.1
Markets in which no coach service was provided in either 1952 or 1948............................	41	203,139	205,204	23.2

Continental also submitted that "total traffic to and from Miami, for the first quarter of 1961, was 12.7% below levels of 1957 . . . while the three markets provided with Air-Bus service by Eastern . . . reflected an increase of 11.2%. . . . Fare levels for this Air-Bus service are approximately 17% below piston coach levels and more than 25% below jet coach levels."

President W. A. Patterson of United called Continental's plan "unjust and unreasonable," "a device to give a temporary advantage," and "a move of desperation," and expressed fear that it "may make it impossible for a large section of the industry to meet its fixed obligations." Continental's President Robert Six charged that United was "satisfied with the *status quo*," and said that in "resisting" the introduction of widespread coach service in the past, it had been shortsighted.

After considering the arguments, the CAB, by a three-to-two vote, suspended Continental's plan because, in the words of the majority, "there is substantial question as to the economic validity of the proposed fares if applied to the industry as a whole."

In August, 1962, Continental submitted a revised proposal for economy

---

[7] *Brief of United Air Lines* (CAB Docket No. 8008).

fares to the CAB. The new proposal was widely interpreted as an attempt to appease those who objected that the original plan would result in lower total profits for the airlines. The revised plan would establish economy fares 20 percent below conventional coach fares, instead of 25 percent as originally proposed, and it would in effect raise conventional coach fares by establishing a nearly identical "business class" with fares about 10 percent higher than the older coach fares. This was a step United had long advocated in the belief that the spread between first-class and coach fares was too wide and not commensurate with the difference in comfort and service. United had argued that higher coach fares would stop the shift from first-class to coach travel. Moreover, the revised plan called for the fares only on the Chicago–Kansas City–Denver–Los Angeles routes, and some flights would still provide the former first-class and coach service at the old rates. In revised form the CAB permitted a six-month "experiment" proposed by President Six, but carefully hedged its approval. According to *The Wall Street Journal,* "the CAB said it's 'uncertain' what 'appeal' the reduced fares would have to the public and we cannot, therefore, forecast accurately the impact of the proposal on the net revenue of the carriers." However, the board added, "a controlled experiment such as has been suggested may provide answers to problems confronting the industry."

EXHIBIT 5–3D

Revenue Passenger-Miles and Fare Yield per Revenue
Passenger-Mile, Domestic Air Traffic, 1946–61

	Revenue Passenger-Miles (in millions)			Average Fare Yield per Passenger-Mile*
Year	First Class	Coach	Total	
1946				4.63¢
1947				5.06
1948				5.76
1949			Coach service introduced	5.76
1950	6,710	1,056	7,766	5.55
1951	8,939	1,272	10,211	5.60
1952	9,775	2,346	12,121	5.55
1953	10,580	3,717	14,247	5.45
1954	10,925	5,321	16,246	5.40
1955	12,501	6,716	19,217	5.35
1956	13,577	8,066	21,643	5.32
1957	15,012	9,487	24,449	5.30
1958	14,391	10,045	24,436 Jet service introduced	5.63
1959	15,853	12,274	28,127	5.87
1960	14,846	14,387	29,233	6.08
1961†	13,700	15,400	29,100	n.a.‡

* Weighted average of fares and miles flown at each fare. Yield can decline either from a price decrease or from a shift of passengers from first-class to coach service.

† Estimated by Continental in early 1961. The total was later revised to 29.3 billion. Actual total was 29.5, according to *Forbes* magazine, May, 1962, p. 20.

‡ Not available.

Among the lines in direct competition with Continental, United and American immediately filed and were granted similar petitions for the Chicago–Denver–Los Angeles routes. United billed its classes as "New Economy First Class" and "New Economy Coach," with fares identical to Continental's. TWA, however, chose not to match the other lines. Instead, it inaugurated "a new Briefcase Commuter Service" featuring bar service and better meals at regular coach fares.

Shortly after the "experiment" started, *The Wall Street Journal* reported: "Several carriers protested [to the CAB] that the experiment would undercut fares far beyond those on the Chicago–West Coast routes and destroy the test by tempting travelers to go out of their way via the cheaper flights." The CAB noted that "restrictions on connecting traffic are more likely to impair than enhance the validity of the experiment," since 36 percent of Continental's traffic normally was connecting traffic.

Continental's experiment was generally acknowledged to be the most important up to that time in attempting to broaden the market for air travel. Other airlines had experimented with reduced fares; but generally, they had dealt with special travel markets. Eastern's Air-Bus, already mentioned, serves as low-cost air transportation to Florida for vacation travelers. Eastern also inaugurated piston-engine "no-reservation shuttle service" between Boston, New York, and Washington in an attempt to be competitive in a heavy travel market. M. A. MacIntyre, President of Eastern, reported in June, 1962, that "since the shuttle service began, total Boston–New York–Washington air traffic has increased 41% . . . [while] Eastern's share . . . has jumped to 60% from 30%." Mr. MacIntyre also reported shuttle service earnings of $700,000 before taxes for the first quarter, while total earnings of the company were $173,000 after taxes.

Allegheny Airlines and TWA also operated a no-reservation shuttle service between Philadelphia and Pittsburgh at a fare of about $15 (in

EXHIBIT 5–3E

Comparison of Economy Fares with Other Air Fares and
Surface Transportation Fares

	Chicago–Los Angeles	Chicago–Denver
Air first class	$131.40	$68.00
Air coach	102.30	53.75
Original economy proposal	77.00	39.00
Accepted "business class"	116.00	61.00
Accepted "economy"	85.00	44.00
Rail first class	85.56	39.95
Rail coach	67.39	31.46
Bus	54.30	24.60

Source: "Business class" and accepted "economy" fares obtained from official Continental Airlines schedule, effective October 28, 1962. All other fares supplied by Continental documents as of 1961.

1960). Regular first-class passengers had priority on the seats, while vacant seats were sold to those who walked on at the low fare. Both air lines in 1960 reported high passenger load factors, with a 60–40 split between first-class and walk-on passengers.

Pacific Southwest Airlines, a local California carrier, operated an extremely low-fare service between San Diego, Los Angeles, and San Francisco. It boasted fares of only 3.8 cents per mile (as opposed to Eastern's 6.5 cents on its shuttle service) and large, fast Electra planes. As a result, the 1½-hour trip between Los Angeles and San Francisco cost only $13.50, compared with $12.65 for train and $9.61 for bus, both of which took ten hours. According to an article in the June 30, 1962, issue of *Business Week:*

> Pacific Southwest insists it has attracted new air travelers. . . . About 30% of its weekend passengers are Navy personnel, most of whom used to ride the bus or else hitch-hike. . . .
>
> On holidays, when business travel is lightest, PSA has been jammed with customers. Last Easter Sunday, it . . . carried an average of 90 per flight

EXHIBIT 5–3F

**Some Selected Comparisons of Air Travel
to Other Modes of Transportation**

INTERCITY REVENUE PASSENGER–MILES, AIR VERSUS
TOTAL COMMON CARRIER*

Year	Percent of Total Common Carrier Passenger-Miles
1940	3
1950	14
1960	49

AUTOMOBILE AND COMMON CARRIERS, 1960*

Mode of Transportation	Percent of Total Intercity Revenue Passenger-Miles
Air	4.2
Rail	2.4
Bus	2.0
Automobile	91.4

REVENUE PASSENGER–MILES (MILLIONS)†

Year	First-Class Parlor and Sleeping Cars	Airlines	Airlines as Percent of Total
1949	9,349	6,753	41.9
1953	7,950	14,760	65.0
1959	3,773	29,269	88.6

* Source: United Air Lines.
† Source: Federal Aviation Administration, *FAA Statistical Handbook of Aviation* (Washington, D.C.: U.S. Government Printing Office, 1960).

(capacity 98) and on the Thanksgiving weekend, it carried . . . 94 per flight.

. . . At the same time it is undoubtedly true that regular air travelers are flying PSA to save money. It gives them a ride almost as fast as the more expensive pure jet, makes a point of being on time and doesn't charge for costly frills. . . . United admits its load factor . . . has dropped about 10% this year.

A survey of reasons given for travel in 1954 led one student of the industry to draw the following three conclusions, which he felt indicated the extent of the problem of finding a mass market for air travel:[8]

1. All reasons can be assigned to either a business requirement, a personal desire, or a genuine emergency.
2. Rarely has a form of common carrier transportation, in and by itself, constituted a bona fide "reason" for travel.
3. The discovery of a "new reason" to motivate passenger travel is rare to the point of nonexistence.

Exhibits 5–3D, 5–3E, and 5–3F present additional information and data pertinent to the airline industry.

Questions

1. Is the market for air travel elastic or inelastic? What factors should be considered?
2. Suppose you were a board member of the CAB who felt that the "economy fare" proposed should be allowed a trial. How would you design an "experiment" to test the theory that the demand for air travel is elastic? That is, what results would you look for, and what controls or limitations, if any, would you put on the test?
3. What has happened to commercial air fares since the time of this report?

CASE 5–4. Problems in Demand Analysis for the Firm

1. You are trying to measure the price elasticity of demand for Qwerts, a typewriter produced by a small independent, Qwerts, Inc. You find that in 1954, at a price of $85, 50,000 units were sold, and that in 1955, at a price of $80, 60,000 were sold. From these data you compute price elasticity and find that it is $-x$.

However, you are certain that "other things" did not remain constant during the years in question, and want to make some allowance for them in your analysis of elasticity. So you make a list of them:

---

[8] Graham H. Aldrich in "Market Analysis of Air Traffic Potential," a paper presented in 1954, as cited by John H. Frederick in *Commercial Air Transportation* (5th ed.; Homewood, Ill.: Richard D. Irwin, Inc., 1961), p. 371.

1.1   Consumer income rose 15 percent.

1.2   Your competitors increased their prices 10 percent.

1.3   You received news from your sales force that for some reason, apparently independent of price or income, they were finding increased sales resistance to Qwerts. They felt that perhaps the company was not improving Qwerts as rapidly as was the competition.

1.4   The proportion of their incomes spent by consumers for products of the typewriter industry dropped rather sharply—30 percent.

a. Indicate *diagrammatically* (do not try to quantify) how much of the change in quantity which you measured was due to the change in price, and how much due to the "other factor." (Treat each event separately; do *not* try to sum them.)

b. In each case, was the measure you calculated greater than, equal to, or less than what was probably the "true" elasticity, that is, elasticity adjusted for the "other" factor? (Be sure to treat each of the four cases *independently.*)

2. Mr. Peck, president of Imperial Zinc Corporation, is approached by his sales manager who suggests that if prices are lowered on Item 345, sales and profits can be increased. At present, when sales are 100,000 units, variable costs are 40 percent of total revenue, the allocated fixed costs are 50 percent of total revenue, and profits are 10 percent. The product at present is selling at $2. The sales manager asserts that if prices are cut by 10 percent, total profits will be one and one-half times what they are now. The president is told that the company has plenty of capacity and that there will be no increase in overhead if sales are as great as predicted.

    a. How many units must be sold at the new price if the sales manager's prediction is to be correct?

    b. What price elasticity is necessary if the sales manager's predictions are to be realized?

3. The Widget Manufacturing Company experienced the following weekly sales.

Week	Price	Sales
1	$1.00	$1,200,000
2	1.10	1,100,000

    a. What is the price elasticity of demand?

    b. What factors could make this estimate incorrect?

chapter **6**

Short-Run Private Costs
of Production

IT IS USEFUL in economics to distinguish between short-run and long-run production possibilities and costs.[1] These periods are defined in terms of the economic events considered to be possible rather than in time as measured by the clock or calendar. Accordingly, the short run may be defined as a period too brief to permit full adjustment of all inputs in an industry to demand for the final product. Adjustment is especially likely to be incomplete if demand for the product or the production technology has recently changed markedly.[2] More precisely, this distinction between long-run and short-run means that some resources cannot be increased without incurring costs in excess of current costs. A new machine could likely be purchased from another firm and installed overnight provided the firm is willing to bear the costs. There are no doubt situations where such a procedure is desirable.

A businessman in a field of manufacturing is ordinarily confronted somewhat infrequently with long-run problems such as changing machines and processes, establishing programs for training labor, or altering plant capacity. He is confronted daily with the short-run problem of determining rate of output and perhaps prices to be charged for output

---

[1] This chapter focuses on private costs of production. Other costs may be incurred as a result of private decision making such as pollution. These are analyzed in Chapter 8.

[2] The distinction between short run and long run is due to Alfred Marshall. He summarized the former as follows: "To sum up then as regards short periods. The supply of specialized skill and ability, of suitable machinery and other material capital, and of the appropriate industrial organization has not time to be fully adapted to demand; but the producers have to adjust their supply to the demand as best they can with the appliances already at their disposal." (*Principles of Economics*, 8th ed. [London: Macmillan & Co., Ltd., 1930], p. 376).

and to be paid for inputs. As pointed out above, short- and long-run problems are intermingled and even difficult to classify. However, fruitful analysis requires simplification and a willingness to hold in *ceteris paribus* (i.e., assume to be unchanged) variables that in practice refuse to hold still as a favor to the analyst. A caution needs to be inserted here, however: the analyst should not assume constancy of a variable which could not conceivably remain constant because it is closely related to a variable that is permitted to change in magnitude in the analysis. For example, the demand for oleomargarine should not be assumed constant when the effect of changes in the price of butter on sales of butter is being considered.

Opportunity Cost

A most important concept in economics is "opportunity cost." This conceives of the true cost of any activity as consisting of whatever is given up in order to carry on the activity. The idea is basic since economics is the science of using scarce resources to satisfy unlimited wants as fully as possible. Resource owners must be paid prices at least as high as they could command in alternative employment opportunities. A successful bid for a resource and its employment in one type of economic activity denies its use for another product.

The opportunity cost idea fits the field of business economics especially well since it suggests the choice which managers must continually make among numerous opportunities for the use of available resources. These are so numerous that they can only be suggested: filling a position with one man costs the firm the potential contribution of another at the same salary; choosing one location for a plant costs the advantages of another site; producing one product costs the income that could have been secured with an alternative product; even choosing to take a vacation costs the income that could otherwise have been earned.

Economic thinking focuses on present opportunities, sometimes in the form of capital values based on present expectations regarding the future. For example, ownership of stock in a corporation entails sacrifice of the opportunity of converting this asset into cash; consequently, the stock should not continue to be held unless the owner would be willing to buy it at today's market price. (Consideration needs to be given, however, to commissions, taxes, and the value of the owner's time in making transactions.) Similarly, if one is calculating the monthly cost of living in a house which he owns, the actual purchase price of the house is irrelevant to the calculation. The same is true of depreciation based on the actual cost. Instead, to operating and maintenance costs, insurance, and taxes the homeowner should add interest on the present sales value and depreciation equal to the expected decline in sales value during the period for which the cost calculation is made.³ The interest rate properly involved in the calculation is a rate attainable with equal risk in an alternate present investment of funds that could be withdrawn from the house by its immediate sale.

While this sort of opportunity cost thinking should be (and in large part actually is) at the heart of managerial decision making, it can sound strange to a student who has specialized in accounting. For tax purposes especially, definite accounting rules must be followed—rules such as evaluating a fixed asset at its actual cost less depreciation according to an acceptable formula. After a period of inflation and other typical

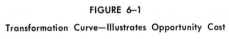

FIGURE 6–1

Transformation Curve—Illustrates Opportunity Cost

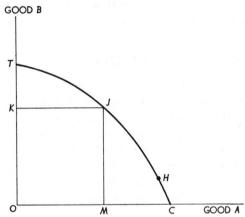

economic changes, the book value of a commercial building is likely to be far below its actual sales value. In general, accountants are moving in the direction of incorporating evaluation of present opportunities in their accounts but are hampered by tax laws and traditional habits of thought.

The idea of opportunity cost can be illustrated by a simple chart, Figure 6–1. If two commodities A and B can be produced with resources available to a firm, the transformation curve TC can be considered to connect all possible output combinations. The company could, during the period, produce OT of good B and none of A, OC of A and none of B, or any combination lying on the curve, such as OM of A and OK of B. The slope of curve TC at any point measures the rate at which B

---

³ The depreciation cost may be negative if appreciation in value is expected. If a better speculative opportunity is seen by the homeowner, the opportunity cost of continuing to own the home includes the expected gain from the (sacrificed) better speculation less the expected gain in the value of the house.

must be sacrificed in order to produce more of A. This "marginal rate of transformation," or opportunity cost, applies to infinitesimal changes along the curve. Applying the idea to finite changes we could say that if point J is an actual combination being produced, the opportunity cost of turning out an additional TK units of B per period would be the OM units of A that could no longer be produced.

The slope of the transformation curve reflects the ability of resources to switch effectively from one product to the other. For example, some of the workers may be more skilled in producing A and others better at tasks associated with B. If the combination at H were being produced, the opportunity cost in terms of product B of increasing the output of A would be large because workers who are quite poor at producing A would have to be diverted from B. If all resources were equally well adapted to both goods, the transformation curve would be linear. Opportunity cost would be independent of relative output rates.[4]

Production Possibilities for a Single Good

In order to understand the meaning of separating production possibilities and costs into "short run" and "long run," it is useful to consider only one good produced with two inputs. For example, in Figure 6–2 good A can be considered to be produced with only labor and capital (both broadly defined), the possible output being larger the greater the input of these factors. Curves labeled I, II, III, IV are "production isoquants," referring successively to larger outputs of A, each curve reflecting a particular output attainable by use of the input combinations which it connects.

The curvature of any production isoquant reflects the possibilities of substituting one input for the other without changing output. Isoquants are concave upward reflecting, for example, the increasing technical difficulty of substituting labor for capital when the ratio of labor to capital is already high.

Figure 6–2 also includes "isocost lines" C_1L_1, C_2L_2, C_3L_3, and C_4L_4, each connecting the input combinations purchasable by the firm for a particular outlay. If no labor were hired, OC_1 would be the number of units of capital that could be purchased per period for a given outlay, OC_2 for a larger outlay, and so forth. Similarly, OL_1, OL_2, and so forth, could be hired for the same outlays if no capital were purchased. In practice both resources would be hired, the objective of the firm being the attainment of maximum output for any given outlay. These maxima are found at the points of tangency with isoquants. Alternatively, the tan-

---

[4] For a fuller but elementary presentation dealing with transformation curve, see Benjamin Ward, *Elementary Price Theory* (New York: The Free Press, 1967), chap. 5.

FIGURE 6–2

Production Isoquants—and Expansion Paths

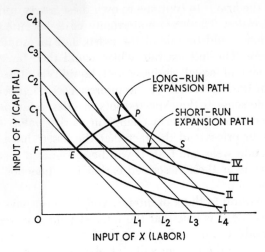

gency points represent the minimum costs of producing a specified output. Line *EP* connects such points of tangency and can be called the "long-run expansion path." The implicit assumption is that any number of additional isoquants could have been drawn so that any combination of inputs along *EP* (or its extension in both directions) would be a possibility provided sufficient time is permitted for adjustment.

In the short run it is useful to assume that capital input is fixed (at *OF*) so that output can be increased only by increasing the use of labor. Since one resource is fixed and hence its costs are fixed, short-run costs are minimized by allowing only the variable input to vary and using the least possible amount of this factor to produce a given output. This restricts the firm to the "short-run expansion path" *FS*.

Fixed and Variable Costs

Short-run cost curves useful in managerial decision making are related to the analysis of production possibilities in Figure 6–2. Corresponding to the fixed input of capital services and variable input of labor services along path *FS* are "fixed costs" and "variable costs" of production. The former are those which can be considered to be unaffected in their total by variations in the rate of use of existing capacity. The latter are those which vary in total with the rate of output.

Fixed costs from an economic point of view are quite different from those to which the study of accounting accustoms us. The reason is the need to ground economics on the opportunity cost idea. Consequently, the basic fixed costs of an enterprise consist of interest and "depreciation" on the present value of buildings and equipment. These cannot be avoided if the firm is to continue to own these assets during the period under consideration. These are opportunity costs because an alternative course of action would be sale of the assets and investment of the proceeds elsewhere. The interest rate which could then be secured on another investment of equal riskiness and liquidity is the one which is appropriate in the calculation of the interest cost. Depreciation as used in an economic sense is the expected loss in sales value over the period under consideration. This loss or change in market value is the result of both changes in prices and the fact that the assets have lost potential service life due to wear and tear. It will be recognized that these principles are the same as those described earlier in connection with the cost of home ownership.

It is quite natural to think of interest which a firm pays on its debt as a fixed cost. While it is true that the interest paid may remain constant over long periods it is not a fixed cost from the economic point of view. Once all interest on the present value of plant has been included in fixed cost it would be double counting also to include interest paid on the bonds which were used in part to finance the purchase of fixed assets.

Certain other costs such as administrative salaries, fire insurance, and license fees are usually considered to be "fixed costs" from a short-run point of view. While important to the accountant these can best be neglected from an economic point of view. They do not affect short-run decisions—there is no alternative opportunity open to the firm which has committed itself for a time to such costs. An exception would occur if the license, for example, could be sold. Then it would be similar to plant which could be disposed of, and the interest lost by holding the license would be a fixed cost during the short period under analysis.

Variable costs are quite similar whether one takes an economic or accounting viewpoint. Labor costs, social security taxes, material costs, cost of fuel, and cost of electric power vary with the rate of output and easily fit in with the idea of variable costs. They are clearly opportunity costs since funds currently expended on these items could alternatively be spent in other ways. Their prices reflect alternative uses to which the resources could have been put.

Relationship of Costs to Production Function

It should be clear that costs of production will be influenced by the shape of the production function. In effect, the production function represents the technological relationships between the input factors and the way in which physical substitution can take place, that is, the exchange of additional machine-hours for labor hours. The production

function is drawn or formulated to illustrate technologically efficient resource combinations. The slope of a production isoquant is called the
"marginal rate of substitution." The interest of the economist or businessman is to choose an input combination which considers not only technological efficiency but also economic efficiency. Hence, the tangency
solution referred to above represents this idea.

It was noted above that in the short run, a firm will vary input use
along the short-run expansion path. Thus, if demand is known, costs will
be minimized by minimizing the variable resource—in this two-input

FIGURE 6–3

Total and Unit Costs—Linear Total Cost

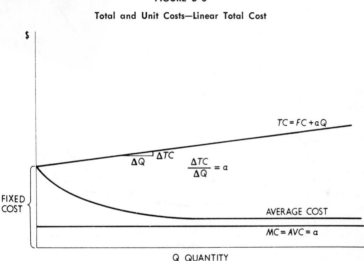

case, labor hours—and using the fixed resource to capacity. The total
cost of a particular output will be the sum of the fixed resource cost plus
the variable cost. If variable costs increased directly proportional to output, then total cost will be a linear function of output: $TC = FC + aQ$,
where TC = total costs, FC = fixed costs, a = variable cost per unit,
and Q = output. Figure 6–3 illustrates a cost curve of this type. Also
shown are the unit cost curves associated with a total cost curve of this
type. As is shown, average variable cost (AVC) and marginal cost (MC)
are constant and equal to a which is the slope of the total cost curve.
Marginal cost is defined as the addition to total cost as the result of an
additional unit of output, or the rate of change in total cost, that is,
$\Delta TC/\Delta Q$. Average variable cost is total variable cost of a given output
quantity divided by that quantity TVC/Q. Average total cost or average
cost is total cost divided by output.

The usual expectation is that as more of a variable input factor is added to a fixed factor, output will first increase at an increasing rate, then level off and then increase at a decreasing rate.[5] This characteristic of the production function translates into total and unit cost curves of the general shapes indicated in Figure 6–4.

Total cost here first increases at decreasing rate and then at an increasing rate. This means that marginal cost first decreases, levels, and then increases. Marginal cost thus varies inversely with marginal product

FIGURE 6–4

Typical Total and Unit Cost Curves

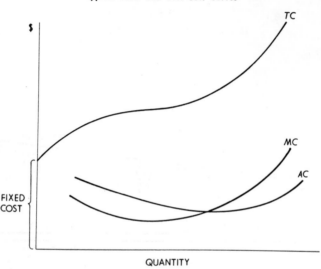

of the variable factor.[6] A very interesting relationship between marginal and average cost is also illustrated in Figure 6–4. When marginal cost is below average cost, average cost is declining. When marginal cost is equal to average cost, average cost is constant. When marginal cost is above average cost, average cost is rising.

---

[5] This change in output as variable inputs are changed is usually called the marginal product of the variable factor, for example, the rate of change of total product for a change in the variable factor holding constant the fixed factor.

[6] This can be shown as follows:

$$MC = \frac{\Delta TC}{\Delta Q} = \frac{\text{Increase in variable factors}}{\text{Increase in quantity}} \times \text{Price of variable factors}$$

since,

$$\text{Marginal product of variable factors} = \frac{\text{Increase in quantity}}{\text{Increase in variable factors}}$$

$$MC = \frac{\text{Price of variable factor}}{\text{Marginal product of variable factor}}$$

Hypothetical Cost Data

A short-run cost schedule for a factory is shown in Figure 6–5, the data being hypothetical and simplified in order to illustrate the basic points. Output is assumed to be capable of varying from 0 to 20 units per day, depending on how much is spent on variable inputs. Total fixed costs (column 2) remain at $32. These consist of interest and depreciation per day on the present value of the plant.

Total variable costs (column 4) rise continually as output increases, rising at first by decreasing increments and later by increasing additions. These increments are shown in column 8 as "marginal cost"—the cost added when one more unit is produced per period. (Marginal cost can be measured either as additional total variable costs or additional total costs.) This pattern of marginal cost is traceable to operation of the famous law of diminishing returns. In the low output range (one to six units) the efficiency of organization of production increases as more labor, materials, and other variable inputs are used in conjunction with the fixed plant. A better proportion is attained between fixed and variable inputs, and this shows up in the declining rate of increase in total variable costs. Above a daily output of seven units, the factory is op-

FIGURE 6–5

Daily Cost Schedule for a Small Factory

(1) Output (no. of units)	(2) Total Fixed Costs	(3) Average Fixed Cost	(4) Total Variable Costs	(5) Average Variable Cost	(6) Total of All Costs	(7) Average Total Cost	(8) Marginal Cost
1	$32.00	$32.00	$ 7.20	$ 7.20	$ 39.20	$39.20	$ 7.20
2	32.00	16.00	12.90	6.45	44.90	22.45	5.70
3	32.00	10.67	17.40	5.80	49.40	16.47	4.50
4	32.00	8.00	21.00	5.25	53.00	13.25	3.60
5	32.00	6.40	24.00	4.80	56.00	11.20	3.00
6	32.00	5.33	26.70	4.45	58.70	9.78	2.70
7	32.00	4.57	29.40	4.20	61.40	8.77	2.70
8	32.00	4.00	32.40	4.05	64.40	8.05	3.00
9	32.00	3.55	36.00	4.00	68.00	7.55	3.60
10	32.00	3.20	40.50	4.05	72.50	7.25	4.50
11	32.00	2.91	46.20	4.20	78.20	7.11	5.70
12	32.00	2.67	53.40	4.45	85.40	7.12	7.20
13	32.00	2.46	62.40	4.80	94.40	7.26	9.00
14	32.00	2.28	73.50	5.25	105.50	7.53	11.10
15	32.00	2.13	87.00	5.80	119.00	7.93	13.50
16	32.00	2.00	103.20	6.45	135.20	8.45	16.20
17	32.00	1.88	122.40	7.20	154.40	9.08	19.20
18	32.00	1.78	144.90	8.05	176.90	9.83	22.50
19	32.00	1.68	171.00	9.00	203.00	10.68	26.10
20	32.00	1.60	201.00	10.05	233.00	11.65	30.00

Source: Albert L. Meyers, *Elements of Modern Economics* (3d ed.; Englewood Cliffs, N.J.: Prentice-Hall, Inc., 1948), p. 158. Reproduced by permission.

erating in the stage of diminishing marginal returns, which causes marginal costs to rise.[7]

Average variable cost can decline even after marginal cost begins to rise. This is apparent at outputs of eight and nine units. When average variable cost is at a minimum it is equal to marginal cost. (This would occur between 9 and 10 units if units were divisible.) Average total cost continues to decline after average variable cost turns up (due to the influence of average fixed cost).

Average and Marginal Cost Curves

It is usually more convenient to work with cost curves rather than a schedule. For many purposes the curves can be sketched without de-

FIGURE 6–6

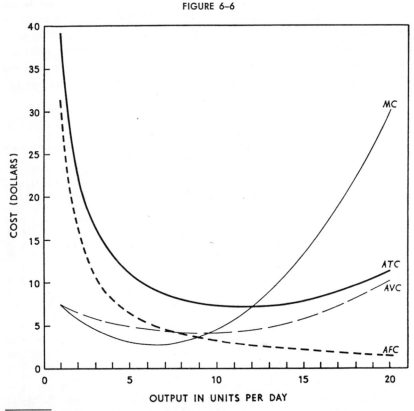

_____

[7] Increasing and decreasing marginal returns can be traced in a chart of the type shown in Figure 6–2. If each higher isoquant represents the same increment in output (e.g., if they were labeled 1, 2, 3, 4,— or 10, 20, 30—), increasing returns to labor input would be reflected in decreasing distances between isoquants along path *FS*; farther to the right the distance between isoquants would increase, reflecting diminishing marginal returns.

fining units along the axes. Figure 6–6, however, shows four cost curves that correspond with the data in Figure 6–5 except that units of output are assumed to be fully divisible rather than discrete. Average fixed cost (*AFC*) is of little importance except as a reminder of the source of high cost per unit when fixed capacity is lightly utilized. Average variable cost is of some importance since it is usually better to shut down than to operate if price does not at least cover average variable cost.[8] Average total cost (*ATC*) is useful in gauging whether returns on capital tied up in fixed plant are adequate. The amount left to compensate for the use of capital consists of total revenue minus total variable costs. This residual is often called "cash flow," and this usage will be followed. Part of the cash flow can be considered to make up for depreciation in value of the plant. Any remainder permits interest to be earned on the plant.

While price minus average total cost is often referred to as "profit per unit" and total returns minus total costs as "profit," this differs greatly from accounting profit. Accountants include only interest on debt as a cost, whereas economists include only opportunity interest earnings. Accountants compute depreciation on original cost according to permissible formulas while expected change in market value of capital assets is in line with the economist's viewpoint. Profit as measured in economics has nothing to do with income tax liability. Instead, the persistence of losses in the economic sense may be a signal to leave the industry, while economic profits tend to attract additional competition.

It should be noted that because of the opportunity cost viewpoint in economics, a high cost firm is not necessarily an inefficient firm. Actually it may be unusually efficient in the sense of being able readily to produce other products. For example, if a skilled surgeon decided to try his hand at commercial fishing for a year he would be a very high-cost fisherman because his time should be charged at the rate he could have earned as a doctor. If he is also a poor fisherman the cost per pound of his catch will be still higher!

Output under Competitive Conditions

Under highly competitive conditions, market price is determined by supply and demand: The individual firm cannot affect this price but does have the problem of adjusting its output rate to this price. The cost curves of Figure 6–6 are useful in understanding this adjustment.

The key curve is that of marginal cost. Ordinarily the firm should

---

[8] The qualification "usually" is inserted because it is not difficult to visualize many possible exceptions to the rule. For example, special shutdown and subsequent start-up costs may exist, costs may have to be incurred to rehire and retrain workers, or customers may be lost who could contribute to later profits.

produce at a rate which equates marginal cost with the market price.[9] This follows logically from the definition of marginal cost as the *additional* cost of increasing the output. Since price of the product shows the added revenue from an extra unit of output, all units should be produced for which marginal cost is below price.

If price is temporarily below the lowest possible average variable cost, the firm should ordinarily cease production (except for additional considerations of the sorts already mentioned). Even if all variable costs are being met but price is below average total cost, the activity is not a good one unless there is an expectation of improvement. It is possible that steps should be taken immediately to alter production processes or to abandon the activity. These possibilities are analyzed at a later point in the book.

All or Nothing Decision

In the ordinary analysis of the relation of cost to output it is assumed that the competitive firm has complete freedom to adjust its rate of output and that it will choose the rate at which marginal cost equals price. The "short-run supply curve" is the marginal cost curve above and to the right of minimum average variable cost because this determines the optimum quantity to supply at any given price.

During a period of seasonal or cyclical slack demand, management may instead be willing to consider an "all or nothing" offer from a buyer. There may be no options open to the producer except to reject or accept the offer. For example, a contract to produce 10,000 suits of a particular variety at $25 per suit may have to be considered even if the tailoring firm ordinarily can sell such garments at $35 each. Under such an all-or-none offer the average variable cost curve, rather than marginal cost, constitutes the supply curve.[10] That is, the offer is worth accepting if average variable cost at that output rate is below $25 since this would leave some cash flow to apply against fixed costs. The offer should be turned down if *AVC* exceeds $25 because the $250,000 revenue would not even cover variable costs. There may, of course, be good reasons apart from immediate revenue and cost which would cause a firm to accept an offer that did not quite cover variable costs. An important reason might be labor turnover costs if present workers would otherwise be laid off.

---

[9] Marginal cost must be rising. If it is falling the output is the *worst* possible since the firm will have produced all units which add more to cost than to revenue and none which add more to revenue than to cost.

[10] In one sense marginal cost still governs the decision since the entire block of 10,000 suits constitutes one unit. Marginal cost per suit is total variable cost divided by 10,000; this is the same as variable cost per suit.

Adaptability and Divisibility of Plant

As a matter of convenience in drawing, curves depicting average total, average variable, and marginal costs are usually made markedly U-shaped. Geometric elegance and economic relevance are often at odds, however, and it should be recognized that many other shapes are quite possible in the real world.

Marginal cost is often approximately constant over a wide range of output. This would clearly be the case for a firm which purchases and resells commodities instead of manufacturing them. If all additional quantities of a good (say TV sets) could be bought at the same price from the manufacturer, the retailer's marginal costs would be nearly the same regardless of the volume. The marginal cost curve would not be completely horizontal, however, because of economies and diseconomies of handling, storage, display, and selling.

If attention is concentrated on producers of goods, it is useful to examine the concepts "adaptability" and "divisibility" as they apply to plant capacity.[11] A plant may be said to be "adaptable" to the extent that it is capable of being used with changing amounts of variable inputs. A piece of farmland, for example, is quite adaptable to different amounts of fertilizer and labor, while a steam shovel is highly unadaptable in that it can be used with only one operator at a time. Plant capacity is highly "divisible" when it contains a large number of identical machines—for example, 20 identical machines for producing concrete blocks, 50 nail-making machines, or 10 printing presses within a single establishment. Complete indivisibility exists when, for example, the plant consists of one long assembly line, each station of which is wholly dependent on the previous ones.

Divisible but unadaptable plants are common in manufacturing since many machines are built to operate at only one rate and require a fixed number of operators and specific amounts of material per time period. In this case, marginal costs are constant over a wide range of output. In order to secure more output, a greater number of machines is utilized, and each requires a fixed complement of labor, power, and materials; consequently, each one adds the same amount to cost as did the previous ones. Reduced output in this case is attained by shutting down a number of machines, and each one which is shut down reduces total variable cost by the same amount.

If plant capacity is indivisible but highly adaptable, a U-shaped marginal cost curve will result. Marginal costs will at first fall, as a better proportion is attained between the indivisible fixed plant and the variable inputs; but eventually, the proportions will become less compatible,

---

[11] See George J. Stigler, "Production and Distribution in the Short Run," *Journal of Political Economy*, June, 1939, pp. 305–27.

and marginal costs will rise. This is the assumption on which Figure 6–6 is based.

If, instead, the plant is divisible but unadaptable—for example, an apparel plant with ten sewing machines each requiring one operator— the marginal cost "curve" will consist of ten horizontal dots, as in Figure 6–7. The same dots will reflect average variable cost. Average total cost will decline, however, as fixed costs are spread over more output.[12]

Still another possibility is an "all or none" output based on technical factors. An atomic reactor may operate at a fixed rate if it operates at all,

FIGURE 6–7

Divisible and Unadaptable Plant—
Marginal Costs Are Constant

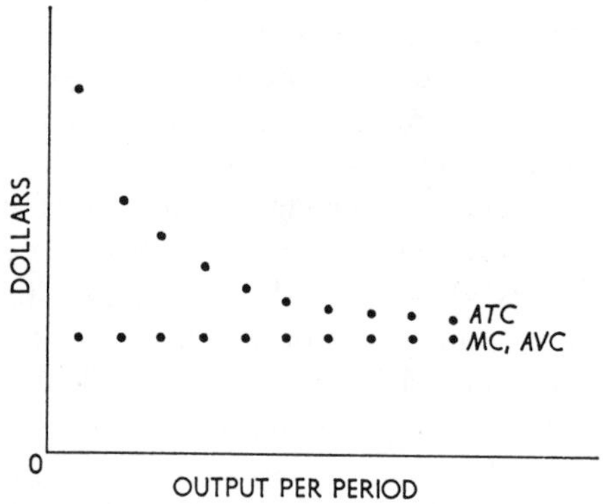

or a blast furnace must either go at full blast or not at all. A legal requirement, for example, an Interstate Commerce Commission order that a certain passenger train be run on a particular schedule, also requires a fixed output (if number of passengers carried does not enter into definition of output).

In these cases plant is both indivisible and unadaptable. Marginal cost and average variable cost become a single (and the same) dot. Average total cost becomes a single dot at the same output, its distance above the other depending on average fixed costs. In general, the progress of technology appears to be moving manufacturing and even farming in the direction of more nearly fixed production coefficients.

Statistical Cost Analysis

Just as statistical analysis often proves useful in the analysis of demand, the statistical technique of multiple regression analysis is often

---

[12] This assumes that fixed costs cannot be eliminated by renting out unused machines or, if the firm does not own the machines, by renting only the number needed.

useful in determining type of cost structure which is present in a business. Of particular interest in pricing and output decisions is the knowledge of whether or not marginal cost is constant as in Figure 6–3 or rising in the relevant range as in Figure 6–4. Regression analysis may provide an answer to this question.[13]

One method of proceeding is to determine whether a linear cost function of the form $TC = a + bQ$ where a is fixed costs and b is variable costs as determined empirically fits better than a curveilinear cost function. One possible curveilinear cost function might be $TC = a + bQ + cQ^2$ where a is fixed cost and b and c are the intercept and slope of a linear marginal cost curve. Since marginal cost is the slope or derivative of TC, it would be $MC = b + 2cQ$ from this equation. If c were positive, the analysis would indicate a rising marginal cost curve. Case 6–5 illustrates another form of nonconstant marginal cost.

APPENDIX A TO CHAPTER 6. Optimal Inventory Policy

A common problem facing many firms is the determination of an inventory policy which minimizes the total costs of carrying inventory. In the simplest case these costs consist of reorder costs and the variable costs of carrying inventory. Reorder costs vary with the number of orders placed, and the costs of carrying inventory vary with size of the average level of inventory.

The inventory carrying cost is directly related to the average level of inventory. If an order is received on the first day of the month and is sold over the month so that none is on hand the last day of the month, the average amount on hand will be equal to the beginning amount plus the ending amount divided by 2. That is, if the order size is equal to Q, then the average inventory is given by

$$\frac{Q + 0}{2} = \frac{Q}{2}$$

If we let i represent the dollar interest and other costs of holding an item in inventory for one year, then the annual carrying cost of holding the average number of units in inventory will be $= iQ/2$.

The reorder costs will be a function of the number of orders per year. The number of orders per year will depend upon annual sales and the size of each order, or if $S =$ annual sales, then the number of orders will $= S/Q$. If the cost per order is equal to $\$b$, then the total ordering cost will $= bS/Q$.

---

[13] See J. Johnston, *Statistical Cost Analysis* (New York: McGraw-Hill Book Co., 1960), for a survey of a large number of industry studies of cost and for helpful information on methodology.

The total inventory costs can now be expressed as the sum of these two costs or

$$TC = \frac{iQ}{2} + \frac{bS}{Q}$$

Figure 6–8 shows a graphic representation of the costs. Average inventory carrying costs increase as the size of the order increases, but the average costs of ordering decreases as the size of orders increases. Thus,

FIGURE 6–8

Inventory Costs—Order Costs and Carrying Costs

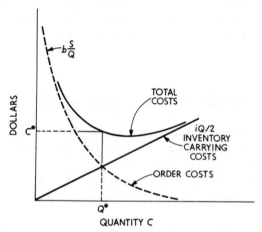

the problem is to find the size of order which minimizes total inventory costs. This size is given by finding the minimum value of the expression above. Taking the derivatives with respect to Q and setting the resulting expression $= 0$ meets the first-order condition for a minimum:

$$\frac{dTc}{dQ} = \frac{i}{2} - \frac{bS}{Q^2} = 0$$

$$Q^2 = \frac{2bS}{i}$$

$$Q^* = \sqrt{\frac{2bs}{i}}$$

Thus the optimal reorder size, Q^*, is given by the square root of $2bS/i$. That is, the optimum size order vary directly with annual sales and reorder costs and inversely with inventory carrying costs.

In this simple formula an optimum order size can be determined. Most inventory systems are more complex and require more complicated variations of the model in order to optimize inventory costs. There are many books which deal with complex inventory problems.[14]

APPENDIX B TO CHAPTER 6. Linear Programming Methods and Cost Minimization

Although linear programming is strictly speaking a mathematical method for either maximizing or minimizing a linear function subject to a set of linear constraints, it has gained such widespread use and acceptance as a tool for business problem solving that it deserves inclusion in a book dealing with business or managerial economics. The exposition here will be concerned with some relatively simple applications of linear programming. The student who wishes to go further is referred to the books listed in the footnote below.[15]

An Example of a Linear Programming Problem

A building contractor is building a small subdivision and can build either brick or frame houses. He estimates that he will make a profit of $800 per house on the frame houses and a profit of $1,200 per house on the brick houses. He, naturally, desires to make the maximum amount of money he can. Since he is limited to these kinds of houses, his profit objective can be expressed algebraically as the equation:

$$\text{Profit} = \pi = 800F + 1{,}200B$$

where F is the number of frame houses and B is the number of brick houses. The $800 and $1,200 coefficients represent the profit contributions per frame or brick house. This equation is called the *objective function*.

Because of long lead times and higher prices if materials are ordered specially, the contractor desires to work with the material that he has on hand. To obtain additional raw materials would increase his costs and reduce the profit margins estimated above. The contractor sets out the

---

[14] See Thomas M. Whitin, *The Theory of Inventory Management* (Princeton, N.J.: Princeton University Press, 1953); and Martin K. Starr and David W. Miller, *Inventory Control: Theory and Practice* (Englewood Cliffs, N.J.: Prentice-Hall, Inc., 1962).

[15] Robert Dorfman, Paul Samuelson, and Robert Solow, *Linear Programming and Economic Analysis* (New York: McGraw-Hill Book Co., 1958); William Baumol, *Economic Theory and Operations Analysis* (3d ed.; Englewood Cliffs, N.J.: Prentice-Hall, Inc., 1972); and George Hadley, *Linear Programming* (Reading, Mass.: Addison-Wesley Publishing Co., Inc., 1962).

requirements and available materials in a table which is reproduced below as Figure 6–9.

The requirements columns in Figure 6–9 are "recipes" for producing these types of houses, incomplete in that they concentrate only on the materials which are in limited supply. Any other materials required are assumed to cause no particular problems. Since supplies of these specific

FIGURE 6–9

Resources and Requirements for House Construction

Resources	Amount Required per House		Amount Available
	Frame	Brick	
Cement (bags)........................	20	35	280
Finish lumber (bd. ft.).................	1,000	500	9,000
Man-hours...........................	500	500	6,000
Bricks..............................	0	4,000	24,000

resources are limited, the use of a resource in the construction of a frame house precludes its being used in a brick house. These four resource limitations can be expressed as linear inequalities as below:

$$20F + 35B \leq 280$$
$$1,000F + 500B \leq 9,000$$
$$500F + 500B \leq 6,000$$
$$0F + 4,000B \leq 24,000$$

The first of these inequalities states that no more than 280 bags of cement can be used in building frame and brick houses; and therefore either 14 frame and no brick, 8 brick and no frame, or some intermediate combination of brick and frame houses which satisfies the equation $20F + 35B \leq 280$ can be built. To formally complete the structure of the problem, two additional constraints are required: $F \geq 0$ and $B \geq 0$. These are called the *nonnegativity* constraints and are designed to insure that a formal solution does not suggest the production of a negative output. The formal problem now consists of three parts:

Objective function: Maximize $\pi = 800F + 1,200B$
Subject to:
Resource constraints:

$$20F + 35B \leq 280$$
$$1,000F + 500B \leq 9,000$$
$$500F + 500B \leq 6,000$$
$$0F + 4,000B \leq 24,000$$

and

Nonnegativity constraints: $F \geq 0$
$B \geq 0.$

A graph in this two-variable case provides a very simple and direct solution method and helps illustrate the concepts. Figure 6–10 shows the effect of the cement constraint on the solution possibilities. Numbers of brick and frame houses are shown on the axes of the graph. The non-negativity constraints are enforced in Figure 6–10 by indicating only zero or positive output of each type of house. The cement constraint line shows the combinations of the maximum number of houses of both kinds which can be produced given the cement constraint. Fewer houses

FIGURE 6–10

"Cement" Constraint Illustrated

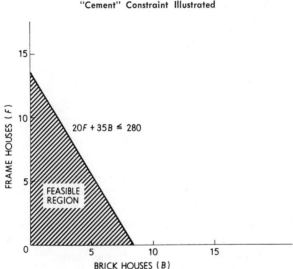

than specified on the constraint line may be produced but would use less than the total supply of cement. The region enclosed by the axes and the constraint line is known as the *feasible region*. This region will alter as the other constraints are taken into account.

In Figure 6–11 the feasible region designated by the cement constraint has been considerably reduced by the addition of further constraints. Each point in this region plus all the points on the boundary lines represent feasible combinations of frame and brick houses which can be built given the constraints of available resources. The contractor now wants to find, within the feasible region, the best, that is, most profitable, combination of houses he can build, using the objective function to define his profit possibilities.

In Figure 6–12, the feasible region has been redrawn to show only those segments of the constraint lines which define the boundaries of the feasible region. As was shown in Figure 6–11, the constraint due to

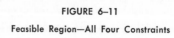

FIGURE 6–11

Feasible Region—All Four Constraints

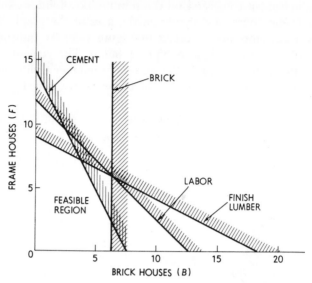

labor is not a restrictive constraint as it lies wholly outside the feasible region. The intersections of the constraint lines which define the feasible region are shown as points (B, F), identifying the numbers of brick and frame houses denoted by those intersections: for example, the intersection $(6, 3.5)$ indicates 6 brick and 3.5 frame houses.[16]

Also shown in Figure 6–12 are several profit lines, each of which represents a set of combinations of brick and frame houses which, respectively, would yield profits of $2,400, $4,800, $7,200, $10,400, and $12,000. Lines representing higher levels of profit are at successively greater distances from the origin. The objective function, Profit $= \pi = 800F + 1,200B$, was used to derive the profit lines; and it is readily apparent that these lines have the slope $-\frac{3}{2} = -\dfrac{1,200}{800}$, which reflects the ratio of profit contributions of brick and frame houses. Since $10,400 is the highest possible profit line which lies within the feasible region, it is

---

[16] The reader may rightfully question the meaning of a possible solution which indicates that 3.5 houses should be built. A realistic solution to this specific problem requires that only complete houses be built. The text will ignore (for sake of ease of presentation) the unrealism of a solution which is not an integer, although there is in fact considerable literature and a methodology available to force integer solutions where they are required.

FIGURE 6–12

Feasible Region and Equal Profit Lines Illustrated

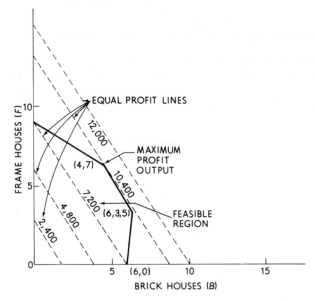

evident that the greatest profit is attained by building four brick and seven frame houses. This point, $(4, 7)$, illustrates the general principle that maximum profit output will be found at either a corner or along a boundary of the feasible region. This reduces the solution to one of checking the corners and choosing the largest profit. In fact, solution methods for more complex problems are simply algorithms for doing just that and providing tests to see that a maximum truly has been reached. These methods, while not difficult, will not be discussed in this text.[17]

This profit maximizing example has illustrated the basic concepts of linear programming. The same methodology can be applied when the objective is to minimize costs subject to certain specifications. The classic example of this type of problem is the so-called diet problem: minimization of total food cost, subject to constraints related to vitamins, caloric, and other food value inputs. Another example is the production of hot dogs which uses a variety of ingredients, some of which are subject to required minimum content. As long as the objective function and the constraints can be reasonably formulated as linear equalities or inequalities, linear programming is an effective solution method. Realistic

---

[17] See Baumol, *Economic Theory and Operations Analysis,* for a very good presentation of the *simplex* method.

problems may involve literally dozens of variables and constraints, requiring computer solutions.

Linear Programming and the Analysis of Production[18]

In Figure 6–13, the axes again represent input factors as in Figure 6–2 in the chapter. However, in this case the production processes are assumed to require fixed proportions of the two input factors. Production, therefore, can take place only along the "process" rays which

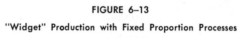

FIGURE 6–13

"Widget" Production with Fixed Proportion Processes

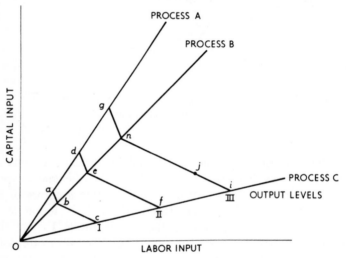

represent the allowable fixed proportion combinations of the input factors. In this diagram only three process rays are shown, indicating that there are only three technologically feasible production processes for "widgets." This assumption may be more realistic than the unlimited substitutibility of labor and capital shown in the production function in the text.

The three processes illustrated show the following input ratios: process A: three capital units for two labor units; process B: one capital unit for one labor unit; and process C: one capital unit for four labor units.

[18] This presentation is similar to that presented in many places in the literature. See particularly Robert Dorfman, "Mathematical, or 'Linear' Programming: A Non-Mathematical Exposition," *American Economic Review*, December, 1953; and Baumol, *Economic Theory and Operations Analysis*, chap. 12.

Let points *a*, *b*, and *c* represent equal outputs of "widgets" using processes A, B, and C, respectively. Since each process utilizes fixed input proportions, doubled output is represented by points *d*, *e*, and *f*, each of which are twice the distance from the origin (*O*) along their respective rays as points *a*, *b*, and *c*. Points *g*, *h*, and *i*, likewise, are respectively three times the distance from *O* as points *a*, *b*, and *c*. Intermediate levels of output may be located in the same manner.

If a larger number of processes and several output levels were shown, the resulting diagram would bear a remarkable resemblance to the production function illustrated in the chapter, the difference being that in this case, production is limited to a finite number of specific processes which utilize the input factors in fixed proportions. Although the number of processes is finite, many combinations of these processes may be derived for a given output. For example, all points along the line segments (*ab*, *bc*, *de*, etc.) connecting equal levels of output on adjacent process rays denote the same output level as the points which are connected. However, production at these intermediate points requires use of a combination of the two adjacent processes, rather than one alone. Consider point *j* on line *hi*. Point *j* represents the same level of output of "widgets" as points *h* and *i*, but will use some ratio of units produced by *both* processes. Division of the output between processes B and C is determined by the way in which point *j* divides the line *hi*. The ratio of *ji/hi* indicates the proportion produced by process B and the ratio *hj/hi* indicates the proportion produced by process C. For example, if point *j* were ⅔ the distance from *h*, ⅔ of the output would be produced by process C and ⅓ by process B.

If there are no limitations on either labor or capital inputs, the total cost of a given output level can be minimized by finding the lowest possible isocost line that just touches a production "isoquant." This point, of necessity, will be either only on one process ray, or lie along the ray connecting two rays at the same output level. This solution is similar in nature to the tangency solution for least-cost output derived in the chapter. The slope of the isocost line is the ratio of the two factor prices. Since $TC = wL + mC$, where w = the price of labor per unit L and m is the price of capital per unit C, then the isocost line is of the form $C = \dfrac{TC}{m} - \dfrac{w}{m}L$.[19] In Figure 6–13, one isocost line is shown which indicates that the least cost way of producing output level II is using process C at level *f*.

---

[19] This slope intercept form of the equation says that if L is zero, $C = TC/m$, the y intercept and the slope is $-w/m$. This isocost line is found in exactly the same manner as the equal profit line was determined in the contractor example.

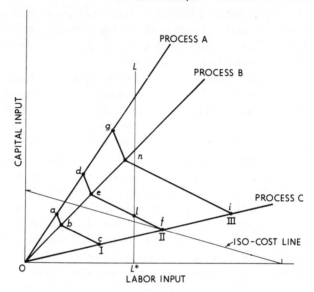

FIGURE 6–14

Production with Fixed Proportion Processes
Limited Labor Input

If one or more factors are limited in supply, then the situation is analogous to the short-run economic analysis with a fixed input factor as discussed in the chapter. Figure 6–14 is the same as Figure 6–13 except that the labor input is limited to the amount shown by the vertical line LL^*. With labor input constrained and with the desire to produce at output level II at minimum cost, the solution of process C at level f is no longer possible. The lowest possible cost will be determined by the intersection of the fixed labor factor and the desired production level. This is at point I and will require the use of both process B and process C. (The proportions produced by each process are determined by the ratios: $el/ef =$ proportion produced by C, and $lf/ef =$ proportion produced by B.) It should be noted that point I lies on a higher isocost line than did point f since the fixed labor constraint prevented maximum utilization of the relative cost advantage of the more labor intensive process C.

This version of the problem was, in effect, a cost minimization problem subject to the constraints of a limited labor supply and a fixed level of output. More commonly, the problem might be one of several limited inputs, but with several possible processes and the desire to maximize profits. A problem of this type would be structured algebraically as follows:

Maximize profits $= \pi_1 P_1 + \pi_2 P_2 + \cdots + \pi_n P_n$

Subject to:
$$a_{11}P_1 + a_{12}P_2 + \cdots + a_{1n}P_n \leq R_1$$
$$a_{21}P_1 + a_{22}P_2 + \cdots + a_{2n}P_n \leq R_2$$
.
.
.
$$a_{i1}P_1 + a_{ij}P_j + \cdots + a_{in}P_n \leq R_i$$
.
.
.
$$a_{m1}P_1 + a_{m2}P_2 + \cdots + a_{mn}P_n \leq R_m$$

and: $P_1, \ldots, P_n \geq 0$

Note: $j = 1, \ldots, n$
$i = 1, \ldots, m$

In this problem, the $P_j's$ represent the production of the product using n different processes. The $\pi_j's$ represent the contribution to profit per unit produced by each process and the small $a_{ij}'s$ represent the amount of resource R_i required to produce a unit of output by process P_j. The $R_i's$ represent the amount of each of the limited resources. The solution will tell what the maximum profits will be and at what level to operate each of the processes. As a general rule, the final solution will involve no more processes than there are constrained resources, and in almost all cases will involve exactly the same number of processes as constraints.[20]

The material presented in this appendix has briefly illustrated the usefulness of linear programming in solving certain kinds of optimization problems. It has also shown the similarity between economic and linear programming analysis of production. However, since we have merely skimmed the surface of linear programming methods, a serious student would be advised to investigate the sources cited earlier.

The Dual Problem

Associated with every maximization linear programming problem is a closely related minimization problem, and vice versa. This "duality" has attracted considerable attention for several reasons. First, many theoretical insights can be reached through analysis of the "dual" problem.

---

[20] This restates what was said earlier—that the optimum solution will always be at a corner. Certain *degenerate* cases, where more than two constraint lines happen to pass through a corner, will result in fewer than m processes in the optimum solution.

Second, some solutions can be obtained more easily through use of the dual than by the original, or "primal," problem. Third, from the economist's viewpoint, interpretation of the dual illustrates many additional parallels between economic theory and linear programming.

The building contractor's problem which was presented earlier provides a convenient example of duality. The two problems are set forth below:

Primal

Maximize $\pi = 800F + 1,200B$

Subject to:
$$20F + \quad 35B \leq \quad 280$$
$$1,000F + \quad 500B \leq \quad 9,000$$
$$500F + \quad 500B \leq \quad 6,000$$
$$0F + 4,000B \leq 24,000$$

and to: $F \geq 0, B \geq 0$

Dual

Minimize $\gamma = 280C + 9,000L + 6,000M + 24,000D$

Subject to:
$$20C + 1,000L + 500M + \quad 0D \geq \quad 800$$
$$35C + \quad 500L + 500M + 4,000D \geq 1,200$$

and to: $C \geq 0, L \geq 0, M \geq 0, D \geq 0$

The symmetry between the dual and the primal is set forth clearly in this example. The objective function of the dual is a minimization function with a new set of variables whose coefficients were the capacity constraints in the primal. The former objective function coefficients have now become the constraints in inequalities whose signs have changed from $\leq$ to $\geq$. The coefficients of the constraints which were read up and down, now read across the rows. Omitting the nonnegativity constraints, the dual has the same number of constraints as were variables in the primal, and the same number of variables as were constraints in the primal. It can be demonstrated that in the solution, the maximum value of the maximization problem (primal) will equal the minimum value of the minimization problem (dual), or vice versa.

The values of the dual variables in a problem such as this are often called "shadow prices." They are, in effect, the profit per input unit attributable to the limiting resources. The total value of the minimization objective function will equal the total profit in the maximization problem. In the dual problem the "profits" are attributed to the limiting input variables; whereas in the primal, profits were attributed to the output variables. A "shadow price" is the upper limit of the price range the contractor would be willing to pay per additional unit of the limited resources. Cement and finish lumber will have nonzero shadow prices since they were used up. The other resources will have zero shadow prices since more are currently available.

While the solution of the dual will not be shown here, it can be determined that the shadow price of cement is $32 per bag and of finish lumber, $0.16 per board foot. In the objective function of the dual the value of

$$\gamma = 280(32) + 9,000(0.16) + 6,000(0) + 24,000(0) = \$10,400$$

which is the same value obtained in the maximizing problem. It is clear that if fractional houses could be built, an additional bag of cement would increase profits from $10,400 to $10,432. The contractor would be advised to buy more cement if he can buy it for less than $32 per bag. Also, if finish lumber were available for less than $0.16 per board foot, profits could be increased. However, if the cement and lumber limits are relaxed, there are obviously limits to the gains that can be achieved because other resource limits may become operative. Sensitivity analysis provides a method of determining these limits.[21]

CASE 6–1. Sunland Tailoring Company

The Sunland Tailoring Company manufactured men's suits and top-coats. Most of their output was sold to men's furnishings stores, department stores, and wholesalers, all of whom distributed the garments under their respective brand names. Sunland did no direct retail selling. From its origin as a tailor shop in 1924, the company had grown to a firm producing approximately 200,000 suits and coats per year.

Actual production of clothing in the plant was concentrated in a period of about nine months each year. Since the company produced no line of summer clothing, there was a period of three months, January through March, when idle capacity was about 90 percent. During this period any needed repairs and renovations were made and a large part of the work force were given unpaid "vacations."

Sunland normally sold suits and coats at an average price of $37.60 each. The price of $37.60 was arrived at by adding approximately 10 percent to total cost per suit, as follows:

---

[21] See Hadley, *Linear Programming,* for a good discussion of sensitivity analysis and for further insights into the dual.

EXHIBIT 6–1A

Labor...............................	$14.00
Material.............................	13.50
Depreciation.........................	1.48
Overhead............................	2.13
Administrative and selling expense.........	1.15
Repairs and supplies...................	1.92
Total cost.......................	$34.18
Plus 10% markup.....................	3.42
Total..........................	$37.60

In October, 1967, the company received an inquiry from the manager of a large chain of department stores operating in the southwestern part of the United States, expressing interest in placing an order for 50,000 men's suits of various specified sizes, for delivery between April 1 and April 15, 1968. It was stated that the order would be confirmed if the price did not exceed $30 per suit.

The chief accountant recommended that the order be rejected. Unwilling to lose this business, the president of the company hired the services of a business management counsel, who prepared a new statement of costs per suit as follows:

EXHIBIT 6–1B

Direct labor..........................	$11.00
Material.............................	12.90
Spoilage.............................	0.60
Total direct costs.................	$24.50
Indirect labor........................	3.00
General factory burden..................	2.20
Depreciation.........................	1.80
Repairs and supplies...................	1.50
Administrative and selling expense.........	1.18
Total..........................	$34.18

In addition to the costs shown above, it was estimated that because of vacations, overtime would have to be paid in the amount of 20 percent of direct labor per unit. Inability of regular sources of supply to provide the full amount of the woolen goods required for this order would force the firm to use other suppliers. One woolen mill was found which was willing to supply the full amount, but the mill refused to grant the usual cutters' discount of 2 percent.

The fee of the management counseling firm was $2,000.

Questions

1. Should the company accept the order for 50,000 suits?
2. Explain which costs are relevant to the decision, and compute the most pertinent cost per suit, justifying your computation.

3. Does average variable cost differ from marginal cost in this situation? Explain.
4. What type of labor cost, not shown in the cost statements, may also be involved?
5. Whatever your decision was, cite some factors that might make the opposite decision wise.

CASE 6–2. Badger and Siegel

Badger and Siegel were two very small producers of a standardized product in a very competitive market. Both priced at the prevailing market price, and both desired to maximize profits. Both plants were about the same size and had a potential capacity of producing 10,000 units per year. Normally, however, both tended to operate at not over 80 percent of capacity, for unit variable costs increased rapidly for any extra production. This increase was caused by the fact that one stage of production required very skilled workmanship. These highly paid workers in consequence worked overtime when production exceeded 80 percent of capacity. Any production between 80 and 85 percent of capacity increased variable costs on this extra output by 10 percent. If production went above 85 percent and not over 90 percent, the *additional* units cost an *additional* 15 percent over the unit variable costs for outputs up to 80 percent. Any units produced over 90 percent of capacity cost 20 percent more than the basic variable costs. At 80 percent of capacity, Badger's unit fixed costs were $3. These costs in total did not change within the range of his production. For outputs through 80 percent capacity, his variable costs were $9 per unit. Siegel did not use quite as much machinery, and his costs at 80 percent capacity were as follows: unit fixed, $2; unit variable, $10.50. In 1959 the price dropped from $12.60 to $12.40. At this price, Siegel was operating at a loss in 1963 when he was working at 80 percent of capacity.

Since Badger and Siegel were friends, Siegel asked Badger what to do under these circumstances. Badger told him that in such a case, he should forget fixed costs and watch variable costs only. Badger said that he watched his variable costs and continued production just so long as his additional costs did not exceed the selling price. Thus, if the price in the market was $12.40, Badger continued to increase output until his additional variable (marginal) costs approximated $12.40.

Siegel, however, insisted that since his costs at normal capacity were $12.50 per unit, he could not possibly reduce his losses by forgetting his fixed costs. He insisted that average costs were the more significant.

In order to settle the argument, Badger and Siegel agreed that they would estimate their costs at various levels of production. They decided to start at 5,000, then estimate them at 7,000, 8,000, 8,500, 9,000, 10,000, and 11,000 units. For production between 10,000 and 11,000 units additional variable costs were estimated at double the level of 8,000 units.

Questions

1. Make this cost-output study for both Badger and Siegel, and indicate how many units each should produce.
2. Assume that there are 50 firms in the industry with Badger's costs and 50 with Siegel's costs. Plot the industry supply schedule.
3. What long-run changes of price and composition of this industry would you predict under the assumptions of pure competition?

CASE 6–3. L. E. Mason Company

In the spring of 1962 the officers of the L. E. Mason Company of Boston, Massachusetts, were concerned about the inventory position of the company's Red Dot line of electrical conduit fittings. The Red Dot line consisted of approximately 180 different fittings made of die-cast aluminum.[22] The fittings were sold throughout the United States by manufacturers' representatives, who took the goods on consignment in 20 warehouses. The company also maintained a factory warehouse in Brockton, Massachusetts, from which shipments were made to the field warehouses and also directly to some customers.

Prior to World War II the L. E. Mason Company was primarily engaged in the bronzing of baby shoes. This activity had led the company to the production by permanent molding of the bases upon which the baby shoes were mounted. With the advent of the war, supplies were no longer available for the bronzing of baby shoes, and the company used its facilities for the production of magnesium castings for incendiary bombs. During the war period the company acquired die-casting

---

[22] Die casting is a manufacturing process in which molten metal is forced into a metal mold or die under pressure. A high-quality casting with excellent surface finish and dimensional accuracy may be produced. Castings are typically made of the lower melting point alloys of zinc, tin, lead, brass, aluminum, and magnesium. Dies are placed into a die-casting machine, which holds them in place with hydraulic pressure. The molten metal is forced into the cavity of the die under pressure. The machine releases the pressure on the die, and the casting is removed. The rate at which castings may be produced depends upon the size of the casting and the pressure required. Small items may be produced very rapidly in large volume through the use of multiple-cavity dies. The castings typically require only simple trimming, tapping and inspection before packing. Dies may range in cost from a few hundred to several thousand dollars. Scrap may be remelted and used again.

equipment. After the war the L. E. Mason Company converted to a proprietary line of gifts and housewares based on the die-casting process, did job-order die casting and resumed the bronzing of baby shoes; in 1958 it decided upon producing the Red Dot line of electrical conduit fittings to make fuller use of its die-casting facilities. In 1962 its business was in three major categories: (1) the Red Dot line, (2) a line of die-cast gift items such as coasters and book ends (some bronzing of baby shoes), and (3) job-order die casting using customer-purchased dies.

Production and Inventory Control

Mr. Kenneth Sullo, chief engineer, stated that his methods of production planning, production scheduling, and inventory control for the Red Dot line were based upon four major criteria: (1) the annual sales forecast for the Red Dot line, (2) the necessary minimum inventory, (3) the desire to make economic production runs on the die-casting machines, and (4) the desire to maintain stable levels of production and employment to avoid the costs inherent in fluctuating production.[23]

The first step in production and inventory planning after receiving the annual sales forecast for the Red Dot line from the sales department was to divide the forecast by 12 to obtain the expected average monthly sales in dollars. This dollar figure was converted into pieces by dividing average monthly dollar sales by the weighted average sales value of a single item to obtain the desired monthly production rate in pieces.

From past sales records, it was possible for Mr. Sullo to determine average monthly sales of each item in the line. These sales varied from almost zero for some items to many thousands of pieces for others. Sales patterns varied somewhat among the 20 warehouses; but the billing clerk, under the supervision of Mr. Sullo, was generally able to allocate the consigned merchandise to the field warehouses in a reasonably satisfactory manner. That is, localized shortages were relatively infrequent.

Inventory records of the field warehouses were maintained at the factory from daily sales reports by the manufacturers' representatives and from shipping records; these records, together with the main warehouse inventory records, were reported in total to Mr. Sullo on about the tenth of each month, accurate as of the first of the month. With this report, Mr. Sullo was able to see quickly which items were in short supply. Those items below a four-month supply were recorded on his production scheduling sheet for further consideration.

---

[23] The recession of 1960–61 had forced layoffs in order to keep inventory levels from becoming too high. When it became necessary to expand production again, it was difficult to get workers, and it took the company approximately six months to regain the former peak level of output.

In general, Mr. Sullo allowed two weeks' time for trimming, tapping, other intermediate operations, and inspection. Therefore, items were scheduled for casting at least two weeks before their inventory was expected to reach the two-month minimum supply limit which is explained below. An item with two and one-half months' supply or less on hand at scheduling time was scheduled immediately. Others were scheduled so that production began two weeks before the inventory was expected to be at a two-month supply. Using a four-month supply as the cutoff for scheduling enabled Mr. Sullo to schedule monthly production in accordance with his two-month supply rule.

Minimum inventory levels were determined by Mr. Sullo on the assumptions that one week's supply was necessary in each of the field warehouses, that it took up to one week to receive sales information from the warehouses, and that shipping time was often as long as a week. An extra week's supply was added for safety, giving a one-month inventory in each of the field warehouses as an order point. An additional month's nationwide supply was desired in the factory warehouse to back up the field warehouses and for direct shipment to customers. Thus the total minimum acceptable level of inventory was a two-month supply.

Through experience, Mr. Sullo found that high-volume items could get as low as one and one-half months' supply without causing great difficulty and that, paradoxically, slow-moving items could be troublesome when the total supply available was at a six-month or greater level. This he attributed to more difficult forecasting for the slow-moving items and to problems of distribution among the warehouses.

In Exhibit 6–3A several items were taken from a typical monthly production scheduling form. Column 1 gives average monthly sales in pieces for the forecast period; column 2, the description or name of the item; column 3, the quantity in inventory in months with supply as of the first of the month; and column 4, the amount to be run (economic run)

EXHIBIT 6–3A

L. E. MASON COMPANY
Production Schedule (selected items)

(1) Average Monthly Sales	(2) Item	(3) On Hand, July 1 (months)	(4) Amount to Run		(5) In Process, July 12	(6) Start Casting Date	(7) Already Packed	(8) Start Packing Date
			Pieces	Months				
800	A	3.6	2,400	3		August 2		August 18
400	B	2.7	1,600	4		At once		July 21*
1,800	C	1.4	7,200	4	2,000	At once		At once
15,000	D	1.9	30,000	2	8,000	Running		At once
50	E	5.0	500	10		July 18		August 1

* Behind schedule, that is, less than two weeks allowed between packing and casting.

in pieces and months. Column 5 gives the number already available (cast and in process since the first of the month); column 6 gives the date to begin casting; column 7 gives the amount packed since the first of the month; and column 8, the date to begin packing.

From the items placed on the production schedule, Mr. Sullo scheduled an assortment that enabled monthly production to equal approximately one twelfth of expected annual sales, taking into account the current inventory levels of the items, the quantities already cast or in process, and any other information available.

An outage in the main warehouse could also cause alterations in the production schedule, depending upon the nationwide supply of the items and its distribution.

If the nationwide supply of the item was sufficient, Mr. Sullo might suggest that shipments be made among the warehouses instead of scheduling immediate production. In some cases, shifting among the warehouses was more costly than scheduling additional production; however, Mr. Sullo believed that this had educational value for the sales department and that employees would become more adept at estimating sales and distribution if they were unable to interrupt production schedules at will.

Economic production-run sizes on the die-casting machines were determined by Mr. Sullo on the primary criterion that it was desirable to run any setup on the machines for at least one three-shift day. Setting up the machines could take up to 15 man-hours in order to get proper temperatures and to obtain quality castings.

Current Situation

In the spring of 1962 the total inventory dollar value in the 20 field warehouses and in the main warehouse was a three-month supply of finished castings at current and expected sales volumes expressed in dollars. Estimated economic order quantities for approximately 60 slow-moving items revealed that these items alone accounted for about two thirds of the value of the three-month supply on hand. Mr. Sullo felt that he really should have a four-month supply on hand in order to service sales properly.

1. Does Mr. Sullo's production control and inventory planning system lead to optimal decisions? If not, what modifications would you suggest?

2. Using the hypothetical information given in Exhibit 6–3B concerning items X, Y, and Z in the line, how many units would you schedule for production in the production period October 10 to November 10?

3. What information should Mr. Sullo call for in order to decide whether or not to increase the total value of his inventory to a four-month supply?

EXHIBIT 6–3B

	X	Y	Z
1961 average monthly sales (units)..............	1,000	25,000	100
Range of monthly sales (1961).................	200–2,500	0–50,000	50–150
Hourly wage rate............................	$2.00	$2.00	$2.00
Inventory on hand (October 10)...............	2,200	15,000	100
Production rate.............................	150/hr.	500/hr.	250/hr.
Material cost per unit.......................	$0.25	$0.50	$0.15
Estimated annual cost of holding one unit in inventory...................................	0.03	0.10	0.02

CASE 6–4. Nordon Manufacturing Company

Nordon Manufacturing Company calculated the following manufacturing costs for one of its two major products:

Materials (8 pounds "BC" at $1.50)......................	$12.00
Labor (6 hours at $2.50, 2 hours at $2)....................	19.00
Manufacturing expense (8 hours at $0.50)..................	4.00
	$35.00

The standard for manufacturing expense (overhead) was calculated at a rate of 80 percent of practical capacity from the flexible budget for manufacturing expense shown in Exhibit 6–4A. Expenses other than manufacturing are $8 a unit at the 80 percent rate ($6 fixed, $2 variable).

Questions

1. What will be the over- or underabsorbed manufacturing expense (volume variance) if operations are at 60 percent of practical capacity? At all other levels of operation? Illustrate graphically on an average cost chart and on a total cost chart.
2. Will a $44 price always result in profits?
3. Will a $42 price always result in losses?
4. Compute the marginal cost curve for output from 60 to 100 percent of capacity.
5. Nordon, which has been operating at 70 percent of capacity (1,640 units per month), with little prospect of a better rate in the next six months, has an opportunity to take a private-brand order for 3,000 units to be delivered at the rate of 500 per month at a price of $36.75 a unit. Assume no effect on other sales, and estimate the effect of accepting this order on Nordon's profits.
6. What advantage is there in working out expense figures at several levels of output for pricing decisions? For operating control?

CASE 6–5. A. W. Jones Manufacturing Company

In early April, 1973, the Jones Company was concerned about costs in manufacturing its major product lines. Of particular concern was that they were experiencing difficulty in making pricing decisions for both regular and special orders. Also, since it was possible to vary production schedules and inventory plans, they were anxious to obtain cost estimates which would enable them to set up alternative production schedules.

To answer these questions, they employed a young economist from a local university to assist them in their analysis. Dr. H. R. Yates visited the company and discussed the problem with a number of company employees. He asked that the company supply him with output and cost data for the production of their principal product line of window air conditioners. There were nine different models produced with the same production facilities. Each model was somewhat different in its requirements for both labor and material.

Dr. Yates determined that a statistical analysis would be required in order to obtain meaningful estimates of production costs. He stated that the validity of a statistical evaluation of short-run costs requires the existence of paired observations on costs and output which meet the following conditions:

1. Within each period, production activity must have proceeded at an approximately uniform rate.
2. Each cost figure should be associated with the corresponding output figure.
3. There should, ideally, be a wide spread in output observations so as to observe cost behavior at differing levels of utilization of the production process.
4. Variations in wage rates and material costs must not be allowed to improperly influence the cost-output relationship.

The first task performed by Dr. Yates and his assistant was to develop a meaningful measure of output which would accurately reflect the total resource requirement for various production mixes. Since plant capacity, wage rates, and material usage for each of the models remained constant over the time period being analyzed, the output measure chosen was *standard labor hours* in production. This rather unusual output measure does reflect the technological efficiencies or inefficiencies which result from changes in the level of utilization. Also, it can be stated in terms of a standard unit—dollars—regardless of the combination of window air conditioners produced within a given production period. Dr. Yates explained this procedure in the excerpt from his report reproduced below.

In order to obtain a measure of aggregate air conditioner output one must develop a method which converts output for each of the nine models into a single number. Since a common manufacturing process is shared, output can be stated in terms of each model's utilization of capacity of the production process. Each model's claim on the production process is hypothesized to be proportional to its standard requirement of the labor input. If one air conditioner requires twice the processing time required by a second model, each unit of the first model would be equivalent to two units of the second in the measurement of final output. Essentially we are using standard labor expenditure as the common denominator for expressing each production mix as a single output measure.

The specific output measure employed is dollar expenditure on standard labor over a four-week period (the cost and output information for the five week months were converted to the four-week basis for the data processing). We expect this measure to be proportional to hours of process time. No adjustment is required for changes in labor costs since wage rates were unchanged during the period of our investigation.

The data on standard labor cost for each model are presented in Exhibit 6–5A. Standard labor cost per item was computed by multiplying total pro-

EXHIBIT 6–5A

Required Expenditure for Standard Labor for
Each Air Conditioner Model

Air Conditioner Model	Required Expenditure for Standard Labor
A113	$ 9.251
A114	9.321
A115	9.219
A116	7.734
B301	7.937
B302	11.459
B303	9.013
C121	9.009
C122	8.628
Parts	0.624

duction cost by the percentage of standard labor in cost (a yearly average was employed for the computation of the percentage of standard labor in cost). As an example, the per unit standard labor requirement for the model A113 was computed as

$$\$9.251 = \$58.79(15.8\%).$$

The relevant cost and output data are presented in Exhibit 6–5B. Row 1 lists the aggregate output of air conditioners for each month contained in the study, where output is defined as expenditure on standard labor per four-week month. This standard labor figure is simply the summation of the expenditure on standard labor for each of the nine

EXHIBIT 6–5B

Output and Cost Data

(production period—four-week months)

	1972									1973				
	Apr.	May	June	July	Aug.	Sept.	Oct.	Nov.	Dec.	Jan.	Feb.	Mar.	Apr.	May
1. Total output* (expenditure on standard labor)	214.5	210.9	187.6	134.6	199.2	190.3	183.1	148.1	125.7	153.5	190.3	232.5	183.1	190.3
2. Total production cost* less standard material	273.7	298.9	279.1	245.9	281.8	269.3	275.5	238.7	256.7	236.9	251.3	237.8	387.7	285.4
3. Per unit cost—1	$1.28	$1.41	$1.48	$1.83	$1.41	$1.41	$1.50	$1.61	$2.04	$1.54	$1.32	$1.02	$2.12	$1.50
4. Total production cost* less total standard cost	71.8	103.2	93.3	113.1	89.8	79.0	87.1	82.6	130.1	91.5	80.0	64.6	n.a.	n.a.
5. Per unit cost—2	$0.33	$0.49	$0.50	$0.83	$0.45	$0.41	$0.47	$0.55	$1.04	$0.60	$0.41	$0.28	n.a.	n.a.
6. Total variable cost* less standard material	235.1	254.9	243.2	204.6	242.3	235.1	199.2	199.2	215.4	195.7	214.5	207.3	n.a.	n.a.
7. Per unit cost—3	$1.10	$1.20	$1.29	$1.52	$1.21	$1.23	$1.28	$1.34	$1.72	$1.28	$1.13	$0.89	n.a.	n.a.

* Thousands of dollars.
n.a.—not available.

models and the "other" category (parts) during the period. Row 2 contains the first of the three cost measures considered in our study. (The major portion of our analysis is conducted using this first cost measure.) We deduct standard material cost from total production costs, leaving standard labor, variance in labor, variance in material, and overhead costs. We expect the average cost measure in row 3 (obtained by dividing the cost variable in row 2 by the output variable in row 1) to exhibit a dependence on the level of activity.

The time period covered by our study is from April, 1972, to May, 1973, excluding March and April, 1973. The rationale behind the exclusion of these two observations is as follows. Initially we found the average cost figure for March to be significantly lower than that expected from an analysis of the other observations. This led us to believe that either costs were understated, output was overstated, or some combination of the two. This hypothesis was further supported when the following observation (April, 1973) was found to have a higher than expected average cost. We then decided to pool the cost and output figure for the two months in order to eliminate the effects of the assumed misstatement. These pooled data *are* consistent with the other observations.

The cost measure in row 4 was obtained by deducting standard labor and standard material from total production costs. The resultant quantity is typically denoted by "variance." Per unit variance (row 4 divided by row 1) is presented in row 5. This second cost measure is also consistent with the assumed economic relationship between cost and output. Row 6 contains the third cost variable, total variable cost less standard material. The variable cost measure was obtained from the accountant's designation of certain costs as fixed or variable within each cost center. Were we secure in this designation of costs (fixed or variable), the resultant average cost measure (row 7) would seem most appropriate. This third cost variable is also consistent with our assumed relationship, we prefer a cost variable which is less a function of the accountant's subjective decision on cost allocation.

Questions

1. Using multiple regression analysis, fit an average cost curve of the form $AC = a + bQ + cQ^2$.
2. Find the appropriate total and marginal cost curves related to the average cost curve derived above. Plot these curves, the average cost curve, and the original data on graph paper.
3. What is the minimum average cost output level per four-week period?
4. The table below illustrates the computation of total production cost from a specific product mix:

Air Conditioner Model	Units Produced	×	Standard Labor Requirement per Unit	=	Expenditure for Standard Labor
A113......	1,000		$ 9.251		$ 9,251
A114......	1,000		9.321		9,321
A115......	1,000		9.219		9,219
A116......	4,000		7.734		30,936
B301......	5,000		7.937		39,685
B302......	1,000		11.459		11,459
B303......	1,000		9.013		9,013
C121......	1,000		9.009		9,009
C122......	1,000		8.628		8,628
Parts......	100,000		0.624		62,400
Total output (round to 199,000)...					$198,921

a. Using the total cost function derived in Question 2, estimate total cost if standard material costs for this output are $1,078,000.

b. If an order is received for 500 additional units of model B301 with standard material costs of $20,568, what will the effect be on total costs of production?

5. Suppose the original output level before the new order was 162,000 units, what would be the additional cost of the order for 500 additional units of model B301? Explain the difference.

CASE 6–6. Problems in Linear Programming

1. A manufacturer makes two products, each requiring the following capacity in hours per unit:

	Product		Available
Shop	X_1	X_2	Hours
Foundry......	6	6	500
Machine......	3	5	420
Finish......	5	2	250

Product X_1 brings in 40 cents per unit profit and X_2, 30 cents per unit.

a. Write the equations.

b. How many of each should the manufacturer produce?

c. What is his total profit?

2. The ABC Company has the option of producing two products during periods of slack activity. For the next week production has been

scheduled so that the milling machine is free ten hours and skilled labor will have eight hours of available time.

Product A requires four hours of machine time and two hours of skilled labor per unit. Product B requires two hours of machine time and two hours of skilled labor per unit.

Product A contributes $5 per unit to profit, and product B contributes $3 per unit to profit.

    a.   Formulate the problem algebraically.

    b.   Solve graphically.

chapter 7

Investment Decisions and Long-Run Cost

EFFICIENT management of a going firm usually requires that consistent attention be paid to long-run affairs such as possible additions to capacity, changes in equipment, and alterations in products. Greatest freedom of choice in such matters exists when an activity is being planned since all opportunities are open (so far as they can be financed). At that point all costs are variable. "Planning curves" or their analytical equivalents relating average costs to the scale of operation, and perhaps to location, are of interest to the businessman trying to set up the most profitable operation.

In terms of the production isoquant chart shown in Figure 6–2 of the previous chapter, both types of input can be varied, and the long-run expansion path *EP* connects the lowest cost combinations of inputs for the attainment of various outputs. These depend on prices of factors as well as on engineering considerations.

The relation between short-run average cost curves for plants of various sizes and long-run average cost can be seen in Figure 7–1. In this illustration only five alternative sizes of plant are assumed to be technically possible due, for example, to the need to use some type of machine which is available only in one size. The five possible plants may be assumed to utilize one to five of these indivisible units of equipment. If the anticipated rate of output during the life of the plant is less than *OM*, it will be most economical to have the smallest size plant (for which $SRAC_1$ is the expected short-run average cost curve). If the expected rate is just a little more than *OM*, it would be possible to use the smallest size plant; but the next larger size plant, utilized at a relatively low rate, would give lower average cost. If anticipated output is between *ON* and *OS*, it will be desirable to build a plant of "optimum" size, associated with curve $SRAC_3$. A larger plant may encounter problems which will increase average costs. It is easy to conceive of a food-retailing store so large that clerks and customers would have to spend an undue amount of time in stocking shelves and finding items. A manufacturing plant may be so large as to create unusually severe automobile, truck, and railroad congestion as well as problems of coordination and supervision within the facility. Curves $SRAC_4$ and $SRAC_5$ reflect the diseconomy of having excessively large plants. The problem of high

FIGURE 7–1

Short-Run Average Cost from a Planning Viewpoint—Cost Depends on Scale of Operations

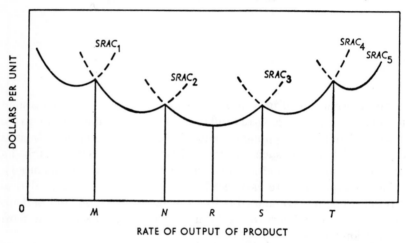

RATE OF OUTPUT OF PRODUCT

costs due to undersized plants which are unable to make sufficient use of specialized machinery, skilled management, and division of labor is much more common. A shortage of capital—owned and borrowed—is especially likely to be the cause of small scale, high unit cost, operation.

The solid line in Figure 7–1 can be called the "long-run average cost curve" since it shows the lowest possible unit cost of turning out any given output per period. This curve is often referred to as a "planning curve" since a firm never actually operates under long-run cost conditions but can use such an analytical framework in choosing the appropriate size of plant to construct. Under competitive conditions it is necessary for survival that unit costs be as low as possible so it is to be expected that the size of plant will be planned to make $SRAC_3$ the short-run average cost curve. Firms possessing monopoly power are also likely to choose plants which minimize unit costs, provided it is to their advantage to sell approximately the least-cost quantity per period. However, this condition may not exist. For example, the demand for electric power in a small and isolated community is likely to be insufficient to permit full economies of scale in production. Similarly, many firms have monopoly power in the production of patented items which they cannot sell at a rate sufficient to secure the cost advantages of large scale production.

In Figure 7–1 it was assumed that some sort of indivisibility of equipment permitted the plant to be built in only five alternative sizes. However, it may instead be possible to build a plant of any desired size; and the long-run average cost curve then becomes a smooth curve, such as

FIGURE 7–2

Long-Run Average Cost—With Complete Divisibility

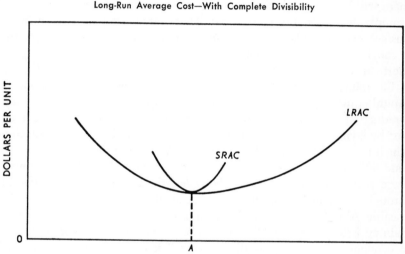

RATE OF OUTPUT OF PRODUCT

LRAC of Figure 7–2. This curve can be conceived as being tangent to all of the possible alternative short-run average cost curves when an unlimited number of sizes of plant is technically possible. It touches the *minimum* point of only one of these curves—*SRAC* in Figure 7–2.

Typically, in manufacturing and trade, anticipated sales per period are much greater than *OA*, the rate at which output can be produced at the lowest average cost by building plant to an optimal scale. In this planning situation a large number of plants, each of the best size, will be built. In the real world, seldom are large numbers of identically sized plants built at the same time. However, some examples can be seen in the fast-food franchise operations such as McDonald's. Usually, many firms will participate in the ownership of these plants, but any or all firms may control many plants. If, however, the advantages of large-scale production are such that the output of one plant of efficient size is a large fraction of the sales of the product in the entire market, it is clear that there will be room for only a small number of plants, and consequently, only a small number of companies. A small city usually has only a few brickyards and a few "ten-cent" stores, for example.

Flexibility of Plant

The plant associated with curve *SRAC* in Figure 7–2 is large enough to take full advantage of economies of scale without being so large as to encounter diseconomies of size. Least-cost output is *OA*. There may, however, be considerable uncertainty as to the average rate at which it will subsequently be found desirable to operate. Or it may be clear that there will be a great deal of fluctuation in the rate of operation due, for example, to seasonality of demand. These circumstances may cause the businessman to build a plant which is quite "flexible" in the sense that it can be operated at nonoptimal rates without greatly increasing the short-run unit cost.[1]

Flexibility can also be obtained by some substitution of labor for capital equipment. If the ratio of labor to capital is kept relatively high, a reduction in output can be effected without much increase in average cost by laying off workers or reducing hours of employment. (A machine which is owned or rented by the firm on a long-term contract cannot be "laid off" in order to reduce fixed costs.) To the extent that guaranteed wage plans are put into effect, however, the achievement of flexibility through the maintenance of a high ratio of labor to equipment is less feasible. Also, labor in which the firm has invested in the form of specific training is to some extent like capital equipment and cannot be laid off as economically as can unskilled labor.[2] This is due to the need to train new workers if the trained worker does not return.

Size of Firm and Cost

The "planning curves" shown in Figure 7–1 pertain to the variation in average costs as the scale of plant is altered. If the firm has only one plant, and if most of its costs are production costs, the best size of firm will be governed almost entirely by the optimum size of plant. If the firm is a multiplant organization, its optimum size may have little relation to the optimum scale of plant. (Large food-retailing companies, for example, are probably somewhat more efficient than smaller firms in this field, although individual plants [stores] are of moderate size.)

---

[1] Flexibility is more important when the commodity cannot be stored or is costly to store since withdrawals from inventory can be temporary substitutes for production.

[2] This idea was developed by Walter Y. Oi, "Labor as a Quasi-Fixed Factor," *Journal of Political Economy*, December, 1962.

It may be necessary for a firm to be large in order to secure the efficient operations of its plants when the efficiency of each plant is related to the operation of the others. This seems to be the situation in the interstate bus business where plants (buses and terminals) are small, but where a large number of buses is needed in order to maintain regular schedules and where the terminals must be numerous if adequate common carrier service is to be furnished. Up to a point, at least, a larger firm enjoys advantages in raising capital, in purchasing, in carrying on research, and in selling. These activities require for their most efficient performance certain specialized personnel, equipment, or procedures which a small firm may be unable to afford. (The possibility of hiring the services of experts who also serve other firms somewhat reduces the diseconomy of small size, however.) A large vertically integrated firm— one which owns plants at different stages in the production process— will probably have lower costs than a nonintegrated company if there is monopoly power at some of the earlier stages, since integration will make it possible to avoid paying monopolistic prices for materials. Unless the firm uses enough materials to make possible their production on an optimum scale, however, integration may be unprofitable. Use of part of the output and sale of the remainder may afford the integrated firm a chance both to avoid high-priced materials and components and to secure an adequate scale of output at the earlier stages.

Limited Production Run

The cost curves shown so far are based on the assumption that production of the good under consideration will continue indefinitely into the future. If it can be foreseen that it will be desirable, or may be desirable, to produce the item for a limited time only, the firm is likely to make a smaller financial commitment for specialized equipment and for specialized training of labor and management.

Suppose an airplane manufacturer has designed a new transport plane and is tooled up for production. A large expenditure will have been incurred for engineering, equipment, recruiting and training of labor, and perhaps for advertising and lobbying. As these sunk costs are divided among more units of output their average per plane will decline. This is one reason the company will hope to sell a large number of units. Another reason is that labor cost per unit diminishes because workers become more adept at their jobs as they continue to produce the same item and as "bugs" in the production process are removed. It was found during World War II that man-hours per military airplane declined approximately 30 percent each time accumulated output doubled. If, for example, the first unit required 100,000 man-hours, the second would take 70,000 man-hours, the fourth would require 49,000 man-hours, and so forth. This permitted dramatic reductions over time in the cost of planes which the armed forces found successful.

Under such conditions the rate of output per month or other time period is very likely to increase. But since a higher rate of output and larger total volume tend to have opposite effects on cost, it is desirable analytically to assume that the monthly rate of output remains constant while the total production run is varied in amount. This is the implicit assumption in Figure 7–3.

FIGURE 7–3

Limited Production Run—Average and Marginal Costs
Decline with Volume

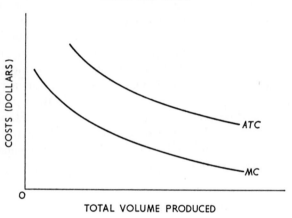

Both average and marginal costs per unit decline as the production run becomes longer. The connection between the firm's ability to sell the item and to produce economically becomes especially close. Quantity discounts are likely to be used to increase total volume since additional sales result in lower costs. If the item is sold to a government agency, active lobbyists and "good connections" can have a similar importance.

In practice it may not be easy to distinguish between a succession of limited production runs and continuous production. If changes are made in the model that require some modification of equipment, part, but probably not all, of the cost reduction due to volume will be lost. Average and marginal cost curves may be similar to those of Figure 7–3 except for upward shifts occurring at the volumes at which model changes are made.[3] If the model change is sufficiently drastic, the limited production run can be considered to be starting from scratch again.

---

[3] Cost curves for finite production runs were developed by Armen Alchian. Various possibilities are described in A. A. Alchian and W. R. Allen, *University Economics* (Belmont, Calif.: Wadsworth Publishing Co., Inc., 1967), pp. 227–38.

Value of Equipment

Whether continuous or limited production is being planned, the businessman is faced with difficult problems related to plant and equipment. For example, he must decide how much and what type of equipment to buy, whether it should be new or used, and when to replace old equipment wholly or partially with new models. Regardless of the care with which calculations are made, judgment plays an important part.

The concept of capitalization is basic to this entire field. Capitalization is the mathematical process of finding the present value of a future stream of income. The calculation is simplest if this income stream is one without end—an income in perpetuity. Suppose a public utility company has paid a dividend of $5 per year per share on its common stock for many years, and will—as far as can be seen—continue to do so indefinitely. The market price of the stock should then depend almost entirely on the interest rate which is considered appropriate for this sort of investment.[4] (This percentage yield will be lower than on most stocks because of the relatively low risk of loss of interest or principal due to the stable nature of the company.) Suppose that the appropriate interest rate is 5 percent per year. The stock would then sell at about $100 per share. This is determined by the capitalization formula for a perpetual income, where V is the present value of a share, I is the anticipated income per annum, and r is the yearly market interest rate on investments of this quality:

$$V = \frac{I}{r}$$

The formula is appropriate only if no change is anticipated in either I or r. Suppose that I is expected to remain at $5 per year but that most buyers anticipate that interest rates in general will rise slightly in the near future. They would then be unwilling to pay quite as much as $100 per share, since they believe that by waiting a while, they can secure a little more than $5 a year on $100 invested in a security of this grade (or even in this same security). On the other hand, if there is a general expectation of a decline in interest rates, the stock should now sell at a little more than $100 a share. This simple capitalization formula is also applicable to evaluation of a piece of land which is expected to yield a steady and perpetual income above taxes and all other costs. For example, the value of a piece of city land recently rented on a 99-year lease to

---

[4] The market price is also affected by the number of dividends paid per year and by brokerage fees and transfer taxes, but these will have a relatively minor effect on market price and are disregarded for purposes of simplification. In periods of rapid inflation, the discount rate may be considerably higher than in a period of expected stable prices. This is due to the loss in purchasing power of the stable dividend.

a dependable firm which pays the owner a yearly rental of $10,000 would be $200,000 if, again, 5 percent were considered the appropriate rate of interest on such an investment. If the land changed hands at this price, the new buyer would, of course, receive a 5 percent return on his investment of $200,000, since this is just another view of the same problem.

The capitalization calculation is somewhat more complicated when the income will be received only for a finite number of years instead of in perpetuity. Income received today is more valuable than the same amount of income received a year from now because if it is received today, it can begin immediately to earn interest for the owner. Therefore, its additional worth is just the amount of interest which it will earn in a year. By the same token, income which is still a year away must be discounted—a year's interest must be taken away—in order to find its present value. If the income is more than a year away, it must be discounted more heavily.

Suppose that a merchant has a claim to three $1,000 payments which are due him one year, two years, and three years from today, respectively. He may wish to sell this claim in order to secure all of the cash immediately (from someone else who will look upon the claim as a suitable investment). The amount for which he can sell the claim depends on the risk which is deemed by potential buyers to be associated with the claim—that is, by the apparent degree of danger of nonpayment or slow payment of an installment when due.

The present value of this claim can be found from the formula:

$$V = \frac{\$1,000}{1+r} + \frac{\$1,000}{(1+r)^2} + \frac{\$1,000}{(1+r)^3}$$

This formula discounts each successive payment more heavily. The first payment is now worth the sum which will build up to $1,000 in one year, without compounding the interest. The second payment is now worth the sum which will build up to $1,000 in two years, with interest compounded at the end of the first year; while the third payment is now worth the amount which would build up to $1,000 in three years if compounded at the end of the first and second years. Suppose r is 6 percent. The first $1,000 installment is now worth $943.40, the second installment is worth $890, and the third is worth $839.62. The entire claim is worth the sum of these amounts, or $2,673.02. This worth would, of course, be greater if the relevant interest rate were deemed to be less than 6 percent, and it would be lower if a higher discount rate were used. Also, the claim would be worth less today if a period shorter than a year were used for compounding interest. (See Figures 7–5 and 7–6 in the appendix to this chapter for present value of a single payment of $1 in future years and of an annual payment of $1 at various interest rates. The calculations in the present paragraph may be checked in Figure 7–6.)

Value of a Machine

The same sort of calculation may be used to determine the present value of a machine. In this case the annual income is the "quasi rent"[5] derived from its productive contribution. Annual quasi rent is found by deducting from the value of the annual product of the machine all variable costs (labor, materials, fuel, etc.) incurred in the same process. No deduction is made, however, for depreciation on the machine or for interest on its cost. The term "cash flow" is often used in this connection in place of "quasi rent." While it brings to mind approximately the correct picture, this term is not an entirely accurate one because in a given year the inflow of funds may take the form of increases in accounts receivable, reductions in liabilities of the firm, or some other change in noncash accounts. In the subsequent discussion the term "cash flow" will be utilized because of its widespread use.

Suppose a machine has three years of productive life remaining and that at the end of that time, it will have no scrap value. Assume also that (like an electric light bulb or, perhaps, a TV picture tube) it gives satisfactory service until it expires, rather than gradually running down or requiring ever-increasing maintenance expenditures. If the product turned out by the machine is worth $4,000 a year and variable expenses of $3,000 a year are incurred in its operation, the machine has a present value of $2,673.02, if a 6 percent rate is used in discounting. (This is the same calculation as made previously—a trick which saves the writers a bit of time.)

Usually, a machine will have scrap value or trade-in value at the end of its productive life. This requires only the modification of adding in the discounted value of this last-ditch contribution of the machine. The scrap value is assumed to be realized as soon as the last output is sold (at the end of the nth year). Letting Q stand for cash flow received at the end of each year and S for scrap value, the formula for the present value of a machine is:

$$V = \frac{Q_1}{1+r} + \frac{Q_2}{(1+r)^2} + \frac{Q_3}{(1+r)^3} + \cdots + \frac{Q_n}{(1+r)^n} + \frac{S}{(1+r)^n}$$

The cash flow need not be the same each year. Normally, it will decrease with time as maintenance and repair expenses connected with the aging machine increase. It is implicitly assumed, however, that the cash flow is maximized each year by operation of the machine at the output rate where marginal cost equals marginal revenue. It has been pointed out that a plant is operated optimally only when marginal revenue and marginal cost are equated, and the same is true of an

---

[5] This name was given by Alfred Marshall to the "income derived from machines or other appliances for production made by man" (*Principles of Economics* [8th ed.; London: Macmillan & Co., Ltd., 1930], p. 74).

individual machine. The correct present value of the machine can only be derived on the assumption that its earnings will be maximized through correct management.

It should be realized that regardless of the arithmetical care with which the present value of a machine is calculated, much uncertainty is present in the calculation. The cash flow will be affected by the price of the output, by prices which will be paid for materials, labor, and so forth, in the future, and by possible breakdowns of the machine itself. Its scrap or trade-in value is probably not definitely ascertainable if the machine has a number of years of life remaining. Also, the selection of the interest rate to be used in discounting requires much information and judgment. Usually, it is correct to utilize an interest rate which reflects the market-determined rate at which the firm could lend its money, the degree of risk being the same.[6]

A further complication involved in estimating V is that the present value of income taxes attributable to the earnings of the machine must be deducted. Perhaps the simplest way to make the necessary calculation is to deduct the anticipated income tax from each year's cash flow before discounting the stream in order to find its present value. If Q_1 is cash flow in period 1 and d_1 is the depreciation charge for that period, we can write:

$$\bar{Q}_1 = Q_1 - [(\text{tax rate}) (Q_1 - d_1)]$$

This formula is based on the deductibility of depreciation for tax purposes. Similar equations would apply to each of the periods of expected life of the asset. The present value becomes:

$$V = \frac{\bar{Q}_1}{1 + r} + \frac{\bar{Q}_2}{(1 + r)^2} + \frac{\bar{Q}_3}{(1 + r)^3} + \cdots + \frac{\bar{Q}_n}{(1 + r)^n} + \frac{S}{(1 + r)^n}$$

An alternative and equivalent expression[7] for cash flow after taxes in period 1 is:

$$\bar{Q}_1 = (1 - \text{tax rate}) \times (\text{revenue} - \text{expenses other than}$$

$$\text{depreciation} - \text{depreciation}) + \text{depreciation}$$

While the same tax rate will ordinarily be used in estimating each year's "after-tax cash flow," the analyst may substitute other rates if he strongly anticipates a change in the tax law. It is also clear that the method of computing depreciation allowances enters into the problem.

---

[6] For more accurate criteria under various conditions, see Harry V. Roberts, "Current Problems in the Economics of Capital Budgeting," *Journal of Business,* January, 1957.

[7] This formula is shown in H. Bierman, Jr., and S. Smidt, *The Capital Budgeting Decision* (New York: Macmillan Co., 1960), p. 105.

Accelerated depreciation tends to increase the present value of assets by lowering income taxes in the early years when cash flows are subjected to smaller discounts. Both the use of accelerated depreciation and the anticipation of lower income tax rates can be seen as favorable to a greater present rate of investment.

Decision to Purchase a Machine

Estimating the worth of a machine involves difficulties but must somehow be accomplished, at least roughly, if a rational decision to purchase or not to purchase a machine is to be made. Once the present value (V) has been determined, it is only necessary to compare this with the cost of the machine. If its value is less than its cost, it should not be purchased; if its value is just equal to its cost, it is a matter of indifference whether it is purchased, since funds invested in the machine will bring the same return as they could earn in an alternative investment. This assumes that sufficient funds are available, and there are not other more attractive uses for the funds. The subject of capital budgeting is considered in the next chapter.

If V exceeds the cost of the machine, it means that according to the best calculation which can be made, the returns from the machine will more than cover all variable costs, depreciation on the machine, and an "opportunity" interest return on the capital tied up in the machine. The investment then appears to be a good one, and management is likely to buy the machine (unless a still better one is available for the job). Sales opportunities may be such that additional machines would also be expected to have a present worth greater than their cost. In this event, management should purchase additional machines as long as the value added by another machine to the present value of the whole stock of machines exceeds the cost of the machine. In this calculation, account must be taken of the fact that each machine which is added may lower the present value of the earlier machines by lowering the market price at which the output can be disposed of. It is also possible that "quantity discounts" can be secured on larger orders for machines, and this further complicates the calculation. These complications are greater than we wish to enter into in this elementary and partial treatment[8] of a difficult subject.

---

[8] An excellent book which should be studied by the reader desiring a thorough training in this subject is Friedrich A. and Vera C. Lutz, *The Theory of Investment of the Firm* (Princeton: Princeton University Press, 1951). Such problems as optimum productive techniques, optimum size of firm, optimum length of life of equipment, and optimum method of finance are treated mathematically. More practical treatments can be found in textbooks in financial management such as James C. Von Horne *Financial Management and Policy* (3d ed.; Englewood Cliffs, N.J.: Prentice-Hall, Inc., 1974).

Should a New Model Be Purchased?

Management faces a slightly different sort of investment decision when confronted with the problem of whether to replace a machine which is still usable with a new, improved model. The problem is similar to that of the fairly opulent family which has to decide each year whether to buy a new-model automobile or to continue to drive the old car. (The firm is more likely than the household to make a rational decision, however.) The development of a dramatically altered model, such as a jet-propelled airliner or an atom-powered ocean liner, can bring this question forcibly before a great many firms at the same time.

It would seem at first glance that a new type of machine which becomes available should be purchased if it will lower the unit cost of production. If investment has already been made in one machine, however, it is often correct to compare the *variable operating costs* per unit using the old machine to the *total cost* per unit using the new machine. Costs which are already sunk should not enter into decisions regarding new steps to be taken or avoided. They are bygones which should remain bygones.

This comparison is not correct, however, to the extent that sunk costs are really not lost because they can be partially recovered through the sale or trade-in of the old machine. As long as average variable operating costs using the old machine are below the selling price of the product, it can continue to yield an annual cash flow. If this cash flow is sufficient to cover interest on its own scrap value plus interest on the difference between the value and cost of a new machine, use of the old machine should be continued.[9]

Like most calculations involving interest, the appropriateness of this formulation is not easy to see. The following may help. If the old machine is continued in use, the firm sacrifices during each time period the interest which could otherwise be earned on its market value. This is one cost of keeping the old machine. Also, by retaining the old machine, the firm sacrifices interest income on the difference between the present value and the cost of the new machine. This interest would actually be secured from the cash flow which would be returned by the new machine over time. If the new machine is markedly superior to the old one, this will be a large item and will make it desirable to replace the old machine with the new one immediately. If, however, the new machine is only a slight improvement over the old one, this will not be a large amount. In that event, it is quite possible that for some years to come, the annual cash flow returned by the old machine will exceed the sum of the annual interest on its disposal value and the annual interest on the difference between value and cost of a new machine. Eventually, of

---

[9] This formulation is given by Lutz and Lutz, *Theory of Investment*, pp. 113–14.

course, the old machine should be replaced, but premature replacement by a model which is only slightly better is both common and uneconomical.

Alternative Formulation of Replacement Criterion

The complex-sounding considerations which have been set forth for deciding rationally between retaining and replacing old machinery can be restated in a somewhat simpler way if "average cost" of a product turned out by the machinery is defined in economic terms rather than as it is apt to be figured by an accountant. Ordinarily, the accountant considers average cost to be made up of variable cost per unit and fixed cost per unit, including in the latter depreciation based on the original cost of the asset. However, it will seldom happen that the market or trade-in value of an old machine will exactly equal its original cost less depreciation as charged off on the books from the time of acquisition to the time at which a decision to keep or replace is to be made.

A direct comparison of the average cost of production using the new machine and using the old machine may be appropriate if three things are done: (1) average cost of producing with the old equipment must include depreciation based not on original cost but on expected decline in market value; (2) interest must be added in as a cost, with its amount being computed on the cost and market value, respectively, of the new and the old equipment; and (3) the average cost calculation using both old and new equipment must be made in each case for the expected optimum output, that is, where marginal cost equals marginal revenue. This may not be the same output in both cases. If it is expected that demand will fall off, replacement of the old machinery becomes less desirable, since a reduction in output will raise average cost of output more sharply for the new machinery than for the old. This is due to the higher fixed costs which will be associated with the new equipment.

In summary, the decision whether to replace existing machinery with new machinery usually cannot be made simply by comparing average cost of production as likely to be calculated by an accountant. Capital will have been sunk in the old equipment, but this historical event is irrelevant to a present decision except to the extent that capital could now be recovered by selling or trading in the old machinery. This requires an economist's calculation of average cost of production using the old machinery. In addition, interest must be included as a cost of production. This is normal procedure for the economist but not for the accountant, except where the interest payment is explicit. Also, the average cost of production using either old or new equipment will depend on the rate of production; consequently, not a single average cost but instead an average cost *curve* should be computed for output from both old and new machinery. The optimum rate of output which is anticipated for each of the two productive processes then determines an average cost for each, and these averages can be directly compared to judge whether replacement is desirable. If *none* of the capital sunk in the old machinery can be recovered by its sale or trade-in, the relevant comparison is simply average cost at the expected output with the new machine versus average variable cost at the expected rate of output using the old machine. Interest and depreciation are elements in the former but not in the latter.

Revenue Considerations

In the preceding discussion, it was implicitly assumed that the revenue received by the firm will be the same whether or not old equipment is replaced. Frequently, however, a better product is turned out by the new equipment, and income is thereby increased. This is especially easy to see in the case of new transportation equipment which will attract customers through greater speed, convenience, and so forth. When revenue is affected, the replacement calculation is more difficult than was indicated by the suggested comparison of average cost of production with new and old equipment. Instead, for the rate of operation expected in each case, net earnings after income taxes must be compared, total income being computed by multiplying output by price per unit and total cost being computed by multiplying output by adjusted cost per unit. (The income tax is computed with the use of accounting costs as permitted for tax purposes, and these will differ from the costs just mentioned.)

The foregoing reduces to the rather obvious statement that old equipment should be replaced by new equipment if annual net income after taxes can thereby be increased. It should be noted, however, that the relevant net income as computed for the alternative of retention of old equipment involves the basic economic concept of disregarding sunk costs based on *previous* decisions. Instead, only *present* alternatives are involved, since average cost is derived in part from the present disposal value of old equipment. In some cases, another firm can make especially good use of secondhand equipment (due perhaps to a very limited capital budget), and in such a case the firm which owns such equipment may have an especially good opportunity to modernize its own plant.

The foregoing discussion of equipment replacement criteria aids the understanding of long-run cost curves such as those of Figure 7–1. First, it emphasizes that these are planning curves prior to commitment of any resources to the activity. If, instead, the operation is already a going one, the relevant planning involves a comparison of average costs per unit of output attainable with new and existing equipment. Second, it should be noted that demand is usually assumed to be independent of cost although this is not always true (e.g., commercial aircraft). And lastly, it becomes evident that while cost curves can be drawn without considering demand, production processes will not actually be established unless prospective sales are sufficient. This is why good schools of engineering usually require that students study some economics.

APPENDIX TO CHAPTER 7. The Abandonment Decision

Almost all of the work of economists on the subject of cost of production pertains either to the short-run problem of operating an existing facility or to the long-run question of planning an efficient plant or firm.[10] For many analytical purposes these concepts are sufficient. However, in the use of economic analysis as a guide to business decisions, it is worthwhile to spell out the criteria for abandonment of an activity that is underway because in many lines of activity there are frequent changes of product. Du Pont, which has shown great concern over the dwindling profit margins which can accompany a mature product line, announced in late 1962 the abandonment of silicon production because of overcapacity in the business and the final termination of rayon production which for over 40 years had constituted an important company activity. Also, smaller firms, at least, frequently go out of business entirely.

If viewed very broadly, the "abandonment decision" embraces a great deal of the science of economics. For example, a purchase requires that money be abandoned in favor of the good. A sale requires that the good be abandoned in favor of money or an account receivable. For purposes of business economics, however, it seems useful to restrict the analysis of abandonment to situations where the sale or alteration of use of fixed assets is involved. Replacement of existing machines with new ones, analyzed in Chapter 7, fits in with the present emphasis, although more stress was placed on acquisition of the new equipment than on the abandonment of the old equipment.

A common occurrence in both California and Florida is the abandonment of citrus fruit growing in order that the land may be sold to real estate developers. When should such an action take place from the point of view of the grower? The sales value of the grove should be compared with the discounted value of the expected cash flow (returns minus variable costs) if citrus production were continued. The discount rate should be the interest rate consistent with the riskiness of this return,

---

[10] An exception is Gordon Shillinglaw, "Profit Analysis for Abandonment Decisions," *The Journal of Business*, vol. 30 (1957).

being higher for greater risk. If the computed present value of the grove is less than the amount offered by a real estate firm, the grove should be sold.[11]

An alternate and equivalent procedure is to consider the cost of the grove to the present owner to be the amount he could receive by selling out to the real estate developer. This "opportunity cost" can be equated to the computed present value of future returns from citrus fruit growing and the "internal rate of return" computed. If the return from the grove were considered to be a perpetual one, r could be computed simply from the equation:

$$C = \frac{Q}{r}$$

where C is the present selling price of the land, Q is the perpetual annual cash flow from producing oranges, and r is the internal rate of return. If this internal rate is unacceptably low (because a higher one is alternatively available), the grove should be abandoned. The higher the offer that is made by the real estate developer, the lower the computed internal rate of return will be and the more likely the grove owner will be to sell out.

In practice many other considerations may be involved. The return from the grove may be considered to be for a limited time only unless expenditures are made to replace trees which no longer bear fruit. If trees are not replaced the cash flow will be a finite one, and the estimated land value at the end should be discounted and added to the present value of the expected cash flow from citrus harvests. (This is similar to the scrap or trade-in value of a machine.) Possibly a higher offer from a real estate firm can be expected later. Or perhaps it is now, or will later be, desirable to retain part of the grove and to sell part of it. As is by now apparent to those who have analyzed actual cases, theory is a guide to thinking about the real world but seldom incorporates all of the relevant variables.

The problem of abandonment of a product can be viewed in terms of the traditional short-run cost curves (see Figure 7–4). These pertain to a firm producing in a competitive market, price being op. If the firm wishes to continue to produce the commodity, ox is the best output. However, unless the situation is expected to improve, management should look around for better alternatives since price is below average cost and this may call for abandonment of the product. This is because the average total cost curve has been constructed so as to incorporate the best alternative opportunity. That is, the interest rate that could be earned on the present selling value of the plant plus expected depreciation of this

---

[11] This may not be true if a still more favorable situation is expected in the near future.

FIGURE 7–4

Returns below Alternatives—May Call for Abandonment

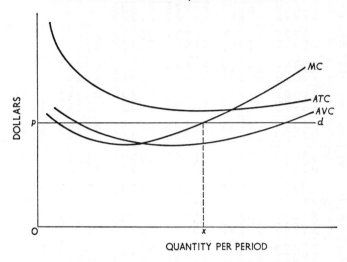

QUANTITY PER PERIOD

value is included as a cost of the commodity for which the chart is drawn. Or, if the best alternative is use of the plant by the *same* firm, the internal rate of return which could be earned on the best possible good becomes part of the fixed cost of turning out the commodity in question.

Consequently, it is quite likely that the firm in Figure 7–4 should abandon the product, either switching to another good and selling unneeded plant, or going out of business entirely. Another possibility is replacement of existing equipment with new equipment if this will lower average cost. Still another is abandonment of the entire company through merger with a stronger firm if the new combination is more likely to earn a "normal" return on this or another product using much the same facilities.

Suppose the fixed plant has no sales value or alternative use. A pipeline might be an example if its salvage value would be no greater than the cost of digging it up. The activity should not be abandoned if price of the product exceeds its average variable cost since this is the only way to secure any return on the fixed asset. That is, the usual alternative of recouping some of the investment by selling the plant or by switching products does not exist. No opportunity cost of utilizing the plant for this product exists. The situation is similar to that described in Chapter 7 where a machine has no sales value. In that case no fixed cost should be considered in deciding whether the machine should be retained.

The same general type of analysis can be applied to "human capital" embodied in an individual because of education, experience, on-the-job training or other investments (see Chapter 10). Alternative employment

FIGURE 7-5

Present Value of $1

Years Hence	1%	2%	4%	6%	8%	10%	12%	14%	15%	16%	18%	20%	22%	24%	25%	26%	28%	30%	35%	40%	45%	50%
1	0.990	0.980	0.962	0.943	0.926	0.909	0.893	0.877	0.870	0.862	0.847	0.833	0.820	0.806	0.800	0.794	0.781	0.769	0.741	0.714	0.690	0.667
2	0.980	0.961	0.925	0.890	0.857	0.826	0.797	0.769	0.756	0.743	0.718	0.694	0.672	0.650	0.640	0.630	0.610	0.592	0.549	0.510	0.476	0.444
3	0.971	0.942	0.889	0.840	0.794	0.751	0.712	0.675	0.658	0.641	0.609	0.579	0.551	0.524	0.512	0.500	0.477	0.455	0.406	0.364	0.328	0.296
4	0.961	0.924	0.855	0.792	0.735	0.683	0.636	0.592	0.572	0.552	0.516	0.482	0.451	0.423	0.410	0.397	0.373	0.350	0.301	0.260	0.226	0.198
5	0.951	0.906	0.822	0.747	0.681	0.621	0.567	0.519	0.497	0.476	0.437	0.402	0.370	0.341	0.328	0.315	0.291	0.269	0.223	0.186	0.156	0.132
6	0.942	0.888	0.790	0.705	0.630	0.564	0.507	0.456	0.432	0.410	0.370	0.335	0.303	0.275	0.262	0.250	0.227	0.207	0.165	0.133	0.108	0.088
7	0.933	0.871	0.760	0.665	0.583	0.513	0.452	0.400	0.376	0.354	0.314	0.279	0.249	0.222	0.210	0.198	0.178	0.159	0.122	0.095	0.074	0.059
8	0.923	0.853	0.731	0.627	0.540	0.467	0.404	0.351	0.327	0.305	0.266	0.233	0.204	0.179	0.168	0.157	0.139	0.123	0.091	0.068	0.051	0.039
9	0.914	0.837	0.703	0.592	0.500	0.424	0.361	0.308	0.284	0.263	0.225	0.194	0.167	0.144	0.134	0.125	0.108	0.094	0.067	0.048	0.035	0.026
10	0.905	0.820	0.676	0.558	0.463	0.386	0.322	0.270	0.247	0.227	0.191	0.162	0.137	0.116	0.107	0.099	0.085	0.073	0.050	0.035	0.024	0.017
11	0.896	0.804	0.650	0.527	0.429	0.350	0.287	0.237	0.215	0.195	0.162	0.135	0.112	0.094	0.086	0.079	0.066	0.056	0.037	0.025	0.017	0.012
12	0.887	0.788	0.625	0.497	0.397	0.319	0.257	0.208	0.187	0.168	0.137	0.112	0.092	0.076	0.069	0.062	0.052	0.043	0.027	0.018	0.012	0.008
13	0.879	0.773	0.601	0.469	0.368	0.290	0.229	0.182	0.163	0.145	0.116	0.093	0.075	0.061	0.055	0.050	0.040	0.033	0.020	0.013	0.008	0.005
14	0.870	0.758	0.577	0.442	0.340	0.263	0.205	0.160	0.141	0.125	0.099	0.078	0.062	0.049	0.044	0.039	0.032	0.025	0.015	0.009	0.006	0.003
15	0.861	0.743	0.555	0.417	0.315	0.239	0.183	0.140	0.123	0.108	0.084	0.065	0.051	0.040	0.035	0.031	0.025	0.020	0.011	0.006	0.004	0.002
16	0.853	0.728	0.534	0.394	0.292	0.218	0.163	0.123	0.107	0.093	0.071	0.054	0.042	0.032	0.028	0.025	0.019	0.015	0.008	0.005	0.003	0.002
17	0.844	0.714	0.513	0.371	0.270	0.198	0.146	0.108	0.093	0.080	0.060	0.045	0.034	0.026	0.023	0.020	0.015	0.012	0.006	0.003	0.002	0.001
18	0.836	0.700	0.494	0.350	0.250	0.180	0.130	0.095	0.081	0.069	0.051	0.038	0.028	0.021	0.018	0.016	0.012	0.009	0.005	0.002	0.001	0.001
19	0.828	0.686	0.475	0.331	0.232	0.164	0.116	0.083	0.070	0.060	0.043	0.031	0.023	0.017	0.014	0.012	0.009	0.007	0.003	0.002	0.001	0.001
20	0.820	0.673	0.456	0.312	0.215	0.149	0.104	0.073	0.061	0.051	0.037	0.026	0.019	0.014	0.012	0.010	0.007	0.005	0.002	0.001	0.001	
21	0.811	0.660	0.439	0.294	0.199	0.135	0.093	0.064	0.053	0.044	0.031	0.022	0.015	0.011	0.009	0.008	0.006	0.004	0.002	0.001		
22	0.803	0.647	0.422	0.278	0.184	0.123	0.083	0.056	0.046	0.038	0.026	0.018	0.013	0.009	0.007	0.006	0.004	0.003	0.001	0.001		
23	0.795	0.634	0.406	0.262	0.170	0.112	0.074	0.049	0.040	0.033	0.022	0.015	0.010	0.007	0.006	0.005	0.003	0.002	0.001			
24	0.788	0.622	0.390	0.247	0.158	0.102	0.066	0.043	0.035	0.028	0.019	0.013	0.008	0.006	0.005	0.004	0.003	0.002	0.001			
25	0.780	0.610	0.375	0.233	0.146	0.092	0.059	0.038	0.030	0.024	0.016	0.010	0.007	0.005	0.004	0.003	0.002	0.001	0.001			
26	0.772	0.598	0.361	0.220	0.135	0.084	0.053	0.033	0.026	0.021	0.014	0.009	0.006	0.004	0.003	0.002	0.002	0.001				
27	0.764	0.586	0.347	0.207	0.125	0.076	0.047	0.029	0.023	0.018	0.011	0.007	0.005	0.003	0.002	0.002	0.001	0.001				
28	0.757	0.574	0.333	0.196	0.116	0.069	0.042	0.026	0.020	0.016	0.010	0.006	0.004	0.002	0.002	0.002	0.001	0.001				
29	0.749	0.563	0.321	0.185	0.107	0.063	0.037	0.022	0.017	0.014	0.008	0.005	0.003	0.002	0.002	0.001	0.001	0.001				
30	0.742	0.552	0.308	0.174	0.099	0.057	0.033	0.020	0.015	0.012	0.007	0.004	0.003	0.002	0.001	0.001	0.001					
40	0.672	0.453	0.208	0.097	0.046	0.022	0.011	0.005	0.004	0.003	0.001	0.001										
50	0.608	0.372	0.141	0.054	0.021	0.009	0.003	0.001	0.001	0.001												

FIGURE 7-6

Present Value of $1 Received Annually for n Years

Years (n)	1%	2%	4%	6%	8%	10%	12%	14%	15%	16%	18%	20%	22%	24%	25%	26%	28%	30%	35%	40%	45%	50%
1	0.990	0.980	0.962	0.943	0.926	0.909	0.893	0.877	0.870	0.862	0.847	0.833	0.820	0.806	0.800	0.794	0.781	0.769	0.741	0.714	0.690	0.667
2	1.970	1.942	1.886	1.833	1.783	1.736	1.690	1.647	1.626	1.605	1.566	1.528	1.492	1.457	1.440	1.424	1.392	1.361	1.289	1.224	1.165	1.111
3	2.941	2.884	2.775	2.673	2.577	2.487	2.402	2.322	2.283	2.246	2.174	2.106	2.042	1.981	1.952	1.923	1.868	1.816	1.696	1.589	1.493	1.407
4	3.902	3.808	3.630	3.465	3.312	3.170	3.037	2.914	2.855	2.798	2.690	2.589	2.494	2.404	2.362	2.320	2.241	2.166	1.997	1.849	1.720	1.605
5	4.853	4.713	4.452	4.212	3.993	3.791	3.605	3.433	3.352	3.274	3.127	2.991	2.864	2.745	2.689	2.635	2.532	2.436	2.220	2.035	1.876	1.737
6	5.795	5.601	5.242	4.917	4.623	4.355	4.111	3.889	3.784	3.685	3.498	3.326	3.167	3.020	2.951	2.885	2.759	2.643	2.385	2.168	1.983	1.824
7	6.728	6.472	6.002	5.582	5.206	4.868	4.564	4.288	4.160	4.039	3.812	3.605	3.416	3.242	3.161	3.083	2.937	2.802	2.508	2.263	2.057	1.883
8	7.652	7.325	6.733	6.210	5.747	5.335	4.968	4.639	4.487	4.344	4.078	3.837	3.619	3.421	3.329	3.241	3.076	2.925	2.598	2.331	2.108	1.922
9	8.566	8.162	7.435	6.802	6.247	5.759	5.328	4.946	4.772	4.607	4.303	4.031	3.786	3.566	3.463	3.366	3.184	3.019	2.665	2.379	2.144	1.948
10	9.471	8.983	8.111	7.360	6.710	6.145	5.650	5.216	5.019	4.833	4.494	4.192	3.923	3.682	3.571	3.465	3.269	3.092	2.715	2.414	2.168	1.965
11	10.368	9.787	8.760	7.887	7.139	6.495	5.988	5.453	5.234	5.029	4.656	4.327	4.035	3.776	3.656	3.544	3.335	3.147	2.757	2.438	2.185	1.977
12	11.255	10.575	9.385	8.384	7.536	6.814	6.194	5.660	5.421	5.197	4.793	4.439	4.127	3.851	3.725	3.606	3.387	3.190	2.779	2.456	2.196	1.985
13	12.134	11.343	9.986	8.853	7.904	7.103	6.424	5.842	5.583	5.342	4.910	4.533	4.203	3.912	3.780	3.656	3.427	3.223	2.799	2.468	2.204	1.990
14	13.004	12.106	10.563	9.295	8.244	7.367	6.628	6.002	5.724	5.468	5.008	4.611	4.265	3.962	3.824	3.695	3.459	3.249	2.814	2.477	2.210	1.993
15	13.865	12.849	11.118	9.712	8.559	7.606	6.811	6.142	5.847	5.575	5.092	4.675	4.315	4.001	3.859	3.726	3.483	3.268	2.825	2.484	2.214	1.995
16	14.718	13.578	11.652	10.106	8.851	7.824	6.974	6.265	5.954	5.669	5.162	4.730	4.357	4.033	3.887	3.751	3.503	3.283	2.834	2.489	2.216	1.997
17	15.562	14.292	12.166	10.477	9.122	8.022	7.120	6.373	6.047	5.749	5.222	4.775	4.391	4.059	3.910	3.771	3.518	3.295	2.840	2.492	2.218	1.998
18	16.398	14.992	12.659	10.828	9.372	8.201	7.250	6.467	6.128	5.818	5.273	4.812	4.419	4.080	3.928	3.786	3.529	3.304	2.844	2.494	2.219	1.999
19	17.226	15.678	13.134	11.158	9.604	8.365	7.366	6.550	6.198	5.877	5.316	4.844	4.442	4.097	3.942	3.799	3.539	3.311	2.848	2.496	2.220	1.999
20	18.046	16.351	13.590	11.470	9.818	8.514	7.469	6.623	6.259	5.929	5.353	4.870	4.460	4.110	3.954	3.808	3.546	3.316	2.850	2.497	2.221	1.999
21	18.857	17.011	14.029	11.764	10.017	8.649	7.562	6.687	6.312	5.973	5.384	4.891	4.476	4.121	3.963	3.816	3.551	3.320	2.852	2.498	2.221	2.000
22	19.660	17.658	14.451	12.042	10.201	8.772	7.645	6.743	6.359	6.011	5.410	4.909	4.488	4.130	3.970	3.822	3.556	3.323	2.853	2.498	2.222	2.000
23	20.456	18.292	14.857	12.303	10.371	8.883	7.718	6.792	6.399	6.044	5.432	4.925	4.499	4.137	3.976	3.827	3.559	3.325	2.854	2.499	2.222	2.000
24	21.243	18.914	15.247	12.550	10.529	8.985	7.784	6.835	6.434	6.073	5.451	4.937	4.507	4.143	3.981	3.831	3.562	3.327	2.855	2.499	2.222	2.000
25	22.023	19.523	15.622	12.783	10.675	9.077	7.843	6.873	6.464	6.097	5.467	4.948	4.514	4.147	3.985	3.834	3.564	3.329	2.856	2.499	2.222	2.000
26	22.795	20.121	15.983	13.003	10.810	9.161	7.896	6.906	6.491	6.118	5.480	4.956	4.520	4.151	3.988	3.837	3.566	3.330	2.856	2.500	2.222	2.000
27	23.560	20.707	16.330	13.211	10.935	9.237	7.943	6.935	6.514	6.136	5.492	4.964	4.524	4.154	3.990	3.839	3.567	3.331	2.856	2.500	2.222	2.000
28	24.316	21.281	16.663	13.406	11.051	9.307	7.984	6.961	6.534	6.152	5.502	4.970	4.528	4.157	3.992	3.840	3.568	3.331	2.857	2.500	2.222	2.000
29	25.066	21.844	16.984	13.591	11.158	9.370	8.022	6.983	6.551	6.166	5.510	4.975	4.531	4.159	3.994	3.841	3.569	3.332	2.857	2.500	2.222	2.000
30	25.808	22.396	17.292	13.765	11.258	9.427	8.055	7.003	6.566	6.177	5.517	4.979	4.534	4.160	3.995	3.842	3.569	3.332	2.857	2.500	2.222	2.000
40	32.835	27.355	19.793	15.046	11.925	9.779	8.244	7.105	6.642	6.234	5.548	4.997	4.544	4.166	3.999	3.846	3.571	3.333	2.857	2.500	2.222	2.000
50	39.196	31.424	21.482	15.762	12.234	9.915	8.304	7.133	6.661	6.246	5.554	4.999	4.545	4.167	4.000	3.846	3.571	3.333	2.857	2.500	2.222	2.000

opportunities tend to decline with age, partly because another employer can anticipate fewer years of productivity. The opportunity cost of remaining with the same employer becomes lower, and the probability that the worker will voluntarily abandon the job becomes smaller. Social security and other retirement incomes can be viewed as incentives to retirement by lowering the cost of job abandonment.[12]

CASE 7–1. Problems in Investment Analysis

1. The AAA Service Company is considering the purchase of a new truck to replace a five-year-old truck which is completely depreciated for tax purposes. The current value of the old truck is estimated to be $500. The new truck can be purchased for $5,000 and is estimated to be worth $500 at the end of five years. Annual operating and maintenance cost for the two trucks are estimated as follows:

	Year				
	1	2	3	4	5
Old..............	950	1,400	1,600	1,600	1,600
New..............	400	400	600	600	700

The firm estimates its cost of capital to be 10 percent and its current tax rate is 48 percent.

Should the new truck be purchased?

2. Bob's Better Bakery is considering an expansion of their baking capacity by purchasing a new computer operated bread-making machine which at a touch of a button loads all the ingredients into a mixing bowl and finished bread comes out five hours later. The equipment costs $2,000,000 but will enable the company to serve 25 fast service sandwich shops exclusively for the next 10 years. Annual sales from the new machines are estimated at $6 million. Labor and raw materials will be $5 million per year. The firm estimates its cost of capital to be 15 percent and its current tax rate is 4.5 percent.

Should the equipment be purchased?

---

[12] More detail on the abandonment decision may be found in M. R. Colberg and J. P. King, "Theory of Production Abandonment," *Rivista Internazionale di Scienze Economiche e Commerciali*, October, 1973.

CASE 7–2. Elberta Crate and Box Company

The Elberta Crate and Box Company was founded in Marshallville, Georgia, in 1905. It was a virtually fully integrated, single-plant operation wholly engaged in making wooden shipping containers for peaches. In 1913 it moved its operation to Bainbridge, Georgia, and subsequently enlarged its product line to include wooden containers for vegetables and citrus fruit. In 1923 an additional plant was opened in Tallahassee, Florida. In 1929 Southern Crate and Veneer of Macon, Georgia, was acquired. Through the years the company has switched production among various types of containers—shook, lugs, hampers, baskets, wirebounds, and so forth—as economic considerations have warranted. In recent years it has concentrated more and more on wirebound containers and is currently the leading producer in this industry.

Throughout its history the company has been raw material oriented, the location of the three plants having been largely determined by the proximity of available standing timber supplies of soft hardwoods and pine of a grade suitable for wooden box construction.

As one type of wooden container after another has come into vogue through the years, the company has switched to the one promising the most remunerative results. For example, in 1962 it was estimated that 1,000,000 hampers could be sold during the coming season, but the production of this number of hampers would completely eliminate production of 1,050,000 celery crates. Since the celery crates provided a cash flow approximately 4 percent higher per unit than did the hampers, a superficial analysis indicated that celery crate production should not be abandoned.

However, it was found that tops and bottoms of hampers could be produced from salvage materials that were available in limited quantities from items other than celery crates. Due to this salvage possibility, the following output combinations were considered to be feasible:

Hampers	Celery Crates
1,000,000	0
850,000	350,000
500,000	650,000
0	1,050,000

Questions

1. Draw a production possibility curve for the firm with respect to output of hampers and celery crates. Assume that only the combinations shown in the table are possible.
2. What output combination appears to be optimum in view of the given information?

3. Suppose Elberta Crate and Box Company were producing the best combination of hampers and celery crates. How low would the cash flow per unit from celery crates have to fall in order to make it desirable to abandon celery crate production? (Express answer as percent of cash flow per unit from hampers.)

CASE 7–3. Robbins Manufacturing Company

Many products can be made either in factories which use automatic machines or in plants using hand assembly by semiskilled workers. Robbins Manufacturing Company, after considerable study, found that it could build any one of three plants: the largest, an almost completely automatic factory; an intermediate one, utilizing an assembly line with some automatic machinery; or the smallest, relying heavily on hand assembly. Estimated costs of producing one type of electronic circuit under these three assumed plant conditions were as shown in Exhibit 7–3A.

EXHIBIT 7–3A

	Plant A Automatic	Plant B Assembly Line	Plant C Hand Operating
Unit costs:			
Materials...................... $	2.00	$ 2.00	$ 2.00
Direct labor....................	0.30	0.60	1.00
Equipment cost*.................	1,000,000.00	300,000.00	125,000.00
Maintenance and overhead:			
Fixed portion.................	300,000.00	125,000.00	100,000.00
Variable costs per unit.........	0.20	0.25	0.60
Annual output capacity (units)†.....	1,000,000.00	500,000.00	250,000.00

* Assume straight-line depreciation over ten years to zero value for each plant and an interest rate on initial investment of 10 percent.

† For outputs greater than the annual capacity of any plant, these plants and their costs would simply be duplicated.

Questions

1. What is the lowest cost plant arrangement for outputs of 100,000, 500,000, and 1,000,000 units? A diagram would be helpful.
2. Your firm has already built plant C, and annual sales for the item have been and are expected to be 100,000 units, at a price of $4 per unit. Should the company continue to produce this item? If your answer is yes, should it use plant C or build another plant?
3. In the light of your analysis in Question 1, explain briefly why a company whose competitors are turning to automation may refuse to take the same step.

CASE 7–4. Macabre, Inc.

Macabre, Inc., had been greatly disappointed in sales of a phosphorescent, plastic skeleton for which it had purchased considerable special equipment (with negligible value for any other purpose), and had annual capacity of 20,000 or more units. The sales manager was certain that annual sales of 16,000 could be achieved through a variety chain if the prices were cut from $9 to $5 as compared with the present 2,000. There was general agreement on the sales volume, but some doubt as to how a product which was losing money at $9 could be profitable at $5.

	Present Average Costs at 2,000 Volume
Labor.	$2.70
Material.	1.70
Depreciation.	2.00
Selling and administrative at 50% of total factory cost.	3.20
	$9.60

Output per man-hour could be expected to rise 50 percent or more for this jump in output. A quantity discount on materials of 10 percent could be taken advantage of. If anything, total selling and administrative effort could be expected to decrease because the item would not require regular sales attention.

Would you recommend that the company drop the item, produce an estimated 2,000 at $9, or 16,000 at $5?

chapter 8

Capital Budgeting and Financing Capital Expenditures

IN THE PREVIOUS chapter, it was pointed out that investment in capital equipment can rationally be made if its calculated present value exceeds its present cost. It is obvious that fairly long-term forecasting is required in order to compute the present value, since it will be remembered, this is the discounted value of cash flows expected to accrue over the entire useful life of the machine (or other form of capital good). If the investment in question is an apartment building with an expected useful life of 50 years, for example, the forecast of rental returns must be made for a period of half a century. Fortunately, the most distant expected cash flows are discounted so heavily that they are not very significant in the calculation of present value, while the near-future returns, which are easier to estimate, have more weight in the calculation.

In order to calculate net present values, not only are long-term forecasts necessary but adequate estimates of the cost of capital are required. Cost-of-capital questions are particularly important when there are many competing capital investment projects which may be undertaken but only limited capital funds are available.

This chapter will discuss the problems involved in ranking investment alternatives and some of the issues in the cost-of-capital area.

Ranking Projects by Rate of Return

As explained previously, the present value of a project can be found from the formula:

$$V = \frac{Q_1}{1 + r} + \frac{Q_2}{(1 + r)^2} + \frac{Q_3}{(1 + r)^3} + \cdots + \frac{Q_n}{(1 + r)^n} + \frac{S}{(1 + r)^n}$$

Comparison of V with the present cost (C) of a machine or other capital good, when the r which is used is a minimum acceptable rate of return to the firm, determines whether the investment is worthwhile. Instead of inserting an "acceptable" r in the previous equation, it is possible to solve for the actual r in the following equation:

$$C = \frac{Q_1}{1+r} + \frac{Q_2}{(1+r)^2} + \frac{Q_3}{(1+r)^3} + \cdots + \frac{Q_n}{(1+r)^n} + \frac{S}{(1+r)^n}$$

The lower the cost of the project, the higher r becomes for any given cash flow and anticipated scrap value. This rate is sometimes called the "internal rate of return" or the "marginal efficiency of capital." If the annual rate of return calculated in this way exceeds the annual rate of cost of capital to the firm, the investment promises to be an acceptable one. The two approaches—comparison of V and C, and comparison of the annual rate of return with the annual cost of capital to the firm—are similar, except in certain cases involving large negative cash flows in later years, because present value will exceed present cost for any project which promises an internal rate of return in excess of the rate of cost of capital. Large negative cash flows in later years may cause the above equation to have multiple solutions. In most cases, however, identical decisions would result under either approach. It should be noted, however, that net present value assumes that cash inflows are reinvested at the cost of capital and the use of internal rate of return assumes that these inflows earn the internal rate of return. It is possible, however, that as cash inflows are received, that there not be investment opportunities available to the firm that would yield a return as great as the so-called internal rate of return.

If a firm has many investment alternatives, the rate of return on each project may be computed. A demand schedule for capital funds can be formed by ranking projects for which such funds are needed, starting with the project which promises the highest return. In a "going" company the very highest rate of return may often come from replacement of a machine or other capital asset which is crucial to the continued use of other equipment that is on hand. Other promising projects may involve expansion of capacity for a product already being produced (e.g., doubling the size of a motel), acquisition of capacity for turning out wholly new products (perhaps by purchasing other companies), acquisition of earlier or later stages in the production-distribution process, or some other activity.

A hypothetical demand schedule for capital funds is shown in Figure 8–1. The arbitrary cutoff point in this schedule is 6 percent; usually a large number of additional projects could be listed at low rates, but these have little prospect of becoming actualities. An implicit assumption made in compiling this sort of schedule is that each project is inde-

FIGURE 8–1

Demand for Capital Funds by a Firm

Project	Expected Rate of Return	Cost of Project (in millions)	Cumulative Demand for Funds (in millions)
A	50%	$ 5	$ 5
B	46	4	9
C	35	10	19
D	24	6	25
E	15	2	27
F	10	10	37
G	8	3	40
H	6	12	52

pendent of those which rank lower. Otherwise, it would not be possible to adopt only projects above any desired point without an effect on the expected rate of return. Projects need not be independent of those which rank higher, since it is assumed that all projects down to the actual cutoff point will be carried out. An investment project which depends on one lower in the scale is not really a separate project and should be combined with the lower one and the combination entered at the appropriate place.

Use of this ranking procedure requires that the decision maker know the cost of capital. It further suggests that the firm has ample funds available at that cost. These assumptions may not always be satisfied in practice. The cost-of-capital concept has been subject to substantial discussion and empirical testing, but a clear-cut case has not yet been made for any one of the several points of view espoused.[1]

Supply of Capital Funds

Concepts involved in an accurate statement of the nature of the supply of capital funds to the firm are more difficult than the concepts on the demand side. The supply curve of funds must be considered to be a curve of the "cost of capital" expressed as an annual interest rate. As long as investment projects promise to yield higher internal rates of interest than the cost-of-capital funds, they should be carried out. The cost of capital to a firm is complicated by the fact that funds for capital in-

---

[1] Among the many articles, the following are of considerable interest: Myron J. Gordon, "The Savings, Investment and Valuation of a Corporation," *Review of Economics and Statistics,* vol. 45 (February, 1962); Franco Modigliani and Merton H. Miller, "The Cost of Capital, Corporation Finance and the Theory of Investment," *American Economic Review,* vol. 48 (June, 1958); and John Lintner, "The Cost of Capital and Optimal Financing of Corporate Growth," *Journal of Finance,* vol. 18 (May, 1963).

vestment may come from a variety of sources and have specific costs which differ from the overall cost of capital.

Sources of Funds

The corporation obtains funds from internally generated sources and may obtain additional funds through outside equity and/or debt financing. Annual depreciation charges by a firm represent (very roughly) the conversion of the firm's fixed assets into liquid or near liquid assets. The depreciation charges themselves are not a source of funds. Rather, they are revenue brought in by the operations of the firm which build up liquid assets; depreciation charges prevent these assets from being paid out as dividends or income taxes. To the extent that these assets are liquid (rather than being in the form of slow-moving accounts receivable, for example), they can be expended for capital goods in a given year in furtherance of the firm's investment program. Similarly, profits earned and retained by the firm during a given year are usually at least partially available for investment. However, this may not always be the case. If the year's profits show up on the balance sheet as a diminution of liabilities rather than in an increase in assets, no actual funds will have been made available for investment, although it may then be easier to borrow again in order to secure capital assets. If additional equity capital has been raised by selling stock during the year, funds will have been made available for investment. The same is true if bonds have been sold or if short-term borrowing from banks has been increased.

Cost of Capital from Specific Sources

For decision making, the relevant costs of capital are future costs, not current or past costs. However, since a firm obtains capital funds from many sources, it is usually not wise to attempt to associate a particular source of funds with a particular capital expenditure outlay. Use of the specific cost of a particular source of capital funds is not wise because increasing the amount of equity funds may result in higher or lower debt costs and hence change the overall cost of capital. Thus, all changes in capital costs should be included, not just those directly associated with a particular source of funds.

In the following sections, costs of capital from specific sources will be discussed first; then, the overall cost of capital. In discussing specific costs, it is implicitly assumed that the mix of debt and equity sources of funds will remain approximately the same.[2]

---

[2] An excellent introduction to the capital structure problem is given by Burton G. Malkiel, *The Debt Equity Combination of the Firm and the Cost of Capital: An Introductory Analysis* (Morristown, N.J.: General Learning Press, 1971).

Cost of Debt

The cost of long-term debt or bonds when the firm receives the face value of the bonds or notes is the interest rate adjusted for the fact that interest is tax deductible. This cost can be expressed as:

$$i_D = (1 - t)R$$

where t is the marginal tax rate and R is the coupon interest rate. Thus with a marginal tax rate of 0.4 and a coupon rate of 6 percent, $i_D = 3.6$ percent.

In many cases bonds are sold at more or less than their face amount resulting in a premium or discount which either lowers or raises the effective interest rate. An approximate formula for calculating the tax adjusted effective interest rate is given by:

$$i_D = \frac{(1 - t)\left[C + \dfrac{1}{n}(P - Q_0)\right]}{\frac{1}{2}(P + Q_0)}$$

where C is the annual dollar interest cost, P is the par or face value of the debt, Q_0 is the proceeds of the issue, and n is the number of years to maturity. This formula is only an approximation as it does not take into account annual compounding. However, it is reasonably accurate for most purposes.[3]

Suppose a ten-year bond with a par value of $1,000 and a face interest rate of 6 percent sells at issue for a net price of $1,030. If the tax rate is 0.4, then

$$i_D = \frac{(1 - 0.4)[60.0 + \frac{1}{10}(1,000 - 1,030)]}{\frac{1}{2}[1,000 + 1,030]}$$
$$= \frac{0.6[60.0 - \frac{1}{10}(30)]}{1,015} = \frac{34.2}{1,015} = 3.37\%$$

For perpetual bonds, this formula simplifies to

$$i_D = \frac{(1 - t)C}{Q_0}$$

Cost of Preferred Stock

In recent years preferred stock has been somewhat in disfavor among corporations seeking investment funds.[4] This is partially because it imposes a debt-like obligation to pay dividends which are not tax deducti-

---

[3] See G. David Quirin, *The Capital Expenditure Decision* (Homewood, Ill.: Richard D. Irwin, Inc., 1967), pp. 100–101.

[4] Gordon Donaldson, "In Defense of Preferred Stock," *Harvard Business Review*, vol. 40, (July–August, 1962).

ble. Even though they are not required, as is interest on debt, dividends are a must if a firm is to successfully issue preferred stock. It is usual to treat dividends on preferred stock as a perpetual requirement, thus, the cost can be expressed

$$i_P = D/Q_0$$

where D is the annual dividend and Q_0 is the proceeds of the issue.

Cost of Common Stock

Equity costs are the most difficult costs to evaluate. One reason is that in order to determine the cost of equity, it is necessary to venture into that highly tentative area of knowledge—the valuation of common stocks. The discussion here will be similar to that of the model proposed by Myron J. Gordon.[5] There is, however, no general agreement that this particular model is the last word on valuation.

The value of a stock to an investor is the present worth of the entire expected flow of income to be derived from owning that stock plus some final liquidating value. Dividends are the income which stockholders receive through owning a stock; thus, at time o, the value of a stock can be expressed as

$$P_o = \frac{D_1}{(1 + i_E)} + \frac{D_2}{(1 + i_E)} + \cdots + \frac{D_\infty}{(1 + i_E)^\infty}$$

$$P_o = \sum_{t=o}^{t=\infty} \frac{D_t}{(1 + i_E)^t}$$

Where P_o is the value of a share of stock at time $t = o$, D_t is the dividend per share expected in period t, and i_E is the market discount factor for the risk class in which the company falls. A risk class is a group of firms which are viewed by the market as having the same risk characteristics, that is, probability distributions of expected dividends. In practice, industry groupings are often used as proxies for risk classes. Cost of equity capital may be defined as the market discount rate, i_E, which makes the present value of the expected dividends equal to the current market price of the stock. By solving the equation, above, for i_E, the cost of equity capital may be computed.

If it is assumed that dividends grow at a constant rate, g, the formula above becomes

$$P_o = \frac{D_o(1 + g)}{(1 + i_E)} + \frac{D_o(1 + g)^2}{(1 + i_E)^2} + \cdots + \frac{D_o(1 + g)^\infty}{(1 + i_E)^\infty}$$

[5] Myron J. Gordon, *The Investment, Financing and Valuation of the Corporation* (Homewood, Ill.: Richard D. Irwin, Inc., 1962).

If i_E is greater than g, reduces to[6]

$$P_o = \frac{D_o}{i_E - g}$$

Solving for the cost of equity capital gives

$$i_E = \frac{D_o}{P_o} + g$$

That is, the cost of capital is equal to the current dividend yield plus the growth rate.

In order to use this cost of equity capital measure, estimates must be made of growth rate, and the user must be willing to accept the assumption of a constant compound growth rate.[7] For example, given a stock currently paying a $2.50 dividend, which is expected to grow at a rate of 5 percent, and whose market price is $50, the cost of equity capital is computed as

$$i_E = \frac{2.50}{50.00} + 0.05 = 0.10, \text{ or } 10 \text{ percent}$$

Several questions are raised by this model. First, how valid is its emphasis on dividends; there are many companies which pay no dividends, yet their stocks trade at high price-earnings ratios. Second, the assumption of constant growth which was discussed briefly above. Third, the implicit assumption of a constant market rate of discount. The problems can be recognized here, but the student should look to his course work in finance for some of the approaches to these problems.

Most companies make a choice between paying dividends or retaining the profits in business. The question of an optimal dividend policy is another interesting question that must be deferred to some other book or course.[8] Investors who buy stock that pays no dividends must expect to sell the stock in the future to some other investors at a higher price even though there are no current dividends. Underlying these transactions must be a belief that some time in the future the corporation will begin to pay dividends. Formally, however, the only element that would enter in the valuation model for such a corporation would be the liquida-

---

[6] Ibid.

[7] Other growth stock models are discussed in Paul F. Wendt, "Current Growth Stock Valuation Methods," *Financial Analysts Journal*, March–April, 1965.

[8] See, for example, Irwin Friend and Marshall Puckett, "Dividends and Stock Prices," *American Economic Review*, vol. 54 (September, 1964); John Lintner, "Distribution of Incomes of Corporations among Dividends, Retained Earnings, and Taxes," *American Economic Review*, vol. 46 (May, 1956); Merton H. Miller and Franco Modigliani, "Dividend Policy, Growth and the Valuation of Shares," *Journal of Business*, vol. 34 (October 1961); Alexander A. Robichek and Stewart C. Myers, *Optimal Financing Decisions* (Englewood Cliffs, N.J.: Prentice-Hall, Inc., 1965); and, James E. Walter, *Dividend Policies and Enterprise Valuation* (Belmont, Calif.: Wadsworth Publishing Co., Inc., 1967).

tion or terminal value. In the formal equation for the cost of equity capital, the firm might substitute the average return that investors might expect to make from market price appreciation.

While the assumption of constant growth may be troublesome, most other assumptions about growth patterns are also troublesome. Often companies grow at high rates in their early years and experience slower growth in their later years. Specific growth assumptions can be used in the valuation model outlined above. Suppose a company's dividend was expected to grow at 10 percent for five years and at 5 percent thereafter. The formula to be solved for i_E would be

$$P_o = \sum_{t=1}^{5} \frac{D_o(1.10)^t}{(1 + i_E)^t} + \sum_{t-6}^{\infty} \frac{D_5(1.05)^t}{(1 + i_E)^t}$$

While these alternative growth assumptions are more cumbersome to work with, computers make the solution of such an equation a relatively simple matter.

Several writers have suggested that since the distant future is more uncertain than the near future, the market rate of discount should be increased for the distant future. A problem is to determine the appropriate adjustment rates to apply. It is more desirable to build the risk elements directly into your analysis rather than make an arbitrary adjustment of the market discount rate. There are a number of books and articles dealing with the treatment of risk and uncertainty in capital expenditure decision problems.[9] Unless there is a radical change in the kind of assets which the firm employs, it seems reasonable to assume that it remains in the same risk class and therefore has a relatively constant cost of equity capital.[10]

Cost of Internally Generated Funds

Funds for investment may be generated internally in a number of ways. Earnings may be retained in the business rather than paid out in dividends. Balances may accrue through the reduction in the level of accounts receivable, or from an increase in the amount of accounts payable (which does not increase costs through lost discounts). Also funds may be retained through a reduction in accounting profits and

---

[9] See David B. Hertz, "Risk Analysis in Capital Investment," *Harvard Business Review*, January–February, 1964; and Wilbur G. Lewellen, *The Cost of Capital* (Belmont, Calif.: Wadsworth Publishing Co., Inc., 1969).

[10] Another approach to the cost of equity capital is by use of the capital-asset pricing model developed by William F. Sharpe, "Capital Asset Prices: A Theory of Market Equilibrium under Conditions of Risk," *Journal of Finance*, vol. 19 (September, 1964). See James C. Van Horne, *Financial Management and Policy* (3d ed., Englewood Cliffs, N.J.: Prentice-Hall, Inc., 1974).

taxes due to the noncash depreciation expenses charges which prevent the payment of taxes and dividends.

These internally generated funds are the largest source of funds available to corporations for new investments. Even though they do not cause an entry on the books to express their costs, it would be a grave mistake to regard them as free. Investments made from internally generated funds at returns below the firm's market rate of discount would reduce the average return on the firm's assets and lower the market value of the firm. Such a policy would reduce the well-being of the stockholders and would certainly be unwise. These funds therefore should earn at least the cost of capital and their opportunity cost would be represented by the average cost of capital.

Overall Cost of Capital

Use of the proportions of the capital represented by the various classes of securities as weights in determining the cost of capital has been suggested by several authors. However, some have suggested using the book value of the securities while others have suggested market value. Book value weights can lead to inconsistent estimates since market values were used in computing the specific costs of capital for each source. Book value for equity may seriously understate the proportion of equity in the capital structure. Market value weights also have some difficulties. They may appear quite different from the book value and investors may perceive the capital structure to be that implied by the book value figures. Such observations may alter the risk perceptions of investors and change their valuation of the stock. Also, market prices are

FIGURE 8–2

Cost of Capital Computations for CFW Corporations—Book and Market Value Weights

Balance Sheet

Assets		Liabilities	
Cash and plant..........	$1,000,000	Long-term debt..........	$ 300,000
		Common stock..........	700,000
Total...........	$1,000,000	Total...........	$1,000,000

Market value of debt....... $ 250,000
Market value of stock...... 1,000,000

Specific cost of debt, $3.00\% = i_D$
Specific cost of equity, $10.00\% = i_E$

Costs of Capital

	Book Value Weights	Market Value Weights
Proportion debt......................	$0.3 \times 3.00 = 0.9$	$0.2 \times 3.00 = 0.6$
Proportion equity....................	$0.7 \times 10.00 = 7.0$	$0.8 \times 10.00 = 8.0$
Cost of capital................	7.9%	8.6%

subject to greater variation than book values and may fluctuate widely making the appropriate weights difficult to choose.

The example shown in Figure 8–2 indicates the procedure for computing the weighted average cost of capital using either book or market value weights. The balance sheet shows debt of $300,000 and equity of $700,000. However, the market values are $250,000 and $1,000,000, respectively. The computations indicate a weighted average cost using book value weights of 7.9 percent but a cost of 8.6 percent when market values are used. Where possible market value weights should be used but care must be taken not to have extreme market fluctuations unduly influence the computations.

Capital Structure

All of the foregoing discussion of the cost of capital has been under the assumption that the capital structure—proportion of debt and equity —was unchanged. As with the other areas discussed, there is considerable controversy over the effect of changing capital structure upon the cost of capital. Modigliani and Miller have shown that under certain assumptions the average cost of capital will remain unchanged with varying proportions of debt and equity. Others have questioned this analysis primarily on the realism of the assumptions and have shown that violations of their assumptions lead to the more traditional view that an appropriate use of debt can reduce the average cost of capital. Thus, the analysis in this chapter has assumed that the optimal capital structure has been found and that additional financing will maintain this structure. In practice, there are periodic departures from optimum capital structures as firms' issue first debt and then equity capital to obtain new funds for capital investment.[11]

Supply Schedule for Capital Funds

The supply schedule for capital funds should relate the average cost of capital and increasing quantities of capital funds. Within fairly wide ranges, the cost of capital to a firm may be fairly constant. A number of scholars have suggested, however, that as the amount of funds sought increases the average cost of capital rises.[12] The shape and position of the curve will depend upon the size and risk class of the corporation. Figure 8–3 shows one possible supply schedule for capital funds on the graph of

---

[11] See Modigliani and Miller, "The Cost of Capital . . ."; and for the traditional view, Eli Schwartz, "Theory of the Capital Structure of the Firm," *Journal of Finance*, vol. 14 (March, 1959).

[12] James S. Dusenberry, *Business Cycles and Economic Growth* (New York: McGraw-Hill Book Co., 1958).

FIGURE 8–3

Demand and Supply of Capital Funds

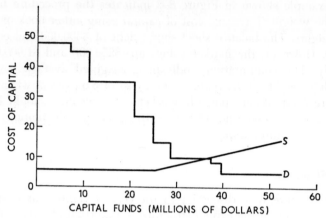

the demand for investment funds derived from a schedule such as that given in Figure 8–1. The flat segment would represent the funds available at a constant average cost from internal and external sources. The rising segment suggests that above some amount, the market is unwilling to supply funds at the same price to this firm. Perhaps, this reflects a market judgment that the firm cannot manage additional investment projects at this time and that it should undertake fewer projects.

The chart in Figure 8–3 suggests that the firm should only invest in those projects up to the intersection of the supply and demand schedules. In practice, there are several problems in using such an approach to capital budgeting analysis. Projects may be contingent upon the acceptance of some other project; they may be mutually exclusive, that is, the undertaking of one project may make another impossible. New methods are being developed to handle these more complex capital investment problems.[13]

CASE 8–1. Problems in Capital Budgeting

1. The XYZ Company has available several investment opportunities with outlays and aftertax cash inflows given as shown in Exhibit 8–1A.

---

[13] See H. Martin Weingartner, *Mathematical Programming and the Analysis of Capital Budgeting* (Englewood Cliffs, N.J.: Prentice-Hall, Inc., 1963); and H. Martin Weingartner, "Capital Budgeting of Interrelated Projects: Survey and Synthesis," *Management Science*, vol. 13 (October, 1966).

EXHIBIT 8–1A

		Cash Inflow by Year				
Project	Outlay	1	2	3	4	5
A........	$ 50,000	15,000	15,000	15,000	15,000	15,000
B........	75,000	25,000	25,000	30,000	35,000	35,000
C........	100,000	75,000	25,000	20,000	15,000	10,000
D........	15,000	5,000	5,000	5,000	5,000	0
E........	90,000	25,000	20,000	20,000	20,000	20,000

a. Compute the internal rate of return on each project.
b. Plot the investment demand schedule.
c. If the cost of capital to XYZ is 10 percent, which projects should be undertaken?

2. The balance sheet of ABC Corporation is given below. ABC has been growing at the rate of 7 percent per year and currently pays a dividend of $2 per year.

ABC CORPORATION
Balance Sheet

Assets		Liabilities	
Plant.................	$1,000,000	Long-term debt.........	$ 500,000
		Common stock.........	500,000
Total...........	$1,000,000	Total...........	$1,000,000

a. If the market price of the stock is currently $75 with 10,000 shares outstanding, what is the cost of equity capital?
b. The company's earnings are such that its marginal tax rate is 0.48 and it can issue new bonds with a coupon rate of 6.5 percent. What is the cost of debt capital?
c. What is the average cost of capital if new stock and bonds are going to be issued so that the proportions of debt and equity remain the same when valued at book? At market, assuming the current debt has a market value of $450,000?

3. Using the annual reports of several corporations, compute the average cost of capital. How does the cost of capital for a utility compare to an industrial? Use both book and market value weights.

CASE 8–2. Imperial Company

The Imperial Company, a small Detroit fruit juice company, was considering two investment alternatives in January of 1962. Both alternatives concerned products with the same seasonal pattern. The time limit on the decision was very short, as both projects required deliveries no later than April 15.

The first alternative considered by the company was the production, packaging, and sale of "chilled orange juice." This juice would be sold directly to retail stores and to dairies for home delivery.

Other brands of chilled orange juice had already secured some brand identification and some measure of success with the trade by quality control of the product and considerable advertising expense. The company felt that it would have to sell its juice under the private labels of dairies and retailers or as an "off" brand. In either case, the company felt, the price it obtained would be somewhat less than that of better known brands.

The company estimated sales volume as shown in Exhibit 8–2A if it entered production.

EXHIBIT 8–2A

1962:

April........................	6,000 units
May.........................	12,000
June........................	18,000
July........................	24,000
August......................	30,000
September...................	30,000
October.....................	24,000
November....................	18,000
December....................	12,000

1963:

January.....................	12,000
February....................	12,000
March.......................	12,000
	210,000 units in first year
	300,000 units in second year

Selling price and direct product costs were estimated by the company to be 24 cents per unit and 21 cents per unit, respectively. Direct product costs were as shown in Exhibit 8–2B.

EXHIBIT 8–2B

Raw materials.....................................	$0.125
Package...	0.025
Labor...	0.010
Overhead (additional only)........................	0.010
Outside container.................................	0.010
Delivery..	0.010
Advertising allowance.............................	0.010
Brokerage...	0.010
	$0.210

The company believed it was impossible to predict profit margins beyond the second year, since the prices of the raw materials fluctuated widely on a yearly basis, depending on crop yields. Imperial felt it could forestall price fluctuations for a period of up to one year by buying ahead, but it pointed out that the risk was considerable in doing this, since prices might be lower in the next year.

The capital investment required to produce and sell the chilled orange juice was easily determined by the company (see Exhibit 8–2C).

EXHIBIT 8–2C

Plate design charges.....................................		$ 350
Packaging machine..	$4,550	
Electrical installation....................................	125	
Transportation..	135	
Spare parts...	240	5,050
Carton inventory...		2,500
Used refrigerated truck..................................		2,500

The company felt that it would wish to retain an inventory of 60,000 finished cartons of juice. It estimated that this inventory would cost $1,500 to maintain for a year. It also pointed out that it expected a base amount of $6,000 of accounts receivable to be outstanding at all times.

The packaging machine required for the chilled juice was a special type designed to handle one type of plastic-coated carton made by one manufacturer. The company pointed out that historically there had been an ever-increasing technological advancement in this type of container packaging. In view of this rapid change the company felt that depreciation charges should be rapid and that useful economic life should be no more than five years.

The company felt that a refrigerated truck was necessary to ship the chilled juice. It was able to purchase a used one and considered its useful life to be four years. Tax rules permitted a 150 percent declining balance to be used to depreciate the truck.

The second alternative under consideration by the Imperial Company was the production and sale of an orange drink placed in half-gallon, nonreturnable decanter bottles. The product was considered of low quality and in the imitation class, the juice content being only 5 percent.

In this field, one or two brands had established only a token following among the trade. Imperial executives attributed this to poor quality control and problems concerning labeling requirements. Each of the two products on the market had been seized more than once within the last year for mislabeling. In addition, Imperial had determined that advertising allowances and expenditures for this product had been very small and not directed to the consumer. Therefore the company concluded that there had been little chance to build a following among retail consumers.

The company had conducted trade research which led it to believe that it could sell orange drink at the same price as that of the market leaders, provided it sold on a guaranteed sales basis. The company executives felt that with adequate quality control, they should be able to establish a brand name in the orange drink line. Under these circumstances, they would be willing to accept a lower than normal profit margin.

Selling price and direct product cost for the orange drink were estimated as shown in Exhibit 8–2D.

EXHIBIT 8–2D

Selling price	$0.31 per unit
Production cost:	
Raw material	0.090
Package	0.100
Cap	0.010
Label	0.010
Overhead (additional only)	0.020
Delivery	0.020
Brokerage	0.010
Advertising	0.010
	$0.270 per unit

The raw material costs for the orange drink, as opposed to the costs for orange juice, were much more stable and presented no problem, the company decided.

The company decided it could expect to obtain the sales shown in Exhibit 8–2E if it adopted the orange drink.

EXHIBIT 8–2E

1962:	
April	4,000 units
May	8,000
June	12,000
July	16,000
August	16,000
September	8,000
October	2,000
	66,000 units in first year
	130,000 units in second year

Capital costs were considerably less than for the investment in chilled juice, with most of the difference attributed to the difference in cost of the two packaging machines and the fact that no truck would be purchased (see Exhibit 8–2F).

EXHIBIT 8–2F

Art charges and plate for label..................		$ 200
Packaging machine..........................	$2,400	
Transportation.............................	125	
Electric installation.........................	125	2,650
Bottles and caps.............................		1,320
Labels.....................................		500

Management figured that an inventory of 8,000 bottles of orange drink would have to be maintained at a cost of $800 per year. The average level of accounts receivable was expected to be about $3,600.

As opposed to the rather specialized packaging machine required for orange juice, the packaging machine for orange drink was designed to handle a large number of sizes and shapes of bottles and was considered a standard machine, having been in production for more than ten years without major modifications. The company management estimated its useful life at ten years.

Delivery of the orange drink could be made in regular company trucks so that no new truck would be needed.

Imperial's management believed that there would be much less of a spoilage problem with the orange drink than there would be with the chilled juice. Temperature was not critical, and the drink could be stored for extended periods of time. The chilled juice was somewhat perishable and could not be stored for long periods of time. It required refrigeration both in storage and in delivery. The company had some excess refrigerator space, however, and management decided that by economizing space, an inventory of chilled juice could be squeezed in without the addition of more lockers.

Questions

1. Which alternative should the Imperial Company management choose?
2. What assumptions have you made about the future?
3. If Imperial could raise up to $20,000 at 6 percent but additional funds would cost 10 percent, should both alternatives be taken? Explain.

CASE 8–3. The Component Manufacturing Company

The Component Manufacturing Company, located in Oakland, California, was a medium-sized producer of parts for the aircraft industry. Prior to 1958, operations were conducted at four plants scattered throughout the city of Oakland.

The dispersion of these plants had been a matter of vital concern to the board of directors for some time. Costs had been rising rapidly and had begun to endanger the competitive pricing position of the company. The board felt that the consolidation of operations under one or possibly two roofs could do much to alleviate the situation.

So, in the spring of 1958 the company entered into a contract with the Acme Construction Company to build a plant on a site in the city of Stockton, 60 miles from the Oakland plants. The financing was arranged through the company's bankers acting as intermediaries with a financial holding company. Under the terms of the deal, the Component Manufacturing Company entered into a 17-year lease agreement with a $250,000 "buy-back" provision. It was contemplated that the transfer of manufacturing facilities and operations would be conducted in phases, with the final move occurring by 1964.

The first section of the new plant was completed, and operations commenced in August of 1960. It had now become apparent that it was not feasible to transfer all operations to this plant. Certain administration and sales functions were better coordinated in Oakland. In addition, it was discovered that the disposal of waste from plating operations could not be handled without a major capital expenditure. So the long-range policy now became firmly established as envisioning a two-plant operation.

To implement this objective, a new plant, contiguous to a super-highway leading to Stockton, was leased for a ten-year period in December of 1960.

Between 1960 and 1962 the company suffered severe losses due to quality problems in the field, training costs at the new plant, and a heavy litigation claim. As a result, the company had a $400,000 carry-forward loss for tax purposes.

By now, operations were conducted in three plants:

Plant No. 1—Owned by the company, encumbered with a $200,000 mortgage. Fully depreciated as war facility. Located in Oakland in generally undesirable area.

Plant No. 2—Leased in December, 1960, Approximately eight years of lease remaining. Located in Oakland.

Plant No. 3—Lease commenced in August of 1960 to continue for 17 years. Located in Stockton.

In September of 1962 the company received an offer of $200,000 for plant No. 1. The offer was considered quite substantial, considering the general deterioration of real estate values in the neighborhood. Further, acceptance would enable the company to consolidate operations into two plants.

EXHIBIT 8–3A

Sale of Building and Move Proposal: Analysis of Cost Savings

	Present Cost	Proposed Cost
Rent	.....	$48,000
Taxes and insurance	$15,200	7,000
Heat	6,800	4,500
Power, light, and water	9,400	8,000
Guards	12,000	4,000
Porters	12,000	9,000
Building repair	4,000	1,000
Parking	900	3,900
Interest	12,000	.....
Maintenance	16,200	2,500
Total operating cost	$88,500	$87,900
Gross cost saving		600
Additional savings:		
Labor rate revision		9,000
Trucking costs		6,000
Plating maintenance reduction		4,000
Companywide improved efficiency		10,400
Net savings from move		$30,000

However, before the consolidation could be accomplished, an extension had to be built on plant No. 2. The treasurer, R. C. Baker, was directed to negotiate this possibility with the owners of the plant. He was further directed to make a thorough study of the cost and cash flow implications of the sale.

EXHIBIT 8–3B

COMPONENT MANUFACTURING COMPANY
Schedule of Capital Expenditures

Item	Amount
Depreciable items:	
Plating department	$43,000
Switchboard	5,000
Laboratory equipment	1,000
Electric wiring	5,000
Total depreciable items	$54,000
Moving costs:	
IBM	$ 4,000
Level plating floor	2,000
Clean up plant No. 1	2,000
Office	3,000
Model room	2,000
Miscellaneous and extras	3,000
Total moving	$16,000
Total expenditures	$70,000

EXHIBIT 8-3C

COMPONENT MANUFACTURING COMPANY
Cash Flow

	Amount Paid Out	Savings before Tax	Less 50% Income Tax	Less Carry-Forward Tax (000)	Savings after Tax	Add Back Depreciation	Net Cash Savings	Adjustment for Less Carry-Forward	Adjusted Cash Savings
Capital expenditures*........	$70,000						$ (70,000)		$ (70,000)
First-year savings.........		$ 30,000	$ 7,000*	0	$ 23,000	$ 5,400	28,400		28,400
Second-year savings........		30,000	15,000	(100)	(85,000)	5,400	(79,600)	$100,000	20,400
Third-year savings.........		30,000	15,000	50	65,000	5,400	70,400	(50,000)	20,400
Fourth-year savings........		30,000	15,000	0	15,000	5,400	20,400		20,400
Fifth-year savings.........		30,000	15,000	0	15,000	5,400	20,400		20,400
Sixth-year savings.........		30,000	15,000	0	15,000	5,400	20,400		20,400
Seventh-year savings.......		30,000	15,000	0	15,000	5,400	20,400		20,400
Eighth-year savings........		30,000	15,000	0	15,000	5,400	20,400		20,400
Ninth-year savings.........		30,000	15,000	0	15,000	5,400	20,400		20,400
Tenth-year savings.........		30,000	15,000	0	15,000	5,400	20,400		20,400
	$70,000	$300,000	$142,000	(50)	$108,000	$54,000	$92,000	$ 50,000	$142,000

* Sixteen thousand dollars of capital expenditure will be written off against current operations. Therefore, 50 percent, or $8,000, is recovered as income tax reduction.

Mr. Baker realized that the tax carry-forward position of $400,000 would be very important in the cash-flow analysis. Selling the building now would result in a $200,000 capital gain, since the plant was fully amortized. Capital gains would be applied to an ordinary loss, and the company would lose 25 cents on the dollar (assuming a tax rate of 50 percent for ease of calculation). This loss would amount to $50,000. If the building were not sold, it would take two years to use up the loss carry-forward.

The owners of plant No. 2 will make the necessary extensions at an annual rental of $48,000, provided Component Manufacturing Company agrees to an extension of the lease to ten years.

On the basis of these preliminary considerations, Mr. Baker decided to analyze two alternatives: (1) sale of the plant immediately and (2) sale of the plant in two years.

Exhibits 8–3A, 8–3B, and 8–3C were prepared by Mr. Baker's staff with the assistance of the industrial engineering department to facilitate the analysis of the two alternatives.

Exhibit 8–3A shows the estimated cost savings from consolidation on a pro forma basis. Exhibit 8–3B is the schedule of capital requirements. Depreciable items are separated from moving costs to facilitate cash flow computations.

Exhibit 8–3C shows the cash flow under the two alternatives. "Net Cash Savings" refers to the first alternative, while the sale in two years is headed "Adjusted Cash Savings." The cash-flow adjustments for capital loss carry-forward were calculated as shown in Exhibit 8–3D.

EXHIBIT 8–3D

	Alternative I		*Alternative II*	
Year	*Profits*	*Cash Flow (taxes 50% after $400,000)*	*Profits*	*Cash Flow (taxes 50% after $400,000)*
1.....................	$400,000*	$400,000	$200,000	$200,000
2.....................	200,000	100,000	200,000	200,000
3.....................	200,000	100,000	400,000*	250,000†
Total.............	$800,000	$600,000	$800,000	$650,000

* Includes $200,000 normal profits plus capital gains.
† Capital gains tax at 25 percent on $200,000.

Question

1. Consider the conversion decision and the sell now or later decision as separate decisions and analyze each. What actions should the firm take? What qualifications are necessary?

CASE 8–4. Diversified Manufacturing Company

In 1947, after 20 years' experience in the field of job-shop manufacturing, Mr. Frederick Burke, Sr., organized the Diversified Manufacturing Company (DMC) in Los Angeles, California. Mr. Burke's sons—Frederick, Jr., and Peter—joined the management of the firm in 1955 and 1962, respectively.

Mr. Burke began by purchasing a 4,000-square-foot building, an adjacent 4,000-square-foot vacant lot, and general-purpose production machinery. The building was expanded in 1954 to 7,500 square feet of production area and 500 square feet of office area.

DMC has been basically a metal-fabricating job shop but has developed a line of metal smoke stands which are sold nationwide through jobbers. It also produces a large share of ice-cream-cone dispensers and -cup dispensers for the ice-cream-cone and -cup industry. DMC has recently become a major supplier of equipment for a leading mobile ice-cream and food-vending company. In 1962 these products accounted for approximately 75 percent of the company's sales. Exhibits 8–4A, 8–4B, and 8–4C show the 1962 balance sheet, income statement, and additional data concerning 1962 operations.

EXHIBIT 8–4A

DIVERSIFIED MANUFACTURING COMPANY
Balance Sheet, December 31, 1962

Assets		Liabilities	
Cash	$ 11,470	Accounts payable	$ 4,736
Securities	5,000	Accruals	2,471
Accounts receivable	18,723	Notes payable	950
Inventory	17,471		
	$ 52,664		$ 8,157
Plant and equipment	64,308	Shareholders' undistributed	
		income*	27,100
		Earned surplus	1,715
		Common stock	80,000
Total	$116,972	Total	$116,972

* DMC is a corporation with a proprietorship tax structure. See Exhibit 8–4B.

EXHIBIT 8–4B

DIVERSIFIED MANUFACTURING COMPANY
Statement of Earnings, December 31, 1962
(in thousands)

Sales	$208
Cost of goods	109
Gross profit	$ 99
Factory burden, sales, and administrative expense	72
Net profit	$ 27

EXHIBIT 8–4C

DIVERSIFIED MANUFACTURING COMPANY
Additional 1962 Data

Average hours per week per man............................	42.7 hours
Total direct labor..	22,300 hours
Average number of production men—22,300/(42.7 × 50)........	10.5 men
Estimated monthly production (at 100% capacity) with present plant and equipment.....................................	$20,000
Estimated average minimum work area per production worker....	500 square feet
Maximum production workers based on space limitations—8,000/500..	16 men
Sales dollars per square foot—$208,000/8,000..................	$28.60 per square foot
Sales dollars per man-hour..................................	$9.35 per hour

EXHIBIT 8–4D

DIVERSIFIED MANUFACTURING COMPANY
Actual and Forecast Annual Sales (1953–65)

Year	Sales
1953................................	$ 91,000
1954................................	80,000
1955................................	89,000
1956................................	93,000
1957................................	101,000
1958................................	95,000
1959................................	107,000
1960................................	121,000
1961................................	142,000
1962................................	208,000
1963................................	275,000*
1964................................	300,000*
1965................................	350,000*

* Forecast. Rapid growth is expected because of an expanded sales promotion plus normal growth.

EXHIBIT 8–4E

DIVERSIFIED MANUFACTURING COMPANY
Monthly Sales, 1961–62
(in thousands)

Month	1961	1962
January........................	$ 7.3	$12.7
February........................	15.4	20.7
March..........................	11.1	19.0
April...........................	18.5	18.9
May............................	12.4	17.1
June...........................	13.0	16.9
July............................	8.4	20.3
August.........................	9.1	7.7
September......................	8.6	8.5
October........................	13.2	18.2
November......................	18.1	27.2
December......................	8.6	20.8

In 1962 the officers of DMC were considering a number of problems concerning the future of the company. Additional manufacturing area was necessary to achieve the forecasted future sales (see Exhibit 8–4D). The financing of the expansion was also a question to be resolved. Several new products were being considered to help even out the rather large monthly fluctuations in production (see Exhibit 8–4E).

DMC determined that a plant with 15,000 square feet of manufacturing area would be sufficient for the next five years. This was derived from the data given in Exhibit 8–4C as follows:

Maximum monthly sales with 8,000 square feet	$ 20,000
Maximum annual sales with 8,000 square feet	240,000
At 80 percent of capacity, annual sales	192,000
Forecast of 1965 sales	350,000

$$\frac{350,000}{192,000} = \frac{x}{8,000}$$

$$x = 14,600 \text{ square feet } (80\% \text{ of capacity})$$

DMC also determined that additional equipment equal to approximately 80 percent of current equipment would be needed by 1965, but that it could be added gradually over the next three years. The replacement value of the current equipment was $40,000. The new building was expected to cost $80,000, the additional equipment $32,000 (80 percent of $40,000); it was expected that the old building could be sold for $40,000. The required financing would then be $72,000. Exhibit 8–4F shows the balance sheet of DMC revised to reflect a $72,000 term loan which the management believed would be repaid from earnings over the next three years if only nominal dividends were declared.

In order to level monthly production, three products were considered, each of which required some additional development. As patents had not

EXHIBIT 8–4F

DIVERSIFIED MANUFACTURING COMPANY

Revised Balance Sheet
(figures rounded to nearest thousand)

Assets		Liabilities	
Cash	$ 11,000	Accounts payable	$ 5,000
Securities	5,000	Accruals	2,000
Accounts receivable	19,000	Notes payable	1,000
Inventory	17,000	Shareholders' income	27,000
	$ 52,000		$ 35,000
Plant and equipment	136,000	Term loan	72,000
		Common stock and retained	
		earnings	82,000
Total	$188,000	Total	$189,000

yet been obtained, these were described only as A, B, and C. Any one or a combination of these products could be produced, as they were independent.

Exhibit 8–4G gives expected additional development and initial mar-

EXHIBIT 8–4G

Product	Cost of Additional Development	Cost of Initial Marketing
A	$2,000	$ 3,000
B	4,000	10,000
C	7,000	15,000

keting costs for each of these products. Exhibit 8–4H shows expected sales and profit contributions for these products.

EXHIBIT 8–4H

DIVERSIFIED MANUFACTURING COMPANY
Proposed Products—A, B, and C

Product	Forecast Sales			Expected Gross Profit		
	1963	1964	1965 and After	1963	1964	1965 and After
A	$10,000	$15,000	$20,000	$1,500	$2,250	$3,000
B	20,000	40,000	40,000	3,000	6,000	6,000
C	......	30,000	50,000	....	4,500	7,500

Mr. Burke and his sons decided to study these proposals and determine what action to take.

Questions

1. What is DMC's estimated cost of capital?
2. Should the expansion be undertaken? Explain.
3. Which, if any, of the filler projects should be used if expansion is justified? If it is not justified?

chapter **9**

Production and Social Costs

CONCERN over environmental deterioration has brought the subject of social costs into great prominence. Virtually all types of production impose some costs on other persons, and firms, in some fields, such as paper, plastics, and nylon production, may impose very large costs on others. Such effects are called "externalities." While some externalities are beneficial—for example, pleasure from a neighbor's flower garden— the ones that cause concern are unfavorable.[1]

As was emphasized in earlier chapters, private costs are taken fully into account by a firm in deciding upon production processes, output rates, plant expansion, contraction, and product abandonment. Costs placed upon others may be partially considered by conscientious executives but are very unlikely to be fully taken into account unless financial rewards or penalties induce such action. As a definitional matter it seems best to let the term "social costs" include the sum of internal and external costs rather than pertaining to the latter alone. The broad problem facing all economies (socialist as well as capitalist) is how to insure that social costs of production will be taken into account by economic units.[2]

---

[1] This is not to say that favorable externalities always require no action. Steven N. S. Cheung, "The Fable of the Bees: An Economic Investigation," *Journal of Law and Economics*, vol. 16, No. 1 (April, 1973), points out that the services of bees and flowers, which often provide uncompensated external benefit, have been marketed since World War I. Bee hives are moved from farm to farm in the western fruit growing areas. In some cases fruit farmers pay for pollination services; in other cases beekeepers pay for nectar extraction.

[2] The USSR is said to have as serious environmental disruption as ours. Marshall I. Goldman, "The Convergence of Environmental Disruption," *Economics of the Environment*; R. Dorfman and N. S. Dorfman, eds. (New York: W. W. Norton & Co. Inc., 1972), p. 294.

Private Bargaining

Under favorable conditions the price system itself can cause firms to consider all costs—not just private costs. Suppose a retail store erects a sign bearing its name on its own property in such a way as largely to obscure the sign of an adjacent theater from passing motorists. The damage is two-way. The store's sign reduces the value of the theater's sign, and the latter's sign reduces the value of the store's sign. Although the second firm to erect a sign may have been somewhat unethical or careless in its decision, subsequent economic behavior is not based on which sign appeared first. A private bargain between the firms under which one firm pays all or part of the cost of moving the other firm's sign is a possibility. The theater owner is likely to be under more pressure from the conflict of signs, since he changes the advertised feature frequently. In the absence of any legal liability the theater owner may bribe the store owner to move his sign to another location.

The store owner should consider the proferred payment as an opportunity cost of leaving the sign in its present location. (Sacrificed income is equivalent to a cost.) An appropriate offer and locational adjustment may remove the external cost imposed by each sign. If he finds it to be cheaper, the theater owner can, of course, move his own sign. If ill will arises between individuals, a private bargain becomes less likely. For example, the store owner may feel it worthwhile to sacrifice some income in order to punish the theater owner whom he does not like.[3] Malevolence can be a powerful economic force.

Not all adverse "neighborhood effects" should be removed. The costs of removing a given amount of noise, traffic congestion, air and water pollution, and litter may exceed the benefits, just as the cost of moving one of the conflicting signs may exceed the benefits.

There is frequently an indirect payoff to the individual who undergoes pollution. For example, an individual may be able to buy or rent a home more cheaply if it is known beforehand that there will be noise from a nearby highway or airport. He may prefer to save on housing cost rather than pay for a quiet environment (especially if he is a bit deaf). This is another example in which the price system may operate in what appears to be an equitable manner.

Pollution and Common Property

The more difficult externality problems facing society and business arise from air and water pollution where many firms and individuals both contribute to, and are adversely affected by, the externality. In large

---

[3] A famous article dealing with the entire problem is Ronald Coase, "The Problem of Social Cost," *Journal of Law and Economics,* vol. 3 (1960).

measure the pollution problem is due to the common property status of most air and water. Any single firm or individual has little incentive to take care of a resource when he cannot appreciable appropriate the benefits of his own conservation. This explains why the same person who carves his initials in a park bench will not do the same with his dining room table. It also helps explain why there is overfishing of popular species such as lobsters which belong to anyone until they enter a trap.

When no charge is made for use of the common environment, firms, municipalities, and individuals can reduce their own costs by using the air, water, beaches, and so forth, as a receptacle for wastes. From a social point of view there is too large an output of commodities that are produced without meeting all costs. In part this may explain why Americans are so well supplied with paper, plastics, cans, and plumbing. From the point of view of the firm, the desirability of having minimal and uniformly applicable restrictions is clear. A firm in a particular industry that is subject to more costly restrictions than its competitors may find itself seriously disadvantaged. The recycling of bottles and aluminum cans may be useful to large companies for its public relations value, even if the process is not inherently very efficient.

Solution by Merger

Under favorable circumstances it is possible to "internalize an externality" through merger of the firm that is harmed and the firm that is polluting. The situation is then improved in that the entire cost will be taken into account by one company. A problem is that the firm that has been able to get rid of some of its costs is not likely to want to absorb them through merger. A more likely situation for merger is found in the "common oil pool case" where pollution is not involved but where firms affect one another's costs. If several different oil companies are pumping from a common oil pool, each has an incentive to pump at an uneconomically high rate in order to maximize its net revenue from the pool. (Each wants to get the oil before it is taken by the others.) A merger of such firms can change the rate of pumping to an optimal one since there will be a single decision maker in a more predictable situation.

The oil pool is an example of an exhaustible resource. In theory the owner of such a resource seeks to maximize its present value, rather than its current production of income. The owner always has the option of selling the property and consequently has an incentive to mine at a rate that keeps the total value at a maximum. It might be thought that this could be done by not working the mine at all but that is not likely to be the case since the owner sacrifices interest income on the valuable resource as long as it remains in the ground.

Present value of an oil pool or other mine is computed from the same formula as the present value of a machine except that the "scrap value" is likely to be zero (assuming that supporting capital equipment cannot be moved), namely:

$$V = \frac{QR_1}{1 + r} + \frac{QR_2}{(1 + r)^2} + \frac{QR_3}{(1 + r)^3} + \cdots + \frac{QR_n}{(1 + r)^n}$$

Quasi rent each period is value of the extracted product less variable costs of mining. Each year's quasi rent (cash flow) is discounted according to its remoteness from the present, with the discount rate being the expected annual interest rate at which cash could be invested elsewhere. (Quasi rents are assumed in the formula to be secured at the end of each year, since even the first year's cash flow is discounted.)

Reference to the formula shows that the present rate of mining should be more rapid: (1) the lower the future price of the product is expected to be; (2) the more variable costs are expected to rise in the future compared with their present level; and (3) the higher the interest rate. (A high interest rate makes distant, heavily discounted receipts less important than near-term receipts.)

If ownership is incomplete, as in the common oil pool situation, variable costs will be increased by the activities of others in drawing down the pool and the total period of exploitation of the resource will be reduced. Both factors put a premium on rapid and immediate mining by any given firm. Merger of the firms involved permits more rational mining activity to be carried out.

Prohibition of Pollution

In the case of air and water pollution and littering, one possible government solution consists of outright prohibition of the act. This can be effective when there are good alternative courses of action. Motorists and boaters may be warned not to litter highways and waterways and threatened with fines for doing so; there are readily available better methods of getting rid of these "bads." However, an absolute prohibition of all air and water pollution by firms is likely to be undesirable, except when an especially dangerous substance is involved. Instead an optimal amount of pollution should be sought, the optimum depending greatly on the natural cleansing capability of the atmosphere, rivers, and oceans. Beyond a point (which is certain to be difficult to determine) the resource cost involved in reducing pollution exceeds the broad benefits of the reduction. Conversely, resources *should* be devoted to pollution reduction as long as marginal social benefits exceed marginal social costs.

Regulation by Authorities

Of far greater importance than outright prohibition of pollution is its regulation by authorities who are established by legislative bodies. In addition to state and local authorities, the Federal Environmental Protection Administration, established in December, 1970, exercises regulatory powers of great significance to business. National air and water quality standards have been set, and E.P.A. is engaged in the difficult and costly mission of securing reductions of emissions by industry, municipalities, and other government units and individuals. Subsidies play an important role. In 1971 over $1 billion was awarded to cities for construction of improved sewage treatment plants.[4] Other devices and weapons used are enforcement conferences, 180-day notices, and civil or criminal suits. Voluntary compliance is sought before suits are filed. Often the firms that are cited will agree before the trial to install the necessary pollution abatement equipment.

E.P.A. is often challenged on technical grounds because a great deal of information about the effects of different levels of pollution is required in addition to knowing what technology is available. There is also a difficult socioeconomic problem, especially because jobs are involved. Some 200–300 mainly small and less efficient factories are expected to shut down by 1976 because of air and water quality standards.[5]

In addition there is now a much greater problem of locating new refineries, pipelines, and utility plants, and this contributes to higher prices and shortages. Delay in construction of the Alaska pipeline because of environmental objections and abandonment of the partially built Cross-Florida Barge Canal on environmental grounds are outstanding examples of the new problem that firms and government agencies now face in addition to the more usual profitability or cost-benefit criteria. The problem viewed broadly is one of balancing all costs against all gains, considering alternative locations and processes. Emotions and guesses may have more weight than careful calculations, especially because valid calculations are so hard to make.

The nature of the problem is illustrated by required emissions standards for cars. Many areas of the country have no serious air pollution, but since automobiles are by nature highly mobile, there is no assurance that a car not equipped with emission control devices will not end up in daily use in a city where smog is prevalent. The awkward administrative solution is to require expensive additional equipment on all new cars, knowing that many will not really need the devices.

---

[4] Y. Cameron, "The Trials of Mr. Clean," *Fortune*, April, 1972, p. 105.
[5] *Ibid.*, p. 103.

Taxes on Pollutants

In the literature of economics the classic form of government intervention when there are important unfavorable externalities consists of a special tax on the polluting firm. If there is a fixed relation between the rate of output of a good and the output of a "bad," it is necessary to curtail production in order to reduce the externality.

Figure 9–1 illustrates the imposition of a specific tax per unit of

FIGURE 9–1

Effluent Tax on All Output

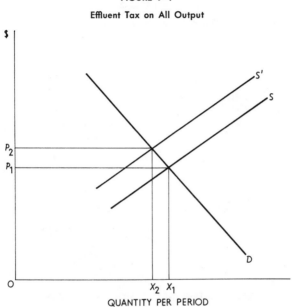

QUANTITY PER PERIOD

product on a competitive industry. The supply curve is S prior to the tax. Because each unit of output will have its marginal cost raised by the amount of the tax, the new supply curve will be S' lying above S by the tax per unit of output. Industry output will be reduced by the amount X_2X_1. This approach is actually used for cigarettes and liquor, to the extent the taxing authorities are trying to reduce adverse social effects rather than simply raising revenue. The effectiveness of the tax in reducing pollution will be greater the larger the tax, the less the negative slope of the demand curve, and the less the positive slope of the supply curve. Since the slope of the supply curve decreases as more time is allowed for adjustment, the long-run effect of the tax in reducing pollution should be greater than its immediate impact.

A more common situation is that the effluent discharge from a plant can be altered by the use of appropriate equipment. Output of the useful product itself is not necessarily affected greatly, although its greater cost will reduce the amount demanded, other things remaining the same. In Figure 9–2 a curve of marginal damages to the community constitutes a sort of demand for pollution reduction. Damages are highest if 100 percent of the effluent is discharged, as indicated by the intersection with the vertical axis. Marginal damages are shown to fall to zero with less than a complete elimination of pollution by the firm in question

FIGURE 9–2

Effluent Charge to Reduce Pollution

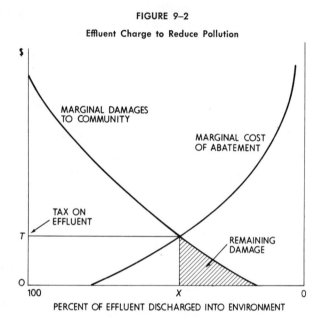

PERCENT OF EFFLUENT DISCHARGED INTO ENVIRONMENT

since the natural cleansing power of water and air will often take care adequately of some effluent discharge. The upsloping curve shows the marginal costs of abatement if carried out optimally by the firm. Complete elimination may be impossible so the curve is stopped short of the right-hand vertical axis. On the other hand, some reduction may be virtually costless, so the marginal cost of abatement is shown to appear only after a small reduction has been effected.[6]

A tax on the effluent will be needed to cause the firm to act. This tax should be set at the level *OT* if the authorities are perfectly informed regarding marginal environmental damages and the firm's marginal

---

[6] The chart is a modification of the one used by Allen V. Kneese and Blair T. Bower, "Causing Offsite Costs to Be Reflected in Waste Disposal Decisions," reprinted in R. Dorfman and N. S. Dorfman, eds., *Economics of the Environment* (New York: W. W. Norton & Co., Inc., 1972), p. 137.

abatement costs. (A big order!) With a flat charge of OT imposed on the discharge, the firm will find it least costly to reduce effluent discharge to point X since it can abate this amount for less outlay than if the tax were paid. The shaded area represents the dollar tab placed on community damages that would still be suffered (but should be endured in the sense that more resources would have to be spent on further cleanup than the cleanup would be worth socially).

It is not difficult to see that a cost-reducing improvement in abatement processes would make possible a greater reduction of pollution and a lower tax. On the other hand a revaluation upward of estimated marginal damages to the community would call for a higher tax and fuller abatement.

Effluent taxes are not in wide use and have been dubbed "a license to pollute" since they are unlikely to stop effluent discharge completely. However, an administrative agency which utilizes direct orders will ordinarily also have to permit less than 100 percent abatement in order not to have devastating effects on firms and on municipalities which own sewage disposal facilities. To that extent the authorities will also indirectly issue "licenses to pollute."

Summary of Some Important Principles

There are few problems that society and many business firms must face that are more difficult than that of reducing environmental damage. The student should train himself to see both sides of the picture—both the value of the product or service that causes pollution and the harmful effects imposed. The social problem is one of maximizing welfare by means of appropriate actions that will usually be strongly supported by some groups and opposed by others, since income distribution is affected.

In some situations private bargaining between involved parties can solve the problem. This solution does not always require that one party be liable for damages. Contrary to the theme of many western movies, it is not always easy to know who is the good guy and who is the bad guy. The upstream rancher who denies water to the new and poorer rancher below may have a large herd that could not otherwise survive. The small rancher below may have purchased his land very cheaply because of the probability of the very water problem that he now encounters. Like some other externalities this one may be happily settled by merger (marriage of the rich rancher's daughter and the poor rancher's son.)

There are some possibilities of useful private bargaining even when a considerable number of persons are involved. An association of upstream manufacturers may be able to bargain with an association of downstream fishermen in such a way that both sides will feel they have gained. Often the "free rider" problem will be encountered, however. Some members of either or both groups will try to obtain the benefits without paying dues, bribes, or other costs.

Government agencies themselves cause much of the pollution problem (municipal waste discharges, dumping by the Navy, sonic booms by the Air Force, runoff from interstate highway construction), but government must often be brought in to alleviate the problem. A great many possibilities for government action exists. These include direct prohibition, liability decisions by the courts, regulation by administrators, education of the public, subsidies, and taxation. In some cases no action should be taken at all. In the words of R. H. Coase, "Nothing could be more 'anti-social' than to oppose any action which causes any harm to anyone."[7]

CASE 9–1. Pollution Problems in the Dairy Industry*

There is a pronounced trend toward fewer and larger dairy plants in this country. Fluid milk plants decreased about 75 percent in number between 1948 and 1958. A marked decline in the number of cheese and butter plants occurred prior to 1948. Ice cream plants have also declined in number.

As dairy food plants become larger, they have a greater need to be located at places having good access to major highways. This increasingly places them near interstate highways and often in the suburban areas of small to medium-sized cities.

The trend is for dairy plants to service larger areas, trucking in raw milk from considerable distances and hauling out packaged products in semitrailers for distances as great as 500 miles.

Where dairy plants utilize the municipal waste treatment facilities they can be major contributors to the load of the municipal systems. The average milk plant of 1980 (250,000 pounds of milk per day) can be predicted to have waste loads equivalent to a population of 55,000 persons unless special efforts are made to pretreat or otherwise markedly reduce these wastes.

The most visible pollutant of the dairy industry is whey. The significance of this is great, since about 20 percent of the total milk produced in this country is converted into whey. Cottage cheese whey represents

---

[7] Coase, "The Problem of Social Cost," p. 35.

* Information is mainly from U.S. Environmental Protection Agency, *Dairy Food Plant Wastes and Waste Treatment Practices*, Water Pollution Control Research Series 12060 EGU, March, 1971.

a more serious problem than sweet whey because of its acid nature which limits its utility as a food or feed.

Surveys have indicated that a great many managers of dairy plants are not aware of the pollution potential of the industry (or just wish the problem would go away).

Exhibit 9–1A shows that surcharges on waste discharge (effluent

EXHIBIT 9–1A

Dairy Food Plants and Effluent Charges

Proprietary Companies in Region	Number of Plants	Plants with Surcharge on Waste Composition
A.................	32	0
B.................	35	2
C.................	9	2
D.................	19	2
E.................	75	2
F.................	10	0
G.................	15	1
H.................	12	1
I.................	5	0
J.................	11	0
K.................	8	0
L.................	27	1
M.................	20	0
N.................	7	Unknown
O.................	15	2
P.................	5	2
Q.................	15	1
Cooperatives		
R.................	9	0
S.................	9	0
T.................	1	0
U.................	27	5
V.................	21	0
W.................	7	0
X.................	23	3

Source: U.S. Environmental Protection Agency, *Dairy Food Plant Wastes and Waste Treatment Practices,* Water Pollution Control Research Series 12060 EGU, March, 1971, p. 20.

taxes) have not yet been heavily utilized in the dairy industry. There have been some instances in which dairy food plants have been closed down after the imposition of surcharges by municipalities.

Questions

1. Assuming that a municipality imposes an effluent tax on a dairy food plant which uses its waste disposal facilities, how would you describe the optimal levy in theoretical terms?

2. Dairy product plants have traditionally been located near large markets, with cheese being produced farther from the market than fresh milk. Explain why. (Reference to Chapter 16 may be helpful.)
3. What developments have tended to change locational determinants for dairy food plants?
4. Milk prices are usually kept artifically high by federal or state marketing orders. Can you think of a plan to redesign this sort of government intervention so as to reduce the pollution threat?
5. When it is possible to convert a "waste product" into salable dairy products, theoretically how far should additional direct processing costs be incurred by a profit maximizing firm?
6. Suppose the dairy plant is otherwise subject to an effluent tax on the waste product. How does this change the theoretical maximizing position with respect to converting the waste product into a salable product?

CASE 9–2. Noise in Moscow*

Many people believe that environmental problems stem mainly from the tendency of private industry to avoid some production costs by discharging "bads" into public waters and air. This belief leads quite naturally to the idea that a centrally planned economy with social ownership of firms would much more easily protect the environment. There is evidence that such is not the case.

Life in Moscow goes on in an often noisy environment. A common sight on the streets is a vendor promoting lottery tickets, excursions or books with a megaphone or a portable public address system. Even the police use loudspeakers to provide lectures and public ridicule to disorderly persons, jaywalkers, etc. The usual level of sound in a Moscow movie house is so high that a moviegoer may leave after a show with a headache and a feeling of fatigue. The big sports stadiums make life difficult for people in nearby housing, especially when spectators in open bleachers express their enthusiasm at soccer matches.

One aspect of the noise problem in any location is the effect noise has on sleep. A Moscow sleep survey involving a 65-question canvas of 5650 people showed that almost half of them suffered from poor sleep and that the majority of these blamed this on external disturbances, primarily noises. Loss of sleep, of course, can have economic as well as social implications in the lowering of labor productivity, a higher incidence of breakage on the job, and other costly malfunctions. The investigators' observation that a fourth of West Germans and a third of Americans suffer from poor sleep implies that they consider sleep disturbance in the USSR to be equal to or possibly greater than such difficulty elsewhere.

---

* Information is from U.S. Environmental Protection Agency, *An Assessment of Noise Concern in Other Nations*, vol. I (December 31, 1971), pp. 38–51.

The law concerning disturbing the peace (hooliganism statute) was adopted by the RSFSR (Russian Federation) in 1966 but the Moscow City Council passed its own stricter version in 1960. A typical public-nuisance ordinance, it applied to all public places, including communal apartments and dormitories, on their balconies, in the streets, etc. It specified that there was to be no loud singing, playing of musical instruments, radios, etc. if it might disturb other citizens, from 11 PM to 8 AM. Fines were up to 100 rubles if the case went as far as the "Neighborhood Commission" of the city council or up to 25 rubles if paid on the spot to the arresting policemen. A similar ordinance prohibiting loud playing of radios, etc. was passed by the Moscow City Council on 11 November, 1969.

Perhaps after the 1969 city ordinance was passed, some enforcement was again temporarily achieved. But despite the 1969 resolution of the city council, applicable noise nuisance ordinances have not been vigorously enforced in the streets; the various sources of street noise such as street vendors and militiamens' megaphones still go unregulated.

The new official emphasis on noise control also seems to be deficient in practice in the area of industrial noise emissions to the community, as a 1971 report from Moscow illustrates. According to this report, a certain electric transformer substation (No. 179) was the constant source of complaints about noise for years in the Moscow "Semenovskaya" neighborhood. The local SES (Sanitary-Epidemological Station) sent a list of offending substations, including No. 179, to the Moscow Power Authority (Mosenegro), and to the national Ministry of Energetics and Electrification with the demand that the transformer noise be abated. The SES also secured a directive from the Moscow City Council (Dec. 1968) that the transformer substation nuisances be abated and that several unenclosed substations, including No. 179, be enclosed in soundproof buildings in the course of the 1969–1971 period. However, these measures achieved nothing except the promise of the director of the Moscow Power Authority that action would be taken. No action was taken.

Questions

1. Explain how the universal tendency of individuals to maximize personal utility contributes to the noise problem in any society.
2. Soviet plant managers often receive bonuses for meeting or exceeding planned output. Explain how this can contribute to noise and other pollution in the U.S.S.R.
3. How is social ownership of firms likely to affect prospects for bargaining between affected parties as a means of removing noise or other disturbing circumstances?
4. In some ways it may be easier and in some ways harder for an environmental protection agency to put pressure on another agency of government than on privately owned firms. Consider this question and apply to the relative problems of the United States and U.S.S.R. in protecting the environment.

chapter 10

Employment of
Human Resources

PAYMENTS for labor services usually make up the largest part of a firm's variable costs. This proportion varies greatly between products, however. Near one extreme is an electric power generating facility where few persons except an occasional skilled attendant can be seen. At the other extreme is the business of gathering unusual sea shells (before the tourists have awakened) by workers who need only ordinary buckets as their capital equipment. With development of improved technology the proportion of the labor force in professional and skilled manual occupations is increasing quite dramatically.

Since a great deal of investment in the individual is required to turn out an engineer, an astronaut, or even a competent automobile mechanic, economists have begun to consider "human capital" to be a factor of production. The term "labor" is becoming less appropriate as a general designation for the human agent. When the term is used it is at least important to keep in mind the tremendous diversity of abilities covered. For analytical purpose it is usually necessary to consider only one reasonably homogeneous type of labor at a time. This approach is similar to the simplification involved in analyzing the single product firm. Usually the principles involved are similar for all the products actually turned out by a firm and for all the types of labor it actually employs.

Marginal Productivity of Labor

Output and input decisions are apt to be made simultaneously in response to the price-cost situation in which the firm finds itself. They are parts of the same optimizing process that the decision makers of the firm are conceived to follow. For the purpose of analytical simplicity, however, it is best to consider output and input decisions separately; consequently the input side is concentrated upon in this chapter.

A unit of labor will be hired by an entrepreneur only if the value of its product is believed to be at least as high as its cost. "Value and cost" are usually measured in monetary terms, although rational calculation may also involve nonpecuniary considerations. For example, a businessman may hire his indolent father-in-law as a way of getting some work out of him if he would have to support him anyway. Or a blond secretary may be hired even if she is not the most efficient worker available at the salary paid.

Judging the contribution of a worker is complicated by the fact that usually he is employed along with capital equipment, materials, supplies, electric power, and other factors. He cannot profitably be paid a wage out of income that is actually attributable to other inputs. The marginal productivity approach offers a logical way out of the dilemma. If all other inputs are held constant the increase in output that would occur if one more unit of labor is hired constitutes the product attributable to that unit. Since all units of labor are considered to be interchangeable any one of the units hired can properly be considered to be contributing this same marginal product. If employing one more worker necessarily entails adding other inputs, such as supplies, the net marginal productivity of labor can be calculated if the cost of this ancillary additional input is deducted from the value of added output. For the purpose of simplification it is usually sufficient to assume all other inputs to be strictly fixed in quantity and to consider only labor to vary in amount.

This is the procedure used in Figure 10–1. The quantity of capital utilized by the hypothetical plant is not shown explicitly but is assumed to be constant while labor input per month can vary from one to ten

FIGURE 10–1

Computation of Value of Marginal Product

(1) Labor Input per Month	(2) Total Output per Month	(3) Marginal Physical Product	(4) Price of Output	(5) Value of Marginal Product
1	25	25	$20	$500
2	53	28	20	560
3	84	31	20	620
4	118	34	20	680
5	155	37	20	740
6	191	36	20	720
7	226	35	20	700
8	259	33	20	660
9	285	26	20	520
10	305	20	20	400

units. The plant's "production function" is reflected in the relation between the fixed capital input, the variable labor input, and the total output shown in column 2. Column 3 shows the marginal physical product of labor, which is simply the increment in total output per month as labor input is increased by one unit. (If labor increments were not exactly one unit in each line of the table, it would be necessary to divide the change in number of units of output by the change in labor input.)

If 6 units of labor were employed, for example, the marginal physical product would be 36 units. This output should not be thought of as the product of the "last man" or the "sixth man" but as the amount of product imputable to any one of the six men employed. Translated into value terms it consequently represents the maximum amount the firm can profitably pay per month to any one of the six men.

The translation of physical product into monetary terms is shown in columns 4 and 5. The firm is assumed to be able to sell any output it wishes at a price of $20 per unit. This means the company is assumed to be too small to affect price by its own actions—it sells in a perfectly competitive market. Value of the marginal product is found by multiplying marginal physical product by $20.

If it is further assumed that the firm is also a price taker (rather than price maker) in the labor market, how much labor should it hire? The answer depends on the monthly wage rate it must pay, and this depends on the entire supply-demand situation in the labor market for the kind of labor needed. Suppose the prevailing wage rate is $600 per month. Eight men appears to be the optimum input. Value of the marginal product at this employment level is $660, but if another man were hired, the addition to the firm's revenue would be only $520 while the addition to wage cost would be $600.

It can be said that optimum input of labor is eight units per month provided it is considered to be worth operating at all. Total revenue from the product will be $5,180 per month (259 × $20) while the total wage bill will be $4,800, leaving $380 to cover other costs. As indicated in an earlier chapter these are (in a simplified explanation) interest and depreciation on the selling value of the plant. If the $380 is not sufficient to cover these costs, the indication is that another use of the firm's plant (perhaps the production of a different product) would be better. If the outlook is for near-future improvement of the price-cost situation for the present product, a switch to another product or disposal of the plant is less likely.

Not all of the information needed for a rational input decision is given in Figure 10–1. All that can be said with certainty is that if a decision is made to turn out the product under consideration, 8 is the best number of units of labor to employ. Other decisions such as whether to switch products, install new equipment, or to sell out altogether require additional information, and some of the relevant principles are stated elsewhere in this book. However, if the prevailing wage rate were $800 per month rather than $600, it can be inferred directly from Figure 10–1 that it would be more economical to shut down. This is because the total value of the product would not be so large as the wage bill at any level of labor input. (In terms of output analysis, the average variable cost would be above the price of the product at all possible output rates.)

Figure 10–1 (like all tables) incorporates finite steps, whereas a diagram such as Figure 10–2 permits consideration of infinitely divisible inputs. Assuming that it is desirable to operate the plant, optimum labor input is *OX* at wage rate *OW*.[1] The total wage bill per time period is *OWKX*. Since total value of the product is the entire area under the *VMP* curve, the area remaining after deduction of *OWKX* represents the "cash flow" available to meet interest, depreciation, and other fixed costs and—if the situation is especially favorable—to yield an excess return above other alternatives to owners of the firm.[2]

Fixed Proportions

Frequently the production function is quite different from those incorporated in Figures 10–1 and 10–2, involving fixed rather than variable proportions between labor and capital. The assumption of fixed proportions is more appropriate to short-run than to long-run analysis, however. The substitution of self-starting automatic elevators for those employing operators is an example of short-run fixity and long-run variability, at least so far as changes in relative cost of labor and capital brought about the change. (Technological knowledge is usually assumed to be unchanged in economic analysis even during long-run adjustments, although economic factors frequently affect the directions in which invention proceeds.)

Suppose a plant is equipped with 10 identical sewing machines, each utilizing one operator. The "curve" depicting value of the marginal product will consist of ten dots at the same height, as in Figure 10–3. This is because each operator-machine combination will add the same amount of product per time period. Diminishing returns do not set in.

---

[1] The *VMP* curve must be falling rather than rising. If the wage rate and *VMP* were equated in the rising portion of *VMP*, labor input would be the worst rather than the best. This is because all units would be hired where the wage was higher than contribution to revenue and none would be hired that added more to revenue than to the wage bill.

[2] Such an excess is usually called "profit," but the desirability of that term is questionable. In a leading analysis of the subject, J. Fred Weston, "A Generalized Uncertainty Theory of Profit," *American Economic Review*, March, 1950, argues that a true profit must be unanticipated. Since receipt of the cash flow shown in Figure 10–2 may be fully expected by the firm, no "profit" is involved, according to this terminology.

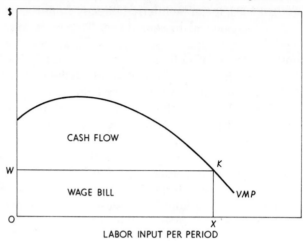

FIGURE 10–2

Optimum Input of Labor—Where VMP Equals Wage Rate

If the prevailing wage rate is *OW*, it appears likely that ten operators will be employed in the production, but, as indicated earlier, this is not necessarily true if we consider a product switch or sale of the plant to be possible as a short-run action. While each machine will yield a return above the wages of its operator, the information given in the chart is not sufficient to tell us whether another product (perhaps bathing suits rather than dresses) should be turned out or whether the entire plant

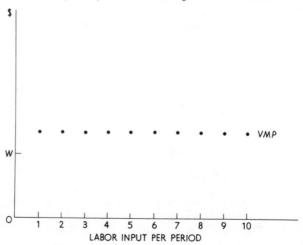

FIGURE 10–3

Fixed Input Proportions—Diminishing Returns Are Absent

should be sold or leased to someone else. Modern technology probably makes short-run fixity of input proportions more common (e.g., three astronauts per space capsule and one policeman per subway train).

Monopolist's Demand for Labor

Only a minor modification of the marginal productivity concept is needed if the firm is a monopolistic rather than competitive seller of output. As a monopolist hires more labor his rate of output will increase and this will lower the price at which he can sell his product. This effect of amount of input on price of output must be taken into account in a rational decision as to how much labor to employ.

In the situation depicted in Figure 10–2, the down-sloping portion of the *VMP* curve reflects operation of the law of diminishing returns. If the firm sold in a monopolistic rather than competitive market, an additional factor—"the law of demand"—would reinforce the law of diminishing returns; that is, price and marginal revenue from output would decline as input increased. The resulting curve is usually called the "marginal revenue product" curve. Mathematically:

$$MRP = MPP \cdot MR$$

(whereas under competitive selling *VMP* equals *MPP* times price of output). Assuming that the monopolistic seller is nevertheless a competitive buyer of labor, his optimum input would be determined as in Figure 10–2, the only difference being that a *MRP* rather than *VMP* curve would be the demand curve. It should be kept in mind that the analysis assumes that one factor (e.g., the amount of land) is kept fixed in amount and only one variable input is used. Alternative assumptions can be made, but the analysis can quickly gain more in complexity than it gains in predictive power.

Monopsony

If a firm is the only buyer of a particular type of labor in a market, it is said to be a monopsonist in that market. Even if there are several firms that hire labor but act in unison in their employment practices, the monopsony analysis is applicable. Actually monopsony power in local labor markets is not very prevalent in the United States according to a careful study made some years ago.[3] This is not to say that it is always unimportant. There has been a tendency in recent years to locate manufacturing plants in rural areas to get away from urban congestion. Such

---

[3] Robert L. Bunting, *Employer Concentration in Local Labor Markets* (Chapel Hill: University of North Carolina Press, 1962).

a plant may be the only large employer within a substantial geographic area and hence possess monopsony power.

Just as a monopolistic seller must consider the effect of his output on the price at which he can sell, the monopsonist must consider the effect of his purchases on the price at which he can buy. (This contrasts with the situation facing an ordinary customer in a grocery store who pays the same price per pound of hamburger no matter what quantity he buys.) The supply schedule of labor to a monopsonist is up-sloping, reflecting the fact that higher wage rates will cause more persons to be willing to supply their labor. In the case of a plant located in a rather isolated area, a higher wage will cause people to drive longer distances

FIGURE 10–4

Computation of Marginal Factor Cost

Labor Input per Hour	Wage Rate per Hour	Total Labor Cost per Hour	Marginal Factor Cost per Hour
1	$2.00	$ 2.00	$2.00
2	2.10	4.20	2.20
3	2.20	6.60	2.40
4	2.30	9.20	2.60
5	2.40	12.00	2.80
6	2.50	15.00	3.00
7	2.60	18.20	3.20
8	2.70	21.60	3.40
9	2.80	25.20	3.60
10	2.90	29.00	3.80

to and from work and will consequently increase the amount of labor supplied.

Corresponding to the important concept of marginal revenue to the monopolist is the idea of marginal factor cost to the monopsonist. Computation of marginal factor cost is shown in Figure 10–4. Suppose the monopsonist were hiring five workers at $2.40 per hour. If a sixth person were hired, he would be available at $2.50 per hour. However, all workers would then have to receive $2.50 per hour to avoid a serious morale problem. Thus the actual extra cost (marginal factor cost) of a sixth worker is $3 even though he is paid only $2.50. It is not necessary to think in terms of movements from one employment level to another. Rather the various employment levels can be thought of as alternatives at a point of time.

The situation of a firm that buys labor monopsonistically is shown in Figure 10–5. The demand for labor is labeled VMP or MRP according to whether the firm is assumed to sell output competitively or monopolistically. Optimum input is OX units of labor per period, determined by the equality of MFC and VMP (or MRP). That is, the monopsonist should hire all workers that add more to his income than they add to his labor cost, but no workers who add more to his labor cost than to his income. In Figure 10–5, the wage rate paid will be *OW*, located on the labor supply curve at the optimum input level. His wage bill will be *OWKX*, and the remaining area under the *VMP* (or *MRP*) curve to the left of *X* measures "cash flow" under the simplified assumption that labor

FIGURE 10–5

Optimum Input for a Monopsonist

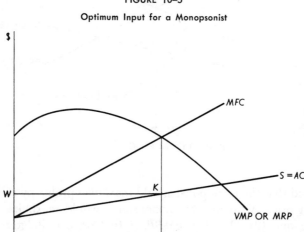

is the only variable input. This is because the total area under *VMP* (*MRP*) measures total revenue.

Bilateral Monopoly

When a single seller of labor or of a product deals with a single buyer, the situation is known as "bilateral monopoly." It is easiest to think in terms of a producer of an industrial product such as automobile headlights selling its entire output to a single automobile manufacturer. As a monopolist the headlight maker will want a high price for its product and will have some monopoly power to attain such a price, while the car maker will want to buy headlights at a low price and will have some monopsony power in this direction.

In Figure 10–6, *MC* is marginal cost of production and *MFC* is marginal to this curve in the same sense as *MFC* in Figure 10–5 is marginal to the supply curve in that figure.

Curve *MRP* shows the additional revenue to the monopsonist from buying different quantities. Curve *MR* is marginal to *MRP* in the same way that *MR* is related to demand in ordinary monopoly analysis. It can

FIGURE 10–6

Bilateral Monopoly

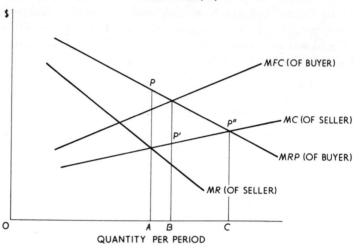

QUANTITY PER PERIOD

then be said that the monopolist would maximize profits by selling quantity *OA* at price *AP* while the monopsonist would maximize his profits by buying quantity *OB* at price *BP*. Actual price is indeterminate between these levels and will be determined by bargaining. A great many factors will enter into bargaining power, including long-run prospects for other sources of supply or for other customers.

A good way to look at the problem of bilateral monopoly is to realize that a monopolist has no supply curve but that the monopsonist would like to be able to buy at the monopolist's marginal cost of production. On the other hand, the monopsonist has no demand curve, but the monopolist would like to sell to him at the full marginal revenue product of the good. In practice, the monopsonist will not be able to make *MC* a supply curve and the monopolist will not be able to make *MRP* a demand curve. However, if the firms should merge into one well-managed company, the quantity exchanged between the divisions would be expanded to *OC; CP* might then be called an "intracompany transfer price" (to be used, perhaps, in cost accounting). The best quantity would be *OC* because a smaller quantity would add more to the firm's revenue than to its cost, while a larger quantity would add more to cost than to revenue.

Bilateral Monopoly in Labor Markets

About one fourth of the labor force in the United States is organized into unions to deal collectively with employers. The percentage is high in many key industries however. In recent years government employees have shown increasing interest in unionism, sometimes to the dismay of the citizens of such cities as New York where a strike by bridge tenders, sanitation workers, subway personnel, or policemen can have devastating effects. Where a single union (monopolist) sells labor to a single employer (monopsonist) the bilateral monopoly case is relevant. It is also applicable in industrywide collective bargaining where one union and numerous firms may be involved. A fairly wide range for the exercise of bargaining between employers and unions may exist. In the case of either private or public workers who are essential to the operation of costly physical plant, *MRP* may be extremely high and inelastic. The primary brake on union bargaining power may then come from the longer run threat of greater automation, reorganization, or relocation. In case of a strike that is deemed to imperil the national safety or health, the President of the United States can obtain a court injunction against the strike good for 80 days. In 1971 this power was invoked against striking longshoremen. This provision of the Taft-Hartley Act tends to reduce union power. However, unemployment compensation and exemption from federal antitrust laws work in the opposite direction. Some strong unions have restrained their use of the strike as a bargaining device, preferring to take a long-run view of what will help their workers. They are wary of political action such as extension of the number of state "right to work" laws under which union membership cannot be a prerequisite for securing a job (although the employee may be forced to join a union to keep his job).

Minimum Wage Laws

Since passage of the Fair Labor Standards Act in 1938, the federal government has set minimum wage rates in "interstate commerce." Coverage has been steadily expanded so that in addition to manufacturing, mining, and wholesaling such activities as retailing, restaurants, hotels, motels, hospitals, laundries, construction, and taxicabs are now included. Agricultural workers on large farms were added in 1966 legislation while domestic workers and government employees were added in April, 1974. The minimum for most workers is $2 per hour as of May 1, 1974, $2.10 as of January 1, 1975, and $2.30 as of January 1, 1976.

The analysis of this chapter can constitute a framework for predicting probable effects of further increases in the legal minimum wage either at the federal level or by the states which have such laws. Many employers are not directly affected because they already pay more than the minimum. Employers of skilled or professional persons are in this category. Employers of low-skilled persons are likely to become more selective in their hiring practices and to lay off the poorer workers who have marginal revenue productivity below the legal minimum wage. Minority groups are especially likely to suffer increased unemployment as their power to compete with majority groups (who may tend to be favored by most employers) is diminished since a floor is put on the wage at which they can offer to work.

If the VMP or MRP curve is completely inelastic due to the need to use labor in fixed proportions to equipment, the firm may not change its employment in the short run but will attempt to automate to a greater extent over time. For example, elevator operators may receive wage increases and suffer no employment losses in the short run but will face greater danger of being replaced eventually by automatic elevators. Companies that have some leeway in their production processes, such as chain food stores, are likely to make immediate laborsaving adjustments such as reducing the number of bag boys employed. (Chain food stores will also have more incentive to consider completely automated checkout systems such as are now available.) In agriculture a higher minimum wage tends to induce a substitution of weed killers, fertilizer, and machinery for hand labor. Many cotton choppers in Mississippi and Louisiana were fired when the federal minimum wage law was extended to cover large farms since it became cheaper to substitute chemical weed killers for their labor.[4]

Training of Workers

In recent years there has been great interest in the idea of investment in the individual as a way to build "human capital" which returns interest to the worker in the form of enhanced future earnings. T. W. Schultz and Gary Becker are the best-known recent contributors to the field, although the general idea is an old one.[5] The emphasis here will be on some of the implications of human capital theory for the firm.

One of the important areas of this sort is the training of employees. The more specific the training to the particular needs of a firm, the more likely the firm is to pay for the training; the more general the training the more likely it is that the individual or government will undergo

---

[4] Numerous statistical studies have been made of employment effects of minimum wages. For example, J. M. Peterson, "Employment Effects of Minimum Wages, 1938–1950" (Ph.D. dissertation, University of Chicago, 1956); H. M. Douty, "Some Effects of the $1.00 Minimum Wage in the United States," *Economica*, May, 1960; M. R. Colberg, "Minimum Wage Effects on Florida's Economic Development," *Journal of Law and Economics*, October, 1960; and Yale Brozen, "The Effect of Statutory Minimum Wage Increases on Teen-Age Employment," *Journal of Law and Economics*, April, 1969.

[5] See especially T. W. Schultz, "Investment in Human Capital," *American Economic Review*, March, 1961; and Gary S. Becker, *Human Capital* (New York: Columbia University Press, 1964).

the cost. The reason is simple. If, for example, a firm pays for a secretarial course for its employees, many are likely to leave the firm after their secretarial capabilities have been built up because there are many places they can work. The company will probably lose much of its investment. If, however, workers are trained to run nylon spinning equipment, the skill acquired cannot often be sold to another company and hence the investment in training is likely to pay off to the company that provides it. Monopsony power in a labor market increases the probability that training of a fairly general nature can usefully be provided by a firm because employment alternatives are scarce. In a "company town" the dominant company may even find it worthwhile to pay for the improvement of reading and arithmetic skills of employees as they would have to leave town to find other substantial employment.

Similarly, although it is usually felt to be wiser to spend money on training young workers in skills specific to a company, it should be kept in mind that their intercompany mobility is greater. This can make investment in older, less mobile employees more desirable than consideration only of the number of years of working life remaining would suggest. Also company-paid programs for training of executives are often worthwhile because the turnover of executives tends to be low. Although the acquisition of general skills (computer programming may qualify) is desirable from the viewpoint of the employee in that it opens up many alternatives for employment, specific training has its values. The employee tends to receive a higher wage than he could earn elsewhere and has greater job security because he will probably be retained in a temporary business slump. If he is lost to the firm it will have to invest in the training of a replacement. From the firm's point of view, specifically trained labor is a sort of fixed capital, and even if the original investment in training is not currently providing the firm a suitable rate of return there is special incentive to continue to employ the worker.[6]

Worker Alienation

One of the famous early descriptions of a factory assembly line is found in Adam Smith's *Wealth of Nations:*

One man draws out the wire, another straights it, a third cuts it, a fourth paints it, a fifth grinds it at the top for receiving the head; to make the head requires two or three distinct operations; to put it on is a peculiar business, to whiten the pins is another; it is even a trade by itself to put them into the paper, and the important business of making a pin is, in this manner, divided

---

[6] This line of analysis was first developed carefully by Walter Oi, "Labor as a Quasi Fixed Factor of Production" (Ph. D. dissertation, University of Chicago, 1961).

into about eighteen distinct operations which in some manufactories, are all performed by distinct hands, though in others the same man will sometimes perform two or three of them.[7]

The extreme specialization and repetitiveness of the assembly line is well suited to many workers who do not like the bother of learning new skills. It may even suit some imaginative people who can think about other things much of the time because a well-learned routine requires little thought. For the most part, however, an increasingly well-educated working force become alienated from jobs that involve routine and repetition. This has led recently to great interest in ways of rearranging work. In some cases it is possible to organize "teams" of workers that perform all of the operations required to turn out a product, with frequent changes in job assignments and with supervisory autonomy. Team members usually willingly fill in when someone is temporarily absent from the job. Where a real *espirit de corps* has been established, productivity has risen markedly.

The Saab automobile plant in Sweden has had encouraging success with new plant and work organization techniques in which production workers (1) are included in development teams; (2) help rebalance jobs; (3) inspect for quality; (4) are responsible for care of equipment they use; and (5) are urged and enabled to learn several jobs. Results have been sufficiently impressive to cause Saab to apply the ideas to a new engine plant opened in January, 1972.[8]

To some extent the steps being taken to decrease worker alienation can be interpreted as methods to give the workers greater "property rights" in their jobs—that is, to make it easier for them to appropriate both pecuniary and nonpecuniary gains from good performance. For example, if a truck driver is assigned to a particular truck to drive rather than being rotated daily to any one of a fleet of trucks, he is certain to be more interested in its maintenance since he can personally benefit from this effort. Also, a team worker who performs different kinds of jobs can more easily develop the professional attitude needed to become a company executive. His personal investment in "human capital" is facilitated.

To a limited degree some American firms are moving toward the "worker-management" system which is a feature of industry in Yugoslavia. In that country, workers' councils have jurisdiction over many aspects of employment, investment, and profit distribution and can even fire the managers. Their wage consists of a fixed sum plus a share in profits. Although production capital is socially owned in all but small enterprises, workers are given a virtual property right in the capital

---

[7] Adam Smith, *The Wealth of Nations*, Modern Library Edition, 1937, pp. 4–5.

[8] Richard E. Walton, "How to Counter Alienation in the Plant," *Harvard Business Review*, November–December, 1972, p. 80.

utilized by their own companies which have to compete with other domestic and foreign enterprise for sales. "Capitalistic" firms that take special steps such as subsidizing stock ownership by employees (Sears, Roebuck is an outstanding example) or delegating some managerial power to production teams are somewhat similarly trying to prevent worker alienation from the job.

Executive Incentives

Although the corporation can be viewed historically as a device by which management has been largely separated from ownership, much of the criticism often heard along this line is unjustified. Many owners of capital do not want to be concerned with management, and officials in a given field may prefer to invest in other areas. Still there is good reason to attempt to secure a partial remarriage of management and ownership in order to give officials a greater incentive to build up profits.

One such device is the supplementing of salaries with stock options. Such options give the right to buy a specified amount of the corporation's unissued stock at a specified price over a designated period of time. If the market price rises the holder can still purchase the stock at the stated price. If it falls sufficiently in price the executive will not exercise the option. If he does acquire the stock he may end up with a capital loss. In the past few years stock options have lost in popularity among corporations officials because of less favorable income tax treatment and because regular salary now is taxed at a maximum marginal rate of 50 percent instead of the previous 70 percent.

Executive incentive plans usually are based on either a straight percentage of net income or on a percentage of profits when profits exceed a designated rate of return on invested capital. Like all formulas these have problems. If bonuses are based on a fixed percentage of net income they are paid even when profits fall off sharply, so long as they are positive, and even if poor decisions were responsible. Bonuses are sometimes based on planned rather than actual profits, being paid only when the plan is achieved or surpassed. This, however, provides an incentive to keep profit plans as low as possible, much as the Soviet production manager is happier with a centrally planned output that is easy to surpass. Or executive bonuses may be paid for improved company performance relative to the industry. This can encounter problems of defining the industry, especially when product mixes change. According to a leading authority in the field, about two thirds of listed companies have incentive plans for executives.[9]

---

[9] Arch Patton, "Why Incentive Plans Fail," *Harvard Business Review*, May–June, 1972, p. 59. Much of the material in this section has been derived from his article.

Virtually every large company in the automotive, retail chain, department store, electrical appliance, office equipment, textile, chemical, and pharmaceutical industries has an executive incentive program. Relatively few are found in public utility, banking, mining, railroad, or life insurance companies.

Bonus plans for executives are more likely to be successful when company results depend heavily on frequently made decisions regarding production, buying, selling, style changes, and the like. They are not needed when results depend mainly on general economic conditions, population movements, actions of regulatory commissions, or on pure chance.

CASE 10–1. General Motors Bonus Plan*

Next week at its annual meeting in Detroit, General Motors Corporation will ask its stockholders to approve continuation of an incentive compensation plan that took $114 million of last year's profits and distributed them to employees. The plan, with a few modifications, is virtually certain to be approved.

And with good reason. Nearly everyone who has had anything to do with forming and executing GM policy has pointed to the incentive system as a major factor in the success of General Motors—the world's largest manufacturing enterprise. About 9 percent of its salaried workers —presently some 15,500 people—participate in the bonus fund, which is one of the industry's oldest plans and probably its largest.

. . . .

Outsiders are well aware of the size of some of the top bonuses. Chairman Frederic G. Donner, for example, drew $590,000 from the incentive plan last year, nearly three times his salary of $200,000. But the bonuses paid to director-officers for 1966 amounted to only 3.2 percent of the total fund.

. . . .

The remaining beneficiaries had annual salaries that under the rules ranged down to $11,700, though some discretion was permitted below that point in cases of exceptional valor. At the same time, there are no minimum payments to eligible employees.

. . . .

Award Time. To make sure that the right persons get the right rewards, GM has an intensive, person-by-person review that carries all the

---

* This case is taken from a longer article in *Business Week*, May 13, 1967, "A Bonus Plan where Performance Counts." Copyright © 1967 by McGraw-Hill Book Company.

way to the top. Eventually, the chairman and president, and then the bonus and salary committee, get to see all the names and bonus suggestions placed in the "book of recommendations."

Final evaluation starts late in the year, when final corporate results can be estimated. At this time, the bonus and salary committee determines how much to award operating directors and heads of divisions and staff functions. (Hard figures must wait until the books are audited.)

The top officers of the company then decide how the remainder of the bonus fund will be split up between the operating divisions, such as Chevrolet, and staff organizations, such as the treasurer's office. The amount any one division gets depends on its total performance, the number of its eligible employees, and even special competitive circumstances.

While all this is going on, supervisors below the level of division head have been reviewing the performance of their personnel. There's no neat form for this. GM tried that once, but dropped it because of the variety of jobs. Performance ratings rest on the judgment of the immediate supervisor, who must defend his recommendation to his superior.

. . . .

Little Change. One measure of the bonus plan's success is its durability. Since 1918, the plan and its administration have undergone no fundamental changes—only adjustments to meet changing circumstances. This year, after stockholder approval, the company will lower the amount made available for the fund because, in practice, the full amount was not being used.

Under the current formula—12 percent of net earnings in excess of 6 percent of net capital—GM could have made $169 million available for bonuses. But it paid out only $114 million—a figure that includes the stock under the stock option plan which this year was valued at $7.2 million.

GM's incentive administrators feel it's a little embarrassing to pay out so much less than possible. So the administrators came up with the new formula: 12 percent of net earnings when net income is between 6 persent and 15 percent of net capital, plus 6 percent of net earnings in excess of 15 percent of net capital. Under this, available funds for last year would have been $129.3 million rather than $169 million, considerably closer to the $114 million paid.

Tax Revision. Another adjustment to be made is in the way bonuses are paid. This would result in quicker payment of smaller bonuses by dividing them into larger annual installments.

Changes will also be made in the stock option plan, in which some 250 high-ranking executives participate. In response to stricter tax rules on capital gains, GM wants to shorten the waiting time for exercising an option from 18 months to 12 months.

Questions

1. What is the present income tax treatment of stock options?
2. On occasion, why may it be desirable for the company to pay a good-sized bonus to an executive who has not actually had a very productive year?
3. What are some implications of the GM bonus plan for intracompany competition?
4. What effects would a bonus plan of this sort have on the families of junior executives?
5. Do you believe this type of plan should be helpful in reducing executive turnover? Explain.
6. Assuming that we are in an era of both high taxes and inflation, would an executive prefer to have a sizable bonus paid immediately or deferred until after his retirement? (Many factors may affect his decision, but analyze only the effects of high tax rates and his anticipation of chronic inflation.)

CASE 10–2. Kaiser Steel Corporation–United Steelworkers of America Long-Range Sharing Plan

During World War II, Kaiser Steel Corporation built near Fontana, California, the only fully integrated steel mill on the West Coast. In 1963 it remained the only fully integrated producer on the West Coast. Its 1962 capacity was three million ingot tons, which put it in the smaller group of large steel companies. Exhibit 10–2A shows for the years 1957 to 1962, Kaiser steel production in tons, net sales, and net income.

Kaiser broke away from the industry bargaining group during the 1959 strike of the United Steelworkers and signed a separate agreement with the union. Among the provisions, this contract provided for the establishment of a committee to study the sharing of gains from productivity.

EXHIBIT 10–2A

Kaiser Steel Corporation

Year	Steel Ingots Produced (tons)	Net sales	Net Income*
1957	1,590,322	$208,307,615	$21,438,507
1958	1,966,278	181,179,192	3,422,271
1959	1,537,802	201,939,440	(7,401,076)
1960	1,706,826	207,116,051	(8,215,842)
1961	1,403,000	265,973,000	17,103,000
1962	1,290,000	232,316,000	(5,207,000)

* Parentheses indicate deficit.
Source: Annual reports of Kaiser Steel Corporation.

In 1962 Kaiser also virtually eliminated the historical differential in steel prices between the West Coast and the remainder of the country. The average price reduction was $12 a ton. Kaiser believed that this would not only make Kaiser more competitive domestically but would assist in meeting the competition from imports.

The following is an announcement and summary of the proposed long-range sharing plan developed by the Long-Range Committee of Kaiser Steel and the United Steelworkers:

LONG-RANGE SHARING PLAN

(Announcement by members of the long-range committee, Kaiser Steel Corp. and the United Steelworkers of America, AFL-CIO, December 17, 1962)

The long-range committee of Kaiser Steel Corp. and the United Steelworkers of America, AFL-CIO, today announced their recommendation of a plan for equitable sharing of economic progress by employees, the company, and the public.

The plan has been accepted by officials of Kaiser Steel and the international union. It will become effective only with approval of employees represented by the union at the Kaiser Steel plant in Fontana.

Announcement was made at a public meeting by Dr. George W. Taylor, chairman of the Committee, by David J. McDonald, president of the United Steelworkers of America, AFL-CIO, and Edgar F. Kaiser, chairman of the Board of Kaiser Steel Corp. The meeting was held at Swing Auditorium on the Orange Show Grounds, San Bernardino, California, and was attended by several thousand employees and their wives and husbands.

Coverage of USWA Employees

The plan will cover all Steelworkers Union employees at the plant, including some 6,500 members of the Production and Maintenance Local No. 2869 and 500 members of Clerical and Technical Local No. 3677, employed at the Fontana steel plant.

Protection against Automation

The plan provides protection against the loss of employment because of any technological advance (automation) or new or improved work methods, and also against the loss of income that an employee might otherwise suffer because of such changes. Appropriate protection is provided against loss of opportunity for employment for all reasons except a decrease in the production or demand for finished steel products, a change in products, and the like. Protection against unemployment for such reasons is already provided by the supplemental unemployment benefits plan and other provisions in the existing collective bargaining agreement.

Monthly Sharing of Savings

The plan provides for a monthly sharing with employees of all savings in the use of materials and supplies, and from increased productivity of labor. The sharing takes place whether the increased productivity comes about by direct effort of employees, by the use of better equipment, newer processes, better materials, or through improved yields. Formula for sharing provides that about one-third of any dollar gains made under the plan will be shared by employees. The balance is shared by the company and by the public through taxes. The plan is not a profit-sharing plan—the amount of sharing is not dependent in any way on the level of company profits.

Minimum Guarantee

The plan guarantees that the employees will receive, as a minimum, any economic improvements which may be negotiated in the future in the basic steel industry. This provision is essential in order to encourage full employee participation and to obtain the maximum benefits from the use of technological improvements, including automation. The parties are confident, however, that this minimum guarantee always will be exceeded because the employees' share of economic gains generated by the plan will be greater than the gains that might result from periodic negotiations between the union and the industry generally.

Industrial Peace

The plan will do away with contract deadlines with respect to economic issues and will contribute greatly to the objective of industrial peace. Normal collective bargaining procedures are retained with respect to all other matters.

Results of Three Years of Study and Research

The plan was developed during nearly 3 years of joint study by long-range committee members and staffs of the United Steelworkers and Kaiser Steel. In addition to committee members named above, also participating in the development of the program were David L. Cole, arbitrator and former Director of the Federal Mediation and Conciliation Service, and Dr. John T. Dunlop, professor, Harvard University, as public members; Marvin J. Miller, assistant to the president, and Charles J. Smith, director of district 38 (West Coast area), for the United Steelworkers of America; and E. E. Trefethen, Jr., vice-chairman of the board, and C. F. Borden, executive vice president, for Kaiser Steel.

Based on Contract Objective

The committee dates back to October 26, 1959, when Kaiser Steel and the Steelworkers ended a 3½-month strike. At that time the company and union entered an agreement to establish a joint nine-man committee representing the public, the company, and the union, to develop a long-range plan for the equitable sharing of economic progress. It was agreed in the contract, "The formula shall give appropriate consideration to safeguarding the employees against increases in cost of living, to promoting stability of employment, to reasonable sharing of increased productivity, labor-cost savings, to providing for necessary expansion and for assuring the company's and employees' progress."

Technological Progress and Protection of Work Practices

The plan recognizes that, in a free enterprise system, economic progress can only be achieved by practical utilization of equipment and materials in order to provide good service and a consistently high quality product. It also recognizes that human values must be conserved in the production process and that the best method of achieving efficiency is by joint effort—not by unilateral change. The plan, therefore, makes no change in existing contractual protections of work practices. It provides, instead, a framework which is designed to lead to increased productivity. This framework consists of the provision for the sharing of gains of increased productivity and the guarantee, which the plan provides, against unemployment due to technological change or such changes in work practices as may mutually be agreed.

Plan Based on Existing Costs

Four steps were taken by the committee in order to meet the requirements for the plan. First step was to establish the present level of costs (not prices) of products that are sold at the steel plant in Fontana in terms of labor costs and material and supply costs for each ton of finished steel produced. This was done in such a manner as to recognize the differences in operating levels as well as in the amount of processing required in producing the various products made by Kaiser Steel. These factors provide the base point or standard against which future improvements in productivity will be measured.

Recognizes Industry and National Economic Factors

The second step was to provide for changes in the price level of purchased materials, for safeguarding employees against cost-of-living increases and comprehending the company's practical ability to pay. The committee chose as the most desirable method of measuring these basic factors two broad economic indexes, which include these considerations. It was agreed that the wholesale price index of industry steel prices and the Consumer Price Index issued by the Bureau of Labor Statistics would fulfill this requirement. Movements of these indexes will be reflected in the standards.

32.5 Percent of Gains Shared by Employees

The third step taken by the committee was the development of a formula for sharing the improvements. The formula is simple and equitable. The employees' share of the total net dollar gains generated under this plan is 32.5 percent. This sharing relationship is consistent with the past ratio of labor costs to total manufacturing costs at Kaiser Steel.

Monthly Sharing by Employees

Finally, the plan provides distribution of the employees' net share in the gains on a monthly basis. The plan thus offers employees potential new sources of income by sharing savings as they occur during the actual course of production. It also permits the parties to agree on the use of a portion of the gains produced by the plan for making improvements or adding to insurance, retirement, vacation, holiday and other benefits not provided generally in the industry. The remaining net gains will be distributed in paychecks directly to the employees each month as an addition to their regular pay, through the receipt of payments under the long-range sharing plan.

Sharing by Incentive Employees

Employees now on incentives may transfer to the long-range sharing plan in a variety of ways.

1. The employees on any incentive plan may decide, by majority vote, to cancel the existing incentive and transfer to the long-range sharing plan.

2. When the company offers, the employees on an incentive plan may decide, by majority vote, to accept a lump sum payment roughly equivalent to 2½ years' incentive earnings and to participate in the long-range sharing plan. If the employees reject the lump sum payment, present incumbents will continue to receive the same incentive earnings as in the past, through conversion of such incentives to plans paying no more than 35 percent and differential payments to equal prior earnings. Any savings made by the company as a result of the acceptance of lump sum payments, or as a result of the elimination of incentive earnings for new employees, will be added to the overall employees' share under the plan.

3. Incentive employees who are not offered a lump sum payment, and who do not elect to transfer to the long-range sharing plan because their incentive earnings, exceed the shares payable under the plan, will continue on incentive and, after two years, will also participate, on an adjusted basis, in the long-range sharing plan.

In Keeping with Basic Agreement

The committee said this long-range sharing plan is in harmony with the spirit and intent of the basic labor agreement. It provides a motivation for insuring the future economic progress of the company and its employees, and at the same time, preserves the normal union and company roles.

Members to Vote on Plan

The plan is in the process of being printed and will be distributed to the membership as soon as practicable. In the meantime, the company and the union have arranged to conduct briefing sessions for both union members and management personnel on details of application of the plan. Voting on the plan by union members will take place after these sessions.

The plan would be effective for a four-year period, subject to review and revision by the company and the union annually. The plan can be terminated by either party on four months' notice, following the fourth anniversary date of the plan.

The proposal was submitted to the locals and ratified by secret ballot on January 11, 1963, by a vote of 3,966 to 1,383. The plan went into effect on March 1, 1963.

In late April, 1963, the first payments under the plan were announced. Total savings over the 1961 rate for the month of March were $962,000, of which $312,000 went to the 3,930 participating workers, with the bonus averaging $79 a man. Not all workers participated, since some chose to remain under existing incentive programs. It was estimated by a United Steelworkers officials that payments varied from 15.1 percent to 45.1 percent of wage rates. The lowest payment was 31.5 cents an hour for an employee in the lowest category earnings $2.10 an hour. An employee in the highest category, earning $3 an hour, received an extra $1.35 an hour.

Questions

1. In what ways could the theory of employment, as developed in this chapter, have been of use to the committee as it developed this plan?
2. What aspects of the plan suggest that the theory is perhaps too narrow for such a dynamic response to changing production techniques?
3. From your own knowledge or from studying the steel industry, are there any factors which might make this plan successful at Kaiser and perhaps not successful at other steel companies? Explain.
4. What alternative solutions are possible to the problems of technological change and automation?
5. What are some shortcomings of the Consumer Price Index as used in this plan?

CASE 10–3. Combatting Worker Alienation*

In a famous moving picture, "Modern Times," Charlie Chaplin satirized the assembly line. After turning the same bolt on successive units of a product all day, he walked out on the street still going through the same bolt-turning motions in a way possible only for a master pantominist.

In recent years, especially, there has been an increasing tendency for blue- and white-collar workers, and to some extent middle managers, to dislike their jobs and resent their bosses. There is less concern about the quality of their product—as suggested by the epidemic of new automobile recalls for correction of defects—and in some cases outright sabotage.

Henry Ford once stated that what the typical worker wants is a job where he does not have to think. Employees today are better educated and accustomed to a considerable amount of convenience and even luxury when off the job. Their organizational commitment is increasingly

---

* Information for this case is from Richard E. Walton, "How to Counter Alienation in the Plant," *Harvard Business Review*, November–December, 1972, pp. 70–81, with permission.

influenced not just by income and security but by the quality of the work experience itself.

Unfortunately, it is more difficult to rearrange work procedures to relieve monotony in the automobile plants and other plants with complex assembly lines than it is in the production of technically simpler products. Nevertheless, such companies as Saab-Scandia and Volvo in Sweden have made major efforts to redesign production processes to counter job alienation. At Saab, the following has occurred:

1. Production workers are also made members of development groups.
2. Responsibility for in-process inspection has been shifted from a separate quality inspection unit to the production workers themselves.
3. Workers take care of their own equipment instead of this being the responsibility of special mechanics.
4. Workers are encouraged to learn several jobs rather than one specialized task in the assembly.

At a new Volvo plant teams of 15 to 25 men are assigned responsibility for particular sections of a car, such as the electrical system, brakes and wheels, and so forth. Within teams, members decide how to allocate tasks. Buffer stocks between work teams allow variations in the rate of work without greatly affecting output of the final product. The revised production setup will cost about 10 percent more than a conventional car plant, but the Volvo management expects this outlay to be more than made up by the greater satisfaction workers find in their jobs.

In the United States a well-known experiment in work rearrangement to promote employee satisfaction has taken place at a Gaines pet food plant. In 1968 the company was planning an additional plant at a new location. The existing facility was encountering problems of worker alienation, and it was decided to attempt to counter these problems at the new plant. The new plant was designed both to accommodate changes in the expectations of workers and to utilize knowledge developed by the behavioral sciences. Nine key features were incorporated in the plant design:

1. Work groups are autonomous. Teams are given responsibility for large segments of the production process. The teams assign workers to tasks, and these are often rotated.
2. Inspection of product and maintenance of equipment are kept within the team.
3. Every set of tasks is designed to include some actions requiring judgment and skill.
4. Pay increases are geared to the mastering by an employee of an increasing number of jobs within a team and then in the plant.

5. Team leaders replace the usual use of specialized supervisory personnel.
6. Production decisions can be made at team levels because economic information and business decision rules are provided at the team level.
7. Rules for plant management were not pre-specified but were allowed to evolve from experience.
8. Differentiating status symbols are avoided. For example, a common decor is used throughout the plant.
9. Management is committed to assess both productivity and employees' satisfaction on a continuing basis.

Early results indicated considerable success. Seventy employees rather than the originally estimated 110 are able to man the plant. Fewer quality rejects and lower absenteeism reduced variable costs. Safety was up, and employee turnover down.

Operators, team leaders, and managers alike have become more involved in their work and also have derived more satisfaction from it. For example, when asked what work is like in the plant and how it differs from other places they have worked, employees typically replied: "I never get bored." "I can make my own decisions." "People will help you; even the operations manager will pitch in to help you clean up a mess— he doesn't act like he is better than you are."

Questions

1. Do you believe that similar innovation would be more difficult, or less difficult, in an old plant?
2. How does size of the work force affect the possibilities of productive innovations along the lines followed by the pet food plant?
3. The plant was not unionized. How would unionization be likely to affect the outcome of a similar attempt at innovation?
4. Name another type of product where somewhat similar innovation might be useful. Name another product where it is unlikely to work well. Justify your answers.
5. Adam Smith said that "specialization is limited by the extent of the market." What other factors may limit the efficiency of specialization?

chapter **11**

The Determination of Prices—Competition and Monopoly

MOST FIRMS have some degree of power to determine the prices at which they will sell and some have a great deal of monopoly power. Still, competition is the most persistent force the businessman must face daily. For this reason economists place great stress on the competitive model of price determination since the model spells out in detail the immediate and ultimate consequences of this force on prices, output, input, number and size of firms, and many other important economic variables. At the same time, anyone with something to sell prefers to be a monopolist because it is more profitable. Consequently, models of competitive and monopolistic behavior together capture much of the essence of what is going on in the business world, although (or rather *because*) the models are simplified and not wholly in accord with any specific real situation. All theory is abstract, and the student must be careful not to shrug it off as "unrealistic." At the same time, he must learn not to apply a model to a situation that it is wholly unsuited to explain. Such a process is truly unrealistic.

COMPETITION

Very Short-Run Supply

Following Alfred Marshall, it is common to distinguish between the "very short run," the "short run," and the "long run" even though, as he recognized, there is no hard and sharp line between these analytical periods.[1] The very short run pertains to the pricing of existing inventories of goods since, analytically, the period being considered is too short to permit production. The analysis is useful for perishing goods and for goods such as housing where the accumulated supply is large in relation to the rate of production.

Services rendered by motels, hotels, parking lots, theaters, and stadia are perishing in that once the structures are built (and the attractions, if any, are scheduled) available spaces are wasted if not used. Very short-run supply curves are vertical in competitive situations where many sellers are providing the same thing to the market, for example, if there are numerous parking lots in a downtown area.

Vertical very short-run supply curves can also exist if the motivation of suppliers is nonpecuniary. Sandlot baseball teams often supply entertainment because they wish to play even at a zero price. The amount of money they raise by passing a hat depends on the number who watch and their willingness to contribute. Charitable and religious services are often provided on a similar voluntary basis, although a degree of compulsion may be present.

The fixed supply case can also arise because of government regulation. The Interstate Commerce Commission may require passenger service on a railroad route that would otherwise be abandoned. Although passenger fares are also regulated, the actual price received per space provided depends on the number of passengers carried. Similarly, the supply of broadcasting services is perfectly inelastic for a station on a regular schedule, and the price collected per hour depends on the amount of advertising sold. In the fixed supply case, competitive price can be considered to depend primarily on demand. This case is illustrated in Figure 11–1.

If the problem under consideration is competitive pricing of an existing stock of a durable good (e.g., houses, oriental rugs, or automobiles), the very short-run supply curve is not vertical—although it can be made so by a special definition, as explained later. A nonperishing nature permits supply to be reserved until a subsequent time period. Also, refrigeration, freezing, drying, smoking, curing, pickling, and other processes permit reservation of supplies of many food products that would otherwise have to be sold quickly.

In the very short run the original cost of production of a durable good should not affect sellers' reservation prices (prices below which they will not sell) but cost of reproduction will do so. Many houses, for example, are worth much more today than their original cost. Owners will not ordinarily sell them for less than comparable houses would cost to build today.

---

[1] Alfred Marshall, *Principles of Economics* (London: Macmillan & Co., Ltd., 1930), p. 379. He also analyzed very long-run or secular movements of prices.

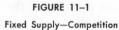

FIGURE 11–1

Fixed Supply—Competition

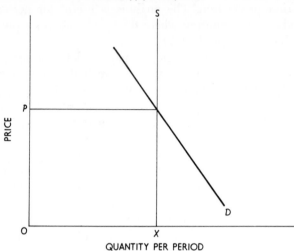

QUANTITY PER PERIOD

If a good is fixed in supply and is not reproducible (paintings of deceased artists, old postage stamps and coins, building sites in specified areas), sellers will have reservations that are unaffected by cost. Satisfaction derived from ownership and anticipation of higher future demand are important in determining reservation prices.

An interesting and useful alternative way of viewing demand and supply for inventories of durable items is to include in demand, rather than in supply, the willingness of owners to retain ownership. That is, a decision to continue to own something of value is equivalent to a decision to buy the good since it involves the opportunity cost of giving up the cash that a sale would otherwise fetch. Viewed in this way, the supply curve for a fixed stock of a durable good is vertical.

Figures 11–2 and 11–3 (the alternative treatment of supply and demand) are drawn side by side in order to illustrate the two alternative ways of dealing with supply and demand for an existing stock of a durable item. The charts pertain to the same situation, but sellers' reservation prices are included in supply in the left-hand figure and in demand on the right.[2] Demand of present owners shown in Figure 11–3 is obtained

---

[2] Philip H. Wicksteed illustrated the inclusion of possessor's stocks in the demand curve and also argued (less successfully) for a similar procedure in short-run and long-run analysis. See "The Scope and Method of Political Economy," *The Economic Journal*, vol. 24 (1914), pp. 1–23. Reprinted in G. Stigler and K. Boulding, eds., *Readings in Price Theory* (Homewood, Ill.: Richard D. Irwin, Inc., 1952), pp. 16–18.

Herbert J. Davenport, *Value and Distribution* (1907), was also an early expositor of this way of viewing demand and supply. See chap. 25, *Reprints of Economic Classics* (New York: Kelley, 1964).

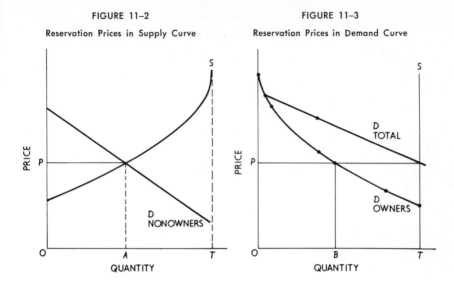

FIGURE 11–2

Reservation Prices in Supply Curve

FIGURE 11–3

Reservation Prices in Demand Curve

by subtracting from total available stock (OT) the quantities along the supply curve S in Figure 11–2. That is, any amount that owners are not willing to supply at any given price they can be considered to be demanding at that price. Market price is OP in both charts. Figure 11–2 shows the amount that changes ownership in the period as the distance OA while the same thing is shown by BT in Figure 11–3. Distance AT on the left and OB on the right show the amount retained by owners. An advantage of the somewhat more complex method of Figure 11–3 is that it brings out more clearly the principle that one should not continue to own a salable asset unless he would be willing to buy it at the market price (except for transactions costs, including the trouble involved). The idea is especially important with respect to securities, the holding of which often becomes more a habit than a rational choice.

Short Run and Long Run

Short-run analysis pertains to pricing and output related to utilization of existing capacity. A great many real-world situations can best be analyzed by means of a side-by-side chart in which short-run adjustments of a typical firm and the entire industry are considered simultaneously and where long-run adjustments can also be shown.

Figure 11–4 is such a chart. The competitive industry is first assumed to be in both short-run and long-run equilibrium with price at OP_1 and output per period at OA. Curve S_1 is the industry's short-run supply function; and LRS, which is drawn horizontally, shows that the industry is one of "constant cost" in the long run in the sense that if enough time is considered to elapse, any quantity—large or small—can be produced at

FIGURE 11–4

Decline in Demand—Causes Short-Run and Long-Run Adjustments

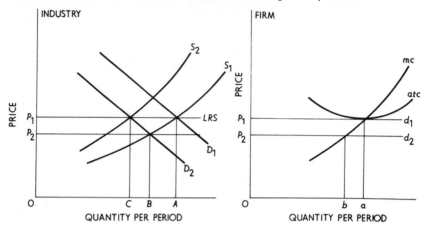

the same unit cost. This, in turn, means that prices of productive inputs will be unaffected by the size of this industry and that such adverse factors as congestion will not set in as the industry expands in size.

The initial equilibrium price and output are determined by the intersection of D_1, S_1, and *LRS*. The firm on the right is a "price taker" being too small to affect industry price. It does possess the power to determine its own output, which will be *Oa*, at the intersection of its own demand curve d_1 and its own marginal cost curve *mc*. That is, the firm will turn out all units that add less to its costs than they can be sold for.

Next suppose demand for the product of this industry suddenly declines to D_2. An immediate reduction of price to OP_2 and of industry output to *OB* would occur. The firm would react to the lower price by reducing its output to *Ob*. (This sort of action by all firms is what reduces industry output to *OB*.) This firm, and the others, will now be suffering economic losses as shown by price being below average total cost (since *atc* includes a return on capital equal to the best alternative employment of the capital). Some firms will leave the industry.[3] A new full equilibrium will be established when enough firms leave the industry to shift the short-run supply curve to the position of S_2 with output *OC* but with price restored to the original level OP_1. Assuming that the firm on the right is one that survives, its output should gradually increase from *Ob* back to the original amount *Oa* as other firms leave and price returns to the level determined by *LRS*.

---

[3] It is not easy to specify *which* firms will leave. In general, those with better alternative uses of capital and entrepreneurial talent and those with more pessimistic expectations regarding this industry will be among those who exit.

The analysis can readily be modified to show the effect of an increase in demand or a change in the level of the *LRS* curve. Perhaps the main lesson to be learned is that a change in demand in a competitive industry, *ceteris paribus,* will cause only a temporary upward or downward change in price. Long-run cost of production will exert a force to bring actual price back to its equilibrium level.

MONOPOLY

As already mentioned, every seller wants to be a monopolist because it is profitable. But monopoly is not a guarantee that profits will be made. For example, thousands of patented items are never produced in spite of the monopoly power conferred by law because the demand-cost situation does not appear to be sufficiently favorable or because the necessary entrepreneurial ability is absent. In a private enterprise system a basic role of government is to establish and enforce a body of rules to frustrate the universal desire to monopolize. Almost needless to say, those who wish to monopolize use their political power to reduce the power of antimonopoly forces.

Where competition is not likely to be an effective regulator of price, as in the case of local electric power production and sale, monopoly may be socially preferable if there are safeguards. Alternative institutional arrangements such as private ownership with public regulation of rates, cooperative ownership, public ownership either with or without regulation by a separate public commission are all possibilities. Selection of the best institutional framework within which to let monopoly operate can make it less objectionable socially.

An interesting example of this idea can be found in the situation of retail liquor stores. In this country it is usually the state or local practice to license such stores, thus holding down their number and securing some public revenue. However, license fees are not closely related to size, profitability, or area within which other stores are excluded. Persons with the political connections to secure licenses at nominal cost from public authorities can often resell the licenses for many times their cost. Indeed, some men are more interested in selling licenses than in the business itself. Alternatively, they may be able to secure monopoly profits from operating the stores. The basic problem is that a valuable business privilege is conferred by representatives of the public at low prices or even at no cost whatever. Since rationing of licenses is not performed by the price system, political favoritism, nepotism, country club or church membership, bribery, or other factors enter as substitutes in their allocation. Scandals connected with the awarding of lucrative television channels dramatize this situation from time to time. The best solution appears to be extension of the price system to the allocation of liquor licenses, television and radio broadcasting privileges, new airline routes, bank charters, and many similar rights. Rights could be awarded in auctions to the highest bidders, thus siphoning off in public revenue a large part of the monopolistic gain that is often available in such fields. Numerous difficulties are inherent in setting up such auctioning schemes—especially in renewing rights—but important social gains, now seldom reaped, are available.

Other Sources of Monopoly Power

In addition to licenses and exclusive franchises, firms may secure monopoly power from patents and copyrights, from exclusive locations, from control of raw materials, from well-known brand names or trademarks, from membership in a cartel, from political connections, from agreements with rivals, and in other ways. Workers can secure monopoly power through unionization; professional associations often do so through unduly restrictive licensing and educational practices. In spite of some check on business firms provided by the federal antitrust laws, as described in Chapter 17, government at all levels appears to do much more to establish and support than to curb monopolistic practices.

Monopoly Demand

Whatever the source of monopoly power, its distinctive theoretical feature is a downsloping demand curve facing the individual firm. This allows the firm to have some choice as to what price to charge. Although a downsloping demand curve implies that some substitution of other goods and services for the one under consideration will occur if price is increased, the monopolist is faced with a demand curve which is not affected by rivals' immediate reactions to his price. This can occur because rivals are so remote (e.g., the local power company has no close rival) or because the firm constitutes only a small part of the (broadly defined) industry. For example, a firm manufacturing ball-point pens may have a distinctive name which it advertises but may not be important enough in the entire pen industry to cause rivals to react to any price change. This situation is often called "monopolistic competition," although analytically it is difficult to separate clearly from monopoly. In both cases the demand curve facing the firm is downsloping from left to right, but under "monopolistic competition" the slope may be less steep and entry of new firms producing close substitutes may make long-run profits less dependable.[4]

---

[4] See Edward H. Chamberlin, *The Theory of Monopolistic Competition* (6th ed.; Cambridge: Harvard University Press, 1950). A leading critic of monopolistic competition as a separate field of theory is George J. Stigler, "Monopolistic Competition in Retrospect," *Five Lectures on Economic Problems* (New York: Macmillan Co., 1949).

Marginal Revenue

A distinctive feature of monopoly analysis is the importance of marginal revenue. Like other marginal concepts in economics, this is the rate of change of an associated total. Marginal revenue is the rate of change in total revenue as sales are altered by a unit (strictly, an infinitesimal unit) per time period. For a competitive firm this is the same as price of the product, but for a monopolist marginal revenue is less than price. This can be seen most easily by considering the following extremely simple demand schedule:

Price	Quantity Demanded	Total Revenue	Marginal Revenue
$10	0	$ 0	$...
9	1	9	9
8	2	16	7
7	3	21	5
6	4	24	3
5	5	25	1
4	6	24	−1
3	7	21	−3

Since the quantity changes by one unit from one row to the next, marginal revenue is simply the change in total revenue as an additional unit is demanded. (If quantity increased by more than one unit at a time, the increase in revenue would be divided by the increase in quantity.) Sup-

FIGURE 11–5

Monopoly Demand—and Marginal Revenue

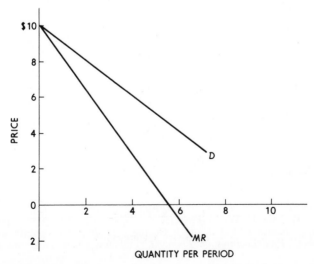

QUANTITY PER PERIOD

pose the monopolist knew the demand situation perfectly. He would know that by charging $9 he could sell one unit per period and that if he charged $8 instead, his gain in revenue would be the $8 secured for the second unit less the $1 cut in income from the first unit (since it will be sold at $8 instead of $9.) Hence marginal revenue of $7 is below the price of $8. The demand schedule and the associated marginal revenue schedule must be understood to represent alternatives at a point in time rather than a series of sales at different prices. What price is actually best from the monopolist's point of view depends on cost and other conditions that will be discussed later.

The foregoing simple demand and marginal revenue schedules are shown graphically in Figure 11–5. Since the demand curve is linear, the marginal revenue curve is also a straight line (with twice as steep a slope).

Monopoly Price for Existing Supply

The simple demand–marginal revenue tools described above lead immediately to useful analysis of some situations in which monopoly pricing occurs. Suppose there are *OS* seats or spaces available in a stadium or parking lot and that the owner wishes to charge a single profit-maximizing price. Assuming monopoly power, the demand curve facing the seller would be downsloping, as in Figure 11–6. What price should he charge? The answer is *OP*, which is the price at which demand is of unitary elasticity. Sales would be *OX* seats or spaces, where *MR* equals zero. It is implicitly assumed that it costs nothing extra to allow

FIGURE 11–6

Monopoly Pricing—of Existing Supply

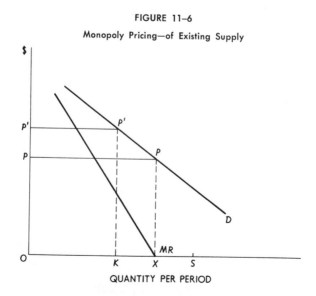

QUANTITY PER PERIOD

additional persons or cars to use the existing facilities—which is close to the actual case. Unsold spaces would be *XS* in amount, since it would "spoil the market" to sell all available spaces.

If the existing supply were much smaller, *OK*, the seller would fill the stadium or parking lot and charge *OP'*. This analysis is approximately relevant for a cartel such as in coffee growing. Favorable growing conditions or inability to control productive efforts of individual coffee growers may easily result in a crop (such as *OS*) which is too large for the good of the industry as a whole. Huge bonfires have been used as a way of destroying the excess coffee (*XS*). In other years no destruction of supply is needed. The above monopoly analysis is not fully applicable if the commodity under consideration is durable, even though fixed in amount. Price policy must then take into account foregone interest and possibly depreciation, maintenance, and storage costs if the existing stock is not sold immediately.

Short-Run Output and Prices

If it is assumed that the monopolist can adjust his rate of production from existing capacity to meet conditions on the demand side, marginal cost must be equated to marginal revenue in order to optimize output and sales. The most profitable single price at which this output can be sold is found at this quantity on the demand curve.

Figure 11–7 is a graphic representation of short-run output and price determination under monopolistic market conditions. Optimum output

FIGURE 11–7

Monopolistic Optimizing—in Short Run

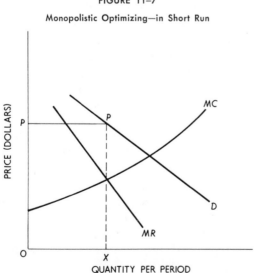

QUANTITY PER PERIOD

is OX, where $MC = MR$. If the monopolist stopped short of this output he would not be maximizing profit because some additional units would add more to revenue than to cost ($MR > MC$). If he produced at a rate greater than OX some units would be adding more to cost than to revenue ($MC > MR$). Only when $MR = MC$ is output optimal. The difficult problem of inventory policy, which exists whenever output and sale need not be simultaneous, will be omitted from consideration here. Consequently, output and sales per period are considered to be equal.

Upward or downward shifts in demand and costs will require output and price adjustments by the monopolist. If entry into the same, or closely related, markets is difficult, demand is less likely to be eroded even over a long period of time.

Long-Run Adjustments

A firm with monopoly power may be maximizing immediate profits but may still be producing on a scale that is too small or too large in view of demand. For example, a motel firm with an advantageous and exclusive location on an interstate highway may be optimizing its situation with respect to the existing facility but be too small to be doing so in a long-run sense. Even assuming that demand will not increase, long-run marginal cost may be below marginal revenue at the existing rate of use, calling for expansion of the facility. The cost of the additional resources needed to construct and operate the new motel units (which reflects their value in alternative opportunities) would then be below the additional revenue derivable from the expenditure.

A monopolistic firm in an optimum short-run position but with too small a plant is portrayed in Figure 11–8. While $SRMC$ is equated to MR at output OX, greater profits could be secured through expansion of capacity since $LRMC$ is below $SRMC$ at output OX. If needed expansion is carried out, OX' will be the optimum output and OP' the optimum price. The expansion will shift the short-run marginal cost curve to the right to the position of $SRMC'$. At output OX' the firm is producing the best output from both a short-run and long-run point of view.

The student may wonder how long-run marginal cost at output OX can be lower than short-run marginal cost when $LRMC$ pertains to *all* resources needed to expand output, while $SRMC$ involves only the short-run variable resources required. That is, such items as opportunity interest on investment and depreciation per time period on new plant are included in $LRMC$ but not in $SRMC$. The answer is that there are assumed to be substantial economies of scale obtainable by having greater capacity. Marginal costs of labor, electric power, materials, and other short-run variable inputs can fall substantially due to the expansion of

FIGURE 11–8

Monopolistic Optimizing—May Call for Plant Expansion

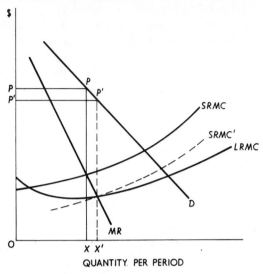

QUANTITY PER PERIOD

capacity; and this reduction can exceed the additional costs attributable to the augmented fixed factor.

Cartels

The analytical apparatus applicable to a single monopolistic seller is useful also for a combination of firms acting in concert to restrict competition. Such a combination is called a cartel by economists, although many businessmen acting legally or illegally to fix noncompetitive prices would be surprised to find the word applied to their own fields. The more spectacular cartels have been international in scope, especially in chemicals and allied products. However, cartel prices are the rule for haircuts within urban areas and are common for dry cleaning, milk, physicians' services, legal services, major brands of gasoline, and some other goods and services.

Cartels which operate over broad geographic areas may allot exclusive marketing territories or assign sales quotas to member firms. It is probably more commonly the case that the cartel fixes price and permits firms to compete for sales. Cartel arrangements are difficult to maintain. Usually "chiseling" generates strains that bring down price or even cause the complete collapse of monopolistic agreements. A basic reason for the strains is that the cartel-determined price usually best fits the needs of a dominant firm, or pleases "representative" companies but is quite poor for some of the firms. Periods of economic recession are especially likely to create disunity by increasing unused capacity.

Figure 11–9 pertains to a single firm subject to a cartel-determined price OP_c. The demand curve is of the "rivals do not match" variety, reflecting potential sales by the firm which is under consideration provided that other cartel members hold strictly to the cartel price. The firm of Figure 11–9 has both short-run and long-run incentives to reduce price

FIGURE 11–9

Incentive to Chisel in a Cartel, Short Run and Long Run

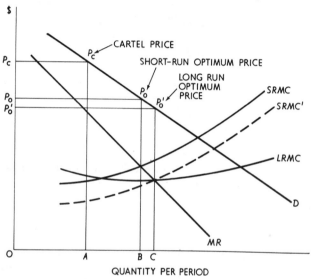

below OP_c, provided its management does not believe its actions will provoke retaliation. (This belief is more likely to be realistic for a relatively small firm.) The immediate establishment of price at P_o, with output and sales of OB, would be better for this firm than the cartel price P_c and sales OA. This is because marginal revenue exceeds $SRMC$ at output OA. However, the firm also has an incentive to add to its capacity because even at price P_o long-run marginal cost is below marginal revenue. Full adjustment—if the firm can get away with it—requires enough expansion to make $SRMC'$ the short-run marginal cost curve, output and sales OC, and price P_o'.

If the firm does not want overtly to violate the cartel price, there are many possibilities for making concessions of a sort less likely to bring retaliation. Some of these devices are special installation and service to customers, money-back guarantees, trading stamps, premiums, high trade-in allowances, entertainment of buyers, and reciprocal purchases at favorable prices. One or more members of a cartel may increase its share of the market so greatly by means of overt or covert price cuts that the more loyal members will cut price or increase concessions to buyers. The process of cartel dissolution may be hastened by the entry of new sellers who remain outside the organization.

The strong arm of government is often enlisted by sellers to strengthen cartel policy. During the depression of the 1930s, the National Recovery Administration encouraged cartel pricing as a (misguided) way of halting price deflation. Even today milk prices are commonly fixed under either federal or state agreements; federal fair trade laws (in periods when they are constitutional) permit manufacturers to set retail prices; and state laws often permit makers of drugs, sporting goods, and other items to make collective decisions on prices. Police power, paid for by the public, is thus enlisted to prevent price cutting.

Taxation of Monopoly Profits

It has already been mentioned that the auctioning of rights to participate in such fields as broadcasting may be an effective means of capturing for the public a portion of monopoly profits. An alternative is to impose special taxes on firms which have clear monopoly power. A "lump-sum" tax, such as a license fee, has the advantage that it should have no effect on the rate of operation or price. This is illustrated in Figure 11–10. Output OX and price OP are best for the monopolist. Area $MPBJ$ is "profit." A lum-sum tax of $MTKJ$ would not affect optimum output or price since marginal cost is unaltered. The "profits" which are taxed away may not have much relation to accounting profits. They constitute instead an income above an alternative return on the fixed capital, since opportunity costs are included in ATC. A sufficiently high lump-sum tax could cause the firm to abandon production, in spite of its monopoly power, and to seek an alternative opportunity.

Competitive auctioning of licenses which convey monopoly power to successful bidders (e.g., for television broadcasting rights) can also be analyzed in Figure 11–10. If the auction is fully competitive, the sum paid will in effect constitute a lump-sum tax in the amount $MJBP$, wiping out monopoly profits. Net income remaining to the monopolist, $OXJM$ would be equal to the total cost, including in cost just a competitive return on capital. It is for this reason that some economists favor a great increase in the distribution of all sorts of exclusive franchises by means of competitive auctions instead of by direct distribution on political and other bases. From the point of view of the businessman who lacks the political power to secure exclusive privileges from public authorities, an auctioning system would open up new business opportunities.

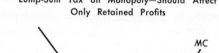

FIGURE 11–10

Lump-Sum Tax on Monopoly—Should Affect
Only Retained Profits

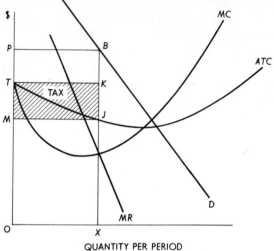

QUANTITY PER PERIOD

APPENDIX TO CHAPTER 11. Pricing under Regulation

It has long been public policy in the United States to regulate public utility and transportation rates on the grounds that "natural monopolies" exist which will otherwise be able to earn exhorbitant profits. Most economists believe that electric power companies clearly fall in the category of firms that should be regulated.[5] Decreasing long-run cost (as scale of plant increases) can make it technically undesirable for more than one company to furnish the service. An exclusive franchise, secured at nominal cost from public authorities, can make the venture highly profitable. The common compromise is to allow monopoly but to give appointed or elected commissioners power over rates, accounting practices, and other aspects of the operation. It is not clear that the whole process is successful since commissioners are usually more in tune to the desires of the companies than those of the public. Prices of many public utility stocks have increased so much in the past quarter century that the long-run effectiveness of commissions in curbing monopoly profits is questionable. (Utility stocks are frequently "split" in order to reduce their price and not call attention to long-run profitability.)

---

[5] There are doubters among the best economists, however. George Stigler and Claire Friedland, "What Can Regulators Regulate? The Case of Electricity," *Journal of Law and Economics,* October, 1965, stress that long-run monopoly power is small in this field and that quality of service remains an important variable that is hard to regulate.

Railroads have been subject to public regulation since the Act to Regulate Commerce of 1887. The most basic provision required that railroad rates in interstate and foreign commerce be "just and reasonable." The Interstate Commerce Commission was set up to administer the act which has had a long history of court interpretations and legislative amendments. By 1920 the emphasis had changed from protection of the public from monopolistic charges to the prevention of rate cutting, since the ICC was permitted to fix minimum rates. Subsequent to 1920, ICC regulation was extended to trucking, pipelines, and water carriers.

Once initiated, regulation is difficult to abandon because many investments and other economic decisions are based on situations engendered by the regulation. Also, many well-paid positions are based on the need of both government and firms to acquire detailed knowledge of legal and economic aspects that affect negotiations between regulators and the regulated. It seems clear, however, that a great decrease in the extent of regulation of transportation, at least, could now be usefully effected, especially in trucking.

Although the airline industry is among the transportation industries that could now be quite competitive, it is subject to rate and route regulation by the Civil Aeronautics Board. As in the case of television station franchises, political contributions and other types of bribery almost inevitably occur in connection with the authoritative allocation of airline routes. Rate regulation of airlines also leads to a serious problem of competition in quality. The most important of these is in the timing of flights, with several different airlines frequently flying out of the same place at about the same favorable hour, headed for the same destination. Quality competition has also taken the form of pretty stewardesses, free or low-cost drinks, lounges in the airports, and free additional travel arrangements. This follows the basic economic truth that where sellers cannot compete freely on a price basis they will be constantly thinking of nonprice concessions in order to attract some of the business of their rivals.

Geometric Analysis of Regulation

The courts have laid down the principle that regulated firms are entitled to a "fair return on the fair value" of their property. Both types of "fairness" have been extremely controversial and have generated an enormous amount of paper work and expert testimony in rate hearings. A fair annual rate of return to an electric utility company is obviously well below that of highly risky fields where principal can easily be lost in a bad period. But exactly what level *is* appropriate? A common (but still nebulous) view is that it should permit the company to compete successfully in the capital markets. "Fair value" is usually based on some combination of original cost and cost of reproduction, but the details of calculation are manifold and controversial. If original cost is used as the sole basis, investors in utility stocks will not secure the capital gains from inflation and growth that usually benefit other investors. If reproduction cost were the sole basis there are knotty questions about such matters as land cost in a hypothetical present purchase and present cost of items that are no longer manufactured.

In a very general way, some dilemmas of regulation by commission are illustrated in Figure 11–11. If the company were unregulated and

FIGURE 11–11

Possible Goals—In Utility Pricing

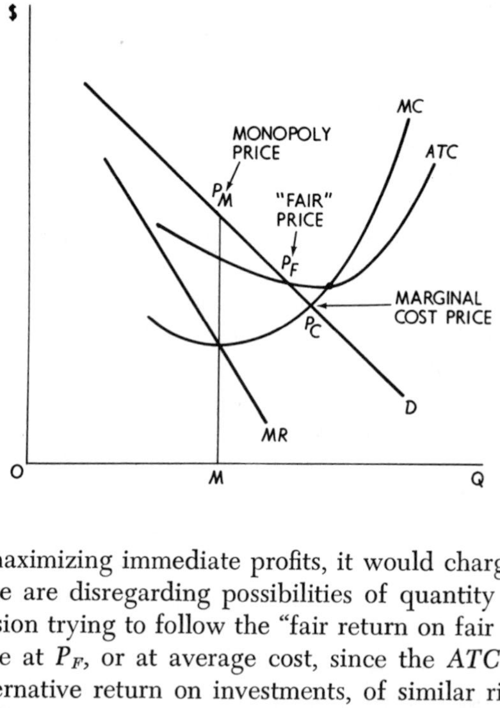

interested in maximizing immediate profits, it would charge a monopoly price MP_M (we are disregarding possibilities of quantity discounts). A utility commission trying to follow the "fair return on fair value" dictum would set price at P_F, or at average cost, since the ATC curve should include an alternative return on investments, of similar riskiness. However, there is also some merit in price P_C, where the marginal cost curve crosses demnad because once the plant capacity is built it can be argued that best use is made of the plant when all units are turned out that could sell at a price that covers only the value of *additional* resources required in production In the situation pictured in Figure 11–11, interest and depreciation on capital could not be covered at price P_C without a government subsidy (or conceivably by voluntary contributions from users). This makes marginal cost pricing an unlikely actual policy of commissioners.

As already implied, the simple graphic analysis of Figure 11–11 omits many of the variables that would be of real-world importance. If the firm sells electric power it is quite certain to use a system of quantity discounts as a means of increasing profits. Buyers with less short-run and long-run elasticity of demand will be charged more than those who have a better opportunity to switch to substitutes. Low rates to large users also secure fuller utilization of capacity. (Such promotional rates have recently come into question as contributing to the "energy crisis.") Also off-daily peak and off-season rates may be lower as a way of smoothing use of existing capacity over time. A certain amount of quality deterioration can be allowed to occur by a utility company as a way of cutting costs or as a way of dramatizing its alleged need for more revenue.

Price and Wage Controls

Although price and wage controls are several thousand years old, their use in the United States has been sparing. Inflationary pressures generated during World War II caused rents and retail prices to be placed under control of the Office of Price Administration. Price controls worked fairly well during World War II due to the large number of paid and volunteer employees and a feeling of patriotism on the part of most Americans. The nature of the pressures can be seen in Figure 11–12 where the amount demanded exceeds amount supplied by the amount KX at the legal ceiling price. One way of equating effective demand and supply is to issue ration stamps in an amount that would cause OK of them to be presented to sellers. If issued in excess or widely counterfeited, ration stamps will often go unhonored; if too few are issued,

FIGURE 11–12

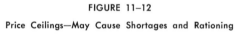

Price Ceilings—May Cause Shortages and Rationing

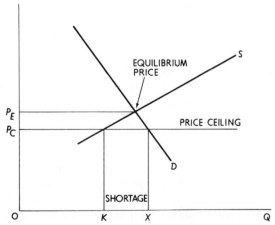

available supplies of goods may go unsold. In the absence of rationing, distribution may be by queue, on the basis of personal relationships, reciprocal favor, or by black-market prices.

Although price controls remained in effect after the termination of World War II, black markets became more prevalent. Even with rationing in existence, ration stamps were often unable to command goods at legal prices. If the law were completely disregarded by sellers, the equilibrium price could become the black-market price. If the price ceiling reduced amount supplied, black-market prices could be even higher.

Rent control during World War II caused a shortage of apartments and the appearance of waiting lists. A large redistribution of income from tenants to building owners was prevented. However, managers often accepted *sub rosa* payments, tenants were forced to buy unwanted furniture, and apartments were undermaintained.

Rent controls remained in effect on existing housing in New York City after the war. The same types of effects as mentioned have been observed, and in addition many buildings have been abandoned entirely (often to become dumps for garbage). Managers of new apartment buildings not subject to rent control have often had to offer tenants special concessions, partly because they rent at rates that seem very high in relation to the controlled segment.

Price controls were reimposed during the Korean War, but the program lacked the vigor of the World War II effort. Since rationing was not instituted it appears that not many price ceilings were actually set below equilibrium prices. Shortages of fuels for heating occurred which may have been due to reductions in supply caused by price control.

Nixon Controls

An unusual experiment in direct controls was announced by President Nixon on August 15, 1971. The main provision of the executive order was that for a period of 90 days prices, wages, rents, and salaries were to be held at levels no higher than existed in the previous 30-day period. At the end of the 90-day period Phase II went into effect. A Pay Board and Price Commission were established. The former was supposed to limit average annual wage increases to 5.5 percent, and the latter hoped to reduce the rate of price inflation to 2.5 percent per year compared with an actual 6 percent the previous year.

Organized labor soon decided that the actual effect of Phase II was to hold down wage rates while "permitting profits to soar." On March 22, 1972, the AFL–CIO members resigned from the Pay Board, making it necessary to restructure the group. The already burdened Internal Revenue Service was charged with the task of policing millions of small businesses. The Pay Board and the Price Commission dealt mainly with big corporations and major wage contracts, trying to keep increases within stabilization boundaries. In order to ease the administrative problem, small businesses and governments with 60 or fewer employees were freed from wage and price controls in early May, 1972. The action was justified on the dubious theoretical grounds that the large companies tend to exert price discipline over the small ones.

Phase III, a greatly relaxed program of control, was instituted January 11, 1973. Voluntary restraints were to replace mandatory ones. Self-administration by businesses and unions was supposed to keep price increases in line only with cost increases and to keep wage increases within the 5.5 percent guideline. Three "problem areas"—food, health care, and construction wages—were kept under mandatory controls. A construction industry stabilization committee was established.

By the spring of 1973 it was clear that the program was not working as such items as precious metals, copper wire, and transformers rose wildly in price. Food prices rose rapidly, soybeans rising so much in price that exports were curtailed, much to the dismay of the Japanese who rely heavily on the United States for this commodity. As a stop-gap measure in preparation for a renewed mandatory effort in Phase IV, prices were frozen on June 13, 1973, with the freeze being for a maximum of 60 days. The freeze was to apply to food after the first processing, but it also affected poultry, fruit, and vegetable growers since they may be unable to sell at profitable prices to processors who are caught in a price-cost squeeze.

The situation of a processor who is caught between a frozen selling price and rising costs is illustrated in Figure 11–13. The firm may be

FIGURE 11–13

Price-Cost Squeeze—May Occur under Price Control

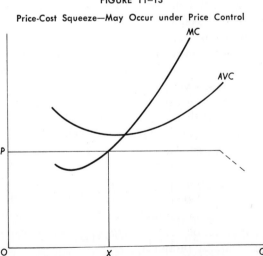

either in a highly competitive field or it may ordinarily possess some monopoly power. (In the latter case a downsloping demand curve might become effective at an output so large that it could not be sold at the ceiling price, as indicated by the dashed line.)

The firm of Figure 11–13 can minimize its losses by shutting down, providing it will not cost too much to start up again after more favorable conditions are restored. If costs of shutting down and restarting an operation are expected to be so high that it is preferable to continue production even with price below *AVC,* the best output rate will be *OX,* where price equals marginal cost. During the summer 1973 price freeze, some poultry producers dramatized the squeeze by destroying baby chicks before the cameras. They claimed that selling costs of poultry would not cover feed and other direct costs of raising them.

Phase IV Controls

Disruptions of supply proved to be so severe that the "60-day" price freeze on food and health care lasted only 36 days. The price freeze in the rest of the economy was allowed to last until August 12, 1973, when Phase IV was to take effect. Beef prices were to remain frozen until September 12, 1973.

The basic rule of Phase IV was that prices were to be permitted to rise only as much as business costs went up. This was similar to Phase II rules except that further markups above cost increases were to be disallowed. As during Phase II, large companies with annual sales of $100 million or more were required under Phase IV to clear all price increases with the federal government. However, some industries were exempt from controls at the outset, including lumber, most regulated utilities, and coal under long-term contract.

A great deal of the economic theory pertaining to the firm is helpful in anticipating problems, methods of evasion, strategy of enforcement, and so forth, in connection with direct controls of the sorts described. It is for this reason that economists are in good demand both by government and business whenever controls are utilized. (The legal field also is helped since lawyers are needed to formulate, interpret, and evade the maze of regulations that define the specifics of control.)

Some of the more evident problems are: What is meant by "cost"? Is it average or marginal cost? How are costs common to many commodities to be allocated? How can true joint costs be allocated? (It is theoretically impossible!) What depreciation formula is allowable? How is a "commodity" to be defined? What if the good is altered slightly in quality? Are advertising costs to be permitted to any degree? How are prices of entirely new goods to be frozen? Are imported goods to be treated differently than domestic products?

Anyone who works in an agency charged with controlling prices is likely to come away with a much greater respect for the work that is usually accomplished efficiently by the price system. Most economists believe that price controls are not a substitute for tighter monetary and fiscal policy as a means of curbing inflation. Temporarily, a program of price control may induce expectations of more stable prices and in this way reduce the upward pressure on prices, wages, and interest rates. In time the expectations are likely to be disappointed. Because of supply disruptions created by unprofitable price-cost relationships during a period of control, prices after decontrol are likely to be higher than if direct controls had been avoided entirely.

CASE 11–1. Prices in Philately[6]

Millions of collectors and many stamp dealers in the United States rely heavily on *Scott's Standard Postage Stamp Catalogue,* which describes and gives prices for over 200,000 stamps in its recent annual editions. After stating that "condition is the all important factor of price. Prices are quoted for stamps in fine conditions," the Scott catalogue goes on to explain its prices as follows:

The prices appearing in this Catalogue were estimated after careful study of available wholesale and retail offerings together with recommendations and information submitted by many of the leading philatelic societies. These and other factors were considered in determining the figures which the editor considers represent the proper or present price basis for a fine specimen when offered by an informed dealer to an informed buyer. Sales are frequently made at lower figures occasioned by individual bargaining, changes in popularity, temporary over-supply, local custom, the "vest pocket dealer," or the many other reasons which cause deviations from any accepted standard. Sales at higher prices are usually because of exceptionally fine condition, unusual postal markings, unexpected political changes or newly discovered information. While the minimum price of a stamp is fixed at 2 cents to cover the dealer's labor and service cost of assorting, cataloguing and filling orders individually, the sum of these list prices does not properly represent the "value" of a packet of unsorted or unmounted stamps sold in bulk which generally consists of only the cheaper stamps. Prices in italics indicate infrequent sales or lack of adequate pricing information.[7]

---

[6] Philately is defined as the "collection and study of postage stamps . . . usually as a hobby" (*Webster's New World Dictionary* [Cleveland: World Publishing Co., 1957]).

[7] *Scott's Standard Postage Stamp Catalogue* (New York: Scott Publications, 1962), p. v.

The Post Office Department at periodic intervals issues *Postage Stamps of the United States,* which gives fuller details on each United States stamp and gives the quantity issued for all commemoratives and airmail stamps. Exhibits 11–1A, 11–1B, and 11–1C give the quantities issued and catalog prices of canceled stamps for three groups of stamps that could be considered "blue chips" because of the wide popularity of U.S. commemoratives and airmails. More recent U.S. commemoratives probably have limited chances of appreciation because of the large quantities issued, usually 120 million, and the very substantial purchases by collectors. Mint commemoratives have been made freely available to all who desired them for a year or two after issue at the U.S. Philatelic Agency. Government policy has also been against allowing the great enhancement of value through the discovery of important errors. When faulty sheets of the Dag Hammarskjold issue were discovered in 1962, the Post Office Department reissued the error for purchase by all who desired it. Thus the spectacular price appreciation of the best-known U.S. error, the inverted airplane in the tricolored 24-cent issue of 1918, seems unlikely to be repeated.

In the early 1970s the government issued commemoratives in large numbers, 32 in 1972. It honored the following that year: Sidney Lanier, poet of the South (one); the Peace Corps (one); National Parks Cen-

EXHIBIT 11–1A

Quantity Issued and Catalog Prices of the U.S. Columbian Exposition Issue—1893

Denomination	Quantity Issued (in thousands)	Scott Catalogue Price, 1949*	Scott Catalogue Price, 1962*	Scott Catalogue Price, 1974*
$0.01	449,196	$ 0.03	$ 0.10	$ 0.15
0.02	1,464,589	0.02	0.05	0.06
0.03	11,501	1.10	2.50	6.00
0.04	19,182	0.35	0.85	2.25
0.05	35,248	0.40	1.00	2.50
0.06	4,708	1.85	3.25	7.00
0.08	10,657	0.50	1.00	2.65
0.10	16,517	0.45	0.85	2.25
0.15	1,577	5.00	7.50	20.00
0.30	617	8.00	13.00	30.00
0.50	244	11.00	17.50	45.00
1.00	55	36.00	50.00	150.00
2.00	46	30.00	50.00	140.00
3.00	28	57.50	90.00	250.00
4.00	26	70.00	110.00	350.00
5.00	27	77.50	220.00	400.00
Total		$299.70	$567.60	$1,407.80

* For canceled stamps.
Sources: *Scott's Standard Postage Stamp Catalogue* (New York: Scott Publications, 1949, 1962, 1974); and *U.S. Postage Stamps, 1847–1957* (Washington, D.C.: U.S. Government Printing Office, 1957).

EXHIBIT 11–1B

Quantity Issued and Catalog Prices of Selected U.S. Commemorative Stamps of the 1920s

Date	Issue	Denomination	Quantity Issued (in thousands)	Scott Catalogue Price, 1949*	Scott Catalogue Price, 1962*	Scott Catalogue Price, 1974*
1920	Pilgrim Tercentenary	$0.01	137,978	$ 0.20	$ 0.50	$ 1.20
1920	Pilgrim Tercentenary	0.02	196,037	0.12	0.35	0.80
1920	Pilgrim Tercentenary	0.05	11,321	2.50	4.50	8.50
1921	Harding Memorial	0.02	1,459,487	0.03	0.06	0.08
1921	Harding Memorial (imperforate)	0.02	770	1.10	1.50	1.75
1921	Harding Memorial (rotary press)	0.02	99,950	0.10	0.20	0.50
1924	Huguenot-Walloon Tercentenary	0.01	51,387	0.25	0.55	1.50
1924	Huguenot-Walloon Tercentenary	0.02	77,753	0.20	0.50	1.25
1924	Huguenot-Walloon Tercentenary	0.05	5,659	2.75	4.50	8.50
1925	Lexington-Concord	0.01	15,615	0.30	0.60	1.65
1925	Lexington-Concord	0.02	26,596	0.45	1.15	3.00
1925	Lexington-Concord	0.05	5,349	2.00	3.00	8.00
1925	Norse-American	0.02	9,105	0.60	1.10	2.00
1925	Norse-American	0.05	1,901	3.00	5.50	9.00
	Subtotal value			$13.60	$24.01	$ 49.73
1929	Nebraska issue†	0.01	8,220	$ 0.12	$ 0.22	$ 0.65
1929	Nebraska issue	0.015	8,990	0.10	0.20	0.80
1929	Nebraska issue	0.02	73,220	0.05	0.15	0.30
1929	Nebraska issue	0.03	2,110	0.50	1.10	3.50
1929	Nebraska issue	0.04	1,600	0.75	1.60	3.75
1929	Nebraska issue	0.05	1,860	0.80	1.60	4.00
1929	Nebraska issue	0.06	980	2.75	4.00	7.00
1929	Nebraska issue	0.07	850	1.50	3.00	6.00
1929	Nebraska issue	0.08	1,480	1.50	4.50	9.00
1929	Nebraska issue	0.09	530	3.75	5.25	9.50
1929	Nebraska issue	0.10	1,890	2.50	4.00	8.50
	Subtotal value			$14.32	$25.62	$ 53.00
	Total value			$27.92	$49.63	$100.73

* For canceled stamps.
† These issues are listed separately since they were regular issues that were overprinted.
Sources: *Scott's Standard Postage Stamp Catalogue* (New York: Scott Publications 1949, 1962, 1974); and *U.S. Postage Stamps, 1847–1957* (Washington, D.C.: U.S. Government Printing Office, 1957).

tennial (eight, including one airmail); family planning (one); American Revolution Bicentennial (four craftsmen); Olympic Games (four, including one airmail); Parent-Teachers Association (one); Wildlife Conservation (four with popular birds and animals); the mail-order business (one); osteopathic medicine (one); Tom Sawyer (one); Christmas (one with angel, one with Santa Claus); the American druggist (one); stamp collecting (one); International Transporation Exposition (one envelope).

EXHIBIT 11–1C

Quantity Issued and Catalog Prices, U.S. Air-mail Stamps, 1918–30

Date	Issue	Denomi-nation	Quantity Issued (in thousands)	Scott Catalogue Price, 1949*	Scott Catalogue Price, 1962*	Scott Catalogue Price, 1974*
1918	Definitive first issue.........	$0.06	3.396	$ 2.00	$ 5.00	$ 12.0
1918	Definitive first issue.........	0.16	3,794	4.50	9.50	21.0
1918	Definitive first issue.........	0.24	2,135	4.00	8.00	20.0
1918	Definitive first issue (center inverted)..........	0.24	0.1	3,500.00	10,000.00	35,000.0
1923	Definitive.................	0.08	6,415	1.40	2.75	7.0
1923	Definitive.................	0.16	5,309	4.00	8.50	21.0
1923	Definitive.................	0.24	5,286	2.25	4.75	12.5
1926–27	Definitive.................	0.10	42,093	0.04	0.15	0.2
1926–27	Definitive.................	0.15	15,597	0.20	0.50	1.2
1926–27	Definitive.................	0.20	17,616	0.12	0.40	1.0
1927	Definitive (Lindbergh).......	0.10	20,379	0.15	1.00	1.8
1928	Definitive.................	0.05	106,888	0.05	0.20	0.5
1930	Definitive.................	0.05	97,641	0.04	0.15	0.4
1930	Definitive (rotary 1931)......	0.05	57,340	0.04	0.15	0.3
1930	Century of Progress.........	0.65	94	18.00	35.00	90.0
1930	Century of Progress.........	1.30	72	35.00	50.00	135.0
˙1930	Century of Progress.........	2.60	61	57.50	95.00	235.0
	Total value (excluding 24¢ in-verted).....................			$ 129.29	$ 221.05	$ 559.0

* For canceled stamps except center-inverted 24-cent stamp, which exists only uncanceled and whose price is quoted ᵢ italics in the Scott catalogue.
Sources: *Scott's Standard Postage Stamp Catalogue* (New York: Scott Publications, 1949, 1962, 1974; *U.S. Postage Stamp 1847–1957* (Washington, D.C.: U.S. Government Printing Office, 1957).

All were low-value stamps, mostly 8 cents. The post office also added albums for current U.S. stamps to its line.

Questions

1. What is the general relationship between price and the quantity issued? What are possible explanations for the price not varying proportionally (though inversely) with the quantity issued?
2. *a.* In what respects does the model for price determination in the very short run fit American postage stamps? In what respects does it differ?
    b. Are the changes in prices between 1949 and 1974 best explained by shifts in supply or demand, or both? Show diagrammatically.
3. Assess U.S. used airmail and commemorative stamps as an investment by calculating rates of return. Assume that you purchased the complete sets of "fine stamps" described in the exhibits in either 1942 or 1962 at 90 percent catalog and sold them in 1962 or 1974 at 70 percent catalog. Consider the inverted airmail as a separate possibility.
4. Another popular way that some collectors have sought to invest in stamps

is to buy sheets of 50 of current commemoratives at face value. For example, one could have purchased 100 sheets of a 1949 3-cent commemorative for $150. In 1974 although the stamps cataloged at 10 cents apiece, they might have been sold to a dealer for 3½ cents. Why would this investment have been the least attractive?

5. Consider whether the post office's policies toward commemoratives is the position of an enlightened monopolist.

CASE 11–2. Southwestern Bell Telephone Company versus City of Houston

The city of Houston and Southwestern Bell Telephone Company have a long history of controversy over local-service telephone rates.[8] In December, 1917, the company filed an application for a rate increase with the City Council and was turned down by the city in January, 1918. However, in September, 1920, the increased rates were finally put into effect after lengthy court proceedings. The final decision was by the Supreme Court of the United States on May 22, 1922.[9]

These rates remained in effect until 1941, when the city was able to obtain a reduction after informal proceedings. The new rates remained in effect until December, 1949, when the telephone company was granted an increase after several days of hearings before the City Council.

In December, 1950, the city passed ordinance No. 5759 terminating the company's franchise effective June 21, 1951, in accordance with the terms of the franchise. In October, 1951, the company filed an application for increased rates. No hearings were set by the City Council, the city taking the position that the franchise question would have to be settled before any action could be taken on the rate application. Conferences were held during the year 1952 by the city and the company; and in December, ordinance No. 8312 was passed, granting the company a new franchise effective January 23, 1953.

In March, 1953, the company filed a supplementary application for increased rates and asked that temporary rates be placed in effect under bond. In April the City Council denied rates under bond and set hearings for the proposed increases for June, 1953.

The hearings before the City Council were conducted from June 1, 1953, through August 20, 1953, and the record contains 2,414 pages of oral testimony and 71 exhibits. On September 9, 1953, the City Council enacted ordinance No. 9236 denying the company's application for an

---

[8] Texas was in 1958 one of two states without a state commission for the regulation of utilities.

[9] *City of Houston* v. *Southwestern Bell Telephone Company*, 259 U.S. 318.

increase in revenues and giving specific findings and conclusions on the issues raised.

The company filed action on October 5, 1953, in the District Court of Harris County, 133d Judicial District of Texas, asking a temporary injunction, a permanent injunction, and the right to place higher rates in effect under bond pending the final determination of the proceedings. The District Court on November 9, 1953, found for the company, and ordered a temporary injunction restraining the city from enforcing the rate ordinance of 1949 and allowing the company to place higher rates in effect under the condition that it file a $12 million surety bond. The company put into effect an increased schedule of rates effective November 10, 1953.

The temporary injunction order was appealed by the city to the Court of Civil Appeals, but the order was affirmed on December 9, 1953, and a rehearing was denied. The Texas Supreme Court refused a writ of error on February 10, 1954.

The company requested that a master in chancery be appointed to receive evidence, hear the issues of fact and law arising in the proceedings, and report findings of fact and conclusions of law to the court. A master in chancery was appointed by the court over the objections of the city, and hearings were held.

The areas of contention were the rate base, the allowable revenues and expenses, and the allowable rate of return. The evidence and findings are presented for each of these areas.

At the outset, the parties agreed that the entire Houston District Exchange, comprising not only the city of Houston but a number of other smaller municipalities, would serve as the basis for the data on plant, revenues, and expenses to be considered. This area is a single operations unit, that is, any local subscriber may call any other local subscriber without payment of a toll.

Rate Base

The basic area of contention between the city and the company on the rate base was in the definition of fair value. The city contended that fair value need not give predominant weight to current cost or reproduction cost. The company felt that current cost should be given predominant weight, particularly since the price level had risen greatly since much of the plant was placed into service.

Exhibit 11–2A shows the computation of the rate base by the company, the city, and the master in chancery. Each is discussed with more detailed discussion following on the questions of depreciation and separations.

Two witnesses for the company testified as to the fair value of the

EXHIBIT 11–2A

Computation of the Rate Base, Houston Exchange, Southwestern Bell Telephone Company
(as of December 31, 1952)

COMPUTATION BY J. B. BLANTON OF THE COMPANY

Current cost of telephone plant in Houston District Exchange (before separations)	$111,475,674
Less: Deterioration and obsolescence (observed)	10,648,707
Current cost of telephone plant less accrued depreciation (before separations)	$100,826,967
Less: Portion allocable to long-distance operations as per "usage method"	17,259,386
Current cost of depreciated telephone plant allocable to local exchange service	$ 83,567,581
Plus: Cash working capital	618,005
Plus: Materials and supplies	971,061
Total Current Worth	$ 85,156,647

COMPUTATION BY JAMES HONAKER FOR THE CITY OF HOUSTON

Gross telephone plant allocable to local exchange service in Houston District Exchange (after separation of portion allocable to long-distance operations according to procedures recommended by Honaker)	$ 71,736,159
Less: A. T. & T. excess earnings through Western Electric Company included in plant	1,240,481
Adjusted gross telephone plant	$ 70,495,678
Less: Reserve for depreciation	13,405,161
Net Telephone Plant as Adjusted	$ 57,090,517

COMPUTATION BY THE MASTER IN CHANCERY

Average original cost of plant in service during 1952 (before separation)	$ 89,334,830
Less: Portion allocable to long distance in accordance with "usage method"	15,231,918
Average original cost after separations	$ 74,102,912
Less: Balance of book reserve for depreciation (based on company's special Houston study)	12,444,474
Average net plant for year 1952	$ 61,658,438
Plus: Adjustment for appreciation of land value	202,054
Fair Value as Determined by Master	$ 61,860,492

Source: *Report of Master in Chancery*, pp. 31, 125.

property. Mr. Jackson Martindell, before the City Council, determined fair value by converting the additions to the plant since 1939 to 1952 dollars by use of the Consumer Price Index, in order to express the value of the plant in terms of the purchasing power of 1952 dollars. By this method, he determined the fair value of the property to be about $83 million. Mr. J. Ben Blanton of the company listed nine elements that he believed should be considered in determining the fair value of the property. These were:

. . . First would be the original cost of the property; by that I mean the number of dollars invested in and subject to all risks inherent to the operation of the business. The second item would be the number of dollars in the reserve for depreciation. . . . The next item, the net investments in the property expressed in terms of the purchasing power of the dollar as of December 31,

1952. . . . The next element that we took into consideration is the current cost of the properties used and useful in rendering telephone service, and by that I mean what it would cost to construct the properties being used in public service at the prices for wages and materials in effect December 31, 1952. . . . The next element is the present condition of the property, that is, whether there is any deterioration or obsolescence existing in the property. The next item to take into consideration is the amount of cash working capital, and the value of the quantity of materials and supplies which are required for the day to day operations of the business. . . . The next item was in the engineering of the property, that is, whether the property had been properly engineered and is adapted to meet the needs of the community. . . . The next item that we look into is to whether there is any existence of nonuseful property, whether there was any waste in the building and the property. . . . The last item which we would recognize and give consideration to, is whether or not Houston is a progressive area, one in which the future of the telephone service will continue into the foreseeable future.[10]

Mr. Blanton's method of appraisal consisted of securing an inventory of all of the assets of the exchange. Equipment other than buildings and land was repriced at prices prevailing on December 31, 1952. Buildings were revalued by the use of building construction cost indices for the Houston area. The buildings were valued as if they were to be rebuilt wholesale rather than piecemeal, as they were actually constructed. Land was valued as appraised in 1949 plus the market price for land added since 1949. For right of way, vehicles, furniture, and work equipment, original cost was taken as the best evidence of the current cost of these items. Observed depreciation was deducted from this total to obtain the present value. The observed depreciation was determined by an engineering inspection of a small sample of the property. An overall percent condition was then determined and applied to the current cost to obtain the depreciated current cost. The long-distance plant was separated from the local plant by means of separations studies which will be discussed later. Both Mr. Martindell and Mr. Blanton used plant as of December 31, 1952, rather than the average plant (see Exhibit 11–2A).

The city, on the other hand, used average annual values for the plant instead of year-end values, and deducted the book reserve for depreciation using the statewide ratio of reserve to depreciable telephone plant. The city used original cost according to the records of the company. The city also used a different separations procedure, which will be explained later. An adjustment was made by the city for alleged excess values of plant equipment purchased from Western Electric Company by Southwestern Bell. (The city contended that because of higher prices, Western Electric was enabled to earn a greater return than a public utility should.) (See Exhibit 11–2A for the rate-base computation.)

---

[10] *Master's Hearing*, p. 728B–735 (transcript of hearing before the master in chancery).

The rate base determined by the City Council after its hearings was $57,292,571. This increase over the rate base presented by the city's witness reflected the appraised value of the land acquired prior to 1949.

The master in chancery determined the rate base in a different manner than either the city or the company. He agreed with the city in the use of average values, in the exclusion of working capital from the rate base, and in interpreting the fair-value statute to permit the use of original cost for property other than land. The master sustained the company with respect to separations, Western Electric Company excess profits, and the use of a special depreciation study for the Houston District Exchange.

The master also found that if as a matter of law he was required to give greater weight to current cost than this, the rate base should be $68,500,000.

Since the disagreement over separation of the toll from local exchange is of fairly great magnitude, and since the question of depreciation is also very important, the evidence on these issues is presented in some detail.

Separations

The National Association of Railroad and Utility Commissioners, acting jointly with the Federal Communications Commission, in 1947 issued a *Separations Manual* designed to provide criteria for the separation of intrastate and interstate plant, revenue, and expenses. This manual was subsequently modified on March 1, 1952, resulting in more equipment being switched to interstate toll. The manual was further modified in 1956, but this last modification does not affect local jurisdiction. This *Separations Manual* was not written for the purpose of separating local exchange from toll, and states that some modification might be required for this use.

The company, using the *Separations Manual*, made studies to separate the plant on the basis of usage. The principal conflict on separations between the city and the company was the group of accounts called station equipment. These include "those telephone facilities which are ordinarily located on the customer's premises, including the apparatus itself, the cost of installation thereof, and the drop wires leading toward the distribution lines on the highways, streets, or utility easements."

The company based its separation of these accounts on a holding-time study which was conducted over a period of several months during representative hours of the day. In this study a team stationed in an exchange timed every call from every phone and determined how long the phone was in use, and noted whether the call was toll or local. An average time for toll calls and an average time for local calls were then determined. These times were then multiplied by the total of each class of calls for the year, and the ratio of toll time to local time determined the percent of joint plant allocated to each category. In this case, this resulted in 4.25 percent of the station equipment being classed as toll and 95.75 percent being classed as local exchange. Much of the rest of the plant can be separated according to actual use. The overall separation factor was 17.65 percent toll and 82.35 percent local exchange on original-cost, undepreciated valuation.[11]

The city, through its witness, Mr. James Honaker, objected to this method of separating the station equipment for several reasons. Most important, it was felt that because toll calls are paid for on a measured basis and because local calls are unlimited under flat-rate billing, naturally much more time will accrue to local calls. Also, Honaker felt that since this equipment was actually in use only about 2 percent of the time, some allowance should be made for "stand-by value," that is, the value of having the phone there even if you are not presently using it. Expenses do not vary appreciably with holding time, especially where dial equipment is used.

For these reasons the city apportioned the station equipment in the same ratio of local to toll as all other plant and equipment. This resulted in 19.7 percent of these accounts being assigned to toll and 80.3 percent assigned to local exchange, a substantial reduction in rate base. The company objected to this method of apportionment primarily because it had a considerable amount of toll equipment located within the Houston District Exchange that served no local purpose, being merely used for switching for toll calls for the surrounding area, resulting in an unjust apportionment of the station equipment.

The city adopted the "Honaker method" of separations in determining the rate base. The master accepted the company's method. He said that the city was not precluded from making its own apportionment, but that in this case it had failed to rationally support its findings. Mr. Honaker had made no local studies, and no adjustment was made for the toll facilities located in Houston for other areas.

Depreciation

Depreciation is important not only in determining the rate base but also in determining expense. The expense question will be postponed until expenses in general are considered.

The company witness for the rate base, Mr. Blanton, used observed depreciation as the basis for the deduction from the valuation. He said that percent condition or observed depreciation should be used

---

[11] *Plaintiff's Exhibit No. 28, Master's Hearing.*

. . . because the amounts in the reserve for depreciation are in there anticipating the ultimate retirement of the property and they are accrued to this investment in a straight uniform method over the service life of the property. The plant itself actually does not deteriorate or become obsolete in a straight uniform line, so to reflect the true condition or the amount which should be deducted for deterioration and obsolescence it has to be done as of a specified time.[12]

The percent condition of each category of plant was arrived at by inspecting a small sample of each and imputing the condition of the sample to the class. For example, out of 72,785 creosoted poles and 183 noncreosoted poles, Mr. Blanton personally inspected 186, and his crew (including himself) inspected a total of 296. Out of 2,505 manholes, 11 brick and 29 concrete manholes were inspected by Mr. Blanton. Some categories of plant were reduced in value for obsolescence, but in no case were they reduced below the book cost less accrued depreciation. The overall percent condition arrived at by Mr. Blanton was 90 percent.

The city, using average original cost as adjusted for its rate base, maintained that the average balance of the reserve for depreciation determined by using the statewide ratio of depreciation reserve to telephone plant should be used as the deduction. (The rates of depreciation are submitted to the FCC by the company engineers and are based upon engineering studies of the service life and expected obsolescence of the various categories of plant and equipment.)

The master followed the city in the case of average depreciation, but without the adjustments which the city had made for alleged Western Electric excess profits.

Revenues and Expenses

Exhibit 11–2B lists the net earnings claimed by the company, the disallowances contended for by the city, and the disallowances which were approved by the master.

EXHIBIT 11–2B

Houston Exchange Earnings as Adjusted by City and by Master in Chancery

Net earnings as claimed by company in its original presentation before city council	$2,341,737
Less: Adjustment to give effect to August, 1953, wage increase not taken into consideration in presentation before city council ($327,824 minus 52% tax credit)	157,355
Adjusted net earnings claimed by company in hearing before master	$2,184,382

---

[12] *Master's Hearing,* p. 970.

EXHIBIT 11–2B (Continued)

Adjustment Contended for by the City	Amount of Disallowance Contended for by City (net after applicable income tax offset)	Amount of City's Claimed Disallowance Not Approved by Master	Amount of City's Claimed Disallowance Approved by Master (net after applicable income tax offset)
a. To give effect to Honaker system of separations............................	$ 318,686	$318,686	
b. To give effect to Western Electric profit disallowance.....	42,204	42,204	
c. To give effect to disallowance of so-called "current cost" depreciation..............	345,928		$ 345,928
d. To give effect to depreciation on annual average plant instead of year-end balances..	53,314		53,314
e. To give effect to disallowances of club dues, expense, and contributions to charitable organizations....................	18,874		18,874
f. To give effect to income tax reduction effected through use of 40–60 debt-equity ratio...............................	128,983	128,983	
g. To give effect to disallowance of certain pension accruals......................	11,598	11,598	
h. To give effect to disallowance of current cost adjustments included in amounts claimed as maintenance expense, including casualty and wiring loss................	71,364	71,364	
i. To give effect to disallowance of certain nonrecurring central office repairs.........	5,513		5,513
j. To give effect to disallowance of certain claimed excessive strike expense..........	2,109	2,109	
k. To give effect to disallowance of certain direct and allocated advertising and business promotion expenses................	14,743	14,743	
l. To give effect to disallowance of certain allocated legal fees and expenses..........	7,599	7,599	
m. To give effect to increased rate of earnings actually enjoyed at 1953 current levels—not identified as to specific items.........	159,619	159,619	
Total disallowances contended for by city.........................	$1,180,534		
Total disallowances contended for by city and not approved by master....		$756,905	
Total disallowances contended for by city and approved by master.......			$ 423,629
Earnings for test period as determined by master........................			$2,608,011

Source: *Report of Master in Chancery*, pp. 146–47.

Items *a* and *b* were discussed previously under the rate base. They were disallowed by the master for the same reasons as before.

Items *c* and *d* both deal with depreciation. Item *d* was disallowed because the master felt that average values should be used since the earnings were based on average plant rather than year-end plant. This was consistent with the deduction of depreciation from average plant rather than year-end plant. The claim for "current cost depreciation" is based upon the theory that depreciation should recover the real physical assets rather than the dollar investment. The master felt that current cost depreciation was too "theoretical" and should not be allowed.

Item *e* was disallowed by the master, as he felt that the stockholders rather than the rate payers should be charged with contributions to charity and club dues. Decisions in Texas cases have been consistently in agreement with the master on this point.

Item *f* was not disallowed because the company actually paid substantially all of this in taxes.

The disallowance of pension accruals was not approved by the master. It is allowed by the FCC as a legitimate operating expense. The courts have uniformly reversed decisions in which this expense was disallowed.

The master felt that item *h* was reasonable. It was based on ten-year averages by both the city and the company, but the company adjusted it to current price levels. The master felt that it was reasonable in that current prices would actually be incurred. The disallowance of item *i* was approved by the master, as it involved the repair of equipment withdrawn from service in the Houston District Exchange. Item *j* was not disallowed by the master because it was less than the increase in the wage bill would have been, had there been no strike.

Item *k* was partly due to differences in allocation methods of the company and the city, and partly due to the disallowance by the city of advertising expense incurred in bill inserts. Since the allocation method of the company was adopted by the master, the only question then is the bill inserts. This amount the master felt to be reasonable. Item *l* was the allocation of a portion of the statewide legal expenses to the Houston District Exchange. Since the actual legal expense in Houston during 1952 was greater than this, the expense was allowed. Item *m* was not allowed, as it was not adequately developed in the record.

Thus, net earnings for 1952 were determined to be $2,608,011 by the master.

Rate of Return

The governing statute does not include any provision as to the rate of return that a utility should be allowed to earn. It is generally assumed that a "fair return" is implied by the statute. The applicable definition of fair return is:

. . . What annual rate will constitute just compensation depends upon many circumstances and must be determined by the exercise of a fair and en-lightened judgment, having regard to all relevant facts. A public utility is entitled to such rates as will permit it to earn a return on the value of the prop-erty which it employs for the convenience of the public equal to that generally being earned at the same time and in the same general part of the country on investments in other business undertakings which are attended by correspond-ing risks and uncertainties; but it has no constitutional rights to profits such as are realized in highly profitable enterprises or speculative ventures. The return should be reasonably sufficient to assure confidence in the financial soundness of the utility, and should be adequate, under efficient and eco-nomical management, to maintain and support its credit and enable it to raise the money necessary for the proper discharge of its public duties. A rate of return may be reasonable at one time and become too high or too low by changes affecting opportunities for investment, the money market, and business conditions generally.[13]

There was extensive testimony as to the fair rate of return, both before the City Council and before the master. The company had two primary witnesses, Mr. Robert Moroney, a Houston investment banker, and Mr. Jackson Martindell, a financial consultant.

Mr. Moroney felt that the current cost of capital provided the best guide to determining the "fair return." To determine the current cost of capital, he made studies of the cost of debt and equity capital. The actual cost of debt capital to Southwestern Bell he determined to be approximately 3 percent. From studies of recent debt issues of other Bell companies, he determined the current cost of new debt capital to be 3½ percent. The prospective cost of debt capital in the next year or two he felt to be 4 percent, because of a long-term upward trend of interest rates. He concluded that predominant weight should be given to the prospective debt cost in determining the current cost of capital.

Mr. Moroney used the earnings-price ratio of the previous 12 months as the best measure of the cost of equity capital. However, since the last direct stock issue of the American Telephone and Telegraph Com-pany prior to this time was in 1931, he did not consider directly the earnings-price ratio of A. T. & T. The conversion of convertible deben-tures into common stock did not adequately represent the true cost of new equity capital to Mr. Moroney because of the "invisible" cost of going into debt incurred by A. T. & T. when it issued convertible de-bentures. Therefore, he considered the cost of new equity capital to the

---

[13] *Bluefield Water Works & Improvement Co.* v. *Public Service Commission,* 262 U.S. 679, 692 (1923).

General Telephone Company, which he determined to be 10.37 percent in 1952 and 11.33 percent in 1953. Also, he determined the cost of new equity capital to electric utilities operating in the same area as Southwestern Bell. This was found to be 9.8 percent, or 10.2 percent after excluding companies which had rate increases prior to a financing, but which was not reflected in earnings.[14] The cost of new equity capital to natural gas companies operating in the area he found to be 9.7 percent. From these results, he estimated the cost of new equity capital to the telephone company to be 11 percent.

In determining the overall cost of capital, Mr. Moroney felt that a 40–60 debt-equity ratio would be the proper one to apply. (The actual A. T. & T. debt-equity ratio was very close to this.) Using this ratio and the capital costs he had developed, he determined the current cost of capital in the three ways shown in Exhibit 11–2C.[15]

EXHIBIT 11–2C

A. At prospective debt cost of 4.0%:

Bonds..........	$ 400,000 × 4.0%..........	$16,000
Stock..........	600,000 × 11.0%..........	66,000
	$1,000,000	$82,000

$82,000 ÷ $1,000,000 = 8.2% cost of new money

B. At spot debt cost of 3.5%:

Bonds..........	$ 400,000 × 3.5%..........	$14,000
Stock..........	600,000 × 11.0%..........	66,000
	$1,000,000	$80,000

$80,000 ÷ $1,000,000 = 8.0% cost of new money

C. At imbedded debt cost of 3.0%:

Bonds..........	$ 400,000 × 3.0%..........	$12,000
Stock..........	600,000 × 11.0%..........	66,000
	$1,000,000	$78,000

$78,000 ÷ $1,000,000 = 7.8% cost of new money

Mr. Moroney also presented an exhibit where he determined the cost of capital on the basis of conversion of convertible debentures but stated emphatically that he did not believe it to be the proper method of determining capital cost. For the period 1950–52 the American Telephone and Telegraph Company obtained equity capital in the amount of $1,863,965,764 from conversion of debentures and sale of stock to employees. This was supported by earnings of $163,455,710, giving an earnings-price ratio of 8.77 percent. Exhibit 11–2D shows how he determined the overall capital cost on this basis.[16]

---

[14] Based on 17 public offerings and 13 preemptive offerings during the period 1948–53.

[15] *Plaintiff's Exhibit No. 45, Master's Hearing.*

[16] *Plaintiff's Exhibit No. 46, Master's Hearing.*

EXHIBIT 11–2D

1. Total money raised by issuance of A. T. & T. stock, three years, 1950–52 . . . . $1,863,965,764
2. Dollars of earnings supporting stock money raised* 163,455,710
3. Relationship of earnings to stock money raised (item 2 ÷ item 1) 8.77%

Debt	$ 400,000 × 3.00%	$12,000
Equity	600,000 × 8.77%	52,620
	$1,000,000	$64,620

$64,620 ÷ $1,000,000 = 6.46%

* Total number of shares of stock issued during each year of the three-year period divided by that year's earnings per share.

Mr. Martindell estimated the current cost of debt capital to be between 3½ and 4 percent, based on the net cost to the issuer of high-grade electric utility securities during 1952–53. He determined the current cost of equity capital from 73 common stock issues of $5 million or more of 40 electric utilities during 1952–53. Some issues were eliminated where they were not underwritten or where the offering price was not set at the latest possible date or where a rate increase was not fully reflected in earnings. Based upon this study, he determined the cost of new equity capital to be between 9½ percent and 10 percent.

The electric utility companies used in the study had an average equity-debt ratio of 35 percent and 65 percent (50 percent debt, 15 percent preferred stock). Mr. Martindell believed the telephone business to be more risky than the electric utility business and therefore, in order to compensate for the difference in risk, he applied a ⅔–⅓ equity-debt ratio to the current costs he had determined. He insisted that this did not reflect his judgment as to the proper equity-debt ratio but was done merely to equalize risks. He based his opinion as to the comparative risks upon a study purporting to show (1) that market changes between 1929 and 1940 showed telephone stocks to be twice as sensitive as electric stocks, (2) that telephone revenues are about 40 percent more sensitive than electric revenues, and (3) that less than one half of electric utility expense is relatively rigid, as compared to three fourths in the telephone industry. Exhibit 11–2E shows how he determined the overall cost of new capital.[17]

Both Mr. Moroney and Mr. Martindell insisted that in order to protect historical stockholders, the current cost of capital should be applied to a current-cost rate base. If a cost rate base were used, then a relatively greater percent return would be required.

---

[17] *Plaintiff's Exhibit No. 51, Master's Hearing*, p. 12.

EXHIBIT 11–2E

Components of Total Capital	Current Cost	Capital Structure Weight	Weighted Components
Debt......................	3.50%– 4.00%	⅓	1.17%–1.33%
Equity....................	9.50%–10.00%	⅔	6.33%–6.67%
Overall current cost of capital...................			7.50%–8.00%

Mr. James Honaker testified as to the fair return for the city. He submitted a study designed to determine the required rate of return to provide $10.50 earnings per average share of A. T. & T. common stock[18] (see Exhibit 11–2F).

EXHIBIT 11–2F

	Capital	Required Earnings
Funded debt:		
Amount............................	$3,748,589,000	
Fixed charges........................		$117,029,000
Publicly held stock of subsidiaries:		
Amount............................	164,392,000	
Dividends and earnings applicable thereto...		11,800,000
American component common stock:		
Amount of stock, premiums, installments, and surplus........................	5,104,870,000	
Dividends and earnings applicable thereto...		373,048,000
Total............................	$9,017,851,000	$501,877,000

Applying the earnings requirement of $501,877,000 to the net telephone plant and other investments total of $8,839,896,000, Mr. Honaker found that a return of 5.68 percent was required to provide $10.50 per share earnings. This same amount would provide a rate of return of 5.57 upon the total capital of $9,017,871,000. A 6 percent return on net plant and other investments would provide earnings of $11.30 per average share, as compared with $11.45 actually earned in 1952. Mr. Honaker determined the historical payout between 1922 and 1952 to be 84.7 percent; and on this basis, $10.63 earnings per average share

---

[18] *Report of Master in Chancery,* District Court of Harris County, Texas, 133d Judicial District, No. 426,913 (*Southwestern Bell Telephone Co.* v. *City of Houston et al.*), p. 153.

were required for 1952. This return would be 5.73 percent on net plant or 5.62 percent on combined capital. If the payout ratio of 90.4 for 1937–52 is considered, then earnings of only $9.95 per average share would be required for 1952, giving a return of 5.45 on net plant or 5.35 on combined capital. Considering this information, Mr. Honaker felt that from 5½ percent to 5¾ percent would be the fair rate of return.

Mr. Edwin Bruhl, an independent certified public accountant, also presented rate-of-return evidence for the city. Mr. Bruhl felt that the debt-equity ratio should be 40–60, even if the interest rate should be very high because of the income tax factor (e.g., for an interest rate of 3½ percent, the net cost to the company is 1.68 cents per dollar of debt capital, whereas it is about 8⅓ cents per dollar of equity capital). Using the imbedded debt cost of 3 percent and an equity capital cost of 7½ percent—the average cost of obtaining equity capital from the conversion of debentures for the period 1945–52—he determined the fair rate of return to be 5.7 percent:

Debt............$ 400,000 × 3.0%............$12,000
Equity.......... 600,000 × 7.5%............ 45,000
$1,000,000 $57,000
$57,000 ÷ $1,000,000 = 5.7%

The master in chancery did not accept any of the methods presented, but instead used his own procedure. The cost of debt capital used was the imbedded cost of the outstanding debt of Southwestern Bell. He did not give any consideration to current debt cost because the company did not plan to issue new debt in the near future, and the replacement of the present debt was still a long way off. To give effect to the 40–60 ratio of debt to equity, he considered the advances from A. T. & T. to Southwestern Bell as debt capital, and he also considered enough of Southwestern Bell's common stock to be debt to bring the total debt component up to 39.719 percent (the actual percentage of A. T. & T.'s capital structure that was debt). This is shown in Exhibit 11–2G. The overall debt cost is therefore 2.936 percent.

In determining the cost of equity capital, the master considered that

EXHIBIT 11–2G

	Debt Component in Dollars	Percent of Total Capital	Rate	Weighted Component
Southwestern Bell debt.......	$175,000,000		2.880%	$5,040,000
A. T. & T. advances.........	35,370,555	25.410%	3.000	1,061,117
Southwestern Bell common...	118,454,654	14.300	3.000	3,553,640
	$328,825,209	39.719%	2.936%	$9,654,757

the actual experience of A. T. & T. should be given greater consideration than Mr. Moroney and Mr. Martindell had given it. Since during the year 1952, total conversions of convertible debentures had been greater than total issues, the master felt that it would be appropriate to consider conversions as though they were an issue of equity capital. The proceeds of conversion for 1952 are shown in Exhibit 11–2H. Average conversion proceeds received by company per share were $137.96.

Thus, he determined the cost of equity capital by using the ratio of 1952 earnings to net conversion proceeds of $11.45 to $138.00, which gave a cost of equity capital of 8.30 percent. With a debt-equity ratio of

EXHIBIT 11–2H

Year of Issue	Par Value of Debenture Converted	Minimum Price at Which Converted	Minimum Proceeds of Conversion
1946	$ 57,968,000	146	$ 84,633,000
1947	57,230,000	140	80,122,000
1949	9,697,000	130	12,606,000
1951	142,360,000	138	196,457,000
1952	260,201,000	136	353,873,000
	$527,456,000		$727,691,000

40–60, the overall capital cost was 6.15 percent. Any return less than this would result in confiscation. If the current cost rate base (as he determined it) were used, then the cost of capital would be 6.00 percent.

In order that a return of 6.15 percent be earned on a rate base of $61,860,492, net earnings of $3,804,420 were required. Earnings for 1952, as determined by the master, were $2,608,011. Therefore, earnings were deficient in the sum of $1,196,409. For the company to earn this amount of net additional revenue, it must collect additional gross revenue of $2,650,046 because of taxes, and so forth.

The master in chancery also submitted a special report in which he recommended that the rates which had been set under bond be reduced to a scale which he proposed. The city suggested an even lower scale. The District Court felt that the proposed rates of the master were too low and that the bonded rates were too high, and said that if the injunction was to remain in effect, the rates should be set halfway between the two scales. The city gave notice of appeal and asked for several extensions. With a change in administration, the city voted to drop the appeal. The company then pledged that the basic phone rates would remain in effect for two years. Pay phone rates were later raised from 5 to 10 cents. Exhibit 11–2I shows the various rate schedules discussed.

EXHIBIT 11–21

Houston Telephone Rates

	(1) 1949 Ordinance	(2) Requested by Company, March, 1953	(3) Set under Bond	(4) Recommended by Master	(5) Set by Court
Business service:					
One party—flat............	$12.00	$18.00	$17.00	$16.00	$16.50
Extension—flat.........	1.50	1.75	1.75		1.75
Semipublic..............	0.25/day	0.35/day	0.35/day		
Extension—noncoin.....	1.00	1.25	1.25		
One party—measured.....	6.00	8.50	8.50		
Extension—measured....	1.00	1.25	1.25		
PBX:					
Commercial:					
Trunks................	18.00	27.00	25.50	24.00	
Stations..............	1.50	1.75	1.75		
Residence:					
Trunks..............	7.13	10.13	9.75	7.88	
Stations..............	1.00	1.25	1.25		
Hotel:					
Trunks..............	12.00	18.00	17.00	16.00	
Stations..............	0.75	1.25	1.25		
Residence service:					
One party..............	4.75	6.75	6.50	5.25	5.90
Two party..............	4.00	5.75	5.50	4.25	4.85
Four party..............	3.25	4.75	4.50	3.25	3.85
Extensions..............	1.00	1.25	1.25		1.25
Rural:					
Business................	7.50*	10.00	10.00*		
Extension.............	1.50	1.75	1.75		
Residence..............	3.25*	4.75	4.75*		
Extension.............	1.00	1.25	1.25		
Government PBX:					
Trunks................	27.00	40.50	38.25	36.00	
Service stations:					
Residence..............	2.00	2.50	2.50		
Business..............	4.00	5.00	5.00		

* Applies within four miles of the base-rate area. For each additional mile or fraction thereof, 25 cents extra. Airline measurement used.

Sources: Columns 1, 2, and 3: *Report of Master in Chancery*, p. 165. Column 4: *Special Report of Master in Chancery*. Column 5: Southwestern Bell Telephone Co.

Questions

1. What should be the goal of the city of Houston in its regulation of the rates of Southwestern Bell Telephone Company?
2. Does or can regulation achieve these goals?
3. What is the relationship between the rate base, the rate of return, and the phone rates which are the end result of the regulatory process? Does the relationship change with changing definitions of the components of the formula?

4. Which of the alternative computations of rate base, rate of return, and expenses would you choose if you were on the Houston City Council or if you were a circuit court judge? Defend your choices.

CASE 11–3. International Air Fares

Air passenger traffic has grown rapidly in the postwar period. The transatlantic route has grown particularly rapidly since the introduction of jet service. Fares have declined as more flights have been scheduled with more airlines participating in the traffic.

Most of the airlines which fly the transatlantic route are members of the International Air Transport Association (IATA), a voluntary organization of airline companies. Any airline with scheduled air services among two or more countries may join, provided it operates under the flag of a state which is eligible for membership in the International Civil Aviation Organization (ICAO), an organization primarily concerned with standardization of technical matters in international aviation.[19]

The IATA provides a means whereby airlines can attempt to solve jointly many problems which they cannot individually resolve.

It is active in the fields of traffic, finance, legal and technical matters, medicine, public information, and the like. In some cases, IATA acts as a central bank of information and technical knowledge for all member airlines; in others, IATA is preparing to publish tariffs and timetables; it conducts such enterprises as the IATA Clearing House; it administers committees of airline experts set up to deal with continuing problems; and it represents the airlines in their dealings with other international organizations.[20]

The IATA also regularly schedules joint rate conferences of scheduled airlines to consider rates. If rate schedules are unanimously agreed upon, they become binding upon the member airlines, subject to the approval of their governments. However, if the agreement is not unanimous, or if all the governments involved do not agree, the result is an "open rate," and members may quote competitive rates. If agreement is reached by all parties, then the member air lines must abide by the conference rates and are subject to fines of up to $25,000 for violations of the agreement. Exhibit 11–3A shows a chronology of actions on fares on the North Atlantic route from 1948 to 1961.

The rapid growth of traffic and the changing character of the service offered is illustrated by Exhibits 11–3B and 11–3C. Exhibit 11–3B shows

---

[19] John H. Frederick, *Commercial Air Transportation* (5th ed.; Homewood, Ill.: Richard D. Irwin, Inc., 1961).

[20] Ibid., pp. 309–10.

EXHIBIT 11–3A

North Atlantic Chronology of Fare Actions

April, 1948   Transatlantic fares increased slightly less than 10%.

First Class	
One Way	*Round Trip*
$350	$630

October, 1948   Special transatlantic excursion fares introduced. Round trip within 30 days for 1⅓ times one-way fare. Good only in winter, October 1, 1948, to April 1, 1949.

October, 1949   Above fare extended over another winter season, good for 60 days.

January, 1950   New excursion fare, 15-day limit. One way plus 10%, January through March.

March, 1950   On-season round trip continued at 180% of one way. Off season set at 133% of one way.

January, 1951   January, 1950, special excursion experiment repeated.

February, 1952   Tourist fares approved and tourist class established.

	First Class		Tourist Class	
	One Way	*Round Trip*	*One Way*	*Round Trip*
On season........	$395	$711	$270	$486
Off season........	395	640	270	417

November, 1955   Off-season transatlantic fares increased.

	First Class	Tourist Class
Round trip.............	$670	$482

November, 1955   Off-season family plan introduced between November 1 and March 31. Head of family paid full fare, wife and children over 12 had the following discounts:

	First Class	Tourist Class
One way..............	$150	$130
Round trip............	300	200

Children under 12 travel at 50% of regular adult fare, as usual.

April, 1956   First-class fare increased.

	One Way	Round Trip
On season..............	$440	$792
Off season.............	440	742

September, 1956   First-class off-season rate reduction eliminated.

October, 1956   Year-round transatlantic excursion fare introduced on tourist class, 15-day limit.

One Way	*Round Trip*
$270	$425

April, 1957   First-class fares reduced.

One Way	*Round Trip*
$400	$720

April, 1958   Economy fare and class introduced. Tourist and first-class fares increased.

First Class		Economy Class	
One Way	*Round Trip*	*One Way*	*Round Trip*
$440	$792	$252	$454

April, 1959   Jet surcharge of $15–$20 instituted.

June, 1961   Flying Tiger offered European groups unprecedented bargain rates on group charters, normal cost of round trip $250–$325; Flying Tiger pro-rated $11,682 over 118-seat Super Constellations. If filled, this means $99 per passenger. Offered only to balance summer season travel, terminated on August 4.

EXHIBIT 11–3A (Continued)

April, 1962	The Board approved an IATA agreement among various U.S. and foreign air carriers which provided for reduced round or circle-trip fares to groups of 25 or more persons traveling in economy-class service on the North Atlantic. Generally speaking, availability of these fares, which amounted to a reduction of 38% from normal fares, was limited to persons having a demonstrated prior affinity.
February, 1963	CAB rejected IATA's proposed reduction in round-trip discounts across the Pacific and North Atlantic . . . This fare increase, which had been agreed upon at the IATA traffic conferences held at Chandler, Arizona, in the fall of 1962, amounted to $27 more for a New York to London flight. . . .
April, 1963	Airlines began operating under an open rate situation over the North Atlantic, Mid-Atlantic, and Pacific. An IATA mail vote had failed to extend pre-Chandler conference fares.
May, 1963	At the meeting held in Montreal on May 24, an agreement was reached by the IATA traffic conference on a compromise proposed to settle the North Atlantic fare dispute. Under terms of the agreement which received Board approval, all carriers were to charge the Chandler fares from May 28 to July 15. On the latter date the one-way economy fare was to be reduced $7 with 5% discount on the round trip. The agreement was to expire on March 31, 1964.
April, 1964	The IATA carriers operating on the North Atlantic routes, though failing to reach unanimous agreement among themselves on international airfares, filed reduced rates effective April 1. . . . Essentially the carriers revised tariffs offered the following reductions for round-trip travel between New York and most European points: 1. First class—$190 reduction all year (20%). 2. Economy class $100.70 reduction (also 20% except 10 summer weeks when reduction was $15.20). 3. 21-day excursion fares—$50 reduction (14%) most of the spring, summer, and fall.
October, 1964	The board approved a $64 reduction in the 14–21 day round trip winter excursion fares on the North Atlantic. The new fare of $335, which was the lowest jet fare ever offered in the winter, was incorporated in an agreement made by the IATA carriers in their meetings in Athens, Greece. Effective November 6 through February 14.
April, 1966	The CAB approved IATA suggested reductions in North Atlantic excursion and all-inclusive tour fares for one year from April 1, 1966.
April, 1967	Economy service to principal European points available at a reduction of 39% to 45% lower than normal fares, provided that ground services as part of a package tour are purchased at an additional minimum price of $70. These fares were available year-round for a 14- to 21-day period except during weekends in June and July eastbound, and August and September westbound.
April, 1968	Approval of the North Atlantic fare structure, which included an introduction of group inclusive tour-basing fares, previously limited through March 31, 1968, was extended for 1 year.
April, 1969	Two-phase fare schedule proposed by IATA carriers. Fares in existence prior to April 1 will remain in force until May 1. At that time, the 5% round trip discount will be eliminated and the 14–21 day excursion will be extended for weekend travel, at an additional cost of $30, and during the peak travel season blackout at an additional cost of $50. In November 1, giant jet fares will be introduced that will enable travel agents to sell New York–London round trip tickets for $175. This promotional fare, called bulk contract, permits the travel agent to buy a minimum of 40 seats to Europe and 20 seats to the United States with two months' notice to the carrier. The $175 charge is for off-season travel. Peak season tickets under the bulk contract concept will cost $220, and normal season travel will be $190.

EXHIBIT 11-3B

North Atlantic Traffic,* 1948–61, IATA Member Carriers
(scheduled flights by class)

Year	First Class			Tourist Class			Economy Class		
	Passengers	Seats	Load Factor	Passengers	Seats	Load Factor	Passengers	Seats	Load Factor
1948	240,472	n.a.†	n.a.	—	—	—	—	—	—
1949	266,535	n.a.	n.a.	—	—	—	—	—	—
1950	311,545	495,561	62.9	—	—	—	—	—	—
1951	329,656	504,185	65.4	—	—	—	—	—	—
1952	243,571	362,289	67.2	188,701	263,559	71.6	—	—	—
1953	186,072	298,452	62.3	320,529	483,285	66.3	—	—	—
1954	169,824	269,103	63.1	380,176	611,835	62.1	—	—	—
1955	189,678	290,530	65.3	462,579	715,962	64.6	—	—	—
1956	208,994	329,172	63.5	576,265	897,689	64.2	—	—	—
1957	228,648	375,274	60.9	739,498	1,075,458	68.8	—	—	—
1958	255,690	451,465	56.6	274,889	450,730	61.0	662,634	1,052,097	63.0
1959	294,160	466,271	63.1	64,362	120,224	53.5	1,008,765	1,484,546	68.0
1960	306,266	581,501	52.7	10,245	24,246	42.3	1,444,261	2,134,901	67.7
1961	244,870	633,701	37.5	—	—	—	1,674,564	3,093,742	54.1
1962	208,175	644,954	32.3	—	—	—	2,063,988	3,761,573	54.9
1963	192,522	648,075	29.7	—	—	—	2,229,745	4,286,884	52.0
1964	235,876	666,874	35.4	—	—	—	2,833,302	4,672,149	60.6
1965	277,661	748,590	37.2	—	—	—	3,333,613	5,612,119	59.7
1966	322,929	804,965	40.1	—	—	—	3,874,621	6,336,392	61.1
1967	354,962	987,532	36.0	—	—	—	4,632,471	7,688,422	60.3

* Between United States–Canada and Europe.
† Not available.
Source: International Air Transport Association, *World Air Transport Statistics* (Montreal, annually), issues of 1957–67

EXHIBIT 11–3C

North Atlantic Traffic,* 1948–61, IATA Member Carriers
(total scheduled flights and charters)

Year	Total Scheduled Flights			Charter Passengers	Total Scheduled and Charter Passengers Carried	Percent Annual Increase
	Passengers	Seats	Load Factor			
1948.............	240,472	n.a.†	n.a.	12,392	252,864	...
1949.............	266,535	n.a.	n.a.	6,102	272,637	+ 7.8
1950.............	311,545	495,561	62.9	5,619	317,164	+16.3
1951.............	329,656	504,185	65.4	11,867	341,523	+ 7.7
1952.............	432,272	625,848	69.1	15,684	447,956	+31.2
1953.............	506,601	781,737	64.8	16,830	523,431	+16.8
1954.............	550,000	880,938	62.4	30,858	580,858	+11.0
1955.............	652,257	1,006,492	64.8	39,543	691,800	+19.1
1956.............	785,259	1,226,861	64.0	49,531	834,790	+20.7
1957.............	968,146	1,450,732	66.7	50,638	1,018,784	+22.0
1958.............	1,193,213	1,954,292	61.1	98,953	1,292,166	+26.8
1959.............	1,367,287	2,071,041	66.0	172,647	1,539,934	+19.2
1960.............	1,760,772	2,740,648	64.2	168,207	1,928,979	+25.3
1961.............	1,919,434	3,747,452	51.2	256,478	2,175,912	+12.8
1962.............	2,272,163	4,406,527	51.6	315,209	2,587,372	+18.9
1963.............	2,422,267	4,934,959	49.1	414,165	2,836,432	+ 9.6
1964.............	3,069,178	5,339,023	57.5	482,010	3,551,188	+25.2
1965.............	3,611,274	6,360,709	57.1	480,496	4,091,670	+15.2
1966.............	4,197,550	7,141,357	58.8	502,896	4,700,446	+14.9
1967.............	4,987,433	8,675,774	57.5	516,941	5,504,341	+17.1

* Between United States–Canada and Europe.
† Not available.
Source: International Air Transport Association, *World Air Transport Statistics* (Montreal, annually), issues of 1957–67.

the total seats available, the number of passengers carried, and the load factor for each of the three classes of service—first class, tourist, and economy. Exhibit 11–3C shows total seats available, total passengers, and also information concerning the number of charter passengers.

IATA conferences in recent years have been uniformly explosive over the rate issue; in fact, open rates have almost resulted several times. An issue which has caused considerable agitation in the rate conferences is the existence of Icelandic Airlines (Loftleider), which, as a nonmember, is free to set whatever rates it chooses between Iceland and the United States, and Iceland and Luxembourg. The other countries force Icelandic to charge the same fares as their state-controlled airlines; but the United States and Luxembourg have no state-owned airlines, so that by adroit scheduling, Icelandic has been able to undercut the IATA members by about 20 percent. Exhibit 11–3D shows some representative Icelandic fares. Icelandic flies no jets; and on the New York to London route, it

EXHIBIT 11–3D

Representative Fares, Icelandic Airlines (Loftleider)
(New York to London)

Date	All Year, One Way	Off-Season Round Trip	On-Season Round Trip
December, 1953	$262.10	$427.20	$427.20
October, 1954	260.40	427.20	427.20
December, 1955	260.40	424.40	469.20
December, 1957	260.40	424.40	469.20
January, 1959	243.40	392.20	438.20
April, 1959	248.40	405.20	447.20
November, 1960	248.40	405.20	405.20
April, 1963	248.40	405.20	405.20
May, 1969	191.10	382.20	464.00*

* Twenty-day excursion fare round trip is $260 off season, $290 on season.

flies from New York to Iceland at an open rate, and then from Iceland to London at the IATA rate, with the net result a very low fare. Icelandic is reported to have a load factor of about 70 percent compared to the 50 percent load factor of the IATA members. Sigurdur Helgason, president of Icelandic Airlines, Inc., has been quoted as saying: "Loftleider's share of the North Atlantic market has remained level at about 2 percent."[21]

Exhibit 11–3E gives some cost and revenue data for international operations by all U.S. airlines which should be representative of the costs of international operations on the North Atlantic run.

A third problem of IATA is the rapid growth of charter flights. This problem has resulted in a rather complicated set of rules for members on the scheduling of charter or group flights. In early 1962 special group fares were permitted only under the following conditions: (1) the group must have been in organization for at least six months prior to the trip; (2) it must have been formed primarily for some purpose other than travel; (3) the group was required to travel together for its entire itinerary; (4) reservations must have been made at least 30 days in advance, with 30 days' notice required for cancellations; (5) the rate did not apply between 7:00 A.M. Friday and 7:00 A.M. Monday on eastbound flights during May, June, and July, and during the same weekend time periods westbound during August, September, and October. However, it was stated that groups that "assemble spontaneously" qualified, provided they were not solicited. Spontaneous groups were eliminated in a later conference. These group fares have been subject to frequent changes over time.

---

[21] *Business Week,* November 24, 1962, p. 45.

EXHIBIT 11–3E

International Operations, All United States Airlines, Passenger/Cargo Carriers

Date	Expense per Available Ton-Mile*	Average Total Passenger Revenue per Passenger-Mile, Scheduled Service	Break-Even Load Factor†	Expense per Revenue Ton-Mile	Passenger Revenue per Revenue Ton-Mile				Rate of Return on International Operations
					First Class	Coach Class	Economy Class	Total Operating Revenues§	
1948	$48.97	$8.01		$86.15	$77.91	...	...	$77.91	7.32%
1949	46.82	7.72		84.29	74.93	...	...	74.93	8.58
1950	44.83	7.28		76.49	70.51	...	...	70.51	5.33
1951	45.69	7.10		70.69	n.a.‡	...	...	69.18	5.98
1952	43.14	7.01		70.44	n.a.	...	...	68.06	3.59
1953	41.20	6.84		67.34	n.a.	...	...	66.86	7.01
1954	38.22	6.76		61.92	86.01	$52.41	...	66.60	9.50
1955	36.16	6.66		56.55	77.36	59.43	...	66.22	5.99
1956	35.59	6.68		55.57	79.11	60.84	...	66.62	8.28
1957	34.49	6.55	59.5	54.54	79.97	59.87	...	65.39	7.88
1958	33.94	6.46	58.0	55.16	82.14	59.82	$47.58	64.51	3.63
1959	34.07	6.29	63.0	52.11	83.39	57.51	48.96	62.92	4.51
1960	31.36	6.35	57.4	52.48	85.82	56.24	55.46	63.48	5.32
1961	28.29	6.08	52.3	51.25	79.23	...	n.a.	60.79	2.84
1962	24.74	5.87	46.7	44.68	78.90			58.52	8.23
1963	22.92	5.82	43.0	43.08	80.55			58.36	12.70
1964	21.53	5.45	45.7	40.22	76.58			54.38	13.29
1965	19.49	5.29	43.7	35.05	71.40			52.61	16.28
1966	18.35	5.16	43.6	31.44	71.21			51.09	15.02

* Represents cost of providing transportation for one ton of cargo (passengers, freight, etc.). Thus, closer seating is one way of increasing tonnage per flight-mile and reducing cost, as well as improved economy in planes.

† Approximated by using an accepted airline rule of thumb of 200 pounds per passenger (weight and baggage) and dividing this into one ton. Thus, one ton equals ten passengers. Average passenger revenue per passenger-mile divided into cost per available ton-mile gives the number of passengers needed for break-even, easily converted to percentage points.

‡ Not available.

§ Includes subsidies until 1954. Also includes revenue from other sources—cargo, mail, and so forth—which are lower per ton-mile than is passenger revenue.

Source: Civil Aeronautics Board, *Handbook of Airline Statistics* (Washington, D.C.: U.S. Government Printing Office, 1962, 1967).

Questions

1. What additional factors do you see that could lead to open rates in international air fares?
2. What steps can IATA take to prevent open rates?
3. What would be the effects on traffic and profits if member airlines were allowed to meet Icelandic fares?
4. From the above data, analyse the future of air fares on the North Atlantic route. Check your predictions against what has actually happened to fares since the data provided in the case.

CASE 11–4. Pressures on the Price Controllers*

The fourth quarter of 1973 demonstrated forcibly the types of problems inevitably faced by government when it attempts to control prices

EXHIBIT 11–4A

Price Spread for Nonferrous Metals

	Excess of World Price Over U.S. Price	
Material	*Jan. 1, 1973*	*Nov. 30, 1973*
Aluminum................	18%	38%
Copper..................	None	65
Lead....................	None	45
Zinc....................	1%	332

in a comprehensive way. During Phase IV more recognition was given to the very different problems produced by different conditions in the various sectors with such fields as petroleum, chemicals, steel, paper, food, and health services posing especially difficult problems. Also during this period of Phase IV there was a movement out of wage and price controls, with actions occurring such as decontrol of fertilizer, some nonferrous metals, portland cement, and automobiles.

Heavy international demand for many basic materials increased the pressures on price control agencies. This was stimulated by a large decline in the international value of the American dollar. The consequence was formation of a two-tiered pricing system as the controls program did not permit domestic prices to increase at the same rate as foreign prices. The resultant increase in exports of many products re-

---

* Source: Cost of Living Council, *Economic Stabilization Program Quarterly Report,* covering the period October 1, 1973, through December 31, 1973.

duced available domestic supplies. The increase in the spread between world prices and U.S. prices for nonferrous metals is shown in Exhibit 11–4A. U.S. prices were held down by means of requiring strict cost justification for price increases. The pressure buildup was reflected in four actions announced by the Cost of Living Council on December 6, 1973.

1. The prices of lead, zinc, and lesser nonferrous metals such as tin, platinum, and bismuth were exempted from controls.
2. Most nonferrous scrap metals were also exempted.
3. Primary aluminum producers were permitted to use the Phase II base price of 29 cents per pound compared with the Phase IV base price of 25 cents per pound.
4. Primary copper producers were permitted a base price of 68 cents per pound compared to the recent price of 60 cents per pound.

During the difficult October 1–December 31, 1973, period the Cost of Living Council received an increased number of requests for exceptions. Exhibit 11–4B shows the "issues" involved in these requests by the manufacturing and service sector.

EXHIBIT 11–4B

Manufacturing and Service Exceptions by Issues, October 1–December 31, 1973

Issue	Number of Requests
1. Requests to increase prices without the requisite cost justification	23
2. Requests for base period profit margin adjustment	16
3. Requests for price relief to permit a firm to continue to manufacture products in short supply whose prices, under Phase IV regulations, do not justify the continued allocation of corporate resources as a result of insufficient return on investment	14
4. Requests to amend the base price or base cost period	11
5. Requests to pass through cost increases on raw materials immediately without cost justification	10
6. Request for relief from Special Rule No. 1 which prohibited price increases on nonflat rolled steel products and noncarbon sheet and strip steel	10
7. Requests for a separate entity treatment for divisions or subsidiaries in a loss position in order to permit a greater than dollar-for-dollar pass through of cost increases	10
8. Requests for adjustment in productivity factor	4
9. Requests which would allow the purchase of and sale of raw or partially processed materials in scarce supply at prices higher than those allowed under the Phase IV regulations	4
10. Requests which would allow firms to increase prices without prenotification	3
11. Requests for relief from the limitations to the maximum price increase which may be implemented on any one item	2
12. Requests for treatment under the Small Business Exemption	1
13. Requests for relief from the provisions of Special Rule No. 2 which permitted price increases for tires and tubes equal to one half of the otherwise cost-justified amounts	1
	109

The difficulty that price control agencies have in denying applications for price relief is shown by the data of Exhibit 11–4C.

EXHIBIT 11–4C

Decisions of Cost of Living Council and Internal Revenue Service Combined, Phase IV, August 12–December 31, 1973

		Number of Decisions		
Sector	Total	Full Approval	Part Approval	Full Denials
Durable goods manufacturing	2,163	1,560	521	82
Nondurable goods manufacturing	2,019	1,484	478	57
Nonmanufacturing	182	143	30	9
Total	4,364	3,187	1,029	148

Questions

1. If "cost justification" is required for price increases by U.S. metal producers, why are domestic prices likely to fall below world prices? (Consider the role of demand in price determination.)
2. Comment carefully on the "issues" shown in Exhibit 11–4B. One problem in control is the difference between accounting cost measurement and the more relevant ideas of economic cost. Comment on this problem.
3. Why is it practically inevitable that most applications for price relief be approved rather than denied?
4. Write a few paragraphs summarizing the work of a system of uncontrolled prices emphasizing the informational advantages possessed by decentralized decision makers.

chapter **12**

Price Discrimination and Price Differentials

DISCRIMINATION is one of those words in the English language that has both highly favorable and unfavorable connotations. Contrast the following sentences: Mr. Johnson is a man of quick mind, impeccable tastes, and keen discrimination; Mr. Robinson advocates discrimination on grounds of race, religion, and national origin. Mr. Johnson's discrimination, an ability to perceive and act on distinctions, seems praiseworthy; Mr. Robinson's discrimination with implications of unjust favoritism in treatment of people entitled to equal treatment is condemned. The economist's view of price discrimination initially is a neutral one. The usefulness of price discrimination depends on whether it contributes to or detracts from the achievement of such goals as efficiency in the allocation of resources. The current legal view starts out by making it unlawful "to discriminate in price between different purchasers of commodities of like grade and quality" and in effect embraces the adverse concept of discrimination, but it then goes on to indicate it is only those differentials that will probably have adverse effects on competition or competitors that are discriminations that will be considered unlawful.

In order to assess price discrimination and price differentials as used by firms, this chapter will ask the following questions:

1. How can price differentials and price discrimination be defined?
2. What are the conditions that make the deliberate use of price discrimination possible?
3. What are the conditions that make the use of price discrimination or price differentials profitable or otherwise acceptable for firms?

337

Definition of Price Differentials and Price Discrimination

It seems almost tautological to state that a price differential exists when units of the identical product are sold at different prices, that is that $P_1 \neq P_2$. It is worth pointing out that the existence of such a price differential is neither a necessary nor sufficient condition for price discrimination which depends upon the price-cost relationship of the two units. For example, in early 1969, many filling stations were selling a composite product made up of gasoline; stamps of various hues which were exchangeable for merchandise and issued in proportion to gasoline purchased; and chances in the particular lottery favored by that service station chain. The price per unit of this package was 39.9 cents a gallon.

Customer 1 was happy to accept the whole package and paid $3.99 for his ten gallons plus. Customer 2 had no use for the particular colored stamps and disapproved of the mild competition the petroleum industry was offering to the gaming tables of Las Vegas and paid $3.99 for the ten gallons period. No price differential existed, but the economist would detect price discrimination. The dealer must pay both for trading stamps and lottery tickets. His marginal costs of serving customer 1 were clearly higher and his gross profit lower in the sale to customer 1.

Economic price discrimination is defined as involving different mark-ups over marginal cost, and more rigorously, as a difference in the marginal rate of return between selling units of a product, that is:

$$\frac{P_1 - MC_1}{\Delta K_1} \neq \frac{P_2 - MC_2}{\Delta K_2}$$

The student may observe that the computation of the differences between price and marginal cost is simpler than figuring out the ΔK's which represent the additional capital investment required for producing and selling one more unit of the product. In short-run problems, this denominator may well be ignored as being irrelevant.[1]

The friendly neighborhood filling station may recognize that while the trading stamp and a casino atmosphere are lures to many customers, that some patrons like customer 2 above may resent the price discrimination. Assume that the dealer has calculated the extra costs of stamps as 1 cent a gallon. He may well ask, "stamps or cash"? and make the sale for $3.89. Ignoring the lottery transaction which legally was supposed to be separate from the sale, he would have eliminated the discrepancy in the difference between price and marginal costs. Whether a price differential

---

[1] Another satisfactory formulation for price discrimination is

$$\frac{P_1}{MK_1} \neq \frac{P_2}{MK_2}$$

The content of the marginal costs will vary, depending on whether the pricing decision is being made in the long run or short run.

has been established is a moot point. The product, gasoline, is not quite identical with gasoline plus games and stamps. In late 1973 and early 1974 games were left to the casinos. Filling stations were more concerned with how to stretch their gas supplies than with amusing customers at considerable expense to themselves. When product differentiation exists and is combined with promotional expenses, price discrimination almost necessarily follows. The faithful customer who will buy without selling efforts will pay the same (or perhaps a greater) price in comparison with the brand switcher who was the object of the promotional expense. Later on other examples of strategies involving somewhat different products sold at quite different ratios of price to marginal cost will be referred to since the strategic considerations are quite similar to those for price discrimination.

Elements of Monopoly and Market Imperfection as Requisites for Discrimination

The conditions of equilibrium under competition are those under which price discrimination is impossible. Only one price known to all buyers and sellers exists for a product. That price under profit-maximizing assumptions is equal to the marginal cost at the output chosen. Additionally, in the long run the price is equal to average costs as well. Each firm is confronted by a horizontal demand curve at the going price which constitutes its MR. Only when the demand curve is downward sloping to the right as in monopoly does the firm have price options. The use of this perfectly competitive model has led to useful predictions of the price level for many markets in which its assumptions are only approximated. As far as price discrimination is concerned, the competitive model's usefulness is in highlighting the departures from it that make discrimination possible; lack of knowledge of prices by consumers; real or imagined distinctions in product quality that make some people willing to pay more than others for a product; dispersion of producers and consumers over geographical space which results in disparities in the additional costs of serving particular customers; the existence of selling costs which reflect possibilities of shaping people's demands toward a particular product; and, as an extreme, full monopoly control of the output of a particular product.

Separation of Markets as a Requisite for Price Discrimination When Price Differentials Are Involved

If price differentials are going to be used, separation of the markets for which the different prices are to be charged is essential. This separation involves two elements: first, a decision upon the classifications of customers who will receive the different prices and second, cost barriers between the markets that will prevent the resale of lower priced units in higher priced markets. This latter provision is, of course, unnecessary if the products are personal services that could not be resold. The used tonsillectomy and appendectomy markets are nonexistent.

In the next section it will be pointed out that for price discrimination to be profitable, the elasticities of demand for the product must be different between the classification of customers that is to receive a higher price and the one that is to receive a lower price. It is worth keeping this point in mind in this discussion of the basis on which markets might be separated. For example, the vendor of a hair shampoo might establish a higher price for blondes as against brunettes. Although this distinction would make it possible to identify the customers (the identification may change from day to day; in this day, "only the hair dresser knows for sure"), there is no reason to think that the basic demands of these groups for shampoos differ in price elasticity. The only justification for a differential in this case would be a difference in cost of production and distribution of the product for different customers. The following list is representative of criteria which reflect classifications based on either a different value of service or a different cost of providing the product or services.

1. Apparent Income or Wealth of Buyer. The man who drives a large car may be charged more for an identical repair job than the owner of a more modest vehicle. The sale of a larger house typically involves a larger commission to the real estate agent since these fees are usually computed at a percentage of sales price and may not reflect an increased effort on his part. Medical men, particularly surgeons, may discriminate in price on the basis of income, although the importance of the discrimination has probably decreased with insurance and government plans that specifiy specific fees.

2. Time of Purchase. Prices are frequently different to those who buy at various times of the day or at different seasons of the year. As later discussion and the Urban Electric case indicate, the cost to firms may differ greatly depending upon the time the product is offered. Electric utilities now typically have lower demands in the winter so that current could be provided for heating with a very small additional cost, whereas electricity used for air conditioning would necessitate an increase in plant with all of the capital costs of the company. The telephone companies similarly face a daytime peak and are willing to offer low long-distance rates at night when excess capacity is available and additional costs are very small.

3. Quantity Purchased by Individual Buyer. There are obvious packaging and distribution economies in the sale of multiple units at once, and quantity discount structures may be primarily tailored to match the prices and marginal costs involved in transactions of a different size. As long as the difference in price is reflected in such cost differences, such discounts would be nondiscriminatory. Differences in the intensity of demand may also be reflected. Large customers may well be able to economically manufacture the good or service for themselves; for example, a large industrial firm could choose to generate its own electricity. Thus the seller may be tempted to offer the services at a differential greater than his cost savings. Such price differences that are not justified by cost differences may be challenged under the Robinson-Patman Act.

4. *Age or Other Personal Characteristics of Buyers.* Youthful and aged persons sometimes receive lower prices than those of intermediate ages. In part this is a way of discriminating according to purchasing power since incomes tend to be lower among the young and the old. The price of motion pictures and rates in amusement parks exemplify discrimination in favor of children. Group life insurance plans, when they provide for payment of the same premium by persons of all ages, discriminate in favor of the older participants for whom mortality rates are higher. The airlines have introduced family fare plans which permit wives and children to accompany the head of the family at reduced fares. Complete market separation may be impossible in some of these cases; a small 14-year-old may receive the 12-year-old price; the executive's secretary could receive the family discount.

5. *Newness of Customer's Business.* Remarkable price concessions have been made by magazines to enlist new subscribers who presumably have not built up habits favorable to using the particular publication. Graduate students often receive lower subscription rates on professional journals than do regular buyers. On the other hand, the long-time customer may receive informal concessions from dealers to whom he is well known. Such informal concessions have helped neighborhood appliance dealers to compete on price with discount or mail-order houses.

6. *Use of the Commodity.* A leading illustration of this method of market separation has occurred in the milk market. Class I, or fluid milk —that is, milk which is sold as fresh bottled milk—commands a higher price than Class II, or surplus milk, which is used for processed milk products such as ice cream, evaporated milk, and dried milk powder. Since the milk is identical, this kind of price discrimination requires record keeping by the milk dealers and processors and has usually been successful only when aided by government regulation. The apparatus required for this type of discrimination emphasizes the first requisite for price discrimination, that is an element of monopoly power.

7. *Location of Buyer.* The geographic separation of buyers often provides a convenient basis for price discrimination. A local producer of a product with substantial transportation costs enjoys a cost advantage with consumers located nearer his plant than that of any competitors. He may well be able to realize a higher effective price at his mill from these customers than he could from shipments to distant buyers on which he must absorb freight. Later in the chapter the discriminatory aspects of "basing-point" pricing will be discussed. Geographic location as a basis for discrimination is apparent in many international transactions. The producers of one country sell their product abroad at lower prices than in the domestic market. The transportation costs and domestic tariffs create barriers to prevent the exported good from undercutting the prices in the domestic market. When a foreign country encourages this process, Americans have termed it "dumping," but the agricultural policies of the United States frequently use a two-price technique with the lower foreign price being one that was designed to get rid of undesired surpluses.

8. Market Function.   The company may choose to sell a commodity at different prices depending upon the economic function that the customer serves. Spark plugs sold to automobile manufacturers as original equipment carry lower prices than those sold to wholesale distributors. The price to wholesalers may be lower than sales made directly to retailers. The failure to give such functional discounts could be illegal; for example, offering a large chain store the same price on a commodity that is offered to independent brokers would fall afoul of Section 2c of the Robinson-Patman Act. Complex legal problems have arisen on the other hand when lower prices are extended to a manufacturer who is also a distributor than to the distributors involved. The legal issues would concern the injuries to competition or to competitors.

9. Product Quality as a Method of Market Separation.   Strictly speaking, the price differentials and price discriminations that have been discussed refer to identical products. A very similar strategy to that of price discrimination is to seek to appeal to different segments of the market by offering products that differ slightly in quality and substantially in price. For example, the manufacturer of a branded aspirin could sell it at a high price to those customers who desired the additional assurance of a quality reputation. At the same time it could bottle the identical aspirin and sell it to a drug or grocery chain at a very much lower price. The price differential would be quite evident; whether or not economic price discrimination existed would have to be established by a difficult calculation as to the marginal costs of advertising. Many consumers are familiar with the various options they have in purchasing automobiles or appliances, options that range from a "stripped" model to a highly deluxe model. Frequently the markup of price over cost is significantly less for the stripped model which incorporates the same basic mechanism as the more luxurious lines. Such models allow the manufacturer both to attract the unusually price conscious among the public and to establish a promotional price that will bring many customers into the store. In the less ethical uses of this strategy the stripped model may be considered "nailed to the floor." The salesman is expected to trade the customer up to higher priced models by stressing the desirable extra features.

Perfect Price Discrimination

It is instructive to consider the extreme case of "perfect" price discrimination in order to understand the motivation behind more practicable schemes of discrimination. Whereas the usual assumption employed in the economic theory of monopoly is that the *single* most profitable

FIGURE 12–1

Perfect Price Discrimination Contrasted with Single Monopoly Price

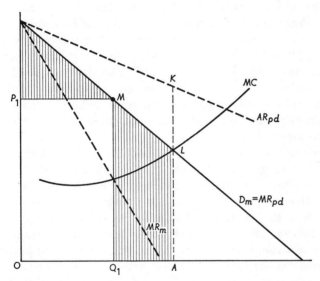

price under existing conditions is charged, the notion of perfect price discrimination is that every unit be sold at a *different* price and that this be the highest price at which that unit will be purchased.

The usual geometrical demonstration of perfect price discrimination is given in Figure 12–1, which contrasts it with one-price monopoly pricing. It should be noted that the demand curve becomes the marginal revenue curve under perfect discrimination. This follows from the assumption that each unit sold is independent of the others; that is, to sell an additional unit, the monopolist does not have to take a lower price on the earlier units. Whatever price he gets for a particular unit adds exactly that amount to his revenue. The average revenue curve lies above the marginal revenue curve, since whatever quantity is considered along the horizontal axis, the earlier units in this quantity will bring a higher price than the later ones and hence will hold the average price above the price at the margin. Maximum profit is secured by selling OA units, where marginal cost equals marginal revenue. Further sales would not be profitable because more would be added to cost than to revenue. Total revenue would amount to OA times AK.

Total revenue under perfect discrimination is also equal to OP_1MQ_1, the revenue under single-price monopoly, plus the shaded areas. The vertically shaded area to the left of M represents the additional amounts paid for units that would have been sold at price M under a one-price system. The shaded area to the right of M is revenue from units that could not be sold profitably under a one-price system since the extra revenue gained from their sale would be more than offset by the loss in revenue due to lower prices on all sales plus the additions to cost.

The student should note that a perfectly discriminating monopolist would extend his production to OA with the last unit sold at the price AL. A condition for allocative efficiency in the perfectly competitive markets is thus satisfied: $P = MR = MC$. The student should also construct a number of possible AC curves and will observe that some of them lying entirely above the demand curve indicate situations where nonsubsidized production in the long run could take place only when there is discrimination.

Our conventional assumption in monopoly analysis is that only one price can be charged and that various price-quantity combinations are alternatives. This assumption would fit cases in which, with no barriers to the transfer of units, any attempt to charge multiple prices would be frustrated by resale of units sold at lower prices and thus the elimination of price differentials. For perfect discrimination, an immediately consumed service would be necessary to eliminate this resale problem. The discriminating monopolist would also have to know for each unit sold the maximum price that would be paid. This could involve charging separate prices to a single customer who purchased multiple units.

Note that in Figure 12–2 marginal revenue under perfect discrimination corresponds with the demand curve and that the AR_{pd} lies above it. Under a one-price system three units would be sold for a total revenue of $24, but under perfect discrimination, five units would be sold for a total revenue of $40.

This perfect price discrimination model illustrates the ultimate in market separation and exploitation of the revenue possibilities from a demand curve. Each unit is sold at the maximum that the "traffic will bear." Approaches to separation of the market into units sold may be found in the oriental bazaar and possibly in the retail automobile market.

In both situations the monopoly element is fairly weak, the advantage of the seller is likely to consist only of the buyer being relatively ill-

FIGURE 12–2

Hypothetical Demand of an Individual Facing a Discriminating
Monopolist

		One Price		Perfect Discrimination			
P	Q	TR	MR	TR_{pd}	MR_{pd}	AR_{pd}	MC
$10	1	$10	$10	$10	$10	$10	$*
9	2	18	8	19	9	9.5	3
8	3	24	6	27	8	9.0	4
7	4	28	4	34	7	8.5	5
6	5	30	2	40	6	8.0	6

* Not specified.

informed and of his preference for dealing with the particular seller because of time and convenience elements.[2] The seller can seek to find out the highest price the buyer is willing to pay in the negotiations and try to get it. Rather than losing the sale he could use his marginal cost as the lower limit. Another case in which the perfect discrimination model could be applicable is in the case of patented capital equipment. The manufacturer could well set up a schedule of charges based on the savings made possible with the equipment. It would be necessary for him to lease rather than sell the machines to avoid the resale problem.

Discrimination by Customer Classification

Instead of attempting to charge the maximum that the demand will bear for each unit, a separation of markets along the demand curve into many submarkets, the firm with some monopoly power may divide customers up by some identifiable characteristics. For specific examples, one may think of adults and children at a movie house, or unrelated individuals and family members on an airline that is using a family plan.

In Figure 12–3 we show the simplest case in which marginal costs remain the same over the relevant output. Panel A shows the conventional monopoly or monopolistic competition price (P) and output (Q) determination by the intersection of MR and MC. The demand curves in panel B and panel C added horizontally at each price equal the total demand shown in Panel A. Panel B depicts the less elastic demand. For example, in airline travel it could show the demand by unrelated individuals, many of whom are flying on business and have no good substitute for such rapid transportation. Panel C shows the more elastic demand. For airline travel, families will find automobiles a conceivable substitute. They are com-

---

[2] Despite its bargaining aspects, the bazaar may well approximate a one-price competitive market when the buyers are experienced rather than being tourists.

FIGURE 12–3

Price Discrimination in Two Separate Markets

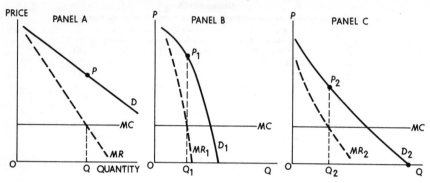

paratively low cost when several people are traveling; the time element is likely to be less important; and family air travel competes with many other forms of recreation. Note that in each of the markets the quantity offered is extended to where $MR = MC$. Note also that under discrimination the total quantity sold OQ_1 plus OQ_2 is greater than that under the one-price system, OQ.[3] Fuller use of capacity is frequently one result of price discrimination.

The profitability of price discrimination has been dependent upon the differing elasticities of demand. If the elasticity had been identical in both markets, MR would have equaled MC at price P in the two markets.[4] Only one price would have been charged.

Figure 12–4 shows the more difficult case in which MC varies with output. Demand in one submarket has been labeled D_1 and demand in the other market, D_2; corresponding marginal revenues are MR_1 and MR_2. Aggregate marginal revenue, AMR, is obtained by the horizontal summation of these marginal revenue curves. The marginal cost of production is shown by MC. Optimum output is OA, determined by the equality of MC and AMR. If the rate of production were above OA, it would be too high because units above OA would add more to the firm's cost than to its revenue, even if units were properly allocated in sale

---

[3] The increase in output occurs because the more elastic demand curve (D_2) is more concave (from above). This is proved in Joan Robinson, *The Economics of Imperfect Competition* (London: Macmillan & Co., Ltd., 1938), pp. 190–93. Mrs. Robinson originated the graphical exposition of price discrimination.

[4] This follows from the definition of the elasticity of demand as $E = \dfrac{-P}{P-MR} \cdot MR_1$ and MR_2 at the most profitable prices are equal to each other as well as to MC. If the elasticities of demand are also equal, then the price must be identical in the two submarkets.

FIGURE 12–4

FIGURE 12–4

Price Discrimination between Two Markets with
MC Varying with Output

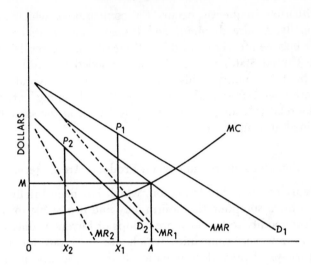

between the two submarkets (that is, allocated so as to equate marginal revenue in each).

Buyers in market 2 receive a substantially lower price (P_2) than buyers in market 1 (who pay P_1). Optimum sales in market 2 are OX_2, determined by the intersection of MR_2 with a horizontal line drawn at the level at which MC equals AMR. Optimum sales in market 1 are determined by the intersection of MR_1 and the same horizontal line. (As a consequence, marginal revenues are equated in the two submarkets.) Prices in the two submarkets are those at which the optimum quantities can be sold; consequently, the prices are found on the demand curves directly above the optimum sales quantities.

In Figure 12–4, demand at any price which is chosen for consideration is considerably more elastic in market 2 than in market 1. This is the reason for the profitability of charging less in market 2 than in the other market. Customers who make up market 2 would desert the firm more extensively as measured by percentages than those in the other submarket if confronted by a high price.

Sometimes a firm divides its sales of a given commodity between a monopolistic market and a highly competitive market. In this case the price is, of course, considerably higher in the former. Marginal revenue is equated in both markets, since the firm will not sell any units in the monopolistic market which will add less to revenue than they would have added if they had been sold in the purely competitive market.

Figure 12–4 can be modified to show this case by extending the horizontal line from M to represent D_1, MR_1, and also the AMR after its intersection with P_2X_2.

This situation frequently occurs for commodities which are traded internationally. As already mentioned, transportation costs create a natural barrier between foreign and domestic markets, and resale by foreigners in the United States may be further impeded by tariffs and quotas imposed by this country. This creates a situation favorable to price discrimination and frequently results in the "dumping" of a product abroad at a relatively low, competitive price while at the same time price is maintained at a higher level at home.

Discrimination and Differentials when Products Are Differentiated

The theory of price discrimination, which has been briefly described, is based on the assumption that a firm may find it possible to sell exactly the same commodity to two or more groups of buyers at different prices. Frequently, however, companies which are in a position to increase profits by means of price discrimination find it necessary or desirable to differentiate products from one another, so that similar—but not quite the same—goods are sold at two or more prices. The distinction in products may act as a barrier between the two markets. When air coach service was first introduced in the late 1940s at a price of 4 cents a mile instead of 6 cents per mile for first-class service, it represented an attempt to add revenue through getting new travelers who would not pay the higher fares. Late night departures and fewer amenities such as meals not only held down cost levels but served to prevent customers from being diverted from first class. The Continental Airlines Case (Chapter 5, Case 5–3) suggests some of the later problems in maintaining sufficient quality differences and small enough price differentials so that the lower priced service would not primarily divert customers from first-class service but would add sufficient revenues to offset additional costs.

Geographic Price Discrimination

Frequently, markets which are subjected to unlike treatment by a firm are separated on a geographic basis—that is, transportation costs impose an economic barrier between markets. The case of "dumping" a commodity abroad at a low price while the domestic price is maintained has already been mentioned. Geographic price discrimination makes its appearance in numerous other forms also. For example, "blanket" freight rates are sometimes charged by the railroads which result in the same charge for transporting a unit of commodity over a wide geographic range, irrespective of the actual length of the haul. An outstanding example has been the movement of California oranges in carload lots from all points of origin in that state to any point between Denver and the North Atlantic seaboard at the same rate. This means, for example, that buyers in Chicago are discriminated against compared with those in New York, in that the former are charged the same price despite the lower marginal cost of production plus transportation involved in placing California oranges in Chicago. More resources are used up in delivering a box of California oranges to New York, but price does not reflect this fact.

Basing-Point Pricing in Steel

A historically important, and still significant, form of geographic price discrimination is known as "basing-point pricing." The most famous example of the practice was the "Pittsburgh-plus" system of pricing used by the steel industry prior to 1924. Under this system, mills all over the United States calculated prices not by reference to their own costs and shipping charges but by reference to the single set of basing-point prices at Pittsburgh, plus rail freight from Pittsburgh to the buyer's location. Thus, steel delivered to Washington, D.C., for example, was priced as if it came from Pittsburgh even if, in fact, it came by boat from nearby Baltimore. The steel industry changed to a multiple basing-point system in 1924 after the United States Steel Corporation was ordered by the Federal Trade Commission to "cease and desist" from the Pittsburgh-plus system. Under the amended system the delivered price at any city was calculated by adding to the mill price the freight from the *applicable* basing point. This was done by calculating the lowest combination of mill price and rail freight for any given buyer. The "applicable basing point" would always be the one from which rail freight was lowest if mill prices were the same, but might not be if mill prices were dissimilar. Any steel mill which wished to sell in a particular locality could offer its product at the delivered price thus computed. This required the absorption of part of the freight charge by more distant steel mills, however.

The portland cement industry was also a well-known practitioner of the multiple basing-point system of pricing; and historically, this system was second only to that of the steel industry in importance to the American economy. Cement prices charged by different companies were thus identical at any point of delivery. During the 1930s, about half of the cement mills were basing points and about half were not. Buyers located near the nonbasing-point mills were forced to pay some "phantom freight," while those near basing points were not at this disadvantage. In 1948 the Supreme Court upheld a Federal Trade Commission order that the portland cement industry "cease and desist" from selling cement at prices calculated in accordance with a multiple basing-point system or using other means to secure identical price quotations for the product of the various companies. Shortly after this decision, both the portland cement and the steel industries abandoned the basing-point method of pricing and adopted systems of f.o.b. mill pricing. They still are permitted to absorb freight to meet competitors' prices. What has been forbidden is the systematic and collusive aspects of multiple basing-point pricing.

Market Penetration

Advocates of basing-point pricing usually claim that the system is highly competitive because each seller can offer his product at the same price in any locality—that is, firms may compete freely for sales but may not compete in price. Any plant which has unused capacity, and whose owners are therefore anxious to increase sales, can offer its wares at the same price as others in any locality, although this may be possible only through "freight absorption," which means a reduction in the "mill net" price realized. Although this may help utilize the excess capacity of the mill which penetrates the usual territory of another mill, it clearly tends to cause excess capacity in the plant whose market is being penetrated. If such freight absorption were not practiced and buyers were instead given prices equivalently lower, the resulting increase in total sales would help avoid excess capacity in both plants.

Market penetration, phantom freight, and freight absorption can perhaps be more easily understood from Figure 12–5. In this chart, A and B are mills producing the same commodity; but B is a basing point (the "applicable" one in the region considered), while A is not. Circles are drawn around B to reflect transportation costs from B; at each point on a circle the delivered price is the same. These delivered prices are shown by the numbers attached to each circle, and are calculated by assuming the mill price at B to be $45 and the transportation cost from one circle to the next to be $1 per unit.[5]

If we assume that freight costs are the same in either direction and that equal distances represent equal freight costs, it is clear that mill A has a very favorable mill net price in selling near home. If mill A sells at point H, for example, the price will be $50, which includes a $5 freight charge from the basing point. Since actual freight from A to H is $1 the "phantom freight" collected by mill A is $4. On the other hand, if mill A sells at point F, the price will be $47, which includes $2 of freight. Since actual freight from A to F is $4, mill A must absorb $2 in freight costs

---

[5] The use of circles assumes that transportation costs are uniform in all directions. Actually, they would be affected by the availability of railroads, highways, and waterways, and by mountains, and so forth; this would cause the isoprice lines to be irregular in shape.

FIGURE 12–5

Mill A Collects Phantom Freight to Left of XY but Absorbs Freight to Right of XY

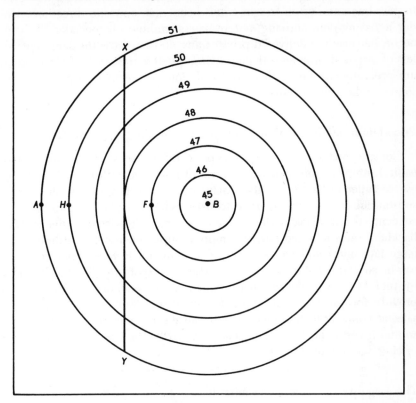

in order to make the sale. On sales anywhere between *A* and the vertical line *XY*, mill *A* will realize phantom freight; while to penetrate beyond line *XY*, it will have to absorb freight. Line *XY* is drawn so as to be equidistant between the two mills.

It is also apparent from the chart that the basing-point mill *B* can penetrate the territory of mill *A* without penalty. If mill *B* sold at point *H*, for example, it would secure the same mill net as on a sale at point *F*, because the delivered price always includes full freight cost from point *B*. Mill *A* could make it more expensive for *B* to get such sales by giving nearby customers an f.o.b. alternative. Its own mill net would be reduced; by how much would depend on the sale price it chose.

Under any system of pricing a certain amount of "cross-hauling" is bound to occur—that is, one mill shipping the same commodity into the natural territory of another mill at the same time the other mill is delivering in the territory of the first mill. This occurs even if the term "cross-hauling" is defined strictly so as to require that a mill in city *A* be shipping a given commodity to a buyer in city *B* at the same time a mill at city *B* is shipping to a buyer at city *A*. The shipments are likely even to pass one another on freight trains headed in opposite directions. Under a basing-point pricing system, cross-hauling is especially likely to occur, because the delivered price at any destination is the same regardless of origin of shipment. If shape, size, quality, and finish of the product are precisely the same, there is an obvious waste of transportation resources when this occurs.

Price Differentials and Discrimination When Marginal Costs Differ

Conspicuous examples of large price differentials are found in such capital intensive industries as electric utilities and railroads. In order to assure fuller utilization of their plant over time they may wish to offer substantial concessions in price to users whose demand is substantially concentrated in slack periods. For example, railroads may give special backhaul rates to avoid moving empty equipment. Electric utilities have large late night and winter troughs in demand. If more kilowatt-hours can be sold at these times, the only additional costs are likely to be those for fuel. Moreover, since their capital costs are dependent on the need to provide for peak demands, the long-run marginal costs of additional sales at nonpeak hours remain low because such sales require little or no capital investment. Case 12–2, The Urban Electric Company, takes up a pricing decision of this type.

The Legality of Price Discrimination[6]

Under the Robinson-Patman Amendment to the Clayton Act price discrimination is made illegal only where the effect "may be to substantially lessen competition" or to "injure competition" with the "granter of the discrimination or his customers." Its basic provisions are enforceable only through civil suits the result of which may be a cease and desist order. Even if injury is proved, the firm may, though experience shows it is difficult, prove that the price differentials made only due allowance for costs or were made in good faith to meet the price of a competitor.

Many forms of pure discrimination are legally acceptable. Identical prices to all customers are not legally considered discrimination even though the economist detects differences in P/MC ratios. Price discrimination in consumer markets is legally acceptable; usually the injury to competition is found in the secondary market when businessmen in competition have paid different prices for the product. Many, if not most, firms have quantity discount schedules that have been unchallenged.

---

[6] Students who are interested in legal and policy issues concerning the law will find the Corwin Edwards' comprehensive study, *"The Price Discrimination Law"* (Washington, D.C.: The Brookings Institution, 1959), illuminating.

The greatest difficulties for management arise in trying to allocate costs to particular units of products. Most firms are multiproduct firms, and the attempt to relate overhead costs to particular products and orders is difficult and frequently involves somewhat arbitrary judgments. The Federal Trade Commission has seemed to favor an average cost approach which requires such allocations rather than clearly identifiable marginal costs.

Case 12–3 on price differentials for Budweiser beer will indicate for a close case the legal questions involved, although it is somewhat atypical in that the injury to competition was alleged to take place in the primary line, beer manufacturing, rather than among customers of Anheuser-Busch. It remains of interest as the displacement of regional and local beers by the national brands has continued into the 1970s.

More legal cases and cease and desist orders have occurred under the heavily criticized Section 2(c) which outlaws granting by sellers of allowances for brokerage to any but brokers.[7]

The Social Acceptability of Price Discrimination

Most of the examples cited in this chapter have been ones that are accepted as fair by the public. What would prove most objectionable would be price differentials that arbitrarily distinguished between individuals. The public may readily accept surgeon's fees based on ability to pay, lower ticket prices for children and special electricity rates for home heating. They might well object to paying a higher price for identical groceries than that paid by equally prosperous persons in front of them in the supermarket line. A one-price system effectively prevails for the most frequent retail transactions for goods. This partially reflects the competitive nature of retailing, but also probably is in part due to attention to the long-run requirement of maintaining good will by firms that have some monopoly power.

CASE 12–1. The Country Doctor[8]

Dr. Young served a rural area a substantial distance by ferry and automobile from other medical facilities. He estimated that to cover his family living expenditures and the fixed overhead connected with his small clinic, he required $15,000 gross income. On purely economic grounds, he could command more income elsewhere. Fifteen thousand

---

[7] One hundred eighteen or 47.6 percent of all orders from 1936–57 occurred under this limited section of the law.

[8] Dr. Young's case is set in the early 1960s before Medicaid and Medicare and the great escalation in medical costs.

dollars plus variable expenses represented a minimum gross necessary for him to continue to supply his services to the particular area, considering his sense of service and other noneconomic factors as well. In addition, he had certain variable expenses which would vary with the number of visits, and he estimated these at $1 a visit. (Obviously using a common unit, the visit, to describe the variety of medical services possible is a great simplification.)

The population of the area consisted essentially of two groups, the new inhabitants and the older inhabitants. The first group was characterized by being mostly retired, generally well off, and primarily attracted by the resort aspects of the community. The second group were permanent residents who furnished services and participated in marginal agriculture and fishing.

EXHIBIT 12–1A

Hypothetical Demand Schedules Confronting
Dr. Young

Price	Visits, Group I	Visits, Group II	Total Visits
$18................	0	0	0
15................	475	25	500
12................	900	100	1,000
9................	1,100	400	1,500
6................	1,300	700	2,000
3................	1,450	1,050	2,500
0................	1,500	1,500	3,000

Assume that the effective demand for Dr. Young's services among the two groups is described by smoothly drawn demand curves through the points in Exhibit 12–1A and that Dr. Young can provide three thousand visits per year.

Questions

1. Evaluate the following pricing alternatives:
   a. A one-price system.
   b. Perfect price discrimination.
   c. A six-price system ($15, $12, $9, $6, $3, $0).
   d. One price for group I and one price for group II.
2. Recognizing that none of the alternatives above are fully possible (Dr. Young would not have the perfect knowledge required for [b] and [c], and would find it professionally difficult to practice [a] and [d] without providing some free services as well), what approach would you recommend?
3. Show that under perfect price discrimination the demand curve becomes

the marginal revenue curve, and construct the new average revenue curve.
4. What are the fundamental economic circumstances that make price discrimination a method for providing an economic service that could not be provided under a one-price system without subsidy? How much of a government subsidy would be required to provide the medical services under a one-price system? Why would one expect price discrimination to be greatly reduced under a comprehensive system of National Health Insurance?

CASE 12–2. The Urban Electric Company

In 1962 the Urban Electric Company, which served both metropolitan and rural areas in the Middle West, found itself in an unfavorable operating position because of the rapid growth of summer air-conditioning load, which had resulted in increased investment in utility plant and equipment without adequate increase in income. Obviously, a compensating type of load was needed to offset the unfavorable system effects of added air-conditioning load. Therefore the president of the company authorized the establishment of a "working" committee to bring in recommendations as to what measures should be taken:

1. To review the data previously prepared in the economic and rate research department to determine whether or not the company should encourage space heating.
2. To estimate the potential rate of growth in the residential space-heating market for the purpose of determining when a balance between summer and winter peaks could again be established.
3. To propose a price policy based on the necessary costs to the company to serve a residential space-heating load.

The committee had as chairman the manager of the rate department and staff representatives from the sales, operating, comptroller, and economic research departments.

During the course of the discussions, committee members developed the following attitudes:

The vice chairman, coming from the sales area, found himself on the horns of a dilemma. His evaluation of market growth, taking into consideration the intense competition to be encountered from the gas and fuel oil interests, was that it was likely to be quite slow; hence a special rate might not be justified at present. On the other hand, competition made it mandatory to be able to offer the lowest possible service rate to gain entrance into the space-heating market; hence a special rate was required.

The representative of the comptroller's office was basically opposed to offering any special rates in the first place, but if a special rate was to be offered, he insisted that investment costs be included in determining company costs of service from the outset.

The representative from the operating department was all in favor of any promotional effort which would at least tend to equalize the rate of growth of summer and winter loads, but was fearful that if domestic space heating once "caught on," it would have a runaway growth similar to that experienced in air conditioning in the postwar period. If this occurred, then the utility would be right back in the position it was about 1930, with winter peaks far in excess of summer peaks. While this situation would be better than a permanent summer peak, it still was an undesirable situation because, on the basis of present knowledge, there would be no compensating summer load to be developed. If this happened, an unbalanced operating condition would become a permanent characteristic of utility operation.

The research analyst from the economic and rate research department, who had been responsible for the basic technical and market research, was inclined to emphasize that the rate of growth of space-heating load seemed almost sure to be slow, while all the evidence tended to prove that the rate of growth of summer air-conditioning load for the next decade was sure to be large; hence, there would be an increasing gap between summer and winter peaks for most, if not all, of the period until 1975. He based his judgment that the rate of electric space-heating growth would be slow on what had actually happened, particularly in northern climatic areas, during the 15 years elapsed since World War II. Electric space heating as the principal source of home comfort heating in the United States really had gotten its start in the Pacific Northwest, where a domestic conventional fuel shortage developed in 1942–43, and in wartime housing developments near military installations. These first systems were poorly engineered and poorly installed, so that electric space heating really had a setback in the first five years after World War II, both from the public and from the utility point of view. It was not until the very rapid rate of growth in summer air conditioning became apparent in the early 1950s that the utilities became concerned with the unbalanced seasonal load that was developing and started taking a genuine interest in electric comfort heating of homes.

The U.S. Census Bureau undertook in 1960 to conduct a housing census on a sample basis, and one item was the fuels being used in domestic comfort heating systems. A condensation of the result of the census survey is shown in Exhibit 12–2A.

If summer and winter growth trends were accurately forecast, space-heating load additions should not be charged with peak responsibility before the mid-1970s; hence a low rate covering direct incremental ex-

EXHIBIT 12–2A

Percentages of Households Using Various Space-Heating Fuels in 1960
(by regions of continental United States)

	Percent of Housing Units Heated by—					
	Gas*	Petro- leum†	Coal	Electric	Liquid Petro- leum Gas	Other‡
1. New England states (6 states)....	12.8	77.8	6.0	0.1	1.5	1.8
2. Mid-Atlantic states (5 states and District of Columbia)...........	28.1	53.8	15.6	0.2	1.0	1.3
3. South Atlantic states (6 states) ...	22.7	39.1	13.3	3.3	8.5	13.1
4. North Central states (12 states)..	45.5	30.2	17.1	0.3	4.5	2.4
5. South Central states (8 states)....	62.7	3.1	9.8	3.5	11.5	9.4
6. Rocky Mountain states (6 states).	73.0	7.6	7.0	1.1	7.4	3.9
7. Pacific Coast states (5 states)....	68.1	16.7	1.8	5.3	3.8	4.3
8. Total United States (including Alaska and Hawaii)...........	43.5	32.6	12.3	1.8	5.1	4.7

* Includes both natural and manufactured gas.
† Includes all grades of petroleum fuels used for heating (except "bottled" liquid petroleum gas).
‡ Includes all types of electric heating where electrical heating is the principal, not the auxiliary, type of heating.
Source: *1960 U.S. Census of Housing.*

penses only would be justified until the winter "valley" was again filled. In his view a new point of equilibrium, assuming no change in general load conditions, would not occur before 20 to 25 years had elapsed. The research analyst therefore favored a low incremental space-heating rate to meet gas competition, and reliance on future general load growth to balance future system peaks.

The chairman showed little interest in any questions but the third, and that from the viewpoint of being able to draw up a rate that would fit into the general rate policies and structure of the company.

The Change in the Seasonal Peak

In the 1930s the Urban Electric Company had a very distinct winter peak. This seasonal concentration of sales plus the late night lows in electric utilization mean the average load factor for the system (the percentage of actual current sold divided by what could have been sold if peak demand was sustained throughout the year) was only 50 percent. Increased industrial activity, the much greater use of electrical appliances in the home, and commercial air conditioning in the summer greatly transformed this pattern (see Exhibit 12–2B) and raised the average load factor to 60 percent.

By 1954 the Urban Electric Company had become concerned enough about the rising summer load to seek giving up certain long-standing rate

EXHIBIT 12–2B

Quarterly Averages of Monthly Maximum Loads Expressed as
Percentages of Previous Winter's Peak Load

	1932	1942	1954
Dec., Jan., Feb..............	95.5	100.0	99.0
Mar., Apr., May............	79.8	90.4	91.2
June, July, Aug..............	66.9	88.8	94.9
Sept., Oct., Nov............	86.4	95.5	94.2

schedules which gave unusually favorable off-peak rates to the users of air-conditioning equipment in the nonwinter months and to customers who established maximum demands outside of the traditional peak period. (See Exhibit 12–2G for such a rate schedule.) The switch to a summer peak was a disadvantage to utilities because the efficiency of utility plant and equipment goes down as ambient temperatures rise. The transmission and distribution efficiency problem is the same for all utilities regardless of whether or not hydro or steam power is used for generation, but the generating efficiency problem is much more acute for steam-generating systems than for the hydroelectric systems. The Urban Company relied exclusively on steam generation and had testified before the state Commerce Commission that its overall plant and equipment efficiency is 14 percent less in hot weather than in cold weather.

Thus, in order to meet customer demands for service, 14 percent more plant and equipment had to be provided to meet summer demands than identically sized winter demands. Therefore, as soon as the differential becomes less than 14 percent, additional capacity would have to be provided on a summer basis rather than a winter basis. The last increment of capacity required to meet annual peak conditions also becomes unused capacity for more than half of the year; therefore, idle capacity was available in the spring, fall, and winter seasons.

Another aspect of the utility operating problem is that whereas, prior to World War II, winter peaks were sufficiently above summer peaks so that generating and transmission equipment could easily be taken out of service for periods of several weeks up to two or three months for heavy maintenance and overhaul, the postwar load developments tended to level off monthly peak demands so that no comparatively long period of the year was really available for planned heavy overhaul and maintenance. This problem was aggravated by the rapid increase in size of generating units in the large utilities from a 100,000- to 150,000-kilowatt capacity to 300,000- to 500,000-kilowatt capacity, with units being planned of from 800,000- to 1,000,000-kilowatt capacity. This increase in size of unit means fewer units and greater efficiency of generation, but it also means increasing total reserve requirements to meet emergency outages as well as normal maintenance and overhaul schedules. For laydowns a 12 percent inoperable reserve would be necessary plus a 5 percent to 10 percent operable reserve for emergencies.

The company was just achieving a comfortable reserve position after the strains of World War II when the shift from winter to summer peaks further embarrassed the operating men because reserve capacity had been planned on a winter, not summer, basis. Exhibit 12–2C shows in index terms what had actually happened to the load conditions being met by the company. The Ratio of Summer Peak to Winter Peak column is

EXHIBIT 12–2C

Growth in Seasonal Peak Demand, 1947–60
(1947 = 100)

| | Relative Growth in Peak Demand | | Ratio of Summer Peak to Winter Peak |
Year	Winter	Summer	
1947 . . . . 100.0		100.0	88.8
1948 . . . . 104.5		104.4	88.7
1949 . . . . 110.1		108.7	87.6
1950 . . . . 120.5		110.6	85.3
1951 . . . . 126.0		115.8	88.1
1952 . . . . 134.2		119.2	89.3
1953 . . . . 138.7		146.2	93.6
1954 . . . . 144.9		154.7	94.8
1955 . . . . 159.2		166.9	93.1
1956 . . . . 169.5		180.2	94.4
1957 . . . . 172.7		196.7	101.1
1958 . . . . 184.3		200.5	96.6
1959 . . . . 201.4		220.2	97.1
1960 . . . . 209.9		240.2	102.5

the important one in this tabulation. In absolute terms, summer peaks were below winter peaks until 1957, but only in 1950 was the differential as much as 14 percent. It was now predicted that this condition could become a permanent situation as summer temperature sensitive load had been averaging about 6.8 percent annual rate growth as compared to a 5.9 percent annual rate of growth for winter temperature sensitive load. (See Exhibit 12–2C.) The spread was widening as air conditioning multiplied in residences in the late 1950s and early 1960s.

Electrical Space Heating

Electric heating had progressed to a point where quality-build equipment was commercially vendable at prices comparable to conventional heating equipment. Current equipment could be depended upon to operate satisfactorily if properly installed by an experienced installer, and if heated spaces were properly insulated. Insulation was extremely important with electric heating, as it does not require the same volume of outside air to supply needed oxygen as was required for flame types of fuel. The cost of operating an electric heating system could vary as much as 50 percent, depending on how well the building was insulated. Storm doors and windows would be a necessity for electrically heated homes, as well as wall, floor, and ceiling insulation.

Room or area control of resistance heating systems had been well developed, and resistance heating had been the fastest growing type of electric space heating in the past decade because it had the lowest installation costs.

Heat pumps for year-round air conditioning were little beyond the pioneering stage. While the component equipment parts were mostly standard items, each job had to be individually engineered and assembled. This made either ground-to-air or water-to-air installations expensive. The big equipment manufacturers came out, about 1955, with the air-to-air heat pump which, while it was the least efficient of the three types of heat pump, was the only one which could be factory-assembled into a self-contained unit. Early air-to-air heat pumps had some operating "bugs" in them but could be produced for a cost low enough to compete with the price of a conventional furnace plus central air-conditioner equipment (about $2,000 for an average-sized installation). Satisfactory "electric" furnaces for hot-air or hot-water heating systems had been available on the market only for the past two or three years and were just beginning to be used.

Off-peak hot-water (or limited heating hour) storage heating systems had been tried but were costly to install, and the large-sized storage tanks occupied considerably more space than a modern furnace. If a satisfactory chemical heat-storage material of small bulk could be found, then off-peak space-heating systems might become popular with both the public and the utilities.

Tolerable Price Differential between Electric and Gas Systems

An analysis of relative operating costs of gas and electric space heating indicated that when the price per BTU[9] consumed for electricity was not more than two to two and a half times the comparable gas price, electric heating could be sold on a nonprice competitive basis because of its greater cleanliness, safety, and flexibility. As noted previously, resistance-heating installation costs, even allowing for extra insulation, were as low as or lower than conventional hot-air or hot-water heating systems, while air-to-air heat pumps could be installed at a cost approximately equal to that of a conventional hot-air furnace plus central air conditioning.

Exhibit 12–2D shows the relative operating cost of heating a 1,200-

---

[9] British thermal unit, the standard measure of heat.

EXHIBIT 12–2D

Comparison of Fuel Cost Ratios for Average Residential Customer under Existing Rates and at Varying Incremental Electricity Rates*

Fuel and Efficiency	Price and Unit	Relative Cost of Heating
Utility gas....................................	8.00 cents/therm	1.00
Fuel oil (80% furnace efficiency)....................	14.30 cents/gal	1.00
Fuel oil (65% furnace efficiency)....................	14.30 cents/gal	1.20
Liquid petroleum gas (80% furnace efficiency)........	14.00 cents/gal	1.60
Liquid petroleum gas (65% furnace efficiency).......	14.00 cents/gal	1.80
Heat pump.....................................	2.45 cents/kwh	2.40
Heat pump.....................................	2.00 cents/kwh	1.95
Heat pump.....................................	1.75 cents/kwh	1.70
Heat pump.....................................	1.50 cents/kwh	1.46
Heat pump.....................................	1.00 cents/kwh	0.97
Resistance heating.............................	2.45 cents/kwh	4.30
Resistance heating.............................	2.00 cents/kwh	3.55
Resistance heating.............................	1.75 cents/kwh	3.10
Resistance heating.............................	1.50 cents/kwh	2.66
Resistance heating.............................	1.00 cent/kwh	1.77

* While the relative cost of heating would hold approximately for a wide range of residences, calculations were based on a well-insulated 1,200-square-foot house. A season including 6,310 degree-days (65 degrees minus average temperature times days) would require an estimated 18,500 kilowatt-hours, and so electric resistance heating would cost approximately $450 as against a little over $100 for gas.

square-foot home[10] with an average heat loss of 50,000 BTU's per hour at approximately current electric and utility gas rates and costs per gallon of fuel oil and liquid petroleum gas.

It also shows how this ratio between electric space heating and utility gas space heating can be lowered if the effective electric heating rate is lowered to 2 cents, 1.75 cents, 1.5 cents, or 1 cent per kilowatt-hour.

Prospects for Reducing Electric-Gas Differential through Rising Gas Prices[11]

Studies of the competitive cost of fossil fuels and electricity, and the probable future price trends of fossil fuels, tended to show that there would not be an acute shortage of natural gas and/or crude oil supply in the United States at least until the 1980s and probably not until after

---

[10] A 1,200-square-foot home is the approximate average size for a four-room, one-floor structure or a five-room apartment, and in the Midwest a 50,000 BTU heat loss per hour is considered average for well-insulated premises of this size.

[11] The higher fossil fuel prices and environmental concerns of the 1970s were not fully anticipated in this forecast. Actually higher fuel prices, when electricity is generated from fossil fuel, work against electric heating, since generating and transmission make the heat/fuel ratio much less for resistance electric heating. In the longer run environmental concerns are likely to favor electric heating as the clean fuels (natural gas and low sulfur oil) become scarce since pollutants can be better removed centrally.

the year 2000. The indigenous U.S. supply was already being supplemented with Canadian gas, and there was talk of building a pipe line from the Mexican gas fields to the United States. Also, new ways were being tried out to liquefy natural gas and transport it in specially built tankers from overseas sources. New ways of producing synthetic or manufactured gas from coal at the mine mouth were being experimented with and might become commercially feasible before the natural gas supply runs out. Finally, chemical fuel cells of various types and midget atomic power plants have been under experimentation.

The conclusion reached from the fuel studies was that even assuming that natural gas rates rise more rapidly than electric rates (as they have in the past 15 years), to hope for equality of rates on a BTU basis between gas and electricity in less than 20 years was unrealistic. In fact, the more likely time for possible equalization of gas and electric rates was thought to be 40 years hence, rather than 20 years.

National Range of Space-Heating Rates

An analysis of the space-heating rates that were offered by private utilities in increasing numbers across the country indicated that the range of the space-heating charges by those companies which were beginning to do considerable space-heating business was seldom higher than 1.5 cents. Rates higher than 2 cents per kilowatt-hour were producing little business.

In analyzing the data of Exhibit 12–2E (shown on pages 364–65), the economic research department was particularly concerned with relating the annual penetration rate into the household heating market to the rates charged. The department recognized that the time the rate had been in effect and the climatic conditions were important factors in interpreting the data that was available.

The second critical relationship was the problem of interpreting the consequences of increased penetration in home heating for the winter peak. Home heating requirements could be expected to have a daily pattern that would be reasonably constant in the current drawn from the system. The relatively minor daily peak could be expected in the morning hours and the demand at the usual winter peak times, 4:30–7:30 P.M., should be expected to be somewhat less than average because of the warming daytime effects and because of household activity in the early evening. On a cold January or February day about 1 percent of annual heating requirements might be required.[12]

---

[12] In the northern Illinois area covered by the Urban's system, annual degree days ranged from 6,100 to 6,500. (A degree day represents the daily difference between a 65° mean temperature and the actual average temperature.) The coldest day to be expected could show a minimum of −10 and a maximum of about 15° or an average of about 2.5. This would represent 62.5° days, about 1 percent of the total.

With these considerations in mind, the following calculations could be made:

Increase in kilowatt-hours generated per 1 percent increase in residential electric space heating saturation would be 1.6 percent (20,000 homes times 18,500 kilowatt-hours heating requirement divided by 23.3 billion kilowatt-hours, the total amount of current transmitted in 1961).

Probable increase in the winter peak load for each percentage increase in heating saturation would be the 1.6 percent times 3.65 percent or approximately 5.8 percent. The 3.65 factor recognizes that on a very cold day the heating demand of 1 percent of the year's requirements would be 365/100 of a load evenly spread throughout the year.

Cost Data

The committee considered three principal ways for determining cost to serve: (1) to charge full annual system peak responsibility to a particular type of load (as was becoming the practice for the air-conditioning load); (2) to average the chargeable responsibility for establishing the monthly maximum demands, and to charge the average monthly demand costs to the new load; and (3) to charge no peak or maximum demand responsibility to space-heating loads. The third method would produce a marginal cost-to-serve figure which includes incremental investment and maintenance charges (if any) directly chargeable to the new load and direct fuel and operating costs for the energy consumed, but does not prorate existing costs over the additional load expected.

The principal difference in these three methods was how peak or system maximum demand charges were assessed against the particular type of load being considered. The method of computing cost-to-serve off-peak night water-heating charges was one form of computation of incremental rates, since it was assumed that night water-heating loads did not add to system investment but rather increased the overall daily usage of utility facilities. In view of the finding that space-heating load was likely to have a slow rate of growth, an incremental method of computing cost to serve might be justified for the foreseeable future.

The average peak-load method of computation was a compromise between the full-peak and the no-peak charge methods. Its use was most suitable when the variation between monthly peaks was so reduced that there would be little chance for scheduling heavy overhaul in any one season of the year, thus requiring increased reserve capacity to provide overhaul periods.

If and when a substantial saturation of electric space heating could be achieved, such load would probably first become dominant during cold spells in January or February. Under already existing system conditions, as extra Christmas lighting was dropped, and early evening commercial lighting loads decreased with the increase of daylight, the time of the

EXHIBIT 12–2E

Saturation of Electric Space Heating in the United States
(as of December 31, 1961)

Effective Date of Current Space-Heating Rate	Name of Electric Utility	Number of Residential Customers in Thousands	Principal State Served	Lowest Block Rate Applicable to Space and Water Heaters		Electric Space Heating Saturation as of Dec. 31, 1961	
				Space (Cents)	Water (Cents)	Heat Pumps —Percent Saturation	Resistance— Percent Saturation
1. NEW ENGLAND STATES							
1961..........	New England Electric System	756.5	Massachusetts	2.00[1]	1.30[2]	0.00	0.10
1958..........	Western Massachusetts Electric Company	125.1	Massachusetts	1.30[2]	1.30[2]	0.00	0.70
2. MIDDLE ATLANTIC STATES							
1958..........	New York State Electric and Gas Corporation	420.8	New York	1.20[2]	1.20[5]	0.00	1.00
1961..........	Public Service Electric and Gas	1,253.1	New Jersey	1.50	1.03[2]	0.00	0.02
1961..........	Philadelphia Electric Company[3]	926.2	Pennsylvania	2.00[4]	1.00[2]	0.00	0.01
1961..........	Baltimore Electric and Gas Company[5]	492.7	Maryland	1.60[4]	1.75[1]	...[6]	0.02
3. SOUTHEASTERN STATES (EXCLUDING TENNESSEE)							
1959[9]..........	Appalachian Electric Power Company	437.7	Virginia	1.50[1]	1.10[1]	0.20	1.50
1957..........	Georgia Power Company	642.1	Georgia	1.00[4]	1.00[1]	0.24	0.41
1962..........	Alabama Power Company[7]	577.0	Alabama	1.00[4]	1.20[1]	0.50	0.80
1962..........	Florida Power Corporation	257.9	Florida	1.60[4]	1.42[1]	3.00	5.40
83 (a). TENNESSEE (TVA)							
1939..........	Electric Power Board of Chattanooga	76.4	Tennessee	0.75[1]	0.40[1]	2.70	52.80
1938..........	Knoxville Utility Board	71.6	Tennessee	0.75[1]	0.40[1]	0.65	43.00
1959..........	Memphis Light, Gas and Water Division[8]	165.3	Tennessee	0.70[1]	0.70[1]	0.05	1.50
1939..........	Nashville Electric Service	117.1	Tennessee	0.75[1]	0.40[1]	0.00	40.00
4. GREAT LAKES AND UPPER MISSISSIPPI VALLEY STATES							
1961[9]..........	Ohio Power Company	418.4	Ohio	1.40[1]	1.00[1]	0.07	1.90
1949..........	Indiana and Michigan Electric Company	200.4	Indiana	1.50[1]	1.00	0.10	3.50
1959..........	Detroit Edison Company	1,177.0	Michigan	2.00[1]	...[10]	...[6]	0.02
1961..........	Central Illinois Public Service Company	203.4	Illinois	1.90[4]	1.40[1]	0.00	0.30
1961..........	Northern States Power Company[11]	654.0	Minnesota	2.00[1]	2.00[1]	0.00	0.07
1960..........	Union Electric Company[12]	550.8	Missouri	1.50[4]	...[12]	...[6]	0.40
5. SOUTHWESTERN STATES							
1961..........	Oklahoma Gas and Electric Company[13]	309.3	Oklahoma	1.20[4]	1.20[4]	0.23	0.12
1960..........	Central Power and Light Company[14]	209.4	Texas	1.00[4]	1.90[2]	0.55	0.27
1952..........	Salt River Power District[15]	92.8	Arizona	1.00[4]	1.00[4]	4.22	1.01

EXHIBIT 12–2E (Continued)

Effective Date of Current Space-Heating Rate	Name of Electric Utility	Number of Residential Customers in Thousands	Principal State Served	Lowest Block Rate Applicable to Space and Water Heaters		Electric Space Heating Saturation as of Dec. 31, 1961	
				Space (cents)	Water (cents)	Heat Pumps —Percent Saturation	Resistance— Percent Saturation
		6. Pacific Coast States					
1961..............	Southern California Edison Company	1,470.7	California	1.40[1]	1.10[1]	0.50	1.40
1961[9]..............	Portland General Electric Company	233.4	Oregon	1.10[1]	0.70[1]	0.10	16.00
1960[9]..............	Tacoma City Light	57.0	Washington	1.20[1]	0.62[1]	0.00	9.60
1960[9]..............	Washington Water Power	129.0	Washington	1.20[1]	0.80[1]	0.03	10.00
1960..............	Idaho Power Company	114.6	Idaho	1.75[1]	0.90[1]	...[6]	0.86
Total for United States.................		36,193.8				0.02	1.10

Notes to Exhibit 12–2E.

[1] Uncontrolled.

[2] Limited usage hours permitted.

[3] Philadelphia Electric Company seasonal space-heating rate is $2 per kilowatt based on 60 percent of connected resistance heating load, plus 2 cents per kilowatt-hour for all monthly usage above 500. Applicable from October through the following May.

[4] Seasonal data, applicable in heating season only.

[5] Baltimore Electric and Gas Company seasonal space-heating rate is applicable for billing months November through May, and provides a low rate of 1.6 cents per kilowatt-hour for all over 600 kilowatt-hours being billed.

[6] Less than 0.01 of 1 percent.

[7] Alabama Power Company's space-heating rate provides for a 0.2-cent reduction in kilowatt-hour charge for all kilowatt-hours consumed over 1,363 per month, November through April.

[8] The contract between the Memphis Light, Gas and Water Division and the TVA was renegotiated in 1959 after Congress refused to pass appropriations for TVA to build a special generating station for Memphis; hence the variation in rates.

[9] Promotional rate in effect before current rate.

[10] The Detroit Edison Company's water-heating rate is a flat monthly charge of from $4 to $7, depending on gallonage of tank. No metering is required, but a time switch is required to control heating hours to 20 per day.

[11] In Minneapolis a 1.5 percent surcharge is applied to all bills. In St. Paul the minimum rate is 2.1 cents per kilowatt-hour. In Winona only, the company has separate water-heating rates which are 1.5 cents per kilowatt-hour for uncontrolled water heating and 1.3 cents for controlled.

[12] The Union Electric Company has established a seasonal flat rate of 2 cents per kilowatt-hour for the four summer billing periods and 1.5 cents per kilowatt-hour during the eight winter billing periods for homes having both electric water heating and electric space heating; off-peak control for either is not required.

[13] Oklahoma Gas and Electric Company allows 0.9-cent discount for all kilowatt-hours consumed over 600 per month for the period from November through April for space-heating installations of 3-kilowatt capacity or over. This, in effect, extends the year-round water-heating rate to space heating during the winter months.

[14] Central Power and Light Company has an all-purpose seasonal residential rate with a bottom charge of 1.25 cents per kilowatt-hour. It also offers an alternate combination of rates: controlled water heating (year-round), 1 cent per kilowatt-hour, and a space-heating rate of 1 cent per kilowatt-hour from approximately November 1 through April. The customer's general usage (lighting, range, appliances, etc.) is charged for on the regular residential rate.

[15] Salt River water- and space-heating rate is applicable from November through April, when water heating and space heating are separately metered. Bottom step of general residential rate applicable to general usage is 1.7 cents.

Sources: "33rd Annual Appliance Survey," *Electric Light and Power*, May and August, 1962. Rate data only: Federal Power Commission, *National Electric Rates*.

daily system peak of the electric system tended to shift in February from a 5:00–6:00 P.M. to a 10:00–11:00 A.M. morning peak produced by industrial load. Space-heating systems loads which would be heaviest in prolonged cold spells could conceivably be the cause for changing the hour of the monthly January or February peak from 10:00–11:00 A.M. to 7:00–8:00 A.M. before other monthly peaks were affected. On the other

EXHIBIT 12–2F

Comparison of Costs to Serve an Average Residential Electric Space-Heating Load during a Normal Winter Season

	Cents per Kilowatt-Hour		
	Full Peak Responsibility	*Average Peak Responsibility*	*No Peak Responsibility*
1. Capacity costs:*			
Generating†	0.435	0.375	. . . .
Transmission‡	0.255	0.180	. . . .
Distribution, including customer costs §	0.450	0.345	0.165
Total capacity costs	1.140	0.900	0.165
2. Operating and maintenance costs:#			
Generating	0.075	0.060	. . . .
Transmission	0.008	0.003	. . . .
Distribution, including meter reading and billing costs	0.045	0.015	0.015
Total operating and mainte- nance costs	0.128	0.078	0.015
3. Fuel costs‖	0.450	0.450	0.450
4. Total cost to serve, excluding certain unallocated executive and financial costs	1.718	1.428	0.630
Percentage ratio of (1) to (2) and (3) to (2)	120.3	100.0	0.441
Percentage ratio of (3) and (2) to (1)	100.0	83.0	0.334

* Capacity costs applied to plant—carrying charges of 12 percent based on a 30-year plant life were applide to plant costs. This percentage, computed by the level-premium method, assumes a 6.5 percent return on equity, a 52 percent debt ratio, a 3.85 percent cost of debt money, and a straight-line depreciation for tax purposes. State and local tax rates vary, depending upon location of plant within the urban area or the suburban areas served by the Urban Electric Company; therefore a weighted average rate of 1.15 percent was applied for the combined state and local rates.

† Generating capacity costs include all costs to build a generating station, including land, structures, and equipment up to and including generating station transformer yards.

‡ Transmission capacity costs include all costs to build and maintain the high-voltage transmission system (66,000 volts and higher) from generating station yard terminals to and including primary distribution centers, where the current is stepped down from high to medium voltage (12,000 to 66,000 volts).

§ Distribution capacity costs include (1) land, structures, and equipment from the primary distribution center terminals through the secondary substations, where voltage is again stepped down from 12,000 volts or higher to 4,000 volts or equivalent thereof; (2) from the distribution substation terminals through the alley transformers, where the current is stepped down from 4,000 volts to 110–20 to 220–40 volts (using voltages) or combinations; (3) company-owned low-voltage equipment on customer premises such as individual service drops and meter equipment.

Operating and maintenance costs, except fuel, are all costs of labor and material used in operation and maintenance of the system, and appertain to the same segments of the electrical system as do the capacity costs. Meter reading, billing, and customer service costs are included under distribution costs.

‖ Fuel charges are the cost of fuel on the kilowatt-hour basis used for generating electricity. They are normally converted to a coal-equivalent basis, although other fuels, such as natural gas and fuel oil, may be used seasonally or only during emergencies.

hand, space-heating load would contribute nothing to July-August-September monthly peak loads, and would be unlikely to change the time of May, June, and October monthly maximum demands until a very high degree of saturation was attained. Therefore, by averaging the expected contributions of space heating for each of the 12 months of the year, a basis for computing investment charges on space-heating load could be established. Such an average charge is more than the incremental cost, but smaller than full-peak responsibility charges.

Exhibit 12–2F, based on an Urban Company space-heating cost-to-serve study, illustrates the comparatively wide spread in results obtained from computing costs on the basis of the three methods outlined. These figures do not include general administrative expenses and certain minor items which were not usually allocated by functions. In determining any rate required to meet the cost to serve, these unallocated expenses were added to the total of itemized costs on an overall percentage basis. They amount to about one eighth of the total.

The Rate Structure

There are various forms in which a winter space-heating rate can be offered. First, it can be a specific single-usage or flat rate which applies only to electric space heating. Such a rate has to be made applicable in conjunction with the appropriate general service rate and also requires separate metering of heating load to administer.

Second, when the block form of rate rather than the demand form of rate is used, a new low block step can be added to an existing general service rate.[13] The problem in this type of procedure for the Rate Committee was to set the volume at which the heating step became effective great enough to insure that the bulk of all other electric services furnished the customer would be charged for at the general-service rate levels during the nonheating season. On the other hand, the effective volume of the space-heating step should be set low enough so that all space heating would fall in the space-heating step, particularly during the heavy heating season (November through March in the geographic area served by the Urban Electric Company). Inasmuch as residential summer air conditioning, per se, tends to increase customer summer usage above winter general service usage levels, the balancing point for applicability of the space-heating step was not easy to determine. The chief advantage of the all-purpose rate was that it required no special metering or billing. The rate (at least theoretically) would be available for any customer using enough kilowatt-hours for any purpose to become eligible for the low steps of the rate.

---

[13] For an explanation of rate forms, see the section entitled "Note on Rates" below.

A third form of space-heating rates was to establish, in effect, a "larger user" rate, but restrict its applicability to customers whose principal means of space heating were all electric. It had all the advantages of the second form of rate, but could adjust the blocks more readily for general-usage and water-heating purposes, without making these adjustments available to all customers. Such a special rate could be offered only for a limited period of time and could then be dropped if found unsatisfactory for any but existing customers without further formal commission procedure.

Notes on Rates

There are three usual forms of general service rates: block, demand, and flat. Governmental rates normally follow the nonresidential form of rates, while so-called "special" rates, when used, can be in any form, but generally are in effect special contracts applying to only one large customer whose usage needs are peculiar to himself. Such special contracts are filed with the utility commission having jurisdiction, but are normally not published as a part of the utility's rate schedule available to the public.

1. Residential rates are generally "block" rates, that is, the total consumption of the customer as recorded by a watt-hour meter is divided into steps or "blocks," with the rate of charge per kilowatt-hour progressively declining for each block as the total consumption increases.

A hypothetical example of a block-type rate schedule is:

First.................	25 kwh at 5 cents per kwh
Next.................	75 kwh at 3 cents per kwh
All over.............	100 kwh at 2 cents per kwh
Minimum bill.........	$1

2. For nonresidential customers the "demand" form of rate is generally used, and it has been tried experimentally for large residential users. This form of rate differs from the block rate in that the two basic components of utility costs are separated and a separate charge is made for each component. The first component is frequently called the "readiness to serve" cost. When a customer is connected to a public utility's lines, the utility by law is required to furnish the customer with any amount of service at any hour of the day or night he desires to use it ("demand" it), up to the capacity of all of his electricity-using equipment. This means that the utility must have generating and distribution capacity available at all times to meet the customers' "demands." The utility calls these basic costs, which are incurred regardless of how much use the customers actually make of electric service, "readiness to serve" costs, or for billing purposes the "demand charge."

The second type of costs borne by a utility are the direct costs of producing and distributing electric energy. The charge made to cover these costs is called the "energy" charge.

Therefore the bill of a customer who is on a demand rate contains two charges: (*a*) for the "demand" he created during the billing period, usually expressed in dollars or cents per kilowatt of demand; and (*b*) an energy charge computed in cents or decimals thereof per kilowatt-hour of energy actually consumed.

A hypothetical example of a demand form is shown in Exhibit 12–2G.

EXHIBIT 12–2G

Rate 13—Industrial Electric Service (Off-Peak)
(extract—includes selected paragraphs only)

AVAILABILITY

This rate is available only to customers receiving alternating current service hereunder at their present locations on November 22, 1954, for all commercial and industrial requirements, and who have not subsequently discontinued doing so. Upon the expiration of the customer's availability period under Rider 21, or upon the discontinuance of service under this rate by the Customer for any reason, whichever first occurs, he shall not again be served hereunder. . . .

EXPLANATION OF RATE

The charge for electric service under this rate is the sum of a charge for the maximum demand created and a charge for the energy supplied. Three operating periods are specified corresponding to load conditions on the Company's system, namely, "peak," "daytime," and "nighttime," and a different demand charge is provided for demands created during each period. The peak billing demand is determined on an annual basis and the off-peak daytime and nighttime billing demands are determined on a monthly basis, as hereinafter provided.

CHARGES

Demand Charge

The number of kilowatts of peak, daytime, and nighttime billing demand shall be charged for in the order named, consecutively through the blocks of kilowatts in the following table, at the prices per kilowatt for the respective demand periods (for example—200 kilowatts of peak billing demand, 800 kilowatts of daytime billing demand, and 100 kilowatts of nighttime billing demand will be charged for at $2.15, $1.00, and $0.55, respectively):

Peak Billing Demand	Daytime Billing Demand	Nighttime Billing Demand		Kilowatts of Billing Demand for the Month
$2.15	$1.35	$0.75	per kilowatt for the first..............	200
1.50	1.00	0.60	per kilowatt for the next..............	800
1.40	0.90	0.55	per kilowatt for the next..............	2,500
1.15	0.75	0.50	per kilowatt for all over..............	3,500

Energy Charge		*Kilowatt Hours Supplied in the Month*
2.49¢ per kilowatt hour for the first...................		6,000
1.14¢ per kilowatt hour for the next...................		24,000
0.90¢ per kilowatt hour for the next...................		70,000
0.68¢ per kilowatt hour for the next...................		400,000
0.59¢ per kilowatt hour for all over...................		500,000

EXHIBIT 12–2G (Continued)

The energy charge for each kilowatt hour supplied in the month is subject to adjustment in accordance with the provisions of the Company's Fuel Adjustment rider.

The gross energy charge shall be ten percent more than the sum of the net energy charge and the "Fuel Adjustment," for the first 100,000 kilowatt hours supplied in the month.

Minimum Charge

The regular minimum monthly demand charge shall be $60.00 for the first month which includes any part of the peak period and for the succeeding four months. For all other months the regular minimum monthly demand charge shall be $40.00.

DEMAND PERIODS

The peak period is the period between the hours of 4:30 P.M. and 7:30 P.M. of each day from each October 15 to the next succeeding February 14, inclusive, except Saturdays, Sundays, Thanksgiving Day, Christmas Day, and New Year's Day.

The Company reserves the right, upon giving the Customer not less than three months' advance written notice, to change the peak period to not more than eight consecutive half-hours between the hours of 8:00 A.M. and 9:00 P.M. of each day in any period of not more than 124 consecutive days, Saturdays, Sundays, and legal holidays excepted.

The daytime period is the period between 8:00 A.M. and 9:00 P.M. of each day, except that it shall not include any period which is within the peak period.

The nighttime period is the period between 9:00 P.M. of each day and 8:00 A.M. of the following day.

Maximum Demands

The peak maximum demand in any month shall be the greater of (*a*) the average of the three highest 30-minute demands established during the peak period, if any, on different days of such month or (*b*) the number of kilowatts by which the daytime maximum demand exceeds 25,000 kilowatts.

The daytime maximum demand in any month shall be the average of the three highest 30-minute demands established during the daytime period on different days of such month.

The nighttime maximum demand in any month shall be the average of the three highest 30-minute demands established during the nighttime period on different nights of such month.

Questions

1. Assuming a flat incremental rate was charged, what rate would you recommend? How could such a rate be administered?

2. Consider the advantages and disadvantages of a flat rate against a new step in block-rate structure. Would it help to restrict the step to October through April?

3. The committee's analysis led it to expect a slow rate of growth in demand. What does this suggest about the relevance for costs of full peak responsibility, average peak responsibility, or no peak responsibility?

4. Would you consider it price discrimination to be charging the kilowatt-hour rate for lighting of 2.45 cents and for space heating of 1.50 cents at the same time of day? Why, or why not? What would the utility lose and gain by setting up a block-rate structure to avoid such separate rates?

CASE 12–3. Anheuser-Busch, Inc., and Federal Trade Commission*

At the end of 1953, Anheuser-Busch, Inc., brewers of Budweiser beer, had completed several years of close contention with Schlitz for the position of number one brewery in national market share. It held about 7 percent of the national market but was first in no major market, and in its home area around St. Louis was fourth in market share behind three regional brewers, one of which, Falstaff, was rapidly growing. (Falstaff was to become the sixth largest brewer in 1954 and fourth in 1955, even though its distribution was limited to 26 states.) After a wage increase in October, 1953, most national brewers increased prices generally by 15 cents a case.[14] Budweiser incurred serious sales losses in several parts of the country, partly because distributors chose to increase the spread between national and local or regional beers by as much as 50 cents a case. In the home market of St. Louis, competitors maintained their pre-October prices of $2.35 a case, and Budweiser's price was held at $2.93.

On January 4, 1954, Anheuser-Busch cut the price of Budweiser by 25 cents. On June 21, with its share up from about an eighth to a sixth of the St. Louis market, the price was cut again to $2.35, the level of competitive beer prices. After the second cut, Budweiser's share moved up to almost 40 percent of the market, and it took first position; all competitors but Falstaff lost heavily in market share. After investigation the Federal Trade Commission issued a complaint charging Anheuser-Busch, Inc., with illegal price discrimination under Section 2 (a) of the Robinson-Patman Act, on the grounds that it "discriminated in price between purchasers of its beer of like grade and quality by selling it to some of its customers at higher prices than to others . . . and the price cut was sufficient to direct business from its competitors . . . and there was a reasonable probability it would substantially lessen competition in the respondent's line of commerce."[15]

In March, 1955, the price of Budweiser was raised 45 cents to $2.80, and that of competitive beers by 15 cents to $2.50. Anheuser-Busch then introduced a new beer, comparable in price to its competitors, without real initial success; and its market share in St. Louis rapidly dwindled to 21 percent by July 31, 1955, and to 17.5 percent by January 31, 1956.[16]

---

* Most of the material in this case is drawn from *Federal Trade Commission* v. *Anheuser-Busch*, FTC Docket 6331; and *Anheuser-Busch* v. *Federal Trade Commission*, 363 U.S. 536 (1960), U.S. 7th Circuit Court of Appeals, April 5, 1959, and January 25, 1961.

[14] A case consisted of 24 12-ounce bottles.

[15] Docket 6331 cited by Circuit Court, April 4, 1959.

[16] Anheuser-Busch has continued this policy of meeting local prices not with Budweiser but with Busch Bavarian, as listeners of the ball games of the Busch-owned St. Louis Cardinals have been well aware.

The changing market shares are shown in Exhibit 12–3A. It also chose to contest the complaint but lost the trial before the Federal Trade Commision, with a cease and desist order being issued against the company in 1957.

The company decided to appeal the order to the circuit court; and in April, 1959, Judge Schnackenberg's decisions set aside the order on the ground that the price cuts had not been discriminatory. "Even if we assume these cuts were directed at Anheuser-Busch's local competitors, by its cuts Anheuser-Busch employed the same means of competition against all of them. Moreover, it did not discriminate among those who

EXHIBIT 12–3A

Estimated Market Shares for Beer in St. Louis Market, 1953–56

	For Periods Ended—				
	December 31, 1953	June 30, 1954	March 1, 1955	July 31, 1955	January 31, 1956
Anheuser-Busch..............	12.5	16.65	39.3	21.0	17.5
Griesedieck, Brothers.........	14.4	12.6	4.8	7.4	6.2
Falstaff.....................	29.4	32.0	29.0	36.6	43.2
Griesedieck Western..........	38.9	33.0	23.0	27.8	27.3
All others..................	4.8	5.8	3.9	7.2	5.8

Notes: In the period ended June 30, 1954, total sales were up by 2.7 percent over the similar period in 1963. Assume that market shares are in physical units and that the period ended December 31, 1953, is for six months (the other periods being inclusive from previous date). Assume also that the sales in the June 30, 1954, period primarily reflect the first price reduction.

Source: Originally FTC Docket 6331.

bought its beer in the St. Louis area. All could buy at the same prices." The decision recognized that the seldom-used criminal provisions of Section 3 of the Robinson-Patman Act specify geographical price discrimination, but the Federal Trade Commission has no jurisdiction under this section. The decision was on the narrow grounds that no price discrimination, as defined by Section 2 (*a*) of the act, had taken place, and so did not consider the company's other defenses of no injury to competition and of meeting competitors' prices in good faith.

This decision was rapidly disposed of when the FTC appealed to the Supreme Court. The Supreme Court's ruling emphasized the law's phraseology, "where the effect may be substantially to lessen competition or to create a monopoly in *any line of commerce*." While congressional concern in enacting the Robinson-Patman Amendment to the Clayton Act was principally with the impact on secondary lines of competition of the bargaining power of large purchasers (notably chain stores), *any line of commerce* included primary competition as well. In this case the primary competition was among the brewers operating in St. Louis, while the secondary competition was among the distributors and retailers of beer.

The court went on to say that a price discrimination is merely a price difference; it was not necessary that different prices be charged to different purchasers in the same market. Here the price differences were between areas—while Budweiser was sold first at $2.93 and then at $2.35 in St. Louis, it was being sold at $3.44 in Chicago and $3.79 in San Francisco. Anheuser-Busch did not attempt to justify these price differences as being justified by cost differences, although with three breweries, some difference in transport costs would necessarily exist. The court then went on to state that there was no flat prohibition of price differentials, since such differentials were but one element in a Section 2 (*a*) violation. "In fact," it said, "Anheuser-Busch has vigorously contended this very case on the entirely separate grounds of insufficient injury to competition and good faith lowering of price to meet competition." The case was sent back to the circuit court for findings on these grounds.

Again, in 1961, Judge Schnackenberg gave a decision on narrow grounds, ruling that there was no injury to competition and in view of this it was not necessary to determine whether the price cut was a good-faith effort to meet competition. He saw the two price reductions as a temporary "experimental method of sales promotion . . . made necessary by competitive conditions" and noted that the two competitors which lost substantial shares had problems other than Budweiser's price cut. Griesedieck Brothers had introduced a new product in 1953 which was "badly named, poorly merchandised, and bitter in taste." Griesedieck Western was purchased by Carling Brewery Company in 1954 after it had been maintaining a highly liquid position at the expense of renewal of production facilities. Thus the court found that the commission failed to prove that the "price reductions in 1954 caused any present-actual injury to competition." The commission had been concerned with potential injury as well, finding that there was "nothing in this record to show that what Anheuser-Busch did in the St. Louis market could not be done in future markets," and that as a nationwide company with assets far greater than local competitors, it could use income from the rest of its business to stabilize possible losses from a price raid. The cricuit court was not persuaded by this argument.

"If the projection is based upon predatoriness and buccaneering it can be reasonably forecast that an adverse effect on competition may occur, . . . [but] Anheuser-Busch exercised a proper restraint in its use of competitive power, not a wilful misuse thereof." This proved to be the last word on this case, though not necessarily the definitive word on the question of business actions that may injure competition.

Questions

1. Do the facts of this case indicate that there was price discrimination in the economic sense?
2. Why do you think the FTC was concerned enough about the business strategy in this case to see it through three court hearings? (Actually, the commission was probably ready for another appeal but was dissuaded by the Solicitor General.)
3. Share elasticity of demand with respect to price has been defined as the percentage change in market share (a percentage of percentage figure) over the percentage change in price. Was the demand indicated to be elastic in this sense as shown in Exhibit 12–3A? What assumptions must be made for this conclusion?
4. What advantages may secondary brands such as Busch Bavarian or Old Milwaukee (Schlitz) have in competition with local and regional brewers?

chapter 13

Price Strategies When Sellers Are Few

A VERY COMMON situation in manufacturing, wholesaling, retailing, and other fields is that of oligopoly, in which the number of sellers of a particular item is so small that each seller must consider his rivals' reactions to his own actions. It has been pointed out that the oligopolist is not faced by a single demand curve but rather that the curve can assume a great variety of shapes (and even a positive slope), depending on the nature and extent of rivals' reactions to its pricing decisions. Both in monopoly and pure competition no such reactions of rivals alter demand; in monopoly there are no rivals, in pure competition the impact of one firm's action is negligible because of its share of the market. Oligopoly thus differs sharply from both monopoly and pure competition, in both of which situations demand can be considered to "stay put" while the firm adjusts itself to the demand-cost situation.

Oligopoly is common in local markets throughout the country. Many towns and cities are large enough to support only a few drugstores, variety stores, department stores, theaters, building materials producers, and so forth. Especially where there is considerable geographic separation between cities, each such seller serves a substantial percentage of the local market and is usually highly sensitive to attempts of competitors to capture larger shares of the market by price cuts or other means.

The larger the market in which a product is sold, the more opportunity there is for a large number of firms (of efficient size) to participate. Nevertheles, oligopoly is common also in industries which serve national and international markets. Here, the situation is usually not literally one of only a "few" sellers; but frequently there are only a few large firms plus a number of small firms, with the dominant companies accounting for a large percentage of total sales. An oligopolistic situation then exists between the large firms, each being highly sensitive to the actions of the others. The small firms in the field may not be directly concerned with rivals' reactions, but the demand for their products and thus their own price-quantity decisions will be conditioned by the interaction of their major rivals.

Reactions to Price Changes under Oligopoly

What are the assumptions that one of the few firms in an industry might make about the reaction of its rivals to a price change it makes? The two simplest ones are, first, that all other firms will promptly follow

FIGURE 13–1

Possible Reactions to Price Change under Oligopoly

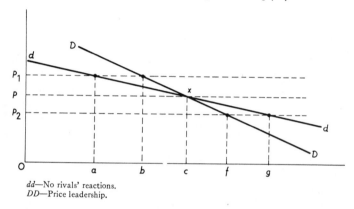

dd—No rivals' reactions.
DD—Price leadership.

the same price change, and, second, that no firms will make any price changes. The demand curves resulting from these two reactions are shown in Figure 13–1. *DD*, labeled the price leadership demand curve, is relatively less elastic than *dd*. Its elasticity can be considered essentially that of the total demand for the commodity insofar as the products of the different firms are homogeneous enough to constitute a commodity. In contrast, *dd* is more elastic since it reflects the gains or losses in sales by competitors who left their prices unaltered. With many firms, perfect information and standard products *dd* would be the demand curve facing the firm under perfect competition and *DD* would be irrelevant. (In that case *dd* would be horizontal.) With very substantial product differentiation so that rival firms furnish only distant substitutes, *dd* and *DD* coincide as the monopoly demand curve. The concept of price leadership would be irrelevant, since there would be no significant rivals to follow.

In Figure 13–1 these four possible demand curves are shown: *dxd*, *DxD*, *dxD*, and *Dxd*. Let us consider them each in turn. First, *dxd* represents the limiting case for oligopoly. The consistent absence of any reaction to a firm's price changes would indicate that it produced a negligible proportion of a standard commodity (pure competition), or was the producer of a differentiated good with either so many close competitors that none was significantly affected by its actions (monopolistic competition) or with such great distinctiveness that no close competitors were present to retaliate (monopoly).

If each firm in this industry could assume that its price changes were always exactly duplicated as indicated by DxD, the monopoly model could be an appropriate approximation for the industry. The equilibrium price might be somewhat different from a single firm monopoly if there were economies or diseconomies of scale because of the difference in the relevant output range for the cost curves. The very condition (of several sellers rather than one) that distinguishes oligopoly from monopoly suggests that the barriers to entry are likely to be lower so that the prices will be set at levels low enough to limit entry and that oligopolies might have more limited prospects of monopoly gains even with strict adherence to the price leaders' choices.

Central to the issue of public policy toward oligopoly situations is the question under what market conditions will it be possible for oligopolists to maintain prices based on the industry elasticity of demand which is reflected in DxD. Firmly established price leadership could be behavior consistent with the hypothesis advanced by Stigler and others that oligopolists wish to collude to maximize joint profits. But as Stigler points out, "such collusion is impossible for many firms and is much more effective in some circumstances than others."[1] Policing the operation of the tacit collusion involved in consistent price leadership is likely to be more difficult the greater the number of firms and the greater the differences in size of firms, in products, and in the purchase requirements of buyers.

The third possible demand curve from Figure 13–1 is dxD, the well-known "kinky or kinked demand curve," initially advanced as an explanation of rigid oligopoly prices.[2] For a change in price upward from p, the dx portion indicates no rivals' reactions. Competitors are satisfied to enjoy the increased quantity of sales available to them since the price of the oligopolist making the price change was a significant determinant of their own demands. (Their respective dd curves were shifted to the right by the action of the firm making the price increase.) For a change in

---

[1] George J. Stigler, *The Organization of Industry* (Homewood, Ill.: Richard D. Irwin, Inc. 1968), p. 39. Reprinted from *Journal of Political Economy*, February, 1964.

[2] The kinked demand curve analysis is associated especially with Paul M. Sweezy, "Demand Conditions under Oligopoly," *Journal of Political Economy*, August, 1939; and in a different form with R. L. Hall and C. J. Hitch, "Price Theory and Business Behavior," *Oxford Economic Papers*, no. 2 (May, 1939).

price downward, the xD portion indicates the price leadership situation of exact retaliation. Other firms would be compelled to respond to the shift of their relatively elastic dd curves to the left by meeting the price cut. To put the problems in terms of equalizing MR and MC, we can recognize a substantial discontinuity in the relevant MR curve at output OC. There is a substantial gap between the high MR associated with the elastic dx segment and the much lower and conceivably negative MR curve associated with the xD segment.

The major prediction of the kinked demand curve analysis is that oligopolistic prices would be comparatively rigid in responding to cost changes (tremendous shifts in the MC curves could be accommodated in the discontinuity between the MR segments below x.) The kinked demand analysis does not assist in explaining the level of the initial price P but it was helpful in explaining price rigidities reported in many studies of the 1940s. In general economic analysis, the kinked demand curve has probably been downgraded in significance with widespread rise in prices including those of oligopolies which has been a feature of the postwar period.[3]

From the standpoint of the managerial economist, the kinked demand curve is a useful construct regardless of its general predictive power. In the postwar period, firms faced with rising costs have had to make provision for the possibility that the emerging of the kink would work against them in raising prices. A common pattern is for a firm to test for its existence by announcing a price rise effective as of a future date. If the other major firms follow it, the results are predicted by xD. If they do not follow, the firm will withdraw its prospective price increase to avoid the loss of market share indicated by the kink.

It is also a construct that illustrates that the favorable results of an aggressive strategy such as a cut in price will hinge upon avoiding or at least postponing retaliation of other firms. Secret price cutting may thus be preferred to open cuts. Major increases in advertising expenditures that could be easily followed may be avoided, while attempts for uniqueness in advertising themes that could be less easily copied may be stressed.

The fourth possible demand curve shown in Figure 13–1, Dxd, has not received the extensive theoretical attention of the others, but it does have an interesting applicability in terms of levels of near capacity operation in an industry accompanied by upward pressures in costs. Why should rivals ignore a downward price change which threatened their sales and

---

[3] As early as 1947, George Stigler published an influential article downgrading the importance of the kinked demand curve on empirical grounds that actual oligopoly prices were not significantly more rigid than others when actual prices charged, not posted prices, were taken into account. See G. J. Stigler, "The Kinked Oligopoly Demand Curve and Rigid Prices," *Journal of Political Economy*, October, 1947.

respond to an increase in prices? At high levels of operations, a firm initiating a price cut would have limited capacity to accommodate increased sales and thus would do little damage to the market position of competitors who may be already faced with the rising marginal costs of near capacity operations. At the same time, especially if there had been a general increase in costs reflecting a new labor contract or price rise in an important material, the expectations of all of the firms would be for higher prices by their competitors and there would be little fear of loss of market position through a price rise.

The four demand curves shown explicitly in Figure 13–1 suggest the following possible quantities sold per time period in response to price changes from P to P_1 or P_2. For an increase in price, the firm is predicted to sell either oa or ob; for a reduction in price, either of or og. The only alternative reactions considered have been that all rivals react exactly and immediately or that none react at all. One range of possibilities ignored so far has been that an initial price cut might produce greater price cuts by the competitors so that even at the lower price less might be sold than the quantity oc associated with price P.[4] In effect, the initial price cut was the signal for a price war in which the motive of the firm's rivals was to discipline the initiator of the price cut and possibly to reduce capacity in the industry by eliminating weaker firms.

Another range of possibilities lies within the areas bounded by the dd and DD curves. Within these areas are points representing the effective demand curves if the reaction is delayed or takes the form of price changes smaller than those of the initiator. The reaction may not necessarily take the form of a price change but could be increased advertising or product improvements by the competitor to reduce his losses and limit the initiator's advantage. Oligopolistic indeterminancy can be illustrated by drawing many possible demand curves through point x; the relevant demand curve depending upon the specific reactions of rivals.

Concentration of American Industry and Oligopoly

A popular statistical device for showing the existence of oligopolistic situations on a national basis is the "concentration ratio." This measure is the percentage of total output, shipments, sales, or employment accounted for by the largest firms in a given industry. Such ratios are published from time to time by the Bureau of the Census and the Federal Trade Commission. The ratios are greatly affected by the broadness or narrowness of industry classification—for example, the "food and kindred products" industry covers such a wide range of activities that it can scarcely show up as concentrated.

---

[4] This possibility is shown graphically in Figure 5–4 of Chapter 5 as curve D_3.

Figure 13–2 shows selected industry concentration ratios based on the percentage of sales accounted for by the largest four and eight firms in the industry. Except for passenger cars, the listing is based on the four-digit Standard Industrial Classification. The selection is more complete for highly concentrated industries with a four-firm ratio of at least 80 percent and an eight-firm ratio of 95 percent. For these the showing of oligopoly is quite conclusive, although market power may be somewhat overstated in some cases because of substitutes from other industries or imports. For example reprocessed aluminum accounts for 20 percent of aluminum product, and imports from Japan and Europe have frequently accounted for over 10 percent of automobiles sold.

Oligopoly behavior in the form of reaction by rivals has characterized the four other industries listed with four-firm concentration ratios of over 40 percent (and eight-firm ratios of over 50 percent). As in the case of steel taken up in Case 13–2, profits may still be relatively low. Even for industries with low concentrations such as cement and brick there are only a few firms serving any one region because of high transportation costs. The majority of the 8,000 newspapers are local monopo-

FIGURE 13–2

1963 Concentration Ratios for Selected Industries

S.I.C. Code	Industry	Four-Firm Ratio	Eight-Firm Ratio	Number of Firms
37151	Passenger cars	99	100	n.a.
3741	Locomotives and parts	97	99	23
3334	Primary aluminum	96	100	7
3211	Flat glass	94	99	11
3511	Steam engines and turbines	93	98	17
3641	Electric lamps	92	96	52
3672	Cathode ray picture tubes	91	95	148
2073	Chewing gum	90	97	20
2111	Cigarettes	80	100	7
3633	Household laundry equipment	78	95	31
3011	Tires and inner tubes	70	89	105
3312	Blast furnaces and steel mills	50	69	162
3522	Farm machinery and equipment	43	55	1,481
3241	Cement	29	49	55
3141	Shoes, except rubber	25	32	785
2851	Paint and allied products	23	34	1,579
2834	Pharmaceutical preparations	22	38	944
2256	Knit fabric mills	18	25	487
2711	Newspapers	15	22	7,982
3251	Brick and structural tile	12	19	401
2086	Bottled and canned soft drinks	12	17	3,569
2421	Sawmills and planning mills	11	14	11,931
3451	Screw machine products	5	8	1,861

n.a.—not available.
Source: U.S. Senate, Committee on the Judiciary, Subcommittee on Antitrust and Monopoly, Report, *Concentration Ratios in Manufacturing Industry: 1963*, Part I (Washington, D.C., 1966).

lies, although they may face intraindustry competition from television and radio and have as indirect competition regional newspapers. Perhaps the most misleading low ratio is that for "bottled and canned soft drinks," an industry that operates with many small, franchised bottlers. The five-digit industry, "flavoring syrups for soft drinks" had a four-firm concentration ratio of 89 percent in 1958, a reflection of the strong position of Coca-Cola and Pepsi-Cola. In the drug industry many monopolistic or oligopolistic positions on patented prescription drugs or widely advertised proprietary products remain unrevealed by the fairly low concentration ratios for "pharmaceutical preparations."

In general, concentration ratios for industries and broad product classes probably understate the degree of concentration in particular product markets. A recent study suggests that as many as 75 percent of 7,000 manufactured products in the finest breakdown compiled by the Department of Commerce may have four-firm concentrations of 50 percent or more of sales.[5] Economists differ substantially in their estimates of what degree of industrial concentration is necessary for oligopoly elements to be significant. A recent study contained data suggesting "that there is no relationship between profitability of concentration if the share of the four largest firms is less than about 80 percent."[6] The list of concentration ratios in Figure 13–2 suggested a 50 percent share for four firms as appropriate, a figure that is in line with other studies of profitability and concentration.[7] Carl Kaysen and Donald F. Turner using a broad grouping of industries set the minimum for oligopoly at an eight-firm concentration ratio of 33 percent and found that 62 percent of all manufacturing shipments in 1954 were then found in such industries.[8]

Pure and Differentiated Oligopoly

Pure oligopoly may be said to exist when sellers of a homogeneous commodity are few in number. This situation is more common among producers of industrial materials than in the consumer goods fields. Most consumer goods are differentiated from one another by means of brand names, trade-marks, and packaging, and usually by some differences in physical characteristics. Materials and components turned out by different companies for use as inputs into production processes are more

---

[5] Dean A. Worcester, Jr., *Monopoly, Big Business and Welfare in the Postwar United States* (Seattle: University of Washington Press, 1967), chap. 4.

[6] George J. Stigler, *The Organization of Industry* (Homewood, Ill.: Richard D. Irwin, Inc., 1968), p. 69.

[7] A recent one is that of David Schwartzman, "The Burden of Monopoly," *Journal of Political Economy*, December, 1960, p. 629.

[8] In *Antitrust Policy; an Economic and Legal Analysis* (Cambridge, Mass.: Harvard University Press, 1959).

frequently indentical. Even if the name of the producer is stamped on the good, this is not apt to influence an experienced industrial buyer if the product is, in fact, identical with that of another firm. Consumers of finished products, on the other hand, are often influenced by brand names and advertising, even where no substantial difference in the commodity actually exists. (Aspirin is a famous example.) As a consequence, "pure oligopoly" may be said to be present in such fields as the manufacture of primary aluminum, primary copper, aluminum rolling and drawing, and certain gypsum products, whereas "differentiated oligopoly" exists for automobiles, cigarettes, hard-surface floor coverings, typewriters, sewing machines, and a great many other commodities.

When oligopolistic firms are few in number and have identical products, their demands are highly interdependent. As concentration of production diminishes and as products are more differentiated, demands are less closely interdependent. If the number of firms selling in a market becomes large enough so that each can disregard the reactions of his rivals to his own price-output actions, the market situation is often designated by economists as "monopolistic competition" or "pure competition," depending on whether differentiated or nondifferentiated products are sold. In each case a single demand curve confronts the firm: in the former case, this is a downsloping monopoly demand curve; while in the latter case, it is a horizontal line. If there are *no* rivals selling the same commodity in the same market, the situation is designated as monopoly. The distinction between "monopoly" and "monopolistic competition" is not a clear one, however, since it encounters the same difficulty of classifying industries as is involved in compiling statistics on concentration. If "industry" is defined very narrowly and products are differentiated, there is only one firm in each industry (e.g., the "Campbell Soup industry"). If the industry is defined more broadly, the Campbell Soup Company becomes instead one firm of a number in the "canned soup industry." On a still broader basis, it is one of a very large number of firms in the "food and food products industry." Whether the company is "oligopolistic" or not depends on whether, in fact, its price adjustments will cause speedy reactions on the part of the other companies. If such reactions would occur, the company can be classified as a "differentiated oligopolist."

The Variety of Oligopolistic Situations as an Influence on Business Decisions

The analysis accompanying Figure 13–1 has been essentially designed to indicate the range of possible reactions that might have to be taken into account by a firm in its price decisions. It is not a simplified presentation of a generally accepted theory of oligopoly pricing. There are many oligopoly models, but there is no such generally accepted theory of oligopoly pricing. The absence of such a theory reflects the wide range of markets which may have some element of the oligopolistic interdependence that we have discussed. Some of the characteristics that may affect behavior in oligopolistic markets are the following (cases in this text are stressed as examples).

Concentration Ratios and Number of Firms. Even when concentration ratios are well above the levels accepted by most economists as oligopolistic, the variations may be great. For example, in the domestic automobile industry General Motors has usually accounted for just over 50 percent of the market and four producers for virtually 100 percent. In the steel industry, United Steel has somewhat over 25 percent, 8 producers have three quarters of the market, but approximately 75 firms produce some primary steel. In contrast, Traditional Department Store (see Case 13–4) faced many competitors on most of its product types but was particularly conscious of the rivalry of two other downtown department stores.

Homogeneity of Products. Compare automobiles that are differentiated in many features with steel ingot or with copper-beryllium alloys (see Case 13–1), both standard products. The close physical similarity of different classes of cigarettes has not stood in the way of strong brand preferences. Were everything else constant, less interdependence would be expected of the differentiated products.

Reliance on Advertising. Cigarettes and beer are heavily advertised; steel very little. Automobiles received substantial advertising, but as a percentage of the very large sales, the industry rates low.

Number of Purchasers of the Product. For example, the smaller the number of purchasers, the greater the advantages of secret price cutting for gaining sales.[9] The automobile industry with thousands of purchasing dealers is in quite a different position than the beryllium industry with a few industrial purchasers.

Economies of Scale in Plant versus Firm. If concentration rests on the economies of scale of single plants, barriers to entry may be larger than when large firms have been built up from many small plants. For example, the distilling industry had a four-firm concentration ratio of 64 percent in 1954 but the four firms operated 54 plants. Its profit record has not suggested that the oligopoly has been effective in maintaining high price-cost ratios.[10]

---

[9] This point is stressed by Stigler, *Organization of Industry*, particularly p. 54.

[10] Stigler, *Organization of Industry*, p. 54 calculated a rate of return on net worth of 7.55 percent from 1953–57 in the industry far below the 23.9 percent for sulfur and 20.3 percent for automobiles.

Rapidity of Technological Development. Unusually rapid techno-logical developments may be productive of cost differences that encourage independent price cuts. An example of a spectacular decline in price was in polyesterfiber which dropped from $1.14 per pound in 1963 to 58 cents a pound in May, 1967.[11]

Other differing characteristics such as the rate of growth of demand could be also cited. Underlying several of the market features above but worth stressing is the importance of barriers to entry in the determination of whether prices can be maintained significantly above the long-run cost levels. Which strategies will be chosen for reducing the uncertainties facing the oligopolistic firm that are discussed in the following sections will in part reflect this variety of market characteristics.

Cartelization or Formal Agreements

That the strictures of the Sherman Act against such restraints have not always been effective has been shown in the electrical price conspiracy case following Chapter 17. Even legal agreements to fix prices often break down since a firm that chooses not to abide by the agreement may have considerable incentive to cut prices if the rivals do not follow.

The experience of international cartels—such as those that have at times operated in such commodities as rubber and coffee—underlines the threat of the entry of new firms which can initially operate under the umbrella of the cartelized price and later, as they gain increased market shares, rupture the agreements. If the Organization of Oil Exporting Countries (OPEC), the oil cartel, continues to be successful in maintaining oil prices far above the cost of production, it will be because of growing demand and the willingness of Arab oil states to restrict production. Such willingness is likely because of the availability of foreign exchange in excess of immediate needs.

The sanction of government intervention frequently has been sought to make effective price and market-sharing agreements. The strong support by drug retailers for fair-trade pricing has been based on their desire that the minimum prices charged by their rivals will be predictable. Part of the past weakness of such price agreements has been that enforcement was left to private litigation and recent proposals for strengthening the McGuire-Keogh Act have been to make the government responsible for enforcement through the Federal Trade Commission. Other legalized cartel arrangements in the United States have been in the fluid milk industry—where prices in most parts of the country are controlled by federal or state commissions—and in sugar production—where import

---

[11] *The New York Times*, October 22, 1967, p. 14 f.

quotas and domestic quotas have been used to limit the supply and maintain a price that is usually far in excess of the world price.[12]

Perhaps the particular price-fixing arrangements most familiar to men who still utilize their services is that of the master barbers associations in many cities. Local business is largely exempt from the federal antitrust laws, and few of the state laws are used. The most extensive government encouragement of price-fixing arrangements was found under the National Recovery Administration (NRA) codes of 1933 and 1934. Although the industry codes were not designed for this purpose, "560 of the first 677 codes contained some provisions relating to minimum prices or costs."[13]

Price Leadership and Other Conventions

An effective method of avoiding price uncertainties and of limiting price competition may be found in the practice of price leadership. There have been antitrust questions raised about a firmly established price leadership convention,[14] but in recent years suits against such parallel action have not been pushed. Under this system of tacitly collusive pricing an important firm is usually the one to decide upon and initiate a price change, automatically followed by the other companies. It is, of course, difficult to generalize with respect to how much consultation takes place between industry officials prior to the initiation of a price change by the leader. If a great deal of interchange occurs, the system may not differ basically from that of overt agreement on price. If, however, the leader initiates the change after little or no advice from others in the industry, the form of collusion is quite different in nature. It is then primarily an "agreement to agree" on price rather than an agreement as to what the actual price should be. Frequently, the largest firm in the industry acts as price leader. If the product is sold in interstate commerce, there is danger in this practice, however, since the pattern may be too obvious to any interested antitrust investigator. For this reason, it may be safer to have other firms initiate the price change from time to time, with the "leader" a temporary follower. To carry out this sort of rotation of leadership, however, may require so much cooperation

---

[12] Students may find it of interest to check the raw sugar prices in the financial pages of their newspapers to note the current price. As of July 2, 1969, the domestic price was $0.0760; its world price was $0.0385 (per pound). This discrepancy will depend on Congress passing new legislation since the Sugar Act was defeated in 1974 to the surprise of many.

[13] Arthur R. Burns, *Decline of Competition* (New York: McGraw-Hill Book Co., 1936), pp. 471–72.

[14] "The essential combination or conspiracy in violation of the Sherman Act may be found in a course of dealings or other circumstances as well as in exchange of words. . .", *American Tobacco Co.* v. *United States*, 328 U.S. 781 (1946).

that the tacit collusion approaches overt price agreement rather than simple price agreement.

Previously in this chapter an exploratory form of price leadership has been discussed. A firm may announce a price rise for a future date and find out whether its rivals go along without risking loss of sales. It can thereby reduce its uncertainty with relatively small costs such as that of bearing the onus of proposing a price rise.

Other conventions that aim at reducing the unpredictability of rivals' responses have been part of trade association activities. Systems of reporting prices at which immediately past sales have been made may well reduce the incentive for price cutting by increasing the likelihood of retaliation, and at the very least can reduce the uncertainties of association members as to prices of competition.

Emphasis on Policies That Are Difficult to Retaliate Against

Market expanding activities of one of few sellers may well emphasize forms of nonprice competition. Both advertising and product differentiation are methods that may both serve to increase sales and by establishing greater distinctiveness for the product lead to less interdependence with the decisions of other sellers in the future.

More is involved in changing price than erasing just one figure. Whole price schedules including quantity discounts, changes for special services, and variations for quality differences frequently must be redrafted. Nonetheless, the changes can be accomplished rapidly and are essentially one-dimensional in comparison with the many alternatives involved in changing product quality or formulating advertising approaches. Prompt, exact retaliation is virtually impossible to product and advertising programs. Basic product innovations can establish a time gap of years. For example, while Ford introduced Maverick, a new small car, in the spring of 1969, General Motor's entry did not come until the summer of 1970.

That nonprice competition can be both a complement and alternative to price competition is discussed more fully in Chapter 14.

Independent Action with Little Concern for Reactions[15]

One way of dealing with the complexity of possible reaction of competitors is to ignore them. Professor Baumol on the basis of his work as

---

[15] In an appendix to Chapter 14, game theory applications are discussed. These applications which call for estimating payoffs that are dependent upon competitors' moves stress the interdependence of decision making under an oligopoly. Nonetheless, if a firm adopts a maximin strategy, that is to maximize the minimum payoff likely under any contingency, it is taking independent action of a sort. By preparing for the least favorable reaction, it is in a position to ignore the actual reaction.

business consultant has concluded that large firms may pay little attention to each others actions except where important long-range decisions must be made.[16] For example, in early 1955 when R.C.A. cut its price on its classical long-playing records, it was primarily convinced "that the mass market was ready for a real assault,"[17] and the response of its competitors was not a real issue.

Three characteristics of this episode are suggestive of circumstances under which reaction of competitors is immaterial; substantial differentiation of the product, the leading firm in the industry, and an aggressive move. The first two of these characteristics are fulfilled by General Motors, and in Case 13–3 it may be noted that its basic pricing formula with its emphasis on costs at a standard volume with a rate of return target is largely independent of competitors' reactions, although the pricing approach does allow for adjustments to meet market conditions.

Companies that are in the top four among the concentrated industries shown in Figure 13–2, and many others in manufacturing, transportation, mining, communications, electric power, banking, and other fields, are often characterized as "big business." Officials of such firms inevitably emphasize the competitiveness of the activities in which they are engaged, and it is true that few are so well insulated from competition, actual and potential, that they can continue to prosper unless management is alert and ready to adapt to changing conditions. At the same time, large firms are in a better position to view profit making over the long run, partly because their financial strength nearly guarantees that they will be in business for a long time. A short-term opportunity to make unusual profits is more likely to be passed up by a very large company if it involves a possibility of damaging its "public image." The long waiting lists for some popular makes of cars following resumption of automobile production after World War II were an indication that sellers were not attempting to maximize immediate profits. (A queue of buyers can always be broken up by a sufficiently high price.)

It is sometimes said that many large firms set price to cover all costs and provide a "target rate of return" on capital. Such target rates can be consistent with profit maximization and may incorporate a longer run view of the effect of current prices on demand, entry of new rivals, union wage demands, and government action in such matters as antitrust, tariffs, and award of contracts. Examination of the pricing policy of large companies is especially difficult partly because many products are typically turned out by a single firm. Different degrees of control over supply, and consequently of price, are likely to prevail for various products. General principles regarding pricing policy of large firms, as far as

---

[16] William Baumol, *Business Behavior, Value and Growth* (New York: Macmillan Co., 1959), chap. 4.

[17] *Business Week,* January 1, 1955.

they differ from the theory of price determination in general, cannot be stated with confidence. Perhaps the most revealing information is obtained by intensive study of particular firms. Two case studies (Case 13–2 and Case 13–3) of pricing by large companies follow.

CASE 13–1. The Riverside Metal Company*

On May 9, 1939, Mr. H. L. Randall, president of the Riverside Metal Company of Riverside, New Jersey, submitted the following statement of price policies to the Temporary National Economic Committee: "The price schedules issued by the Riverside Metal Company are contingent upon the prices published by the larger units of industry. From time to time these larger units publish their scale of prices, and our company has no alternative except to meet such published prices in order to compete."

Beryllium is an element which can be combined with copper, nickel, and certain other metals to produce alloys which possess great qualities of hardness, lightness, and strength. The principal industrial form in which this metal is used is in the alloy, beryllium copper, which consists of about 2 percent beryllium and 98 percent copper. The chief advantages of beryllium copper are the combination of extraordinary high-fatigue properties with good electrical conductivity. Beryllium alloys have many industrial uses, such as parts for electric motors, telephone instruments, diamond drills, and airplanes. Altimeters used in airplanes have beryllium copper diaphragms because these are more sensitive than other materials. Beryllium alloys are also used in bushings on machine parts.

Beryllium metal is derived from beryl oxide-bearing ores, which are refined by a relatively simple process. For technical reasons, refiners sell beryllium in the form of a master alloy, which contains 3.5–5 percent beryllium, with the remainder copper. Fabricators melt the master alloy and add copper to bring the final beryllium copper alloy to the desired weight, frequently 2 percent in beryllium content.

In 1939 beryllium master alloy was being produced from ore by two principal companies, the Beryllium Corporation of Reading, Pennsylvania, and the Brush Beryllium Company of Cleveland, Ohio. These

---

* Material for this case was derived largely from *T.N.E.C. Hearings,* Part 5, 76th Cong., 1st sess. (Washington, D.C.: U.S. Government Printing Office, 1939).

Of the 51 cases in the original edition of *Business Economics*, this is the only one that appears in substantially the same form as it did in 1951. The original authors, Richard M. Alt and William C. Bradford, have been replaced, the number of chapters have increased from 8 to 17, and more words are printed on each page. It is pleasant to think that although much has been in flux, some business issues remain the same.

companies also fabricated the master alloy into sheets, strips, castings, and other products. Both companies sold master alloy to fabricators of beryllium alloy products. The largest of these fabricators was the American Brass Company of Waterbury, Connecticut. The Riverside Metal Company was one of the smallest fabricating firms in the beryllium alloy industry.

The following testimony from the hearings of the Temporary National Economic Committee[18] describes some aspects of price policies used in the industry (see also Exhibit 13–1A).

EXHIBIT 13–1A

Beryllium Copper Base Prices, 1935–39

	Riverside Metal Co.				American Brass Co.		
Date	Sheet	Wire	Rods	Date	Sheet	Wire	Rods
February 25, 1935..........0.97		1.25	0.97	February 6, 1935..........0.97		1.25	0.97
June 28, 1935..........0.96		1.24	0.96	June 27, 1935..........0.96		1.24	0.96
August 22, 1935..........0.96½		1.24½	0.96½	August 20, 1935..........0.96½		1.24½	0.96½
September 19, 1935..........0.97		1.25	0.97	September 17, 1935..........0.97		1.25	0.97
October 27, 1936..........0.98		1.26	0.98	October 27, 1936..........0.98		1.26	0.98
November 7, 1936..........0.98½		1.26½	0.98½	November 7, 1936..........0.98½		1.26½	0.98½
December 15, 1936..........0.99		1.27	0.99	December 15, 1936..........0.99		1.27	0.99
December 31, 1936..........1.00		1.28	1.00	December 31, 1936..........1.00		1.28	1.00
January 14, 1937..........1.01		1.29	1.00	January 14, 1937..........1.01		1.29	1.01
February 16, 1937..........1.02		1.30	1.02	February 16, 1937..........1.02		1.30	1.02
February 22, 1937..........1.03		1.31	1.03	February 22, 1937..........1.03		1.31	1.03
March 8, 1937..........1.05		1.33	1.05	March 8, 1937..........1.05		1.33	1.05
March 31, 1937..........1.06		1.34	1.06	March 31, 1937..........1.06		1.34	1.06
April 6, 1937..........1.05		1.33	1.05	April 6, 1937..........1.05		1.33	1.05
April 20, 1937..........1.04		1.32	1.04	April 20, 1937..........1.04		1.32	1.04
October 26, 1937..........1.03		1.31	1.03	October 26, 1937..........1.03		1.31	1.03
November 23, 1937..........1.02		1.30	1.02	November 23, 1937..........1.02		1.30	1.02
January 20, 1938..........1.12		1.30	1.12	January 20, 1938..........1.12		1.30	1.12
January 28, 1938..........1.11½		1.29½	1.11½	January 28, 1938..........1.11½		1.29½	1.11½
May 20, 1938..........1.10½		1.28½	1.10½	May 20, 1938..........1.10½		1.28½	1.10½
July 5, 1938..........1.11		1.29	1.11	July 5, 1938..........1.11		1.29	1.11
July 25, 1938..........1.11¼		1.29¼	1.11¼	July 25, 1938..........1.11¼		1.29¼	1.11¼
September 19, 1938..........1.11½		1.29½	1.11½	September 19, 1938..........1.11½		1.29½	1.11½
October 10, 1938..........1.11¾		1.29¾	1.11¾	October 10, 1938..........1.11⅞		1.29⅞	1.11⅞
October 13, 1938..........1.12		1.30	1.12	October 13, 1938..........1.12		1.30	1.12
April 20, 1939..........1.11		1.29	1.11	April 20, 1939..........1.11		1.29	1.11

Source: *T.N.E.C. Hearings*, Part 5, 76th Cong. 1st sess. (Washington, D.C.: U.S. Government Printing Office, 1939), pp. 2284, 2287–88.

MR. COX: You are the president of the Riverside Brass Co.?

MR. RANDALL: Riverside Metal Co.

MR. COX: What is the business of that company?

MR. RANDALL: The business of the Riverside Metal Co. is the fabrication of nonferrous alloys into rod, wire, sheet, and strip. We supply the manufacturer with a raw product.

MR. COX: You buy the master alloy and fabricate the material?

MR. RANDALL: That is correct.

· · · · · · ·

---

[18] *Ibid.*, pp. 2084 ff.

We make nickel silvers, phosphor bronzes, some brass; I think altogether we have an alloy list of over 80 different alloys.

Mr. Cox: Are all of the alloys which your company makes alloys which are also made and sold by the American Brass Co.?

Mr. Randall: I think that would be true.

Mr. Cox: How large a company is your company? Will you give us your capitalization?

Mr. Randall: Our capitalization is one and a half million dollars, and we are almost the smallest unit in the industry; there may be one or two smaller, but I think we are almost the smallest.

Mr. Cox: Can you give us any approximate figure to indicate what percentage of the industry your company controls?

Mr. Randall: Less than one and a half percent.

. . . . . .

Mr. Cox: From whom do you buy the master alloys?

Mr. Randall: We buy the master alloys from the Beryllium Products Corporation.

Mr. Cox: That is Mr. Gahagan?

Mr. Randall: Mr. Gahagan.

Mr. Cox: Have you always bought all of your master alloy from that company?

Mr. Randall: Practically all; yes.

. . . . . .

Mr. Cox: Mr. Randall, would it be correct to say that there is a well crystallized practice of price leadership in the industry in which you are engaged?

Mr. Randall: I would say so.

Mr. Cox: And what company is the price leader?

Mr. Randall: I would say the American Brass Co. holds that position.

Mr. Cox: And your company follows the prices which are announced by American Brass?

Mr. Randall: That is correct.

Mr. Cox: So that when they reduce the price you have to reduce it too. Is that correct?

Mr. Randall: Well, we don't have to, but we do.

Mr. Cox: And when they raise the price you raise the price.

Mr. Randall: That is correct.

Mr. Cox: Do you remember that in February 1937, Mr. Gahagan's company reduced the price of the master alloy from $30 to $23 a pound?

Mr. Randall: I didn't know it at that time.

Mr. Cox: You did know there was a price decrease.

Mr. Randall: I do now.

Mr. Cox: Weren't you buying from Mr. Gahagan?

Mr. Randall: I think we were buying from them but it was quite some time after that I got the information that the price had gone down.

Mr. Cox: After the decrease in the price of the master alloy, it is a fact, isn't it, that there was no decrease in price of the fabricated product which you made?

Mr. Randall: I don't remember about that, I don't know, because I don't know when that decrease took place.

Mr. Cox: Looking at your sheet prices for the year 1937, you started at $1.01 a pound on January 14, 1937, and rose progressively until you reached $1.06 on March 31, and then on April 6, 1937, they dropped to $1.05. You remember those.

Mr. Randall: Yes; I remember those. That was copper.

. . . .

Mr. Cox: But you do know there was about that time a decrease of $7 a pound in the price which you were paying to Mr. Gahagan.

Mr. Randall: Yes; I do know that.

Mr. Cox: I will put this question to you, Mr. Randall. Why didn't you reduce the price of the fabricated product following that decrease in the price of the master alloy?

Mr. Randall: Well, of course I would not make a reduction in the base price of beryllium copper unless the American Brass made a price reduction in beryllium copper.

Mr. Cox: And the American Brass Co. made no reduction at that time?

Mr. Randall: If they did, we did, as indicated on that sheet.

Mr. Cox: Assuming you didn't make a price change then, the reason you didn't was because the American Brass Co. didn't.

Mr. Randall: That is correct.

Mr. Arnold: You exercise no individual judgment as to the price you charged for your product, then, in a situation?

Mr. Randall: Well, I think that is about what it amounts to; yes, sir.

Mr. Arnold: When you say you have to follow, you don't mean anybody told you you had to follow?

Mr. Randall: No sir; I don't mean that at all.

Mr. Arnold: But you have a feeling something might happen if you didn't?

Mr. Randall: I don't know what would happen.

Mr. Cox: You don't want to find out, do you?

The Chairman: Well, as a matter of fact, Mr. Randall, if the American Brass Co. raised the price would the Brass Co. consult you about raising it?

Mr. Randall: No, sir; not at all.

The Chairman: You would, however, follow them without exercising any independent judgment as to whether or not it was desirable.

Mr. Randall: That is correct.

The Chairman: Suppose the American Brass Co. raises its price, but you are satisfied with your output and with the profit that you are making at the old price. Why is it necessary for you to increase your price to your customers, who are already paying you a price sufficient to give you a profit that is satisfactory to you?

Mr. Randall: I don't know that it is necessary; as a practical matter, if we didn't raise our prices the American Brass Co. or other companies, whoever they might be, would put their price back to where it was.

Mr. Chairman: That wouldn't bother you, because you were making a profit at the old price.

MR. RANDALL: Not on beryllium copper.

THE CHAIRMAN: Why do you do it?

MR. RANDALL: It is the custom of the industry, at least of the smaller companies, to do that.

THE CHAIRMAN: And other small companies do the same thing?

MR. RANDALL: Yes, sir.

THE CHAIRMAN: Is there any reason outside of custom for it?

MR. RANDALL: No, sir.

THE CHAIRMAN: Isn't it likely to reduce the amount of business that you can obtain?

MR. RANDALL: I don't think so.

THE CHAIRMAN: Well, if a competitor raises the price for an identical product, isn't it likely to believe that the producer who does not raise the price would get more business?

MR. RANDALL: I imagine it would, if the other price stayed where it had been raised to. I think that might work out over a period of time.

THE CHAIRMAN: You see, I am trying to get some understanding of the exact reasons why this price policy is followed, and it is not an answer—understand me, I am not criticizing your answer—that carries conviction merely to say it is the custom of the industry. There is a reason for customs. What, in your opinion, is the reason for this custom to follow the leader?

MR. RANDALL: Well, of course, that is a custom which has been prevalent, I think, in the industry for many, many years prior to my entry into it.

THE CHAIRMAN: Oh, yes; we hear a lot about price leadership, but I am trying to get the picture of this practice as you see it, and why you follow it.

MR. RANDALL: Well, I don't think I have ever given the matter very much consideration. We simply, when the new prices come out, print them just as they are. We don't give the matter any consideration. The prices are published and we print those prices.

THE CHAIRMAN: Is there any sort of compulsion, moral or otherwise?

MR. RANDALL: Absolutely none.

THE CHAIRMAN: Do you think it is a good practice?

MR. RANDALL: Well, I have never given the subject very much consideration.

THE CHAIRMAN: Now, of course, it is one of the most important subjects in your business.

MR. RANDALL: Yes; it is, of course.

THE CHAIRMAN: The price that you get for your product.

MR. RANDALL: I can't answer that question. I don't know whether it is a good practice or whether it isn't a good practice. I know that it has been the custom of the industry for years on end, and I know that it is what we do, that's all.

THE CHAIRMAN: A moment ago, in response to either Mr. Cox's question or my question, you answered that if you did not follow the price up, then the American Brass Co. or some other company would come down again.

MR. RANDALL: I don't think I said they would. I said they probably would or they might. I don't know what they would do.

THE CHAIRMAN: Then I made the comment that that would not be a disturbing result, because it would mean merely the restoration of the old price. I could imagine, however, that you might start a price war, and that the other companies might go below you. Is there a possibility that that is what you have in mind?

MR. RANDALL: I didn't have it in mind until this moment. That is a possibility; yes.

THE CHAIRMAN: So you want the committee to understand that so far as you and your company are concerned, this price-leadership question is one to which you have never given any real consideration, and you have boosted your prices along with the American Brass Co. just as a matter of custom?

MR. RANDALL: Yes.

. . . .

MR. ARNOLD: . . . but if this policy is continued, you will continue to follow the American Brass regardless of what your costs are, won't you, so that won't be an element in the picture?

MR. RANDALL: Of course, to be perfectly frank, on that subject we don't know what our costs are on beryllium.

MR. ARNOLD: It wouldn't make any difference if you did, so far as the present prices are concerned, would it?

MR. RANDALL: No, sir; I don't think it would.

MR. ARNOLD: In other words, there is a situation here where there is a lot of competitors and no competition.

MR. RANDALL: Well, we simply, as I said before, follow the prices that are published, and that is what we have been doing for a good many years.

. . . .

At the conclusion of Mr. Randall's testimony, Mr. John A. Coe, Jr., general sales manager of the American Brass Company, was called to the stand. His testimony follows:

MR. COX: What is the nature of the business of the American Brass Co.?

MR. COE: The American Brass Co. is engaged in the production of copper, brass, bronze, and nickel silver in wrought forms, including sheet, wire, rods and tubes and other fabricated forms.

MR. COX: What is the capitalization of the company?

MR. COE: The American Brass Co. is a wholly owned fabricating subsidiary of the Anaconda Copper Mining Co.

MR. COX: Can you tell us what the capitalization of the company is?

MR. COE: I do not know what it is.

MR. COX: You heard Mr. Randall testify that his company did less than 1½ percent of the business in which he was engaged. Can you give us any approximate figure as to the percentage of the business which your company does?

MR. COE: Approximately 25 percent.

. . . .

MR. COX: You heard Mr. Randall's testimony with respect to the system of price leadership which prevails.

MR. COE: Yes.

MR. Cox: Would you agree with his description of that system insofar as it denoted your company as the price leader?

MR. Coe: I wouldn't agree with that statement.

MR. Cox: You wouldn't agree with the statement?

MR. Coe: No.

MR. Cox: In other words, it is your position that your company is not the price leader in the industry?

MR. Coe: We are not the price leader of the industry.

MR. Cox: It is a fact, is it not, that your prices for beryllium copper have been substantially the same as those of Mr. Randall for a period between 1934 and the present time?

MR. Coe: So far as I know, they have been practically the same.

MR. Cox: Practically the same prices. Now, you say you are not the price leader. Is there any price leader in the industry?

MR. Coe: There is none.

MR. Cox: Then how do you explain the fact that the prices are the same?

MR. Coe: We publish our prices; they are public information; anybody who wishes to, may follow those prices at his own discretion.

MR. Arnold: They all wish to apparently, don't they?

MR. Coe: They do not, sir.

MR. Arnold: You mean they have not been following those prices?

MR. Coe: On our product they have not, sir.

MR. Arnold: I got the impression, I may be wrong, that the prices of competitors and your prices have been substantially identical.

MR. Coe: To some extent they have been identical. There are always variations in many prices.

MR. Arnold: You said that anyone who wishes to might follow. Some of them certainly wish to.

MR. Coe: Some of them do wish to.

MR. Arnold: And some of them did follow.

MR. Coe: That is correct.

MR. Arnold: And therefore to that extent you have been the leader.

MR. Coe: To some extent we have been the leader in that we have put out our prices. However, others have put out prices and we have followed them at times.

MR. Arnold: What other companies would you put in the position of price leadership aside from your own?

MR. Coe: Practically any member of the industry.

MR. Cox: Including Mr. Randall?

MR. Coe: Including Mr. Randall.

. . . .

MR. Arnold: I take it that the prices are fixed generally by someone following someone else, and that sometimes they follow you and other times you follow others.

MR. Coe: May I ask what you mean by "fixed"? We publish our prices; they become our prices; they are public information. In that way the prices of the American Brass Co. are fixed by us.

MR. Arnold: Then you understand what we mean by "fixed" and I repeat my question: Is it true that prices are fixed in this industry either by someone following you or by your following others?

MR. COE: Not in all respects. Many times we do not follow others in all respects; many times they do not follow us in all respects.

MR. ARNOLD: But there is a following on the part of the various companies in the industry?

MR. COE: A general following; yes, sir.

THE CHAIRMAN: Not that you impose your ideas as to what the price should be upon anybody else, or that anybody else imposes it upon you, but when any company makes a change in price, the tendency is for all to follow that change?

MR. COE: That is the tendency.

THE CHAIRMAN: And how long has that been the system?

MR. COE: As far back as I have been with the company that has been in vogue; water seeking its own level.

. . . .

THE CHAIRMAN: What factors go into the determination of the price?

MR. COE: The cost of our raw metals going into the alloys, plus our manufacturing differentials. The latter is determined by our price committee.

THE CHAIRMAN: And if the price of the raw material should go down, then one would naturally expect the price of the finished product to go down, unless there was some countervailing change in some other factor?

MR. COE: There are other factors to be taken into consideration; yes, sir.

THE CHAIRMAN: Well, now, would you say that the price fluctuates in the same degree that the price of these countervailing or these other factors fluctuate?

MR. COE: That is a difficult question to answer. I don't quite know what you mean by that.

THE CHAIRMAN: Well, I tried to make it simple. The price of the finished product would naturally, one would suppose, depend upon the cost of the various factors which go into making the finished product?

MR. COE: That is correct.

THE CHAIRMAN: Well, now, do you want the committee to understand that always the price of the finished product is determined by these other factors and by no other consideration?

MR. COE: The price is determined by the price of raw materials going into those products, plus our cost of manufacturing.

THE CHAIRMAN: Yes; those are the other factors?

MR. COE: Those are the other factors.

THE CHAIRMAN: And there is no other consideration that goes into the determination of the price?

MR. COE: That is correct.

THE CHAIRMAN: And how about this leadership, why do you follow somebody else's lead sometimes?

MR. COE: We can get no more for our product than other people can get for theirs; will charge for theirs.

THE CHAIRMAN: Here is another outfit which is supposedly competing with you, which is not as efficient as you are, and therefore which finds for example that there is a much heavier plant charge, let us say; therefore, it is not able to produce this finished product at as low a price as you, and because it doesn't produce it at as low a price as you, it has to raise the price, but according to your testimony when such a company raises the price, then you follow and raise your price, although your costs have not changed.

MR. COE: We have not necessarily raised our price.

THE CHAIRMAN: Oh, now, let's drop the word "necessarily." You have just said that you have done that and that other companies follow you occasionally. Now, Mr. Coe, we are merely trying to get the facts here; we are not laying the basis for a case against the American Brass Co. I am trying to get through my mind this picture of price leadership in industry.

Now, you have told us as explicitly as it can be told that in some cases other companies in the same business as you follow the price that you fix, and you have told us how you determine that price, and then you say in other instances you followed the price of other companies, and when you do that necessarily you do it upon factors that are not reflected in your business, but on factors that are reflected in the business of the company which raises the price. Now why do you do it?

MR. COE: We can get as much for our product as any competitor can get for his product.

THE CHAIRMAN: Now we are getting somewhere. If some other company raises the price and is getting that price, then you think you had better come up and equalize it?

MR. COE: I feel that our product is as good as any made by the industry.

THE CHAIRMAN: It may be better.

MR. COE: I hope it is.

THE CHAIRMAN: But the point in determining the price thing is that you base it not upon the actual costs of manufacture in your plants, but upon the highest charge that anybody in the industry makes by and large, isn't that the effect of this price leadership policy?

MR. COE: It is usually predicated on the lowest price that anybody makes.

THE CHAIRMAN: Well, of course, there was an old familiar saying that the price the companies charge is what the traffic will bear. Now isn't that the motto which guides those who follow the practice of price leadership?

MR. COE: It depends on what you mean by "traffic." Of course we have to compete with many other things besides brass and copper.

THE CHAIRMAN: Well, would you say the American Brass Co. puts its product out at the lowest possible price, bearing in mind all of these factors of cost?

MR. COE: It is necessary when we get our products to the ultimate consumer as low as we reasonably can, and still at a fair margin of profit, in order that we will not be—that our products will not be supplanted by substitutes.

THE CHAIRMAN: But under this plan of price leadership, is it not inevitable that the tendency would be to raise the price so as to cover the cost of the less efficient member of the industry?

MR. COE: The tendency has been just the opposite. The tendency has been to lower the price.

Questions

1. Was the price policy of the Riverside Metal Company based on sound economic reasoning? What assumptions about retaliation had Mr. Randall made—to a price set above that posted by American Brass? To a price set below that of American Brass?
2. Can you suggest an alternative price policy that might prove more profitable for the Riverside Metal Company?

CASE 13–2. United States Steel and the Abortive 1962 Steel Price Increases

One of the first acts of newly inaugurated President Ford was to call for a council to monitor but not control significant price and wage decisions. This action in the summer of 1974 when prices were rising at an annual rate of over 10 percent suggested that managements in leading firms of concentrated and important industries could expect continued scrutiny of their pricing decisions.

You may be discussing these cases at a time when some version of the wage-price guideposts have been reintroduced as an attempt to help meet cost-push inflation. In 1962 they were announced as follows:

The general guide for noninflationary wage behavior is that the rate of increase in wage rates (including fringe benefits) in each industry be equal to the trend rate of over-all productivity increase. General acceptance of this guide would maintain stability of labor cost per unit of output for the economy as a whole—though not of course for individual industries.

The general guide for noninflationary price behavior calls for price reduction if the industry's rate of productivity increase exceeds the over-all rate—for this would mean declining unit labor costs; it calls for an appropriate increase in price if the opposite relationship prevails; and it calls for stable prices if the two rates of productivity increase are equal.[19]

The 1962 confrontation may well have helped establish the apparent record of success for the guideposts in the 1962–66 period when wage and price rises were unusually low for a period of rising employment and profits.[20]

---

[19] *Economic Report of the President*, January, 1962, (Washington, D.C.: U.S. Government Printing Office, 1962), p. 168. It was recognized that various exceptions would be necessary for equity and efficiency, and in 1964 a specific figure of 3.2 percent was announced for trend productivity.

[20] In "The Wage Price Issue—The Need for Guideposts," Hearings before the Joint Economic Committee of Congress, January, 1968, are econometric studies by G. L. Percy and G. Fromm that indicated that wage rises during this period were distinctly smaller than would be expected from such explanatory variables as low

The majority of economists in 1969 attributed the inflation to the failure to control excess demand. With inflation the effectiveness of voluntary guideposts backed only by the sanction of public opinion vanished. As the Council of Economic Advisors put it in January, 1969, "Once consumer prices started to move up sharply, increases in compensation no larger than the productivity trend would not have led to any improvement in real income. Workers could not be expected to accept such a result, particularly in view of the previous rapid and consistent rise in corporate profits."[21]

Nonetheless it stressed, "Since the economic consequences of private price and wage decisions bear so importantly on the public welfare, it is important for Government to point the way in which these individual decisions can serve the public interest." The student may be the judge of how closely the performance of this role in the 1970s resembles that of the steel pricing decision of 1962.

After a price increase in 1957, there was a much smaller general increase in 1958 and only selective price adjustments from 1959 through 1961, with the overall change in the last two years being slightly downward. It can be noted from Exhibits 13–2A, 13–2B, and 13–2C that production, employment, profits, and exports were all substantially down from the levels of the middle 1950s. Man-hour productivity had risen substantially in 1959 and 1961, while employment costs were rising more slowly than before. Most of the industry had been subjected to a prolonged strike running from the early summer of 1959 to January, 1960.

On March 31, 1962, congratulations were extended to the steelworkers and to the steel industry for their "early and responsible settlement," well in advance of the June 30 deadline, and the earliest settlement in the quarter-century relationship between the industry and the union. This early settlement contrasted with the 1959 negotiations, which included a 116-day strike. President Kennedy, in a telephone message to David J. MacDonald, president of the United Steelworkers, said:

> When I appealed to the Union and to the industry to commence negotiations early in order to avert an inventory buildup—with consequences detrimental to the nation at large as well as to the industry and its employees—I did so with firm confidence that the steelworkers' union and the industry would measure up to their responsibility to serve the national interest.
>
> You have done so through free collective bargaining, without the pressure of a deadline or under the threat of a strike. This is indeed industrial statesmanship of the highest order.

---

unemployment and rising profit levels, and through the influence on unit labor costs the rise in prices also was significantly less than would have been expected from 1947–60 relationships.

[21] *Economic Report of the President,* January, 1969 (Washington, D.C.: U.S. Government Printing Office, 1969), p. 119.

EXHIBIT 13–2A

Productivity, Employment Costs, and Prices in Steel Industry, 1940–61

Year	(1) Ingot Production (millions of tons)	(2) Total Wage-Hours Worked (millions)	(3) Ingot Tons ÷ Hours Worked (1 ÷ 2)	(4) Annual Percentage Change in (3)	(5) Average Total Employment Cost per Hour	(6) Annual Percentage Change in (5)	(7) Steel Products Price Index	(8) Annual Percentage Change in (7)
1940	67.0	858	0.0781	....	0.905	....	100.0	....
1945	79.7	1,009	0.0790	0.2*	1.307	7.0*	103.1	0.6*
1946	66.6	837	0.0792	0.3	1.404	7.4	112.2	8.8
1947	84.9	984	0.0863	8.9	1.563	11.3	130.8	16.6
1948	88.6	1,029	0.0861	0.0	1.679	7.4	148.8	13.8
1949	78.0	885	0.0881	2.3	1.753	4.4	161.1	8.3
1950	96.8	1,023	0.0947	7.5	1.908	8.8	169.2	5.0
1951	105.2	1,133	0.0946	0.0	2.114	10.8	182.8	8.0
1952	93.2	971	0.0960	1.5	2.315	9.5	186.8	2.2
1953	111.6	1,119	0.0997	3.9	2.440	5.4	201.0	7.6
1954	88.3	901	0.0980	(1.7)†	2.512	3.0	209.7	4.3
1955	117.0	1,062	0.1102	12.5	2.722	8.3	219.5	4.7
1956	115.2	1,027	0.1122	1.9	2.954	8.5	238.0	8.4
1957	112.7	990	0.1139	1.5	3.216	8.9	260.7	9.5
1958	85.3	756	0.1128	(1.0)	3.513	9.2	269.8	3.5
1959	93.4	769	0.1215	7.7	3.798	8.1	274.3	1.7
1960	99.3	840	0.1182	(2.7)	3.820	0.6	273.9	(0.2)
1961	98.0	775	0.1267	7.2	3.989	4.4	272.8	(0.4)

* Annual average over five years.
† Parentheses indicate negative changes.

Notes: Column 2 was obtained by dividing aggregate payroll of wage employees by hourly total payroll cost. Column 3, as a measure of man-hour productivity, could overstate the increase if the proportion of salary to wage workers increased and understate it if more processing was given to steel shipments. Column 5 includes payroll costs plus pension, insurance, S.U.B., and social security.

Source: American Iron and Steel Institute, particularly *The Competitive Challenge to Steel* (Pittsburgh, 1963), p. 82.

EXHIBIT 13–2B

Comparison of Steel Industry Return on Net Assets with Average Rate of Return for Leading Manufacturing Industries

Year	Average Return on Net Assets		Percent by Which Steel Industry Return was ABOVE (+) or BELOW (−) Average Rate of Return for Leading Mfg. Industries	Steel Industry Ranking among Leading Manufacturing Industries	Number of Leading Industrial Categories Covered
	Steel Industry	Leading Manufacturing Industries			
1940.	8.5%	10.3%	−18%	32d	45
1941.	9.6	12.4	−23	40th	44
1942.	6.5	10.1	−36	45th	45
1943.	5.6	9.9	−43	43d	44
1944.	5.2	9.8	−47	44th	45
1945.	5.0	9.1	−45	44th	45
1946.	7.5	12.1	−38	41st	45
1947.	11.3	17.0	−33	42d	45
1948.	14.0	18.9	−26	38th	45
1949.	11.5	13.8	−17	24th	45
1950.	15.3	17.1	−10	28th	45
1951.	12.3	14.4	−15	25th	46
1952.	8.8	12.3	−28	35th	46
1953.	11.6	12.5	−7	21st	46
1954.	9.4	12.4	−24	32d	46
1955.	15.2	15.0	+1	14th	41
1956.	13.9	13.9	0	17th	41
1957.	13.2	12.8	+3	17th	41
1958.	8.2	9.8	−16	27th	41
1959.	8.4	11.7	−28	35th	41
1960.	7.8	10.6	−26	29th	41
1961.	6.4	10.1	−37	33d	41

Source: Computed from First National City Bank, *Monthly Letters*, April issues. See Exhibit 13–2A.

EXHIBIT 13–2C

United States Imports and Exports of Steel
Mill Products (net tons)

Year	Imports	Exports
1950	1,013,600	2,638,634
1951	2,176,996	3,136,639
1952	1,201,435	4,005,248
1953	1,702,991	2,990,751
1954	770,822	2,791,886
1955	973,155	4,060,998
1956	1,340,746	4,347,903
1957	1,154,831	5,347,678
1958	1,707,130	2,822,910
1959	4,396,354	1,676,652
1960	3,358,752	2,977,278
1961	3,164,256	1,989,179

Note: In ingot equivalent, each ton of steel mill products
represented about 1.35 tons of ingots (figure varied from 1.32
to 1.37 in last five years).

Source: American Iron and Steel Institute, *Foreign Trade
Trends* (1962). See Exhibit 13–2A.

The settlement you have announced is both forward looking and responsible. It is obviously noninflationary and should provide a solid base for continued price stability.

An industry statement said the new benefits would increase employment costs by about 2½ percent during the first year. This compares with an average annual increase of 3½ percent to 3¾ percent under the contract negotiated in 1960, and with 8 percent a year in the period between 1940 and 1960. R. Conrad Cooper of U.S. Steel, chief industry negotiator, said that the settlement cost did not fall wholly "within the limits of anticipated gains in productive efficiency." The industry statement estimated the cost of the settlement exceeded by about 50 percent its productivity gain. Cooper added that the accord represented real progress in the development of voluntary collective bargaining in the steel industry.

Steps in the Negotiation

The 1960 steel contract provided for several wage increases, the last of which was scheduled for October 1, 1961. Prior to that date, executives of major steel companies were hinting at a general rise in steel prices to coincide with that wage increase. On September 6, 1961, President Kennedy wrote the heads of 12 steel companies, expressing his concern with stability of steel prices. Mr. Kennedy wrote:

. . . the steel industry, by absorbing increases in employment costs since 1958 has demonstrated a will to halt the price-wage spiral in steel. If the industry were now to forego a price increase, it would enter collective bargaining negotiations next spring with a record of three-and-a-half years of price stability. It would clearly then be the turn of the labor representatives to limit wage demands to a level consistent with continued price stability. The moral position of the steel industry next spring and its claim to the support of public opinion will be strengthened by the exercise of price restraint now.

EXHIBIT 13–2D

Steel Industry Capital Expenditures, Depreciation,
Depletion, and Amortization, 1946–61
(millions)

Year	Capital Expenditures for Additions, Improvements and Replacements	Depreciation, Depletion and Amortization
1946	$ 365	$169
1947	554	239
1948	642	302
1949	483	278
1950	505	327
1951	1,051	374
1952	1,298	450
1953	988	614
1954	609	670
1955	714	737
1956	1,311	748
1957	1,723	766
1958	1,137	673
1959	934	665
1960	1,521	698
1961	978	729

Source: Annual statistical reports of the American Iron and Steel Institute.

He eventually received replies from all 12 companies. The reply from Roger Blough for U.S. Steel denied that the cause of inflation would be found in the levels of steel prices and profits. Blough's letter noted that the President's letter "does raise questions of such serious import, including the future of freedom of marketing, that I feel impelled to include a word on that score also, for whatever value it may be." He wrote of "the admittedly hazardous task which your economic advisers have undertaken in forecasting steel industry profits at varying rates of operation. . . . Moreover, it might reasonably appear to some—as, frankly, it does to me—that they seem to be assuming the role of informal price setters for steel—psychological or otherwise."

In January, 1962, President Kennedy urged an early agreement to avoid the upsetting uncertainty of a possible strike, and especially the speculation which precedes a strike deadline, such as heavy buying by steel users. At his news conference on January 15, Mr. Kennedy said that Secretary of Labor Arthur J. Goldberg, would be available "for what ever good offices he may perform." In reply to a question at the conference the President stressed his desire for a settlement which would not force an increase in steel prices, that is, the cost of the wage increase

EXHIBIT 13–2E

Average Hourly Earnings per Hour Paid For (BLS)
(steel versus other industries)

	Dollars per Hour Paid for—		
Year	*Steel Industry*	*All Manufacturing*	*Auto Industry*
1940	$0.84	$0.66	$0.94
1941	0.94	0.73	1.04
1942	1.02	0.85	1.17
1943	1.12	0.96	1.24
1944	1.16	1.01	1.27
1945	1.18	1.02	1.27
1946	1.28	1.08	1.35
1947	1.44	1.22	1.47
1948	1.58	1.33	1.61
1949	1.65	1.38	1.70
1950	1.69	1.44	1.78
1951	1.92	1.56	1.91
1952	2.02	1.65	2.05
1953	2.19	1.74	2.14
1954	2.23	1.78	2.20
1955	2.41	1.86	2.29
1956	2.57	1.95	2.35
1957	2.73	2.05	2.46
1958	2.91	2.11	2.55
1959	3.10	2.19	2.71
1960	3.08	2.26	2.81
1961	3.20	2.32	2.87

Source: U.S. Bureau of Labor Statistics.

should not exceed the savings resulting from increased productivity. The President's economic report to the Congress, released the following week, went so far as to urge that average productivity gains for the general economy be used as guidelines for wage settlements. The report of the Council of Economic Advisers recommended that the overall increase in output per man-hour of 2½ percent to 3 percent a year be taken as the measuring rod for higher wages and fringe benefits in any industry. If efficiency of a specific industry was going up faster, this would call for price reductions.

One of the strongest statements about the role of government in collective bargaining was Secretary Goldberg's "definitive" statement of the Kennedy administration's labor-management philosophy to the Executive Club of Chicago, on February 23. Goldberg said that in the past when government officials assisted in collective bargaining, their only aim had been to achieve a settlement. But today, in the light of the nation's commitments at home and abroad, government and private mediators must increasingly provide guidelines to the parties in labor disputes. Such guidelines should insure "right settlements" that take into account the public interest as well as the interests of the parties. Goldberg said he did not mean that government should impose the terms of a settlement, but he claimed that "everyone expects the government to assert and define the national interest."

Anonymous steel industry sources took exception to the Goldberg position:

The moment the government goes beyond being a policeman or offering its service as mediator, it has an impact on the outcome of collective bargaining and converts it from an economic to a political process. From a broad philosophical standpoint, most businessmen feel that in a competitive system you serve the national interest in pursuing your private interest. Government exertion of its influence prevents the system from operating as it should. From a practical standpoint, labor represents more votes than businessmen, so businessmen feel that any settlement that is a political settlement is likely to be more pro-labor than pro-management.

George Meany, president of the American Federation of Labor and Congress of Industrial Organizations, also brusquely rejected Secretary Goldberg's "definitive" statement. Mr. Meany said:

I don't agree with it. The government's role is mediation, conciliation or anything else it can do to help industrial peace. When he says the role of the government is to assert the national interest, he is infringing on the rights of free people and free society, and I don't agree with him whatsoever. This is a step in the direction of saying the federal government should tell either or both sides what to do, and I don't agree with that.

Support for Secretary Goldberg came from Joseph L. Block, chairman of Inland Steel, who was at the speaker's table when Goldberg spoke (Block was a member of President Kennedy's 21-man Advisory Committee on Labor-Management Policy):

I heartily endorse Mr. Goldberg's concept. It is the government's function to elucidate the national objectives, to point out what the national needs are. Those guidelines should be taken into account in collective bargaining. A contest of strength where the stronger side wins doesn't prove a thing. Each side has to represent its own interest, but neither side must be unmindful of the needs of the nation. Who else can point out those needs but the government?

A. A. Berle, Jr., also supported the Goldberg view and the work of the Council of Economic Advisors, contending that there is an unwritten "social contract" holding both sides to certain responsibilities as well as granting both the privileges that make this power possible, and that under this social contract the government can—and perhaps must—intervene when economic power in private hands threatens the economic community of the United States. Berle sees the "emerging relationship" as this: "When the wage and price levels markedly affect, or threaten to upset, the economy of the country, the government claims power to step in on behalf of the 'public interest.'" The difficulty is in telling what the words "public interest" mean. Berle sees the Council of Economic Advisors as the future key agency here, for "its views on acceptable wage and price levels are, and should be, extremely important":

The council can advise the President—and through his authority advise both big labor and big corporations—about where the peril points are. It can advise the President when the government should intervene to modify private decisions based on power, either of labor to tie up plants by strike, or of management to set prices by administration. It can and indeed does keep a close check on these allegedly private decisions, taken in company offices or union headquarters. It could communicate to either or both when it sees a peril point approaching. And it can advise the President when intervention is needed in the "public interest"—that is, when employment, production and purchasing power under free competitive enterprise are likely to be weakened, when inflation becomes a danger, when economic stability generally is likely to be threatened.[22]

U.S. Steel's annual report, released on March 20, 1962, pointed to its holding of the price line in 1961. Mr. Blough's statement to stockholders said that in 1961 "the inexorable influences of the market place in our competitive free enterprise system continued to dictate the course of U.S. Steel's pricing actions." No reference to pricing plans for 1962 appeared in the report, but Blough indicated deep concern about competition and slack demand. Robert C. Tyson, chairman of the U.S. Steel's Finance Committee, called "unsatisfactory" the idea that productivity is a criterion for setting wages. "The notion appears to be that if an enterprise or industry learns how to produce more efficiently, then it can pay more to its employees without raising its product's prices. If we can do this, it is proper to force us to do so." Mr. Tyson said this theory is unsatisfactory because if more money is paid to those with jobs, there is less available for rehiring those workers without jobs. Unemployment becomes chronic,

---

[22] A. A. Berle, Jr., "Unwritten Constitution for Our Economy," *The New York Times Magazine,* April 29, 1962.

and the incentives for creating new jobs are stultified. Productivity, he went on, is useful as a method of describing economic facts, rather than as a measure for determining wage rates. It indicates only that a price increase or widespread unemployment must result if the average wage level rises faster than productivity. "No increase in employment costs in excess of the nation's long-term rate of productivity increase can be regarded as noninflationary." (At this stage in negotiations the industry was holding out for employment cost increases not exceeding 2 percent annually, coinciding with the annual productivity increase as figured by the companies for recent years.)

Steel Prices Go Up—and Come Down Again

U.S. Steel signed the labor contract agreed upon at the end of March on April 5. This contract provided for costs (not in direct wages but in other benefits) which were subsequently estimated at 10.6 cents an hour, or a total of $159 million a year for the industry, with some 520,000 workers. On April 10 the company announced an average increase of $6 a ton in the price of steel, accompanying the announcement with a statement signed by Leslie B. Worthington, president, explaining this increase:

Since our last over-all adjustment in the summer of 1958, the level of steel prices has not been increased but, if anything, has declined somewhat. This situation, in the face of steadily mounting production costs which have included four increases in steel-worker wages and benefits prior to the end of last year, has been due to the competitive pressures from domestic producers and from imports of foreign-made steel as well as from other materials which are used as substitutes for steel.

. . . .

In the three years since the end of 1958, United States Steel has spent $1,185,000,000 for modernization and replacement of facilities and for the development of new sources of raw materials. Internally, there were only two sources from which this money could come: depreciation and reinvested profit. Depreciation in these years amounted to $610,000,000; and reinvested profit, $187,000,000—or, together, only about two-thirds of the total sum required. So after using all the income available from operations, we had to make up the difference of $388,000,000 out of borrowings from the public. In fact, during the period 1958–1961, we have actually borrowed a total of $800,000,000 to provide for present and future needs. And this must be repaid out of profits that have not yet been earned, and will not be earned for some years to come.

During these three years, moreover, United States Steel's profits have dropped to the lowest levels since 1952; while reinvested profit—which is all the profit there is to be plowed back in the business after payment of dividends—has declined from $115,000,000 in 1958 to less than $3,000,000 last year. Yet the dividend rate has not been increased in more than five years, although there have been seven general increases in employment costs during this interval.

. . . .

In all, we have experienced a net increase of about 6 percent in our costs over this period despite cost reductions which have been effected through the use of new, more efficient facilities, improved techniques and better raw materials. Compared with this net increase of 6 percent, the price increase of 3½ percent announced today clearly falls considerably short of the amount needed to restore even the cost-price relationship in the low production year of 1958.

In reaching this conclusion, we have given full consideration, of course, to the fact that any price increase which comes, as this does, at a time when foreign-made steels are already underselling ours in a number of product lines, will add—temporarily, at least—to the competitive difficulties which we are now experiencing. But the present price level cannot be maintained any longer when our problems are viewed in long-range perspective. For the long pull a strong, profitable company is the only insurance that formidable competition can be met and that the necessary lower costs to meet that competition will be assured.[23]

President Kennedy was informed of U.S. Steel's price increase at a meeting requested by Roger Blough at 5:45 P.M. on April 10. Mr. Kennedy spoke at his news conference the next day in "a tone of cold anger" in reading a long indictment of the steel companies' actions:

The simultaneous and identical actions of United States Steel and other leading steel corporations increasing steel prices by some $6 a ton constitute a wholly unjustifiable and irresponsible defiance of the public interest.

In this serious hour in our nation's history when we are confronted with grave crises in Berlin and Southeast Asia, when we are devoting our energies to economic recovery and stability, when we are asking Reservists to leave their homes and families months on end and servicemen to risk their lives— and four were killed in the last two days in Vietnam—and asking union members to hold down their wage requests at a time when restraint and sacrifice are being asked of every citizen, the American people will find it hard, as I do, to accept a situation in which a tiny handful of steel executives whose pursuit of private power and profit exceeds their sense of public responsibility, can show such utter contempt for the interest of 185,000,000 Americans.

If this rise in the cost of steel is imitated by the rest of the industry, instead of rescinded, it would increase the cost of homes, autos, appliances and most other items for every American family. It would increase the cost of machinery and tools to every American businessman and farmer. It would seriously handicap our efforts to prevent an inflationary spiral, from eating up the pensions of our older citizens and our new gains in purchasing power. It would add, Defense Secretary Robert S. McNamara informed me this morn-

---

[23] *The New York Times,* April 11, 1962.

ing, an estimated $1,000,000,000 to the cost of our defenses at a time when every dollar is needed for national security and other purposes.

It will make it more difficult for American goods to compete in foreign markets, more difficult to withstand competition from foreign imports and thus more difficult to improve our balance-of-payment position and stem the flow of gold. And it is necessary to stem it for our national security if we're going to pay for our security commitments abroad.

And it would surely handicap our efforts to induce other industries and unions to adopt responsible price and wage policies.

The facts of the matter are that there is no justification for an increase in steel prices.

The recent settlement between the industry and the union, which does not even take place until July 1, was widely acknowledged to be non-inflationary, and the whole purpose and effect of this Administration's role, which both parties understood, was to achieve an agreement which would make unnecessary any increases in prices.

Steel output per man is rising so fast that labor costs per ton of steel can actually be expected to decline in the next twelve months. And, in fact, the Acting Commissioner of the Bureau of Labor Statistics informed me this morning that, and I quote, "employment costs per unit of steel output in 1961 were essentially the same as they were in 1958." The cost of major raw materials—steel scrap and coal—has also been declining.

And for an industry which has been generally operating at less than two-thirds of capacity, its profit rate has been normal and can be expected to rise sharply this year in view of the reduction in idle capacity. Their lot has been easier than that of 100,000 steelworkers thrown out of work in the last three years.

The industry's cash dividends have exceeded $600,000,000 in each of the last five years; and earnings in the first quarter of this year were estimated in the Feb. 28 *Wall Street Journal* to be among the highest in history.

In short, at a time when they could be exploring how more efficiency and better prices could be obtained, reducing prices in this industry in recognition of lower costs, their unusually good labor contract, their foreign competition and their increase in production and profits which are coming this year, a few gigantic corporations have decided to increase prices in ruthless disregard of their public responsibility.

Price and wage decisions in this country, except for a very limited restriction in the case of monopolies and national emergency strikes, are and ought to be freely and privately made. But the American people have a right to expect, in return for that freedom, a higher sense of business responsibility for the welfare of their country than has been shown in the last two days.

Sometime ago I asked each American to consider what he would do for his country, and I asked the steel companies. In the last twenty-four hours we had their answer.[24]

By the time President Kennedy had issued the above statement at his

---

[24] As reported in *The New York Times,* April 11, 1962.

news conference on April 11, the majority of the larger steel producers had followed U.S. Steel's lead: Bethlehem, Republic, Jones & Laughlin, Youngstown, and Wheeling. A major administrative strategy was to attempt to persuade other important companies to hold the line.[25] By the end of April, only Inland Steel, Kaiser Steel, and Armco were in this category of holdouts, and firms with an estimated 16 percent of capacity had not increased prices. On Friday morning, April 13, Joseph Block, chairman of Inland's board, announced from Kyoto, Japan: "We do not feel that an advance in steel prices at this time would be in the national interest," and the official company announcement followed shortly thereafter:

Inland Steel Co. today announced that it will not make any adjustment in existing prices of its steel mill products at this time. The company has long recognized the need for improvements in steel industry profits in relation to capital invested. It believes this condition, which does not exist today, will ultimately have to be corrected. Nevertheless, in full recognition of the national interest and competitive factors, the company feels that it is untimely to make an upward adjustment.

Shortly after noon, Kaiser announced it would maintain prices, and at about the same time the Defense Department announced an award of $5 million of armor plate to Lukens Steel Company, one of the smaller holdouts. At 3:20 P.M., Bethlehem unexpectedly rescinded its price increase; and at 5:28 P.M., U.S. Steel withdrew its price increases just 71 hours and 58 minutes after its original announcement.

The following week, after the prices had come back down, the joint Senate-House Republican leadership issued a statement summarizing nine governmental actions used by the White House, and deploring their use:

1. The Federal Trade Commission publicly suggested the possibility of collusion, announced an immediate investigation, and talked of $2,000 a day penalties.

2. The Justice Department spoke threateningly of antitrust violations and ordered an immediate investigation.

3. Treasury Department officials indicated they were at once reconsidering the planned increase in depreciation rates for steel.

4. The Internal Revenue Service was reported making a menacing move toward U.S. Steel's incentive benefits plan for its executives.

---

[25] Wallace Carroll in "Steel: A 72-Hour Drama with an All-Star Cast," *The New York Times*, April 23, 1962, states: "According to one official who was deeply involved in all this effort, the over-all objective was to line up companies representing 18 percent of the nation's capacity. If this could be done, according to friendly sources in the steel industry, these companies with their lower prices soon would be doing 25 percent of the business. Then Big Steel would have to yield."

5. The Senate Antitrust and Monopoly subcommittee began subpoenaing records from twelve steel companies, returnable May 14.

6. The House Antitrust subcommittee announced an immediate investigation, with hearings opening May 2.

7. The Justice Department announced it was ordering a grand jury investigation.

8. The Department of Defense, seemingly ignoring laws requiring competitive bidding, publicly announced it was shifting steel purchases to companies that had not increased prices, and other Government agencies were directed to do likewise.

9. The F.B.I. began routing newspaper men out of bed at 3.00 A.M. on Thursday, April 12, in line with President Kennedy's press conference assertion that "we are investigating" a statement attributed to a steel company official in the newspapers.

Taken cumulatively these nine actions amount to a display of naked political power never seen before in this nation.

Taken singly these nine actions are punitive, heavy-handed and frightening.

.   .   .   .   .   .

We condone nothing in the actions of the steel companies except their right to make an economic judgment without massive retaliation by the Federal Government.

Aftermath

Whether or not the steel executives who wore buttons bearing the words "I miss Ike" and in smaller letters "I even miss Harry" had removed them by the spring of 1963 could not be scientifically determined. In any case the administration did not quarrel with a price rise covering about 20 percent of the industry's products and resulting in about a 1 percent increase in the overall steel products price index. It was led by such smaller producers as Lukens, who later modified some of the rises to take into account lesser increases by U.S. Steel. President Kennedy stated that the steel producers "have acted with some restraint in this case."

Questions

1. Explain Mr. Kennedy's strong reaction to the price increase in 1962. Would you agree or disagree with his position?
2. Do you think the failure of U.S. Steel's price increase in 1962 was primarily because of political considerations, economic considerations, or a combination of both?
3. What is the rationale for the wage-price guideposts? Why is a firm like U.S. Steel particularly subject to them?

CASE 13–3. Price-Level Determination by General Motors

For many years, General Motors seems to have been following the same pricing procedures.[26]

1. The preliminary product planning, so that a car such as Chevrolet may be sold within a general price range.
2. The establishing of standard prices on the basis of standard costs and a standard return at a standard volume.
3. The setting of the prevaling or list price. (Actually, this price has been set at a retail level, with the price to the dealer allowing a margin of from 20 percent to 25 percent on a car with standard equipment.)

The following material is from the *Hearings before the Senate Subcommittee on Antitrust and Monopoly of December, 1955.*[27] Mr. Burns was counsel for the committee, and Mr. Bradley and Mr. Donner were vice presidents and directors of General Motors.

MR. BURNS: I would like to ask you some questions with respect to those principles, and the source of my information is the articles by Donaldson Brown, which I believe were published in 1924, entitled "Pricing Policy in Relation to Financial Return."

You are familiar with those articles?

MR. BRADLEY: Yes.

MR. BURNS: And do they express in broad terms the pricing policies which have been used by the corporation since that time?

MR. BRADLEY: That is correct.

MR. BURNS: Mr. Brown also made this statement with respect to attainable annual return and the pricing formula,

> The formulation of the pricing policy must be with regard to the particular circumstances pertaining to each individual business. When formulated, it is expressed simply in the conception of what have been defined as standard volume and the economic return available.

Now, would you explain for the benefit of our record what is meant by the term "standard volume"?

MR. BRADLEY: Yes; I think I might illustrate the standard volume.

We endeavor in planning for capacity to—we take the number of days there are in the year, and then take out the Sundays and holidays, and then we take out the minimum number of days we produce this over a period of time to turn around—I mean, to bring out new models.

---

[26] The most detailed exposition of the method is probably in Homer Vanderblue's article, "Pricing Policies in the Automobile Industry," *Harvard Business Review*, Summer, 1939, pp. 1–17. Other references are Kaplan, Dirlam, and Lanzillotti, *Pricing in Big Business* (Washington, D.C.: Brookings Institution, 1958), pp. 48–55, 131–35; and Joel Dean, *Managerial Economics* (Englewood Cliffs, N.J.: Prentice-Hall, 1951), pp. 448–49.

[27] Washington, D.C.: U.S. Government Printing Office, 1956.

From that, we find there are 225, taking out all the Sundays, holidays, and Saturdays, and 15 full days, or 30 half days, for turning around, giving 225 days which we would like to run the plants, year in and year out.

But we don't use 225, we use 80 percent of that as a standard volume, because ours is a business that you might call cyclical, and while it has been on the upswing for a number of years, there have been times when we had downswings—in fact, for a number of years we averaged below standard volume.

So, to allow for that cyclical factor and other conditions beyond our control, we take 80 percent of that 225 days, times the rated capacity per hour. So that gives us 180 days. And that, multiplied by our daily capacity, gives us a standard volume, which we work up by divisions, and which we hope to average.

Well, we have had years below it, and years above it.

MR. BURNS: How long a planning period do you use in your consideration of standard volume?

MR. BRADLEY: Well, except for the number of days for the turnaround, we haven't changed our standard volume. The 80 percent of the rated daily capacity times 225 days, that has remained constant over the years.

MR. BURNS: When you are planning—

MR. BRADLEY: Excuse me. We use that in planning capacity.

MR. BURNS: Now, when you are making your projections for either new models or plant expansion, do you use any particular length of time as a planning period?

MR. BRADLEY: Well, of course, we make our economic studies for several years ahead, but they are not firm. They are subject to revision at any time. I mean, for example, we did not plan for as big a volume as we have had in the last 2 or 3 years. With the national income, which has grown faster—the gross national product—with the movement out to the suburbs, and so on, so the big market has been bigger than we anticipated, but we try to look ahead a number of years and plan accordingly. We have to plan at least 2 years ahead or we would not have the capacity.

MR. BURNS: Well, now, what profit margin or attainable return have you used in pricing policy in recent years?

MR. BRADLEY: Well, actually in the back of our minds we have a standard, but one of the factors referred to there was competition. And the net profit may be below standard, or what we hope to have—the economic return attainable may be bigger in one business—one activity or one division than another. But we can always compare with what we expected.

We have not changed our general sights in a period of over 20 years.

MR. BURNS: What have been the general sights?

MR. BRADLEY: Ours is a fairly rapid turnover business, and our operations will yield between 15 or 20 percent on the net capital employed over the years. . . .

. . . .

SENATOR O'MAHONEY: . . . What is this general overall percentage which is added to the cost of the car for overhead for the general staff?

MR. DONNER: The figure I haven't got in my mind. Maybe I can get it in a minute. It isn't a high percentage at all. I don't think it would be 1 percent.

SENATOR O'MAHONEY: Let me ask you this way, then.

What are the basic elements of cost that enter into fixing the price of the car that is sold to the average automobile purchaser in the United States?

MR. DONNER: Sixty percent of the cost is materials that we buy. Some thirty-odd percent is payroll.

SENATOR O'MAHONEY: That includes all payrolls, the mechanics and the—

MR. DONNER: Right up to the president.

SENATOR O'MAHONEY: Right up to the president?

MR. DONNER: There is a couple of percent depreciation—

SENATOR O'MAHONEY: Yes, sir.

MR. DONNER (*continuing*): And I think a couple of percent for taxes other than Federal income taxes.

Now, that roughly adds up to a hundred percent of the cost.

. . . .

(After putting in the record S.E.C. figures for 1954 that showed profits after taxes as 9.9 percent of stockholder equity for all industry and 14.1 percent for motor vehicles and parts, Mr. Burns continued:)

I also would like to place in the record some figures from Moody's of the percentage of net income to net worth:

General Motors, 1948, 24.47; 1949, 31.37; 1950, 34.94; 1951, 20 percent; 1952, 20.59; 1953, 20.05; and their figure for 1954 is 24.43 percent. (1955 showed a 31 percent return.)

Competition in Price in the 1960s and 1970s[28]

In a statement prepared for a Senate Subcommittee in October, 1968, General Motors elaborated on some of the steps in its pricing policy as follows:

The MSP (Manufacturer's Suggested or list Price) represents a complex balancing of many and sometimes opposing factors. These include the competitive advantages the manufacturer believes his new product line offers in relation to his and other prior models, his estimate of the customer appeal of new competitive products, the prices of his competitors, his estimates of change in the cost of production and his appraisal of the market potential . . .

As an example the report indicated how Chrysler had rolled back its average announced increase of $84 per car on 1969 models to $52 after General Motors announced increases of only $49 per car. Such modifications by Ford and Chrysler took place several times in the 1960s.

General Motors noted that the wholesale price index for cars declined about 2.5 percent between 1959 and 1968, although GM's hourly employment costs rose 63 percent, the costs of steel and copper rose 9 percent and 58 percent respectively, and the wholesale price index for all in-

---

[28] The quotations in these sections are from *The Automobile Industry, A Case Study in Competition* (General Motors Corporation, October, 1968), pp. 33, 37, 43.

dustrial commodities rose 8 percent. ". . . In these ten years, General Motors countered its rising costs with imaginative efforts to increase efficiency and to develop and sell 'more car per car'—more optional equipment and a higher proportion of top-of-the-line models. For the first several years, our results were further favorably influenced by a rapidly expanding market as car sales doubled from 1958 to 1965 . . ."

The report went on to emphasize that GM's pricing methods are not of a mechanical cost-plus nature and indicated that the cost was frequently adjusted to the price range through product variations: ". . . The key test is whether a product of the type specified can be produced at a cost which will enable the manufacturer to sell at a profit in the defined areas of the price structure . . ."

A Target Rate of Return in the 1960s and 1970s

General Motors' operating results from 1961 to 1973 have been quite consistent with these statements as to their pricing policy and their stated target rate of profits. Mr. Bradley's testimony above suggested that "their operations will yield about 15–25 percent on the net capital employed over the years."

Let us assume that General Motors' target from 1961 through 1973 was an 18 percent return on shareholder investment, and that this goal was expected to be achieved when the company achieved 100 percent of standard volume. In Exhibit 13–3A the last column estimates the ratio of

EXHIBIT 13–3A

Operating Results for General Motors, 1961–73

Year	Sales (millions)	Net Income (millions)	Share-holders' Investment* (millions)	Unit Sales, Cars and Trucks (thousands)	Profit as Percent of In-vestment	Actual Unit Sales ÷ Standard†
1961	$11,395	$ 893	6,026	3,150	14.8	0.85
1962	14,640	1,459	6,650	4,223	21.9	1.08
1963	16,494	1,591	7,121	4,662	22.4	1.14
1964	16,997	1,734	7,599	4,560	22.8	1.06
1965	20,734	2,125	8,237	5,696	25.8	1.27
1966	20,208	1,793	8,726	5,195	20.6	1.11
1967	20,026	1,627	9,261	4,799	17.6	0.98
1968	22,755	1,732	9,756	5,410	17.8	1.06
1969	24,295	1,711	10,227	5,260	16.7	0.99
1970	18,752	609	9,854	3,591	6.1	0.65
1971	28,264	1,936	10,805	5,767	17.9	1.01
1972	30,435	2,163	11,683	5,740	18.5	0.96
1973	35,798	2,398	12,567	6,512	19.1	1.07

* Year-end.
† Based on long-run linear trend, standard has been computed as $S = 3,700 + 200t$; t is taken as 0 in 1961; units are thousands of cars. Thus S for 1968 when $t = 7$ would be 5,100 thousands of cars.
Source: GM *Information Handbook*, 1968, and subsequent annual reports.

actual volume to standard volume, the latter being calculated by a long-run trend. The first five columns are from GM's statements, and we properly assume that these results were dominated by domestic car and truck operations although recognizing they include appliance and international results.

The first step is to calculate as a percentage of sales the markup needed to achieve an 18 percent return on investment. That markup would depend on two factors: the proportion of sales at standard volume to stockholder investment, and the proportion of income before income taxes to the aftertax income. The following is the required formula:

$$\text{Markup} = \text{Target return} \times \frac{\text{Stockholders' investment}}{\text{Sales at standard volume}} \times \frac{\text{Pretax income}}{\text{Aftertax income}}$$

From 1961 to 1968 sales at standard volume were double or slightly more than double stockholder investment, so that the second term on the right had the value of one half or a little less. Income taxes were from 45 percent to 52.5 percent of GM's income, averaging about 49 percent, so that the third term on the right had a value averaging slightly over two. For the company during this period the last two terms roughly cancel out and the required markup was between 15 percent and 18.5 percent of the sales price. In subsequent years the ratio of stockholder investment to sales dropped (probably because of inflation which would raise sales more than the value of such assets as plant and equipment) so the required markup on sales was approximately 13 percent from 1971 to 1973.

It can be expected that profits would increase more than proportionally with volume because unit costs would drop as fixed costs are spread over more units. In Mr. Donner's testimony cited earlier in the case, he estimated fixed costs at 15 percent of total costs at standard volume. Exhibit 13–3B shows the implications of this for average total costs and for margins. *ATC* is taken to equal unit at standard volume. Price is taken to be 1.18 which represents at markup of just over 15 percent of price which is about average for the period.

EXHIBIT 13–3B

Prices, Costs, Margins at Various Outputs

	Ratio of Actual Volume to Standard Volume						
	0.65	*0.80*	*0.90*	*1.00*	*1.10*	*1.20*	*1.30*
Price..............	1.180	1.180	1.180	1.180	1.180	1.180	1.180
ATC..............	1.081	1.038	1.017	1.000	0.986	0.975	0.965
AVC.............	0.850	0.850	0.850	0.850	0.850	0.850	0.850
AFC..............	0.231	0.188	0.167	0.150	0.136	0.125	0.115
Price—*ATC*........	0.99	0.142	0.163	0.180	0.194	0.205	0.215
Predicted profits.......	6.4%	11.4%	14.7%	18%	21.3%	24.6%	28.0%

Since, coincidentally, the margin of 0.18 at the standard volume corresponds with the target rate of return on investment, the predicted profits as a percentage of investment given in the last row can be obtained by multiplying the ratio of actual to standard volume by the margin, that is, price minus ATC, which is given in the next to last row.

Questions

1. Are the actual profits as a percentage of investment of General Motors reasonably consistent with a target return of 18 percent at standard volume? (Compare the figures in Exhibit 13–3A with those in the last row of Exhibit 13–3B.)
2. Show diagramatically how increases in volume increase both dimensions of the rectangle of profits $[(P\text{-}ATC)Q]$. Use figures of Exhibit 13–3B.
3. What markup on sales would be called for to get a target return of 18 percent in 1962, in 1969? (The ratio of pretax income to aftertax income in each year was approximately 2.)
4. General Motors' approach has been termed "sophisticated cost-plus pricing." How does GM break the circle that prices determine volume and volume determines cost and cost determines price? How can GM bring demand considerations into its pricing approach?
5. Could the other automobile manufacturers successfully use a similar approach to pricing? What modifications might be necessary? (The student will find it helpful to examine the operating results of at least one other car manufacturer to see if a target return of 15 percent to 20 percent on investment would have been practical.) Do you think other firms could be as independent in their pricing as General Motors?

CASE 13–4. Traditional Department Stores, Inc.

Traditional Department Stores, Inc., was a medium-sized chain of department stores located in the Middle West, with stores in ten cities.[29]

Mr. Marshall Jennings, the chief menswear buyer for the largest store in the chain, was explaining the manner in which his buyers operated in ordering and pricing men's clothing. Mr. Jennings was a college classmate of William Griffin, who was a professor of business and economics at a nearby university. Professor Griffin was interested in determining how price and "output" decisions were made by a retail organization.

---

[29] This case is based in large part upon the research of Dean R. M. Cyert and Professor J. G. March of the Graduate School of Industrial Administration, Carnegie Institute of Technology, as reported in *The Behavioral Theory of the Firm*, © 1963. Adapted by permission of Prentice-Hall, Inc., Englewood Cliffs, N.J.

Professor Griffin knew that Mr. Jennings' store competed with two other large men's clothing stores in the trading area.

Mr. Jennings was quick to point out at the beginning of the conversation that while he could only talk in detail about his department, the general practice that he and his buyers followed was a more or less standard procedure used quite widely in all departments and in most department stores.

Professor Griffin suggested that Mr. Jennings first explain how the buyer determined what quantity of goods to order (and thus what quantity the store had to sell) and then discuss normal pricing and special pricing practices.

Ordering

Mr. Jennings began by explaining that there were two kinds of orders —advance orders and reorders. The size of the advance order depended largely on the estimated sales for the season for which the goods were being ordered, but also depended on the amount of "risk" involved in advance ordering. When items were highly seasonal in nature, so that selling an overstock after the season was difficult, advance orders as a percent of total orders were kept low, Mr. Jennings explained. Also, clothes of a very faddish or stylish nature presented a risky situation, since tastes could change easily and it was difficult to predict ahead of time what would sell well. Mr. Jennings estimated for Professor Griffin the percentage of estimated sales placed in advance orders for each of the four major buying seasons (see Exhibit 13–4A).

EXHIBIT 13–4A

Season	Percent	Order Dates	
Easter	70	January	15–20
Summer	50	March	10–15
Back to school	65	May	20–25
Holiday	75	September	20–25

The basic estimates of sales volume for each period were based on sales for the last period and adjusted for shifts in the timing of holidays, special sales, and so forth. Predictions were deliberately reduced somewhat from the last year's sales in order to decrease possible overforecasting, a mistake that was held against the buyer in judging his performance. Estimated sales forecasts did not have to be very accurate for ordering purposes, since the size of reorders could be varied to correct estimating errors.

By relying on reorders during the selling season, the buyers were able to utilize the most recent information on demand trends in terms of ovrall volume and specific items. Mr. Jennings warned, however, that the buyers had to balance this advantage against the disadvantages. Manufacturers required lead times for production, with the result that "out of stocks" might occur before the reorder was delivered. Moreover, since the manufacturer based both the type and the amount of recuttings on early reorders in order to decrease his risk of obsolete inventories, the buyer who waited till too late in the season to reorder might not be able to get the required amount or the exact styles and colors he desired.

Mr. Jennings outlined the following method of determining reorder amounts. Shortly after the selling season began, the buyers checked each of their product style lines against that same line during the previous year, and then applied this ratio to the previous year's sales. For instance, if sales during the first two weeks of an item were 80 units, and sales during the same period of the previous year were 100, then the buyer calculated that sales for the remainder of the season would be 80 percent of last year's sales during the remainder of the season.

Once this new estimate of sales was determined, the inventory on hand was subtracted from this figure and any inventory desired at the end of the season added to it in order to calculate the reorder quantity. In some cases where sales had been much less than initially expected, the inventory on hand might be so large as to yield a negative reorder quantity by this calculation. In this case, past orders might be canceled or the price cut in order to move more merchandise. Once the selling season was under way and the reorder made, such a calculation was made every week to determine whether part of the reorder should be canceled, whether the price should be cut, or whether more should be ordered. This weekly check served as a control mechanism which prevented extraordinary overstocks on stock "outs" on each line.

Mr. Jennings stressed the importance of having a routinized method for handling the order problem. If each buyer had a free rein to buy as much as he wanted whenever he wanted to do so, on hundreds of items, each coming in different styles and colors, the problem of controlling purchases, sales, and inventory levels would be tremendous.

Mr. Jennings confessed that during the last year his staff had had more difficulty than usual in predicting sales volumes accurately, with the result that the department had had to cancel orders, sell goods at cut prices, and sell after the seasons were over. But occasionally, the store also found itself with too little stock. The trouble came from a new large discount store that had opened on the edge of the city, about four miles from the center of the business district. This store, according to Mr. Jennings, constantly engaged in special promotions and low markups.

Mr. Jennings said he did not know how to take this store's behavior into account in forecasting sales for any one line. Prior to the opening of the discount store, he stated, he had not felt much need to take his competition into account in ordering, since the estimating method, which ignored these competitors, had in general worked satisfactorily. Professor Griffin then asked if he might see a record of an item with which Mr. Jennings had experienced trouble. Mr. Jennings had one of his assistants pull the records on men's Bermuda shorts (see Exhibit 13–4B).

EXHIBIT 13–4B

Sales and Competition Report
(men's Bermuda shorts)

	Number of Pairs Sold	Tra-ditional	Young's	Olds-field's	Shopper's Discount
$4.95 summer line:					
1961:					
Easter.....................	121	$4.95	$4.95	$4.95	—
Summer...................	459	4.95	4.95	4.75	—
Back to school.............	315	4.25	4.25	4.50	—
1962:					
Easter.....................	110	4.95	4.95	4.95	$3.95
Summer...................	200	4.95	4.95	4.95	3.95
Back to school.............	300	3.95	3.95	3.75	3.75
$7.95 summer line:					
1961:					
Easter.....................	60	7.95	7.95	7.49	—
Summer...................	180	7.95	7.95	7.95	—
Back to school.............	120	7.95	7.95	7.95	—
1962:					
Easter.....................	20	7.95	7.95	7.95	5.95
Summer...................	100	7.95	7.95	7.49	5.95
Back to school.............	220	5.95	5.95	5.95	5.95

Normal Price Determination

Mr. Jennings next described for Professor Griffin the concept of retail "price lining." The store carried only a limited number of different-quality items in the same product group. This simplified choice for consumers, resulted in stable product categories for manufacturers to produce in, and ultimately increased the retail stability of prices. Since the various price lines were reasonably well standardized, as were retail markups, the manufacturer knew the maximum his costs could be in order to sell his product at a particular price in the retail market. Likewise, each retail firm knew that the cost differences were not great for merchandise in any given price line, and thus that prices in that line among different stores would not vary significantly unless intended. Thus, price lining resulted in comparability for manufacturer, retailer, and shopper, according to Mr. Jennings.

Once price lines were selected, a large part of the pricing problem was solved. Merchandise was purchased to sell within a given price line and yield a "normal" markup. Normal markup for the menswear and boyswear department as a whole was 40 percent. This markup had been in existence in the industry as standard for 40 or 50 years, Mr. Jennings said. As a result of price-line standardization, the department was able to operate for the most part from a schedule of standard costs and standard prices. The schedule for the boy's section was as shown in Exhibit 13–4C.

EXHIBIT 13–4C

Traditional Department Stores, Inc.
(boyswear—normal markup)

Standard Costs	Standard Price*	Effective Markup
$ 3.00	$ 5.00	40.0%
3.75	5.95	37.0
4.75	7.95	40.2
5.50	8.95	38.5
6.75	10.95	38.3
7.75	12.95	40.1
8.75	14.95	41.5
10.75	17.95	40.0
11.75	19.95	41.0
13.75	22.95	40.0
14.75	25.00	41.0
18.75	29.95	37.4

* Calculated from the following rule: "Divide each cost by 60 percent (one markup), and move the result to nearest 95 cents."

The selection of price lines was an infrequent policy decision. Such a decision by high-level buying and administrative personnel was based on a wide range of factors—competitive lines in other stores, the economic characteristics of the community, the store's desired image, and so forth. For most decisions and to most buyers the price-line structure was a "given." The problem for the buyer, then, was to find goods that could be assigned prices that would enable the department to attain or improve the markup goal.

Although the average normal markup for the department was 40 percent, each product group had its own normal markup, which varied somewhat among product groups and which in general tended to be higher:

1. The greater the risk involved with the product.
2. The higher the costs (other than product cost).

3. The less the effect of competition.
4. The lower the price elasticity.

Risk was involved, for example, where the department dealt with foreign manufacturers. Products often varied in quality, and deliveries were not so dependable. As a result, the markup was increased 50 percent on these items, or to 60 percent of retail cost.

Another exceptional markup occurred when the store handled a product on an exclusive arrangement. Since the consumer was not able to make comparisons, the price and margin were set higher according to the following company rule: "When merchandise is handled on an exclusive basis, calculate the standard price from the cost, then use the next highest price on the standard schedule."

Markups were also higher on large items which used up a great deal of floor space, and on items that required considerable personal sales attention. In both cases, costs were higher.

Price decreases were automatically made to match lower prices by the store's two major competitors, although when a competitor's plans to feature an item were known in advance, the store often did not stock and never displayed the identical item. The store also met the prices of lesser competitors such as drugstores if these stores actively promoted and displayed the product. (Information about competitors was gained through newspaper advertisements, manufacturers' salesmen, customers, and professional shoppers.) Mr. Jennings stated that last year he had felt it necessary to feature a month-long "back to school" sale on many summer clothes in order to clear out large inventories built up during the spring and summer months. He blamed these overstocks on the discount house. "To tell the truth," Mr. Jennings stated, "we were all a little surprised at the results of the sale. We were actually caught short of stock after two and a half weeks, and had to rush through a special order to continue the advertised sale."

Sales Price Determination

Mr. Jennings stated that a completely different set of rules governed sales pricing in order to achieve a price appeal. Special sales were limited in number. Usually, they occurred when a buyer was able to make arrangements for lines that were exclusive in the immediate market at lower than normal cost—in other words, at a special discount.

The management had promulgated certain policy directives for the buyers to follow:

1. Whenever the normal price falls at one of the following lines, the corresponding sale price will be used:

Normal Price	Sale Price
$1.00...............	$0.85
1.95...............	1.65
2.50...............	2.10
2.95...............	2.45
3.50...............	2.90
3.95...............	3.30
4.95...............	3.90
5.00...............	3.90

2. For all other merchandise, there must be a reduction of *at least* 15 percent on items retailing regularly for $3 or less and at least *16⅔* percent on higher priced items.
3. All sales prices must end with a zero or a five.
4. No sale prices are allowed to fall on price lines normal for the product group.
5. Whenever there is a choice between an ending of 85 cents and 90 cents, the latter ending will prevail.
6. Use the standard schedule of sales pricing for prices that are slightly higher (by 5 cents) than the listed values. Thus, if the price is $3 retail, assume it is the same as $2.95 in computing the sales price.
7. The smaller the retail price, the smaller must be the increments between sales price endings, in order to approximate as closely as possible the desired percentage reduction. Therefore, after determining the necessary percentage reduction from normal price, carry the result down to the nearest ending specified below:
   a. Retail price greater than $5, reduce to the nearer of 90 cents or 45 cents.
   b. Retail price less than $5 but greater than $2, reduce to the nearest of 90 cents, 65 cents, 45 cents, or 30 cents.
   c. Retail price under $2, reduce to the nearer of zero or 5 cents.
   d. Reduce 5 cents more if the sale price is the same as another price line in the same product category.
8. When the special discount cost from the manufacturer is over 30 percent less than normal, pass some of the savings on to the customer by using the following formula:

$$\frac{\text{Special discount cost}}{1 - \text{Normal markup}}$$

if the resultant sales price using the normal rule is greater. [Mr. Jennings stated that "this usually happens when our relationship with the manufacturer has been one of long standing."]

When Professor Griffin asked if competitors' reactions were considered in setting sales prices, Mr. Jennings replied that they were not. He did say, however, that his store always met the sales prices of competitors on comparable items if their prices were lower, and competitors in turn would do likewise. The store had a firm policy, however, against raising prices to match competitors' prices when they were higher than those of Traditional.

Markdowns

Mr. Jennings next went into markdown pricing procedures. He explained: "We generally consider a markdown to be a decrease in price that the buyer feels will be permanent. However, there are exceptions in practice to this definition."

Mr. Jennings said that he liked to look on markdowns as a kind of "emergency device" which the department used in its efforts to maintain sales and inventory control. Their use, he explained, could be roughly grouped into two categories—special cases and general routines.

Special Cases

Competition. When it was determined that a recognized competitor was selling an item at a lower price, the department would mark down the item to equal the competitor's price. However, explained Mr. Jennings, if the department had reason to believe that the price was the result of a mistake, a check would be made with the competitor first before reducing the price. "Frequently," according to Mr. Jennings, "it develops that the price discrepancy is unintentional, and the competitor's price is increased."

Customer Adjustment. A returned defective item was marked down to zero and eliminated. Soiled or damaged merchandise was reduced in price. Merchandise that was returned by a customer after the line to which it belonged had been reduced in price was reduced accordingly.

Premature Depletion. If the stock for a sale was prematurely depleted, regular stock would be transferred to the sale racks and be marked down to sale price.

Promotion Item. At times during the year, as a stimulant to business, items which were in excess and also available in a large and balanced assortment were marked down by 4 percent.

Obsolescence Differential. Some items were suitable only for one season because of a particular style, color, or material, and could not be sold in the succeeding season. To accelerate the sale of these items, they were marked down one or two dollars near the peak of the season. Said Mr. Jennings: "We view this reduction as small enough to avoid antagonizing recent purchasers of the items but large enough to stimulate sales."

Drop in Wholesale Price during Season. When this happened, all items in stock, regardless of when they were purchased, were reduced to the appropriate level based on the new wholesale price.

Substandard Merchandise. Items which did not meet the quality standards of the original samples were either sent back to the manufacturer or, if this was not convenient, reduced in price and reimbursement sought from the manufacturer.

General Routine

This category accounted for the largest amount of dollars of markdown, according to Mr. Jennings. The items were marked down when some signal (inventory figures, reports from salesclerks, etc.) indicated that excess inventories existed. The exact nature of the price reaction depended on an analysis of the reasons for failure. Mr. Jennings outlined the pricing procedures followed for each of several common causes of excess inventories.

Normal Remnants. These were the odd sizes, less popular colors, and less favored styles remaining from the total assortment of an item which sold satisfactorily during the season. These items were considered normal, since it was impossible to order precisely the right assortment. "In fact," commented Mr. Jennings, "the complete clearance of the stock of an item by the end of the season is taken as an indication that the buyer did not buy heavily enough and that he probably suffered lost sales."

Overstocked Merchandise. These are items for which the buyer was overly optimistic—which had normal sales but still remained in a well-balanced assortment of styles and sizes at the end of the season with many acceptable items included.

Unaccepted Merchandise. This was merchandise that had "unsatisfactory" sales. During the season the sales personnel tried to determine whether the lack of acceptance was due to overpricing or poor style, color, and so forth. "The distinction is usually made," remarked Mr. Jennings, "by determining whether the item was ignored or whether it got attention but low sales."

The Markdown Process. Usually, Mr. Jennings said, items were not marked down right away but were mentally "stored" in an "availability pool" until the store or department had a general clearance sale. However, Mr. Jennings pointed out, there were times during the year when the department could not wait till the next scheduled clearance due to lack of space or lack of funds. In this case, immediate markdowns were ordered, such as the "back to school" sale of overstocked Bermuda shorts mentioned previously.

Items were marked down $33\frac{1}{3}$ percent in the first markdown, except in special conditions where space was extremely tight, when they were reduced 50 percent. Mr. Jennings remarked that the 33⅓ percent off approximated the cost of the merchandise, plus 10 cents to cover past handling costs, but that 33⅓ percent off was an easier rule to follow. All marked-down merchandise was advertised "at least one third off." The 33⅓ percent rule was developed into a standard "first markdown price" schedule with prices *reduced further* to the nearest 85 cents (to distinguish markdown from scale prices which ended in 90 cents). (See Exhibit 13–4D.)

EXHIBIT 13–4D

Boyswear Section

Regular Retail Price	*First Markdown Price*
$ 5.00	$3.85
5.95	3.85
(6.95)*	(4.85)
7.95	4.85
8.95	5.85
9.95	5.85
10.95	6.85
12.95	7.85

* Not considered a regular retail price.

There were two exceptions to the above rule, according to Mr. Jennings. Higher priced items were marked down by 40 percent or more. Experience had indicated that these items (over $15) did not have high rates of obsolescence, so that when they were marked down, they were more soiled than were lower priced goods.

The second case involved manufacturers' closeouts of remnants of odd styles, sizes, colors, and so forth, which were purchased at low cost. In this case the department tried to sell these items for one season at the regular pirce, and then cut the price by one half.

Second markdowns, for merchandise still not cleared by the initial markdown, followed no rule and were left to the buyer's discretion.

Questions

1. How does the actual pricing practice of Mr. Jennings' department square with traditional price theory? In what ways do economic concepts apply? In what areas do they seem not to apply?
2. To what extent did these pricing practices seem to be influenced by the number of sellers?
3. What do you think is the reason for having such well-defined pricing practices? Do you think the buying and price decisions of this department could be made with a computer? Why, or why not?
4. Do you see any conflict between the "best"—that is, optimum—economic behavior of the firm and the practical needs of the organization? Explain.

chapter 14

Nonprice Aspects of Competition

FREQUENTLY the term "nonprice competition" has been used to designate rivalry between firms in product specifications and in selling and advertising efforts. But this usage can be quite misleading. In one situation the competing firms may be charging identical prices and may take particular care that they always "meet competition" in price. As a matter of fact the major restraint against a firm's decision to cut prices is the probability of immediate retaliation by its rivals, as discussed in Chapter 13. The cigarette industry is one in which differences in wholesale prices sufficient to encourage a retail price differential are not tolerated. In a second situation a firm may charge a price that has little apparent relationship with that of other producers of similar products. The Rolls Royce at $17,000-plus is an illustration. Many other examples can be found in between these cases. For example, in many regions of the country less-advertised brands of gasoline have typically sold for 2 cents per gallon below the standard brands. An attempt by an independent to increase the differential is likely to lead to retaliation. With favorable price differentials, private brands of bread, frozen orange juice, margarine, and canned vegetables have outsold nationally advertised brands both in corporate and voluntary food chain stores.[1]

The basic point is this: under most market structures that are intermediate between pure monopoly and pure competition, firms will be concerned simultaneously with the effects of price, product quality, and advertising on the quantity demanded. Nonprice rivalry does not take place without some attention to price. To paraphrase marketing experts,

---

[1] Jules Backman, *Advertising Competition* (New York: New York University Press, 1967), pp. 57–58.

firms aim at a satisfactory or optimal "mix" of product features, advertising, and price.[2]

Firms may agree, conspiratorially or tacitly, on price and at the same time leave the issue of quantity and relative market shares open to quality and advertising efforts. On the other hand, Rolls Royce may set a price figure that has so little relation to automobiles most nearly comparable with it that there is little point of making price changes when, say, Cadillac makes a price change. When price is taken as a given determinant of the quantity demanded, managements' concentration on product improvement and selling efforts to better meet or to shift consumer preferences represents nonprice aspects of market competition. They are methods of increasing sales that are alternatives to reductions in prices.

But it must be recognized that price changes, product improvements, and advertising may be complements in market rivalry. In a world of imperfect knowledge of market alternatives, advertising can make price and product decisions more effective. As examples: almost any retail grocery advertisement is essentially a price list; Polaroid plugs its new $14.95 (suggested retail price) zip camera; the cigarette companies launch advertising campaigns to present the virtues of new longer filter brands.

Competition in Services and Other Terms of Trade

The close relationship between price and nonprice aspects of competition can be shown by examining the many terms of trade and collateral services which closely resemble price differences. Many concessions such as freight allowances, discounts, and trading stamps or coupons with definite cash value can of course be translated into price terms.

The inability of business to compete in price because of legal barriers or private price or cartel arrangements has frequently led to ingenious nonprice methods of competition. Under the NRA, when minimum prices in many industries were controlled by code provisions, the Division of Industrial Economics of the National Recovery Administration listed more than 200 devices that were used. These included such product improvements as product and maintenance guarantees, special labels, sales on approval, and installation and erection of equipment. They also included such selling aids as display material, the provision of sales help, and such miscellaneous concessions as gifts and entertainment, split shipments, and acceptance of buyer's capital stock.

---

[2] For simple mathematical models, see I. R. Dorfman and P. O. Steiner, "Optimal Advertising and Optimal Quality," *American Economic Review,* December, 1954, pp. 822–36.

Types of Product Competition

In relatively few markets today are firms engaged in selling completely standardized products. This is especially true of final consumer goods, for which competition in quality, style, and design is a pervasive form of nonprice competition.

The concept of "quality" is by no means simple. It involves numerous variables, some of which can be measured; others defy measurement. Any one product can involve several quality variables. An automobile, for example, can be appraised as to horsepower, durability, gasoline consumption, probable frequency and cost of repairs, comfort, riding qualities, safety, and ease of handling.

Competition in some industries has served to give the consumer substantial improvements over the years, with part of the gain reflected in lower prices and the rest in better quality. For example, since World War II, automobile tires have been both improved greatly in quality and lowered in price. Economy of operation is another aspect of quality competition which can be measured approximately. According to tests made by the Procurement Division of the United States Treasury in 1931, the average consumption of five makes of 6-cubic-foot refrigerators was 44 kilowatt-hours per month. A test based on 14 makes in 1938 showed average electricity consumption to have declined to 35 kilowatt-hours per month.[3] By 1954 this amount of current was sufficient to operate the average 8.3- to 9.6-cubic-foot refrigerators for a month, according to tests by Consumers Union.[4] For later developments see Case 14–1.

Although many quality changes are physically measurable in terms of performance, as a rule it is impossible to translate these changes into price equivalents.[5] Where quality changes are of the intangible sort involving design, taste, and style, not even measures of physical performance are available. Yet these intangible elements are often the chief determinants of consumer choice. In women's clothing, for example, the indefinable element of style is far more important than are thread count, tensile strength of the cloth, or quality of workmanship. The success of a new model of automobile frequently has been determined more by the design of the hood than by the efficiency of the motor, though gasoline mileage has become more important since 1973.

The degree to which quality competition emphasizes measurable elements of the product varies with commodities. Where industrial buyers

---

[3] *Price Behavior and Business Policy,* TNEC Monograph No. 1, 76th Cong., 3d sess. (Washington, D.C.: U.S. Government Printing Office, 1940), p. 64.

[4] Calculated from data given in *Consumer Reports,* September, 1954, p. 403.

[5] Andrew T. Court made an interesting attempt to develop a price index for automobiles which would reflect changes not only in price but also in weight, wheel base, and horsepower, expressed in terms of price (cf. A. T. Court, *Dynamics of Automobile Demand* [New York: General Motors Corp., 1939], pp. 99–117).

constitute the chief market, there is a tendency to stress such features as operating economy, tensile strength, and durability. In consumer goods markets, sellers find it desirable to emphasize the intangible elements of quality, style, and design because these are less easily copied. Sellers of food products seldom mention their conformity with government standards of quality; sellers of dresses do not usually emphasize fiber content; and distributors of cosmetics do not ordinarily refer to the quality of ingredients of their products. Flavor, style, and attractive containers are more important selling features.

Varieties of Sales Promotion

As an alternative or complement to varying the product, many business companies compete by incurring selling expenses which are directed primarily at creating demand. Collectively, these expenditures can be called "sales promotion," including advertising, which involves outlays for newspaper and magazine publicity, direct mail, catalogs, television and radio programs, window displays, and billboards. The basic characteristic of these expenditures is that they are undertaken with a view to influencing the buyer, though some changes of the physical form of the product, as in packaging, may also be involved. Obviously, in some cases, it is difficult to distinguish changes in the product expressly designed for their effect on the consumer from those which have substantive utility. Who is to say whether a catsup bottle which is conveniently designed for table use may not also be the one whose contours catch the consumer's eye on the supermarket shelf?

Related to advertising is the use of trademarks and brand names. The purpose of these is to furnish an easy means of identifying a particular seller's product. It is conceivable that brands might be employed merely to enable the buyer to identify products embodying certain measurable quality differences. But usually, sellers combine the use of brands with advertising which attempts to persuade buyers that the product has certain desirable intangible characteristics which are unique or which it possesses in greater degree than competing goods. The brand is built into a limited monopoly, with a regular following created by advertising.

The effectiveness with which trademarks and brands can protect a product against price competition varies with different lines of goods. In fields in which comparisons are relatively simple, or in markets where buyers are well equipped technically (as in many industrial goods markets), there is a strong tendency for buyers to switch to competing brands as soon as substantial price differences appear. On the other hand, where the consumer is unable to compare rival brands intelligently, the effective use of brands and trademarks frequently permits wide price differentials to be maintained between virtually identical products. A lack of correspondence between price and U.S. Department of Agriculture grade for particular food products often exists. In the case of grocery products the element of taste is so subjective that comparisons among brands are very difficult; as a result, sellers are presented with an opportunity to create demand through nonprice competition. Striking illustrations of the insulation from price competition afforded by brand names are in the drug and cosmetic field. The consumer is almost completely uninformed as to the merits of rival products; few are aware of the significance of specifications of the United States Pharmacopoeia. Advertising-sales ratios are higher for proprietary drugs and cosmetics than for any other industry.[6] In addition, elaborate sales promotion efforts are directed at physicians to encourage prescriptions by brand names.

Other devices of sales promotion include personal selling,[7] free distribution of samples of the product, give-away contests, and other methods such as the use of coupons exchangeable for other products. With regard to personal selling, it should be noted that some use of salesmen's time is for "production," such as making estimates, giving instruction in the use of the product, handling complaints, and making collections. But it cannot be doubted that an important use of salesmen is for promotion of demand for the product. As such, personal selling is an alternative or a supplement to other means of sales promotion.

The Magnitude of Product and Selling Competition

What is the cost of these product and selling efforts? The total spending for industrial research and development was estimated for 1965 at $13,825 million about half financed by government and half by industry.[8] Much of this was on process research (which frequently is connected with product changes); a great deal went into basic, military, or space research and development which scarcely fits the framework of this chapter. We will conclude only that a few billion annually could have been involved in commercial product innovations and variations.

Other production costs will also be affected. At a later point in the chapter an economic model will be presented indicating that for differentiated products, potential economies of scale may be unrealized. Costs of hundreds of millions have been incurred in the automobile industry alone for annual style changes.

---

[6] For 1957 they were estimated at 14.7 percent for toilet preparations and 10.28 percent for drugs. Lester G. Telser, "Advertising and Competition," *The Journal of Political Economy*, December, 1964, p. 543.

[7] Avon Products with its horde of housewives selling cosmetics door to door was one of the great growth stocks of the 1960s and early 1970s.

[8] The source of this figure is the National Science Foundation. It was cited in Backman, *Advertisng Competition*, p. 23.

A comprehensive series for advertising expenditures in the United States has been published by *Printer's Ink* magazine. In both the prewar and postwar periods advertising amounted to about 2.25 percent of GNP and 1.5 percent of total corporate sales. It has increased in proportion to consumption expenditures from about 3 percent to 3.5 percent. Advertising is only a fraction of total marketing costs, which include personal selling and the costs of physical distribution as well. For example, in a sample of 127 industrial companies total marketing costs were found to be 15.1 percent of sales, of which advertising and sales promotion was 2.2 percent, or less than one seventh of total marketing costs.[9] On the other hand, for one of the most highly advertised consumer products, breakfast cereals, advertising and sales promotion expenditures were 17 percent of sales in 1964 while other components of marketing costs were 10 percent.[10]

Many marketing costs, those related to the physical distribution of products, would be considered production costs rather than selling expenditures designed to increase the demand for the product. Personal selling costs may well involve such production functions as physical delivery of the product but also may be intended to influence demands for products. An example of how personal selling may be substituted for advertising is that of Avon products. While the cosmetic industry was estimated in 1963 to spend 15 percent of sales on advertising, Avon with its house-to-house representatives spent only 2.7 percent.[11] No attempt will be made here to assess the demand-influencing component of costs of nonprice competition. The results are also substantial in terms of the product choice offered the consumer and in the rate of product change over time.

An Economic Model of Product Differentiation

Product differentiation is one result of product and sales competition. Products can be said to be differentiated if some buyers are willing to pay more for one firm's version of a commodity than for another firm's version.

Under the assumption that there are a large number of firms producing products that are tolerable but at the same time distinguishable substitutes for each other, the demand curve for the firm in Figure 14–1 can be drawn with the assumption that all other prices are held constant

---

[9] *Industrial Marketing—1963* (New York: McGraw-Hill Book Co., June, 1964).

[10] *Studies of Organization and Competition in Grocery Manufacturing, Technical Study 6*, National Commission on Food Marketing (Washington, D.C., June, 1966), p. 147.

[11] Penelope Orth, "Cosmetics: The Brand Is Everything," *Printers' Ink*, November 1, 1963, p. 30.

FIGURE 14-1

Initial and Equilibrium Position for Firm with Differentiated Product and Free
Entry into Industry

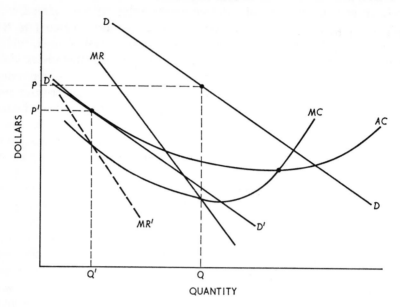

including those of competitors. Assume that initially the price is at P, the
profit-maximizing position with output Q where $MC = MR$. If free entry
exists this is not an equilibrium position for the long run, since the high
profits will attract new firms producing similar but not identical products. The effect of their entry is to shift the firm's demand curve to the
left as its customers find the products of the new entrants more appealing. It is conceivable that this process could go on until the firm's
demand was at $D'D'$. At this point its profit-maximizing price would have
dropped to P' and the quantity produced to Q'.

This is not necessarily the only equilibrium position. A degree of
product uniqueness and appeal could be postulated for the particular
firm that could leave it with continuing profits despite the possibilities of
entry into the industry. This latter case would approach that of monopoly. In fact there is no clear line between monopoly and monopolistic
competition. The issue hinges on the ease of substitution of competing
products.

One generalization that has come out of the analysis of the type of
Figure 14-1 is that where (*a*) product differentiation exists and (*b*)
entry into the production of similar products is easy, then firms in the
group or industry will be operating below the most efficient scale of
production. This would necessarily be true when all profits were elimi-

nated by the entry of new firms. A downward-sloping demand curve can be tangent only to a downward-sloping average cost curve.

Examples most frequently cited are from the retailing field. The product differentiation in the service station industry is associated with location, the brand of gasoline, the cleanliness of washrooms, and the friendly smiles (or lack of them) of the station personnel. The gallonage of gasoline sold at many stations may be well below that possible at optimal capacity. More resources of land, labor, and capital are devoted to the function of pumping gas than would be necessary with fewer stations. This extra use of resources may of course result in a locational convenience not otherwise available. Opponents of "fair trade" have pointed out that the druggists' hope for greater profitability under price-maintenance agreements is likely to be thwarted as long as entry is uncontrolled. The greater number of drugstores entering the business results in each encountering higher unit costs.

Sales Promotion and Economic Growth: An Illustrative Model

In addition to stressing its role in making consumers better informed, defenders of advertising have emphasized its role in promoting economic growth. The introduction of new or substantially modified products is frequently associated with marketing costs that are very large in proportion to sales for the first year or two.[12] Figure 14–2 shows a situation in which additional advertising permitted a large expansion of output, a lower price, and increased profits.

DD and *AC* represent the demand and average cost curves without advertising after a new product has been on the market for three years. D_aD_a and AC_a represent the same functions after three years with advertising at the rate of $1 million per year. Without advertising, profits are approximately $80,000 at a price of $1.08 and a volume of 1 million units. With advertising, profits would be maximized at a volume of 4.4 million units and a price of about 93 cents. The effect of the advertising program is shown by the shift of the demand curve to the right. As a result of economies of scale at the higher volume, unit costs including promotional expenditures are substantially lower than the average production costs without advertising.

Two points should be made about the illustration in Figure 14–2. First, a cumulative effect can be expected from the advertising and from the demonstration effects of the use of the product by others. The demand developed in the first year might be only two million units, and

---

[12] For selected food products these were 57 percent for the first year and 37 percent for the second, in a study by Robert D. Buzzell and Robert E. Nourse, *Product Innovation, the Product Life Cycle and Competitive Behavior, Selected Food Processing Industries, 1947–1964* (Cambridge, Mass.: Arthur D. Little, Inc., 1966).

FIGURE 14–2

The Hypothetical Effect of Advertising on a Firm's Price, Output, and Profits

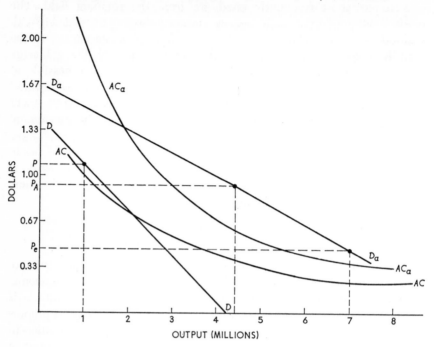

OUTPUT (MILLIONS)

at a price of 93 cents large losses would be sustained. As the demand continues to shift to the right, a break-even point is reached at an output of three million units—this might occur some time within the second year. Second, the indicated profits and costs at the profit-maximizing output are such as to make it highly tempting for new entrants. Production cost including return on capital is indicated at 40 cents per unit, advertising at 23 cents, and profit about 30 cents per unit. Other firms would have much leeway to use either sales promotion or a price emphasis or both to break into the market. Unless the original firm were protected by very strong barriers to entry such as a strong patent position or technical mastery of a complex production process, it would be likely that at some time during the introductory period it would have selected a price like P_e (just under $0.50). It then would be producing seven million units with profits of about $700,000. This strategy would act as a deterrent to easy entry by other firms and the resulting leftward shift of the demand curve shown in Figure 14–1.

What is the relationship, then, of sales promotion to economic growth? In the first place, by gaining rapid consumer acceptance for new products and product improvements, sales promotion may result in volume production and thus lower real costs (increased factor productivity) much sooner than without such sales stimulus. Secondly, profit prospects may be greatly increased, as indicated in Figure 14–2, and this could act as a stimulus to entrepreneurship and investment that would not otherwise take place.

In this example advertising has served to build up a larger market by attracting customers to a particular version of a product. This may offset the tendency in markets with differentiated products toward fragmentation and consequent production at well below optimum scales. Figure 14–2 could be used, however, to indicate less favorable possibilities. Suppose the firm set the price P_a and new entrants were attracted. It could maintain D_aD_a only by increasing its advertising budget and shifting its AC_a to the right; competitors then would presumably have increased their own efforts. One can easily envision an eventual equilibrium at a price as high or higher than P_a with no profits and with costs at a high level. One check to such a development could be oligopolistic restraint by the sellers, recognizing that selling efforts would be retaliated against. Such retaliation is by no means as certain as that against an aggressive price move. The basic check is that of the entry of other firms which choose to emphasize a low price. It was reputedly Clair Wilcox who said approximately this: "Competition in the United States is two-thirds oligopoly and one-third Sears, Roebuck." Such firms as Sears, Roebuck and Company, and A & P have been particularly diligent in seeking out manufacturers who are willing to supply goods on a cost of production basis and to leave the distribution problem to them.

A Marginal Approach

How far should advertising or product quality be carried consistent with the maximization of profits? To examine advertising expenditures as a variable, the firm can select a particular price and quality of product. With the price given, a marginal revenue curve can be constructed at that price as in Figure 14–3. For a given quality of product, a marginal cost curve for production can be determined (technology and factor prices are assumed constant). If the price were determined in a purely competitive market, the intersection of the MR and MC_p curves in Figure 14–3 would indicate the profit-maximizing output. (Sales promotion expenditures would be neither necessary nor helpful with identical products that could not be differentiated by the consumer.)

The origin in Figure 14–3 represents a base quantity which could be either the quantity sold at price P with no advertising, or that quantity sold with the minimum of advertising required to enter the market at all. With differentiated rather than identical products, the quantity demanded at P may be increased by additional amounts of advertising

FIGURE 14–3

The Determination of Advertising Expenditures with Given Price and Product

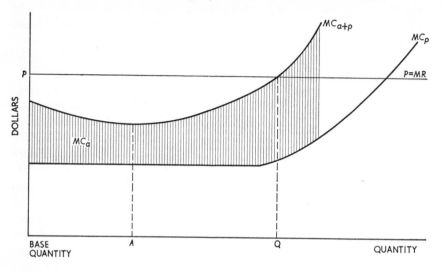

(thus shifting a downward-sloping demand curve to the right). The shaded vertical distances indicating MC_a first show increasing returns in unit sales per dollar of advertising. This could reflect such factors as increased cumulative impact with greater frequency of advertising, cheaper advertising rates for greater quantity, or the use of more expensive and more effective media. To obtain sales beyond point A, decreasing returns are to be expected as additional or more expensive messages produce fewer added sales per dollar of expenditure. Finally at point Q, where the marginal costs of producing and of promoting an additional sale equal the added revenue per unit, further increases in advertising become unprofitable.

Analysis similar to that of Figure 14–3 can deal with the problem of quality improvement with advertising and price held fixed. There would be only one marginal cost curve, which would represent the added costs of production for selling one more unit of a product, but the specifications of the product would be changing with each increase in quantity. Assume that ten units of a standard quality could be sold and the average variable cost per unit is $1. Under the same conditions 11 units of a slightly improved product could be sold with an AVC of $1.05. The relevant marginal cost of selling one more unit by improving quality would be $1.55, not $1.05, since total variable costs would now be $11.55.

Few firms probably draw the thousands of graphs of the type of Figure 14–3 to take into account all the possible permutations of price, advertising, and product in order to locate the optimal combination of price and nonprice factors. It is a practical framework only for incremental moves with most of the elements of the marketing mix taken as given. The analysis rests essentially on the requirement that to maximize profits, all activities should be pushed to that point where the marginal return is equal to the marginal cost.

Consumerism, Product, and Promotion Policies

In Chapter 1 consumerism was cited as a challenge for business decision making. Essentially it calls for honesty and candor in product and promotional decisions. The rule of caveat emptor (let the buyer beware) may have tolerably served a marketplace where choices were few and products were simple. It is less appropriate for the changing and complex choices that consumers must make today. There is an asymmetry between the potential expertise of the producer and seller about the product he offers and the consumer's knowledge about the many goods and services he must buy that places a particular responsibility upon the seller to fully disclose material facts about his wares.

Three approaches to consumer protection that represent constraints on business decision making constitute the main thrust of consumerism. One is litigation under the legal doctrines of implicit warranty or of fraud. The second is through legal regulation, either of product standards (as in building codes and motor vehicle safety requirements) or of the honesty or fullness of disclosure of promotion. The third is through private exposure such as the product information offered by Consumers Union in *Consumers Reports* or in the recording of abuses by a Nader task force. All three can be thought of as supplements to the provision of consumer alternatives in the marketplace.

It is not within the scope of this chapter to take up government restraints in general (some amplification is contained in Chapter 16). Rather it is to concentrate on the interplay between managerial decisions and consumerism in particular but reasonably representative situations— Case 14–1 with refrigerators and Case 14–2 with cigarettes.

The refrigerator case is of particular interest in the 1970s because its facts gave impetus to Senator Tunney's "truth in energy act" which was before Congress in 1974. Through the mid-1950s as indicated on the third page of this chapter, refrigerators had become larger, cheaper, and more economical in energy usage. They continued to become larger and cheaper in original price and offered new features such as no-frost operation and automatic icemakers. But by the 1970s the average refrigerator required four times as much energy to operate. The energy shortages of 1973–74 focused attention on the advantages for society of reducing energy demand, and more specifically on the fact that appliance purchasers were being offered little or no information on the energy cost of appliances, although these typically exceeded the purchase price. The prospect was that higher energy prices would make electricity or gas consumption information even more important for rational choice by consumers.

A latent consumerist issue had become a very active one. The approach of the "truth in energy act" was to require an estimate of annual operating costs in the labeling of refrigerators, freezers, ranges, air-conditioners, clothes dryers, and water heaters. The supervision would be by the Federal Trade Commission and the National Bureau of Standards. The Association of Home Appliance Manufacturers opposed the operating cost provisions (presumably favoring energy usage), the administration had a voluntary alternative, others suggested the inclusion of other appliances. Refrigerator manufacturers faced not only the issue of what bill to support but what their own product and promotional policies should be concerning energy usage.

Another aspect of consumerism, the concern for product safety, is brought out in Case 14–2, "Upheaval in the Cigarette Industry." Such leaders in the antismoking campaign as the American Cancer Society may deplore the increase in the total number of cigarettes sold but can point to the decline in pounds of cigarette and tobacco products smoked, the sharp reduction in the percentage of men who smoke cigarettes, and the increased recognition of the rights of nonsmokers such as in various bans on smoking in public places. A triumph of sorts for women's liberation is suggested by the observation of Dr. Horn, director of the National Clearinghouse for Smoking and Health (an agency of HEW) who stated that "the girls have been keeping up with the boys" in cigarette smoking.[13] Significant contributions of the consumer advocates have been the publicizing of medical findings on smoking hazards, the exposure of the poor performance of cigarette filters in the 1950s, and the pressure on public agencies to act rather than to evade the health issue. A tangible gain has been the significant reduction of the tar content of cigarette smoke in the two decades after 1954. The requirement that tar and nicotine content, as determined by the FTC, be a part of all advertising is likely to mean further reductions. The specified warning that "The Surgeon General Has Determined That Cigarette Smoking Is Dangerous to Your Health" has added candor previously missing from national cigarette advertising.

The Game Theory Approach

An appendix to this chapter deals with game theory and considers simple applications to business situations. The idea is intriguing as ap-

---

[13] As quoted in *U.S. News & World Report,* December 17, 1973.

plied to the market strategies of the few rivals in many of our own oligopolistic industries. Clearly the managements of the firms can be thought to be playing a complex game rich in the variety of price and nonprice moves that each can make. For each move, the rival may have a countermove. The discovery of guiding principles for action from an analysis of game-playing would indeed be helpful. The material is placed in a separate position from the main text because the grasp of the fundamentals is time-consuming and because the clearest theoretical developments have been with simple two-person games that are poor approximations of the more complex business games.

APPENDIX TO CHAPTER 14. Game Theory and Business Decisions

Suppose you are invited to be a spectator at a meeting of the board of directors of a large corporation. And suppose that soon after the meeting is called to order, each director, at the request of the chairman, begins to toss a coin into the air and to record the resulting heads and tails on a piece of paper. You will probably conclude that the assembled officials have suddenly felt an irresistible urge to gamble or else that the hectic pace of modern business has finally proved to be too much for the human mind. Actually, however, the directors may be engaging in a new and quite rational method of decision making according to the theory of games developed principally by a famous mathematician, the late John von Neumann.[14] As will be explained later, the purpose of the coin tossing may be to secure guidance of a pure chance (hence, unpredictable) nature as to an important business move. They may be taking the steps necessary to minimize the likelihood that their opponents will be able to guess their next move, since they themselves will not know what they are going to do until the coin-tossing ceremony is over. In the words of von Neumann and Morgenstern: "Ignorance is obviously a very good safeguard against disclosing information directly or indirectly."[15] The executive coin tossing is carried out, however, as only a part of a carefully calculated process of making a decision and differs sharply from the action of the motorist who tosses a coin to decide which fork of the road to take when he is completely lost.

---

[14] The theory is set forth in most complete form in John von Neumann and Oskar Morgenstern, *Theory of Games and Economic Behavior* (Princeton: Princeton University Press, 1944). An application of game theory to competition and oligopoly is Martin Shubik, *Strategy and Market Structure* (New York: John Wiley & Sons, Inc., 1959).

[15] *Theory of Games and Economic Behavior*, p. 146.

Since its original promulgation the theory of games has attracted much attention in military planning circles because of its implications for certain situations encountered in war. Theoretically, it can also be useful to the gambler in guiding his play in such games as poker and in the more purely intellectual activity of chess playing. However, its actual application to such complicated games is extremely difficult and not likely to prove of practical help to the players.[16] It is especially difficult to visualize the tough, gun-toting poker player of the western movies sitting patiently while one of the players is running off on his portable electronic computer the calculations necessary to decide whether to raise, call, or drop out.

Certain simple games, however (which might conceivably be suitable for gambling), can readily be handled by means of the theory of games. The player who uses the system indicated by game theory is playing conservatively. He assumes that his opponent is skilled rather than stupid. In the words of J. D. Williams, game theory "refers to a kind of mathematical morality, or at least frugality, which claims that the sensible object of the player is to gain as much from the game as he can, safely, in the face of a skillful opponent who is pursuing an antithetical goal."[17]

Often, the business situation in which an executive decision is required is so complex that application of the theory of games is not likely to be considered feasible. When there is a clean-cut conflict of interests between one firm and another, however, or between one firm and all other close rivals taken as a group, an optimal sort of business behavior may be calculable by the use of game theory. Even where an actual solution cannot be reached, the "way of thinking" about a problem which is suggested by game theory may be useful to the business executive. And as was suggested earlier, some knowledge of game theory should at least cause one to appreciate the possible virtue of basing an important decision on the outcome of some apparently frivolous action such as the toss of a coin or the throw of a pair of dice or a single die.

The Game of Hul Gul

This appendix will not attempt to give any systematic or comprehensive explanation of the elements of game theory (such as is given in mathematical terms by von Neumann and Morgenstern, and more simply by J. D. Williams), but will instead apply the theory to certain simple

[16] Von Neumann and Morgenstern devote a considerable amount of space to analysis of a simplified version of poker and conclude that "the mathematical problem of real poker is difficult but probably not beyond the reach of techniques which are available" (ibid., p. 219).

[17] J. D. Williams, *The Compleat Strategyst* (New York: McGraw-Hill Book Co., 1954), p. 23. This book gives a simple and humorous exposition of the elements of the theory of games. The present appendix is heavily indebted to this work.

conflict situations in such a way as to enable the reader (it is hoped) to analyze some simple business cases by this method.[18] This simple introduction may kindle some interest in further study of the theory and its possible business applications. An old game called Hul Gul, which is reputedly played by children, will first be investigated. By using the results of the analysis, one should be able to win a considerable amount of candy from even an extremely intelligent child, unless the child is too bright to stake his sweets on the outcome of the game.

The game of Hul Gul is played with beans or other small objects. In the simplest version, only two beans are used. One player holds his hands behind his back, then brings forth one fist in which he holds either one or two beans. The other player must attempt to guess the number of beans. If he does so correctly, he gets the beans or other remuneration— otherwise, he pays an amount equal to the difference between what he guessed and the actual number of beans held. It is quite obvious that the first player will wish to hold one bean more often than two beans, since when he holds only one, that is all he can lose; whereas when he holds two beans, he may lose two. He cannot hold one bean every time, however, for his strategy would quickly be figured out. To find out what proportion of the time he should hold one bean and what proportion of the time he should hold two beans in order to lose the smallest amount to a clever opponent is a suitable task for the theory of games. The holder of the beans is at a disadvantage compared with the guesser, since part of the time he will lose two beans on a particular play, whereas the guesser cannot lose more than one bean on a play. Consequently, a realistic objective of the holder is to minimize his loss, and a proper objective of the guesser is to maximize his gain by means of scientific play. The proportion of the time that the guesser should call "one bean" and "two beans" can also be determined by game theory.

Payoff Matrix

The first step is to arrange gains and losses (payoffs) in matrix form, showing who pays how much to whom under various possible circumstances. The holder of beans will be called "North," and the guesser will be called "West." Figure 14–4 shows this matrix, with positive numbers indicating payments by North to West and negative numbers denoting payments by West to North. For example, if North holds two beans and West guesses two, West receives the two beans from North. Conse-

---

[18] We shall be concerned only with "two-person zero-sum games." In such a game the interests of the players are diametrically opposed, and one player gains only at the expense of the other. The fact that collusion is unprofitable simplifies the game. On this point, see D. Blackwell and M. A. Girshick, *Theory of Games and Statistical Decisions* (New York: John Wiley & Sons, Inc., 1954), p. 10.

FIGURE 14–4

Two-Bean Hul Gul

	NORTH HOLDS		
	1	2	ROW MINIMA
WEST GUESSES 1	+1	−1	−1
WEST GUESSES 2	−1	+2	−1
COLUMN MAXIMA	+1	+2	

quently, the number +2 is in the box corresponding to "North holds 2" and "West guesses 2." The propriety of the other payoffs can as readily be seen.

Solution of the Game

The first step in finding the solution to the game, once the payoff matrix has been set up, is to find the minimum figure in each row and the maximum figure in each column. These are entered alongside and under the table, respectively. If the larger of the row minima were equal to the smaller of the column maxima, the game would have a "saddle point" which would immediately indicate the best strategy for each participant. (This will be explained later.) In the game of two-bean Hul Gul, however, the larger row minimum is −1, while the smaller column maximum is +1, so the game does not have a saddle point, and further calculations are necessary.

In a "two-by-two" zero-sum game, these further calculations are simple. First, subtract each figure in row 2 from the number immediately above. This gives +2 and −3. Signs are then disregarded, and these numbers are switched so that the 3 is associated with the left-hand column and the 2 is associated with the right-hand column. This solves the game for North, the bean holder. He should hold one bean three times and two beans two times out of five plays, on the average. In order to avoid falling into any sort of predictable pattern, he should ideally use a chance device of some suitable sort. For example, if North owned a miniature of the Pentagon Building in Washington, D.C., he could mark three of the sides with a 1 and two of the sides with a 2, and roll the replica on its side before each play. Each time a 1 came up, he would hold one bean; and each time a 2 came up, he would hold two beans. (It would be important, of course, to roll the building behind his back, so that his opponent would not also know the answer.)

It is also simple to find the relative use which West should make of his two alternative guesses. Subtract each figure in column 2 from the figure just to the left in column 1 to get +2 and −3. Disregard signs, and switch the numbers, so that the former is associated with the second row and the latter with the first row. This indicates that West should guess "one bean" three times out of five plays and "two beans" two times out of five plays, preferably using a suitable chance device to guide his calls also. It will be noted that this appeals quite readily to one's reason. Since North is going to hold one bean three times out of five, West should have the greatest success in guessing by using the same proportions. This helps one see how game theory is based on the assumption that each participant is intelligent. It is, of course, possible to devise a strategy superior to that suggested by this theory if one is playing with someone who "tips his hand" in any way.

Value of the Game

Even if both players follow the rules of good play as determined by game theory, the game may be biased in favor of one player or the other. The game of two-bean Hul Gul is disadvantageous to the holder and is stacked to favor the guesser, as was observed earlier. The value of the game is found by a calculation which uses the best mixture of either player against the results of either alternative action of the other player and involves an averaging process.

North's best mixture is three of "hold 1" to two of "hold 2." Used in conjunction with "West guesses 1," this gives the following calculation of average payoff:

$$\frac{3(1) + 2(-1)}{3 + 2} = +\tfrac{1}{5}$$

Alternatively, the value of the game could be calculated by using North's best mixture with the "West guesses 2" alternative, as follows:

$$\frac{3(-1) + 2(+2)}{3 + 2} = +\tfrac{1}{5}$$

Or the value of the game can be calculated by using West's best mixture against either of North's alternatives:

$$\frac{3(+1) + 2(-1)}{3 + 2} = +\tfrac{1}{5}$$

$$\frac{3(-1) + 2(+2)}{3 + 2} = +\tfrac{1}{5}$$

The value of the game comes out $+\tfrac{1}{5}$ in each of the four alternative calculations.[19] A positive value denotes that the game is unfair to North. If both players play "correctly," West will gain an average of $\tfrac{1}{5}$ (of

---

[19] Actually, the first and third equations are the same, and the second and fourth are the same, but each of the four equations is derived in a different way.

whatever the unit of payoff may be) per play. In 20 guesses, for example, West will win an average of 4 units, and North will lose this amount.[20]

Saddle-Point Solution

As already mentioned, the game of two-bean Hul Gul does not have a saddle point—the maximum of the row minima does not equal the minimum of the column maxima. However, the matrix shown in Figure 14–5, which is not related to any particular game, meets these require-

FIGURE 14–5

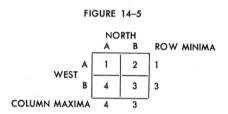

ments. Here, 3 is both the maximum of the figures to the right of the matrix and the minimum of those below the matrix. Payoffs are from North to West, so North wants to keep the payoff as low as possible, and West wants to make it as high as possible. West will always select alternative B, since both of the possible payoffs are superior to those in row 1. North will also always select alternative B, since he assumes West to be intelligent and is therefore convinced that West would choose alternative B and gain 4 if North used alternative A. The solution of the game is, therefore, that North always uses B, and West always uses B. It would do North no good to mix his choices between A and B because, since West will stick to B, this would merely result in West's gaining more than 3 on some plays. The value of the game is 3, since that is the payoff to West each time; 3 is called the "saddle value."

Business Situation with a Saddle Point

The theory of games seems to hold more promise of being useful in guiding executive decisions in repetitive situations such as pricing and advertising than in one-time decisions. It may, however, logically be applied to the latter type of decision also. Suppose that there are two large—but not entirely modern—motels so located between a mountain range on one side and a national park on the other that while they are in vigorous competition with one another, they are well isolated from other accommodations for motorists. (This assumption makes a zero-sum game

---

[20] It is, of course, possible (but extremely improbable) that all guesses will be wrong in a series of 20 guesses. In that case, West's loss would be 20 units. But the longer they play, the more likely it is that West will come out ahead.

solution quite plausible, since the gains made by each will be mainly at the expense of the other.) The motels will again be named North and West.

Aware of the luxury demanded by American motorists, both motel owners begin to ponder the desirability of installing free television in all rooms and/or building a swimming pool on the premises in order to take business away from the rival firm. By chance, both hire the same management consultant, who, after considerable study, furnishes each manager with estimated payoffs from various combinations of actions. Payoffs are estimated increases and decreases of weekly net profits, positive figures being profit gains by West and negative figures being profit gains by North. Each entrepreneur learns that the other has access to the same payoff information, and each regards the other as an astute businessman (see Figure 14–6).

FIGURE 14–6

The Motel Game

		NORTH INSTALLS				
		TV	POOL	BOTH	NEITHER	ROW MINIMA
	TV	+2	−10	−20	+10	−20
WEST INSTALLS	POOL	+10	+4	−10	+15	−10
	BOTH	+15	+5	+6	+20	+5
	NEITHER	−5	−10	−15	0	−15
COLUMN MAXIMA		+15	+5	+6	+20	

It will be noted that the installation of TV, a swimming pool, or both is somewhat more favorable to West than to North. This may be because North's location is somewhat lower and shadier than West's location, which will force North to erect higher antennas, and which will make swimming somewhat less attractive to the guests. Nevertheless, it will not pay North to abstain entirely from these improvements. The matrix has a saddle point at "install both" for West and "install pool" for North.[21] North's weekly loss of net profits (after costs, including the new maintenance, repair, and depreciation) will be $5, because of the new investment by the two motels. However, if West installed both TV and a pool while his rival did nothing, he could deprive North of an estimated $20 a week in net profits.

Business Situation without a Saddle Point

In the motel game just described the situation called for a one time investment by each firm. More interesting applications of game theory in-

---

[21] The saddle value is $5 because this figure is both the maximum of the row minima and the minimum of the column maxima.

volve repetitive moves carried out according to a computed mixed strategy.

Suppose that two firms, which we shall again call North and West, are grocery stores located in the same area but well isolated from other sellers. This makes them close rivals who watch each other's prices and selling activities warily. Every Thursday evening, each entrepreneur turns over his advertising copy to the local newspaper; included in the advertised items is a loss leader designed to attract customers to his store and away from the rival store. Experience has shown, we shall assume, that coffee and butter are the most satisfactory loss leaders; each Thursday, each manager chooses one of these to be the special bargain during the Friday-Saturday period. Suppose further that historical experience has taught each seller that the gains and losses from various possible actions are as shown in Figure 14–7, positive payoffs being gains in total

FIGURE 14–7

A Loss-Leader Game

| | | NORTH USES AS LOSS LEADER | | |
		BUTTER	COFFEE	ROW MINIMA
	BUTTER	0	+100	0
WEST USES AS LOSS LEADER	COFFEE	+150	−50	−50
	COLUMN MAXIMA	+150	+100	

dollar sales by West and losses of sales by North, and negative payoffs being gains in dollar sales by North at the expense of his rival, West.[22]

It is apparent that the whole practice of using loss leaders is more favorable to West than to North. However, experience has shown North that it is not wise to run no loss leader at all, in view of West's consistent policy of using leaders.[23] A glance at the row minima and column maxima shows that there is no saddle point. It is clear that it would not be desirable for West to use butter each week as the loss leader because North would do the same and no sales advantage would accrue to West. It would be undesirable for West to use coffee as the leader each week because North would also do so and would take $50 in sales away from

---

[22] This assumption makes it a zero-sum game. Actually, it is quite possible that total sales will be somewhat increased by the loss leaders for the two stores taken together and that the gain of one will not be entirely at the expense of the other. If the assumption is close to the truth, however, the game theory solution may be of practical utility.

[23] The strategy on North's part of using either butter or coffee as a leader may be said to be "dominant" over a strategy on his part of using no leader at all. If a third column labeled "No Leader" were added to the matrix, the payoffs might be, for example, +80 and +200 in rows 1 and 2, respectively. This strategy is clearly so inferior from North's viewpoint that it should never be followed. Therefore, it can be eliminated from the matrix.

West. Similarly, it would be foolish for North to settle on a policy of using butter each week as the leader because West would use coffee as the leader and gain $150 in sales at North's expense. It can similarly be seen that a constant strategy of using coffee as the leader would be unwise for North. Clearly, a mixture of strategies by each grocer is called for, with the loss-leader special for each week being kept a secret until it is too late for the rival firm to change its advertising copy in the newspaper. The optimal mixture of the two alternative actions can be calculated as in two-bean Hul Gul, since this too is a two-by-two matrix without a saddle point.

Subtracting each figure in row 2 from the figure just above it, we get -150 and $+150$, which means that North should use each loss leader half of the time, perhaps tossing a coin once a week and using butter as the leader when heads turns up and coffee when tails turns up.

To obtain West's optimal mixture, subtract each figure in column 2 from the figure just to the left. This gives -100 and $+200$. Disregarding the sign and switching the numbers, it turns out that West should use butter twice for each time he uses coffee as a loss leader. His choice on any particular Thursday should be determined by using a chance device which has twice as great a probability of indicating butter as it has of indicating coffee. He might, for example, shake a cocktail shaker containing two yellow marbles and one brown marble of equal size, close his eyes and withdraw one—and then use butter as the loss leader if he comes up with a yellow marble and coffee if he picks out the brown one.

The value of the loss-leader "game" can be calculated by using the best mixture of either seller against the results of either alternative strategy of the other. The average payoff according to the four methods of calculation is as follows:

$$1. \quad \frac{1(0) + 1(+100)}{2} = +50$$

$$2. \quad \frac{1(+150) + 1(-50)}{2} = +50$$

$$3. \quad \frac{2(0) + 1(+150)}{3} = +50$$

$$4. \quad \frac{2(+100) + 1(-50)}{3} = +50$$

Since the value of the game is positive, it is "unfair" to North and favorable to West. West should continue to use loss leaders, and this forces North to do so also. North should try to convince West that it would be better to discontinue these special bargains and even offer West some valuable consideration if he will discontinue using loss leaders (so long as this consideration is not more damaging to his net profits than the loss of $50 a week in sales). Another possibility is that North will hire a group of people to buy only the loss leader from West for a period of time, hoping to discourage the loss-leader practice. (This strategy would change the payoff matrix, and North would hope to make West believe the change to be permanent.)

Some Other Possible Applications

It has been suggested by other writers that two firms that share a market where the demand is more or less fixed might use game theory in deciding whether to use radio, television, or printed advertising. Depending on the calculated gains and losses, they may arrive at a saddle point solution where they stick to one medium each (not necessarily the same one) or follow a mixed strategy.[24] The latter bears a resemblance to the loss-leader game which has been described. The saddle point situation is similar to the motel game of this appendix.

The U.S. Army has made use of game theory in the assignment of personnel. The payoff matrix is derived from evaluation of the suitability of various persons in various jobs. Presumably an amateur radio operator will not end up as an army cook if the evaluations make sense.

Nonzero-sum games, where the gains of one player are not wholly at the expense of the other player, are potentially more useful. Unfortunately, the theory has not been fully worked out. It is, however, possible to set up some simplified models that can be useful in solving business problems. For example, a firm bidding on government contracts and possessing some knowledge of its competitors may be able to randomize its bids in such a way as to maximize its probability of winning only as many contracts as it has capacity to fulfill. Price wars, where survival depends heavily on the asset position of participants, expected demand, and other economic data have been analyzed as nonzero-sum games.

Checkerboard land buying, which may be just within the financial capability of a firm wishing to acquire a large tract of land, has also been the subject of analysis. The danger is that competitors may buy up strategic strips for later sale at high prices. The company must design its checkerboard buying pattern in such a way as to make competitor's holdings as costly as possible. The game is likely to be more successful when competitive buyers are financially weak and are consequently unable to hold out for long.

General Observations on Game Theory and Business

A main difficulty in applying game theory to business decisions is getting reasonably accurate estimates of payoffs under various condi-

---

[24] Martin Shubik, "The Uses of Game Theory in Management Science," *Management Science*, October, 1955, p. 339. Some of the other examples of possible uses of game theory are taken from this article.

tions. These estimates need not be perfectly accurate, but if they err too greatly may lead to incorrect actions. In these respects the estimates do not differ from calculations made to guide executives in nongame situations, for example, whether to build a new plant when it is clear that rivals will not react. Any decision based on inadequate work by statisticians, accountants, engineers, and other experts is apt to be nonoptimal. Acquiring information is itself costly, however, so an excessive research effort is also nonoptimal. It is easy to say that research should be carried to the point where marginal gains equal marginal costs, but application of the principle is usually difficult.

Another problem is choosing the best payoff criterion. In business this is usually assumed to be net profits to the firm. Sometimes, however, maximization of short-term profits is incompatible with maximizing longterm profits. In the case of the loss-leader problem of the appendix, payoffs were in terms of gains and losses of sales by the two stores. This tacitly assumes that profits are positively correlated with storewide sales. Otherwise sales do not constitute a rational payoff criterion—unless short-run sales are considered to be positively correlated with long-run profits through their power to mold consumers' buying habits.

According to J. C. C. McKinsey,[25] "the most crying need" in game theory is the development of a more satisfactory theory of nonzero-sum games and games where the number of players exceeds two. Nevertheless, game theory in its present state has been characterized by McKinsey as an important "intellectual breakthrough."[26]

CASE 14–1. Refrigerators and Kilowatt-Hours

Even before the energy "crisis" of the fall of 1973, the average price paid by consumers for a kilowatt-hour of electricity had started to rise. It's low had approached 2 cents per kilowatt-hour in 1969 and 1970. The extrapolation used in the M.I.T. study[27] that is the source for much

---

[25] J. C. C. McKinsey, *Introduction to the Theory of Games* (New York: McGraw-Hill Book Co., 1952), p. 358

[26] A very interesting criticism of the Von Neumann–Morgenstern theory of games is contained in an article by Daniel Ellsberg, "Theory of the Reluctant Duelist," *American Economic Review*, December, 1956. He points out that the conservative actions indicated by game theory are more appropriate for one who is forced to engage in the game than to one who enters a two-person conflict situation willingly in the hope of a big payoff to himself. Applied to business, this suggests that the best strategy may be to try to confuse an opponent, to find out his strategy by wiretaps or otherwise, or to tempt him into a situation where a big "killing" is possible. This is particularly the case where only one "play" is to be made, as Ellsberg points out.

[27] *The Productivity of Serving Consumer Durable Goods* (The Center for Policy Alternatives M.I.T.—Report No. CPA–74–4, 1974).

of the data in this case is for a doubling of the kilowatt-hour price by 1980. This prospect for higher prices, together with an increased public awareness of a social interest in energy saving, represented a challenge to the product and related policies of refrigerator manufacturers and distributors.

In many respects the consumer had been served well by vigorous and innovative competition in the industry. The average price for a refrigerator as expressed in constant dollars (1958) dropped from $320 in 1958 to $200 in 1972. The current dollar average price in 1972 was about $290, a demonstration that some prices do come down in a generally inflationary period. The cost index per cubic foot which adjusts for the fact that refrigerators were becoming larger showed an even more dramatic drop to 56 percent of its 1959 value. The service call index had dropped to less than half of its 1959 value. Performance characteristics such as "pulldown," the ability to cool food rapidly, had increased materially. Refrigerators took less overall room per unit of usable space; there were more "features" such as automatic icemakers and ice-water dispensers; and the proportion of low-temperature freezer space had been increased.

In one respect, however, the average new refrigerator of the model years of the early 1970s was distinctly more expensive than that of the 1950s; the average kilowatt-hour usage had increased from just over one to four per day. For the economy as a whole home refrigeration has been estimated to use from 14.1 to 20 percent of total residential usage of current, which in turn is close to one third (32.7 percent) of total domestic usage of electric power. Thus household refrigeration accounts for between 5 and 7 percent of total usage of electricity in the United States. Its estimated annual growth rate of 8.3 percent is slightly above that for the total U.S. load.

Life-Cycle Costs

Over the service life of a refrigerator, the household must incur three major types of costs: the initial purchase price, the costs of servicing, and the power costs. This concept was illustrated in a special study for the M.I.T. project[28] by estimating the costs for a 15-cubic-foot no-frost refrigerator of 1972 over its lifetime. The purchase price was taken to be $270, the power consumption was estimated as 1,840 kilowatt-hours a year, and the annual cost for outside servicing was assumed to be $9. The additional assumptions of the table below are: a life of 14 years, which has been the average scrappage age for many years; an increase

---

[28] W. S. Chow and G. Newton, Jr., "Energy Utilization of Refrigerators and Television Receivers," Special study in *Productivity of Serving Consumer Goods*, pp. 175 f.

EXHIBIT 14–1A

Discounted Life-Cycle Costs of No-Frost Refrigerator
(15 cubic feet—1972)

	At $0.03 per Kilowatt-Hour			At $0.05 per Kilowatt-Hour		
	Annualized Life-Cycle Costs	*P.V.* of Life-Cycle Costs*	*Per-cent*	*Annualized Life-Cycle Costs*	*P.V.* of Life-Cycle Costs*	*Per-cent*
Purchase.............	$ 32.75	270	32	$ 32.75	270	22
Energy...............	55.20	455	54	92.00	758	69
Service maintenance....	12.84	106	13	12.84	106	9
Total...........	$100.79	831	100	$135.59	1134	100

* P.V.—present value.

of 50 percent in the servicing cost for years 11 to 14; a $3 imputed cost for the hour of annual time the household might spend on cleaning: two different prices per kilowatt-hour of electricity, 3 cents and 5 cents; and an interest rate of 8 percent. The life-cycle costs are given in Exhibit 14–1A.

The same study contrasted the cost of a no-frost refrigerator of the 1970s with a hypothetical "early" manual defrost machine. It assumed the same size and purchase price but the early machine would have just one door and a smaller freezer space, say 1.5 cubic feet against 4.5 cubic feet. The "early" refrigerator would use only 790 kilowatt-hours annually but would require five extra hours of user maintenance (four hours for defrosting and an extra hour for cleaning). The results are given in Exhibit 14–1B.

Clearly one way of reducing the life-cycle cost of refrigeration to the household would be the purchase of the early 15-cubic-foot machine and then the life-cycle cost advantage is almost doubled to $337 at the $0.05

EXHIBIT 14–1B

Discounted Life-Cycle Costs of "Early" Manual Defrost Refrigerator
(15 cubic feet)

	At $0.03 per Kilowatt-Hour			At $0.05 per Kilowatt-Hour		
	Annualized Life-Cycle Costs	*P.V. of Life-Cycle Costs*	*Per-cent*	*Annualized Life-Cycle Costs*	*P.V. of Life-Cycle Costs*	*Per-cent*
Purchase.............	$32.75	270	41	$32.75	270	34
Energy...............	23.70	195	29	29.50	325	41
Service mainte-nance*.............	24.50	202	30	24.50	202	25
Total...........	$80.95	667	100	$96.75	797	100

* Service is assumed to be only $6 a year instead of $9 for years 1–10 and 50 percent higher for years 11–14.

per kilowatt-hour price that could prevail during the lifetime of a new refrigerator.

The M.I.T. study thought this an unlikely solution: "So, in spite of the lower cost of manual-defrost machines with their inconvenient small freezer volumes, it would seem to be an exercise in futility to try to promote a return to the horse-and-buggy days of the refrigerator business."[29] (The authors assume the housewife puts nonquantifiable values on things like aesthetics and convenience irrespective of the economics of the purchase.)

A course more likely to be successful in reducing energy usage in the study's judgment was to make engineering changes in the no-frost models. Two relatively simple changes were suggested as well as a tentative program that speculated on the cost effectiveness of several design changes made in combination. All the proposals had the effect of increasing the initial purchase price but of reducing energy requirements from the current estimated level of 1,840 kilowatt-hours. The increase in purchase price is estimated at double manufacturer's cost, to reflect profit and distributor margins, in Exhibit 14–1C.

EXHIBIT 14–1C

Estimated Impact on Purchase Price and Energy Consumption of Engineering Changes for 15-Cubic-Foot No-Frost Refrigerator

Change	Increase in Purchase Price	Decrease in Annual Energy Use (kilowatt-hours)
(a) Substitution of polyurethane insulation for fiberglass	$14	438
(b) Increase efficiency of compressor motor from 65% to 75%	20	245
(a) and (b) together	34	625
(c) Tentative program including (a) and (b) and four other changes (increase in evaporator and condensor surfaces, etc.)	90	990

Competition in the Refrigerator Industry

During most of the postwar period, refrigerator production has had a four-firm concentration ratio of between 60 percent and 70 percent: (Whirlpool—the usual supplier for Sears' Coldspot line; General Motors with Frigidaire; General Electric—Hotpoint; and plain Westinghouse.) The top 11 producers have accounted for 80 percent to 90 percent production.

A number of factors have intensified competition. Substantial overcapacity was present from 1951 until the late 1960s. This stemmed di-

[29] Ibid., p. 183.

rectly from expansion to meet the postwar demand which led to a peak production of over six million in 1950, a total not again reached until 1972. Distributors with their own brands, conspicuously Sears, were in strong rivalry with the national manufacturers which sold through independent dealers as well as discount chains. Imports, particularly from Italy, became a competitive factor in the late 1960s, although the number, 874,000 in 1971, overstates their direct competitive importance. Most were of the smaller size serving mobile home, trailer, and so forth, market. Imports represented only 4 percent of the dollar volume of U.S. production.

Alan F. Fusfeld has summarized various market surveys on refrigerator demand substantially as follows:[30]

1. Approximately 70–80% of all purchases are from new household formation or replacement due to unsatisfactory performance from age or reliability.

2. Price per cubic foot is the primary basis of brand choice for 45% of consumers.

3. Features provide the primary basis for approximately 35% of cases. . . . For those replacing units less than 10 years old in satisfactory condition (approximately 15% of demand) feature innovation has a stronger effect.

4. The elasticities are such that product-improvement efforts would be channeled towards improvement of costs per cubic foot and features.

It is not surprising that the peak period of product innovation, the mid-1950s to the mid-1960s, corresponded with the low household formation that reflected the low birth rates of the 1930s. In a saturated market demand primarily rested on new household formation and replacement. *Electrical Merchandising Week* (January, 1960) stated, "The problem of the industry is to continually create more design and performance innovations to dramatize the superiority of today's merchandise over antiquated boxes still throbbing away in millions of kitchens."

The general pricing policy of the industry has been to charge more for larger, feature-laden models than constant markup over cost would otherwise suggest, thus putting a profitability premium on product innovation. Some indication of this policy can be noted in Exhibit 14–1D showing the Sears' refrigerator lines as listed in the Fall-Winter catalogs for 1973 and 1974.[31]

Technological Change in the Product

While competitive pressures can keep prices in line with costs, cost-cutting changes in technology were required to reduce the constant dollar price of refrigerators. Scale economies are not a generally applicable

---

[30] *Application of the Technological Progress Function to Consumer Durable Products*, M.I.T. Report, p. 225.

[31] The indication is that the price in dollars rises more rapidly than weight in pounds. This would be conclusive only if costs were proportional to weights.

explanation since the industry and firm volume has not materially increased since 1950. The major product change that reduced costs was in thin-wall, straight-line construction that cut material usage per cubic foot of space drastically between 1956 and 1968. This change also yielded a feature attractive to consumers since the straight-line design cut down on exterior dimensions and saved space in the kitchen.

A feature that rapidly swept the market was no-frost, a totally frostless system requiring no maintenance by the consumer for either the fresh-food or the freezer section. It was available on 10 percent of the models in 1960 and on 90 percent by 1967.[32] It substantially replaced both the manual defrost and a cycle-defrost system that reached peak popularity in the 1950s. The combination of materials savings, larger inside volume, and the increased proportion of low-temperature freezer space, together with the no-frost feature, accounts for most of the increased energy consumption.[33]

Two other production features of significance were the popular automatic ice-makers and the magnetic door seal from which even a small child could force a way out. There were other marketing features that did not really represent technological changes, such as the side-by-side style for freezer and fresh foods, ice-water dispensers, humidifying drawers, and shelf changes.

Refrigerator Lines

It is interesting to compare the refrigerator lines of the leading distributor, Sears, Roebuck and Company, as they appeared the summer before and the summer after the energy "crisis" of 1973–74. This is done in Exhibits 14–1D and 14–1E. Several changes between the two years follow previous trends. Constant-dollar unit prices are down—the typical $5 to $10 increase in the catalog price amounts to a much smaller percentage than the approximately 10 percent rise in the Consumer Price Index. Shipping weights are generally lower, a probable reflection of further economies in use of materials. The featured, top-of-the-line model (H in the exhibit) with 22.2 cubic feet of internal space continued the trend toward larger refrigerators. The 34 percent of its space devoted to a freezer section continued the development toward greater freezer capacity. Increasing size was also suggested by the dropping of two small manual defrost models imported from Italy in 1973.

---

[32] *Application of the Technical Progress Function,* p. 230. Fusfeld notes that the period of 1956–64 was that of greatest innovative activity and that this corresponded with the period of greatest competitive pressure.

[33] Inside volume went from an average of 8 cubic feet in 1950 to 15 cubic feet in 1972; low-temperature freezer space went from less than 20 percent of total space in 1959 to almost 30 percent in 1965 and later models.

EXHIBIT 14–1D

Sears' Refrigerator Line: Fall–Winter, 1973, and Fall–Winter, 1974, Catalogs[1]

	Fall–Winter, 1974, Specifications								Comparable 1973 Model			
	Catalog[2] Price	Total Inside Cubic Feet	Percent Cubic Feet in Freezer	T/S[3]	Insulation[4]	Ice maker[5]	De-frost[6]	Shipping Weight (pounds)		Catalog[2] Price	Shipping Weight (pounds)	Other Differences
A.	$289.85	15.2	28	T	F	Opt.	F	302	A.	$279.95	306	None noted
B.	319.95	17.1	28	T	F	Opt.	F	307	B.	314.95	313	None noted
C.	364.95	19.3	30	T	F	Opt.	F	312	C.	359.95	320	None noted
D.	249.95	13.0	27	T	F	Opt.	F	271	D.	239.95	286	None noted
E.	339.95	15.2	28	T	F	Yes	F	310	E.	329.95	315	None noted
F.	369.95	17.1	28	T	F	Yes	F	322	F.	364.95	321	None noted
G.	449.95	19.2	30	T	U	Yes	F	332	G.	429.95	385	No insulation specified
H.	599.95	22.2	34	S	U	Yes	F	379	H.	No comparable model		
I.	509.95	19.0	33	S	U	Yes	F	345	I.	509.95	349	Copper tubing supplied
J.	409.95	19.1	33	S	U	Opt.	F	335	J.	399.95	336	None noted
K.	369.95	17.1	32	S	F	Opt.	F	338	K.	359.95	333	None noted
L.	379.95	19.0	34	S	F	No	F	323	L.	379.95	323	Ice-maker option noted
M.	319.95	19.0	28	T	U	No	F	291	M.	No comparable model		
N.	299.95	17.0	n.a.	T	U	No	F	271	N.	No comparable model		
O.	219.95	12.0	23	T	U	Opt.	M*	198	O.	199.95	208	No insulation specified
P.	189.95	12.4	10	T	U	No	M	185	P.	No comparable model		

[1] Generally exterior dimensions were slightly less in 1974 than 1973. The 1973 line contained two Italian imports: 7.7 cubic feet, one-door, M defrost for $139.95 and 8.5 cubic feet, two-door, M* defrost for $169.95. Both were dropped in 1974. Both years offered a refrigerator, stove, sink combination at $364.95 (the refrigerator having 5.6 cubic feet and manual defrost), and a 1.6 cubic-foot den-office refrigerator and ice maker at $189.95.

[2] This is understood for all models with ice maker since copper tubing costing $6.79 in 1974 and $5.29 in 1973 must be ordered. Color options cost $5 extra. Shipping costs must be added.

[3] T = top freezer; S = side freezer section.

[4] F = fiberglass; U = polyurethane frame.

[5] Ice-maker option added $40 to price and 14 pounds to shipping weight both years.

[6] Defrost system indicated by F for frostless or no-frost, M for manual, M* manual for freezer and automatic cycle for refrigerator.

EXHIBIT 14–1E

Catalog Listings of Economy Models in Sears Fall–Winter Catalogs for 1973 and 1974

1973   1974

12.0-cubic foot Refrigerator-
Freezer with provision
for adding an Ice Maker

$199⁹⁵

Lighted 9.2-cubic foot automatic-defrost refrigerator
section with 3 shelves, 2 crispers with shelf-cover. Door
with egg rack, butter keeper, 2 shelves. Manual defrost
2.8-cubic-foot freezer holds 96 lbs., ice cube trays. Shelf
and juice rack on freezer door. Adjustable cold control.
White acrylic-finish cabinet 57⅛x29x23⅞ inches wide.
Right-hand doors with magnetic gaskets. Allow 3
inches air space above.
  *Order Ice Maker below, copper tubing on page 1253. See
  Guarantee and Note on page 1261*
46 G 63201N—Shipping weight 208 lbs.............$199.95
Ice Maker for above. 130-crescent capacity bucket.
46 G 8070—Shipping weight 14 lbs...................$40.00

Our lowest-priced Coldspot Refrigerators

Our most compact Top-freezer
Refrigerator .. 12.0 cu. ft.
 • Provision for adding Ice Maker
 • Efficient polyurethane foam insulation

White $**219**⁹⁵   Colors $**224**⁹⁵

Lighted 9.2-cu. ft. automatic-defrost refrigerator
section has 3 adjustable shelves, 2 crispers. Egg
rack, butter keeper, 2 shelves on door. Manual-
defrost 2.8-cu. ft. freezer section with 2 ice trays.
Shelf, juice can rack on freezer door. Flush-
hinged right-hand doors with magnetic gaskets.
Plastic liner. Acrylic-finish cabinet 56¾x24x
30⅝ inches deep including handles. Allow 3-inch
air space above. *Order Ice Maker 46 H 8070,
page 1116. See Guarantee, Note, page 1120.*
Shipping weight 198 pounds.
46 H 63201N—White...................$219.95
46 H 63202N—Coppertone............. 224.95
46 H 63204N—Avocado................ 224.95
46 H 63206N—Tawny Gold............. 224.95

*Even at this low price, a 12.4-cu. ft.
single door Refrigerator-Freezer
with POLYURETHANE INSULATION*

Only $**189**⁹⁵

Lighted 11.2-cubic foot refrigerator section has 2
stationary shelves, 2 crispers with covers that
act as third shelf. Butter keeper, egg rack, 2
shelves on door. Manual-defrost, 1.2-cubic foot
freezer section. Adjustable cold control, plastic
liner. Flush-hinged right-hand door with magnetic gasket. Acrylic-finish cabinet 56¾x24x
30⅝ inches deep including handles. Allows 3-
inch air space above. *See Guarantee and Note on
page 1120.*
46 H 63121N—Shpg. wt. 185 lbs.........$189.95

Sources: Sears Fall–Winter Catalog, 1973, p. 1251; Sears Fall–Winter Catalog, 1974, p. 1121.

None of these developments suggested a product strategy aimed at
minimizing life-cycle costs or one that reflected increased concern with
energy consumption. In no case did the Sears catalogs suggest economies
in energy consumption. On the other hand, the catalogs specified polyurethane as the insulation in eight of the 1974 models as against two in
1973. These included the four highest priced and the two lowest priced
economy models illustrated in Exhibit 14–1E. The use of polyurethane
insulation was put in headline captions in 1974 (for the low-priced
models) rather than being buried in the text as in 1973. The two models
in which the price rose the most (by $20) represented switches from no
insulation specified to polyurethane. This move was consistent with the
higher costs the M.I.T. study suggested for polyurethane insulation.

Questions

1. Which of these three strategies (with what ever variations you wish to
    include) would you suggest for a refrigerator producer in the mid-1970s.

a. Ignore the problem of increasing energy and life-cycle costs on the grounds that consumers will continue to respond most to new features and to lowest purchase price per cubic foot.

b. Increase proportion of models with polyurethane and maintain at least one economy model (with manual defrost, polyurethane, and other changes) that was designed to minimize life-cycle costs; but don't raise energy issue directly in promotion.

c. Adopt and promote energy cutting changes that would minimize life-cycle costs for each size of refrigerator. Encourage the American Home Appliance Association to adopt energy-rating systems and/or laws requiring energy usage labeling.

2. Evaluate the contribution the engineering changes proposed in Exhibit 14–2C could make toward minimizing life-cycle costs. First, assume 14 years life, 8 percent interest rate, and then a more conservative 10 years life, 10 percent interest rate.

3. Would you favor labeling laws requiring average usage requirements to be stated? Would you favor laws limiting energy usage or controlling product specifications in a way to limit such usage?

4. What developments have taken place since 1974 on the kilowatt-hours used by refrigerators? Trade journals and catalogs (particularly Sears) would be a helpful source as well as visits to a friendly appliance dealer.

CASE 14–2. Upheaval in the Cigarette Industry

Four significant transformations have taken place within the cigarette industry in the 20th century. First was the dissolution in 1911 of the "tobacco trust," the American Tobacco Company, after its Sherman Act conviction, into 16 successor companies, 4 of which were to be significant in the future of cigarettes: the American Tobacco Company (now American Brands), the R. J. Reynolds Tobacco Company (now R. J. Reynolds Industries), P. F. Lorillard (presently a subsidiary of Loew's), and Liggett & Myers.

The second change was the conversion of an almost insignificant appendage to snuff, smoking tobacco, and cigars into a national cigarette habit. Modest-sized, multiproduct producers became large, highly profitable advertisers with one dominant brand each. By 1930 one could "walk a mile for a camel," "reach for a Lucky Strike instead of a sweet," or possibly "prefer Chesterfield." A minor late comer, Old Gold, scarcely challenged the over 90 percent of the market held by the Big Three.

Probably "upheaval" is too strong a term for the serious incursions made into the share of the Big Three in the thirties by the price competition of the 10-cent brands. But the persistence of the smaller companies in hanging on to almost one fifth of the market and the gaining of small footholds in the market by Brown & Williamson and, particularly, by

Philip Morris were omens for the future. By 1947 matters seemed almost back to the three-brand dominance of the 1920s. The low-priced brands had been almost extinguished by higher incomes, higher taxes, and higher tobacco prices which accompanied the war. The companies had been little damaged by the defeat in a new antitrust suit.

The upheaval with which this case is primarily concerned was under way by 1950 with increased publicity about new medical findings in the relationship of cigarettes and health. By 1975 the following were among the changes:

1. A peaking of per capita cigarette consumption in 1963 after a half century of almost continuous growth.
2. A significant drop in the percentage of male cigarette smokers so that equal participation in the habit by men and women seemed assured.
3. The decline of the regular size cigarette responsible for over 95 percent of sales as late as 1947 to 6 percent of the market, and the rise of filter tips to 85 percent of the total sold.
4. An approximate halving of the nicotine and tar content of cigarettes between 1954 and 1972.
5. The conversion of single brands per company to multiple brand lines and of single variety brands to brand umbrellas which could cover, as with Marlboro, six product varieties.
6. The transformation of tobacco products companies into substantially diversified firms.
7. The replacement of swinging TV commercials with printed advertisements made austere by tar-nicotine listings and the Surgeon General's warning.
8. The decline of the Big Three into the first, fourth, and sixth of a less concentrated six. Only the position of Reynolds was relatively unaltered.

The concern of this case is with advertising, product, and price competition during these changes; how they have served as alternatives and complements in competitive strategies; how such strategies have been influenced by economic forces such as the Great Depression and exogenous factors such as the findings on smoking and health; and with the policy choices in advertising, product policy, and price as they present themselves in the late 1970s.

The Rise of the Big Three

When the original American Tobacco Company was dissolved in 1911 as a consequence of antitrust action, only three of the successor companies, American Tobacco, Liggett and Myers, and P. Lorillard, were allocated any significant position in cigarettes, a product that constituted only 6 percent of tobacco sales but whose use was growing. The continuation of this oligopolistic structure and particularly the dominance of three brands from World War I through 1931 and again briefly in the years following World War II reflected the strategy of a fourth successor firm, the R. J. Reynolds Company, in introducing the Camel brand in 1913. The strategy was this:

1. To heavily advertise one brand only (in a standard package of 20 cigarettes); and
2. To produce a mild cigarette largely from domestic tobaccos.

This combination of product and advertising policy was well suited to gain new smokers in an extremely unsaturated market. Later experience was to reveal that year-to-year brand loyalties were strong with only 10 percent to 15 percent of smokers shifting brands in particular years.

Reynolds' share of the cigarette market rose from 0.2 percent in 1913 to 40 percent in 1917 and 45 percent in 1925. Noting the success of Camels, the Liggett & Myers Company similarly concentrated advertising on its brand, Chesterfield, which had been launched in 1912. American Tobacco Company followed with the Lucky Strike brand in 1917. In 1926 the P. Lorillard Company attempted to enter the field with its Old Gold brand. It embarked on an ambitious advertising campaign, financed by the flotation of a $15 million issue of debenture bonds in 1927. Despite large advertising expenditures, which exceeded $1.5 million by 1938, the Old Gold brand failed to increase its share of the market beyond 6 percent. In January, 1933, the Philip Morris Company launched a new blend of 15-cent cigarettes under the brand name Philip Morris after substantial product testing to select the particular blend that met the greatest consumer favor. By 1939 expenditures for advertising exceeded $1.5 million, and the company was firmly entrenched in fourth place.

The Rise of the 10-Cent Brands in the 1930s and Decline in the 1940s

Relying on an inelastic demand for the product, the leading tobacco companies raised the wholesale price of cigarettes from $6 per thousand to $6.40 in October, 1929, and to $6.85 in June, 1931.[34] These wholesale prices resulted in retail price increases on the more popular brands of 14 and 15 cents per package. The maintained high prices of the leading brands encouraged transference of demand, particularly after June, 1931,

---

[34] This decision in 1931 which was made in a deepening depression when tobacco prices were at record lows was justified by Reynolds because "Courage was needed in the U.S.," by American "as an opportunity to make money," and by Liggett and Myers to get "more money for advertising." William H. Nicholls, *Price Policies in the Cigarette Industry* (Nashville: Vanderbilt University Press, 1951), p. 83.

to 10-cent cigarettes. Prior to 1931 there were only two 10-cent brands of significance—Coupon, sold by Liggett & Myers, and Paul Jones, sold by Continental Tobacco Company.

After June, 1931, several other companies entered the field: in September, Larus & Brothers, Inc.; in March, 1932, Brown & Williamson Tobacco Company reduced the price on its Wings brand to put it in the 10-cent class; in May, 1932, Sunshines, manufactured by the Pinkerton Tobacco Company, were put in the 10-cent class; in June, 1932, Axton-Fisher entered its new brand, Twenty Grand; during the same month, Scott & Dill came into the scramble; and in September, Stephano Brothers brought out Marvels. The rise in sales of the 10-cent brands during the depression was phenomenal. Starting almost from nothing in 1931 they accounted for over 20 percent of the domestic cigarette market for a few months during the fall of 1932. On January 3, 1933, the Big Three reduced wholesale prices to $6 per thousand, and a month later to $5.50. Retail prices fell to 12.5 cents, then to 10 and 11 cents. With the price differential for the leading brands practically removed, sales of 10-cent cigarettes fell from 21.3 percent of total sales in December, 1932, to 6.4 percent in May, 1933. In January, 1934, the Big Three increased wholesale prices to $6.10 per thousand and in January, 1936, to $6.25, with resulting increases in retail prices to 12.5 and then 13.5 cents a package. The 10-cent brands responded by increasing to a share of the total market which ranged from 10 percent to 12 percent. By 1939 this share had increased to over 17 percent.

In 1936 most of the companies producing 10-cent cigarettes swung over to advertising. Although it was clear that their margins could not permit the extensive advertising employed by the standard brands, they thought that a limited amount was desirable to build volume.

Although advertising expenditures of each of the Big Three were vastly in excess of those of other companies in the field in the period 1930–39, the three leaders did not hold the same relative positions throughout the period. Over this ten-year period, Chesterfield spent an average of 5.4 cents a carton; Camel spent 4.1 cents; and Lucky Strike, 4.0 cents. By contrast, the 10-cent brands spent only 0.5 cents per carton of cigarettes sold.

Basic external factors influencing the market strategies of the cigarette companies throughout the postwar period were, first, high levels of income and employment, and, second, high and increasing per unit taxes. Together they doomed the low-priced brands that had drastically reduced the dominance of the Big Three. The war and postwar prosperity made price appeal less compelling and the high unit taxes (8 cents per pack for the federal government and from 4 to 11 cents a pack by states in 1967) limited the percentage significances of a few cents margin.

In 1947, as shown in Exhibit 14–2A, the market shares of the Big

EXHIBIT 14–2A

Shares of Domestic Market for Leading Cigarettes

(all brand varieties with over 2½ percent of market in selected years are listed)

Company and Cigarette*	*Percentages of Domestic Sales*						
	1931	*1947*	*1953*	*1959*	*1962*	*1967*	*1973*
R. J. Reynolds							
Camel **R**	28.4	30.4	25.6	14.0	13.2	7.6	4.2
American Tobacco							
Lucky Strike **R**	39.5	29.5	16.8	9.5	7.8	4.0	(2.0)
Liggett & Myers							
Chesterfields **R**	22.7	20.8	12.5†	3.6†	(2.0)†	(0.8)	(0.2)
P. Lorillard							
Old Gold **R**	6.5	4.3	5.0†	2.5†	(0.2)†	(0.1)	(0.0)
Philip Morris							
Philip Morris **R**		6.9	7.2†	2.5†	(0.8)†	(0.2)	(0.1)
American Tobacco							
Pall Mall **K**		3.4	·12.4†	14.1†	14.4	10.7	6.8
Brown & Williamson							
Kool **M-R**			3.0	3.0†	(0.7)†	(0.5)	(0.2)
American Tobacco							
Tareyton **K**			3.6	2.5†	(0.6)†	(0.2)	(0.1)
Liggett & Myers							
Chesterfield **K**			3.5	2.5†	(2.4)†	(1.6)	(1.0)
R. J. Reynolds							
Winston **F**				9.5	12.1	13.2	12.1
Winston **F**100						(1.9)	2.6
Brown & Williamson							
Viceroy **F**				4.7	3.8	3.7	2.6
Liggett & Myers							
L & M **F**				5.5	4.9	3.2	(1.8)
Philip Morris							
Marlboro **F**				4.6	5.1	6.0	11.9
P. Lorillard							
Kent **F**				8.0	7.0	5.4	3.7
R. J. Reynolds							
Salem **M-F**				7.0	9.1	7.9	6.1
Philip Morris							
Parliament **F**				2.5	(2.0)	(1.6)	(1.7)
Brown & Williamson							
Kool **M-F**						4.9	8.0
American							
Tareyton **F**						3.3	(2.1)
Brown & Williamson							
Raleigh **F**	—	—	—	—	—	2.7	(1.9)
Total share of cigarettes with 2½% plus	97.1	95.3	89.6	86.0	77.4	72.6	58.2
No. of varieties with 2½% plus	4	6	9	16	9	12	9

* The letters R = Regular, K = King-Size, M = Mentholated, and F = Filter Tips. Parentheses denote less than 2½ percent for brands that were once on list.

† Indicates that other types of same brand are omitted from figure. Since by 1973 all leading brands had multiple types, daggers are omitted.

Sources: For 1947–68 data various December issues of *Business Week*. For 1931, the *American Tobacco Co.* v. *U.S.* (328 U.S. 781). For 1973 data, see Exhibit 14–2C.

Three had been restored to over 80 percent of the market. Philip Morris maintained the beachhead it had established in the 1930s. A harbinger of the product competition to come was the 3.4 percent share of Pall Mall, a "king-size" cigarette.

The Medical Findings

The key external factor that was to influence strategies of the 1950s, 1960s and 1970s was discussed largely in scientific journals and medical meetings. But by 1953 and 1954 the basic findings of the strong statistical association of lung cancer, heart disease, and generally higher death rates with cigarette smoking were well established:

1. Correlation studies indicated that the rapid rise in lung cancer in the various countries of the world followed the establishment of widespread cigarette habits. The best of these studies made allowance for such other factors as urban rather than rural residence.
2. Retrospective studies of lung cancer victims indicated that the vast majority were regular cigarette smokers. These studies had become more persuasive as better control groups were set up that showed these victims differed from the rest of the population primarily in their smoking habits.
3. Human pathological findings found significant changes in the lungs of smokers that indicated precancerous conditions.
4. Experiments indicated that cancer could be induced in laboratory animals by components of the cigarette smoke.
5. Prospective studies, in which large samples of middle-aged men were classified as to smoking and other characteristics and were followed through several years to observe the time and cause of death, indicated death rates from lung cancer for heavy cigarette smokers of approximately 20 times that of nonsmokers. These prospective studies broadened the health issue from simply lung cancer to generally excessive mortality rates, particularly from coronary artery diseases, and confronted the public with such findings as the fact that heavy cigarette smokers in their late forties and fifties die at rates of men who are seven or eight years older among nonsmokers.

Presumably influenced by the public health agitation and declining sales, 14 tobacco companies, including all of the majors, formed the Tobacco Industry Research Committee to study all phases of tobacco use, and from 1954 through 1962 contributed $6.25 million for about 400 grants to research men. The public position taken by both it and the Tobacco Institute formed by the same companies in 1958 to advance public relations has been that the causative role of cigarettes in disease has not been proved and that more experimental research is needed.

It was plausible to maintain this position through 1963 because the origins of cancer remained obscure, the causes seemed to be multiple, only long-continued cigarette smoking was the culprit pointed to by the studies, and the bulk of the evidence continued to be statistical.

The Filter Revolution

Judging from the product revolution that took place between 1952 and 1960, substantial proportions of the smoking public felt that tangible reassurance was important. In 1953, as shown in Exhibit 14–2A, no filter brand qualified with $2\frac{1}{2}$ percent of the market; as a matter of fact, the handful of then existing brands taken together constituted less than 2 percent of the market. The greater length to "travel the smoke" of the king-sized cigarette seemed to be supplying whatever soothing effects cigarette smokers needed in face of the disagreeable statistics. The continuing growth of king-sized brands had cut the share of the five "regular" leaders from 92 percent to 67 percent since 1947; and Old Gold, Philip Morris, and Chesterfield had come out with the larger versions. As it turned out, the nonfilter king-sized category had almost reached its apex, and no brand but Pall Mall was to do well (as can be noted in Exhibits 14–2B and 14–2C, Pall Mall had a 78 percent share of the category in 1967 and 1973).

By 1959 almost 50 percent of consumption was of filter cigarettes and the brand structure of the industry had been drastically transformed—no less than 16 brands had approximately $2\frac{1}{2}$ percent of the market or more, as against 4 in 1931, 6 in 1947, and 9 in 1953. The seven additions were all filter cigarettes, representing all of the six major companies except American Tobacco, which, however, possessed the new-brand leader, Pall Mall. No one brand had as much as one seventh of the market.

The splintering process continued in the next decade. Seven of the 16 leading brand types in 1959 dropped well below 2.5 percent (2 king-size, 6 regular, and 1 filter brand) and were replaced by 3 filter brands; Kool, the mentholated king-size filter cigarette which displaced its regular counterpart; the Tareyton filter which replaced the Tareyton king-size; and Raleigh, an established brand which featured coupons but never had attained a 2.5 percent in either its regular or king-size version. The dramatic change can be visualized in looking at Exhibit 14–2A and noting that six leading brand types had 95.3 percent of sales in 1947 and that by 1973 the 8 leaders had only 58.3 percent. Similarly, Exhibit 14–2B shows 61 varieties of 23 brands in 6 distinct segments of the market, including the growing 100 mm plain and mentholated filter markets, a far cry from the 5 regular brands that dominated the market in 1947.

EXHIBIT 14-2B. 1967 Sales ($ billions); Percent Share of Market and 1962/1967 Comparison of Advertising Expenditures by Cigarette Manufacturers

| | Standard Filters | | | | 100 mm Filters | | | | Nonfilters | | | | Advertising Cost in Cents per Carton | |
| | Plain | | Menthol | | Plain | | Menthol | | Regular | | King-Size | | | |
	Sales	Share	Sales	Share	Sales	Share	Sales	Share	Sales	Share	Sales	Share	1962	1967
All cigarettes sold	239.9	45*	94.1	17.5*	39.6	7.5*	13.1	2.5*	69.1	13*	72.9	13.7*		
R. J. Reynolds:														
Winston	70.0	29			10.1	25	2.5	19					5.0	8.5
Salem			41.9	44.5			2.7	20					6.8	9.3
Camel	3.4	1.4	0.3	0.3					40.0	58			2.9	5.8
American Tobacco:														
Pall Mall	2.1	0.9			11.1	28	2.0	15			57.0	78.2	3.6	7.0
Lucky Strike	17.4	7.3	0.8	0.9	0.4	1.1	0.4	3					2.8	7.7
Tareyton	1.0	0.4			2.9	7.3					1.1	1.5	10.3	15.3
Carleton													New	42.2
Silvas					0.1		1968						New	n.a.
Brown & Williamson:														
Kool			26.0	27			1968		2.5	3.6			5.7	10.6
Viceroy	19.6	8.2			1968								7.5	11.0
Raleigh	14.6	6.1									3.7	5.1	5.3	5.7
Belair			8.9	9									66.7	11.7
Philip Morris:														
Marlboro	31.1	13	1.1	1.7	2.1	5.3							7.2	10.5
Benson & Hedges	0.5	0.2			8.8	22.1	3.0	23					n.a.	25.0
Parliament	8.7	3.6											13.2	8.4
Philip Morris	2.8	1.7	0.6	0.6					1.4	2	2.8	3.8	6.3	11.1
Alpine			2.6	2.7									20.7	10.9
Virginia Slims					1968		1968						New	New
P. Lorillard:														
Kent	28.7	11.5			1.6	4							7.5	8.9
Newport			7.7	8.2			0.4	3					15.5	18.8
True	4.7	2	2.6	2.7									New	34.1
Old Gold	4.1	1.7									0.5	0.7	9.3	12.8
Spring			0.3	0.3			0.7	5.3					n.a.	19.6
Liggett & Meyers:														
L & M	17.1	7.2			1.4	3.5	1.4	11.7					9.0	14.0
Chesterfield	2.1	0.9	0.5	0.5	1.0	2.5			0.5	0.7			6.2	11.2
Lark	8.2	3.4			1968						8.3	11.4	New	18.8

n.a.—not available.

* Represents share of total market; obviously shares of each category would equal 100 percent.

Note: An entry of "1968" in the 100 mm cigarette groups means the brand introduced such a version then.

Sources: Business Week, December 15, 1967 (sales); Advertising Age, September 15, 1967 (shares); expenditures and rates...

It is worth giving some attention to the advertising and product strategies and tactics, and to the external pressures under which they were used during this period of rapid change. After being relatively stable in 1954 and 1955, advertising expenditures increased by 40 percent in 1956 and did not stabilize again until a 1959 level was reached double that of six years earlier. Another surge in advertising expenditures took place between 1962 and 1969, as shown in Exhibit 14–2E, and in the advertising per carton figures of Exhibit 14–2B.

1954–63: The Era of the Comforting Advertisements. After a two-year decline in per capita[35] cigarette consumption in 1953 and 1954 from 3,509 to 3,216 cigarettes, consumption rose to its all-time peak of about 4,300 in 1963. The general outlines of the product changes and increased advertising that were associated with this gain have been sketched in Exhibits 14–2A to 14–2E and in the preceding section. It is important to recognize the industry strategy and the government policies which conditioned these strategies.

The Formulation of Advertising Standards. In the late 1930s, long before the publicity on lung cancer and cigarettes, the cigarette companies had started to use health appeals to promote their brands, and these themes continued in the postwar period. For example, in 1939, Philip Morris was claiming that "Philip Morris cigarettes are much better for the nose and throat, a superiority recognized by eminent medical authorities." This advertising emphasis may well have eased the way for the king-sized cigarettes, whose greater length was tangible evidence of further screening for the throat. Pall Mall was utilizing this appeal in 1949 with "Guard against throat scratch . . . enjoy smoother smoking. Pall Mall's greater length of fine tobacco travels the smoke further, filters the smoke and makes it mild."

In 1950 the Federal Trade Commission was finally able to issue cease and desist orders against three of the companies against the use of various health claims ending litigation which had begun in 1942 and 1943.[36] In view of the widely published medical findings on cigarette smoking, the FTC felt it was vital to have a more expeditious method of dealing with health claims so in September, 1954, the following standards were proposed:

1. No claims be made that cigarettes are beneficial to health in any respect, or that they are not harmful or irritating; and no reference to the presence or absence of any physical effect should be made.

---

[35] Per capita figures somewhat unrealistically use the population 18 and over as a base reflecting the many state laws that forbid sale to those under 18. Since somewhat less than half of the over 18-year-olds smoked cigarettes in 1963, a consumption of well over a pack-a-day of those with the habit was indicated.

[36] P. Lorillard used the humorous approach after it was barred from low-nicotine and less irritation claims with the well-known, "Okay mother, if you want a treat instead of a treatment, treat yourself to Old Golds."

EXHIBIT 14–2C.   Unit Sales ($ billions); Total Market Shares; Market Segment Sha

and Number and Type of Brand Varieties, 1973

Company and Brand	Number and Type Brand Varieties	Total Company and Brand		85 mm Fi Plain	
		Sales	Share	Sales	Sh
All cigarettes sold............	95	575.0	100	240.4	41
R. J. Reynolds................	13	179.1	31.2	85.3	35
Winston....................	4 H, L*	87.7	15.2	69.5	28
Salem......................	2	48.5	8.4	—	—
Camel......................	2	29.8	5.2	5.8	2
Vantage....................	2 T	7.2	1.3	6.2	2
Doral......................	2	5.9	1.0	3.8	1
American Brands..............	19	92.9	16.0	16.8	6
Pall Mall...................	4	52.5	9.1	0.9	0
Lucky Strike...............	3 T	12.9	2.2	1.2	0
Tareyton...................	3 Ch	19.3	3.3	12.0	5
Carleton...................	3 T	2.5	0.4	2.5	1
Silva Thins.................	2	4.7	0.8	—	—
Iceberg 10's.................	1 T	1.0	0.2	—	—
Brown & Williamson...........	14	100.7	17.6	26.0	10
Kool......................	4 L, H*	56.2	9.8	—	—
Viceroy....................	2	18.4	3.2	14.9	6
Raleigh....................	4 C, L	16.4	2.9	11.1	4
Belair.....................	2 C	9.6	1.7	—	—
Philip Morris.................	22	121.9	21.2	78.7	32
Marlboro...................	6 2H	78.2	13.6	68.8	28.
Benson & Hedges...........	5 T, Ch	23.0	4.0	2.4	1.
Parliament..................	3 H, Ch	9.6	1.7	7.4	3.
Philip Morris...............	2	2.2	0.4	—	—
Alpine.....................	1 C	1.7	0.3	—	—
Virginia Slims...............	2	7.2	1.3	—	—
Lorillard (Loew's).............	14	49.0	8.5	31.4	13.
Kent......................	4 H	30.0	5.2	21.2	8.
Newport...................	3 H	4.5	0.8	—	—
True......................	2 T	8.8	1.5	5.9	2.
Old Gold...................	4 C	5.2	0.9	4.3	1.
Liggett & Myers..............	13	29.6	5.1	15.3	7.
L & M.....................	4 H	13.2	2.3	10.2	4.
Chesterfield.................	5 C	8.3	1.7	0.3	0.
Lark......................	2 Ch	6.6	1.1	4.8	2.
Eve.......................	2	1.5	0.3	—	—

† Represents share of total market; obviously shares of each category would equal 100 perce
Notes on other brand varieties: H = hard box; L = additional low-tar variety; C = coupo
Ch = charcoal; T = tar specified on package; * intro. in 1974; ** included under plain.
Source: *Barron's*, October 29, 1973, pp. 11–15.

2. No claims be made that length of cigarette or filter causes less nicotine, tars, resin, and so forth, unless scientifically and conclusively supported by an impartial party.

3. No reference be made to lungs, larynx, or any part of the body, or to digestion, nerves, energy, or doctors.

| Menthol | | 100 mm Filters | | | | Nonfilters | | | |
| | | Plain | | Menthol | | Regular | | Kings (85 mm) | |
s	Share	Sales	Share	Sales	Share	Sales	Share	Sales	Share
.6	17.8†	86.3	15.0†	43.8	7.6†	38.8	6.7†	49.7	8.6†
.3	37.3	16.3	17.4	15.2	34.7	24.0	61.2	—	—
	—	16.3	17.4	1.9	4.3	—	—	—	—
.2	34.3	—	—	13.3	30.4	—	—	—	—
	—	—	—	—	—	24.0	61.2	—	—
.0	1.0	—	—	—	—	—	—	—	—
.1	2.0	—	—	—	—	—	—	—	—
.4	1.4	21.1	24.4	3.8	8.7	11.5	29.6	39.4	79.2
	—	11.0	12.7	1.7	3.9	—	—	38.9	78.2
	—	0.2	0.2	—	—	11.5	29.6	—	—
	—	6.8	7.9	—	—	—	—	0.5	1.0
	**	—	—	—	—	—	—	—	—
	—	3.1	3.6	1.6	3.7	—	—	—	—
.0	1.0	—	—	*		—	—	—	—
.7	51.3	1.9	7.9	11.7	26.7	1.4	3.6	1.9	3.8
.9	44.7	—	—	8.9	20.3	1.4	3.6	—	—
	—	3.5	4.0	—	—	—	—	—	—
	—	3.4	3.9	—	—	—	—	1.9	3.8
.8	6.6	—	—	2.8	6.4	—	—	—	—
.8	2.7	28.0	32.4	10.3	23.5	0.4	1.0	1.8	3.6
.9	0.8	8.5	9.8	—	—	—	—	—	—
.2	0.2	13.2	15.3	7.2	16.4	—	—	—	—
	—	2.2	2.5	—	—	—	—	—	—
	—	—	—	—	—	0.4	1.0	1.8	3.6
.7	1.7	—	—	—	—	—	—	—	—
	—	4.1	4.8	3.1	7.1	—	—	—	—
.9	6.7	8.2	9.3	2.1	4.8	0.1	0.3	0.3	0.6
	—	7.7	8.7	1.1	2.5	—	—	—	—
.0	3.9	—	—	0.5	1.2	—	—	—	—
.9	2.8	*	—	*	—	—	—	—	—
	—	0.5	0.6	—	—	0.1	0.3	0.3	0.6
.0	0.0	5.6	6.5	1.3	3.0	1.4	3.6	6.0	12.1
	—	2.3	2.7	0.7	1.6	—	—	—	—
.0	0.0	0.6	0.7	—	—	1.4	3.6	6.0	12.1
	—	1.8	2.1	—	—	—	—	—	—
	—	0.9	1.0	0.6	1.4	—	—	—	—

4. No implication be made of medical approval of a brand or of smoking in general.

5. Advertising be limited to discussion of taste, quality, flavor, enjoyment, and matters of opinion.

6. No unsubstantiated claims of comparative volume be made.

7. Only testimonials which are current, genuine, and do not violate other rules be used.

8. No false disparagement of another cigarette be made.

The Significance of the Standards for Business Policy. It is not difficult to understand the willingness of the cigarette firms to go along with these standards. Strident claims of less damage to health would probably injure industry sales in view of the virtually impossible job of demonstrating that filters would reduce the long-range harm done by cigarette smoking.

With the industry's consent, the FTC published substantially these standards as guides for evaluating cigarette advertising on September 2, 1955. An explicit recognition was made of filters by stating that "words, including those relating to filters or filtration which imply the presence or absence of any physical effort or effects are considered subject to this guide." Standard number five above was modified so as not to be an absolute prohibition, and its amendment was promised, "when facts and circumstances permit."

The advertising themes chosen in 1956 raised no apparent issues:

Loved for gentleness. Some people are known—and loved—for being gentle. So is this new cigarette. New Philip Morris, made gentle for modern taste.

Only Camels taste so rich yet smoke so mild.

Light up a Lucky; it's light up time! Men, this is it! No cigarette in the world ever tasted so good. You see, Lucky Strike means fine tobacco—mild good tasting tobacco that's TOASTED to taste even better.

Like your pleasure big? Smoke for real—smoke Chesterfields.

Only Viceroy has 20,000 filters for the smoothest taste in smoke. Twice as many filters as the other two largest selling filter brands.

You get a lot to like—the easy drawing filter feels right in your mouth. It works but doesn't get in the way. (Marlboros.)

Winstons taste good! Like a cigarette should! Get your flavor and filter too—this finer filter works so effectively.

Say, have you tried new Salems? A new idea in smoking—take a puff . . . its springtime.

While the FTC seemed tolerably satisfied with the compliance with the new advertising guides, serious questions were developing about what function the filter in a filter cigarette was serving. What miracle, for example, was the "miracle tip" of the L&M cigarette performing? What were "all the benefits of a filter" claimed by Kool? What did the "real filtration" of the Tareyton signify? And why should Viceroy have "twice as many filters"?

The Consumers Union Reports. In March, 1957, CU reported that its tests showed little difference in nicotine content of the smoke between filter cigarettes and those with no filters and only "somewhat less tar" from the filter cigarettes. They also found that the average nicotine and tar levels of filter-tip cigarettes had risen over the 1955 level. As an extreme example, though its advertising still claimed the "micronite filter," Kent cigarettes showed eight times as much tar as the original 1952 Kent and one third more than the Kent of 1955.

The American Cancer Society Study. In June, 1957, the conclusions of the elaborate Hammond and Horn study on the relation between smoking and death rates among men from 50 to 70 years of age were announced to the American Medical Association. A major conclusion was that the death rate of the cigarette smokers (in their sample of 190,000 men traced for 44 months) was 68 percent higher than the death rate of a comparable group of men who never smoked, age being taken into consideration.[37] The death rate from lung cancer ran from 3.4 per 100,000 per year for men who never smoked to 217.3 for men who smoked over two packs a day.

The **Reader's Digest** *Articles.* *Reader's Digest* had an independent consulting chemist run tests similar to those of CU. The magazine wrote up the results in somewhat more dramatic fashion. It pointed out that smokers switching from the regular cigarettes of the Big Four to the filter cigarettes rated lowest in tar and nicotine would gain tar reductions of only 7 to 17 percent. But a switch to such leading sellers among filters as Marlboro, Winston, and L&M might actually lead to an increase in tars and nicotine. The article concluded: "It's entirely possible to manufacture filter tips much more efficient than any now on the market" and asked: "Why aren't these improved filter tips available?"[38]

In a second article in August the magazine gave Kent cigarettes a tremendous sales boost in an article entitled "Wanted—and Available—Filter Tips That Really Filter." The re-engineered Kent had been tested and found to deliver about 40 percent less tar than the regular nonfilter cigarettes, and P. Lorillard's successful exploitation of this finding was widely copied by other companies with similar claims.

The Congressional Hearings. Congressman Blatnik of Minnesota, the chairman of the Legal and Monetary Affairs Subcommittee of the House Government Operations Committee, opened the July hearings by announcing that "our hearings today are concerned with the advertising of cigarettes—particularly filter tip cigarettes." The hearings opened with Dr. E. C. Hammond testifying about the American Cancer Society report. Plans were to call later upon representatives of the tobacco industry; but none appeared, with the exception of Dr. Clarence C. Little, the Scientific Director of the Tobacco Industry Research Committee.

---

[37] *False and Misleading Advertising (Filter-Tip Cigarettes)*, Hearings before a Subcommittee of the Committee on Government Operations, House of Representatives, 85th Cong., 1st sess. (Washington, D.C.: U.S. Government Printing Office, 1957), p. 312.

[38] Ibid., pp. 609, 612.

Dr. Little's basic position was that "I would like to get more facts before I am able to say whether there is any relationship between smoking and cancer. . . ."[39]

Dr. Wynder of the Sloane-Kettering Institute for Cancer Research recommended regulations that would encourage or perhaps even require the filter cigarette manufacturers to reduce their tar and nicotine content to 40 percent below that of the standard regular-size cigarette. He admitted that at the present state of knowledge the filter could not selectively eliminate cancer-causing agents but simply could quantitatively reduce the intake of all tobacco smoke. He also summed up the result of a survey of 500 patients who had switched to filters: "We found that more than 70 percent of them had switched because they thought they were getting health protection or because of advertising which indicated they got health protection."[40]

The Committee wound up its testimony with Mr. Blatnik expressing regret that the tobacco industry "for some reason won't voluntarily come before us—a free, responsible public body in a public forum and tell us what is superior about their filter, or justify at least in some measure the claims they are making before the entire American audience at great expense to themselves in promotion of the filter tips. . . ."[41]

The "Safer" Cigarette (*1957–59*). The changes toward reduced tars and nicotine in the smoke that took place from 1957 through 1959 were substantial. The major physical changes were in greater porosity and in venting of the cigarette paper and in the use of more resistant filters. Associated with these was the increased use of flavoring agents, including menthol, to make the reduced smoke intake more palatable. Regular Old Golds were shifted to a blend of low-nicotine, low-tar tobaccos, a move opposite to the use of stronger tobaccos which probably accounted for some of the increase of tars in filter cigarettes noted in 1957.

One manifestation of the change was the influx of new high-filtration brands, including Duke, Life, Spring, and Alpine. Duke, with a long filter and a paper overwrap which made it look even longer, produced only half the tars of the regular Kents, which were low in 1958. Even more important in terms of the 1959 market was the decline in tars and nicotine of the leading sellers among the filters: L&M, Marlboro, Viceroy, and Salem. Even Winston, the leader of them all, whose filter had been reported to have a practically indiscernible effect on tars and nicotine, showed a decrease of 15 percent. Its slogan of "Its what's up front that counts" had been ironically valid.[42]

While filtertips gained slightly in market share, *Business Week* ob-

---

[39] Ibid., p. 48.

[40] Ibid., p. 279.

[41] Ibid., p. 277.

[42] As reported by Consumers Union in *Consumer Reports*, January, 1960.

served that they "seem to have peaked out at just under 50 percent of the total market."[43] Neither of the two publications conducting the best-known tests on cigarettes predicted the end of the swing toward "safer" products. *Consumer Reports* noted difficulty in providing "the latest results in the low-tar, low-nicotine race," since "with solid rewards of gold waiting, many cigarette companies are juggling and working over their products in the frantic manner associated with style changes in the garment industry."[44]

The *Reader's Digest* commented: "The tobacco industry will not admit publicly that it is seeking safer cigarettes. Indeed it continues to deny that any tobacco-health problem exists. . . . The men of the to-bacco industry are not being fooled. They know that their task now is to get the gun unloaded before a new generation of customers decides that the game is silly, the stakes too high."[45]

The FTC Ends the "Tar Derby". Besides being encouraged toward modest filter improvements, some gradation in the advertising claims for filtered cigarettes, and the introduction of new high-filtration products, some manufacturers made strident claims for the low tar of their ciga-rettes. These constituted the so-called "tar derby" in which conflcting claims about what brands eliminated the most tar or nicotine were wide-spread.

In December, 1959, the FTC brought its first complaint since setting up standards and seeking voluntary compliance. It charged that the ad-vertising claim that Life cigarettes are "proved to give you least tar and nicotine of all cigarettes" was not true, that representations of U.S. gov-ernment endorsement were false (advertisements stated the figures were "on file with an agency of the United States Government"), and that a television commercial showing liquid being poured into Life's "millicel super filter" and into that of another cigarette did not give "proof how Life gives least tar and nicotine."

Brown & Williamson did not choose to fight. Instead, after consulta-tions with the industry the chairman of the FTC announced that in the absence of a satisfactory uniform test and proof of advantage to the smoker, there be no more tar and nicotine claims in advertising. Duke and Life, the truly high-filtration cigarettes, left without the weapon of advertising their only significantly advantage, dwindled into obscurity.

What has been called the "tar derby," when widespread and fre-quently conflicting claims about the tar and nicotine elimination were made, particularly in 1958 and 1959, had ended. No longer was the consumer faced with claims like "up to 43 percent higher filtration,"

---

[43] *Business Week,* December 26, 1959, p. 68.

[44] *Consumer Reports,* January, 1960, p. 18.

[45] "The Search for 'Safer' Cigarettes," *Reader's Digest,* November, 1959, pp. 44–45.

"now lower in tars and nicotine than any leading cigarette," and "Life filters best by far." Its major legacy was an improvement in the filtration quality of most filter cigarettes. Accordingly to the periodic studies of Consumers Union, the average tars in smoke per cigarette had dropped from 35 milligrams to 21 and from 40 to 27 for regular filter and king-sized filter cigarettes between March, 1957, and Januray, 1960. A speech by the chairman of the FTC on February 5, 1960, confirmed that industry agreement had been reached that tar and nicotine claims should cease for the time being. (The FTC left open its possible resumption at some future date when it was satisfied with testing procedures.) One can understand why the companies went along as long as they were assured that all advertising for cigarettes would stress sweetness and light, with no unpleasantness about tar, nicotine, and shorter life-spans for smokers.

After the Surgeon-General's Report, 1964–

In 1964 the Surgeon-General of the United States officially recognized cigarette smoking as a threat to the health of Americans. The medical findings were not new, but the authority of the office assured the industry that the habit it fostered would be under continuous rather than sporadic fire from regulatory bodies and private health interests such as the American Cancer Society and American Health Association.

The policy issues the industry as a whole were forced to face were: what voluntary or compulsory restrictions should it accept in advertising and in product labeling? Its initial decision was to continue voluntary compliance with the guides agreed upon with the FTC in 1960, with a few additions to placate public concern with television advertising aimed at young people, such as the use of obviously adult rather than youthful models. Three companies, American, P. Lorillard, and Stephano Brothers dropped out of the code agreement with FTC approvals so that they would be better able to inform the public of the low-tar qualities of Carlton, True and Marvel (once a leading 10-cent brand).

The industry strongly resisted pressures from the FTC that health warnings should be required in all advertisements, and were able in 1965 to obtain a congressional prohibition on any such FTC restrictions, effective until June, 1969. The price paid by the industry in this deal was a modest one, the requirement that the warning, "Caution, Cigarette Smoking May Be Hazardous to Your Health," be printed on every package. The industry along with the National Association of Broadcasters challenged the Federal Communication Commission ruling that broadcasters accepting cigarette advertising should provide time for anti-smoking commercials. (The guideline ratio of one "anti" for three "pro" was worth about $75,000,000 of advertising time in 1968.) Their case was lost in the Court of Appeals and appealed to the Supreme Court.

In 1969 the industry sought to extend until 1975 the legislation that would prevent the Federal Trade Commission from requiring strong health warning in all advertisements. The legislation was buried in the Senate. In July it proposed a voluntary industry agreement to remove cigarette advertising from the broadcasting media by September, 1970. The National Association of Broadcasters had put forward a much more gradual program to phase out such advertising by 1973, a program that would give the broadcasting industry more time to recoup losses.

At this time the Federal Trade Commission acted. First, all television ads were banned from TV. Second, all printed ads were required to carry the warning: "The Surgeon General has determined cigarette smoking is dangerous to your health." After the Commission had set up regular testing procedures all advertising was required to carry the tar and nicotine content of the cigarette as determined by these tests. This seemed to many a desirable reversal of the previous FTC standards that virtually barred such information. These measures had some advantages for the cigarette companies. The required antismoking commercials had apparently played a part in the sharp reduction of per-capita smoking in 1969 and 1970—many fewer could be expected now that they were voluntary. Television advertising had become terribly expensive as indicated in Exhibit 14–2E. Finally, the presence of the warning could be helpful in warding off private damage suits for lung cancer deaths.

The Strategies of the Cigarette Firms in the 1970s

Brand-share data is given in Exhibits 14–2A to 14–2D and company share data is included in Exhibit 14–2C. It should be clear from these that the critical decisions as to whether firms gained or lost share concerned their willingness and ability to establish strong filter brands in the 1950s. If we examine the changes from 1967 to 1973 in market share, it can be seen that they reflect far earlier decisions. The large gainers were Philip Morris 12.4 percent to 21.2 percent and Brown and Williamson from 14.2 percent to 17.6 percent. The large losers were American from 22.2 percent to 16.0 percent and Liggett & Myers from 8.3 percent to 5.1 percent. The declines of Reynolds from 32.3 percent to 31.2 percent and P. Loillard from 9.7 percent to 6.5 percent were much less serious. Philip Morris had been able to develop established but minor filters into contention very quickly (and one, Marlboro, became the world's leading cigarette in 1973); Brown & Williamson had converted its small mentholated brand, Kool, quickly as it became clear menthol could compensate in taste for that filtered out. American, on the other hand perhaps overconfident because of success of king-size Pall Mall, the leading brand in 1958 and 1962, developed the smallest share of the six in plain 85 mm filters and along with Liggett & Myers was a negligible factor in the mentholated 85 mm filters.

What the product should be is the first strategic decision. One clear direction in the mid-1970s was toward the 100 mm length with the market share rising from 10 percent to 22.6 percent for plain and mentholated taken together. Less clear was the potential demand for really low tar and nicotine cigarettes discussed under the advertising question. The continuation of historically low levels seemed assured. The American Cancer Society reported that while 90 percent of all cigarettes sold in 1954 were in a range from 35 to 53 milligrams of tar, that a similar range in 1960 was 19 to 35, and in 1972 was 14 to 29. Filters seemed destined to remain more than mere mouthpieces.[46]

What theme to advertise? The critical question in the choice of appropriate advertising themes was product-oriented. Should the companies place emphasis on high-filtration products and advertise their qualities or should they stick with the good taste of fine tobacco in a setting of romance, virility, or swinging youth? Only P. Lorillard and American chose to promote high-filtration products such as True, initially and Carleton and Silva Thins with statements on low-income and tar content, and with the sanction of the FTC they withdrew from compliance with the industry standards. Other brands such as Lark and Tareyton displayed their charcoal filters but most chose to ignore the health question.

In 1974 Carlton (1 mg to 4 mg tar) simply stated Carlton is lowest. Lorillard advertised the new True 100's (12 mg tar) as "lower in both tar and nicotine than 99% of all other 100's sold." Other brands that chose to specify tar and nicotine content on packs took the middle position between taste and tar. Reynolds predicted Vantage (11 mg tar) to be "the lowest one your friends will enjoy." Ads for Lucky 100's and Tens suggested "cut your tar in half," since these brands with 10 mg tar were about halfway between the lowest (1 mg) and the "bestselling regular size" (23 mg). Raleigh was representative of what was an increasingly common product-advertising strategy. Introduce an additional lower tar variety to your line, perhaps 13 mg in tar as compared with 16 to 20 mg. for other brand varieties, and simply claim "lowered tar." Raleigh's new variety was called "extra mild"; Winston's, Marlboros', and Kool's used the designation "light."

The bulk of the leading selling filters (15 to 22 mg tar) stressed such themes as "excitement" (Viceroy), "pleasure" (Newport), "rugged man in rugged country" (Marlboro), "doing it right" (Winston), "black eye signifying brand loyalty" (Tareyton), and "America's favorite cigarette break" with picture of broken cigarette (Benson & Hedges 100's).

How many product varieties of cigarettes should be produced? Should these have separate brands or should each brand be sold in several varieties? As shown by Exhibits 14–2B and 14–2C, each company has chosen to enter all six market segments (classified by length, the

---

[46] *U.S. News & World Report*, December 17, 1973, p. 84.

presence of a filter, and by mentholation). The one apparent exception resulted from R. J. Reynolds' withdrawal of Brandon, an entry in the king-size, nonfilter market that was even less successful than other challengers to Pall Mall.

In the 1950s, when all firms decided that they must enter the filter and mentholated filter markets, proliferation of both product varieties and brands occurred (see Exhibit 14–2A). The vehicles used to enter the filter market were separate brands. The leading brands of the 1940s maintained their nonfilter identity, although Philip Morris, Chesterfield, and Old Gold did offer a second king-size variety.

EXHIBIT 14–2D

Concentration Ratios for 1973 in Sub-categories of the Cigarette Market

Subcategory	Sales (billions)	Cumulative Percent of Sales by Brands				Leading Brands
		1	*2*	*3*	*4*	
85 mm plain filter........	240.4	28.9	57.5	66.3	72.5	Winston, Marlboro
85 mm menthol filter.....	102.6	44.7	79.0	85.6	89.5	Kool, Salem
100 mm plain filter.......	86.3	17.4	32.7	43.4	55.8	Winston, Benson & Hedges, Pall Mall
100 mm menthol filter....	43.8	30.4	50.7	67.1	74.2	Salem, Kool, Benson & Hedges
Regular................	38.8	61.2	90.8	94.4	98.0	Camel, Lucky Strike
King..................	49.7	78.2	90.3	94.1	97.7	Pall Mall, Chesterfield
Hard-box..............	44.8	82.1	89.2	95.5	97.4	Marlboro
Couponed..............	41.7	39.3	62.3	82.1	95.8	Raleigh, Belair, Chesterfield Old Gold
Charcoal filter..........	29.9	63.0	85.0	92.5	99.4	Tareyton, Lark
Specified tar and nicotine..............	23.3	37.9	68.8	79.3	89.3	True, Vantage

Notes:
1. Last four categories cross boundaries of first six and cannot be added to total sales.
2. Firm concentration ratios are distinctly higher for first four categories (see Exhibit 14–2c) and for couponed cigarettes in which B. & W. has first two brands.
Source: *Barrons,* October 29, 1973, pp. 11–15.

In 1967 the once Big Three were being offered in no less than 13 varieties including 5 separate renditions each by Lucky Strike and Chesterfield. Each of the early entrants into the 100 mm filter field was an additional variety of an established brand. Pall Mall, the first entrant in 1966, had been the industry leader through 1965 with only its king-size version (a category that had begun to decline). Benson & Hedges was the next, also in 1966, a long-established, premium-price brand owned by Philip Morris. One executive in explaining Chesterfield's extension into the field stated, "Unless you've got a completely new product with a unique sales story, it pays to bring out a line extension nowadays. For one thing, you benefit from the economies of advertising. For another, cigarette smokers are extremely brand-loyal."[47]

How much advertising? Exhibit 14–2E shows that total advertising expenditures more than quadrupled between 1955 and 1967. An important reason for this increase was the growth in the number of brands. For example, to establish Benson & Hedges in the 100 mm filter field, the Philip Morris Company increased expenditures from less than half a million dollars in 1965 to over $15 million in 1967. R. J. Reynolds was able to hold its expenditures to the lowest (4.2) percent of sales, largely

EXHIBIT 14–2E

Cigarette Advertising Expenditures and Percent of Sales*
(expenditures in millions of dollars)

	1955*	1958*	1965	Percent Sales	1967†	Percent Sales	1972	Percent Sales
R. J. Reynolds..............	20.1	28.5	69.8	4.1	78.4	4.2	78.2	2.6
American Tobacco..........	21.3	32.0	58.0	5.8	71.5	5.2	57.0	1.9
P. Lorillard.................	12.3	23.7	34.7	7.6	41.8	7.9	42.0	5.2
Brown & Williamson........	5.8	21.4	32.9	6.4	38.0	6.7	52.2	6.0
Philip Morris..............	10.1	19.1	37.7	6.8	44.4	5.5	61.0	2.9
Liggett & Myers............	13.0	17.6	35.5	7.7	37.5	6.9	37.0	4.9
Total (*Printers' Ink*)*.....	$82.6	142.3	—		—		—	
Total (*Advertising Age*)...	71.9	127.6	268.8		311.6		327.4	

* The major difference between the *Printers' Ink* figures given by company for 1955 and 1958 and the *Advertising Age* figures are that the former includes a miscellaneous category estimating such items as company advertising department expenditures while the latter concentrates on media payments only.

† Television expenditures in 1967 constituted from 64.2 percent (American) to 87.6 percent (B.&W.) of total. Radio expenditures from 0 percent (P.M.) to 13.5 percent (P. Lorillard); Magazine expenditures from 3.1 percent (Lorillard) to 21.8 percent (American); and newspapers from 0.3 percent (B.&W.) to 7.8 percent (American).

Sources: *Printers' Ink*, October 30, 1959; *Advertising Age*, June 4 and June 25, 1962; late August summary issue 1966, 1968, 1973.

reflecting its concentration on three major brands. A critical question facing the industry with the static market of the 1960s was whether costs per unit could be held down where increases in advertising expenditures must probably be met from increased prices or reduced profits, with total sales remaining constant.

Exhibit 14–2B shows how high costs had become per carton for newer smaller brands. The drop in advertising expenditures with television banned was smaller than some investors had hoped. Exhibit 14–2E underestimates the real drop that did occur sinces prices were rising and advertising in noncigarette fields was increasing. The great beneficiaries of the shift were the general magazines and billboards. One effect on product policy of the changed media was likely to be fewer new

---

[47] *Business Week*, December 3, 1966, p. 143.

brands, since television, while costly, also could launch a new name rapidly.

Should the firms diversify by merging with companies in other industries? If so, what other industries? Five out of the six leading firms had actively sought and found such merger opportunities by 1969. Only Brown & Williamson, with the greatest relative gain in market share, had done little diversification (although its parent, the British-American Tobacco Company, also sold ice cream). American Tobacco Company became American Brands, Inc., and R. J. Reynolds Tobacco Company became R. J. Reynolds Industries, Inc., in May, 1969, when their sales outside of the tobacco industry rose to over 25 percent of their totals. The industries chosen by all five firms were mainly in the consumer goods field; biscuits, liquor, chewing gum, oriental foods, fruit punch, and pet foods. Evidently attracted by the relatively low stock price/earnings ratio, Loews Theatres, Inc., acquired P. Lorillard Corporation.

How dramatic the change was for an industry with only 8 percent of its employment outside of tobacco products in 1958 is suggested by the following increase in the number of subsidiaries for the five American companies between 1964 and 1972 (figures in parentheses are the percent of 1972 sales that were of nontobacco products:[48]

American Brands (29%) . . . . 4 to 74
Phillip Morris Inc. (20%) . . . . 8 to 62
Liggett & Myers (59%) . . . . 4 to 21
R. J. Reynolds, Ind. (27%) . . . . 3 to 10
Loews (Lorillard) (31%) . . . . 5 to 130

It is true that some of the new subsidiaries represented expansion in tobacco abroad, but since most of the foreign sales are in tobacco, the percentages given understate the share of domestic business that is in other products.

Could price be used as a weapon? The use of direct price appeals seemed more inhibited than ever by high unit taxes and by the oligopolistic nature of the industry that threatened retaliation. The introduction of the new long cigarettes at standard prices (after the introductory phase, their retail prices were from 0 to 2 cents higher) embodied in part a more-for-your-money appeal. The inclusion of coupons had been a long-time feature of Raleigh's merchandising, and about 8 percent of the cigarettes sold in 1973 used coupons (see Exhibits 14–2C and 14–2D). These indirect price cuts did not break the firm pattern of close to identical pricing that prevailed during most of the postwar period. The ability of the industry to raise prices together and so to pass on increase costs meant that its above-average profitability continued despite trying events. The fortunes of the various firms varied fairly closely with the changes in their market positions.

---

[48] *Moody's Industrials* and Company Reports, 1965–73.

For the Future

There will be further interplay between government agencies and the policies of cigarette firms including interrelated price, product, and advertising strategies. The strength of ingrained smoking habits including brand preferences is such that the industry makes long-run adjustments slowly and it can scarcely be said to have fully adjusted to the consequences of the smoking-death rate findings in the middle of the 1970s, and new shocks in the forms of government regulation, scientific findings, and technological changes may well face it.

The student has excellent opportunities to observe events subsequent to 1974. Because of the federal excise tax, excellent estimates are available on brand shares. The most available source is one of the December issues of *Business Week* each year, or alternatively of *Barrons* in late October to December. Advertising changes can be found in *Advertising Age* (an August issue of the latter has good data). Further government hearings are almost a certainty.

Questions

1. Consider the relationship of price, product and advertising policies to the state of the industry, the economy, and of the society in the following periods: the 1920s, 1930s, the 1940s, the 1950s and the 1960s.
2. To what, if any, extent do you think the cigarette firms have failed to meet public responsibilities in connection with the medical findings since 1953? Do you see any shortcomings as primarily a failure of management or of the public and its regulatory authorities?
3. The demand for cigarettes has generally been considered highly inelastic, thus making the industry a prime candidate for reliable added tax revenues. Can this generalization be squared with the experience of the 1930s?
4. How did the very strength of the Big Three's position in nonfilter cigarettes contribute to their declining market shares?
5. Optional. Look up changes in the most recent year for Exhibit 14–2C and 14–2D. Analyze as well as you can shifts in market shares and changing strategies. (This could be a term paper.)

CASE 14–3. Problems in Nonprice Competition

A. Industry Variations in Advertising-Sales Ratios

In a study of 41 consumer-goods industries (manufacturing), 11 were found with advertising-sales ratios of over 3 percent and 9 with ratios of under 1 percent (based on 1957 data).[49] The median industry (car-

---

[49] The data in this problem has been derived from Lester G. Telser, "Advertising and Competition," *The Journal of Political Economy*, December, 1964, p. 543.

pets) showed a 2.05 percent ratio. In the list below, these 20 high and low industries are listed alphabetically. The four-firm concentration ratio (the percent of industry sales by the four leading firms) for 1958 is given in parenthesis.

1.	Appliances........... (43)	11.	Millinery............ (6)
2.	Beer and Malt......... (29)	12.	Motor Vehicles........ (88)
3.	Cereals............. (83)	13.	Other Tobacco (cigarettes).... (77)
4.	Clocks and Watches...... (49)	14.	Parts and Accessories...... (33)
5.	Confectionery......... (37)	15.	Periodicals.......... (31)
6.	Drugs.............. (30)	16.	Perfumes............ (29)
7.	Furs.............. (5)	17.	Petroleum Refining....... (32)
8.	Hand Tools........... (33)	18.	Soaps............. (63)
9.	Meats............. (28)	19.	Sugar............. (65)
10.	Mens Clothing......... (15)	20.	Wine............. (35)

Questions

1. Separate the high advertisers from the low advertisers, giving reasons for your choice. You can check your choices against the list at the end of the case.

2. Did you find any relationship between concentration ratios and advertising? Explain.

B. "Dynamic" Product Competition

One of Jules Backman's conclusions in a study of advertising was that "the proliferation of brands has reflected dynamic competition and has resulted in significant changes in market shares. These developments indicate that the degree of market power which supposedly accompanies product differentiation indentified by brand names and implemented by large scale advertising is much weaker than contended."[50]

Among the illustrations were the following:

Dial toilet soap (Armour & Company) in the six years following 1959 became the leading brand with 19 percent in a market in which Lever Bros. and Proctor & Gamble had had 52 percent of total sales.

Three of the five leading dentifrices in 1965 included the number one brand (a fluoridated paste) were not in the list before 1956.

In 1964 no fewer than 459 branded deodrants of eight types were available.

The number of soaps and detergents offered for sale in a sample of grocery stores increased from 65 in 1950 to 200 in 1963; frozen foods available went from 121 to 350; paper products from 52 to 145.

The Merck & Company "Cortone" was the only Corticosteroid tablet available in 1950. By 1959, 29 companies were selling similar steroid products.

---

[50] Jules Backman, *Advertising and Competition* (New York: New York University Press, 1967), p. 80. The examples that follow appear from pp. 62–76.

The four leading brands of 28 food items averaged 20.7 percent market shares in 1948 while the 4 leaders for each product in 1959 averaged 16.4 percent.

Products introduced after 1963 represented 70 percent of Procter & Gamble's sales, 60 percent of Bristol-Myers (drugs), 90 percent of Alberto-Culver's (cosmetics), and 33 percent of Campbell Soup's which continued its 90 percent share of the wet soup market.

From 1950 to 1963 per capita consumption of ready-to-eat cereals increased from 4.05 to 5.72 with presweetened (such as Sugar Frosted Flakes) and nutrition (such as Total) types accounting for 1.21 and 0.40 pounds respectively.

Private brands outsold manufacturer's brands from 1960 to 1963 in a sample of corporate food chains in such products as white bread, frozen orange juice, and margarine. For independent stores over a wide range of food products (canned fruits, coffee, bacon, etc.), private brands exceeded a 25 percent share in all categories studied and exceeded 50 percent for bakery and dairy products and frozen vegetables and fruit juices.[51]

Questions

1. In most of the examples above, what seemed to be a prerequisite for substantially altered market shares?
2. Is "product proliferation" an unmixed blessing to the firm, to economy? What checks are there on burgeoning advertising?

C. A Great American Advertising Program

An advertising program of $500,000 permitted General American Consolidated, Inc., to increase volume, make larger profits, and charge a lower price to maximize profits on its major product. Show diagrammatically the demand and average cost curves and indicate profits. Discuss economic circumstances that would make such a happy combination of events possible.

An Ending Note About Problem A

Industries 1, 2, 3, 4, 5, 6, 8, 13, 16, 18 and 20 were the high advertisers. You earn a double demerit for failing to include 16, 6, 18 and 2 on your list which led with ratios of 14.7, 12.3, 7.9, and 6.9 percent; a similar demerit is awarded for including 11 or 19 on the high list Their percentages were 0.33 and 0.28. The third low industry, periodicals (15), with 0.30 is a surprise; evidently the many mail appeals for subscriptions were excluded from the advertising totals.

---

[51] Ibid., p. 56.

CASE 14–4. Fine Foods, Inc.*

Fine Foods, Inc., is a large multiplant food-processing and merchandising company. Fine Foods executives were searching for standards to guide them in the selection and allocation of trade deals among their many sales districts throughout the United States. Up to the present time, the decisions as to what districts should get trade "deals" in support of their sales effort and how much, and what kind each trade deal should be, were made subjectively by Mr. Fox, head of the promotion department, in consultation with the regional sales managers, each of whom had responsibility for four or five sales districts. A consultant suggested that the company might use either a game-theory or a decision-matrix model to make its selection and allocation of trade deals, since Fine Foods faced only one large competitor who, along with Fine Foods, accounted for more than 90 percent of the market in any sales district. Mr. Fox believed that the following items might be pertinent to the use of game theory or decision theory:

1. The existing company policy towards trade deals was that they were undesirable from a merchandising point of view, but a necessary evil since competitors used them extensively and large supermarket chains expected them from manufacturers. Mr. Fox had been told by an executive that if Fine Foods' competitors stopped using trade deals, Fine Foods would never use them.

2. Fine Foods, for most of its products, held the largest market share of that product class. However, since the competitors had started using trade deals, they had steadily encroached on the Fine Foods brand share. *The major goal of Fine Foods, in trade dealing, had been to stop the decline in market share and maintain the status quo.* Previously, Mr. Fox had guessed as to the type and amount of deal to be offered by the competitor, and then estimated the kind of deal needed to stop the decline.

3. Mr. Fox and the regional managers had subjectively decided which districts should get promotion funds, then deals were decided on. Mr. Fox tried to allocate deals to districts in which Fine Foods' brand share was very high (for protection), where it was relatively low (to gain a more "normal" share), and where competitors had dealt heavily in the past.

4. Each competitor typically favored certain types and amounts of deals. The types and amounts of deals varied from product to product and district to district, but within each district, on any given product,

---

* This case is intended for use with the appendix to this chapter. It was prepared by Mr. Harry Lavo under the supervision of Professor Gilbert R. Whitaker (Washington University, St. Louis, Missouri). It is not designed to present illustrations of either effective or ineffective handling of administrative problems.

EXHIBIT 14-4A

Fine Foods, Inc.—Atlanta District

	Fine Foods' Response to Deals by Brand Y					Brand Y Deals		
	Direct Account Promotion Payment Offer (P.P.O.)			Free Goods 1 with 5	No Deal	Direct/Account Payment/Promotion Offer	Direct/Account Buying/Allowance	Probability
	$0.25	$0.40	$0.60	$0.37				
Gross profit	$10,000	$12,000	$13,500	$10,500	$0	$0.25		0.10
Cost	$ 8,000	$10,000	$13,000	$ 7,500	$0			
Market share	+0	+2	+5	+4	−1			
Gross profit	$ 8,000	$18,000	$21,000	$12,000	$0	$0.50		0.20
Cost	$ 7,000	$20,000	$21,000	$ 9,000	$0			
Market share	−1	+0	+1	+0	−3			
Gross profit	$ 2,000	$ 6,000	$10,000	$ 6,000	$0	$0.75		0.10
Cost	$ 2,000	$ 4,000	$ 8,000	$ 3,500	$0			
Market share	−4	−2	+0	+2	−6			
Gross profit	$ 8,000	$10,000	$12,000	$ 4,000	$0		$0.40	0.25
Cost	$ 8,000	$10,000	$15,000	$ 5,000	$0			
Market share	−1	+0	+2	+0	−2			
Gross profit	$ 6,000	$ 8,000	$10,000	$ 4,000	$0		$0.60	0.15
Cost	$10,000	$12,000	$13,000	$ 4,000	$0			
Market share	−3	−1	+0	+2	−4			
Gross profit	$ 8,000	$10,000	$11,000	$10,000	$0			0.20
Cost	$ 4,000	$ 7,000	$ 9,000	$ 6,500	$0			
Market share	+0	+2	+3	+1	−1			1.00

* Boxes denote deals which are estimated to prevent changes in market share for each Brand Y deal possibility.

Mr. Fox felt he could judge what deals might be used and the relative probabilities of their use. However, in some districts where little competition had occurred until recently, Mr. Fox admitted to himself that he didn't really know which type deal would be favored.

Upon the advice of the consultant, and with the help of the accounting and research departments, Mr. Fox proceeded to estimate the results from possible deals on Fine Foods' "Luscious" brand of soup and common types of retaliations by brand Y, the only competing brand. For each combination of strategies, Mr. Fox estimated the resulting cost, gross profits, and effect on market share. Exhibit 14–3A contains these estimates for the Atlanta District sales territory.

Questions to Be Answered

1. Design a game-theory matrix for the Atlanta District and choose the best strategy.
   a. What assumptions must be made in order to utilize this method of choice?
   b. Do you see any possible conflicts between game-theory choice and the policies of Fine Foods?
2. Design a decision-theory matrix (see Chapter 1) and choose the best strategy.
   a. Explain the assumptions that lie behind your choice of a payoff measure. Behind your decision rules.
   b. Is any particular payoff measure or decision rule particularly suited to Fine Foods' trade deal policies?
3. Which of the two types of quantitative decision models do you prefer? Why?

Questions to Be Considered

Assume that you have used matrixes such as these for many sales districts. What alternative ways might a set amount of "trade deal funds" (from which deal costs must be covered) be allocated to the districts? In other words, how would you decide which districts get money and which did not? Does the way in which you allocate the "money" depend upon the assumptions behind the choice of either a zero-sum game or a decision-matrix model? Does it depend on your payoff measure? On your decision rules, when you use the decision-matrix model?

chapter **15**

Product Line Policy

Most of the discussion thus far has been concerned with demand, output, and cost for a single commodity produced by a firm or industry. This is obviously an unrealistic assumption for virtually all firms engaged in the wholesaling, retailing, or transporting of goods. Manufacturing establishments more frequently specialize in only one good (e.g., bricks, portland cement, a soft drink, airplanes, wheat, or tobacco) but, even so, usually produce the good in various sizes, models, packages, and qualities, so that it is not entirely clear whether they should be called single-product or multiple-product firms. In recent years, there seems to have been a particular emphasis on product diversification on the part of manufacturers—single-product firms becoming multiple-product producers and those already handling multiple products adding even more lines.[1]

The assumption of one product to a firm is a simplifying abstraction which is useful in developing numerous principles applicable to multiproduct companies as well. For the most part, the profit-maximizing entrepreneur handling many commodities should make short-run and long-run calculations in the same way as is suggested by economic theory for the single-commodity firm; he should equate marginal cost and marginal revenue in short-run operational decisions with respect to every product, and should anticipate at least covering average costs (including normal returns to self-employed factors) when making new investment pertaining to any product.

The multiproduct firm is often a member of several industries when "industry" is classified according to the federal government's statistical procedure. It is equally appropriate, though usually less useful, to con-

---

[1] This trend is interestingly described by Gilbert Burck in "The Rush to Diversify," *Fortune,* September, 1955, p. 91.

sider the firm to be a member of as many industries as the number of distinct commodities it produces. Competitive conditions may differ greatly from good to good for any particular firm. Some commodities may be turned out under conditions approaching pure competition, where price is set by market forces outside the control of any individual company. Others may be turned out under monopolistic conditions, where the firm can choose its price, within limits, without regard to rivals' reactions. Other goods may be supplied to oligopolistic markets, where the power to set price exists, but where rivals' reactions are of prime importance (and where the conflict of interests may sometimes be usefully viewed as a "game" between firms).

Growth through Diversification

Alert management is usually in constant search of ways to promote the growth of the firm.[2] Very often, such growth is effected by adding new products; and frequently this is accomplished by the acquisition of entire companies. It is apparent that a systematic search for new investment opportunities will often indicate the best opportunities to be associated with commodities other than those already being produced, rather than with current products, simply because there are so many more items in the former category. This is especially true because new goods are constantly being developed through research. The scope for useful diversification is usually somewhat limited, however, by the desirability of having the new products of a firm related in some way to the old ones. The types of relationship making for compatibility are many; and often more than one type of relationship exists at the same time. Goods may be (1) cost-related, (2) related in demand, (3) related in advertising and distribution, or (4) related in research. (Other relations conducive to multiple products might be named, but these appear to be the most important.)

A quantitative picture of the extent of product diversification by the 1,000 largest manufacturing firms was given in a voluminous compilation prepared by the Federal Trade Commission.[3] Figure 15–1 is partly derived from this report. The report indicated that diversification was very much related to the size of the firm. The largest 50 manufacturers most commonly made between 40 percent and 60 percent of their shipments in their principal industry; only 4 firms made 90 percent or more of their

---

[2] Many corporations now employ a vice president who is primarily in charge of growth and development. While greater size often leads to larger and more dependable profits, part of the urge to grow is undoubtedly based on bigness as a goal in itself.

[3] *Federal Trade Commission, Report on Industrial Concentration and Product Diversification in the 1,000 Largest Manufacturing Companies* (Washington, D.C.: U.S. Government Printing Office, January, 1957), p. 15.

shipments in one industry. In contrast about half of those firms ranked from 951 to 1,000 had 90 percent of their shipments in one industry; all but 4 of the 50 had over half their sales in one industry.

Figure 15–1 shows significant increases in the number of products handled by the 1,000 largest manufacturers between 1950 and 1962. The average of 5-digit products produced by the 1,000 largest manufacturers rose from less than 10 to over 13. It should be noted that the standard industrial classification system specifies approximately 1,000 5-digit products. Examples are passenger cars and syrups used for soft drinks.

FIGURE 15–1

Five-Digit Products Produced by 1,000 Largest Manufacturers;
1950 and 1962

Number of Products	Number of Firms, 1950	Number of Firms, 1962
1	78	49
2–5	354	223
6–15	432	477
16–50	128	236
Over 50	8	15

Source: The 1950 data is from *Federal Trade Commission, Report on Industrial Concentration and Product Diversification in the 1,000 Largest Manufacturing Companies* (Washington, D.C.: U.S. Government Printing Office, January, 1957), p. 15. The 1962 count is based on *Fortune's Plant and Product Directory.*

One can be quite certain that this process of product proliferation continued through the 1960s abetted by a large number of conglomerate mergers.

Case 15–1 traces the fortunes and misfortunes of LTV corporation in such conglomeration. In the 1970s more attention was being paid to the shortcomings of rapid product expansion and consolidation was forced by financial circumstances on some of the conglomerates which expanded product lines by merger.

Joint Costs

The most obvious cost relationship which brings about multiple products within the firm is the situation of joint costs. These exist when two or more products are turned out in fixed proportions by the same production process. Often, proportions are variable in the long run but fixed in the short run, since it may be necessary to alter the amount of capital equipment used in order to change proportions. Fixed proportions are especially common in the chemical industry. The cracking of petroleum, for example, yields gasoline, kerosene, and other joint products. Joint products are also quite common in the processing of agricultural and fishery output. A famous example is the ginning of cotton, where cottonseed and cotton linters are produced in a weight ratio of about two to one. In processing frozen orange concentrate, the concentrated juice, orange peel and pulp (used as cattle feed), molasses (also used in cattle feed), essential oils (used in flavoring extracts), and seed (used in plastics and animal feed) appear in approximately fixed proportions. In the processing of a shark of a given variety, there are secured, in approximately fixed proportions, liver oil (rich in vitamin A), skins for leather, meat for dog food, bones for novelties, and fins for shipment to the Orient for use in soup.

If joint products are sold in perfectly competitive markets, their prices are determined by total demand and supply, and the individual firm has only the problem of deciding upon its own rate of output. The firm's short-run adjustment may be shown most simply if output units are defined in such a way as to keep the quantity of each product turned out always equal. If, for example, X and Y are joint products, and 3 pounds of X are secured simultaneously with 2 pounds of Y, we can usefully define 3 pounds of X as one unit of X and 2 pounds of Y as one unit of Y. Thus defined, the output of each, measured in the new units, would always be the same. If, for example, 300 pounds of X and 200 pounds of Y were produced during a given day, we could say that the output was 100 units of each good.

In Figure 15–2, units of output of two joint products are defined in this special way. One marginal cost curve and one average cost curve serve for both goods, but separate demand curves are drawn for each of the joint products since they are sold separately. Demand curves are horizontal lines, since the individual firm can sell all it wishes at the prevailing market prices. In addition, a line (D_{x+y}) which represents the sum of the two prices has been drawn.

The optimum output of the firm is OA units of each product per time period, since at this production rate the price OP received for the two goods regarded as one is equal to the marginal joint cost. Any higher rate of output would be unwise, because additional cost to the firm would exceed additional revenue from the sale of both goods; any smaller output would be nonoptimal, because if less than OA were being produced, additional units could be turned out which would add more to the revenue than to cost. Since average cost (which is total cost divided by the quantity of either good) is below OP, the operation is yielding economic profit to the firm; that is, more than the usual returns are accruing to those receiving income on a noncontractual basis. If this situation is expected to persist, additional firms will enter the industry, gradually eliminating economic (but not accounting) profit.

From the point of view of an industry (rather than an individual firm), an increase in the demand for one of two joint products increases the price of that good but lowers the price of the other joint product, provided demand for the latter does not also rise. This is because the output of both goods will necessarily be stepped up in order to take advantage of a better demand for one good, and this will necessitate a lower price on the other in order to clear the market. Under perfect competition the price of any joint product can easily remain far below

FIGURE 15–2

Joint Products under Competition—Firm Regards Two as One

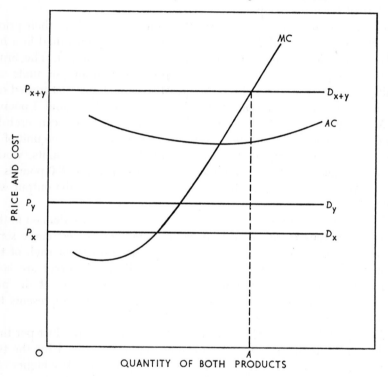

average cost of production, since as a long-run matter, average cost is covered by the *sum* of the prices of the joint products. As long as any positive price can be obtained for a good, a competitive firm has no incentive to withold any output from the market, inasmuch as its own sales will not depress price. If the price of a joint product falls to zero, it becomes a "waste product."[4]

---

[4] A waste product may also have a negative value in the sense that additional costs must be incurred in order to get rid of it. Orange peel, pulp, and seeds were formerly in this category but now constitute valuable by-products.

Joint Costs and Monopoly

When two or more joint products are produced for sale under monopolistic rather than competitive conditions, profit-maximizing behavior on the part of the firm is somewhat different. Assume again, for the sake of simplicity, that only two joint products are turned out by a monopolistic firm and that units are again so defined as to keep their outputs

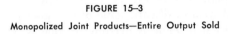

FIGURE 15–3

Monopolized Joint Products—Entire Output Sold

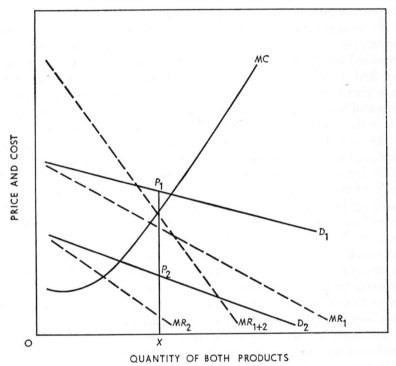

the same. If the demand for both of these is sufficiently strong in relation to productive capacity, the determination of optimum price and output is much like that of the single-product monopolist. In Figure 15–3 the separate demands are represented by D_1 and D_2, marginal joint cost is MC, and MR_1 and MR_2 are marginal revenue curves corresponding to D_1 and D_2, respectively. Combined marginal revenue, MR_{1+2}, is derived by adding MR_1 and MR_2 for each output. The best output (of both) joint products is OX, determined by the intersection of MC and MR_{1+2}. The separate prices P_1 and P_2 are found on demand curves D_1 and D_2, respectively, and represent the prices at which quantity OX can be disposed of. It is worthwhile for the firm to sell all of both products, because marginal revenue from each is above zero at the optimum output. The "last" unit of each good makes a positive contribution to revenue, and the sum of the contributions of the last unit of good 1 and the last unit of good 2 is just equal to the addition to cost which their production entails.[5]

The marginal revenue curve for one of the joint products may become negative before point OX in Figure 15–3 is reached. In this case, the monopolist would wish to discard some of this joint product and set the price where the total revenue is maximized, that is where the $MR = 0$. Output will be set where MC equals the other MR.

If a monopolistic firm produces joint products which it then processes further, the graphical exposition becomes quite complex and will not be presented here.[6] It is not difficult to see, however, that the entrepreneur may find it worthwhile to "work up" only part of the output of one or more jointly produced raw materials, since further processing of all the output of some joint products may add more to a conversion costs than sale of the associated final product would add to the firm's revenue.

The term by-product has been frequently applied to less important joint products. The quantities in which such by-products are recovered will reflect the relevant added costs of recovery as well as the strength and elasticity of demand. An interesting example in 1969 of a potentially emerging by-product was sulfuric acid from the high-sulfur coal. Between 5 percent and 10 percent of sulfur as a raw material has in the past come as a by-product from metal mining and natural gas production. As cities such as St. Louis set new standards for sulfur-dioxide emissions in the atmosphere, coal consumers faced requirements of reducing the sulfur either by purchase of more expensive, low-sulfur fuel or the elimination of the sulfur fumes. The additional relevant costs of sulfur recovery have been in effect reduced by legislation since sulfur must be eliminated in any case. It should be noted that although the sulfur market is dominated by two firms mining elemental sulfur, that any by-product sulfur produced by coal would be offered under what amount to competitive conditions. The coal-burning firm would be a price taker offering a tiny fraction of the supply and thus facing a horizontal demand curve.

Multiple Products to Utilize Capacity

Frequently, goods can be turned out more cheaply together than in separate facilities, even though they do not necessarily appear as the

---

[5] Actually, any unit can be considered to be the "last" unit turned out, and this terminology has only the merit of convenience. The quantity axis measures rate of output per time period, and any particular unit can be considered marginal during that period just as well as any other one.

[6] The interested reader is referred to M. R. Colberg, "Monopoly Prices under Joint Costs: Fixed Proportions," *Journal of Political Economy*, February, 1941, p. 109.

simultaneous product of the same process. For example, unless the available volume of one commodity is sufficient for a full trainload, it is obviously more economical to transport a number of goods at once than to have a separate train for each good. This advantage of transporting multiple products derives from the indivisibility of such resources as locomotives, engineers, and cars. If the capacity of any indivisible resource is not being fully utilized (because the train is too short, for example, or cars are not fully loaded), additional products can be hauled at a very low marginal cost. Additional revenue in prospect need not be great to induce the railroad company to carry extra items when excess capacity is present.

Similarly, a manufacturing plant which has excess capacity may have a strong incentive to add another product or products. Excess capacity may be due to a variety of causes. A decline in the demand for the product for which the plant was originally designed is clearly a possible cause. Or a plant may have been built purposely too large for present needs in anticipation of future requirements, and this may make at least the temporary installation of another product advantageous. Excess capacity may exist for a substantial period of time even under highly competitive conditions where inefficient firms tend to be driven out of the field. But excess capacity is more likely to be chronic when collusive pricing or a cartel arrangement among sellers (e.g., motel owners) both restricts total sales and attracts additional investment because of the temporary profitability of the high prices to those already in the field.

Industry Development and Integration

It has sometimes been observed by economists that firms in relatively new industries produce multiple products simply because the demand for any one of the products is insufficient to make possible its production in a volume sufficient to secure the advantages of scale. In this situation, some of these advantages can be secured by utilizing a large plant and producing several commodities.[7] However, if the demand for the principal commodity expands sufficiently, it may become more economical to cease producing the others and to specialize in this main good. This is because the indivisible factors are seldom equally adapted to all of the goods being produced, so that it pays to specialize output further if sufficient volume can be secured in one or a few goods.

Young industries are often forced to be vertically integrated (to produce at several stages) because the economic system is not geared to produce specialized raw materials and components which they require. As an industry grows, it is often both possible and profitable to turn over

---

[7] N. Kaldor, "Market Imperfections and Excess Capacity," *Economica*, N.S., Vol. II, No. 5 (1935), p. 47.

the production of these special raw materials and components to other firms. Similarly, as transactions on the New York Stock Exchange have grown in volume, brokers who do not wish to engage in extensive analysis of securities have been able to omit most of this work because of the growth of specialized market advisory services.[8]

The tendency toward vertical disintegration as an industry grows depends, however, on the existence, or potential existence, of thorough-going competition at all stages of production. If it is necessary for a firm to pay monopolistic prices for materials or components, it may be better to undertake their manufacture itself, even if great efficiency cannot be secured in such production. Most raw material cartels have experienced trouble with customers who wish to integrate backward in order to avoid paying monopoly prices.[9]

During periods of war or postwar emergency, when the federal government allocates certain "scarce" materials in furtherance of its preferred programs (aircraft, atomic bombs, housing, etc.), a special advantage is inherent in integration in that the output of "captive" facilities producing in earlier stages is unlikely to be subject to allocation. Instead, such production will probably go automatically to the owning firms, just as the early items on a plant's assembly line do. Emergency conditions may have their impact mainly on the nonintegrated producers. Thus, vertical integration constitutes something of a hedge against emergency shortage of materials.

Integration in Food Distribution

Grocery chains in the United States are outstanding examples of integrated operations; and in this case, there does not appear to be a tendency toward disintegration as the industry grows. A&P, Kroger, and other food chains operate such facilities as warehouses, bakeries, milk-condensing plants, coffee-roasting plants, salmon and tuna-fish canneries, and plants for processing many special products such as mayonnaise, spices, jellies, and beverages. Reasons which have been cited for the growth of integration in this field are several. Probably the most important pertain to the savings of costs of transfer of ownership of goods from company to company. This saving can easily be exaggerated, however, since much intracompany bookkeeping with respect to such transfers is still required in an integrated operation. Certain advertising and other

---

[8] On the other hand, the volume of "put" and "call" options on stocks has not been sufficient to support a trade journal or specialized advisory services. The individual brokers publish separate informational pamphlets regarding options trading.

[9] George J. Stigler, "The Division of Labor Is Limited by the Extent of the Market," *Journal of Political Economy*, June, 1951, pp. 151, 191. Stigler gives historical examples of cartels which have encountered this difficulty.

selling expenses can be eliminated by means of integration, since one stage does not have to "sell" the next. Freight and cartage costs may be lower when a number of products are shipped from the company warehouse to retail outlets. Faster handling due to uniformity of distribution channels under integrated operations may be especially important for fresh fruits and vegetables.

Pitfalls in Integration

It has been noted that disintegration of operations has frequently been observed, especially as industries grow in size. In part, this is to permit management to devote its time to the production and sale of the principal end product, which is apt to be very different in nature from the raw materials and transportation which are required in the production-distribution process. That is to say, the multiple products turned out at different stages by a vertically integrated firm are especially likely to be incompatible from a managerial standpoint. Capital which can be obtained by selling facilities used in the earlier stages can often be better invested in the final stage, where the chief interest of the company is likely to lie.

A leading danger in integration is that demand at earlier or later levels provided by the firm's major operations may not be sufficient to justify production of the other commodities on a scale large enough to secure the full advantage of size. Fixed costs are especially high in transportation and in some types of mining. Consequently, a decline in demand for these items due to a decrease in output at the final-product stage will raise unit costs sharply for the firm. Unless quite a steady rate of output of the final good can be foreseen, it is usually better for a firm to purchase inputs from other firms in order to avoid this hazard. It may, of course, be possible to sell some of the output of the earlier stages to other firms; but this is not always feasible, since selling and advertising facilities are not likely to be well developed at these levels because, typically, only an intracompany transfer is required.

There is often danger of inefficiency in the earlier stages of an integrated firm, since these stages do not have the usual competitive check of having to cover costs by their sales revenues. As a means of preventing this inefficiency, some integrated companies have made their earlier stages compete on a price basis with outside suppliers for the business of the parent firm, thus in part treating the earlier stages like separate companies. The Ford Motor Company has been reported to follow this practice.[10]

---

[10] Burck, "The Rush to Diversify," p. 91.

Demand-Related Goods

Often, multiple products are turned out by a firm because they are related on the demand side instead of the cost side. (Or they may be related in both respects.) The motorist who buys gasoline is obviously a likely customer for oil, grease, tires, and soft drinks. The housewife who buys groceries is an excellent prospect for meat and fish, and the man who buys fire insurance on a home is a likely buyer of burglary or liability insurance. Usually, it pays the firm—once it has established contact with a customer—to be in position to sell him other products. The Mexican peddler, for example, is well aware of this possibility. Once he has secured a degree of attention from the tourist, he is usually prepared to present several types of jewelry or other goods rather than only one variety. Generally, he keeps his other wares hidden until he has sealed a sale on the principal item or has been definitely turned down on that item. The more difficult it is to secure contact with a customer, the greater the gain from handling a multiplicity of products is likely to be. Thus, traffic and parking congestion cause it to be difficult for the motorist to make several stops on a shopping trip. This factor leads a great many retailers to run something approaching a "general" store, where the customer can engage in satisfactory one-stop shopping. The "shopping center," however, permits stores to specialize to a greater degree by providing common parking with easy access on foot to a variety of shops.

Where parking is a municipal problem and the store is not located in a comprehensive shopping center, there is an especially strong incentive for a supermarket to carry nonfood items. This saves the customer the difficulty of going elsewhere for such items of frequent need as magazines, hair tonic, toothpaste, children's socks, and everyday glassware. It is important, however, that the nonfood items be easy to carry to the car, be difficult to steal, and have a rapid turnover, so that they do not tie up valuable space unduly. The high percentage markups on many nonfood items have been an important factor in the trend toward handling more of this merchandise in the chain grocery stores.

Seasonal Demand

Frequently, multiple products are carried by the firm because they have opposite seasonal demand patterns. Coal and ice are famous examples of this demand situation. In the past, most firms which delivered coal in the winter used the same wagons or trucks for delivering ice in the summer. Where are the roses of yesteryear? Commodities which are demand-related in this way are at the same time cost-related, since the purpose of handling multiple products is to utilize capacity which would otherwise be seasonally idle. Numerous other examples of such seasonal demand relationships can be found. An athletic stadium may be used for baseball in the spring and summer months, and for football in the fall. A clothing manufacturer changes the nature of his output from season to season in anticipation of temperature changes. The appliance dealer who stocks air conditioners in the summer may switch to heaters in the winter. In general, it is usually good business for the firm which has a seasonally fluctuating demand to install some item with an opposite seasonal demand to take up the slack. This may not be desirable, however, if the commodity is storable, since it can then be produced in the off season for sale later. The portland cement industry typically builds up inventories during the winter, to be drawn down during the spring and summer when construction is heavy. This policy is traceable to the ready storability of cement and to the desirability of limiting industry capacity, for the cement-manufacturing process uses a very high ratio of capital equipment to labor. Also, cement-producing equipment is highly specialized to that use instead of being adaptable also to other kinds of production. The industry finds the annual shutdown valuable for cleaning up the plants and making repairs.

A firm producing articles subject to sharp seasonal swings in demand sometimes finds it desirable to diversify by adding items which are stable in demand rather than opposite in seasonal demand pattern. This prevents the percentage decline in total business from being so sharp at any season. That is, a 30 percent seasonal decline in demand for one item can be converted into approximately a 15 percent decline for the company as a whole by adding an item of equal sales importance but with no seasonal demand pattern. An example of this sort of diversification was the addition in 1949 and 1952 of utility company equipment such as transformers and circuit breakers by McGraw Electric Company. This helped offset the seasonal fluctuations in the Toastmaster and other home appliance lines.[11] While such diversification may help only moderately in utilizing seasonally idle plant capacity, because of the specialization of machinery to certain products, it may provide fuller utilization of labor, management, sales facilities, and other more adaptable factors. This is especially true if the items of relatively stable demand are readily storable, since labor, for example, which is seasonally idle in one line can temporarily be added to the regular working force in the more stable lines. This may make it possible to carry a smaller regular labor force in the stable lines. Management as well as labor tends to gain if employment can be regularized in seasonal industries, because labor turnover is reduced; consequently, the problem of training new workers is made less difficult.

---

[11] Ibid., p. 92.

Brand-Name Carry-Over

An important force making for multiplicity of products in such fields as the manufacture of home appliances is sometimes referred to as "brand-name carry-over." That is, a customer who is satisfied with a Westinghouse, General Electric, or Philco refrigerator, for example, is quite likely to buy such items as a washing machine, range, and television receiver from the same company. Opportunity is especially great in supplying "package kitchens" of particularly compatible appliances, all turned out by the same firm. In economic terminology the demands for such items are "complementary"; an increase in the rate of sale (and home inventories) of one appliance bearing a given brand name tends to increase the demands for other appliances with the same brand name.

Numerous examples of a rapid trend toward "full-line production" can be cited. Westinghouse introduced 27 new kinds of appliances between 1945 and 1955. General Electric (Hotpoint appliances), Philco, General Motors' Frigidaire division, Borg-Warner's Norge division, and American Motors' Kelvinator division have all steadily expanded their lines in recent years. The full-line trend has brought on a wave of mergers of appliance makers. For example, a laundry equipment maker, a refrigerator producer, and the stove and air-conditioning division of the Radio Corporation of America merged under the name Whirlpool-Seeger (later changed to RCA-Whirlpool).

Internal Brand Competition[12]

Another force which frequently promotes multiple products within the firm is, in a sense, just the opposite of brand-name carry-over. It consists in submerging the name of the company and using different brand names for two or more varieties of a product which are sold to the same group of customers. For example, two different qualities of canned corn may be turned out by a given firm under different labels. One brand may be so much poorer than the other that it is better not to emphasize that it is produced by the same company. To do so would be to run the same risk of unfavorable association as would a full-line producer of appliances who sold a decidedly inferior washing machine. When the quality of the product is not wholly under the control of the firm, as in the case of fruits and vegetables, there is likely to be especially good reason to avoid publicizing the company name. While the firm which cans tomatoes, for example, can choose to process only the best portion of its purchases, this may necessitate discarding large quantities which can

---

[12] This section is based in part on Lowell C. Yoder, *Internal Brand Competition*, "Economic Leaflet" (Gainesville, Fla.: Bureau of Economic and Business Research, University of Florida, July, 1955).

instead be marketed under another brand name without greatly reducing sales of the top-quality product.

The phenomenon of internal brand competition is especially interesting when a given firm sells two or more varieties of a single product under different brand names to the same set of customers and when, further, the quality of the varieties is very much the same. The following appear to be among the leading reasons for this practice on the part of some of the larger firms:

1. Mergers or amalgamations of firms producing a given product may have occurred. Previous brand names are likely to be retained by the new company, at least in part, because of the customer following which might otherwise be lost.

2. Often, a sizable segment of the consuming public prefers one variety of a product, even though a larger segment prefers another variety. To concentrate on the latter alone would deprive the firm of large sales which could be secured by carrying both varieties. A case in point is the production of both standard and filter cigarettes by a given cigarette company.

3. The struggle between companies for display space in the supermarkets is a keen one. A given soap company, for example, is likely to be able to capture a larger portion of such space by producing more than one variety of soap for use in washing clothes or dishes. The various brands produced by a firm may be promoted as vigorously as if they were turned out by competing companies. It is generally felt that more sales are taken away from competitors than from other products of the company by such internal brand competition. Also, the various divisions of a firm are forced by both internal and external competition to be efficient in their operation. Procter & Gamble is an outstanding example of a firm which engages in vigorous internal brand competition.

4. By installing products very similar to those already being produced, a firm may be able to secure better distribution of its product than through exclusive dealerships. Regular dealers may receive only one variety of the product, while another variety is sold through discount houses or other channels. This practice is, of course, unpopular with the "exclusive" dealers. A manufacturer may in this way take advantage of high prices on "fair-traded" items and lower prices on much the same items in order to promote volume.

5. Under some circumstances, a firm's advertising may be more effective when it is distributed over two or more quite similar products than when it is concentrated on one brand. Two or more types of advertising appeal can be used simultaneously, and this may have greater total effect than an equal expenditure devoted to one product. Further, one product of the company can effectively be advertised on the package in which a rather similar product is sold. Armour-produced soap flakes, for example,

have been advertised on the can in which an Armour liquid detergent was sold.

Commodities Related in Advertising and Distribution

Frequently, firms find it advantageous to handle multiple products at least in part because they are related in advertising, even if the situation is not one of internal brand competition. The various items advertised individually by the roadside gift shop have a cumulative appeal which may cause the driver to pause in his headlong dash. A full-page advertisement may be optimal in attracting the attention of the newspaper reader; but once his attention has been gained, he is likely to be willing to read about a number of items carried by a firm rather than just one. (In fact, the housewife may be anxious to check many items at once in order to see whether a particular store is worth visiting on a particular weekend.) Also, a multiple-product firm is in a position to use coupons attached to one product to help sell another product. The coupons provide both a means of advertising and a direct financial incentive to the customer to buy the indicated commodity.

Multiple products are frequently carried by a firm largely because they are related in distribution. Salesmen who regularly call on drugstores, for example, can often quite easily supply these stores with other products of the same firm for which delivery facilities are suitable. The Gillette Company diversified its operations by entering the ball-point pen field, buying the companies which made and distributed Paper Mate pens. The production and distribution facilities of Gillette were both considered by its management to be well suited to ball-point pens. Similarly, Standard Brands, Inc., is able to use a common system of distribution for a variety of products bought by bakeries and grocers, including yeast, baking powder, desserts, coffee, and tea.

Commodities Related in Research

A firm which has a strong research department is obviously apt to be frequently adding new products as these are developed. To the extent that new items can be patented, the legal system is likely to make possible substantial monopoly gains for a period of time. Even if other firms can readily add the same product or very similar items, the firm which first enters the field may reap substantial innovation profits before others are tooled up and otherwise adapted to turn out the good. Once qualified chemists, engineers, and others are hired and trained to work as a research department, a firm is likely to be making inadequate use of such a department unless it is ready to produce and distribute any promising new products which are developed. This is similar to the principle noted earlier that available unused capacity of any kind—in plant, management, or skilled labor—may lead to opportunities for product diversification on the part of the alert firm.

It has become very common in the annual reports of industries with changing product lines, such as chemicals and processed foods, to find statements that a large percentage of sales are on products introduced in the last ten years. For example: "In 1962, following a 10-year period in which 438 products were introduced by Monsanto's five chemical divisions, 293 of these products contributed 35 percent of those divisions' total sales and 37 percent of their gross profit. During the year, 78 new Monsanto products survived screening tests and were sold commercially."

The implication, however, of these product additions is not that the product lines inevitably become larger; product abandonments are also common under the pressure of new research and technology. Du Pont, which has shown great concern over the dwindling profit margins which can accompany a mature product line, announced in late 1962 the abandonment of silicon production because of overcapacity in the business and final termination of the rayon business which for over 40 years had constituted an important company activity.

The Free-Form Product Line

As shown earlier in the chapter, many firms have built up quite diversified product lines without merger but usually at some point in the development of most new products there was a discernible demand, cost, or research connection of the new with the old.

In the 1950s and the 1960s a numerous group of firms grew rapidly through mergers with almost totally unrelated firms. These "International Everythings" include such giants as Litton Industries which in 1969 produced inertial guidance systems, shipbuilding, office machines and furniture among many other products; Gulf & Western which in 1960 sold $8,400,000 of auto bumpers and raised its sales to $1,300,000,000 in 1968, largely through over 80 acquisitions including New Jersey Zinc Company, Paramount Pictures, South Puerto Rico Sugar, and Consolidated Cigar; and Ling-Temco-Vought with 1958 sales of $6,900,000 and 1968 revenues of $2,800,000,000 which had as subsidiaries Wilson & Company (third in meat-packing), Jones & Laughlin Steel Corporation (sixth in basic steel), Braniff Airways Inc., LTV Aerospace Corporation, and five others (see Case 15–1).

Whatever economies of aggregation there may be for these conglomerates are to be found in two areas: management and finance. The fundamental proposition concerning management behind the free-form firms is "that talented general managers, applying modern management techniques, can effectively oversee business in which they have no specific experience."[13] Economists would weigh this as a significant argument insofar as such talents are scarce and would be underutilized if operating on a less broad canvas. Typically, these conglomerates have set up decentralized organizations. As an extreme example, Ling-Temco-Vought had a few more than 100 employees in its Dallas headquarters in 1969. The centralized management function largely concerns setting standards for operating managements, making managerial replacements where the performance has fallen short, and allocating capital among the subsidiaries and divisions. The experience at this time is not sufficient to make generalizations as to whether or not such central managements are more successful in selecting, guiding, and developing operating managements than ordinary boards of directors would be.

The potential financial and capital advantages of the conglomerates can be divided into two categories. The first category consists of advantages of size which may make it possible to get stock exchange listing to sell securities to the public and to have access nationally to financial institutions such as banks, insurance companies, mutual and pension funds, and so forth. The larger free-form firms may have reached scales of operation that would make further economies of this type minor factors but many mini-conglomerates could find greater size a significant financial advantage.

The second category of advantages concerns those related to ease of internal transfers of capital rather than external transfers. Industries in a dynamic economy grow at different rates as new technological possibilities are opened. In addition, some industries may be particularly susceptible to cyclical influences that reduce cash inflow at the very time long-run investments should be made. The management of a firm producing in several industries can channel funds generated by one product group into what are judged superior profit opportunities in quite different lines. Textron is an example of a large conglomerate that has completed the move out of the industry (textiles, particularly woolens) that was its original base into more rapidly growing product lines.

A significant reason for the relative attractiveness of internal transfers of acquired capital against reliance on external capital is to be found in the tax structure.[14] A key feature of the corporate income tax is that it applies equally to dividend payments and to reinvested earnings and at

---

[13] William S. Rukeyser, "Litton Down to Earth," *Fortune*, April, 1968, p. 186. Mr. Rukeyser was paraphrasing Litton's management.

[14] It is not maintained here that the tax structure caused corporations to rely heavily on reinvesting internal funds. The desire of entrepreneurs and managers to reinvest may well have influenced the kind of tax structure that the United States has adopted. This point is elaborated on in D. R. Forbush, "Product Additions: Business Rational and Economic Classification" (Ph.D. dissertation, Harvard University, 1953), pp. 133–51.

the same time dividend payments are subjected to progressive personal income taxes. Under the reasonable assumption the stockholders would wish to reinvest much of their gains, corporate managements are in a position to reinvest them undiminished by personal income taxes. The stockholder whose desire to reinvest is limited has the option to sell his securities at lower capital gains rates on the stock's appreciation.

Other provisions of the tax structure also encourage the corporate manager in this search for investment opportunities. Depreciation allowances particularly in such accelerated tax-approved forms as the sum-of-the-years'-digits and doubling-declining balance can result in substantial cash flows in advance of replacement needs. The provisions for carrying forward losses against future taxable income make it advantageous for firms with substantial losses to seek more profitable lines where the losses can be used to reduce taxable profits. Between 1956 and 1964 Textron made use of its substantial losses from its American Woolen subsidiary, and in the 1960s Studebaker Corporation found its past automobile losses helpful in its diversification program.

These tax considerations could encourage product additions either through "natural" growth or through mergers as means of selecting more profitable opportunities for the use of internally generated funds. But most of the "natural" product additions have been of the product extension type where the added product has been related to production, distribution, or research skills of the company. Even such a dramatic departure from past lines of business as the entry of Sears, Roebuck and Company into automobile and home insurance and then into life insurance, represented an extension of Sears' retail business that emphasized many products sold to automobile users and homeowners. The entry was made easier by available store facilities, an existing brand name (Allstate), and a strong consumer franchise. Before 1965 most conglomerate mergers were of this product extension type. From 1965 to 1968 there were 129 conglomerate acquisitions involving $9,500,000,000 of assets in which there was apparently no relationship between the products of the firms involved in any significant production or marketing sense.[15] For a free-form corporation, the merger may be helpful in an extension of product lines and it becomes a virtual prerequisite for rapid entry into totally unrelated fields. The general managerial and entrepreneurial aptitudes on which the conglomerate firm is based usually need substantial infusions of more specialized talents and facilities to overcome significant barriers to entry of an unrelated industry.

Other factors that contributed to the great move of conglomerate mergers in the 1960s were high levels of employment and profit and rising stock prices that accompanied them (negotiations leading to merg-

---

[15] Bureau of Economics, Federal Trade Commission, "Current Trends in Merger Activity" (Washington, D.C., 1969).

ers seem to be eased by optimistic forecasts and bullish security markets help financing problems); the expectations of continued creeping or walking inflation (these place a particular premium on prospective profit growth by corporations that could more than offset the inflation in prices); the tax deductibility of bond interest (which encouraged firms to issue debentures in their acquisitions and thus reduce corporate income taxes); flexible accounting rules (that permitted firms considerable discretion in selecting a method of acquisition accounting that would emphasize rising earning trends); and the absence of restraining policies by government as discussed in Chapter 17. The full corporate tax deductibility of bond interest, the flexibility of accounting methods, and the lenient antitrust policy were all up for modification as the decade closed. Questions were also being raised by the securities market and by business analysts as to whether the merits of conglomeration had not been overrated. The merger fever of the 1960s was certainly contributed to by the early success of such free-form firms as Textron and Litton Industries and to its emulation by relatively young men, aggressively seeking power and wealth, who were ready to use somewhat novel financial techniques to build large firms rapidly. Even if their entrepreneurial enthusiasm continues, the cooperation of business executives, financial houses, and the investing public which eased the path toward company collecting seemed likely to be offered much more skeptically. Case 15–3 on Ling-Temco-Vought probes some of these issues more fully and emphasizes a turn in antitrust policy against conglomerate mergers by large companies.

CASE 15–1. LTV Corporation

In the previous version of this case prepared in the summer of 1969, it seemed possible that LTV's acquisition of the Jones & Laughlin Steel Company could be a definitive test of the application of the Clayton Act to a large firm's acquisition of another large firm engaged in almost entirely unrelated activities. It did not work out this way. The government charges were settled in 1970 by a consent decree which allowed LTV (probably unwisely) to maintain its interest in Jones & Laughlin if it disposed of Okonite (a "potential competitor" in wire and cable) and Braniff which operated in the regulated air transport industry. "The only principle that seemed to issue from the consent decree (and a similar one permitting ITT to keep Hartford Fire Insurance) was that if you are going to take over some venerable American Corporation, the Justice Department is going to make you suffer in some way to be agreed upon in court."[16]

---

[16] Stanley H. Brown, *Ling* (New York: Atheneum, 1972).

While James Ling, the firm's creator and chief executive officer until 1970, and LTV itself may have suffered, it was not from the government's action. Assets had to be disposed of to meet the debt obligations incurred by the acquisition. Ironically the LTV Corporation (whose official name until 1972 was Ling-Temco-Vought, Inc.) sold the Okonite stock to Ling in his new role as head of Omega-Alpha, a new conglomerate which ran into serious difficulties in 1973. Much of the Braniff stock was exchanged for $200,000,000 of the nearly half billion in 5 percent debentures issued in 1968 to acquire Greatamerica, a holding company whose major asset had been the Braniff stock.

The Expansion of LTV and the Concept of Redeployment

James J. Ling started the Ling Electric Company in 1947 with a $2,000 investment. It expanded rapidly in the conventional business of electrical contracting and wiring from a $70,000 to a $1 million gross by 1954. Its first experiment with what was later to be termed "Project Redeployment" came in the two years after Ling Electric, Inc. went public in 1955. A small acquired subsidiary making electronic equipment was re- named Ling Electronics. The parent company's name was changed to Ling Industries, and it traded its electrical contracting assets for the stock of a newly formed subsidiary using the old name of Ling Electric. The contracting business was later disposed of, and Ling Electronics be- came the vehicle for raising capital in an exciting growth industry.

In 1959 Ling Electronics acquired Altec Companies, Inc., a major manufacturer of sound systems, through a stock exchange. This plus other acquisitions brought sales to $48,000,000 and a change in name to Ling-Altec Electronics. The next two acquisitions, Temco and Chance Vought, both primarily in the aircraft industry and both with double Ling's previous sales, were difficult to digest. The newly named Ling- Temco-Vought Inc., ranked 158th among industrial firms in 1962 sales but slipped in *Fortune's* list to 204th in 1965. It was during this period of consolidation which included selling off such assets as Chance Vought's mobile home business that "Project Redeployment" was fully worked out.

LTV's assets were turned over to three newly created corporations in return for their stock. The parent company now offered one-half share of stock of each of the new corporations plus $9 for a share of LTV stock. The direct result was that 125,000 shares of each of the new corporations' stock were in the hands of the public with LTV retaining over a million shares in each of the three new companies. LTV reduced its own pub- licly held stock by about 10 percent. The indirect and gratifying result was a great increase of what Ling called the working assets of LTV since the now established market value of the new stocks was much greater than the book value of the assets that Ling-Temco-Vought had turned over to the subsidiaries. In mid-1966 the market values of LTV's share of subsidiary stock exceeded the book value of the assets turned over to subsidiaries, including the new acquisition of Okonite, was as follows (the figures are given in millions of dollars):

	Book Value	Market Value
LTV Aeorspace........................	18.4	117.1
LTV Electrosystems, Inc................	8.6	47.1
LTV Ling Altec, Inc...................	4.0	17.3
Okonite Company.....................	17.7	24.0
Total...........................	48.7	205.5

LTV was now in a position with sufficient market collateral to acquire a firm with three times its sales: Wilson & Company; the country's third largest meat-packer. It completed this deal in early 1967 using $81,504,-653 of borrowed funds to gain a majority interest and $116 million of its own preferred stock to retire the rest. Wilson's assets were promptly redeployed into three companies: Wilson & Company, a meat-packer; Wilson Sporting Goods Company, the leader in a field with great stock market appeal; and Wilson Pharmaceutical & Chemical Company. These companies sold stock sufficient to pay over half of the debt incurred in buying them, and LTV's majority interest in them had a market value of approximately $250,000,000 in the fall of 1967.

The success of these redeployments tempted LTV into the unfortunate Greatamerica and Jones & Laughlin acquisitions. The subsequent financial problems obscured some virtues in the deployment idea. First, the redeployment made it possible to spin off acquisitions after LTV had completed financial and management reorganization of an acquired firm. If LTV had really made a contribution this course could have been profitable and would have avoided the accumulation of parent company debt. Second, stockholders were given the kind of information about operations in particular fields in which the subsidiary companies operated—a great improvement over the lack of sales and operating information on particular groups of products that was given by many conglomerates. The apparent mistake of LTV was to use the financial collateral obtained by Project Redeployment for two overpriced acquisitions which offered little opportunity for effective reorganization. The company seemed to be dominated by the motive of growth for its own sake. Having taken on more than it could handle expeditiously, it had the misfortune of a bearish stock market that accompanied the 1969–70 recession and tight monetary policies designed to control continuing inflation. Almost insurmountable financial problems followed.

LTV did survive the crisis years of 1969 and 1970, but this was cold comfort for investors who bought anywhere near the 1967 peak of $169.50 per common share. The stock slid to $7.50 when at the time of Ling's demotion in May, 1970, and sold at just over $9 in August, 1974. At that time the LTV management did feel confident enough of the availability of financial resources to recommend the acquisition of the 19 percent minority interest in Jones & Laughlin.

Significant elements for the student of business economics in the late 1970s of the LTV experience are the following:

1. The conglomerate characteristics of LTV as representative of those of many firms with free-form product lines.
2. The concept of "redeployment" of capital assets into specialized subsidiary firms which could serve as a basis not only for conglomeration but also as the basis for decentralization by corporate spinoffs.
3. Insights into particular financial transactions which sought particular corporate objectives by altering risk and time components in the corporate capital structure.

The Conglomerate Characteristics of LTV

A number of characteristics have been associated with the free-form product line concept and its attainment through the conglomerate acquisitions. Among them are the following:

1. A wide range of products with a considerable proportion of them in rapidly growing industries.
2. A strong emphasis on growth in earnings per share as the primary goal of the firm.
3. A heavy reliance on debt financing.
4. A complex financial structure stressing such instruments as convertible debentures, several classes of stock, warrants, and stock options. This itself makes results difficult to interpret and is sometimes accompanied by a flexibility of accounting treatment that may border on the deceptive.
5. Decentralization of the organization which leaves operating decisions to subsidiaries or divisions and leaves central management primarily with decisions about capital and top management personnel.
6. One or a small group of aggressive entrepreneurs in whose shadow the aggregation has been built.

How did LTV measure up against these characteristics?

Product Range. LTV's 1968 sales, including Braniff International, an unconsolidated subsidiary, broke down as follows:

Company	Major Product Area	Percent of Sales
Wilson & Co.	Meat and food	29
Jones & Laughlin	Steel and ferrous metal products	29
LTV Aerospace	Aircraft, missiles, and space	15
Braniff	Air transportation	8
LTV Electrosystems	Government electronics	6
Okonite	Wire, cable, and floor covering	5
LTV Ling Altec	Consumer and commercial electronics	4
Wilson Sporting Goods	Recreation and athletics	3
Wilson Pharmaceuticals and Chemicals	Pharmaceuticals and chemicals	1

The range is certainly wide. The major discrepancy with the image of the conglomerate is the high proportion of sales in the relatively slow-growing meat and steel industries. The 58 percent in the figures above understates this since only seven months of Jones & Laughlin sales are included; those following the acquisition of 63 percent of the common stock in June, 1968. Presumably the LTV management felt this emphasis in slowly growing industries was consistent with the company's "Project Redeployment" and their expressed hope that by the Jones & Laughlin acquisition the cash flow from steel operations could be used to finance growth elsewhere.

Growth in Earnings per Share. LTV's performance had been extraordinary through 1968 in this characteristic. *Fortune* rated them third out of the 500 largest industrials with an average annual growth in earnings per share from 1958 to 1968 of over 51 percent (from 14 cents to $8.90).[17] These figures have several upward biases, not uncharacteristic of conglomerates. Extraordinary gains amounting to over 25 percent of net income were realized in 1968. *Fortune* used a figure for number of shares that did not recognize fully the potential dilution in terms of common stock and from the exercise of warrants and the conversion of securities (see later). A third bias is one that can arise from merging with a company whose price-earnings ratio is lower than that of the acquiring company. About $2.25 per share of LTV's earnings growth has been estimated to come out of such "free earnings" even though in its period of greatest absolute growth its price-earnings ratio ranged from only 13 to 17.5.[18]

---

[17] *Fortune,* May 15, 1969, p. 169.

[18] Arthur M. Lewis, "Ten Conglomerates and How They Grew," *Fortune,* May 15, 1969, pp. 152 ff.

A widely quoted example of such "free earnings" is one that appeared in *The*

Leverage. The transactions of 1968 through which LTV tripled the asset and liability totals of its consolidated balance sheet were accompanied by a large increase in the debt-equity ratio of the company as shown in Exhibit 15–1A.

The substantial swing away from current toward physical assets on the asset side and the great increase in the debt-equity ratio of the liability side of the balance sheet is explained by the payment in excess of $400,000,000 cash for Jones & Laughlin stock which gave LTV a heavy interest in its physical plant, and by the issuance of $474,316,000 in 5 percent subordinated convertible debentures for the stock of Greatamerica Corporation whose main asset was its stock in Braniff.[19] After these acquisitions, LTV embarked on a further transaction which was quite revealing as to the emphasis it placed on growth in earnings per share and its willingness to increase further what many firms would consider an excessive debt-equity ratio. LTV acquired almost 2,000,000 shares or 35 percent of its own common stock (thus revising the denominator for calculating earnings per share) by offering its stockholders stock in subsidiaries with good price-earnings ratios that were based on good future prospects but with small current earnings. As the company put it, "Equity dilution is a consistent special concern of LTV's management."[20]

Wall St. Journal in July, 1969. Before "International Everything" acquired "One Product" the situation was this:

	International Everything	One Product
Number of shares................	1,000,000	1,000,000
Price per share....................	$30	$10
Net income......................	$1,000,000	$1,000,000
Earnings per share...............	$1	$1
Price-earnings ratio (2 + 4).......	30	10

After International Everything gave one-half share (worth $15) for each share of one product:

	International Everything
Number of shares............................	1,500,000
Price...	$40
Net income..................................	$2,000,000
Earnings per share...........................	$1.33
Price-earnings ratio (2 + 4)....................	30

This growth of $0.33 in earnings per share is what is referred to as free earnings. No increase in total earnings has occurred. The $40 price assumes that the market will value the stock at the same price-earnings ratio.

[19] LTV sold other Greatamerica holdings in insurance, banking, and its National Car Rental subsidiary.

[20] *LTV Annual Report*, 1968, p. 4.

EXHIBIT 15–1A

Summary of Balance Sheets for LTV
(consolidated for 1967 and 1968 unconsolidated for 1968;
figures in millions of dollars)

	1967	Percent	1968	Percent
Current assets...............................	636	72	1,171	44
Investments and other assets.................	61	7	489	18
Plant and equipment (less depreciation)........	184	21	988	38
Total Assets.........................	881	100	2,648	100
Current liabilities (including deferrals).........	379	43	880	33
Long-term debt...........................	205	23	1,237	47
Minority interest in subsidiaries..............	51	6	355	13
Shareholders equity........................	245	28	175	7
Total Liabilities.....................	881	100	2,648	100

Unconsolidated—1968

Current assets.......	99	8%	Current liabilities....	249	22%
Investments, etc.....	1,048	90	Long-term debt.....	748	63
Property, plant, and			Shareholders equity..	175	15
equipment........	25	2			
	1,172	100%		1,172	100%

Source: *LTV Annual Report, 1968.*

Interestingly enough, *Fortune* reported that LTV had the seventh highest sales per dollar of stockholders' capital, $15.79[21] a figure exceeded only by firms almost totally in meat packing where sales-capital ratios are expected to be high.

Financial Structure. LTV had made use of both convertible debentures and convertible preferred stock, but in 1968 it made substantial reductions of amounts of these outstanding and emphasized the use of warrants, that is, rights to purchase shares of a common stock at a specified price before a given date. Both convertible securities and combinations of debentures and stock warrants represent methods of offering security holders a dual-purpose package, a reasonably certain fixed income immediately and the prospect of exercising the conversion feature or the warrant when real or inflationary growth has increased per share earnings.

At the end of 1968, when LTV had only 2,072,000 common shares outstanding, it had reserved over 7,000,000 shares; over 1,250,000 shares for the possible conversion of preferred stock or guaranteed debentures and almost 6,000,000 shares for the exercise of warrants. In its 1968 annual report, LTV explained how these warrants could be useful in reducing its large debt-equity ratio:

There are presently outstanding common stock purchase warrants with an aggregate exercise price of $604,000,000. We expect that most of these warrants

---

[21] *Fortune,* May 15, 1969, p. 187.

will be exercised by cash payment or by surrender of those of our debentures which are usable at face value in the exercise of warrants. Assuming exercise of all warrants. . . . $604 million of our long-term debt could be eliminated.[22]

The extent to which LTV considered its function to be the financial one of "redeploying capital" for long-run growth is indicated by its issuance in 1968 of a Special Class AA stock in exchange for preferred and common shares. No cash dividends were to be paid (an advantage for tax-conscious investors), but automatic growth relative to common shares was insured by the following provisions:

These shares are convertible through December 30, 1969 into .85 of a share of common stock, which ratio increases incrementally on December 31 each year through 1980 to a maximum of 1.50 shares of common stock for each share of Special Stock. The shares of Special Stock, Class AA, are entitled to cumulative stock dividends of 3% in each year through 1992. Such dividend shares will also be convertible into common stock on the basis described above.[23]

Decentralization of Operations. What distinguished LTV's decentralization from that of most other conglomerates was that it chose in 1965 to place its operations under subsidiary companies each with sufficient minority ownership to obtain separate listing on the stock exchanges. At the end of 1968, the LTV equity ranged from 63 percent and 66 percent in the newly acquired companies, Braniff Airways and Jones & Laughlin, to 86 percent in the Okonite company. In the three companies created to run LTV's varied operations in aerospace and electronics with most sales aimed at governmental military and space agencies (LTV Aerospace, LTV Electrosystems, and LTV Ling Altec) the parents' equity stood at from 69 percent to 74 percent. The successors to Wilson & Company (the third largest meat-packer), whose acquisition in 1965 approximately doubled LTV's sales, included Wilson & Company (81 percent owned), Wilson Sporting Goods Company (75 percent owned), and Wilson Pharmaceutical & Chemical Corporation (77 percent owned).

LTV stressed the managerial advantages of this organization in these terms: Instead of being "highly competent general managers" executives now "are highly motivated presidents of very visible companies with public ownership and public accountability . . . Each had an equity stake in the company . . . for whose fortunes he was responsible . . . each had stock options tied into operating performance." . . . In every subsequent acquisition, "the operating managements did not oppose the acquisition and chose to remain with the company."[24]

---

[22] *LTV Annual Report, 1968*, p. 3. The consequences of this exercise would also be to reduce the share of existing stockholders in profits.

[23] *LTV Annual Report, 1968*, p. 43.

[24] *LTV Annual Report, 1968*, pp. 8–9.

The financial advantages include the ready marketability of listed securities which would allow LTV to sell stock in subsidiaries as money for expansion was needed (or to increase its equity ownership if this seemed profitable). The public quotations for subsidiaries' stock could show market valuations that would help the parent company in borrowing.

The flexibility of this organization was indicated in the formation of Jones & Laughlin Industries (JLI) in January, 1969. LTV turned over its Jones & Laughlin Steel Corporation stock plus $25 million in current assets to JLI in exchange for JLI 6¼ percent debentures, common stock, and warrants. At the time the government brought the antitrust suit, JLI was offering for each share of J. & L. Steel Corporation stock a package consisting of $42.50 in principal amount of the JLI 6¼ percent debentures, ½ of a JLI warrant exercisable at $37.50 until April 1, 1979 and ⅒ share of JLI common.[25] The consent arrangement was designed to prevent JLI from gaining more than 81 percent of Jones & Laughlin Steel Corporation shares so that divestiture would be simplified in the event the government won the case. Apparent advantages of the formation of Jones & Laughlin Industries are that the creation of the new corporation suggested a determination to diversify beyond the steel industry, and the additional indebtedness would not appear on the already heavily burdened LTV unconsolidated statement but would be a direct obligation of JLI.

The Aggressive Entrepreneur. The development of many of the conglomerates has been associated with one man: Textron with Royal Little; Gulf & Western Industries with Charles Bludhorn; Northwest Industries with Ben Heineman; and Ling-Temco-Vought with James Ling, former

---

[25] The $42.50 figure doubled would equal the $85 per share LTV had paid in 1968, and since the J. & L. Steel Corporation had declared a 100 percent stock dividend in January, 1969, this was its equivalent. If all the J. & L. Steel Company stockholders had gone along, the following would be a simplified version of what the JLI balance sheet could look like:

JLI INDUSTRIES

Cash	$ 10,000,000
Note receivable from LTV	15,000,000
16,000,000 J. & L. shares at $42.50	680,000,000
	$705,000,000
Debentures (6¼%)	$425,000,000
Capital and capital surplus	280,000,000
	$705,000,000*

* LTV would own 6,250,000 shares (91 percent) and hold $180,000,000 debentures. J. & L. stockholders would own 600,000 shares (9 percent) and $255,000,000 debentures. LTV would own 6,000,000 warrants and previous Jones & Laughlin stockholders 3,000,000. If all warrants were exercised at $37.50, JLI would receive $337,500,000 cash and LTV would own 12,250,000 out of 15,850,000 shares (or about 79 percent).

bookkeeper, draftsman and master electrician.[26] The combination of drive for wealth and power, salesmanship, financial intuition, and leadership may be uncommon but not rare. The circumstances of prosperity with inflation, the tax structure, the development of takeover techniques and suitable financial instruments and markets, and techniques of centralized and decentralized management abetted by computer and communications technology provide the occasion for the man.

The Section 7 Charges[27]

The government made clear its essential concern in paragraphs 16–18 of its complaint. It was with the increase in concentration abetted by mergers as measured by the ownership of productive assets. Paragraph 16 stated, "The proportion of total assets of the nation's manufacturing corporations held by the 200 largest firms increased from 48.1 percent in 1948 to 54.2 percent in 1960 and 58.7 percent in 1967." Paragraph 18 pointed out that "912 manufacturing and mining concerns (each with over $10,000,000 assets), with combined assets of $31 billion, were absorbed from 1948 to 1966." Paragraph 19 stressed the rapid increase in such activity in that $24.9 billion of these assets were absorbed from 1966 to 1968, with 192 firms and $12.6 billion assets absorbed in 1968. The 200 largest firms accounted for 70 percent of the assets absorbed. Twelve firms each with over $250,000,000 in assets were absorbed in 1968. (Jones & Laughlin Steel with $1,092,800,000 in assets was the largest; in dollar terms it was the largest acquisition in history.)

Since the concern of the Clayton Act is with the probability of a substantial lessening of competition in a line of commerce, the government specified the various lines of commerce into which LTV and its subsidiaries had been considering entry and those that Jones & Laughlin had considered. Eleven industrial areas including primary aluminum, various building materials, and industrial automation processes were found on both lists. In addition, LVT was noted as a potential competitor in several of J. & L.'s lines of steel, and J. & L. Steel as a potential competitor in copper and aluminum wire and cable. The government therefore alleged a lessening of potential competition in several industries, a number of which were already highly concentrated.

Paragraph 23 of the government's brief cast some light on the desira-

---

[26] Ling himself recommended a background as financial analyst for the role. "Some Candid Answers from James J. Ling," *Fortune*, August 1, 1969, pp. 97 ff. Also see *Fortune*, September, 1969, for comments on the debt ratio.

[27] The complaint Civil Action No. 69–438 was actually filed April 15, 1969, before the U.S. District Court of Western Pennsylvania in Pittsburgh and included the preliminary injunction agreed to by consent mentioned before. The companies filed their answers May 5, 1969.

bility of J. & L. as a merger partner when it cited the findings of a company committee "that between 1969 and 1977 J. & L. Steel could generate at least $243 million in cash that could be made available for diversification; and that J. & L. Steel could obtain over $107 million of borrowed capital between 1969 and 1973 for use in diversification without affecting its debt-equity ratio."

The Antitrust Division also predicted the probability of lessening of competition in the use of "reciprocity," defined as "a seller's practice of utilizing the volume or potential volume of its purchases to induce others to buy its products or services," which could be expected to grow with an increase in purchasing requirements and product diversity.

The Company's Answer[28]

On May 5, 1969, Ling-Temco-Vought submitted an answer to the complaint outlining four defenses:

1. That the government averments did not make out a violation of the Clayton Act.
2. That the acquisition of Jones & Laughlin stock was for investment only and that the intent of LTV was to maintain Jones & Laughlin as a separate corporation with separate management.
3. That a determination that LTV had violated the act "would represent such an abrupt and fundamental shift in doctrine as to amount to an improperly retrospective application of Section 7."
4. That the government charges were mistaken in vital particulars. For example, as to potential competition, "the entrance barriers into steel production were not merely high, but effectively prohibit any entry through internal expansion into the integrated steel industry." It denied the relevance of reciprocity since "such practices are contrary to LTV's recorded and effective policies."

Questions

1. What economic functions was Ling-Temco-Vought serving?
2. Why might it have considered a particularly appropriate target for a test of the application of Section 7 to the conglomerate firm?
3. What advantages are there in the type of organization and financing that LTV selected for the achievement of its purposes?
4. Why did its financial structure make it very vulnerable to disappointing earnings by Braniff and JLI in 1969?

---

[28] Answer of Ling-Temco-Vought, Inc., in Civil Action No. 49–438, U.S. District Court, Western District of Pennsylvania.

CASE 15–2. Zenith Radio Corporation

The stockholders of the Zenith Radio Corporation received the following letter in February, 1950:

February 8, 1950

To Our Shareholders:

You have no doubt seen news items in the daily press (copy enclosed) to the effect that Zenith will shortly discontinue the manufacture of auto radios. I feel that you are entitled to a direct first hand statement as to the reasons for this decision which should have a far-reaching effect on your investment in our company.

When we originally went into the manufacture of auto radios for the automobile manufactures, it was on the basis that such production would absorb some of our overhead and keep our people employed during the "off season," for household radio. Up until the war, when production of all radios was stopped, the anticipated results from this business were accomplished.

However, since the resumption of production at the end of the war, the auto radio business has not worked out as satisfactorily for us, due to several factors, which I will explain as follows:

The auto companies now require their peak requirements of radios at the *same* period of the year that our home radio and television are in greatest demand with the result that we have not been able to take full advantage of the overwhelming demand for these products from our distributors, dealers and the public. The terrific demand for television has greatly complicated our problem.

Immediately following the war we were limited in our pricing of auto sets by OPA restrictions, with the result that we operated at a loss on this business for the first two years. With the removal of these restrictions, and with the cooperation of the auto manufacturers, we were able to reprice our sets to them on a basis which has enabled us to recover our postwar loss.

However, the present competitive situation does not now warrant our using large valuable manufacturing space and some of our most highly skilled engineering and production personnel for this type of manufacturing at the expense of the much more lucrative television and radio production so much needed by our distributors and dealers.

We have, therefore, decided to concentrate our efforts on home radio, television and hearing aid production for which we expect Zenith will enjoy continued high public demand.

The quarter just finished January 31st, was the highest in volume of sales in our history, approximately $33 million and will, I expect, show the largest profit, when the figures are completed.

Present demand and orders on hand indicate a continuance of our present high rate of production for the next two months, with no indication as yet of any appreciable decline thereafter.

The future of our company was never brighter and we are determined to make the most of our opportunity.

E. F. McDonald, Jr.
President

The automobile radio business represented about $20 million of Zenith's $77,146,881 sales, April 1, 1948, to April 1, 1949. Zenith sales subsequently rose to $110 million in fiscal 1950 and $137 million in calendar year 1952. By 1961, when Zenith and RCA Victor were contending for the largest market share in television, sales reached $274 million and an 18.2 percent return on net worth of $98.6 million was achieved.

Television production rose from 178,500 sets in 1947 to 945,000 in 1948 and 3,000,000 in 1949. The 1950 industry output of 7,557,000 had only been exceeded once through 1961. (The rivalry between Zenith and RCA continued into color television with Zenith the leader in 1973.)

Questions

1. In what way did the economically relevant cost to Zenith of producing automobile radios change from the prewar to the early postwar period (1946–48)?
2. How had the relevant costs changed from early 1948 to 1950?
3. How did both long-run and short-run considerations enter the decision? Consider Zenith's market position in your answer.
4. Suppose that Zenith had prepared a cash flow analysis for the next ten years that assumed:
   a. During 1950 and 1951 the before tax income would be reduced by 2 million a year as a result of margins on auto radios that were lower than on TV sets and as a result of extra expansion of facilities needed to continue auto radios.
   b. That from 1952 through 1959 a two million a year contribution from auto radios would be partially offset one million less from TV as a result of failure to get as strong a market position as would have been possible because of continued auto radio production.
   c. A pretax cost of capital of 20 percent.
   Would analysis under these assumptions indicate the radios should be dropped?

The Plant
Location Decision—
Domestic and
Multinational

ALTHOUGH the problem of where to locate a new plant arises infrequently for most firms, it is clearly a matter of great importance whenever it must be faced. Economic consultants are often brought in to study the problem of location and to advise management on this subject. While company officials are usually expert in the day-to-day operations of the firm, they may feel much less at home with the problem of finding an optimum location, since this involves such questions as the relative availability and cost of labor, capital, and materials at various places at which they may have had no business experience. Executives employed by large retailing "chains" are more likely than most officials to be in close touch with locational problems because of the frequency with which new outlets are established. There is seldom only one suitable location for a plant; instead, numerous locations are likely to be satisfactory, though some may be decidedly better than others. Some locations, of course, are so poor that their selection alone would insure failure.

Nonpecuniary Factors in Location

Most theorizing about the behavior of firms assumes that the goal of management is to maximize the excess of receipts over costs during a period of time (or, more accurately, the present value of such net receipts). Economists are paying increased attention, however, to nonpecuniary gratifications and costs as a motivating force in decisions, and this seems to be true also for locational decisions. A plant may be located so as to be convenient to the home of the owner even if this would not otherwise be considered the best site. Or plants may locate near such cities as New York, New Orleans, or San Francisco for the convenience of executives and visitors interested in urban divertissement. In other cases an urban location is carefully avoided because of city problems. Frequently plants are located in Florida or California because of favorable climatic conditions which may be sought by officials. Pecuniary and nonpecuniary motivations become intermixed, however, when favorable climate also makes it possible to pay lower wages or salaries to employees or to secure better personnel at any given rate of pay.

Personal considerations are more likely to be important in the location of plants belonging to small firms than to those of large, multiplant companies. Questionnaire studies of reasons for locational decisions are quite popular, but special care must be taken with respect to evaluating responses dealing with personal considerations. One reason is that factors which appeal to the owner or manager may also affect costs or receipts by appealing also to employees or customers. Another reason is that a businessman may not be willing to leave his home community but in locating a new enterprise there he will select one which is compatible with that location. His response may then fail to emphasize the basic economic factors which made the location favorable.[1]

Cost

In location theory main emphasis is usually given to the cost side. The most favorable location for production is often said to be at the place where the unit cost of gathering materials, processing them, and delivering the finished product is minimized. This formulation is somewhat vague because it does not say *how many* units are produced and sold. Nevertheless, it is a useful approach for a large class of locational decisions where demand is large in relation to the output of a plant of economical size so that the main problem is one of producing at low cost.

A simple chart which usefully emphasizes some of the key variables is shown as Figure 16–1. This pertains to a plant turning out a single product made of one important raw material and sold in a single market. Processing costs, consisting of such expenses as wages, utility charges, depreciation of plant and equipment, and actual or opportunity rent on land are included in the line labeled P. Since these vary with the rate of output, the line pertains to an expected long-run average rate of production. Processing costs are apt to be higher in urban locations due to

---

[1] This is pointed out in Hugh O. Nourse, *Regional Economics* (New York: McGraw-Hill Book Co., 1968), p. 10.

FIGURE 16–1

Optimum Location in a Simple Case
(material source provides lowest cost)

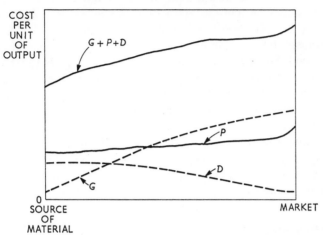

higher land values and wage rates. Since it is assumed that the market is an urban area, the P line is highest at that end of the chart. Material-gathering costs (G) per unit of output are lowest if the plant is located at the material source (e.g., a paper mill near the forest) and highest if the material must be brought all the way to the market before manufacture. The cost of transportation per mile is assumed to diminish with distance—a common feature in railroad rates, for example.

The D line pertains to the cost per unit of transporting the finished good to market. This is lowest if the plant is located at the market (e.g., a soft drink plant in a city) and higher if the plant is located farther from the market.

The top line, found by vertical addition of P, G, and D, should indicate the lowest cost location—at the material source as Figure 16–1 is drawn. The principal determinant of the best location is usually the relative change in height of curves G and D over the range between material source and market. That is, if curve G rises more than curve D falls over this range (as it does in Figure 16–1), location at the material source is apt to be more economical; if curve D had declined relatively more, location at the market would probably have been indicated. These locational forces can, of course, be overcome by processing advantages of other locations. For example, a town between the material source and market may have an especially favorable labor supply situation, a river to provide essential cooling or transportation, or other decisive advantage.

Suppose the material source and the market are 500 miles apart. The amount of raw material per unit of product may be an important determinant of the relative change in the G and D curves over the 500-mile distance. If 10 pounds of material were needed to make 1 pound of finished product, the material gathering cost curve would go up much more than the product delivery cost curve would decline. That is, the cost of transporting 10 pounds of material 500 miles would probably greatly exceed the cost of moving 1 pound of product that distance. The smelting of most ores, the ginning of cotton, the crushing of cane sugar, the production of fruit juices, and the canning of crab meat, tuna, and salmon are examples of "weight-losing" processes where it would be uneconomical to locate near the market, since this would mean incurring heavy transportation expenses on substances which are wasted or burned up in processing. A dramatic example of extreme weight loss is found in the processing of gold-containing ore, where almost all of the weight is lost. This processing takes place, of course, right at the mines.

Market Orientation

In other cases, it would cost more to move the finished product a long distance than it costs to move the material(s) the same distance. This promotes location at the market. An example is the baking industry. Flour and other components can be transported quite cheaply to the city; but bread, pies, and cakes are costly to transport. Also, the need for freshness reinforces the desirability of urban location. The farm machinery industry tends to locate in farming areas rather than near steel mills and other sources of components, because such bulky machinery is expensive to transport compared with components. The same force has led to the establishment of regional automobile assembly plants, especially by General Motors and Ford. The form, perishability, and unit value of finished products have a great influence on freight rates, and hence on location. For example, the waste space necessarily involved in transporting tin cans and bottles fosters their production near the market rather than near sources of materials.

Products which use "ubiquitous" materials—those which are available nearly everywhere—tend to locate at the market. In terms of Figure 16–1 the principal raw material source and the market are the same place (the market) so that no other location need be considered. Such products as soft drinks, beer, and ice are manufactured in cities, since it would be uneconomical to transport the water incorporated in these commodities very far. At the same time, such manufacturing is usually not carried on in the very heart of cities because the competition of other uses (clothing stores, drugstores, banks, etc.) makes rental costs in central areas excessive for businesses which do not sell directly to large numbers of consumers. Sulfuric acid, an extremely important industrial material, is produced near the market. The production process adds weight, and the expense of long-distance transportation of a corrosive substance is relatively high.

Location near the market is also promoted by the production of "style goods." The demand for such products as ladies' hats and dresses is so capricious that producers must be ready to alter the nature of their output on short notice. By locating in such cities as New York and Miami, style goods producers are able to reduce inventory losses by keeping their fingers on the pulse of demand. The locational importance of this factor has been somewhat reduced by the utilization of highspeed air transportation for style goods.

Location at Both Ends

Where the principal raw material loses very little weight, or where the higher transportation rate on the finished product quite closely compensates for the lower weight of the finished product, it may make little difference whether processing takes place near the raw material source or near the market. In terms of Figure 16–1 the G and P curves would rise and fall about the same distance so that the $G + P + D$ curve might be at about the same level at the market and at the material source. An example is the oil-refining industry, which has processing facilities both near the oil fields and near the large cities. The utilization of a very large part of the crude oil for a great variety of products means that processing is not greatly weight-losing; consequently, oil may be refined at the market. At the same time, the finished products are economically transportable (by pipe line, tank car, and tanker, for example), so that processing at the source is also feasible.

The slight weight-losing property of wheat when milled into flour is quite closely compensated by the higher transportation rate for flour. Consequently, flour milling occurs both near the wheat fields and near the markets. Changes in the relative cost of transporting wheat and flour can quickly alter the relative desirability of milling near the material source or near the market.[2]

Milling-in-Transit Privilege

There is a tendency for location to be most economical either at the source of the principal material or at the market due to the downward

---

[2] D. Phillip Locklin, *Economics of Transportation* (7th ed.; Homewood, Ill.: Richard D. Irwin, Inc., 1954), p. 61, points out that the relationship between transportation rates on wheat and flour has at times determined whether flour to be consumed in Europe should be milled in the United States or abroad. Shipping rates for wheat and flour on the Great Lakes greatly affect the desirability of milling flour for the eastern markets in the Midwest or in the East.

concavity of curves *G* and *P* in Figure 16–1—that is, to the fact that freight rates usually increase less than proportionally with distance. While a location between the material source and the market would secure some of this advantage of rate "tapering" with distance for *both* the material and the product, it would not secure so great a *total* advantage in transfer cost as location at either end. To offset this tendency, the railroads frequently grant "transit" privileges, under which a through rate is paid on both the raw material (e.g., grain) and the finished product (e.g., flour). This is usually the rate applicable to the raw material. The through rate replaces the combination of rates which would otherwise be charged; that is, it neglects the fact that a stop is made for purposes of processing.

In terms of Figure 16–1 the transit privilege would cause *G* + *P* to be horizontal over the entire range. As a consequence, any location between the source of the material and the market would be equally feasible from a transportation point of view. It should, however, be noted that from a *social* point of view the transit privilege is not desirable, in that more resources must be devoted to transportation to the extent that location is artifically influenced by this sort of rate. That is, if the concavity of the *G* and *P* curves is consistent with the actual cost savings due to long hauls, the transit privilege, by causing *G* + *P* to be horizontal, distorts "natural" patterns of location. It would also tend to hold down land values at the material source and at the market, and to increase land values at intermediate points.

Transit privileges apply to a large number of commodities and to quite dissimilar forms of "processing." Shippers of livestock may use the privilege to rest their stock and to test the possibilities of local sale. Soybeans and cottonseed may be converted into oil and meal under this rate system. Lumber products may be milled, iron and steel stopped for fabrication of certain kinds, and agricultural products stopped for storage under the transit privilege.

Multiple Sources of Materials

Frequently, a manufacturing process uses two or more materials in large quantities. When both are weight-losing in the process, the optimal location may be between the principal sources of these materials. If one of the materials—for example, fuel—is more weight-losing than the other, this material will tend to exert more influence on the minimum transfer cost location. At the same time, the attraction of the market may also be significant.

The steel industry provides an interesting example of this situation. It is also an extremely important example because of the attraction of steel itself to a great variety of steel-using manufacturing activities.[3] Steel plants are usually located between deposits of coking coal and iron ore. Much the greater influence has been exerted by coal, in part because of low-cost water transportation available on the Great Lakes for ore from the Lake Superior region and on the eastern seaboard for imported ore. The market exerts perhaps an even greater influence than fuel, especially since cities are the main source of the scrap used in steelmaking. That is, the best markets are also important sources of an important material. Economies recently introduced in the use of coal in blast furnaces have somewhat diminished the attraction of fuel as a locational factor for steel mills and have increased the relative locational pull of the markets.

Processing Costs

In many industries, transportation is not highly significant, constituting but a small part of the total cost of putting the product into the hands of the consumer. Improvements in highways and transportation technology are tending to increase the number of such industries. This may lead to the establishment of a relatively small number of large plants designed to serve national or even international markets. Examples of such commodities are typewriters, alarm clocks and watches, razor blades, and bobby pins. For such goods the location which minimizes processing costs is apt to be optimal.

If labor were perfectly mobile between different geographical areas, regional differences in wage and salary rates would not be an important factor in plant location.[4] Under this assumption, workers would move until no further advantage in terms of real wages could be secured. (If this is to be strictly true, real wages must be considered to reflect—as positive or negative items—such factors as climate, cultural advantages and disadvantages, traffic congestion, and recreational opportunities.) In the real world, however, some types of labor are slow to move in adequate numbers. This is a basic reason for the "farm problem" and for the low earnings of many families in such areas as the Appalachian South. Well-educated persons tend to be much more mobile, however.

The existence of regional differences in the wages of potentially equally productive workers may exert a powerful locational pull in industries where labor costs are a large part of total processing cost. Many

---

[3] According to Richardson Wood, "Where to Put Your Plant," *Fortune,* July, 1956, p. 101, the existence of the steel belt stretching from Buffalo and Pittsburgh to Detroit and Chicago is the main reason why 70 percent of the industrial labor force of the country is found in less than 10 percent of the nation's territory.

[4] "Perfect mobility" does not necessitate a readiness of *every* worker to move. It implies only such readiness on the part of a sufficient number of laborers to equate wage rates for a given type of work at different places.

textile and woolen mills have moved to the South and to Puerto Rico to take advantage of lower wage rates. The shoe industry has shown a tendency to establish plants in small communities in the South, especially to utilize female labor. Frequently, firms which move to low-wage areas to take advantage of this cost saving are careful to conceal the fact, in view of the rather general feeling that there is something reprehensible in this sort of action. Actually, the only way in which low-wage areas can rapidly improve their economic lot is through the increase in capital in relation to labor. Each plant which is located to take advantage of relatively low-cost labor helps raise the real income of workers in that area.

There is, however, much resistance to the "natural" process of permitting relative labor surplus areas to attract industry by paying lower wages. Labor unions attempt to equalize wage rates throughout the country by means of industrywide collective bargaining and by pressing politically for an ever higher and broader federal minimum wage. They are joined in these efforts by congressmen and some businessmen from high wage areas who fear the competition of lower wage areas. Paradoxically, the federal government tends to price many low productivity persons out of the labor market by raising legal minimum wage rates while operating "depressed area" or "area redevelopment" programs designed to bring new plants to low-income areas. A great many state and local programs, many providing subsidies, attest to the tremendous interest in attracting new industry. While manufacturing facilities are usually more spectacular, local unemployment can also be relieved by bringing in wholesale, retail, recreational, and government facilities.

Land Rent

The purchase price which must be paid by a firm for the land on which it erects a plant—or alternatively, the rent which must be paid on a long-term lease for the use of land—may be an important locational factor. For convenience, we shall speak of the rent on land, since this keeps the cost on an annual or monthly basis comparable to wage and interest payments.

Land rent, like the return to any factor of production, arises from its value productivity. This productivity stems from the fertility of the soil in agricultural uses, from the minerals which it may contain, and from its location, especially with respect to markets. The last-named factor is of principal importance in location theory.

A German economist, Johann Heinrich von Thünen,[5] was the first to

---

[5] *Der Isolierte Staat in Beziehung auf Landwirtschaft und Nationalökonomie* (3d ed.; Berlin: Schumacher-Zarchlin, 1875).

describe the pattern of land use and rents which would tend to evolve from the unhampered workings of the price system. He considered a large town in the middle of a wide plain, where the land was everywhere of equal fertility. The plain was assumed to be isolated from other places of economic activity by a wilderness. The town was considered to supply the farmers with manufactured items in exchange for raw materials and food.

Von Thünen concluded that the rent of land would decline with its distance from the town. Within a circle nearest the town, such commodities as green vegetables and milk would be produced. Intensive cultivation of forest lands for fuel and building materials would take place in the next circle. Such activities as grain and cattle raising would occur in the outer circles. In the most remote zone the most extensive land use— hunting—would take place. The basic principle is that different uses of land vary in their ability to bear rental costs relative to transportation costs. Such items as milk and vegetables are perishable and are transported to market frequently. They are better able to stand high yearly rental costs than the high yearly transportation costs which would be associated with more distant hauls to market. Grains, on the other hand, are transported to market less frequently and in larger lots, so they can better bear high transfer costs than high land rents. The aim of each user of land is to minimize the sum of land rental and transportation charges per time period.

Although based on highly abstract assumptions, the von Thünen theory discloses factors which are of importance both for agricultural and industrial location. If fertility, land contours, and other natural features are fairly uniform, rent per unit of land tends to decline with distance from the market. Since this decline is due basically to the cost of transportation from plant or farm to the market, any change in the structure of transportation charges tends to affect land rents. It was pointed out earlier that the milling-in-transit privilege tends to increase land rents at points more remote from the market and material source by giving the same through rate from material source to market regardless of where processing actually takes place. A general increase in freight rates tends to increase rental values near the market and to decrease the value of the more remote sites. Von Thünen's pattern of location of various activities can still be observed, although it tends to become less obvious as population centers become less isolated.

Demand as a Locational Factor

Although location theory tends to emphasize cost of transporting raw materials and final products and, less frequently, variations in labor cost from place to place, many locational choices are based more importantly on demand. This is clearly true where convenience to the buyer requires a downtown or shopping center location for jewelry stores, banks, clothing stores, or theaters.

For industrial plants the demand factor is often difficult to separate from that of transportation cost on final products. A plant locating in a rapidly growing urban community is likely to be choosing a transportation cost minimizing site if its product is weight gaining in nature. Still, total demand may also be greater because buyers can easily visit the plant and because there are advertising and other sales values in being a local firm. Producers of style goods can more easily judge shifts in demand if located at the market. The demand factor does not, of course, dictate location only in the large markets. A firm may be better advised to locate in a market of limited size where it is an important supplier than in a much larger market where the number of competitors is also large and where profit possibilities are easier to detect.

The rate of growth of a local market appears to be a particularly important locational determinant. Rapid growth of population and income provides much protection to existing firms because new rivals must enter at a rapid rate in order to reduce the sales volume of earlier entrants. This was an outstanding reason given by businessmen for selection of South Florida for new manufacturing facilities.[6]

Demand Interdependence

Some useful location theory bears a strong resemblance to price theory in oligopolistic markets in that close rivals may react to one another's decisions. The substantial, and sometimes prohibitive, cost of relocating, however, usually means that a new entrant will give more consideration to the location of an existing plant than owners of an existing plant will give to reacting locationwise to a new rival's choice.

Because of the large number of possibilities with respect to the nature of price competition, costliness of changing location, and assumptions which a firm may make as to rivals' reactions, it is necessary to specify clearly the set of assumptions on which any theory of locational interdependence is based. It is also a convenient simplification to consider the market to lie along a straight line rather than having a circular, hexagonal, or irregular shape, as it usually would have in reality. Despite this simplification (or rather *because* of this simplification), it is possible to see some interrelationships of real-world significance.

The following assumptions make possible the study of a simple model of locational interdependence:

---

[6] M. L. Greenhut and M. R. Colberg, *Factors in the Location of Florida Industry* (Tallahassee: Florida State University, 1962), p. 66.

1. The market is linear and bounded at both ends.
2. At each point, there can be only one delivered price. The total amount purchased at that point is sold by the firm with the lower delivered price. The lower the delivered price, the greater the physical volume of sales.
3. There are two rival firms, A and B, selling the same product.
4. Marginal costs are constant, so that the desirability of increasing sales is not limited by rising production costs.
5. Freight rates per unit per mile decline uniformly as the haul increases.
6. Sales are made on an f.o.b. mill basis, so that delivered price at any point is equal to the mill price plus freight.
7. Each plant can be moved to any point, without cost.

FIGURE 16–2

Optimum Locations for Two-Plant Monopoly
(fall at quartiles A and B)

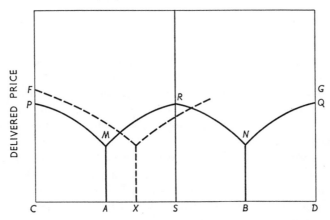

Figure 16–2 represents the linear market by the distance CD.[7] If a mill is located at point A, the f.o.b. mill price is AM; delivered prices to the left and right of A are shown by the lines MP and MR, respectively. These price lines are drawn concavely downward, to reflect the tapering of rates with distance. If a mill is located at point B, the mill price is similarly represented by BN, and delivered prices by NR and NQ. Points F and G represent the highest price at which any sales can be made. It is clear that if demand curves are similar and downsloping at all points in the market, greater quantities will be sold near the mills than at a dis-

---

[7] Chart and analysis are a modification of Arthur Smithies, "Optimal Location in Spatial Competition," *Journal of Political Economy*, June, 1941, p. 426.

tance, but it will pay to make additional sales which can be secured, since the consumer is assumed to pay the freight.

If it is assumed that a single firm owns both plants—that is, that the firm is a monopolist in the market—it is not difficult to see that the locations A and B are optimal. These locations are at the quartiles, so that distances CA, AS, SB, and BD are all equal. Maximum sales could be secured by these locations, since lower average delivered prices can be charged than with any other locations. This can be seen by considering what the situation would be if plant A were closer to S than is now shown. Suppose it were located at point X, plant A could then undersell plant B in the territory just to the right of S (as indicated by the dotted price line), but this would not help the firm, since it owns both plants. To the left of A, plant A would sell less than before because delivered prices (as shown by the dotted line) would be higher. While the same amount as before could be sold between A and X, the decreased sales to the left of A would cause a diminution in total sales. The firm would, consequently, be better off with its plants at the quartiles.

Competition in Location

If the two plants are owned by separate companies, and if each firm believes that the other will match both its price and its location, the quartiles will again be the equilibrium location. Suppose that plant A considers a move to the center of the market in an effort to control a greater territory. Under this assumption the locator would know immediately that plant B would also move to the center. If the moves were made, both firms would then still control only half the market (as before) but would have diminished sales, since the long hauls toward C and D would reduce the quantities which buyers would purchase. The best thing for both plants to do would be to stay at the quartile locations, since they would anticipate poor results from any movement toward the center.

Under altered assumptions as to rivals' reactions the quartiles will no longer be the likely locations. If each competitor erroneously believes he can increase his sales territory by moving closer to the center because his rival will not change location, both will locate closer than the quartiles to the center. Plant A, for example, may first move from A to X. This will cause plant A to take sales away from plant B, which will move a comparable distance toward S, or even farther. (That is, the belief that plant B would "stay put" turns out to be erroneous.) Plant A will then locate symmetrically, or go even closer to the center. Where the move toward the center will stop depends on how quickly the competitors revise their original expectation of locational independence as they notice declining sales brought on by the rival's movements. Once they have moved toward S, locating at equal distances on either side, they will not retreat to the quartiles, since each would fear that the other would not also move away from the center. The wisest thing for the firms to do would be to come to a cartel-like agreement to move back to the quartiles. In this case a monopolistic agreement as to location (but not as to mill price) would be socially beneficial.

Location along a Highway

Those great modern institutions—the automobile and highway—create numerous interesting locational problems. In this case the buyers transport themselves to the goods offered by the gift shop, restaurant, filling station, motel, or other roadside facility. The most important consideration is locating and advertising in such a way as to stop a sufficient number of cars. Location at or near the intersection of highways may be advantageous not only because of the greater number of cars passing such a point but also because of the lower speeds which the intersection imposes on drivers.

Gift shops which also sell candy, soft drinks, and other items of interest to motorists often locate along a long stretch of highway well away from all other structures. This permits the economical purchase or lease of a substantial plot of land with ample parking space. Where the highway is divided or where it is a heavily traveled two-lane road, most cars will stop only on the right-hand side of the road. This may make it important to measure the average rate of flow in both directions before arriving at a locational decision. A gift shop located along a barren stretch of road will usually advertise heavily for many miles in order to build up demand. In this situation the optimal strategy for a competitor is to locate on the same side of the road but at a point which will be reached a little sooner by the traffic stream. This permits the invader to take over part of the demand which the other firm's advertising has built up. Adoption of a quite similar name for the shop (Jones' Gift Shop versus Jane's Gift Shoppe) and the handling of similar commodities are also useful. If the first firm then adds a shop on the other side of the highway some miles away, the rival firm can again set up a shop near to it, but reached sooner by the stream of traffic. While the first firm might retaliate by erecting a third facility in front of its rival, this may not be economically feasible, since aggregate capacity could easily become too large for the market. Relocation of an existing shop and associated advertising is costly, so a situation of being outflanked by a new rival is apt to be serious.

It is well-known that motels and restaurants are complementary facilities, each increasing the demand for the other. To a lesser extent, theaters, bowling alleys, and drugstores exert useful complementarity. A location one day's drive from a tourist center such as Miami Beach or Walt Disney World is especially attractive to motels. Unfortunately for some investors, new interstate highways can extend the distance typically covered in one day as well as causing much traffic to bypass motels on older roads.

Agglomeration of Sellers

Location theorists make frequent use of the term "agglomeration" in referring to the tendency of firms or plants to locate adjacent to one another. A principal motive in agglomerating is the saving of transfer costs between facilities. An extreme example is location of a can producing plant next door to a soup company, with conveyor belts transporting the cans between the plants. One reason for the growing popularity of industrial parks is the ability of some firms to cooperate with others because of proximity. Technical personnel, for example, may be able more easily to communicate regarding common problems.

Modern shopping centers, which include stores selling items that customers are likely to buy on the same trip, demonstrate vividly the advantages of agglomeration. The same is true of a wholesaling center such as the huge Merchandise Mart in Chicago. Well-informed and alert buyers are able to compare available merchandise more easily on a single trip. It is interesting, however, to note that life insurance companies do not agglomerate in order to help the consumer secure the best buy. They prefer, in fact, to do business as far away as possible from competitors, namely, right in the homes of prospective buyers.

MULTINATIONAL BUSINESS

When firms establish plants on foreign soil the locational forces already described apply but their relative importance is altered and some new considerations come into play. Multinational corporations have grown rapidly in number and size in recent years. They are, however, not a new idea. Such enterprises as the East India Company, the Virginia Company, and the Massachusetts Bay Company operated as multinational companies as early as the 17th and 18th centuries. In the United States multinational companies existed as early as the 1850s.[8]

Multinational corporations are usually large companies. *Fortune* magazine regularly publishes a list of the 500 largest U.S. companies and the 200 largest foreign companies. These lists include most of the important multinational companies. The U.S. Department of Commerce reported in 1968 that 60 percent of U.S. private foreign investment was accounted

---

[8] National Association of Manufacturers, *U.S. Stake in World Trade and Investment*, (1972), p. 2.

FIGURE 16-3

Leading Multinational Companies

Company	Base	World Sales (billions)	Company	Base	World Sales (billions)
General Motors	U.S.	$28.3	ITT	U.S.	$7.3
Exxon	U.S.	18.7	Gulf Oil	U.S.	5.9
Ford Motor	U.S.	16.4	British		
Royal Dutch/Shell	Britain–Netherlands	12.7	Petroleum	Britain	5.2
General Electric	U.S.	9.4	Phillips	Netherlands	5.2
IBM	U.S.	8.3	Volkswagen	Germany	5.0
Mobil Oil	U.S.	8.2	Westinghouse		
Chrysler	U.S.	8.0	Electric	U.S.	4.6
Texaco	U.S.	7.5	Du Pont	U.S.	3.8
Unilever	Britain–Netherlands	7.5	Siemens	Germany	3.8
			Imperial Chemical	Britain	3.7
			RCA	U.S.	3.7

Source: *Newsweek*, November 20, 1972, p. 96.

for by the 50 largest corporations, 70 percent by the 100 largest, and 90 percent by the 300 largest corporations.[9]

The biggest multinational companies are not all American based, as shown in Figure 16–3, which lists the 20 largest on the basis of world sales. The tremendous importance of the automobile is illustrated by the prominence of car manufacturers and oil companies.

Figure 16–4 gives supplementary data for some of the U.S. multina-

FIGURE 16–4

Importance of Foreign Investment to Some Leading U.S. Multinationals

Company	Total Sales in 1967 (thousands)	Number of Countries with Production Facilities	Percent of Total Assets Abroad
General Motors	$20,026,252	24	15†
Exxon	13,266,015	45*	56
Ford Motor	10,515,700	27*	40
Chrysler	6,213,383	18	31†
Mobil Oil	5,771,776	38*	46
IBM	5,345,291	14	34
Gulf Oil	4,202,121	48*	38
Dupont	3,102,033	16*	12
ITT	2,760,572	60	47

* Includes unconsolidated affiliates and manufacturing franchises.
† Excludes Canada.
Source: *Fortune*, September 15, 1968, p. 105.

---

[9] *Survey of Current Business,* October, 1968.

tional firms listed in Figure 16–3. The number of countries in which investment has occurred and the magnitude of assets located abroad is shown to be especially large for such companies as International Telephone and Telegraph, Exxon, Gulf Oil, Mobil Oil, and Ford Motor Company.

It should be remembered that the United States also secures a large amount of direct investment from other countries. For example, the Pechiney Aluminum Company of France invested in the United States in order to take advantage of the lower cost of capital and electric power.[10] Imperial Chemical Industries of Britain recently took over the Atlas Corporation, a Delaware firm, making ICI the world's largest chemical company.[11] British Petroleum has become a major operator of filling stations in the United States and has made a successful bid for concessions in the new Alaskan oil fields. This is not just a recent trend since the early American railroads were built largely with British capital. A Japanese owned aluminum smelter and a West German steel plant in the United States are recent examples of foreign capital moving to this country.

Most multinational companies were not initially established to operate facilities internationally. Instead, they usually intended to participate in ordinary export markets. Their multinational character has usually evolved over time as profit-maximizing adjustments were made to changing domestic and international economic and political conditions.

Labor Costs

Higher labor costs in the United States, due in part to the prevalence of labor unions in major industries, often provide the primary incentive for American firms to move some operations abroad. In the nonunionized sectors of the economy federal minimum wage laws sometimes have the effect of keeping wage rates of relatively low-skilled workers above levels that would make them competitive with foreign labor.

For example, in order to compete at all in the production of many electronic products that are turned out in the Orient with low-cost but hard-working labor, it is necessary for American firms to own facilities in such countries as Taiwan and South Korea. Frequently such countries are relied upon for low-cost components which are assembled in the United States. Even the Japanese are turning to South Korea, Taiwan,

---

[10] *The Multinational Corporation: Studies on U.S. Foreign Investment,* U.S. Department of Commerce, Bureau of International Commerce, vol. 1 (March, 1972), p. 15.

[11] Lester R. Brown, *The Interdependence of Nations,* Headline Series, No. 212, Foreign Policy Association (October, 1972), p. 13.

and Hong Kong for components as their own workers enjoy higher wage rates with economic development.

The U.S. federal minimum wage law seems to be an important reason for an estimated 300 U.S. firms having plants in Mexico where the labor-intensive aspects of their operations can be carried out more economically.[12] Some of these plants are located just over the Mexican border to escape the minimum wage law while remaining fairly close to U.S. markets and material sources. An authoritatively imposed minimum wage can offer a particular threat to producers who use low-skill workers in that large increases in required wage rates may occur on short notice whereas competitively determined wage rates move up more predictably.

Tariffs and Quotas

Tariff barriers erected by foreign nations that would otherwise be good markets for American products provide another important incentive for direct U.S. investment abroad. Prohibitive tariffs can often be circumvented by locating a facility behind the tariff wall. The growth in size and importance of the European Economic Community stimulates other countries to locate plants within the E.E.C. (Belgium, Denmark, France, West Germany, Ireland, Italy, Luxembourg, the Netherlands, and the United Kingdom as of early 1973). The reason is that this common market provides free trade within its borders but tends to erect protective tariffs against competitive products from the outside world. As the European Common Market grows in size, the sales potential of foreign firms which locate within its borders tends to grow.

Import quotas tend to be even more restrictive than tariffs. If an increase in demand in a foreign market causes the price of a good to rise there, exports to that country will increase in spite of a tariff. A rigid import quota, however, will not permit an increase in the quantity of the good entering the country. The inference, so far as foreign investment is concerned, is that it is even more important to locate behind quota barriers than behind tariff barriers. Quotas, either alone or in addition to import duties, can make it necessary for U.S. firms to establish foreign facilities in order to make substantial sales abroad. This has occurred in the automobile business, especially in South America.

Income Tax Advantages

Income tax advantages may accrue from multinational corporate operations. Most countries have lower corporate income tax rates than the

---

[12] Ibid., p. 17.

present 48 percent of profit (above the first $25,000) in the United States. If profits earned abroad are reinvested abroad, they are not subject to taxation in the United States. The combination of a lower foreign tax rate and a company policy (possibly imposed by the foreign government) of reinvestment of net income abroad can consequently produce a tax saving.[13]

If an American-based multinational corporation does return foreign-earned profits to the United States, a direct credit against American income taxes in the amount paid the foreign government is allowed. This is more favorable than the treatment given to a state income tax which is permitted only as a cost deduction rather than as a direct offset to the final tax. It has consequently been argued by opponents of multinational enterprise that it is more favorable to have a plant located abroad than in a state that has a corporate income tax (as almost all do).

Proximity to Market

In some cases the desire to be near the market causes firms to locate facilities abroad. This is similar to the locational factor mentioned earlier in the chapter, namely that producers of "style goods" prefer to be close to the market to permit quicker detection of changes in consumers' tastes. This is even more important when sales are made to foreign customers because changes in their tastes may be less discernable at a distance. It should be remembered that sales are made to industrial and governmental buyers as well as to final consumers. Nearness to the relevant business and government officials is useful in adjusting the product to changes in their needs.

Government Regulations

Another motive for U.S. international investment may be a desire to get away, at least in part, from government regulations. These may include the antitrust laws, because dispersion of facilities on a worldwide basis tends to keep a company from appearing too large in any one market.

Or regulations (apart from tariffs, quotas, and minimum wages already discussed) imposed by a foreign government may make it necessary to produce in that country in order to meet legal standards. It is

---

[13] Income tax law related to foreign income is becoming increasingly complex. The statements in the text give the general situation as of early 1973 but necessarily omit many of the legal complexities. These are related to such matters as percent of ownership, foreign holding companies, specific methods of computing taxable foreign income subject to taxation, and differences in treatment of countries considered to be "undeveloped." See, for example, Robert S. Rendell, "Developments in Foreign Tax Credit: How It Affects Doing Business Abroad," *The Journal of Taxation,* November, 1972.

necessary, for example, to produce drugs in France for sale within that nation in order to meet their inspection regulations.

As antipollution laws become stricter in the United States and more costly to comply with, there can be an incentive to establish a plant in a country where such regulations are less stringent or are not enforced. The consequences to the environment can be drastic, as in northern Italy where rivers and the Adriatic Sea have been seriously polluted, even by atomic waste. The polluting firms in Italy are not all foreign based, but there is special danger that absentee owners will be less considerate than domestic firms in this respect. Underdeveloped countries are usually more interested in new capital than in environmental protection and may compete for plants on the basis of leniency of antipollution measures. This is not necessarily irrational: each case must be considered separately on the basis of all benefits and all costs. An immaculate environment is not of great comfort to a hungry population.

When the favorable aspects of investing abroad appear to outweigh the unfavorable ones, such as political risk (both from foreign and domestic politicians), financial regulations, and the difficulties of adjusting to a different cultural setting a company is likely to go multinational or increase its scope in this regard.

Where to Invest

The wide world may offer a great many alternative locations for manufacturing and sales facilities. The alternatives for oil or mineral extraction are more limited. Among the many questions to be considered in selecting the country for a manufacturing facility are:

1. Will the market be large enough to permit sufficient economies of scale to be attained? This question may be of particular significance if the location is based heavily on getting into a territory protected by tariff or quota walls.
2. Is the investment climate favorable? Is foreign ownership really welcomed or is expropriation of foreign capital a likelihood?
3. Is repatriation of profits and eventually of capital investment permitted and likely to continue to be permitted?
4. Are foreign-owned firms subject to bothersome controls that are not imposed on domestic business?
5. Are domestic prices and exchange rates sufficiently stable to make it possible to plan and operate a normal business rather than to be primarily concerned about speculating on commodity price changes and on currency values?

Once the country has been selected it is necessary to select a specific place within the country. Here the traditional location determinants given earlier in the chapter are relevant. There may well be others, however. For example, national authorities may limit location to places considered to be relatively underdeveloped or less endangered by pollution or congestion. If this is not the case particular attention may be paid to the divertissement of executives. (If other things are more or less equal, why not locate in Paris?) A well-developed infrastructure (transportation facilities, schools, dwellings, utilities, etc.) can be of special value to a foreign firm which may not have the political connections needed to secure supporting government or private expenditures along these lines.

A broad picture of which countries have attracted the most American investment in manufacturing is provided in Figure 16–5. The importance

FIGURE 16–5

U.S. Direct Investment in Manufacturing
As of December 31, 1970
(billion dollars)

Country	Book Value
Canada	$10.1
United Kingdom	5.0
Germany	2.8
France	1.9
Australia	1.7
Venezuela	0.5

Source: *Trends in Direct Investment Abroad by U.S. Multinational Companies, 1960 to 1970*, U.S. Department of Commerce, Office of International Investment (February, 1972), p. 6.

of Canada and the United Kingdom is evident. According to well-known authorities rates of return on American investment abroad appear usually to have been higher than on domestic investment, although the differential is narrowing.[14]

American firms are just beginning to invest in the Socialist countries. Yugoslavia is the outstanding prospect since it has provided legal authorization for the forming of joint ventures between its domestic firms and firms from both capitalist and socialist nations. The leading joint venture to date is with Italy in the production of Fiat automobiles in Yugoslavia. Over 50 other joint venture contracts were in force in early 1973, a few of them with American firms. A very important stimulus will be provided by a 1972 decision of the U.S. government to underwrite private investment in Yugoslavia and Rumania through the Overseas Private Investment Corporation. Insurance rates are the same for all

---

[14] Judd Polk, Irene W. Meister, and Lawrence A. Veit, *U.S. Production Abroad and the Balance of Payments* (The Conference Board, 1966), p. 42.

countries: 0.3 percent against inconvertibility of currencies; 0.6 percent against expropriation; and 0.6 percent against war risk, a total of 1.5 percent per year. Since these are among the major risks faced by multinational firms, the insurance should stimulate investment abroad by U.S. firms and especially facilitate investment in approved Socialist nations. The prospect is that the trend toward multinational corporations will break down some of the economic barriers not only among countries with similar systems but even among those with unlike economic systems.

CASE 16–1. Kaiser Aluminum and Chemical Corporation*

The late Henry J. Kaiser edged into the aluminum industry in 1946 with three beat-up war-surplus plants he first leased and later bought from the government. Today, Executive Vice-President Stanley B. White, who heads the aluminum division, can point to a chain of 37 plants in 16 states, plus 31 in 19 foreign countries.

In the early days, Kaiser was strictly a sandlotter in a major league dominated by three companies: Aluminum Company of America, the Canadian company now known as Alcan Aluminum, Ltd., and Reynolds Metal Company. With experience and sophistication, however, Kaiser has made significant contributions to the technology, logistics, and vitality of the business. The company is known as a rugged competitor. Furthermore, it has carved out a strong position in raw material sources. In Jamaica, Kaiser has an estimated 40-year supply of bauxite, and in Australia a one-half interest in the world's largest known reserve.

Power Play. Thirteen years ago, Kaiser put a backspin on aluminum logistics. The company built a new ingot capacity in the Ohio River Valley instead of expanding its Spokane and Tacoma, Washington, plants. Cheap hydroelectric power was by then no longer the dominant consideration; proximity to markets—meaning shorter freight hauls—made Ravenswood, West Virginia, an attractive site, despite the need to use higher cost thermal energy.

Now Kaiser is again reversing the spin. Ready (the president) is pouring new money into the Tacoma plant, shut down as 'inefficient' in 1958, and installing expensive new continuous heat-treating furnaces at the Spokane rolling mill. The reason: availability of Australian alumina. Kaiser's half interest in the Australian bauxite deposits is backed up by a 52 percent interest in the company that processes the ore. Total value of the Australia ventures is $250 million.

Instead of paying $12 a ton for shipping alumina refined from Jamai-

---

* This case is taken from a longer article in *Business Week*, February 17, 1968, "Kaiser finds catalyst for growth."

can bauxite 3,100 miles by rail from the New Orleans area to the North-west, Kaiser pays less than $3 a ton for the Australian equivalent shipped 6,500 miles by water to Tacoma. The saving translates into 1 cent per pound on ingots that bring 25 cents a pound in the domestic market. On a ton of product like coiled strip, that 4 percent saving amounts to $20.

Questions

1. What are the three most important determinants of location of Kaiser's aluminum ingot plants?
2. Suppose the automobile industry should sharply increase its use of aluminum per car. How might this influence the location of new aluminum capacity?
3. Suppose atomic generation of electric power became less costly than hydroelectric generation. Would Jamaica become a likely country in which to locate an aluminum ingot mill?
4. What locational effects are associated with the light weight of finished aluminum?
5. How would you characterize the competitive situation in aluminum?

CASE 16–2. Reed, Waite, and Gentzler

The firm of Reed, Waite, and Gentzler had for many years been engaged in the production and distribution of a line of work clothes sold under the brand name "RWG." The line consisted primarily of denim overalls and jackets, denim trousers (more popularly known as "blue jeans"), cotton twill trousers and shirts, and plain cotton trousers and shirts. A line of work hosiery was also included. These products were sold nationally, and the line was well known and popular. They were sold by department stores, chains, and specialty shops, and in smaller towns and villages were found in the "dry goods" stores.

The company operated three plants to supply its market. The shirt factory was located in a city of approximately 80,000 population in New Hampshire. The trouser factory was located in a suburb of Philadelphia, Pennsylvania. This factory produced trousers, overalls, and jackets. The hosiery mill was located in central Pennsylvania in a community of about 110,000 population. The executive and sales offices of the firm were located in New York City. Sales officers were also maintained in Chicago and Los Angeles. The location of headquarters in New York City was dictated by the long-established custom in the trade of buyers converging upon New York. There had been some modification of this practice since 1947; for this reason, sales offices had been opened in both Chicago and Los Angeles.

Like practically all industries in the postwar period, the textile industry had expanded to meet both accumulated demand and new demand
resulting from population increases. It appeared, however, that the industry as a whole suffered from chronic excess capacity, which was
reflected in keen price competition. A large part of the industry was
affected by frequent style changes which, at the manufactured clothing
level, sometimes resulted in drastic price cutting. Firms whose products
were sensitive to these factors found it essential to maintain locations
where such changes in demand could be most quickly perceived. The
so-called "work clothes," while not subject to such frequent style
changes, were nevertheles highly competitive. There were several large
firms competing with Reed, Waite, and Gentzler, as well as a number of
smaller firms serving regional and local markets.

In addition to the production of RWG-brand clothes, the company
produced a number of private brands under contract with department
stores and chains. The capacity of the company's plants was, therefore,
geared to a demand consisting of RWG products plus private brands
produced under contract. Placing of orders for private brands by purchasers was usually handled by competitive bidding. Securing such
contracts was almost entirely a problem of competitive costs. Reed,
Waite, and Gentzler experienced no more than the usual problems
associated with the sales estimates of its own brands of clothing. Production of RWG clothing was planned according to sales estimates plus
inventory control, and the balance of capacity was filled to the greatest
possible extent by production of private brands. Certain items of work
clothing—such as blue jeans, blue cotton shirts, olive-drab twill trousers,
and olive-drab cotton and twill shirts—were considered staples. These
items could be produced for inventory when there was stability in the
market for finished goods. Materials and labor were the two largest
components of production. Instability in the finished goods market,
however, seriously complicated the inventory problem.

Until 1950, Reed, Waite, and Gentzler had been fairly successful in
obtaining sufficent contracts for private brands to keep the trouser
factory near Philadelphia operating at or near rated capacity. Early in
1950, there was some noticeable idle capacity which had caused a
reduction in the labor force. The outbreak of the Korean War in June of
that year had resulted in the procurement of some military contracts
which kept the plant occupied until April of 1951. Again, idle capacity
began to appear. A similar situation existed among competitors of the
company. This condition was reflected in keener competition for bids on
private-brand production. Reed, Waite, and Gentzler were unsuccessful
bidders on several contracts which they had obtained on many occasions
in the past. The company reduced its bids on future contracts but still
lost several to its competitors. On the latest contracts which had gone to

competitors, the firm felt that it had submitted the lowest possible quotations consistent with its costs of operations. The loss of these contracts was also causing the unit costs of its own brands to rise to such an extent that competition was jeopardizing the market for RWG clothing.

An investigation of the problem was undertaken, and the following facts were revealed:

Labor Costs. It was easily and quickly determined that the labor costs of Reed, Waite, and Gentzler were higher than the costs of several of its larger competitors. Philadelphia had long been known as a "needle trades" city. During the time that a large part of the total labor force of the area had been engaged in the needle trades, the level of wages for the area as a whole had been strongly influenced by wages in the trade. While the supply of labor was adequate, there was little demand on the part of other industries to put upward pressure upon wage rates. The clothing industry had long been unionized except for a number of very small firms, so that the wage structure for the community as a whole had remained fairly stable, although it had tended upward. With the growth of "hard goods" industries in the Philadelphia area, however, the needle trades workers had become a proportionally smaller part of the labor supply, and their influence upon the wage structure had diminished accordingly. The growth of the area as an industrial center during and following World War II had diminished the influence of the trade even further. It was now quite apparent that the rise in wages of textile workers was influenced by the labor demands of other industries rather than exerting an influence upon them. To some extent the pressure of textile workers' unions was an effort to maintain their wage level consistent with that of the area. In the postwar period, growth of new industries and expansion of older ones had placed heavy demands upon the labor supply, in spite of a large population increase in the area.

The same situation existed in other textile areas of the Northeast. This was not true in all areas, however. In some isolated New England textile areas, this condition had not developed, so that some textile mills were able to enjoy a wage advantage due to the local situation. Of greater effect, however, were the differentials in wages within the clothing industry itself. During the decade of the thirties, there had begun a migration of the textile and clothing industry to the southern part of eastern United States. Some of the firms which had relocated in the Carolinas, Georgia, Tennessee, and Alabama were experiencing lower wage scales than plants of the same firms in the north. To some extent, this was because many of the workers in southern plants were not organized by labor unions, and the effects of local labor-supply situations permitted lower wages. The union had at the present time undertaken the organization of southern workers; but even where some workers were organized, there were still wage differentials as compared with the North.

Productivity. Of equal, if not greater, importance was the differential in productivity between southern and northern mills. While the differentials varied between plants and regions, it was clear that productivity was greater, on the average, in southern than in northern plants. Some of this greater productivity could be traced to more modern plants and equipment, but there were also indications that some was due to the workers themselves. In the North, productivity had actually declined with the growth of more restrictive practices negotiated by collective bargaining.

Materials. There appeared to be little differential in material costs between the two regions. In some cases of individual bargaining between clothing manufacturers and individual mills, there was some shading of prices, but the general practice of price quotations on wide regional bases tended to prevail. There was, however, one notable exception on the Pacific Coast. This area was accessible to Japanese mills, and many kinds of cotton finished goods could be obtained more cheaply than in the eastern United States, although there was some tariff protection.

Markets. Analysis of sales of Reed, Waite, and Gentzler on a regional basis indicated that there had been a considerable shift in the past 25 years. For many years the firm had marketed the greater share of its output in the East, the Northeast, and the Midwest, and since 1947 had moved to the Pacific Coast. The rapid growth of chain stores in smaller cities and towns in rural areas had enabled the company to grow into a national market. With the growth in the production of private brands the output of the firm was further diffused. The chief markets at present were the Atlantic seaboard, the upper Midwest and the Mississippi Valley, and the Pacific Coast. The company had always sold its merchandise f.o.b. factory. This practice should perhaps be examined, since transportation to the Pacific Coast was an important factor on RWG brands. On private brands, transportation had become more important with the population shift to the Pacific area.

Following this investigation, the company considered the relocation of the trouser factory from Philadelphia to a point which would improve the company's competitive position. Three locations—designated as cities A, B, and C—were suitable as possible choices. Location A was a city of about 55,000 population in western Tennesee. This city was provided with adequate rail and highway transportation, and was within a radius of 200 miles of several textile mills producing the kinds of finished cotton goods used by the trouser factory. Currently, there was in this city a firm producing inexpensive women's dresses. There were also several small firms assembling light electrical goods, and a soap factory. The nearest city of comparable size was 83 miles distant. Surrounding city A was an agricultural area of near-marginal productivity. The city streets, water supply, and similar services were considered adequate for the needs of the immediate future. There was no indication that the city would experience any considerable growth within the next 10 to 20 years. Land was available both within the city and just outside the city limits. The trouser factory in Philadelphia currently employed about 450 persons. It was believed that this number of workers could be recruited from the present population of city A without serious effect upon the existing labor supply.

Location B was in northeastern Mississippi in a city of approximately 18,000 in an area served by the Tennessee Valley Authority. At present, there was a small hosiery mill located there, as well as a meat-packing firm, a mirror factory, a lumber mill, a small electronics plant, and two canneries. City B was located on the main line of the Illinois Central Railroad and was served by two arterial highways. This city, in contrast to the others, had been actively engaged in a program of attracting industry, and was prepared to offer a number of concessions as to land and taxes. In three instances the city had bonded itself to erect the buildings, and it had leased the buildings to the firms currently occupying them. Upon learning of the interest of Reed, Waite, and Gentzler, similar approaches had been made. City B, however, had grown rapidly within the past ten years. Its population had increased almost 4,000 within that period, and there were indications that growth would continue, but perhaps at a less rapid rate. About 22 miles distant was another city of 12,000 population; and Memphis, Tennessee, was 125 miles away. Jackson, the capital of Mississippi, was at a distance of 92 miles. An extensive program of street paving, sewer construction, and school building had been projected, but only the early stages had been completed. The area immediately surrounding the city was agricultural, and there appeared to be noticeable migration from this area into city B.

Location C was in Georgia, about 15 miles from Atlanta. City C was also well located as to rail and highway transportation. Since the end of World War II, however, the countryside between city C and Atlanta had developed to such an extent that highway travel between the two areas was regulated by traffic lights and highway patrols. Nearer Atlanta were large housing developments. Toward city C, there were both housing and industry. The population of city C was approximately 24,000 and was still increasing. To relieve the traffic congestion, a new superhighway had been planned and approved for construction between city C and Atlanta. A number of firms had located their plants in city C in the past ten years, and several more were currently interested. Beyond city C the area was agricultural. There was evidence of union activity in city C,

EXHIBIT 16–2A

Comparison of Actual and Estimated Costs of Denim Trousers
(per dozen)

Item	Philadelphia	City A	City B	City C
Materials.............................	$ 3.13	$ 3.14	$3.13	$ 3.11
Labor.................................	3.21	1.53	1.49	2.04
Waste................................	0.59	0.61	0.60	0.60
Factory overhead*....................	4.08	2.97	2.27†	2.74
Indirect labor........................	2.01	1.62	1.65	1.81
Administration expense................	0.40	0.41	0.41	0.41
Total cost.........................	$13.42	$10.28	$9.55	$10.71

* Includes amortization of new plant; does not include book value of Philadelphia plant.
† City B proposed certain tax and land concessions, which are taken into account.

and many firms in Atlanta and city C were now organized. Where comparisons could be made, there still appeared to be lower unit costs in city C than in plants in the North performing similar operations with organized labor. There was little doubt that the facilities of city C would require improvement and expansion within the next five years.

Exhibit 16–2A shows costs of producing blue denim trousers at the Philadelphia factory as compared with costs at the three proposed locations. Costs in the proposed locations are estimates based upon surveys of the areas. Exhibit 16–2B shows the railroad transportation cost from the various points per dozen pairs of blue denim trousers. While these costs are not paid by Reed, Waite, and Gentzler, they are part of the delivered cost to the purchaser and thus are a competitive element of delivered price.

The market for Reed, Waite, and Gentzler is divided approximately as follows: 40 percent is sold in the Atlantic seaboard division, 50 percent in the Midwest and the Mississippi Valley, and 10 percent in the Far West and Pacific Coast region.

EXHIBIT 16–2B

Average Railroad Freight Rates to Selected Cities from Philadelphia
and Proposed Locations (per dozen)

Destination	Freight Rates—			
	From Philadelphia	From City A	From City B	From City C
New York.....................	$0.39	$1.01	$1.14	$0.39
Chicago.......................	0.86	0.99	0.99	0.86
Los Angeles...................	1.52	1.31	1.49	1.52

Questions

1. Which location would you recommend? Why?
2. Would your answer be the same for both the short and the long run? Explain.
3. Is the lowest cost location always the best? Elaborate.
4. How would industrywide collective bargaining with labor affect the location of firms like Reed, Waite, and Gentzler?
5. What considerations other than those explicitly taken up in the text may influence the choice of a new location for the trouser factory?

CASE 16–3. Jaye and Compton, Inc.

The plant of Jaye and Compton was engaged in the printing business. For a number of years, it had confined the major part of its activities to the printing of several national magazines, mail-order catalogs, and city telephone directories. In addition, it filled large color-printing orders on a job basis. Only in certain cases did the company accept any orders for quantities under 10,000 copies.

The firm of Jaye and Compton was located in Chicago; and from the time the partnership was formed until 1937, the company had operated in leased quarters in an industrial building. In that year the partners decided that the rental on the space had reached such proportions that it would be more economical to occupy its own plant. The firm then moved to a building which had been erected in 1928 for a machine-tool company. It was four stories high and had been constructed so that all floors, including the basement, would support heavy equipment. It was equipped with two freight elevators and had its own steam power plant. The machine-tool company had failed during the depression, and the building had been unoccupied for three years prior to its purchase by Jaye and Compton. The purchase price was considerably less than its original cost, and in 1937 the building could not be duplicated at the price paid for it. Considerable renovation had been necessary, and some new equipment was acquired, but it was believed that the building would be adequate for several decades. At the same time, the company had acquired five vacant lots across the street from this building. Upon removal to these quarters the partnership was incorporated.

The present building, which occupied one city block, was fully occupied by the firm in 1953. The vacant lots, which for many years had been used as parking space for employees, were now occupied by three buildings. The company had grown to the point where it now had 4,700 employees, 3,450 of whom were working in the shops on two shifts. One of the buildings constructed on the vacant lots was used entirely for storage, while another had been constructed in 1941 as an employee cafeteria. In addition, two other buildings several blocks away had been leased for storage of paper and supplies, which were transferred by truck to the main building as needed. Four blocks from the main building the company was presently leasing, on an annual basis, a large vacant lot which had been improved for employee parking.

In the main plant itself, printing operations were carried on in the basement and on the first three floors. The top floor was used for office space. Because of lack of space on any one floor, it had not yet been possible to devise a system where any one job could be initiated and completed on the same floor. In some cases a given job would require operations on all floors. This necessitated a great deal of handling and movement from one floor to another, much of which had to be done in small lots because of the narrow space between machines. Very little power handling equipment could be used because of the crowded conditions .

Since 1947 business had been increasing, and it was anticipated that there would be further increases. Several of the national magazines which the company had printed for many years were increasing in both size of issue and quantity, which further complicated the problems of the already crowded scheduling department. The actual and prospective increases in business volume were also a strain on the apprentice-training program which the company felt it was forced to expand in order to provide adequate trained personnel. After a survey of these operational difficulties, the conclusion was reached that additional space or an entirely new plant would be necessary.

A firm of industrial engineers was retained to make recommendations for a solution. The first step was an investigation of additional space and retention of the present quarters.. This line of inquiry was not very promising. There was no space available within 20 blocks of the present plant. The space which was available could be reached only by automobile and truck, and it would be necesary to travel streets which were currently overloaded with traffic. It was feared that additional space at such a distance would result in rising costs per job, a situation which was to be avoided, since it might affect bids on contract jobs. This avenue of investigation was quickly abandoned, and efforts were concentrated upon the location of an entirely new plant.

Quickly discarded was the possibility of moving out of the Chicago area entirely. This was considered, but the chief limitation was the procurement of trained personnel in a new location. A demand for approximately 3,500 printers, pressmen, typesetters, and color-press operators was one which it was felt that no one community could provide immediately. The nature of Jaye and Compton's business was not such as to permit a reduction of any size and a gradual building up over the long run. There were some communities in which the supply of skilled workers was adequate, but they would have to be drawn away from present employment. This would probably lead to substantial increases in wages in the long run and high turnover in the short run.

A search was undertaken for a location in the Chicago area. The present plant was easily accessible by public transportation as well as private automobile. Employees of the company lived in all sections of Chicago and did not appear to be concentrated in any one particular area. A survey revealed that approximately one half of the workers used public transportation; the remainder used private cars or car pools. The company was completely unionized, except for white-collar workers, and labor problems had been negligible. The average period of service for skilled workers was 14 years. In view of these findings, it was felt that the new location would have to be one of relatively easy access and one which would not materially increase travel time for a substantial majority of the workers.

The industrial engineering firm suggested two possible plant sites. One was located in a suburb northwest of Chicago, approximately 17 miles from the present location, which was on the west side of Chicago about 2 miles west of the downtown business area. On this proposed location the company could erect a one-story plant, in which machinery could be assembled so as to minimize the amount of material handling. Conveyor belts and power handling equipment could be used. The storage section of the plant would be two or three stories and would also be suitable for power handling equipment. This section would be connected to the printing area by conveyor belts. The office portion would be four stories in height and would also house the cafeteria, lounges, and recreational space. There was adequate space for parking up to 4,000 automobiles. The suburban railroad station was the equivalent of four city blocks distant. The community was primarily residential, although a number of light industries were located there. The larger share of the population of 31,000 was employed in the city of Chicago. One of the features of commuting was that Jaye and Compton employees would be riding on suburban trains at a time when the rush hour was in the opposite direction. This location would, however, entail a journey of approximately $1\frac{1}{2}$ hours for employees living on the south side of Chicago. For employees living on the west side, it would increase their travel time by approximately 20 to 30 minutes. For employees living on the north side the increased travel time would average about 10 minutes.

The second location was within the city itself, on the far west side and slightly south of the main business section of Chicago, about 7 miles distant. This location was much more accessible by public transportation, being served by both bus and train. The difference in travel time for employees, compared to the present location, would be negligible. The amount of land was limited, however. The printing operations would again be housed in a building of at least three stories, but the layout would be improved so as to reduce a substantial portion of the handling which occurred in the present plant. In order to provide adequate parking space the storage facilities would be four stories in height; while the office building, with space for the cafeteria and recreational facilities, would be six stories high. This location would be more accessible for the negotiation of business, a great deal of which originated in the Chicago business area. There would also be easier access to railway transportation, since this site was adjacent to the main line of the Pennsylvania and Santa Fe railroads. The other site would be provided with a railway siding, but because it was on a railroad leading out of Chicago to the Northwest, there would be a delay of one day in delivery of freight cars to rail lines to the east and south of Chicago.

Exhibit 16–3A is a brief summary of the report of the industrial en-

EXHIBIT 16–3A

Item	Northwest Suburban Site	City of Chicago Site
Cost of new plant	$20,400,000	$23,575,000
Property taxes new plant (per year)	961,000	1,315,000
Reduction in miscellaneous costs (per year)	1,422,000	978,000
Estimated annual reduction in total payroll at current volume of business*	3,200,000	2,465,000
Estimated number of employees at current volume of business	4,100	4,275

* This figure includes not only the actual reduction in numbers of employees but also the increased productivity of remaining employees due primarily to new layout and use of additional equipment.

gineering firm. The net earnings of Jaye and Compton before federal income taxes for the year 1953 were $8,543,291.

The firm had ample resources to construct either of the proposed new plants without any external financing. It was estimated that the present plant could be sold for approximately $3.25 million.

The president of Jaye and Compton preferred the Chicago site for the new plant. He was quite concerned over employee reaction to the more distant location. Several of the directors, however, preferred the suburban location. They were of the opinion that the distance factor could be overcome to a large extent in the long run. Since it was a. suburban community, the workers could be encouraged to move to the suburbs. Two directors even proposed that the company undertake the financing of the purchase of new homes for employees who had five or more years of service with the company. This would involve the commitment of about $10 million of company funds for an average period of approximately ten years. As an added inducement the interest rate could be set at about 1 percent below the present mortgage-money market. The company at present had almost $20 million in securities, from which these funds could be taken if necesary. This commitment would not jeopardize the construction of a new plant from internal funds.

Questions

1. Which location would you recommend? Why?
2. Would you consider it profitable for the company to undertake financing of employee homes, as proposed by the two directors?
3. To what extent do transportation costs affect this proposed change of location?
4. Which considerations appear to be more important in this case—long run or short run?
5. Does a publishing firm usually locate near the source of its principal raw materials or near the market? Explain.

CASE 16–4. Dow Chemical in Europe*

Dow Chemical has shown that it *is* possible to make money as a basic chemical producer. In 1967, with total sales of $1.4 billion, Dow was the only large American chemical producer to show an upturn in profits, which reached $131 million, and in 1968 it bettered that record. In building up its European business, which now runs to $250 million, Dow was careful to establish strong marketing positions through exports before investing too heavily abroad. Such exports included both ethylene oxide and styrene, which goes into the making of the plastic polystyrene. With these selling positions established, Dow set up a manufacturing complex at Terneuzen, Holland, on the Schelde River near Antwerp, where it now makes most of the products it formerly shipped from the United States. For some years Dow has relied on European sources for its basic feedstocks such as ethylene and benzene, but this dependency is ending. This year the company will bring on stream a $60 million cracker at Terneuzen that will supply all of its current needs, and more besides. It will buy naptha from the oil companies, but in other respects it will be self-sufficient.

Dow, in short, has accomplished the "backward integration" toward

---

* Selected portions of an article by John Davenport, "The Chemical Industry Pushes into Hostile Country," *Fortune,* April, 1969, reprinted with permission.

petroleum that Carbide hesitated to try. Dow is confident about its prospects precisely because it has paid so much attention to broadening its markets. "The point about a modern cracker," one of its experts explains, "is that it throws off not one product but many—ethylene, of course, but also benzene and propylene. If you can use only one of those products, backward integration does not pay. But if you can use all of them, as we can, there is a very considerable cost saving." In addition, Dow has wangled a long-term contract from the big Belgian company, Solvay, for its excess ethylene.

Questions

1. Why do multinational companies usually start as domestic firms and branch out later?
2. What are some common dangers in backward integration? Why may they be of particular concern to a firm operating away from its home country?
3. Why is backward integration likely to pose special problems when the earlier stage turns out many joint products, as in petroleum cracking?
4. What effect should the expansion of the European common market have on Dow's European market?
5. Does the 1973 devaluation of the U.S. dollar tend to make it more important or less important for U.S. firms to set up production facilities in Europe?

CASE 16–5. Computer Machinery Corporation Goes Multinational*

Computer Machinery Corporation was only 13 months old, with only 75 employees and $2 million in total capital, when it launched a European venture in 1969. CMC's purpose in going multinational was to forestall fierce competition by establishing a foothold before the competition had a chance to do so.

What makes inexperience so dangerous for smaller companies is the fact that they cannot afford many mistakes. Slips that would hardly cause a 3M or RCA any worry can spell disaster for a little company with limited resources. . . . If immediate profit and loss questions had been the only consideration, CMC would not be in Europe today. But our market research showed that Europe represents a sales potential of fully 50% that of the United States. . . .

If one or more of our larger competitors—or even those our size—became established in Europe before we did, we might never be able to penetrate that

---

* Taken from James K. Sweeney, "A Small Company Enters the European Market," *Harvard Business Review*, September–October, 1970, with permission.

market. Our move into Europe, although expensive now, would be even more expensive—and riskier—later. . . .

A small U.S. company operating in Europe has some advantages over a larger one. Because the little fellow has far less impact on the host country, he is more likely to be left alone by the government than is the giant whose every move generates economic repercussions. . . .

As part of the plan to maintain a low profile overseas, we will hire only nationals wherever we go. This is true not only in the case of workers and technical personnel, but also managers.

Questions

1. Which of the traditional factors applicable to domestic locations appears to have been most important to CMC's European venture?
2. There has long been discussion of the "brain drain" from Europe to the United States. What effects are multinational companies likely to have on this movement?
3. CMC has opened a sales and service facility in France, a country that has shown alarm over the penetration of American products. Would you expect this to be an important worry of CMC?
4. What factors do you believe were especially instrumental in causing CMC to locate an international facility first in England?
5. Are the Socialist countries now "out of bounds" for a computer company?

chapter **17**

Antitrust Limitations on
Business Decisions

THE INTEREST of business economics in government regulation in general
and in the antitrust laws in particular is in the framework they establish
and the constraints that they set upon the firm's decisions. The emphasis
of this chapter is on the antitrust laws which are relevant for most
American businesses. The main body of the chapter concentrates on their
relationship to managerial decisions. The basic laws that may act as
restraints on such decisions are the following: the Sherman Act (1890);
the Clayton Act (1914); the Federal Trade Commission Act (1914); the
Robinson-Patman Amendment to the Clayton Act (1936); the Wheeler-
Lea Amendment to the Federal Trade Commission Act (1938); and the
Anti-Merger Amendment to the Clayton Act (1950). The basic provisions of these laws are presented as an appendix to this chapter.

The Prohibition of Price Fixing and Related Agreements

The particular antitrust provision that probably has had the greatest
effect on business decision making is Section 1 of the Sherman Act that
states, "Every contract, combination in the form of trust or otherwise, or
conspiracy, in restraint of trade or commerce among the several states or
with foreign nations is hereby declared to be illegal." This provision was
the first to be effectively applied in decisions against the Trans-Missouri
Freight Association and the Addystone Pipe & Steel Co. in 1899. The first
case held illegal railroad price-fixing agreement and the second rendered
invalid a pooling agreement by cast-iron pipe manufacturers who sought
to reduce competition by sharing markets.

In later litigation, the reasonableness of particular restraints has frequently been an issue, but agreements to fix prices to restrict production

and to divide markets have generally been illegal per se, or in themselves. The classic statement on the illegality of price fixing was delivered in the Trenton Potteries Case in 1927. Producers of vitreous pottery fixtures for use in bathrooms and lavatories were members of a trade organization which had been found guilty of fixing prices. They appealed on the grounds that the prices were reasonable. Justice Harlan Stone of the Supreme Court in finding against the firms stated, "The aim and result of every price-fixing agreement, if effective, is the elimination of one form of competition. The power to fix prices, whether reasonably exercised or not, involves the power to control the market and to fix arbitrary and unreasonable prices. The reasonable price fixed today may through economic and business changes become the unreasonable price of tomorrow."[1]

What this has meant for the business firm is that to act legally in important market and production decisions, it is called upon to act independently. For the broad range of American firms, cartelization is effectively prohibited. This has not meant that firms never, in fact, fix prices collusively, but rather that the ability to do so openly and with legal sanctions to back the agreement is impossible. In Chapter 13 we recognized that when sellers are few, tacit agreements based on such conventions as consistent price leadership may well be common. Trade association activities which may approach price fixing will be discussed below. Nonetheless, the United States has encompassed into law prohibitions to meet the observation of Adam Smith that "people of the same trade seldom meet together, even for merriment and diversion, but the conversation ends in a conspiracy against the public or in some contrivance to raise prices."[2]

Case 17–1 which touches upon what has been called the "Great Electrical Price-Fixing Conspiracy" has indicated that sanctions may be severe. Several businessmen who agreed in clandestine motel meetings to fix prices on bids for electrical equipment were sent to prison in 1961 and their companies paid many millions of dollars in damage suits to public and private utilities.

Exceptions from the Prohibition on Price Fixing

While the thrust of antitrust policy is for independent market decisions, there have been a number of significant exceptions. Perhaps the most debated are the fair-trade laws. Enforcement of the Sherman Act covered not only agreements between competitors but price-fixing agreements between manufacturers and dealers. In the 1930s when downward

---

[1] *U.S.* v. *Trenton Potteries Co.*, 273 U.S. 392 (1927).

[2] Adam Smith, *Wealth of Nations*, Book I, Chap. 5.

price pressures resulting from excess capacity were great, many states (finally all but three) passed legislation permitting manufacturers to require their dealers to maintain particular prices on products with trademarks. A legal justification for such a requirement was found in the idea that the manufacturer owned the trademark and that widespread price cutting on such an identified product could diminish the reputation of the product and thus the property value of the trademark.[3] Such legislation stood in conflict with the Sherman Act prohibitions on agreements when applied to interstate commerce. It was necessary that Congress pass legislation to exempt such agreements from the Sherman Act prohibitions. In 1937 the Miller-Tydings Act exempted interstate contracts fixing resale prices within states where fair-trade laws had been enacted.

In order to be effective, the state fair-trade laws contained nonsigner's clauses that simplified the task of the manufacturer. An agreement with a single retailer was sufficient to set the fair-trade price for all retailers under such clauses, thus saving the manufacturer the laborious task of getting agreements from all retailers. The Miller-Tydings Act contained no provision referring to these clauses and was held inapplicable in 1951 in a case involving sales of Calvert and Seagram Whiskey at $3.35 instead of the fixed price of $4.24.[4] With the strong support of the American Fair Trade Council, and particularly the retail druggists, the McGuire-Keogh Act promptly restored the antitrust exemption with the nonsigner's clause permitted. Nonetheless, fair-trade agreements have continued to lose ground as in state after state the nonsigner's clause was nullified on grounds of conflict with state constitutions. Manufacturers found the obtaining and enforcement of thousands of price-fixing agreements not worth the time and cost and the "suggested list price" has succeeded such agreements in most industries with the conspicious exception of drugs, where retailers have been most cooperative.

A second exemption to antitrust prohibitions against price agreements occurred in the enactment of N.R.A. legislation in 1933. General price deflation was associated with the depression and the National Recovery Act encouraged industry codes which permitted firms to get together to draw up specifications as to fair market behavior and frequently included price-fixing agreements. The Blue Eagle symbolizing the N.R.A. had a short life. The major permanent effect of the legislation was in the encouragement of trade associations whose discussions of mutual industry problems such as production rate and prices have sometimes led to antitrust violations. Whether such activities constitute illegal agreements to fix prices has depended upon whether the price information collected

---

[3] *Old Dearborn Distributing Co.* v. *Seagram Distillers Corp.* 299 U.S. 183 (1936).

[4] *Schwegmann Bros.* v. *Calvert Corp.* and *Schwegmann Bros.* v. *Seagram Distillers Corp.* (341 U.S. 384).

refers to present and future rather than past prices, whether its dissemination is limited to members of the trade association, and whether any recommended list prices agreed to were in fact effective.[5] Most associations are discreet enough in discussions they may have on price so that the government is not provided with written evidence as to price collusion. The courts have found that one or two letters between company presidents as to agreed-upon prices are legally far more convincing than hundreds of pages of economic testimony indicating that the similarity in price changes was not purely coincidental.

Legislation has also been passed exempting particular groups from the antitrust strictures on price-fixing and market-sharing agreements. The Webb-Pomerene Act of 1919 was designed to exempt price-fixing agreements that involved only the export activities of American firms. The justification for this exemption was that American firms were frequently placed in competition with foreign cartels and could need to form a united front. Agricultural and labor organizations were exempted by the Clayton Act. One approach toward the agricultural problem was to encourage increased market power among farmers. That this approach was not very successful is indicated by a succession of later government interventions into agricultural markets. A final example of an exemption is that of the Reed-Bulwinkle Act of 1948 that exempted the rate-making activities of railroad traffic bureaus.

It is worth noting that permission to make price agreements is not necessarily effective in raising prices when market structures approach that of pure competition. Many ingenious forms of price cutting were found to bypass the N.R.A. codes;[6] only in a few agricultural industries where producers are relatively few have farmers been effective in setting prices by agreements. Fair trade has proved satisfactory for only a few lines of commerce where the support of the idea is virtually unanimous, as with retail druggists.

Monopolization

Not only did the Sherman Act prohibit price agreements but it also prohibited monopolization in Section 2, which stated that "every person who shall monopolize, or attempt to monopolize, or combine or conspire with any other person or persons, to monopolize any part of the trade or commerce among the several States, or with foreign nations, shall be deemed guilty of a misdemeanor. . . ." This particular section was of little legal force until the 1946 decision concerning Alcoa.[7] Earlier cases

---

[5] These are among the distinctions between illegal and legal activities in the case, *Tag Manufacturers Institute* v. *F.T.C.*, 774F.2d452 (1st Cir., 1949).

[6] See Chapter 14 for a listing of some of these.

[7] *U.S.* v. *Aluminum Company of America, et al.*, Court of Appeals, Second Circuit, 148F.2d, 416 (1945).

against firms with monopoly power largely rested on records of predatory practices and specific restraints of trade they were using to build monopoly power. As a concomitant to discouraging cartelization by its firm line on agreements, Sherman Act enforcement encouraged the building of dominant firms by merger that eliminated the necessity for continuing agreements between separate firms.

The building up of monopoly power is not the result of a particular business decision, except in the relatively rare case where all significant firms in an industry simultaneously agree to merge. It usually is the result of a series of decisions including some mergers and some successful innovations which may have initially been protected by patents. Strong monopoly positions outside of the regulated utilities are comparatively rare. In determining monopoly power, court decisions have concentrated on the power to fix prices and to exclude competitors. Monopolizing embraces something more than monopoly alone. To be guilty of monopolizing, the firm, must know what it is doing and act in a way that tends to preserve or enhance its monopoly power.

What does this mean for decision making by firms? If a firm is approaching a two-thirds share of a significant market, decisions that might result in further enhancement of its market position could well bring about an antitrust prosecution. In the du Pont Cellophane Case a market share of about 75 percent together with actions that showed du Pont was active in setting and keeping this position was held to constitute monopolizing of the cellophane market. Du Pont's acquittal depended upon satisfying a majority of the Supreme Court that cellophane was merely one of a number of flexible wrapping materials and thus did not constitute the relevant market upon which to judge the workability of competition.

As an influence on decision making of most firms, Section 2 of the Sherman Act is of less moment than Section 1. The case brought against International Business Machines in 1969, which stresses its share of over 70 percent of computer sales, is exceptional. While this case[8] could run on for many years, if it goes to trial, it may well be settled as was the case charging IBM with monopolization of the tabulating machine and tabulating card industry. In a consent decree[9] IBM agreed to such provisions as the sale as well as lease of its machines, the licensing of past patents without charge, and a reduction of its IBM tabulating card share to below 50 percent by necessary aids to competitors.

The complaint cited IBM's 76 percent share of the general-purpose digital computer market in which total revenues were estimated at over $3 billion. As anticompetitive acts associated with this market position

---

[8] Civil Action No. 69 Civ. 200, U.S. District Court for the Southern District of New York filed January 17, 1969.

[9] Civil Action 72–344, U.S. District Court for the Southern District of New York, January 25, 1956.

it emphasized IBM's single-price policy that included software (programs, etc.) and support items along with computers, and its action in entering segments of the market where competitors had carved out significant positions. Control Data Corporation and three software companies also filed private suits against IBM in early 1969. The Control Data case was settled privately with the controversial provision that the plaintiff destroy the documents it had prepared for the litigation. The Telex Company received a multihundred million dollar award of damages which was being appealed at the end of 1974.

The student may have the opportunity and interest to follow later developments of these significant suits through press reports.

In addition it has often been claimed that General Motors cannot compete as vigorously as its relatively low costs would permit since with a market share ranging between 50 and 60 percent of the automotive market, it is approaching a situation where monopolizing charges could be brought. But it is difficult to find other firms in General Motors' position.

Another application that some firms must take into account is the extension of the patent privilege which permits the legal exclusion of competitors to a point where an industry is deemed to be monopolized. Case 17–3 on American Telephone & Telegraph illustrates this consideration.

Even though there are several important markets where a few firms control over 70 percent of the market, and while recommendations have been made that the antitrust laws should be strengthened so that the dominant position of a few firms could be reduced, they do not at present come under legal prohibitions of Section 2. In a few cases, of which the most prominent example was the suit against the major tobacco companies that was settled in 1946,[10] monopoly convictions have been obtained where the actions of a group of dominant firms was held to be sufficient to exclude competitors or to fix prices.

The kinds of policy questions that are of considerable concern to the managements of many large and powerful firms are not so much the current legal threats to existing market positions but questions concerning social responsibilities associated with market power.

Price Discrimination

The antitrust law that has probably been the most criticized is the Robinson-Patman Act, which prohibits discrimination "in price between different purchasers of commodities of like grade or quality . . . where the effect of such discrimination may be substantially to lessen competi-

---

[10] *American Tobacco Co.* v. *U.S.*, 328 U.S. 781 (1946).

tion or tend to create a monopoly in any line of commerce, or to injure, destroy or prevent competition with any person who either grants or unknowingly receives the benefit of such discrimination or with customers or with either of them."

As a restriction on business decisions it should be noted that all price discrimination is not prohibited, and in Chapter 12 we have been concerned with the situations in which it is economically and legally justified.

The price discrimination involved in such delivered price systems as the basing point system has been successfully attacked where the government in addition has been able to demonstrate collusive agreements to enforce the system. The economics of such pricing arrangements were also discussed in Chapter 12.

Objections to the Robinson-Patman Act have centered on its test of injury to competitors rather than to competition and on such *per se* provisions as 2c, that makes it unlawful for a firm to receive a discount because it chose to deal directly with the manufacturer rather than through a broker. This brokerage provision was aimed directly at the chain stores which sought to introduce economies of vertical distribution in retailing and which were prepared to bypass traditional distribution channels.

Exclusion of Competitors

In a competitive economy, the very success and growth of some firms is likely to eliminate competitors from the market. A number of the provisions of the antitrust laws are aimed at particular practices that suggest that the exclusion is unfair.

The most specific prohibition on business tractics is Section 3 of the Clayton Act which made unlawful tying agreements and exclusive dealing contracts which "may substantially lessen competition or tend to create a monopoly in any line of commerce." Such tying arrangements require that a purchaser or lessor must purchase one commodity as a condition for the purchase or lease of another. For example, a firm that required the use of its material along with the purchase of a patented machine could be risking an antitrust prosecution. An exclusive dealing arrangement requires the dealers to purchase only from a specified manufacturer. Conspicuous examples in our economy have been in contracts that require a service station to purchase all its gasoline from a particular refiner, or an automobile agency to purchase all of its automobiles and spare parts from a particular manufacturer.

The restrictions have not been so tight as to make it impossible for many firms to bind their customers quite closely to them. For example, in the automobile industry, the threat of losing a dealer franchise together with considerable advantages in concentrating·on a particular automobile line has produced a retail system in which most dealers in fact handle only Chevrolets or only Fords. Many other franchising arrangements that amount to exclusive dealing are made in competitive markets such as the roadside restaurant business where the probability of lessening competition is remote. Serious antitrust questions, however, have been raised concerning tying arrangements such as those between IBM cards and the business machines that they were designed to be used with. As a matter of fact, IBM was called upon as part of the settlement of a Sherman Act case against it to recreate competitive conditions in the card business, in which its name had become generic, and to reduce its market share in "IBM" cards to less than 50 percent.

Attempts to exclude competitors by disparaging their products has been condemned as an unfair practice by the Federal Trade Commission Act. "Squeezing" customers by raising the price of a raw material in which a vertically integrated firm has a dominant production position has been ruled in restraint of trade under Section 1 of the Sherman Act. An illustration of this occurred in the Alcoa Case in which Alcoa, who was ruled to have monopoly power in the production of aluminum ingot and who also fabricated ingot into final products, raised the price on ingot while leaving the price on final products the same. The possibilities of this tactic for squeezing out independent fabricators are evident.

The Decision to Merge

In the late 1960s the United States was in the ironic situation in which available legal weapons against certain types of mergers had become very much stronger and at the same time the number and the size of corporate acquisitions were at all time peaks.

The first real merger movement in this country came immediately after the passing of the Sherman Act. The climax of this merger movement was the formation of U.S. Steel—a combination of several previous combinations of steel producers and fabricators. Three hundred other combinations occurred between 1890 and 1904 creating dominant firms in many industries. The Sherman Act proved ineffective in dissolving many of these combinations, although the dominant positions created in many industries were eroded away by the entry of new competitors. The Clayton Act in 1914 sought to remedy the situation by prohibiting stock acquisitions that may substantially lessen competition between the two firms or tend to create a monopoly, but its effectiveness was limited by the fact that it was not applicable to merger through the purchase of assets and because its application to vertical mergers was unclear. A second merger movement of considerable size took place in the prosperity of the 1920s and ended with the depression. In 1950 at what seemed the peak of a new postwar merger movement, the Clayton Act was amended to make it clear that all types of mergers regardless of the method of accomplishment were prohibited if the effect of the acquisition "may be substantially to lessen competition or to tend to create a monopoly in any line of commerce in any section of the country." The enforcement agencies were relatively slow in using their new powers, and the first major case to be decided was that of the Bethlehem-Youngstown proposed merger (Case 17–4). Subsequent decisions have made it clear that there is a real antitrust risk wherever a horizontal or vertical merger involves a modest percentage of a particular line of commerce. The most definitive decision has been the Brown Shoe Case[11] in which the Brown Shoe Company's acquisition of G. R. Kinney Company was ruled void. Brown Shoe had produced about 4 percent of the total shoe output and Kinney produced 0.5 percent, although it retailed more, about 1.2 percent. The court noted that in a large number of cities the combined share of the two companies exceeded 5 percent. This figure may guide future decisions, although the Supreme Court made it clear that other circumstances such as a trend toward vertical integration by several companies which tended to foreclose retail outlets from competitors was a factor. In commenting on the significance of the case, David Dale Martin stated, "In essence the new policy is simple: both vertical and horizontal mergers are likely to be held illegal unless companies can demonstrate that mergers are likely to increase competition and thus promote the public interest."[12]

The government has also been successful in dissolving such product extension mergers as the acquisition of Clorox, the leading bleach producer, by Procter & Gamble on the grounds that Procter & Gamble's significant power in related products could result in a lessening of competition in the bleach market.[13]

Merger activity accelerated through 1968 as shown by Figure 17–1. The number of manufacturing and mining firms acquired in 1968—2,442 —was more than double that of any previous year except 1967 (with 1,496 such mergers). Similar increases also took place in trade and service mergers to bring the total number in 1968 up to 4,003. This proved to be a peak as both the number and assets of mergers fell off, influenced by the bearish stock market of 1969 to 1974 and the financial difficulties of hastily expanded conglomerates typified by LTV (see Case 15–1).

Not only was the number of mergers up but the size of acquiring and acquired firms was larger. One hundred ninety-two acquisitions of mining and manufacturing firms in 1968 were of firms with over $10 million

---

[11] *Brown Shoe Co., Inc.* v. *U.S.* 370 U.S. 294 (1964).

[12] David Dale Martin, "The Brown Shoe Case and the New Antimerger Policy," *The American Economic Review*, June, 1963, pp. 340–58.

[13] *F.T.C.* v. *Procter & Gamble*, 386 U.S. 568 (1967).

FIGURE 17–1

Number of Manufacturing and Mining Concerns Acquired,
1940–68

Period	Number	Period	Number
1940	140	1955	683
1941	111	1956	673
1942	118	1957	585
1943	213	1958	589
1944	324	1959	835
1945	333	1960	844
1946	419	1961	954
1947	404	1962	853
1948	223	1963	861
1949	126	1964	854
1950	219	1965	1,008
1951	235	1966	995
1952	288	1967	1,496
1953	295	1968	2,442
1954	387		

Source: Federal Trade Commission, "Current Trends in Merger Activity, 1968" (F.T.C. 1969), p. 9.

in assets; in 1955 the number had been 68. Seventy-four of the acquisitions were by the 200 largest firms in assets; in 1955 the number was 41. The total amount of assets acquired was $12.6 billion, a figure that was equal to 44.6 percent of new investment in manufacturing and mining; in 1955, the peak year before 1967 in this significant ratio, the total amount of new assets of $2.1 billion, a figure that was equal to 17.2 percent of new investment in manufacturing and mining. In 1968 nine mergers involved acquisitions of companies with over $250 million in assets. Only six such mergers had occurred in the postwar period prior to 1967 and only two prior to 1965.

Why so much merger activity in the face of stringent legal barriers? The significant mergers of 1968 were essentially conglomerate mergers in which there is no important vertical relationship of supplier and customer or horizontal relationship of offering similar products in the same market. In 1968, 84 percent of the number and 89 percent of the assets involved for the acquisitions of firms with over $10 million of assets were of this type; a great increase in recent years.

Donald F. Turner, the head of the Antitrust Division under President Johnson, felt that these mergers were essentially unreachable under the existing law which specified as unlawful "mergers which may substantially lessen competition in any line of commerce." The problem was to find a line of commerce shared by companies in different industries. In 1969 the Nixon administration with John Mitchell as Attorney General and Richard W. McClaren as head of the Antitrust Division, challenged the conglomerate merger movement with several suits including the challenge to the stock acquisition by Ling-Temco-Vought, Inc., of Jones & Laughlin Steel Corporation on three basic grounds:[14]

1. The increase in manufacturing concentration so that the 200 largest corporations controlled 58 percent of total manufacturing assets in 1968 as against 48 percent in 1948, which was abetted by mergers. The trend "leaves us with the unacceptable probability that the nation's assets will continue to be concentrated in the hands of fewer and fewer people."
2. The decrease of potential competition since Ling-Temco-Vought was a potential competitor in "cold rolled sheet stainless steel wire" and Jones & Laughlin was a potential competitor in "copper and aluminum wire and cable." Both firms were potential competitors in a number of concentrated industries such as primary aluminum and gypsum.
3. The increase in the probability of reciprocity, that is for Jones & Laughlin and Ling-Temco-Vought to make purchases from each other, or to use their combined purchasing power to increase their sales to the detriment of competition.

Attorney General Mitchell laid down this guideline for firms contemplating mergers:[15]

1. The Nixon Administration "may very well" file suit to prevent mergers among any of the largest 200 manufacturing firms or firms of comparable size in retailing and other industries.
2. "Will probably" file suit if any of the 200 seek to merge with any "leading producer in any concentrated industry."
3. and "of course will continue to challenge mergers" that regardless of the size of the companies involved may substantially lessen "potential" competition or develop a situation of substantial potential of reciprocity.

In the mid-1970s there was evidence that antitrust strictures against mergers might be loosening. McClaren had resigned as head of the Antitrust Division to take a federal judgeship after Nixon had opposed his prosecution of I.T. & T. in its acquisition of the Hartford Fire Insurance Company, a case settled by consent decree.[16] A more conservative

---

[14] Case is included in Chapter 15 elaboration on this point. Complaint was filed before the U.S. District Court, Western District of Pennsylvania (1969). Direct quotations are from that complaint and from Attorney General Mitchell's speech which is cited below.

[15] Attorney General Mitchell's speech of June 6, 1969, before the Georgia Bar Association as quoted in *The Wall Street Journal*, June 9, 1969, p. 4.

[16] Nixon told Kleindienst, "I don't want McClaren to run around prosecuting people, raising hell about conglomerates. . . . Now you keep him the hell out of that . . . Don't file the brief." Kleindienst denied this pressure in his confirmation proceedings for Attorney General and in 1974 was convicted of a misdemeanor for this denial. From White House tapes as reported in the *Boston Globe*, July 7, 1974.

Supreme Court with four Nixon appointees found against the Antitrust Divisions in several bank merger cases involving the issue of substantially lessening potential competition. The acquisition of the United Electric Coals Companies by General Dynamics was allowed to stand despite, "government figures showing the substantial percentages of the coal mining business in various markets controlled by the merged companies."[17]

Setting a Plane for Competition

The price, product, advertising, and production policy of business are increasingly affected by legislation demanding higher and fairer standards of honesty and awareness of the noncommercial consequences of business actions. In simpler, primarily agricultural economies, the rule of caveat emptor, that is, let the buyer beware, was reasonably appropriate. The consumer choice between commodities was limited to those that were fairly familiar. Most transactions were with acquaintances rather than with strangers. On the few occasions that the buyer made unfamiliar transactions, he could act with an attitude of distrust. With the growing complexity of consumer choice and with a rapidly changing technology that continually results in new options, the consumers must be able to act with reasonable trust and confidence. Perfect knowledge of all alternative product characteristics, and of relative prices has become impossible.

The basic antitrust law in this area is Section 5 of the Clayton Act that forbids "unfair" competitive practices with the Wheeler-Lea Amendment which forbids "deceptive" practices (1938). In a number of ways, legislation has proved inadequate; and in the 1960s there was continuing pressure for greater consumer protection which led to such legislation as the Cigarette Labeling Act in 1965, the Fair Packaging and Labeling Act of 1967 and the Truth in Lending Act of 1968.[18] Other legislation that does not really fall under the heading of antitrust also has been concerned with the problems of honesty in labeling and advertising or with more complete knowledge for the consumer. For example, the Food and Drug Administration has been concerned with adulteration, misbranding and the safety of food and drug products under a succession of legislative acts starting with the Food and Drug Acts of 1906. In

---

[17] "Tipping the Scales, High Court Favors Business More Often in Antitrust Cases," *The Wall Street Journal*, May 21, 1974.

[18] That more might be done is discussed in *The Dark Side of the Marketplace*, (New York: Prentice-Hall, Inc., 1968), by Senator Warren G. Magnuson and Jean Carper.

1962 drug amendments were passed that, among other things, made it necessary that a manufacturer in applying for approval of a drug must prove not only that it is safe but also that it is effective and that drug labels and advertisements must contain information of injurious side effects. The impetus for this legislation came from the thalidomide disaster that resulted in the birth of more than 7,000 European babies without arms or legs. The United States had been saved a similar experience by the resoluteness of Dr. Frances Kelsey, an FDA examiner. To keep the pill off the market, she resisted heavy pressure from the drug industry. In a different field, the Security and Exchange Commission is responsible for seeing that full disclosure is made of the relevant facts on new issues of securities.

The amended FTC legislation leaves manufacturers considerable leeway for puffing in advertising which can be quite misleading. The FTC may obtain a stipulation with the company's agreement that it will discontinue what the FTC considers misleading advertising, but the company is not penalized further nor are the past effects of the advertising removed. If such an agreement cannot be made, the FTC can issue a cease and desist order against the advertising themes. This order can be challenged in the courts, and a period of several years may elapse before a legal injunction against the advertisement is obtained. By this time it is quite likely that the company will want a fresh approach and would give up the advertising in any case. The cigarette industry case in Chapter 14 illustrates this process.

The legal constraints under which business firms must operate have set a minimal but rising plane for competition. Many business firms may well wish to select higher standards of candor. It is important that they lead the way since the long-run acceptability of any economic arrangements is likely to rest on their fundamental honesty in meeting society's needs.

Different types of standards quite outside the scope of the antitrust laws are also being developed. Their economic justification is sufficiently similar to make them worth mentioning here. These standards seek to make competitive firms consider the social costs in the form of environmental pollution of their choice of products and production methods. Examples are specifications for exhaust emission of automobiles, for the amount and chemical composition of smoke placed into the atmosphere, and for discharges of pollutants into rivers and lakes. Most of these regulations require increased costs by producers and, unless required by the federal government and thus applicable to all firms in an industry, are likely to be infeasible for firms operating in competitive sectors of the economy where additional costs for an individual firm would jeopardize its survival. Constructive leadership in meeting these problems and in developing acceptable standards that eventually will be mandated by the government is a challenge to managerial policy making for the inframarginal firm.

APPENDIX TO CHAPTER 17. The Antitrust Laws

The Sherman Antitrust Act (1890)

An Act to protect trade and commerce against unlawful restraints and monopolies.

Be it enacted by the Senate and House of Representatives of the United States of America in Congress assembled.

Sec. 1. Every contract, combination in the form of trust or otherwise, or conspiracy, in restraint of trade or commerce among the several States, or with foreign nations, is hereby declared to be illegal. Every person who shall make any such contract or engage in any such combination or conspiracy, shall be deemed guilty of a misdemeanor, and, on conviction thereof, shall be punished by fine not exceeding five thousand dollars, or by imprisonment not exceeding one year, or by both said punishments, in the discretion of the court.

Sec. 2. Every person who shall monopolize, or attempt to monopolize, or combine or conspire with any other person or persons, to monopolize any part of the trade or commerce among the several States, or with foreign nations, shall be deemed guilty of a misdemeanor, and, on conviction thereof, shall be punished by fine not exceeding five thousand dollars, or by imprisonment not exceeding one year, or by both said punishments, in the discretion of the court. . . . [The fine limit is now $50,000.]

Sec. 4. The several circuit courts of the United States are hereby invested with jurisdiction to prevent and restrain violations of this act; and it shall be the duty of the several district attorneys of the United States, in their respective districts, under the direction of the Attorney General, to institute proceedings in equity to prevent and restrain such violations. Such proceedings may be by way of petition setting forth the case and praying that such violation shall be enjoined or otherwise prohibited. When the parties complained of shall have been duly notified of such petition the court shall proceed, as soon as may be, to the hearing and determination of the case; and pending such petition and before final decree, the court may at any time make such temporary restraining order of prohibition as shall be deemed just in the premises. . . .

Sec. 7. Any person who shall be injured in his business or property by any other person or corporation by reason of anything forbidden or declared to be unlawful by this act, may sue therefore in any circuit court of the United States in the district in which the defendant resides or is found, without respect to the amount in controversy, and shall recover threefold the damages by him sustained, and the cost of suit, including a reasonable attorney's fee.

Note: Section 3 makes the act applicable to territories and the District of Columbia, Section 5 deals with subpoena power of court; Section 6 gives right to seize property of violators in transit; and Section 8 defines "persons" to include associations and corporations.

The Federal Trade Commission Act (1914)

An Act to create a Federal Trade Commission, to define its powers and duties, and for other purposes.

Be it enacted by the Senate and House of Representatives of the United States of America in Congress assembled, That a commission is hereby created and established, to be known as the Federal Trade Commission (hereinafter referred to as the commission), which shall be composed of five commissioners, who shall be appointed by the President, by and with the advice and consent of the Senate. Not more than three of the commissioners shall be members of the same political party. The first commissioners appointed shall continue in office for terms of three, four, five, six, and seven years, respectively, from the date of the taking effect of this Act, the term of each to be designated by the President, but their successors shall be appointed for terms of seven years, except that any person chosen to fill a vacancy shall be appointed only for the unexpired term of the commissioner whom he shall succeed. The commission shall choose a chairman from its membership. . . .

Sec. 5. That unfair methods of competition in commerce are hereby declared unlawful.

The commission is hereby empowered and directed to prevent persons, partnerships, or corporations except banks, and common carriers subject to the Act to regulate commerce, from using unfair methods of competition in commerce.

Whenever the commission shall have reason to believe that any such person, partnership, or corporation has been or is using any unfair methods of competition in commerce, and if it shall appear to the commission that a proceeding by it in respect thereof would be to the interest of the public, it shall issue and serve upon such person, partnership, or corporation a complaint stating its charges in that respect, and containing a notice of a hearing upon a day and at a place therein fixed at least thirty days after the service of said complaint. The person, partnership, or corporation so complained of shall have the right to appear at the place and time so fixed and show cause why an order should not be entered by the commission requiring such person, partnership, or corporation to cease and desist from the violation of the law so charged in said complaint. . . . If upon such hearing the commission shall be of the opinion that the method of competition in question is prohibited by this Act, it shall make a report in writing in which it shall state its findings as to the facts, and shall issue and cause to be served on such person, partnership, or corporation an order requiring such person, partnership or corporation to cease and desist from using such method of competition. . . .

If such person, partnership, or corporation fails or neglects to obey such order of the commission while the same is in effect, the commission may apply to the circuit court of appeals of the United States, within any circuit where the method of competition in question was used or where such person, partnership, or corporation resides or carries on business, for the enforcement of its order. . . .

The findings of the commission as to the facts, if supported by testimony, shall be conclusive. . . .

Sec. 6.   That the commission shall also have the power—

(a) To gather and compile information concerning, and to investigate from time to time the organization, business, conduct, practices, and management of any corporation engaged in commerce, excepting banks and common carriers subject to the Act to regulate commerce. . . .

(b) To require, by general or special orders, corporations engaged in commerce to file with the commission in such form as the commission may prescribe annual or special reports or answers in writing to specific questions, furnishing to the commission such information as it may require. . . .

(c) Whenever a final decree has been entered against any defendant corporation in any suit brought by the United States to prevent and restrain any violation of the antitrust Acts, to make investigations, upon its own initiative, of the manner in which the decree has been or is being carried out, and upon the application of the Attorney General it shall be its duty to make such investigation.

(d) Upon the direction of the President or either House of Congress to investigate and report the facts relating to any alleged violations of the antitrust Acts by any corporation.

(e) Upon the application of the Attorney General, to investigate and make recommendations for the readjustment of the business of any corporation alleged to be violating the antitrust Acts, in order that the corporation may thereafter maintain its organization, management, and conduct of business in accordance with law.

(f) To make public from time to time such portions of the information obtained by it hereunder, except trade secrets and names of customers, as it shall deem expedient in the public interest; and to make annual and special reports to the Congress and to submit therewith recommendations for additional legislation; and to provide for the publication of its reports and decisions in such form and manner as may be best adapted for public information and use.

(g) From time to time to classify corporations and to make rules and regulations for the purpose of carrying out the provisions of this Act.

(h) To investigate, from time to time, trade conditions in and with foreign countries where associations, combinations, or practices of manufacturers, merchants, or traders, or other conditions, may affect the foreign trade of the United States, and to report to Congress thereon, with such recommendations as it deems advisable. . . .

Sec. 10.   That any person who shall neglect or refuse to attend and testify, or to answer any lawful inquiry, or to produce documentary evidence, if in his power to do so, in obedience to the subpoena or lawful requirement of the commission, shall be guilty of an offense and upon conviction thereof by a court of competent jurisdiction shall be punished by a fine of not less than

$1,000 nor more than $5,000, or by imprisonment for not more than one year, or by both such fine and imprisonment. [Maximum is now $50,000.]

The Clayton Act (1915)

An Act to supplement existing laws against unlawful restraints and monopolies, and for other purposes.

Sec. 2. That is shall be unlawful for any person engaged in commerce, in the course of such commerce, either directly or indirectly, to discriminate in price between different purchasers of commodities, which commodities are sold for use, consumption, or resale within the United States or any Territory thereof or the District of Columbia or any insular possession or other place under the jurisdiction of the United States, where the effect of such discrimination *may be to substantially lessen competition or tend to create a monopoly in any line of commerce:* Provided, That nothing herein contained shall prevent discrimination in price between purchasers of commodities on account of differences in the grade, quality, or quantity of the commodity sold, or that makes only due allowance for differences in the cost of selling or transportation, or discrimination in price in the same or different communities made in good faith to meet competition: And provided further, That nothing herein contained shall prevent persons engaged in selling goods, wares, or merchandise in commerce from selecting their own customers in bona fide transactions and not in restraint of trade.

Sec. 3. That it shall be unlawful for any person engaged in commerce, in the course of such commerce, to lease or make a sale or contract for sale of goods, wares, merchandise, machinery, supplies, or other commodities, whether patented or unpatented, for use, consumption, or resale within the United States or any Territory thereof or the District of Columbia or any insular possession or other place under the jurisdiction of the United States, or fix a price charged therefor, or discount from, or rebate upon, such price, on the condition, agreement, or understanding that the lessee or purchaser thereof shall not use or deal in the goods, wares, merchandise, machinery, supplies, or other commodity of a competitor or competitors of the lessor or seller, where the effect of such lease, sale, or contract for sale or such condition, agreement, or understanding may be to substantially lessen competition or tend to create a monopoly in any line of commerce.

Note: Sections 4 and 5 provide, respectively, for triple damage suits by private injured parties and for final judgments in a suit brought by the government as being prima-facie evidence in private suits in the matters involved.

Sec. 6. That the labor of a human being is not a commodity or an article of commerce. Nothing contained in the antitrust laws shall be construed to forbid the existence and operation of labor, agricultural, or horticultural organizations, instituted for the purposes of mutual help, and not having capital stock or conducted for profits, or to forbid or restrain individual members of such organizations from lawfully carrying out the legitimate objects thereof; nor shall such organizations, or the members thereof, be held or construed to be illegal combinations or conspiracies in restraint of trade under the antitrust laws.

Sec. 7. That no corporation engaged in commerce shall acquire, directly or indirectly, the whole or any part of the stock or other share capital of another corporation engaged also in commerce where the effect of such acquisition may be to substantially lessen competition between the corporation whose stock is so acquired and the corporation making the acquisition or to restrain such commerce in any section or community or tend to create a monopoly of any line of commerce. . . .

Sec. 8. . . . That from and after two years from the date of the approval of this Act no person at the same time shall be a director in any two or more corporations, any one of which has capital, surplus, and undivided profits aggregating more than $1,000,000, engaged in whole or in part in commerce, other than banks, banking associations, trust companies, and common carriers subject to the Act to regulate commerce, approved February fourth, eighteen hundred and eighty-seven, if such corporations are or shall have been theretofore, by virtue of their business and location of operation, competitors, so that the elimination of competition by agreement between them would constitute a violation of any of the provisions of any of the antitrust laws. . . .

Sec. 11. That authority to enforce compliance with sections two, three, seven, and eight of this Act by the persons respectively subject thereto is hereby vested: in the Interstate Commerce Commission where applicable to common carriers, in the Federal Reserve Board where applicable to banks, banking associations, and trust companies, and in the Federal Trade Commission where applicable to all other character of commerce. . . .

Sec. 14. That whenever a corporation shall violate any of the penal provisions of the antitrust laws, such violation shall be deemed to be also that of the individual directors, officers, or agents of such corporation who shall have authorized, ordered, or done any of the acts constituting in whole or in part such violation, and such violation shall be deemed a misdemeanor, and upon conviction therefor of any such director, officer, or agent he shall be punished by a fine of not exceeding $5,000 or by imprisonment for not exceeding one year, or by both, in the discretion of the court.

Sec. 15. That the several district courts of the United States are hereby invested with jurisdiction to prevent and restrain violations of this Act, and it shall be the duty of the several district attorneys of the United States, in their respective districts, under the direction of the Attorney General, to institute proceedings in equity to prevent and restrain such violations. . . .

Robinson-Patman Amendment to the Clayton Act (1936)

An Act to amend section 2 of the Act entitled "An Act to supplement existing laws against unlawful restraints and monopolies, and for other purposes," approved October 15, 1914, as amended (U.S.C., title 15, sec. 13), and for other purposes.

Be it enacted by the Senate and House of Representatives of the United States of America in Congress assembled, That section 2 of the Act entitled 'An Act to supplement existing laws against unlawful restraints and monopolies, and for other purposes' approved October 15, 1914, as amended (U.S.C., title 15, sec. 13), is amended to read as follows:

'Sec. 2. (a) That it shall be unlawful for any person engaged in commerce, in the course of such commerce, either directly or indirectly, to discriminate in price between different purchasers of commodities of like grade and quality, where either of any of the purchases involved in such discrimination are in commerce, where such commodities are sold for use, consumption, or resale within the United States, or any Territory thereof or the District of Columbia or any insular possession or other place under the jurisdiction of the United States, and where the effect of such discrimination may be substantially to lessen competition or tend to create a monopoly in any line of commerce, or to injure, destroy, or prevent competition with any person who either grants or knowingly receives the benefit of such discrimination, or with customers of either of them: Provided, That nothing herein contained shall prevent differentials which make only due allowance for differences in the cost of manufacture, sale, or delivery resulting from the differing methods or quantities in which such commodities are to such purchasers sold or delivered: Provided, however, That the Federal Trade Commission may, after due investigation and hearing to all interested parties, fix and establish quantity limits, and revise the same as it finds necessary, as to particular commodities or classes of commodities, where it finds that available purchasers in greater quantities are so few to render differentials on account thereof unjustly discriminatory or promotive of monopoly in any line of commerce; and the foregoing shall then not be construed to permit differentials based on differences in quantities greater than those so fixed and established: And provided further, That nothing herein contained shall prevent persons engaged in selling goods, wares, or merchandise in commerce from selecting their own customers in bona fide transactions and not in restraint of trade: And provided further, That nothing herein contained shall prevent price changes from time to time where in response to changing conditions affecting the market for or the marketability of the goods concerned, such as but not limited to actual or imminent deterioration of perishable goods, obsolescence of seasonal goods, distress sales under the court process, or sales in good faith in discontinuance of business in the goods concerned.

'(b) Upon proof being made, at any hearing on a complaint under this section, that there has been discrimination in price or services or facilities furnished, the burden of rebutting the prima-facie case thus made by showing justification shall be upon the person charged with a violation of this section, and unless justification shall be affirmatively shown, the Commission is authorized to issue an order terminating the discrimination: Provided, however, That nothing herein contained shall prevent a seller rebutting the prima-facie case thus made by showing that his lower price or the furnishing of services or facilities to any purchaser or purchasers was made in good faith to meet an equally low price of a competitor, or the services or facilities furnished by a competitor.

'(c) That it shall be unlawful for any person engaged in commerce, in the course of such commerce, to pay or grant, or to receive or accept, anything of value as a commission, brokerage, or other compensation, or any allowance or discount in lieu thereof, except for services rendered in connection with the sale or purchase of goods, wares, or merchandise, either to the other party to such transaction or to an agent, representative, or other intermediary therein where such intermediary is acting in fact for or in behalf, or is subject to the direct or indirect control, of any party to such transaction other than the person by whom such compensation is so granted or paid.

'(d) That it shall be unlawful for any person engaged in commerce to pay or contract for the payment of anything of value to or for the benefit of a customer of such person in the course of such commerce as compensation or in consideration for any services or the processing, handling, sale, or offering for sale of any products or commodities manufactured, sold, or offered for sale by such person, unless such payment or consideration is available on proportionally equal terms to all other customers competing in the distribution of such products or commodities.

'(e) That it shall be unlawful for any person to discriminate in favor of one purchaser against another purchaser or purchasers of a commodity bought for resale, with or without processing, by contracting to furnish or furnishing, or by contributing to the furnishing of, any services or facilities connected with the processing, handling, sale, or offering for sale of such commodity so purchased upon terms not accorded to all purchasers on proportionally equal terms.

'(f) That it shall be unlawful for any person engaged in commerce, in the course of such commerce, knowingly to induce or receive a discrimination in price which is prohibited by this section.'

Note: Section 3 of the act, which has not been used, prohibits regional price discrimination for the purpose of "destroying competition or eliminating a competitor."

Wheeler-Lea Amendment to the Federal Trade Commission Act (1938)

To amend the Act creating the Federal Trade Commission, to define its powers and duties, and for other purposes.

Sec. 3.   Section 5 of such Act, as amended (U.S.C., 1934 ed., title 15, sec. 45), is hereby amended to read as follows:

'*Sec. 5.*   (a) Unfair methods of competition in commerce, and unfair or deceptive acts or practices in commerce, are hereby declared unlawful.'

Sec. 4.   Such Act is further amended by adding at the end thereof new sections to read as follows:

'*Sec. 12.*   (a) It shall be unlawful for any person, partnership, or corporation to disseminate, or cause to be disseminated, any false advertisement—

'(1) By United States mails, or in commerce by any other means, for the purpose of inducing, or which is likely to induce, directly or indirectly, the purchase in commerce of food, drugs, devices, or cosmetics, or (2) By any means, for the purpose of inducing, or which is likely to induce, directly or indirectly, the purchase in commerce of food, drugs, devices, or cosmetics.

'(*b*) The dissemination or the causing to be disseminated of any false advertisement within the provisions of subsection (*a*) of this section shall be an unfair or deceptive act or practice in commerce within the meaning of section 5.'

Antimerger Amendment of 1950

To amend an Act entitled 'An Act to supplement existing laws against unlawful restraints and monopolies, and for other purposes,' approved October 15, 1914 (38 Stat. 730), as amended.

Be it enacted by the Senate and House of Representatives of the United States of America in Congress assembled. That sections 7 and 11 of an Act entitled 'An Act to supplement existing laws against unlawful restraints and monopolies, and for other purposes,' approved October 15, 1914, as amended (U.S.C., title 15, secs. 18 and 21), are hereby amended to read as follows:

'No corporation shall acquire, directly or indirectly, the whole or any part of the stock or other share capital and no corporation subject to the jurisdiction of the Federal Trade Commission shall acquire the whole or any part of the assets of one or more corporations engaged in commerce, where in any line of commerce in any section of the country, the effect of such acquisition, of such stocks or assets, or of the use of such stock by the voting or granting of proxies or otherwise, may be substantially to lessen competition, or to tend to create a monopoly. . . .'

CASE 17–1. The Electrical Price Conspiracy Cases and General Electric Directive 20.5*

On February 6 and 7, 1961, Judge J. Cullen Ganey, in the U.S. District Court in Philadelphia, fined 29 corporations engaged in the manufacture of electrical equipment a total of $1,787,000 (General Electric paying $437,500; Westinghouse, $372,500). In addition he fined 44 executives of these firms $137,500, and sentenced 30 of these men to 30 days in jail. All but seven were given suspended sentences "reluctantly," Judge Ganey said, because of the defendant's age, health, or family situation. The seven ordered to jail the following week included three men from GE, two from Westinghouse, and one each from Cutler-Hammer, Inc., and

---

* The authors acknowledge the assistance of Clarkson students John Thorne and David Banker in securing material for this case which has been prepared from various news and other sources of the time and from General Electric's Policy Directive 20.5.

Clark Controller Company. (Eight of the suspended jail sentences went to GE men.)

The sentencing by Judge Ganey brought to a close the first phase of the antitrust suits brought a year earlier in Judge Ganey's courtroom by Attorney General William Rogers and his Antitrust Division head, Robert Bicks. The sentences ended the criminal cases brought by the federal government, but still remaining were civil suits concerned with the same offenses. Companies involved in criminal cases may be fined up to $50,000 for each offense; individuals may be fined up to $10,000 and sentenced to a year in prison, or both. Most of Judge Ganey's sentences were less than those recommended by the government prosecutors. No testimony about the alleged offenses had been heard by Judge Ganey, since all defendants had pleaded either guilty (in the seven suits regarded as "major" by the Department of Justice), or nolo contendere (no contest, admitting no guilt but not fighting the charges) in the remaining 13 suits. Yet to be filed were numerous suits by purchasers of equipment against the manufacturers as a consequence of the sentences. Such suits would allege overpayments by these purchasers coupled with a demand for reimbursement and perhaps for treble damages as well.

The case had begun with the empaneling in 1959 of a grand jury in Philadelphia to hear evidence presented by the Antitrust Division, subpoena documents (since it was to consider the return of criminal indictments), and subpoena individuals. A second grand jury was empaneled in mid-November, 1959. More and more evidence was presented to the two grand juries; and on February 16 and 17, 1960, they handed down the first 7 indictments, charging 40 companies and 18 individuals with fixing prices or dividing the market. Thirteen more indictments followed during 1960. The Justice Department filed a deposition opposing the acceptance of nolo pleas, and Judge Ganey so ruled at the arraignment on the first seven indictments in April, 1960. At that time, Allis-Chalmers and its employees pleaded "guilty"; most others pleaded "not guilty." As more evidence came to the attention of the companies involved, however, an effort at rapid settlement was made. On October 31, 1960, attorneys for the companies and for the Justice Department worked out a package of guilty pleas in the seven major cases and nolo pleas in the others. These pleas were heard and accepted by Judge Ganey in December, 1960, and the stage was set for the sentencing in February, 1961.

In announcing the sentences, Judge Ganey stated:

This is a shocking indictment of a vast section of our economy, for what is really at stake here is the survival of the kind of economy under which America has grown to greatness, the free enterprise system.

The conduct of the corporate and individual defendants alike, in the words of the distinguished assistant attorney general [Bicks] who headed the Antitrust Division of the Department of Justice, have flagrantly mocked the image of that economic system of free enterprise which we profess to the country and destroyed the model which we offer today as a free world alternative to state control and eventual dictatorship. Some extent of the vastness of the schemes for price fixing, bid rigging and job allocations can be gleaned from the fact that the annual corporate sales covered by these bills of indictment represent a billion and three-quarter dollars. . . .

It is not to be taken as disparaging of the long and arduous effort the Government has made, and even more the highly efficient and competent manner of its doing, that only in these instances where ultimate responsibility for corporate conduct amongst those indicted, vested, are prison sentences to be imposed. Rather am I convinced that in the great number of these defendants' cases, they were torn between conscience and an approved corporate policy, with the rewarding objectives of promotion, comfortable security and large salaries—in short, the organization or the company man, the conformist, who goes along with his superiors and finds balm for his conscience in additional comforts and the security of his place in the corporate set-up."[19]

Some Facts Concerning the Price Conspiracies

The electrical conspiracy involved numerous independent agreements to fix prices on particular types of electrical equipment. At the time of the initial jury investigation, some of the conspiracies had been in operation for as long as eight years. Twenty-nine manufacturers of electrical equipment were involved including such firms as General Electric, Westinghouse, and Allis-Chalmers. Prices were fixed on electrical equipment ranging in size and value from $2 insulators to multi-million dollar turbines. As indicated by Judge Ganey's summary, annual sales of the products involved at one time or another in the charges was $1,750,000,000.[20]

Economic reasons for the price fixing included these: During the 50s the entire industry was plagued with overcapacity. The major manufacturers were faced with increased competition from smaller manufacturers who began broadening their product lines. The industry's position was further weakened by the wide usage of the competitive sealed bid. Competitive bidding in some cases had resulted in price quotations on heavy equipment that gave discounts as high as 50 percent off list. General Electric, the major company involved and the one without which the conspiracy could not have taken place, faced organizational problems.

The company had been reorganized into a decentralized structure in

---

[19] These introductory paragraphs were prepared by Dr. John A. Larson from contemporary news reports as an introduction to case MR216R1 of the Northwestern University School of Business.

[20] "The Incredible Electrical Conspiracy," *Fortune,* April, 1961, p. 132 summarizes many of these.

1950 when Ralph Cordiner took over as president. General Electric was divided into 110 nearly autonomous companies. The head of each company was given responsibility for operating results as well as the price level on goods his branch produced. Under Cordiner, the company heads were faced with strong pressure to increase profits as a percentage of sales and at the same time to increase sales volume. Given the intense competition and overcapacity, these goals were incompatible. One approach accepted by several General Electric managers was to meet with officials from other companies and to predetermine price levels. An important example involved price fixing on switch gear equipment. Between 1951 and 1958 the conspiracy affected some $650 million worth of sales. Sales were broken down into two categories—sealed and open bids. The sealed bid business was divided among four companies (the only producers in the United States at that time) on a fixed percentage basis. General Electric was allotted 45 percent; Westinghouse, 35 percent; Allis-Chalmers, 10 percent; and Federal Pacific, 10 percent. Meetings were held periodically to determine who would get what bids and what the price should be for the prechosen successful bidder.

The open bid market was controlled by upper level executives (general managers and vice presidents) who met to set book prices. (Attendance lists at these meetings were called Christmas card lists and meetings were called, oddly enough, "choir practices." Each company was given a code number; GE–1, Westinghouse–2, Allis-Chalmers–3, Federal Pacific–7, to be used for telephone communication. The companies were tempted to and often did break the rules by secretly setting lower prices on bids. Occasionally one of the companies would become dissatisfied with its market share and would go it alone on the open market for a period of time. In late 1953 General Electric dropped out of the conspiracy. In 1954–55, the famous "white sale" occurred in which prices on all types of electrical equipment were discounted by as much as 45 percent off book. Hard hit by the sale, the General Electric switch gear division decided to reactivate the old cartel arrangements which were reasonably successful in 1956 and early 1957. These arrangements broke down in 1957 when a discount violating the agreement by Westinghouse instituted a chain reaction that resulted in a price war similar to that of 1954–55.

In 1958 the cartel was reborn with revised shares for sealed bids. General Electric was reduced from 45 percent to 40.3 percent, Westinghouse from 35 percent to 31.3 percent and Allis-Chalmers from 10 percent to 8.8 percent. Federal Pacific was increased to 15.6 percent, and I-T-E received a 4 percent allotment. This last stage relied upon a formula based on the phases of the moon to determine successful bidders and prices.

The year 1959 was the beginning of the end for the electrical conspiracies. The T.V.A. had become extremely suspicious concerning the almost identical bids and rapid price hikes on turbine generators and had informed the federal government of its suspicions. The Antitrust Division was able to build up evidence by using relevant documents that had been obtained under subpoena to get testimony from individuals with lesser involvement. The ultimate object was to determine whether the major manufacturers and top executives were active participants in the conspiracy. As William Maher, chief of the Antitrust's Division at Philadelphia, put it, the idea was to "go after the biggest fish in the smallest companies, then hope to get enough information to land the biggest fish in the biggest companies."[21]

General Electric Directive 20.5

General Electric had a specific, written "Directive Policy," which could not be rescinded or changed by any member of management, for compliance with the antitrust laws. It had originally been issued in 1946 and in an amended version at the time of the antitrust trials it was a one page document. It briefly stated the need for a Directive Policy because of the decentralization of the company and of the substantial injuries to the company that could result from "expensive litigation, treble damage liability, and injunctions or orders affecting its property and business."

The Directive Policy itself was a few short paragraphs stating:

It is the Policy of the Company to comply strictly in all respects with the anti-trust laws. There shall be no exception to this Policy nor shall it be compromised or qualified by anyone acting for or on behalf of the Company.

No employee shall enter into any understanding, agreement, plan or scheme, expressed or implied, formal or informal, with any competitor, in regard to prices, terms or conditions of sale, production, distribution, territories or customers; nor exchange or discuss with a competitor prices, terms or conditions of sale or any other competitive information; nor engage in any other conduct which in the opinion of the Company's counsel violates any of the anti-trust laws.

Each employee responsible for the Company's conduct or practices which may involve the application of the anti-trust laws should consult and be guided by the advice of counsel assigned to his component.

Where an employee who has acted in good faith upon the advice of counsel for the Company nevertheless becomes involved in an anti-trust proceeding, the Company will be prepared to assist and defend the employee through attorneys representing the Company in the case. However, if an employee is convicted of violating the law, the Company cannot as a matter of law save the employee from whatever punishment the court may impose upon him as a consequence of such conviction.

---

[21] *Fortune,* May, 1961, p. 163.

It is the obligation of each employee of the Company in his area of responsibility to adhere to the above stated Policy.

The fact that the policy had not been a complete success was indicated by 36 successful antitrust suits against General Electric since 1941.

Dealing with the Convicted Executives

One of the troublesome issues that Ralph Cordiner, then chairman of the board of General Electric, had to face was that of company sanctions against the executives involved. In January, 1960, he stated that after careful consideration,

I came to the only possible conclusion: that the Company could not ignore such flagrant disregard of the Company Directive Policy 20.5. . . .

A man who is General Manager has tremendous ethical responsibilities. He must also be held accountable for his own performance and the performance of his Component. Thus I concluded that the persons responsible for these violations of Company policy must be disciplined by such penalties as resignations from their officership, removal from their present assignments, demotion in rank, decrease in pay, and assignment to positions where the offenders can have no authority or responsibility for pricing. These penalties are being imposed as rapidly as the cases of violation can be fairly reviewed and as the restaffing can be carried out consistent with maintaining service to customers and protecting the jobs of innocent employees.[22]

Within two months of the time of the sentencing, all 16 executives of General Electric had resigned from the company, and later interviews indicated that at least some of the resignations were forced. Other corporate defendants were much more lenient than General Electric, and in most cases their convicted executives continued their roles with the company. They justified this leniency on the grounds that the executives had been punished sufficiently and had essentially been acting in their companies' interests as they saw them.

Top Management's Responsibility

One of the most embarrassing aspects of the case to the top management of General Electric were the questions raised as to how it could have been unaware of price conspiracies that were so widespread. Senator Estes Kefauver addressed Mr. Cordiner after a congressional hearing in which Cordiner had testified as follows: "It is hard to understand how you in sales and executive positions did not find out and know about or

---

[22] Speech of Ralph G. Cordiner at General Electric Management Conference, Hot Springs, Va., January 5, 1960.

were not put on your suspicion about these meetings with competitors until so late in the game."[23]

John Brooks wrote a satirical article, "The Curious Wink," for the *New Yorker*[24] whose theme was the apparent difficulty of communication in General Electric and raised the question of whether the administration of Directive Policy 20.5 was sometimes conducted with a wink.

At the 1961 stockholders' meeting, resolutions offered by James B. Carey, president of the International Union of Electrical, Radio and Machine Workers were decisively beaten. One proposed:

Resolved that the Directors of General Electric Company appoint an impartial committee of recognized integrity, none of the members of which is an officer, director or employee of the Company, to investigate and determine (1) whether the Chairman of the Board, any other directors, or any officers of the Company reasonably should have known of the existence of the conspiracy to violate the Federal anti-trust laws prior to the 1960 indictments; and (2) whether the Incentive Compensation Plan or any other incentive policies of the Company serve to encourage its officers and employees to engage in such conduct. . . .[25]

The Civil Suits and Consent Decrees

In addition to the criminal suits, the electrical companies were subject to 18 civil suits covering the conspiracies. The government's purpose was to get court injunctions against the practices involved that would permit quicker and more rigorous action since future violations could be adjudged as being in contempt of court. Rather than going to trial, the companies chose to negotiate consent decrees. After tough bargaining with the Justice Department, all 18 suits were settled by consent decrees on September 25, 1962; General Electric agreed to such provisions as the issuance of new price lists, independently arrived at, for each of the 18 product lines (involving about $500,000,000 in annual sales), the submitting of affidavits swearing each sealed bid to the government was made independently, and the selling of component parts to less integrated manufacturers.

The Private Treble Damage Suits

Altogether 2,000 suits were filed, mostly by utility companies. Proving damages was not simple particularly since there was no trial record

---

[23] Hearing of the Subcommittee on Antitrust and Monopoly of the Senate Judiciary Committee, June 5, 1961.

[24] John Brooks, "The Curious Wink," *New Yorker*, May 26, 1967.

[25] *General Electric Notice of Annual Meeting and Proxy Statement*, March 17, 1961, pp. 23–24. This notice included a lengthy review of the antitrust cases.

because all of the criminal cases had been settled by "guilty" or "nolo contendere" pleas. The basic principle was to try to establish the difference between what prices would have been without the conspiracy and with it. The first settlement by General Electric was for $7,470,000 on government purchases mostly by the T.V.A. This represented a little over 10 percent of purchases of $69,600,000 of GE products covered by the suits. General Electric did not concede that customers had been damaged but pushed a policy that it was worth money to compromise to get cases settled. By 1965 most of the major suits were settled. General Electric had paid out $225 million and estimated that this would be 99 percent of the total. (About $110 million had been paid by Westinghouse and $45 million by Allis-Chalmers.)[26]

Company Policy 20.5, as of June 8, 1964

This postconspiracy version of the directive was expanded to four pages with two additional pages outlining the procedures for compliance. It included an acknowledgment sheet for the employee to sign. This indicated his understanding and compliance. A second signature was required by a manager who thus indicated he had reviewed the policy with the individual. Along with the directive were 19 pages summarizing the provisions and giving guides for compliance with Sections 1 and 2 of the Sherman Act; Sections 2 (as amended by the Robinson-Patman Act), 3, and 7 (as amended in 1950) of the Clayton Act; and Section 5 of the Federal Trade Commission Act.

Added provisions to the Directive Policy itself that seem to reflect the convictions of 1961 include:[27]

As to Need:

The character of our free society and the unmatched success of the economy of the United States is based solidly on the concept of a free and competitive market. The future of the General Electric Company depends upon the continued existence of such a free, competitive market. Our growth and success will reflect the extent to which we are able to innovate, to provide superior products and services to our customers and to show competitive initiative in all areas of the Company's business. In General Electric, the only effective and enduring business philosophy is one of fair, vigorous competition. As a matter of good business judgment, there is no excuse for collusive activities in violation of the antitrust laws. As a matter of economic, ethical and legal principle, it is the unequivocal policy of the Company to avoid actions which in any way restrain or restrict competition in violation of the antitrust laws.

---

[26] "The High Cost of Price-Fixing," *Time,* September 10, 1965.

[27] "Directive Policy on the Compliance by the Company and Its Employees with the Antitrust Laws," June 8, 1964, General Electric Co., pp. 1–3, 7, 15.

As to Application:

The provisions of this Directive Policy prescribe mandatory courses of action upon all Company officers and managers. No employee has any authority to act in any manner inconsistent with the provisions of this Directive Policy, to qualify or compromise it, nor to authorize, direct, or condone violations of its terms by another.

As to Relationship with Competitors:

. . . no employee shall give to or accept from a competitor, nor discuss with a competitor, any information concerning prices, terms or conditions of sale, or other competitive information.

As to Company Discipline:

Any employee who violates, or who orders or knowingly permits a subordinate to violate, this Policy, shall be subject to severe disciplinary or other appropriate action, including discharge.

Similarly the Procedure for Compliance provisions seemed influenced by the case in the following provisions:

As to Auditors:

At the request of the General Counsel and in consultation with him, the Comptroller has devised and put into effect a continuing program whereby the Traveling Auditors on his staff expand the scope of their regular audits to examine in depth any records which may indicate the failure of employees to abide by the Company's Directive Policy 20.5.

As to Supervision:

Furthermore, it is the basic responsibility of each Manager to ask each employee, directly, any specific questions concerning the subject matter of, and compliance with, Directive Policy 20.5 which may seem appropriate in the light of the duties of the particular employee. . . . It is one objective of this procedure to develop at an early state information on any areas of operations which are generating doubts among our own people before such doubts arise outside the Company. . . .

Careful examination and inquiry will continuously be made by each General Manager into any circumstances which might evidence lack of vigorous competition in the business of any Department.

Guides to Compliance:

For Section 1 of the Sherman Act the following guides to relationship with competitors were given:

Compete vigorously and independently at *all* times and in *every* ethical way.

Maintain your own freedom to compete by avoiding any kind of agreements or "gentlemen's understandings" with representatives of competitors . . .

Act at all times so your customers, the public and the trade press will know that you are competing vigorously . . .

Secure from the market place—and not from competitors—as much "competitive intelligence" about your competition as you ethically can.

Vigorous competition frequently produces or compels similarity or identity of competitor's prices, programs or policies. Your business records should be such as to demonstrate that decisions concerning your prices, policies and programs are the result of your *independent* judgment, and not agreements or understandings with others.

Questions

1. What three legal weapons were available to the government and injured parties under Section 1? What decisions did General Electric have to make upon how to confront each?
2. The production of electrical equipment involves heavy capital and other fixed costs. Discuss the apparent demand and cost situation in the 1950s that made conspiracy particularly tempting.
3. How might the revisions in policy statement 20.5 make it more effective?

CASE 17–2. Telex versus IBM: The Problem of Plug Compatible Peripherals[28]

"In the constellation of multinational corporations," wrote William Rodgers, "International Business Machines illuminates the economic firmament more than any other."[29] In early 1974, IBM's 575,000 stockholders owned 146,061,750 shares with a sale value of $36.5 billion. IBM was marketing its products in four out of every five nations on earth. It ranked sixth among U.S. corporations in total revenue. Predicted by some to become the world's largest corporation by the end of the century, IBM's net income for the second quarter of 1974 was up 35 percent from the year before, the highest such increase in the company's history.

This was hardly the description of a firm in trouble. Yet in recent years, IBM has undeniably fallen in uncomfortable straits. Its most serious problems have been of a legal nature and, ironically, stem to a large degree from its own incredible success. By a combination of marketing genius, technological wizardry and both proved and alleged anticompetitive business practice, IBM has captured and maintained between 70

---

[28] In the technical jargon of the day, plug compatible peripherals are ancillary equipment such as memory units that can be used with, that is, plugged into, the main computer unit. The body of the case was written by Daniel H. Forbush, and the authors express their appreciation for his permission to edit and use it.

[29] William Rodgers, "IBM on Trial," *Harpers,* May, 1974, p. 79.

percent to 80 percent control of the domestic computer business and half the world market. IBM has become a potential antitrust defendant.

The Antitrust Assault

The assault came on two main fronts. The first attack came from the Justice Department on the last business day of the Johnson administration. For monopolizing the electronic data processing industry, and particularly the mainframe market, the government sought a radical restructuring of IBM into "several, discrete, competitive entities."

It was not the first time that IBM and the Justice Department have confronted each other. In 1935 IBM was found guilty by a federal court of illegally requiring lessees of its tabulating machines to buy punch cards exclusively from IBM. In 1952 the Justice Department charged IBM with monopolizing the tabulating-machine business itself but a trial was averted when IBM accepted a consent decree from government lawyers four years later.

A less drastic but costly threat to IBM is the second source of legal attacks the giant must defend itself against—its bloodied competition, Control Data Corporation, which pioneered the development of huge computers, filed against IBM in late 1968, a month before the Justice Department. It charged IBM with, among other things, attempting to ruin Control Data's market by announcing large computers it had no intention of producing (as Control Data put it, "paper machines and phantom computers"). The case was later settled out of court with IBM paying Control Data roughly $110 million and Control Data turning over to IBM the $3 million index of internal IBM documents it had made in preparation for the case. Since then, other firms have followed Control Data's lead. In the spring of 1974, a total of 12 punitive and triple-damage suits were pending against IBM, seeking a collective $4.3 billion.[30]

Large as that sum may seem, it could go higher. IBM lost a monopolization suit to the Telex Corporation in 1973 and was assessed $259 million in damages. It faces a rash of additional suits from other manufacturers of computer accessories if the verdict withstands IBM's appeal. As many as 40 firms, according to a 1974 estimate, were in position to file. With a catalogue of IBM's anticompetitive practices already on the record as a result of the Telex action (it obtained 40,000 internal IBM documents to make its case), all a potential litigant needs, "is a Xerox machine and a month of discovery to bring the record up to date."[31]

---

[30] Ibid., p. 81.

[31] The estimator and source of the quotation is Jack Biddle, executive director of the Computor Industry Association, as quoted in *Business Week*, September 22, 1973, pp. 18–20.

The Telex case involved a far narrower issue than the Justice Department suit. While the government accused IBM of a broad range of monopolistic practices in a number of computer markets, the Telex decision dealt only with IBM's dominance and marketing practices in accessories for IBM's own computers. These accessories are such peripheral "plug compatible" products as magnetic tape and disk storage devices (upon which information is stored and fed into the "mainframe" or "central processing unit"), main memories, printers, and communication controllers.

In further contrast to the government's suit, which considers IBM's behavior over an extended period, the time frame of the Telex suit is just four years—1969 through the recession in 1970 and 1971 to recovery in 1972. This was a critical time for the industry, bringing the first serious sales downturn it had ever suffered. Revenue rose 6 percent or less in 1970 and 1971 compared to regular annual increases of 10 percent before 1969. Total shipments of new equipment actually dropped slightly in 1970. IBM was additionally pressed by the infant independent peripheral manufacturers who, offering products equivalent to IBM's at lower prices, found ready acceptance by budget-conscious computer users. For its attempt to "destroy" this new competition by predatory pricing practices and market strategy "bearing no relationship to technological skill, industry, appropriate foresight, or customer benefit," Judge A. Sherman Christensen found IBM in violation of Section 2 of the Sherman Act.

The Plug Compatible Problem

The origin of IBM's plug compatible competition was uncomplicated. Du Pont, discontented in 1966 with an IBM refusal to lower its price on a tape drive, asked Telex, a relatively small communications outfit based in Tulsa, Oklahoma, to copy the device. Others spotted their opportunity in the field and moved in. Output grew rapidly in the latter part of the 1960s, and the independents moved into production of the newer, faster disk drives in addition to the tape units. By the turn of the decade, plug compatible equipment was recognized as an important market in itself.[32]

"Their business strategy was magnificently simple," says *Fortune* magazine of the peripherals. "Copy and, where possible, improve upon an IBM design, and undersell IBM to its own customers."[33] Through "reverse engineering," which meant simply purchasing a device from IBM, disassembling it, and erecting an assembly line to produce a similar

---

[32] Except when other citations are given, text material is based on the opinion of Judge A. Sherman Christensen handed down in the United States District Court, Tulsa, Okla. (September 17, 1973).

[33] Louis Beman "IBM's Travails in Lilliput," *Fortune*, November, 1973, pp. 148–50.

machine, the independents offered savings of about 20 percent on IBM equivalents. Frequently they offered a better product as well. While IBM, making its pitch as a "total systems vendor," hung on to the large majority of the market share, sophisticated users turned increasingly to the independents.

For the independents, 1970 was a heady year. In that year they shipped half of all disk and tape drives they had ever installed. The purchase value of the plug compatible manufacturers doubled in the period, from $150 million at the end of 1969 to more than $300 million by the end of 1970. Of the tape drives attached to IBM mainframes in 1976, 13 percent had been installed by independents, while 6 percent of the disk drives had been installed by independents. This was in a market that only a few years before had been 100 percent IBM's.

How did the independents penetrate the once exclusive province of IBM so quickly? For one thing, IBM's pricing policies, which yielded profits as high as 50 percent on some items, created an umbrella wide enough for the peripheral manufacturers to slip beneath. In addition, IBM failed to devote the same development effort to its peripherals that it did to the development of its mainframes. As a result, most of IBM's peripheral products were regarded as inferior, even by IBM management. In a frank evaluation of 26 pieces of equipment in its own product line, IBM judged 16 as deficient, 4 superior, and 6 as equal to the competition.[34]

The incursion by the independents might seem to testify against IBM's possession of undue market power. But it was not until 1970 that IBM took steps to counter the problem. When the U.S. Budget Bureau advised government agencies to switch to non-IBM peripherals in early 1970, concerned IBM executives became alarmed. In February, the peripheral problem was designated a "key corporate strategic issue," and a month later a "peripherals task force" was appointed to, among other things, recommend product strategies to impede the growth of the competition.

The task force urged counteraction in the form of faster development of its peripheral products including improvements midway through a product's life cycle. Called "mid-life enhancements," the improvements were intended to make competitors' inventories obsolete. The task force further recommended consideration of price changes. This advice was put into effect in September, 1970, when IBM announced a new bargain-priced disk drive publicly called the 2319A. Internally, however, it was known as "the Mallard" and actually was nothing more than a reworked disk drive first delivered over three years earlier. But this time the device was priced about 25 percent lower and was available only to customers

---

[34] Rodgers, "IBM on Trial," pp. 82–83.

buying or leasing new systems. It fit only one new IBM computer. The object of Mallard was to reach those customers who were looking for lower prices—and who were thus most susceptible to buying from IBM's competition—without cutting prices for all users. That route would have reduced IBM's revenue by an estimated $120 million a year.[35]

By the fall of 1970, a second peripherals task force had concluded that Memorex and Telex were IBM's strongest competitors in disk drives. It was demonstrated that should IBM cut prices on its other disk drives to a point below the price of the plug compatible equivalents, Memorex and Telex too would have to cut prices with a "very serious impact" on the profits and revenues of both.

In December, IBM broadened its price reductions to all its disk devices. As expected, the independents dropped their prices and, as expected, they were hurt. But from February 12 to April 9, 1971, they increased their installation of disk drives more than 50 percent and threatened to erode IBM's control over printers and memories. Telex still appeared to IBM as a "viable" competitor that could "manage impressive earnings." Clearly, a stronger remedy was required.

It came in late May in the announcement of the "Fixed Term Plan," which called for extended leases of IBM peripherals at sharply reduced rates. To offset the losses in revenue, IBM called for a 3 percent to 8 percent increase in the price of its central processing units. Under FTP, for customers willing to lease IBM peripherals for one or two years, the saving was 8 or 16 percent respectively. For some users, the saving went as high as 30 percent because extra-use charges on IBM computers were also eliminated. "It's a shocker," said a New York securities analyst at the time. "IBM is just wrecking the profitability of the whole area."[36]

FTP was indeed strong medicine. As it turned out, it was also the cure. IBM's Commercial Analysis Section, described as "a kind of corporate CIA," reported happily at the end of the year that the monthly sales of the plug compatibles were off 48 percent in disks and 62 percent in tapes. Badly battered, Telex filed suit against IBM on January 21, 1972.

Provision of the Judge's Decision

The day Judge Christensen announced his decision in Tulsa's District Court—September 17, 1973—the level of IBM stock plunged 26 points. The firm was in shock. From its point of view, the plug compatibles were parasites who would not even have had a market if not for IBM's mainframes. Cutting prices and temporarily lowering profits—swallowing "whatever financial pills are required . . . irrespective of financial considerations of one or two years," as Chairman Thomas Watson, Jr. urged

---

[35] Beman, "IBM's Travails in Lilliput."

[36] *Business Week*, September 22, 1973, p. 19.

in a particularly damaging memo—seemed natural to IBM if that would make its competitors reluctant to challenge its dominance again. According to *Fortune* magazine, IBM's lawyers were so certain of their legal grounds they made no serious effort to settle out of court with Telex.[37] The Greyhound Corporation, after all, had filed charges against IBM in 1970 and the judge not only dismissed the complaint but complimented IBM for its diligence and competence. Christensen rejected IBM's contention that the relevant market in the case was the entire electronic data processing industry. Instead, he limited it to peripheral devices plug compatible with IBM central processing units.

"If the percentage of a relevant market controlled by an alleged monopolist is high, an inference of market power may be drawn," he ruled. "Market power," he said, "was simply the economic ability to charge unreasonable high prices and to exclude competition." According to its own documents, IBM in 1970 sold or leased 80 percent of the tape drives, 94 percent of the disk drives, and 99 percent of the impact printers that were plugged into its central units. These shares of the relevant submarkets combined with testimony concerning the effects of IBM's predatory practices on its plug compatible competition led Christensen to the guilty verdict:[38]

To ". . . obviate the found monopoly, and to restore a healthy competitive climate within a reasonable time," Christensen ordered IBM to do the following:

—Pay Telex $352 million (this was later revised to $259 million).
—Price all the functionally different devices that go into a computer system separately and to apply "substantially uniform" markups over actual costs of development, manufacture, and marketing of each unit.
—Establish separate prices for existing central processors and memories, which previously had been priced together.
—Eliminate all penalty payments on customers for premature termination of long-term lease agreements, providing customers give 90 days' notice of termination. This provision shall be limited to a three-year period and is intended to open the market for competitive substitution.
—Refrain from all predatory pricing, leasing, or other practices or strategies intended to obtain or maintain a monopoly of the market for equipment compatible with its computers, or any relevant submarket.

---

[37] Beman, "IBM's Travails in Lilliput."

[38] Actually, both parties were found guilty, IBM of the anticompetitive practices already ennumerated and Telex of violating copyrights and misappropriating trade secrets. For its transgressions, Telex was ordered by Judge Christensen to pay IBM damages of $21.9 million. In January 1975 the U.S. Court of Appeals reversed the decision, ruling that IBM had only followed ordinary marketing methods. Telex planned an appeal to the Supreme Court.

Questions

1. How do the business operations of Telex and similar equipment manufacturers serve the economy?
2. How can IBM's actions be interpreted as vigorously competitive actions? How did its dominant position in computers indicate to the court that this action, nevertheless, would reduce competition?
3. Given the past reluctance of the courts to order dissolution of technology-based monopolizers, it seems likely that the Justice department case may settle for a consent decree. From the Telex experience, what restrictions on future activities in peripherals and software might be acceptable to both IBM and the government? (You may be able to check your answer with the terms of a completed settlement.)

CASE 17–3. The 1956 Consent Decree of American Telephone & Telegraph Company

Introduction

The consent decree (a court order issued without trial with the consent of all parties) has become the method of settling the majority of the recent civil suits brought under the antitrust laws, and several leading firms, including American Can Company and International Business Machines, have agreed to the compulsory licensing of long lists of patents. The American Telephone & Telegraph consent decree of 1956 falls into this category, in which part of the government's contention is that the sheer aggregation of patents in a field of technology adds up to more monopoly power than the individual patents were designed to grant. Both the government and management face interesting decisions in their willingness to accept such decrees. The government must weigh economy and quicker, surer relief against the possibilities of losing an effective precedent for subsequent cases, of failing to develop a record that would provide a basis for private treble-damage suits, and of settling for limited remedies. Management may gain from the avoidance of more severe penalties from public or private litigation, from better public relations, and from a friendlier climate for establishing standards of conduct in the "gray" areas left by the uncertainties in the meaning and application of antitrust laws. These gains must be weighed against the stringency of the remedies it accepts.

The Concentration of Patents and Compulsory Licensing. Action to monopolize patents through agreement between separate companies has been long considered illegal. The Hartford-Empire case in 1945 was the first that called for compulsory licensing of the patents by decree of the Supreme Court. Even more recently has the undue concentration of patents by one firm in an industry been found illegal. The government charged the United Shoe Machinery Company, in a case decided in 1953, with being "engaged in a program of engrossing all patents and inventions of importance relating to shoe machinery for the purpose of blanketing the shoe machinery industry with patents under the control of United and thereby suppressing competition in the industry." It was required to grant patents at reasonable royalties.

Several consent decrees have been concluded since the war with leading firms in various industries with compulsory licensing provisions. The typical decree has required royalty-free licensing of past patents and licensing at a reasonable royalty of future patents. The trend has been toward provisions that require the furnishing of the necessary know-how as well, through manuals, drawings, and technical personnel.

The Complaint. The consent decree signed in *United States* v. *Western Electric and A. T. & T.* (1956) involved 8,600 patents of the Bell System. The original complaint, issued in 1949, had charged violations of Sections 1 and 2 of the Sherman Act. Among other specific charges, it maintained that Western Electric had monopolized the production of telephonic apparatus and equipment "by acquiring substantially all basic patents in the field of wire telephony." The Justice Department sought the remedy of dissolution of Western Electric into three companies, to be followed by competitive bidding in the purchase of telephonic equipment. One effect of such dissolution might be to alleviate a regulatory problem brought out in the FCC investigation. Western Electric had been alleged to manufacture about 90 percent of the telephonic equipment in the FCC report. The FCC had concluded that excessive charges made by Western Electric for equipment entered into the operating expenses and property valuations of the regional telephone companies. Rates were then set that yielded somewhat more than a fair return.[39]

Provisions of the Consent Decree[40]

IV. A. The defendants are each enjoined . . . from commencing and after three years . . . continuing . . . to manufacture . . . any equipment which is of a type not sold or leased or intended to be sold or leased to companies of the Bell System. . . .

V. The defendant A. T. & T. is enjoined . . . from engaging . . . in any business other than furnishing common carrier communications service . . . [except where made for government contracts, experiments on new communication devices]. . . .

[39] Federal Communications Commission, *Investigation of the Telephone Industry in the United States,* House Document 340 (Washington, D.C.: U.S. Government Printing Office, 1939), particularly chap. xviii.

[40] *United States* v. *Western Electric and A. T. & T.* (U.S. District Court for New Jersey, January 25, 1956).

IX. Western is ordered . . . to maintain cost accounting methods . . . that affords a valid basis . . . for determining the cost to Western of equipment sold to A. T. & T. and Bell operating companies. . . .

X. The defendants are each ordered . . . to grant . . . to any applicant . . . nonexclusive licenses under . . . all existing and future Bell System patents. . . . Such licenses . . . shall be royalty free under all patents prior to date of the Final Judgment [about 8,000 patents were involved] and to be at reasonable royalties to persons under all other existing and future Bell System patents [but on the condition that such persons will grant licenses to defendants on all patents over which they have control at reasonable royalties]. . . .

XIV. The defendants are each ordered . . . to furnish . . . technical information [relating to use of patents]. . . .

What the Antitrust Suit Consent Decree Means[41]

These questions and answers were prepared as being of interest to the Bell System managers:

1. *What was the government's reason for starting the Antitrust Suit?* When the Federal Government in January 1949 filed its Civil Antitrust Suit under the Sherman Act against AT&T and Western Electric, it alleged that the two companies have unreasonably restrained and monopolized commerce in telephone equipment and supplies.

    The complaint asked that AT&T sell Western and that Western be broken up into three separate companies, that the Bell Companies be restricted to buying their equipment and supplies by competitive bidding, that working relationships between AT&T and the associated companies provided under the license contract be discontinued, that it be made compulsory for AT&T, Western and the Labs to license all patents to all applicants on a nondiscriminatory basis, and that they be required to furnish technical information to licensees under such patents.

2. *What was our answer to this complaint?* AT&T and Western filed an answer asking that the complaint be dismissed. The companies stated that they believe the charges are without foundation. Furthermore, the companies pointed out, the existing relationships and arrangements between the associated companies have been and are of the highest value to the users of the telephone service and to the public generally. We maintained at that time—and we still maintain—that we have done nothing illegal. Entry of this decree does not constitute any evidence or admission to the allegations in the complaint.

3. *What developed after this complaint was filed and we answered it?* This case never actually came to trial. Since 1949 the Bell System has furnished the Justice Department with thousands of pages of documents and exhibits. Discussions over an extended period of time among representatives of AT&T, Western and the Federal Government resulted in the consent decrees, or final judgment, of January 24, 1956.

---

[41] *Management Topics No. 6,* public relations brochure of Northern California area of Pacific Telephone, February 6, 1956 (San Francisco). Some deletions and rearrangements have been made.

4. *Does this decree settle this antitrust matter once and for all?* Yes. In the absence of changed conditions, the issues from the point of view of both the Government and the Bell System are settled.

5. *What effect does the decree have on the organization of the Bell System?* The decree does not affect the general relationship among AT&T, Western Electric, Bell Telephone Laboratories and the associated companies that has been successfully serving the communications needs of our nation and the National Defense for almost 80 years.

    The decree does confine the activities of the System to common carrier communications services. This means those services which are subject to public regulation, with certain specified exceptions.

6. *Does the decree affect our relationships with the Bell Telephone Laboratories or limit in any way the research activities of the Bell Labs?* No, it has no effect at all on our relationships with the Labs—and does not in any way curtail the Labs' activities.

7. *Can Western Electric continue to work on defense jobs, such as NIKE, SAGE, the DEW Line, etc.?* Yes, the decree specifically excludes from the regulation requirement any and all services performed by any unit of the Bell System for the U.S. government and its agencies.

8. *Will the decree adversely affect Bell System revenues?* Revenue losses will not be great in relation to total revenues.

9. *What does the decree specify on Bell System patents?* The decree specifies that W. E. and AT&T are to license all their present and future U.S. patents to all applicants, "with no limit as to time or the use to which they may be put." This makes mandatory our present licensing policy.

    United States patents issued prior to January 24, 1956—and there are about 8,600 of them—are in almost all cases to be licensed royalty-free to all applicants. Any patents issued subsequent to January 24, 1956, are to be licensed to any applicant at reasonable royalties.

10. *Can the Bell System continue to obtain needed licenses under the patents of others?* Yes, applicants for licenses under Bell System patents can be required to grant to the Bell System any licenses the latter wants for use in its common carrier communications business, subject to reasonable royalties.

11. *What important patents are covered by the royalty-free provisions?* A number of basic patents including patents covering such items as transistors, microwave systems, vacuum tubes, carrier systems, coaxial cables and special tubes used in electronic "brains."

12. *What does the decree say about making "technical information" available?* It states that W. E. and AT&T must, in addition to patents, make associated with patents that have been licensed. This information includes Western's manufacturing drawings and specifications relating to equipment that it makes for the Bell System.

13. *How does Bell System management feel about this final judgment?* In commenting on the decree, C. F. Craig, President of the American Telephone and Telegraph Company, said:

    During the seven years since this suit was brought, the Bell System has furnished the Government with extensive information.

While the terms of this decree are stringent they do recognize the position we have held from the beginning that supervision by Federal and State regulatory bodies safeguards the public interest.

We believe the long-standing relationships among the manufacturing, research and operating functions of the Bell System are in the public interest and under the decree they remain intact.

To a very large extent, it is the unique combination and teamwork of the operating companies, the Bell Telephone Laboratories and the Western Electric Company that, over the years, has produced for the people of this country the finest, most widely used and progressive telephone service in the world.

Questions

1. From the admittedly limited presentation available, why were the managements of AT&T and Western Electric willing to accept a consent decree?
2. Has the government a legitimate objection to the mere aggregation of many legal patents by one firm?

CASE 17–4. The Proposed Merger of Bethlehem and Youngstown

The merger proposal of the Bethlehem Steel Corportion and the Youngstown Sheet and Tube Company in 1954 stirred up considerable excitement on the good American grounds of being big and of promising not only one but possibly two major struggles, one between the government and the companies, and the second between Bethlehem and United States Steel.

The merger promised to be the biggest yet in terms of dollar assets— $2.3 billion. Such are the mathematics of growth and inflation that this figure is 50 percent greater than the $1.5 billion (including "water") of the merger creating U.S. Steel in 1901. While 1954 had a bumper crop of big merger proposals, such as Olin Industries–Mathieson Chemicals ($584 million), W. R. Grace & Company–Davidson Chemical ($384 million), Nash-Kelvinator–Hudson ($341 million), and Burlington Mills–Pacific Mills–Goodall-Sanford ($428 million), all of them involved less than one quarter of the assets of the steel merger proposal.

Antitrust and Steel Mergers. The Antitrust Division opened fire by getting a temporary injunction against the merger under the amended Section 7 of the Clayton Act. Its previous record against mergers in the steel industry had not been successful, although it had lost some close decisions. In 1920, nine years after litigation began, its attempt to break up the U.S. Steel combination in a Sherman Act case failed by a four-to-three decision in the Supreme Court. The Federal Trade Commission dropped its Clayton Act case against Bethlehem's acquisition of the Lackawanna Steel Company and of the Midvale Steel and Ordnance Company in the 1920s. After more than doubling its capacity in these mergers, Bethlehem was blocked from taking over Youngstown in 1930 not by the Antitrust Division but by minority stockholders in Youngstown. The government's most recent defeat on the steel merger front had been in the Columbia Steel case, when it charged U.S. Steel with attempting to monopolize when its subsidiary Columbia acquired Consolidated Steel, a West Coast fabricator. The five-to-four setback in the Supreme Court, however, proved helpful in getting Congress to close the loophole in Section 7 of the Clayton Act which, while barring stock acquisitions which may substantially lessen competition or tend to monopoly, permitted the merger of assets.

The second potential struggle which added interest to the Bethlehem-Youngstown proposal was the prospect of Bethlehem invading the Chicago area market and challenging U.S. Steel. Since U.S. Steel had recently opened its Fairless Mills in the eastern seaboard area where Bethlehem had been the leader, the situation had elements of "tit for tat." In its antitrust case, Bethlehem was to lay considerable emphasis on the increase in competition which might follow from its invasion of steel production in the Chicago area.

The Industry and Concentration in Steel Ingot Capacity

The steel industry is usually defined as consisting of the integrated companies which produce pig iron, steel ingots, and rolled steel (of the 24 such companies in 1956, the 15 largest had 86 percent of the total ingot capacity); of the semi-integrated companies (56) that do not produce pig iron; of the nonintegrated companies (128) that buy crude and semifinished steel for rolling; and of the merchant pig iron producers (12) that sell to foundaries and steel makers. There were also about 3,000 iron and steel foundaries in 1956.

The "Big Eight." A picture of considerable stability in concentration is obtained by examining the share of the largest eight producers in steel ingot capacity, which rose from 71 percent in 1904 to 79 percent in 1940 and then declined to 76 percent in 1956 (see Exhibit 17–4A). Actually, since U.S. Steel, with only 48 percent of the capacity, was producing 63 percent of the ingots in 1904 (much of the independent capacity was apparently obsolescent), the indicated rise in concentration after its formation should be discounted.

This statistical stability in concentration has been produced by opposing tendencies. Paramount in the reduction of the share of the largest eight has been the decline in the share of U.S. Steel, a decline that may

EXHIBIT 17–4A

Steel: Share of Leading Companies in Steel Ingot Capacity,
1904–56 (percent)

	1904	1916	1928	1940	1948	1956
Largest firm..................	48.0	47.3	39.7	34.1	33.1	30.6
Next two....................	8.8	9.1	18.7	23.6	23.8	23.6
Next five...................	13.9	15.0	14.3	21.3	20.8	22.0
Largest eight...............	70.8	71.3	72.8	79.0	77.7	76.1

Sources: American Iron and Steel Institute, *Directory of Iron and Steel Works of the United States and Canada* for earlier years, and *Annual Capacities of Coke Ovens, Blast Furnaces and Steelmaking Furnaces as of January 1, 1955, by Companies, States and Districts (United States and Canada)*, pp. 13–15 (as compiled in Simon N. Whitney, *Antitrust Policies* [New York: Twentieth Century Fund, 1958], p. 290).

be coming to an end. Moderate-sized firms have been able to expand vigorously, though no firm through internal growth has been able to add over 4 percent to its share of the market (the size of Inland Steel, which has been the least dependent of the "Big Eight" on mergers). Under the pressure of wartime and regional needs, four firms were able to hurdle the substantial investment requirements and join the ranks of integrated producers since 1940 (Kaiser, Detroit, McLouth and Lone Star).

Forces working to increase concentration have been those behind the decline in the number of companies making steel or pig iron from 500 in 1904 to 220 in 1956. Associated with the needs of advancing technology, integration and larger plant size has been substantial merger activity. For example, Bethlehem which was not in the first ten in 1904 absorbed the third, fourth, sixth, and eighth largest firms of that year. Thirteen acquisitions of Republic Steel during the 1915 to 1945 period accounted for 64 percent of its additions to assets.

The Companies' Case for the Merger: (a) The Affidavit of Arthur B. Homer, President of Bethlehem Steel[42]

[*Growth of Chicago Market.*] Bethlehem's reasons for desiring the merger are simple. They are legitimate business reasons, completely devoid of any anticompetitive or monopolistic intent.

The greatest growth in demand for steel products over the next 15 or 20 years is expected to take place in the Mid-Continent Area, particularly in the region in and around Chicago. For many years the demand for steel products in that region has substantially exceeded the capacity of the plants located there, and it is anticipated that such demand will increase materially with the opening of the St. Lawrence Seaway. The products which are in the shortest

---

[42] This and the following section are excerpts from "Affidavits on Behalf of the Defendants in Opposition to the Plaintiffs Motion for Summary Judgment," September 26, 1957. The government sought and lost the motion.

supply in that region are heavy structural shapes and plates—products which Bethlehem has had wide experience in producing and selling and which are produced in the Mid-Continent Area in a complete range of sizes by only one producer—United States Steel Corporation (U.S. Steel).[43] There also have been recurring shortages in the entire Mid-Continent Area for other products such as tin plate and hot rolled sheets.

Bethlehem, as a major steel producer, has a legitimate desire to serve the Mid-Continent Area, particularly the region of which Chicago is the center, and to be a substantial participant in its growth. It cannot do so effectively from its existing plants in the East and far West because of the freight dis-advantages involved in shipments from those plants to destinations in the Mid-Continent Area. The tonnages that Bethlehem now ships into the Mid-Continent Area constitute a relatively small percentage of the steel products consumed in that Area, and the competition in that Area is dominated by the companies with plants located there. The market in and around the whole Chicago region is virtually out of reach of Bethlehem's Eastern plants as an area of effective competition.

[*Acquisition Only Feasible Approach.*] For sound business reasons, the acquisition by Bethlehem of the Youngstown plants is the only feasible way in which Bethlehem in the foreseeable future can become an effective and substantial competitor in the Mid-Continent Area and help carry out the expansion in that Area which it believes necessary to satisfy the needs of the steel consumers there. Neither Bethlehem nor Youngstown, alone, will be able to provide the expansion that is envisioned as a result of the merger. Under the expansion program as presently projected by Bethlehem, if the merger is carried out, the steel-making capacity of the Youngstown plants would be expanded by 2,588,000 ingot tons annually (602,000 at the Youngstown Plant and 1,986,000 tons at the Chicago Plant).

The existing area of the Chicago Plant is inadequate to accommodate the full expansion scheduled for that plant. Bethlehem has, however, acquired additional property on Lake Michigan which will provide adequate space for the continued expansion of the Chicago Plant. In order to take advantage of the lower cost of expanding existing capacity, finishing facilities will be erected on the new property, which will be supplied with semi-finished steel from the expanded facilities on the existing plant area.

[*Expansion Costs.*] It is estimated that the cost of such expansion of the existing Youngstown plants would be approximately $358,000,000. Because the new capacity would be obtained by expanding existing plants, the cost per ingot ton of such expansion would be approximately $135, and such expansion could be carried out by the merged companies within the present price struc-ture of the industry and within their available financial resources.

The reason why Bethlehem, or any other steel producer, cannot under pres-

---

[43] Of the total, 2,225,000 tons of industry capacity in the Chicago region for plates, U.S. Steel has 54.7 percent and Inland Steel Company (Inland) has 29.7 percent and of the total 1,890,000 tons of industry capacity in that region for struc-tural shapes, U.S. Steel has 55.7 percent and Inland has 24.9 percent. Both U.S. Steel and Inland are in the process of expanding their capacities in the Chicago region for structural shapes and U.S. Steel is also expanding its capacity there for plates.

ent conditions build a large new integrated steel plant in the Chicago region is that the tremendous cost of such a plant would prohibit profitable operations for many years to come. Such a plant, including capacity for the production of raw steel and finishing facilities for a normal range of products, would cost about $300 per ingot ton at today's prices. The average net profits earned in 1956 by the producers with more than 93 percent of the steel-making capacity in the United States (including Bethlehem and Younngstown) were $8.64 per ingot ton of capacity, after average charges per ingot ton of capacity of $5.87 for depreciation and $0.58 for interest. On the basis of capital costs of $300 per ton of ingot capacity for a new plant, depreciation charges on a 4 percent basis would be $12 per ton of ingot capacity and, assuming 60 percent debt financing at a 5 percent rate, interest charges would be $9 per ton of ingot capacity. Depreciation and interest charges for a new plant would thus be $14.65 more than the average of such charges for existing facilities. A new plant would also require a substantial addition to working capital and would entail large nonrecurring expenses customarily incurred in starting up new facilities.[44]

It is easy to see, therefore, why the one feasible way to accomplish large-scale increases in capacity is through the expansion of existing plants. That is the only way in which in the last ten years companies other than U.S. Steel have been able to keep the cost of their expansion within manageable bounds. That is the only way in which it will be possible in the future for Bethlehem, and companies smaller than Bethlehem, to create significant new capacity without completely distorting the cost of capital facilities. It is, of course, in the public interest that new capacity required to supply the demand for steel be provided at the lowest possible cost, because, in the end, the cost of facilities must be repaid by the public through the prices paid for steel products or otherwise.

U.S. Steel several years ago was able to build a new integrated plant at Fairless Hills, Pennsylvania, which has a present ingot capacity of 2,200,000 tons and is estimated to have cost upwards of $600,000,000. But the cost of that plant was much smaller in relation to the total physical and financial assets of U.S. Steel than the cost of such a plant would be in relation to Bethlehem or any other steel producer; hence it did not distort U.S. Steel's financial situation to the same degree as it would in the case of any other producer. Furthermore, U.S. Steel received Government aid (not now available to the rest of the industry) in constructing the Fairless Hills Plant, in the form of rapid tax amortization for approximately $468,000,000 of the total cost of that plant.

A smaller, less costly plant is not the answer. The necessity for both size and diversity of finishing capacity indicates a sizeable plant. There are substantial economic obstacles to building a small plant for the production of such basic items as structurals, plates, sheets, and bars.

[*Inability of Youngstown to Carry Out Expansion.*] As appears in Mr. McCuskey's affidavit, Youngstown is not in a position alone to carry out the

---

[44] "Financial Analysis of the Steel Industry for 1956," *Steel Magazine,* April 1, 1957.

above outlined expansion program of its plants projected by Bethlehem. The total book value of Youngstown's existing plants, buildings, machinery, and equipment (including construction in progress) is less than $200,000,000, or about $32 per ingot ton of capacity.

Furthermore, Youngstown has not had any previous experience in the heavy structural and plate businesses.

[*Strengthening of Competition.*] Far from having a tendency to lessen competition or to create a monopoly, the merger appears to be the only feasible way in which in the near future necessary substantial additional capacity for the production of steel products in the Mid-Continent Area can be made available *as a new competitive force in the hands of a steel producer other than the existing strongly entrenched companies already dominant in that Area.*

The steel industry today has only one nation-wide steel company—U.S. Steel—which is larger than the next three companies combined, which has important steel production and finishing facilities in all parts of the country and which is in a position to exert strong competitive force in every market area. The merger will result in another company capable of waging effective competition in many of the markets of U.S. Steel, to the benefit of suppliers, customers and the public alike.

The merger will result in salutary strengthening of the forces of competition in the steel industry, and do so without impairing, or even tending to impair, the vigor of competition in any market area and without tending to create a monopoly.

The Companies' Case for the Merger: (b) The Affidavit of George McCuskey, Vice President for Finance, Youngstown Steel

Youngstown desires to consummate the merger with Bethlehem for sound business reasons which are in the public interest and are the complete antithesis of any anticompetitive or monopolistic purpose, objective or result.

[*Geographic Expansion.*] In the first place, the consummation of the merger would enable stockholders of Youngstown to participate in the geographic markets located in the Eastern and Western Areas and also to obtain the benefits of the broad diversification of products now enjoyed by Bethlehem. Bethlehem produces some 35 classes of steel products which Youngstown does not produce.

. . . The complementary aspects of the locations of the Youngstown plants in the Mid-Continent Area and the Bethlehem plants in the Eastern and Western Areas (as well as the locations of their respective geographic areas of effective competition) and of their respective product lines, are unique in the entire steel industry. No two other major steel companies complement each other so completely.

Unless the proposed merger is carried out, Youngstown will not be able to compete effectively in the Eastern and Western Areas without the construction of new basic integrated steel facilities at new locations in those Areas. It is estimated that the cost of constructing such facilities would be approximately $300 per ton of ingot capacity. These facilities would have to compete with existing steel plants which were constructed at a much lower relative cost. It is clear that, under the steel price structure now prevailing and foreseeable, the broadening of the geographic areas in which Youngstown can effectively compete, by the construction of new basic steel plants in new locations, would be unprofitable for many years. It is also clear that the construction of such plants is beyond Youngstown's ability to finance.

Youngstown's other major interest in the merger is that it will provide the greatly increased financial resources necessary to permit the full and prompt development of Youngstown's strategically located properties in the Mid-Continent Area.

[*Diversification Sought, Particularly into Heavy Structurals.*]   For many years Youngstown's management has recognized that it would be desirable and beneficial to increase Youngstown's capacity substantially so as to meet deficits in the local supply of various products in the respective natural markets of Youngstown's Chicago and Ohio plants. Not only would this increased capacity, as such, be of obvious public benefit, but the diversification of products contemplated would have many advantages. Diversification of the product line of a steel plant, such as the Youngstown plant at Chicago or in Ohio, substantially increases (1) the efficiency and economy of plant operation, (2) the stability of plant earnings and employment and (3) the ability of the plant to serve consumers. A broadening of the product line of a steel plant makes it possible more fully and continuously to utilize its steel making or ingot capacity by increasing its production of some, and decreasing its production of other, finished products as the relative volume of the requirements of consumers from time to time shifts among the various finished steel products. . . .

Indicative of this fact, Youngstown's Chicago plant operated at a rate of only 83.0% of capacity during the first six months of 1957, whereas its neighbor, Inland Steel Company, was able to operate at 102.5% of capacity due primarily to its facilities for the manufacture of heavy plates, structurals, and other items in short supply. For the same reasons the Lackawanna and Sparrows Point plants of Bethlehem were able to operate at 97.6% and 102.8% of capacity, respectively, during the same period.

Notwithstanding temporary periods of adequate supply, the demand for important steel products in the home market of Youngstown's Chicago plant has in many years substantially exceeded the capacity of the plants located in the Chicago area. It is estimated that in the next 15 or 20 years the largest growth in the demand for steel products in the United States will be in the Mid-Continent Area and particularly in the Chicago region. This growth will be greatly accelerated and increased by the opening of the St. Lawrence Seaway. . . .

Heavy structural shapes and plates, which Youngstown does not and cannot now make, have been and are in especially short supply in the Chicago region. In that region these products are made by only two large producers—U.S. Steel and Inland Steel—and U.S. Steel alone produces a complete range of sizes. . . .

[*Youngstown's Limited Ability for Financing.*]   To enlarge the facilities of

Youngstown's Chicago and Ohio plants so as to provide the needed increase in capacities and diversification of product lines will require very large capital expenditures. Recent studies indicate that the cost of expanding Youngtown's present facilities to the extent necessary to provide such product diversification and increased capacities would be approximately $350 million.

At the present time Youngstown has a net worth of approximately $400 million. Its present funded debt totals $98 million, in addition to which it has an indirect obligation with respect to 35% of the $308 million funded debt of Erie Mining Company incurred to finance the development of a tremendous taconite project in Minnesota. Even though Youngstown has maintained a strong financial position, it would be manifestly impossible for it alone to secure the necessary financing for a project of the magnitude to be undertaken if the merger is consummated. . . .

[*Contributions to National Defense and Efficiency.*] In my opinion the proposed merger will also result in a substantial increase in the capacity of this country to carry on our national program. Bethlehem has had considerable experience over a period of years in providing our Government with different lines of necessary defense materials and products. This know-how, coupled with the existing and expanded production facilities of Youngstown, will constitute a combination of experience, manpower and plant which will greatly enhance the capabilities of this country to produce materials necessary either for national defense or war.

Another substantial, although less important, result of the proposed merger will be to effect savings in operating costs and to promote efficiency. For example, the merger will eliminate or reduce cross-hauling of iron ore by making it possible to divert Bethlehem's ore production at the head of the Great Lakes to the Youngstown plants in the Mid-Continent Area and to divert Youngstown's ore production in Labrador and Quebec to Bethlehem's plants in the Eastern Area.

[*The Effect of the Merger in Increasing Competition and Serving the Public Interest.*] Contrary to Plantiff's claims, the merger will increase competition and guard against monopoly in the steel industry and will promote the interests of the public and of the companies involved, in the following ways:

First: The merger will make economically feasible the diversification of the product lines and the increase of the capacities of the Chicago and Ohio plants of Youngstown through expansion of their respective facilities, as shown above. The immediate program for expansion of Youngstown's plants upon consummation of the merger is designed to relieve at least in part the present and prospective undersupply of important steel products in the respective home territories of those plants. . . .

Second: In the Chicago region, heavy structural shapes and plates are made by only two producers, of which only one produces a complete range of sizes. Their combined capacities do not nearly meet the local demand for such products. The merger will provide additional effective competition in those products in the Chicago region and is the most feasible means by which a new competitor can enter this market in the near future.

Third: The program for expansion of facilities at the Chicago and Ohio plants of Youngstown which is projected upon consummation of the merger, will provide permanent employment for a large number of persons. . . .

Fourth: Consummation of the merger will not result in the closing of any plant or in curtailing the capacity or production of any plant. . . .

Fifth: Consummation of the merger will enable Youngstown stockholders to share in important markets in the Eastern and Western Areas (in which Youngstown plants cannot effectively compete) and in the benefits of much wider product diversification. It will enable Bethlehem stockholders to share in important markets in the Mid-Continent Area (in which Bethlehem plants cannot effectively compete) and in the benefits of a somewhat broader diversification of products.

The merger will also strengthen the national defense capabilities of this country and will make possible saving in operating costs, illustrated by elimination or reduction of cross-hauling of iron ore. . . .

The Government's Case

The government's brief was a simple one. It had to show that "in any line of commerce" and "in any section of the country" the merger "may substantially lessen competition" or "tend to monopoly." The amended Clayton Act made it clear that the phrase "in any line of commerce" applied to the lessening of competition rather than only to the phrase "tend to monopoly" as in the original act.

Market Share of Shipments of Common Products. The government concentrated on market shares in terms of common finished steel product shipments. It contended that "market shares are the ultimate results of all competitive forces" and that "actual shipments are more significant than plant locations inasmuch as sales achieved represent an ability to overcome 'natural barriers.'"

Since Bethlehem's and Youngstown's production were primarily of common products, although Bethlehem was in heavy structurals and Youngstown was not, and Youngstown emphasized pipe more than Bethlehem, and since both companies shipped to several common areas (this overlap was largely due to Bethlehem's Lackawanna plant at Buffalo and Youngstown's mills at Youngstown), the government was able to present the data shown in Exhibit 17–4B. Figures are percentages of industry total for products produced by both companies.

EXHIBIT 17–4B

	Bethlehem	Youngstown	B-Y
United States	15	5	20
Northeastern states (plus Chicago)	15	5	20
Northeastern states (including Michigan and Ohio)	20–21	3–4	20–25
Michigan, Ohio, Pennsylvania, New York	16–17	4	20–22
Michigan–Ohio	7–9	6	13–15
Michigan	12	3	15
Ohio	5	9–10	15

The government then went on to present evidence that for particular product categories, such as cold-rolled sheets, both Bethlehem and Youngstown were shipping substantial amounts to common customers in common county locations. The government concluded that 7 percent of Bethlehem's sales of all finished steel products and about 8 percent of Youngstown's were of the same products to the same customers in the same states (these percentages take in only the shipments to Michigan and Ohio of sheets and bars, although the denominators are all United States shipments of the respective companies).

The basic government case, then, was simply that if a firm buys out another firm which is making a substantial proportion of its shipments in the same products to the same customers in the same places, it follows that the probability of substantial lessening of competition has been established within the meaning of the Clayton Act. The buyer has one less independent source of supply competing for his trade.

Other Government Arguments. The Antitrust Division supplemented this basic argument based on market shares and numbers with several other points. It pointed out vertical dangers of the merger in such products as wire rope. Bethlehem was integrated to produce and sell wire rope, Youngstown produced rope wire for sale to nonintegrated rope companies and bought wire rope for sale from such companies. The merger could wipe out an independent source of supply for them. It stressed the fact that Bethlehem had always maintained or increased its market share after previous mergers, so that the increase in concentration could be expected to be permanent. No new entrant of Youngstown's size could reasonably be expected in the steel industry.

Antitrust emphasized the irrelevance of the defendants' expansion plans. They might change them unless the court sat in as "an administrative supervisor of the projected expansion," a procedure "foreign to legislative intent." An inquiry into the motives for the merger would mean "no limit to the number of interesting and highly speculative lines of inquiry" which conceivably belong in a Sherman Act proceeding but have no place in a Clayton Act case if the act is to have any meaning. "Finally, insofar as heavy structurals are concerned, why should Youngstown be sacrificed as an important independent competitor in light steel products for the purpose of further entrenching the duopoly of Bethlehem and U.S. Steel in heavy structurals that now exists in the United States (the two had over 75 percent of structural capacity)?"

The Rebuttal of the Companies

Bethlehem and Youngstown sought to combat the government's case not only by stressing the possibilities of meeting U.S. Steel more effectively in Chicago but by suggesting that the government's use of market shares and regional breakdowns exaggerated any negative effects on competition. Their case concentrated on plant locations in three broad regions, the Eastern (15 Atlantic seaboard states), the Mid-Continent, and the Western (seven Far Western states). Bethlehem operated only in the Eastern and Western; Youngstown only in the Mid-Continent, which included Michigan and Ohio. They argued that mills were effective competitors only near the plant because of the high ratios of transportation cost. "In their own territories, the mills set the standards (including price) which distant producers must meet; in serving distant territories, on the other hand . . . to a much greater extent, they merely supply deficiencies in production in those territories rather than fix or influence the setting of standards of competitive performance."[45] The Pittsburgh producing center, with its excess of capacity over local demand, was held to ward off the Eastern and Mid-Continent producers from effective competition with each other.

While the Pittsburgh barrier was not much of a factor for the Lackawanna plant at Buffalo, Lackawanna's advantage was held to be in the Detroit area, while the mills at Youngstown competed effectively in western Michigan.

In dealing with the government's shipment data, the companies emphasized the large shares of other companies in Michigan and Ohio, used years other than 1955, when the overlap in sales had been somewhat higher than usual because of the booming automobile demand, and stressed the Mid-Continent area rather than the government's choice of the Northeastern states. Their conclusion was that "the merger will not materially reduce effective alternative sources of supply" because of a "sufficient number of other producers in a strong competitive position."

United States v. Bethlehem Steel Corporation and Youngstown Sheet Tube Company[46]

To sum up the court's conclusions as to the impact of the merger, it is clear that the acquisition of Youngstown, by Bethlehem, would violate Section 7 in that in each of the relevant markets considered the effect may be substantially to lessen competition or to tend to create a monopoly.

[*Substantial Competition Eliminated.*] The proposed merger would eliminate the present substantial competition between Bethlehem and Youngstown in substantial relevant markets. It would eliminate substantial potential com-

---

[45] This quotation and much of the argument of this section is from the affidavit of C. H. H. Wikel, September 16, 1957 (Civil Action 115–328 before U.S. District Court, Southern District of New York).

[46] U.S. District Court, Southern District of New York, Civil Action No. 115–328, reproduced as the conclusion of Judge Weinfeld's opinion enjoining the proposed merger of the two companies. Opinion delivered on November 21, 1958.

petition between them. It would eliminate a substantial independent alternative source of supply for all steel consumers. It would eliminate Youngstown as a vital source of supply for independent fabricators who are in competition with Bethlehem in the sale of certain fabricated steel products. It would eliminate Youngstown as a substantial buyer of certain fabricated steel products.

[*The Argument as to Beneficial Aspects of the Merger.*]   One final matter remains to be considered. The defendants urge earnestly that in considering the impact on competition of the proposed merger the court take into account what they point to as its beneficial aspects. Any lessening of competition resulting from the merger should be balanced, they say, against the benefits which would accrue from Bethlehem's plants thus creating new steel capacity in an existing deficit area and enhancing the power of the merged company to give United States Steel more effective and vigorous competition than Bethlehem and Youngstown can now give separately.

We pass for the moment the question of whether or not this contention is anything more than an expression of good intention and high purpose.

[*The Shortage of Steel in Chicago Area.*]   The substance of their argument is: the steel mills in and around the Chicago area lack sufficient plant capacity to satisfy demand in that area, especially for heavy structural shapes and plates; these have been in critical short supply for years and the lag has been supplied by distant steel producers at excessive freight costs and premium prices. The defendants contend that the situation will become more acute in the years ahead and that the shortage has already resulted in new steel-consuming industries locating their plants in other regions of the country—a "kind of chain reaction [which] is a wasteful drag on the country's economic resources." The defendants say a remedy is sorely needed "and that the merger will unquestionably provide that remedy." In essence this summarizes their justification for the merger.

[*The Proposal for Expansion in Chicago.*]   What is planned under the proposed merger is an expansion of the ingot capacity of Youngstown's two existing plants, one at Chicago and the other at Youngstown, by 2,588,000 tons, and a new plate mill and a new structural shape mill at Youngstown's Chicago plant with combined capacity of 1,176,000 tons. The plan also provides for a modernization program which would increase capacity to roll certain products at the Chicago and Youngstown plants. This part of the plan is unrelated to the structural shape and plate program.

It is undoubtedly easier and cheaper to acquire and develop existing plant capacity than to build entirely anew. Each defendant in urging the merger takes a dim view of its ability to undertake, on its own, a program to meet the existing and anticipated demand for heavy structural shapes and plates in the Chicago area.

Youngstown claims it is without the know-how, the experienced personnel or the requisite capital to enter into the structural shape and plate business. Bethlehem, acknowledging it has the know-how and the experience in that field, contends that the construction of an entirely new fully integrated plant in the Chicago area of 2,500,000 tons of ingot capacity is not economically feasible. It estimates that such a new plant would cost $750,000,000 (or $300 per ton of ingot capacity) as compared to $358,000,000 (or $135 per ton ingot capacity) for expansion of Youngstown's existing plants under the plan outlined above. Bethlehem also rules out as uneconomical the construction of a new plant in the Chicago area limited to structural shape and plate mills.

The defendants' apprehensions, which, of course, involve matters of business judgment and, in a sense, matters of preference, are not persuasive in the light of their prior activities and history, their financial resources, their growth and demonstrated capacity through the years to meet the challenge of a constantly growing economy.

[*The Expansion Record of Bethlehem.*] Over the decades Bethlehem has grown internally; it has not only maintained but bettered its position in a highly concentrated industry; it has never lacked the financial resources or the effective means required to expand and keep pace with the increased demands of our national economy.

From an ingot capacity of 212,800 tons in 1905 Bethlehem's capacity reached 23,000,000 by January 1, 1958. During the nine-year period from January 1, 1948, to January 1, 1957, it expanded its ingot capacity from 13,800,000 tons to 20,500,000 tons, an increase of 6,700,000 tons or 48.6 percent. Over the five-year period from 1953 to 1958 the percentage increase was 30.7 percent.

The fact is that within one year of the commencement of this action to enjoin the merger, Bethlehem increased its steel capacity by 2,500,000 tons. The significance of this increase is apparent when it is noted that as of January 1, 1957, there were in the United States eighty-four companies with steel ingot capacity, of which seventy-five had a total capacity of less than 2,500,000 tons.

[*The Expansion Record of Youngstown.*] Youngstown no less than Bethlehem has demonstrated ability to keep pace with the demands of our growing economy. Youngstown expanded from an ingot capacity of 806,400 tons in 1906 to 6,500,000 tons by January 1, 1958. During the nine-year period from January 1, 1948, to January 1, 1957, it expanded its ingot capacity from 4,002,000 tons to 6,240,000—an increase of 2,238,000 or 55.9 percent. Over the five-year period from 1953 to 1958 its ingot capacity grew 31.4 percent.

Youngstown, too, has been a vigorous factor in the steel industry. Its position as No. 6 casts it in the role of one of the giants of that mammoth industry. Through the years it has carried on a regular expansion program. In 1955, without regard to the merger, it projected a comprehensive future development plan, part of which has already been put into effect. During the 10-year period, 1947–56, Youngstown made capital expenditures of $530,000,000.

[*Youngstown as a Successful Firm.*] A fact not to be overlooked—indeed one to be underscored—is that no adverse factor justifies Youngstown's participation in the proposed merger. Indeed for a number of years the return on its invested capital was greater than that earned by either United States Steel or Bethlehem. No financial stringency, present or threatened, justifies its absorption by Bethlehem.

[*Alternatives for Meeting Chicago Demand.*] The Court is not persuaded that the proposed merger is the only way in which the supply of plates and shapes in the Chicago area can be expanded. Other steel producers are capable of meeting the challenge. In fact both United States Steel and Inland are in the process of expanding their capacities in the Chicago area for structural shapes and United States Steel is also expanding its capacity for plates in that area.

[*The Failure of the Defendants' Argument.*]   In essence, the defendants are maintaining that a proposed capacity increase of 1,176,000 tons in the Chicago area for plates and structural shapes counterbalances a merger between companies which produced over 24,000,000 tons of ingots and shipped almost 15,000,000 tons of a great variety of finished steel products in 1955. It has already been noted that hot rolled sheets, cold rolled sheets and hot rolled bars are the three most important products of the iron and steel industry and that Bethlehem and Youngstown are substantial and important factors in the production of these key products.

Plates and structural shapes are substantially less important in terms of tonnage than hot and cold rolled sheets and hot rolled bars. Assuming the relevance of the argument, the defendants have failed to establish counterbalancing benefits to offset the substantial lessening of competition which would result from the merger.

Not only do the facts fail to support the defendants' contention, but the argument does not hold up as a matter of law. If the merger offends the statute in any relevant market then good motives and even demonstrable benefits are irrelevant and afford no defense. Section 7 "is violated whether or not actual restraints or monopolies, or the substantial lessening of competition, have occurred or are intended."

[*The Objectives and Application of the Clayton Act.*]   The antitrust laws articulate the policy formulated by Congress. The significance and objectives of the Clayton Act and the 1950 amendment are well documented. In approving the policy embodied in these acts, Congress rejected the alleged advantages of size in favor of the preservation of a competitive system. The consideration to be accorded to benefits of one kind or another in one section or another of the country which may flow from a merger involving a substantial lessening of competition is a matter properly to be urged upon Congress. It is outside the province of the Court. The simple test under Section 7 is whether or not the merger may substantially lessen competition "in any line of commerce in any section of the country."

Any alleged benefit to the steel consumer in the Chicago district because of reduced freight charges and an increased supply cannot, under the law, be bought at the expense of other consumers of numerous other steel products where the effects of the merger violate the act. A merger may have a different impact in different markets—but if the prescribed effect is visited on one or more relevant markets then it matters not what the claimed benefits may be elsewhere.

And for that matter, with respect to oil field equipment and supplies, as separate lines of commerce, the contention itself is by its own terms unavailing. Amended Section 7 as stated in the committee reports ". . . is intended [to prohibit] acquisitions which substantially lessen competition, as well as those which tend to create a monopoly . . . if they have the specified effect in any line of commerce, whether or not that line of commerce is a large part of the business of any of the corporations involved in the acquisition. . . . The purpose of the bill is to protect competition in each line of commerce in each section of the country."

[*Dangers of Chain Reaction.*] The merger offers an incipient threat of setting into motion a chain of reaction of further mergers by the other but less powerful companies in the steel industry. If there is logic to the defendants' contention that their joinder is justified to enable them, in their own language, to offer "challenging competition to United States Steel . . . which exercises dominant influence over competitive conditions in the steel industry . . ." then the remaining large producers in the "Big Twelve" could with equal logic urge that they, too, be permitted to join forces and to concentrate their economic resources in order to give more effective competition to the enhanced "Big Two"; and so we reach a point of more intense concentration in an industry already highly concentrated—indeed we head in the direction of triopoly.

[*Congressional Purpose—No Distinction between Good Mergers and Bad Mergers.*] Congress in seeking to halt the growing tendency to increased concentration of power in various industries was fully aware of the arguments in support of the supposed advantages of size and the claim of greater efficiency and lower cost to the ultimate consumer. It made no distinction between good mergers and bad mergers. It condemned all which came within the reach of the prohibition of Section 7. The function of the Court is to carry out declared Congressional policy. "Though our preference were for monopoly and against competition, we should 'guard against the danger of sliding unconsciously from the narrow confines of law into the more spacious domain of policy.'" The Court must take the statute as written.

The proposed merger runs afoul of the prohibition of the statute in so many directions that to permit it, is to render Section 7 sterile. To say that the elimination of Youngstown would not result in "a significant reduction in the vigor of competition" in the steel industry is, in the light of its history, to disregard experience.

[*Lines of Commerce with Reasonable Probability of Substantially Lessened Competition.*] The Court concludes that there is a reasonable probability that the merger of Bethlehem and Youngstown would, in violation of Section 7, substantially lessen competition and tend to create a monopoly in:

1. the iron and steel industry,
2. hot rolled sheets,
3. cold rolled sheets and
4. hot rolled bars, in
    a. the United States as a whole,
    b. the northeast quadrant of the United States,
    c. Michigan, Ohio, Pennsylvania and New York,
    d. Michigan and Ohio,
    e. Michigan, and
    f. Ohio,
5. buttweld pipe,
6. electricweld pipe,
7. seamless pipe,

8. oil field equipment,
9. oil field equipment and supplies,
10. tin plate,
11. track spikes, and
12. wire rope.

[*Court Instructions.*] Submit decree within ten days, in accordance with the foregoing and the further enumerated findings of fact and conclusions of law filed herewith, enjoining the proposed merger as violative of Section 7 of the Clayton Act.

Shortly afterwards the companies announced that there would be no appeal and that the merger proposal had been dropped.

Addendum

Despite reduced profits from 1958 through 1961, the Bethlehem Steel Corporation did not abandon its goal of a location in the important midwestern market. In December, 1962, it formally announced plans to spend $250 million over three years in building a steel-rolling and -finishing plant at Burns Harbor, Indiana. Its capacity was announced as 592,000 tons of plate a year, 284,000 tons of tin plate, 720,000 tons of cold-rolled sheet, and 354,000 tons of hot-rolled sheet.

Production began in 1964. Construction of raw steel capacity began in 1965 with an annual capacity of 2,000,000 ingot tons planned for 1970. Total investment in the new plant will total $1,000,000,000 with another $150,000,000 necessary to double ingot capacity by 1975.[47] According to the company, "every element of each facility at Burns Harbor embodies the most advanced technology. This goes beyond steel production to include smoke control, water cleaning systems, and power facilities. Computers control key functions of the plant's operations."[48]

Both Bethlehem and Youngstown increased production of raw steel by about 60 percent in the decade after the merger was abandoned in 1958. Bethlehem spent $2,222,000,000 and Youngstown $668,700,000 in capital from 1959 through 1967, with financing being primarily through internal cash flow.[49]

Questions

1. Were there strong business reasons for the Bethlehem-Youngstown merger? What did each company have to gain? Why may the companies have decided not to appeal the decision?

---

[47] "The Bethlehem Story," *The Magazine of Metals Producing*, December, 1968. pp. 55–56.

[48] "The Burns Harbor Plant," Bethlehem Steel Publications, 1968.

[49] "The Bethlehem Story," *The Magazine of Metals Producing*, December, 1968, p. 29.

2. What was the government's case? What meaning did it seek for such key phrases of the Clayton Act amendment as "in any line of commerce" and "may substantially lessen competition"? Did it prove that the "net competitive effects" of the merger would be adverse?

3. Why was the government so confident and the companies so modest about the companies' capabilities for expansion in the Chicago area? Does Bethlehem's announcement in late 1962 of expansion tend to support the government's contention?

4. It has been argued that Bethlehem's postmerger expansion adds weight to the importance of considering "potential competition" in merger cases and that the end result of the merger decision has been favorable. Is this argument justified?

Index of Cases

Index

*This book has been set in 10 and 9 point Cale-
donia, leaded 2 points. Chapter numbers are
18 point Spartan Light and 48 point Onyx.
Chapter titles are 24 point Spartan Medium.
The size of the type page is 27 by 45½ picas.*